Philharmonic

A History of New York's Orchestra

Also by Howard Shanet

LEARN TO READ MUSIC

PHILHARMONIC

A History of
New York's Orchestra

HOWARD SHANET

Doubleday & Company, Inc., Garden City, New York 1975

ISBN: 0-385-08861-2
Library of Congress Catalog Card Number 72–96256
Copyright © 1975 by Howard Shanet
All Rights Reserved
Printed in the United States of America
First Edition

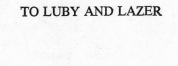

TO LUBY AND LAZER

Acknowledgments

Those who helped were many.

At the New York Philharmonic Society, Amyas Ames, the Chairman of the Board, David M. Keiser, the Honorary Chairman, and Carlos Moseley, the President, despite their justifiable anxiety that I might not always say things the way the Philharmonic would like them said, put at my disposal most of the Society's records, including a great many materials of a confidential nature. Other members of the Philharmonic's present and past administrations who were never too busy to satisfy my insatiable requests for information were: Bruno Zirato, Advisor to the Board; Helen M. Thompson, Manager, and William Weissel, Assistant Manager; Frank Milburn, Press Director and Music Administrator, and Joan Barton, Ken Miller, Wesley DeLacy, and Walter Van Thiel of his department; Winston Fitzgerald, Administrative Assistant; Maynard Steiner, Controller; Eleanor V. Capria of the Radio Department; Sophie G. Untermeyer, Fund Raising Director; Alice Kyne and Josephine Carpenter of the office staff; and Diane Thompson and Carlotta Wilsen of the Archives. The musicians of the Philharmonic Orchestra whom I consulted on one subject or another are too numerous to be thanked separately, but they have all been told how grateful I am for their help. The encouragement of Axel Rosin, a member of the Philharmonic's Board of Directors and President of the Book-of-the-Month Club, strengthened me at several moments when the path seemed long and the going rough, in the twelve years (twelve years!) during which I worked at this book.

From only one source did I receive financial aid. Columbia University, several years ago, gave me a grant from its Faculty Research Fund for certain kinds of secretarial and research assistance, thanks to the recommendations of Jacques Barzun, then Provost, and Lawrence H. Chamberlain, then Vice-President, of the University. Dr. Barzun, without knowing it, has given me another kind of assistance: his book *The Modern Researcher* (written with Henry F. Graff) was compass and sextant whenever I drifted from the historian's true course.

I owe the thrill of seeing the original Prospectus of the Philharmonic, dating from 1842—long believed to have been lost—to Harold Lineback of St. Louis, one of the most resourceful collectors of American historical materials, who also put at my disposal a number of rare pictures and concert programs, and other items from his collection. When Harold Lineback gives scholars access to such of his holdings as the diaries of Ureli Corelli Hill and Anthony Reiff, the history of the Philharmonic's early years will have to be rewritten.

In the uncharted wilderness that the history of nineteenth-century American music still remains, my research helpers had to be trained as jungle fighters. I hereby award medals for gallantry in action to Patsy Rogers, Phyllis Mason, Kay Jaffee, Elizabeth Mears Kurtz, Thomas C. Day, Darrell Panethiere, and Robert F. Willis. For raw-typing much of my manuscript I thank Myrtle Turner, and for fine-typing it I thank Lee Powell. The doughty team of Miriam Baumgarten, Thomas W. Baker, and Richard Koprowski helped to proofread the book by reading aloud to me every word and punctuation in it.

Without the tireless race of librarians every musicologist would flounder helplessly. I pay my special tribute to those of the Columbia University Music Library and the Music Division of the New York Public Library, but I also received aid from the Library of Congress, the British Museum, the Henry E. Huntington Library, and the New-York Historical Society. To James B. Dolan, who was orchestra librarian for the NBC Symphony when Arturo Toscanini was conducting it, I am indebted for the opportunity to examine many of the markings and adjustments that Toscanini made in orchestral scores.

A great deal of information about European orchestras, which enabled me to compare their histories and operations with those of the New York Philharmonic, was generously supplied to me by the administrative officers of the Royal Philharmonic Society of London, the Meiningen Theater Orchestra, the Weimar State Orchestra, the Orchestra of the Société des Concerts du Conservatoire of Paris, the Royal Liverpool Philharmonic Orchestra, the Hallé Orchestra of Manchester, the Gürzenich Orchestra of Cologne, and the Philharmonic Societies of Vienna, Budapest, Munich, Bordeaux, and Brussels. That Dr. C. B. Oldman, Honorary Librarian of the Royal Philharmonic Society of London, who knew me only from the favors that I asked of him, took days of time from his own work to search the records of the Society for the hundred bits of information that I requested leaves me as astonished as I am grateful.

Mrs. Artur Rodzinski and Mrs. Janos Scholz (formerly Mrs. Ernest Schelling) have let me examine large collections of the correspondence and other papers of their late husbands, Artur Rodzinski and Ernest Schelling, both of whom played important parts in the history of the New York Philharmonic.

Among the hardy souls who read all or part of my manuscript and gave me those helpful criticisms that are so painful and so necessary for a writer were my wife, Bernice, my sister, Julia Koob, Leonard Bernstein, Carlos Moseley of the New York Philharmonic, Barbara Novak O'Doherty of Barnard College, H. Wiley Hitchcock of Brooklyn College, and Ken McCormick and Lisa Drew of Doubleday & Company.

I have tried to mention, in the text or in the notes to it, the many people who have written me about Philharmonic matters. If there are others who have helped me, whose names I have not cited, I take this opportunity to offer them one great collective thank.

Howard Shanet

Preface

"The history of the Philharmonic Orchestra is the history of music in America," wrote the distinguished critic and journalist James Gibbons Huneker in 1917.

This statement sounds so grand that it is always being trotted out for quotation on ceremonial occasions.* But Huneker and those who quote him have failed to see that some of the most significant and character-istic aspects of the Philharmonic's history have been the ways in which it was *not* the whole of American music, nor even, at times, part of its mainstream. The history of the Philharmonic Orchestra, after all, is not the history of opera in America, nor of choral music, chamber music, church music, folk music, popular music, musical comedy, dance music, band music, theater music, music instruction, or music publishing. And even if Huneker had limited his assertion to orchestral music, it would still be untrue. The history of the Philharmonic was far from being the history even of orchestral music in America at any number of moments:

–in 1842, when there already existed an old musical culture, varied and vital enough to *give birth* to the Philharmonic,

–in the 1850s, when American composers filled the press with com-plaints that the Philharmonic did not represent them,

* Huneker used it in his account of the Philharmonic, written on the orches-tra's seventy-fifth anniversary. I find that the idea was not original with him, however. Fourteen years earlier, Arthur Laser, in an article in the German peri-odical *Die Musik,* had said: "The 'History of the Philharmonic Society of New York' coincides almost completely with the history of music in America."

–in the 1870s, when the Theodore Thomas Orchestra, rather than the Philharmonic, was molding the tastes of the nation,

–in the 1890s, when it was the Boston Symphony that was demonstrating how a subsidized orchestra should be run,

–and especially in Huneker's 1917, when Walter Damrosch's Symphony Society rivaled the Philharmonic, when half a dozen other American cities boasted their own great orchestras, and when two of the most brilliant of them, Stokowski's Philadelphians and Muck's Bostonians, regularly invaded New York territory, bold as Cortés among the Mexicans.

Least of all would it be so today, when the much discussed explosion (and fragmentation) in the nation's musical life has gone beyond any degree known in the past.

Is the historian of the Philharmonic trying to belittle its role? No. I have been worrying Huneker's error so much because it is a widespread one, stemming not from too great pride but, strange as it may seem, from undue modesty—from the timid tacit assumption that the Philharmonic, and indeed all "serious" music in America, must live in a little byway of the world, separate from the daily business of life. It is only in such a narrow byway that the Philharmonic can seem to be equatable with all American music. But if Huneker had taken a wider view, he could have said, with more truth and greater daring: "In the history of the Philharmonic Orchestra can be seen a reflection of American life in its time." For the Philharmonic, though only one part of music in America, *has* been a cultural mirror, reflecting—sometimes dimly, sometimes clearly—the social environment, the economic conditions, the ethnic changes, the urban growth, the political events, and the educational state of its community. And like other mirrors (to risk carrying the figure of speech a step further), in addition to reflecting, it has sometimes focused the energies that reached it so that they acted back upon the world around it.

It is in this broad sense that I propose to examine the development of the New York Philharmonic, relating it whenever possible to the society in which it has functioned.

It follows from this that I am not writing an "official" or "authorized" history, like the ones that were issued on the Philharmonic's fiftieth, seventy-fifth, and one hundredth anniversaries, by Krehbiel, Huneker, and Erskine. They were excellent little books, full of valuable information, but they belonged to the class of self-congratulatory publications that large institutions put out on their anniversaries. The time has come to do more than that for the historic Philharmonic. The oldest orchestra in America and one of the oldest in the world no longer needs the petty gratification of being told that it has been very well-behaved. What it needs and deserves is a reckoning of its participation in the changing cultural patterns of American life over its historic span of a century and a quarter.†

I had better admit at the outset, however, that in making this reckoning I shall have an ax to grind: *I am determined to do what I can to combat the vast, and largely unjustified, inferiority complex that has oppressed American music throughout its history, and continues to do so today.* This attitude I adopt not out of chauvinism, which is always an unreasonable posture, but in order to redress the balance, to catch up, after all the years of *anti*-Americanism $(= \frac{1}{\text{chauvinism}})$, which have been infinitely more unreasonable. For the moment, I am not talking about the mysterious managerial procedures that import third-rate singers and conductors from abroad while first-rate Americans languish unused. I am talking about the fact that most American historians, musicians, and musicologists pretend to themselves, by a peculiar suspension of everything they know about historical processes, that their country's music has no history. Our most widely used college textbook of music history does not recognize the existence of the United States before the late nineteenth century. America gets four pages after that. A respected member of the American Musicological Society, proposing to his colleagues a "Profile for American Musicology," finds European music from Renaissance madrigal to Bulgar folk song satisfactory subject matter for musicology, but knows of nothing suitable in all American history. "Unfortunately," he writes, "American music has not been interesting enough, artistically, to merit from us that commitment." In this cavalier assertion he dismisses in advance three centuries of a nation's music that have hardly begun to be heard or studied.

I became painfully aware of the plight of American historical studies in music as I pursued my researches for this history. I found that many of the older authorities on American music could not be trusted either for factual material (not their fault—the primary sources were just beginning to be collected) or for critical evaluation (their fault—any-

† Actually, the period that I have set myself to cover in this book is more like a century and three quarters—from the Philharmonic's antecedents in the forty or fifty years before its founding in 1842 to the moment of Pierre Boulez's accession as Music Director in 1971.

one's half-baked comments were accepted as gospel if only they met the requirement of being condescending enough about American music). Among my own contemporaries only a handful of maverick scholars dared to insist, at the risk of professional quarantine, that American music history should not be an exotic study in America. It is symptomatic of the condition that this first full-length history of our greatest orchestra must be written by a conductor out of missionary zeal rather than by a historian out of professional involvement.

That is why I must grind my ax, clearing away the historical undergrowth, if I am to tell the story of the Philharmonic in its natural context. And you who read these pages must scrape away the cultural brainwashing of a century, to examine with ordinary common sense the historical evidence that I lay before you. If I tell you that New York had a Philharmonic Society as early as Vienna, do not brush aside the achievement as a quaint freak of history, but rather ask what rich cultural background must have existed in old New York that it could match the imperial city in this respect. If I tell you further that New York's early Philharmonic was healthier than Vienna's, and better appreciated by its community—that indeed the Vienna institution collapsed twice between 1850 and 1860, giving no concerts at all for six of those years, while the young New York orchestra continued to grow—do not look for rationalizations by historical sleight of hand, but recognize the obvious truth that the social, economic, and cultural requirements for the presentation of symphonic music must have been better developed in New York in the 1850s than they were in Vienna. To understand the evolution of the Philharmonic against the background of its own society is surprisingly difficult for most educated Americans, who have been indoctrinated to evaluate their musical life by Procrustean standards that have no organic relation to it. You can get so tied up with Renaissance madrigals and Bulgarian folk songs that you no longer find anything artistically interesting in all American music. And it is not easy to give up your cultural cigarettes, though you know that they cause intellectual cancer.

Look back at that sentence of Huneker's: "The history of the Philharmonic Orchestra is the history of music in America." Huneker was a sensualist and a man about town (see his racy novel *Painted Veils*) who had heard every kind of music that the metropolis had to offer. Only by censoring out nine tenths of what he knew was there could he equate the history of the Philharmonic with the history of American music. He was certainly no puritan, but that was just what he did.

Contents

PART III: AN ORCHESTRA IS BORN
(1842–43)

PART IV: YOUTH
(1843–79)

PART V: MATURITY
(1879–1909)

PART VI: A NEW LEASE ON LIFE
(1909–58)

PART VII: REBIRTH
(1958–   )

EPILOGUE
The Future

BACKNOTES

BIBLIOGRAPHY

APPENDICES

INDEX

Illustrations

Figure

IN THE TEXT

GRAPHS

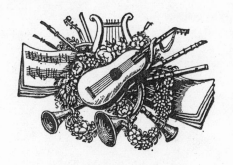

Tableau

The First Concert of the New York Philharmonic (December 7, 1842)

It is a little before eight o'clock on a wintry Wednesday evening in December of 1842, and we are entering a large hall that can be rented for public entertainments in the building known as the Apollo Rooms, at 410 Broadway (east side of the street, between Canal and Walker). The place has an air of unaccustomed elegance tonight. The seats are the usual plain wooden benches, but we are led to them by impeccably dressed young men, wearing white gloves and carrying slender white rods of wood as symbols of their office. They are not ordinary ushers but members of the orchestra, selected for this special duty because of their manners and appearance.

I wish we could report either that the cream of New York society has turned out for the Philharmonic's first concert or that the democratic masses, hungry for culture, are clamoring at the gates; but neither would be true. The hall is almost full, but a great many of those present are the families, friends, or pupils of the orchestra players. There is a great deal of German being spoken in the audience and some strong foreign accents even among those who are speaking English. More than 40 per cent of the players in the orchestra are of German origin and a considerable part of tonight's audience has been drawn from the city's rapidly growing colony of German-Americans. It is all more than respectable by bourgeois standards—no common laborers or people of low class—but it is not high society.

There must be 600 or 650 people in the hall, which can accommodate at least 700. An advertisement in today's newspapers has informed the public that "There are vacancies for but few more subscribers, who alone are admissible." Six hundred may not seem to be a very large number of persons to be attracted to an event of this importance in a city of 350,000 population. But this is the Society's first concert—nobody knows what to expect—and money is very tight this year. The tickets, although reasonably priced, are not cheap. A subscription covering four tickets for each of the three concerts of the season costs $10; that comes to $3.33 for one set of four tickets, or 83¢ per ticket. For 83¢ in 1842 you can provide your family with 15 pounds of beef, lamb, or mutton, or you can hire a carpenter for six hours of skilled work. The Park Theatre, where you can see the best theatrical entertainment in town, is charging only 50¢ for the boxes, 25¢ for the pit, and 12½¢ for the gallery. Then, apart from the question of price, there are still some people in New York who consider any music outside a church to be the work of the devil and no less sinful than dancing.

It is eight o'clock now and the concert is about to begin, but there is still no sign of the orchestra. The stage is empty, except for the music stands, each with its tin candlestick, a piano with its chair, and seats for about fifty musicians. The seats are really something of a luxury since the whole orchestra will stand throughout the performance of each piece, as is done in London and at the celebrated Gewandhaus concerts in Leipzig. Only the violoncellists will be seated, anatomy and art making it difficult "for cellists to stand like the rest of a band."

I spoke of the stage a moment ago, but "stage" is not quite the right word. The Philharmonic has gone to considerable expense for the building of a so-called "orchestra," a wooden structure designed especially to accommodate the players and singers for these concerts. The bill for the construction of the "orchestra" and forty music stands comes to $173.49, but it should pay for itself in a few seasons. Already several individuals and organizations have inquired about renting it at $5 per use.

The Philharmonic will have no fewer than three conductors in the course of the evening, and they will follow the new method that London has been using for instrumental music during the past ten years or so—instead of the conductor's being seated at the piano and dividing his duties with the "leader" or principal violinist (as is customary in New York concerts), he will stand, with a baton in his hand, and assume direct control of the orchestra. The program names the three men who will share the honor of conducting the first concert of the Philharmonic Society of New York. They are Messrs. Ureli Corelli Hill, Denis G. Etienne, and Henry C. Timm.

The orchestra enters now in such orderly fashion and in such dignified silence that a hush falls over the audience. Not a sound from the players—none of that scraping of fiddles and tootling of horns that you would hear from these same musicians if they were warming up in one of the theater orchestras where many of them play. They need not even break the silence to tune their instruments; that was done in the anteroom, before coming on stage, when Mr. U. C. Hill, the President of the Philharmonic Society and the conductor of the first piece, politely requested the first oboist to sound his A.

Hill is a tireless organizer who deserves much of the credit for the launching of the new Philharmonic. For that matter he seems to have something to do, either as conductor or violinist or teacher, with every aspect of New York's musical life. As he stands before us on the platform, his determined face framed in undisciplined whiskers, a fanatic glint in his eye, he has the look of a spiritual leader—we almost expect him to break into a religious exhortation. He lifts his arm, ready to begin.

The first piece on the program is going to be Beethoven's Fifth Symphony. The only previous performance of this symphony in New York was almost two years ago, in February 1841. It is said to have been a good one, but the concert was a strictly German affair, given by the German Society of New York for the benefit of needy German immigrants. So a great many of tonight's listeners will be hearing Beethoven's Fifth Symphony for the first time.

The impact of those thunderous opening tones is overwhelming after the silent dignity of the orchestra's entry on stage and the hushed anticipation of the listeners. Some of the more conservative members of the audience may prefer the gentler styles of Mozart and Rossini, with which they are more familiar, but no one denies the power and grandeur of this music.

It is music that seems appropriate, moreover, to this momentous occasion. With this concert New York can take its place among the few cities of the world that have their own permanent orchestras. Even Vienna, the musical Jerusalem, the home of Mozart, Haydn, and Beethoven, is reported only now to be organizing its own Philharmonic

Concerts (the first official performance should have taken place ten days ago, on November 27, but it is too soon for any account of it to have reached America). Now there will be a New York Philharmonic, too, to prove that an energetic and resourceful young land knows how to appreciate the finest things in life.

As the second work on the program, Antoinette Otto is to sing an excerpt from Weber's *Oberon*. At least one sympathetic critic has called her "the most brilliant vocalist in America." For Madame Otto's number, Yankee U. C. Hill has left the conductor's desk and Hamburg-born H. C. Timm has taken command. Timm, as the program indicates, will direct all the vocal music in the concert. Since he is a wizard as a piano accompanist—one of those all-around useful musicians who can read anything at sight—he is always in demand to work with singers at the piano, and they feel comfortable with him as their director when an orchestra is available.

The program has the variety that listeners, in Europe as well as in this country, expect in an orchestra concert. After the grand symphony and the colorful operatic excerpt, there is to be still another kind of music—a well-known chamber-music composition, which will give several of the musicians a chance to shine as individuals. It is the Quintette in D minor, Opus 74, by Johann Nepomuk Hummel, for piano, violin, viola, cello, and double bass, played by Messrs. Scharfenberg, Hill, Derwort, Boucher, and Rosier. To appreciate the special meaning of this portion of the program for tonight's audience, you must know that William Scharfenberg, the brilliant young pianist of the quintet, only twenty-three years old but generally considered the best keyboard player in the city, was actually a pupil of Hummel's in his native Germany; and that Hummel, who died only five years ago, in 1837, was the pupil of Mozart and the successor of Haydn (at Prince Esterházy's court), and just about their equal in fame until very recently. For a New York audience it is thrilling to think that the young pianist to whom they are listening at this moment is the direct musical descendant not only of the world-famous composer whose Quintette he is playing, but also (at a distance of only one generation) of such legendary giants as Mozart and Haydn. The public's involvement in the performance is heightened, moreover, by the fact that Scharfenberg and the other players in the quintet are among the most popular music teachers in New York; their pupils are applauding proudly everywhere around us. If there were any doubts about the wisdom of ending the first half of the program with a piece for only five players rather than for full orchestra, it can now be seen that these misgivings were unjustified.

Intermission. It is a welcome and even necessary respite, for the air has grown stale, as it tends to do in most theaters and concert halls. It is not that it is too warm (the temperature outside is about 27 degrees tonight, with a light snow falling) but just that the ventilation is inadequate. This is a problem that plagues the designers of all public buildings. The Capitol at Washington is notorious for its unwholesome air which has been blamed for sickness and even deaths among the members of the House of Representatives. As for theatergoers, they seem to take foul air for granted: many ladies and gentlemen accept headache as a necessary concomitant of public entertainment, and fainting in public places is quite common. There are several places on Broadway, it is said, where the poisonous exhalations of the audience are dense enough to dim the lights in the upper parts of the house. Conditions are not that bad in the Apollo Rooms, but a breath of fresh air is certainly welcome.

The outside of the building is narrow, only 20 feet wide at the front, and only three stories high, but the façade is appropriately classical: a triangular pediment, decorated with a rising sun, is supported from below by four Ionic columns, and crowned above with three statuary figures. Across the face of the building, just below the representation of the rising sun, are the words "THE APOLLO" in huge letters. A flagpole tops the whole.

It is not a palatial edifice. The street floor has the look of a storefront. But it is a dignified structure, well-kept and more than respectable. In fact, any hesitation about its use by the Philharmonic seems to have been on the landlord's side: he is said to have asked for his money in advance, if we are to believe Anthony Reiff the bassoonist, who is also Vice-President of the Society. The rent for the season, including the three concerts and all the rehearsals, comes to more than $135.

Inside the concert hall again. You would never guess its shape from the front of the building. The façade, as we have said, is narrow, but the structure flares out behind No. 410 to make room for this large hall. Except for the orchestra's platform and the rows of "pews" for the spectators, the hall is quite bare. But the brightly flickering gaslight of the chandeliers, and the noisy animation of the crowd—the ladies in their off-the-shoulder gowns, the men tail-coated and waistcoated—lend the scene a festive excitement.

The orchestra is entering now for the second half of the program. It has its share of remarkable personalities. S. Milon in the cello section, for example, always takes *two* cellos into the orchestra with him and seems to switch from one of his instruments to the other from time to time. This peculiar behavior is due not to caprice but to necessity, and the story behind it is a romantic one. Milon was a junior officer in Napoleon's army; in the bitter retreat from Moscow in the winter of 1812 his left hand was frozen and parts of three fingers had to be amputated. Milon, stubborn old soldier, has worked out a method of tuning and fingering, employing two cellos, tuned differently from each other so that the second instrument can be used in keys that are difficult on the first.

Louis Wiegers, of the violin section, is not only a fine instrumentalist, but also a good conductor and a gifted arranger. Unfortunately for Wiegers's career, however, there are persistent rumors about his "habits of life"—it seems likely that he drinks rather more than he ought to.

As for the Dodworth family, when they are on stage you hardly need the rest of the orchestra. There are four Dodworths in the Philharmonic —Harvey B. plays the violin, as does Allen; C.R. plays the piccolo, and Tom the trombone. But all the Dodworths can double on brass instruments. In fact, they are the hub of New York's military-band music. Dodworth's Band, which may number as many as fifty performers for special occasions, is in demand for all sorts of civic events, from parades to dances. Tomorrow, for instance, is Thanksgiving Day, December 8, and the Dodworths will be playing for the Grand Thanksgiving Ball at the Tivoli Saloon. Their reputation goes beyond New York—Dodworth's Band has already played for the inaugurations of three Presidents of the United States: Van Buren, Harrison, and Tyler.

The conductor for Weber's *Oberon* Overture appears. It is neither Mr. Hill nor Mr. Timm this time, but the respected piano teacher D. G. Etienne. Quite apart from his long experience—he has been playing and conducting in New York since 1816—there are practical reasons for giving him such a prominent role in this first concert: Etienne has a large following of potential subscribers among the music lovers and music students of the city, and he is the dean of the small but vigorous French clique which watches jealously the inroads of the Germans on New York's musical life.

Charles Edward Horn enters now to sing the Rossini duet with Madame Otto. Horn may be famous both here and in England as singer and composer, but he is fifty-six years old and the truth of the matter is that he has lost his voice. He cracks on the first note he sings! He is notorious, moreover, for forgetting the words when he performs and faking them in a sort of gibbering double-talk. Nevertheless, the public applauds him warmly for the duet and for the *Fidelio* excerpt that follows it. New York audiences put up with Horn's physical inadequacy because they recognize his basic artistry and respect his record of achievements. When he came to America in 1827 he had already composed and produced more than twenty English operas in London. His songs, such as "Cherry Ripe," are heard everywhere. In New York, as a theater music director, he has presented any number of English-language operas, including his own American opera, *The Pilgrim of Love,* based on a story by New York's favorite son, Washington Irving. Many of the Philharmonic's musicians have worked in Mr. Horn's productions at the Park Theatre and elsewhere, and H. C. Timm, who is his conductor tonight, was formerly chorus master under him at the National Opera-House.

The vocal portion of the program concludes with Madame Otto singing the "Aria Bravura" from Mozart's *Belmont and Constantia* (*The Abduction from the Seraglio*), with Mr. Timm directing. Now Timm has the privilege of conducting the crowning work of the concert —the first American performance of the *New Overture in D* by the contemporary Bohemian composer Jan Václav Kalliwoda. Kalliwoda is regarded as one of the most gifted of Europe's composers, whose very name, as the New York *Albion* commented in Saturday's issue, "is a passport for the favorable reception" of his work. The noted German critic Robert Schumann has reviewed Kalliwoda's recent music in phrases filled with admiration: "unique in the symphonic world" . . . "full of artistic, finely worked out details" . . . "a still green and fresh branch in the German forest of poet-musicians." (Schumann, himself a composer, has also paid Kalliwoda the compliment of dedicating some piano pieces to him.)

The overture ends with a resounding clangor—the rich, sure sound of a "numerous and powerful" orchestra. For years U. C. Hill and his colleagues have dreamed of a permanent, professional orchestra in New York. Certainly the new Philharmonic—mounted securely astride its own specially designed platform, playing a brilliant contemporary work from its own library on its own music stands for its audience of subscribers—promises to be both professional and permanent.

Part I

The Scene
(1841–42)

Chapter 1

"A Little River and Harbor Town . . .
A Dull, Dark Age in Our History"

What business had a town like New York with a Philharmonic Society in 1842—the same year that Vienna, one of the music capitals of the world, organized its Philharmonic Concerts, almost forty years before Berlin established its concerts, sixty years before Warsaw, Copenhagen, Prague, and Stockholm founded theirs, and three quarters of a century before Rome, Milan, Barcelona, and Madrid?

That an American town of 350,000, only half a century out of colonialism, should have outstripped all these European centers of culture has seemed to most observers, American as well as European, to border on presumption. "In the land of the dollar," asked Oswald Garrison Villard rhetorically, "a great orchestra seventy-five years old?" (It was 1917 and, as President of the Philharmonic, he was delivering an address at Carnegie Hall in celebration of the orchestra's seventy-fifth anniversary.) "The assertion is at first one to be denied, or doubted as an impossibility, or an anachronism." For New York in 1842, Villard reminded his listeners, was but "a little river and harbor town" and the 1840s in general "a dull, dark age in our history."

This is still the generally accepted image of "old New York": a quaint enough little town, but a backwoods in matters of culture.

It is an image that is false on both points.

By the standards of 1842, New York, with its population of about 350,000, was not "a little river and harbor town," but one of the most populous communities of the world. Certainly London and Paris were much larger—the former with approximately 2,000,000 people and the latter with almost 1,000,000—but no other cities of Europe were in this class. St. Petersburg, the next in line, was under 500,000. Vienna was of about the same size as New York, as were Moscow, Naples, and Berlin. Manchester, Amsterdam, Liverpool, Birmingham, Glasgow, Lisbon, Madrid, and Dublin were smaller. And Brussels, Rome, Venice, Budapest, Warsaw, Copenhagen, Bordeaux, Hamburg, Milan, Prague, Munich, Stockholm, Dresden, Athens, and Leipzig were not even in the same league with the great metropolis of the New World. *In 1842 New York was the seventh largest city in the Western world!*

Beneath the temporary discomfort of a financial depression that had dragged on since 1837, it was also a wealthy city.

In the entire history of the United States there has been no decade in which the material conditions of the country developed more dramatically than in the ten years from 1830 to 1840. It was the period when the nation's railroad mileage grew from 23 miles to 2,800, when anthracite coal was applied to locomotives and to the manufacturing of iron, when regular steamship service across the Atlantic was instituted, when the American system of express companies began to take shape, and when the steamboat, exploiting the growing network of navigable rivers and canals, could convert a little frontier fort like Chicago in a matter of six or seven years into a flourishing town with eight steamers joining it to Buffalo—and thereby to New York.

New York City profited greatly from the nation's improvements in communication and production, and particularly from the opening of the Erie Canal in 1825. The canal made New York the gateway from the Atlantic to the interior of the country and, as railroad lines were built to supplement the older means of communication, New York inevitably became the chief rail terminal of the East Coast as well.

The merchants and manufacturers of the city prospered. When Moses Yale Beach, the owner of the *Sun,* drew up a list of the wealthiest New Yorkers in 1842, he was able to count 14 men with fortunes of a million dollars or more (John Jacob Astor, the richest of them all, he put down for $14,000,000), 34 with more than a half-million dollars, and 599 with more than a hundred thousand; even if Beach's estimates are not entirely accurate, his list makes its point.

It was not only the millionaires who benefited from New York's growing wealth in the 1830s and early 1840s. Despite the nationwide financial panic of 1837 and subsequent hard times in 1839 and 1842, many thousands of New York homes were made more citified throughout this period by the introduction of gas and anthracite coal for lighting, heating, and cooking, by supplies of pure water moved to the city in great aqueducts, by pretentious imitations of Greek architecture on the outside, and by very comfortable furniture and appointments on the inside.

And the city was as rich culturally as it was materially. "A dull, dark age"? On the contrary, as the next two chapters will show, the New York of 1842 had a varied and often sophisticated artistic life. The arts, moreover, were not insulated from each other. The same people who took theater tickets also bought books and engravings, went to see exhibitions of paintings, attended concerts, and made music for themselves at home. The 1842 diaries of men as far apart as Philip Hone (sixty-two-year-old "leader of the *ton*," self-made business man, and former mayor of the city) and George Templeton Strong (twenty-two-year-old Columbia College graduate and solicitor) show them both in constant cultural motion, from theater to lecture to bookshop to art gallery to music performance. Ordinary New Yorkers, neither rich nor educated, heard fine orchestral overtures with their plays at the theaters, saw ballets with their concerts and refreshments at the summer "gardens," and, in the bulging museums of the city, sampled under one roof music and painting, lectures and sideshows, scientific exhibits and poetry. Admittedly, the artistic offering varied in quality from the masterly to the trivial, as it does in any age and place, but its vitality and its diffusion throughout the city's population were remarkable.

In this ground, the Philharmonic put down its roots.

Chapter 2

New York's Cultural Life

A sense of the colorful artistic environment in which the founding of the Philharmonic took place can be conveyed by a bird's-eye view of what was happening in New York in the theater, in literature, in visual art, and in music, in that historic season of 1841–42. As the various arts are surveyed, certain patterns common to all of them will emerge: the sheer abundance of what was available, the munificence with which the public rewarded its favorites, the ambivalence toward native talent (pride in its accomplishment, tugging against a desire for European approval), and the typically American endeavor to reconcile fashionable exclusiveness with popular acceptance.

THEATER

In 1841–42 New York supported at the box office four full-time repertory houses with stock companies of actors and singers, a German-language theater, two museums whose offerings mingled entertainment and education, an endless round of lectures and poetry readings, a full season of circus attractions, and several summer gardens which offered diversions ranging from ballets and comedies to balloon ascensions.

This was in addition to the concert and opera activities.

Of the theaters, only one, the Olympic, was small. The Park, the Bowery, and the Chatham each had a capacity of about two thousand —more than double the average Broadway theater of today. Yet a successful play frequently ran for eighteen or twenty nights in a row and a real hit might roll up forty or fifty performances in the course of the season. Even if the houses were not always full, these figures are impressive for a city of 350,000.[1] *

And what were the staples of the theatrical diet, the everyday fare that the managers served the public between the hoped-for hits? They were the works of Shakespeare. In 1841–42, the three large theaters produced among them at least fifteen of Shakespeare's plays.[2] Nor was the interest in Shakespeare confined to the upper classes. On the contrary, the fashionable Park Theatre did fewer of his plays than the more proletarian Bowery and Chatham, which catered to the rougher element in the city's population—only six for the Park as compared with ten at the Bowery and nine at the Chatham. Even the lowly circus paid its homage to the Bard—on horseback. A glance ahead at the season of 1842–43 discovers that Welch's Circus would present C. J. Rogers, equestrian, "with correct and superb costumes, and music" in "a Tribute to Shakespeare, in which the rider would personate Sir John Fallstaff, Shylock, and Richard III."

So common was the Shakespearean currency that everyone could recognize its counterfeit. William Mitchell at his little Olympic Theatre kept his audiences roaring with laughter by burlesquing the great tragedies. *Richard No. III,* a take-off on *Richard III,* was such a hit when it was introduced in 1842 that it was performed twenty-nine times in succession and forty-three times in the season. Only a public completely familiar with the revered original could take such joy in the Olympic's literary sacrileges.[3]

In addition to the plays of Shakespeare, another substantial area of the repertory, also derived from British sources, consisted in 1842 of such fine old comedies as Sheridan's *The Rivals* and *The School for*

---

* The number in small type indicates a backnote in the section beginning on page 413. The backnotes are numbered consecutively from 1 to 238, and at the beginning of each backnote will be found the number of the page that it refers to. The backnotes consist, for the most part, of supplementary information (often documentary or bibliographical) that might interrupt the text if included in it. Whenever it seems that a note has more immediate interest—that the reader might want to see it in conjunction with the text—it is given at the bottom of the page as a footnote, like this one.

Scandal, and Goldsmith's *She Stoops to Conquer.* The Park Theatre, with its fashionable public, paid more attention to these literate, word-conscious plays than did the other houses, but the programs of the Bowery and the Chatham showed them with great frequency too.

The New York theater was strongly oriented toward England. This orientation was based, of course, on the common language of the two countries, but it was reinforced by other factors. Most of the New York theater managers were British, and they tended to import both plays and players from the mother country. The theaters of London, Dublin, Edinburgh, and other cities produced an abundant supply of tested wares, ready packaged for export. It seldom took more than one season for a London hit to find its way to New York and it sometimes did so in a matter of months or even weeks. Such importations were facilitated by the great strides that were being made in trans-Atlantic travel. By the 1840s packet boats were regularly crossing to Europe in fourteen or sixteen days, and faster crossings were not unknown.

The "popular" theaters, such as the Bowery and the Chatham, gave their share of Shakespeare and Sheridan, but they also gave generous servings of the so-called melodramas—sensational, romantic plays, liberally sprinkled with music in the form of songs, choruses, and orchestral accompaniments. The ground for the growth of the melodrama (and other popular entertainments with music) was prepared by a peculiarity in the English theatrical tradition: English law had long confined "legitimate" drama to the theaters protected by royal patent (Covent Garden and Drury Lane in London); all other theaters were restricted to spectacles not regarded as regular stage plays, and were consequently led to incorporate large amounts of music into their productions. In their search for genres that would not violate the law, the non-privileged theaters mated the popular ballad opera with the Gothic horror romance and other elements, and came up with a mongrel form so successful that the royal theaters were eventually forced to adopt it too: the melodrama. In America, the public appetite for melodrama was insatiable—new offerings were constantly in demand and American creative talents were encouraged to make their own domestic variations on the formula. Since that formula emphasized music, it tended to make the American theater heavily musical from an early period in its growth. But it also tended to make Americans associate their native musical theater with the "illegitimate" background of the melodrama, thus intensifying the cultural inferiority complexes already present in the

former colonies—Americans could turn out this vulgar and sensational
stuff well enough, but for "art" one had to go to Europe. Legacies of
these complexes will rise to haunt us at many a point as we pursue this
history. To this day, Americans quite unreasonably think of their
musical theater as categorically lower in the cultural scale than "legitimate" plays that have not been contaminated by music.

The theaters that served the "common people" (and under this heading we must include, in varying degrees, not only the Bowery, the Chatham, and the Olympic, but also the museums and circuses and some
of the lecture halls) also had two peculiarly American specialties which
were less likely to be found at the more exclusive Park although they
were already being exported to Europe with great success. These were
the so-called "Ethiopian" entertainments and "Yankee" characterizations, both associated with American vernacular music. The former
were imitations of Negro song, dance, and speech, often exaggerated or caricatured, by white actors in blackface makeup—a genre
that was soon to settle into its classic form as "negro minstrelsy." The
most famous of these Ethiopians in 1842 was T. D. ("Jim Crow")
Rice. The leader in the field of Yankee characterizations was George
Handel Hill (brother of Ureli Corelli Hill). In 1842 "Yankee" Hill
had already been regaling New Yorkers for at least a dozen years with
his comic songs, Yankee stories, and "lectures on the habits, customs
and manners of Down Easters"; many pieces were written especially to
provide characteristic roles for him—*The Vermonter* and *Josh Horse-
radish,* for example. And like T. D. Rice he had won triumphs with his
American folk art in London.

At the Park Theatre, which claimed to attract the most refined elements among the city's theatergoers, the two great successes of the
1841–42 season were both elegant importations: from London, the comedy *London Assurance* by the precocious Irish playwright Dion Bouci-
cault (not yet nineteen years old), and from the continent, the return of
the dazzling Austrian dancer Fanny Elssler. *London Assurance* made a
sensation with its method of staging, in which lavish drawing rooms were
represented not by painted views but by realistic three-walled rooms,
actually furnished in the latest style of home decoration. The divine
Fanny, in her New York debut in 1840, had created the greatest furore
that the American stage had known; after her 1842 engagement, she was
said to be taking $150,000 out of the country with her, in a time of

financial depression. She left behind her a wake of adoring audiences and ruined theater managers.

In 1842, although the taste of the upper classes for things European was becoming more marked, the difference between the fancy Park Theatre and the others in New York still resided less in what you saw and heard on the stage than in whom you saw next to you in the audience. *London Assurance,* for example, made its sensational success at the Park, but it was copied by both the Bowery and the Chatham before the season was out. New Yorkers of all social classes were exposed to very similar theatrical experiences (including theater music), though they might be exposed in different buildings or on different levels of the same building, according to their social and financial condition. A common vocabulary of theater, and of theater music, was widely understood by rich and poor alike.

New York's entertainment world offered a profusion of other delights:

¶Mitchell's impish satires and zany farces at the Olympic Theatre (which attracted a truly democratic audience, ranging from the newsboys and bootblacks in the pit to a "fashionable attendance," as well as that greatest of compliments in the theatrical world, the actors from other companies).

¶The German Theater with its performances of Kotzebue, Nestroy, and others, as well as concerts and opera.

¶Barnum's American Museum, Peale's New York Museum, and the National Museum of Wax Figures, with their smorgasbord of Indians, freaks, serious lectures, Ethiopian and Yankee impersonations, scientific exhibits, musical performances, ballets, acrobatics, complete plays, circus acts, puppet shows, works of art, magicians, fortunetellers, trained fleas, mermaids, hypnotists, daguerreotypists, wax figures, Maelzel's mechanical dancing figures, and (as the New York Museum advertised) the six thousand curiosities of the museum itself.

¶The circuses at the Bowery Amphitheatre and the Arcadian Garden (horsemanship acts, acrobats, gymnasts, performers on the elastic cord and the flying rope, "Negro" specialties, strong men, clowns, musicians, comic pantomime, grand entrees and spectacles).

¶The summer gardens—the fashionable Niblo's, the Vauxhall, the Tivoli, the Atlantic, Castle Garden—where the remarkable Ravels (nine of them) sparkled in their melodramatic-pantomimic-acrobatic ballet-plays, excellent comedians offered "vaudevilles" or light plays,

Lauriat made his balloon ascensions, and one could always count on a promenade musicale, fireworks, and cooling refreshments.

From Shakespeare to fireworks, and at prices from 6¼ cents to a dollar, every New Yorker could find his theater.

It was in the orchestras of such theaters that the Philharmonic would find many of its musicians. It was in the audiences of such theaters that the Philharmonic would find many of its listeners.

LECTURES

Halfway between theater and literature lay the flourishing domain of lectures. Or even closer than halfway: some of the lectures advertised in the New York newspapers in 1842, particularly by the commercial museums, were really plays in disguise. That small group of New Yorkers who still thought it improper to be seen in a theater attended without any twinges of conscience regular plays presented at the New York Museum as a series of "comic lectures" by actors from the Olympic Theatre.

But apart from these conscious or subconscious subterfuges, there was a deluge of real lectures in the auditoriums of the city. Dickens, who visited New York in 1842, later satirized this craze for lectures in *Martin Chuzzlewit;* his New York ladies, above domestic drudgery, go to courses of lectures on the Philosophy of the Soul, the Philosophy of Crime, the Philosophy of Vegetables, the Philosophy of Government, and the Philosophy of Matter. Many of these may have been as superficial as the satirist implies, but he would certainly have to except—in the year of his visit, alone—Ralph Waldo Emerson's great series on "The Times,"[4] Jared Sparks's course of eight lectures on the "Events of the American Revolution," Dr. Francis Lister Hawks's series at the New-York Historical Society, and perhaps even Dr. Dionysius Lardner's popularizations of such scientific subjects as the "Solar System," "Modern Methods of Physical Research," and "The Moon," and the numerous demonstrations of animal magnetism or mesmerism. Under the heading of lectures was also understood in 1842 the endless stream of poetry and elocution readings, given sometimes by professional actors but just as often by talented "ladies and gentlemen"—particularly ladies. Not only the omnipresent Shakespeare, but also works of Scott and Byron, and of such contemporary Americans as Longfellow and

Halleck could be heard at these lectures, sometimes with critical or interpretative comments.

The astonishing appetite for lectures was not dulled even during the economic depression, when the theaters were having financial troubles. Jared Sparks's course on the American Revolution attracted such crowds, Philip Hone reported in 1841, that the chapel of the recently built New York University could not hold them, and they had to adjourn to the huge Tabernacle, "the omnium gatherum and holdall of the city" (Hone-ese for "the largest hall"). A possible explanation for the flourishing of the lecture system in a time of depression is that lectures were relatively inexpensive to put on—no scenery, no costumes, no large casts, no orchestra in the pit, no stage machinery, lower auditorium costs. Even a small turnout for a lecture could mean a profit, whereas the same size of audience for a costly play or opera might spell ruin.

But the fact that the lecture circuits were already growing before the depression (there were about three thousand lyceum lecture associations in the United States by 1835) and continued to prosper long after the bad years were over indicates that there must have been a deeper reason for their success. Surely it was the hunger of the middle classes of the young nation, and to some extent of all its social strata, to be "cultivated" and "educated." What the book clubs and the record clubs and the educational radio and television programs are for the culture-hungry public of today, the lectures seem to have been for the New Yorkers of the mid-nineteenth century. In such a public the new Philharmonic Society could also expect to find eager followers.

LITERATURE

When Charles Dickens visited New York in 1842, a great dinner and a grand ball in his honor were arranged by committees of the most distinguished men of the city. The ball was held in the Park Theatre, where the whole area of the stage and pit was floored over to make an immense ballroom for the occasion. Something like 2,200 tickets (more than the capacity of the house) were sold at $10 each, but, what with committee members sneaking their friends in through back ways, about 2,500 "Boz" admirers managed to crowd in. The splendid decorations, paintings, and tableaux vivants were based on favorite passages in Dickens's works.

All this fuss and adulation was predicated on a wide public acquaintance with Dickens's writings. Although, at the age of thirty, he was still young in his career, his books were sold by the thousands in America, and the New York stage had been presenting theatrical versions of *The Pickwick Papers, Nicholas Nickleby,* and *Oliver Twist* for years. The same was true of Sir Walter Scott and Bulwer-Lytton: tens of thousands of copies of their novels were imported to America or reprinted here, and all their best-known works were converted into dramatic versions for the New York stage. Similarly, the works of Byron, Moore, Southey, Wordsworth, Keats, Shelley, Coleridge, Burns, Mrs. Browning, Mrs. Hermans, and every other important British author were reprinted and sold in the United States in large editions. Half the books printed in the United States before the middle of the nineteenth century were British.

British writers were not always overjoyed by their American popularity, for, in the absence of any copyright agreements, Yankee publishers printed the whole English literature free, without any payment either to author or to original publisher. But the educational and sociological consequences of this literary freeloading were of incalculable importance. With only the actual costs of production to worry about, American printer-publishers were able to bring the writings of the best authors to all classes of the population at very low prices—in 1842, novels in a cheap format could be bought for as little as 6¼¢ and 12½¢. Since so many of the books were British, the unifying force of the English language was reaffirmed in American life at a crucial moment—the moment when great waves of immigration brought new languages to these shores. "Our vernacular tongue, the English language," toasted the Reverend Mr. Henry Bellows at the Dickens dinner, "a recovery from the confusion of Babel, destined yet to build a tower which shall reach to Heaven."

Against the British background, a distinct American literature had begun to make itself felt even before the 1840s, and New York was a principal center of its activity. Washington Irving's comic *History of New York* (pretended to be written by "Diedrich Knickerbocker") had succeeded as early as 1809, and his *Sketch Book* of 1819 had won him fame in England as well as here; by 1842, with many more titles to his credit, including several works on the American West, Irving was the respected dean of New York's literary community and so much of a national hero that, as a sort of acknowledgment of his services, he was appointed Ambassador to Spain. James Fenimore Cooper's angular novels of romantic adventure had been a success in the United States and the rage on the continent from the time of the publication of *The Spy* (1821).† William Cullen Bryant (a New Yorker by residence, though born in Massachusetts), already admired for his precocious *Thanatopsis,* had been acclaimed both here and in London since his *Poems* of 1832. Yet in all these cases, part of the measure of the accomplishment was success in Europe. New Yorkers had conflicting feelings about European recognition. On the one hand they were anxious to assert their democratic independence and originality as Americans, and on the other hand European acceptance remained a test of artistic achievement. Certainly New York felt the influence of the American frontier democracy to the west, but in many of its manners and aspirations it was at least as close to the big cities of Europe and Britain. Despite the popular European image of an America of coonskin caps and tomahawks, New York in 1842 had not been a frontier society for 100 or 150 years, and Irving, Cooper, and Bryant were not the sons of deerslayers but of a merchant, a lawyer, and a doctor.

New York readers were devouring huge amounts of poetry in those days, in periodicals, in separate volumes, and in collections like Rufus Griswold's *Poets and Poetry of America,* issued in 1842. Among the New York poets, in addition to Bryant, Joseph Rodman Drake, author of *The Culprit Fay,* was still remembered, and Fitz-Greene Halleck was held in high regard (fifteen years after the composition of his satirical poem *Fanny,* admiring college students were still borrowing a rare copy from each other). Nathaniel P. Willis—flowery, smooth, sentimental, professional, turning out verse and prose with journalistic ease—was typical of the littérateurs of the "Knickerbocker" period. But already Edgar Allan Poe was pointing the way to a sharper criticism; in his essay of 1842 on the poems of J. G. C. Brainard he insisted that Americans must no longer praise all their literature indiscriminately out of a fear that the rest of the world might look down on them: "We

† When Berlioz exchanged batons with Mendelssohn in Leipzig in 1843, he wrote him a witty dedication that took for granted their mutual acquaintance with the Cooperese jargon: "To Chief Mendelssohn. / Great chief! we promised each other to exchange tomahawks. Here is mine, it is crude; yours is simple! / Only Squaws and Palefaces love ornate arms. Be my brother! And when the Great Spirit will have sent us to the happy hunting grounds, may our braves hang our tomahawks together at the door of the council chamber." (Berlioz, *Voyage Musical,* I, p. 80, and *Le Musicien Errant,* p. 32.)

have, at length, arrived at that epoch when our literature may and must stand on its own merits, or fall through its own defects. We have snapped asunder the leading-strings of our British grandmamma, and, better still, we have survived the first hours of our novel freedom— the first licentious hours of a hobbledehoy braggadocio and swagger."

The writers of other parts of America interacted, of course, with those of New York. New England authors, for example, often visited New York (as we have seen Emerson doing for his lectures of 1842), but even when they did not come in person, their works were promptly known and discussed in the city. One effect that this traffic had on the New York literary scene was to intensify an already existing penchant for German and other foreign elements. Many New England influences pulled in this direction: the intellectual and social connections that Harvard and Boston maintained with the continent, directly and by way of England . . . the scholarly methods that New Englanders like George Ticknor and George Bancroft had brought back with them after studies abroad . . . translations, like the *Specimens of Foreign Standard Literature* that George Ripley began to issue in 1838, or Sarah Margaret Fuller's version of Eckermann's *Conversations with Goethe.*

At the same time, interestingly enough, New England writers were not deaf to the almost opposite demand from many quarters for a literature striving to express the new American spirit, and in this movement, too, their influence was felt in New York. Emerson, Hawthorne, and Longfellow had already begun to think along these lines in the late 1830s, and no one will deny that Emerson, at least, had succeeded in finding an American expression—independent, personal, self-reliant, liberally humanitarian, peacefully revolutionary—for his American ideals. Meanwhile, John Greenleaf Whittier, who spent 1837 in New York working for the anti-slavery cause, dealt equally in his fiery prose and verse with national issues of the day and the stories of his region's past.

The tug of war between the foreign and the domestic showed with particular clarity in the field of historical writing. George Bancroft chose to apply the exacting standards of German scholarship to a patriotic theme in his gigantic *History of the United States,* which had been appearing, volume by volume, since 1834. But other American historians of intellectual interests deliberately and almost ostentatiously sought subjects that were not immediately concerned with the United States. William H. Prescott had made his name with his *History of the Reign of Ferdinand and Isabella* in 1837, and John L. Motley would soon begin his exhaustive studies in the history of the Dutch Republic. It was a matter of great pride to educated Americans that the works of these gifted men were translated into the principal European languages.

Americans themselves, however, were ready to honor their talented authors. Washington Irving's appointment as Ambassador to Spain in 1842 was a reward for cultural achievement. At a single ceremony in 1837 Columbia College had given honorary degrees to three Knickerbocker authors: Halleck, Bryant, and Charles Fenno Hoffman. And Longfellow was the object of such adulation, in the early 1840s, that Poe feared he would be spoiled by it.[5]

The volume of sales of serious and learned books is an index of the healthiness of the intellectual community. Prescott's *Ferdinand and Isabella* had gone through eight editions between 1837 and 1842 and was still selling strongly. James Kent, the New York jurist—the venerable "Chancellor" Kent—told Philip Hone, as the new year of 1843 began, that his *Commentaries* had brought him a profit of $5,000 a year ever since the work had come out in 1830 (that would make about $60,000), and added that he did not "apprehend any diminution of the profits of the sale for twenty years to come." The books of John L. Stephens of New York, the great explorer, earned fantastic sums of money; his *Incidents of Travel in Central America, Chiapas, and Yucatan* was published in July of 1841, and by October of the same year he was reported to have cleared $15,000 on it.[6]

New York in 1842—welcoming all the authors of Old and New England, providing a public and a field of action for Irving, Cooper, Bryant, and Poe, sprouting poets in every periodical—was far from a literary backwoods. And the same cultural matrix that fed its literature helped to sustain its music. It will be no surprise, after one of the Philharmonic's early concerts, to find a New York music lover wondering whether "Weber . . . couldn't be compared to Coleridge, and Beethoven to Carlyle."[7]

PAINTING

In the 1840s Americans, and New Yorkers in particular, were buying American art more readily than at any other time in the nation's history.

An important factor in this healthy situation was a remarkable institution called the American Art-Union, which grew out of the earlier Apollo Association. The most striking aspect of its operation was its distribution of art works by a sort of lottery. The system was simple and extremely successful: the Union bought the work of contemporary American artists and showed it at the gallery it maintained in New York; for a $5 annual fee, a member received a large steel engraving, four small ones, and copies of the published *Transactions* and *Bulletin;* but most exciting of all, he also had the chance of winning one of the original paintings, for, as the Union purchased new paintings, it distributed the old ones to the subscribers by lot. Unfortunately, jealous enemies of the organization brought suit against it in 1851 for violation of the state lottery laws and by 1853 the last works of art had been auctioned off. But during the short period of its activity the Union had distributed about 150,000 engravings and 2,400 original works by more than 250 American artists. At its peak, it had had 18,960 subscribers.

Another important institution where New Yorkers could see the works of their countrymen exhibited was the National Academy of Design, organized in 1826 under the leadership of Samuel F. B. Morse, who was soon to become even more famous as inventor of the telegraph than he was as painter. For many years there was also the more old-fashioned American Academy of Fine Arts, but it was in protest against its restrictive policies that Morse founded the National Academy, and by 1841 the older institution was out of the running.

America had a long and proud tradition in painting, going back to the middle of the eighteenth century. Benjamin West of Pennsylvania, as the world knew, had become President of the Royal Academy in London. John Singleton Copley and Gilbert Stuart were names that were known wherever genius was valued. And there was a continuity to the tradition: West and Copley had helped to guide the talents of other American painters—Ralph Earl and Charles Willson Peale among them.

But in 1842 these were names of the past. Who were the American painters whose works the New York public looked at, paid for, or talked about?

First of all there was an older generation, Europe-oriented in its training and frustrated by the apparent inability of America to respond to its Old World standards: the self-centered and short-tempered octogenarian Colonel John Trumbull; John Vanderlyn, angrily seeking the country's recognition while he denounced its artistic insensitivity; and romantic Washington Allston, who had been torturing himself and his unfinished canvas of *Belshazzar's Feast* since 1818 without being able to complete it.[8] There was Samuel F. B. Morse, too—Allston's favorite pupil—but he was spending more time in 1842 on his telegraph, his daguerreotype projects, his National Academy, and his professorship at the young New York University than he was on his painting. And there was the English-born Thomas Sully, living in Philadelphia but well-known in New York, whose portrait style seemed to be diluted by the techniques he brought back from a return visit to London.

None of these artists held the center of the stage, however. The cynosure of New York's art world was Thomas Cole. His paintings of the "wild" and unspoiled American landscape and the allegories he set in similar backgrounds were rightly admired by Americans of all ages and all social classes. Half a million visitors saw Cole's *Voyage of Life* series at the Art-Union and when the Union included them among the pictures that could be won in its lottery of 1848 its membership shot up seven thousand above the preceding year. Although Cole was English-born—he came to America at the age of eighteen—he was lovingly adopted by his new country, and his friend, William Cullen Bryant, even stretched a point in a poem addressed to him by calling America his "native land."[9] Another American painter who was highly regarded in New York was Asher B. Durand, who also celebrated the glories of the American landscape, actually doing his painting out of doors instead of working in a studio from pencil notes.‡ And William S. Mount of Stony Brook, Long Island (an out-of-doors painter, too, who designed a special artist's wagon, with large glass windows, to paint in during bad weather), was much admired for his genre pictures of Long Island farm life.

It was a period when some American artists, at least, were beginning to overcome their fear that America was too unrefined to provide subject matter for anything as elevated as art. By the 1830s and early '40s Cole, Durand, Mount, and many others were turning eagerly to the native landscape and people. Certain painters and engravers, indeed, were creating an American style and technique, organically related to their American subject matter, though their achievements were seldom taken seriously as "art," even by the artists themselves, but rather as utilitarian or decorative craft work (and continue to be so regarded in

‡ See the reproduction of his *Kindred Spirits* in Figure 17.

certain formalistic circles to this day). Under this heading fall many of
the prints that became the standard wall decorations in the parlors of
the nation, engraved illustrations for the fancy Keepsake and Treasure
volumes that embellished the parlor tables, political cartoons, book
illustrations, scene paintings for theaters, huge descriptive panoramas of
distant or exotic places, and much of the work of practical portraitists—
in other words, the "vernacular" art absorbed by the general public.*

The vernacular touch had been present in some of the more polished
American painters too, ever since colonial days, though perhaps more
in the choice of subject than in its treatment: Copley's *Watson and the
Shark* could hardly have come out of any other part of the world than
America, and the same could be said for several paintings by Ralph
Earl and Charles Willson Peale. In the 1820s and '30s a continuation of
this strain can be discerned in several artists who, relatively untrained,
worked out their own styles, with even less concern for the aesthetic
requirements of the European art world and its sophisticated imitators
in the United States. John James Audubon, the great portrayer of the
birds of America, found in his mixture of crayon and water color a
homemade technique that suited to perfection his mixture of science and
art. George Catlin, the Barnum of the art world, recorded the life of
the American Indians in hundreds of vivid paintings and then exhibited
them in the United States and London in Wild West shows complete
with live Indians. Erastus S. Field of Massachusetts, despite a brief
exposure to the formalism of Samuel Morse in New York, evoked in
his portraits the stiff charm of the so-called American primitives of a
century before.

Perhaps the most original of all—so original that he could not succeed with the New York cognoscenti of his time—was John Quidor
(1801–81), undervalued and neglected by his countrymen to this day.
Quidor may have had to paint parade banners and decorate fire en-
gines to eke out his living, but in his canvases, particularly in those
based on the stories of Washington Irving, his comic exaggeration and
exuberant drawing produced masterpieces of wildly humorous characterization that are even more distinctively American than the tales
that inspired them.

* The most striking manifestation of vernacular art, as John Kouwenhoven has
insisted in his *Made in America*, lay outside the field of painting, in that of
technological design—the designs of buildings, weapons, tools, machines, clocks,
ships, locomotives, stoves, furniture, and the hundreds of other objects required
by and produced for a democratic society with "an expanding machine economy."

Finally there were the painter sons of Charles Willson Peale—Rembrandt, Rubens, Raphaelle, and Titian Peale—who absorbed some of their father's peculiarly American inventiveness.[10] Rubens had continued his father's experiments with public museums of art, science, and "curiosities." Rembrandt was working on a system of teaching drawing and penmanship in the public schools. Titian had adapted his talents to the uses of science on expeditions to Florida, South America, and the South Seas. All the Peales, including not only Charles Willson and his sons but also his brother James and the latter's three daughters, had pioneered in still life from the earliest decades of the century, and Raphaelle had achieved a perfection in this field that would have made him outstanding in any age and any land. The Peales were based in Philadelphia, but they and their work were well-known in New York. In fact, Rubens was running Peale's Museum in New York at the very moment of the Philharmonic's conception in the spring of 1842, and some of the people who patronized the one also attended the other.

The healthiness of New York's and the nation's attitude toward painting in this period lay in the willingness of all levels of the public to encourage and reward the native artists, and the willingness of most of the artists to create for the practical and aesthetic needs of the public. As early as the 1820s Rembrandt Peale's *Court of Death,* which he publicized as "an appeal to the public taste by a native artist," was taken directly to the people on tour, special buildings being constructed where necessary for the display of the huge canvas of 24 by 13 feet. It was visited by more than 32,000 Americans who paid $9,000 for the privilege, and 100,000 colored engravings of it were prepared for sale at a dollar each. The Common Council of New York came in a body to see it; nor was this unusual—the work of American artists, particularly when it dealt with the country's history or heritage, was viewed as a source of national pride, and public-spirited officials and citizens came forward eagerly to admire and pay homage. Not only the members of the Common Council, but the mayor, the newspaper editors, Daniel Webster, and other public figures were pleased to attend Catlin's Gallery of Indian paintings and artifacts on a single morning in 1837. Philip Hone, appreciating the success with which Cole had captured the American landscape, went so far as to say: "I think every American is bound to prove his love of country by admiring Cole." Hone was in some ways a cultural pretender, always concerned with presenting a good front and always worried about what Europeans would think, but whatever his motives may have been, he nevertheless bought Cole's paintings for his back parlor and filled the pages of his diary with discussions of Vanderlyn, West, Trumbull, Stuart, Mount, Morse, Greenough, Catlin, Audubon, Allston, Inman, Weir, the National Academy, and the American Academy.

Rich men financed the studies of young Americans abroad, and bought and commissioned paintings of native artists. Cole's famous allegorical series of four paintings, *The Voyage of Life*, was made for Samuel Ward (senior), the banker, and another series, *The Course of Empire*, for Luman Reed. Reed's son-in-law, Jonathan Sturges, gave Asher B. Durand the financial help that permitted him to go abroad in 1840. David Hosack owned a whole collection of canvases by Trumbull. George Washington Strong was only a moderately wealthy man, but he commissioned two genre paintings of William S. Mount. Colonel Stevens of Hoboken engaged Morse, Vanderlyn, Sully, Doughty, and Cole to do pictures for his steamboat *Albany*.

Most painters, it is true, relied on portrait work for some part of their livelihood, particularly in the early stages of their careers, but when they ventured into other types of painting they were often very generously paid for their work. The Art-Union in New York might give $500 for a landscape and $2,000 for a large painting of special interest. The price that Samuel Ward had agreed to pay Cole for the *Voyage of Life* series was reported to be $5,000, and some said as much as $12,000. The Philadelphia Academy bought the late Benjamin West's celebrated *Death on the Pale Horse* for $8,000, and New York enviously crowded to see it when it was displayed at the Academy of Fine Arts in 1836. What these prices signify about the regard of New Yorkers and other Americans for their own artists can be judged from the fact that only $3,000 was being asked in 1837 by a New York dealer for an alleged Rembrandt (van Rijn, not Peale).

A special kind of painting, designed expressly for exhibition to the public at large, was the panorama, which enjoyed a tremendous popularity for more than half a century and was at the very peak of its success in the 1840s. There were two principal types: in the earlier of the two, a huge landscape painting covered the inside surface of a cylindrical building so that the observer standing at the center was completely surrounded by what he saw, very much as he would be in a real landscape; in the later type, motion was added by presenting the painting on long strips of canvas which were wound (either by hand or by steam engine) from one roller to another, usually to the accompaniment of an explanatory lecture and sometimes with background music provided by a pianist or a band.

The "moving" panoramas had been tried in various forms even in the eighteenth century, but they made their sensational successes in the late 1830s and early 1840s. At that time John Rowson Smith, a theater scene painter, prepared a highly successful one of the *Mississippi River*. Shortly thereafter John Banvard of New York did another panorama of the Mississippi, using one continuous strip of canvas which he claimed was three miles long. It thrilled not only the great public, but the intellectual elite of New York and Boston as well: Longfellow, who was working on *Evangeline*, attended several Boston performances in order to study the Louisiana landscape. In England the panoramas of Banvard and Smith were honored by command performances for Queen Victoria, and 600,000 people saw Banvard's alone. In New York, in the period around 1842, panoramas and dioramas could be seen at five or six different establishments; some of these productions had been on view for years, visited by thousands upon thousands of paying customers.

The emphasis in the foregoing paragraphs has been on New York's (and the nation's) vigorous interest in the works of American painters because this was such a characteristic and remarkable attribute of the period, but of course the attentions of buyers, viewers, and students were not wholly confined to the native painters. The American Academy of the Arts, until its demise in 1841, exhibited many fine old European paintings. There were weekly auctions at Gourlay's and at Levy and Harrison's. Wealthy New Yorkers put together their own collections and kept track of the holdings of collectors in nearby cities— the princely Colonel Perkins in Boston, Charles Abrahams in Philadelphia, Robert Gilmor in Baltimore; in their catalogues figured Claude Lorrain, Hals, Hobbema, Holbein, Murillo, Poussin, Ruisdael, Titian, Velázquez. If original old masters were too expensive for some pocketbooks, copies had to do; and many a young American painter earned his way through Europe by duplicating the greats of the past for patrons back home.

Trumbull, Vanderlyn, and Allston; Morse and Sully; Cole, Durand, and Mount; Quidor, Audubon, Catlin, and Field; panoramas, prints, and engravings; exhibitions and collections; the Art-Union and the National Academy; and a whole family of Peales! As in the theater and in literature, so also in painting, the profusion and variety of the New York offering were matched by the eagerness of the public's response.

An obvious question remains to be answered. Was there an equivalent excitement in the *music* world of the city at the crucial moment that preceded the birth of the Philharmonic?

Chapter 3

The New York Music World

The musical life of old New York equaled the other cultural activities in its vitality.

Can a New Yorker of today fail to be impressed, for example, by the information that Beethoven's opera *Fidelio,* when it was first produced in New York in 1839, was given for fourteen nights in a row at the 2,000-seat Park Theatre, and then revived twice in the same season —in a city of 312,000 inhabitants? We all know that neither the Metropolitan Opera nor the New York City Opera could come anywhere near such a run of the Beethoven work in our present city of 8,000,000 people. And the *Fidelio* of 1839 was not considered a great success: the cast was so-so and the scenery and costumes poor. A real hit, like the *Cinderella* of a few years before, would play fifty times in a season, be repeated tirelessly in subsequent years, and along the way give birth to a burlesque or comic take-off with a long run of its own at a smaller house.

Opera was a favored entertainment among all classes, from those who paid $1 for a box ticket to those who paid 25¢ for the gallery. In the depression year of 1841–42, there was less opera in New York than in some previous seasons; but in spite of the hard times the Park Theatre was able to offer: Bellini's *Norma* and *La Sonnambula;* Adam's *Postillion of Longjumeau;* Auber's *Fra Diavolo* and *The Bronze Horse;*

Hérold's *Zampa;* and a new opera, *The Maid of Saxony,* with music by
C. E. Horn (who was to appear as vocal soloist in the Philharmonic's
first concert) and a libretto by G. P. Morris of the New York *Mirror.*
Some of these operas, such as *Norma* and *The Bronze Horse,* enjoyed
four or five performances each, and the new American work, *The
Maid of Saxony,* managed to chalk up ten. In addition to this series of
operas, the Park presented such musical works as Bishop's *Clari* (which
contains the perennial favorite "Home, Sweet Home") and the three-
act "musical play" *The Carnival at Naples.* But in this it was not alone,
for all the New York theaters regularly offered the less pretentious musical pieces of this sort—ballad operas, musical comedies, plays with
musical numbers interspersed—every week of the season.

In fact, the Park was not alone even in the field of formal opera. The
German company at the Franklin Theatre gave two of Weber's works:
Preciosa and *Der Freischütz.* They also did Nestroy's comedy with
songs and dances, *Der böse Geist Lumpacivagabundus.*

Meanwhile, an illegitimate offspring of New York's opera tastes was
flourishing at William Mitchell's Olympic Theatre, in the form of bur-
lesques of the standard operas. *Zampa, or the Red Corsair* became
Sam Parr, with the Red Coarse Hair; Norma became *Mrs. Normer*
(married to Polony, "a Rum'un, overflowing with gall"); *La Gazza
Ladra, or the Maid of Palaiseau* became *The Cat's in the Larder, or
the Maid with a Parasol; La Sonnambula* became *The Roof Scrambler.*
In assaying the culture of New York of that period, it should not be
forgotten that this sort of fooling presupposed a public already familiar
with the operas being caricatured, just as Mitchell's "travesties" of
Hamlet or *Richard III* took for granted a knowledge of the Shakespearean originals, and some of his burlettas assumed an acquaintance
with classical mythology and history.

The city's appetite for opera, at the time when the Philharmonic
was being conceived, was only part of its zest for music. A tally shows
that in the New York of 1841–42 there was some sort of public performance of music—opera, concert, musical play, religious music—
practically every day of the year, and concerts alone averaged two to
four per week throughout the season from September to May. This
tally, moreover, covers only those events that were wholly or primarily
musical. The number is multiplied many times when one adds the
numerous occasions on which music was more or less incidental—ballet
or dance programs, background music for plays, theater entr'actes,

church services, circuses, variety shows, parades, official ceremonies, museum presentations, puppet shows, even art exhibitions—for it was a rare public offering that had no music at all.

In the regular instrumental and vocal concerts, as well as in the opera, New York heard each year representatives of the principal European countries. Among European musicians it was common knowledge as early as the 1830s that the American public rewarded generously with applause and money those who fed its hunger for music. A steady stream of singers and instrumentalists came from the Old World to perform and teach in the New, some remaining for months, some for years, and some settling permanently. There were celebrities among them and unknowns, geniuses and incompetents, but it is hardly necessary to point out that all of them made the arduous crossing of the Atlantic because they believed that there was something for them to do here. In short, they came to make music or money or both, in a society in which a great many practitioners could expect to do so. A performer who caught the fancy of the New York public could easily attract audiences for three or four concerts in the course of one season, and might also share the platform with other artists in as many more. The season of 1841–42 had its share of successful visitors from abroad. John Braham, England's most famous male singer (short, fat, and sixty-nine years old, but still singing magnificently), gave no fewer than seventeen concerts in New York and Brooklyn in that single season. This number was matched by the Rainer Family, who performed in native Tyrolese costume their repertory of songs, ballads, and Alpine melodies, with orchestra accompaniment. Eufrasia Borghese, the Italian operatic soprano, was able to appear in six concerts in her first month in New York, and two more after that. Madame Spohr-Zahn, daughter of the great composer Louis Spohr, enjoyed four appearances in the season. Like most democracies, the United States was dazzled by aristocratic titles—a musical Almanach de Gotha paraded across the New York concert stage in 1841–42: Voizel, "tenor of the private music of the King of France," Billet, "first violoncellist of the Music of the Emperor of Russia," Signor John Nagel, "first Violin to the King of Sweden," G. Knoop, "Concert-Meister of the late King of England, William IV." And despite the hard times, they all found their listeners. "Mr. Knoop fiddles and Braham sings to large audiences, whose $400 or $500 a night is made as easily as a banker's commissions," Philip Hone noted in his diary. Within the next two seasons,

even greater successes would be enjoyed by the violinists Ole Bull and
Vieuxtemps, and the soprano Castellan.

Notwithstanding the number of the imported artists, however, it was
of course the local, resident musicians, both native and naturalized,
who had to form the core of the city's musical life. The best of them
gave concerts of their own and shared the soloist's limelight with the
visiting artists, but they also made up the orchestras that supported
the featured performers on such occasions and that played regularly in
the theaters, and they were also the music teachers of the city. They
were the ones who stayed put—who could be counted on for every
kind of musical event that the growing community required. To make a
living from their profession, they had to be busy constantly. They
learned how to organize concerts as well as how to perform in them,
how to be cooperative as well as competitive. Those who survived this
educational ordeal were a breed of exceptionally stable and self-suf-
ficient artists. They were the material from which a Philharmonic Society could be formed. Henry Timm seemed to be accompanist for
everyone in New York, trained choruses, and conducted too; in the
1841–42 season, there were few concerts that he did not appear in.
U. C. Hill was constantly turning up throughout the year as leader of
the violin section, or as conductor. C. E. Horn taught platoons of singers, composed operas and oratorios, sang in as many performances as
Timm accompanied, and served as a theater music director. J. Kyle
and Ernst, the flutists, were other regulars, as were the pianists Scharfenberg, L. Rakemann, King, Alpers, and Heinrich, the violinists Rapetti, Wiegers, and Marks, the cellist Boucher, the bassist Rosier, and
the trumpeter Wolter. And the numerous resident singers—Madame
Otto, Mrs. Horn, Mrs. Loder, Austin Phillips, Dempster, and scores of
others—contributed to the year's music-making an astonishing variety
of vocal music, from popular ballads to oratorio and opera.

What music did all these musicians, foreign and domestic, perform
here? Very much the same music that was being given in the theaters
and concert halls of Europe, with a leavening of local material. New
Yorkers heard all the currently fashionable theater pieces of Rossini,
Boieldieu, Auber, Bellini, Weber, Mozart, Hérold, Bishop, and Donizetti, and concert pieces by these composers, plus Handel, Purcell,
Arne, Haydn, Beethoven, Spohr, Mendelssohn, and dozens of lesser
men. Of composers living in New York, the smoothly professional

Charles Edward Horn and the wildly original Anthony Philip Heinrich reached large audiences.

Listeners with a taste for the grand in the New York of 1841–42 could attend the oratorio performances of the Sacred Music Society. Beethoven's *Christ on the Mount of Olives,* conducted by U. C. Hill, was so enthusiastically received that a repeat performance had to be scheduled in the capacious auditorium of the Broadway Tabernacle, which could accommodate more than 2,500 persons. Even more successful was the Society's presentation of *David and Goliath* by the Chevalier Sigismund Neukomm (a favorite pupil of Haydn's, now virtually forgotten as a composer, but then internationally admired), which had to be given four times.

For more relaxed moods, Niblo's (on Broadway at Prince Street) offered a series of delightful *Concerts d'Hiver à la Musard,* "wintergarden" concerts in the style of those that Philippe Musard, the quadrille king, had given with great acclaim at Drury Lane in London. An extensive promenade was decorated with plants and shrubbery of every variety—in the depths of winter—to give the impression of a garden. Fine vocal soloists of the caliber of Giubilei and Seguin and an orchestra of eighteen with the ever-present Timm at the piano performed a varied selection of music—there might be Mozart, Rossini, Bellini, Weber, and the dances of Lanner and Strauss.* At Ferdinand Palmo's new Saloon, "decorated in the most gorgeous style of Eastern grandeur," the New York voluptuary, resting on a luxurious sofa, could enjoy his concert and his refreshments simultaneously. Palmo's and Niblo's were only the most elegant of a large number of musico-refectorial establishments. At a lower rung on the social ladder were places like the Rainbow, which advertised "Musical Parties" with Kavanagh (one of the city's very useful but not very illustrious singers), and Weidemeyer's beer hall, which boasted concerts with entertainers from the Franklin Theatre's German company. In the summers such entertainments were even more widespread, mingled with pantomimes, ballets, plays, fireworks, and balls. Then a musical New Yorker could choose among a promenade musicale with fireworks at Niblo's Garden, Dodworth's Band at the Atlantic Garden, vaudevilles and assorted diversions at the Vauxhall or Tivoli Gardens or at Castle Garden, and

* The borrowed Frenchiness of the title *Concerts d'Hiver* ("Winter Concerts") was a natural target for William Mitchell, the punster of the New York theater; he promptly announced for his Olympic Theatre *Un Concert d'Enfer* ("A Hell Concert").

concerts three times a week with *"Speisen und Getränke von bester Qualität"* at the Spring Garden on Seventeenth Street.

The churches must not be forgotten in any account of the year's music-making. Although there were still some within the Protestant churches who held any but the simplest music in the service to be a distraction, their number was dwindling, and one could hear admirable music at St. Thomas's and several other places. As for the Catholic churches, St. Patrick's and St. Peter's were the envy of musical Protestants. On Christmas Day St. Peter's was jammed, there were a choir of fifty or sixty thoroughly drilled singers and a full orchestra, and one might hear anything from a Mozart mass to Handel's *Messiah*.

Less glamorous than concerts and opera and the other public performances of music, but of great importance in the musical culture of the city, were the study and practice of music in the home. Almost all the New York musicians we have mentioned were teachers as well as performers, and many of the visiting artists from abroad were not above giving lessons while they were here. Hill, Horn, and Heinrich—the three H's of New York music—among them gave sound instruction in violin, piano, singing, and composition to several generations of students. The pedagogical influence of William Scharfenberg, another of the Philharmonic's founders, reaches even further: some of his editions of piano music were still in the catalogue of the New York publishing firm of G. Schirmer, Inc., in the 1970s. Music students and amateurs had been springing up like Cadmus's legions since the 1820s. Many of the students, amateurs, and professionals met in each other's homes or formed clubs for the enjoyment of music. Such was the "Beefsteak Club," which met once a month for a pleasant evening of dinner and music-making. By the 1840s this home market had encouraged the growth in New York of a prosperous piano-manufacturing industry—the firms of Nunns, and Dubois and Stodart, and Raven, among others—and the bringing in of additional pianos made by Chickering of Boston, Boardman and Gray of Albany, and Knabe of Baltimore.

Theaters full of operatic and musical life, concerts ranging from ballads to grand oratorios, visiting virtuosos and native talents, dancing gardens, singing churches, amateurs, teachers, makers of instruments— is it not evident now that the New York of 1842 was ready for its Philharmonic Society?

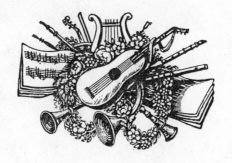

Part II

Antecedents
(Before 1842)

Chapter 4

The Two Earlier Philharmonics
(1799–1827)

In such a flourishing culture, it would begin to seem, a Philharmonic Society should have been attempted even *earlier* than 1842.

It was. At least twice. And under the very same name.

On December 7, 1799—forty-three years earlier than has generally been reckoned—New Yorkers read in the *Daily Advertiser* the announcement of their first Philharmonic: "The members of the St. Ceecilia [misprint for "Cecilia"], and Harmonica [misprint for "Harmonical"] Societies are informed that a junction of these two has been formed under the name of the PHILHARMONIC SOCIETY, the punctual attendance of each member is particularly requested at Delacroix,* Broadway, on Thursday Evening next at half after six, as business of importance will there be laid before the Society."

The *Advertiser's* spelling and punctuation leave something to be desired, but its information is valuable. It tells us that even the Philharmonic of 1799 did not start from scratch, but built upon the work of still earlier musical societies. The St. Cecilia Society, according to the New York directory of 1796, "was instituted in 1791, with a

---

* Joseph Delacroix ran a catering establishment at his home, No. 112 Broadway, which was a popular place for meetings and concerts and the ice cream and punch that went with them.

view to cultivate the science of music, and a good taste in its execution. The concerts are held weekly on Saturday evenings; the principal professors of music in the city are members, and performers at these concerts." The same directory carries a terse reference to the Philharmonic's other parent: "Harmonical Society for the approvement [sic] in music, meet Tuesday," and the 1797 directory informs us that "This Society was instituted March 17th, 1796, for the purpose of cultivating the Knowledge of Vocal and Instrumental Music."

The St. Cecilia and Harmonical Societies were not the only musical societies in New York before 1800, nor were they the earliest. A Musick Club is mentioned by Dr. Alexander Hamilton of Annapolis, who visited New York in 1744. The *Mercury* of April 12, 1773, in announcing a concert "to be conducted, and the first Violin perform'd, by Mr. [Hermann] Zedtwitz (A Capital Performer from London),"[11] adds: "The other Instrumental Parts, by the Gentlemen of the Harmonic Society." (This is not the same as the Harmoni*cal* Society, which, as has just been seen, was not instituted until 1796.) Between 1789 and 1799 we find frequent mention in the press or the city directories of the Musical Society of the City of New York, the Haydn Society, the Columbian Anacreontic Society, the Uranian Musical Society ("instituted for improvement in sacred vocal music"), the Calliopean Society, the Polyhymnian Society, and the Euterpean Society—all meeting regularly and making music in a city of fewer than 60,000 inhabitants.

The titles of these organizations, with their echoes of a classical education, reflect both their high cultural aims and their social exclusiveness. Although the founders and members were sincere in their zeal for musical "improvement" and "cultivation," they were also aware of the social advantages of a private musical society as compared with a public concert. In a society, you knew who was sitting next to you and exercised some control over his admission. A society's members were people of similar social background and interests, who enjoyed sharing with each other at regular intervals not only a musical experience but also such pleasures as conversation, refreshments, dancing, and, in general, "belonging."

Still, the 1799 Philharmonic Society was democratic in its government, as befitted a cultural institution in a young republic. It had a Constitution and Bye-Laws that contained clear provisions for amendment, and for elections of officers and members. The officers, in addition to a President, Vice-President, Treasurer, Secretary, and Standing Committee, included also a Leader (principal violinist). It was the Leader's duty to conduct the performance of the music selected by the Standing Committee for each concert and to take care of the Society's instruments and music; in compensation for his services he was paid annually the sum of $150. Each member paid $12 a year to the Society and new members paid, in addition, an admission fee of $8.

The 1799 Philharmonic Society had three kinds of performances, Weekly Concerts, Monthly Concerts, and Annual Concerts. The Weekly Concerts were not public but were restricted to the members themselves. They were apparently more like readings than like concerts in the modern sense. There is no evidence that there was any group preparation for the weekly meetings, though the players could borrow the music in advance—and woe betide the one who did not bring it back for the next meeting: he was fined $5, and if he lost or damaged the music he could be expelled unless he made proper restitution.

The last concert in every month was called the Monthly Concert. It was semi-public. Each member was entitled to three or more tickets to admit the ladies of his family. Careful measures were taken for social protection: each lady's ticket bore her name and the member's endorsement; if a member were actually performing in the orchestra, he could have an extra ticket for a gentleman, presumably to sit with the ladies while he played; and there was provision "that any Member introducing an improper character, shall upon proof before the Society be expelled."

The Annual Concert, held in December of each year, was public in that a certain number of tickets was sold to outsiders, the proceeds above the costs of the concert being reserved for the use of the Society or sometimes given to charity.

No smoking was permitted at the Annual or Monthly Concerts (i.e., when ladies were present) "under the penalty of two dollars for each offense." There is a glimpse of the pleasant social atmosphere that prevailed at these meetings in the provision, considered important enough to be entered as a separate bylaw, "That the Treasurer shall provide Brandy and Water, Beer, Crackers and Cheese, for the refreshment of the Society at the Weekly and other Concerts." To distinguish them at the concerts, members were required "to wear on the left breast a Mazarine blue rose, with a small one of Coquilicot [sic] in the middle, as the badge of the Society." Officers wore, suspended by a coquelicot ribbon around the neck, silver medals with the words "PHILHAR-

MONIC SOCIETY" encircling appropriate devices: for the President,
Apollo with his lyre; for the Vice-President, a harp; for the Treasurer,
two crossed keys; for the Secretary, two crossed pens; for the Leader,
a music book and violin; and for each of the Standing Committee, a
lyre.

The old Philharmonic Society had the honor of participating in the
funeral ceremonies for George Washington in 1799. When the news
reached New York that Washington had died on December 14, the
entire city rose to honor him. On December 24 the *Commercial Advertiser,* its pages dressed for mourning by broad bands of black between the columns, carried a call to the members of the Philharmonic
Society from their Secretary:[12]

> ### Philoharmonic Society
>
> The Members of this Society are particularly
> requested to be punctual in their attendance, at
> the usual place of meeting, on Thursday evening
> the 26th inst. in order to make arrangements in
> concert with the other Societies towards paying
> suitable honors to the memory of George Wash-
> ington.   *ISAAC G. OGDEN,* Sec.

Observe that the name of the Society is spelled "Philoharmonic" on
this occasion. Four days later, however, when further instructions for
the members were given in the same newspaper, the spelling was
"Phil'harmonic." And on December 30, the day before the procession,
it was finally "Philharmonic":

> On arrival of the Front, at the Church, on a Signal given, the whole
> will halt, and open to the right and left—The BIER preceded by the
> Music, Anacreontic and Philharmonic Societies, Clergy—and Girls in
> white robes—will pass through the Procession, into the Church, the re-
> mainder of the Procession moving after the Bier in reversed order—

The Anacreontic and Philharmonic Societies were described the next
day as being "In complete Mourning—the Grand officers bearing
Wands, decorated with crape—the Members wearing their Badges
with Crape and Bows of Love Ribbon."

The Philharmonic of 1799 was as lively as it was well organized.
It gave more concerts per year than the later Philharmonic (of 1842)
would be able to give in any of its first thirty seasons. The columns of

the *Commercial Advertiser,* the *Evening Post,* and the *Morning Chron-icle* carried frequent notices of its activities from 1800 to the fall of 1816. The Society could honestly claim to offer "Vocal and Instrumental Music by the most celebrated performers in the City." The English-born James Hewitt, one of New York's most active musicians, often served as Leader, and other participants, who were well-known to the music lovers of old New York, were A. Gautier† (clarinet), D. Lynch (flute), and C. Gilfert (piano), together with such favorite singing actors from the theater as Pardi, Perrossier, Miss Dellinger, and Mr. and Mrs. Hodgkinson. The programs at the concerts of the old Philharmonic were very much like those that were being heard in London and not too different from what was being played in Paris or Vienna. There were concertos, overtures, minuets, and sinfonie by Haydn, Pleyel, Gyrowetz, Wranitzky, Steibelt, and Kreutzer, plus vocal pieces, usually by English or local American composers.

It has generally been assumed that our later New York Philharmonic, in 1842, took the idea for its name from the London Philharmonic Society. H. E. Krehbiel, in his history of the New York Philharmonic, speaking of its founding in 1842, says: "Doubtless one stimulus was that to which tribute was paid in the naming of the society: the artistic impulses of the day came from London, and London had a Philharmonic Society." But the London Philharmonic was not founded until 1813, and when we know that New York already had a society of the same name in 1799 it makes no sense to look to the England of 1813 for the model. This is not to imply that London borrowed the name from New York; the probability seems to be that both New York in 1799 and London in 1813 derived their titles from the "Philharmonick Society" that was in existence in London during the first half of the eighteenth century.

The first Philharmonic seems to vanish from the New York musical scene after 1816. The last evidence of its activity that I know is a concert and ball for the benefit of the Orphan Asylum on December 17 of that year at Washington Hall, with the versatile P. N. Utt (listed

† The large number of French names in New York's public activities at this period can be attributed to the French Revolution and the upheavals in Haiti; among the refugees were many musicians, artists, dancing masters, and fencing masters. William Dunlap, who had known them personally, singled out the musicians, in his *History of the American Theatre,* as a particularly skillful and colorful group, most of them "gentlemen who had seen better days, . . . some of them nobles, some officers in the army of the king."

in the city directories variously as musical instrument maker, ship-master, tavern-, porterhouse-, and coffeehouse-keeper, and "teacher of musick") as flutist, and George Geib (merely music dealer and teacher) as pianist.

But the city did not have to go many years without a Philharmonic Society. A second Philharmonic—today as unjustly forgotten as the first—was founded in 1824. A New York Philharmonic Society at that date might reasonably be expected to follow the pattern of London's (which had been in existence since 1813), but, surprisingly, it was based on almost opposite principles. The London Philharmonic had been established by professional musicians, and all its Directors, Members, and Associates were required to be professionals. The second New York Philharmonic, on the other hand, was the creature of wealthy and socially prominent laymen, who went so far as to provide in their Constitution: "No Professor of Music, or Teacher of Music, shall be a Governor of the Institution." (The intention was probably to prevent ambitious professionals from using the Society as a spring-board for their careers.)

The Philharmonic of 1824 does, on the contrary, show traces of descent from the defunct New York Philharmonic of 1799. It even seems likely, for at least one section of the 1824 Constitution, that the framers had the 1799 Constitution before them as they worked. Almost identical words are used in prescribing the insignia to be worn by officers and members—the rosettes, the ribbons, and the silver lyres, harps, and keys [see page 45]—down to the same misspelling of "coquelicot" as "Coquilicot" and the same grammatical misuse of "cross keys" for "crossed keys." Such traditional patterns may ultimately have been descended from British and European practices, but in New York they could be inherited by the second Philharmonic directly from the first one.

The second Philharmonic was not very democratic in its administration. It was neither the musicians nor the Subscribers but the so-called Governors who ran all its affairs. A Governor was a contributor of $50 plus an annual subscription of $5; he had the privilege of taking two ladies with him to all concerts and rehearsals, and it seems only fair that he should get more for his $50 donation than an ordinary Subscriber of $5 annually, who was entitled to admission for himself and *one* lady to the Public Concerts only. But, beyond that, only a

Governor could become a Director of the Society, or an Officer, or a member of the Sub-Committee that managed all performances, personnel matters, and finances, or one of the Trustees who took care of properties and funds. The Constitution could not even be amended except by vote of the Governors.

In that kind of privileged atmosphere, it is not surprising that the list of Governors of the second New York Philharmonic, published at the end of the Constitution, reads like a roll call of New York's fashionable society. A small sampling includes an Astor, a Brevoort, Philip Hone (who would be mayor of the city in 1825–26) and two more Hones, Clement C. Moore (son of the Episcopal Bishop of New York, professor of theology in the General Theological Seminary, and author of " 'Twas the night before Christmas . . ."), E. Malibran (the merchant whose marriage to the great singing star, the Signorina Maria García, in 1826, would give her the name that she was to make worldfamous), six Joneses of varying degrees of wealth, three of the patrician Schermerhorns, three Delafields, a Rhinelander, and a Roosevelt.[13]

If the second Philharmonic was not democratic, it was at least benevolent. The Constitution and By-Laws outlined two imaginative projects that had not even been approached by the 1799 Society. One was a sort of insurance system for professional musicians. "In order to foster and encourage the science of Music," the Society guaranteed that, for all professors or teachers of music who engaged to give their "best services" to the Society at all concerts and rehearsals for three years, it would pay the sum of $150 to the widow, orphans, or heirs of the musician if he should die within that period. If he agreed to serve for a period of five years, the benefit would be $500, for seven years $800, and for ten years $1,000—unless he should "by immoral or improper conduct render himself obnoxious to the Society."

The other benevolent project was a plan for encouraging local composers by premiums or prizes of money. Seven categories were set up— song, vocal duet, glee, piano concerto, violin concerto, overture and sinfonie, and "other orchestral pieces"—and two of them were to be chosen for the prizes each year. Monthly meetings were established for performing the music submitted for these prizes and also for the purpose of "practising and of encouraging Amateurs, by affording opportunities and facilities for playing and singing in concert."

The second Philharmonic was in advance of most musical societies of its time in an important point of musical organization: it had appointed a permanent conductor for the season, instead of choosing a new one for each concert.[14] His name, D. Ettienne (this is Denis G. Etienne, slightly misspelled), was printed along with those of the Directors, facing the first page of the Constitution. Etienne was a highly respected pianist, conductor, and teacher—also horn player when necessary—who had been one of the leaders of the city's musical life since 1816 and would remain active in it until the 1850s.

For more than three years, from March 1824 to the end of 1827, the second Philharmonic was an important force in New York's musical life. Announcements of its meetings and concerts appeared frequently in the *American,* the *Post,* and other newspapers, and they represent a great deal of excellent music-making. Some of the best New York musicians were involved with the second Philharmonic in one capacity or another. Diligent conductors and organizers like Etienne, E. C. Riley, and P. H. Taylor were subscribing members. The young U. C. Hill, already considered one of the city's finest musicians, played violin in the orchestra. The popular soprano Louisa Gillingham made an exclusive agreement in 1824 not to appear in public "other than in the orchestra of the Philharmonic Society." Other musicians were invited to perform under the Society's sponsorship—Miss Kelly of the Park Theatre, Madame Brichta, the much admired contralto, Gilles, the cellist. The Philharmonic made some effort to keep abreast of the times in its programs. The concerts, in the style of the day, alternated orchestral works and opera selections with solo and chamber pieces, and much of the music stemmed from the preceding fifteen or twenty-five years—from Rossini, Méhul, Boieldieu, and some of the English and German composers of the period. But among the contemporaries who were played on Philharmonic programs was also Beethoven, part of whose Second Symphony was given in the very first Public Concert, on December 16, 1824—one of the earliest concert performances of a Beethoven orchestral work in New York—and more of whose music was performed at subsequent concerts.[15] The second Philharmonic Society had a certain amount of competition from other musical organizations of the city, such as the Sacred Music Society, the Euterpean Society, and the Choral Society, but it seems for the most part to have been a healthy and friendly competition.[16]

The really serious competition, affecting not only the Philharmonic

Society but all musical performances in New York, came from outside the city, in the second season of the Society, in the form of the
Italian Opera Company of Manuel García, which opened on November 29, 1825, with Rossini's *Il Barbiere di Siviglia*. The great sensation
of the company was García's young daughter, the Signorina Maria
Felicitá García, soon to be called affectionately by the New York public
just "the Signorina." It was the moment in New York's cultural history
for the fashionable upper classes, the theater lovers, and the music
lovers to appreciate a skillful Italian troupe that offered the snob appeal
of performance in a foreign language, and the genuine attractions of
good acting and the Signorina's superb voice. The success was perhaps
the greatest that the New York stage had known. The Philharmonic
Society had had some unofficial connections with the opera company
from the start: Etienne, the conductor of the Philharmonic, "presided at the piano" in the excellent twenty-five-piece orchestra employed for the opera, and at least half a dozen other players in the
opera orchestra were regular subscribing members of the Society. But
when the Philharmonic recognized the magnitude of the Garcías' triumph, it adopted the only possible strategy—it invited the Garcías to
appear officially in the Society's concerts. It was considered a great
coup when the Philharmonic secured them for its concert of December 22, 1825, at the City Hotel. The advertisement in the *Post* included the phrases of traffic instruction that New Yorkers recognized
as a sign that a very large and very elegant crowd was expected: "All
carriages . . . will range with their horses heads down Broadway; and
on returning for the company, will take their station on the side of the
street opposite to the Hotel. No carriage will be suffered to draw up to
the door, until required by the party for whom it is in attendance. An
efficient police will be engaged to enforce the regulation." The Garcías,
with the entire Italian company, appeared twice more in that season
"under the patronage of the Philharmonic Society."

In spite of its excellent organization and its apparent success, the
second Philharmonic was unable to survive. In the fall of 1827 a
meeting was announced for November 3 in foreboding terms: ". . . the
further continuance of the Society will depend on the results of this
meeting." The press did carry word of another meeting set for December 1, but after that the Society seems to have given no more public
concerts and it is not even clear whether its private sessions lasted out

the season of 1827–28. The New York *Mirror,* looking wistfully backward several years later, on January 3, 1835, remarked that the Philharmonic Society had given "several excellent concerts, and was of infinite service to the cause of music, by manifesting to the public what effects a powerful band were enabled to create; but, from some cause, this society died, what we may well term, an unnatural death; it ceased to exist from want of support, and from the apathy of those who should have sustained it."

There are several possible explanations for the "apathy" and "want of support" that characterized the disappearance of the second Philharmonic.

The great flowering of home music-making was distracting the concert public to the point where audiences were dropping off noticeably from 1827 on. The *Albion* of January 26, 1828, tells us that such name singers as Horn, Pearman, and Mrs. Austin had drawn only about two hundred persons for one of their finest performances, and it then attempts (with just a touch of sarcasm) to analyze the situation: "The spread of music and the general introduction of the piano into private families, lessens the keenness for the theatres—for who will be at the trouble and expense of going to a theatre to hear a bad song, when they can be admirably accommodated with the same thing at home." The period from 1827 to 1831 seems to have been one of satiety with all public performances except the most exciting and sensational. It brings to mind the drain that television made on public attendance in the 1950s.

A peculiar craze, moreover, flooded New York in the season of 1828–29, drawing off the energies and resources that would otherwise have gone into musical entertainments and the theater. This was a mania for masquerade balls. It seems to have begun with parties in private homes, but soon spread to the theaters, which converted themselves into ballrooms by flooring over the pit even with the stage. These alterations and the fancy decorations that went with them were so extensive that a theater was usually not available for ordinary performances the night before a ball. When the Park Theatre gave a Grand Fancy Masquerade Ball on March 3, 1829, the preparations forced the cancellation of the appearance of C. E. Horn and Mrs. Austin, which had been scheduled for March 2. Balls were sponsored not only by the Park, but also by the Bowery, Chatham, and Lafayette Theatres, Masonic Hall, the City Hotel Assembly Room, and by a number of dancing masters. While the masquerade mania lasted, it unquestionably hurt the concert business.‡

For such a moment in New York's musical history, the second Philharmonic's plan may have been at once too sober and too ambitious. What with its prizes for local composers, and its "life insurance" benefits for the orchestra musicians, it would have required a huge financial and civic commitment.

But perhaps the most powerful and invincible force competing with the second Philharmonic was at the opposite pole from the encouragement of domestic musicians or the simple pleasures of making music at home. It was the importation of exotic entertainments from abroad—Italian and French opera and ballet—to which the New York fashionables, including the class from which Governors of the Philharmonic had to be drawn, succumbed increasingly from 1825 on, turning away from the plainer attractions of concerts. The public, said the *Mirror* in 1828, "like practised *gourmands* have lost all relish for simple, wholesome food." This worked so deep a change in New York's musical habits and tastes that it made some of the old Philharmonic's aims meaningless and others futile. What point could there be in giving prizes for American compositions, when the ideal compositions had become European? What point in encouraging local performers with "insurance," when the public was being trained to wait only for the next glamorous import?

For about fourteen years after the disappearance of the second Philharmonic, New York had no Philharmonic Society. But they were not sterile years. They were years of ferment and transition that helped to prepare the way for the founding in 1842 of a third Philharmonic. They were the years in which the musical orientation of the city began to shift from English-American to continental, in which New York developed a corps of experienced orchestra personnel equal to the demands of the nineteenth-century repertory, and in which the social and economic foundations of the 1842 Philharmonic were laid.

‡ Masquerade prices were purposely set high in order to keep the company "select." But apparently respectability was not maintained: in the spring of 1829 the state legislature passed a law against masquerades in theaters and public places, imposing a penalty of $1,000 against the proprietors for each violation. By the next year, the law may have been somewhat relaxed or at least broadly interpreted, since the Park Theatre on February 17, 1830, gave a masquerade ball for which four hundred gentlemen subscribed, at $5 for a gentleman and two ladies, each gentleman signing in twenty-four hours in advance so that inquiry could be made about him.

Chapter 5

The Changing Tradition

Throughout the first quarter of the nineteenth century, that is, until about the time of the second Philharmonic, the prevailing musical atmosphere in New York had remained heavily English and heavily vocal. Within that English-American tradition, however, a considerable increase in sophistication had taken place by 1825 in the expanding public that could afford to cultivate music. At the beginning of the century, the musical taste of the citizenry had been strongly influenced by the Yankee singing masters (themselves descendants of an old English tradition), with their vernacular arts of psalmody and ballad singing, and the peculiar nasal tone that was their earmark. But an increasingly genteel New York was aching to dispel "the utter barbarism into which we all had innocently been plunged,"[17] and in 1817 two very polished British singers, Charles Incledon and Thomas Philipps, introduced a subtler style that revolutionized the city's taste. For many years afterward, New Yorkers divided their musical history into "before Incledon and Philipps" and "after them." These two artists replaced the rigid repertory and the provincial twang of the singing masters by a varied art that required sensitive nuancing and phrasing, judicious embellishment, and a clear, round tone. They applied it to both opera and concert. By the time that another fine English singer, Pearman, came to New York in the fall of 1823, the new style had won the field and the best people in town had made themselves its champions.

This was the point in the evolution of New York taste that had been reached when the second Philharmonic was founded in 1824. It was still very much an English taste. Incledon, Philipps, and Pearman made their theatrical successes in such English operas as Bishop's *The Devil's Bridge* and Dibdin's *The Waterman*. A typical concert (in which both Incledon and Philipps performed), on July 24, 1818, at the Park Theatre, was built around British songs and duets by Arne, Bishop, Braham, Hook, Jackson, Kelly, Storace, and Webb, and a Scottish national air. The orchestral Overture and Sinfonie (no composers named) that began the first and second halves of the concert may possibly have come from other countries, but if they did, they were likely to have stopped in London for approval.

It was not just music or aesthetics that won the day for the suave art of Incledon, Philipps, and Pearman. Powerful social pressures were at work. Young men and women found that they could use the supple new style to circumvent social restrictions—"to awaken in young hearts and communicate from one to another the softest and most tender feelings. Sentiments which, in a plain dress of prose, could not have appeared in any company, now stole in every where under the winning disguises which the artist had woven for them."[18] Just as the waltz owed some of its popularity to its liberties of physical contact—to the fact that it permitted a man and a woman, in effect, to embrace in public—so did the new musical taste feed on its liberties of sentimental communication, which permitted a man and a woman to court each other through "the artifices of poetry and music."

The new style had another social force in its favor—fashion. "A more elegant and fashionable audience have never assembled in the Park Theatre," sang the press after one of Pearman's performances. This is a comment that recurs with the regularity of a refrain in the newspapers of the period. Elegance, modishness, and refinement were qualities that were becoming important to a society in which more and more people had the time and the money to spend on such edifications. And English-language opera and concerts, now that they were being offered on a high artistic level—far removed from the embarrassing crudities of the Yankee "Twangoros"—were more than acceptable as a "source of rational and refined enjoyment." Accordingly, a whole literature of English pieces, stamped with London's endorsement, was welcomed in New York, and important foreign-language operas, like *Der Freischütz*, were presented in English versions.

From the social and artistic success of the English musical culture

in New York, it seemed that it should be a natural and a short step
to a specifically *American* musical culture that also used the English
language. Elegance and refinement were still compatible with a kind of
cultural nationalism in 1824. The patrician second Philharmonic was
trying earnestly at that very moment to encourage local composers and
performers with prizes and insurance benefits. The signs of the hopeful
nationalism were everywhere. When Samuel Woodworth's *La Fayette,
or, the Castle of Olmutz* was announced in 1824, George P. Morris
himself, the founder of the New York *Mirror,* initialed an article ex-
horting "all who wish to *encourage dramatic writing in America,* . . .
to attend the theater on this occasion. The only way to *make authors*
in this country, is to encourage every well-meant *effort,* and thus induce
a *perseverance* which may ultimately reflect honour on our country."
The rewards of such encouragement had already begun to show in
1825, when the *Mirror* of September 17 could proudly announce:

> *American Opera.*—We perceive by the play-bills, that a new pastoral
> opera is in rehearsal at Chatham Theatre, entitled the *"Forest Rose, or
> American Farmers."* It was written by a gentleman of this city [Samuel
> Woodworth again]; and the MUSIC, (which is entirely *original,*) com-
> posed by JOHN DAVIES, ESQ. well known as a professor, and formerly
> leader of the orchestra in Chatham Garden. [Davies was also a member
> of the Philharmonic Society.] The piece is, therefore, truly an *American
> production,* and the second entire opera, we believe, that has ever been
> composed on this side the Atlantic. Being favored with a perusal of this
> piece, and permitted to be present at the rehearsal of the overture, to-
> gether with several songs, duetts, trios, &c. we did propose giving our
> opinion of them; but have been expressly prohibited both by the drama-
> tist and composer, from anything that can possibly be construed into a
> *puff.* They both insist upon the propriety of letting the production rest
> upon its own intrinsic merits, if it possess any. We are, consequently,
> only permitted to say, that the *Forest Rose* is comprised in two acts,
> abounding with original songs, calculated to elevate the character of
> *American Farmers,* and excite in our citizens a taste for rural recreations,
> and domestic enjoyments. The scene lies in New Jersey, near the beauti-
> ful village of Newark, a distant view of which, we understand, will be
> presented on the stage . . .

The next month the same periodical, in reporting a benefit performance of the opera, had the pleasure of invoking for an American
production New York's classic incantation of success: "A more numer-

ous assembly of beauty, fashion, and taste, has never before crowded within the walls of Chatham." Beauty, fashion, and taste! Then American musical art had made the grade—it was accepted by the arbiters of New York's elegance.

The *Forest Rose,* as an individual work, was to remain popular for many decades. It is possible that, if the school that it represented had been nurtured with the full support of its community, an indigenous American musical theater might have had something like a natural growth in the nineteenth century. In many ways the American comic opera was ready, as the German *Singspiel* had been in a somewhat analogous situation, to expand into a national Romantic opera on its own terms. But within less than three months after the opening of the *Forest Rose,* the very foundations of the vernacular musical theater were shaken by the spectacular success and the artistic revelations of García's Italian opera company. The second Philharmonic was severely shaken, too, as we have seen, and managed to recover its balance— for a short time—only by the expedient of leaning on the Italian opera company for support.

From this point on, New York's musical orientation would continue to shift from an English-American to a continental European direction.

"We were at a loss which to admire most," exulted the press after the opening of the Italian opera, "the powerful vocal talents of the operatic corps, or the galaxy of fashion and beauty that listened with admiration and applause." It was significant that the reporter was at a loss which to admire most. It meant that the musical triumph was once again reinforced by the social power of fashion. But this time the foreign transplant was siphoning off the sustenance that local art, including the second Philharmonic and the English-language opera, required in order to live. In the spring of 1826 it was reported that some prominent citizens were getting together to talk about establishing Italian opera as a permanent and separate institution in the city, and a few observers began to fear that they might have welcomed a Trojan horse within their walls. "We are sorry to observe," complained the *Mirror* on June 17, 1826, "that the Italian opera threatens to exclude the English from the stage . . . Though we were much gratified to witness the liberality with which the foreign opera was patronized on its first introduction into this city, we did not expect to see it so wholly engross the attention of the public, as to leave the music of our own language neglected."

Even home music was affected by the taste for the foreign. Since the advent of the Italian opera, reports the *Mirror,* "every lady warbles delightful, unintelligible Italian. English is getting out of fashion; and while the unsuspecting old folks are sitting back on the sofa, congratulating themselves on their daughter's proficiency in music, what all those fine flourishes are about is best known to the glowing girl, and peradventure to the very agreeable young gentleman who leans over her shoulder to turn the leaves, and who is very much astonished when the clock strikes eleven."[19] Our writer teases, but he is basically sympathetic with the attitude that ties elegance to foreignness.

To keep the account just, it should be mentioned that the Signorina herself—the star around whom the Italian opera company revolved— appeared also in English opera. When her husband, Malibran, suffered business losses, she took an engagement at the new Bowery Theatre at $500 a night, opening with tremendous success in *The Devil's Bridge.* This was received, however, less as the great goddess giving her talents to the vernacular theater than as her *elevating* it to her own level of refinement. On the evenings when she performed, the price of admission was doubled to make the audience "select," and arrangements were made "to prevent the audience of the upper tiers admittance to the lower tier." Her farewell performance, on October 29, 1827, illustrates the internationalization that had taken place in New York's music and theater. Compare it with the 1818 program of Incledon and Philipps (described on page 55), in which almost everything was British. The Signorina appeared first in Boieldieu's *John of Paris.* Then there were five numbers in Italian, two in French, one in German, and one in Spanish. Finally, she came forward to the footlights to accompany herself on the harp in a farewell song in English, written for her by her colleague Keene.*

The departure of the Signorina did not by any means signal the end of the foreign influence. The visits of French performers had been growing in frequency and success since 1826. In the summer of 1827 a company from New Orleans gave highly praised presentations of opera by Boieldieu, Auber, Dalayrac, Bochsa, Fétis, Cherubini, and Weber. The *Mirror* found the troupe far above mediocrity, its success

---

* But she was too moved to play—she rose, and the ubiquitous Etienne, still presiding at the piano (and presumably still conductor of the second Philharmonic at that date), accompanied her as she sang.

assured by the large foreign population of the city "—in conjunction with two such powerful auxiliaries as fashion and curiosity."

These powerful auxiliaries were joined by another at least as powerful—sex—when, in February 1827, the Bowery Theatre presented Madame Francisque Hutin in a season of French ballet, preceded by provocative reports that she was very scantily clad when she danced. This proved to be no exaggeration, according to New York's standards of 1827, and at her first bound onto the stage "the cheeks of the greater portion of the audience were crimsoned with shame, and every lady in the lower tier of boxes immediately left the house."[20] Fashion, curiosity, and sex were more than a match for pudency, however, and it was not long before New York was as much at ease with the conventional ballet undress of Madame Hutin, Madame Achille, Celeste, and other French dancers, as with the music they danced to.[21]

Throughout the 1830s the French and Italian performers continued to charm the paying public in the theaters, and often in the concert halls as well. And always the inescapable determining word was "FASHION." By 1833 a number of wealthy and socially prominent New Yorkers were so anxious to acquire what the press constantly referred to as a "refined musical taste" that they built expressly for an imported Italian opera company—of mediocre quality—the most sumptuous theater that the country had ever known. *What is significant for Philharmonic history is that a large part of the money that supported the new venture came from the pockets that had formerly maintained the second Philharmonic!* Among the box subscribers for the Italian opera, mentioned by Philip Hone in his diary entry for September 16, 1833, are the following individuals and families who had been Governors of the 1824 Philharmonic: Hone, Schermerhorn, General Jones, James J. Jones, Coster, Howland, Prime, Ray, Lynch, and Hall.

The private boxes in the new opera house cost $6,000 each. Philip Hone attended the opening performance, *La Gazza Ladra,* on November 19, 1833, and found it tiresome. He was nevertheless willing to suffer through four hours of it at huge financial cost because it was "splendid and refined." The "proprietors" of the opera house (the gentlemen who had subscribed its costs) tried to outdo each other in the magnificence with which they decorated their private boxes: some of the boxes were painted in fresco; some had rich silk hangings and ornaments; some had gilded panels and cornices; and all were furnished with luxurious sofas and armchairs. While the city's wealth and fashion

were preoccupied with this exclusive and glamorous toy, it was very unlikely that they would find a Philharmonic Society as interesting as it
had seemed to them in 1824.

If the Philharmonic could no longer have the patronage of the few,
the fancy Italian opera was not for the many. Shortly after the opening
of the new house, the *Mirror* (which, only seven years before, had
cautioned against a foreign take-over) tried to shame the public into
attending with the warning that if the Italian experiment failed it
would signify that the Western Hemisphere was not ready for the
spread of a refined musical taste. That seemed to be the case. Half
a century later, when the identification of the foreign with the musical
was complete in New York, it would be possible with the aid of the
aspiring wealthy to sustain whole seasons of opera that were linguis-
tically and culturally almost incomprehensible to the listeners.[22] But
in the mid-1830s the Italian opera sank under the weight of its own
extravagance and snobbishness. The wealthy clique was not quite able
to carry the enterprise alone, and it made no sense for ordinary citizens
to patronize the Italian opera house. The prices were too high. The
singers were not as good as many they had heard before, or could hear
right then in English at the Park Theatre. And the lavishly decorated
private boxes, with their cushioned sofas and armchairs, offended the
democratic sensitivities of those who had to sit in the plain seats of
other parts of the house.

Upon the departure of the Italian opera company in 1835, the fashionable audience was reluctant to leave its opulent theater for the ordinary Park Theatre, but it soon readapted and the Park, with its
English opera, became the rage again. With the advantage of hindsight
one can see, however, that each foreign invasion left the Anglo-American tradition a bit weaker, both in concert and in opera. The second
Philharmonic had been unable to function at all after 1827. But the
English-language opera, elastic because of its strong roots in a popular
culture, made several temporary recoveries, particularly when gifted
singing actors were imported from England—Mrs. Edward Knight in
1826, Charles Edward Horn in 1827, Mrs. Austin in 1828, the queen
of English vocalists, Mrs. Wood, in 1833, and others throughout the
1830s. New York heard, and heard often, in those years, English
versions of operas by Rossini, Bellini, Donizetti, Mozart, Weber, Beethoven, Auber, Boieldieu, Meyerbeer, Arne, Horn, Bishop, Watson,
Davies.[23]

Meanwhile, in addition to the French and the Italians, German musicians had begun to make their presence felt, especially in instrumental music. In the 1830s (and increasingly after 1835) skilled German pianists and players of wind and stringed instruments were taking jobs in the theater orchestras, giving lessons, and occasionally appearing on concert programs. Orchestral works of Haydn, Mozart, Weber, Beethoven, and other German-Austrian composers had long been coming to America by way of England, but additional and more recent examples now began to arrive directly from the continent, along with much piano and chamber music. The German community of New York had its own Concordia society for the cultivation of instrumental and vocal music. In fact, the bulk of New York's German population remained culturally segregated from the rest of the city—there were not likely to be many non-Germans around when beer and a concert were sociably mixed at Schilling's Salon at "6 Strasse Tompkins." But certain well-schooled German players, like Timm and Scharfenberg, were eagerly accepted by the city's other musicians and by a small, select circle of the local intelligentsia and lovers of music. These German artists made music with some of the best musicians of the city in various private homes and sometimes in public concerts, and their influence, focused on such effective portions of the community, was penetrating even before their numbers were large.

New York's music world, which until about 1825 had been strongly Anglo-American, had become, in the short space of ten or fifteen years, a cosmopolitan mixture. For a while, the vernacular tradition continued side by side with the foreign ones, occasionally jealous of them, but more often dreaming of building a solid American art by the proven American method of combining the best native elements with the best imported ones—from England, Italy, France, Germany, or anywhere else. But the mixture was not socially stable. As the use of the vernacular in music declined, it was inevitable that some of the broad popular audience for concerts and opera would be lost, and that those activities would come to be considered "high-brow." The gallery customers who had paid 12½¢ or 25¢ to enjoy the familiar idiom of their musical theater in English could not be expected to pay four to eight times that much to listen to singers whose language they could not even understand; they sought out their own "lighter" musical entertainments. And it was equally inevitable, since vernacular vocal music was falling in prestige, that segments of the wealthy or intellectual upper classes should ally themselves instead with foreign instrumental music, especially the German, which was the most impressive school of instrumental music at the time. In 1839 or 1840, the separation between the "foreign-serious" and the "native-popular" was still far from complete, but the affinity of the wealthy and the educated for the foreign was growing, and anything as refined as a Philharmonic Society would now be expected to have a strong infusion of the European in it from the outset.[24] The new conditions were, in fact, favorable for the formation of a new style of Philharmonic, devoted chiefly to the kind of instrumental music for large orchestra that was currently being cultivated in Europe, and avoiding vernacular vocal music on principle, as well as because it was not organically suited to performance by such an orchestra.

The very changes in tradition—from English-American to continental European—that had helped to subvert the second Philharmonic socially and economically, by luring away its audiences and its financial support, were now, in an ironic reversal, helping to make possible a third Philharmonic.

Chapter 6

Bigger and Better Orchestras
(1825–39)

In the same fifteen years that saw the shift toward continental musical traditions, New York was also developing the players who would be necessary for an orchestra capable of handling the literature of the Romantic era. And once again an apparent rival of the second Philharmonic—the musical theater, both imported and domestic, with all its spectacular seductions—turned out, in the long run, to be an ally of the cause. There was seldom a sharp line, in the first half of the nineteenth century, between theater performers and concert performers. The theater orchestras built up a reservoir of concert musicians in the city by providing jobs for them. And from the opposite direction, the concert activities provided additional income and additional performing experience for the singers and instrumentalists of the theater staffs.

The handful of histories of American music that have been written exaggerate the shortage of instrumentalists in New York City before 1830. García has usually been given credit for introducing the first proper theater orchestra in his Italian opera performances of 1825–26. He may well have elevated the artistic level, but he did not bring his orchestra with him. It was made up of New York musicians—who were already so well-known in the city that their names were used as an attraction in the advertisements for the opera. Many of them, in fact, were members of the Philharmonic Society of 1824, including Etienne, the Philharmonic's conductor, who presided at the piano in García's orchestra.[25]

Each New York theater, long before García and long after him, had a small but permanent orchestra, which not only played appropriate supporting music for the dramatic action in every play, but often performed overtures and other instrumental pieces between the two or more plays that made up an evening's program. For example, when the great Charles and Fanny Kemble appeared in 1832 in such plays as Shakespeare's *Hamlet* and Sheridan Knowles's *The Hunchback,* the playbills advertised that the orchestra would play the overtures to Rossini's *Semiramide,* Mozart's *Don Giovanni,* and Weber's *Oberon,* and a "New Overture" by Bishop. In this way the players in the theater orchestras gained experience in certain areas of the concert literature and helped to educate their audiences in that literature too. The theatergoing public knew by heart—much more than the corresponding public does today—the standard overtures and many other pieces of the most respected composers, to which they were exposed night after night. It reached the point, around 1830, where the press actually carried complaints of too much repetition of the familiar pieces. The *Mirror*'s critic, on October 23, 1830, praises the Park Theatre for its excellent operatic music but scolds that "the music played by the band on ordinary nights [as incidental music for plays] is worn out." Three or four overtures are used too much, he says—Mozart's *Marriage of Figaro,* Weber's *Der Freischütz,* Auber's *Masaniello,* and Boieldieu's *Caliph of Bagdad.* A correspondent who signs himself by the reassuring name of Joseph Steady writes to the paper on December 22, 1832, that a person of his acquaintance, who has a season ticket, is inclined to believe "that the various fiddles and flutes of the band could play everything in that set of books without the aid of the men; and that the musicians go to sleep frequently, entrusting the music entirely to the instruments!"

The permanent pit orchestras in the theaters were necessarily small, not because of a shortage of musicians in the city, but because the theaters could seldom afford either the space or the money that large orchestras required. The Park Theatre in the mid-1830s usually had about 18 players. Montresor's Italian opera company at the Richmond Hill Theatre in 1832–33 had 20. At all New York theaters, enlarged orchestras were sometimes advertised for special occasions or for specially weighty compositions, but in theater work a larger orchestra might even prove a disadvantage—it could mean trouble with acoustics and balances. The orchestra of the beautiful Italian opera house that was built in 1833 was only slightly larger than Montresor's, with 25 or 27 men,[26] but it was criticized by the *Evening Star* as "rather too powerful for the size of the house"—a house which, with its much-vaunted carpets and upholstery, should have been better able to absorb large volumes of sound than most other New York auditoriums. For most purposes, and for many years, 18 or 20 men was considered a reasonable size for a theater orchestra.*

These little orchestras tended to ingrain some good habits and some very bad ones in their musicians. Since every man had to pull his full weight through the unpredictable hazards of musical theater performances, he had to be independent, resourceful, musically alert, and a good sight reader. But he also grew accustomed to playing loudly and roughly much of the time, and out of tune some of the time; he was likely to appear in public with insufficient rehearsal, and to ignore the subtleties of blending into an artistic ensemble. In the rosters of such theater orchestras can be found many—indeed, most—of the musicians who would soon help to make possible the third Philharmonic, and they would inevitably bring to the early efforts of that organization both the defects and the virtues of their theater training.

As for concert orchestras, the brief lull at the end of the 1820s, when the second Philharmonic seems to have disappeared, was followed by a busy intensification of concert activities in the 1830s. Though the Philharmonic succumbed, some of New York's other music societies managed to recover; moreover, almost all the theater musicians took part in concerts, which generally involved an orchestra of some kind, and enterprising individuals continued to organize the charmingly variegated programs characteristic of the period, enlisting both the professional and the amateur talents of the city. Many of the same people who had been active in the old Philharmonic turn up in the concerts of the Sacred Music Society, the Musical Fund Society, the

---

* Ritter tells us (*Music in America,* p. 213) that in 1837–38 the regular pit orchestra at the Park Theatre consisted of 21 musicians. He lists them as: 6 violins, 2 violas, 2 cellos, 2 basses, 1 flute and another flute to cover the oboe part, 2 clarinets, 2 bassoons, 2 horns, 1 trumpet, 1 trombone, and drums. But Ritter, as Krehbiel sums him up, "is a historian who must be read with extreme caution in all things"—anyone who can make that list of instruments add up to 21 is as good a mathematician as Ritter.

Amateur Musical Fund Society (separate from the preceding), and the Euterpean Society, which, in the long view, can also be seen as connecting links with the greater Philharmonic that would be founded in 1842.

Take as an example the concert that the New York Musical Fund Society gave at Masonic Hall on June 10, 1830. One of the soloists was Louisa Gillingham, who will be remembered from 1824 for her agreement to perform exclusively with the Philharmonic; in the orchestra of twenty-eight players we can recognize Etienne (playing horn this time!) and at least three others as subscribing members of the old Philharmonic. But equally significant is the presence in the same pivotal orchestra, in 1830, of half a dozen musicians who would be playing twelve years later in the third Philharmonic: Ureli Corelli Hill as leader, W. H. Sage, violin, D. Walker, cello, A. Reiff, clarinet (he played bassoon in the later Philharmonic), W. Plain, trombone, and W. Wood, drum.

The orchestras that played at these concerts were not permanent organizations, but rather what are spoken of today as "pickup" orchestras, made up of free-lance musicians assembled for each occasion. Many of the musicians who played with the Sacred Music Society may be found also in the concerts of the Musical Fund and Euterpean Societies, and of course they were often the same men who played in the theaters. "The orchestra will embrace all the talent in the city," runs one of the constantly recurring advertising formulas of the day.

Throughout the 1830s, these concert orchestras were increasing in skill over the standards of the preceding decade, and growing in size at the same time (as the theater orchestras could not). An orchestra of 35 players was considered a sizable one in Europe as well as in the United States—Mendelssohn used about that number in his world-famous Gewandhaus Orchestra in Leipzig after 1835—yet larger ones were found frequently in New York concerts in the 1830s. The New York Musical Fund employed a professional orchestra of 38 for a concert in 1834. In the same year, the New York Sacred Music Society gave Handel's *Messiah* (with Mozart's additions to the score, of course), using an orchestra of 42 instruments and a chorus of 135 voices. Or, jumping a few years to January 30, 1839, we find the Euterpean Society enjoying a particularly fine and well-balanced orchestra of at least 40 musicians at its fortieth anniversary concert.[27] And the quality of the players was higher than has usually been supposed. When U. C. Hill visited Europe in 1835 he noted in his diary that some of the players in Spohr's orchestra in Kassel were not up to New York standards. We know the names of the men who supplied the leadership for these New York orchestras.† It is not surprising that they are the same men who, within a few years, would be building the third Philharmonic.

Paralleling the technical advances were aesthetic and educational ones, preparing the kind of atmosphere in which a Philharmonic Society could eventually thrive.

Music criticism, although it retained the candor and asperity characteristic of New York's newspaper style (it must have taken courage for a critic to walk the streets unprotected after calling a musician "inferior," a "thumper," a "sad bungler at the violin," or a "torturer of catgut"), was becoming considerably more knowing. When an English musician named Gear, who had settled in New York, organized a concert on May 27, 1831, the *Mirror's* man called it "altogether . . . one of the best we have attended in America," but he let nobody get away with anything. He observed that the violins did not use mutes as the score required in a *scena* from *Der Freischütz;* that Rossini's *Guillaume Tell* Overture calls for a minimum of six cellos in its first movement and that Mr. Gear, who couldn't get that many, used four violas to make up the difference; and that the solo in Rossini's second movement, played on a clarinet in this concert, was really written for the *corno inglese,* "an instrument of beautiful and peculiar quality, and totally unknown in this country."‡ As for Mr. Gear, Sr., who performed on the double bass (he had been principal bass of the second Philharmonic), he "played Handel's air, the 'Harmonious Blacksmith,' *a la Dragonetti,* with no particular effect but that of making himself extremely warm."

Audiences, as well as critics, were growing more sophisticated. A single example will illustrate how discriminating they had become in their choices. In the summer of 1834, both Niblo's Garden and the Vauxhall Garden, popular entertainment resorts where refreshments

† Alfred Boucher for the Musical Fund concert, William Penson for the Sacred Music Society's *Messiah,* Dr. J. M. Quin (aided by Boucher, U. C. Hill, M. Rapetti, and W. H. Sage) for the Euterpean Society.

‡ Not quite. In a concert given by Anthony Philip Heinrich on May 4, 1821, in Philadelphia, there was a *Divertimento (alla Marcia)* of his composition, for timpani and eleven wind instruments, including a "Corno Inglese, [played] by an Amateur."

and music were mingled, gave whole series not just of regular concerts but also of Sacred Concerts of the music of Handel, Haydn, Mozart, and Beethoven, and ordinary New Yorkers thronged to hear them at an average admission price of 25¢. Emboldened by these successes, the Vauxhall, with its excellent but small forces, announced a complete production of Beethoven's *Christ on the Mount of Olives*. Then, as the *American Musical Journal* (October 1834) related approvingly, the "public seemed to be aware of the absurdity of attempting to perform the splendid choruses of Beethoven with ten or a dozen chorus singers, and wisely staid away—a decided proof of their good judgment . . . [When] an entire Oratorio is offered, they naturally inquire into the capability and resources of the establishment to produce it in a proper manner."

With orchestras, between 1830 and 1839, growing toward the levels required for the grand symphonic literature of the nineteenth century, and audiences and critics keeping pace with the professional growth, it would take only a final spurt of activity, in the three years from 1839 to 1842, to carry the development to its natural resolution in another Philharmonic Society.

Chapter 7

The Final Spurt
(1839–42)

On June 8, 1839, a young German-Jewish musician named Daniel
Schlesinger died in New York.[28] His death, at the age of thirty-nine,
after less than three years in his new country, evoked a response of
astonishing depth and extent in New York's music community. A committee of fifteen gentlemen organized on an imposing scale a "Grand
Musical Solemnity," or memorial concert, which enlisted the services
of an impressive array of the musicians of the city, attracted an audience of at least two thousand people who jammed the cavernous
Broadway Tabernacle "almost to suffocation," and raised close to
$3,500 for the family that Schlesinger left behind him. Tradition has it
that the Grand Musical Solemnity, given on June 25, 1839, made such
an overwhelming impression on the musicians and the audience that it
"was largely responsible for forming the Philharmonic."[29]

This is an exaggeration, of course. Common sense tells us that a
single successful concert in 1839 cannot be largely responsible for the
establishment of a society in 1842. What can be correctly said is that the
development of orchestral forces that had been taking place throughout the 1830s accelerated greatly around 1838 and 1839, and that the
Schlesinger Solemnity was one of several exciting events that capped
that development. After it came other steps of equal importance on the
road that led to the third Philharmonic Society.

At first glance, the extraordinary excitement that the Schlesinger Solemnity aroused in audience and performers is hard to understand. The concert seems to differ little, in program or personnel, from many others that were being given in New York at that time. The program (reproduced on page 71) was *not* "largely orchestral in character," as has generally been assumed, but the usual blend of choral, chamber-music, solo, and orchestral pieces; only three numbers were for orchestra, and of those three, two could not have seemed very special to New York ears in 1839—both Beethoven's Second Symphony and Weber's *Freischütz* Overture were old favorites.[30] As for the orchestra players, they were the same pickup musicians, from the theaters and other sources, that New Yorkers were accustomed to seeing at all their big concerts, and so many of them were busy with other engagements that the concert had to be put on with only one rehearsal.[31]

What then was so different about the Schlesinger memorial concert that set it off from all the other concerts of its period and made such an emotional impact on its audience that the birth of the great Philharmonic Society three years later could (rightly or wrongly) be attributed to its reverberations? Only one thing: the *size* of the orchestra. The advertisements promised that there would be sixty performers—half again as many as even large orchestras ordinarily had—and the sheer power of the orchestra had an overwhelming effect on its audience. At the end of the *Freischütz* Overture the applause was so insistent that U. C. Hill, who was serving as leader for the second half of the concert, repeated the piece. The nineteen-year-old George Templeton Strong, who was among the listeners, said that he supposed he had heard the overture before but "perhaps the different style of perform-ance made it seem another piece. It was glorious. & I don't wonder the Audience encored it in a perfect hurricane & thunder of applause."[32]

The Schlesinger Solemnity was not the only steppingstone on the way to the Philharmonic. Between 1839 and 1842 performances with large orchestra continued to grow in frequency. When the Sacred Music Society presented the Chevalier Sigismund Neukomm's oratorio *David* on March 31, 1840, there was an orchestra of forty-three players, and the performance was so successful that it had to be repeated twice in the same season. Even popular entertainments began to go in for large orchestras. In January 1841 the Park Theatre announced in the *Herald* a series of "Concerts (à la Musard) as now given at the Theatre Royal, Drury Lane, London"; for these winter promenade concerts,

MUSICAL SOLEMNITY,

IN MEMORY OF

DANIEL SCHLESINGER.

JUNE 25, 1839.

PROGRAMME.

PART I.

1. GRAND OVERTURE—Full Orchestra. Composed expressly for the London Philharmonic Society; *its first performance in this country,* — D. Schlesinger.
2. CHORUS—Das Deutsche Vaterland—The Concordia.
3. ARIA—" Was sag ich," as sung by v. Weber's request, at his last Concert— Madame CARADORI ALLAN, - - - - - - - - v. Weber.
4. SOLO—Violin—grand variations from La Norma—Mr. Halma, - - Bellini,
5. CHORUS—Kyrie Eleison—The Concordia, vi Haweg.
6. ARIA DI BASSO—from il Flauto Magico—by an Amateur, - - - Mozart.
7. "THE SPIRIT SONG,"—*Mr. C. E. Horn,* - - - - - Haydn.
8. ALLEGRO of the celebrated Quatuor in C minor, for piano, tenor, Violin, Violincello,—Messrs. Scharfenberg, Hill, A. T. K. & Boucher, - - D. Schlesinger.

PART II.

1. GRAND OVERTURE—Der Freyschutz—full Orchestra, - - - - v. Weber.
2. DOUBLE QUARTETTE—Wanderlied—The Concordia, - - - - Schöns.
3. ELEGIE—Violincello—Mr. Boucher, - - - - - - - Parofka.
4. ARIA—Parto ma tu ben mio—from the Clemenza di Tito—Madame CARADORI ALLAN, with Clarionet Obligato, by Mr. Christian, - - - Mozart.
5. VRIATIONS—Flute—"Through the Forest"—From Der Freyschutz, Mr. Kyle, Nicholson.
6. GRAND CHORUS—Der Herbst am Rhein, with orchestral accompaniments— The Concordia.
7. AIR DE DUPREZ—from Guido and Ginevra, br the first time in America—Mr. Halma, - - - - - - - - - - - - - - - Halevy.
8. FINALE OF THE GRAND SINFONIA IN D MAJOR—full Orchestra, - Beethoven.

Director of the Concert, - - Mr. ETIENNE,
Who will preside at the Piano-forte.

Leader of the First Part, - Mr. HUGHES,
By permission of Mr. Simpson.

Leader of the Second Part, - Mr. HILL.

Narine & Co's Print, 11 *Wall St.*

promised the announcement, the orchestra "will be augmented to 45 performers, and consist of the most distinguished artists."

Some of the largest concerts, marshaling strong forces of soloists, orchestra players, and chorus singers, were benefit performances for charitable causes. The Schlesinger Solemnity was of this kind. And it was another benefit concert, early in 1841, that provided the next historic link in the chain that led to the Philharmonic. There was in New York City a German Society, founded by Baron Steuben in the 1790s, that devoted itself to aiding German immigrants. Around 1840 Germans were beginning to come to New York in such numbers that a concert was planned, in conjunction with the Concordia music society, to raise money for sending the immigrants on to the Far West. This concert, which was given on February 11, 1841, with a "full and effective" orchestra, "comprising the best talent in the city," had a larger proportion of orchestral music than the Schlesinger Solemnity had had. (Compare the programs on pages 73 and 71.) The city's German community turned out in force (George Templeton Strong, although he enjoyed the performance, could not resist remarking in his Diary that the hall was "jammed with Dutchmen like a barrel of Dutch herrings"). The concert "was universally called the best since the great one in honor of the lamented Schlesinger."[33] Its success, following on that of the Schlesinger Solemnity, brought home to New York musicians that, if they were interested in orchestral concerts on a large scale, they had better take into account the eager audiences and the skillful players that the city's German element could supply. This practical lesson was not lost on U. C. Hill, who had served as leader in both concerts, when he was stirring up the organizers of the Philharmonic Society a year later. Nor did he forget an important musical experience that he had gained in the German Society concert: Beethoven's Fifth Symphony, which he had prepared with great care for that concert, was also to be the central work of the Philharmonic's first program on December 7, 1842, led once again by Hill.*

There was no question that serious concert music was attracting more and more attention in New York City. "We are in the midst of a

* The German Society performance may have been the United States premiere of Beethoven's Fifth Symphony; the *American,* on the day of the concert, spoke of the symphony as being performed on this occasion "for the first time in this country." (It added that "as the fourth movement is the most admired, our friends will do well to remain until the end." Impatient audiences of 1841, like those of more recent years, tended to make for the exits shortly before the end of a concert.)

THE public is hereby informed that the GRAND
CONCERT FOR THE BENEFIT OF THE
GERMAN SOCIETY of this city, will take place
on Thursday, the 11th February, at the Broadway
Tabernacle, on which occasion the following eminent Solo performers have, in the kindest manner,
tendered their valuable services:

MRS. MARONCELLI, MR. ALFRED BOU-
CHER, MR. L. RAKEMANN, and MR. W.
SCHARFENBERG; together with the members of
the " Concordia," as also a number of other distinguished Ladies and Gentlemen Amateurs.

The Orchestra having voluntarily offered its assistance, and comprising the best talent in the city, will
be full and effective.

Leader of the Instrumental department,
MR. U. C. HILL.
Do   do   Vocal   do,
MR. L. RAKEMANN.
PROGRAMME.
PART I.

1 Overture—" Egmont," grand orches-
tra,   L. Van Beethoven
2 Chorus—" Jagers Abschied," by the
members of the Concordia,
Mendelsohn Bartholdy
3 Fantasia—Violoncello Solo, 1st time
here, Mr Alfred Boucher,   A Batta
4 Duetto—" Deh Conte," from Norma
Signora Maroncelli and an amateur
lady,   Bellini
5 Chorus by the Concordia.
PART II.

6 Overture—" Die Felsenmuhle," grand
orchestra,   Reissiger
7 Aria—" Al desio," with violoncello
obligato, Signora Maroncelli and
Mr Rosier,   Mozart
8 Sextetto—For 2 pianos concertante,
by Messrs Scharfenberg and Rakemann, with accompaniment of the
clarinetto, horn, bassoon and contra
basso, by Messrs Fleming, Woch-
ning, Reiff and Jacoby,   Ferdinand Ries
9 Chorus—" Der Rhein," of the " Con-
cordia," with orchestra accompaniment,   Panny

PART III.

10 Grand Simfonia in C Minor,   L. Van Beethoven
1st movement—Allegro con brio.
2d   do   Andante con moto.
3d   do   Menuet and Trio.
4th   do   Allegro and Presto finale.
Performance to commence at 8 o'clock precisely.
Tickets, at One Dollar each, to be had at the Music Stores of Messrs Dubois, Bacon & Chambers, 285
Broadway; Stoddart, Worcester & Dunham, 361
Broadway: C. F. Hoyer, 301 Broadway; J. F. Atwill, 201 Broadway, and of the following members of
the Committee:

T. Achelis, 44 Beaver street; C. W. Faber, 44
Broad street; W. Kobbé, 40 Beaver street; C. H.
Sand, 49 Stone st; E. Unkart, 36 Pine st; T. Vietor,
36 Exchange st; C. F. Grosheim, 78 William st; F.
S. Schlesinger, 49 Beaver st; O. Camman, 26 Wall
st; Dr. C. Henschel, 138 Chambers st; M Vogel, 59
Broad st; Dr. H. Senff, 89 Leonard st; F. A. Spies,
13 South William st; H. Koop, 39 Liberty st.
F. S. SCHLESINGER, Chairman.
C. F. GROSHEIM, Secretary.   fe6 6t

Advertisement in the New York *American* of February 10, 1841, for the
German Society concert of the following day.

most singular movement connected with the sentiment, philosophy, finance and morals of theatricals in the United States," marveled the *Herald* of April 1, 1841: the legitimate drama was dying, "and the taste of the educated and intelligent classes have [sic] merged into music of the very highest order, and an occasional patronage of opera . . . [T]he attention of the *elite* is turned exclusively at present to music, and will be for some time to come." One after another, in the season of 1841–42, came the concerts presented by vocalists and instrumentalists from every country of Europe and from New York's own community of musicians. "Rich and varied, far in excess of former standards," is the way the musical season is characterized by Odell, the annalist of the New York stage.

Late in that season, Anthony Philip Heinrich[34] was responsible for the grandest milestone of all on the road to the Philharmonic's first concert. In the spring of 1842, his supporters announced:

THE HEINRICH MUSICAL FESTIVAL

It should be extensively known that preparations are being made for a grand musical festival to be held in this city. . . . In England, and on the continent, since the grand commemoration of Handel, such meetings have been frequent, when the most eminent performers combine their efforts, talent and skill in presenting to the public the great compositions of the giant masters.

The Heinrich Concert has been projected on a magnificent scale, corresponding in some degree to those assemblages in Europe. . . . We are not aware that any combination of musical talent has yet taken place in our country under such circumstances as to justify the designation of a Musical Festival.

If, however, an orchestra, which will number nearly 100 of the best performers in the United States, and a choir of sixty selected vocalists, trained and drilled by an efficient and competent chorus master; combined with the brightest stars that corruscate in our musical horizon, constitute material for a Festival—then is Mr. Heinrich prepared to give an entertainment which shall be referred to, in after times, as the first American Musical Festival.†[35]

---

† Strictly speaking, the Heinrich Festival was not the first in America nor even in New York City. Heinrich must certainly have known about the several "Union Performances of Sacred Music" led by U. C. Hill in 1839 at the Broadway Tabernacle, with nine hundred to a thousand singers plus orchestra each time; these were numerically many times larger than his festival, though less ambitious artistically.

Heinrich may not have realized fully his plan of a hundred players, but he certainly came closer to it than anyone had so far done in America. A pretty good idea of the size of his orchestra can be gleaned from the issue of *Brother Jonathan* of April 16, 1842, in which it was indicated that Heinrich's music required an orchestra of "Six Double Basses, six Viloncello [sic], eight Violas, twenty four Violins, primo and secondo, four Trumpets, four Horns, one Cornetto, one Bombardo, one Ophicliede [sic], one Serpent, one Bass Horn, three Tromboni, one Contra Fagotto, two Fagotti, two Oboes, three Clarinetti, one petite Clarinet [sic], two Flauti, one Piccolo, Timpani, Bass and Side Drums, Tambourins, Cymbals, Triangle, Gongs, &c." This adds up to seventy-nine players, even without allowing for the possibilities of the final "&c."[36]

Heinrich's program (see Figure 9) was, of course, designed chiefly as a showcase for his own compositions, yet it managed ingeniously to offer a varied sampling of genres and national styles that were then cultivated in New York. Of Rossini there were a duet from *Tancredi* and the "Inflammatus" from the *Stabat Mater*. There was an aria from Haydn's *The Seasons*. There was a song with double-bass obbligato by Vincent Novello. And the finale was a choral *Hallelujah* by Beethoven.[37] As for Heinrich's own compositions, no fewer than seven were listed on the program: two big works, each in several sections, from his mammoth creation for orchestra and chorus entitled *The Pilgrim Fathers,* two songs and a vocal duet and quintet, all with texts in English, and a "Motetto Concertante" in Latin.

Heinrich's Festival was the most promising demonstration of musical creativity that New York City had yet known. It was appreciated too. "On Thursday evening we had the gratification of witnessing the complete triumph of a veteran musician," said the reviewers.[38] There had been a thousand people in the audience at the Tabernacle, a great orchestra and choir, the most eminent musical talent in the country, and over all had presided "the genius, enthusiasm, and wonderful power of the old composer." Of Heinrich's *Grand Overture:* "the melodies were good, but the harmony was magnificent." Although some of its passages "were upon too scientific and German principles" to be understood by any except musical connoisseurs, the general effect must nevertheless have been highly satisfactory, "for at the conclusion of the piece the composer was honoured with repeated rounds of applause from the thronged audience who had listened to it. It was a grateful sight, though an oppressive one, to witness the emotions of the veteran upon receiving the unequivocal testimony to his taste and talent. It shook the old man out of his composure, but we trust that after his excitement shall have subsided, . . . he will remember last Thursday evening with peculiar satisfaction." Heinrich had summoned the musical talent of the land around him, and it was "most honorable to those composing it that they promptly responded to the call, and volunteered their services."

That "eminent talent" included many who, only six months later, would be participating in the first concert of the New York Philharmonic.[39] And Heinrich himself had an important connection with the Philharmonic: on April 2, 1842, at the very time when he was planning and preparing his Grand Musical Festival, he was chosen chairman of the meeting that was called to organize the Philharmonic Society of New York. It is unlikely that this was sheer coincidence; it seems a reasonable conjecture that Heinrich, engaged in putting together as imposing an orchestral concert as New York could imagine in 1842, and known to have had a long lifetime of experience as violinist, pianist, organist, composer, and conductor, was felt to be a good man to entrust with the chairmanship of the organizational meeting for the new orchestra.

No fluke of gestation is necessary to explain the birth of the Philharmonic in 1842. The natural growth of concert life in New York City, and the social and economic conditions that nourished it, had reached the point where a third Philharmonic—different from the Philharmonics of 1799 and 1824, as it was different from the London Philharmonic, yet related by heredity to all of them—was inevitable.

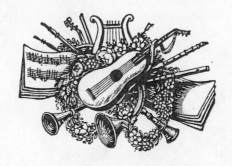

Part III

An Orchestra Is Born
(1842–43)

Chapter 8

Founding

Many forces converged to make the early 1840s a propitious time for the founding of the new kind of Philharmonic.

The economic circumstances were right. The community was now numerous enough and wealthy enough to fill the large concert rooms in which orchestral performances must be held. Although 1842 was still a depression year, the same hard times that were discouraging all but the greatest hits in the expensive gamble of theatrical productions made concerts seem more practical, from a managerial viewpoint, since they entailed a smaller investment. In December 1842, when the Park and Bowery Theatres could ask only 50¢ for a box seat, and 12½¢ for the gallery, a good concert ticket could still command $1; this meant that the theaters needed bigger audiences (i.e., bigger and more sensational successes) than did the concert halls in order to make ends meet.

The social environment was right, too, for the establishment of the new Philharmonic. The "professors of music" had evolved into enterprising musical craftsmen, willing and able to take the responsibility of organizing themselves into an efficient cooperative and (thanks in some degree to the Jacksonian revolution) possessing the political know-how to do so. The first Philharmonic, in 1799, had been, essentially, a club of subscribers. The second Philharmonic, in 1824, although apparently another such club, had really drawn the line more sharply between its wealthy Governors and the musicians toward whom they observed a benevolent paternalism. But the third Philharmonic was to be a democratic and even "communistic" association of musical artisans, running their own performances and dividing the profits among themselves at the end of each season. The new Philharmonic, like many social institutions of its era, would seek to strike a balance between the exclusiveness of subscription membership (modeled after the examples of its two predecessors in New York City) and control by the musicians themselves (after the pattern of the London Philharmonic Society).

From the subscribers' viewpoint such exclusive concerts had also the merit of social respectability. This was a very important consideration at the period of which we are speaking. The flight of the best people from the theaters to the concert halls was due in no small measure to their disapproval of the moral condition of the theaters. This was not based, as many people today imagine, on the assumption that all actors and actresses were dissolute. On the contrary, the best of them were as acceptable—and even as sought after—in good society as Broadway and Hollywood stars in a later era. The poor moral reputation of the theaters arose primarily from the fact that prostitutes, in almost all English and American theaters, were given a special section to use as a market place for their wares. William Dunlap in 1832 made the abolition of this evil a principal theme of his *History of the American Theatre*. He protested against the "improper, indecent, and scandalous practice of setting apart a portion of the boxes for this most disgusting display, . . . present[ing] to the gaze of the matron and virgin the unabashed votaries of vice, and tempt[ing] the yet unsullied youth by the example of the false face which depravity assumes for the purposes of enticing to guilt."[40] The concert halls, and sometimes the opera, were free of this taint in the 1840s. "Facilities for hearing music constitute the greatest attraction of the city to me . . . ," wrote L. Maria Child in one of her *Letters from New York* in 1844, making special mention of the new Philharmonic Society and of the Italian opera: "no degraded corner is reserved for unveiled vice."[41] A Philharmonic Society restricted to subscribers promised protection against the loose women who offended respectable people in the theaters.

The ethnic forces in New York's music world, moreover, were momentarily in a working balance that was favorable for the founding of an orchestral society. English, French, Italian, American, and German elements could be found side by side in the orchestras, and to some extent in the audiences, of the city. The German element, bearers of a flourishing school of instrumental music, had swelled sufficiently to encourage the formation of an orchestral society, but had not yet overwhelmed the other national groups whose cooperation was needed in order to get the society started.

Finally, the artistic and educational level of the city's musical life signaled its readiness for the new institution:

The conductors were ready—such musicians as Hill, Timm, and Etienne, thoroughly trained and experienced in the old dual system of "leader plus someone presiding at the pianoforte," but able to conduct in the modern manner when required.

The repertory was ready—to the substantial body of Classical orchestral music, European composers were adding a rich Romantic literature of overtures, symphonies, and concertos, suitable for big audiences in big auditoriums, and much of this music was already being imported to New York. Local composers, too, both émigrés and natives, in addition to writing for the theater, the church, and other utilitarian outlets, were making their contribution to orchestral "art" music. We have already seen Heinrich at work, and the young New Yorker George Frederick Bristow was also putting notes on paper with professional skill.

The orchestra players were ready—men who had learned, in the hard school of the theater pit and the "one-shot" concert, how to work in a large ensemble.

And the public was ready. It had learned to appreciate large and well-balanced orchestras. It knew many of the great works of the European musical culture practically from memory: Handel and Haydn oratorios, several of Beethoven's compositions, a great number of instrumental and vocal works of Mozart, Haydn, Hummel, and Weber, all the latest French and Italian operas, all the English operas and a number of German ones, and some of the newer music of Mendelssohn, Thalberg, and Spohr. Everyone was playing or singing, or paying to hear others do so. There was a hunger for self-improvement, partly because it was believed to contribute to advancement in a democratic society, and partly for the sake of "culture." Articles about music, magazines devoted to it, and educational books were multiplying. Current aesthetic attitudes held music to be a "rational and refined amusement," and even the strait-laced were coming to accept it as such.

Into this promising situation stepped Ureli Corelli Hill and his fellow musicians.

For years they had been talking about a professional orchestra large enough and good enough to play great orchestral pieces as their composers intended them to sound. Now the times were auspicious. On April 2, 1842, Hill, aided by several of his colleagues, succeeded in assembling at the Apollo Rooms a very large number of the city's musicians for the express purpose of forming such an orchestral society.[42] Heinrich was chosen chairman of the meeting. A committee of five was appointed to draft a Constitution to be submitted at a meeting two weeks later, on April 16. They did their work so well that the Constitution was adopted at the next meeting, on April 23.* As soon as the Constitution was adopted, the first officers were elected in accordance with its provisions: U. C. Hill, of course, as President; Anthony Reiff, the bassoonist, Vice-President; F. W. Rosier, Secretary; Allan Dodworth, Treasurer; and W. Wood, the timpanist, Librarian. At a fourth meeting on May 7, the number of officers was increased by two so-called Assistants ("Directors" would probably have been a more accurate description of their rank), and A. Boucher, the cellist, and H. Otto, the violinist, were elected to fill these positions.

Ureli Corelli Hill, musical pioneer, chief begetter of the New York Philharmonic, and one of the most intriguing personalities in the cultural history of the United States, was born around 1802 or 1803, but whether in New York, Massachusetts, or Connecticut is not certain. His father, Uri K. Hill, though he was described as a rigid music master of the old school, showed a touch of unconventionality in naming his son. He manufactured "Ureli" by combining his own first name, Uri, with that of a friend, Dr. Eli Todd (which suggests that Ureli should probably be pronounced "ū-rē′-lī," i.e., yu-ree′-lye), and he added "Corelli" as a middle name to express his admiration for the great Italian composer.† U. C. Hill—that was how Ureli Corelli was commonly known—became a professional musician when he was still in his teens, giving lessons busily, and playing violin in New York's theater orchestras (including those that took part in the historic engagements of Edmund Kean and of the García-Malibran opera company in the

---

* They deserve to be remembered for it: the committee consisted of Hill, Daniel Walker, the cellist, F. W. Rosier, the double-bass player, and William Penson and Allan Dodworth, the violinists (Dodworth, like all members of his family, was talented on several instruments, but he was enrolled as a violinist in the Philharmonic).

† In the same baroque spirit, he named Ureli Corelli's brother George Handel.

1820s). His qualities of leadership were soon recognized and most of
his engagements began to be as a concertmaster, rather than as an
ordinary violinist. He led the New York Sacred Music Society for some
time and attracted particular attention with a full-scale performance of
Handel's *Messiah* in 1831. It is surprising, therefore, to find him at the
Tremont Theatre in Boston in 1835 not as leader but as first violin
under Ostinelli; perhaps he was content to serve in that capacity because the Tremont band had the reputation of contriving to obtain
from Europe "all the latest works, of the best masters." Shortly thereafter Hill went to Europe where he studied with the renowned Moritz
Hauptmann, and with the even more renowned Ludwig Spohr, who
praised him as a "capable artist and good and amiable man." He met
Mendelssohn in Leipzig, heard Habeneck's superb orchestra in Paris,
and played in the Drury Lane Theatre orchestra in London. In May
1837, an announcement in the New York *American* informed the city
that Hill had "arrived from his Musical tour in Germany, France, and
England," intended to fix his residence in New York, and would teach
violin, piano, and composition. He was soon the principal violin teacher
and orchestra leader of the city, and remained so throughout the period
of the Philharmonic's creation and early consolidation. Sometime between 1848 and 1852, he went West in the hope of making his fortune,
but seems not to have succeeded in this venture. Upon his return to
New York, he tried to market a pianoforte that he had invented which
was guaranteed never to go out of tune because little bells had been
substituted for the strings, but this, too, failed to make him a rich man,
as did also some real estate deals in New Jersey. He made what living
he could from playing in theater orchestras and occasional concerts,
but his imagination was always at work on grand and original schemes
—generally too grand and original for practical acceptance, like his
plan for an auditorium capable of accommodating forty thousand listeners for the celebration of Beethoven's one hundredth anniversary
in 1870. Despite the discouragements that he suffered, and his increasing age, he continued to play in the Philharmonic until 1873 and to
serve as a Director until 1875. But then he could take no more. On
September 2, 1875, at his home in Paterson, New Jersey, he killed
himself by swallowing morphine. There are touching lines in his farewell letters to his wife: "Why should or how can a man exist and be
powerless to earn means for his family . . . '—I'd rather be a toad'
[he quotes from Shakespeare's *Othello*] than live so." And in his ultimate moment of misery he made one more attempt, characteristically

noble and characteristically insufficient, to take care of his wife's practical needs, reminding her to ask the Philharmonic Society, the Musical Protective Union, and the Musical Fund for the $50 that she would be entitled to from each of them as his widow. To "the outside world," Hill wrote sadly but firmly: ". . . my divine Father knows how much I have been sinned against, and he will judge me."

New York has waited too long to pay sufficient and suitable honor to its musical martyr, Ureli Corelli Hill. In December 1834, when Hill was still a young man, the *American Musical Journal* prophesied: "He is one of the most eminent of our native musicians, and one whose genius is yet destined, we believe, to reflect honor on his country." One day, when his whole story has been told, it will be seen that he fulfilled that prophecy.[43]

In the Constitution that Hill and his colleagues adopted in April 1842 can be recognized their concept of what the new Philharmonic Society should be, and it is a concept that inherits much from three earlier institutions: the London Philharmonic of 1813 and the New York societies of 1799 and 1824. A four-way comparison—New York Philharmonic of 1842 with each of the others—reveals some of the lines of descent:[44]

Like London's was the all-important provision that "the members shall be professors of music." Like London's was the declaration that the Society's object would be "the advancement of Instrumental Music," vocal music being accepted only grudgingly. Like London's was the limiting of admission to subscribers and their families and a small number of their friends; outsiders were not welcome, and it was not until 1851 that the xenophobia of the New York Philharmonic relaxed sufficiently for a bylaw to provide that "a limited number of tickets may be issued to strangers at one dollar and fifty cents each."

Like the 1799 Philharmonic's was the "Government," headed by a President and Vice-President in both cases. This seems such a natural arrangement to the American reader that it may surprise him to learn that the London Philharmonic had no such officers, being ruled by seven Directors instead. When it is observed, moreover, that the 1824 Philharmonic in New York was similar to those of 1799 and 1842 in this regard, one wonders whether all three New York Philharmonics may not have reflected the example of the United States government and Constitution, of which Americans were so proud.[45]

Like the 1824 Philharmonic's was the assumption that the Society should offer financial benefits to its performers, and even, under certain circumstances, to their families: "Each member of the orchestra," stipulated the third Philharmonic's Constitution, "shall receive $25 for his services at all the concerts and rehearsals during the season," and an early amendment authorized a "sinking fund for the relief of distressed members, their widows and children." One aim of these measures, as of the 1824 "insurance" system, was to encourage permanent, or at least long-term, membership in the orchestra. The 1842 Constitution provided that the orchestra was to consist of fifty-three professional musicians, drawn from the seventy Actual Members, and it even specified the proportions of the instrumentation.[46] Again, the reader who imagines such efforts toward permanency to be common to all orchestral societies of the period should understand that the London Philharmonic had no such provisions in its Laws.‡

Its organization completed, the new Philharmonic, in the summer of 1842, issued a prospectus that caused great excitement in New York's musical circles. The list of members given in the prospectus included most of the city's best instrumentalists, and the succinctly outlined plan promised to set a new standard for orchestral music in New York:

The PHILHARMONIC SOCIETY have the honor to announce their intention to give, during the ensuing season, THREE VOCAL AND INSTRUMENTAL CONCERTS, *upon a plan similar to those so celebrated in the principal cities of Europe.*

The First Concert to take place about the end of November, 1842.
The Second   "   "   "   "   "   "   March, 1843.
The Third   "   "   "   "   "   ".   May, 1843.

The most eminent Vocalists in the city at the time of the Concerts will be engaged,* *and no pains spared to render the Instrumental talent of the Society effective by frequent playing together; and the chief object will be, to elevate the Art, improve musical taste, and gratify those already acquainted with classic musical compositions, by performing the Grand Symphonies and Overtures of Beethoven, Mozart, Haydn, Spohr, Mendelssohn, and other great Masters, with a strength and precision hitherto unknown in this country.*[47]

The New York *Mirror* cooperated with a long "puff" on August 20. The new musical society, said the *Mirror,* would effect "a vast improve-

‡ In fact, to this day, as the Royal Philharmonic Society, it does not have a permanent orchestra of its own, but engages one or more orchestras for each season of its concerts. Its original policy in 1813 had been the extreme one that "no Member or Associate . . . shall receive any pay" for performing at the Society's concerts, but this had proven impractical after the first few years.

* Although the Constitution adopted a few months before had given the object of the Society as "the advancement of Instrumental Music," the New York Philharmonic, like the London, found it expedient almost from the start to interpret this self-imposed restriction loosely, ignoring it completely when the glamour of a vocal soloist seemed necessary in the competition with other attractions.

ment in the present taste for that delightful art. . . . The principles upon which this Society has been organized are those, in our opinion, best calculated to place the Society upon a firm and lasting basis; its array of talent is very promising; its objects are good; and the respectability and business-like habits of its committee of management unexceptionable."

Nihil obstat. Everything was now ready for the debut of the biggest and best Philharmonic that New York had ever known. Subscriptions were coming in, the orchestra had been rehearsing regularly on Saturday afternoons, and the first concert was scheduled for Monday evening, November 7, 1842.

Chapter 9

First Season

As the date of the first concert approached, paid advertisements began to appear in the press. *The Albion* printed this one just two days before the concert date:

The Albion. *November 5,* 1842.

PHILHARMONIC SOCIETY.—The Committee of Management respectfully announce to the Subscribers, that the FIRST CONCERT of the Society will take place at the Apollo Saloon, on Monday evening, November 7th.

The Committee would at the same time state to the Public, that Subscription Lists have been opened at the following Music Stores:—Firth & Hall's, No. 1 Franklin Square; Atwill's, 201 Broadway; James L. Hewitt & Co., 239 Broadway; C. P. Hoyers, 301 Broadway, and at Thomas Dodworth's, 402 Broadway.

Oct. 15.   F. W. ROSIER, Secretary.

Then came a crisis—triggered, ironically, by the same expansion of theater music that had helped to make the Philharmonic possible. What happened was that the Park Theatre had an unexpected hit, and since some of the Philharmonic's best musicians were earning their livings by playing at the Park, the opening concert had to be postponed. The Park's hit was *The Israelites in Egypt, or, The Passage of the Red*

Sea, with music taken from both Rossini and Handel, "the drama written and the music adapted by" M. Rophino Lacy.[48]

It opened on October 31, "in a style of splendor unexampled on this side of the Atlantic." The orchestra (according to *The Union*) had "at least double the number of performers than on ordinary occasions." The libretto lists by name thirty-five of the principal players of this expanded orchestra, and twenty-two of them are Philharmonic men; it would have been impossible for the new Society to have given its first concert without them.[49]

Not until the beginning of December was the coast clear again. This time the concert was set for December 7, 1842, exactly a month later than the date that had originally been planned. Again, the advance "puffs" began. The *Albion* of December 3 promised that New York audiences would be "astonished at the effects which so large and well-practiced a band can produce" and that "the gems of instrumental compositions to be given on this occasion . . . will gladden the hearing of musical critics." Again there were paid advertisements in the days just before the concert—this time in the *Sun,* the *American,* the *Evening Post,* and the *Commercial Advertiser,* sometimes listed under "Amusements," though sometimes in the miscellaneous columns of public notices and merchandise bargains. The advertisements assured potential subscribers, who might have been skeptical because of the November postponement, that "The First Concert will positively take place at the Apollo Rooms on Wednesday, 7th of December."

How the concert succeeded and how the orchestra played can be judged from a review published in *The Albion* three days after the concert:

CONCERTS.

First Philharmonic Concert.—We must undoubtedly reckon Wednesday evening last, as the commencement of a New Musical Era, in this western world. The concert which was then given, at the Apollo Rooms, was the first of an attempt to form an approved school of instrumental music in this country, after the manner and upon the principles of the celebrated Philharmonic Society of London, and well, "excellent well," indeed, have the members commenced. We do not mean to flatter them, nor do we think they desire it, by saying that they have come up to their sister society, but we see no reason to doubt that they may do so, if they continue with the spirit, zeal, and energy with which they have begun.*

The first part consisted of Beethoven's Grand Symphony in C minor, played throughout [i.e., in its entirety], and with a precision and care which gave evident proof of the anxiety of every artist there, to promote the good cause, and do honour to his own talents; *Madame Otto* then sang a *"Scena"* from "Oberon," after which the part concluded with a splendid Septuor by *Hummel,* arranged as a Quintette for the Pianoforte, Violin, Viola, Violoncello, and Contra Bass. It was played in capital style, the obligato piano part being charmingly played by *Scharfenburg* [Scharfenberg]. The original arrangements of this Septett are for the Pianoforte obligato, Clarionet, Oboe, Flute, Alto, Violoncello, and Double Bass; it was a great favourite of the distinguished composer himself, who used to take pleasure in playing the Piano part in public.

The second part commenced with Weber's Overture to "Oberon," which was followed by a duet of *Rossini,* sung by *Madame Otto, and Mr. Horn,* and two vocal solos by them, and the concert was concluded with a new overture by *Kalliwoda.*

There were about fifty-four performers on the occasion, placed upon a handsome orchestra [platform], the property of the society. *Mr. Wolfe* [Woolf] led [as concertmaster], seconded by *Mr. Marks;* the first part was concluded [conducted?] by *Mr. U. C. Hill;* the second part by *M. Etienne;* the concluding overture, and all the vocalism by Mr. Timm, and all these conductors did their duty carefully and well. It was quite delightful to observe artists who have distinguished themselves as musical *Stars* and whose solo performances have given unmixed satisfaction, quietly taking their places, simply as members of the orchestra in their several department[s], thus shewing that it was the general cause of music, and not personal distinction, which actuated them in the performance.

Being well assured that every individual of this excellent society is solicitous for its prosperity, we are confident that a few observations given in candour and good feeling will be received in that spirit. There was attention paid, *but not enough,* to the *pianos* and *fortes,* that is to the elocution of the music. The flute and the clarionet were somewhat too flat, and the violins behind the leader were not in good tune together after the first piece. We also perceived that the energies of the

* *The Albion,* as its name prepares us to expect, was an English-oriented periodical that automatically assumed the complete derivation of New York's Philharmonic from London's. In evaluating this aspect of its commentary, the reader should note that the subtitle of the publication was *"British, Colonial and Foreign Weekly Gazette."* Actually, as Elkin explains in his history of the Royal Philharmonic Society (pp. 37–41), the London Philharmonic had sunk in 1842 to the lowest point in its artistic and managerial fortunes.

performers, being so intensely strung in the beginning were relaxed a little toward the end; this, however, was to be expected on a first night, but they will do well to be *very* careful throughout. Again, as it will conduce to the dignity as well as permanency of the society, we would recommend that attempts be made to let the business of each night go as regularly as clock-work, not allowing any signs of confusion; and that the members of the orchestra refrain from all unnecessary conversation whilst in their places.

That this Society is calculated to flourish, and to give a tone to musical taste here, we can well believe, and it has our most fervent wishes as it has our most confident expectations for public sympathy with its objects.

George Templeton Strong, then twenty-two years old, was a passionate music lover and a bit of an intellectual snob. He was one of the original subscribers to the Philharmonic, and his Diary has an entry about the first concert, made the next night, that depicts vividly its effects as experienced by a sensitive young man:

Heard the first Philharmonic Concert last night. The instrumental part of it was glorious—Beethoven's Symphony in C minor was splendidly played—& the Overture to Oberon still better if possible—I never knew before half the grace & delicacy of the 'composition'—. An orchestra of over 60, most perfectly drilled, & composed of all the available talent in the city, gave an effect to it very different from what I've heard on former occasions when it's been performed. But what put it into the heads of the Socy to bring forward Mad. Otto & Mr. C. E. Horn as the sole vocal performers—? Both were poor enough—the former sang like a [hand?] organ;—in the progress of human ingenuity automatons will doubtless be made at some future day to sing with just as much expression—and the latter can't sing at all.—In the very first note he gave in his Duet from—something—his voice broke most horribly.—

As for the audience, its size can be estimated from the ticket sales. The First Annual Report shows that 139 subscriptions were sold in advance, each entitling the subscriber to four tickets for the concert; that makes a maximum of 556 persons who could have been present on subscription. To this should be added from 50 to 100 possible listeners, because something like $50 to $100 worth of "extra" single tickets were sold to subscribers and orchestra members. So the first Philharmonic audience must have numbered around 600 or 650.

It is even possible to name the principal members of that audience, for the Third Annual Report of the Philharmonic included a retrospective list of all the subscribers, season by season, for the three years that the Society had been in existence. (See Appendix I, page 487.) Since only subscribers and Actual Members were permitted to buy extra tickets for their families and friends, this list gives a very good idea of the social structure of the audience. Only a few of the names could be considered important in the wealthy or socially prominent strata of New York society—August Belmont, perhaps, as representative of the great international banking house of Rothschild; James W. Gerard, the respected lawyer; Oroondates Mauran, rich in money as in name; Clement C. Moore, professor in the Theological Seminary; and perhaps De Rham, Rhinelander, Ward, and a few others. A large number of those on the list were professional members of the Philharmonic Society; and others, like Luis and Maroncelli, were music dealers or teachers. Most of the remainder were just nice people, brought into the fold either by a real interest in music or by a relationship as a friend, pupil, or parent of pupil with one of the members of the Society. There is no Astor, no Brevoort, no Schermerhorn, no Hone, and not even one Jones. Of the "good" families, it is worth observing, many are carry-overs from the Governors and Subscribers of the aristocratic 1824 Philharmonic.[50]

This brings us to another list—the honored roll of the musicians who made up the original membership of the Philharmonic. During the summer of 1842, a prospectus was issued which shows the official membership list just before the first concert. Even if a few members dropped out or joined, as they seem to have done, in the time between the printing of the prospectus and the giving of the actual performances, this list can probably be taken as the membership roll for the beginning of the first season:[51]

PHILHARMONIC SOCIETY OF NEW YORK
First Season.—1842–43

VIOLINS: Apelles, Chubb, Chatel, Dodworth, A., Dodworth, H., De Luce, Ensign, Gunther, Helfenritter, Herzog, Hill, Knæbel, Lehman, Marks, Martini, Meyrer, Otto, Phillips, Sage, Wiegers, Woolff. TENORS [VIOLAS]: Derwort, Goodwin, Grebner. Clapdau [Clapdor], Heinrich, Johnson. VIOLONCELLOS: Boucher, Boocock, Hegelund, Walker. DOUBLE BASSES: Jacoby, Pirsson, Rosier, Schneider. FLUTES: Kyle, J., Ernst. PICCOLO: Dodworth, C. CLARINETTS [sic]: Göller, Grönefeldt [Groenevelt]. OBOES: Sauer, Stark. BASSOONS: Reiff, Kyle, A. HORNS: Munson, Nidds, Trojsi, Wöhning. TROMBONES: Timm, Schutz, Plane [Plain]. TRUMPETS: Mason, Wolter. DRUMS: Wood. CONTRA FAGOTTO:

Dodworth. PIANISTS, &c.: Alpers, Etienne, Hodges, Mus. Doc., Horn, King, Kopowski [Kossowski], Metz, Scharfenberg and Timm.

A glimpse of the inner workings of the Philharmonic in its first season is afforded by the Society's two-page statement of Expenditure and Receipts [see pages 94 and 95].† In the Expenditure section, each performing member is shown to have received $25 [line 9] as his dividend for the year—his share of what remained after the expenses of the season had been paid. The amount of $25 for the season's work may provoke a smile today, but it was not low for 1842. It was the equivalent of $8.33 for each of the three concerts, whereas standard "orchestral rates" were only $5 or $6 per concert. Under "Professional aid" [line 6] appear the three paid soloists for the season, at $25 each, and an orchestra player hired from the outside to cover an oboe part, at $6 for a concert. Soloists who were members of the Society performed without any extra pay, as did the various conductors. Adam Fecher, the "Porter and Messenger" [line 8], did all the dirty work at the rehearsals and concerts for about thirty years, during which period he was almost always the highest-paid man in the organization; in this first season he made $122, five times as much as any soloist or orchestra member (including the conductors). It is saddening to recognize that "Charity to Mr C——" [line 7] probably refers to poor Clapdor, who died before he could enjoy a second year with the Society. A seemingly trivial item of "Sordini" or mutes for the stringed instruments [line 13] is of symbolic importance: the mutes were purchased in 1842 at the time of the first concert, though the only part of the program that required mutes was the first twenty measures of Weber's *Oberon* Overture—the new Philharmonic was determined to perform the great orchestral pieces exactly as their composers had conceived them in every detail.

On the Receipts side of Secretary Rosier's ledger, the largest single entry is the $1,390 received from 139 subscribers [line 1].‡ But a

† In examining the statement, however, it would be well to know that Rosier, the Secretary, was a bit loose in keeping his records and accounts. It is not without reason that he inserts the disclaimer "Errors excepted" at the end of the financial report, below the date of 9th September, 1844. The date itself is wrong—it should have been 1843!

‡ The Third Annual Report, however, as shown on page 488, gives the total number of subscribers for the first season as 141, rather than 139. The explanation seems to be that there were 139 subscriptions, but in two cases a pair of friends (presumably "close" in more than one sense of the word) took a single $10 subscription between them, and the Society paid them the courtesy of counting their names separately.

substantial portion of the Philharmonic's receipts came, in one form or
another, from the professional members themselves. Thirteen of them
had taken subscriptions, and in addition to that the members bought
twice as many extra tickets as the subscribers [lines 4 to 7]. When
the annual taxes or dues, and the fines for absences, are added in, the
members account for about 35 per cent of their own Society's income.[52] The figures for fines [lines 8 and 9] may mask an incipient
problem: fines for absence from a performance, at $5 each, seem to
indicate only eight cases of missed concerts, but those for absence from
a rehearsal, at 50¢ each, must represent 235 attendance violations—a
warning that a serious difficulty may be brewing.

At the conclusion of its first season, however, the young Philharmonic
was an unquestioned success. It was financially solvent, had paid a
small dividend to its members, and had every prospect of increasing
its subscriptions for the next year. Even more important, it was becoming a potent influence on the city's musical taste. Although the Philharmonic gave only three concerts in its first season, and those open
only to the restricted circle of its subscribers, its members gave large
numbers of public concerts of their own, disseminating the style, the
literature, the artistic standards, and the technical skills of its competent band of players in widening circles. So, when Madame Otto announced a concert for March 17, 1843, after having appeared as soloist
in the first two Philharmonic concerts, *The Pathfinder* called attention
to the relationship: "Besides the vocal talent, she has the attraction of
most of the members of the Philharmonic Band, which the public have
as yet had no opportunity of hearing." So also, F. W. Rosier, the
Philharmonic's Secretary, advertised for his own program of May 10
"the two splendid Overtures," Mendelssohn's *Midsummer Night's
Dream* and Weber's *Jubilee,* that had been the hits of a Philharmonic
concert only a few weeks before.[53] In many people's minds the Philharmonic was coming to be associated with an "elevated" musical taste
and was getting much of the credit for maintaining and promulgating
it. When Scharfenberg gave his concert in the spring (every artist
worth his salt could be counted on, as surely as the change of the
seasons, to give at least one concert per year that was treated as his
display case or benefit vehicle), *The Pathfinder* of April 15 found
that the music was "of a very high order, and was performed in a
manner that reflected great credit on all concerned; most of the Philharmonic Society were there, and the overtures of Egmont and William
Tell, the former conducted by U. C. Hill, the latter by W. Alpers,

were extremely well played." The Philharmonic was acting as a musical stimulant in the community. It stirred up a few jealousies, particularly among those who felt that the German clique was taking over too much of the music establishment, but the good feelings that it awakened were far more numerous than the bad.

The Philharmonic's programs were still organized according to the old tradition—a symphony, a vocal solo, an overture, a chamber-music piece, more vocal music, an instrumental solo or two, and a favorite overture to end with—but newer composers began to be fitted to the format, and the music selected was generally of high quality and sometimes even challenging. Each of the three concerts of the first season began with a Beethoven symphony (Nos. 5, 3, and 2). The overtures

Expenditure.   PHILHARMONIC SOCIETY,

Cost of Orchestra and Forty Music Stands........		$173 49
Advertising		45 00½
Rent of Room, Rehearsal and Performance.......................................		135 25
Printing		35 50
Purchase and Copying of Music..		60 50½
Professional aid, Mrs Loder, $25; Mrs Otto, $25; Mr. Horn, $25; Mr. Weise, $6................		81 00
Charity to Mr C———, by vote of the Society......................................		20 00
Mr. Fecher, Porter and Messenger..		122 00
Fifty-eight Members received $25 each..	$1450 00	
Two Members received $6 each...	12 00	
		1462 00
Engraving Ticket Plate and Printing Tickets......................................	$41 75	
Books and Stationery..	18 75	
Sundries, Sordini, Cartage, Tickets, Box Lock for Music Closet, &c., &c., &c................	20 87½	
		81 37½
In favour of the Society...		16 56½
		$2,232 75

STILL DUE

From Mr. Timm, carried to account of 1843-44....	$7 50
From Mr. Alpers, carried to account of 1843-44....................................	5 50
From Mr. Loder, carried to account of 1843-44....................................	6 00
From Mr. Kossowski, no account...	7 00
From Mr. King, no account..	8 50
From Dr. Hodges..	1 75
From the Euterpean Society...	10 00
	$46 25

Financial Report of the Philharmonic Society for its first season, 1842–43, as prepared by F. W. Rosier, Secretary. In line 1 of the *Expenditure* page, and line 10 of the *Receipts* page, the word "Orchestra" refers to the specially constructed platform on which the performers were placed. Rosier's figures were by Weber, Kalliwoda, Rossini, and Mendelssohn. There were chamber music, instrumental solos, and vocal (including choral) music by Haydn, Mozart, Hummel, Beethoven, Romberg, Rossini, Bellini, Weber, and Spohr. The performances were not all of equal polish and refinement, but the members had all to be competent professionals before they could even be admitted, and there could be no doubt, even in the first season, that the Philharmonic Society was giving New York as a matter of course the kind of balanced instrumentation and careful execution that the city had previously enjoyed only on the rarest special occasions.

On May 6, 1843, two weeks after the final concert of the Philharmonic's first season, *The Pathfinder,* recognizing the cultural impor-

FIRST SEASON, 1842-43.	*Receipts.*	
One hundred and thirty-nine Subscribers at $10 each..		$1390 00
Taxes upon Members..		192 00
Taxes upon Members who from leaving the City, or other causes, ceased to be so.....................		3 75
Extra Tickets—Subscribers to First Concert..	$15 00	
Extra Tickets—Subscribers to Second Concert..	66 50	
Extra Tickets—Subscribers to Third Concert..	67 50	
Extra Tickets—Members to the Three Concerts..	305 50	
	———	464 50
Fines for Absentees from Rehearsals..	$117 50	
Fines for Absentees from Performance..	40 00	
		157 50
Use of Orchestra on five occasions.—Mr. Scharfenberg, Mr. Otto, Mr. Rosier and The Euterpean Society twice...		25 00
		$2,232 75
Balance...		$16 56½
Treasurer in advance...		29 68

New York, *9th September,* 1844.

    Errors excepted.

       F. W. ROSIER, *Secretary*

indicate that the four lines for Extra Tickets (under *Receipts*) should add up to $464.50, but their sum is actually $454.50; perhaps the second of the four lines should be $76.50 instead of $66.50.

tance of the new institution, devoted more than two columns of its space to a summary and analysis of the Society's first season. "We do not think any thing has ever been attempted in this city," said the article, "that will more conduce to the advancement of musical taste, than the formation of the above society . . . Already has its influence been felt . . . We, ourselves, in many houses have seen Beethoven's Symphonies arranged as duetts on the Piano Fortes of young ladies, where we used to see Quicksteps and Gallops . . . " The chief defect of the orchestra was the want of a pianissimo. One cause of this was that money-saving theater managers and others who employed orchestral players generally expected each man "to do the work (that is make the noise) of four, and we may say, en passant, in too many instances to be remunerated in an inverse ratio," so that the musicians tended to get into the habit of rasping. As for the last concert of the season, the Beethoven Septet would have been too long for a chamber work on an orchestral program "even had it been as well played as in reality it was played badly," but Mendelssohn's *Midsummer Night's Dream* Overture had been a delight and Weber's *Jubilee* Overture a triumph. "The enthusiasm of the audience at the conclusion of the Jubilee Overture, exceeded every thing we recollect to have witnessed, many rising spontaneously to their feet, and the unanimous call for its repetition was promptly responded to by the Society, and thus concluded the first season of this very meritorious Association."*

The birth of a living creature midst the fearful hazards and the protective mechanisms of natural generation must always seem to combine the miraculous and the inevitable. So does the birth of a living institution. The Philharmonic had had a long, hard struggle for life, but it had stubbornly survived the trauma of birth and infancy. An orchestra that could end the first season of its new life with the enthusiastic listeners "rising spontaneously to their feet" in a "unanimous call" for an encore would seem finally to have a good chance for lasting success. It was probably just as well at that moment that no soothsayer could look ahead to tell the founding fathers the stern truth:

The next hundred years would often be harder.

---

* For the full text, never before reprinted, of this contemporary evaluation of the Philharmonic's initial impact, see Appendix III.

Part IV

Youth
(1843–79)

Chapter 10

The Young Cooperative
(1843–54)

From the start of the second season, there were signs that the Philharmonic was beginning to interest the fashionable society of the city. George Templeton Strong made an excited entry in his Diary for the opening concert of the season, on November 18, 1843: "Great crowd: all the aristocracy and 'gig respectability' and wealth and beauty and fashion of the city there on the spot an hour beforehand."* He might have noticed that William B. Astor had now subscribed, as had several other rich or prominent persons: Henry Brevoort, Samuel B. Ruggles, Goold Hoyt, B. L. Swan, P. A. Schermerhorn, John D. Wolfe, and Robert L. Stevens. The performance, moreover, was so successful that Weber's *Jubilee* Overture had to be encored, as it had been at the last concert of the previous season. Throughout its second year, the orchestra continued to gain in artistic as well as social prestige. "Even your Boston critics admit that some of the best productions of the art are brought forward with superior talent and skill [by the New York Philharmonic]," observed the distinguished author Lydia Maria Child, herself a former Bostonian, at the end of the season.[54]

* Looking down from his seat in a little side gallery of the Apollo Rooms, he saw Fanning C. Tucker, the wealthy musical amateur, "trying to devise outlets for his legs and barking his knees on the bench next in front of him [Tucker was almost 7 feet tall], and Mr. Wilmerding [the prosperous auctioneer] dozing off regularly at the soft passages and waking with a jump at the loud ones . . ."

Encouraged by its reception during its first year, the Philharmonic lengthened the series of the second year from three to four concerts— and it managed to do so without raising the subscription price, which remained at $10 for a whole season. This was accomplished by a clever reshuffling of the admission system. In the first season, the subscriber had received a total of twelve admissions for his $10—four tickets to each of three concerts. In the second season, he still received twelve admissions but they were distributed differently—*three* tickets to each of *four* concerts. Apparently the patrons were satisfied with the new arrangement. The income from subscriptions and extra tickets rose from $1,855 in the first year to almost $2,500 in the second, and each performing member could be paid a dividend of $32 for his work in presenting the concerts.

The only embarrassing episode for the young Philharmonic—and it was a minor one—was the falling from grace of F. W. Rosier, the organization's Secretary. At the end of the first season Rosier had felt called upon to say to the members: "The enthusiasm for the well doing of the Society may not be known to the members generally, but it will be gratifying for them to be informed that they themselves, in Subscriptions and extra Tickets, supported the undertaking to the amount of about $600"; what the members discovered, to their chagrin, before the end of the second season, was that they had also supported Rosier himself to the amount of about $100. He was impeached and tried on April 15, 1844, for having put into his pocket about $42 worth of tickets charged to members of the Philharmonic and $50 worth of subscriptions that he had collected. With a few other driblets of indebtedness, it turned out, Rosier owed the Society $103.75. Nevertheless, with scrupulous fairness, they credited him with three quarters of the $32 dividend to which, as a member, he was entitled for the season—three quarters because after his trial, of course, he could not play the last of the four concerts of the season.†

† After this scandal Rosier seems to disappear from New York. This must have been a loss to the city's cultural life, for he had been a leader among musicians and blessed with other talents besides. It was only a year and a half since the *Mirror* of August 6, 1842, under the heading of "Musical Gossipings," had paid him a public compliment: "Mr. Rosier, a musician of unusual ability, a fine writer, a sweet poet, a popular composer, and altogether a modest, unpretending man of merit, will, we hope, soon become as well known and appreciated by the many as he already is by the few." His name comes to my attention again in the Civil War when a Confederate naval song, *The Alabama,* bears the attribution "Music by F. W. Rosier."

In its second season the Philharmonic remained a cooperative society whose members were all professional musicians. The nucleus of the organization was the group of Actual Members, limited to seventy "professors." When, at the beginning of the second season, the Constitution was modified to add a class of so-called Associate Members, they too were required to be professionals. Unlike subscribers, Associate Members were allowed to attend rehearsals as well as concerts, and were given preference for actual membership when vacancies occurred. The purpose of establishing this class was a double one: to give professional musicians, who might be working at the hour of the concerts, a chance to hear the programs at the rehearsals, and also to line up a reserve force of instrumentalists for the orchestra. For their privileges Associate Members paid only $5 per season, but they had to be formally elected to membership, in the same manner as Actual Members.‡ Within a few years, the new kind of membership was to provoke unexpected alterations in the nature of the Philharmonic's public, but in 1843–44 it attracted little attention: only five of New York's musicians enrolled as Associate Members.

It was in the 1843–44 season, too, that the first Honorary Members were elected to the Philharmonic: the celebrated violinists Henri Vieuxtemps of Belgium and Ole Bull of Norway, both of whom were then appearing in New York. Neither of these great artists was above performing at the Park Theatre on the same programs with ordinary farces and comedies, and, although actors were playing to small audiences that year, the virtuoso violinists packed the house. Early in December, both Vieuxtemps and Bull also gave sensationally successful concerts of their own in other auditoriums. For Vieuxtemps's concert, Washington Hall was jammed and the audience "wrought up . . . into a state of furor"; for Ole Bull's, at the Tabernacle, four thousand tickets were sold and even people who arrived an hour in advance had to stand all through the

‡ That such democratic procedures were not without their problems can be seen from the report of William Wood, Secretary of the Society, on September 14, 1844. It seems that the property of the Philharmonic at the end of the first season had included 60 white ballot balls and 38 black balls, used in elections. To these had been added, during the second season, no white ones but 60 additional black ones. This should have made a total of 60 white and 98 black, "and yet at this time," says the perplexed Annual Report, "there are 65 white balls and only 62 black ones remaining." That some of the members might have pocketed the 36 missing black balls as reminders of their veto power is understandable, but where the five extra white balls came from may remain forever a Philharmonic mystery.

performance. A few days later, on December 16, 1843, the New York Philharmonic made the timely move of naming Vieuxtemps and Bull Honorary Members of the Society, obviously in the hope that this might induce them to appear as soloists on Philharmonic programs. Vieuxtemps did so, without any financial reward, on May 18, 1844, but Bull was harder to pin down. The committee of members designated to present him with his certificate of honorary membership at the end of the season could not even catch him in order to give him the document, and finally contented themselves with leaving it at his lodgings at the Astor House.[55]

By the end of its fourth season, the Philharmonic was showing clear signs of stability and progress. The finances were in good shape. The budget for the year amounted to $3,328, as compared with $2,233 for the first year. The annual dividend for each performing member had risen from $25 to $37. The sinking fund for the help of the needy was deposited in a savings bank.[56] The library was growing with purchases and contributions of music. With some satisfaction, and with an awareness of its cultural responsibility, the Society entered in its Annual Report the historic record of all the programs it had given in its four years. It was a record of which any orchestra of the time, anywhere in the world, could be proud. Each program was anchored by a full symphony and balanced with vocal and instrumental pieces, chamber music, and overtures, by the principal classical and contemporary composers. Not only Beethoven, but Mozart, Haydn, Mendelssohn, Spohr, and Weber were old friends to the subscribers, as were Rossini, Bellini, and Donizetti, and the newer names of Berlioz and Verdi had also found their way onto the programs by 1846. American composers could take encouragement from a bylaw, added to the Constitution, that held out the promise of one American composition being performed each season, if it were approved by a committee set up for that purpose.[57]

With the progress came ambition. As early as the third season, U. C. Hill extended invitations to two of Europe's greatest composer-conductors, Spohr and Mendelssohn (both of whom he knew well from his European tour), to come to the United States to direct a great musical festival involving a combination of the Philharmonic's personnel with choral forces. Spohr was eager to accept, but he could not obtain the necessary leave of absence from the Elector of Hesse-Cassel, whom he served; he wrote Hill that during the past few years he had been refused shorter leaves for engagements in England and Germany, and did not dare even to ask for the three months that the trip to America would require. Mendelssohn had complete freedom to go where he wished, but he had to decline because of poor health, as he explained in a characteristically warm reply in excellent English.[58] Though neither Spohr nor Mendelssohn was able to come to New York, the Philharmonic won some reflection of their glory by adding them to the list of Honorary Members in 1845–46; and both of them thrilled the members by sending letters of acknowledgment from Europe.*

Something of the festival plan survived to combine with another ambition of the young Philharmonic in the fourth season. Already there were plans for a Philharmonic Hall, "a splendid musical edifice . . . fully commensurate with the wants of the New York public," and a special Festival Concert was organized in the hope of raising money for such a building. "This concert," promised the Philharmonic's advance announcement, "will be given . . . on the most magnificent scale ever attempted in this country: combining the principal musical talent, vocal and instrumental, in and about New-York. There will be between **300** and **400 PERFORMERS,**" continued the announcement, its fervor transporting it into capital letters and boldface type, "and **Beethoven's Choral Symphony, No. 9,** will be given, making this an era in the musical world." To present Beethoven's Ninth Symphony for the first time in America was, indeed, a significant cultural venture. In that same spring of 1846, Richard Wagner's plan to perform this symphony at a Pension Fund Concert in Dresden aroused the bitter opposition of the orchestra committee, which protested to the General Director that the work "stood in ill repute and assuredly would keep the public from the concert." Yet the New York Philharmonic had the vision to recognize the work as a

---

* Two other Honorary Members were elected in 1845–46: Leopold de Meyer and Joseph Burke. De Meyer, who styled himself the "Lion Pianist," had a penchant for hokum in his publicity and in his stage antics, but he was nevertheless a brilliant virtuoso—the first in the succession of romantic European glamour-pianists who dazzled New York in the middle of the nineteenth century. He was probably expected to respond to the honor that the Philharmonic bestowed on him by appearing as soloist on one of the Society's programs, but he never did so. The amazingly versatile Joseph Burke—known in his boyhood as "Master Burke, the Boy Phenomenon"—made his New York debut as musician and actor in 1830 at the age of eleven, playing virtuoso violin solos, conducting the orchestra in overtures, and acting dramatic roles that ranged incredibly from Irish dialects to Shakespeare's Shylock and Richard III. By the time that he appeared with the Philharmonic in 1846, however (in a concerto by his teacher, de Beriot), he was devoting himself to the violin with such success that he was invited to return as Philharmonic soloist five more times within the next ten years.

masterpiece and the daring to propose it as a popular attraction. The concert took place on May 20, 1846, at Castle Garden,[59] under the direction of George Loder and U. C. Hill. But it did not, alas, raise enough money for the hall; 116 years more would have to go by before that dream of the Philharmonic's pioneers could be realized.

The drive for a concert hall was one of several financial pressures behind a campaign to obtain an Act of Incorporation for the Philharmonic from the state legislature in Albany. "The Act is important to us for ordinary business and necessary for building the Hall, and for collecting debts due the Society," the officers explained to the members in 1846. In the very first season, already annoyed by hard-to-collect debts, the Government of the Philharmonic had suggested "the propriety of immediately obtaining an Act of Incorporation, as without it the Society will continue to labour under many disadvantages." The annoyance grew with each year: in the third season the Annual Report complained of various members and subscribers "from whom, notwithstanding all exertion, the amount of subscription has as yet not been possible to collect." Accordingly, an application for incorporation was made in 1844–45, but it failed to pass the legislature, whereupon the Philharmonic's Government decided that it would have to resort to lobbying— or, as it was phrased in more formal language, that "it would be well to have some prominent member of the Society deputised for interesting in this matter the members of the Legislature at Albany." Of course, the man for the job was U. C. Hill. Aided and guided by three public-spirited lawyers of the city (J. W. Gerard, J. Y. Westervelt, and Henry Nicoll), who gave their services without charge, Hill almost succeeded in securing the incorporation in 1846; this time Albany seemed sympathetic, but simply did not get around to the matter because of the pressure of other public business. It was not until February 17, 1853, in its eleventh season, that the Philharmonic Society finally obtained the Act of Incorporation that it had long needed for the management of its finances. "But let us not be actuated too much by a mercenary spirit in the matter," moralized the officers with commendable self-discipline for a moment of such triumph, "but rather let our thoughts be directed to the elevation of the Society to its proper position, by the greatest excellence in our future performances."

There was a danger period for the Philharmonic in the three years from 1846 to 1849, when the Society's artistic and economic progress was threatened. On the artistic front, there were some who warned that the orchestra was beginning to bog down because it needed a permanent conductor, instead of the constantly changing succession that had led it since its founding. The *United States Magazine and Democratic Review* in a strongly worded article in April 1847 cited as evidence recent performances of two Beethoven symphonies. When Alfred Boucher of the Philharmonic's cello section conducted the Seventh Symphony, complained the article, the Society "lost more in his violincello [sic] playing in the *Allegretto* than they gained by his conducting." And H. C. Timm, who had led the *Pastoral* Symphony, though unsurpassed as a pianist, lacked "the necessary nerve and immobility for the conductor's stand." "Why should not this society have a perpetual director?" the critic asked. "The Philharmonic Society of London has tried it with the greatest success, having, under COSTA's direction, attained an excellence, and developed resources before unknown to itself.† . . . Let this society but elect a man whom their own judgment will point out to them as fittest for their constant director; one who will work, and who will make the society work . . . and they will resume the progressive march in which we are sorry to say they have halted, and seem inclined to stand at ease." To this plea the Society hearkened, but very slowly and cautiously. Until 1847 there had never been fewer than three conductors in a season and sometimes as many as five or six. Over the next five years, the number was generally reduced to two conductors, and finally in the eleventh season, 1852–53, Theodore Eisfeld became the first conductor to do an entire season for the Philharmonic.[60]

Meanwhile, the Philharmonic had to face another danger. Its economic position was being undermined by competition from two European imports—operatic stars and virtuoso instrumentalists. While New York's fashionables were running to hear the imported opera performances and the visiting instrumentalists, the Philharmonic's income dwindled. The officers sounded worried in their yearly reports. The "opening for the entire season of a new and elegant Opera House in the upper part of the city, by a very large Italian Operatic Company, expressly and exclusively engaged for it," they said in 1848, was a principal cause of the falling off in subscriptions. And the arrival of two or three small but very good orchestras, which gave their own series of concerts at low prices (the officers explained a year later), "made it necessary for the Committee of Management to use all the means in their power to cause

† Michael Costa had been engaged as the first permanent conductor of the London Philharmonic only the year before, in 1846.

the Society to be patronized as it had hitherto been." They tried moving from the Apollo to the somewhat larger Chinese Rooms (Broadway near Spring Street) for the comfort of the listeners; they did what they could to entice into the orchestra some of the city's good professional players who had been hanging back; they exhorted "the Members individually, to use their influence amongst their scholars and friends to become Associate Members"; they resorted to direct solicitation, pep talks, appeals to cultural duty—anything to win back the profession and the general public to an interest in the Philharmonic's concerts. Nothing seemed to help. Receipts for the sixth and seventh seasons, 1847–49, fell below the income of the very first year.

Then an unmistakable reversal of the trend began to be felt. Attendance started to climb, at first steadily and then spectacularly. Ticket receipts went from a low of $1,590 for the seventh season to $2,100 for the eighth, $9,259 for the fourteenth, and no less than $14,234 for the fifteenth season. This was not due, initially, to any planned campaign by the Philharmonic. Indeed, no one was more surprised and even bewildered than the poor-again rich-again Philharmonians. After declaring that the "patronage of the Society almost equals its palmiest days," the Eighth Annual Report in September 1850 went on to confess that "this improved state of its prospects was not caused by any special effort on the part of the Government during the last year, but appears to be of natural consequence."

In retrospect, it can be seen that several forces had combined to rebuild the Society's fortunes. From the fourth season on, a drastic realignment had been taking place within the structure of the Philharmonic's membership and patronage. The category of Associate Members had originally been established for the benefit of professional musicians. However, since Associate Members could attend rehearsals, they had in a sense an advantage over regular subscribers who could attend only the concerts, and some non-professionals also began to ask for rehearsal privileges. When the Society agreed to admit amateurs and ordinary music lovers to the rehearsals for the same $5 fee that other Associate Members paid, many people joined as Associates instead of as subscribers. In the third season there had been only 12 Associate Members, all professionals,[61] as compared with 220 subscribers. But in the fourth season the number of Associates jumped to 56, most of them *non*-professionals, and the subscribers fell slightly but prophetically to 210. After that, the number of Associate Members increased with astonishing rapidity, while the number of subscribers gradually decreased.

This transformation was accelerated by the Philharmonic's decision, in 1847, to admit ladies as Associate Members, a step that was eventually to affect all the social relationships of the Society to its community. Reminiscing in a letter to the *Evening Post* in 1892, on the fiftieth anniversary of the Philharmonic, "An Old Member" (presumably Mrs. Francis G. Shaw, whom Huneker called "the first woman to attend our rehearsals") described how she had attended the last concert of the season in 1847, had seen in the program a notice about associate membership to be arranged at the music shop of Scharfenberg and Luis, and had called on Mr. Scharfenberg in October, only to be told that ladies did not go to the rehearsals. She had insisted, however, and in a few days had received her printed notice of admission as an Associate Member of the Philharmonic Society with the privilege of attending "the twelve rehearsals and four concerts, and for the modest sum of five dollars." When she went to the first rehearsal of the season, the story continues, the conductor arose and said, "Gentlemen, I presume now that we have agreed to admit ladies as Associate Members, you will agree with me that we should throw away our cigars." The next week, our old member reports, there were twenty or thirty ladies at the rehearsal, and at the third, at least one or two hundred.

It is a charming story and one that has been much repeated in Philharmonic annals, but, at the risk of seeming callous toward a lady who later became a generous benefactor of the Society's Pension Fund, we must correct a few details in it. Mrs. Shaw did not have to insist over Philharmonic opposition that a lady should be able to attend rehearsals; the notice about membership that she saw at the concert of April 17, 1847, openly invited ladies to join. In fact, as of January 1847 the Constitution had been amended to provide specifically (Article XXXIII) that "Ladies may be elected as Associate Members with the privilege of attending all the Concerts of the Society, and the three Rehearsals immediately preceding each Concert, on payment of five dollars per annum in advance." It seems unlikely, too, that the conductor would have asked members to give up their smoking for the sake of the new Associate Member, since Article II of the bylaws of the Society already prohibited smoking.

There were 19 women among the 132 Associate Members of the 1847–48 season. Several of them were professional musicians them-

selves, but it was their non-professional sisters who would swell the
Philharmonic audiences in the future and contribute to that feminine
presence which has ever since been so much heavier in American
than in European orchestral affairs. The associate membership afforded
ladies the opportunity to indulge in a respectable daytime social entertainment (attendance at rehearsals), either unescorted or with "the other
girls." By the mid-1850s the *majority* of the Associate Members were
women.

Young people, too, were attending in increasing numbers. The Philharmonic provided a chance for the younger generation, shielded under
the socially and culturally acceptable umbrella of the rehearsal and concert, to meet publicly on a level of easy closeness that would otherwise
have been considered scandalous. A staff columnist who wrote on music
for *The Albion* over the signature of "GAMMA" sent a reporter to the
Philharmonic concert of March 1, 1856. It was a stormy enough night
"to have frightened the most enthusiastic votary of music," he reported,
yet the theater was "full to the very ceiling" three quarters of an hour
before the concert; curious to know "what was passing amid the multi-
tude who appeared so eager for harmony," he walked up and down,
listening and observing:

> "Well! I declare to you that I came away convinced that 'passional
> attraction' was far more to them than the attraction of harmony. You
> would think so, too, if you had heard: 'Aren't you ashamed of yourself'—
> 'Hush!'—'Oh dear!'—'Don't speak so loud'—'love'—'ice cream'—re-
> peated as many times as I did; but at all events it was evident that for two
> thirds of the public, the grand object of the event was to go and eat
> ices at Maillard's under other eyes than those of mamma and papa. I
> even saw"—

"Enough! enough! my friend," GAMMA pretended to break in on him,
"cease to calumniate young America in that way."

Though the immediate incentives to increased attendance may have
been such worldly considerations as an escape (for the young), a di-
version (for the ladies), and a bargain (for all the Associate Members),
the underlying reason for the Philharmonic's popularity and prosperity
in the 1850s was the basic soundness of what the orchestra was doing:
it was filling a need in the community by supplying proper performances of the rich literature of instrumental music; and it was educating
its audiences (by admitting them to rehearsals) to understand that

music and want more of it. Under these stimuli, both the mundane and the idealistic, the number of Associate Members shot up from 56 in 1845–46 to 1,773 a decade later.

As the material and artistic position of the Philharmonic grew more solid, the forms that the consolidation took were strongly affected by the German element in the city and in the orchestra. Between 1850 and 1860 about 15 per cent of New York's population was German-born— not just of German descent, but actually born in the old country. To get the "feel" of what 15 per cent meant in the city, imagine that 1,200,000 German immigrants were living in New York today. The proportion of adult males among the immigrants, moreover, was larger than in the general population, for the males tended to come over first and then, when they had become established, either to send for their families or to begin families here. And the Germans were men of aggressive ideas in politics, in the arts, and in education—aggressive enough to have impelled them to leave their native land. They brought strong pressures to bear on each of these aspects of the city's life. Within the orchestra the percentage of Germans was even higher than in the city at large. In the first year of the Philharmonic there were already twenty-two Germans among the fifty-three performing members, that is, about 42 per cent. By the thirteenth season, in 1855, there were fifty-three Germans out of sixty-seven performing members, making an increase to 79 per cent. The ethnic consolidation showed in the roster of conductors too. The nine conductors of the first decade had been of various national origins—American (Hill and Bristow), French (Etienne and Boucher), English (Loder), Austro-Bohemian (Maretzek), and German (Timm, Alpers, Wiegers, and Eisfeld). But by 1852, when Eisfeld became the first man to take a full Philharmonic season, the conducting responsibility had been narrowed down to one man, and that one a German. For half a century afterward, every conductor of the New York Philharmonic would be of German birth or background.

This German-staffed and German-led organization favored German music. Although it was true that the German-Austrian composers had contributed some of the cornerstones of the available orchestral repertory, the leaning of the Philharmonic toward German-Austrian compositions, it must be admitted, exceeded the proportion that might be expected. The Philharmonic's repertory seldom contained less than 70 per cent of music by German-Austrian composers. One could expect a great many compositions of Beethoven, or of Mendelssohn, on any orchestral program in the nineteenth century. But it took a certain amount of *parti pris* to justify the inclusion of a Gumbert, a Heinemeyer, or a Schindelmeisser, when equally talented American composers were clamoring for attention and being ignored. Once again (as had been the case a quarter of a century earlier when García and his Italian opera company had made their conquest of the city), conditions were favorable for a European invasion of New York's music world. The well-organized and well-trained German musicians, reared in a culture that encouraged instrumental music, and bearing their treasure of German-Austrian repertory, were prepared for dominant positions in the shaping of the Philharmonic's course. And they could be welcomed and supported not only by their fellow immigrants but by certain native American groups within the community, particularly those with intellectual or social pretensions, who hoped to make it clear that they were able to appreciate the best that the Old World could offer.‡

The foreign orientation of the Philharmonic was being strengthened at just the time when prosperity was beginning to smile upon the Society. The Philharmonic was growing less American as it grew more fashionable.

‡ A surprisingly large segment of New York's concert public was drawn from the Jewish part of the city's population. Although Jews were not often accepted in fashionable society, they were taken for granted as an inevitable part of the musical audience. In 1845 our constant informant, George Templeton Strong (who would one day be President of the Philharmonic), commented on a concert that he attended: "As usual, three-fourths of the assembly were children of Israel: the author of *Coningsby* [Disraeli] certainly right in claiming for his brethren a higher development of the musical sense than is common to mankind." [Diary, February 23, 1845.] The influx of German Jews after the European revolutions of 1848 added fresh numbers to New York's musical audience.

Chapter 11

The American Composer Protests

Less American—more fashionable.

This was an explosive combination and it burst into public attention in a critical dispute in 1854. There was in New York, in the season of 1853–54, a brilliant orchestra assembled by the French showman-conductor Louis Antoine Jullien. On Christmas Eve of 1853 Jullien introduced a composition by the American composer William Henry Fry entitled *Santa Claus: Christmas Symphony*. In a review in the *Musical World and New York Musical Times* on January 7, 1854, Richard Storrs Willis spoke of the symphony in terms that, although generally favorable, were not enthusiastic enough to please the composer.* Fry was hurt by what he considered to be Willis's frivolous attitude toward his work. In a Gargantuan letter, eleven columns long, published in the *Musical World* on January 21, 1854, and quoted shortly thereafter in *Dwight's Journal of Music* in Boston, he asked for better treatment of

* "Mr. FRY's 'Santa Claus' we consider a good Christmas piece: but hardly a composition to be gravely criticised like an earnest work of Art. It is a kind of *extravaganza* which moves the audience to laughter, entertaining them seasonably with imitated snow-storms, trotting horses, sleigh-bells, cracking whips, etc. Moreover, in the production of these things there is no little ingenuity displayed. The discordant winds are most discordantly well given; and among the graver features of the piece, our Lord's Prayer (as given in musical recitative), is marked and impressive."

Americans by Americans, especially since "the Philharmonic Society of this city is an incubus on Art, never having asked for or performed a single American instrumental composition during the eleven years of its existence . . ." The next week the *Musical World* carried a reply from Willis. Three weeks later Fry had a reply to the reply, and the week after that Willis had a reply to the reply to the reply. By this time (February 25) the Philharmonic really began to get involved, for Willis included a letter from a Philharmonic member stating that American works *were* played.

Then George Bristow, who only a few months before had been elected an officer of the Philharmonic, joined the fray on the side of his fellow composer Fry, with a sarcastic letter in the *Musical World* of March 4:

> As it is possible to miss a needle in a haystack, I am not surprised that Mr. Fry has missed the fact, that during the eleven years the Philharmonic Society has been in operation in this city, it played once, either by mistake or accident, one single American composition, an overture of mine . . . this single stray fact shows that the Philharmonic Society has been as anti-American as if it had been located in London during the Revolutionary War, and composed of native-born British tories . . .
>
> It appears the Society's eleven years of promoting American art have embraced one whole performance of one whole American overture, one whole rehearsal of one whole American symphony, and the performance of an overture by an Englishman stopping here—Mr. Loder—(whom your beautiful correspondent would infer is an American) who, happening to be conductor here, had the influence to have it played. . . .

Now the letters to the *Musical World* came thick and fast. The Philharmonic's Treasurer, Scharfenberg, answered Bristow on March 11, and the issue of March 18 carried a defense by H. C. Timm, President of the Philharmonic, and the Philharmonic's Board of Directors. Including "native or adopted citizens" and public rehearsals as well as concerts, wrote Timm, stretching a point or two, the Philharmonic had played a considerable number of compositions by Americans. He then proceeded, inexplicably, to weaken his own argument by giving the various nationalities of his "Americans" in parentheses after their names: G. Loder (English), H. Saroni (German), F. G. Hansen (German), T. Eisfeld (German), G. F. Bristow (American, two pieces),

F. E. Miguel (French), Knaebel (German), Dodworth (American), W. Mason (American), W. V. Wallace (Irish, songs), and A. P. Heinrich (German†—who, however, withdrew his compositions before they were used). An impartial observer cannot escape the feeling that the list is padded, in any case. Of all those named, only Loder, Wallace, Bristow, Dodworth, and Mason had been heard in real public performances, rather than rehearsals, and of these, Loder was an Englishman who had already left the country, and Wallace was an Irish visitor who soon would. In fact, when an official review was made by the Philharmonic, at the end of the season, of "all the grand instrumental pieces, such as Overtures and Symphonies" that had been performed since the beginning of the Society, only one performance of one American work (Bristow's *Concert Overture*) was listed in the total of 145 performances of 74 different compositions. Sensing the discomfort of the orchestra's position, the politic U. C. Hill, though he was Vice-President of the Philharmonic, wrote on March 25 to say that his name should not have appeared on Timm's letter, since he endorsed neither side completely.

Bristow still burned, however. On April 1 he announced his intention—in view of the Philharmonic's "systematized effort to extinguish American music"—to form an American Philharmonic to play mainly American works. "Who are the men," he asked rhetorically, "who told you that Americans cannot write up to the standard of the New York Philharmonic Society? They are the same style of illuminati that in the London Philharmonic, after attempting to rehearse it, kicked Beethoven's C Minor Symphony under their desks and pronounced the composer a fool or a madman." Then on April 15 the *Musical World* reprinted a bantering article from *Dwight's Journal,* suggesting that New York needed not only an American Philharmonic but a Chinese Philharmonic to take care of the musical interests of the immigrants from that country, and painting a comic scene of the Philharmonic's fifty-five or fifty-six German members in military combat with its seven or eight non-Germans. This teasing was too much for Bristow; furious that his life's work should be made a matter for jest, he wrote his most scorching letter the next week: "From the commencement there has been on the part of the performing members and the direction of the Philharmonic Society little short of a conspiracy against the art of a country to which they have come for a living; and it is very bad taste for men to bite the hand that feeds them. If all their artistic affections are

† He was really Bohemian by birth.

unalterably German, let them pack up and go back to Germany, and enjoy the police and the bayonets . . . where an artist is a serf to a nobleman . . . What is the Philharmonic Society in this country? Is it to play exclusively the works of German masters, especially if they be dead? . . . or is it to stimulate original art on the spot?"

What had started as a quarrel between Fry and Willis about the *Santa Claus* Symphony had brought to a head the impatience of the American composer with his treatment by American performing organizations. The year before, Fry had written bitterly, in connection with a projected concert of works of his colleague A. P. Heinrich: "A composer in this country may as well burn his compositions for any opportunity he has for making himself heard. Our Opera Houses and Musical Societies are worse than useless so far [as] they foster American Art." Now he and Bristow were shouting their discontent. "I thought the time had come," Fry declared, "to say something for American Art, seeing how much attention is given to foreign Art, while our own is ignored; that the applause of Philadelphia is quite as good as that of Vienna— each for its 'native Art' and of the two I prefer that of Philadelphia."[62] John S. Dwight, from the pontifical perch of his *Journal of Music* in Boston, questioned with wily exaggeration whether Fry would succeed "in proving the love of Handel, Mozart and Beethoven sheer affectation, slavish idolatry, pedantry and 'old fogyism' and in demonstrating the huge strides by which 'Young America' has put all that far behind it." Nevertheless he was forced to admit his admiration for Fry's audacity, for his "smart eccentric spicy talent . . . evident knowledge of the science, history and practice of his Art, and a wonderfully quick and quaint suggestiveness of thought that must make this apology for *Santa Claus* against the classics, and for musical young America against musical old Europe a memorable document of the present queer stage in our musical history. It sums up and intensifies to an almost burning focus the arguments and aspirations of this would-be-all in music as in all things—this ambitious and irreverent young giant Jonathan."[63]

The Fry-Willis dispute, as Dwight sensed, marked a critical point not only in the history of the New York Philharmonic but also in the history of American musical culture. Pleading and scolding, Fry and Bristow asked that the Philharmonic, as the leader among our musical societies, actively cultivate American music. Like Ralph Waldo Emerson, they held that an American art must grow organically from native materials.‡ For the American composer, it was not only a matter of an occasional performance of a composition, but of "keeping it before the public for a sufficient time necessary to make himself understood . . . Comparisons drawn between me and another," Fry said, "have no meaning until performances are as freely and frequently given to one as the other." With regard to the Philharmonic this observation was especially significant since its subscribers were every year enlisting in greater numbers as Associate Members who would hear three or four rehearsals for each performance. No single performance of a new work could compete with the educational power of this system.

Fry's fears and complaints were to some extent justified. There *were* composers in New York turning out ambitious works—operas, symphonies, orchestral pieces, oratorios—often on a grand Romantic scale, calling for large colorful orchestras and full-voiced choruses; but the Philharmonic was not playing their music. Fry himself had written an opera and three symphonies, Heinrich a mountain of music for all possible forces, and Asahel Abbot imposing oratorios. Not a note of all this was ever given by the Society. There seems to have been a moment of hope in 1850 when the Annual Report admitted that "the provisions in the Constitution for the encouragement of composers of instrumental music in this country do not appear to be at all satisfactory; and as it is right and just that we should extend every assistance in our power to this department of the art, which we profess to be aiming to advance, the Government recommend that a competent committee be appointed to reconstruct that part of our Constitution." But the very next year, instead of improving the situation, the Philharmonic made it worse: the bylaws had specifically provided for the performance of large orchestral works, composed in this country, that might be presented to the Society; in 1851 the qualification "composed in this country" was significantly dropped. When Friedrich Schneider, a German composer, dedicated a symphony to the members of the New York Philharmonic

‡ "Our houses are built with foreign taste; our shelves are garnished with foreign ornaments; our opinions, our tastes, our faculties, lean, and follow the Past and the Distant," Emerson had protested in his essay on *Self-Reliance* (1841). ". . . [If] the American artist will study with hope and love . . . the climate, the soil, the length of the day, the wants of the people, the habit and form of the government, he will create a house in which all these will find themselves fitted, and taste and sentiment will find themselves satisfied also."

Society, they were proud to give it its first performance on one of their regular concerts, and to acknowledge the dedication in self-satisfied phrases. But when the prolific Heinrich dedicated his *Wanderer's Adieu* to the Philharmonic, it was politely and quietly accepted and filed in the library. Bristow was the composer of a symphony, overtures, and a variety of other instrumental and vocal compositions; probably because he was a member of the orchestra, he *had* had one piece performed by them in 1847—a *Concert Overture,* "respectfully dedicated to the subscribers of the Philharmonic Society"—but, as we have seen, he resented the Philharmonic's using that isolated performance as its defense against the charges that it neglected American music.

It is important to recognize that the Philharmonic, in ignoring American music, did not speak for all segments of the city's musical life. There were other individuals and organizations that figured importantly in New York's music world and that were not above playing the music of local composers. Indeed, it was another orchestra, it will be remembered, that had sparked the Fry-Willis quarrel with its performance of the *Santa Claus* Symphony. The orchestra of Louis Antoine Jullien was giving New York in 1853–54 a series of concerts on a level of technical proficiency that could probably not have been excelled in any city of the world at that time. For Jullien had culled the best performers of the principal European cities for his orchestra—such men as Bottesini, the world's greatest virtuoso of the double bass, and Lavigne, prince of oboists[64]—and had added to them every talented New Yorker who was available and could make the grade. With his stunning collection of one hundred players—about thirty more than the Philharmonic could muster at that time—Jullien presented programs that were a colorful sampling of the whole orchestral repertory. There were grand overtures, symphonies, and opera and oratorio excerpts by Handel, Mozart, Beethoven, Cherubini, Mendelssohn, Rossini, Donizetti, and Wagner; there were showpieces for the soloists, who included not only a platoon of his brilliant orchestra men but also the internationally celebrated singer Anna Zerr; there were Jullien's own fabulously successful quadrilles, waltzes, polkas, and galops, which had to be repeated over and over again by popular demand from one concert to the next; occasionally there was a sensational stunt worthy of P. T. Barnum, such as the notorious *Fireman's Quadrille,* in which terrifying flames were simulated in the hall while an incendiary orchestra and a fire-fighting chorus roared through their descriptive music.*

And there were contemporary American compositions. By the time Jullien was ready to leave the country in 1854, he had given over two hundred concerts from Boston to New Orleans in less than a year (in the same period of time the Philharmonic gave only four), performing works of Fry, Bristow, and other local composers not once but repeatedly and at modest admission prices. He was particularly partial to Fry. Fry's "New Descriptive Symphony" entitled *A Day in the Country* was repeated many times, as was *The Breaking Heart;* and the *Childe Harold Symphony,* composed expressly for Jullien, was also presented. As for the controversial *Santa Claus: Christmas Symphony,* Jullien performed it more than forty times in New York and on tour. In all of the nineteenth century the Philharmonic did not play any single work forty times—not even Beethoven's Fifth Symphony, let alone the work of a struggling American composer. Of Bristow's music, Jullien gave at least a dozen performances of excerpts from three different symphonies. Bristow, as a tribute, later entitled one of his compositions *Jullien Symphony,* and when the Philharmonic did perform it in the spring of 1856 *The Albion* took the occasion to chastise the Society for its neglect of American music and to compare it unfavorably with Jullien in this respect:

> But do you know how much is expressed by those two little words the *Jullien Symphony?* They mean simply that Jullien did more for Concert music in three months, than the Philharmonic Society has accomplished since Mr. U. C. Hill created it and brought it before the world. He [Jullien] gave us Mozart, Beethoven, and Mendelssohn, as we have never heard them interpreted in New York. He taught us the art of

* ". . . red and blue fire visible through the windows of the dome; . . . some admirable pieces of instrumentation meant to imitate the thundering, quivering, shuddering rush and roar of falling walls . . . a clamorous chorus shouting 'Go it, 20,' 'Play away, 49,' 'hay-hay,' and so on." So did George Templeton Strong describe in his Diary "the conjunction of Barnum and Jullien at the so-called 'Musical Congress with 1,500 performers'" at the Crystal Palace in June of 1854. But he also noted that Jullien played on the same program four choruses from Handel's *Messiah,* Rossini's *William Tell* Overture, Wagner's *Tannhäuser* Overture, and part of Beethoven's Fifth Symphony. And the audience for this concert, Strong reported, was so enormous (estimated at fifteen thousand by some and forty thousand by others) that he was "seriously exercised about the possibilities of falling galleries and panic-stricken multitudes."

shades and effects in music, and has rendered the metronome and all mechanical music hateful to us for ever. He revealed to us the powers of Bristow, Fry, and Eisfeld, and did far more for their reputation than was ever done by the Society, which owed so much at least to the first and last of these noble and courageous musicians. And this is the true meaning of Bristow's Symphony.

Jullien even found room on his programs for the folklike idiom of Stephen Foster at the very moment when American snobs were learning to be ashamed of their own vernacular music. The serious-minded New York correspondent of *Dwight's Journal* warned in 1854 that Jullien's soloist, the great Anna Zerr, "shame to say, had stooped to pick up one night and sang 'Old Folks at Home' for the b'hoys; one would as soon think of picking up an applecore in the street."[65]

Since New York composers were not always willing to wait with the performances of their works for "the accidental presence of . . . M. Jullien," as Fry put it, and since they were not likely to be played by the Philharmonic, they frequently found ways to put together big concerts of their own. Only a year earlier, beginning in November 1852, Fry himself had presented a series of eleven huge lectures on music, using his own compositions (*A Day in the Country, The Breaking Heart,* and others) as part of the illustrative material. These concert-lectures, given at Metropolitan Hall, employed a chorus of one hundred, an orchestra of eighty of the best instrumentalists in the city, Dodworth's Band and the Seventh Regiment Band to demonstrate military music, and a corps of soloists. The leader or concertmaster was U. C. Hill. The orchestra was conducted by Fry's fellow composer George Bristow.

This lecture series, for which Fry had been collecting material for several years in Europe and in this country, constituted one of the most imaginative educational experiments that the history of American music has ever known. Illustrating with his orchestra, bands, chorus, and soloists, Fry investigated just about every aspect of the theory, history, and sociology of music from the most ancient times to his own day.[66] And of course he seized every opportunity to champion the cause of American music. This was a much broader musical education than the Philharmonic was giving its subscribers, even if an important motive on Fry's part, in presenting the series, may have been the public performance of his own musical compositions. And, although he lost $4,000 on the venture (at prices of $5 for the entire course and $1 for a single lecture, he could not cover the costs of his army of performers), he reached audiences of one to three thousand people for each lecture.

Anthony Philip Heinrich had also for years been organizing concerts for the display of his own music. His Grand Musical Festival at the Broadway Tabernacle on June 16, 1842, has been discussed above as one of the Philharmonic's precursors. Heinrich produced another concert "upon a scale of grandeur seldom equalled in this or any other country" on May 6, 1846, again at the Tabernacle, this one with a program made up entirely of ten of his own compositions, including *A Monumental Symphony—"To the Spirit of Beethoven"—An Echo from America, to the Inauguration of the Monument at Bonn,* the *Embarcation March and Chorus, "The Adieu of the Pilgrims,"* and *"The Washingtoniad, or The Deeds of a Hero"—An American Festive Ouverture.* His concerts, like Fry's, were imposing affairs in the number and quantity of the performers. For the 1846 program Heinrich had orchestra, chorus, organ, vocal soloists—"the Best Vocal and Instrumental Talent of the City." The conductor was George Loder, who only two weeks later would conduct the New York Philharmonic in the first American performance of Beethoven's Ninth Symphony. Elaborate program notes were prepared by Henry C. Watson, one of New York's leading critics. Again, on April 21, 1853, shortly before the visit of Jullien's orchestra to New York, Heinrich presented at Metropolitan Hall a Grand Valedictory Concert as his musical farewell before a visit to Europe. This time Heinrich shared the direction of the concert with Theodore Eisfeld, the current conductor of the Philharmonic. About half the program was made up of Heinrich's works, and the other half of compositions of William Vincent Wallace, E. J. Loder, Hobbs, Weber, and Mozart. Heinrich's concerts brought out large audiences, the first one (in 1842) more than a thousand people, the second (in 1846) about fifteen hundred, the third (1853) about two thousand, and elicited warm and enthusiastic responses from the public and the press. The solo artists were among the favorite New York musicians of the time—Madame Otto, Timm, W. A. King (the respected organist of Grace Church)—and for the most part they generously donated their services so that the composer could be the beneficiary of whatever profits might be made from the concerts. In sum, these performances of the music of a local composer were an important and organic part of the musical life of the community.[67]

The rosters of musicians for the concerts of Fry and Heinrich and

even Jullien contained many of the same names that appeared in the
Philharmonic programs. Since the number of fine professional musicians in a city the size of New York was not unlimited, there was likely
to be a certain duplication of names in any series of artistic performances
of a high level. But it was not the Philharmonic as such that participated
in these performances of New York composers, and indeed the same
men who played conservative and European-oriented programs within
the regular Philharmonic series tended to play more contemporary
American music when they performed under less pretentious auspices.
Dodworth's Musical Festival, for example, at Metropolitan Hall on
February 20, 1852 (band of fifty performers, tickets popularly priced at
only 50¢), makes a striking comparison with the Philharmonic subscription concert of February 28. Philharmonic members appeared in central
roles in the Dodworth concert: Harvey B. Dodworth was listed as
Director, and his brother Allen as cornet soloist, and George F. Bristow
would "preside at the Piano Forte." Their program included the first
American performance of Mendelssohn's *Grand Military Overture,*
and works by Verdi, Rossini, Bellini, Ernst, and others; but it also
offered four pieces by New York composers: an excerpt from Bristow's
opera *Rip Van Winkle,* another of Bristow's vocal works, a *Grand
Polka* "composed expressly for this occasion" by Thomas Coates, and
a *Quickstep* by Harvey Dodworth himself. And among the featured
artists, Henry Squires was identified as "The American Tenor." No
Philharmonic program in 1852 presented four works by local composers
and proudly called attention to the fact that a soloist was American.
The program that the Philharmonic would present a week later, on
February 28, was made up of a symphony of Beethoven, two vocal
excerpts and an overture by Weber, a Mendelssohn concerto, a Mozart overture, two Schubert songs, and a piano solo by Kalkbrenner.
This was the program that the same Dodworths and the same George
Bristow would play in their capacities as Philharmonic members, and
it is a very different program from the one that they put together when
left to their own devices eight days earlier.[68] Without considering the
question of the quality of the music in each program, it is easy to see
from an objective viewpoint that the Philharmonic's concert is more
"serious" and more Central European, the Dodworth Festival more
popular and more American.

The Dodworth concerts were not alone in their alliance between the
popular and the American. Jullien's programs showed the same charac-

teristic, and it is safe to make the generalization that by the 1850s American composers were more likely to find themselves on programs of a "lighter" nature, frequently in company with some of the favorite excerpts from Italian operas, than on programs that were intended as serious symphonic presentations.

Chapter 12

Consolidation
(1852–67)

The Philharmonic, meanwhile, was becoming intrenched as the symbol
of musical dignity, stability, and sobriety. Though it gave only four concerts per season, it was the quasi-official symphonic organization of the
city. This position was won for the Philharmonic by a combination of the
German musical establishment of the city with two small but influential
segments of the native population—the socially ambitious and the intellectually ambitious. Under this morganatic union the Philharmonic
prospered. Surveying the Society's first ten years, the *Musical World* of
November 13, 1852, commented:

> . . . [The] Philharmonic has been steadily growing in public favor, in
> numbers, in skill and in wealth, until it has become incomparably the
> best musical society on this continent; its rehearsals and concerts being
> looked forward to with eager anticipations by lovers of a high order of
> music, while those whom fashion compels to *affect* a love for such music,
> no more dare stay away from a PHILHARMONIC performance, than they
> would dare to be caught in town in mid-summer.

The Philharmonic's audiences grew so in size that by the tenth season
the concerts had to be moved from the Apollo Rooms to more spacious
accommodations at Niblo's, and by the fifteenth season to the even
grander precincts of the Academy of Music at Fourteenth Street

and Irving Place.

The wave of the Society's prosperity reached its crest in that fifteenth season. For its first concert at the Academy of Music, on November 22, 1856, there was a "crowd unprecedented in the annals of that society," as one experienced concertgoer reported. "The building was packed full half an hour before Eisfeld rapped for his forces to come to order. We almost abandoned the quest of seats in despair; only the most indefatigable exertions obtained them at last. A great change from the old scene in the Apollo rooms . . ."[69] Even before any single tickets were sold, the different kinds of season subscribers (Associate, Professional, and Subscribing Members) could fill most of the hall. The Associate Members alone numbered 1,773—a dramatic increase from the 317 of only five years before. The newer category of Professional Members had been established in the eleventh season to attract resident artists and teachers into the Society by admitting them to the rehearsals and concerts for only $3 per annum; starting with 58 members, it had grown to 213 by the fifteenth season. Only the number of Subscribing Members was decreasing, but this the Philharmonic considered to be "a favorable omen for the cause of Art," since Subscribing Members were those who obtained tickets only for public performances and not for rehearsals. "These persons," said the Annual Report, "are gradually being merged into the more desirable number, who value the rehearsals as well as the more formal concerts, for purposes of musical culture." (See table, Backnote 70.)

As the Society grew, it shed some of its quaint old ways. For one thing, the orchestra finally sat down. In its issue of December 3, 1853, the *Musical World and Times* remarked impatiently that it could not "account for the necessity of the performers *standing*. Aside from being uncomfortable to them, this looks bad and impresses the spectators uncomfortably." And not long afterward the practice of standing was abandoned. The charming old custom of the most personable members of the orchestra serving as ushers, with their white wands of office, had to yield to progress too; Ritter, in his *Music in America*, tells us that paid ushers began to be employed in 1854, and the Society's financial records seem to confirm this, although "Doorkeepers" were paid even before that.* While old customs were fading, new ones were coming in.

---

* Krehbiel explains in his Philharmonic book that the custom of ushering with white wands was given up "because of the opportunities for amusement which it afforded to some of the younger attendants whose ebulliency of animal spirits sometimes overcame their sense of decorum."

By the fifteenth season, for example, opera cloaks, those badges of high society, were beginning to be seen in the audience.

Glorying in the success of that fifteenth season, the Society asked Richard Storrs Willis (the same Willis who three years earlier had offended Fry by criticizing his *Santa Claus* Symphony) to prepare a statement of its position for the Annual Report. "The root of our success," rhapsodized Willis, "is *not* fashion—although this animating exterior sunshine, we admit, very lavishly has visited us; it is not the spirit of clique and nationalism—are not our ranks open to all nationalities, and have we not already the representatives of many such among us? . . . it is not pelf or annual dividend—our increasing numbers and expenses holding very much in check the individual dividend from an increasing pecuniary success; . . . but it is *Art* . . ."

Of course the roots that Willis felt it necessary to disclaim—fashion, clique, money—were precisely the ones that some knowing New Yorkers had been associating with the Philharmonic's improving fortunes for the last few years. The same sophisticated concertgoer who had exclaimed that the packed Academy of Music was "a great change from the old scene in the Apollo rooms," went on to add "and not wholly for the better. Nine-tenths of this assemblage cared nothing for Beethoven's music and chattered and looked about and wished it was over. A smaller audience of appreciative people would have been far more agreeable, even to the orchestra, for it would have applauded with more sympathy and intelligence. However," he went on, resignedly, "it's well to bring masses of people into contact with the realities of music; it helps educate their sense of art, and Heaven knows they need it." Willis, himself, in his official statement for the Annual Report, acknowledged the danger from those whose attendance "may be based, perhaps, less on a sincere love of Art than the musical fashion of the hour." But the Philharmonic had educated the public in the past, he hastened to assure the members, and would continue to educate newcomers and to absorb them into the main body. "It is only while the process of assimilation is going on, that such an outside influence is unfavorably felt." To put it bluntly, some of the new listeners had musical bad manners. "The inattention, and heedless talking and disturbance of but a limited number of our audience, are proving a serious annoyance at our Philharmonic performances . . . If each little neighborhood would take care of itself, and promptly frown down the few, chance disturbers of its pleasure, perfect order would soon be secured . . . In foreign audiences, it is ever, effectually done."

One of the sources of the problem was that, beginning in 1855–56, all members were given the privilege of buying extra tickets for their non-subscribing friends at only 50¢ for rehearsals and $1 for concerts. The response was so overwhelming that even Niblo's Concert-room (for rehearsals) and the large hall known as Niblo's Garden (for concerts) proved insufficient to accommodate the crowd of new Associate Members and their guests, and the sale of extra tickets for rehearsals had to be stopped until the next season, 1856–57, when the Philharmonic was able to move to the capacious Academy of Music. In that year extra tickets were sold to the unprecedented amount of $4,330. The flood of new subscriptions and extra-ticket sales carried into the Philharmonic's audience many of the relatively untutored listeners, mostly young, whom Willis was reproving for their lapses from good manners.

It should not be assumed, however, that the difficulty with the new audience resulted from American provincialism. The situation was quite the same in most European concerts. Observe that Willis, in advising the members to frown down the disturbers, assured them that "[in] foreign audiences, it is ever, effectually done"—implying, of course, that the same problem existed abroad.† Indeed, in earlier days a certain amount of conversation and social activity was assumed to be part of the pleasure of concertgoing, and it was only as the cult of seriousness settled over the musical world toward the middle of the nineteenth century that a vice seemed to be defined where only a practice had existed before. The Philharmonic concerts, since their audience represented a relatively closed society of subscribers, members, and their invited guests, were more staid in their atmosphere than were popular concerts open to the general public, either in New York or in most European cities. We do not ordinarily hear, for instance, of pickpockets

† At the London Philharmonic in 1842, confesses Foster's history of that Society (p. 173), "complaints were received from people that someone disturbed them greatly by hissing Thalberg [the celebrated composer-pianist], and by flirting loudly with his female friends during Thalberg's Fantasias. The offender's name, they said, was M–cf–rr–n!" Presumably this was the composer George Alexander Macfarren, at that time already twenty-nine years of age and a professor at the Royal Academy of Music, and the occasion was a concert conducted by no less a personage than Mendelssohn.

or brawlers being a nuisance at Philharmonic concerts as they were at
so many other public entertainments.

Having settled comfortably into its attitude of moderate conservatism,
and having shaped its public largely to agree with its policies, the Philharmonic was able to move ahead satisfactorily on its chosen path
for another decade. There were occasional setbacks but none serious
enough either to overturn the organization or to persuade it that its
direction should be modified.

The first of the reverses occurred immediately after the triumph of the
fifteenth season (1856-57) in which receipts and membership had
broken all Philharmonic records. A jealous providence in the very next
season took its revenge for so much happiness. First there was the terrible financial Panic of 1857, which toppled more than five thousand
banks and railroads in a year; in a city darkened by unemployment
and hunger meetings, a luxury like the Philharmonic was bound to
suffer. Then the manager of the Academy of Music not only presented
some concerts of his own which drew off part of the public, but had the
effrontery to use the name of "Philharmonic Concerts" for them. The
growing popularity of opera performances had been making competition for the Society for several years; in the period of great prosperity
that the city and the nation had just been enjoying, this pressure had
been easily absorbed, but now it made itself painfully felt. Adopting
a much humbler tone than it had taken in its season of glory the year
before, the Philharmonic administration complained and explained: "In
regard to the solo performers, we have endeavored to obtain the best
talent available, both vocal and instrumental; but it must be borne in
mind that we labor in this respect under great disadvantages, from the
well known fact that celebrated artists, who pass the winter in our city,
invariably come here under a previous engagement with some operatic
manager, by which they are debarred from appearing at any other
than the manager's own public performances. For instance, during the
last season the services of Messrs. Vieuxtemps [violinist], Thalberg
[pianist] and Formes [singer] were promised, but could never be obtained when an opportunity for making good the promise presented itself." There may even have been some feeling of competition from the
formation of a new Philharmonic Society in the neighboring city of
Brooklyn, although the New York Philharmonic went out of its way in
1858 to offer its best wishes for success and to suggest that the new
society "undoubtedly owes its origin to the mother Institution of New-

York." Dark backstage machinations lurked also in the following bitter lines from the Sixteenth Annual Report: "The Lessee of the Academy having declared, that on no account will he allow the Philharmonic Society again to occupy the said building—for reasons which the reader must deduce for himself, as they are not known to us—our choice remains between Cooper's Institute, Burton's or Niblo's Theatres, and the City Assembly Rooms, one of which places will probably be selected until a regular MUSIC HALL, so much needed in our city, shall have been built."‡ The intransigence of the Academy's lessee hurt all the more because the Philharmonic had gone along with a sizable increase in rent, from $1,600 to $2,500, during the difficult year that had just passed. (How steep a jump this was can be judged from the fact that in the old Apollo Rooms the rent had ordinarily ranged from $100 to not more than $250 for an entire season.)

In short, everything seemed to be going wrong in the stormy sixteenth season. The number of subscriptions, which had been 2,034 the year before, fell to 1,490, and to make matters worse, more than fifty of them were not paid up by the end of the season. The sale of extra tickets declined painfully, from $4,330 to $2,388. Probably hoping, in the face of these difficulties, to make the next season as attractive as possible, the Board of Directors announced that it had decided "to give during the coming season FIVE instead of four concerts, with the usual number of rehearsals, WITHOUT INCREASING *the price of subscription*. At the same time, it has been found necessary to pass a regulation to the effect, that henceforth all subscriptions must be paid in advance."

The setback was only temporary, however. Even in this difficult season, the total membership was greater than in any year except the boom season of 1856–57; and the financial receipts had begun to climb again during the next few years when another reverse was caused by an outside force—the Civil War.

The War took its toll of the Philharmonic only indirectly. Fearing that the Society would not be able to fill the Academy of Music under wartime conditions, the Directors moved the concerts, for the two seasons of 1861 to 1863, to the smaller Irving Hall (around the block, at the southwest corner of Irving Place and Fifteenth Street), which cost them only $800 in rent for the season as compared with the $2,500 that had been paid at the Academy. This was a mistaken economy.

‡ The concerts were indeed moved to Niblo's Garden for the next year, 1858–59.

The smaller hall was filled during those two years, but it meant a temporary drop in the number of members that could be accommodated and, consequently, in receipts.[71]

The fears of a wartime slump, it soon became clear, were unjustified. On the contrary, as frequently happens in time of war, attendance at all sorts of entertainments, including concerts and opera, began to rise. In November 1862, William Henry Fry, writing as critic of the *Tribune,* had said, "In these times of doubt and desolation, of war and waste, it is too much to expect a fine opera, rich in all the appointments of novelty, excellence, amplitude, contrast. A regular season is not possible . . . ." But by the spring of the next year his tune had changed: "The week has been one of the most brilliant prosperity for the Academy. The Man in the Moon suddenly visiting us, and going to the Academy now, would never suppose that we were engaged in a desperate civil war, where the stakes were Liberty or Slavery, Union or Disunion. Least of all would he suppose that we are spending some two million dollars a day for the war; a sum greater than the total cost of the Federal Government for a year under the administration of Washington." In the fall of 1863 the Philharmonic was able to move back to the Academy of Music. "The Academy was filled on Saturday evening," *Dwight's Journal* could report on November 14, 1863, "on the occasion of the first Philharmonic Concert of the season. It must have been very gratifying for the Board of Directors to see their new enterprise so nobly sustained. It was a venture on their part to assume the expense of the Academy, but the attendance on the night of their first concert dispelled all doubts as to the feasibility of the plan. The audience was large, brilliant, and appreciative, and the rendition of the . . . programme painstaking and successful." By the time the War was over, in the twenty-fourth season (1865–66), the Philharmonic had surpassed its previous peak for financial receipts with a total of $13,926 taken in from memberships and extra tickets.[72]

From these heights of prosperity came an unexpected plunge in the very next season, the twenty-fifth-anniversary year of 1866–67. (See graph, page 130.) The dip, although a large one, was only for that one season, after which the receipts rebounded just as suddenly to their previous high. These changing fortunes resulted from an accident. On the night of May 21, 1866, the Academy of Music was gutted in a great fire that burned all the north side of Fourteenth Street from Irving Place to Third Avenue, and the Philharmonic had to move to Steinway

Hall, one block west on Fourteenth Street, for the new season. The orchestra did not suffer seriously from the fire itself (in fact, it collected $494.25 in insurance "for instruments lost by conflagration of the Academy"), but it did suffer from the smaller capacity of Steinway Hall. Rent at Steinway was only $1,000, as against the $2,750 that the Academy had recently been taking for a season, but the savings were negligible alongside the loss in ticket sales, which fell from $13,900 to $9,500 in that single season.* As soon as the concerts could move back to the Academy once more, in 1867–68, the receipts shot up again to $14,000.[73]

Except for the loss caused by the burning of the Academy, the Philharmonic's financial returns seem to climb steadily through the Civil War and immediately after it, from about $6,000 in 1861–62 to $14,000 in 1867–68. But, surprisingly, while the amount of income was going up, the number of members of all kinds was falling off sharply. Of the 1,339 members in 1863–64, only 457 remained by 1867–68! (See table, Backnote 74.) This apparent contradiction has a rational explanation. Philharmonic audiences, like the New York public in general, were always sensitive to money matters. The number of subscribers declined because subscription prices were raised steeply in 1863–65 and again in 1867–68. The membership thinned so far that the Society's income would have shrunk to a fraction of its previous level, even at the higher prices, if it had not been for a compensatory factor: *extra* tickets (for non-subscribers) were now such good value by comparison that the increasing number of people buying them outweighed the decline in regular membership. Between 1862 and 1868 the share of the Philharmonic's income that came from sales of extra tickets rose spectacularly from 23 to 65 per cent, while the share from season memberships fell reciprocally from 77 to 35 per cent. All of this implied changes in the Philharmonic's outlook. When an orchestra sells more single tickets for separate concerts than it does season subscriptions, it must seek more brilliant attractions that will ensure full houses even without the security of advance subscribers.

It is no surprise, after this analysis of the Philharmonic's income, to

---

* An innocent casualty of the move to Steinway Hall was the pianist James Wehli. He had enjoyed a considerable success as soloist with the Philharmonic the year before and was scheduled to perform again in 1866–67. But a letter from the Secretary on December 2, 1866, informed him that the Society would have to cancel his appearance because he used a Chickering piano and Steinway would not permit it.

NEW YORK PHILHARMONIC
FINANCIAL RECEIPTS, 1842–1868

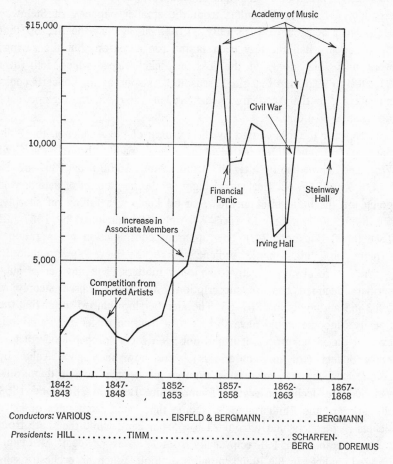

Conductors: VARIOUS . . . . EISFELD & BERGMANN . . . . BERGMANN

Presidents: HILL . . . . TIMM . . . . SCHARFEN-
                                                            BERG   DOREMUS

find equally drastic changes taking place in its expenditures. Such items
as advertising, and salaries for special personnel, inevitably loom larger
in the budget of an organization whose income depends on holding the
public's attention from one performance to another. The Philharmonic
began to engage attractive soloists, and even orchestra players from
outside the organization, on a much larger scale than previously. "Extra
professional services"—that is, outside players called in when needed—
had formerly been an item of a couple of hundred dollars, at the most,
in the budget, and soloists' fees had been $50 or $100 a season, if the
artists were not prevailed upon to donate their services for nothing; in

1862–63, for example, these two items together came to about $300. But they jumped to more than $1,700 in 1863–64 and 1864–65, and to $2,686 in 1865–66—an increase of 800 per cent over 1862–63. Bergmann, the conductor, who had previously received no remuneration except the glory of his position and an annual dividend like that of any player in the orchestra, was paid a real conductor's fee of $500 in 1865–66—the first annual salary to a conductor in the Philharmonic's history.† The budget for advertising had usually been about $150 for the season—occasionally a little more—but in 1865–66 it went over $600.[75] Clearly the Philharmonic was making an effort to change much of its mode of operation.

It was creating what advertising circles today would call a new image.

---

† In the full flush of the triumphant fifteenth season, 1856–57, Theodore Eisfeld, as the captain who had led his men to victory, had been voted a gold watch and chain valued at $145.75 as a testimonial from his colleagues in the Society. In the sixth season, 1847–48, the Society had given U. C. Hill a "Tribute of Merit" in the form of a gold snuffbox valued at $143. But neither Eisfeld nor Hill had been paid a regular conductor's salary.

Chapter 13

Growth After the Civil War
(1867–70)

The new image became clear for all to see from 1867 on—expensive soloists, fashionable auditorium, liberal advertising, salaried conductor, enlarged orchestra.

What was happening was that the Philharmonic was trying to meet competition in its chosen field of serious, German-oriented concerts. The greatest threat came from Theodore Thomas who had assembled a fine professional orchestra of his own, rehearsed it carefully, and won over a large section of the public and the press. But there was also, strange as it may seem at first glance, competition from some of the orchestra's own people. The Philharmonic personnel could not be expected to make a living from five concerts a year. Eisfeld, Bergmann, and the orchestra men had all been taking part in other series of concerts since the 1850s. It was as violinist in Bergmann's Sacred Concerts that Theodore Thomas had learned some of the ropes of concert giving. For that matter Thomas himself remained a member of the Philharmonic until 1869, while his own performances were rivaling those of the Society. Even the Brooklyn Philharmonic, which in one sense helped the New York orchestra by using some of the same personnel and thereby providing them with extra jobs, also constituted a kind of competition, if only because it represented another call on the services of the same conductors and players and therefore competed for dates, repertory, and soloists, though not for the same audience. For several years, too, the press had been aggravating the competitive tensions by carping at the Philharmonic's methods and standards, and calling for change. "The antiquated, old-fogyish New York Philharmonic Society," needled *Dwight's Journal* from Boston in December 1864, "long since distanced by the Brooklyn society in the matter of novelty, variety and general excellence, will soon have another formidable, and I trust, successful rival in a series of 'Symphonic Soirees,' under the vigorous management and leadership of THEO. THOMAS."

The Philharmonic's twenty-fifth anniversary was naturally a time for self-examination, and perhaps it was a good thing, in the long view, that the season was financially a poor one—it provided the incentive for speeding up the reforms that had been in the making for a few years. The move to the small Steinway Hall in that twenty-fifth season, it will be remembered, had caused money problems, and a gala extra concert to celebrate the anniversary on May 4, 1867,[76] had netted only the disappointing sum of $517.92. Since Scharfenberg, the President of the Philharmonic, had anyway resigned early in the season because he was moving to Havana (Bristow had been elected to fill out his term), it seemed a strategic moment for a change of regime. The man who has been given most of the credit for the new look that the Philharmonic now assumed was Dr. R. Ogden Doremus (1824–1906), the distinguished professor of chemistry at the New York Free Academy (City College), who was proposed for the Society's presidency in 1867. Doremus was highly regarded in both the intellectual and the social circles of the city, and his mission to France a few years earlier to help in the perfection of a gunpowder for Napoleon III had lent him even a public glamour. Doremus had had an associate membership in the Philharmonic since 1845 (his name can be found in the Fourth Annual Report, concealed behind the phonetic misspelling "Derimus"), but he was not a professional musician, and this was an obstacle to his becoming President of the Society since the Constitution required the presidency to be filled from among the professionals who constituted the Actual Members. So strongly was it now felt, nevertheless, that a man of his position and talents was necessary to guide the orchestra in changing times that the Constitution was actually amended to permit him to be elected.

Doremus promptly went to work to make the Philharmonic what New Yorkers of the last century called a "high-class" institution. In the three years of his tenure from 1867 to 1870 he augmented the orchestra from the seventy-eight or eighty performing members that it had previously been drawing upon to a grand Romantic size of more than one hundred performing musicians.[77] He put pressure on the Society to make its programs more attractive so that they could better compete for the public attention with the offerings of Theodore Thomas and other musico-artistic events. A great fuss was made, for example, in May of 1869, about his persuading the celebrated actor Edwin Booth to read Lord Byron's *Manfred* in the musical setting by Robert Schumann—its first performance in America. But most characteristically of all, he set out on a deliberate campaign to interest the fashionable elements of New York's social world in the Philharmonic concerts to a greater degree than ever before. He counted on the power of money, of glamour, and of advertising. For each of the three years of his administration, the Society spent approximately $1,000 on advertising; this was two or three times what it had spent in most previous seasons. Bergmann's salary as conductor went from $500 for a season to $600 and then to $1,000. Soloists and featured artists were chosen with an eye to the box office. Fewer of them were expected to be content with the glory of the performance as remuneration, and a currently successful singer or actress could now hope for a fee of $300 to $500 for an appearance with the Philharmonic. Choruses no longer had to volunteer their services. In Doremus's last year with the orchestra, the Arion Chorus was paid $850, and another $3,279 was spent for soloists and extra orchestra players. Beginning in 1867–68, the Philharmonic proudly listed in summary at the end of each of its Annual Reports the names of the soloists who had adorned the year— Madame Parepa-Rosa, Madame Camilla Urso, and eight others in that season alone—and in subsequent years the list was to include the most glamorous of the touring virtuosi: Rubinstein, Wieniawski, Wilhelmj, Rivé, Remenyi, Lilli Lehmann.

All of this paid off in ticket receipts, which set new records every year—$14,061 in 1867–68, $23,636 in 1868–69, and $25,507 in 1869–70. There had been an anxious moment in the first of those years when the cost of an associate membership for the season was raised from $8 to $10 and the number of members in the money-sensitive Philharmonic community promptly dropped to 399, the lowest it had been in fifteen years. But Doremus's high-pressure methods had so increased the sale of extra (non-subscription) tickets that a very satisfactory sum was realized for the whole season; and the situation

was saved for the next year by increasing the number of concerts from
five to six, which carried the ticket and subscription sales in all categories to new heights. Finally, a new system of auctioning off the box
seats at the Academy of Music had such snob appeal that it brought in
a tidy sum of fresh money beginning in the season of 1869–70.

Bigger orchestras, bigger halls, bigger audiences, bigger budgets were
all inextricably bound up together. The composers of the Romantic
era, from the middle of the nineteenth century on, wrote for an orchestra that was larger and louder than that of the Classical masters of an
earlier age. The woodwind and brass instruments had been improved
by the invention of key and valve systems which gave them a new
agility. The stringed instruments had met this threat to their preemi-
nence by improvement in technique, particularly in the higher registers,
by changes in the style of playing to emphasize great sonority, and by
a simple increase in numbers to compensate for the growing power of
the other sections in the orchestra. Composers like Berlioz and Wagner
specified carefully the number of string players that they required to
prevent imbalance in the orchestra—"at least 16 first violins," "at
least 12 violoncellos" were frequent indications in their scores. New
instruments, such as the bass tuba, were added to the orchestra's ar-
senal. Older ones, such as the harp, were radically improved. Woodwind
instruments that had formerly been considered "extra," such as the
piccolo, the bass clarinet, the English horn, and the contrabassoon, became accepted and expected parts of a large orchestra. The percussion
section expanded to include, as standard equipment, instruments that
had once been thought of as exotic—the "Janizary" instruments (bass
drum, triangle, cymbals), the gong, the tambourine, the xylophone,
castanets, bells. The piano, with the steel frame that was developed
by the Steinway company and other manufacturers, became the powerful solo instrument of great virtuoso performers, ready to match the
orchestras of the day.*

As orchestras developed in size, complexity, and the level of their

* It is not surprising, therefore, to find piano manufacturers, including Steinway,
Knabe, Weber, and others, functioning as the impresarios and music patrons of
a large part of the city's musical life in the second half of the century, for business
reasons as well as philanthropic or artistic ones. Music publishers, for their part,
took over music journals and periodicals for their advertising value; Dexter Smith's
Musical, Literary, Dramatic, and Art Paper boasted itself in 1873 "the only
Musical Monthly in the United States which is not issued by a Music Publishing
House as an advertising medium."

players, forceful artistic leaders were obviously required to integrate them—the emergence of the "artist-conductor" was inevitable. The old practice of temporarily elevating one or another orchestra member (sometimes a talented one, but sometimes merely a faithful or an industrious one) to lead his peers could no longer be adequate. Yet, until the years following the Civil War, the Philharmonic seemed conservatively reluctant to recognize this reality.[78] For the first ten years of its existence, as we have seen, despite the grumblings of the press and the connoisseurs about the importance of entrusting the musical direction to a single conductor, it persisted in its patchwork pattern of two to six different conductors every season. Then for thirteen more years, until the end of its twenty-third season in 1865, it vacillated between Theodore Eisfeld and Carl Bergmann as conductors, sometimes giving a whole season to one of them, but more often dividing a season between them. Yet Theodore Eisfeld had demonstrated in the several seasons for which he had had full responsibility that he was a thoroughly schooled musician and artist,[79] a strong leader, and attractive to the public. He had also had the initiative and the educational foresight to pioneer in the presentation of chamber-music series in the city, had had the distinction and the publicity of conducting some of the fabulous Jenny Lind concerts, and had been one of the founders and the first conductor of the sister Philharmonic in Brooklyn. In spite of these obvious qualifications, the Philharmonic seems to have hesitated to turn over its direction entirely to him. Krehbiel implies that Eisfeld never recovered physically, spiritually, or financially from an experience that he underwent in 1858–59 when, on his return from a visit to Germany, the ship that bore him, the S.S. *Austria,* burned at sea and he found his way back to New York, by way of the Azores, only after much suffering. But it seems unreasonable to lay too much of the blame on this ordeal by water, since Eisfeld successfully carried almost two thirds of the Philharmonic's concerts for half a dozen years after it.† When he retired to Germany in 1866, however, the stage was left clear for Bergmann to take over as permanent conductor.

The role of artist-conductor was waiting for Bergmann, and Berg-

---

† Krehbiel also says that the Philharmonic "exhausted its Sinking Fund" with a loan of $500 to Eisfeld to make possible his trip to Germany, and that it eventually forgave him part of the debt; but there is no record of this in the Treasurer's Reports of the period, the Sinking Fund holding $863.39 in 1858 and $910.11 in 1859, all safely earning interest in the Bowery Savings Bank and the Seamen's Savings Bank.

mann was ready for it. When he came to the United States in the fall of 1849 (fleeing from Europe because of his involvement in the 1848 revolution), he had already, at the age of twenty-eight, worked with orchestras in Breslau, Vienna, Pesth, Warsaw, and Venice. In this country he had gone through the mill of orchestral experience for four more years, first as cellist and then as conductor for the little traveling orchestra known as the Germania. Then, settling in New York in 1854, he had become conductor of the Männergesangverein Arion (Arion Men's Chorus), and by 1855 was alternating with Eisfeld as conductor of the Philharmonic. At the same time he served as cellist in the famous Mason-Thomas chamber-music concerts. He also presented, on his own, a long series of Sacred Concerts with orchestral programs as impressive as, and more adventurous than, those of the Philharmonic. He had already conducted Wagner's *Tannhäuser* Overture with the Germania orchestra in Boston in 1852, and had given an entire Wagner Night there in 1853 "to gratify the public curiosity about Wagner," and after he had taken up his residence in New York, his name continued to be associated with the "new music" of Wagner, Liszt, and Berlioz. Bergmann's championing of Wagner was pioneering work, and successful pioneering at that. When Wagner himself conducted his *Tannhäuser* Overture and some *Lohengrin* excerpts with the London Philharmonic in 1855, the press of that city still found him "a desperate charlatan," *Lohengrin* "an incoherent mass of rubbish," and the *Tannhäuser* Overture "one of the most curious pieces of patchwork ever passed off by self-delusion for a complete and significant creation." Yet Bergmann's performance of the same *Tannhäuser* Overture, on April 21 of the same year, with the New York Philharmonic (his first appearance with the Philharmonic, replacing Eisfeld who was ill), evoked a thunderous ovation; and later in the same season he was encouraged to play more Wagner, a *Lohengrin* excerpt and the *Rienzi* Overture, in a Grand German Musical Festival at the Metropolitan Theatre. Indeed, Bergmann's *Tannhäuser* performance was so well received by critics, musicians, and public that it made his career—on the basis of that one concert, the Philharmonic's Directors gave him the chief credit for the orchestra's improvement during the season, and he was engaged as conductor for all the concerts of the next season, the beginning of his twenty-year association with the Society. The comparison with London says much for Bergmann, for New York, and for the Philharmonic. To a progressive artist in the third quarter of the nineteenth century, Wagner, Liszt, Berlioz, Schumann, and even Brahms and Tchaikovsky were "causes," and all of them were represented in the New York Philharmonic programs under Bergmann's baton. His performance of Brahms's Second Serenade in 1862 was one of the earliest in America, he introduced Wagner's *Tristan* Prelude to New York in 1866, and he had programmed the American premiere of Tchaikovsky's *Romeo and Juliet* for a concert which he was never able to give, in 1876, the last year of his life.

Looking back from the vantage points of Germany and the year 1880, Max Goldstein, a knowledgeable commentator, summed up: "Principally Bergmann communicated to the Americans their first regular acquaintance with the symphonies of Schumann, [and] numerous creations of Liszt, Berlioz and Wagner, and created for America a kind of tradition in the comprehension and rendering of the nine symphonies of Beethoven."[80] Thanks to the musical evangelism of Bergmann and his co-workers, the tradition of German-serious music was now so firmly allied with "high-class" music-making and concertgoing in New York that it could embrace the new music with the old, the futurism of Wagner with the classicism of Beethoven and Mozart. When an outsider like Berlioz seemed to be accepted in this exclusive, orthodox circle, it was largely because, and to the extent that, he had already been accepted in Germany, and the "Scène d'Amour" from the French composer's *Romeo and Juliet* appears in a Philharmonic program of 1872, in English-speaking New York, under the hybrid-German title of "Liebes scene."

Chapter 14

Loss of the Native Heritage

The German domination of symphonic music in New York, and indeed everywhere in the United States, has too long been underestimated. It is a domination that has largely determined the aesthetics and the sociology of orchestral concert giving in this country.

It was in the years after the Civil War that the victory of the German tradition was confirmed. When, in 1852, *Dwight's Journal* said of the New York Philharmonic: "The members are all inspired by the same sympathies,—mostly Germans, they believe in the German Composers," the American composer, represented by Fry and Bristow, could still fight back proudly and fiercely, and the Philharmonic still felt obliged to issue an apologia. But by the Bergmann era, the American composers no longer struggled to assert themselves on the musical scene. From one point of view they can be said to have been defeated; from another, it can be said that the Germanization had developed so far that it had now become the American national style for "serious" music. Anthony Philip Heinrich, Louis Moreau Gottschalk, William Henry Fry—the peculiarly American ones—were out of the running. Heinrich, once heralded as the "Beethoven of America," had come to be regarded in his old age as a lovable eccentric to be humored in a kindly fashion, but not to be taken seriously; and he was completely forgotten as soon as he was dead in 1869. Yet this was the man whom

Oscar Sonneck, the pioneer American musicologist, has properly called
"easily the most commanding figure as a composer in America before
1860." Gottschalk did enjoy a great success in this country as a pianist
—it would have taken deaf ears not to have recognized the quality of a
performer whom Chopin had hailed as a "king of pianists," and who
had been showered with praise by Berlioz, Liszt, and the other magistrates of European musical taste—but as a composer he had to seek
his appreciative audiences abroad, in the Latin American countries of
the Caribbean and of South America. Fry, in the mid-1860s, was a
pathetic figure, a sick and aging man, still complaining about the senseless anti-Americanism of the American musical world. Only George
Frederick Bristow, of this group of American composers, managed to
shape something of a career for himself, and this he could do because
in the first place he tended by nature and background to sound more
like the acceptable models of Mendelssohn and Schumann, in the
second place he had the good fortune to outlive the other three, and
the time, therefore, to learn to reconcile himself to the now accepted
European style, and in the third place he held important positions
throughout his life, in the New York Philharmonic, in the public school
system of the city, and as a choral conductor, which gave him a secure
foothold, and provided him with performance outlets for his music.

Between the Italianization of the opera world and the Germanization of the symphonic world, there was not very much room for an
indigenous American style. New American composers in the generations after the Civil War were valued to the degree that they sounded
like the current European products, with an occasional little touch of
Americanism accepted and even expected—in the form of a title, an
alleged Indian theme, or some similar minor gesture. It is touching
to read Fry's stubborn but hopeless protests, sprinkled throughout his
critiques in the *Tribune* in the years just before his death in 1865. "To
see . . . seventy or eighty musical gentlemen . . . ," he wrote of the
New York Philharmonic in 1863, "content to advertise year in and year
out, pieces of foreign production . . . is a sorry sight . . . no other
country is so wanting in artistic pride." Our musical societies claimed
to be elevating the cultural level, but they were "devoted to the distant
and the dead." Twenty years ago, he pointed out, there had been
societies, half amateur and half professional, it is true, but "glad to
play original compositions; and in one or two instances [they] struck
medals in honor of the composer"; whereas in 1864 an American

composer had to present his music at his own cost if he wanted it to be heard, and American musical art that was known to the public was, in consequence, "as scarce here in New York as on the Western prairies." The Italian opera might be fashionable now, but Fry sighed for the time when opera in English had flourished in New York, when the great Malibran, and Mrs. Austin, and Mrs. Wood, and the Seguin company, and a host of others had not scorned to sing in English. Now, in the 1860s, if you heard singing in English, it was likely to be the "sham Negro minstrelsy" which had become the "lyric-democratic idea of the age."

The separation between "serious"-European and "light"-American music had become so accepted a fact of New York's musical life by the mid-1860s, as Fry astutely observed, that the long tradition of musical theater in the English language was dying and forgotten. It has never been remembered since then. To this day, those few historians who can overcome the intellectuals' prejudice against American popular musical theater in English persist in calling *The Black Crook* of 1866 America's first musical comedy. The truth of the matter is that the history of our musical comedy extends back in an unbroken line at least to the eighteenth century.[81] What can properly be dated from somewhere around 1866 is the entrenchment of the musical and social bigotry that assigned our native musical theater to an artistic ghetto, isolated from the fashionable society of imported opera and the quasi-religious atmosphere of German serious music of the nineteenth century.

It was not entirely coincidence that these developments came forward in the years immediately after the Civil War. The war helped to establish the position of recent immigrants in American society. Immigrant farmers and craftsmen made money because of the war; their young men served in the Union Army, often replacing for money a citizen who was able to buy his way out of the draft, and the long duration of the War strengthened the ties of the newcomers to the rest of the population, with whom they shared experiences and anxieties. But, interestingly enough, while the Germans were assimilating rapidly into the post-Civil-War, money-making American society, new German immigrants were necessary to fill the musical ranks. For native Americans already considered music the province of foreigners, and even the sons of immigrants looked often to other fields, where there was more money to be made, in order to lift themselves into the new American society. As the second half of the nineteenth century moved on, the New

York Philharmonic became more German than it had ever been before. "The members of the orchestra," wrote Krehbiel in his *Memorial* in 1892, "are now, with but few exceptions, either musicians of German birth or German parentage. . . . The people of the United States have not learned to look upon the profession of music as the Germans do, with whom it is not only an art or a pastime but also a trade. Orchestral instruments, like the oboe, clarinet, trombone, French horn, and double-bass, are no more studied in 1892 by the native population than they were in 1792. For players upon them we are still dependent either on foreigners or the children of naturalized citizens." Krehbiel did not exaggerate: of the approximately one hundred musicians who made up the Philharmonic in 1892, only three were not German.

These were the years, in the latter part of the nineteenth century, when pro-Germanism was spreading through many areas of the English-speaking cultural world. In England Carlyle and his followers, in America Emerson and Bancroft had long been admirers of German culture. Even before the Civil War a small but growing number of educated Americans had become acquainted with German writers— Bürger, de la Motte Fouqué, Heine, Hoffmann, Lessing, Schiller, the Schlegels, Uhland, and of course Goethe—either in the original language or in translation. In 1850 more than twenty English translations of Goethe's *Faust* were already in existence. But it was in the second half of the century that translations of the artistic quality of Bayard Taylor's version of *Faust* "in the original meters," and of Longfellow's and Leland's renderings of German lyric poems, impressed a wider American public with the importance of German literature. In higher education, the painstaking scholarly methods of the Germans were being adopted by American universities. In political philosophy, Hegelian influences competed with the English tradition. As perceptive a statesman and historian as Bancroft, the great chronicler of American democracy, could be sufficiently blinded by his admiration for Bismarck's new Germany to expect from the Iron Chancellor's dictatorial regime in 1870 "the most liberal government on the continent of Europe." The English historian Edward Augustus Freeman (who endeavored in his literary style to use as far as possible only words of Teutonic origin) was merely expounding a generally accepted Romantic theory when he taught, in his lectures to American audiences in 1881, that both England and America owed their tradition of liberty to their common ancestors in the forests of ancient Germany.

Yet even those Americans who were sympathetic to German culture sometimes feared that the assimilation might not be proceeding with equal satisfaction in all provinces. "We may well ask," warned Josiah Strong in 1885, in *Our Country: Its Possible Future and Its Present Crisis,* "whether this in-sweeping immigration is to foreignize us or we are to Americanize it." Walt Whitman, sad, wise, somewhat disillusioned, yet still hopeful, regretted in his *Democratic Vistas* of 1871 that, since the War, European models had dominated American life and art, and deplored the self-conscious "culture" that he recognized everywhere around him in artistic matters—culture "for a single class alone, or for the parlors or lecture-rooms," with no "eye to practical life" or to the realities of the great America.

In music, both these fears had already been justified. We have taken note, in the preceding chapter, of Carl Bergmann's contribution to the Germanization of New York's music. Toward the end of Bergmann's life, and in the years immediately after his death in 1876, two other conductors, Leopold Damrosch and Theodore Thomas, carried on the process of educating the New York public in the German-Austrian canon. Comparing them in their rivalry for the leadership of the city's orchestral activity, Max Goldstein made a subtle distinction between them: "In the former, Germany is in America; in the latter, America is in Germany!"[82] By the late 1870s, in other words, New York had only the choice of being conquered by the German musical style or of submitting to it. The German domination, moreover, was based not on the pleasant entertainment values of the Mozart-Haydn period, but on the self-important seriousness that characterized German music of the second half of the nineteenth century. As the German states prospered and advanced economically and politically, there grew up within them a cultural clique that became more assertive and more influential with every year, especially after the great military and psychological victory in the Franco-Prussian War. These earnest and generally well-educated music lovers had a snobbish disdain for the old school of brilliant virtuosity-for-its-own-sake, which had seduced the Parisian audiences in the first half of the nineteenth century, and for the socially relaxed mood of earlier days of concertgoing in Germany and the United States. They recognized, by common agreement, a body of great and monumental musical literature, emphasizing particularly the imposing works of Beethoven, and for the first time in the history of music a large part of the performing instrumentalists preferred to devote themselves principally to composers of the past. So unmistakably German was this attitude that musicians of the serious type—the great Russian pianist Anton Rubinstein, for example—were frequently referred to by the German title of Herr, even when they were of other nationalities. Repelled by the very commercialism which gave their society unprecedented opportunities for enjoying music, they tried to be noble in art, above sordid money-making, avoiding the vulgar "trash" that satisfied lesser souls. These self-righteous attitudes were shared by a small but determined part of the listening public, who sometimes seemed to constitute a semireligious congregation; by a large number of professional performing musicians, who functioned as artist-priests; and by certain composers, who, if we carry our figure a bit further, seem inescapably to have aspired toward some degree of divinity: Wagner and Liszt are obvious examples.

Cultured Englishmen and Americans embraced this German austerity eagerly. The Eleventh Edition of the Encyclopaedia Britannica, published just before the First World War, gives a retrospective insight into this development in its article on APPLAUSE: "The reverential spirit which abolished applause in church has tended to spread to the theatre and the concert-room, largely under the influence of the quasi-religious atmosphere of the Wagner performances at Baireuth. In Germany (e.g. the court theatres at Berlin) applause during the performance and 'calling before the curtain' have been officially forbidden, but even in Germany this is felt to be in advance of public opinion." In any city in the United States that had a concert life, Max Goldstein pointed out, it was the Germans who ran the concerts.[83] They might begin as popular musicians or theater men, but they would soon combine these breadwinning occupations with performances of serious choral works (presented in conjunction with the omnipresent German singing societies, such as the Arion or Liederkranz), and would eventually turn their attention to the enshrined "standard" literature of the great masters of the past, centering around the Nonalogue of Beethoven, and to the complexities of the Wagnerian "music of the future," all the more prized for the intellectual difficulties it posed. As in any cult, the public did not always come for pleasure, and the practitioners did not always come for profit; indeed, they seemed often to be participating in an artistic penance. A whole mythology of pseudophilosophy and pseudomorality grew up around this highbrow musical culture, often confused, but always espoused with ardor by its self-appointed champions. "A symphony orchestra shows the culture of a community, not opera," said Theodore Thomas. "The man who does not know Shakespeare is to be pitied; and the man who does not understand Beethoven and has not been under his spell has not half lived his life. The master works of instrumental music are the language of the soul and express more than those of any other art. Light music, 'popular' so called, is the sensual side of the art and has more or less devil in it."[84]

Here in a single indigestible statement are the clichés of half a century. Even today American musical life has hardly begun to free itself of them.

Chapter 15

Crest and Trough
(1870–79)

The regime of Dr. Doremus as President of the Philharmonic, although it lasted only three years, was long remembered as a golden age in the Society's annals. Twenty years later, Krehbiel still paid Doremus tribute in his history of the Philharmonic, and half a century after that, Erskine repeated all his praises in the book that he prepared for the hundredth anniversary of the orchestra. In an age which admired commercial success and scientific achievement, Doremus—man of science, yet man of affairs—had brought financial prosperity to the Philharmonic at the same time that he had increased its artistic prestige. The men in the orchestra were always interested in the size of their dividends, but they also enjoyed their increased importance in the city's life, and they had enough romantic idealism to bring a certain amount of missionary spirit to their participation in the Philharmonic. As a matter of fact, the players did not profit so exceptionally in dollars during the Doremus years. The largest dividend that they received in this period was only about $25 per man for a concert with all its public and private rehearsals. They had done almost that well several times in the past, and had done considerably better in the memorable fifteenth season (1856–57) when they had averaged over $35 per man per concert. The value of

the dividend had to be sharply discounted in the Doremus era, moreover, because the cost of living was extremely high—something like 45
per cent higher than it had been ten years before.

Golden ages are usually more golden in retrospect. At the peak of
the success of the Doremus-Bergmann consulship, there were grumblings from certain sections of the public about the administrative
methods and the programs. James Francis Ruggles, a socially prominent
New Yorker who was a regular concertgoer, complained in October of
1869 that Dr. Doremus issued tickets far beyond the capacity of the
Academy of Music and let his friends in by some back stairs, so as to
half fill the house before its doors were opened to the common herd of
subscribers. (The Doctor publicly denied the latter charge.) A conservative bloc chafed at the large quantities of Liszt and Wagner that the
zealous Bergmann forced them to listen to, and many of them found
the full houses of new converts that Doremus and Bergmann now
crowded into the Academy of Music a questionable improvement. If the
audience was smaller in the old days, it had at least consisted of the
right people, who knew how to behave at a concert, and who could
always find seats for themselves without pushing and pressing. One of
the most articulate of the conservatives was George Templeton Strong.
"Doremus wants to make the Philharmonic concerts 'draw,' and he has
succeeded," commented Strong at the beginning of Doremus's last season. "He has made them pay better than ever before. That is to say,
he has increased the annual dividend to each member of the orchestra
by perhaps as much as five dollars, but he has made the Society and its
concerts worthless."[85]

It certainly seems more than coincidence that Doremus resigned "on
account of some miff or tiff," as Strong confided to his diary in the
spring of 1870, and that Strong was promptly offered the presidency
by the Philharmonic Board. Probably Strong's opinions as a spokesman
for the conservative element had combined with his reputation as an
avid music lover and his success as founder of the high-toned Church
Music Association (which was being discussed in some circles as a possible rival of the Philharmonic) to make him a logical candidate. At
any rate, he was notified on May 31, 1870, of his unanimous election
as President of the New York Philharmonic.

Krehbiel and Erskine, the historians of the Philharmonic, have given
Dr. Doremus all the credit for the successes and the innovations in the
shaping of the Society's new image. But this is an exaggeration. The

new direction was already evident in Scharfenberg's presidency, before Doremus, and continued to develop even more strongly under George Templeton Strong, after Doremus. It was in Scharfenberg's time, way back in 1863, that the concerts were moved to the Academy of Music, the best hall in town. It was in Scharfenberg's time that the number of concerts was increased to five, with a special sixth concert added in two of the seasons; that Bergmann was given a regular annual salary as conductor; that the expenditures for advertising and for outside professional help began to increase; and that the receipts from the popular sale of extra tickets became a major part of the Society's income.

Strong, as we could have predicted from his criticisms of Doremus, sought to make the Philharmonic's public even more exclusive and its programs even more conservative than they had been. At his very first meeting, three days after his election, with "the seven Philharmonic and Teutonic directors," as he called them with affectionate condescension, he brought up the question of reserved seats. Until this time, all seats had been on a first come, first served basis, and one had had to arrive early in order to get the best ones, unless he could pull strings with someone high in the Society. The reserved-seat experiment, introduced for 1870–71, was a success; every seat in the Academy, except a few far back in the balcony, was sold weeks before the first concert, and when the boxes were auctioned it was found that the revenue from these privileged subscribers was three times as great as it had been in Doremus's best year. Moreover, the income from Associate Members' subscriptions also rose by about 25 per cent, so that, by the end of Strong's first season as President, the Philharmonic had surpassed all of its previous records for financial success. Only the sale of "extra" tickets went down, and this may well have pleased Strong, for the extra tickets represented a less "select" audience than that sustained by subscription.

Strong was particularly proud of the improvement that was becoming evident in audience manners at rehearsals and concerts. He felt that he had begun this progress with the educational campaign that he had conducted for the concerts of his Church Music Association, but that it had now spread to the Philharmonic and to other New York concerts. There was less talking and giggling, the audience was more likely to be silent and attentive, and a regulation was established (difficult to enforce, it was true, despite a "strong printed notice") against the snobbish practice of entering while the music was going on. Anyone who has followed the Metropolitan Opera's struggle with the same practice in recent years will understand Strong's difficulties a century ago in requiring latecomers to wait for a pause in the music before entering the hall.

As for program-making, Strong slyly proposed to the Directors early in his first term that a circular be sent to the subscribers asking what works they would like to hear in the next season; it would give an interesting picture of their taste, he suggested, and would make them feel as though they had some share in making up the program. Also, one suspects, Strong hoped that it might lead to less Wagner, Liszt, Berlioz, and Schumann, all of whom he could hardly abide. Back in 1866, when Strong was just an ordinary subscriber, a Philharmonic program that included Wagner's *Lohengrin* Prelude and Berlioz's *Roman Carnival* Overture had goaded him to remark that "Wagner writes like an 'intoxified' pig, Berlioz like a tipsy chimpanzee." The "galvanic Abbé Liszt" he considered "trash," and he pretended never to remember whether the name was spelled L-i-s-z-t, or L-i-z-s-t. He left at the intermission of one concert in order to avoid hearing Schumann's *Manfred* Overture, and Schumann's Piano Concerto he found "inane and long winded." Though he held Beethoven ordinarily above all other composers, he felt obliged to say even of that composer's Ninth Symphony: "Its spasms and oddities foreshadow the degradation Beethoven's peculiarities have undergone at the hands of those who think themselves his scholars and successors." Wagner he found queer but clever. The Prelude to *Lohengrin* he defined as "two squeakinesses with a brassiness between them. It seems uncommon nonsense," he went on, "but with an occasional gleam of smartness, like the talk of a clever man who is just losing his wits. I do not suppose, however, that Wagner is a half-crazed genius. I take him to be a composer of considerable ability and of plodding industry, and that he writes like a lunatic in order to attract the notice he could not secure by putting his conceptions, such as they are, into the forms of plain sense and artistic propriety."

These opinions Strong carried over into the period of his presidency, but he had less luck in making repertory changes to suit his taste than he did in other aspects of the Society's conduct. For one thing, the Philharmonic's Constitution did not give the President powers over the program-making; for another, Bergmann, the conductor, who was in practice the strongest single influence on the nature of the repertory, was a passionate supporter of the new music, and a sizable portion of the public seemed willing and even determined to pay for tickets to hear it. Indeed, Strong had to use some of his energies to counter unexpected difficulties at the other end of the spectrum, where U. C. Hill, though no lover of Wagner, wanted to remove a Haydn symphony from a program as "obsolete."* And a special all-Beethoven concert which the orchestra had organized for December 17, 1870, to honor the one hundredth anniversary of the composer's birth, sold so few seats that complimentary tickets had to be given away on a large scale, in the twenty-four hours before the concert, in order to guarantee an audience.

Great excitement, on the other hand, surrounded the appearance with the Philharmonic of the illustrious pianist, composer, and conductor Anton Rubinstein. When he arrived in New York on September 12, 1872, looking (said Strong) like a "long-haired Kalmuck," an orchestra of Philharmonic men serenaded him with performances of a Wagner overture, Meyerbeer's *Fackeltanz,* and the Andante of Beethoven's Fifth Symphony. A great crowd gathered in Fourth Avenue to witness this romantic gesture. Rubinstein played with the Philharmonic on November 16, and it was generally agreed that he was the best pianist that had been heard in New York within memory. But the Rubinstein mania almost led to the disruption of the orchestra later in the same season. The Philharmonic had agreed to pay $1,000 to Maurice Grau, the impresario, for the appearance of Henry Wieniawski, the Polish violinist, and Rubinstein, conducting his own *Ocean* Symphony, to finish the season gloriously on April 19, 1873. But late in March it was discovered, as Strong tells the story, that Grau was advertising Rubinstein and his symphony for a prior concert speculation of his own. Bergmann and most of the Board members were furious. The question had to be referred to a meeting of the full Society for fear that the orchestra might be too exasperated to play properly under Rubinstein. Some were for repudiating him, others were ready to resign if this were done, and Strong had to deliver a ten-minute oration to calm the passions. Rankling to both sides, beneath the surface of the argument, was the irritating awareness that Theodore Thomas, with his

---

* Old U. C. Hill seemed to be going through a voltaic phase in 1871. Strong reports on January 9 that Hill solicited his subscription for a benefit concert that he proposed to offer at the Academy, in which he would give Beethoven's *Pastoral* Symphony with the storm in the third movement illustrated by flashes of electric light and an improved thunder machine of sheet iron. Strong advised him that it might be well "to consider the expediency of this somewhat maturely."

private orchestra, had already presented excerpts from the coveted symphony on January 2 as part of a brilliant series of Rubinstein-Wieniawski-Thomas concerts in New York and Brooklyn. The fuss was smoothed over in time for the concert, and the great magician, conducting without a score, hypnotized public and orchestra alike. At the Philharmonic's annual meeting and election, at the close of the season, Rubinstein was made an Honorary Member, and Strong was applauded into the presidency again.

The Philharmonic had reason to be pleased with the four years of Strong's presidency, from 1870 to 1874. The audience had been cultivated to new heights of refinement. Materially, the orchestra had never been so prosperous. In Strong's first two years ticket receipts set a new record for the Society, and the average for the four years was the highest of any administration in the Philharmonic's history. The same was true of the dividends paid to the men in the orchestra. There were fringe benefits too. For example, Strong's cultivated and wealthy friend Edmund Schermerhorn had been running a series of chamber-music "matinees" at his home on certain afternoons for an audience of about fifty of the right people; in 1872 and 1873, he advanced from quartets and sextets to an orchestra of about twenty-five players, mostly "picked Philharmonickers" who welcomed the additional income that these pleasant afternoons brought them. At the end of George Templeton Strong's second year as President, the members of the Philharmonic, in gratitude for his achievements, elected him an Honorary Associate Member.† To all appearances, it was a time for rejoicing and congratulations in the Philharmonic.

But beneath the appearances of health and prosperity, the roots of trouble and hard times were already growing.

For one thing, in the midst of the most successful era in its history, the Philharmonic was alienating large sections of the press and the public. Strong's election to the presidency of the Philharmonic had originally been greeted with approval by the New York press, and the usual complimentary "puffs" had appeared in the newspapers. But in the

---

† There were only two other names on that select list—Dr. R. Ogden Doremus, Strong's predecessor, and Edwin Booth, the tragedian. The class of Honorary Associate Members had been created by amendment to the Philharmonic's Constitution, toward the end of Dr. Doremus's last term in office, in order to honor him (as a non-professional he was not eligible for regular honorary membership), and Edwin Booth, who had performed for the Society's benefit at Dr. Doremus's request, had also been admitted.

fall of 1870 the Philharmonic's Directors decided to advertise in only six dailies instead of the more than twenty that they had formerly patronized, and also to cut down on free tickets and other privileges for the press. Strong warned nervously that the newspapers would attack in retaliation, and they did. Within a matter of weeks the editors of the *Herald* were making war on the Philharmonic: they criticized the spacing of the concerts, which had been just about the same, as far as anyone could see, for the past twenty years; they complained that the programs lacked novelty; and they referred pointedly to the management of the Society as "formerly" efficient. When the first concert of the season came around, the hall was really crowded and the orchestra was pleased with the success of its experiment with reserved seats, but the *World* and the *Herald* said that the Academy was "not so full as usual." That the Philharmonic was right and the newspapers wrong can be seen from the ticket receipts, which were the highest that the Society had ever known. Now that their share of complimentary tickets and reserved seats had been curtailed, the critics were seldom satisfied. "Whenever we play Beethoven or Mozart," observed the Philharmonic's President, "they denounce us for producing 'hackneyed' compositions, and when we bring out some 'novelty' of Raff's or Rubinstein's, they deplore our neglect of the great old classical models."

The public joined the press in accusing the Philharmonic of snobbishness, of favoritism in the distribution of tickets, of greed in money matters, and of catering to a narrow clique in its program-making. Krehbiel, the Philharmonic's proud historian at the end of the nineteenth century, felt obliged "in the interests of truth" to reprint the following amusing verses, "which gave expression to the extreme wing of a considerable number of malcontents":

> The German Philharmonic
>   Rules the music of this town;
> It plays for pet subscribers—
>   The public is done brown.
> Its Music of the Future
>   On every pure ear palls;—
> Subscribers sit—the public stands,
>   As cattle stand in stalls.
> Then sing the Philharmonic,
>   Where Art-love reigns o'er all!
> When the Dollar looks almighty large
>   And Music very small!

There were also protests of gross fraud and dishonesty in the sale of Philharmonic seats at Heuser's and Schirmer's music shops. Such scandals were common in business and politics in the cynical, money-minded years that followed the Civil War, and now they were cropping up in the world of music too.[86]

On top of these difficulties came the terrible financial Panic of 1873. Many causes have been suggested for the Panic and the depression that followed it—overspeculation and overexpansion in mines, railroads, manufacturing, and grain farming, in Europe, the United States, and South America; the aftereffects of the Civil War and the Franco-Prussian War; the huge losses that were suffered in the great Chicago and Boston fires, and the strain that they imposed on New York insurance companies; the unsettling effect on international trade of the recently opened Suez Canal. The American crash was precipitated by a crisis in Vienna which caused Europeans to recall loans in the United States. The financial world in America had begun to be nervous in April 1873, when the Atlantic Bank failed. Other banks went down in early September, but the really big shock was the failure on September 18 of the supposedly impregnable New York house of Jay Cooke, which had been the principal financier of the Civil War, and which even then was building the Northern Pacific Railroad. Panic broke out among the Wall Street stock gamblers and speculators. Every day saw more runs on banks. The Stock Exchange judiciously closed down entirely for ten days. Factories were shut, railroad construction stopped, the stream of business slowed to a trickle. In New York City the unemployed battled the police.

For the Philharmonic the repercussions from this financial disaster were sharp and immediate. People do not rush to spend their money on orchestra subscriptions when the whole economy is unstable and confused, and unstable and confused it remained for almost six years of depression and deflation. In a single year the Philharmonic's ticket receipts fell more than $6,000. The boxes, which had been distributed by auction for several years, now went at panic prices, and many were not sold at all. For the first concert of the thirty-second season, on November 15, 1873, the Academy of Music seemed very full but, as the President confessed, "It would be indiscreet to enquire what was the percentage of deadheads"; he himself had given away some half-dozen boxes. The hard times also stirred up unrest in the ranks. In the first year of the depression, our old friend "the ancient and garrulous U. C. Hill," as Strong called him, reported that the Philharmonic men were disturbed. In a way they were as much employers as employees, since the Philharmonic was a cooperative,[87] but they could not be happy in either capacity—with the ticket sales spoiled by the Panic, the musicians grumbled that their dividend would be smaller. There was talk of a new Board of Directors and of dissatisfaction with Bergmann, the conductor, who was said to be "lazy and negligent and always overcharged with lager." Indeed, Strong began to get the impression that Hill was hinting to him that he ought to decline reelection as President. Under these circumstances, though Strong was reelected by a vote of forty out of sixty-six, he decided to decline because there seemed to be too many dissenters to his holding the office. Hill wrote to Strong, at this juncture, begging him to accept, but Strong questioned his sincerity. "I think the politic U. C. Hill tried to elect Doremus," he confided to his Diary. "He is a slippery fish."

So a new President, Henry G. Stebbins, was inducted, though Bergmann remained as conductor, while ticket sales and the morale of the orchestra continued to plunge downward. Stebbins lasted one year as President of the Philharmonic and was succeeded by Edmund Schermerhorn, the music patron. "An admirable choice for the Society," commented Strong, who was a very sick man now and probably suffering just a little from sour grapes as well, "but bad for Edmund."

It was a bad time for everyone involved. The talented Bergmann, who had made the Philharmonic into a great orchestra in the German image, was now professionally so sloppy, spiritually so depressed, physically so decayed, and continually so drunk that only the great affection that his men bore him kept him in his post. Finally, for the general rehearsal and concert of March 17 and 18, 1876, it became impossible for him to go on, and the conductor's stand had to be taken over at short notice by Bergmann's faithful henchman, the violist George Matzka. Six days later the Philharmonic asked for Bergmann's resignation, and the last concert of the season, on April 22, had also to be conducted by Matzka. Nothing would ever go right for Bergmann again. The death of his wife, his severance from the Philharmonic, and his sickness plunged him into an extreme melancholy. "From that time," reads his obituary in the New York *Tribune* of August 14, 1876, "he rapidly declined in health and spirits, living a solitary and retired life, and shunning the company of his former associates. About a week ago he was obliged to seek refuge at the German Hospital, where he died on Thursday night at 11 o'clock."[88] The final rites, held not in a church but in the Aschenbrödel Hall on East Fourth Street, bore the marks of the transplanted German culture of which Bergmann had been one of the chief champions in America. "His funeral took place on Saturday under the auspices of the Aschenbrodel Society, of which he was a member," reported *Dwight's Journal* on August 19, ". . . The services were entirely musical; no minister was present and no burial service was read. As the coffin was borne from the house the members of the Arion Society entoned Bergmann's favorite song, the 'Pilgrim's Chorus' from Wagner's Tannhäuser, accompanied by a band from the Aschenbrodel Society." Bergmann's obsequies, like his whole life, ended in a pathetic decrescendo: "Through some misunderstanding, the news of his death did not reach many of his musical associates, who would otherwise have attended the funeral, and therefore the number present was comparatively small."[89]

The Philharmonic's affairs were at a low ebb. Its conductor was dead. Ticket receipts had fallen to only $10,000 for the season, and each player's dividend was a mere $30 for the whole series of six concerts with all their rehearsals. The orchestra had watched helplessly as its musical standards had been lowered during the period of Bergmann's decay. And in this weakened condition the Philharmonic had to face its greatest problem of all, its bogey, the competition of Theodore Thomas.

Ever since 1863, when Thomas had assembled an orchestra to present ten "matinees" at Irving Hall, he had been giving long series of concerts with an orchestra of symphonic proportions. After the Irving Hall matinees, there were his Symphony Soirees (later called Symphony Concerts), beginning in 1864, and a gigantic number of so-called Garden Concerts of a popular nature, given from 1865 on, in Belvedere Lion Park, Terrace Garden, and Central Park Garden. Thomas always had a first-rate orchestra. He picked his men carefully, rehearsed them almost daily, and maintained a strict discipline. He made the work artistically worthwhile for the best musicians by giving them opportunities to play solos whenever possible, and financially worthwhile for all the men by obtaining as many engagements as possible. When Thomas was appointed conductor of the neighboring Brooklyn Philharmonic Society in 1866, he saw to it that his men were engaged for those concerts. And, after 1868, he traveled more and more with the orchestra in order to keep them gainfully employed.

All of this meant several kinds of competition between Thomas and the Philharmonic: competition for the services of the best orchestra players in the city, competition for the best dates in the calendar, competition for the attention of the public, competition for the favors of the press, competition for the most brilliant soloists, and competition for interesting pieces in the repertory. In most of these, Thomas was coming out ahead. Krehbiel, in his Philharmonic *Memorial,* says flatly, "Mr. Thomas depleted the ranks of the Society of many of its best players." Thomas, in his *Autobiography,* brands this an untruthful statement, but he is not being completely candid. The personnel records and the programs reveal that numbers of the best Philharmonic players were lured away from time to time by artistic or financial bait or by the temptation to appear as solo performers with Thomas's fine orchestra.‡ One reason that the Philharmonic had to spend more money for "extra professional services," that is, outsiders hired as substitutes for missing members, throughout the administrations of Doremus and Strong was the Thomas competition. When it was not a question of actually losing a present member, it sometimes meant that the Philharmonic had to be content with a lesser man for some instrument because the best players in town had been won over by the more attractive conditions of working with Thomas. Once in a while, too, Thomas's concerts fell on the same dates as Philharmonic concerts. On January 22, 1876, for example, Thomas was giving one of his Symphony Concerts at the same time that Bergmann was conducting a Philharmonic performance. And on March 18 of the same year, the sad day when the crumbling Bergmann could no longer function and Matzka had to take over for him, Thomas was conducting a concert of the Brooklyn Philharmonic Society—a particularly poignant comparison, since Bergmann had once been conductor of the Brooklyn Philharmonic and New York musical insiders believed that Thomas had squeezed him out of the job.

The rivalry between Thomas and the Philharmonic was a recognized fact of New York musical life. Already in 1866 the *Neue New Yorker Musik Zeitung* had hinted that it was Thomas's success that had prompted Bergmann to include such "progressive" composers as Liszt,

---

‡ F. Letsch, the trombonist, and H. Schmitz and T. Lotze, the horn players, were on the Philharmonic rolls for 1869–70, but on November 27, 1869, while the Philharmonic was presenting a concert in New York, they were making music with Thomas in Chicago. (Bergmann, still the Philharmonic's conductor at that time, must have had mixed emotions about his three absentees when, a few days later, in one of Thomas's Chicago concerts they took part in a trio composed by Bergmann himself.) The next year the names of Letsch and Schmitz were qualified in the Philharmonic roster by the phrase "did not perform," but anyone attending the Thomas concerts in Boston in October of 1870 could have heard them there.

Wagner, and Berlioz in the Philharmonic programs.* And *Dwight's Journal,* on October 13, 1866, after repeating the *Musik Zeitung's* intimation, had added its own comment on the rivalry: "The [Philharmonic's] first public rehearsal takes place on October 20, the same day on which Theodore Thomas gives his first symphonic soiree. . . . Certainly the programmes of both parties have many novelties in common. But Thomas is the bolder of the two, and has undertaken to do in five concerts work that might well tax the energy of an orchestra for a couple of years." Similarly, in 1871, a critic, taking the Philharmonic to task for the "general lack of finish in much that was done," added that "this was the more noticeable by contrast with the recent concerts given by Theodore Thomas's orchestra, which were, in every respect, superior to those of the Philharmonic Society."[90] During 1873 and 1874, when George Templeton Strong was President of the Society, he took note of the problem on several occasions:

> I begin to perceive in the Philharmonic Society, what I suppose a shrewder person would have perceived long ago, namely, an intense jealousy of Theodore Thomas and his orchestra . . . My Philharmonic friends are evidently perturbed by the triumphs of Theodore Thomas. He has cut out Bergmann as conductor of the Brooklyn Philharmonic, and his garden concerts are growing in brilliancy and in public favor . . . Thomas's people rehearse daily. If our society would consent to do likewise, it could beat them out of sight, being numerically so much stronger than they; and if we would treat the candid and sagacious "critics" of the daily press a little more liberally in the matter of complimentary tickets and reserved seats, they would be more civil to us, though that is no great matter. . . . [The] Society feels sore because of Theodore Thomas's triumphs and of the praises showered on him by the newspaper critics whom he knows how to manipulate.

---

* The hint, though typical of New York's musical sport of pitting Thomas against the Philharmonic forces, was an unjust one. Bergmann had been conducting whole Wagner programs when Thomas was still a teen-ager, and it was Thomas who had learned a great deal about serious program-making from Bergmann when he had served as concertmaster for Bergmann's series of eleven Sacred Concerts in 1856—concerts which had included (six years before Thomas's first orchestral concert) the American premieres of two Berlioz overtures and three major works of Schumann. In April 1859, when the young Thomas was conducting standard operas for the impresario Ullmann, Bergmann gave the first performance in America of an entire Wagner opera (*Tannhäuser,* at the New York Stadt-Theater, April 4, 1859).

Finally, at the beginning of the 1874–75 season, when Strong had stepped down from the presidency and the orchestra seemed to be sinking in spirits as in profits, he summed up sadly: "The Philharmonic season opens dull. I fear my friends of that Society have not the vigor and enterprise to hold their own against Theodore Thomas."

Having struggled unsuccessfully for so many years to meet Thomas's challenge, the Philharmonic finally decided that the only way to handle him was to hire him. According to Thomas's *Autobiography,* "prominent members" of the Philharmonic had talked with him, even before Bergmann's death, about combining his orchestra with theirs so that he could become conductor of the Philharmonic. They were unable to come to an understanding, Thomas says, because they made it a condition that he give up his own series of Symphony Concerts. In 1876, when Bergmann died, Thomas was approached again with the same proposals and again he turned them down. "I refused to accept any conditions," are his proud words.[91]

Now the Philharmonic Directors were in a quandary. They had taken the logical step of inviting Thomas to be their conductor, in the hope of winning his talents for their side, only to find him unwilling to give up the very series of concerts that constituted the Philharmonic's most serious competition. In desperation they tried to engage a foreign conductor, but the effort failed, as Krehbiel tells us. Looking around for someone who might already be active on the New York musical scene, the Philharmonic members elected (it should not be forgotten that the conductors of the Society were chosen democratically) Dr. Leopold Damrosch for the season of 1876–77.[92]

The result was a financial catastrophe. The receipts for the season came to hardly more than $8,000—the lowest they had been in fifteen years—and the individual dividend to each player was only $18 for the whole season of six concerts and all rehearsals, even less than the $25 that each man had received at the end of that first pioneering season of 1842–43. President Schermerhorn and the Philharmonic Board may not have expected Damrosch to outdraw Theodore Thomas, but neither had they been prepared for so complete a debacle. Damrosch, after all, had held a respected position in New York's music world since 1871, when he had come here from Germany at the age of thirty-nine to conduct the Arion male chorus. It was the Philharmonic, on May 6 of that same year, that had given him his formal New York debut as a violinist in the Beethoven Concerto.[93] About two years later, with the encouragement of the great Anton Rubinstein and the cooperation of the

Knabe Piano Company, he had established the Oratorio Society. In Europe, he had been concertmaster of the Weimar Court Orchestra under Liszt, had known Wagner, von Bülow, and most of the other important musical figures of Germany, and had conducted the Breslau Orchestral Society.

When it was announced in 1876 that Damrosch would be the new conductor of the Philharmonic, the professional press was not unfavorable, but with the figure of Theodore Thomas looming up before him, and the shadow of the late Carl Bergmann hovering darkly behind him, Damrosch was caught between the quick and the dead. The editor of the Steinway Hall Programme Notes (*not* the Academy of Music where the Philharmonic played, but Steinway Hall where its rivals held forth) went out of his way to refer to Damrosch and the Philharmonic in a subtly patronizing sentence as "a thoroughly capable and conscientious conductor . . . who, it is hoped, will put a little fresh vim into the Society." And in the middle of the season, *Dwight's Journal* commented with condescending kindness: "Although the performance of the Philharmonic orchestra under the direction of Dr. Damrosch has been praised by some of our critics, rather more than the performance seem [sic] to warrant, it cannot be denied that there has been much improvement under the new conductor. There is more clearness and precision of attack in the violins and less of eccentricity on the part of the wind instruments than last season; and the performance of Schumann's great work [the Second Symphony], if not specially inspired, was not marred by any glaring inaccuracy." In the same publication (January 20, 1877) another reviewer remarked: "The orchestra of the Philharmonic has improved greatly under the new leader, Dr. Damrosch, who is a very particular director, but who inspires his orchestra with something of his own musical fire and taste"; this would have been fine if the writer had not, typically, felt obliged to go on at great length not about Damrosch but about Bergmann ("long may the Philharmonic continue to cover his memory with glory!") and Thomas ("all music lovers must be grateful to Mr. Thomas for all he has done for Music in New York, and should encourage him as he nobly deserves").

As for the programs that the Philharmonic offered under Damrosch, a learned German coterie found them models of program construction, but the general public was scared away, straight into the arms of Theodore Thomas. In the single season of 1876–77, Damrosch presented, of the new music, the first American performances of substantial ex-

cerpts from Wagner's *Walküre* and *Götterdämmerung,* of Saint-Saëns's
G-Minor Piano Concerto, of Goldmark's *Rustic Wedding* Symphony,
and of a big chunk from Berlioz's *The Trojans,* as well as compositions
by Schumann and Liszt; and, of the old masters, works of Handel,
Haydn, Gluck, and Beethoven—of the last named, not only the familiar favorites, but also the *Choral Fantasy* and the music to *The
Ruins of Athens.* The little group of devotees said that such serious and
earnest programs had never been heard in New York, and praised the
new conductor for his courage; the general public said that such serious
and earnest programs had never been heard in New York, and stayed
away.

Humbled, the Philharmonic elected Theodore Thomas conductor for
the season of 1877–78, without requiring that he give up his own
Symphony Concerts. Immediately the ticket receipts for the season shot
up by more than 50 per cent, from $8,291 under Damrosch to $12,499
under Thomas, and the orchestra players' dividend from $18 to $82!

If any doubt remained that the Philharmonic owed its improved
fortunes to Theodore Thomas, it was resolved the next year when, to
the Society's distress, Thomas left New York to accept a position as
head of a new College of Music in Cincinnati. The Philharmonic had
to engage another conductor. Having burned its fingers once on Leopold Damrosch, the Society would not elect him again; it gave Adolf
Neuendorff forty-six votes to Damrosch's twenty-nine. Neuendorff,
though only thirty-five years old, had already made a considerable reputation for himself as a theater conductor, had composed some respectable music of his own, and had conducted the first New York
stagings of Wagner's *Lohengrin* and *Walküre.*[94] But he was not Theodore Thomas. The ticket receipts had been pathetically low under
Damrosch, but under Neuendorff they fell even lower, to not much
more than $7,000 for the entire thirty-seventh season. The individual
player, for his work in six concerts and all attendant rehearsals, took
home a paltry $25 at the end of the year.

Fortunately it was a good moment to rush right back to Theodore
Thomas, who was finding in Cincinnati that life as director of the College of Music was not all he had hoped it would be. He agreed to
commute between Cincinnati and New York (no mean trick in those
days) in order to conduct the Philharmonic's six concerts and six public
rehearsals of 1879–80, and settled in New York again for the next

year.† Immediately, even while Thomas was living in Cincinnati and traveling to New York for each Philharmonic concert, the receipts rose like a great financial cheer from $7,158 under Neuendorff to $18,736 under Thomas. The dramatic changes in the Philharmonic's financial fortunes can be seen in the following graph, covering the periods of Bergmann's glory and decline, of Damrosch and Neuendorff in distress, and of Theodore Thomas to the rescue.

The Philharmonic had finally been forced to face realistically the fact that it needed a big-time conductor if it were to become a big-time orchestra.

NEW YORK PHILHARMONIC
FINANCIAL RECEIPTS, 1867–84

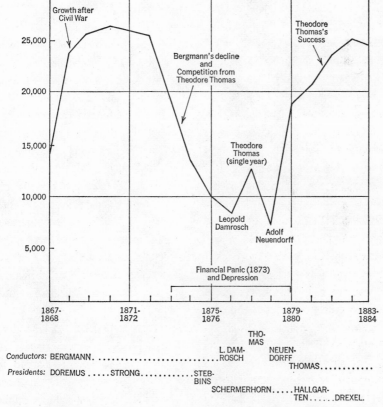

† To everyone's relief, since it was known that he had meanwhile been offered the conductorship of the London Philharmonic in June, 1880.

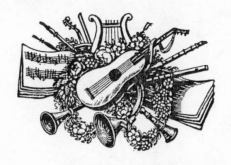

Part V

Maturity
(1879–1909)

Chapter 16

King Theodore
(1879–91)

Financial prosperity, artistic progress, and civic respect marked the subsequent reign of Theodore Thomas over the New York Philharmonic from 1879 to 1891.

Money, always an index of one kind of organizational health, began to flow more freely in the Philharmonic's fiscal veins. Between Thomas's first year and the time he left the orchestra in 1891, the ticket receipts and the dividend paid to each orchestra player more than doubled.

Halfway through the Thomas era, in 1886, the Philharmonic was once again prosperous enough and fashionable enough to feel that it had outgrown its fine auditorium, the Academy of Music, and to look around (as it had thirty years earlier when it had moved *to* the Academy) for the best theater in town. When the orchestra selected the new Metropolitan Opera House, at Broadway and Thirty-ninth Street, which had been opened only three years earlier by some of the most aggressively wealthy elements of New York's society, it was willing and able to pay a much higher rent—as much as two thirds more than at the Academy—as the price for its stylishness.

The Philharmonic's new status was reflected also in the payment of its soloists. Most of them could now expect $150 to $350 for a single program; after 1885 individual fees of $500 and more began to appear for celebrated singers like Lilli Lehmann, Schröder-Hanfstängel, and Nordica, and the total spent for soloists in a season might be as much as $1,500. Only a few artists, like the brilliant pianist Rafael Joseffy, who was made an Honorary Member in 1883, performed without any fee, just for the pleasure and prestige that a solo appearance afforded.*

Theodore Thomas himself drew $2,500 a year, the highest salary that had ever been paid to a conductor by the Philharmonic. He says, moreover, in his *Autobiography,* that during all the years that he was the conductor, he never took the full amount of salary to which he was entitled by his contract. This was true. Thomas's contracts gave him not a fixed sum but twenty dividend shares each year, and, thanks to his success, his twenty shares were generally worth much more than $2,500—as much as $4,000 or $4,500 in some seasons—but he generously turned back the difference to the Philharmonic's treasury each time.[95] The orchestra men, in their turn, knew how to do things right when occasions arose to show their regard for the "Meister." When a music stand was to be procured for him, it was specially constructed at fifteen times the cost of an ordinary one. When Thomas was married for the second time, at the age of fifty-five, toward the end of his Philharmonic tenure, the orchestra spent $600 on a wedding gift from Tiffany's ("a highly ornamental clock with two candelabers," as the Society's Minutes described it). For his last concert the conductor's stand was decorated with flowers, and a laurel wreath was presented to him that both he and Mrs. Thomas valued and preserved to the end of their days for the sentiment it held.[96]

Though Thomas was proud of the prosperity that he brought to the Philharmonic, he would have been the first to remonstrate that he should be judged not by material gains but by artistic and educational ones. First of all, he improved the orchestra as a musical instrument. As soon as he was ensconced at the Philharmonic conductor's desk, he saw to it that the principal players of his private orchestra became members of the Society. In fact, although Thomas continued to give a

---

* Joseffy kept playing without pay, year after year, from 1883 to 1889, while others were receiving generous honoraria. Eventually, we are relieved to note, in 1889-90, he was given a payment of $300—but he never played with the Philharmonic again after that. Was it just that the great pianist had stopped playing in public? Had he finally found out that the others were being paid? Or was the $300 an acknowledgment of past services at the moment when he was about to appear with the Philharmonic for the last time?

great many concerts in New York and elsewhere, apart from the six concerts and six public rehearsals in the Philharmonic series, he tended to think of them all as given by one orchestra—"his" orchestra—and it is frequently difficult to tell in his *Autobiography* whether he is talking about the Philharmonic or not. In a way, he was justified in this, for he reshaped the Philharmonic according to his own rigorous standards. Rehearsal and concert routines were professional and efficient. The men were trained to respond instantly to every demand of their conductor. The tone quality was vastly improved.

Theodore Thomas educated his public as well as his orchestra. "Throughout my life," he wrote to the directors of the Brooklyn Philharmonic Society in 1874, "my aim has been to make good music popular, and it now appears that I have only done the public justice in believing, and acting constantly on the belief, that the people would enjoy and support the best in art when continually set before them in a clear and intelligent manner."[97] The phrase "good music" is the key to Thomas's attitude. He is usually said to have done more than anyone else to educate the American public to good music; this must be translated to mean that he did more than anyone else to establish the German-serious style as the proper high-class style for music in America. Carl Bergmann and others had already carried this process far. Thomas confirmed and expanded their work and made the stylistic victory complete by the huge number and the high quality of his performances, by ubiquity and persistence as well as excellence. He did not merely help the cause of good music; he defined it. Thomas believed that he knew what was good for the public and he taught it to them. In a way it was a kind of musical brainwashing. "Even those who did not thoroughly understand his work," his adoring biographer, George P. Upton, assures us, "were proud of it when they saw that European artists were eager to appear at his concerts, and European composers were equally eager that he should perform their new works."[98] In an interview in 1882 Thomas enunciated his "Philharmonic Creed":

To endeavor always to form a refined musical taste among the people by the intelligent selection of music; to give, in order to accomplish the desired result, only standard works, both of the new and old masters, and to be thus conservative and not given to experimenting with the new musical sensations of the hour. I may exemplify this further by saying that while Berlioz, Liszt, Rubinstein, Brahms, and others may be, and will be given, such masters are never allowed representation to the exclusion, even in a degree, of Beethoven and Mozart. Nor would the first mentioned be permitted on the programme if the great symphonies were not thoroughly understood by the public.[99]

In this statement we find most of the basic tenets of the "serious" approach—the duty of the musical leader to guide the people to an elevated musical taste, the assumption that there exists a recognized body of "standard" works of which a great musical society like the Philharmonic should be the conservator, and the assignment to the venerated Beethoven and Mozart of unquestioned priority over such newer and lesser masters as Berlioz, Liszt, Rubinstein, and Brahms, who must patiently wait their turn until the great symphonies of the older masters have been taught to the public. Thomas certainly meant every phrase of this creed *in principle*. But his dicta, like those of many a strong-minded man, must be taken with a grain of salt. *In practice,* while Beethoven did hold the central position in his repertory, accounting for about a fifth of all the music he played, Berlioz, Liszt, Rubinstein, and Brahms fared very well for men on probation, while Wagner and Schumann, whom he had not even mentioned, but who were considered at least as radical, received more attention than any of the old masters except Beethoven. Mozart, on the other hand, was not played as much by Thomas as his statement would lead us to believe. A tally reveals that in the thirteen years that Thomas conducted the New York Philharmonic he gave only seventeen performances of pieces by Mozart. The seventeen performances represented only eleven different pieces, some of the pieces having been played more than once. Of the eleven pieces only four were symphonies (receiving a total of nine performances); the others were one piano concerto (performed once), the Adagio and Fugue for strings (performed once), and five vocal excerpts (including an aria from the Italian opera *Figaro,* sung in German, and an aria from the German opera *Die Zauberflöte,* sung in Italian). That is all out of the whole Köchel catalogue. In the same thirteen years, by comparison, Thomas gave twenty-seven performances of works of Schumann, including all four of his symphonies (fourteen performances) and half a dozen of his other major works (thirteen performances). As for Wagner, Thomas gave him thirty-four performances

—exactly twice as many as Mozart. It would seem that, the "Philharmonic Creed" notwithstanding, some newer masters *were* "allowed representation to the exclusion, . . . in a degree" of Mozart.

Within the restricting framework of the German-serious approach,
and with a few excursions outside it, Thomas did nevertheless present
a remarkably well-balanced and well-rounded repertory. He had
learned a great deal about practical program-making in his years of
violin playing in the Jullien, Bergmann, and Musard concert series.
(One should not take too seriously Thomas's deprecating remarks about
Jullien and Bergmann in his *Autobiography.* Like Wagner and many
another self-centered man of genius, Thomas was often most antago-
nistic to those to whom he owed the most.) Then had come the experience of presenting hundreds upon hundreds of concerts in the
Brooklyn Philharmonic series, the Irving Hall Matinees, the Symphony
Soirees, the New York Garden Concerts, and the far-flung tours. By
the time Thomas settled down at the New York Philharmonic he was a
master of the art of constructing programs that challenged his audiences a little more each time without ever going so far as to alienate
or lose them. Not only Beethoven and Mozart, not only Berlioz, Liszt,
Rubinstein, and Brahms, not only Schumann and Wagner, but also
Haydn, Schubert, Weber, Chopin, Mendelssohn, Spohr, Dvořák,
Tchaikovsky, Cowen, Goldmark, Raff, Saint-Saëns, Strauss, the "re-
discovered" Bach, and even an occasional American piece were in his
repertory. (See the table in Backnote 100.)

"Occasional American piece" may be too generous a description.
In his thirteen years with the Philharmonic Thomas did only one
American composition worth mentioning: John Knowles Paine's *An
Island Fantasy,* in 1890. He played other American compositions in his
Brooklyn Philharmonic programs and in some of the free-lance concerts that he conducted in New York, but he seemed to regard the
Philharmonic as too conservative a forum for such music. The programs
of his "light" summer concerts and matinees in New York and other
cities had sometimes contained American names, but many of these did
not represent real orchestral works but solo pieces interpolated in an
orchestral program when the composer could be present as performer—
piano pieces by L. M. Gottschalk and J. N. Pattison, for example,
which displayed their authors more as instrumentalists than as composers. For the "serious" programs of his later years, whether in New

York or elsewhere, the proportion of major American compositions that Thomas presented was not very large—perhaps 1 or 2 per cent of the music he performed. "I played all there were," said he laconically.†[101]

In the history of the New York Philharmonic Theodore Thomas can be seen as the bridge between an older type of conductor whom we have labeled with the compound term artist-conductor, and a newer kind of virtuoso conductor whom we might call the interpreter-conductor, who was to dominate the musical scene in the latter part of the nineteenth century and the beginning of the twentieth century. The transition was a gradual one. Carl Bergmann, the most impressive of Thomas's predecessors, exemplifies the artist-conductor. Bergmann was much more than a mere time-beater. He was a real conductor who controlled artistically all the elements that go into a fine performance by an orchestra of a hundred men. There was something of the educator and the missionary in Bergmann too, and we have seen that he was an ardent champion of the difficult "new" music of Berlioz, Liszt, and Wagner.‡ Theodore Thomas's relationship with the Philharmonic Society had many points in common with Bergmann's. They had both come up through the ranks, Bergmann as a cellist and Thomas as a violinist, and they both continued to be listed as Actual Performing Members of the Philharmonic throughout the years that they conducted

† Now and then, in the course of his career outside the Philharmonic, Thomas did offer "American Nights," with larger amounts of American music, particularly on special occasions of national significance, such as the Philadelphia Centennial of 1876, celebrating the one hundredth anniversary of American independence. Even for that patriotic event, however, although he invited two American composers to write works for the opening ceremonies, he awarded not to an American but to Richard Wagner the outsize commission of $5,000 for a Centennial Inauguration March. The result, as Elson remarked in *The National Music of America*, was "about as national as a performance of 'Rienzi' would have been." Wagner himself is reported to have commented cynically: "The best thing about that composition was the money I got for it."[102]

‡ An anecdote from R. O. Mason's *Sketches* of 1887 (p. 199) illustrates Bergmann's attitude:

"But Mr. Bergmann," said some one as they were selecting a programme for the coming concert, "the people don't like Wagner." "Den dey must hear him till dey do," said Bergmann.

It is amusing to find the same anecdote applied almost verbatim to Theodore Thomas by the editor of his *Autobiography*, G. P. Upton, in 1905 (Vol. I, p. 235):

When . . . he was told that people did not like [Wagner's compositions], he coolly replied: "Then they must hear them till they do."

it. Both of them were chosen by election, that is, they owed their positions to the votes of the orchestra members. But here some points of difference begin to be apparent. Bergmann did not yet have a free choice in selecting the music for the programs and he did not have the all-important power of hiring or firing the musicians. Thomas, although he also was an elected conductor, was so desperately needed by the Society that he was able to accept and hold the position on his own terms. His was the decisive voice in choosing the repertory and an important one in all matters of personnel, partly because he continued to maintain his own private orchestra to which some of the Philharmonic's key players belonged and on which they depended for their livings. He was, in any case, a strong-willed, uncompromising man who usually ended up having things his way.

In Europe, a new breed of Romantic interpreter-conductor had been developed under the influences of Jullien, Wagner, Liszt, and von Bülow—a conductor who made other men's music conform to *his* interpretation, who changed tempo radically from one measure to the next as the spirit moved him, who demanded the highest technical standards of his orchestra players, whose histrionic gestures in conducting were often as extreme as his readings, and who tended to excite either adulation or revulsion in his listeners rather than calm attention. Theodore Thomas, as a young man, had seen at least the outward trappings of this extroverted style in Jullien's New York concerts of 1853 and 1854, in which Thomas had played violin, and he had met von Bülow and Liszt during his visits to Europe in 1867 and 1880. But he frowned upon the excesses of the interpreter-conductors and, in his own conducting, assimilated only as much of their aesthetics and methods as was compatible with his sober personality. He too wished to impose his taste on orchestra and public, or at least to train them to accept it, but since that taste was not so exaggerated as the extremists', and his manner of presenting it more dignified, he sometimes gave the impression of being less "modern" (i.e., less Romantic) than he really was. On the podium Thomas was neither fiery nor elegant, but authoritative and forceful. His Boswell, George P. Upton, has given us a picture of Thomas in the concert room: "He walked in an easy but dignified way to the desk, turned and made a graceful bow to his audience, then turned to his players who were always in readiness, simply lifted his arms, gave the signal and the work began. There was no fuss, no disorder, no desk rappings, no instructions to his concertmeister, no waiting for this man or that man to get his instrument ready, no nervousness, no hesitation. You could settle down to your seat with the absolute conviction that everything was right and everything was going right. Everything he did was sure, strong, sane, healthy. It was never necessary for his hearers to feel anxious about results." There were no "extraordinary demonstrations with the baton," said Upton, no "jack-in-the-box jumpings, or sensational motions of the head, arms, and feet . . . Mr. Thomas was the least demonstrative of all the great leaders of his day, but he was the most graceful, dignified, and easy of them."[103] Upton's taste, of course, had been molded in Thomas's school; but to most people not so prepared, as Upton admitted, "Mr. Thomas appeared impassive and unemotional in the concert-room." The composer-conductor Jacques Offenbach, whose orientation was more French than German, watched Thomas at work in New York in 1876 and came away with mixed reactions. Though he gave Thomas credit as an orchestra builder and propagator of classical music, he found that "as actual conductor, Thomas did not live up to the reputation that has been given him." He could be dull, and he could be clumsy. On the one hand, he interpreted so-called light music of Rossini, Auber, Verdi, and Hérold without fire and without spirit, and on the other, "when by chance he wishes to inject a little energy, he conducts with both arms at once, which, from behind, makes him look like a great bird trying to take flight."[104] Thomas's imperious manner, always dignified, often stolid, the faithful saw as healthiness, the critical as heaviness.

Thomas's avoidance of the sensational mannerisms of the extreme Romanticists has contributed to a historical tradition that portrays him as more conservative and scholarly than he was in practice. His pronouncements about interpreting each old masterwork "exactly as the composer intended that it should be interpreted" have been taken at face value, chiefly because of their authoritarian tone. John H. Mueller writes: "He was not . . . a Nikisch or a Seidl who revelled in personal interpretation. He was rather a conservative, ever 'faithful to the score.' His claim to be the only conductor who executed the Bach embellishments according to traditional specifications was typical."[105] Thomas did indeed make a study, particularly during the last few years of his life, of the eighteenth-century embellishments as described by Leopold Mozart, C. P. E. Bach, and J. Quantz. But this did not ensure or even imply faithfulness to the score. He *talked* about authenticity when he proclaimed in his autobiography: "Our art is old enough to warrant the representation of every period, as far as possible under its own conditions, by using the same instruments as those for which the composer conceived his work."[106] But what he actually *did*, throughout most of his life, was to adjust the works of Bach to the large and thick performing forces that the Romantic taste favored. In the cantata *Ein feste Burg*, for example—as he performed it with the entire New York Philharmonic and a chorus of 480 singers in 1881, and with more than double those instrumental and vocal forces in a New York festival concert the next year—he "substituted modern instruments for the obsolete ones which Bach used, . . . filled in harmonies, transposed where it was necessary for a modern instrument, divided the instruments variously, and augmented where strength was effective." "By a thousand little devices," as his widow fondly phrased it, "he had enriched the classic scores and modernized them."[107] It was only around 1900, when he was sixty-five years old (and after he had left the New York Philharmonic), that he underwent a sort of aesthetic conversion: instead of trying to "adapt Bach to the modern orchestra," he began "adapting the modern orchestra to Bach." But he never went all the way. He restored such old instruments as the oboe d'amore, but not such others as the Baroque trumpets; he conscientiously worked out the sort of ornamentation that an eighteenth-century player might have improvised, but then imbedded it rigidly in whole orchestral sections; he attempted to preserve the relative numbers of woodwind, brass, and stringed instruments that Bach had used, yet increased the absolute size of the orchestra beyond even the inflated standards of the late nineteenth century. For a performance of Bach's B-Minor Mass in 1902 he used 131 instrumentalists. On the very page of his *Autobiography* that exhorted sincere musicians to employ "the same instruments as those for which the composer conceived his work," Thomas described certain of his procedures that did just the opposite:

. . . I used the method of the modern orchestra palette for the three so-called trumpet parts, and by a discreet rewriting of these parts for four D cornets for the first and second, and two trumpets in A for the third, and duplicating these with four D and two A clarinets—according to compass—I obtained a characteristic color of the trumpet parts, and at the same time made them powerful enough to blend with sixteen [or more] first violins, twelve flutes, twelve oboes, etc.[108]

Even with such compromises, Thomas's efforts in the direction of stylistic purity were ahead of what most European and American conductors were doing at the turn of the century. He was not a full-fledged Romantic interpreter-conductor. But Thomas was not above some Romantic hocus-pocus in his declarations of faithfulness to the old traditions. "This combination," he said of the trumpet-woodwind-string arrangement described above, "also enabled the players to give the original ornamentations of the composer, which one might call to-day a secret language, and which were fully written out in all the parts." Of course "this combination" enabled nothing of the sort—Thomas's instrumental impasto had nothing to do with the ornamentations, which could be performed with uniformity not because of his changes in orchestration but simply because they had been copied out in modern notation in all the parts. "The effect of Bach's music played by an orchestra thus proportioned," he concluded, "is entirely different from that which is produced when played by the orchestra ordinarily used in modern times." It was—but it was also different from the effect produced by the orchestra ordinarily used in Bach's times.

In the same spirit, with one foot planted firmly on the classics and the other striding forward with Romantic grandiosity, Thomas performed a symphony of Mozart with an orchestra of three hundred men though he knew that it had been conceived for an orchestra of a fraction of that size. He explained with relish how he went about it: "I had placed the players on stage so as to form a triple orchestra, similar to an organ with three manuals, which could be played on either singly or in combination, at the pleasure of the conductor. . . . I made use of my combinations with good effect in the concerts, and accomplished some unusual shading by manipulating my triple orchestra, even in such works as Mozart's 'Jupiter Symphony.' " And this was one of those symphonies of Mozart that he had promised in his Creed to make "thoroughly understood by the public"! For Handel's *Israel in Egypt,* in the same series of festival concerts, the "conservative" Thomas carried his Romantic gigantism even further: to his orchestra of nearly three hundred players, he joined a chorus of nearly three thousand voices.[109]

Theodore Thomas, self-made leader, rugged individualist, musical moralist, impure purist, was the child of his era.

Chapter 17

Abdication and Succession
(1891–98)

In 1891, at the peak of the Philharmonic's prosperity and his own personal success, Theodore Thomas left New York.

His move came as a surprise to many people, but it should not have. He had been threatening to leave for years. Not content with the part-time nature of the Philharmonic, unwilling to submit any longer to the physical, mental, and financial strain of keeping up his private Thomas Orchestra, jealous of the support and attention being given to the Metropolitan Opera and to rival concert conductors, Thomas insisted that a great city like New York should be able to provide him with what he called a "permanent" orchestra. "What I wished," he explained many years later in his *Autobiography,* "was a large orchestra, sufficiently subsidized to enable it to hold the rehearsals necessary for artistic performances, its object and aim to be to attain the highest artistic performance of master-works, and to set a standard for the whole country, and give New York one of the greatest orchestras of the world. This would have been progress, and the time was ripe for it." When he had finally moved to disband his Thomas Orchestra in 1888, he and his men had really thought "that New York would not allow our organization to be abandoned after so many years of service, but

would raise an endowment fund and make it a permanent institution."
But the hoped-for offer was not forthcoming. Thomas seems then to
have issued a sort of ultimatum. "I made a plain statement to my
friends and the Philharmonic Society," he asserted, "that I should wait
two years to see if any thing would be done in New York toward a
permanent orchestra, and if nothing were done, I should then leave. So
I waited, but beyond personal offers made to me by friends, of from
three thousand to ten thousand dollars, nothing came of it."[110]

Meanwhile, Thomas watched with envy as Boston built up the kind
of orchestra that he dreamed about; but Boston already had its own
brilliant conductor, Artur Nikisch, at the time when Thomas was
ready to leave New York. He would probably have been interested in
developing a permanent orchestra in Cincinnati, with its solid German-American cultural community, but Cincinnati and Thomas had
tried each other in 1878 and had found it impossible to get along together. When the Chicago Orchestral Association invited him to establish a new orchestra in that city and guaranteed its finances for three
years beginning July 1, 1891, Thomas accepted.

In a relatively undeveloped Chicago, Theodore Thomas was eventually able to demonstrate what he had intended for a ripe New York.
Conditions were all wrong in Chicago for the establishment of a great
permanent orchestra, but by a combination of stubborn dedication,
technical knowledge, talent, hard work, and money, Thomas sur-
mounted the problems. Chicago had no adequate supply of fine players—so he took with him from New York a completely balanced orchestra of sixty men, able to function as a traveling orchestra, to which
were added twenty-four to thirty Chicago musicians to make the full
orchestra. Chicago was not so rich as New York—but with the aid of
his new wife, the former Rose Fay of Chicago, and her brother, C. Norman Fay, Thomas marshaled some of the most influential names in
the city (Sprague, Armour, Potter, McCormick, Field) to assure the
orchestra's finances. The immense Auditorium was unsuitable as a concert hall—a new Orchestra Hall was made possible by a public subscription of nearly $750,000 from more than eight thousand contribu-
tors. But even more remarkable than these material accomplishments
was the intellectual structure of public taste that Thomas reared in
Chicago. His greatest problem at the outset had been what he called
"the indifference of the mass of the people to the higher forms of
music." Unlike the New York public, Chicagoans had not yet been

trained to like the kind of music that Thomas wanted them to like.
But he persevered, "notwithstanding all opposition, until finally the intelligent and influential minority were ready to give up their trifles for
broader forms, carrying with them the rest of our musical world."* By
the time of his death in 1905, Theodore Thomas had established in
Chicago one of the strongest of the citadels of German-serious music
with which he garrisoned America.

Back in New York, to everyone's surprise, the Philharmonic found a
conductor who was able not only to match Theodore Thomas's brilliant
financial and artistic record with the Society, but to surpass it. Anton
Seidl, in background and personality, had the makings of a glamorous
interpreter-conductor. Hungarian by birth—in itself an exotic passport
to the American artistic world—he was even rumored to be the illegitimate son of Franz Liszt. That he was said to be an atheist and a
freethinker was actually to his advantage in public relations—for an
ordinary American citizen it might have been reprehensible but for a
Hungarian artist it seemed romantically in character. Besides, he had
such personal fire that many who disagreed with him nevertheless admitted his fascination. Dvořák, who criticized him as a "wild rebel and
an atheist," became his fast friend during his stay in New York. After
leaving the Leipzig Conservatory in 1872, Seidl had actually lived in
the household of Richard Wagner for a number of years as one of the
young musicians who helped to prepare the score and parts of *The
Ring of the Nibelung*. It was Wagner himself who had recommended
him, after that, as conductor for Angelo Neumann's Wagner Theater.
Seidl came to New York in 1885 as conductor for the new German
Opera which had been "orphaned" by the death of Leopold Damrosch,
but he also began to give concert programs almost from the start with
sufficient success to arouse the jealousy of Theodore Thomas. Ordinarily
the Seidl Orchestra gave only five or six concerts in a season, but in
the late 1880s the Brighton Hotel Company hired Seidl with his orchestra of sixty-four musicians to give two concerts daily at the Brigh-

---

* A chilling insight into Thomas's powers of musical indoctrination, more sug-
gestive of Orwell's 1984 than of Thomas's 1904, may be gained from a paragraph
by his biographer, G. P. Upton:
   In conversation with Mr. Thomas about a year before his death, I asked
   him why he had discontinued making "request" programmes. He replied:
   "Because it is no longer necessary. My audiences no longer request. They
   are satisfied with what satisfies me." In this statement he referred to the regular patrons. "Transients" sometimes sent in requests, but he paid no attention to them. [Theodore Thomas, *Autobiography*, Vol. I, p. 171.]

ton Beach Music Hall at an admission price of only 25¢. In a summer
season of three months they gave 172 concerts.[111] By the time Seidl
replaced Thomas as Philharmonic conductor in 1891, he had won an
enthusiastic following in the concert hall as well as the opera house.

Seidl, the disciple of Wagner, was one of the new race of conductors
who played on the orchestra as a virtuoso pianist played on his instrument. He could make the orchestra "sing and sigh and whisper,
exult, plead, and threaten, storm, rage and overwhelm, as no other
conductor could," rhapsodized his admirer, Henry T. Finck, the critic
of the *Evening Post*. Bergmann and Thomas had come up through the
ranks of the orchestra as cellist and violinist, but Seidl, a pianist like
many of the new conductors, came to the Philharmonic from outside,
with none of the inhibitions of an orchestra man's tradition with respect
to the standard repertory. Indeed, it was said that he was conducting
certain classic compositions for the first time in his life when he did
them with the New York Philharmonic.

One can guess that, with this background and temperament, Seidl
performed a great deal of the new music of his day; but the total
amount, interestingly enough, was rather less than is generally believed.
By actual count, his repertory even represents a slight falling-off in the
performance of living composers, as compared with the repertory of
Theodore Thomas. Although Seidl was the champion of the "new"
music of Wagner and Liszt, it should be observed that both of them
had been dead for several years by the time Seidl came to the Philharmonic in 1891. They were, in fact, on the way to becoming an established part of the modern sector of the orchestral repertory, and that
repertory in general was tending to assume more and more the aspect
of an accepted body of past music with only some leavening from the
new. Seidl's orchestra library shows him to have had a balanced collection of great breadth, covering the principal orchestral works from
the time of Haydn to his own day. At the end of Seidl's first year, in
1892, the Philharmonic's official historian could safely affirm the view
of the Society with regard to repertory: "I should say that it has conceived its duty primarily to be the conservation of musical compositions
which the judgment and taste of the cultured would have admitted to
the first rank. Only secondarily has it made propaganda for new and
progressive composers who have widened the boundaries of the
art."[112]

A special case among composers then living was that of Dvořák, who was resident in New York at the time; the excitement of his presence, added to his evident genius, made for a very high number of performances of his compositions by the Philharmonic, of which he was named an Honorary Member in 1894. When the Society gave the premiere of his *New World* Symphony at the public rehearsal and concert of December 15 and 16, 1893, under Seidl's baton, conductor, orchestra, audience, and press were equally enthusiastic. "The people applauded so much," wrote Dvořák to his publisher Simrock, "that I had to thank them from the box like a king!? alla Mascagni in Vienna (don't laugh!)."[113]

Seidl's innovations were not so much in the choice of music as in his freedom of interpretation of any piece, whether old or new, that he put on his programs. For the interpreter-conductor, the composer's indications in his score were only the starting materials from which he molded a living performance. From Wagner, Seidl had learned how to use constantly shifting tempos, even where the composer had written nothing of the sort, to inject a new kind of animation into the old masterworks. "Is it any wonder," asked James G. Huneker in his defense, "that he saw as if with freshly anointed eyes; saw that the old had been superseded by the new; and that even a Beethoven symphony might be mended out of all resemblance to its original shape and gait."[114]

At first Seidl's controversial methods divided the public and the critics into two battling camps. But by the time his second year as Philharmonic conductor had begun, it was clear that Seidl was the victor. The Society thereafter enjoyed, with Seidl as conductor and E. Francis Hyde as President, a period of unprecedented prosperity—such prosperity that a serious financial depression from 1893 to about 1897 did not affect the Philharmonic in any way. All the indices with which we are familiar from earlier examples—ticket receipts, orchestra players' dividends, artists' fees—went up steadily from year to year. The income from ticket sales and subscriptions, which had been considered high during the Thomas regime at something over $28,000 for a year, went over $29,000 in Seidl's very first year and then moved on to $32,-000, to $34,000, and finally, in 1897–98, surpassing all previous records, to $49,691. The dividend paid to each orchestra player went up correspondingly, reaching in that last year $380 per man; even allowing for the fact that the number of performances was increased in that year from six concerts and public rehearsals to eight, it still meant something like $47.50 per program for each player. This seemed a generous reward indeed to the New York musician of that day, when free-lance players as a rule received only $7 for a concert including one rehearsal, and $2 for each extra rehearsal.[115] Seidl's own salary was a sliding one, computed as the equivalent of twelve orchestra player's shares, so he also profited materially from the great success that he brought to the Society; in his last year his salary came to $4,560, as compared with the $2,500 that Theodore Thomas had regularly drawn.

Already under Thomas the Philharmonic had begun to adopt the methods and manners of a modern orchestra "of the highest class," and now the process accelerated. Internationally famous soloists came to be expected regularly for every season, and big fees were paid to get them—noted singers drew $500 to $600 for a public rehearsal and concert, and in 1897–98 the admired Belgian violinist Ysaÿe received $700, the highest amount the Philharmonic had ever paid an individual soloist. (Of course, mere composers like MacDowell and Busoni could still be had for $100 and $150 respectively, and Victor Herbert, since he was a member of the Philharmonic, played his own Cello Concerto without any fee at all.) Expenditures for advertising had gone ahead slowly but steadily under Thomas until they exceeded $1,700 in his last year; under Seidl they rushed on to reach $3,700. Regular program notes, or "descriptive programmes," as they were called, were now commissioned by the Society; A. Mees wrote them from 1887 through 1896 at $15 a concert, after which the distinguished critic Henry Edward Krehbiel took on the job at a fee more in keeping with his position in the musical community—$25 a concert. Symbolic of the Philharmonic's growing sense of its own style and importance was the publication in 1892, on its fiftieth anniversary, of the first history of the Society, written by Krehbiel under the title of *The Philharmonic Society of New York: A Memorial.*† In his brief but thor-

---

† Krehbiel worked out a complicated deal with the Society, whereby he not only wrote the book, but had it printed (by C. J. Krehbiel & Co.!), and then delivered to the Philharmonic at a modest price the entire first edition of 2,000 copies which they could resell at a profit. The Philharmonic, in turn, contracted with Novello, Ewer, & Co. to sell the books to the public at a higher price, in return for a share of the profits. But after several years nearly 1,600 of the 2,000 copies were still on the shelves, and Novello, Ewer & Co. requested the Philharmonic to take them back. For some time the members of the Society tried to unload the books by various means, all equally unsuccessful, until President E. Francis Hyde came up with one of those beautifully simple solutions that can occur only to the strong man in a family. His brother Clarence bought all the remaining Krehbiel books from the Society—almost 1,600 of them—for $1,500.

ough book, Krehbiel emphasized the Philharmonic's position as "the most conspicuous, dignified, and stable musical institution in the American metropolis," and characterized its audiences as "the fine flower of the city's music lovers." When the President of the Philharmonic, E. Francis Hyde, was visiting in London in 1892, he could proudly present copies of the *Memorial* to the Directors and conductor of the London Philharmonic Society.

Although the Philharmonic during Seidl's tenure still did not own a permanent home of its own, it rented the finest concert hall in the city for its performances—the new Music Hall, at Seventh Avenue and Fifty-seventh Street, built by Andrew Carnegie in 1891 and later known by his name. The Metropolitan Opera House, where the Philharmonic had played since 1886, had questionable acoustics for orchestral music, but it had been the most fashionable hall in town and it had offered the practical advantages of a very large seating capacity and of storage space for the orchestra's library and equipment. That was why Theodore Thomas had put up with it, though he considered the hall and its stage too large for the best artistic results. The Metropolitan's attractions, social and practical, were strong enough so that the Philharmonic had stayed on there even after Carnegie's Music Hall, with its superior acoustics and seating arrangements, had opened. And the orchestra would probably have remained at the Met even longer if that building had not obligingly burned on August 27, 1892, forcing an immediate shift for the next season to the Music Hall.

With such high-class conductors, high-class soloists, high-class programs, and high-class auditoriums, it is not surprising that the Philharmonic under Thomas and Seidl began to attract an increasingly high-class clientele. Concealed in the cold figures of the subscription lists is evidence of the important social change that was taking place in the Philharmonic's audiences. For some time the orchestra had been giving each program twice—first at a so-called public rehearsal on Friday afternoon, and then at the regular concert on Saturday evening. The Friday afternoons had been patronized by certain special groups, including professional musicians and others who might be occupied on Saturday evenings, patrons from out of town who would have been put off by the prospect of returning home late at night from a regular evening concert, and unaccompanied ladies who could venture forth by day with more propriety than they could by night. The regular subscribers, as might be expected, favored the formal Saturday nights.

That was the case until 1888–89. But in that year, subscriptions for the public rehearsals actually exceeded subscriptions to the regular concerts, and indeed the trend persisted and intensified for many years to come, as can be seen from the graph below. On the other hand, single extra tickets (as distinguished from subscriptions for the whole season) behaved in just the opposite manner—that is, began to bring in *less* at public rehearsals than at evening concerts. These changes are significant. They mean that an increasing share of the Philharmonic's

COMPARISON OF TICKET SALES FOR AFTERNOON AND EVENING PERFORMANCES NEW YORK PHILHARMONIC, 1883–1909

(See also table in Backnote 116)

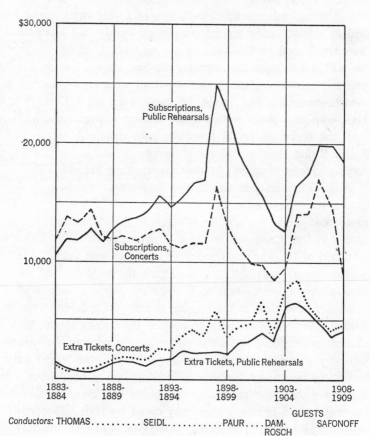

public, after 1885, was made up of that affluent class of ladies and gentlemen—especially ladies—that could afford to spend Friday afternoons at a concert, away from work or home, and that they ensured their privilege by taking full-season subscriptions in advance for the afternoon events. "Society" was staking an increasing claim on the Philharmonic.

From this point on, the names of the rich and the prominent are associated even more than before with the affairs of the Philharmonic. In the preceding period the presidency of the Society had been filled by well-to-do music lovers like George Templeton Strong. But beginning in 1881 the Presidents were men whom all New Yorkers recognized as public figures of extremely great wealth. Joseph W. Drexel, the international banker, was President from 1881 until his death in 1888. E. Francis Hyde, brilliant corporation lawyer and philanthropist, was President from then until 1901. And after that the President would be no less a figure than Andrew Carnegie. In his essay "The Gospel of Wealth," in 1889, Carnegie expressed a concept of the duty of the man of wealth to which Drexel and Hyde, as their actions demonstrated, could also have subscribed: ". . . to consider all surplus revenues which come to him simply as trust funds, which he is called upon to administer, and strictly bound as a matter of duty to administer in the manner which, in his judgment, is best calculated to produce the most beneficial results for the community . . . The best means of benefiting the community is to place within its reach the ladders upon which the aspiring can rise—parks, and means of recreation, by which men are helped in body and mind; works of art, certain to give pleasure and improve the public taste, and public institutions of various kinds, which will improve the general condition of the people—in this manner returning their surplus wealth to the mass of their fellows in the forms best calculated to do them lasting good."[117]

Several of the philanthropists were touched by the plight of the aged or sick members of the Philharmonic, and there was much talk in the 1880s about setting up some sort of trust fund for their benefit. The Philharmonic had always tried to take care of its needy members with whatever money could be spared from its meager budget. In the very first season, 1842–43, there was an expenditure of $20 for "charity to Mr. C——, by vote of the Society," and small appropriations for widows and the sick were frequent in the Philharmonic accounts—

not to mention an occasional loan from the Sinking Fund to special member U. C. Hill when he was in special trouble. But there had been no proper Pension Fund. In February 1888, however, when President Drexel was himself in such ill health that he asked the Philharmonic to replace him as President, he selflessly thought to offer $5,000 for what he called the "sick fund" as soon as a plan should be put into shape. The Philharmonic replied that they wanted him as their President, sick or well, and refused to accept his resignation, but he died before the season was over and before he could launch the fund. A Pension Fund was nevertheless started shortly thereafter, in May of 1890, when Elkan Naumburg, banker and patron of the arts, gave the Philharmonic $5,000 to be deposited at interest as the nucleus of a fund. Within the next few years Mrs. Drexel added the $5,000 that her late husband had intended for this cause, and Mrs. F. G. Shaw‡ contributed $1,000. Mrs. Shaw formed the habit of making smaller gifts to the Pension Fund every Christmas and left the orchestra another $1,000 for the Fund when she died.[118] Anton Seidl, acting somewhat in the spirit in which Theodore Thomas had yearly renounced part of his salary in the interests of the orchestra, more than once donated one of his dividend "shares" to the Fund. Beginning in 1895, the orchestra members themselves voted to turn over to the Pension Fund each year the equivalent of one dividend share plus all fines and taxes collected from the players during the year. Consequently, by the season of 1895–96 the Pension Fund had grown to the point where $11,000 could be invested in an interest-bearing mortgage. Modern business methods, befitting the era of a Drexel, a Hyde, and a Naumburg, were finally being applied to the Philharmonic's welfare fund.

As the style of the Philharmonic grew more expensive, the wealthy Presidents and other patrons were sometimes called upon to make contributions for various needs apart from the Pension Fund, but until the turn of the century the amounts involved were small, measured in hundreds of dollars rather than thousands. When President Hyde, for example, guaranteed the Philharmonic against loss in three special festival concerts to celebrate the Society's fiftieth anniversary in 1892, the total deficit that he had to make up—after all the orchestra men and soloists

‡ The same Mrs. Shaw who, in 1847, had been one of the first women to request associate membership.

had been paid, and all costs of advertising and production had been covered—was $493.61.* The public-spirited supporters of the Philharmonic did not seem to be faced with serious financial problems.

On March 28, 1898, at the height of this period of the Philharmonic's social, financial, and artistic success, New Yorkers were horrified to learn that Anton Seidl had suddenly died at the age of forty-seven.[119] Seidl's funeral, one of the most remarkable that the city has ever known, tells much about the place that he had made for himself in the life of New York. The obsequies were held in the Metropolitan Opera House. The orchestra pit was floored over, and the coffin placed upon it. Tickets were prepared for the occasion, and nearly 12,000 persons applied for them, although only 4,000 could be squeezed into the theater. Outside, where 150 members of the Musical Union played Chopin's *Funeral March,* Broadway was clogged for seven blocks with a "surging mass of people." Inside, many wept openly during the playing of two works that they associated with Seidl's memory, the Adagio lamentoso from Tchaikovsky's *Pathétique* Symphony, and "Siegfried's Death" from Wagner's *Götterdämmerung.* Among the pallbearers were famous musicians (Eugène Ysaÿe, Rafael Joseffy, Edward MacDowell, Xavier Scharwenka), respected critics (Henry Krehbiel, H. T. Finck), and prominent citizens (Richard Watson Gilder, E. Francis Hyde, Carl Schurz). A funeral address was delivered by the Reverend Merle St. Croix Wright and, counterbalancing this message from the church, Krehbiel read a telegram from Robert G. Ingersoll, "the great agnostic." James Gibbons Huneker unintentionally captured some of the bizarrerie of the occasion, along with its grandeur, when he wrote: "His funeral was more impressive than any music drama I ever saw or heard at Bayreuth."[120]

Seidl died on March 28, 1898, and the Philharmonic was scheduled for a public rehearsal and concert a few days later, on April 1 and 2. In such esteem was Seidl held that the Directors of the Philharmonic decided to postpone the concert—a step which had been taken only

---

* Hyde was even able to extend his generosity to other Philharmonics than his own—the London Philharmonic Society has in its possession a letter from him, dated July 18, 1892, which ends on the following note of casual liberality: "P.S. If it would not be presuming for one not a resident to join in your guaranty fund, I should be glad to become associated with your other subscribers in this matter, and I have accordingly signed the enclosed blank form." And he continued his London contributions for many seasons.

once previously in the Society's history, in 1865 after the assassination
of Abraham Lincoln. The postponement was not actually made this
time, however, reportedly because Carnegie Hall was not available for
another suitable date. There was a flurry of protests to the press and
threats of boycott, but the public rehearsal and concert were given at
the scheduled time under the baton of the American-born conductor
Frank Van der Stucken.[121] It happened that both programs, the one
after Lincoln's death and the one after Seidl's death, included Beethoven's Ninth Symphony, and in both cases it was felt that the "Ode to
Joy" at the end of the symphony would be inappropriate under the
circumstances. Accordingly that movement was omitted and another
and more suitable piece added to the program as a tribute. It is a comment on the cultural changes that had taken place between 1865 and
1898 that the added composition in the earlier concert was the "Funeral
March" from Beethoven's Third Symphony, and in the later one "Siegfried's Death" from Wagner's *Götterdämmerung*.

Chapter 18

Slump and Counter-Slump
(1898–1909)

With the death of Seidl it became painfully clear how much the Philharmonic had been dependent for its success on its glamorous interpreter-conductor. It was almost impossible for any other conductor to fill the place of the idolized leader. After an unsuccessful attempt to engage the Belgian violin virtuoso and conductor Eugène Ysaÿe, the Philharmonic took Emil Paur, who had been conducting the Boston Symphony Orchestra.[122] Paur was a more than competent conductor, but he could not arouse and inflame the public as his predecessor had done. Under Seidl the ticket receipts had climbed to unprecedented heights in the midst of a severe financial depression; under Paur, in comparatively good times, they began to fall again. In the four years of his tenure, from 1898 to 1902, the orchestra's income dropped from the $50,000 level, at which Seidl had left it, to approximately $35,000. What was particularly discouraging was that, although single ticket sales for individual concerts went quite well, season subscriptions for the public rehearsals and concerts—the part of an orchestra's income that gives it security because it can count on it in advance—fell off badly. It was as though the public was saying, "We may buy tickets for each concert, as we look it over and see who the soloists are and what the program may be, but we do not have enough confidence in you to commit ourselves in advance for the whole season." Naturally the orchestra players' dividends went down too, and in the Philharmonic this was fatal for a conductor, since he was elected by the orchestra players.

Meanwhile, in Paur's fourth and last year, E. Francis Hyde had found it necessary to resign as President of the Philharmonic Society, but had paved the way for Andrew Carnegie to succeed him. So deeply was Hyde loved and respected that the members continued to come to him as to a father for help and advice, even after Carnegie had replaced him. When, for example, the orchestra was planning extensive amendments to the Constitution and By-Laws in 1902, the proposed changes were submitted for final criticism not to President Carnegie but to ex-President Hyde. Nevertheless, if Hyde had to leave, it seemed that the Philharmonic could hardly ask for a more impressive successor to the presidency than Andrew Carnegie, multi-millionaire, philanthropist, and builder of Carnegie Hall. Those who dreamed, however, that Carnegie's millions would be promptly placed at the disposal of the Philharmonic to produce a new era of orchestral glory were to be disappointed—in his first season as President, 1901–2, the whole of Carnegie's financial aid to the orchestra consisted of a contribution of $456 to help balance the regular budget.

But Carnegie was a man who made his influence felt beyond the exact measure of his financial contribution. He was fond of Walter Damrosch, son of Leopold Damrosch, and the knowledge among the Philharmonic members of Walter's good relations with Carnegie contributed to his election as conductor of the Philharmonic for 1902–3.[123] Although Paur, setting aside his pride, sent word to the election meeting of his interest in retaining the conductor's position, Damrosch defeated him by a vote of forty-six to thirteen.

Financially, Walter's season was almost as bad as his father's had been in 1876–77. He seemed unable to attract the public. Subscriptions zoomed downward even further than they had under Paur, and the single-ticket sales went with them. The orchestra players' dividend fell to $116 for the entire season, that is, only $14.50 for a public rehearsal and concert, including all the necessary preparatory rehearsals. Damrosch's own salary was the lowest that a Philharmonic conductor had had in a long time, $1,392 (even Paur had averaged a little over $2,500 per season). And he had no one to blame but himself, for the conductor's salary, computed as twelve orchestra dividends or shares, rose or fell with the success that the conductor brought to the season.

From this low point the Philharmonic made one of the most remarkable recoveries in its history. And Walter Damrosch, strange as it may seem, was directly responsible for that recovery although the path that it eventually took was quite the opposite of the one that he had planned for it.[124] Damrosch may not have had the power to excite the audience, but he was imaginative and resourceful. On December 18, 1902, early in his season with the Philharmonic, he explained to a specially convened meeting of the members an important step that he had taken toward relieving the orchestra's difficulties. He outlined the situation as follows: The subscription to the concerts had decreased considerably, and the competition of rival organizations with backing of unlimited wealth (everyone knew that he was referring particularly to the Boston Symphony Orchestra, supported munificently by Major Henry L. Higginson) could no longer be met by ordinary methods—"the only way to successfully compete and keep the Society in the position of the foremost New York orchestral organization financially and artistically, [was] to acquire a subsidy or fund." With this object in view, he had approached the President, Andrew Carnegie, and had achieved the following result (I quote from the Minutes of the meeting):

> Mr. Carnegie expressed his willingness to head a fund with five thousand dollars, this fund to be subscribed to by others to raise it to ten thousand dollars or more and this fund to be renewed each year for the coming four years. The Fund to be called The New York Philharmonic Society Orchestra Fund, and this Fund to be used for the artistic and material improvement of the Society.

Carnegie had very strong ideas about philanthropic giving. In his essay on "Wealth," he had written: "In bestowing charity, the main consideration should be to help those who will help themselves; . . . to assist, but rarely or never to do all. Neither the individual nor the race is improved by alms-giving." Accordingly, he had imposed the condition that the Philharmonic members pledge themselves to contribute to the Fund 5 per cent of the dividends that they derived from their regular series of eight public rehearsals and concerts. The Fund, Damrosch said, was to be put in the charge of a committee of trustees consisting of Carnegie, Richard Arnold (Vice-President and concertmaster of the

Philharmonic), Damrosch, E. Francis Hyde (the Philharmonic's former President), and Elkan Naumburg (the founder of the Philharmonic's Pension Fund).

Damrosch's speech was received with applause, and the Society unanimously adopted resolutions accepting the Fund, endorsing the trustees, and subscribing 5 per cent of the yearly dividends, without further delay, from that very same year. Damrosch offered to apprise the trustees of the action of the Society. Delighted with their conductor's cleverness in arranging and manipulating all this, the Philharmonic Society tendered Walter Damrosch a vote of thanks in recognition of his services.

So far so good. But less than three weeks later, on January 5, 1903, Damrosch had a meeting with "several of [his] friends and some old subscribers and friends of the Philharmonic," a meeting at which a rather different plan was outlined. A much larger fund—the sum mentioned by Damrosch in *My Musical Life* is $50,000 a year for the four years—was proposed as the beginning of an endowment for a "permanent orchestra" of which the Philharmonic Society was to be only the nucleus. This Permanent Orchestra Fund was to be administered by a board that would adequately represent the financial backers and would *not* be under the control of the Philharmonic Society. "The terms of the deed of trust under which the fund was to be held," Damrosch explains, "were to be determined by a committee of three, consisting of Mr. Samuel Untermeyer, Mr. John Notman, and Mr. E. Francis Hyde." Moreover, since the Philharmonic was to be only the nucleus of the city's new permanent orchestra, it was obvious that some of its players would be replaced.

Samuel Untermeyer communicated the propositions of the Sub-Committee of the Permanent Orchestra Fund to the Philharmonic; the Philharmonic had them printed and distributed to all the members and then called a special meeting of the whole Society on February 18 to act on them. The Philharmonic members had an uncomfortable impression that they were being asked to make very definite pledges on behalf of their Society, without a very clear idea of what they were being offered in return; they feared, moreover, that the proposed conditions and changes conflicted with the Charter, Constitution, and By-Laws of their Society as then constituted. Nevertheless, since the Philharmonic Society was "heartily in sympathy with any movement to improve upon the condition of orchestral matters in New York," they appointed a Committee of Five, to whom was added the Vice-President, Richard Arnold, ex officio, to discuss the propositions in detail with Mr. Untermeyer or the Sub-Committee of the Permanent Orchestra Fund.

Ten days later the Philharmonic's Committee, still smoldering, reported the "sum and substance" of what had apparently been a warm interview with Mr. Untermeyer. He had made it clear that his proposals and conditions were to be taken as an ultimatum, and in fact demanded "that the entire affairs of the organization, financial, governmental and artistic be placed in the hands of a Board of Directors as set forth in his paper." It was now understood, moreover, that it was the intention of the Permanent Orchestra Fund Sub-Committee, among other changes of personnel, to demote Richard Arnold, the concertmaster, who was also the Vice-President, and to retire August Roebbelen, violinist, who was also the Secretary of the Society, both of whom were considered to be affected by advancing age. Since both Arnold and Roebbelen were members of the Philharmonic's Committee, sent to treat with Mr. Untermeyer, it can be imagined that the plan did not sit well with that Committee. The outraged Roebbelen asked whether Damrosch had not made very different proposals at that first meeting on December 18, and called for a reading of the Minutes in substantiation. Where was Mr. Carnegie's $5,000? Where was his Committee of Trustees? One of the Orchestra Committee members reported that, at the conference with Mr. Untermeyer, he had requested information about this and was answered "that this sum had been merged with the Permanent Orchestra Fund and that the Committee of Trustees as endorsed by the Society had ceased to exist as a Committee." Angered, the Society then voted unanimously to send a letter to Mr. Harry Harkness Flagler, who was now serving as representative of the Sub-Committee of the Permanent Orchestra Fund, in the form of the following resolution:

The Philharmonic Society of New York has carefully considered the propositions of the Committee representing ladies and gentlemen who are interested in providing a permanent orchestra for the City of New York with the Philharmonic Society as a nucleus. The Society, however, is constrained not to concur in the Amendments to its Constitution proposed by the Committee, on the general grounds that these Amendments so change the nature of the Society as to seriously interfere with

the control of its affairs by its members which has always been its vital
principle, and that the future prosperity of the Society would be thereby
imperiled.

Finally, to counter the slur on Richard Arnold's professional reputation, contained in the Sub-Committee's plan to demote him, "a motion
to tender Mr. Richard Arnold an official expression of confidence as
concert master of the Philharmonic Society was made, seconded and
carried unanimously."

The Philharmonic and Richard Arnold may have been growing old,
but the assumption of their imminent demise was soon shown to be
premature. Goaded by the threat that they had just faced, they sprang
into vigorous action. As Arnold analyzed the situation, in order to
"compete with rival organizations, and to overcome the growing opposition of a portion of the Press, the Philharmonic Society [needed]
a European celebrity for a conductor and one of the first rank at that."
This meant that they needed funds and friends. They found both
through their beloved ex-President and Honorary Associate Member,
E. Francis Hyde. With his aid, working swiftly and quietly, they put
together a Conductor's Fund, subscribed by Andrew Carnegie, John D.
Rockefeller,[125] James Loeb, Elkan Naumburg, Grant Schley, Hyde,
and his brother, Clarence M. Hyde.

Then in a sensational move they engaged not one but seven celebrated conductors from as many different parts of the world—Edouard
Colonne of Paris, Gustav Kogel of Frankfurt, Henry Wood of London,
Victor Herbert of Pittsburgh,[126] Felix Weingartner of Munich, Vassily
Safonoff of Moscow, and Dr. Richard Strauss of Berlin. Exploiting the
presence of Weingartner in New York, they gave an extra concert
under his direction in the middle of the season. The whole plan worked
so well that it was repeated with slight variations in the next two
seasons. In 1904–5, Kogel, Colonne, Safonoff, and Weingartner returned, and Karl Panzner of Bremen was added to the list. Theodore
Thomas had been invited also, to make what was planned as a sentimental and triumphal return from Chicago, but he died before the
assigned date for the concert and was replaced by Kogel. In that season
Weingartner gave two extra performances, a public rehearsal and an
evening concert. In the next year, 1905–6, Safonoff and Victor Herbert
were back again, and to them were added Willem Mengelberg of
Amsterdam, Max Fiedler of Hamburg, Ernst Kunwald of Frankfurt,

and Fritz Steinbach of Cologne. By now the Philharmonic's system of guest conductors was doing nicely, and Safonoff in particular had become such a favorite that he was asked to conduct two extra performances beyond the regular series of eight evening concerts and eight afternoon concerts (called that now, instead of public rehearsals). The ticket sales rose gratifyingly to almost $39,000 in 1903–4, and then to approximately $50,000 in each of the next two seasons, finally matching the record that had been set in Seidl's last year.

The guest-conductors coup had captured the public's interest and had put the Philharmonic back on its feet again. Now it seemed that the podium could once more be entrusted to a single conductor for an entire season, and for 1906–7 it was turned over to the guest conductor who had enjoyed the most brilliant success, Safonoff. Vassily Ilyich Safonoff had a many-sided talent. Director of the Moscow Conservatory and conductor of the Symphony Concerts of the Imperial Russian Music Society, he was also a fine pianist (pupil of Leschetizky) and a respected teacher (Josef Lhevinne and Alexander Scriabin were among his pupils). Tchaikovsky had dedicated a composition to him. He had the fiery temperament and the volatile personality that the public expected of the son of a Cossack general. When he put aside the baton to conduct with his bare hands (Safonoff was one of the earliest of the modern conductors to try conducting without a stick), particularly in his extroverted performances of the music of his countryman Tchaikovsky, the New York audiences felt that a new excitement had come to the Philharmonic. He was said to be paid $20,000 a year, by far the largest amount that any Philharmonic conductor had ever received. Gone were the days of youthful innocence when a conductor could be rewarded for several years of service by the gift of a gold watch and chain.

Another sign of the new energy in the management of the Philharmonic's affairs was the attempt to add extra concerts in each season. This had begun in the three guest-conductor years and continued in Safonoff's three years, from 1906 to 1909. In the first two years that Safonoff conducted there were sixteen regular concerts each season (eight afternoon and eight evening), an extra pair of concerts at Carnegie Hall each season, and a mixed handful of other performances, some at Carnegie Hall and some elsewhere—one at the vast New York Hippodrome (it could seat over five thousand people) at 756 Sixth Avenue, one at the home of William K. Vanderbilt at 660

Fifth Avenue, one with the MacDowell Association, one with the American singer Lillian Nordica, one for the Goethe Celebration of the Liederkranz Society. In Safonoff's third year as regular conductor of the Philharmonic, Gustav Mahler was invited to conduct an extra pair of Carnegie Hall concerts.

Safonoff, and most of the guest conductors who preceded him, belonged to the class of virtuoso interpreter-conductors. In their repertory, selected in collaboration with the elected Directors of the Philharmonic, there was a striking decline in the number of living composers performed and a lesser decline in performances of German-Austrian compositions. This had already begun under Seidl but became much more marked in the years that followed his death. The slight drop in the German-Austrian division reflects the competition of the rising schools of Slavic composers, especially Dvořák and Tchaikovsky. The big drop in the percentage of living composers represents a much more significant development—the settling of the international symphonic repertory into an established literature of music of the past. Some of this established literature was old music, the enshrined masterworks of the late Classic and early Romantic periods; some of it was of more recent vintage— Wagner and Tchaikovsky, for example. An interpreter-conductor requires a certain standardization in the literature that he performs; how will the listener recognize and appreciate the conductor's unique and individualistic interpretation if he is not familiar with the material that is being worked over? The interpreter insists that you hear *his* Beethoven and *his* Mozart. As for American composers, they received about the same percentage as they had in the past—close to zero. Indeed, American composers of proper academic training could usually do better in Europe than they could at home. The large works of Edward Mac-Dowell, who was generally accepted as the most important American composer of the time, were published in Germany, not in the United States. A sizable group of musical expatriates began to be evident at this time: Templeton Strong (whose father had been President of the Philharmonic) lived in Switzerland after 1892, Blair Fairchild in Paris after 1903, Arthur Byrd in Berlin after 1886, Louis Campbell-Tipton in Paris after 1905, Bertram Shapleigh in England for a number of years after 1904. The late Otto Kinkeldey, reminiscing at the MacDowell Celebration in New York in 1961 about his studies with MacDowell at Columbia University in 1902, told how MacDowell had advised him to go to Europe to work; there was nothing that he could learn in Germany that he couldn't be taught equally well in the United States, the composer explained, but he would live in a musical atmosphere there that he could not find in the United States at that time. MacDowell himself had had only two pieces played by the New York Philharmonic, each of them just once, and both of them in Seidl's day.[127]

In Safonoff's first year the dollars rolled into the Philharmonic box office: when the regular and extra concerts were added together, the total ticket sales came to more than $55,000 for the season. In the second year the sum was just a bit lower, around $50,000, but still very satisfactory. But in the third year the receipts were under $40,000 and nervousness began to set in. Richard Arnold and his fellow members of the Philharmonic had done a remarkable job of reinvigorating the old Society, with the aid of E. Francis Hyde and his phalanx of philanthropists, but it now began to appear that Walter Damrosch—and for that matter Theodore Thomas before him—had been right in insisting that the Philharmonic would have to undergo serious reorganization if it were to be placed on a permanent basis. The glamour and the excitement of the interpreter-conductors—from Seidl, through the years of guest conductors, to Safonoff—had temporarily outweighed and concealed certain inherent weaknesses of the Philharmonic's structure. A decade after Seidl's death it became apparent that serious problems that had been facing the Philharmonic even in his time had not yet been solved.

Chapter 19

Competition
(*The New York Symphony Society*)

The Philharmonic's most conspicuous problem in its effort to "go big-time" was the mounting competition from others with the same goal in mind—a competition whose roots went back at least to the days of the Thomas Orchestra. When Theodore Thomas was persuaded to become conductor of the Philharmonic in 1877, it was imagined that the problem would be solved, for it was the Thomas Orchestra that had been the Society's most dangerous rival. But they both reckoned without Leopold Damrosch. After his one disastrous season with the Philharmonic in 1876–77, when it was clear that Thomas had won that field from him, Damrosch energetically put together an *ad hoc* orchestra of his own with which he gave several series of afternoon and evening concerts in 1877–78—even managing to steal the first American performance of Brahms's First Symphony from the Philharmonic by performing it a week before Thomas had scheduled it. New York at that time had a reservoir of about twelve hundred orchestra musicians, of whom several hundred were of the first rank by the strictest international standards, and it was possible to "pick up" a full orchestra for individual concerts or series without too much trouble.

The next year, 1878, was the year that Theodore Thomas went to

Cincinnati, and Leopold Damrosch seized the opportunity to establish his own concerts more securely in New York. Using all his organizational and social talents, as well as his musical ones, he founded the Symphony Society of the City of New York. The Minutes of Proceedings of the Board of Directors are frank about the relationship of the Symphony Society's origin to Theodore Thomas. An entry for the meeting of October 22, 1878, reads: "The general desire for a continuance of Symphony Concerts in this City, an interruption of which was threatened by the departure of Mr. Theodore Thomas for the city of Cincinnati, induced several music loving gentlemen to form a preliminary organization for the purpose of satisfying the demand for Music of the character usually given at those Concerts." The Symphony Society even took over the dates that had been held at Steinway Hall for the Thomas Orchestra, with the idea that some of Thomas's public would come with the dates. In the Symphony Society's charter, its field of activity was wisely defined to include "Instrumental and Vocal Music, both Sacred and Secular." This distinguished it from the Philharmonic and gave it the possibility of acquiring a personality and a following of its own, since Damrosch had at his disposal the forces of the Oratorio Society, which he had founded, and other choral groups. When Thomas, disappointed in his Cincinnati venture, began to work in New York again in 1879 and 1880, the New York Symphony Society was well enough established to continue its work in rivalry with him and the Philharmonic, moving its concerts from Steinway Hall to the Academy of Music, where the Philharmonic was then playing. By 1883–84 the Symphony Society had become so ambitious an enterprise that it was considering the idea of building its own Hall of Music for its concerts.

In 1885 Leopold Damrosch died and his son Walter, only twenty-three years old, took over the direction of the Symphony Society and the Oratorio Society. Walter's social gifts were even greater than his father's when it came to enlisting the aid of the wealthy and the socially prominent for artistic ventures. By 1886 he had Andrew Carnegie on his Board (long before the Philharmonic was able to catch him, it will be noticed) and by 1891 he had added the support of J. P. Morgan, John D. Rockefeller, Collis P. Huntington, three Vanderbilts, and half a dozen other rich patrons, who subscribed an annual guarantee fund of $50,000 "for the purpose of making the orchestra of the Society a permanent organization, the members of which shall be engaged by the year, and shall be constantly under the training and direction of the same conductor."

It is fascinating to observe how closely Walter followed in the footsteps of his father. The reason for his spurt of organizational activity in 1891, as it had been for his father's in 1878, was that Theodore Thomas, the despot of the New York musical scene, was leaving town again—this time for Chicago. The guarantee fund of 1891 gave out after several years, however, and from 1898 to 1903 the Symphony Society did not function as such, although Damrosch tried to find as much employment as he could for his men. In 1902–3, again like his father, he had had a one-year chance with the Philharmonic, which had turned into the second Damrosch debacle. Then, once again in his father's pattern, when it was clear that the Philharmonic could not be his, he built his own orchestral forces. With the aid of Harry Harkness Flagler and other moneyed friends, he reorganized the Symphony Society of New York in 1903.

In building up his orchestra, Damrosch frequently imported gifted musicians from Europe. In this he had an advantage over the Philharmonic, which, as a cooperative society of local orchestra musicians, was naturally reluctant to bring in its own competition from abroad. The Philharmonic ordinarily stood by the so-called "six-months rule" of the Musical Mutual Protective Union, which provided that a foreigner could not become a union member, and therefore could not accept a position, until he had resided in the United States for half a year. But Damrosch seemed to take a positive delight in testing and stretching the union's regulations. In 1891, when he was hastening to strengthen his orchestra to take advantage of Theodore Thomas's departure for Chicago, he persuaded the union to waive the six-months rule so that he could bring in the Russian violinist Adolf Brodsky as concertmaster. But in 1893, when he tried to do the same thing with the Danish cellist Anton Hegner, the orchestra actually walked off the stage in protest, and the audience had to go home without any concert. This is generally considered to have been the first strike in a regular symphony orchestra in the United States. Damrosch ended up paying a fine to the union. Again, in 1905, Damrosch imported five French orchestra players, claiming that he could not find comparable musicians here. He had to pay another fine, but the five Frenchmen were permitted to remain and to join the union, since they were deemed not to blame for the position in which they had been placed.

Damrosch's musical performances were severely criticized in many circles and were seldom considered superior to the Philharmonic's, but his program-making was often more adventurous. It was the Symphony Society, not the Philharmonic, that brought Tchaikovsky to New York in 1891 for the opening season at Carnegie's Music Hall. It was the Symphony Society, not the Philharmonic, that cultivated the music of Debussy in the first few years of the twentieth century as a refreshing change from the omnipresent German repertory. It was the Symphony Society, after Gustav Mahler had come to New York to conduct at the Metropolitan Opera, that presented him as concert conductor in the 1908-9 season, before the Philharmonic could do so. Under both Damrosches, father and son, the Symphony Society was a continuing challenge to the Philharmonic.

The Symphony Society was not the only force that the Philharmonic had to contend with. The Philharmonic conductors and players were always competing with themselves, even more than they had done in the 1860s. Since they could not make a living from their six or eight pairs of annual concerts, they had always to be on the lookout for other engagements—indeed, had to create other engagements, which inevitably distracted attention from the work of the Philharmonic itself. As an example, not by any means the most extreme that could be cited, in the season of 1885-86, when Theodore Thomas had already given up the series of Symphony Concerts which the Philharmonic had so dreaded, he nevertheless presented in New York—in addition to his Philharmonic concerts—twenty-four Young People's Matinees, twenty-four Popular Concerts, and two Liederkranz Concerts. He also gave sixteen Brooklyn Philharmonic Concerts, eight Brooklyn Popular Matinees, six Philadelphia Symphony Concerts, three or four concerts each in Jersey City, Newark, New Haven, and Orange, a great music festival in Cincinnati, and five weeks of Summer Night Concerts in Chicago, as well as single performances in various other cities. Since he used his New York men for all these out-of-town engagements, which were necessary for their economic survival, the Philharmonic sometimes had to take second best. In 1887, for example, the Philharmonic gave its last concert of the season on April 9, instead of April 23, because Thomas would be on the road at the later date and, as the Secretary of the Philharmonic agreed in a letter to him, "we would consequently not be able to count on the participation of those members engaged by your Orchestra." Anton Seidl also had his own private orchestra, which gave a regular series of winter concerts as well as long ones of summer concerts. When Safonoff was engaged as conductor on a generous annual salary, after 1906, the Philharmonic could reserve the right to grant him permission for outside performances only when they did not conflict with the interests of the Society, but for the orchestra players the problems remained the same as in the old days. Beginning in 1904 the Russian Symphony, conducted by Modest Altschuler, provided more competition. And always, after 1883, there was the running counterpoint of the Metropolitan Opera, draining off much of the city's wealth by the appeal of the opera world to fashion, and much of its attention by the appeal of the star system to sensation.

It was doubly irritating to the Philharmonic to find another kind of competition coming from cities that had taken the inspiration or even the actual "cadres" for their orchestras from New York—either from the Philharmonic or from the Thomas Orchestra. In Boston, music enthusiasts like John S. Dwight had held up the Thomas Orchestra and the Philharmonic as incentives for the founding of their own orchestra. "We are falling behind New York. We will become provincial without it!" complained *Dwight's Journal* in September 1880. But when Henry L. Higginson established the Boston Symphony Orchestra in 1881, with musicians and conductor engaged by the year, and the payment of an anticipated annual deficit of $50,000 guaranteed in advance, yet with no attempt to interfere with the conductor's artistic and professional responsibility, Boston provided for its orchestra, in a single step, conditions that New York could not begin to match. Every time the secure, well-drilled, permanently organized Boston Symphony Orchestra came to New York on its concert visits, the New York Philharmonic winced under the inevitable comparison. The Chicago Orchestra had been built by Theodore Thomas, after he had left the Philharmonic in 1891, around a nucleus of sixty New York musicians, but Chicago also provided a subsidy for its orchestra, making possible a season three times as long as the Philharmonic's. By 1896 Thomas felt ready to show what could be accomplished under a permanent orchestra system by bringing his Chicago Orchestra to New York for seven concerts, and the mission succeeded well enough to justify a return in 1898 for seven more. Pittsburgh provided another case. Victor Herbert, formerly of the New York Philharmonic, conducted the Pittsburgh Symphony Orchestra from 1898 to 1904. Pittsburgh's seventy players, generously supported as something close to a full-time orchestra, also reached New York on tour.

It must have hurt to hear Victor Herbert's Pittsburgh Symphony Orchestra described as "more than New York has."

The strain of all these competitions and rivalries grew more difficult for the Philharmonic to meet after the loss of the dynamic Seidl as conductor in 1898. But historians have gone too far in depicting the condition of the orchestra from Paur to Safonoff as one of complete decline. Even J. H. Mueller, author of the most penetrating study of the American orchestras, speaks of the Philharmonic at this period as "constantly subject to odious comparison with the Boston orchestra, . . . eking out a threadbare existence, at the point of death from sheer inanition. No first-rate conductor," he concludes, "could be attracted under such hopeless conditions."[128] Yet it was Boston's own conductor, Emil Paur, who was glad to come to New York for four years at precisely that moment! And after Paur, the Philharmonic was able to attract the most famous conductors of the world as its guest conductors, the most celebrated performing artists as its soloists, and the great millionaires of the country as its financial supporters; and it was able to interest a public that sustained ticket sales sometimes above those of the Seidl period and seldom far below. Nor should Safonoff be disparaged as a "more or less obscure Russian," or a "musical Tartar . . . , aberrant, and irresponsible."[129] He was an outstanding conductor, pianist, and teacher, and his "fistic style of direction, vehement and theatrical," was only his personal version of the emotional and histrionic style characteristic of most of the interpreter-conductors from Wagner to Seidl.

The corroding problem of the Philharmonic was that, even while it was attracting such sensational conductors, such eminent soloists, such wealthy patrons, and such substantial audiences, it was disintegrating internally. Backnote 130 gives the evidence. It shows the number of Actual Members who performed in the orchestra during each season, as compared with the amount of money spent for "extra professional services," that is, for hiring outside players as substitutes when the regular members of the Society did not play for one reason or another. The figures tell a sad, clear story. In the comparatively healthy years from 1867 to 1870, so many of New York's professional musicians wanted to be members of the Philharmonic that it could always find the one hundred players that its largest concerts required (column C) in its pool of Actual Members (column B). As the competition of the Thomas Orchestra and other concerts began to be felt in the 1870s, both the number of Actual Members enrolled and the number that performed in the concerts went down slightly, and of course the amount spent to hire outsiders as substitutes (column D) had to go up somewhat, but the differential was not yet alarmingly large. From 1883 to 1909, however, the amount spent for substitutes rose from the neighborhood of $2,000 to more than $8,000 per season. The number of registered Actual Members fell from ninety-two to fifty-seven, and the number performing in the orchestra to thirty-seven. Only thirty-seven real Philharmonic members playing in an orchestra of one hundred men! They hardly had the right to be called an orchestra any more; one could say that they functioned more as a cooperative concert management of thirty-seven men who hired the performers necessary to put on a series of concerts.

Ultimately the Philharmonic's problems of cruel competition and internal deterioration had to be reflected in financial troubles. Trying to support a glamorous outside with a crumbling inside, the orchestra was balancing its budget only on paper. Annual dividends continued to be paid to the men, but after 1903 the conductors' salaries did not come from the regular budget: in the three guest-conductor years from 1903 to 1906, E. Francis Hyde raised something like $50,000 out of his own and his friends' purses to pay for the imported big names. The Philharmonic was discovering that a high-class, competitive orchestra had high-class, competitive expenses. Advertising in newspapers and concert programs had to be increased to $5,000 or $6,000 a year. The principal wind players petitioned for extra pay to match what rival organizations were doing. The rent for Carnegie Hall climbed from $4,000 to about $6,700 for the season. The overhead expenses began to take on a modern tinge: a press agent and a press-clipping service were hired, and allowances for "typewriting" and "telephone" appeared in Philharmonic budgets. The soloists of international fame, necessary to satisfy a demanding public, were costing more every year: Mesdames Schumann-Heink and Gadski drew $800 apiece for solo appearances, and the violinist Ysaÿe asked even more than that. The Ysaÿe story gives us a glimpse of what it meant to bargain in the celebrity market at the beginning of this century. Ysaÿe's manager informed the Philharmonic that his fee would be $1,500. The Philharmonic replied that they would pay $750 for him as a soloist, but they might be interested to know what terms could be arranged for Ysaÿe to appear also as conductor. For a box-office attraction like Ysaÿe, the manager demanded no less than $2,400 for a double appearance as both conductor and soloist. The Philharmonic answered coldly that it would be willing to pay $750 for him as soloist. What is our surprise, then, to find that in 1904–5 the Philharmonic did actually give Ysaÿe a fee of $1,400 for playing the Bruch G-Minor Violin Concerto! What had happened to the tone of steel in which the manager had been given his $750 answer? What had happened was that the Knabe Piano Company had offered to give the Philharmonic a rebate of $600 on Ysaÿe's fee if a Knabe piano were displayed prominently on stage at the violinist's performance. The Philharmonic had agreed.

It was becoming more and more difficult for the Philharmonic members to make ends meet. Trying to lift themselves up by their own bootstraps, they made desperate efforts to expand their seasons with additional concerts. There were perennial hopes for a series at the Brooklyn Academy of Music and talks with the concert manager Loudon Charlton about traveling engagements, but both these projects fell through. Safonoff was offered a contract for twenty-five to thirty concerts in a season—on paper—but when it came to concrete arrangements, only the usual eight pairs materialized. An orchestra in which only thirty-seven players out of a hundred are regular members cannot have a very high morale. It is touching to see these once proud musicians being treated almost like charity cases. Even the extra concerts that were arranged by one means or another in these years, gala as some of them seemed to the public eye, had a "make-work" quality about them for the men in the orchestra; they seldom meant more to the Society than an extra night's pay for the players, and many of those were outside men, picked up for the occasion. For the extra concert at the home of William K. Vanderbilt at 660 Fifth Avenue in 1908, the stipulated orchestra of sixty Philharmonic members could not be assembled and twenty-two outsiders had to be hired to make up the number. A mention of "drummers' traps," moreover, in the Philharmonic's records of the Vanderbilt engagement suggests that some of the members may have stooped to providing dance music after the concert that evening. For "high-class" musicians, at that time, this had demeaning professional and social connotations. "My men are all ruined," Theodore Thomas had complained when he was forced to disband his private orchestra in 1888, "by constant playing at balls and dances, for a living. A nice state of affairs, truly, that after a lifetime of hard work the members of my orchestra must play for *dancing* in order to live."[131] Two decades later, the state of affairs seemed to have grown even worse.

Richard Arnold and his colleagues had waged a stirring but futile campaign to save their beloved cooperative society. They had tried everything that experience and ingenuity suggested—they had raised extra funds, they had imported some of the world's greatest soloists and conductors, they had tried to lengthen their seasons, they had modernized their advertising, their press relations, and their office management—but as long as their affairs were managed collectively by a membership that drifted in and out of their handful of concerts each year, while they earned their livings elsewhere, they could not compete with the big-business methods of the great subsidized orchestras that were being built by the wealthy of America. When two extra concerts were announced for the end of the season of 1908–9, it was not the Philharmonic's regular conductor Vassily Safonoff who led them, but Gustav Mahler. The music world learned then that Safonoff was on his way out and Mahler on his way in. But this was not merely the replacement of one man by another. It was the end of one way of musical life and the beginning of a new one. After sixty-seven years, the cooperative society of professional musicians, democratically deciding who their conductor would be, what music they would play, where they would play it, and how much they would charge for the privilege of attendance at their performances, was to be converted into an orchestra hired and administered by a little group of wealthy citizens that undertook to support it as a public service.

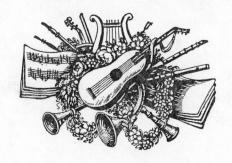

Part VI

A New Lease on Life
(1909–58)

Chapter 20

Reorganization
(1909–11)

"Like many another private enterprise," comments J. H. Mueller on the reorganization of the Philharmonic in 1909, "it was taken over by society as soon as it was affected with the public interest."[132]

The Philharmonic in 1909, however, was taken over not by "society," but by "high society." In the season of 1908–9, while Safonoff was still the conductor, Mrs. George R. Sheldon, wife of a prominent banker, and a number of other public-spirited citizens began to organize a group of so-called Guarantors of the Fund for the Permanent Orchestra of the Philharmonic Society of New York. Their object was to raise enough money to rebuild the Philharmonic into an orchestra of the first rank, paying sufficient salaries to the players and to the conductor to enable them to give their full time to the orchestra during the concert season. By the early part of 1909 large sums were being pledged by some of the old and a great many new supporters of the Philharmonic. These were not the subscriptions of $10 or $15 on which the Society had relied in years past for balancing its budget, nor even the donations of several hundred or several thousand dollars that a few men had made since 1903 for paying the conductors. They were promises of as much as $10,000, $15,000, and in a couple of cases even $30,000 each, and they came from a long list of people whose names meant wealth or position in New York's social and business circles—J. P. Morgan, Thomas Fortune Ryan, Joseph Pulitzer, John D. Rockefeller, E. J. de Coppet, Mrs. Harry Payne Whitney, Miss Dorothy Whitney, Alex Smith Cochran, Mrs. Samuel Untermeyer, Arthur Curtiss James, and many others.

On February 6, 1909, Mr. and Mrs. Sheldon and four of their friends,* acting for the Guarantors, were able to send the Philharmonic the following historic proposition—in effect an ultimatum—destined to revolutionize the orchestra's career:

¶It was proposed to organize in New York an orchestra of the highest order, under the exclusive direction of a fine conductor, the members of the orchestra to devote their time to its work for at least twenty-three successive weeks a year.

¶The corporate frame of the Philharmonic *could* be used for this purpose (the implication was that, if the Philharmonic did not cooperate, an orchestra might be formed without it), but this would require "radical changes in its organization and methods," especially in the commitment of every player to give his time to the orchestra for the full season, in return for a stated salary.

¶The Guarantors would undertake to make good any deficits for the three seasons 1909–12, and hoped, moreover, in that period, to raise an endowment fund to give the orchestra a permanent basis, but they would insist on having the entire control of the affairs of the Society. The Philharmonic would no longer be governed by its democratically elected Board of Directors. Instead, a powerful Committee of the Guarantors would designate the Directors (of whom three, however, would always be orchestra men), and would control all their actions, including the choice of officers, conductor, and manager, and the making of contracts. Some of the present members of the Society might even be dismissed from the orchestra, for each player would have to be accepted by the new conductor, with the approval of the Guarantors' Committee.

¶To underline the readiness of the project, a list of Guarantors and Donors was appended, with the actual amounts that each pledged.[133]

The Society acted swiftly to accept the proposition. On February 12, 1909, it suspended all bylaws that might conflict with the terms of

---

* They were Ruth Dana Draper, Henry Lane Eno, Ernest H. Schelling, and Nelson S. Spencer.

the offer, stipulating only that no performer be paid less than $35 per week under the new system, and that all contracts be carried out in accordance with the rules of the New York musicians' union. By the end of the month a Guarantors' Committee, with Mrs. Sheldon as Chairman, was meeting regularly,† and the wheels of the Philharmonic's new machinery were beginning to turn.

Like most revolutions this one proceeded gradually. The Guarantors, for example, did not actually depose the officers and Directors of the Society, and in fact the elected ones continued in office until 1912. But from the beginning of 1909 the Guarantors' Committee took over the practical administration of the Philharmonic's business affairs. So much was this so, that the annual meetings of the entire membership of the Philharmonic, at which the election of officers and Directors ordinarily took place, were not even held in 1910 and 1911, and when Andrew Carnegie resigned from the presidency in April 1909, the office was simply left vacant. Carnegie had anyway never been deeply involved in any personal way with the organization, and had always left the actual chairmanship of meetings to the Vice-President, Richard Arnold. But Mrs. Sheldon and her group of Guarantors—especially the ladies, who had the time and the interest to attend meetings regularly and pursue the business that grew out of them—threw themselves into the work with enthusiasm. Fortunately they also had energy and ability. The records of their formal meetings show that they knew how to make the committee system work. For the season of 1909–10, they supervised the organization and contracting of a full symphony orchestra, engaged one of the world's most distinguished musicians, Gustav Mahler, as conductor, increased the number of concerts from the eighteen of the preceding season to forty-six, arranged the orchestra's first tour outside the city, and raised more than $118,000 to cover the deficit that these activities incurred.

The transition from cooperative society to subsidized orchestra was smoothened by the retention of two of the Philharmonic's ablest officers, Richard Arnold, its Vice-President, and Felix Leifels, its Secretary, veterans of the heroic but hopeless struggle to save the old system. At one of the first meetings of the Guarantors' Committee in 1909, they were placed on annual salaries, in charge of the business

† The Guarantors' Committee included, in addition to the four associates of the Sheldons mentioned in the preceding footnote, three members of the orchestra: Richard Arnold, Felix F. Leifels, and Henry P. Schmitt. Leifels was Secretary of the Committee.

management of the Society's affairs. Arnold and Leifels constituted a bridge between the old regime and the new, Arnold holding the office of Vice-President until his death in 1918, and Leifels serving as Manager and Secretary until 1921.[134]

For the men in the orchestra, the increase that the Guarantors were effecting in the number of concerts must have seemed at least as impressive as their prowess in raising money. Even in the declining days of the old cooperative system, after all, the Philharmonic had already known how to obtain financial aid from E. Francis Hyde's rich friends, including some of the same people that Mrs. Sheldon was now approaching. The Society's receipts from an average concert, moreover, had actually been much higher under the cooperative than they were during the first two years under the Guarantors—about $2,600 per concert in 1906–9, as compared with $1,400 in 1909–11. But under the old system the concerts had been too few to permit the men to make the Philharmonic their principal occupation, and players who had constantly to be out looking for other jobs could not attend rehearsals regularly enough to maintain a high artistic level. The need for job security and the yearning for artistic excellence on the part of the orchestra men were among the most important forces leading them to accept the control of their society by the Guarantors, who could assure them of forty-six concerts in 1909–10 and sixty-five concerts in 1910–11, as compared with the eighteen of 1908–9.

Gustav Mahler, composer and conductor, whom the Guarantors had selected to lead the orchestra, was forty-nine years old in 1909, and his reputation as an inspired artist but a fierce and uncompromising taskmaster was firmly established both in Europe and in America. In Budapest, Hamburg, and Vienna, he had not merely conducted but had reshaped operatic and symphonic institutions for two decades; and at New York's Metropolitan Opera, even in the short time since 1907, he had brought new life to standard works from Wagner to Mozart. The Philharmonic's Guarantors had reason to hope that he would have both the firmness and the fire to guide the reorganization of their orchestra.

Mahler began to stir things up immediately. He brought in a new concertmaster, the American violinist Theodore Spiering.[135] He changed most of the important players in the woodwind and brass sections, favoring in the woodwinds the highly regarded French school. He adjusted the string section to his taste, cutting down the number of basses from fourteen to eight and engaging some fine new cellists from other orchestras.

When the reformed Philharmonic gave its first concert, on November 4, 1909, the new order was received with cautious optimism, but by the second and third concerts even Mahler's enemies had to agree that he was welding his forces into "a joyfully responsive and flexible instrument," capable of expressing every nuance of his highly personal style.

Fortunately, Mahler shared the desire of the orchestra players and the Guarantors to expand the number of concerts in the season. The symphony, he told a *Tribune* reporter upon his arrival from Europe for his first season with the Philharmonic, was the basis on which the musical education of a people must stand, and he intended, therefore, to devote his time to his symphony work rather than to the opera. In addition to regular subscription series on Friday afternoons and on Thursday evenings (the latter replacing the old Saturday evening concerts), the reorganized Philharmonic was offering several series with an educational tinge: a Beethoven cycle, a "historical" cycle, and Sunday concerts with programs of the more popular selections, so that "all, no matter what their means, should have the chance of hearing the best music." There were also a Brooklyn series, two concerts in Philadelphia, and a short tour—the first that the Philharmonic had ever made—that took the orchestra to New Haven, Springfield, Providence, and Boston. And Mahler was willing to conduct them all.

Most Americans assume that Mahler's expansion of the New York Philharmonic's activities represented a transplantation of his Vienna practice to a sparsely cultivated New York. But in Vienna, where Mahler had conducted the Philharmonic Concerts from 1898 to 1900, he had never had the number and the variety of concerts that he now dared to present in New York. As a matter of fact, the Vienna Philharmonic in the 1970s does not offer as many performances as Mahler did in New York in 1909. Then as now, European cities, with a few exceptions, had long opera seasons, but short symphony seasons; their symphony concerts—notwithstanding Mahler's characterization of the symphony as "the basis on which the musical education of a people must stand"—have always been a subordinate activity of the same orchestra that plays for the opera. In the expanded New York Philharmonic seasons Mahler had a symphonic vehicle that he may have dreamed of, but had never realized, in Europe.

Mahler embraced his new work with passion, but almost from the beginning the marriage was not a completely happy one. Although the orchestra shaped up beautifully, there were difficulties from three other quarters—the press, the audiences, and the Guarantors.

An important part of the press was hostile to Mahler, as composer and conductor. In particular, he had a strained and strange relationship with Henry E. Krehbiel, who, as music critic of the *Tribune,* was one of the city's most influential magistrates of musical taste. Krehbiel, the author of the first history of the Philharmonic, had also been writing the Philharmonic's program notes for many years, and considered himself a guardian of the Society's standards. He was strongly opposed to a great deal of what Mahler was doing as conductor and as composer, and, since he was an honest man, he was sometimes unable to conceal his disapproval even in the official program notes. He greeted Beethoven's *Consecration of the House* Overture, the opening work on Mahler's first program of the 1909–10 season, with these unenthusiastic lines in the program pamphlet: "This is a composition written 'to order' for a special occasion and therefore belongs to the class awkwardly called 'occasionals,' of which, as a rule, little is expected." In his newspaper columns Krehbiel was much more severe. After the New York premiere of Mahler's First Symphony, on December 16, 1909, Krehbiel went to the trouble of writing for the New York *World* (not his own paper) an exhaustive discussion of the symphony. Mahler had become such a potent influence in the musical life of the city, and indeed of the world, he said, that his symphony could not be "as summarily dismissed as we are inclined to think that it ought to be." Krehbiel's chief criticism was that the symphony was essentially descriptive or "program" music from which the programmatic story had been arbitrarily removed, and that the music no longer made sense in this stripped condition. But he also found fault with many other aspects of the composition, and even when he was trying to be sympathetic, seemed incapable of expressing his sympathy without throwing in a whack or two to preserve discipline: "There is no reason why [Mahler] should be a prophet of the ugly, as he discloses himself in the last movement of the Symphony in D. He makes that plain by interrupting a painfully cacophonous din with an episode built on a melody which is exquisitely lovely and profoundly moving." Of the series of historical concerts, Krehbiel questioned the accuracy and the adequacy, pointing out, for example, that to present as a Bach Suite a pastiche made up of three movements from one suite and two in the wrong key from another suite "militated somewhat against

the educational value of the scheme."[136] But most of all he was outraged by the liberties that Mahler took with the texts of the great masters of the past; for Krehbiel, an unjustified alteration in a score of
Beethoven was lèse-majesté if not sacrilege. Krehbiel was, of course, a
better scholar than Mahler, who, as an interpreter-conductor in an
advanced stage, presented performances of Beethoven and Schubert
that would shock any well-educated musician of today. Who can doubt,
for example, which side he must espouse when he reads Krehbiel's
critique of a Mahler performance of Beethoven's Fifth Symphony:

> . . . The first evidence of erraticism occurred in the famous cadenza, in
> the first movement.
> This Mr. Mahler phlebotomized by giving it to two oboes and beating
> time for each note—not in the expressive adagio called for by Beethoven,
> but in a rigid andante. Thus the rhapsodic utterance contemplated by the
> composer was turned into a mere connecting link between two parts of
> the movement. Into the cadence of the second subject of the third
> movement, Mr. Mahler injected a bit of un-Beethovenian color by chang-
> ing the horn part so that listeners familiar with their Wagner were
> startled by hearing something very like Hagen's call from "Götterdäm-
> merung" from the instruments which in the score simply sustain a har-
> mony voice in octaves. In the finale Mr. Mahler several times doubled
> voices (bassoons with 'cellos) and transposed the piccolo part an octave
> higher. Here he secured sonority which aided him in building up a thrill-
> ing climax, but did not materially disturb Beethoven's color scheme. The
> question of the artistic righteousness of his act may be left to the decision
> of musicians.[137]

Mahler was always helping composers along in their orchestration, to
Krehbiel's distress. In Beethoven's *Pastoral* Symphony, "Mr. Mahler is
not satisfied with the thunder of Beethoven's kettledrum, so he has
added another pair with a part of their own. The fact that Beethoven
was in his day an innovator in the use of the kettledrums, and might
have written three parts or four if he had been so disposed, might be
offered as a plea for the preservation of the purity of the classic text.
But under present conditions it would be idle to offer it."[138] In
Schubert's *Unfinished* Symphony "there was considerable violent ac-
centuation of dynamic contrasts, and it was not necessary to be a purist
to make one deplore the loss of refinement which came from the frequent doubling of the voices of the wind instruments." In Beethoven's

Coriolanus Overture, "the performance . . . was dramatically lurid. All through the evening the tympanist bombarded the ears of the hearers."[139] It did not help the relationship between the two men that Mahler had forbidden Krehbiel to write any program notes about his compositions. Mahler was known to disapprove of all such printed aids. "At a concert," Krehbiel reported him as saying, "one should listen, not look,—use the ears, not the eyes."[140] Krehbiel deferred to Mahler's wishes, but he grumbled about it occasionally in his newspaper reviews with a certain petulance, as of a wounded annotator.

So embittered did Krehbiel become that, although he was ordinarily correct in his behavior, he published at the time of Mahler's death in 1911, when others were writing respectful or admiring obituaries, a violent attack on the defenseless departed. The pianist and conductor Ossip Gabrilowitsch, supported by many other prominent persons, felt obliged to issue a pamphlet in reply.

Audiences of today may think wistfully what a thrill it must have been to have heard Mahler conducting the New York Philharmonic, but in 1909 and 1910 the audiences that took advantage of the opportunity were small ones—"probably the smallest that ever attended a Philharmonic concert in fifty years" and "perhaps the smallest in number that ever gathered at a Philharmonic concert" are typical descriptions. It was, after all, the first time that the Philharmonic had tried to give so many concerts in one season, and it took time for a sufficient public to develop. Some of the old guard found Mahler too radical both as composer and conductor. They agreed with Krehbiel: "If Mr. Gustav Mahler were not the conductor of the Philharmonic Society, and if his programmes and performances were not significant of a tendency which has been foreign to concerts of that organization during the two generations in which it has cultivated high class music, the production of his symphony . . . could be disposed of with very few words indeed."[141] One should not assume too quickly that this was a narrow-minded attitude. Johannes Brahms too had spoken of Mahler as "the most incorrigible revolutionist."[142] It was not that Krehbiel and some of his contemporaries in New York failed to appreciate Mahler but, on the contrary, that they grasped the revolutionary "dangerousness" of his compositions, which dared to experiment with materials that had formerly been considered vulgar, and of his performance methods, which appealed to a public that seemed undiscriminating to those who had been patrons of the old Philharmonic. At the other extreme, the "masses" seemed to find the various educational series unattractive; this was a disappointment to Mahler, who had talked at the beginning of the season of popular-priced concerts that would give everyone the chance of hearing the best music. Some sophisticated New Yorkers, moreover, resented Mahler's assumption that they had to be educated. They reminded him that a good part of his repertory had long been familiar to concertgoers in the city, that he tended to repeat pieces like Beethoven's Fifth too often in a single season, and that the Boston Symphony Orchestra and Damrosch's Symphony Society had already played in the same season several of the pieces that he was making such a fuss about. For Mahler's second year, the Philharmonic decided that it had better drop the Beethoven and historical cycles. There was also exceptional competition from opera during Mahler's term with the Philharmonic, when the Metropolitan Opera and Oscar Hammerstein's sensational company were vying with each other for New York's attention‡ Finally, there was about Mahler's music-making an atmosphere and a spirit almost of religious fanaticism; and some of the public were simply not in the same church.

Mahler and the Guarantors' Committee did not always get along well with each other either. He apparently found it difficult to take suggestions from the strong-willed ladies who were so important on the Committee. He had very clear ideas, for instance, about the music that he wanted to perform, but the Guarantors' Committee, in his second season with the Philharmonic, appointed a formal Program Committee of six of their members (four ladies, two musicians) to supervise the selection of music for the concerts. There was a serious dispute, too, about Mahler's contract, as can be seen from a letter that he wrote from Munich to his concertmaster, Spiering, on June 21, 1910, before the beginning of his second season with the Philharmonic:

> I am completely without news from America. As you know, at my urging a regular Manager was engaged,* who, however, to my great displeasure, has proposed sixty-five concerts and asserts that without this

‡ The Metropolitan could boast Toscanini and Caruso among its many star attractions. At Hammerstein's Manhattan Opera House, on West Thirty-fourth Street, artists of the brilliance of Garden, Melba, Nordica, and Tetrazzini, in a repertory refreshingly different from the Metropolitan's, were enjoying such a dazzling success that the Met found it worthwhile to buy Hammerstein's silence for more than a million dollars in 1910.

* This clause may explain the replacement of Leifels by Loudon Charlton, described in Backnote 134.

huge stepping up of the work schedule he cannot guarantee any success. I asked, for this colossal increase in output, a small increase in my honorarium (contractually I am obligated only for forty-five concerts), which demand, however, was denied by the Committee, so that I now am simply falling back on my contractual rights and obligations.

This I have now communicated to the Committee, but have since heard nothing from them.[143]

The dispute dragged on into the middle of the new season. Finally, Samuel Untermeyer agreed to act as arbitrator between Mahler and a committee representing the Guarantors' Committee. Mahler demanded an additional $5,000 for conducting an extra twenty concerts during the season. The arbitrator decided against the Committee, but Mahler agreed, at Untermeyer's suggestion, to reduce his claim to $3,000. At the same time, although the New York public assumed that Mahler had been engaged for three years, the Committee was sounding out other conductors in case Mahler became too demanding. Franz Kneisel, better known as violinist than conductor, had been approached, but would not leave his current work for the one-year contract that was being discussed with him. So manager Charlton was instructed to ask Mahler unofficially what his terms for the next year would be. Mahler said that he would conduct ninety to a hundred concerts, far more than the forty-six of his first year and the sixty-five of the season then in progress, for the sum of $30,000. The Committee thereupon discontinued negotiations with Kneisel, and asked Mahler to put into writing his terms and conditions for the conductorship for the next season. When he did, his proposition was rejected and the Executive Committee was given power to continue negotiations with Felix Weingartner, to whose agent a cable had previously been sent. If the Committee failed to complete a contract with Weingartner, it was to reopen negotiations with Mahler![144] Neither side would have been well advised to buy a used car from the other.

Much of the unpleasantness was Mahler's own fault. He had always been a difficult man, complex, tense, high-strung, but since 1907 when he had suffered a double blow—the death of his daughter, and the information that his heart condition did not leave him long to live—he had been even more difficult. Mahler's widow, the late Alma Mahler Werfel, in an interview in 1960, described how she sometimes went to the last part of a Mahler rehearsal with the Philharmonic and "took him home afterwards in order to save him." Asked what she meant by "save him," she replied:

You see, Mahler had a peculiarity, a special characteristic—he listened to the gossip and intrigues of the orchestra men. It was so in Vienna, and it was so here in New York, too. In every orchestra there is at least one musician who lives on such plots, and Mahler would listen to him and become upset about some real or imagined injury. If I were there at the end of the rehearsal, the trouble-makers couldn't do anything, but if bad weather or some other reason kept me away, he would be sure to come home angry from some poison they had put in his ear. The greatest men are sometimes like children, they have no weapons to defend themselves. And Mahler was so insecure (not musically—no one was more secure there—but personally) that he was ready to listen to anyone. But in all this, you must understand, he was an innocent, a complete innocent.[145]

A typical Mahlerian contretemps occurred when Mahler imported the prominent Hungarian pianist Joseph Weiss, a pupil of Liszt's, to appear as soloist with the Philharmonic in the Schumann Concerto. "At Saturday's rehearsal," reported the *Evening World* of January 31, 1910, with tongue halfway into cheek, "Herr Weiss suggested that the oboes play a little softer in a certain place. Herr Mahler suggested that Herr Weiss confine himself to his own instrument and not talk so much. Herr Weiss remarked that he was as good a pianist as Herr Mahler was a conductor, seized his music and stalked out." The next afternoon Weiss presented himself at Carnegie Hall, ready to play the concert, but the angry Mahler would not have him; the conductor grew so excited, one newspaper confided, that an "explosion" was only narrowly averted. "Mrs. Mahler tried to act as peacemaker," added the *Telegraph,* "and suffered the inevitable consequences." The press was clearly delighted by the antics of the temperamental foreign artists, but for the Philharmonic Society it was an embarrassing affair.[146]

It is a question how successfully the relationship between the difficult Mahler and the determined Guarantors' Committee could have continued, but the resolution was taken tragically out of their hands. Mahler fell seriously ill in February and March of 1911 and his faithful concertmaster, Theodore Spiering, had to conduct the last quarter of the season—sometimes with no warning until the day of the concert, since Mahler thought each time that he would be well enough to resume his duties. But others could see that Mahler was a very sick man. On March 22 the Guarantors' Committee delegated one of its members to visit Mahler and to express the sympathy of the Committee on his illness. Mahler returned to Vienna by slow stages, suffering all the way. By May 18, he was dead.

The period of Mahler's tenure tested the Philharmonic as a modern American orchestra with a long season addressed to a broad public. It is true that each of these elements was in an early stage of development—the Philharmonic was only slightly more modern, slightly more American, with a somewhat longer season, addressed to a relatively broader public, than in the days before 1909. Nor were the special features of the new regime original, either with Mahler or with the Guarantors' Committee—Jullien, Bergmann, Thomas, and a number of conductors and orchestras in cities other than New York had long ago explored the mysteries of extended seasons, historical concerts, famous-composer programs, popular concerts, and out-of-town tours. But Mahler's two years represented the first time that the conservative Philharmonic, which formerly had stood like a great rock in the midst of the swirling waters of change, had made an effort to move with the new currents and even to influence their course. For Mahler the experiment had often been a stormy experience, but for the orchestra there was no question that it had begun to succeed. In the first year of the reorganization the number of concerts was three times as great as it had ever been before, and in the second year it was four times as great. The deficit was very large, it is true, but there were generous citizens not only willing to pay it, but also to give their time and skills to the cause, and in the second year they had narrowed considerably the gap between the orchestra's expenses and its earned income. The expressed policy of the Guarantors' Committee was "to reconcile the commercially possible with the artistically desirable," and the Committee now knew, after its two instructive years with Mahler, that an expanding Philharmonic was compatible with the most exacting artistic standards.

The force of the revitalized Philharmonic under Mahler was felt even outside New York. The out-of-town tours in Mahler's two years, although short, were of great cultural impact. Unlike other orchestras, including the Boston Symphony Orchestra, which cut their forces to about two thirds of regular strength for traveling purposes, the Philharmonic traveled with its full complement of ninety-two men. Mahler was not one to compromise in such matters. If the stage of Infantry

Hall in Providence was too small for the orchestra that Berlioz and Strauss required, it had to be built out until it was the right size. Many a listener learned for the first time in the course of these short tours what the sumptuous orchestral works of the great Romantic composers could be like at the hands of a first-rate professional orchestra, shaped and led by an inspired conductor. The tours were good for the morale of the Philharmonic men too. There was a satisfaction in being the grand New York Philharmonic, led by one of the most famous musicians in the world and representing New York City in the style that lesser communities expected of it. Audiences were small at first, but they were enthusiastic, and for many years after Mahler's departure the Philharmonic would find it worthwhile, artistically and spiritually, if not always financially, to carry its music to a widening circuit of cities. The Philharmonic was now of more than local interest. There would be times in the future when, with a powerful personality at its head, it would seem to be as much a national as a metropolitan institution.

In the life story of the Philharmonic, Mahler's brief term marks a moment of great historic significance—the moment when the new rubbed abrasively against the old, clearing a path for the future. But Mahler did *not,* as is generally supposed, sweep aside with one brusque gesture the shaky structure of an old Philharmonic to begin his work with an orchestra built entirely of new materials and on new principles. His period of service can better be seen as a period of transition and he as an instrument of change—a change that had been gradually prepared, inside and outside the Philharmonic, for many years before he appeared on the scene. There had been Theodore Thomas's plans and demands for a "permanent" orchestra and his successful demonstration in Chicago of how it should be accomplished. There had been Walter Damrosch's proposal of the Permanent Orchestra Fund, which outlined in 1903, before Mahler even came to America, much the same plan that was finally put into effect in 1909. And there had been, for six years before Mahler's term, the Conductors' Fund that Richard Arnold and E. Francis Hyde had raised from some of the same people who would later support the Guarantors' Fund. By the time that Mahler took over the Philharmonic, much of the way had been prepared for him.

Just as gradual as the preparation of the new was the fading of the old. Many elements of the pre-1909 Philharmonic survived in Mahler's period. Throughout his term, for example, and on into the year

after it, the Philharmonic remained legally the same corporation that
it had been before 1909, with the same Directors who had been elected
by its Actual Members under its old bylaws.[147] The Society did sur-
render the day-to-day running of its affairs to the Guarantors' Committee, but it had three orchestra representatives on the Committee, as
we have seen, and two of them, Richard Arnold and Felix Leifels,
retained important roles in the orchestra's administration. In the actual
music-making, Arnold was unseated from the concertmaster's chair
when Spiering was engaged, but Leifels played at the first desk of
double basses during both of Mahler's years; of the six other old-
timers on the Board of Directors, five continued to play in the orchestra under Mahler. Too much has been made, in general, of Mahler's
hiring new players for the orchestra. Most of the wind players were
new, it is true, but the strings were largely the same, including even
August Roebbelen, whom Damrosch had singled out for dismissal in
1903 as having "passed his time of usefulness," but whom Mahler
apparently found acceptable in 1909–10 and again in 1910–11. A
comparison of the orchestra lists for the end of Safonoff's conductorship and the beginning of Mahler's shows that only six of the old
Actual Performing Members did not come back and that at least twenty-
six of the "new" players in the orchestra were the same New York
musicians that the Philharmonic had hired in 1908–9 as extras to fill
out its thinning ranks. The difference was that they were now hired
for a long season.

The new players, particularly the winds, were a welcome addition
to the orchestra, but it was not the quality of the individual musicians
that made the Philharmonic a different institution after 1909 than it
had been before, nor even its artistic leadership, which had already
been beyond reproach in the days of Bergmann and Thomas. What
made it different was the expanded basis of its operations—the guaranteed salaries for the orchestra players, the full seasons, the varied
types of concerts, the efforts on the one hand to reach and on the
other hand to educate a somewhat broader public, the tours, the recognition by the wealthy of a responsibility to put the Philharmonic's
cultural riches within the reach of their less fortunate fellow citizens.
And it was a basis with a future because it fanned out in so many
directions that it permitted, and invited, further expansion for a long
time to come.

Chapter 21

Expansion
(1911–23)

Mahler's successor as conductor, whoever he might be, would have to live and work in the Philharmonic's new atmosphere of expansion. He would be expected to conduct more concerts in one season than the typical European orchestra gave in five years. He would have to vary his programs for the different publics that all these concerts served. He would have to be interested in the education of the community, but not condescending about it. He would have to please a good part of the press. He would have to be physically and psychologically prepared to travel American distances—computed on a different geographical scale from European distances—on his orchestra's tours. He would have to understand, in order to get along with the wealthy group that guaranteed the orchestra's finances, either how to adapt to their ideas or, if he were a strong enough personality, how to make them adapt to his. And while he was juggling these five or six balls in the air, he would have to maintain artistic standards that would satisfy a self-conscious metropolis convinced that the eyes of Europe were fixed critically upon it and determined that its orchestra would be (in Mahler's words) "the best in the country and the equal of any in the world."

The man who took over this many-sided task in the fall of 1911 was Josef Stransky. He was of Bohemian origin, thirty-nine years old at the time he came to the Philharmonic, a man of attractive appearance and good general education (he had studied medicine in Prague and Leipzig at the same time that he was studying music). He was not an international celebrity like Mahler, but he had an impressive professional background as opera and concert conductor in Prague, Hamburg, Berlin, and Dresden, and as guest conductor in Holland and England.

He turned out to be the right man for the job. In his first season Stransky conducted more concerts than any previous Philharmonic conductor had done in one season—a total of 84, including 31 on tour. Two years later the Board of Directors, in a public statement, declared that this, together with 115 rehearsals during the twenty-three-week season, represented "about the limit of what would seem physically possible without the sacrifice of musical excellence." Yet in 1919–20 Stransky went beyond that limit to give 98 concerts, including 32 on tour; and the next year a coast-to-coast tour swelled the traveling schedule alone to 94 concerts.

This record of numbers was matched by an equally impressive record of variety. In his twelve years as conductor of the Philharmonic (ten years full-time, two more shared with other conductors), Stransky conducted more different types of concerts than the Philharmonic's public had ever enjoyed before. There were, of course, the regular subscription concerts, which had grown into four distinct series, on Thursday evenings, Friday afternoons, Saturday evenings, and Sunday afternoons. There were afternoon and evening series in Brooklyn. There was the Philharmonic's first Young People's Concert, in January of 1914, which was such a success that two more were given the next season and Brooklyn had to have one of its own. There were, for those who signed up as members of the Philharmonic Society, such special privileges as Orchestral Lectures by the composer Rubin Goldmark, illustrated by the orchestra, Evenings of Light Music, *Concerts Intimes,* and An Oriental Evening with Roshanara. There were special performances at Columbia University, at the Cooper Union, and at army camps. And then there were the annual tours, numbering from nineteen to ninety-four concerts in different years, and reaching not only into New York, New Jersey, and the New England states, but also to the cities of the South, the Midwest, the Pacific coast, and Canada.[148] In all this work Stransky had only occasional aid from an assistant or associate conductor.

Stransky was a great popular success. Not since the days of Anton Seidl had there been such warm and spontaneous applause, such sold-out houses, and such satisfying box-office returns. Stransky may not have quadrupled the ticket sale, as his most exuberant admirers claimed, but he did double it. At the conclusion of his ninth season the management could announce officially that the concerts had enjoyed "the largest subscription since their inauguration."

Sold-out houses, however, did not mean balanced budgets. The Philharmonic's expenditures, under Stransky, were creeping up in all the familiar departments—salaries, tour expenses, hall rental, advertising, administrative costs—and some completely new financial burdens were being incurred. Stransky's contract, negotiated in the months after he opened his first season, gave him $20,000 a year for three years, plus several fringe benefits, such as the transportation of his baggage to and from the ship on his arrival and departure each season (it was taken for granted in the New York of 1911 that a proper conductor was not a permanent resident of the city, but a European who arrived and departed each season). Stransky's income tax was paid by the Society. An official Assistant Conductor—the Philharmonic had never had one before—was engaged for him; Fritz Stahlberg, a violinist in the orchestra and a composer, was the first to hold the position.* That a regular Manager was advisable for the Philharmonic had already been recognized by Mahler; for the swelling activities of the Stransky period such a functionary became indispensable, and Felix Leifels was appointed to the post. A number of free concerts, given as a public service, brought in no revenue, but cost the Philharmonic almost as much as regular subscription concerts to put on. The prices of soloists and leading orchestra players were rising in the American market as more orchestras grew up all over the country and competed for musical artists—at the beginning of Stransky's term, the Philharmonic was already bidding against Damrosch's Symphony Society and several others in New York and against major orchestras in Boston, Chicago, Cincinnati, Philadelphia, Minneapolis, and St. Louis; by the end of his

* Stahlberg was succeeded by William H. Humiston, a composer who had been one of Edward MacDowell's students and who also wrote the program notes for the Philharmonic for many years. After 1920 Stransky had the American composer Henry Hadley as Associate Conductor (the distinction between an Associate and an Assistant being apparently that the Associate actually conducted some public performances, whereas the Assistant merely helped behind the scenes).

term, San Francisco, Cleveland, Detroit, Baltimore, and Los Angeles had been added to the list of enterprising cities that were maintaining fine symphony orchestras and contributing to the demand for musicians.

The financial pressure on the Philharmonic was relieved a bit by one of those bequests that orchestras (and private individuals) dream about. Late in 1911 it was learned that Joseph Pulitzer, the newspaper publisher, who had died on October 29 of that year, had remembered the Society in his will. Pulitzer had been a lover of orchestral music; he was known to have had an entire orchestra of Philharmonic men brought up to his estate at Bar Harbor to play for him. His will gave the Philharmonic $500,000 as a permanent endowment fund, plus certain other sums, not to exceed an additional $500,-000. The fund was to be used, Pulitzer had provided,

> to perfect the present orchestra and to place it on a more independent basis and to increase the number of concerts to be given in the City of New York, which additional concerts I hope will not have too severely classical programs and to be open to the public at reduced rates . . .

There must have been a nervous moment in Philharmonic circles when it was reported that Pulitzer required his favorite composers to be played, but the Society could heave a corporate sigh of relief at the information that the favorites were Beethoven, Wagner, and Liszt, a more than acceptable trio. There were also some legal conditions, however, that necessitated changes in the very organization of the Philharmonic Society. The bequests to the Philharmonic were made

> contingent on that Society's becoming, within three years after my death, a membership corporation under the laws of New York, representing the general public, with a membership of not less than one thousand paying dues, and on said Society's receiving the approval of my executors. If the above conditions be not complied with, I revoke the bequests to said Society absolutely.

The Pulitzer bequest was not the cause of the Philharmonic's finally changing its structure—the forces of change had been working for a long time—but it certainly hastened the process. Vice-President Arnold and Secretary Leifels promptly called meetings of the Philharmonic's members and of the eight musicians who still constituted the Board of Directors under the old rules. Mrs. Sheldon called a meeting of the Guarantors' Committee. Both groups appointed subcommittees which met with each other, with legal counsel, and with the executors of the will. In order to comply with Pulitzer's conditions, the bylaws had to be completely revised and two delicate legal technicalities had to be worked out: the existing Pension Fund had to be abolished and its assets distributed among the members in an acceptable manner, and the Society's certificate of incorporation had to be amended by striking out as one of its objects "the relief of distressed actual members, their widows and children." The reason for this was that under New York State law a membership corporation—which Pulitzer required the Society to become—could not also be subject to the Insurance Law, and it was questionable whether the orchestra's Pension Fund and its relief of distressed members and their families would not bring it within some of the provisions of the Insurance Law. Nelson S. Spencer, the Guarantors' legal adviser, together with William Hornblower, counsel for the executors of the will, and Hector W. Thomas, counsel for all the old members of the Philharmonic Society,† unraveled all this to everyone's satisfaction. Finally, on March 16, 1912, the full Philharmonic Society and its Board of Directors assembled, accepted the new bylaws and administrative arrangements, and in effect voted themselves out of power.

Immediately, the administrative authority was redistributed in accordance with the new bylaws. About one hundred persons who had contributed very large sums (the minimum was set at $1,000) were elected Sustaining Members, and a new Board of Directors was nominated to consist of twelve persons, in the significant proportion of nine Sustaining Members to three Musical Members. Of course several pillars of the Guarantors' Committee reappeared among the new Directors as Sustaining Members—Mrs. Sheldon, Mrs. Cheney, Rudolf Flinsch, Nelson Spencer—and the Musical Members were our old orchestra stalwarts, Arnold, Leifels, and Schmitt, the former Vice-President, Secretary, and Treasurer of the Society.[149]

As with all large wills, it took a while for the Pulitzer money to be handed over, but finally in November 1913 a good part of it—$775,-000 in cash—was paid to the Philharmonic's Treasurer. The new Board of Directors was quick to point out to the public that the cash-in-hand value of the gift was less than the layman might imagine from the

---

† Hector Thomas was the son of Theodore Thomas. It seems fitting, in retrospect, that the lawyer who acted for the orchestra members in accepting the endowment bequest should have been the son of a man who had dreamed of making the Philharmonic a permanently endowed orchestra.

sound of "half a million dollars" or "three quarters of a million dollars": what the Philharmonic really had to work with was the income from the investment of the bequest, and that might range from $35,000 to $45,000 per annum.[150] Today, as a matter of fact, although the Philharmonic still enjoys the benefits of Pulitzer's gift, the annual income is even less; the expendable portion of the bequest, which eventually came to about $400,000, was long ago used up in covering deficits, and the permanent endowment of half a million dollars produces interest of something over $22,000 a year.

The significance of Pulitzer's gift to the Philharmonic, however, reached beyond its exact financial worth. It is said to have been the first permanent endowment of an American symphony orchestra by a grant of investment capital, as distinguished from year-to-year contributions to take care of annual deficits. The Philharmonic's Guarantors, since their earliest announcements, had been calling for "an endowment fund which would establish the orchestra upon a permanent basis," and the Pulitzer bequest made a substantial beginning in that direction. Moreover, Pulitzer sounded a new kind of democratic note in his insistence that the Philharmonic give more concerts at lower rates and enlist at least a thousand dues-paying members. The Philharmonic might be less democratic in its administrative machinery under the new system than it had been in the days when the orchestra players decided all questions by vote, but it would be much more democratic in its social goals and in its public membership. Pulitzer helped to prepare for the day when one or two extremely wealthy men could no longer be expected to maintain an orchestra for a great city, and when a broader support would have to be solicited.‡ Symbolic of the change was the Monster Music Festival of music by Wagner and Tchaikovsky, conducted by Stransky on December 21, 1913, in the old Madison Square Garden at Twenty-fourth Street; there were 12,682 persons at the concert, which was announced as part of the *Evening Mail*'s "Campaign for Classic Music at Popular Prices / In cooperation with the Wage Earners' Theatre League and Theatre Centre for Schools."

Both Stransky and the Board of Directors were glad to widen the Philharmonic's public as the Pulitzer bequest encouraged them to do— Stransky because he was an affable man who enjoyed his popularity, the Board because expanded audiences were good for the budget, and

‡ A day that was hastened by the heavy income taxes that were made possible by the Sixteenth Amendment to the United States Constitution in 1913.

both of them for idealistic reasons as well. This was reflected in the choice of music for the Philharmonic's programs, which were now slanted more toward a broad "anonymous" audience than toward a known elite of connoisseurs. But even without pressures from the Pulitzer will and from the Directors, Stransky's musical tastes were catholic enough to accommodate a wide spectrum of listeners. *The repertory of music that Stransky presented was by far the most varied and the most comprehensive—and the liveliest—that the Philharmonic had known under any conductor since its inception.* He did offer large doses of the Wagner and Liszt that Pulitzer had prescribed, and of his ever-popular countryman Dvořák. But, in addition to these, his seasons always had their share of Bach, Haydn, Mozart, Beethoven, and Schubert, of Weber, Mendelssohn, Schumann, and Brahms, of Berlioz, of Richard Strauss, of Tchaikovsky. He played the French-Belgian composers, from Lalo, Franck, Chabrier, and Godard to Massenet, Saint-Saëns, Debussy, Dukas, Charpentier, Widor, Roussel, and d'Indy. He played the English—Delius, Elgar, Stanford. He played the Russians —Borodin, Rimsky-Korsakov, Rachmaninov, Glazunov, Kalinnikov. He played the Norwegian, Grieg. Of course he played such fellow Czechoslovakians as Smetana, Novak, and Fibich. He played the still controversial music of his predecessor Mahler. He introduced early works of Stravinsky (*Fireworks,* in 1914) and Schoenberg (*Pelleas and Melisande,* first American performance, in 1915). He played others of his contemporaries from every part of the world—Alfvén, Bloch Grainger, Korngold, Reger, Respighi, Sibelius. And he programmed more performances of American compositions than all his predecessors on the Philharmonic podium put together: Bingham, Chadwick, Foote, Gilbert, Goldmark, Hadley, Herbert (born Irish, but American by adoption), Humiston, Kramer, MacDowell, Daniel Gregory Mason, Morris, Paine, Powell, Rogers, Schelling, David Stanley Smith, Sousa, Sweet, Whithorne, Wilson; what is more, he played many of them repeatedly.

A little of the variety in Stransky's concert repertory, it must be admitted, can be traced to the influence of the First World War. German-Austrian music, which in the prewar years had been providing about 65 per cent of all the music played, fell precipitously to about 40 per cent when it became the music of the enemy in 1917–18. In compensation, the performances of American music and the music of our allies (England, Russia, France) went up in the balance. It was more a question of emphasis, however, than of substantive change; the same kinds of variety can be found in Stransky's programs before 1917, but with slightly different proportions. Unlike conductors in some other cities, Stransky did not yield to the clamoring of extremists for the complete elimination of German-Austrian music from American concert performances. He continued to serve generous helpings even of Wagner, who for many anti-Germans had become symbolic of Teutonism. Richard Strauss was dropped completely for a few years, however, because he was a *living* German composer who would theoretically have been entitled to royalties for performances of his works, and very few Americans would have been so liberal as to agree to that during the war. Although some of these wartime gains and losses in the repertory evened off by 1922, the prewar proportions were never restored; in the long view the amount of German-Austrian music played by the Philharmonic continued to decline slowly after 1922, while, on the other hand, performances of American and Russian music never fell back to their previous low levels.

The war affected the Philharmonic in other ways also. At first, while the United States remained neutral, the conflict seemed remote—a European war. Count Johann von Bernstorff, the German Ambassador, was still as welcome as any other Philharmonic boxholder in 1915–16. When occasionally the war impinged on the music world, it was at second or third hand, as in the following notice which appeared in programs of the New York Philharmonic in 1915:

KNITTING
During Performances.

THE PHILHARMONIC SOCIETY fully appreciates the spirit that prompts charitable assistance in the great world's calamity caused by the European war, but many complaints have been received from patrons of the concerts who are annoyed by knitting during performances, and the Directors respectfully request that this practice, which interferes with the artistic enjoyment of the music, be omitted.

FELIX F. LEIFELS, Manager.

But on April 6, 1917, President Wilson and Congress proclaimed a state of war, and before the end of the year the music world was feeling the repercussions. Ernst Kunwald, the conductor of the Cincinnati Symphony Orchestra (he had been one of the guest conductors of the New York Philharmonic in the season of 1905–6), was arrested in December 1917, interned in Fort Oglethorpe, and eventually deported; the conductors who completed the season in Cincinnati were safely English, American, Russian, and Belgian. Karl Muck, the conductor of the Boston Symphony Orchestra, was arrested and interned in March 1918 and returned to Germany after the Armistice. The names of Muck and Kunwald were quietly dropped from their American record labels during the war. In New York, the Philharmonic's President, Oswald Garrison Villard, though native-born, was tragically affected by the wartime prejudices. He had to sell his newspaper, the New York *Post,* in 1918, because his opposition to the United States' entry into the war caused the sales to fall off, and he resigned from the presidency of the Philharmonic and from his positions as Trustee and Director of the Society when it was made clear to him that "pacificism and music would not mix in wartime." Rudolf Flinsch, the Treasurer, who had been a member of the Guarantors' Committee in the Mahler days, resigned with him. The Philharmonic had no President for the rest of that season, nor for the next one, when it was even without a Vice-President because of the death of Richard Arnold. (It was not until 1919, when Henry E. Cooper took over the presidency, that the Philharmonic's highest office was filled again.) Stransky, however, had no serious difficulties from the war; he was apparently accepted as a Czech, not a German, and besides, he took out his first citizenship papers in 1918. In some cities—Boston, for example—not only the conductors, but also the German orchestra players had their wartime troubles. But the New York Philharmonic, by the time of the First World War, was much less German in its personnel than it had been at the turn of the century. In 1909, just before the orchestra was reorganized, though all but two or three of the Actual Members were still German, the extra players who had to be hired to complete the orchestra already included some Frenchmen, some Italians, and some of the Jewish immigrants from Russia and Central Europe who were beginning to take a larger role in the city's musical life. Under Mahler, who Gallicized the woodwind section, and under Stransky, the de-Germanizing process had continued further. It was the war, nevertheless, in 1918, that finally converted the Philharmonic's concertmeister into its concert*master*.

It was under Stransky, at this period, that the Philharmonic reached outside the concert hall toward another audience through its first phonograph recordings. Between January 1917 and October 1919 about twenty-five pieces, mostly old favorites, were recorded by the acoustic method for Columbia Records. There were overtures, symphony movements, dances, marches, and various characteristic pieces by Beethoven, Mozart, Haydn, Weber, Berlioz, Dvořák, Brahms, Liszt, Tchaikovsky, Saint-Saëns, Ambroise Thomas, Moszkowski, Rimsky-Korsakov, Victor Herbert, Flotow, Suppé, Waldteufel, Ippolitov-Ivanov, Elgar, Massenet, Sullivan. The blurb in the Columbia catalogue read:

PHILHARMONIC ORCHESTRA OF NEW YORK—
Josef Stransky, Conductor

(Exclusive Columbia Artist.)

THE New York Philharmonic Orchestra has been called "the symphonic keystone in America's temple of music." The exclusive Columbia Records of this famous orchestra under the baton of Josef Stransky is only an additional proof of the reputation of Columbia orchestral recordings. The first public concert of the New York Philharmonic Orchestra was on December 7, 1842, the first composition performed, Beethoven's Fifth Symphony, which fittingly enough was the first Columbia recording of the orchestra.[151] The Philharmonic Orchestra of New York is one of the particular prides of the Columbia catalogue.

Stransky was warmly supported by a large part of the press; Henry T. Finck, the critic of the *Post,* admitted openly that he had been his "unofficial press-agent.[152] But another faction, led by Richard Aldrich of the *Times,* began to oppose Stransky with equal fervor, complaining that he catered to the public taste for the most easily accessible music. By the season of 1916–17 the President of the Philharmonic Society felt obliged to defend it, in his annual address to the members, against the allegation in "the columns of a certain newspaper" that the Philharmonic was "losing the support of those of the highest musical taste in the community and drawing in the less critical public." Stransky's friend Finck said that "once every other year there was a regular *Philharmonic Drive.* It consisted of an obviously preconcerted attack. Dozens of letters (mostly unsigned) were printed in certain newspapers, conveying the impression that Stransky and his orchestra were seventeenth rate—a positive disgrace to the country." Finck hinted darkly that one of the leaders of these attacks was a disgruntled composer whose works Stransky refused to play, and also that Stransky's $30,000 salary (Finck padded it—it was only a little over $20,000) aroused the jealousy of other conductors who joined the opposition.[153]

The truth about Stransky's abilities and artistic standards probably lay somewhere between the two extremes. He won great crowds of new adherents to the cause of orchestral music, but he alienated many of the most sophisticated and most earnest music lovers who had once constituted an important element among the Philharmonic patrons. He offered a varied and colorful array of compositions, but he tended to favor the immediately pleasurable over the controversial or complicated. Some of the greatest artists of the world—and most of them appeared with the Philharmonic during Stransky's regime—musicians of the rank of Kreisler and Paderewski, lavished superlatives on him, yet even his strongest defender, Finck, admitted that "he was by no means always at his best at these concerts. Sometimes he conducted in a slovenly way that quite justified adverse criticism." Although Stransky undoubtedly had real deficiencies, the negative side of the story seems to have survived much more strongly than the positive in the memories of music historians and journalists. Half a century after Stransky's time, books that deal with American music are still harping almost vindictively on his "mediocrity," without citing any evidence of it.[154] In Stransky's own day, even his severest critics agreed that he had improved the orchestra's personnel and raised its technical level, yet some of the adverse propaganda of the clever opposing faction is still remembered and believed to this day. Every New York musician knows, for example, the anecdote about a rehearsal of Tchaikovsky's Fourth Symphony in which, when the second theme of the finale was reached, the orchestra, instead of playing the melody, sang it, with these words:

"Ev-'ry-bo-dy knows   it but   Stran-sky."

If the incident took place at all (which seems unlikely), it could only have been as a playful prank, and would testify to the great affability of the man in an age when the relationships between orchestra players and conductor were not yet so easy as they are today. But it is impossible to believe, as we are asked to believe, that the musicians were accusing Stransky of not knowing Tchaikovsky's Fourth Symphony, one of his trusted warhorses, which he conducted from one to fifteen times in almost every season. (If Stransky had an obvious fault in his year-to-year programming, it was that he repeated relentlessly a few of his and the public's favorite pieces, among them Chabrier's *España*, Dukas's *The Sorcerer's Apprentice*, and Tchaikovsky's Fourth.)

Whether the criticisms were justified or not, they were successful. Stranksy was eased out of his position in one of the smoothest operations in the oily history of orchestral-conductorial politics. In 1919, when Stransky had already been suffering for several years from the attacks of his enemies, a new orchestra had been founded in the city (Finck speaks as though its establishment had been for the express long-term purpose of getting Stransky out of the Philharmonic, but this is probably an exaggeration) with the composer Edgard Varèse as its first conductor. Varèse was not only a musician of remarkable talents and passionate dedication to new music, but he was also an extremely handsome young man, and with this combination of attractions he had succeeded in enlisting the cooperation of some of the best orchestra musicians and some of the wealthiest women in town. This was the reason for the strangely bifurcated name of the new organization: The New Symphony Orchestra, Inc. [rich ladies] of the Musicians' New Orchestra Society [good players]. Varèse was able to give only two performances of a single program with the New Symphony Orchestra (April 11 and 12, 1919) before his financial guarantors recognized with shock that all this new music that sounded so fascinating when he talked about it was difficult for most of their listeners to take. His one program consisted, after a seldom-played instrumental excerpt from a Bach cantata, of four unfamiliar modern works—compositions of Debussy, Casella, Bartók, and Dupont—in their first New York performances. Varèse had announced two more pairs of concerts, made up entirely of music of recent composition (Whithorne, Sibelius, Griffes, Loeffler; Tommasini, Satie, Busoni, Roussel, Ravel), but they were never given.[155] Instead, for the next season, the New Symphony Orchestra was conducted in more conservative programs by Artur Bodanzky of the Metropolitan Opera, and after that, in the season of 1920–21, also by Willem Mengelberg, the Dutch conductor who had been one of the imposing set of guests who had led the Philharmonic in 1905–6.

Now, the National Symphony Orchestra (this name had been adopted, instead of New Symphony Orchestra, for the 1920–21 season of the organization) was lavishly financed by Clarence Mackay, president of the Postal Telegraph Company, and Adolph Lewisohn, the copper magnate.* They paid for everything that Mengelberg needed in the way of players and rehearsal time, and Mengelberg, whose conducting style was anyway much more impressive than Stransky's, was able to dazzle the New York concertgoers. It seemed a shame to the Directors of the Philharmonic to be missing out on so much talent and so much money. For the season beginning in the fall of 1921, the National Symphony Orchestra was merged with the Philharmonic, with Henry E. Cooper of the Philharmonic remaining President, but Mackay of the National being named Chairman of the Board. Since Stransky was still called Conductor and Henry Hadley Associate Conductor, while Mengelberg and Bodanzky were listed only as guest conductors, it looked as though Stransky had withstood the attack of the opposition after all. But Mengelberg's guest-conducting stint was a long and successful one, amounting to about half the season, and for the next season (1922–23) Mengelberg and Stransky were announced equally as Conductors, with Hadley still Associate Conductor, and a compatriot of Mengelberg's, Willem van Hoogstraten, as guest conductor for one pair of concerts. The next moves, for the season of 1923–24, were obvious to any chess player: Mengelberg and van Hoogstraten to Conductors, Hadley remaining Associate Conductor, Stransky checkmate—out of a job. During the next two years, Stransky made an attempt to give concerts with a newly formed State Symphony Orchestra, and then abandoned the podium to become a dealer in oil paintings.

---

* Lewisohn, donor of the Lewisohn Stadium to the College of the City of New York, was actively interested in music at the time of the New Symphony Orchestra's founding—though he was already in his seventies, he began to take singing lessons, and entertained his guests with German *Lieder*.

Chapter 22

Mergers and Gambits
(1923–28)

Although Stransky had abdicated, Mengelberg never had the throne entirely to himself. In each of the nine seasons that he worked with the Philharmonic, he conducted only about half of the concerts. Just as the merger of the Philharmonic with the National Symphony Orchestra had involved a division of administrative responsibility between the officers of the two orchestras (the President, Henry E. Cooper, coming from the Philharmonic, and the Chairman of the Board, Clarence Mackay, coming from the National Symphony), so also did it entail a division of the conducting responsibility between Stransky and Mengelberg, and this pattern of division continued after Stransky's departure. The table in Backnote 156 shows how Mengelberg shared the conductor's position with others from 1921 to 1930. This arrangement seems to have been perfectly satisfactory to him. It permitted him to devote the rest of each year to his European engagements, especially his Concertgebouw Orchestra in Amsterdam. Besides, like most European conductors, he may not have been interested in subjecting himself to the strain of a whole New York Philharmonic season of more than one hundred concerts. To do such long seasons in one city demands a huge and constantly changing repertory of new and old works. It is a physical and mental hazard and exposes the conductor too constantly to the critics and the public—the former tend to find chinks in his armor, and the latter to weary of him. So it is not surprising that Mengelberg was willing to take only half a New York season.

For the Philharmonic's long-term needs, however, the division of leadership was of questionable soundness. While Stokowski in Philadelphia and Koussevitzky in Boston were building orchestras in the 1920s that reflected the powerful personalities of their leaders, the Philharmonic suffered from conductorial schizophrenia. Though Mengelberg drilled the New York players into an ensemble of almost military discipline, he did not provide the Society with a unified artistic policy that would carry it forward through the periods of his absence.

Fortunately the Philharmonic had, among the wealthy laymen who served as its officers and Directors and helped to support it financially, a number of intelligent and conscientious administrators with talent and experience in running large organizations. With the same idealism that the Guarantors' Committee had shown in the reorganization of 1909, *they* formulated a policy that promised to guide the Philharmonic still further in the direction of expanded service to the community. One of their leaders was Clarence Mackay, who had become Chairman of the Board after the merger with his National Symphony Orchestra. Over his name as Chairman, the Board of Directors announced, before the opening of the 1922–23 season, a "plan to secure for the Philharmonic Orchestra a wider popular audience." There were a number of remarkable features in the program, but two of them stood out from the others: "a definite policy for the advancement of American music," and an extensive plan for "the education of a new public."

The first project was described by Mackay himself as the "Greater Americanization of the Philharmonic," and his announcement outlined its implementation in specific terms:

The Directors have felt that the development of music in America has reached the point where an organization such as the *Philharmonic*, should offer definite encouragement to the native American composer of orchestral music. With this idea in mind, they have engaged MR. HENRY HADLEY as *Associate Conductor*, with instructions to examine the scores of compositions submitted by American composers and to perform at certain concerts of the year those scores which, in his judgment, seem to merit presentation. . . . Adequate rehearsals will be given to works and the concerts at which they will be played will give them the widest possible hearing.

The second project, the educational one, encompassed a series of five concerts in the Great Hall of City College, five concerts in Carnegie Hall, five at Cooper Union, four at the Commercial High School in Brooklyn, and a series of single concerts in such colleges as Princeton, Yale, Vassar, Smith, Mount Holyoke, and Connecticut. The concerts at City College and in Carnegie Hall would be given in cooperation with the faculties of City College and Hunter College. Courses in music appreciation had been established, and in addition to the ten orchestral concerts there would be a series of lectures and smaller concerts at both colleges. There was an imaginative extension to the plan: the five concerts at City College were to be broadcasted by radio—this was 1922, remember—so that colleges, high schools, and other educational institutions "within a radius of 1,500 miles" might profit by the concerts, and coordinated arrangements were being made for the students in these institutions to "listen in" on the nights of the concerts. The five concerts at Cooper Union were designed to reach (Mackay explained with an unconscious and certainly forgivable touch of benevolent paternalism) "the very large public which exists below Twenty-third Street." The Brooklyn concerts and the college concerts were extensions of previous activities, but they had now been made part of what could certainly be called with some pride "a definite educational policy."

The most astonishing thing about these ambitious plans is that they were actually carried out with reasonable success. Hadley did perform an American work on each of six concerts. Although the total of American music played was not conspicuously greater than it had been under Stransky before the new policy was announced, and although the composers chosen reflected Hadley's conservative tastes (Gilbert, Converse, Deems Taylor, Chadwick, Hadley himself), the process was more orderly than before and the very announcement of the policy of encouraging native composers was of value. As for the educational concerts, the whole imposing series was given as announced, and some of them were broadcasted, as promised, by radio station WEAF. This was the beginning of the broadcasts of Philharmonic concerts which continued in one form or another for fifty-five years, until 1967.

These experiments were not exceptional, moreover, but typical of a new sense of cultural responsibility that seemed to mark the activities of the Philharmonic after the merger with the National Symphony Orchestra.

For example, a serious and educational slant in the Philharmonic's phonograph recordings dates from that period. Of the very first Philharmonic recordings, the thirty sides made under Stransky from 1917 to 1919, most had been "light" music and some had been abridged. But higher aesthetic aspirations distinguished the Philharmonic recordings conducted by Mengelberg for the Victor label between 1922 and 1926, which included unabridged performances of such solid works as Beethoven's *Coriolanus* Overture, Liszt's *Les Préludes,* Wagner's *Flying Dutchman* Overture, and Schelling's *A Victory Ball,* on two to four sides each. Of course, practically all record makers of the day abridged some of the compositions they recorded, in order to adapt the music to the four-minute length of a record side, but the conscientious ones tried to avoid such amputations when they were dealing with major works of art. In this spirit of selective conscientiousness, the Brunswick Company in 1926 proudly advertised the Philharmonic's recording of Tchaikovsky's *Marche Slave,* with Mengelberg conducting, as "the only record of this composition without cuts or omissions," though Mengelberg and Brunswick did not hesitate to make cuts in two Strauss waltzes that they released in the same season. Brunswick recorded all of these by their new electrical process (slogan: "Electrical Recording Compares with Mechanical Recording as Electric Light Compares with Candle Light"), as they did also a highly praised issue of the Scherzo and Nocturne from Mendelssohn's *Midsummer Night's Dream,* with the Philharmonic under Toscanini's baton. Toscanini was very cautious about committing his art to phonograph records, but by 1929, as the interest in a substantial repertory increased and the quality of the sound reproduction improved, he was persuaded by Victor to record with the Philharmonic such classic monuments as Haydn's *Clock* Symphony and Mozart's *Haffner,* as well as works of Gluck, Rossini, Mendelssohn, Verdi, and Dukas; and Mengelberg, although he did not lead the orchestra in concerts after 1930, continued to record important works with it for a number of years thereafter.

Meanwhile, in 1926, the Philharmonic had participated in a massive educational project sponsored by Ginn & Company, the Boston book publishers, combining recordings with the printed word. This was a Music Appreciation Course, for use in elementary and junior-high schools, centering around a series of sixty double-faced records with a handsomely printed and illustrated volume for the guidance of the teachers. The phonograph records were made under the direction of Henry Hadley, the Philharmonic's Associate Conductor. Although the old acoustic process was used, rather than the new electrical one, no effort was spared to achieve the highest quality of recording and performance;

but it may have been because the acoustic method required all the performers to be crowded into a limited space directly in front of the recording horns that only thirty-nine or forty of the Philharmonic men were used. Photographs taken at the time of the recording show the shirt-sleeved players disposed according to a strategic floor plan—some on specially constructed high chairs, some in low seats, some standing, some with their backs to the recording horns and the conductor, some pointing their instruments straight at the recording horns, some reading their music from sheets hung from the ceiling—while Hadley, also in shirt sleeves, mounted on a very high platform, gesticulates strenuously to coordinate his forces. It must be admitted that the musical content of the course was uneven: lots of music by Helen S. Leavitt but practically nothing by Bach, Haydn, Mozart, or Beethoven; lots of "easy" short pieces from the most familiar portions of the nineteenth-century repertory but practically nothing that was really modern in 1926. The compilers of the Music Appreciation Course may have gone too far in claiming that "the central place, which in the study of literature is held by the works of the great authors, is held in this course by standard music." But their cultural and pedagogical aims were of the highest, and Hadley could speak for all associated with the project when he said that they were "imbued with the idea of musical service to the rising generation."[157]

From the same progressive time in the Philharmonic's history stemmed its low-priced summer concerts at the Lewisohn Stadium. Actually, outdoor concerts of this kind had been going on at the Stadium since 1918, but at first they had no formal connection with the Philharmonic. Their humble origins have been traced by Sophie Untermeyer (daughter of "Minnie" Guggenheimer, lifelong pilot of the Stadium Concerts) in her book *Mother Is Minnie*.[158] It seems that in the summer of 1917, at a free band concert given in St. Nicholas Park under the sponsorship of the city's Parks Department, a prankster threw a clump of sod right into the bell of the tuba. This made it clear to City Chamberlain Louis Fehr, who was present as a representative of the mayor, that a more sheltered location was needed for outdoor concerts, and he recommended for that purpose the nearby Lewisohn Stadium, the walled athletic field of City College. A brief series of free band concerts was given there, most of them led by Arnold Volpe, a Lithuanian-born musician who had been active as conductor and teacher in New York for some years. Volpe was an ambitious man and he had an ambitious wife. Encouraged by the success of the free band concerts, they proposed a much bolder project for the Stadium: concerts with symphony orchestra instead of band, at very low admission prices—no ticket more than 50¢, soldiers and sailors to be admitted free (we were in the midst of World War I). To underwrite such a project they needed wealthy and public-spirited supporters, and it was obvious that Adolph Lewisohn, who had donated to City College the stadium in which the concerts were to be given, should be asked for a contribution. At this point, Aaron Barron, a music critic for the Yiddish press, gave the Volpes some good advice. He suggested that the right middleman between the Volpes and Lewisohn would be Mrs. Charles S. Guggenheimer, whose son Randolph was taking violin lessons from Volpe, and who had known Lewisohn since her girlhood. Mrs. Guggenheimer succeeded in interesting Lewisohn in the concert fund, and then went on, with the aid of many of the city's social leaders (especially Mrs. Newbold LeRoy Edgar, later the Countess Mercati), to raise the money for season after season of Stadium Concerts throughout almost half a century.[159] As Mrs. Guggenheimer grew older she seemed also to grow more eccentric, relishing her role as Minnie, the lovably zany Mrs. Malaprop of New York's music world. Of the endless store of Minnie anecdotes, a single characteristic one will have to suffice as illustration: how, preparing to introduce the Crown Prince of Sweden to the Stadium audience, she invited him onstage by snapping her fingers and calling "Here, Prince, Prince!"

At the start of the Stadium symphony series in 1918, the musicians had been recruited from the Metropolitan Opera Orchestra, the New York Symphony Society, and other sources, as well as from the Philharmonic, and the management had been independent of the Philharmonic's. Of the conductors during the first four summers, only one, Henry Hadley, was directly connected with the Philharmonic. What is more, when an official Stadium orchestra was named for the 1920 season, it was not the Philharmonic but its chief rival, the National Symphony Orchestra, that was selected; and in 1921 the Stadium players were drawn chiefly from the Philadelphia Orchestra.*

---

* It had been planned that summer to use Philharmonic, National, and perhaps some other New York musicians, but less than a week before the opening night of the season the New York local of the musicians' union had withdrawn the orchestra, accusing the Stadium of being affiliated "in some way" with the National Symphony Orchestra, which had just been disbanded after a dispute with the union. In a sensational coup, Arthur Judson, who had recently been engaged as chief manager of the Stadium Concerts, assembled an entirely new orchestra within twenty-four hours.

The turning point came in 1922, when the Philharmonic was installed as the Stadium orchestra, Arthur Judson served as Manager for both the Philharmonic and the Stadium, and even the program notes were written for both organizations by the same man, Lawrence Gilman; and the dovetail was strengthened in 1923, when Willem van Hoogstraten was named co-conductor of the Philharmonic and chief conductor of the Stadium. Some of these bonds lasted longer than others[160]—but the public continued to think of the Stadium Concerts as the Philharmonic's summer season, and even after 1951, when the Philharmonic's name ceased to be used for the Stadium Concerts, it was hard to erase the association from New York minds. In the early years of the relationship, the Stadium series seemed particularly close to the new spirit of popularization and democratization that we have recognized in so many of the Philharmonic's efforts from about 1922 on. Tickets for Stadium performances could be had for as little as 25¢, and a favorite program might attract an audience of twenty thousand people; yet many of the greatest conductors and performers of the world were brought to these "people's" concerts in a repertory of breadth and variety. To the optimistic and the socially conscious, the Stadium Concerts seemed to prophesy "how large Philharmonic audiences might be, in favorable circumstances."[161]

It was in this era, too, that the Philharmonic's Young People's Concerts, which had been tried on a small scale in Stransky's time, were expanded into a substantial series by the American pianist-composer-conductor Ernest Schelling.[162] He was aided in this endeavor by two generous and efficient ladies—typical of the laymen who were helping the Philharmonic to shape its goals and make them come true—Mrs. E. H. Harriman and Mrs. Charles E. Mitchell, who became chairmen of the Philharmonic's Educational and Children's Concerts Committees. Schelling had often talked with them, and with Franklin Robinson of the American Orchestral Society, about his "plan for the symphonic education of the young," although he did not at first envisage conducting the concerts himself. When Clarence Mackay, Chairman of the Philharmonic's Board of Directors, asked him what he considered the best strategy for enlarging the orchestra's sphere of influence, he pointed out that symphonic concerts for children and young people could "form the taste of the future Philharmonic audiences." It is characteristic of the attitude of most cultivated musicians of the time that Schelling believed such concerts also to be "of paramount importance to fight the influence of jazz" on the young (though he himself is said to have been interested in jazz and even to have played it on occasion); Walter Damrosch, too, hoped that "some popular substitute could be found for the interminable jazz that is ravaging not only our own country but all Europe."[163] The principal object of the Children's Concerts, however, as Schelling explained whenever he wrote or spoke on the subject, was: to excite the imagination and the interest of children so that, when they reached adulthood, they would be sensitive enough to *enjoy* symphonic music, and enlightened enough to *support* it. To Mackay's question of how to ensure a following for the Philharmonic, Schelling replied with a touch of playfulness: "Catch that following when they are young (and cannot defend themselves, some might say!)."

With the launching of Schelling's Children's Concerts on January 26, 1924, the Philharmonic immediately found itself the nation's cynosure in symphony concerts for the young. This was somewhat unexpected. Although New York had a respectable history in this branch of music —Theodore Thomas had given educational concerts with his own orchestra in the 1880s, Stransky had conducted his Philharmonic Young People's Concerts for several seasons from 1913–14 on, and Frank and Walter Damrosch had been presenting a highly successful series almost continuously since the 1890s—many cities of the Midwest had forged ahead of New York by 1924. The symphony orchestras of Chicago, Cleveland, St. Louis, Kansas City, and Minneapolis, for example, had long been cooperating with the schools in the presentation of educational concerts, while the New York schools were "scored and ridiculed on the lecture platform in the West for being content to remain at the last of the procession," as the chairman of the Philharmonic Children's Concerts wrote in 1924.[164] But once Schelling's plan was under way, he and the Philharmonic became leaders in the field. In the very first season each of the five programs had to be given twice, some of New York's "best" private schools began to encourage parents to subscribe, and Schelling came into demand as a guest conductor for children's programs in other cities. At the end of the first season, Boston contracted to copy the series as a "package," using only its own orchestra of Boston Symphony players, but bringing in Schelling as conductor, with his Philharmonic programs, lectures, and illustrative materials. Philadelphia soon followed suit, and Schelling eventually conducted children's or young people's concerts† in seventeen American and European cities. In 1927–28 the New York performances, which had been taking place at Aeolian Hall, on Forty-second Street near Fifth Avenue, were moved to Carnegie Hall; the original purpose of this move seems to have been to economize on production costs by combining the two Aeolian Hall series (of five concerts each) into one series in the larger auditorium, but in the peak years of 1928 to 1931 the demand for the concerts was great enough to require not one but three Carnegie Hall series, totaling fifteen or sixteen concerts each season.[165] Requests for information on the preparation of such concerts came from near and far. Felix Weingartner, one of the most respected conductors of his age, wrote to Schelling from Basel: "It is really wonderful how you have organized the Children's Concerts. I am, with my present efforts here . . . a small child in comparison with what you do. The idea which took root so marvelously with you spreads much more slowly and inadequately on the European continent. / I will learn a lot from your performances . . ."[166] And when the Palestine Symphony Orchestra was inaugurated under Toscanini in 1936, the founder of the orchestra, Bronislav Huberman, wrote to Schelling for advice about organizing their children's concerts.

Of all the varied means that Schelling used for capturing the children's attention, the most admired was his collection of lantern slides; he had five thousand of them, hand-colored on glass, and valued at more than $25,000—pictures of musical instruments of all ages and countries, of composers and how they lived, and of every other subject that lent itself to visual illustration in connection with his programs. His contemporaries, in their accounts of these concerts, were inclined to speak of the slides in the tone in which a medieval traveler might describe the magical machines of some exotic land, concentrating on them to the exclusion of the other methods that Schelling employed. But Schelling himself was not so narrow; he exploited—in addition to the rich musical resources of the Philharmonic—all the pedagogical devices of his day. Songs were introduced into the programs to give the entire audience a chance to participate. Notebooks were handed in by the children, and the best ones were given prizes at the end of each season. (Some of the notebooks were so imaginative that they attracted international attention;

† Sometimes one name was used and sometimes the other. Schelling's New York series began as "Children's Concerts" but later became "Concerts for Children and Young People" and then "Concerts for Young People."

they were put on exhibition in the United States, Germany, Czechoslovakia, and South Africa, and were requested for examination by the
educational authorities in Soviet Russia.) The responsibility of writing
the program notes was sometimes turned over to whole classes or even
schools of children. Talented youngsters performed as soloists alongside
the experienced professionals. Efforts were made to involve the parents,
who frequently became devotees in their own right. Programs were often
centered around special instructional themes—"Fiddles, Little and Big,"
"The Overture," "American Composers."‡ Of course, each age has its
styles in education as in art, and music educators today might swallow
hard at the carefree musicology that Schelling sometimes allowed himself
in attempting to simplify complex matters. But Schelling did not present
himself as an educator or musicologist; "I *avoid* every possible attempt,"
he said, "to make these concerts a course of study. It would be plainly
impossible to do this in the limited time at my disposal." He hoped only
to awaken the child's imagination, "to leave some thought about music,
or *because* of music, that will start a train of thought . . . an opening to
a wide horizon." Schelling's musical and personal gifts lent his performances their special quality, and the correspondence files bulge with letters from children, parents, and musicians that bear witness to the in-
spirational values of the Children's and Young People's Concerts.

In 1937 Schelling suffered a serious eye injury, resulting from an accident in his speedboat. When it became clear that he would be unable
to conduct the Young People's Concerts for 1937–38, John Barbirolli
(then the Philharmonic's regular conductor) substituted for him at the
first performance and Schelling's friend Rudolph Ganz took over the remainder of the season, both working from Schelling's programs and
materials in order to ensure continuity. Schelling was able to resume his
activities the following season, but it was to be his last: he died very
suddenly on December 8, 1939. The Philharmonic made its next
Young People's Concert, on January 20, 1940, a Schelling Memorial
Concert, in which his familiar techniques of presentation—lantern slides

---

‡ The Children's Concerts under Schelling were ahead of the Philharmonic's
adult concerts in the proportion of American compositions performed. "I have
made a special point," wrote Schelling in a report to the Society in 1933, "of
giving as many American compositions as possible, as I wished our young people
to realize that we have in our midst many distinguished composers whose works
can well equal, if not surpass, many of the modern compositions that come to us
from Europe."

and all—were used touchingly by his successor, Rudolph Ganz, to survey "Uncle Ernest's" own life and works. But Schelling's most impressive memorial, and the best testimonial to the solidity with which he built the Young People's Concerts of the New York Philharmonic, is the continuance of the concerts in an unbroken line from his first series in 1923-24 to the present day.

All the forward-looking ventures on which the Philharmonic embarked in the 1920s—the Young People's Concerts, the low-priced summer concerts at the Stadium, the radio broadcasts and phonograph recordings, the educational programs, the Americanization project—were in addition to the regular subscription series, which, for their part, had developed into the most imposing array of such concerts in the orchestra's history. Here, for example, is the list for 1922-23:

    14 Thursday evenings at Carnegie Hall
    18 Friday afternoons at Carnegie Hall
     6 Saturday evenings at Carnegie Hall
    12 Sunday afternoons at Carnegie Hall
     8 Tuesday evenings at the Metropolitan Opera House
     4 Sunday afternoons at the Metropolitan Opera House
     6 Sunday afternoons at the Brooklyn Academy of Music

In this upsurge, the merger with the National Symphony Orchestra in 1921 gave the Philharmonic welcome reinforcements on more than one level. On the audience level it brought in the entire list of National Symphony subscribers as potential Philharmonic customers; it was to accommodate them and to take advantage of their availability that the two new series of concerts in the Metropolitan Opera House were inaugurated in 1921-22. It was on the executive level, however, that much-needed financial and administrative resources were to be found, and here the Philharmonic acquired from the National a group of the most generous and most energetic music patrons in the city, some of whom were to remain active in its affairs almost to the present day. In addition to Clarence H. Mackay, the telegraph magnate, who became Chairman of the Philharmonic's Board of Directors, there were Otto H. Kahn, the banker, who became a Vice-President, and Alvin W. Krech, another banker, Honorary Secretary.* Also from the National

---

* Mackay was so influential in the city's musical and social life that, when Oscar Hammerstein made the mistake of antagonizing Mrs. Mackay in 1909, New York "society" withdrew its support almost entirely from Hammerstein's Manhattan Opera Company, eventually contributing to its collapse (Mrs. Mackay's friends were responsible for 30 to 40 per cent of the subscriptions to box

came several key members of the Philharmonic's Auxiliary Board: Mrs. Vincent Astor, its Chairman, Mrs. Charles S. Guggenheimer, Mrs. Newbold LeRoy Edgar, Mrs. Arthur Sachs, and Charles Hayden (still another banker). The Auxiliary Board was a brainchild of Mackay's. In 1921–22 he asked Mrs. Astor to form an "Advisory Board," chiefly to marshal the wealthy and influential women of the community who might give their time, and their husbands' money, for the orchestra's cause. At first the new Board was not entirely female (Walter W. Price, the financier, was Associate Chairman), but after 1923–24, when its name was changed from Advisory to Auxiliary, it functioned as the women's arm of the Society's administration. Mrs. Astor (who was later Mrs. Lytle Hull) did so brilliant a job of organizing the Auxiliary Board that she remained its natural and necessary Chairman until 1961 and has been its Honorary Chairman since then.† For a short time after the National Symphony and the Philharmonic Society were merged, Henry E. Cooper, one of the Philharmonic's old officers, remained President, but it was Mackay as Chairman of the Board who called the plays, and in 1922 Cooper retired from the presidency and was succeeded by Frederic A. Juilliard, the textile merchant (who was a trustee of the $20,000,000 Juilliard Music Foundation established by the will of his uncle, Augustus D. Juilliard). Nourished by fresh social resources, the Board of the Philharmonic became, within a few years, a very impressive body of civic personages, including, in addition to those already mentioned, such men as Nicholas Murray Butler, President of Columbia University, Elihu Root, ex-Secretary of State and winner of the Nobel Peace Prize, Charles Triller, successful businessman, and Marshall Field, investment banker. (With that kind of social

---

and orchestra seats, as J. F. Cone explains in *Oscar Hammerstein's Manhattan Opera Company*, pp. 222–23).

Mackay served the Philharmonic as Chairman of the Board for seventeen years, until his death in 1938. His ties with the music world were unusually varied—he was a Director of the Metropolitan Opera Association, his daughter was married to composer Irving Berlin, and his second wife was the soprano Anna Case, who had sung in the American premieres of Mussorgsky's *Boris Godunov,* Monteverdi's *Orfeo,* and Strauss's *Rosenkavalier,* and who appeared as soloist with the Philharmonic on more than one occasion.

† The Philharmonic awarded Mrs. Hull honorary membership in the Society (of which she is also a Vice-President and a Director) in 1968. Leonard Bernstein made the presentation at the concert of March 7, 1968, at Philharmonic Hall, giving Mrs. Hull as a memento from the Society a unique copy of the opening chapter of this book, hand-lettered on vellum and bound in morocco leather.

makeup, the new administration, despite its sincere democracy of purpose, could not entirely escape a north-of-Twenty-third-Street mentality: in Mackay's first flushed announcement in 1922 about the policy of educating a "new public," all the Directors were listed in alphabetical order, except for the two who were orchestra players, Scipione Guidi and L. E. Manoly, whose names came trailing along as an afterthought at the end of the list—a faux pas that was quickly corrected and never repeated.)

One other transfer from the National Symphony Orchestra deserves special mention. Lawrence Gilman, who had been both Secretary and program annotator for the National (and for its progenitor, the New Symphony Orchestra), now took over the program notes of the Philharmonic, which he wrote until his death in 1939. His style—learned, elegant, yet playfully imaginative—gave them a distinction that they have not often had before or after his time. It is curious, however, that one quality that is evident in his New Symphony notes seems to be suppressed in his Philharmonic notes—sexiness. In the earlier set of notes Gilman uses Beethoven's Fifth Symphony as an opportunity to demonstrate that the great thunderer was not "a chaste saint," or goes out of his way to share with his readers his enjoyment of Schubert's and Wagner's lapses from conventional morality. In his Philharmonic days this preoccupation disappears or at least is sublimated. Apparently he found that *quod licet iuveni, non licet Iovi*—what was permitted to the youthful New Symphony might not be becoming to the lordly Philharmonic.

In the orchestra itself the merger with the National Symphony was not greeted with joy. The heartbreaking truth was that more than fifty of the old Philharmonic players lost their jobs in the first year of the amalgamation, 1921–22, and several more each year after that as the Mackay-Mengelberg faction continued to assert itself. From the National came a new concertmaster, Guidi, a solo cellist, Van Vliet, a first-desk violist, Fishberg, a solo contrabassist, Fortier, a solo bassoonist, B. Kohon, and many others. The same tactic was employed in replacing key orchestra personnel that was used in replacing Stransky by Mengelberg as conductor, and Cooper by Juilliard as President—first a new man was appointed to a position jointly with the old occupant, then after a year or so the old name disappeared from the list and the new one remained alone. Thus the Philharmonic had two solo clarinets, two solo bassoons, and two solo horns in 1921–22, but by 1923–24, the old-timers were no longer in the orchestra and the new men were safely ensconced. In the advance announcement for 1920–21, the Philharmonic's manager had asserted the indivisibility of Stransky and the orchestra musicians: "Mr. Stransky and the personnel of the Philharmonic Orchestra present an exceptional unity. The development of the ensemble is remarkably interwoven with the magnetism, conscientious effort, and interpretative genius of its leader." Yet by the end of that same season, half of the remarkably interwoven exceptional unity had been turned over to Mengelberg and in two more years Stransky was out of it completely. In those two years the Philharmonic became practically a new orchestra. It was no wonder that Stransky could not hold his own with the orchestra players against Mengelberg. They were not the same musicians that he had hired and trained. They were Mengelberg's men.‡

The Philharmonic was just recovering from its exertions in swallowing the National Symphony when it was faced with another upstart orchestra. In the season of 1922–23 a group of wealthy people headed by Senator Coleman DuPont had put up about $180,000 to underwrite a season of symphony concerts under an ambitious conductor named Dirk Foch. Foch (whose name was originally Fock, but who apparently found the Dutch form to be inadvisable in America) was a man of excellent background and great charm. He was born in Java, where his father was the governor general of the Dutch East Indies, studied with the revered Nikisch, and had conducted in Holland, Germany, Sweden, and elsewhere, before he came to New York. Foch and his City Symphony Orchestra gave nearly fifty concerts in the course of their season, but their total income for all the concerts was barely $21,000 and the guarantors had to cover a deficit of about $156,000. Nevertheless, since one of their stated purposes was to bring music "to the multitude" as a public service, they might have gone on with a second season if Foch had not made a tactical error. In March of 1923 he antagonized his employers and backers in a clash over the rights to the name of The City Symphony Orchestra, Inc. The Board of Directors summoned him to a meeting, brought pressure on him to relinquish his claim, and then promptly went into conference with Arthur Judson, the new Manager of the Philharmonic (who, with commendable managerial efficiency, had been waiting in the next room

‡ Could this be a clue to the "Everybody knows it but Stransky" story, recounted on page 231 above?

until Foch's departure), about the possibility of combining the City Symphony Orchestra with the Philharmonic in some way.

In May of 1923 officials of the two societies reached an agreement that attested to Judson's great skill in negotiation. It provided, in essence, that:

The Philharmonic would *not* take over the orchestra personnel, conductor, or other employees of the City Symphony, and would not assume any of its debts.

Mrs. Louise Ryals de Cravioto, who had functioned as a very efficient fund-raiser for the City Symphony, would agree to raise $50,000 for the Philharmonic in the next year "from sources not [already] contributing to the Guarantee Fund of the Philharmonic."

The Philharmonic would recognize the former backers of the City Symphony "in some official way to be determined by the Philharmonic Society."

All subscription lists and similar resources would be turned over to the Philharmonic.

Mrs. de Cravioto worked with the Executive Committee of the Philharmonic's Auxiliary Board for many years afterward (indeed, she continued to do so until 1970, under the name of Mrs. Bartlett Arkell), and the Philharmonic recognized the former backers of the City Symphony by creating for a number of them the title of Honorary Vice-President of the Auxiliary Board.[167]

In the complicated adjustments that the Philharmonic made in its business operations in the 1920s, the chief administrator was Arthur Judson, the new Manager of the Society. He was well prepared for his many-sided job. "Once a music-hungry youth in a 'musically ignorant' small town" (his own characterization of his early years in Dayton, Ohio, where he was born in 1881), he had gained experience, as a young man, in such varied occupations as playing the violin, running the music department of a small college, and doing editorial and advertising work for a music magazine. But it was in 1915, when he was appointed Manager of Stokowski's Philadelphia Orchestra, that he found his life's calling as a concert manager, or, to use a description that he proudly adopted, "a salesman of fine music." And already at that early stage of Judson's career, the boldness of his touch could be felt: at the same time that he was managing Stokowski's orchestra, he started his own musical booking agency in Philadelphia, and within a few years he had opened a second booking office in New York. By the time that Judson became Manager of the New York Philharmonic and Executive Secretary of its Board of Directors in 1922, his special gift for handling any number of musical undertakings at one time had been raised to a new level: he was able to hold his double post in New York (really a triple post if one counts the managership of the Stadium Concerts in the summers) while he continued *simultaneously* as Manager of the Philadelphia Orchestra for thirteen more years and Advisory Manager of the Cincinnati Symphony for five of those years, and ran his private managerial enterprises too. Resourceful and aggressive, trained in music and skillful in business, Judson perceived at this period that audiences could be enlarged beyond what most people imagined and that the increase could be beneficial both to his private ventures and to the Philharmonic. He entered willingly into the plans for the Philharmonic's educational series and low-priced summer events, designed to reach a new public. Meanwhile, recognizing what radio could mean as a medium for the diffusion not only of the Philharmonic's performances but of all music, he organized in 1926 the Judson Radio Program Corporation and then the network of the United Independent Broadcasters, Inc., which led in 1928 to the Columbia Broadcasting System (of which Judson remained a major stockholder). With the same knack with which he handled mergers of broadcasting systems and of symphony orchestras, he also absorbed five of his principal competitors in concert management into his own firm, forming Columbia Concerts Corporation in 1930. And at about the same time, he took part in the founding of Community Concerts, which worked up markets for music in towns that had previously had little or no concert life. By the 1930s Arthur Judson had become the most powerful figure in American music management. Since Judson's flair for making money out of music led him constantly to seek expanding audiences, he could honestly combine profit-making with democratic ideals of public service and reconcile his private business interests with his administration of the New York Philharmonic.

With the city's orchestral forces in better balance, after the neutralization of the National and City Symphony Orchestras, it seemed that Mengelberg[168] might have a chance to enjoy his position as the Philharmonic's leading conductor. He was then at the height of his reputation as a builder of orchestras and a perfectionist in orchestral performance. Mengelberg had a gift for dictatorial rule that communicated itself to audiences as well as to orchestras, and elicited from critics such phrases as "thorough control" (New York, 1905), "overpowering force" (London, 1911), and "the most spectacularly well-trained orchestra in America" (the New York Philharmonic under his direction in the 1920s).[169] He made his performances exciting by the precision that he exacted of the players, by his awesome control over his great orchestral instrument of a hundred human beings, which he could make respond with the flexibility that a virtuoso pianist of the Romantic style might bring to his interpretations. Yet his methods as conductor were not in themselves sensational. In fact, it was a common joke among orchestra men that Mengelberg's secret rehearsal weapon was *talk*—endless, boring talk. He sometimes wasted so much rehearsal time in speechmaking that extra rehearsals had to be called for the real work of bringing the orchestra up to his genuinely high standards of music-making. His long lectures to the players, moreover, were often primitive and repetitious; the useful fraction of their content could have been communicated in a few sentences. They were not without a certain didactic value, however—like a military drill sergeant Mengelberg *dulled* his men into routine conformity with his requirements. "There was no need to depend on impalpable factors like inspiration or personal feeling," says Winthrop Sargeant, who played violin in the orchestra. "By the time Mengelberg had thoroughly rehearsed a maneuver, the Philharmonic could carry it out automatically by itself."[170] Mengelberg's uneconomical rehearsal habits may also help to explain why he tended to repeat certain works over and over again in his programs: it took so many rehearsal hours to prepare each piece that, once one was ready, it was likely to see service in more than one concert. Strauss's *Ein Heldenleben,* which the composer had dedicated to Mengelberg, was a particular favorite, cropping up several times in every season, but Philharmonic audiences found it almost as hard to escape Liszt's *Les Préludes.* Though Mengelberg was widely admired for his meticulously prepared (but willfully personal) Beethoven performances, his affinities were more for the high Romantic composers of the second half of the nineteenth century. He managed, nevertheless, to find room in his Philharmonic programs for more of the music of his own time than he is usually given credit for—it should not be forgotten that Mahler, Strauss, and Debussy, all of whom he championed, were his contemporaries, and he also played such Americans as Schelling, Goldmark, Hadley, Taylor, and Hanson, such

Italians as Casella and Respighi, something of Honegger, Tailleferre, and Milhaud, a dozen composers from his native Holland, occasional pieces by Bloch, Tansman, Szymanowski, and Kodály, and "easy" Stravinsky compositions like the *Firebird* Suite. Schoenberg and Hindemith he ignored. Bartók he attempted once, with unhappy results: the work was the First Piano Concerto, which the composer himself was engaged to play with the Philharmonic in the 1927–28 season, but Mengelberg considered the concerto too difficult for the amount of rehearsal time available, and Bartók was obliged to substitute an earlier work, his Rhapsody, Opus 1. Even this easier piece, however, received a "groping accompaniment" from Mengelberg and the Philharmonic, according to the press, and the Philharmonic's embarrassment was underlined by the bold stroke of Fritz Reiner, then conductor of the Cincinnati Symphony, who presented the concerto in New York, with Bartók as a soloist, only a month after Mengelberg had dropped the work.

Such reverses were rare for Mengelberg, however. The critics may occasionally have grumbled at his lapses, but they regularly extolled his virtues. The orchestra men may have joked about his eternal speech-making, but they respected him as a musician and were proud of the level of proficiency to which he had raised them. Some segments of the public may have missed the performances of the ousted Stransky, in which "thrills chased one another in squads down [one's] medullary nerves" (as H. T. Finck expressed it), but they quickly found neurological solace in Mengelberg's performances, "which converted one's spine into a sort of electromagnetic field" (as Vincent Sheean expressed it).[171] Mengelberg's position seemed so unassailable that he could afford to bring in as guest conductor his compatriot Willem van Hoogstraten, who took the first part of each season from 1923 to 1925.[172]

Van Hoogstraten was not a serious challenge to Mengelberg's pre-eminence. But the Board of Directors had dropped Stransky in order to satisfy the demands of certain portions of the press and the public for more stimulating musical fare, and they began now to invite other celebrities from the European music world, in addition to Mengelberg, as guest conductors for part of each season. For 1924–25 there were two of them, Igor Stravinsky and Wilhelm Furtwängler. Although Stravinsky conducted three performances of a program of his own works, and appeared as pianist in his own Concerto for Piano and

Wind Orchestra, he was of course regarded primarily neither as conductor nor as soloist, but as a composer. Furtwängler recognized Stravinsky's presence in the city by giving the Philharmonic and its audiences their first taste of his *Rite of Spring* (not a typical item in Furtwängler's otherwise conservative repertory). Furtwängler himself, however, had such a warm reception as conductor that the possibility of his taking over the directorship of the Philharmonic from Mengelberg for the whole season of 1925–26 was privately discussed with him. Since his European commitments left him only two months for New York, he divided the next two years, 1925 to 1927, with Mengelberg, but there was a feeling in the air that he might one day become permanent conductor of the Philharmonic.

Meanwhile Mackay, the energetic Chairman of the Board, who had been angling for another internationally celebrated conductor—Arturo Toscanini—announced triumphantly that he had caught him for 1926. Toscanini's first engagement with the Philharmonic was a short one, from January 14 to February 17, but it was a gigantic success. The way had been prepared—Toscanini had already impressed the public, the press, and the musicians, in the years between 1908 and 1915, with his work at the Metropolitan Opera, and in 1920–21, immediately after the war in which Italy had been our ally, he had made a goodwill tour of the United States with the orchestra of La Scala. Now his Philharmonic appearances generated tremendous excitement. He was immediately reengaged as guest conductor for the next year, 1926–27, and although illness prevented him from conducting all but three of his concerts (all-Beethoven programs), those won such unqualified approval that the Philharmonic considered itself fortunate when Toscanini agreed to become one of its regular conductors for 1927–28, sharing the season with Mengelberg.

To hire conductors like Toscanini, Mengelberg, and Furtwängler took money. And it took more money to engage a continuing flow of additional guest conductors, to enlarge the orchestra to 111 players, to extend the season to twenty-eight weeks, to send the orchestra on tour, and to keep outbidding other symphony societies in the competitive market for the services of top-notch orchestra men—a market that had become tighter as the new immigration laws limited the supply of European musicians and the new movie palaces offered trained musicians attractive salaries. The Philharmonic's budget rose relentlessly with every year. The total expenses for operating the orchestra climbed from about $183,000 in 1909–10, the season of the Philharmonic's reorganization, to almost $700,000 in 1927–28. (See table in Backnote 173.) Of course, the earnings of the orchestra increased too with its greater activity, but there was a deficit every year of $100,000 to $150,000 that had to be made up by those who volunteered to be guarantors, and it was clear that this sum might soon rise even higher.

In 1924 Mackay, as Chairman of the Board of the Philharmonic, invited the patrons and the managers of a number of the nation's important orchestras to New York to discuss their common deficit problems. The New York contingent was the largest, including Mackay, Frederic Juilliard, Otto Kahn, and Marshall Field of the Philharmonic's supporters, and Harry Harkness Flagler of the Symphony Society, as well as the Philharmonic's Manager, Arthur Judson; but Philadelphia, Chicago, Cleveland, Los Angeles, and Minneapolis were also represented. Flagler had particular reason to be interested in the subject of the meeting—from 1914 on he had undertaken to guarantee the seasons of Damrosch's Symphony Society to the tune of about $100,000 a year, and in 1920 he had personally paid the bills for sending Damrosch and the entire orchestra of about ninety players on the first European tour made by any American symphony orchestra. He could look forward to making up more than a million dollars in Symphony Society deficits, all by himself, in the period from 1922 to 1928 alone.[174]

As the financial pressures increased, the Philharmonic and the Symphony Society began to listen more attentively to the suggestions, made frequently and from many sides, that the two orchestras should combine, instead of competing with each other. (As early as 1910, during Mahler's time with the Philharmonic, there had been rumors of such a combination.) The marriage of the two societies was agreed upon in February of 1928 and the name of the Philharmonic Society of New York was legally changed on June 8, 1928, in time to prepare for the new season in the fall, to the Philharmonic-Symphony Society of New York, Inc.

As with the earlier mergers, there were some significant changes in the power structure of the Philharmonic's Board of Directors. Mackay (who had come to the Philharmonic in 1921 as a result of the amalgamation with the National Symphony Orchestra) remained Chairman of the Board, but Flagler, the angel of the Symphony Society, now became President of the Philharmonic, replacing Frederic A. Juilliard, for whom the new title of First Vice-President was created. The two Vice-Presidents of the Philharmonic, Marshall Field and Otto H. Kahn (another alumnus of the National), retained their positions but two new Vice-Presidents were named in addition: Paul D. Cravath, the distinguished lawyer, and Henry Seligman, the banker, whose family had been patrons of the Symphony Society since the days of Walter Damrosch's father, Leopold. Other new members of the Board of Directors, all of them names that commanded respect, were John W. Davis, who had been the Democratic candidate for President of the United States in 1924, Felix Warburg, of the banking firm of Kuhn, Loeb, and Company, and Henry W. Taft and Edwin T. Rice, prominent lawyers (Taft was the brother of ex-President William Howard Taft).[175] The Auxiliary Board, now composed entirely of women, gained a number of active new members at the time of the merger, but quietly dropped the long list of Honorary Vice-Presidents who had been named in connection with the absorption of the City Symphony Orchestra in 1923. Mrs. Vincent Astor, the able chairman of the Executive Committee of the Auxiliary Board, kept that position but also moved up to the Board of Directors of the Philharmonic-Symphony Society, of which the only other female member was Mrs. E. H. Harriman.

For the infantry—the men who actually did the playing in both orchestras—this merger, like the earlier one with the National Symphony Orchestra, was not entirely an occasion for celebration. Part of the deal required that about twenty of Damrosch's men from the Symphony Society be taken into the Philharmonic. This meant, on the one hand, that all the rest of their colleagues would now have to go out and seek other jobs for themselves, not an easy task in a city that was purposely reducing the number of its orchestras, and on the other hand, that about twenty of the old Philharmonic players would have to be dismissed in order to make room for the newcomers. In the end, all the first-desk men of the Philharmonic kept their places but twenty-five of their fellow musicians were not rehired for the 1928–29 season. (Actually, thirty-two new men were engaged, instead of twenty-five, since the orchestra was slightly enlarged in the reorganization.) In the files of the Philharmonic there is a very efficient and very understanding letter of Harry Harkness Flagler's, dealing with the sad story of the dismissal of a number of men who would "find it most difficult to get new positions." Moved by the plight of the many Symphony Society players who were not to be taken over by the Philharmonic, Flagler and members of his family created a fund from which payments were made to each "retiring" musician according to his length of service.[176] Winthrop Sargeant, who was playing violin in the Symphony Society at the time of the merger, says that Flagler also presented to each of the members a pair of solid-gold cuff links; the occasion, he remarks, "thereafter became known among us ruefully as 'the day we got the cuff links and lost our shirts.' . . . The only note that relieved the desperate gloom was an announcement by one of the woodwind players that he had found a place where we could sell our solid-gold memorial cuff links for fifteen dollars in cash."[177]

John H. Mueller correctly observes[178] that the mergers of the 1920s in New York brought into the Philharmonic Flagler of the New York Symphony Society and Mackay of the National Symphony Orchestra, "thereby effecting an important consolidation of financial forces." This must not be taken to mean, however, that all the resources of the Symphony Society, the National Symphony Orchestra, the City Symphony Orchestra, and the Philharmonic were now pooled together, making the Philharmonic four times as rich as it had been before. The annual deficit, that is, the gap between the cost of running the orchestra and the income that it earned, remained of about the same order after the 1928 merger as it had been before it—generally between $110,000 and $150,000 per annum, with an occasional spurt to around $180,-000—and of this amount, after income from investments and a few additional sources had been taken into account, the wealthy patrons could usually expect to be called upon for about $100,000. Some years it was a little more and some years it was a little less, but it is not unfair to say that the combined philanthropic backers of the four orchestras were now required to carry a burden not much larger than any one of the orchestras would have carried before the mergers. The city, moreover, did not hear more concerts under the new system. In 1927–28, before the merger, the Philharmonic presented a total of 114 concerts of all kinds in New York City and that number remained essentially the same for thirty years to come. In other words, the city *lost* the number and the variety of the concerts that had formerly been contributed by the rival orchestras.

What the Philharmonic gained was the unified patronage of the subscribers and concertgoers who had previously been divided among the several orchestras. The Philharmonic could now count on fuller houses and more income from subscriptions and ticket sales, so that it could better afford the steadily rising cost of its operations. The Directors and other wealthy supporters of the Philharmonic did give money, moreover, for special projects, such as tours, which would not have been feasible within the regular budget of the Society and which extended the period of guaranteed employment for the men in the orchestra. They also contributed to the orchestra's endowment funds, Pension Fund, and educational budget. And they were always, both men and women, remarkably generous with their time and managerial talents, not only in the central work of the Board of Directors and the Governing Board of the Auxiliary, but in all the constantly proliferating activities of the Society.

Perhaps the most significant result of the mergers was that the Philharmonic-Symphony Society became for all practical purposes the official orchestra of the city of New York and the focus of the city's orchestral activity—acquiring thereby the stability of organization that enabled it to survive the worst days of the Depression of the 1930s, and accepting as inevitable the social and cultural responsibilities that previously had been voluntary indulgences by one or another of the three or four orchestras that had co-existed in New York.

The merger meant a shake-up for the conductors too. Damrosch was now sixty-five years old, and he knew perfectly well, in any case, that he could not compete with such stars as Toscanini and Mengelberg. At a concert given in his honor in March 1927, with both the Philharmonic and the Symphony Society participating, he himself had indicated that he intended in the future to "let the other fellow do the rehearsing." After the merger, he was engaged as one of six guest conductors for the new season, but it was for a period of little more than two weeks, and Damrosch and everyone else in New York's music world knew that it was intended as a gesture of homage and good will—a parting gesture that was not likely to be often repeated in the future.

The real contest was between Mengelberg and Toscanini, and it became evident over the next two years that Toscanini was winning. For the first season of the amalgamation, although Toscanini took only about a month and a half of concerts toward the end of the season's schedule, he was given the chief role in selecting the players for the merged orchestras. Mengelberg, who knew what this privilege had meant to him at the time when his orchestra was merging with Stransky's, cannot have been very comfortable as he watched the highly disciplined—some said Prussianized—orchestral instrument that he had built up according to his own musical methods and aesthetic principles being rebuilt and retuned by an even more domineering personality than his own. His discomfort must have increased at the beginning of the 1929–30 season when he found that, although he and Toscanini were both listed simply as "conductors," Toscanini's name was given first—just as his own name had been listed first in the good old days when van Hoogstraten had been unquestionably his subordinate. His fears must have been confirmed when the Philharmonic, planning its first tour of Europe for the spring of 1930, turned all of it over to Toscanini. Besides, it could not have escaped him that everyone connected with the Philharmonic, from Mackay and Flagler to the men in the orchestra, spoke of Toscanini as though he were "the" conductor of the orchestra, with all others merely tolerated guests. In any case, before the end of that season it had come to an open fight, and Mengelberg was not among the conductors who were engaged for the next year. Just as Mengelberg had come in nominally as a guest conductor under Stransky, then had shared a season with him, and finally had taken over completely, so had Toscanini come in as a guest conductor under Mengelberg, then had shared the orchestra with him, and had ended by taking it away from him. Toscanini had pulled a Mengelberg on Mengelberg.

Chapter 23

The Master Conductor
(1926–36)

"Here, truly, is the Master not only of the orchestra, but of all the orchestra conductors."

The quotation is from Émile Vuillermoz, critic of *L'Excelsior* in Paris, extolling Toscanini's performances with the Philharmonic-Symphony during the European tour of 1930, but similar superlatives could be found in the press of every city in which the Maestro conducted. In the mind of the average man the name of Toscanini was as much a label for all music as that of Einstein was for all mathematics. The New Yorker, watching the traffic cop waving his arms in the middle of the street, could heckle him with "Who do you think you are? Toscanini?" in the assurance that his gag would be understood, though neither he nor the cop might ever have attended an orchestral concert. Toscanini became a legend in his own lifetime.[179]

The primary basis for the legend was, of course, his superb musicianship, which the professional could analyze in technical terms but which even the layman could recognize subjectively. The best Toscanini performances with the Philharmonic had a precision and a clarity that set them off from other conductors' performances with the same orchestra. Every entrance of a group of instruments was cleanly accurate and perfectly "together," each strand in the music's texture balanced against each other one, the loudness or softness of each instrument or section just right in proportion to all the others. Everyone knew about Toscanini's fabulous musical memory: not only did he always conduct in public without a score, but it was common knowledge that he learned even the most difficult of those scores, including whole operas, in a few days of reading them through—the notes held just three or four inches from his nearly blind eyes. There were a dozen well-known stories about his writing out from memory, note-perfect, whole compositions that he had not seen for years, and there were hundreds of other stories about the remarkable sharpness of his hearing, which could pick out an error, a crudity, or a case of poor intonation anywhere in the depths of the orchestra. The rhythm of a Toscanini performance was always strict, yet alive, energetic, yet controlled. Orchestra men—even the few who hated him—would attest that it was easier to follow Toscanini's articulate and communicative hands than those of an ordinary conductor. The rigor of his style, the feeling of purity that it gave, was widely admired, especially for the music of Beethoven. He was a strict, indeed tyrannical disciplinarian, content with nothing less than perfection. Yet there was an electric intensity in his best rehearsals and performances that excited orchestra and audience alike.

On top of that, there was the attraction of his person and his personality. His classically contoured head seemed to grow even handsomer as he aged. All musicians and a good part of the general public had heard about his eye for the girls, his rumored love affairs with women half his age. As for his Terrible Temper, it had a historiography of its own; every orchestra player, every journalist, every teller of anecdotes at cocktail parties, every father whose little boy was learning to play the violin, helped to keep in circulation the tales of rehearsals at which watches were smashed against the wall, batons were shattered, music stands were kicked over, scores were dashed to the ground, violin bows were snapped in the faces of their owners (Toscanini was sued for assault in 1919 by an Italian violinist whose eye he had injured in an outburst of anger), and full orchestras were punished for imperfections in their playing by being abandoned on stage while the Maestro stomped off to sulk.

Bold gestures and colorful episodes in his life also caught the popular fancy. He was known as the man who had imposed a Pax Romana on the otherwise unruly prima donnas of the Metropolitan Opera. He

had dared to defy Mussolini's regime and in consequence had been
mauled by Fascisti in Bologna in 1931. When a protest was sent to
Hitler, in 1933, against the persecution of Jewish musicians by the
Nazis, Toscanini asked that his name head the list of signers, and later
that year he refused to conduct at the Wagner theater in Bayreuth
because of the "lamentable events which have wounded my feelings
both as man and artist." Musicians relished, as long as someone else
was the object of the attack, the juicy Italian invective with which he
abused his musical enemies. And the public enjoyed vicariously the
huge salaries that the Philharmonic was reported to be paying him.

In short, Toscanini was natural journalistic material. He was not a
publicity seeker—on the contrary, he was personally shy, disliked being
interviewed, and could not stand photographers' flashbulbs—but he
seemed to make good copy without even trying, and Dorle Jarmel, the
Philharmonic-Symphony's Press Representative, was able to exploit the
opportunities with skill and tact. The full flowering of the Toscanini
cult came later, during his time as conductor of the NBC Symphony,
when the National Broadcasting Company supplied its airwaves and
its rich resources for public relations, but a good start had already been
made in the Philharmonic years.

Toscanini's apotheosis has made it difficult to give a rational interpretation of the subsequent history of the Philharmonic. His age may
well have been the Golden Age of the orchestra, as it has often been
called, but it cannot be taken as divine perfection without ignoring
some of the recorded facts and without setting up misleading guideposts
for the understanding of what came after him. It becomes necessary
for the historian—risking the ire of the true believers—to debunk some
aspects of the legend in order to clear the way for intelligent discussion.

First, there is the dogma that Toscanini purged orchestral performance of the subjectivity that prevailed among the conductors of his
time, and ushered in a new epoch of literal faithfulness to the composer's score. "The fashion threatened at times to use written notes as
a springboard rather than as a text. Toscanini recalled us to artistic
integrity," said John Erskine in his Philharmonic history, and many another commentator has accepted the illusion that Toscanini was the
musical purist who preserved and defended every note in the works of
the great classic masters and particularly of Beethoven. Toscanini *spoke*
constantly of the importance of playing these works exactly "as written" (as Theodore Thomas had talked of Bach in an earlier genera-

tion), but in practice he tampered with the scores to almost the same degree as his fellow conductors. The impression of a closer adherence to the Beethoven text on Toscanini's part arose largely from the fact that his musical personality had so much in common with Beethoven's—the same brusque clarity and controlled storminess—that his alterations of a Beethoven score tended to be less conspicuous than those made by other hands. But they were there. Many a sharp-eared musician found to his surprise, when he compared a Toscanini performance with the composer's score, that some particularly felicitous detail of execution had been achieved not by rehearsing until every note of the given text was heard as Beethoven had written it, but by the simpler expedient of changing Beethoven's text until it gave the desired result. A typical case would be measures 220 to 223 in the *Coriolanus* Overture, where Toscanini made the first beat of each measure come through more forcefully by adding cellos and kettledrum to Beethoven's scoring of double basses and bassoon. Small though this adjustment may seem, it is liable, like most such tinkerings, to affect the music's meaning. There is no doubt that Toscanini's instrumentation makes the downbeats stronger and cleaner than Beethoven's. But in doing so it tends to underline the *first* beats in a series of measures in which the composer indicates explicitly (by **sf** symbols) that he is seeking to emphasize the *later* beats.[180]

Kettledrum and cellos added here by Toscanini

The other Beethoven overtures and symphonies were peppered with Toscanini's additions and changes, especially in the winds and the kettledrums; every orchestra man who played under him enjoys citing his favorite instances. Most of Toscanini's contributions, as has been ___sted, were grafted so naturally and tastefully onto the Beethoven stock that they have gone largely unnoticed, but a few produced artistic anomalies. In the first movement of the Eighth Symphony, at the point where the cellos, basses, and bassoons bring back the principal theme as loudly as they can (measure 190), Toscanini actually tried doubling the melody with pounding kettledrums supported by extra brass, a vulgarity so out of character with his own standards of artistic simplicity that it is surprising to find him still experimenting with it in his late days with the NBC Symphony.[181] As for the Ninth Symphony, Toscanini "helped" its composer in many of the same places where other conductors did, and in a few of his own. A good example is afforded by the measures from 93 to 108 (and the similar passages from 330 to 345, 623 to 638, and 860 to 875) in the second movement, where Toscanini strengthened Beethoven's woodwind lines with the blare of two trumpets and four horns—thus inverting the character of the passage from one of woodwinds with brass support to one of brass with woodwind support. (See the reproduction of the score in Figure 49.) That this line of "improvement" was not original with Toscanini, but stemmed from no less a figure than Richard Wagner, and that other great conductors have indulged themselves in something like it too, does not alter the fact that Toscanini, in adopting it, made just as free with the score as any of his colleagues did.[182]

Toscanini has been credited with correcting mistakes in the standard editions of Beethoven's scores. Some of these corrections bear testimony to what Warren D. Allen called "Toscanini's musicological instinct,"[183] but others turn out to have been questions of Toscanini's personal taste and judgment, and not necessarily the final word either artistically or musicologically. One of them, for example, was in the final Presto of the *Leonore* Overture No. 3, in which Toscanini changed the initial note from C to D, probably to make it agree with the similar passage in the *Leonore* Overture No. 2. This "correction" (also made by von Bülow before Toscanini) is debatable, however; Sir Donald Tovey, in his *Essays in Musical Analysis,* even cites the two different beginnings as evidence of Beethoven's sensitivity in distinguishing between the different formal demands of the two overtures. Toscanini, who was a studious man, certainly knew, and had considered, the arguments for and against each version; but once he formed an opinion his worshiping followers promptly accepted it as ultimate truth and endowed it with the sanctity of ecclesiastical law.

Toscanini's emendations were not confined to Beethoven. At one point he decided that, in Ravel's orchestration of Mussorgsky's *Pictures from an Exhibition,* a section of the last movement ("The Great Gate of Kiev") was not satisfactory, and he concluded therefore, according to his biographer Howard Taubman, that it "had not been orchestrated by Ravel"! So he redid seventeen measures of the orchestration. (Yet, as Taubman records, when Toscanini saw that another conductor had marked a mere slowing-down at one point in this score, he wrote near it, *"Perchè? Vergogna!"* ["Why? For shame!"].) In the opening measures of Tchaikovsky's *Manfred* Symphony, Toscanini inserted a clarinet part to reinforce the bass clarinet, thereby defeating the obvious intention of the composer, who had already assigned no fewer than three bassoons to the line to produce the special tone color that he desired. In Smetana's *Vltava* (*The Moldau*) Toscanini added trumpet to a voice that seemed to him to need strengthening. In the Third Symphony of Schumann, he did just about as much reorchestrating as most other conductors of his time had done, and that was a great deal. When Toscanini constantly repeated his injunction to other conductors to "play as written! do as written!" he reserved to himself the right to make *his* changes in the score. To this day his former librarian for the NBC Symphony, James B. Dolan, carries on a voluminous correspondence with musicians who want to copy for their own use "the Toscanini changes" in the standard repertory. One can argue on stylistic grounds either for or against the particular alterations that Toscanini made, but there can no longer be any argument as to whether he made them. He did. And it is time to brush away, like the historical cobweb that it is, the myth of his absolute observance of the composer's instructions.

An important distinction must be made, however, between the methods of Toscanini and those of the nineteenth-century interpreter-conductors. Unlike the extreme representatives of the older group, who used every score as a vehicle for personal expression, Toscanini unquestionably strove with all his remarkable skill, energy, and devotion, to serve the interests of the composer. There is no doubt that he believed sincerely, when he adjusted the scores of the composers whom he admired, that he was helping to bring out their original intentions more clearly. Uncompromising in his professional requirements, as severe with himself as with the musicians under him, he studied and restudied the masterworks of the music literature with a genuine humility, seeking always to understand the music more completely and changing his interpretations willingly when the evidence seemed to warrant it. (When he worked on Beethoven's Seventh Symphony with the NBC orchestra toward the end of his life, he criticized certain details of their earlier performances together: "*I* was stupid; *you* were stupid," he said to the orchestra men, "Only Beethoven was not stupid.") Perhaps, to distinguish Toscanini from the unbridled interpreter-conductors, we should speak of him as one of a newer breed of "master-conductors"—sovereign, absolute in authority, yet always using their powers to serve the art they loved—a breed that included also such of Toscanini's younger contemporaries as Koussevitzky, Walter, and Beecham, and a little later Klemperer and Furtwängler.

Toscanini's incorruptible artistic conscience had at its service, in achieving the musical results for which he was famous, natural gifts and technical abilities that came close to perfection. But even the folklore surrounding his gifts and abilities must not go unchallenged if he is to be admired for what he really did as one of the greatest conductors in the history of the art.

For example, though Toscanini's musical ear and memory were extraordinary, some of the traditional tales told about them by overenthusiastic admirers are silly enough to be embarrassing. The importance of Toscanini's phenomenal gifts lay in his use of them to sort out and balance every thread in the musical texture until a piece of music was as clear to the listener as it was in the written score. He set standards of accuracy, precision, and clarity for the Philharmonic-Symphony that were salutary models for the whole world of music performance. And certainly the dozens of anecdotes of his detecting the most minute slips in orchestral playing (a single note left out by a woodwind player in an orchestral tutti!) are intriguing footnotes to his art. But when miracles of technical virtuosity are seen in the Maestro's most commonplace acts, or when careless reminiscences are served up as authentic history, Toscanini's achievement is cheapened. Typical of such misleading interpretations (often fostered by fine professional musicians who really know better but who derive a spiritual satisfaction from persuading themselves that they have been witnesses to feats of magical genius) is the anecdote about the Philharmonic-Symphony rehearsal of a new cello concerto during which the soloist, in repeating a certain passage, changed one small detail in the fingering. The story goes that Toscanini's ear promptly caught the difference: "I like it better when you play the D with the third finger instead of the fourth," he remarked. The story is essentially true—it took place in January 1935, at a rehearsal for the premiere of Castelnuovo-Tedesco's Cello Concerto, with Gregor Piatigorsky as soloist—but it is not remarkable. The change in fingering involved a shift from the A-string to the D-string, familiar to the ear of any cellist, and Toscanini, in addition to being one of the great conductors of all time, had once been a good cellist.[184] Even the most experienced music critics and journalists have not always escaped the fairy-tale inconsistencies of the Toscanini legends. What are we to think when, of three respected writers telling an often repeated tale of Toscanini's musical prowess, (1) the first describes a crestfallen double-bass player who reported during the intermission of a concert that his E-string had just broken and who was reassured by Toscanini, after a few moments of concentrated thought, that he needn't worry because the E-string wasn't needed in any of the pieces that remained to be played that night, (2) the second tells the same fable about a *bassoon* player with a broken E-flat key ("before a concert," this time), and (3) the third tells it about a troubled trombonist with a bad low note ("just before an opera performance")?[185] Can all the low-pitched instruments in Toscanini's orchestras have been hexed?

Another matter is more serious. One of Toscanini's most valuable contributions to the art of musical performance in his time was his repeated demonstration that, in music of regular metric pattern, a right tempo could be found for each piece and then maintained steadily, without capricious deviations from the composer's indications. It was Toscanini's happy choice of tempo and unshakable security of rhythm that laid the foundations for the masterpieces of musical architecture that his performances became. Yet it cannot be ignored that it was in this same field of rhythm that Toscanini suffered from a technical defect—perhaps his only one but not the less real for that: he was very easily confused by the intricate rhythms, especially those with changing meters or displaced accents, that many important composers began to write toward the end of the nineteenth century and the early part of the twentieth. Any competent orchestra player or conductor who watched Toscanini conducting Strauss's *Till Eulenspiegel* could see that he was "swimming" in the passage just before No. 24. It was the skill of the orchestra men that saved the situation; with a lesser orchestra there would have been collapse or, at the very least, raggedness, but the men of the Philharmonic (and in later years of the NBC Symphony) knew this music too well to be thrown. Toscanini had similar difficulties with rhythm in certain sections of Ravel's *Daphnis and Chloe,* of Copland's *El Salón México,* of Stravinsky's *Petrushka,* and of d'Indy's *Istar.* This would have been a minor weakness if it had not been for the likelihood that it contributed to Toscanini's avoidance of many kinds of new music and thereby limited the repertory that he offered the public.

Still another aspect of Toscanini's conducting practice calls for stern criticism rather than the tolerant chuckle that it usually evokes. The celebrated temper tantrums, which were so exciting and amusing to read about or hear about, were childish indulgences that wasted the time and money of the orchestra and insulted the dignity of its players. Samuel Antek, in his *This Was Toscanini* (pp. 89–90), has described one of the Maestro's rages, occasioned, as well as anyone could tell, by a single phrase in the cellos that he thought was too listless: "With a torrent of insults he broke his baton, picked up the score, began to pound it, tore it up, kicked at the stand, and then pushed it off the stage. Then, bellowing at the top of his lungs,* he began to claw at his collar until his hand caught in the chain of the watch he carried in his breast pocket. With a furious wrench he pulled it away, glared at it with unseeing eyes, and, in a vicious lunge, smashed it to the ground where the watch spattered in all directions." Any pediatrician will recognize the syndrome. These oubursts may have been helpful to Toscanini as an emotional catharsis, but they were no help to the orchestra musicians, who would have profited more from the efficient and pointed corrections that Toscanini knew better than anyone else how to give when he was behaving like a mature man. At one point the musicians' union discouraged the Philharmonic from admitting listeners to rehearsals for fear that Toscanini might insult and embarrass the players in their presence. Toscanini himself was aware of this failing; he often showed that he was sorry after a temper fit, and he tended to exclude visitors from rehearsals, especially when he was angry, quite independently of the union, the orchestra management, or any other influence. This was a serious disappointment to the music students of the time, who would have given anything to watch the master at work—particularly since Toscanini's rehearsals frequently produced more perfect music-making than his public concerts, when the accumulated tensions were sometimes so great

---

* "The only sound that comes to mind to equal it," says Antek, "is the horrible shrieking of stuck bulls in a slaughterhouse I once visited as a boy in Chicago."

that they might cause things to go wrong. The Philharmonic men could understand what *Musical America* had reported of Toscanini years before, in 1915, when he had stormed out of his Metropolitan Opera position: "that his great talent and mastery . . . were offset by his frightful irritability and his habit of perpetually abusing the artists, the chorus and orchestra during rehearsals . . . by the end of the season half the company was in a state of nervous collapse."

One wonders indeed why the Philharmonic-Symphony players submitted to the reign of terror. There were several reasons. They admired Toscanini's musicianship and leadership, which brought out the best that was in them, and made them partners in performances of which they could be proud. They respected him for his integrity as man and artist. They understood that his outbursts were not attacks on them, but defenses of the music—Toscanini knew so clearly how he wanted the score to sound that every deviation from the ideal pained and infuriated him. They were set on fire by his burning devotion to music. They loved him for the goodness that was in him: the childish anger had its complement in a childlike warmth and directness. Moreover, musicians in the 1920s and early 1930s, no matter what their artistic pretensions, generally had much more modest ideas about their social and professional positions than do their counterparts of today: there was a great gulf between the ruling maestro and the men who played under him, and they accepted its existence. But the most important reason of all was simply that they were afraid of losing their jobs. The early 1930s were years of terrible financial depression, and Toscanini had the power to hire and fire like an absolute monarch; that terrible temper could oust a man on the spur of the moment—in the midst of a season, in the midst of a phrase. Toscanini's ousters were seldom permanent, but the terrified musician could never be sure.

It has often been said that Toscanini brought great financial prosperity to the Philharmonic, but this is not borne out by the records. It is true that he aroused extraordinary excitement in the city's musical circles and that many of his concerts attracted very big crowds for a time of depression, but in all his years with the Philharmonic he never conducted more than half a season, and the very enthusiasm engendered by his appearances sometimes made for a letdown at the box office in the other half of the season, even for well-known conductors who were otherwise attractive to the public. In fact, the receipts tended to go *down* throughout the Golden Age, while the deficits went up. (See table in Backnote 186.)

Of course, Toscanini was not the kind of man to be concerned about the box office; when the perfection of a performance was at stake, he did not consider what it would cost or what it was likely to bring in. Nevertheless he was always careful to collect every cent of his own ample salary. The exact amount that Toscanini received was not revealed, but it was known to be approximately $100,000 for ten weeks of concerts. Howard Taubman relates that one year when the amount should have been $102,000, Clarence Mackay, the Chairman of the Board, had made it a round figure of $100,000. "Why didn't you make it $110,000?" Toscanini complained. "That is also a round number." And $110,000 was what he received on that occasion. Europeans who were in the know laughed at these salaries—or envied them; other famous conductors, such as Bruno Walter and Otto Klemperer, were paid by the Philharmonic at a third or a quarter of that rate, and it was certain that Toscanini himself asked for and received nothing like it when he conducted in Milan or Vienna.† Even in the depths of the Depression, when the Philharmonic's orchestra men agreed to a cut of 10 per cent in their salaries so that the orchestra could go on—giving them an average of about $90 a week for a thirty-week season, or, to put it another way, an annual income of $2,700—Toscanini continued to take $80,000 to $90,000 from the Society for ten weeks of work.

The financial position of the Philharmonic had become so difficult by 1934 that the Society had to launch a special campaign to raise $500,000 from the public. It succeeded in collecting almost that amount, but meanwhile serious proposals were being made that both the Philharmonic and the Metropolitan Opera (which had been having its own financial troubles) could effect important economies by merging. The idea was that the Philharmonic would replace the Metropolitan orchestra for the opera performances, and the artistic and business management of the combined organizations would be directed by Toscanini and the managers of the Philharmonic, Judson and Zirato, probably with the collaboration of certain representatives of the Metropolitan. (Gatti-Casazza, the manager of the Metropolitan, was retiring at the end of the 1934–35 season.)

It can be imagined that the Metropolitan orchestra players were not

---

† In Philadelphia, however, Stokowski was being rewarded with similar American munificence.

too pleased at the prospect of being replaced by the Philharmonic. By the fall of 1934 they and certain other elements opposed to the merger had formed the Metropolitan Opera Association Protective Committee, which attacked the plan bitterly on the grounds that it would throw out of work not only the hundred men of the Metropolitan orchestra but also, in consequence of dividing the season between symphonic and operatic performances, hundreds of dancers, chorus singers, stagehands, and other employees. "The suggestion that Mr. Toscanini could successfully replace Mr. Gatti," the Committee went on angrily, according to a report in the *Musical Courier* of December 1, 1934, "is absurd and ridiculous, as this gentleman has in the last few years repeatedly asserted that he will not conduct opera; as the same person has absolutely no managerial ability but is well known for his dislike of American music, his manners, his partiality, his despotic temperament —and sundry other peculiarities which make him quite unfit for anything except as concert conductor." The Committee recommended "that the members of the Philharmonic Symphony be advised to look into the affairs of their own institution as conducted by their managers (Messrs. Judson and Zirato—two highly remunerated artists' representatives and concert managers) and by Mr. Toscanini (of $100,000 fame and salary). It is quite certain that the $500,000 fund subscribed by the American public, early this year—were it to be properly used—should make possible at least five seasons of concerts instead of three." It also urged "that the press, the various unions and the music-loving public prevent any concert bureau or artists' manager, such as the above mentioned (with their multiple interests at stake) from obtaining an almost complete control of these important institutions in the American musical world."

Toscanini was in Italy at the time, but Bruno Zirato, the Philharmonic's Assistant Manager, laid the whole story before him. Zirato cabled his report to Arthur Judson:

Had several talks with the Maestro. Find it rather difficult to convey his views by cable. He believes that the merger would not help either organization artistically. Giving concerts at the Metropolitan, the Philharmonic would lower its standards achieved so far. He believes it impossible that only forty performances of ten operas would satisfy the public. Anyway, he never could recommend giving concerts at the Metropolitan on account of the acoustic conditions there, despite proposed stage improvements. [It had been proposed that the symphony concerts be given in the opera house to save the cost of renting Carnegie Hall.] The Maestro, however, wishes you to tell the members of the board that this honest opinion should not carry any weight in their minds, or arrest any negotiations if they still consider advantageous a merger with the Philharmonic.[187]

Toscanini's veto was sufficient. The merger was abandoned.

Such skirmishes hardly scratched the Toscanini legend. In the singing of his praises during his eleven years with the Philharmonic there were seldom any dissenting voices. The only aspect of his art that was criticized with any frequency was the rather limited nature of the repertory that he performed. The standard works of Beethoven, Brahms, and Wagner (excerpts from the operas) made up 40 per cent of his programs with the Philharmonic—about a third more space than most other American orchestras were allotting to those composers. He gave a good deal of attention to Italian music in the form of half a dozen Rossini overtures, played frequently, and a long list of other Italian composers, some of them very deserving, but others obviously just his friends and acquaintances. In order to placate those who complained that he did not perform enough contemporary music, he spotted around in his programs an assortment of modern pieces that were relatively easy to take. He did more of these than his critics acknowledged—his very first program with the Philharmonic in January of 1926 included Respighi's *Pines of Rome,* and a week later he did parts of Stravinsky's *Petrushka*—but he admitted openly that his heart was not with the new music. As for American music, he would occasionally make an impatient gesture in its direction by programming a light or uncontroversial composition. In the eleven seasons of his regular association with the Philharmonic, he conducted only five pieces by American composers. And when he led the Philharmonic on the first European tour in its history in 1930, he took no American conductor or soloist with him and played not a single American composition on any of the programs.

Toscanini had a ready excuse for his conservatism. He was not a young man—when he came to the Philharmonic in 1926 he was almost sixty years old and when he left it in 1936 he was almost seventy—and his coevals were really composers like Strauss and Debussy, whom he did play with some frequency. He had done his share of first performances earlier in his life; let the young conductors play the young composers. Nevertheless, Koussevitzky and Stokowski were finding it possible to grow with their times and to present a constant flow of new and provocative musical ideas, including those of the vigorous young American school that was beginning to clamor for attention. Walter Damrosch, though older than Toscanini and of much more modest gifts as performer, kept his interests broad enough and his mind open enough to commission a jazzy piano concerto of George Gershwin or to give the first performance of an adventurous symphony by the young Aaron Copland in the mid-1920s. And when Damrosch took his Symphony Society on a concert tour of Europe in 1920 (ten years before Toscanini's tour with the Philharmonic), he gave featured roles to the American violinist Albert Spalding and the American composer-pianist John Powell—unlike Toscanini, who gave Europe no sign that the Philharmonic was an American orchestra.[188]

There are some, indeed, who have questioned whether Toscanini's repertory would have been sufficient "if, like Theodore Thomas, Frederick Stock, Stokowski, Koussevitzky, Monteux, and others with long tenures he had had to risk boring his audiences by conducting concert after concert, year in and year out, with only minor midseason vacations";[189] they point out that Toscanini was always seen at his best in New York, since he never had to undergo the strain of a full season. But this seems an unwarranted challenge. All who worked with Toscanini have marveled at the sheer quantity of music that he was familiar with, from opera and oratorio to symphony and chamber music, from Mozart and Wagner to Verdi and Stravinsky. Moreover, most of the other European conductors who came to this country had had no previous experience with the long seasons of American orchestras, and many of them had started with more limited repertories than Toscanini's. They learned to expand them "on the job," and with Toscanini's fabulous ability to devour new scores there is no doubt that he could have done so too, even at his age, if he had wished to. What is doubtful is that the orchestra could have survived a full season of Toscanini wear and tear.

The effects of this fantastic Toscanini on the history of the Philharmonic lead to one judgment if examined at close range and to a very different one if taken in the long view. The immediate effects were unmistakable. Such was the power of Toscanini's musicianship and personality that for the first time since the days of Anton Seidl the Philharmonic was able to capture the full support of the New York public, to rouse up an artistic esprit de corps within its own ranks, and to meet the excitement of the Boston Symphony Orchestra and the Philadelphia Orchestra. Toscanini had made of the Philharmonic—by teaching it, inspiring it, and terrorizing it—a musical instrument that New York could proudly believe to be the greatest in the world. No longer did sophisticated New Yorkers have to prove the refinement of their tastes by letting it be known that they preferred the Boston Symphony Orchestra to their own. No longer did the Philharmonic musicians, underpaid though they were, have to feel like spiritual charity cases; an orchestra that had been whipped into shape by Toscanini wore the scars of its flagellation in artistic honor.

It was this kind of excitement that Clarence Mackay had in mind when he gave it as his opinion at the Philharmonic's Annual Meeting in 1927 that "the engagement of Mr. Toscanini as a regular conductor was one of the most important events in the history of the Society." But what had happened to the progressive program that Mackay himself had so farsightedly outlined in 1922—the encouragement of American music, the education of a great new public? In the very next sentence after his pronouncement of the importance of Toscanini's appointment, Mackay had added that "the educational policy of the Society had not been definitely settled so far for the next season." The sad truth is that it ground to a halt while the "cult of personality" was fostered.

Toscanini did not determine Philharmonic policy alone, even during the Golden Age, but he was a powerful influence on it, and the outward symbol of it. So all-important a decision as the scrapping of the merger with the Metropolitan Opera hung on Toscanini's "No," or at least the Board of Directors was willing to let the public think so. Ultimately it is the Directors who must be given the responsibility for allowing themselves to be diverted from their high purposes by the remarkable talents of the Maestro—or perhaps we should say of all the master-conductors, for Toscanini was only the most conspicuously successful of many similar conductors who shared the seasons of the Golden Age with him. But just as he is always given the credit, both inside and outside the Philharmonic, for the achievements of the Golden Age, so must he also answer for its losses.

And the losses were many.

Henry Hadley's noble dream that the Philharmonic might finally ally itself with the American composer (had not Mackay called it the

"Greater Americanization of the Philharmonic"?) died while the glamorous conductors were the focal points of the concerts. In the first year of the plan, 1922–23, Hadley presented five American works at his six concerts; in 1923–24 he did four more pieces, and in 1924–25 a few more; but in 1925–26, when the Toscaninis and Furtwänglers began to crowd the schedule, he was given only the sop of conducting one of his own compositions on a program that was really led by Mengelberg, and the next year he was reduced to conducting in exile, at two out-of-town colleges, a piece by Rubin Goldmark. After that Henry Hadley's name no longer appears on the roster of Philharmonic conductors.

Undaunted, Hadley continued his work outside the Philharmonic, with an organization called the Manhattan Symphony Orchestra, presenting dozens of American compositions in the three years that he conducted it, from 1929 to 1932. The Manhattan Symphony Orchestra had a policy of performing an American composition, conducted by the composer whenever possible, on each of its programs. Ticket prices were purposely kept within a modest range, from 50¢ to $2, with a special price of 25¢ for music students; moreover, some concerts were given absolutely free and others were broadcasted over radio station WOR. This was the kind of project that Hadley had hoped to clothe with the prestige and the permanency of the Philharmonic.‡

Since before the World War a concern about American music had been making itself felt. It was intensified, naturally, during the patriotic days of the war and persisted after it. A keynote was the belief that, as the encouragement of repeated performances was given, important American composers would spring up. The restlessness and the hopes expressed themselves in a variety of idealistic efforts. Mackay's "Greater Americanization of the Philharmonic" and Hadley's

‡ In the summers of 1934 and 1935 Hadley led another inventive project involving New York Philharmonic players—an outdoor symphonic festival at Stockbridge, Massachusetts. Although these Berkshire Symphonic Festivals consisted of only three concerts in each of the two summers, Hadley found room on the programs for four American compositions: a piece of his own, and works by Edward MacDowell, John Powell, and Burnet C. Tuthill. The Berkshire Symphony Orchestra was described in the first year as "composed of 65 members of The New York Philharmonic-Symphony Society Orchestra" and in the second year as "composed of 85 members of The New York Philharmonic-Symphony and other Orchestras." In 1936, however, Koussevitzky and the Boston Symphony Orchestra became the performers for these concerts, from which the Berkshire Music Festival and Berkshire Music Center at Tanglewood are descended.

Manhattan Symphony programs were not isolated cases. Stransky offered composers informal readings of their manuscript music at special rehearsals of his short-lived State Symphony Orchestra after his departure from the Philharmonic in 1923, and Howard Hanson of the Eastman School started his American Composers' Concerts in 1925. Some of the same motivations led to the founding of the Society for the Publication of American Music in 1919* and of the League of Composers in 1923. The cause found its verbal outlets in a torrent of magazine articles, newspaper stories, and books. Some of the authors were writers with an interest in music, and others were musicians with an interest in writing. But there was general agreement among them that America's musical health required composer, performer, and public to move closer to each other, and general optimism that a school of American music with such sound roots was not far off. Henry F. Gilbert† in 1915 made the point that our European-trained conductors, even when they had the best of intentions, tended to choose for performance those American compositions that sounded the most European. Walter R. Spalding in 1918, discussing "The War in Its Relation to American Music," was sure that our national music would rise up, vigorous and fanciful, when we freed ourselves from our "servile reliance upon foreign methods" and particularly from our dependence on Germany. Carl Whitmer in 1918, in an article bearing the strange title of "The Energy of American Crowd Music," protested that we had been "so artistically reticent or intellectually snobbish that our large output of ladylike works tied with baby ribbon is entirely out of proportion to our other qualities, so elemental for the most part." Ezra Pound, though a voluntary exile in Europe, made himself the propagandist for the young American composer George Antheil, who, he believed, had found "an aesthetic of machinery" appropriate to a twentieth-century America of cities and machine shops.[190] The composer Louis Gruenberg, calling "For an American Gesture," asked us not to scorn such resources as jazz, Negro spirituals, and the various kinds of local

---

* By Burnet C. Tuthill, son of William B. Tuthill, the architect of Carnegie Hall. It may be taken as a small sign of the change in the city's cultural mood in just one generation that in 1891 William Tuthill's great music hall could be inaugurated without a single American composition on the program, and in 1919 Tuthill's son could be the founder of a society devoted exclusively to American music.

† For bibliographical information on the writings mentioned in this paragraph, see the authors' names in the Bibliography (page 467).

color that the immigrants brought us, which could be blended into something decidedly American, recognizable the world over as such, just as surely as were the immigrants themselves. William Treat Upton in 1928 tried to retrieve for us "Our Musical Expatriates" by proudly summarizing their accomplishments abroad. Daniel Gregory Mason in 1928 studied *The Dilemma of American Music,* giving both horns (the polyglot parroting of Europe, and the dangers of an American nationalism) a hard time. William Arms Fisher in 1929 was one of the many who looked ahead to "The Great American Symphony." As for jazz, in the 1920s everyone from Louis Armstrong to Aaron Copland was publishing his opinions on its place in American music.

Most important of all, the American composers could already back up all the ferment with a substantial stock of music. The pioneers—Heinrich, Bristow, Fry, Gottschalk—had been forgotten, and the later school of Romantic composition, represented by Chadwick, Goldmark, MacDowell, Hill, or Mason, might seem tamely conservative. But by the end of the 1920s a conductor could choose, according to his tastes, from a wide sweep of actively creative musicians, offering every degree of caution or daring he might desire, and all thirsting for performances of their music. There were Howard Hanson, Leo Sowerby, and Randall Thompson; there were Frederick Shepherd Converse, John Alden Carpenter, John Powell, Emerson Whithorne, and Louis Gruenberg; there was George Gershwin; there were Aaron Copland, Douglas Moore, Roy Harris, George Antheil, Virgil Thomson, Roger Sessions, Walter Piston, Quincy Porter, Wallingford Riegger, and Henry Cowell. There could even have been Charles Ives, if only ears and eyes could have opened to him.

Once more, in the 1920s, the American composer was raising his voice, as he had already done three quarters of a century before, when Fry and Bristow had cried to the Philharmonic for attention to themselves and their colleagues. Once more the Philharmonic had the opportunity to link the American performer organically with the American creator of music. And once more—this time even after recognizing and defining its natural role—the Philharmonic allowed itself to be distracted by considerations of glamour and prestige. Toscanini had shaped the Philharmonic into the most glorious musical instrument in America, but as far as its relevance to the musical needs of New York at that moment was concerned, it might just as well have been in Berlin or Vienna or Milan. Its superb performances were being used on the one hand to reinforce the already overbalancing weight of the German-Austrian music of the past in the background of the New York public, and on the other hand to parade before the jealous ears of American composers the works of Respighi, de Sabata, Tommasini, Martucci, Sinigaglia, Pizzetti, Busoni, Castelnuovo-Tedesco, Wolf-Ferrari, Bossi, and Sonzogno. It was such uses that provoked even the conservative composer Daniel Gregory Mason, a self-announced classicist, to complain in 1931 that these concerts should be more than "museums of the masterpieces of musical art in the past," and to scold enviously that "the fashion-enslaved, prestige-hypnotized minds" that kept Toscanini at the head of the "rich and reactionary Philharmonic-Symphony" were "totally devoid of any American loyalty to match the Italian loyalty that is, after all, rather likeable in him."[191]

Mackay's elaborate plan for systematic educational concerts suffered its losses too during the master-conductor era, but it fared rather better than the Americanization project (perhaps because its roots went back a little further into the Philharmonic's past—already in Stransky's early seasons, a decade before Mackay's plan, a bloc of 250 "Students' Tickets at 25¢ each" had been made available for certain concerts). After the year of 1922–23, the Philharmonic dropped its educational series at the Cooper Union, at City College, and at the Brooklyn Commercial High School. But another of its educational series, the one at Carnegie Hall that had begun as part of the Philharmonic's collaboration with City College, was not a complete loss; it was turned into a so-called Students' or Popular Series, which was a substantial set of Carnegie Hall concerts, with the same conductors who were featured for the fancier subscription series of the season, but with lower prices. Until 1948 these concerts continued to be referred to either as Students' Concerts or Popular Concerts, but as far as their programs were concerned, they were really regular Philharmonic-Symphony concerts at lower rates. These performances reached and even created a wider public, but under a system which required anywhere from four to eight conductors to split the season among them, they could have no coordinated educational plan. The innocent public was educated in the "non-pattern" of whatever programs of the regular season happened to fall on the dates designated as Students' Concerts. Similarly, the radio broadcasts that had begun as part of the educational plan of 1922 continued and even multiplied, but they too were soon transmuted into ordinary Sunday afternoon concerts that were not specifically designed for their educational mission. John Erskine, taking stock officially for the Philharmonic-Symphony in 1942, after two decades of broadcasts, questioned frankly "how far the Sunday programs have until now been planned with the special needs of this audience in mind," and admitted that "few conductors, few touring concert artists, have the forethought to inquire what music the boys and girls in the local school system have been studying . . ."[192] The schools and colleges, from their side, did not presume to affect the content or the manner of presentation of the so-called educational programs; their students and teachers were expected to take gratefully whatever cultural handouts they were offered by an artist of Toscanini's or Walter's stature, and for the most part they accepted their passive role unquestioningly. Only rarely did a disappointed critic or educator dare to speak up. In 1934, during the Philharmonic's special campaign to raise $500,000, W. J. Henderson of the New York *Sun* charged that "prima donna conductors" had diverted the public taste from the music itself to the conductor's idiosyncrasies:

> Critical comment . . . is almost entirely directed to the "readings" of mighty magicians of the conductor's wand . . . Can [the public] ever again be trained to love music for its own sake and not because of the marvels wrought upon it by supermen?[193]

And Professor Douglas Moore of Columbia University, at about the same time, criticized Toscanini's Philharmonic for its artistic and educational policies. "We are being asked to raise $500,000," he chided, ". . . And what for? To develop new music? No, but to keep alive a great institution that is a symbol of the past, conducted by a man who admits that he has no understanding or care for modern music. Certainly it is a great thing to keep alive the music of the past, but the Philharmonic . . . [stands] unalterably opposed to any progress in the new principles of music." As for the radio broadcasts, said Moore, undoubtedly they had been of educational value, but the gain was "slight compared to what it might be."[194]

In short, the "definite educational policy" ended up as something much less than the glorious promise of the Mackay manifesto. Fortunately some parts of the educational work continued to be cultivated, and for this the ladies of the Auxiliary Board deserve unstinted praise. The chairmen and vice-chairmen of their Educational Committees raised money to keep the Popular Concerts at popular prices, arranged for poor students to study with Philharmonic orchestra players, tried to maintain meaningful contacts with the colleges and the public schools, and helped Ernest Schelling with his Children's and Young People's Concerts. The educational seeds that had been planted in 1922 never died, but they were obscured in the heliotropic flowering of the master-conductors. It would be a long time before they would grow as they could have grown.

Chapter 24

And After the Master?
(1936–43)

Toscanini's departure from the Philharmonic stage, in a special farewell concert on April 29, 1936, was as glorious an occasion as was to be expected for the "Master of all Masters of Music" (*magister magistrorum musices* Georgetown University had called him in conferring an honorary degree on him). Prices for a box seating eight were raised to $200 for this concert—under ordinary conditions that would have been the cost of a subscription for a whole series of ten concerts—and there were reports that speculators and scalpers were getting even more for tickets at the last moment. The program, a characteristic one for Toscanini, was constructed entirely of Beethoven and Wagner: Beethoven's *Leonore* Overture No. 1 and Violin Concerto (Heifetz, soloist), and four of the best-known excerpts from the Wagnerian operas. A crowd of a thousand queued up for standing room, although they knew in advance that only a few lucky ones could be admitted. Outside Carnegie Hall the brilliant dress of the arriving guests, and the uniforms of mounted police and patrolmen on foot—more than fifty had been assigned to the event—added to the color. The excitement was compounded by the widespread belief that this would be the great conductor's last concert in America.

The drawback to this kind of exit by a master-conductor is that it can always be upstaged by another master-conductor. The next month Leopold Stokowski, resigning from his post as chief conductor of the Philadelphia Orchestra, capped a grand cross-country tour with a farewell concert not at Carnegie Hall but in Madison Square Garden, drawing an audience of about twelve thousand, more than four times the capacity of Carnegie Hall.

Was it only accident that the rise of the totalitarian conductors in the 1920s and 1930s coincided with the rise of the totalitarian political leaders? It is ironic that, although many of the conductors were passionately opposed to political dictatorship, exposing themselves to danger in order to defy it,* they nevertheless enforced their own dictatorships in their own smaller worlds. The consequences were sometimes predictably similar too. Whole platoons of masterlet conductors tried to ape the methods and the mannerisms of the greats. The imitators of Toscanini began to conduct from memory without a score, often with disastrous results (he did so because he was almost blind and had a remarkable memory, but his copiers generally had neither the excuse nor the resource), or to vibrate the left hand like a cellist's to suggest warmth of tone to the orchestra, or to churn the air with a circular motion of the right hand for passages that moved ahead, or to cow their orchestras in rehearsal with abusive language. The imitators of Koussevitzky wore their coats capelike over their shoulders, or emulated his espousal of the works of living composers, often with surprisingly good results. The imitators of Stokowski could seldom duplicate his fertile inventiveness, but they tried his experiments in rearranging the seating plans of orchestras and threw away their batons to conduct with the hands alone, as he did—generally with no marked change in their work, either for the better or for the worse.

At the opposite extreme from imitation, the dictatorship of the virtuoso master-conductors, like other dictatorships, occasionally produced a rebellion against all centralized authority, which took the form of attempting to give orchestral performances without any conductor. It is significant that it was in the 1920s and 1930s that most of these at-

---

* Mussolini personally kept track of Toscanini's political transgressions, withdrawing his passport in 1938 when wiretapping revealed that the Maestro had attacked the Duce's anti-Semitic policy as "medieval stuff." Koussevitzky, while living under the Bolshevik government, dared to denounce it in a letter to the press as "the harshest, most despotic and violent regime that has ever reigned over us." (See G. Ciano, *Ciano's Hidden Diary*, and A. Lourié, *Sergei Koussevitzky*.)

tempts were made in Russia, Germany, and the United States. In New York the American Symphonic Ensemble (later known as the Conductorless Symphony Orchestra) was founded in 1928 "to permit the listeners to focus attention on the music"—the antithetical phrase "instead of the conductor" being unmistakably understood.

Another school of musicians, reacting against the master-conductor syndrome, began to show an interest in chamber orchestras of modest proportions (as an antidote to the grandiosity of the master-conductors); in music of the Baroque and earlier eras and of the more venturesome composers of their own time (as a change from the predominantly Romantic repertory favored by the celebrated international conductors); and in a performance practice, for old music, based on historical and musicological research (rather than on the arbitrary intuitive determinations of the older generation of "interpreters"). The Philharmonic itself had an offshoot that reflected these interests. In 1935–36, Toscanini's last season, a Philharmonic-Symphony Chamber Orchestra was founded under the conductorship of Hans Lange, who had been the Philharmonic's Assistant Conductor from 1928 to 1933 and a guest conductor after that, and with the assistance of the composer-conductor Otto Luening, who was then head of the Music Department of Bennington College. It was a semi-official organization, made up of sixteen of the principal players of the Philharmonic, with the Philharmonic's Assistant Manager, Bruno Zirato, as Manager. It presented at Town Hall, under the auspices of Bennington College, a neatly planned series of "Five Centuries of Chamber Music," offering music for small orchestra from the sixteenth century to the twentieth, and managing to include in this handful of concerts five works by living American composers and three more by contemporary composers of England, France, and Germany. The programs were given, moreover, with an attempt at authenticity that the big Philharmonic had seldom approached. A real harpsichord was brought in for Baroque music instead of the doctored piano that had been used in Philharmonic concerts.† The size of the performing group was adjusted to the practice of the historical period, instead of vice versa. And some effort was made to employ current musicological knowledge in such difficult matters as the ornamentation in Baroque and Classic music. The series was a success with

† One should not be misled by the appearance of the word "harpsichord" in the Philharmonic programs of Mahler and Mengelberg; the instrument they actually used was a gelded Steinway piano, its hammers or action altered in one way or another to imitate the tone of a harpsichord.

both press and public, and a second season of five concerts was organized for 1936–37, again with Otto Luening as Lange's artistic and administrative assistant behind the scenes. For one of the concerts of the second season, Luening took over the baton from Lange with such excellent results that he was announced as Associate Conductor for 1937–38, dividing the series equally with Lange. Unfortunately, that third season failed to be realized because of the usual financial problems that beset young orchestras. But while the Philharmonic-Symphony Chamber Orchestra lasted, it opened the minds of many New Yorkers to a musical literature and an aesthetic viewpoint that the parent orchestra had not been able to present under the rule of the master-conductors.[195]

For the Philharmonic the withdrawal of the imperial figure of Toscanini left open the possibilities of imitation or reaction—that is, either his replacement by another greatest-living-conductor or the engagement of a younger talent without any pretensions to patriarchal authority. Choosing the first possibility, the Philharmonic invited Wilhelm Furtwängler.

Furtwängler was no stranger to the Philharmonic. He had first worked with it as a guest conductor in 1925, and had then served as co-conductor with Mengelberg for the two seasons from 1925 to 1927, always with critical success and a warm reception from the public. Now, at the age of fifty, he was one of the most sought-after and respected conductors of Europe. He had held important posts in Vienna, in Berlin (as successor to Richard Strauss), in Mannheim (as successor to Mengelberg), and in Leipzig (as successor to Nikisch). He was one of the few men who could conceivably dare to appear as the successor to Toscanini. Like Toscanini, he had both musical authority and a striking personality. He was a man who was single-mindedly dedicated and consecrated to music. If Toscanini had been the Imperator of New York's music world, Furtwängler would be its Pontifex Maximus. The words that were most frequently applied to his interpretations and his conducting style, both in Europe and in America, were profundity and forcefulness. Yet he was colorful enough to be a good subject for the journalists, and although his deification had not yet reached Toscaninian proportions, there were signs that a satisfactory Furtwängler legend was forming. His spastic beat was part of the shop talk of the international music world. (Orchestra men knew the anecdote of a London performance of Beethoven's Fifth Symphony in which one player leaned over and asked another how he could tell from Furt-wängler's beat when to begin playing at the opening of the symphony. "After the thirteenth wiggle," replied the experienced player.) On the podium he made wild gesticulations, shook like an epileptic, scowled angrily (to the delight of the audience) when anything went wrong, spat profusely, and stamped his feet so loudly that at Bayreuth it was suggested that a mat be put under them to muffle the noise during per-formances. From a technical viewpoint his conducting gestures, unlike Toscanini's, were poor, and orchestra players everywhere complained that they could not follow them, but audiences loved what his devoted ex-secretary Berta Geissmar described as "the expressive directing movements of his wonderful hands, which seemed to paint the music on an invisible screen or form it out of an unseen piece of clay."[196] Yet eventually it was not only the easily seduced audience but the orchestra too that was carried along by his immersion in his art, by the penetra-tion of his musical understanding, by his burning intensity—and by adequate rehearsal time.

Furtwängler's appointment as conductor of the Philharmonic-Sym-phony was announced late in February 1936, shortly after the an-nouncement of Toscanini's resignation. But New Yorkers were puzzled to read in their newspapers immediately thereafter an Associated Press report that Furtwängler had just been reappointed to his former posi-tion as chief of the Berlin State Opera. It seemed unlikely that he could take either of these jobs so casually as to imagine that he could do them both at the same time. The puzzlement began to change to suspicion as word got out that the Associated Press report had come from official sources in the German government. Many Americans had felt for some time that Furtwängler was cooperating too closely with the Nazi authorities and, in effect, lending them the prestige that his name carried in artistic and intellectual circles. Now their fears seemed to be confirmed. A cable from the Philharmonic brought the following reply: "I am not chief of Berlin Opera but conduct as guest. My job is only music. WILHELM FURTWÄNGLER."[197]

Nevertheless the Associated Press continued to insist that official circles in Berlin confirmed their original report. Whether the announce-ment had been made with or without Furtwängler's permission, it in-dicated that the Nazi government was very much involved in his affairs. The matter was still being hotly debated in the music world when news reached New York on March 7 of an open letter published in the Manchester *Guardian* by the violinist Bronislav Huberman, formerly a friend of Furtwängler's, reminding the public that it was two and a half years since the conductor had assured him that all "real Germans" condemned the Nazi brutalities, and upbraiding Furtwängler and all German spiritual and intellectual leaders for having spoken no "word of liberation" since then. On the same day, March 7, 1936, an event occurred which triggered a barrage of protests against Furtwängler's appointment: Hitler marched into the Rhineland. Newspapers, cultural groups, private individuals, and unions (including the musicians' union) came out against him. On March 15 Furtwängler sent another cable:

> Political controversy disagreeable to me. Am not politician but exponent of German music which belongs to all humanity regardless of politics. I propose postpone my season in the interest of Philharmonic Society until the time public realizes that politics and music are apart. FURTWÄNGLER.

The few supporters that Furtwängler still had in New York must certainly have been alienated by the arrogance of that last clause, which presumed to scold the New York public for mingling politics and music in a case that had been precipitated by his government's doing just that.‡ Berta Geissmar recounts that the next thing she heard from him was a warning that "people in Berlin were spreading the rumor that [she] . . . had incited the Jews of New York against him!"

With Furtwängler out of the running as a new Toscanini, the Philharmonic tried the opposite possibility: modesty and retrenchment. The Directors engaged two considerably younger and less famous conductors, John Barbirolli, thirty-six years old, and Artur Rodzinski, forty-four years old. Rodzinski was already known to them from a two-week engagement with the Philharmonic in the fall of 1934. It was Barbirolli, however, whom they seemed to be testing for the principal position. He was given the best and longest part of the season,

‡ Although Furtwängler was officially absolved in 1946 of the charges of pro-Nazi activity that had been made against him, there is no doubt that he had been on close terms with some of the highest Nazi leaders. In an interview reported in the New York *Times* on October 26, 1969, Albert Speer, "Hitler's personal architect, master builder and wartime Armaments Minister," introduces an anecdote (in which he and Furtwängler address each other by their first names) with the remark: "All Berlin knew that I was very friendly with Wilhelm Furtwängler, the directer of the Philharmonic."

the first ten weeks; and the program for the opening concert of the season carried a laudatory biographical sketch. Barbirolli was English (no political problems here), of mixed Italian and French family (Toscanini, the first Italian conductor in the Philharmonic's history— who, like Barbirolli, had started as a cellist—had not done too badly within recent memory), and he had already had a good deal of experience in both opera and concert for a conductor of his age. He had begun his conducting career at the age of twenty-five by founding his own chamber orchestra, but his first important "break" had come from one of those last-minute substitutions that can make an artist's name in the theater or in the music world. Sir Thomas Beecham had been scheduled to conduct the London Symphony Orchestra in a program that featured Pablo Casals as soloist, and when Sir Thomas had fallen ill, Barbirolli had been called upon to replace him, on only two days' notice. Barbirolli's background as a cellist had stood him in good stead, for his accompaniment in the familiar Haydn Cello Concerto had been so comfortable that it had won the praise of the great Casals. Barbirolli had gone on to become one of the conductors of the London Symphony Orchestra, of the Royal Philharmonic Society, and of the Covent Garden opera seasons, and to appear as guest conductor with numerous British and continental orchestras, from Liverpool to Leningrad. Then, in the depths of the international depression, he had taken over the Scottish Orchestra of Glasgow and the Leeds Symphony Orchestra and had succeeded in arousing such interest that both orchestras, which had been in danger of going down because of public indifference, had actually been able to extend their seasons. The hope was that the Philharmonic might be "discovering" a new talent; no pretense was made that it was presenting a new Toscanini.

Before the season of 1936–37 was very old—indeed, before Rodzinski's part of it had even been reached—the Directors had decided that Barbirolli had passed his tests well enough to be entrusted with the full conductorship. For the four years from 1937 to 1941 Barbirolli was the official conductor of the Philharmonic-Symphony Society, sharing his seasons only with the guest conductors who came for a few weeks of each year.

Meanwhile, since 1936–37, the Philharmonic's Directors had been making some attempts at answering those critics who had accused the Society of paying insufficient attention to contemporary music. Instead of engaging internationally known virtuoso conductors to fill out the

season, as they had been accustomed to doing in the past, they had
announced for 1936–37 three "composer-conductors" from different
countries who had led the orchestra for two weeks each: Carlos Chávez
of Mexico; Igor Stravinsky, Russian in background though a French
citizen since 1934; and Georges Enesco, the Romanian violinist-com-
poser-conductor. The many-talented Enesco (his musical memory as
prodigious as Toscanini's; his piano, organ, and cello playing as sensitive as his violin playing; his teaching as highly prized as his performing) had such a success that he was kept on as guest composer-conductor (the only one) for the next two years. He was even announced for
another year after that, along with Serge Prokofiev of the Soviet Union
and Albert Stoessel of the United States, but those plans had to be altered at the eleventh hour—Enesco fell ill with pneumonia on his
way to America and Prokofiev cabled that the Russian government
would not give him a visa, whereupon the Philharmonic had to arrange
for Barbirolli and Stravinsky to cover their dates. Another project was
intended to encourage American composers: Philharmonic-Symphony
Awards of $1,000 for a work of symphonic length and $500 for a
shorter work were announced for the seasons of 1936–37 and 1937–
38. The winners of Awards and Honorable Mentions for the first year
were Gardner Read, Quincy Porter, and Philip James, and for the
second year David Van Vactor, Charles Haubiel, and Robert Sanders,
and their winning compositions were performed in the regular concert
series. It seemed almost as though the departure of Toscanini had been
a signal for increased attention to contemporary music and American
music.

That the overcoming of the American national inferiority complex
was far from complete, however, in spite of this effort, was clearly
shown in the concerts that the Philharmonic-Symphony gave in connection with the World's Fair of 1939. These included, in addition to
an Inaugural Concert of international cast, Norwegian, Polish, Brazilian, Romanian, American, Swiss, British, and Czechoslovakian concerts. The Norwegian concert consisted entirely of Norwegian music;
the Polish concert entirely of Polish music; Brazil presented two programs, one all-Brazilian, the other all-Brazilian except for the *Faust*
Symphony of Liszt; little Romania put on an all-Romanian program;
little Switzerland an all-Swiss program; of course, Czechoslovakia, which
had been known as "the conservatory of Europe" since the eighteenth
century, offered a whole program of Czech music. Only the two Eng-

lish-speaking countries, the United States and its cultural mother, Great Britain, were diffident about presenting the music of their own composers. The United States concert consisted chiefly of Beethoven's Ninth Symphony, prefaced by two short American pieces, one by the young Samuel Barber and the other by Walter Damrosch, who conducted the concert. (The two British concerts each had about half a program of British music.) Yet this was the time when the WPA Federal Music Project was finding hundreds of American compositions to perform—in fact, to make up for the lack of American music at the World's Fair, the New York Composers' Forum-Laboratory of the Federal Music Project gave twenty-two concerts, mostly in the WPA Auditorium at the Fair, in which no fewer than 201 works by 41 composers living in America were presented. A lively new school of American composition was manifesting itself in spite of all obstacles, but the Philharmonic was still making only an occasional cautious move in its direction in the late 1930s by programming a few of the sure-fire American composers, such as Samuel Barber and Deems Taylor. Even Aaron Copland enjoyed only one Philharmonic performance during those years. A Philharmonic-Symphony subscriber could hear lots of English music at Barbirolli's hands, and an astonishing quantity of Romanian music (Enesco, Otesco, Alessandresco, Mihalovici, Golestan, Andrico, Rogalski, Lipatti, Dragoi) at Enesco's hands, but he was not likely to hear anything by Marc Blitzstein, Paul Bowles, Henry Brant, Henry Cowell, David Diamond, Arthur Farwell, Howard Hanson, Charles Ives, Wallingford Riegger, William Schuman, Roger Sessions, or Virgil Thomson —or even George Gershwin. Yet he could have heard all of those American composers, and many more, at the Composers' Forum performances in New York between 1935 and 1939.[198]

When the Philharmonic had decided, for 1936–37, to retrench from the prestige class of Toscanini and Furtwängler to that of Barbirolli and Rodzinski, it had accompanied the change by a parallel retrenchment in its business affairs. The length of the season had been cut by 20 or 25 per cent, from 30 weeks to 24 weeks, from 122 concerts to 92. The orchestra had been pared down from 107 players to 102. And expenditures had been slashed by more than a quarter, from $725,000 in the last year of the Toscanini period to $534,000 in Barbirolli's trial year, most of the savings being effected in the salaries paid to conductors and performers. These curtailments succeeded in bringing down the financial deficit for 1936–37 to the lowest figure that had been shown in ten years. Over the next several seasons, as Barbirolli gained the confidence of the Society, the valves were gradually opened. The number of concerts was allowed to increase, year by year, until it first regained and then exceeded its former level; and the annual budget was permitted to go up to its previous height too.[199] The Philharmonic's Directors were no longer economizing on Barbirolli.

But even the substantial material resources that the Society was now putting behind Barbirolli could not solve the problems inherent in his situation. The stock comment on that situation is that Barbirolli faced the insuperable difficulty of competing with the record left by Toscanini. This is a gross understatement of his task and his achievement. At half Toscanini's age and with half his experience, Barbirolli was called upon for *double* the job that had been asked of the older man. Toscanini came to New York each year for only half the season, though he was accorded all the attentions and privileges of a permanent conductor. He was never required, as Barbirolli was, to sustain the burdens of a full New York season, with its steady grind of rehearsal after rehearsal and concert after concert from fall to spring, with its demands for a huge list of constantly changing programs, with its pressures from all the public and private groups that expected a permanent conductor of the Philharmonic-Symphony to accept responsibility for its policy, and with its unremitting, full-time exposure to the music critics of the New York newspapers. From 1937 to 1940 Barbirolli bore the full weight of the schedule on his own shoulders; the guest conductors relieved him of only two to four weeks in each season. He was a willing servant of the orchestra, too, taking it on sizable tours in 1939 and 1940 for the first time in half a dozen years, and even stepping in to take over a Young People's Concert in 1937 when Ernest Schelling had to undergo his eye operation. Considering the difficulties of his position and the embarrassment of having to solve them in the public eye in New York City, Barbirolli was doing very commendably —it would have been an accomplishment if he had done no more than get through each season—but all his work had to be done in the atmosphere of "letdown" that Toscanini notoriously left behind him when he had finished with any post. After living in the environment of permanent artistic crisis that Toscanini carried with him, the orchestra players, the management, the Board of Directors, and even the public had to relax. This had been true wherever Toscanini had worked throughout his life—an exhilarating artistic experience while he was there, followed by a slump as soon as he was gone. In New York the cult of The Maestro had been instilled into musicians and public, but now the central figure toward which the cult had been directed had been taken away. What was worse, it had actually been given to a rival: after the establishment of the NBC Symphony in New York in 1937, Barbirolli and the Philharmonic had to compete not only with the memory of Toscanini but with the Maestro himself in the flesh and on the air.

The simple question that was being asked of the Philharmonic by 1940 or 1941 was "Where do we go from here?" But nobody seemed to have a very clear answer, and it is not unfair to say that for the two years from 1941 to 1943, as far as its over-all policy was concerned, the Philharmonic drifted.

Barbirolli was being eased out as gracefully as possible. Already in 1940–41 there was some encroachment on the length of his New York season. First, under a kind of barter arrangement, the Chicago Symphony Orchestra gave a pair of concerts on the regular subscription series in exchange for Philharmonic-Symphony appearances in Chicago. After that, Dimitri Mitropoulos and Bruno Walter (and Walter Damrosch for two concerts devoted to his own opera *Cyrano*) conducted for a total of almost two months, before Barbirolli came back to finish the season. Then in 1941–42, when the Philharmonic was celebrating its one hundredth anniversary, Barbirolli became only one of ten conductors invited for the centennial season. He still had the largest number of concerts of any of the conductors but he had to share the podium with Stokowski, Walter, Rodzinski, Mitropoulos, Busch, Goossens, Koussevitzky, Damrosch, and Toscanini himself. It can be seen from the list of names that the Philharmonic's Directors were once again thinking of glamorous master-conductors, and in this company Barbirolli took on the unpromising character of a glamour conductor with less glamour than most of the others.

Of all the conductors of the Philharmonic's 1941–42 season, Serge Koussevitzky of the Boston Symphony Orchestra made the biggest hit, and the musical gossip of New York had it that he might be the next conductor of the Philharmonic-Symphony. In his brief two weeks as guest conductor, he had succeeded in stamping his own personality on the orchestra—critics and audiences were astonished to find that the famed Boston Symphony tone was really the Koussevitzky tone and that the Philharmonic had it too when he conducted. "There is no question," summed up Virgil Thomson in the *Herald Tribune*, "that with standard Philharmonic equipment Mr. Koussevitzky has produced the best all-around result of the year . . . Everybody else who has led the Philharmonic this season has been, by comparison, a blind date." Koussevitzky's guest engagement with the Philharmonic-Symphony had been accepted at the request of the Boston Symphony trustees. Ordinarily he and the trustees alike had shown little interest in his appearing as guest conductor with other American orchestras, but an exception had been made because of the one hundredth anniversary of the Philharmonic. Nevertheless the impression began to get about that, if he were offered the conductorship of the Philharmonic-Symphony, he might be in the mood to accept it. The whole period was so darkened for Koussevitzky, it was known, by the death of his wife, Natalie, on January 11, 1942, that he was susceptible to any forces that would keep him from an immediate return to the scene of their life in Boston.

It is tempting to guess what the future of the Philharmonic-Symphony might have held if Koussevitzky, with his burning idealism and his practical gift for making his dreams come true, had been named the Society's conductor in 1942—would there have been New York equivalents of the Berkshire Music Center and the summer festivals at Tanglewood? performances of the new music that Koussevitzky encouraged wherever he worked? commissions for composers of symphonic, choral, and operatic music? the great educational academy that he envisaged for the development of young talent in music and all its sister arts? But the negotiations with Koussevitzky were not consummated,* and the Philharmonic, still without a principal conductor, announced that the 1942–43 season was "planned along the same general lines as the past one." This meant that there would be another imposing array of star conductors and it also meant, for those who could read between the lines, that Barbirolli's share would be whittled down a little further. There were eight different conductors in 1942–43 before the season was over. Toscanini, Walter, Rodzinski, Mitropoulos, and Barbirolli returned from the preceding season, and to them were

---

* The Philharmonic's records reveal an earlier relationship with Koussevitzky— quaint, in retrospect—that also failed of consummation. In January of 1909, when the Philharmonic was still a cooperative society and Koussevitzky was better known as contrabass virtuoso than as conductor, the members engaged him for two appearances as doublebass soloist at a fee of $150. But the performances never took place; Germaine Schnitzer, pianist, played instead.

added Howard Barlow, Fritz Reiner, and Efrem Kurtz. But now Barbirolli's share of the season's concerts was only of the same order as Rodzinski's, Mitropoulos's, and Reiner's, and it was Bruno Walter who took care of more of the concerts than any of the others.

Clearly this heterogeneous group could not shape a coherent artistic policy, yet some force was doing so in no uncertain fashion, for the repertory of music performed by the Philharmonic showed at this point some of the most startling changes in the orchestra's history. Performances of American music, which had formed an infinitesimal part of the programs in the early life of the Philharmonic and had hovered somewhere around 4 per cent of the total in recent years, suddenly went up to 15 per cent of all music played. At the same time the proportion of music by living composers of all national origins went above 30 per cent for the first time in recent history. And finally, the performances of German-Austrian music fell from the usual norm of somewhere around 60 per cent to an all-time low for the Philharmonic of only 40 per cent.

The powerful force that effected in so short a time changes in listening patterns that a hundred years of cultural development had not been able to produce was World War II, into which the United States had finally been plunged after the attack on Pearl Harbor on December 7, 1941. At the beginning of the war the attitude of the New York Philharmonic-Symphony, and probably of most American intellectuals, was that German and Austrian music should not be suppressed merely because Hitler had made those countries our military enemies. Wagner and Strauss continued to appear on Philharmonic programs, and the opening motif of Beethoven's Fifth Symphony had become the symbol for Allied victory, and not only because its rhythm happened to coincide with the Morse code pattern for the letter V but also because Beethoven remained for many the archetype of the democratic and individualistic artist. "There must be no black-out of music during the ordeals now facing a war-torn globe," wrote Marshall Field, President and Chairman of the Board of the New York Philharmonic-Symphony, in his foreword to John Erskine's book about the Society in 1943. Yet in the very year of his writing, the wartime distaste for all things German, combined with the patriotic urge to boost our own American composers and those of our Allies, had already been sufficient to decrease the Philharmonic's performances of German-Austrian music by about a third and to increase its performances of American music more than threefold. (See the graph on page 293.) And before the war was over, many American intellectuals, repelled by the Nazis' interference in art in general, and by Hitler's personal predilection for the Wagnerian music dramas in particular, were to abandon the liberal doctrine of the neutrality of music. Paul Henry Lang, at that time probably the most respected of the younger musicologists in America, wrote an article for the *Saturday Review* in 1945 in which he denounced Wagner's works as "Background Music for *Mein Kampf.*" Of the rise in the number of Philharmonic performances of living composers (to about a fifth more than it had been), a substantial part must be attributed to the compositions of Prokofiev and Shostakovich. Their increase in popularity was only partly due to the fact that Russia was our partner in the struggle against fascism. Their aesthetic-stylistic quality was anyway in the ascendant just then, as that of Wagner and Strauss was anyway in its decline. But the political and emotional pressures of the war years did accelerate the process.

When the war ended, the Philharmonic repertory changed almost as radically in the opposite direction—the number of performances of American composers and of all living composers slumped back toward the prewar levels and the number of performances of German-Austrian music promptly rose again. But there was some residual effect from the war's influence. The German-Austrian music went up only to 48 per cent of the total, not all the way to its former 60 or 65 per cent, and it seemed unlikely that it would ever again have quite the unquestioned domination of the Philharmonic's repertory that it had enjoyed before the two World Wars.

The Philharmonic did its part in the nation's war effort during World War II. The members of the orchestra, with Dimitri Mitropoulos, gave two fully equipped ambulances to the Red Cross. The Society helped with the scrap-metal campaign, and donated books, money, and recordings for armed forces libraries. But since the thing that the Philharmonic did best was the giving of musical performances, its most conspicuous contribution took the form of "concerts for military and civilian morale." There were about twenty such concerts—at army camps, on board the USS *Prairie State,* for the benefit of the American Red Cross, for the cadets of the Military Academy at West Point, for the wounded at Halloran Hospital. And of course a number of orchestra members and Directors of the Philharmonic served in the armed forces—the printed programs, during the war years, generally

REPERTORY OF NEW YORK PHILHARMONIC, 1842–1970
Performances of Music of German-Austrian, Living, and
United States Composers
(Only selected years are shown)

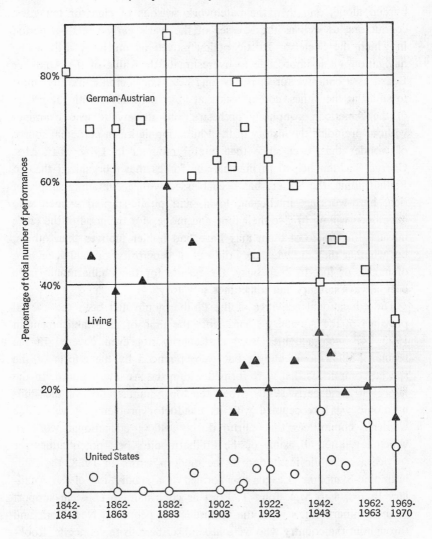

listed ten or twelve of the personnel who were on leave "in the service of the United States."

For the motley period in the Philharmonic's history from 1937 to 1943, which saw first Barbirolli's brave efforts to support his Atlantean burden alone, and then the patchwork seasons of eight or ten guest conductors, as well as the stresses of the war's early years—a period in which the Society's artistic policy moved as much by drift as by navigation—it is impossible to overestimate the value of the Auxiliary Board as a cohesive force. It has long been considered culturally smart to smile at the ladies' committees that busy themselves with the affairs of the American symphony orchestra, but to anyone who examines without prejudice the history of the Philharmonic it is a perpetual source of wonder that, ever since that fateful moment in 1909 when Mrs. George Sheldon helped to marshal the forces that reorganized the old Philharmonic, the Society has been blessed with an unfailing supply of rich, hard-working, intelligent, loyal, and public-spirited women who have been willing to give their time and money for the good of the city's musical life. Some of them may have had nobler motives than others, but whether they did what they did out of generosity, or vanity, or love of music, or just to keep busy, the results for the Philharmonic have been always salutary and sometimes salvatory.

The educational activities of the Philharmonic had been the special province of the Auxiliary Board from the time of its establishment in 1923–24. Such activities were customarily not even covered in the regular Philharmonic budget but were financed by the efforts of the special committees that were formed within the Auxiliary Board. In the late 1930s and early 1940s, when the top administration of the Philharmonic was preoccupied with its conductor problems, it was these women's committees that nurtured the selfless educational work in which lay, after all, some of the Philharmonic's best potentialities for service as a public institution in the modern sense. In 1938, the Philharmonic-Symphony League was formed as a subdivision of the Auxiliary Board, with Mrs. John T. Pratt as chairman, to enlist in support of the Philharmonic's work the multitudes of people in New York and throughout the country who were *not* subscribers to the concerts. Looking far ahead with intelligence and optimism, the League planned not only for the already large radio audience (estimated a few years later in 1942 at nine million listeners for the weekly broadcasts) but also for a television public that they knew must one day come into being.

The hope was expressed that as new listeners swelled the ranks, ticket prices would go down and the Philharmonic would face the pleasant need for a great new auditorium, many times the size of Carnegie Hall, to accommodate the public that it had bred. The immediate realization was much less exciting than the heady dreams, but it was important that someone was doing the dreaming while the eight or ten guest conductors were carrying on their contest on the Philharmonic's podium.

Meanwhile the other committees (all made up of women who paid substantial sums as a sort of initiation fee for the privilege of performing these public services) busied themselves with the Young People's Concerts, the Pension Fund for the orchestra players, the scholarships to enable needy public school students to take lessons with the first-desk men of the Philharmonic, the concert tickets provided to college and high school students at nominal prices and to underprivileged music students absolutely free, the subscriptions for organized groups, especially those that might never have attended concerts before, and the Popular (Students') Concerts. Mrs. Charles S. Guggenheimer, the Popular Concerts chairman, kept a sharp eye on the ticket prices to make sure that they remained inexpensive enough to meet the stipulation of some of the donors that tickets be held within the reach of students and teachers.

What the orchestra still lacked in 1943 was strong artistic leadership. After two years of guest conductors, the Philharmonic had learned again the old lesson that a fine orchestra cannot be guided with twenty hands on the reins. For 1943–44 the Society gave the musical control to one man. Artur Rodzinski, already known in the profession as a trainer of orchestras (he had molded the Los Angeles Philharmonic and the Cleveland Orchestra into shape and had prepared the NBC Symphony for Toscanini) was appointed Musical Director.

Chapter 25

The Musical Director
(1943–49)

Not just conductor, but Musical Director.

Damrosch had called himself Musical Director of the old Symphony Society, and Toscanini had been fleetingly referred to as General Musical Director of the Philharmonic-Symphony at certain moments during his last two seasons when it had seemed politic to distinguish him in rank from the other conductors, but except for that the Philharmonic had not used this title before. "Musical Director" suggested a position that was far from any of the meanings that "conductor" had held in the Philharmonic's past:

—far, certainly, from the kind of *ad hoc* conductor that the Society had known in its earliest days, when the orchestra had been content to choose several of its regular playing members to split the conducting of a program among them,

—far from the artist-conductor of Bergmann's vintage, a professional conductor but one who was elected by a majority vote of the orchestra's members and held his office only at their pleasure,

—far from the interpreter-conductor of a later date who, whether he owed his position to election or appointment, dominated the music-making by the romantic force of his personality,

—far from the competent but compliant conductor of Stransky's type, who allowed the tides of popular taste to pull him in their direction,

—far even from the great master-conductors of more recent years who, taking their brief turns, dictated their wills and whims to their worshiping minions for a few weeks of the season.

Rodzinski was not to be any of these kinds of conductor, but the Musical Director. He would still have to work with the stick in hand and the score in head, but his most characteristic tool would be the plan in mind. It was assumed that he would supervise all musical and artistic aspects of the Philharmonic's activities. He would control the personnel of the orchestra. He would choose assistant and guest conductors. He would select soloists. He would plan the repertory for each season, coordinating the programs of guest conductors with his own. "On him," the Society announced in its prospectus for 1943–44, "will fall the major responsibility for the design of the season." He could be expected, moreover, to provide the long-term direction—not just for a single season but over a span of several—that the Philharmonic had so sorely lacked in recent years.

Rodzinski seemed well prepared for this responsibility. Born in 1892 of Polish parentage in Spalato (at that time Austria, later Yugoslavia), he had had an excellent general as well as musical education, and had received a degree in law from the University of Vienna before becoming active as concert and opera conductor in Poland. In 1926, still in his early thirties, he had been engaged as assistant conductor to Stokowski for the Philadelphia Orchestra. Three years later, having outgrown the assistant class, he had been named conductor of the Los Angeles Philharmonic, and by 1933 he had become conductor of the Cleveland Orchestra, which he had raised to a high level of efficiency. His first New York Philharmonic engagement had been a brief one of two weeks in the fall of 1934, but two years later, when he had had a longer one, he had proven his professional excellence—in fact, one music critic had remarked with rue that, if the Philharmonic's Directors had not been in such a hurry to appoint Barbirolli as their conductor at the beginning of that season, they could have found a man of "overwhelming superiority" to him in Rodzinski. Instead, Rodzinski had gone on to the task of shaping the new NBC Symphony for Toscanini, and this had stamped the ultimate cachet on his reputation as a builder and mentor of orchestras. He was also considered to be intellectually alert to new ideas in music—he had given the American premiere of Shostakovich's sensational opera *Lady Macbeth of Mtzensk,* had been among the first to think of offering operas in concert form, had introduced the works of many contemporary composers . . . In temperament, experience, and abilities, he seemed to be the man who could give the Philharmonic the firm directorial hand it needed.

Rodzinski's directorial hand proved to be even firmer than had been anticipated. Hardly had his appointment been made public when he fired fourteen of the Philharmonic's players, among them the concertmaster and six other first-desk men. "These changes," read a statement released by the Philharmonic-Symphony on February 18, 1943, "are necessary for the good of the orchestra and to insure a better balance in its various sections." The action caused a scandal. It was hard for most people to understand why the dismissals should be necessary. After all, the Philharmonic remained essentially the same orchestra that had been warmly—sometimes even rapturously—received during the preceding two years when it had been in the hands of Toscanini, Koussevitzky, and a number of other conductors, including Rodzinski himself. In an orchestra of this caliber it was difficult to believe that fourteen musicians had suddenly been discovered to be incompetent.* Those who were at all sympathetic to Rodzinski's action assumed that he wanted in particular to bring with him into the Philharmonic some of the outstanding players that he had counted on in the Cleveland Orchestra (such as Leonard Rose the cellist and William Lincer the violist) and in general to man all positions with players who would create a matched ensemble. Since the dismissals were made known in February 1943, but were not to take effect until the end of the season, there was a lame-duck interval of several awkward months during which the "fired" musicians had to play out the rest of the season alongside their more fortunate colleagues, and the conductors (Barbirolli, Kurtz, Reiner, and Walter) had to contend with the morale of an orchestra in which a seventh of the musicians knew that they were to

---

* The most puzzling of the firings was that of Rodzinski's friend Mishel Piastro, the Assistant Conductor and concertmaster of the Philharmonic-Symphony, who had been chosen for the concertmaster's position in 1931 by no less an authority than Toscanini. In a conversation shortly before his death in 1970 Piastro insisted that, after more than a quarter of a century, he still did not know the reason for his replacement, but he maintained, with a broad-mindedness that seems remarkable under the circumstances, that Rodzinski must have felt it necessary or he would not have allowed it, and that it had never interfered with their personal friendship.

be dropped. The *Sunday News* quipped that for Barbirolli, who had survived seven submarine attacks in a transatlantic voyage the year before, "dodging Nazi subs again will be a relief after the guerrilla warfare of the Philharmonic-Symphony Orchestra." Meanwhile, the controversy had been carried to the musicians' union, where the orchestra's shop committee, led by one of the dismissed musicians, asked for a trial of Rodzinski by the American Federation of Musicians on the grounds that he had damaged the reputations of the dismissed players "and endangered their musical livelihood." The trial was never held because the union's executive board upheld the Society's right to fire the musicians; this so outraged some of the members of the shop committee that they filed impeachment charges against the leaders of Local 802, but the charges were not taken up by the union membership. Instead, the complaints against Rodzinski were withdrawn in April "in the interests of reaching an amicable settlement and in order to insure future co-operation and harmony between Dr. Rodzinski and members of the orchestra." This prepared the way by mid-May for a compromise in which five of the fourteen ousted men were restored to their places, and the minimum salary of orchestra members was raised from $90 to $100 a week for the regular twenty-eight-week season.† As a gesture of harmony the agreement was announced in a joint statement signed by Marshall Field as President of the Philharmonic-Symphony Society, Jacob Rosenberg as head of Local 802 of the union, and Rodzinski.

In spite of this initial encounter, which could be expected to make the orchestra uncomfortable, Rodzinski thereafter enjoyed excellent relations with the players. His manner in rehearsal was always considerate; to men who had served under the Toscanini tirades it was a pleasant surprise to find that the stern-looking Rodzinski was never even sarcastic in rehearsal. He had a tendency, which some members of the orchestra found appealing, to let his personal life touch theirs in little ways. When his son Richard was born, he celebrated the event with the Philharmonic by programming the *Toy* Symphony (the one formerly attributed to Haydn). He encouraged Mrs. Rodzinski, who

---

† A few days later the Society let it be known "in about the most casual way possible" (as the New York *Sun* commented) that the new concertmaster to replace Piastro would be John Corigliano, who had been assistant concertmaster at Piastro's side since 1935; this was done not in a special press release—presumably to avoid stirring up the Piastro affair again—but simply by listing Corigliano, in the routine announcement of soloists for the next season, with the title of "concertmaster" before his name.

counted all the orchestra men among her admirers, to help form a club of the players' wives. Rodzinski was known to cut a rehearsal in half (always a welcome gesture in the busy Philharmonic schedule) because it was a "nice day and I'd like to take my little boy out . . . you probably like a walk, too." The orchestra made its gestures also: on the birth of Rodzinski's son, a group of the musicians played a serenade at his home.

There was a touch of modernity in Rodzinski's orientation, as compared with that of any of his predecessors, that showed itself both in the choice of music for each season and in his ideas on the interpretation of that music. Rodzinski's style of conducting was plainer, more straightforward, less Romantic than that of the interpreter-conductors. His tempos were always steady and the beats were always shown clearly, so that the orchestra was sure of where it was at every moment. He seldom added to a composition the ritardandos and accelerandos that more Romantic conductors used to stamp their interpretations on the work of the composer. In rehearsal he would read a piece through until a bar or two before the end, then go back and make those corrections that were absolutely necessary, but without trying to add any personal touches; what he did strive for constantly was what he called a "clean" sound. To ears attuned to the subtleties and refinements of some of the older conductors, this style sometimes seemed sterile and uninflected, but there was no denying its solidity and security. It was a somewhat more streamlined, more modern style than a good part of the public, and even of the orchestra musicians, had been taught to expect. Yet it was so obviously right for Rodzinski and so clearly related to the newer face that the arts had taken on in the world that it was accepted comfortably and with general satisfaction by all concerned.

The Philharmonic's repertory under Rodzinski's guidance, and the artists and conductors chosen to help him in presenting it, took on much of the same personality. Clean-cut conductors like George Szell and Pierre Monteux, and adventurous ones like Leopold Stokowski, began to appear more frequently as guests; and more composers, and more progressive ones, were invited to conduct their own compositions—in addition to Stravinsky, who was already a familiar figure in the concerts, there were Villa-Lobos, Tansman, Rosenthal, Milhaud, Thomson, Kreutz, Harris, Hanson. Rodzinski's repertory, like his conducting style, had a craggy aspect: there was always plenty of Beethoven, Brahms, and the other solid standards, and among the moderns he leaned toward the heavier and more forceful compositions—although he was intellectually curious about the experimenters in contemporary music, the modern composers likely to appear on his programs were men like Bartók, Hindemith, Harris, Schuman, Martinů, Prokofiev, Shostakovich, Rathaus, Bloch, Roussel, Walton. One can contrast his tastes with those of Bruno Walter, who had been appearing frequently as a Philharmonic guest conductor since 1941. When Walter wanted to do something of Schoenberg's, he chose the early and romantic *Verklärte Nacht,* but Rodzinski chose the newer and more radical *Ode to Napoleon,* which had been enlarged by Schoenberg from chamber-music proportions at Rodzinski's suggestion. Walter celebrated his fiftieth anniversary as a conductor by a performance of Beethoven's Ninth Symphony; Rodzinski marked a birthday anniversary by a reading session of new American music, including part of the Fourth Symphony of the then seldom played composer Charles Ives.‡

Rodzinski's musical style has been described as straightforward, but his personality also had a hot emotionalism in it. It was an emotionalism that could sometimes be sublimated into artistic fire (he was praised for his fervor in Strauss's *Elektra* and Wagner's *Tristan*) but that seemed at other times to verge on eccentricity. A veteran of the Philharmonic's staff recalls how, infuriated by some real or imagined offense, Rodzinski would prepare a lacerating letter for her to send. "Now that you've written it, Dr. Rodzinski," she would have to say to him, "tear it up." His deep involvement in the Buchman Moral Re-Armament movement struck many of the Philharmonic musicians as strange, as did his practice of reading his philosophical thoughts to the orchestra at rehearsal.

Even stranger tales were told of Rodzinski's volatile behavior toward his young assistant conductors, but whether they were true or not seems unimportant now by comparison with the fact that he gave two talented young Americans the Philharmonic openings that started their professional conducting careers.[200] Having begun his own American career in 1926 as assistant conductor to Leopold Stokowski, Rodzinski

‡ Rodzinski seems to have had a blind spot, however, for the American popular music with which the teen-agers of the 1940s were obsessed. He liked the older popular music well enough when it was dressed up in symphonic guise—he played Gershwin often for instance, and had commissioned Jerome Kern to write his *Scenario for Orchestra on Themes from "Showboat"*—but on a much publicized occasion in January of 1944, in connection with a Philharmonic concert for soldiers at Camp Kilmer in New Jersey, he was reported as linking Frank Sinatra with the nation's juvenile delinquency problem. "Nuts," replied Sinatra.

was sympathetic toward the need of young American conductors for some sort of practical training opportunity, since this country does not have the chain of opera houses that provides that opportunity in many European countries. When he became Musical Director of the Philharmonic he reestablished the position of Assistant Conductor, which Hans Lange had occupied from 1928 to 1933 but which had been vacant since that time.[201] Rodzinski appointed as his assistant in 1943 the young Leonard Bernstein, whom Koussevitzky had recommended to him. Even the gentlest and most generous of assistant conductors dreams about the day when a famous conductor will be unable to go on and the young assistant will have a chance to show what he can do. Bernstein's chance came when he substituted for a guest conductor, Bruno Walter, at one of the regular Sunday afternoon concerts on November 14, 1943, won an ovation from the audience, and made the front page of the next day's New York *Times*. Before the season was over, Bernstein had conducted the Philharmonic eleven times, substituting for, or sharing concerts with, Rodzinski, Barlow, and Walter, and conducting his own *Jeremiah* Symphony with such success that he won the Critics' Circle Award for it. By the next year, having shed the assistant's cocoon, he was engaged as a Philharmonic guest conductor. The year after that, 1945–46, Rodzinski gave the Assistant Conductor opportunity to another young American, Walter Hendl, who held the position until 1949, when he graduated to the conductorship of the Dallas Symphony Orchestra.

Although the number of concerts and the size of the orchestra remained approximately the same throughout Rodzinski's term, the Philharmonic's budget rose sharply in all departments, until it finally crossed the million-dollar line in 1946–47.[202] Some of the growth was only on paper, reflecting the general rise of prices in the nation's economy during those years. But not all of it. The Philharmonic's budget grew at least 7 per cent more than the consumer price index in the four years from 1943 to 1947.

An important factor in the increased budget was a new Pension Plan for orchestra members and office employees, which became effective in 1944. Previously there had been no retirement benefits at all for office workers and admittedly inadequate ones for musicians. These, such as they were, had been kept afloat by informal and sporadic fund-raising efforts, valiantly led by one of the ladies' committees. Under the new system, though "benefit" concerts continued to be a valued support for the Pension Fund, the Society undertook to pay about $80,000 a year toward retirement costs (about five times what the participating employees contributed). A Philharmonic musician, in consequence, could look forward to a modest but guaranteed allowance at the age of sixty; wind-instrument players, indeed, "because of the greater physical demands on them," could retire when they were only fifty-five. (Office employees would not be retired until the age of sixty-five.) At the same time that the Plan protected the players, it helped to ensure that the quality of the orchestra would not be endangered by musicians whose playing was beginning to suffer because of their age.* The maximum allowance of $1,200 a year, for thirty or more years of service, would seem very small today, but in 1944 the Philharmonic's Pension Plan represented "the most liberal retirement provision created by any of the orchestras" of America.

Two ventures during the 1943–47 period brought the Philharmonic to new audiences. The first was a series of summer broadcast-concerts on Sunday afternoons, carried from coast to coast over the full network of 118 radio stations of the Columbia Broadcasting System, under the sponsorship of the United States Rubber Company. Since the Sunday concerts were already being broadcasted during the fall-winter season, the Philharmonic was now being heard on the radio every Sunday the year round. In addition to the millions of radio listeners, moreover, the summer concerts had "live" audiences (generally in Carnegie Hall) who obtained their tickets free by requesting them of the United States Rubber Company. The programs of these concerts, directed toward a nationwide radio public, favored the respected orchestral standbys of the Classic and Romantic eras. The conductors, however, were of the same caliber that the Philharmonic-Symphony chose for its regular winter concerts—not only Rodzinski, but also Walter, Monteux, Stokowski, Reiner, Szell, Ormandy, Mitropoulos, Golschmann, Steinberg, Iturbi, and Barlow; and there were soloists of equal rank—Rubinstein, Schnabel, Serkin, Horowitz, and Hofmann among the pianists; Milstein, Stern, and Morini among the violinists; Traubel and Kipnis among the singers. The series, which began in the summer of 1943, reached its climax in the spring of 1947 in a tour that could boast

---

* Musicians of today are apparently of tougher stuff than those of 1944: the retirement age is now sixty-five for all Philharmonic-Symphony employees, whether they are office workers or wind-instrument players, and it may even be stretched to sixty-eight in some cases. Dollar benefits are now more than five times what they were in 1944.

Stokowski, Ormandy, Szell, and Mitropoulos as the conductors, and Traubel as the soloist, and that took the orchestra to seventeen states.

The other venture into a popular medium came at about the same time. On May 1, 1947, the Society was able to offer, for the benefit of the orchestra's Pension Fund, a preview of Boris Morros's film *Carnegie Hall,* "Featuring / THE PHILHARMONIC-SYMPHONY ORCHESTRA / and / BRUNO WALTER / LEOPOLD STOKOWSKI / WALTER DAMROSCH / FRITZ REINER / ARTUR RODZINSKI / JASCHA HEIFETZ / GREGOR PIATIGORSKY / ARTUR RUBINSTEIN / LILY PONS / RISË STEVENS / JAN PEERCE / EZIO PINZA." Though Harry James, the jazz trumpeter, and Vaughan Monroe and his orchestra had important parts in the film, the invitation did not mention them, presumably because they were not considered to be of equal dignity with the Philharmonic-Symphony Orchestra and its conductors and soloists. The plot of the movie was more tolerant; it dealt with a boy who chose to be a jazzman rather than a "serious" musician, but who nevertheless succeeded in getting to the stage of Carnegie Hall with a performance of a *57th Street Rhapsody.*

The radio series and the movie were not originated by Rodzinski, but he participated in them personally and they added to the air of busy music-making that enveloped the Philharmonic during his tenure as Musical Director.

When the contributions of Rodzinski's term were summed up—the well-designed seasons, the orchestral discipline, the strengthened repertory, the encouragement of young American conductors—it seemed that the Philharmonic had not enjoyed such a period of artistic security and purposefulness for as far back as anyone could remember. Said Virgil Thomson: "Today the Philharmonic, for the first time in this writer's memory, is the equal of the Boston and Philadelphia orchestras and possibly their superior. . . . Artur Rodzinski has done more for the orchestra in that respect than any other conductor in our century has done. Mahler and Toscanini were greater interpreters, were not such great builders. If Stokowski and Munch, also great interpreters, have been able . . . , as guests, to play upon the orchestra in full freedom and to produce from it sonorous and expressive beauties of the highest quality, that achievement has been made possible by Rodzinski's . . . careful training."[203]

It took everyone by surprise therefore—the orchestra, the public, and probably even most of the Philharmonic's Board of Directors (who had just offered Rodzinski a new three-year contract)—when Rodzinski suddenly resigned in the middle of the 1946–47 season, accusing Arthur Judson, the Society's Manager, of interfering with his artistic privileges and responsibilities. "The three pillars of a soundly run orchestra," he told reporters, "are the board, the manager, and the musical director. As the New York Philharmonic is run, these three pillars are not of equal importance, as they must be. The board and musical director revolve around the manager as if they were satellites." The press worked the matter over thoroughly, mostly taking Rodzinski's side. Some attempts were made at reconciliation, but they were not successful. After February 3, 1947, the line "ARTUR RODZINSKI, Musical Director," which had appeared on all Philharmonic programs since August 1, 1943, was dropped. Rodzinski accepted a new position as head of the Chicago Symphony Orchestra, and the New York Philharmonic was once more without a leader.[204]

The Philharmonic was now understandably sensitive about giving anyone else the title of Musical Director, but the Rodzinski years, despite their drawbacks, had taught the Board the important lesson that the artistic direction had to be coordinated by some authoritative and qualified figure, even if a different title had to be given him. The prospectus for 1947–48 began with the following announcement:

THE PHILHARMONIC-SYMPHONY SOCIETY OF NEW YORK announces, for its 106th year, the appointment of the distinguished conductor Bruno Walter as Musical Adviser. In this capacity Mr. Walter will supervise the personnel of the orchestra, the choice of fellow-conductors and soloists, and the general over-all planning of programs to insure a balanced and brilliant season. . . .

In accepting the post of Musical Adviser—a title he himself chose—Bruno Walter stated: "When the Philharmonic-Symphony Society, in 1943, honored me with an invitation to become its Musical Director, I felt obliged to answer that, because of my age, I did not feel able to fulfill the manifold obligations connected with such a position and especially to cope with the very extensive concert schedule of the Society . . . But, in this situation, as a friend of the Philharmonic-Symphony Society and in view of my many years of association with the orchestra, I feel I have a moral obligation to put my services at the disposal of the Society."

The second paragraph of this statement seemed designed to inform the public that Walter had been offered the position of Musical Director, and had declined it, *before* Rodzinski had been offered it. Walter, seventy-one years old and one of the most eminent conductors of his time, was entitled to stand on his professional dignity. Born in Berlin in 1876, he had become assistant to Gustav Mahler in Hamburg when he was still in his teens. At the age of twenty-four he had been appointed conductor at the Royal Opera House in Berlin, but had chosen to leave that post to serve again with Mahler at the Vienna Opera. Since 1913 he had worked as opera and concert conductor in the principal cities of the world, earning a name for himself as an interpreter of the German-Austrian music of the Classic and Romantic eras, and especially of Mozart and Mahler. Fleeing the Nazis in 1938, he had taken refuge first in France and then in the United States, of which he had recently become a citizen. Although his first guest-conducting appearances in the United States, in 1923, had been with Damrosch's Symphony Society, he had conducted the Philharmonic-Symphony often in the early 1930s and again since 1941. In New York he had also worked, with outstanding success, for the NBC Symphony and the Metropolitan Opera. He was highly regarded as pianist and accompanist, too, and was the author of several books on music, one of which (the autobiographical *Theme and Variations*) had just been issued in the year before his appointment as Musical Adviser of the Philharmonic. In 1947 Bruno Walter was one of the great personages of the world of music.

During the next two years Walter, whose international reputation was built on his smoothly rounded interpretations of the standard German-Austrian works, made an exceptional effort (no doubt in an attempt to ward off anticipated criticism) to diversify his repertory. He still gave most of his program time to his familiar favorites—Beethoven, Brahms, Bruckner, Mahler, Richard Strauss (Mozart was surprisingly absent). But he also found time in the 1947–48 season for symphonies by Daniel Gregory Mason, Douglas Moore, and Paul Hindemith, and in 1948–49 for a composition of Norman Dello Joio's (he had no more room for novelties in that year because a Beethoven cycle took up no fewer than nineteen of the twenty-six concerts that he conducted). Compared with his extremely conservative record in his earlier seasons as conductor and guest conductor of the Philharmonic, this may have represented a certain liberalization. But Walter's tastes remained confined for the most part to the German-Austrian late-Romantic literature, and when he ventured to play anything either a little newer or a little older—the twentieth-century compositions that we have just menioned, for example, or the Mozart for which he was renowned—he flavored it with a German-Austrian late-Romantic performance style. His Mozart had a lot of Mahler in it. This was an important ingredient in the secret recipe that led John Erskine, as a spokesman for thousands of others, to marvel at the special revelations of "Bruno Walter . . . who uncovers fresh wonders in Mozart." That Walter was in his seventies at this time does not in itself account for his conservatism; Koussevitzky and Stokowski at the same age (to apply again the gauge that we have already used to measure Toscanini's conservatism) never tired of satisfying their intellectual curiosity and that of their listeners with a constant flow of new music and new sonorities. One must simply say that Walter, in an age of specialization, had chosen to act as curator of one small wing of music's museum.

As a guest conductor Walter had the artistic right to indulge his specialized preferences, but as Musical Adviser for the principal orchestra of one of the world's music capitals, he had the responsibility to see that a balanced schedule was made available to the public. In this he succeeded admirably. The repertory for the whole season was much more varied than one would guess from Walter's own programs. This was accomplished over the two seasons from 1947 to 1949 by wisely encouraging the conductors who shared the work with him to indulge their very different and very individual talents. They were Mitropoulos, Stokowski, Szell, Munch, and the orchestra's Assistant Conductor, Walter Hendl; and among them—each contributing according to his own tastes and aptitudes—they enlivened the concerts with an assortment of composers of many schools and periods. Even a partial list for the two seasons reveals the variety. Of the older composers there were Rameau and Vivaldi. From the nineteenth century there were Chabrier, Bizet, Lalo, and Chausson among the French, and Mussorgsky and Borodin among the Russians, as well as Verdi and Tchaikovsky, who, much as they were played elsewhere, would not have been likely to appear on Walter's own programs. Of composers who straddled the nineteenth and twentieth centuries, there were Debussy, Rimsky-Korsakov, Fauré, Saint-Saëns, Griffes, Satie, d'Indy, Charpentier. For the twentieth century there were composers from every part of the world (many of whom had ended by living in the United States)—Bartók, Bloch, de Falla, Honegger, Khachaturian, Krenek, Martinů, Menotti, Messiaen, Milhaud, Poulenc, Prokofiev, Rathaus, Ravel, Roussel, Schnabel, Schoenberg, Shostakovich, Stravinsky, Walton, Webern; and native American composers of various age groups—Barber, Bauer, Copland,

Dello Joio, Gershwin, Gould, George, Harris, Mennin, Schuman, Scott, Siegmeister, Thomson, Cowell, Diamond, Hanson, Herrmann, Kreutz, Luening.

Such a list of American composers requires a qualifying observation if it is not to be misleading. It gives no hint that the turnover in American pieces was so rapid that, although there might be lots of American names on the list, no one piece was likely to become familiar enough to win a place in the standard repertory. This was so not only in Bruno Walter's time but throughout the Philharmonic's history (it is only a little less true today), and not only in the Philharmonic, for that matter, but in most of the nation's orchestras. The habits of American musical life have tended to produce a class of "distinguished but seldom-played composers." Except for the works of a few of the most prominent composers, such as Copland, Gershwin, and Barber, an American composition was not ordinarily played more than once or twice by the same American orchestra. Many a work was given its first performance in a New York Philharmonic concert but was never again heard by the same public. Yet so much prestige attached to even a single performance by the New York Philharmonic-Symphony that it was often sufficient to establish the composer as "known." The result was that he could be respected as a name for the rest of his life on the basis of one or two such performances, and yet never really function as a composer in living communication with a public, because there were not enough repetitions of his music to allow audiences to accept it as a regular part of their listening experience. Examples of highly talented professional composers who were treated in this way—honored but not heard—are David Van Vactor and the late Quincy Porter, both of whom wrote symphonies that were given Philharmonic-Symphony Awards and first performances in the 1930s but were never played again by the Society after that. Douglas Moore's Symphony in A (to take one of the pieces conducted by Bruno Walter in 1948) did have one more performance by the Philharmonic, in 1954, but only because Columbia University hired the orchestra in that year to present a program of music by its faculty members as part of the celebration of the university's bicentennial.

The seasons that Bruno Walter supervised were as lively as most of the Philharmonic's subscribers cared to have them. Nevertheless it was at this time that the young Leonard Bernstein, who had taken over Stokowski's New York City Symphony at the City Center, was finding a new public of extremely enthusiastic supporters among those for whom the programs of the Philharmonic and of Toscanini's NBC Symphony were not adventurous enough. It was an early sign, not fully appreciated at the time by the musical seismologists, of tremors to come.

Although Bruno Walter was the Philharmonic's Musical Adviser from 1947 to 1949, he did not have the largest share of the concerts. The most active roles were taken by Stokowski and Munch in the first year, and Stokowski and Mitropoulos in the second year. Those who were speculating as to who might be the next conductor of the Philharmonic could eliminate Walter, who had already indicated years before that he considered himself too old for the job, and Munch, who became the regular conductor of the Boston Symphony Orchestra in 1949. It looked, therefore, as though either Stokowski or Mitropoulos might be the choice. The Philharmonic played it safe for 1949–50 by appointing *both* as a transitional step.

Chapter 26

The Old Order Changeth
(1949–58)

The double conductor was a device that the Philharmonic had used in the past as a bridge between two regimes. There were the Stransky-Mengelberg years that paved the way for Mengelberg's take-over. There were the Mengelberg-Toscanini seasons that prepared for Toscanini's assumption of power. And Barbirolli had shared a season with Rodzinski before being named conductor. Now Stokowski and Mitropoulos were both designated as conductors for 1949–50, each conducting about a third of the season, with smaller batches of concerts being taken by guest conductors.

Mitropoulos[205] had appeared with the Philharmonic-Symphony for the first time in 1940–41, and had returned many times since then. He had succeeded, during those visits, in winning over the musical "vanguard" of the city by his attentions to new music and by his technical gifts (especially his prodigious powers of memorization), without losing the favor of the general public, which was attracted by the emotional abandon of his conducting style. As he worked with the Philharmonic-Symphony in 1949–50, it became clear to the management and the Directors that he was building up both a "musical reputation and [a] personal following," and in the next two years his role and his rank were increased, step by step. For 1950–51 he alone held the title of Conductor, carrying half of the season by himself, with four guest conductors dividing the remaining concerts among them. And for 1951–52 he was given three fifths of the concerts and was also appointed Musical Director, with all the prerogatives and responsibilities that had been assumed to go with that title since Rodzinski's time.[206]

Both Mitropoulos and Stokowski were "musical directors" by temperament and belief, in any case, with or without the title; both had the broad interest in many schools of music, from old to new, the imagination to take a long view, and the desire to reach a widening portion of the city's public. This fortunate circumstance guaranteed, even while they were joint conductors, that the Philharmonic's programs would have the breadth and variety that resulted from their colorful personalities and lively musical curiosity. With the added contribution of the guest conductors, the Philharmonic may not have had a neatly unified program, but it certainly had one that represented some of the most varied currents, from conservative to modern, in the musical stream.

Inside music and outside it, the time after World War II was a time of change. The forces of reform—economic, social, and political—that had been released in the New Deal of the 1930s accelerated during and after the war. The wartime boom, which was interrupted only by mild recessions in the long period from 1939 to 1953, was combined with a sufficient redistribution of the nation's wealth to give lower-income groups the means for enjoying some of the cultural goods that had previously been considered the exclusive property of the affluent. Along with this, and often inseparable from it, went a social and political democratization. A big bloc of the population felt that it was newly enfranchised, not only economically, politically, and socially, but also culturally. Paperback books, exploited as an economic expedient during the war, were changing the reading habits of the nation. Schools and colleges of all kinds were flooded with applications for admission, first because of the encouragement of the GI Bill of Rights (the educational benefits that Congress provided for ex-servicemen) and later because of the bumper crop of war babies. Higher education, formerly the preserve of the wealthy, became (for that very reason, as well as for its inherent value) a desired hunting ground for those with a certain amount of new money in their pockets. In the arts this expansion meant a new public, a new student body, and a new market.

The world of music reflected these changes. It was a time of musical crosscurrents, some of them within the traditional sphere of the Philharmonic, but many of them beyond its boundaries. There was a growing insistence on the part of composers that the great symphony orchestras, if they were really to be the institutions of public service that they had for some time been claiming to be, could no longer favor so predominantly the conservative elements that made up the bulk of their repertory. But the variety of the claimants for attention was dizzying. There were the twelve-tone and serialist composers, the more or less folksy nationalists, the atonal expressionists, the neo-Classicists (soon dividing by fission into neo-Baroque, neo-Romantic and Neo-everything-else schools), the partisans of symphonic jazz, and the musical left of the avant-garde with its various Trotskyite factions. Meanwhile, outside the formal communities of symphony and opera, "popular" music and jazz were splintering in a dozen directions, with their own affinities and antagonisms and snobberies, from bop to rock and roll, and from wildflower to hydroponically cultivated folk music. The scene was full of contradictions. Within ten or twelve years after the war, the number of symphony orchestras in the United States, ranging from the New York Philharmonic to community and college orchestras, had reached approximately one thousand, most of them founded since 1940; yet there was not one of them that did not complain about its financial condition. There were dozens upon dozens of opera companies and "workshops" in conservatories, colleges, and theaters around the country, yet there was not one full-time opera house in all the United States—even the Metropolitan ran for only a fraction of the year—and at the same time American singers of the finest professional quality were being grown in such numbers that they had to be exported to Europe, where shrewd impresarios staffed their opera houses with them. It was demanded on the one hand that the established musical institutions, such as the Philharmonic, the Boston Symphony, and the Metropolitan Opera, accept educational responsibilities, and on the other hand, that they step down (or up—according to some viewpoints) to the level of "the people."

Mitropoulos and the Philharmonic were caught up in the maelstrom of the changing times. There is a revealing statement of Mitropoulos's attitude in an Introduction that he wrote in 1952 for a book entitled

Ten Operatic Masterpieces (by Olin Downes, then music critic of the New York *Times*):

> Although I am a conductor specializing in symphonic music, I must confess that my heart since my childhood has been very close to the theater as a whole and naturally also to that delightful, artificial, stylized musical theater, that enchanting conventional life called opera. I must confess also that I have always felt, besides the desire to give my services as a devotee to my art, the ambition of taking the attitude of an educator and cherished the dream of bringing music to greater numbers of people. In playing symphonic music, let us say, abstract music, which is in itself an architectural delight of sounds but is addressed to an already initiated audience of music lovers and therefore to a minority, I have always felt myself kept afar from reaching large numbers of people. Therefore, every time I have an opportunity to conduct an opera, I feel immensely happy, because that is the moment and the opportunity for me to reach more people and come closer to their hearts—through music which describes the feelings of life, together with words, actions, and dramatic situations. That is the opera, and it is a pity that here in the United States there are, in proportion to its size, so few operatic enterprises.

Mitropoulos had the opportunity to court both of these audiences —the opera public, and the "greater numbers of people" that he had always dreamed of reaching—even before he was given the full rank of Musical Director. In December of 1949, when he was still sharing the conductorship with Stokowski, he gave a performance of Strauss's *Elektra* in concert form that was so successful that for the following season he was encouraged to present in concert form three more works that were originally intended for the theater: Berg's opera *Wozzeck,* Ravel's opera *L'Heure Espagnole,* and Milhaud's music for the Aeschylus-Claudel play *Les Choéphores.* In subsequent seasons he added Schoenberg's "monodrama" *Erwartung,* Monteverdi's *Orfeo,* Busoni's *Arlecchino,* Milhaud's *Cristophe Colomb,* and substantial portions of Mussorgsky's *Boris Godunov* and Wagner's *Die Walküre* and *Götterdämmerung.*

All of these were still intended for a sophisticated audience, but the "greater numbers of people" were approached in September 1950 when Mitropoulos and the Philharmonic-Symphony appeared as the stage attraction, four shows a day, at the Roxy Theatre for a program featuring on the screen Tyrone Power and Orson Welles in the romantic film *The Black Rose*. This idea seems to have been worked out with Spyros Skouras, who was an important figure in film circles and had become a member of the Philharmonic's Board of Directors when his fellow Greek Mitropoulos became active in its affairs. The concerts were billed as the "First Broadway Appearance" of the Philhar-monic-Symphony Society of New York, the word "Broadway" being used in the sense of "popular theater"—geographically speaking, the Philharmonic had appeared on Broadway many times, including its earliest concerts at the Apollo Rooms at 410 Broadway. The full orchestra of 104 musicians was employed, with Eileen Farrell as so-prano soloist. Throughout a two-week period, the Philharmonic gave four forty-five-minute concerts a day. Four partially different programs were used (that is, some numbers were repeated from one program to another), each being given for about half a week. The programs were made up, for the most part, of tested popular favorites. Here are two of them by way of sample:

September 8 through 11, 1950
Smetana—Overture to *The Bartered Bride*
Tchaikovsky—Two movements from Symphony No. 5
Verdi—Aria, *"Pace, pace, mio Dio"* (Eileen Farrell)
De Falla—Three Dances from *The Three-Cornered Hat*

September 12 through 14, 1950
Weber—Overture to *Euryanthe*
Prokofiev—*Classical* Symphony
Verdi—*"Pace, pace, mio, Dio"* (Eileen Farrell)
Wagner—Overture to *Tannhäuser*

Two more weeks of Roxy performances were given at the end of the same season, in May 1951, this time with young Michael Rabin (the fifteen-year-old son of one of the Philharmonic musicians) as violin soloist, and with Edouard Nies-Berger, the Philharmonic's organist, playing Bach before the orchestra was put on stage by a specially built, mechanized ten-ton car. On the screen was *I'd Climb the High-est Mountain,* starring Susan Hayward and Bill Lundigan.

The reactions to the Roxy engagements were surprisingly favorable. The public turned out in great numbers though the films offered were not extraordinary; for the September appearances alone, 205,000 people at-tended—the equivalent in audience numbers of one hundred concerts at Carnegie Hall. The critics seemed to be so thrilled by the social implications of these democratically oriented concerts that they did not bring up the questions that some of the city's conservatives and sophisticates were asking: whether it was not demeaning for the Phil-harmonic-Symphony to serve as the added attraction to a movie (there was disagreement even among the Society's Directors on this point), whether the public would be educated to respect the Philharmonic's work by programs that leaned so far toward the pop side and were not truly representative of the Philharmonic's repertory, whether it was right that not one American piece should have been played on any of these concerts. On the contrary, the critics rejoiced in the full and responsive houses, the quality of the performances, and even the pro-gram-making. And in the last analysis, with or without critical approval, the Philharmonic had certainly taken a significant step. It had ventured outside its familiar privileged halls, not just to go slumming, but to tell "the others" that it was willing to work for them, if they were ready to buy its services.

The Roxy engagements also had another purpose—to make more work for the Philharmonic's players. The attitude of orchestra men toward their own profession was beginning to change at this time. They thought of themselves as musical artists, but they also felt that they were entitled to the kinds of benefits that ordinary unionized working-men were gaining for themselves in the changing American society. The management and the Directors of the Philharmonic were in gen-eral sympathetic to the needs of the musicians and sometimes even solicitous for their welfare. In 1944, when the Society had modernized its Pension Fund, the official announcement had declared: "This step not only insures the maintenance of the orchestra at the highest pos-sible artistic level, but is also consonant with sound social thinking. The fact that the society is a non-profit institution should not deprive its loyal employees of the benefits they would receive were they em-ployed in industry." The minimum weekly salary was raised for the season 1948–49 from $110 to $125, for 1951–52 to $130, and for 1954–55 to $145. All the principal players earned much more than the minimum—a number of them even double the minimum—and the salary scales seemed quite respectable on paper until one observed that the contracts ordinarily guaranteed only twenty-eight weeks of work out of the year. Even counting the Lewisohn Stadium concerts which the men could play in the summers, there would be only thirty-four to thirty-six weeks of employment in the year—and the pay scale was lower in the summer than in the regular season. That is why the orchestra men were constantly pressing for longer seasons and why the administration was pleased to obtain such extra engagements as the Roxy concerts or the subsidized tours that were made possible from time to time. The utopian dream of every Philharmonic man was that one day he might have a year-round job as other respectable citizens did. In the meantime, he had to spread the income from thirty-four or thirty-six weeks over the expenses for fifty-two, and a large part of the wage increases was eaten up by steadily rising prices.

The total budget of the Philharmonic had crossed the million-dollar line in 1947 and again in 1949; and throughout the seven years that Mitropoulos was conductor, from 1950 to 1957, it was always between a million and a million and a half dollars. Ticket sales usually covered only about half of this. If you added to them the smaller amounts earned from phonograph recordings and radio, and some income from invested funds like the old Pulitzer endowment, the Philharmonic could take care of about four fifths of its budget. The last fifth, however, had to be made up from gifts and contributions of all sorts, from the Directors, the Auxiliary Board, the Guarantors' Fund, and other sources. Each year it was possible to scrape together without too much difficulty about half the amount necessary to cover that deficit. But the securing of the final portion, the net deficit, which might easily come to $150,000 for a typical season, seldom failed to provoke its annual crisis, regularly relieved by the generosity of a few of those interested individuals with whose friendship the Philharmonic had been blessed for most of its existence.

But times were changing in the 1950s. "Because of high taxes," read an announcement that was printed in the programs of the spring of 1951, "large gifts have all but disappeared. Meanwhile expenses continue to mount. No orchestra in the United States can maintain its musical standards and charge enough for tickets to cover its costs. Even so, the Federal admissions tax of 20% precludes considering higher prices under present conditions." To broaden the base of contributions for meeting the deficit, a new group of supporters was formed, known as the Friends of the Philharmonic-Symphony Society. To the astonishment of the skeptics, the Philharmonic succeeded by this simple plan in rounding up another reserve of public-spirited music lovers. In the very first campaign in 1951, 53 chairmen assisted by

301 workers were able to raise $79,565 from 2,730 contributors. All that the contributors received in return, except for the satisfaction of their good deed, was an invitation to two of the orchestra rehearsals. For the 1952 campaign the figures went up to 75 chairmen, 589 workers, 3,426 contributors, and $110,678 taken in. Further financial assistance came with the repeal, effective November 1, 1951, of the 20 per cent Federal admissions tax on concert tickets, and with liberalization of the income tax law in 1952 and 1954 to permit larger deductions for contributions to organizations like the Philharmonic.

Yet the officers of the Society knew very well that the expenses were likely to continue their climb, while the revenues had a top limit that could not easily be exceeded. At the beginning of the season of 1952–53, Floyd G. Blair, the President of the Society, addressing its annual meeting, had reminded the members that along with the continuing economic boom there was a continuing inflation which had to be taken into account in interpreting the big amounts in the orchestra's budget. Between the decreased buying power of the dollar and the growing emancipation of the musicians as professionals, all orchestra costs were mounting. But, Blair emphasized, "although expenses increase, Carnegie Hall's seating capacity cannot be enlarged. Nor can ticket prices be raised to compensate fully for increased costs. If pushed too high, receipts begin to fall off. Our experience indicates that while the public attending the concerts may be counted on to pay one-half or perhaps more of the great cost of maintaining an orchestra, the other half must be met by gifts or special sources of revenue." He was afraid that at some time in the not too remote future the orchestras of the country might have to turn to the government as the only source of help that was left to them. He personally was against outright government subsidies, but if some sort of government help became essential to the continued life of our musical organizations, he felt that it would be "better to accept it than to see them shrink in importance and many perhaps pass out of existence."

In the face of all these difficulties the Philharmonic tried nevertheless not to curtail the natural expansion of its activities where they seemed to be for the good of the public and the orchestra. It had become so expensive for the orchestra to travel, for example, that tours were certainly not justifiable from a business viewpoint. But they provided extra weeks of work for the men, they added to the orchestra's prestige, and they served educational and cultural purposes; therefore they were

continued either with private financing or, after the inauguration of the
State Department's cultural exchange program in 1954, with some government support. There had been tours to the Midwest and the South
under Stokowski and Walter in 1948–49. There was a brilliant series
of fourteen concerts at the Edinburgh Festival in Scotland, under
Mitropoulos and Walter, just before the 1951–52 season began, which
also carried the sound and name of the New York Philharmonic to
millions of radio listeners in Great Britain and Western Europe through
BBC broadcasts. There was another tour of southern cities of the
United States in the spring of 1954, under Mitropoulos, which worked
out so well that the Philharmonic was encouraged to undertake for the
next year its first cross-country trip since Stransky had led one in 1921
—a tour of thirty-one concerts, under Mitropoulos and Guido Cantelli, through the Midwest to California and the Pacific Northwest.

These tours, especially the trip across the Atlantic to Edinburgh,
suggested to many that the orchestra might serve as a cultural "weapon"
for the government. In the fall of 1955, under the sponsorship of the
U. S. Department of State and the American National Theater and
Academy (ANTA), the Philharmonic visited fifteen European cities
in which it played twenty-seven concerts, most of them conducted by
Mitropoulos but a few taken by Szell and Cantelli. The cities were
Edinburgh again, Vienna, Brussels, Berlin, Paris, Geneva, Basel,
Berne, Zurich, Milan, Perugia, Rome, Naples, London, and Athens (a
triumphal home-coming for Mitropoulos, who had not conducted in his
native Greece since 1938 and now returned in glory as Musical Director of one of the world's greatest orchestras). It was the first continental European tour by the Philharmonic since Toscanini's in 1930,
and this time, at least, several American composers (Gould, Barber,
Copland) and native or naturalized American soloists (Byron Janis,
Grant Johannesen, Nathan Milstein) were presented.[207] The 1955
tour was the first of several overseas journeys in which the Philharmonic
was of service to the United States as a cultural and diplomatic instrument.

The orchestra was also something of an educational instrument, on
the home front. Its weekly radio broadcasts, carried regularly by the
Columbia Broadcasting System since 1930, brought the concerts to
millions of people throughout the United States—fifteen million in a
single month was the estimate in 1956–57. Thousands of these people
became Radio Members by making small financial contributions to the

Philharmonic (in return they received the program notes by mail in advance of the broadcasts); at the peak, in 1954–55, there were more than twenty thousand Radio Members. Some of the listeners were at great distances from Carnegie Hall; in fact California vied with New York for the largest number of Radio Members. The commentators who supplied the radio audience with spoken program notes—since 1930 the list had included Olin Downes, Leonard Liebling, Pitts Sanborn, Lawrence Gilman, Deems Taylor, and James Fassett—became familiar musical guides to a nationwide public.[208] On the practical side, the income from the Radio Members and the sustaining fee from the Columbia Broadcasting System were welcome, but they were modest in amount; it was only in the years when the broadcasts were sponsored commercially by one of the industrial giants of the nation—the United States Rubber Company, the Standard Oil Company of New Jersey, Willys Overland Motors—that the added revenue to the Society and to the men of the orchestra was really large. In any case, money was not the principal consideration in the radio programs; in the mid-1950s, when America had more radios than families, the broadcasts were bound to have educational value for the public and prestige value for the Philharmonic. Similarly the royalties from phonograph recordings were not of critical importance in the Philharmonic's budget, but the recordings were valued as instruments of cultural dissemination and as winners of national and international fame for the Philharmonic.

Both radio and recordings had at first been regarded with suspicion, as dehumanizing machines, by the artists and the intellectuals. "It seems only yesterday," wrote John Erskine on the Philharmonic's one hundredth anniversary in 1942, "when to inveigh against canned music was the correct thing among the cultured." Some musicians, moreover, had feared that they were committing economic suicide by recording music to compete with their live performances. The American Federation of Musicians had authorized an expenditure of a million dollars in 1930 to fight the abhorred canned music, and ASCAP (the organization that licenses for a fee the performances of the music of member composers) had published *The Murder of Music* in 1933 to warn against the dangers to composer and performer of the mechanization of music. This was not just a paranoid fear. Within two years after recorded sound began to be successfully used in "talking" movies in the late 1920s, some eighteen thousand theater musicians had lost their jobs. As the radio stations and the jukeboxes exploited recorded music in the next decade, more live musicians had found themselves out of work. In 1942 the American Federation of Musicians, convinced that commercial use of recordings was destroying its members' employment opportunities, imposed a ban on all recording in the United States; and by 1944 the record industry, unable to hold out against this pressure any longer, had been forced to agree to the union's terms—that royalties on every record sold be paid to the union for the help of unemployed musicians. But the Taft-Hartley Act of 1947 made such royalty collections illegal, and the union, therefore, defended its interests by ordering another ban at the beginning of 1948. This time the dispute was settled by the creation of the Music Performance Trust Funds; the producers of phonograph records (later joined by the producers of television films) agreed to make cash contributions to the Trust Funds, which would be spent by an impartial trustee to employ musicians for performances open to the public without charge. Thanks to the Solomon-like wisdom with which the trustee, Colonel Samuel R. Rosenbaum, presided over the Funds, the industry and the musicians remained at peace, but the system was generally conceded to be a makeshift that would one day have to be replaced by an adequate plan of compensation to performers for the use of their talents on recordings.

In the meantime the voracious public of music consumers that had been growing since World War II was fed in the 1950s by radio (AM and FM), long-playing records (which had chased the old 78-rpm records from the field by the middle of the 1950s), and to some extent by television (30 per cent of all households in the United States owned television sets by 1952). There is no doubt that the massive infusion of music and entertainment through these media cut down the size of the paying audience in theater and concert hall. For the Philharmonic, the number of persons attending the regular concerts fell from 252,000 in the season of 1949–50 to 228,000 in 1955–56.[209] This is not to say that it was the spread of recorded and artificially disseminated music that directly reduced the live concert audience. It may have been a TV soap opera that competed with the concert, not another musical attraction. The hope was that in the long run the wide distribution of symphonic music by recordings and by radio would create new audiences and stimulate the interest of the old ones so that live attendance would actually go up. In 1954 it was estimated that Americans bought $70,000,000 worth of recordings of so-called classical music, as compared with about $750,000 in 1934.[210] It was impossible to conceive of all those records as being merely force-fed into a great public maw, never to be tasted or digested. Presumably some of those record buyers already attended live concerts and others, now that they were being familiarized with the diet, would soon want to do so. When the Philharmonic-Symphony engaged André Kostelanetz as guest conductor for the first time in 1953–54, the prospectus explained that his three special concerts would "introduce good music to new non-subscription audiences attracted to Carnegie Hall by the wide popularity of Mr. Kostelanetz on recordings and radio, as well as in concert." Radio and recordings, which once had seemed to symphonic musicians to be monsters inspiring fear, now seemed to be potentially generous creatures inviting exploitation for a higher good.

The Philharmonic took advantage, to some extent, of the expanding public for radio and recordings, and even made one venture into television—a program called *The Anatomy of a Symphony Orchestra,* showing a rehearsal under Mitropoulos, on the CBS "See It Now" program of Edward R. Murrow in 1954—but it cannot be said to have exploited them as educational media or to have explored their full potentialities. For the most part the Philharmonic merely funneled to the radio and phonograph publics the material that it was anyway using at the moment. Nor was it more adventurous in its formal educational programs, those aimed directly at children and students. The Young People's Concerts that Wilfrid Pelletier conducted from 1953 to 1957 were not conspicuously different from those that Ernest Schelling had presented three decades earlier. The number of performances was generally about the same and occasionally even smaller—two or three "elementary" concerts at Town Hall for children between the ages of five and nine, and five concerts at Carnegie Hall for those between nine and fifteen. The subject matter and the style of presentation varied somewhat with the conductor, but never so much that a parent in 1955 would fail to recognize the Young People's Concerts of his own childhood.[211] Newer were the concerts, two to four in number each season, that had been given in school auditoriums since 1952 for senior and junior high school students, in cooperation with the New York City Board of Education; these were arranged by the Philharmonic's recently formed Coordinating Committee for Music Education (part of the women's Auxiliary Board). And for adults, as a double stimulus, part educational and part promotional, the Subscription Committee chairman in 1955 started a series of lecture-discussions, "Backstage at the Philharmonic," open only to Philharmonic subscribers, with Dr. Carleton Sprague Smith as moderator.

But the scale of these efforts seemed much too small for the biggest musical organization in the biggest city of America, in a period of purported educational and cultural explosion. The officers and Directors of the Philharmonic, who were, after all, men and women of more than ordinary intelligence and good will, could not fail to sense this for themselves. Their difficulty (in addition to the inescapable fact that new activities would require new money) was that they were expected to bring to the Philharmonic's problems the artistic insights of professional musicians as well as the administrative abilities of intelligent laymen. Nevertheless in 1955–56 they took the risks of some important decisions. The central one was the commitment to join with the Metropolitan Opera Association and other artistic organizations in the creation of the new Lincoln Center for the Performing Arts, which would include a concert hall built expressly for the Philharmonic. In connection with this there was a realignment of officers: Floyd G. Blair (banker), who had been President for six years, became Chairman of the Board, and David M. Keiser (of the Cuban-American Sugar Co.), who had been a progressive force in the Society's affairs for ten years, succeeded him as President; Arthur A. Houghton, Jr. (Steuben Glass, Inc.), was elected to the newly created post of Vice-Chairman. There was also some new blood: Gerald F. Beal, a banker who had joined the Board of Directors only the year before, became Treasurer, and Amyas Ames (of the investment firm of Kidder, Peabody & Co.) was elected to the Board. All of these were men who looked forward eagerly to the "greatly expanded artistic and educational potential" that they believed the new Center would offer the Philharmonic. Houghton and Keiser represented the Philharmonic on the committee, headed by John D. Rockefeller 3rd, which had been organized to develop Lincoln Center.

The new officers took action on several fronts simultaneously. To make sure that the projected Philharmonic Hall turned out right, they arranged for visits to existing halls in the United States and Europe and for meetings with officials of other orchestras. They launched a study of activities that might be opened to the Philharmonic by location in the new Center and by closeness to other performing organizations. In a spirit of self-examination they engaged a management consultant firm, Cresap, McCormick and Paget, to survey the operations of the Society and make recommendations for their improvement. A Music Policy Committee was formed to look into the selection of repertory, conductors, and soloists.

These efforts at reform were not quite strong enough, not quite clear enough, and not quite soon enough. Some of the most powerful newspaper critics and a small but articulate segment of the public had grown impatient with what they considered to be the Philharmonic's failure to face realistically the conditions of mid-twentieth-century musical life in New York. In the spring of 1956 they attacked. Howard Taubman led with a full-page critique of the Philharmonic's modus operandi in the New York *Times* of Sunday, April 29. An eight-column headline read: THE PHILHARMONIC—WHAT'S WRONG WITH IT AND WHY. Systematically and mercilessly Taubman examined the Society's weaknesses. The orchestra, he said, was demoralized and its playing second-class. Mitropoulos he found to be "overmatched by the requirements of the Philharmonic post": weak in some of the most important areas of the repertory, and inadequate as an orchestral drillmaster. The choice of guest conductors and of soloists was too narrow. The program-making was haphazard and without over-all design. The Board of Directors did not include enough professional musicians and, although unquestionably well-intentioned, seemed to lack a "vibrant, up-to-date philosophy." It was questioned whether the Managers of the Society, Arthur Judson and Bruno Zirato, should be permitted to divide their interests between their Philharmonic positions and their commercial involvements with the powerful Columbia Artists Management, Inc.* Taubman made some positive recommendations: appoint a new Musical Director capable of rebuilding the orchestra; make the selection of the programs the core of the season's plans and then choose the conductors and soloists required by the music; do much more to reach a wider public. To turn the tide, the

* This criticism seemed to flare up whenever a Philharmonic crisis aroused partisan emotions. Judson's dual role had been challenged, for example, by the players that Rodzinski fired in 1943, and then by Rodzinski in his turn when he had to leave the Philharmonic four years later. The critic Cecil Smith, however, defended Judson in his book *Worlds of Music* in 1952: "In the past few years, at least, statistics do not bear out the assertion that Judson uses his orchestral position to further his private managerial interests . . . Over half the Philharmonic soloists [engaged for 1952–53] had no connection with either Judson or Columbia, though roughly two-thirds of the most eligible orchestral soloists are Columbia's clients."

Board would have to "lead the way in producing a fresh, enlarged policy."

Paul Henry Lang of the *Herald Tribune* was just as severe in a series of three Sunday articles in the month of June. "It becomes more apparent with each season," he wrote, "that our orchestra, the New York Philharmonic-Symphony, is a deteriorating artistic institution." Some of the blame he too threw on the shoulders of Mitropoulos. But even more of it he allotted to "the domination of the Society by the commercial management," that is, by Arthur Judson. "It is indefensible," he argued, "for a person involved up to his neck in the exploitation of the concert industry to serve at the same time as the paid manager of what to all intents and purposes is a public trust." Lang volunteered half a dozen examples of imaginative approaches that could be taken to improve the organization. "The forward looking members of the Board, together with the musicians," he counseled, "should take the initiative, clean house, install their own management, and do some fresh thinking. By the time the Philharmonic moves to its new quarters [in the Lincoln Center] it should be a completely rejuvenated, active, and optimistic artistic society. There is no point in having a modern plant for an outmoded institution."

There were others who complained of the "holy trinity" of guest conductors, Bruno Walter, George Szell, and Guido Cantelli, who had been engaged every year from 1951 through 1956. Their continual presence, it was said, had not left sufficient room for the variety of guest conductors from all over the world that a great city like New York and a great orchestra like the Philharmonic were entitled to. All three of them, moreover, despite their outstanding abilities, were considered to be very conservative in their program-making, Walter and Szell confining themselves principally to the most familiar masterworks, and young Cantelli, Toscanini's protégé, limiting his repertory almost as much as his protector did.

The officers of the Philharmonic accepted these devastating criticisms with astonishing humility. "At the close of the season," President Keiser and Chairman Blair informed the members in their Annual Report for 1955–56, "the Society received considerable notice in the press containing valuable recommendations for which the Society, as a public institution is always grateful. Many of the items brought up by the press were at that time, and are, under active consideration by the Society's Directors. Rather than answer the articles directly, it is hoped that the ultimate results of the Society's actions will speak for themselves." This was on September 10, 1956. By the time the Philharmonic gave its first concert of the new season on October 18, the result of one of the actions was already evident. Arthur Judson, who had still been listed as a Manager at the time of the report, had retired,[212] and Bruno Zirato had been given the new title of Managing Director. (George E. Judd, Jr., remained his assistant.)

In the conducting department no revolutionary changes could be anticipated, since most conductors make their commitments at least a year in advance. Mitropoulos would have to remain as Musical Director at least for 1956–57. A new look in the list of guest conductors seemed to be a response to the newspaper criticisms but it actually reflected arrangements made by the Society before the concerted newspaper attacks of May 1956. Leonard Bernstein was back after five years of absence from the Philharmonic podium, and there were also Paul Paray, the French conductor who was Musical Director of the Detroit Symphony, Max Rudolf of the Metropolitan Opera, and Igor Stravinsky as conductor of his own works. Of the old familiar faces, Bruno Walter and Guido Cantelli were scheduled to reappear, but the tragedy of Cantelli's death—he was killed in an air crash in November 1956, shortly before his first scheduled concert of the season—made it necessary for other conductors to take over his concert dates; the Hungarian conductor Georg Solti and the Brazilian composer Heitor Villa-Lobos were among those who did so. A few months after Cantelli's death it was announced that the eighty-year-old Bruno Walter would "cease his regular guest conducting activities" at the end of the season. But these changes proceeded from natural causes; they were not responses to the criticisms.

Evidence of a real shake-up in the conducting situation came in the spring of 1957 when the preliminary announcement for the 1957–58 season was issued. Mitropoulos was no longer Musical Director. Instead, he and Leonard Bernstein were listed equally as Principal Conductors; Bernstein, moreover, was given the additional title of Musical Director of the Young People's Concerts. There could be little doubt about the significance of these arrangements: once more the Philharmonic was using the double-conductor play, and the outcome was predictable. Although there was an impressive line-up of guest conductors, none of them was in the running for the principal post.[213] And Mitropoulos, though he was dividing the season with Bernstein, could not be taken seriously as a candidate. Certainly he had not been demoted from Musical Director to co-conductor only to be promoted up again. Howard Taubman, in a New York *Times* article of May 12, 1957, evaluating the plans for the season of 1957–58, questioned even Mitropoulos's ability to maintain proper standards of orchestra discipline, morale, and execution during the approaching year. "He has had ample opportunity," wrote Taubman, "and has failed. One does not question his sympathies for certain modern schools and his gifts of temperament and personality. But he appears to have neither the interest nor the special talent for the meticulous training or sustained leadership which inspires an orchestra to live up to its highest potentialities, whatever the music." Mitropoulos was actually a great favorite with the orchestra men for his kind, warm, democratic manner, his generosity in making contributions for their financial needs, and his almost religious dedication to his art. His tastes for opera and for certain of the recent American and European composers exposed the orchestra to a considerable amount of music that it had not played before and that it therefore found interesting, at least for a while.[214] His remarkable memory filled the musicians with awe: when he rehearsed without a score, he knew by heart each player's part down to the last sharp and flat, the last sixteenth note, and even the rehearsal numbers. Yet there were some observers who recognized that it was more a visual than an aural memory. In fact, Mitropoulos did not seem to be very sensitive or very demanding in his aural standards: the Philharmonic often played uncomfortably out of tune under his direction, and in the Romantic and modern literature, when he was carried away by his emotional involvement in the music, the orchestral tone was frequently very rough and the lines were sometimes out of balance. The breadth of Mitropoulos's musical interests and his acceptance of the conductor's responsibilities as educator had led to hopes that he would prove himself a real Musical Director, but these hopes had remained partially unfulfilled. The simplicity and naïveté that were so charming in him as a man were sometimes unbecoming in a cultural leader of one of the world's most sophisticated cities. For Mitropoulos to go on performing Baroque music, for example, without the basso continuo and with all the stylistic baggage of nineteenth-century Romanticism was no longer acceptable in a city in which Paul Henry Lang, one of the world's leading musicologists, was music critic of the *Herald Tribune* and in which every postwar college boy knew the conventions of eighteenth-century music performance from his required music course.

"The Bach Suite in D (No. 3)," wrote Lang of a Mitropoulos performance in November 1956, "struck me like one of those amusing maps entitled 'A New Yorker's idea of the West,' where geography is distorted in fantastic fashion. There was a lot of fast sawing by a huge orchestra, the contrapuntal lines were lost, the cadences testified to the rugged individuality of the members of the orchestra, the timid trumpets contributed a bit of color instead of proudly dominating the scene, the oboes could not be heard, and of course the absence of the harpsichord or piano (the latter was on the stage!) resulted in holes in the harmony."

Hardly six weeks of the season of 1957–58 had gone by with Mitropoulos and Bernstein as joint conductors when it was announced that Bernstein had been named Musical Director of the New York Philharmonic-Symphony, with a contract for the next three years. David Keiser, the President of the Philharmonic, had invited the press to the Century Association to hear the announcement, but it was Mitropoulos who actually made it. He said with evident sincerity that he was "abdicating with joy," and that Bernstein was his choice to take over the full responsibility of the orchestra's direction. Although the press had had such a large role in what he dubbed his "abdication," there seemed to be no bitterness in his suggestions that critics should give more support to the Philharmonic. "It is all right to write what you believe," he said, "but sometimes, you should also think that when you write something disagreeable it doesn't only hurt the conductor; it also hurts the Philharmonic. The Philharmonic needs more support and less criticism. If too many critical things are printed, the public loses faith." Bernstein's appointment, said Mitropoulos, was a sign that America was now so grown up musically that it could offer such an important post to an American-born and American-trained musician. Mitropoulos probably knew as little about America's music history of the past century as most European musicians do, but he had (no doubt inadvertently) phrased his comment to make a point of great sociological importance. The sign of America's musical maturity was not that it could *produce* a musician capable of filling this important post (it had long been able to do so) but that it had finally developed the self-confidence and security to *offer* its most honored musical position to a native son. It was touching to hear the kind, generous, and well-intentioned artist make his unconsciously condescending remark from his position of weakness. Bernstein, with his feeling for the dramatic, seemed to sense these relationships. "The situation," he said, obviously moved, "is at once heartbreaking and yet it fills me with such a sense of responsibility. Mr. Mitropoulos is a great genius and I hope I'll be worthy to follow him."

The announcement came so early in the season, November 20, 1957, that every occurrence for the rest of the season tended to be interpreted as though Bernstein were already in complete charge, although officially he was still sharing the position with his senior, Mitropoulos. It was remarked that Bernstein's term had been set for three years to ensure continuity of leadership as the orchestra prepared for its move to Lincoln Center for the Performing Arts. His first televised Young People's Concert, at the beginning of 1958, was analyzed and praised not only for itself but also as an earnest of the new Philharmonic policy. "What counts," wrote Howard Taubman, now apparently an enthusiastic supporter, "is that as the incoming musical director of the New York Philharmonic, he regards this task [children's concerts] as vital and is willing to take on some of it instead of delegating it entirely to a guest or assistant conductor. Mr. Bernstein's point of view is symptomatic of the new look that members of the Philharmonic official family have been taking at their responsibility to young audiences. There are encouraging signs that in this area, too, the Philharmonic Society is waking up." When the orchestra left on another ambassadorial tour in the spring, under the auspices of the President's Special International Program for Cultural Presentations, this time spending seven weeks in South and Central America, it was hard not to regard it as more Bernstein's tour than Mitropoulos's, since the new conductor had twenty-eight of the concerts to the old one's eleven.

Some of Bernstein's innovations for 1958–59 were released to the press as early as February of 1958, and for the rest of the season New York musicians and concertgoers discussed the controversial changes as though they were already abreast of them. "Bravo for the New York Philharmonic!" cried Howard Taubman in the *Times,* perhaps with some proprietary interest, after playing the orchestra's gadfly so assiduously. "What looked like a somnambulistic organization two years ago has been transformed into an institution with ideas and imagination. The plans announced for next season reveal a progressive purpose and a creative point of view. / Leonard Bernstein, the new musical director, has not hesitated to think big in designing a blueprint for an entire season, and he has had the wholehearted support of the Board of Directors. Give Mr. Bernstein credit for the vigor and daring of a man intent on high adventure. Give the Board credit for its willingness to take risks and to break with traditional procedures."

What Taubman considered of the greatest general importance was the assumption behind everything that Bernstein was doing, that music should be an exhilarating experience. But he singled out for special praise two new ideas. The first one was that the Thursday evening concerts would be turned into informal "Previews," in which the conductor would feel free to talk to the audience about the music or about any subject that would add to the enjoyment and understanding of the program. Since the music critics would not review the program until it was repeated the next afternoon, Bernstein would, in effect, have the advantage of an extra run-through, in the presence of a live audience, before the press made their comments; Taubman thought it was very clever of Bernstein to make so interesting an invention from his necessity. The personable and articulate Bernstein would be in his natural element at these Previews. Taubman seemed a little less certain how the announced guest conductors—Dimitri Mitropoulos,[215] Sir John Barbirolli, Herbert von Karajan, and Thomas Schippers—would manage when their Thursdays came around.

The second point that Taubman lauded was the idea of giving the whole season's program an over-all plan. For example, in Bernstein's eighteen weeks as conductor he would present a survey of American music, and the guest conductors would have other themes binding their programs together. This, Taubman felt, was as it should be: he interpreted it to mean that the music would be chosen first and such details as the engagement of suitable guest artists would follow from it.

"Much remains to be done, but the Philharmonic is awake," he concluded. "It is behaving at long last as if it knows that it is functioning in the middle of the twentieth century."

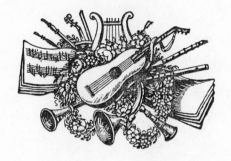

Part VII

Rebirth
(1958–)

Chapter 27

"In the Middle of the Twentieth Century"
(*The Philharmonic Changes, 1958–69*)

What a difference a few spirited men can make in a great institution!

Under Leonard Bernstein's directorship the Philharmonic finally began to adapt its habits to the conditions of the postwar world. Indeed for the first time in its history it made a start toward becoming what it had missed becoming at the several previous opportunities in its life span: a representative of American musical art, and a dispenser of musical culture to a democratic society. Bernstein did not personally invent most of the new steps that were taken—the Board of Directors and the management of the Society deserved the credit for some of the most important ones, the newspaper critics (especially Taubman of the *Times* and Lang of the *Herald Tribune*) had provoked others, and the evolving social and economic circumstances themselves produced still others —but when Bernstein was not the cause of change, he was often its instrument or its symbol. Though he actually conducted only a large fraction of the Philharmonic's new schedule, the public tended to associate his vivid personality with all of it.

Behind the scenes, meanwhile, the planning and organizing were being done by the officers, Directors, and managers, led by another of those cadres of public-spirited citizens that the Philharmonic has succeeded in mustering at several critical periods in its modern history. David M. Keiser, President of the Philharmonic from 1956 to 1963, and Chairman of the Board after that, was a successful businessman (his sugar company was thriving again, despite Fidel Castro's expropriation of the Cuban part of it) who had also been trained in music in his youth (he kept up his piano-playing well enough to take one of the solo parts of a Bach triple concerto in a Philharmonic concert). This combination of business competence and musical competence fitted him well for the position of chief executive of a symphony orchestra. When Keiser found, in 1963, that his intense involvement with the Philharmonic as President was taking more of his time than he could spare, he shifted to the less onerous office of Chairman of the Board, and Amyas Ames, who had been a Vice-President since 1958, was elected President in his stead. Ames did not have as much musical background as Keiser, but he had other virtues: a way with people (a calm, reasonable man, he seemed to be able to make others work together cooperatively), a way with money (he was a senior partner of the banking firm of Kidder, Peabody & Co., and had been raising money for the Philharmonic since 1959 as General Chairman of the Friends of the Philharmonic), and an indomitable zeal for improving the quality of life in the city at a time when, as he once admitted, most people thought that everything was "going to hell in a hack." Arthur A. Houghton, Jr., Chairman of the Philharmonic's Board from 1958 to 1963, was a man whose great wealth (he was President of Steuben Glass, Inc., and Director of Corning Glass Works) was matched by his concern for the public good; he worked not only for the Philharmonic but for a host of other civic and cultural organizations—museums, libraries, educational institutions. The professional Managing Director of the Philharmonic, when Bernstein was engaged as Music Director in 1958, was the genial Bruno Zirato, who had been with the orchestra since the Toscanini days; but in 1959 he was named Advisor to the Board, and the Associate Director, George E. Judd, Jr., took the chief managerial post. Judd was only thirty-four years old at the time, but he had been a professional manager since his early twenties; generous, high-minded, and quietly efficient, he had an important hand in the shaping of the Philharmonic's vigorous new style in the two years that were allowed him before his death. His successor as Managing Director in 1961 was his former Associate Managing Director, Carlos du Pre Moseley. Moseley was a professional musician by education: he was a good pianist (when David Keiser took part in that Philharmonic performance of a Bach triple concerto, Moseley was another of the soloists—the third was Leonard Bernstein), he had been director of the School of Music of the University of Oklahoma for five years, and he had served the United States government in several positions involving music administration here and abroad. At the Philharmonic, he had been in charge of press and public relations before getting into the managerial department, and had shown in that work the same quick mind and soft-spoken diplomacy ("the velvet hand inside the velvet glove," one musician called it) that made orchestra players and Philharmonic Directors alike feel that Moseley understood their problems. These were some of the many officers and officials whose administrative abilities and sense of social responsibility complemented Bernstein's musical talents and showmanship in the remarkable changes that the Philharmonic underwent between 1958 and 1969.

It was in the summers that the Philharmonic eventually showed its new face most clearly, and the most striking feature of that new face— the one that differed most from the way the Philharmonic used to look —was the series of free concerts that the orchestra began to give in the city's parks in 1965.

70,000, YES 70,000, HEAR PHILHARMONIC IN PARK

That was the headline on the front page of the New York *Times* on August 11, 1965. It was reporting the first of the free concerts, which had taken place the night before in Central Park. Some skeptics had doubted that blasé New Yorkers would turn out in any numbers for a free concert (the traditional attitude in New York has been that there must be something wrong with it if it's being given away for nothing). The program, moreover, was a rather heavy one, consisting of the first performance of a fanfare by William Schuman, Wagner's *Meistersinger* Overture, and Beethoven's Ninth Symphony, and the conductor was William Steinberg, not the popular idol, Bernstein. But the managers and the officers of the Society knew that when the Philharmonic had given an outdoor park concert in Milwaukee in 1964, it had drawn a serious, attentive audience of 30,000 people. The Philharmonic is more of a novelty in Milwaukee than it is in its own city, but on the other hand Milwaukee is only a tenth the size of New York.

The Philharmonic—and especially Carlos Moseley, the Managing Director—had been working on the plan for outdoor concerts for about three years. At first it had been intended to give them in Lincoln Center's Damrosch Park and the Ford Foundation had been approached for financial support, but this plan was dropped when it was learned that Damrosch Park could not be completed in time. Then it was suggested to Mayor Robert F. Wagner that the huge Sheep Meadow in Central Park be the site for the open-air concerts; he was enthusiastic but urged the Philharmonic to find a way of going to all five boroughs of the city. This meant some kind of movable stage, and Christopher Jaffe designed one that could be carried by four nine-ton trailers or, to put it more accurately, that was formed when the four trailers backed up to each other and locked together. The Philharmonic offered to find the money for all the artistic personnel and the musical expenses, if the city would take care of building the shell and moving it from borough to borough. This was agreed and the Philharmonic's burden was eased by a contributon of $57,500 from the Jos. Schlitz Brewing Company, which had sponsored the successful Milwaukee park concert. Altogether, the City of New York spent about $100,000 for the stage and other equipment and $90,000 more for operating them, and Schlitz and the Philharmonic gave almost $120,000 for the remaining expenses.* The trailerized shell was named the "Minnie" Guggenheimer Shell in honor of Mrs. Charles S. Guggenheimer of the Philharmonic's Board of Directors and Auxiliary Board, who had been a leader in presenting outdoor music in the city at the Lewisohn Stadium Concerts. The twelve Park Concerts of the Philharmonic were spread equitably among Central Park in Manhattan, Prospect Park in Brooklyn, Crocheron Park in Queens, the Botanical Garden in the Bronx, and Clove Lake Park in Staten Island.

When the second season of Park Concerts was given, in the summer of 1966, the opening one, with Leonard Bernstein conducting Beethoven's *Eroica* Symphony and Stravinsky's *Rite of Spring,* attracted the largest audience of which the Philharmonic had any record. Thomas P. F. Hoving, who was then Commissioner of Parks, estimated it at 75,000, but another official said that 90,000 would be closer.

These free concerts worked a revolutionary change in the meaning of the Philharmonic's service to the community. For all 115 of its subscription concerts of 1965–66 the Philharmonic had a paid attendance of about 325,000 admissions, but the 12 Park Concerts of 1965 alone

* The city's Department of Parks also supplied the unsung, essential, and apparently amiable cleanup squads that went to work after each performance. "These people leave the nicest trash of all," one worker remarked appreciatively to a Philharmonic official.

had an attendance of 457,000, and those of the next four seasons, though plagued by bad weather, were attended by an average of about 300,000 people each year. A handful of summer concerts had found a public equal in size to the *total* of all the subscription concerts that the Philharmonic played!

Another summer public—and a paying one—was found for the Philharmonic by the informal Promenades, conceived and directed not by Bernstein but by André Kostelanetz. For these pleasantly relaxed programs, begun in 1963, the rows of seats were removed from the parquet level of Philharmonic Hall and replaced by tables and chairs. Here the listeners could enjoy beer, wine, and champagne along with the music. (The actual serving of the refreshments was done before and after the concerts and during intermissions, but never while the orchestra was playing.) Although Kostelanetz prepared these concerts in about half the rehearsal time that an ordinary Philharmonic performance got, the programs were not ordinary "pops" material. A Russian Promenade was likely to have excerpts from a seldom-heard opera of Rimsky-Korsakov in addition to the expected Tchaikovsky favorites; a Viennese Promenade might have as many rarities of Mozart as it did Strauss waltzes; an American Promenade might offer a little-known work of the nineteenth century or the premiere of a contemporary composition. Encores, frowned upon at other Philharmonic concerts from the earliest days, were welcomed in the informal atmosphere of the Promenades; sometimes there were four or five of them. Exhibits—of paintings, costume designs, photographs, sculpture—were on view in the Hall during the Promenade season. There were nineteen or more Promenade concerts each year, usually in June.

And still another summer public came for the Festivals at Philharmonic Hall—intended as a kind of indoor, urban, air-conditioned equivalent for what other orchestras offered in the more bucolic surroundings of a Tanglewood or a Saratoga. A French-American Festival, presented in cooperation with the French government, opened on Bastille Day, July 14, 1965. Bernstein's fellow composer-conductor-pianist Lukas Foss was named Artistic Director for the Festival, which consisted of ten orchestral concerts and four chamber-music programs, with composers, conductors, singers, and instrumentalists of both nations. A Festival of Stravinsky—His Heritage and His Legacy, with ten orchestral programs and three chamber-music performances, again under Foss's direction, was the original idea for the summer of 1967; and in

the next two summers, although the Philharmonic did not put on festivals of its own, it took part in the ambitious ones that Lincoln Center
sponsored. The festival programs, intellectually more challenging than
the Promenade programs, were presumably designed to attract sophisticated audiences.

The summer projects were not isolated events. The Philharmonic, in
the "Bernstein era," was spreading out in every direction in which it had
room to spread out:

It tripled the size of its audience. In 1955–56 the total attendance for
the season had been about 250,000; by the late 1960s it had risen to an
average of 780,000 a year. Part of this increase came from the free concerts in the parks, but for the paid concerts, too, capacity crowds became the rule. Throughout the 1960s at least 90 per cent of the seats
were sold out by subscription, long before each season began, for all
Philharmonic series, including the Young People's Concerts. In fact, the
saturation point was reached: the concerts could easily have been 100
per cent subscribed in advance, with a waiting list for each ticket offered,
but the management deliberately held back a small number of seats for
"single" sale at the box office. Of these, almost all were usually sold.
Once or twice a season, a few of the single tickets might go untaken at
the box office for a program that failed to catch the public's fancy; but
ordinarily the only unsold seats for Philharmonic performances were
the handful that might occasionally be left vacant by a public so accustomed to sold-out houses that it was not optimistic enough to try for the
last few tickets just before concert time. The raising of subscription
prices in 1965–66 and again in 1967–68 did not dampen the public ardor in the least.

It became more adventurous in its tours. Extensive tours were not
new to the Philharmonic, but those that Bernstein led had a style and a
scope that set them off from their forerunners. He lent them a peculiarly
American kind of high spirits. Even when he was still co-conductor with
Mitropoulos, in the spring of 1958, he had dominated the tour of Central and South America, and had characteristically programmed a work
by a United States composer on each of his concerts. And the next
year, when he took the orchestra on a Grand Tour of Europe and the
Near East—fifty concerts in seventeen countries, from Lebanon and
Turkey to Finland and Norway, and from Russia and Yugoslavia to
Luxembourg and England—the world could tell at last that the Philharmonic was an American orchestra. Bernstein and the two conductors

who helped him on the tour, Thomas Schippers and Seymour Lipkin, were all "American-born and American-trained"; the repertory included compositions by seven American composers (Barber, Bernstein, Copland, Diamond, Gershwin, Ives, and Piston), at least one of which was heard at each concert; and the soloists were Bernstein and Lipkin as pianists, and three of the regular first-desk players of the orchestra: John Corigliano, violin, Laszlo Varga, cello, and John Wummer, flute.

In subsequent seasons the orchestra continued to take its music to new audiences in distant places—Hawaii, Alaska, Japan, Canada (coast to coast), England, Israel, and nine countries of Western Europe. In the decade between 1958 and 1968 Bernstein conducted the Philharmonic in thirty-three countries around the world. Of course there were travels in the continental United States too: twice across the whole country from ocean to ocean (in 1960 and again three years later), to eastern states (1966) and to midwestern ones (1967). And in most seasons there were quick out-of-town forays for smaller numbers of concerts, amounting to miniature tours, that were squeezed into openings in the orchestra's calendar; these were usually to communities within easy reach of New York, but swift hops to places as far away as Milwaukee and even Berlin were not unknown.

On the longer journeys the travel expenses for orchestra, equipment, and staff were much more than could be covered by ticket receipts alone, even with the sold-out houses that the Philharmonic had come to expect. Fortunately the glamour of Bernstein and the orchestra attracted financial aid from a number of sources—the governments of the United States and some of the visited countries, large industrial concerns, and private donors. The Columbia Broadcasting System, for example, sponsored the 1960 tour of continental American cities and Hawaii, and the 1961 tour of Japan, Alaska, Canada, and some cities of the southern United States; the President's Special International Program for Cultural Presentations sponsored the 1959 Grand Tour of Europe and the Near East; the Ford Motor Company flew the Philharmonic to West Berlin for two concerts in 1960; the Canadian Centennial Commission helped with the bills for the 1967 transcontinental tour of eleven performances in Canada (which became part of that country's celebration of its one hundredth anniversary); and both Trans World Airlines and the United States Department of State contributed generous sums to make possible the twenty-four concerts in Israel and Western Europe in 1968.

In Bernstein's first visits to Europe with the Philharmonic, his flamboyant conducting style rubbed some of the music critics the wrong way,
though the public, in Europe as in America, was captivated by him from
the start. But before long even the critics were on his side. Harold Schonberg of the New York *Times,* who had often been impatient with him in
the past, summarized the change at the end of Bernstein's Philharmonic
decade: "Now when Mr. Bernstein takes his orchestra on tour, . . . he
makes a series of triumphant processionals."

**The Philharmonic's new activities swelled the total number of its con-
certs.** In sheer quantity the orchestra was producing more performances
than in the past. In the 1930s and 1940s, when Toscanini, Barbirolli,
Rodzinski, and Walter held sway, the average number of concerts in a
season was 120; under Mitropoulos, from 1950 to 1957, it was 131; but
under Bernstein the average rose first to 165 and then (for the last five
years of his directorship) to 192 concerts per season. Although Bernstein did not conduct all of these himself, he nevertheless conducted
more concerts during his tenure as Music Director than any other conductor in the history of the Society, a total of 835 concerts in the period
from 1958 to 1969.†

The Philharmonic found a new ally in television. Television had been
feared by many for the competition that it offered to all live performance, and it had been blamed for part of the drop that Philharmonic attendance had suffered earlier in the 1950s. In the Bernstein period,
however, the Philharmonic's audiences and activities expanded in spite
of the continuing competition. Television may even have *helped* the
Philharmonic fill its hall, for Bernstein's TV programs had made him
the best-known musician in America, and his popularity on the screen
must certainly have been reflected in the auditorium. Bernstein was already a well-known TV personality before his appointment as Music
Director of the Philharmonic. Beginning in 1954 he had made for the
"Omnibus" television series a succession of programs in which he had
treated musical subjects with his characteristic blend of the entertaining
and the instructive; and in 1957–58, when he was still dividing the Philharmonic conductorship with Mitropoulos, but had already been given
the title of Musical Director of the Young People's Concerts, his first
season of four Philharmonic children's programs had been presented on
the Columbia Broadcasting System television network. By the next year

† He had also led 104 Philharmonic concerts as guest conductor before he became Music Director in 1958.

he had a second CBS series going, "Leonard Bernstein and the New York Philharmonic," but although it continued for a number of years, it was the Young People's Concerts that made the most lasting success. They won every award that was given in the field of educational television. They continued, year after year, on CBS's nationwide hookup (in color from 1966–67 on), capturing a wide enough public to make them attractive to commercial sponsors, such as the Shell Oil Company, the Bell System, and the Polaroid Corporation. The estimate was that ten million people in the United States alone saw and heard each of the orchestra's telecasts—without setting foot in Carnegie Hall or Philharmonic Hall, they added a huge new public to those already served by the Philharmonic. A large number of the programs, either as video tapes or as 16mm. films, were made available to schools on loan, rental, or purchase, or were syndicated for foreign TV showing. In 1969 they could be seen in twenty-nine countries, "including Sweden and New Zealand, Ireland and Israel, Iceland and Portugal, Surinam and Australia," as the Philharmonic announced with justifiable pride.

Bernstein took these television programs very seriously. They were the one Philharmonic activity that he did not interrupt during his sabbatical leave of 1964–65. There were forty-seven shows between 1958 and 1969, and Bernstein conceived, wrote, narrated, and conducted all of them himself. The subjects covered a wide range—sonata form, the music of Charles Ives, musical intervals, impressionism. "I don't talk down to them," Bernstein said of the children, and a very large number of adults found that the programs held *their* interest too. There were only four different programs in a season, but each was given twice on the same day in the concert hall, the first performance serving also as a run-through rehearsal for the telecast, and the second one being taped for later showing. Naturally, for those who could be present in the hall, the excitement of participating in an internationally famous telecast made the experience doubly rewarding. The waiting list for subscriptions was so long that some parents enrolled their children at birth.

The Philharmonic's recordings broadened its influence. Like the telecasts, the Philharmonic's phonograph recordings reached listeners both in New York City and outside it. Bernstein's popularity made it worthwhile for Columbia Records to issue well over two hundred albums—comprising many times that number of separate compositions—of his performances with the Philharmonic. In a typical year, record royalties might bring in $150,000 or $175,000 for the Society.

Consider that this represented almost 400,000 records sold each year, that each record was played over and over again, and that each playing was likely to be heard by more than one person, and you begin to appreciate how much the Philharmonic's recording program contributed to the general "spreading out" of the orchestra's influence.

The Philharmonic diversified the rosters of its guest conductors and soloists. In all Mitropoulos's years as Musical Director, the list of guest conductors had centered around Walter, Szell, and Cantelli, with smaller assignments, in one season or another, for Bernstein, Golschmann, Kostelanetz, Kurtz, Monteux, Paray, Rudolf, de Sabata, Schippers, Solti, and the composer-conductors Stravinsky and Villa-Lobos. During the Bernstein period, between 1958 and 1969, there were return engagements for most of these and for Mitropoulos himself, but dozens of other conductors were engaged as well, so that the public was given a broader sampling of the field. (See list in Backnote 216.)

The same sort of variegation showed in the roster of soloists for Philharmonic concerts, where it reflected the loosening-up of the repertory and, consequently, of the performers required to present it. This had already begun to some extent under Mitropoulos in the fifties, but it went much further under Bernstein in the sixties. Without looking into the details of who the soloists were, we can see one sign of the diversification in some unusual categories of performers—from the exotic to the vernacular—that stand out from the standard ones of piano, voice, the principal orchestral instruments, and chorus, which are the traditional guests in symphonic circles. In the 1950s there had already been occasion to use narrators and a jazz ensemble (for a composition by the Swiss composer Rolf Liebermann, conducted by Mitropoulos), as well as the Japanese koto and the Austrian zither (for Kostelanetz's concerts). But after 1958 one could find in Philharmonic programs:

- harpsichord, lute, viola da gamba, and oboe d'amore, for performances of Baroque music;
- tape recorder, *ondes Martenot,* "solo" string quartet, xylophones, Japanese *biwa* and *shakuhachi,* and several different kinds of jazz groups and chamber ensembles, for various contemporary works;
- much more use of narrators and of choruses (sometimes six or eight in a season);
- military band;
- dancers, pantomimists, and puppeteers;

• and various kinds of musical comedy performers—actors, singers, dancers—for the musical theater pieces that Bernstein sometimes incorporated into his concerts.

A strong factor in the liberalization of the repertory, and consequently of the featured performers' list, was the greater participation of André Kostelanetz as conductor after 1962, when the summer Promenades were added to his Special Saturday Night Concerts. Bernstein was enlivening the subscription concerts, but on Saturday nights and in the summers it was Kostelanetz who came up with week after week of intriguing innovations.

A special flurry of diversification was occasioned by the celebration of the Philharmonic's 125th anniversary, for which several extraordinary steps were taken in 1967–68. (The 1967–68 season was actually the 126th, but the 125th anniversary of the historic first concert of December 7, 1842, fell within it.) Conductors who had been very closely associated with the orchestra in one way or another were invited as guest conductors. Works that the Philharmonic had introduced to American audiences in the course of its long history were performed again in "a season of commemorative programming"—the definition being interpreted broadly enough to include works introduced by the orchestra's old rival, the New York Symphony Society, before it had merged with the Philharmonic in 1928. A special "birthday" concert, on December 7, 1967, repeated the first Philharmonic program (the one that is described in the Tableau that opens this book) before what the New York *Times* described as "one of the most illustrious audiences in New York musical history." A Gala Opening Night Concert had as its guest performer not an individual artist but the entire Vienna Philharmonic (founded, like the New York Philharmonic, in 1842). Eighteen new compositions were commissioned of composers of many different countries (thanks chiefly to a gift from Francis Goelet of the Philharmonic's Board of Directors) and eleven of them were finished in time to receive their world premieres during the anniversary year.[217]

The Philharmonic extended its educational activities. The postwar era, as was brought out in the preceding chapter, saw a hunger for education, sometimes for its own sake, sometimes as an aid to advancement in the world, and sometimes for "culture." Typical of the movement to bring to the millions some of the educational advantages that had previously been reserved for the thousands was the televising of the Young People's Concerts, which would otherwise have benefited only the relatively small number of children and parents physically and financially able to get into Carnegie Hall or Philharmonic Hall.

This was not the only educational service that the Philharmonic provided. Ever since the Society's surge of public spirit in the early 1920s, high school and college students had been given the privilege of buying tickets at reduced rates for certain regular subscription concerts; in the 1960s about five thousand such tickets were sold every year at $1.50 each, the difference between that and the value of the ticket being underwritten by the Society.

When Lincoln Center was established, its Constitution provided for "educating the general public" with relation to musical and performing art, and in 1960—before a single building of the Center was completed—a Lincoln Center Student Program was started. Under it the Center covered all costs for a series of Philharmonic performances (from three to eight of them) for high school students; the ticket price was never more than $1.50 and the houses were always sold out. So eager was the Center to get going on its educational program that it did not wait for the construction of the new Philharmonic Hall on its own ground, but generously sponsored the first two years of these concerts on what some people might have thought to be rival territory at Carnegie Hall. Another Lincoln Center project gave Student Awards of two or three tickets for regular subscription concerts of the Philharmonic (the Center paid for the subscriptions) as a sort of prize to one thousand outstanding high school seniors each year.

In a different line of endeavor, but still an educational one, the Philharmonic collaborated with various organizations—the American Symphony Orchestra League, the New York State Council on the Arts, the American Conductors Project, the Leventritt Awards, the Naumburg Foundation, the Mitropoulos International Music Competition—in seminars, workshops, and contests for musicians. It was from the Mitropoulos Competition that the Philharmonic drew its Assistant Conductors. Bernstein took not one but three young conductors every year as his assistants, in order to spread the educational benefits of the apprenticeship, and he helped to pay for this program through his Leonard Bernstein Foundation.

In a broad sense, Bernstein generally gave an educational slant even to his concerts for adults: his Preview concerts, for example, involved explanations of the music to the audience. And the subscription programs of each season were interrelated by didactic themes that continued through whole series of concerts. There were surveys of American, French, British, and Scandinavian music, of the concerto, of theater music, of twentieth-century problems in music, of Schumann and the Romantic movement, of the Gallic approach and the Teutonic approach, of the avant-garde, of symphonic forms in the twentieth century, and of the works of Mahler, Pergolesi, Handel, and Sibelius. These surveys were given less emphasis after 1962–63, but they were not by any means abandoned. The one on symphonic forms in the twentieth century, begun in 1965–66, ran on into the next season.

The printed program notes for such concerts naturally tended to assume an educational quality of their own. This was underlined by the appointment of university-connected scholars as program annotators for the Philharmonic: first Howard Shanet of Columbia University, in 1959, and then (when he resigned the next year in order to write this history of the Society) Edward Downes, formerly of the University of Minnesota and subsequently of Queens College in New York. Almost all the Philharmonic's previous annotators had been well-known music critics and journalists by profession. (For the complete list see Backnote 218.)

The Philharmonic increased its use of the orchestra and improved the terms of its employment. The salaries of the orchestra men rose steadily between 1957 and 1964—the minimum went from $155 to $200 a week—and at the same time the number of weeks of guaranteed employment in each season rose from thirty-two to forty-two. Nevertheless, the men yearned for something more—for the security of a year-round job. In July 1959, in the midst of all the excitement connected with the building of Lincoln Center, Alfred J. Manuti, President of Local 802 of the American Federation of Musicians, had argued that, at a time when more than $75,000,000 was being raised for the completion of Lincoln Center and when the budgeted cost of Philharmonic Hall was being increased from $8,500,000 to $9,500,000, there was no reason why the "increased needs of human beings" could not also be budgeted. Planning should begin immediately, he had said, to employ both the Philharmonic and the Metropolitan Opera orchestras on a year-round basis:

For the first time in America, let us have two orchestras whose members can finally have the economic security and peace of mind that only guaran-

teed full employment can bring. For the first time, let us be able to say
that we have given the same careful consideration to the needs of the performer, as we do to the needs of the place of performance.[219]

In the fall of 1961 the Philharmonic musicians had actually gone out
on strike over this and other issues, but after one week they had decided
to accept a contract that assured them of forty-two weeks of employment by 1963–64. Finally, in the spring of 1964, the Philharmonic and
the union were able to announce jointly that they had reached agreement on a contract for year-round employment with four weeks of paid
vacation—"this important goal," Amyas Ames, President of the Philharmonic, called it, "which has long been the dream of symphony
orchestra associations and orchestra musicians throughout the country." When the new contract went into effect for the 1964–65 season it
was the first time that an entire symphony orchestra in the United
States had operated on such a fifty-two-week formal contract, but it was
only a matter of time before the others followed suit (the Philadelphia
Orchestra, in fact, had already announced a similar contract, but it was
not to go into operation until the 1965–66 season).

In the Philharmonic's next three-year contract, negotiated just prior
to the opening of the 1967–68 season, the advances continued: by the
end of the contract period, the minimum salary—important players
received much more—was $15,040 a year ($270 per week, plus a
guarantee of $1,000 annually for making records), paid vacations were
lengthened to six weeks, and the administration of a new Pension Plan
was put into the hands of six trustees, three of them orchestra players
elected by their fellow musicians and three of them officers of the
Society. A member who retired under the new Pension Plan was entitled to an annual benefit of $200 for each year of service; a musician
with thirty-five years of service, for example, would receive a pension
of $7,000 per year.

The expansion of the season of employment went hand in hand with
the expansion in the concert activities, each stimulating the other. With
all those man-weeks of music available, the Philharmonic could now
push ahead with its plans for summer festivals in Philharmonic Hall
and open-air performances in the parks of the city. In a sense it *had*
to do so in order to justify the full-year contracts.[220]

For the orchestra men, better pay and better benefits—together
with the satisfaction that came from the Philharmonic's growing useful-

ness to more of the city's people—made for better morale. The musicians' ordinary interests as working citizens, and their special ones as artists, were being recognized as they had never been before. The full-year contract was as much a matter of principle as of money; in fact, a clause in the contract gave the musicians the option of *not* working for certain weeks of the summer season if they preferred (and if the orchestra could spare them), and a number of them exercised that option. But the whole orchestra was elated by the feeling, which the Park Concerts gave them, of breaking through to the community. "Even if a little is lost in the translation," said one of the violinists, referring to the artificial amplification of sound that the great outdoor spaces required, "it brings the orchestra to the people, and that's the important thing."

The continuing social emancipation of the orchestra revealed itself in two other signs, faint but not to be ignored—the appointment of a Negro violinist (Sanford Allen in 1962) and two female string players (Orin O'Brien, bass player, in 1966 and Evangeline Benedetti, cellist, in 1967). The Misses O'Brien and Benedetti were not the first women to play in the orchestra—there had been several harpists—but they were the first to serve as full members of the string section. And it seems likely that Sanford Allen was the first Negro in the entire history of the Philharmonic to be engaged as a full-time member.[221] Of course there had been Negro *soloists* with the Philharmonic in the past, but in this category, too, there was change: the number leaped upward in the Bernstein period, when Negro artists were heard in every season, without exception.‡

The Philharmonic enlarged the American element in its repertory and its personnel. Performances of American compositions rose from the usual 4 or 5 per cent that had been typical of the early 1950s to about 15 per cent of all performances in the 1960s. For Bernstein's own concerts the proportion of American works was even higher—close to 30 per cent—but the average for all Philharmonic performances was kept down by the largely European repertories of some of the other conductors. Among the soloists employed, both instrumental and

‡ One of the earliest Negro soloists with the Philharmonic was the Cuban violinist José White (his first name was sometimes given as Joseph or Josef), who played the Mendelssohn Concerto and the Bach Chaconne at a Philharmonic concert on December 11, 1875, with such success that he was reengaged in the same season (on March 18, 1876) to play the *Ballade et Polonaise* by Vieuxtemps and also to repeat the Chaconne, "by request."

vocal, there was a great increase of the American-born-and-trained, with at least half, and in some seasons two thirds, of the total number falling in this category. "It's more than just a symbolic gesture," said the Philharmonic's Managing Director, Carlos Moseley, in a newspaper interview shortly before the opening of Philharmonic Hall, "that all our soloists on opening night there will be Americans or Canadians." In the orchestra itself, 83 of the 106 musicians, or 78 per cent, were American-born in 1969. When John Corigliano, the American concertmaster, retired in 1966, he was replaced by another musician born and educated in the United States, David Nadien.[222] Only in the conducting department was the proportion of Americans (other than Bernstein) still on the low side: Wallenstein and Schippers were frequent guests, and Maazel was sometimes lured from his base of operations in Europe, but that was about all; even the few conductors of American birth and education who had managed to establish themselves in permanent positions in other cities were hardly ever invited for the Philharmonic's subscription concerts. Of course, an orchestra that had Bernstein as its principal conductor may have felt less need to seek out other Americans. And the Philharmonic was certainly doing better in this direction than it had done in the past, and probably better than most of the other large-city orchestras were doing. It was the younger American conductors whose legitimate expectations the Philharmonic failed to satisfy. It seemed at first that they would enjoy the three assistant conductorships that were established in 1959, with the help of the Koussevitzky Foundation and the Leonard Bernstein Foundation, to give "outstanding members of the younger generation of conductors . . . the experience of working with a major symphonic organization." Since promising Europeans had plenty of opportunities for conducting posts in their own countries, common sense suggested that the Philharmonic jobs would be used to train Americans. In the first few years this did begin to happen, but in 1963 it was decided that the Philharmonic's assistant conductorships would be given as prizes each year to the winners of the Dimitri Mitropoulos International Music Competition—a contest open to conductors from all nations—and the result was that thereafter 90 per cent of the Philharmonic's Assistant Conductors were non-Americans.

The Philharmonic was accorded wider recognition by officialdom— international, national, state, and local.

¶When the orchestra returned from its Grand Tour of Europe and the Near East in 1959, its opening-night concert at Carnegie Hall was attended by the Secretary-General of the United Nations and diplomatic representatives of each of the countries visited on the tour.

¶President Eisenhower came to New York for the ground-breaking ceremony at the site of Philharmonic Hall in 1959; Bernstein was invited to bring a chamber orchestra of Philharmonic men to Washington on the occasion of a state dinner for the visiting President of Colombia in 1960;* Mrs. Kennedy represented the White House at the opening of Philharmonic Hall in 1962; certain of the Philharmonic's tours abroad, as we have noted, were sponsored by the Federal government.

¶On the state level, the New York State Council on the Arts, in its efforts to spread the cultural riches of New York City to other parts of the state, sent the Philharmonic, conducted by Bernstein, to Troy, New York, in 1962, to give a concert for seven thousand school children. (A less official recognition of the Philharmonic's prestige in state circles could be observed during the gubernatorial election campaign of 1966, when an imaginative political group took it on itself to print and hand out, at the Philharmonic's free outdoor concerts in Central Park, program notes that bore the credit line, "Young New Yorkers for Rockefeller.")

¶On the local level, the New York City Board of Education worked with the Philharmonic on educational concerts and student admissions; and for the big free concerts in the parks of the five boroughs, the city provided the performance areas and the specially designed equipment that made the concerts possible. When Bernstein was given the Key to the City of New York, upon the Philharmonic's return from its overseas tour in 1959, he was said to be the "first figure in the cultural world" to receive that honor.

There was no mistaking the stirring-up that characterized the rebirth of the Philharmonic after 1958. More conspicuous than any of the specific changes, however, was the sheer excitement that centered around Leonard Bernstein. It sparked many of the new developments

* How deeply ingrained was the American habit of "thinking un-American" with regard to concert music was shown by the printed program for this occasion, which volunteered the following information with reference to Bernstein: "When he assumed his position with the Philharmonic in 1958, it marked the first time that a native-born and trained United States musician had held such a prominent post." Imagine boasting, instead of being ashamed, that it had taken 118 years for an American to be appointed to a prominent American post—and boasting it, of all places, in the White House before distinguished visitors from abroad!

and provided the atmosphere for all of them. When some of the innovations turned out to be disappointing and others aroused opposition, the feeling of vitality was not lost and may even have been heightened by the controversy.

Controversy there certainly was. Some of the projects that the newspaper critics had recommended or endorsed when they were ripping the Philharmonic apart from 1956 to 1958 proved to be of permanent value, but others merely reflected the critics' personal tastes and caused new complaints when they were adopted. The press had given a warm greeting to the Previews, at which the conductor could explain the music to his audience, but many listeners were irritated by the pedagogical condescension that the system seemed to encourage in any conductor who was interested enough to use it, and the Previews atrophied within a few seasons. Howard Taubman of the *Times* had demanded some over-all design for the programs of each season and had applauded Bernstein's plan to thread "themes" through groups of programs; but Taubman's successor, Harold Schonberg, found that didactic themes were not to be equated with program planning and shot some of his most sarcastic barbs at the surveys that his predecessor had endorsed. All the critics had clamored for Mitropoulos's replacement on the grounds that he was stylistically too specialized and extreme, and technically not a good enough disciplinarian, but most of them at one time or another came to say exactly the same thing about Bernstein, whose appointment they had originally approved. A revolution had been called for and a revolution had taken place, but not always on the anticipated terms. It had been insisted, for instance, that reform demanded a Philharmonic management free of entangling alliances with the commercial world of music; yet when Arthur Judson left the Philharmonic, in 1956, he was replaced not by an outsider but by his co-manager, Bruno Zirato; and he, in turn, was succeeded in 1959 by George Judd, Jr., whose father was Manager of the Boston Symphony Orchestra and whose brother was Arthur Judson's partner in the firm of Judson, O'Neill and Judd, a division of the huge Columbia Artists Management, Inc. Nevertheless, the reform proceeded smoothly under Zirato and Judd, without any suspicion of special interest. Similarly, the social makeup of the Board of Directors remained substantially the same throughout the period of expansion as it had been in 1955–56, the critics' demand that representatives of the orchestra players be restored to the Board being ignored; yet it must be admitted in all fairness that the old kind of board proved as liberal and progressive as a newer kind had been expected to be. On the other hand, although the choice of soloists, guest conductors, and programs was vastly modified along the lines of greater variety that criticism had cried for, there was just as much dissatisfaction with it as there had been before—as any student of human nature could have predicted.

These were small matters. The one big disappointment in the Philharmonic's career under Bernstein—the one contraction where an expansion had been hoped for—came in its radio broadcasts, and this was attributable neither to Bernstein nor to the Philharmonic but to changing economic and social circumstances. Over the years the Philharmonic had built up a radio following of millions of people, first on stations WEAF and WOR in the 1920s, and then, since 1930, on the network of the Columbia Broadcasting System. In 1960 there had been some nervous fears that all might not be well when Arthur Hull Hayes, President of CBS Radio, in two brief talks during the intermissions of Philharmonic broadcasts, challenged the members of the radio audience to give evidence of their existence by writing to CBS— challenged them "to stand up and be counted," so that the network could judge whether there was a sufficiently large audience to justify continuing the broadcasts in future years. But these fears had been allayed by March 1963 when CBS celebrated the one thousandth broadcast of the New York Philharmonic with a barrage of publicity extolling "the continued loyalty of the national radio audience to the orchestra's broadcasts" and citing the eleven thousand letters written in response to Hayes's intermission talks as a "striking expression of the bond between the orchestra and its radio listenership." It came as a shock when, only two months later, in May 1963, CBS announced that after thirty-three years of broadcasting of the Philharmonic concerts it was dropping the series because of a "constantly diminishing audience." This had been brought about, Hayes said, by "the availability of good music, including performances of the Philharmonic, from so many other sources at times of the listener's own choosing" (presumably on recordings and broadcasts of recordings) and by the natural pride of some radio stations in offering their own local orchestras instead of the Philharmonic. The time had come, he said, when CBS had to "accede to the realities of the day."

Acting with speed and imagination, the Society organized its own

New York Philharmonic Radio Network in time for the 1963–64 season.† By 1967 the Network included 104 stations in the continental United States, Canada, and Puerto Rico. But in spite of this courageous effort, the radio broadcasts were not able to survive. The number of Radio Members had fallen so low by the spring of 1967 that the revenue they brought to the Society was less than the cost of sending out the printed program notes, and that part of the project had to be dropped. Then, in the summer of 1967, the orchestra men, dissatisfied with the financial arrangements for their broadcasts, voted not to continue them on the same basis. In 1967–68, for the first time in forty-five years, there were no regular Philharmonic broadcasts. Of course, the Philharmonic's *recordings* continued to be heard on radio stations all over the country and all over the world, but the live performances —at least for the time being—were lost from the airways.

The loss of the radio broadcasts, like the criticisms of some of the innovations, did not seriously dampen the success of the Bernstein regime. The sense of excitement sustained the interest even of those who disagreed. The Philharmonic was alive. The Board of Directors and the management knew how to go along with Leonard Bernstein's ideas, and he knew how to go along with theirs. Together they brought about the expansion of the orchestra's public, the creation of vital new services for that public, the year-round employment of the musicians, the increased Americanization, the heightened prestige and morale of the whole organization, the television series, the worldwide tours— all the moves that reanimated the Philharmonic. The resilient officers of the Society, who were able to bounce back after each critical attack, and the resourceful managers, who had to administer without any precedents the biggest symphonic operation that the world had ever known, made a lively team with their spectacular conductor.

---

† Within a day after CBS dropped the Philharmonic broadcasts in 1963, Mayor Robert F. Wagner offered the Society the facilities of the municipal broadcasting station, WNYC, for broadcasting the concerts and distributing tapes to radio stations around the country. The Philharmonic Network eventually used WOR and then WQXR, but Wagner was the first to come forward.

Chapter 28

The Spectacular Conductor
(1958–69)

Spectacular-conductor, did we say? It is a temptation to classify Bernstein with that label, much as we have called others artist-conductors, interpreter-conductors, and master-conductors. "Spectacular," in all its different dictionary meanings, seemed to fit the Bernstein of the 1950s and 1960s. He was spectacular in the literal sense that he "made a colorful spectacle or show" of his performances. He was spectacular in the colloquial sense that he "stood out strikingly and sometimes sensationally" from those around him. And it was more than coincidence that some of his greatest successes were elaborate television programs of the kind known in the trade as spectaculars—educational or cultural spectaculars, his might be called.

But this would understate Bernstein's role. If ever the Philharmonic had a conductor who deserved the title of Music Director, he was that conductor.* Bernstein stamped his lively, and often controversial, personality on every aspect of the orchestra's music-making: the repertory,

* At Bernstein's request the title of his job was changed from Musical Director to Music Director. It seemed superfluous to describe the leader of the Philharmonic as "musical," whereas "Music Director" defined the area of his responsibility as all matters dealing with music, as differentiated from business matters, which were handled by the Managing Director.

the themes that bound together the programs of each season in an over-all plan, the selection of soloists and guest conductors, the public relations of the orchestra, its educational functions, its recordings. Sometimes, indeed, Bernstein seemed to be Music Director not just for the Philharmonic but for all America. "The N. Y. Philharmonic's Leonard Bernstein has been a one-man task force in increasing public interest in symphonic music over the past few years," said the January 1967 issue of *Allegro,* the official publication of the New York local of the musicians' union. At the other extreme, the smallest detail might claim his attention. At one point he had the dress of the Philharmonic orchestra redesigned, experimenting with a specially created costume for the Previews that was not as formal as full evening dress. ("You look like a bellhop at the Astor," one Philharmonic musician needled another, the first time they wore the new uniform. The conventional dress was resumed before the season was over.)

The spectacular element in Bernstein was naturally the one that caught the public eye most readily. But it was a result, not a cause. The moving force behind almost all his public acts was an all-embracing love of music—and of the people who give and receive music—of a kind that is more often found in the ardent amateur than in the hardened professional. Bernstein was aware of this himself. In his book of collected writings, *The Infinite Variety of Music* (1966), he declared: "I am a fanatic music lover. I can't live one day without hearing music, playing it, studying it, or thinking about it. And all this is quite apart from my professional role as a musician; I am a fan, a committed member of the musical public." Bernstein's driving love of music—which, like all love, hoped always for requital—worked to the benefit of the Philharmonic and the public. It spurred him to use his great and varied talents to create new music, to re-create old, to explain and to persuade, by every means available to him. Not content to win the audience in one concert hall, he carried his musical love to the hundreds of millions who heard and saw him on television, on recordings, and on his tours of America and the world. He serenaded them as pianist and conductor; he wrote and read them love letters as composer, author, lecturer, and teacher; he wooed them in the musical theater.

Bernstein's musical love affair made him flamboyant and sensational, a democrat and a popularizer; he asked everyone to love him in return. Together with his innate gifts, it made him a "natural" for the newspapers, the magazines, and television. As his professional fame grew, his every move became public property. His clothes and his social life were described in the press. Fans told each other that his wife gave him his haircuts. They knew that he was on first-name terms with President Kennedy, and at the opening of Philharmonic Hall in 1962 the television-watchers of the nation saw him kiss the First Lady on camera. He was always accomplishing the unexpected in his art: the public never knew whether his next appearance would be as conductor, pianist, symphony composer, teacher, or musical comedy composer. Like Toscanini in his day, Bernstein became the symbol of The Musician for the American public—though there were different meanings behind the symbols: Bernstein's easy personality and his use of the television medium made him an intimate and entertaining visitor in the viewer's home, whereas Toscanini had remained the remote, awe-inspiring representative of imported high art.†

Throughout the early years of Bernstein's professional life, the events in his career unfolded as though they were scenes in a well-directed theatrical performance. This was already so in his first season with the Philharmonic in 1943–44, when as a twenty-five-year-old Assistant Conductor, he made his sensational debut as a replacement on short notice for Bruno Walter, and built his success unerringly throughout the season.‡ It was not just that a talented young man had substituted, in the classic pattern, for a celebrated older one, and had made good. It was also that it was the right time—in the midst of

---

† Some years ago the little daughter of another American conductor was attending a concert conducted by her father. Asked what she thought of it, she replied, "Mr. Bernstein was wonderful!" Anyone conducting a concert had become for this little girl a Mr. Bernstein—even her own father!

‡ Before that, Bernstein had studied at the Boston Latin School and Harvard University (where Walter Piston and Edward Burlingame Hill had been among his music teachers), and at the Curtis Institute of Music in Philadelphia (piano with Isabelle Vengerova, conducting with Fritz Reiner). He had also "scrounged around" New York, as he later put it in an interview, working on comedy skits with Adolph Green and Betty Comden, and doing arrangements of popular music under the pen name of Lenny Amber. ("Amber" is the English translation of the German or Yiddish word "Bernstein." A variant of the name appears in Amberson Enterprises, Inc., which was formed in more recent years to handle some of Bernstein's television and film projects.) Meanwhile he had been Koussevitzky's pupil in conducting at Tanglewood in the summers. Koussevitzky recommended him to Rodzinski, in 1943, for the post of Assistant Conductor of the New York Philharmonic-Symphony, and it was in that capacity that he substituted for Bruno Walter (who had been scheduled to appear as guest conductor) on November 14, 1943.

the war against Hitler—for the public to welcome and appreciate a young conductor who was American, proudly Jewish, and an original composer. Berstein was so responsively attuned to what was timely in the worlds of art and theater that he seemed to sense exactly when his artistic projects had to veer from one direction to another. Concert pieces of intellectual cast dovetailed neatly in his output with easily accessible theater music—the biblical seriousness of the *Jeremiah* Symphony with the jazziness of the ballet *Fancy Free*—the *Serenade* for violin and small orchestra, inspired by Plato's *Symposium,* with the boisterous musical comedy *Wonderful Town.* And always the threads of conducting and teaching were interwoven with those of writing and composing. From 1945 to 1947 Bernstein conducted his own appealingly youthful orchestra, the New York City Symphony, in three seasons of refreshing performances of old and new works, boldly learning his repertory under the noses of the New York critics and public. After that, guest engagements made him a familiar figure as performer in the principal cities of Europe and America; as teacher, in those years, he was associated with Tanglewood, Brandeis University, and the "Omnibus" television programs. It all seemed to converge around 1957: that was the year when he shared the post of Principal Conductor of the New York Philharmonic with Mitropoulos, when his first Young People's Concert was televised, and when his immensely successful musical, *West Side Story,* was produced. By the next year, at the age of forty, he was Music Director of the Philharmonic. Then, for eleven years (with a slight relaxation only in the sabbatical season of 1964–65), the demands of the conducting and the educational work took priority over the writing of music. He was busy with the Philharmonic concerts in New York and on tour, more than eight hundred of them, the lovingly prepared educational programs on television, more than forty of them, and the guest conducting of concert and opera all over the world.[223]

How was it that this rare talent (many would say genius) did not enjoy unanimous acclaim? How was it that, at the height of Bernstein's success, he remained the target for sporadic attack? How was it that one critic would praise him while another condemned him—that, in fact, the same critic might praise and condemn him in a single article?

"The New York Philharmonic is fundamentally and potentially one of the truly great orchestras, but at present it has no character. It seems some-

what doubtful that its amusing, brilliant, stubborn, charming and altogether provocative principal conductor, Leonard Bernstein, has the will
or perhaps the capacity to develop in the orchestra such a character, such
a recognizable spirit." (Paul Henry Lang, New York *Herald Tribune,*
November 5, 1961)

"There is no reason why under his leadership, with his genuine musical
gifts, the New York Philharmonic could not be one of the greatest orchestras in the world." (Paul Henry Lang, same article)

"It was in the slower moments [of Mahler's First Symphony] that the
interpretation was obvious and even vulgar. . . . He dawdled and he
underlined and he pampered the music and spread himself all over the
place. . . . Will Mr. Bernstein ever strike the mean between objectivity
and the sort of adolescent heart-on-sleeve sentimentality he now favors?"
(Harold C. Schonberg, New York *Times,* May 5, 1962)

"Mr. Bernstein conducted it [Brahms's Second Symphony] in his usual
fashion—with great emphasis on tonal values, with a tendency to linger
lovingly on the sentimental aspects of the music . . . for a child of the
twentieth century, Mr. Bernstein has some tendencies that are decidedly
atavistic. When he can control them, and he did on this occasion, the result can be a singular combination of contemporary orchestral logic and
nineteenth-century emotional freedom." (Harold C. Schonberg, *Times,*
two weeks later)

At first glance these writers would seem to be inconsistent. But some
of the inconsistency reflected Bernstein's own musical personality, which
was a mixture of the most varied—and sometimes the most contra-
dictory—ingredients. There was passionate emotional commitment,
and there were sudden bursts of frivolity. There were his phenomenal
gifts as composer and performer, and there was his brash showmanship.
There was his orthodox educational background, and there was his
razzle-dazzle background in jazz and show business. There was his
nostalgic affinity for his European cultural heritage, and his joy in the
American vernacular. There was Bernstein the conductor, joined like a
Siamese twin to Bernstein the composer. "That's one of the reasons,"
Bernstein himself declared in a televised Young People's Concert in
1960, "why I'm so sympathetic to Mahler: I understand his problem.
It's like being two different men locked up in the same body."
   The results of mixing such divergent elements showed up in his

Philharmonic performances. In a Bernstein performance the inflections of phrasing and nuance might be extremely subtle or they might be emotionally intensified to the point of exaggeration; the actor in him might tempt him to ham. Intellectually he knew better than most other conductors how to plan the total layout of a piece, yet his eagerness to communicate his pleasure in a favorite passage could lead him to stress it more than his own plan required. Sometimes he enjoyed the act of music-making so much that he seemed not to care about polishing every detail. Problems of rhythm did not exist for him—he delighted in rhythmic complications—but he might toy with the simplest rhythms until more restrained musicians complained of distortion. Bernstein's personal excitement and energy in performance could be overwhelming; when everything was right, the orchestra, too, caught fire, but at other times there might be an uncomfortable gap between the exuberance of the conductor and the matter-of-factness of his players.

Bernstein's repertory for his Philharmonic concerts was wide-ranging, from the Baroque and Classic, through the Romantic, to most of the moderns, and even the avant-garde. But he was perhaps not equally suited for all of these styles. In his early years with the Philharmonic he was criticized for sometimes performing Baroque music in a Romantic style, without sufficient regard for current musicological research. If his performances of old music were more Romanticized than the best current usage endorsed, his performances of the Romantic literature might have been expected to please; but ironically, though they would probably have pleased the nineteenth-century Romanticists themselves, they were branded as extreme by some contemporary critics and listeners. The moderns of the first half of the twentieth century, everyone agreed, Bernstein did brilliantly, though even here some composers and their partisans resented the personal imprint that he placed on everything he performed—"Don't interpret my music," one composer was said to have grumbled, "just play it." Bernstein had an unmatched "feel" for the syncopations and other rhythmic and metric complications of the music of that period, and he was particularly good at the American nationalist style of Gershwin, Copland, and Harris, and of the age group just after that (Schuman, Diamond, Blitzstein, Fine), including the jazz and popular-music elements. He played some of the avant-garde composers and some of the serialists out of a sense of duty, but he was not personally sympathetic to most of their music.

But the greatest part of the public was not concerned either with scholarly accuracy or with avant-garde experiments—it was thrilled by the spectacular Bernstein, who "gave himself" in every performance, and it rewarded him with packed auditoriums and willing ovations. And not only in New York. Almost everywhere that Bernstein conducted, either with the Philharmonic or as guest conductor, though the critics and the musicologists might find fault, the audiences were won over. In Vienna the Bernstein chemistry worked perhaps more powerfully than anywhere else. Even when he dared to bring the Viennese their own music—Strauss's *Rosenkavalier,* Mahler's *Lied von der Erde,* Beethoven's *Missa Solemnis*—he was given one triumph after another. What higher honor could Vienna bestow on a foreign musician than to ask him to conduct a special production of Beethoven's only opera, *Fidelio,* in the historic Theater an der Wien (where the opera's first performance took place in 1805), during the celebration of the two hundredth anniversary of Beethoven's birth?

A rehearsal, since it was a more intimate affair than a performance, was even more revealing of the atmosphere that surrounded Bernstein. Almost everyone at a rehearsal, from the musicians to the administrative staff, addressed Bernstein as "Lenny." Joseph Fabbroni, the personnel manager of the New York City Symphony when Bernstein was its conductor in the late 1940s, had been distressed by this and had tried unsuccessfully to insist that the conductor be addressed as "Maestro." "At least 'Maestro Lenny,'" he had finally pleaded, but he had failed even in that compromise. Bernstein did not mind being called Lenny by people he was working with, or even by strangers when it was clearly just a sign of popular affection. "Cabdrivers shout 'Hey, Lenny!' to me," he told a *Times* interviewer in 1968. "I love people, so that doesn't bother me." But he resented it when the press made a public affectation of it. Whether he liked it or not, however, this sort of intimacy was encouraged by his sociable disposition and his theatrical sense of humor. In 1962 there was a teen-age fad for sweat shirts with life-size heads of Bach, Beethoven, or Brahms imprinted on the front; Bernstein playfully appeared at a Philharmonic rehearsal on April 4, 1962, wearing his Brahms sweat shirt. A Bernstein rehearsal, however, was basically a very serious working session, though it might be sprinkled with witticisms and gags, and the conductor's explanations might be colorful or metaphorical. The musicians were comfortably relaxed in their response, but their interest was held by the musical or intellectual content of what was happening. A typical Bernstein program was likely, in any case, to contain enough material that was a bit off the familiar path to keep the players involved during rehearsal. And Bernstein always knew the scores thoroughly and brilliantly.

The Philharmonic men were not easily impressed—most of the world's conductors had passed in review before them—but they spoke admiringly of Bernstein's natural and technical gifts, such as his musical ear and memory. Bernstein heard most of what happened in the orchestra, though he was not the kind of conductor who fussed over the faintest gradations of the last desk of the second violins; artistically he was seldom interested in that kind of discrimination. His musical memory was among the most remarkable that the musicians had ever encountered, and it was an aural memory, not a visual one, a memory for the sounds themselves, not just for their symbols on paper. The players had their fund of anecdotes about the memory stunts of Toscanini and Mitropoulos, but the Bernstein stories matched any of them. A well-authenticated one was told by a musician who had been at Tanglewood one summer when Bernstein was giving a lecture on contemporary American composers, illustrating profusely at the piano with examples from their orchestral compositions. The musician, who happened to be sitting next to Aaron Copland, remarked to him that it was amazing that Bernstein had found the time, in his heavy conducting schedule, to look up all the scores of new music that he was quoting and then to practice and memorize them. "Look up? Practice?" laughed Copland. "Most of that music isn't even published. The symphony of Roger Sessions he's heard just once."

By temperament and by choice, Bernstein did not limit his conducting motions to the strictly functional: some gestures served as much for personal expression, or to illustrate the music, as to communicate meaning to the players; but this was *in addition* to what the orchestra required for clarity, which was always present as a substructure. For many years the flailing beat of his arms and the choreographic use of his body were so florid that they were dizzying to the orchestra men; the busy motion was exciting to the players at first encounter, but after a few weeks of the season they would discount much of the movement. This is what Paul Henry Lang was referring to in 1962 when he said that "the gestures become exaggerated, and, especially when he begins to conduct from the hips and does some rope skipping, the spectacle can be embarrassing." After 1964 or 1965, however, Bernstein's podium manner grew more reserved, breaking out into its old flamboyance only occasionally. Some part of the greater economy of gesture may have been connected with his adopting the use of a baton; formerly he had conducted without one, but, after injuring his back, he found that the baton saved some of the physical exertion.

Bernstein was usually considerate of the orchestra players, did not insult them in rehearsal, as many a dictatorial maestro has been known to do, and praised them when he was pleased with their work. Considering the informality that he permitted, and even encouraged, in his relationships with the players, the discipline was excellent. Most of the men appreciated the warmth of his affection for the orchestra. Many of them recognized the brilliance of his intellect and the breadth of his cultural interests. Some were impressed by his literary productions (by 1969 comprising three volumes of collected short pieces), his serious musical compositions, and his musical comedy and film scores. The older and more conservative ones may have felt remote from his excursions into "popular" music, but they still admired him for the success of those ventures—and for the money he made from them. And all the men were aware that Bernstein's presence had been the fructifying agent that had led to their new positions of importance in the city's cultural life. Characteristic of the easygoing relationship between conductor and players was Bernstein's leave-taking in the spring of 1964, before he went on sabbatical for the following season. The entire orchestra toasted him at a luncheon at the Tavern-on-the-Green, and Bernstein responded with two couplets that he had made for them:

> Love one another and sing while you play
> And be good to mother while daddy's away.

> So forward, my hearties, with courage and cheer
> To a season with ninety-eight weeks in the year.

"No one gets as much out of the Philharmonic as he does," wrote Raymond Ericson admiringly in the New York Times of December 29, 1966, a year after Bernstein's return from his sabbatical. Ericson had long been one of Bernstein's supporters, but the whole New York press grew noticeably more favorable toward Bernstein from 1966 on. For one thing, his style was increasing in sobriety. For another, some of those who had formerly been irritated by the explosive mixture of his personality recognized, as the evidence accumulated, how generous were his intentions and how real was his contribution to the city's musical life. Harold C. Schonberg had for years been scolding Bernstein in the tone of one who feels that he must be severe because the object of his criticism is worth saving. But in May 1966, looking back at the season that had just ended, he found that "it was seldom . . . that Bernstein fell back upon his old tricks—those distortions of musical line, those too-obvious spellings-out, the general over-emphasis with which he used to approach music . . . Thus he is developing into the kind of interpretive musician that his extraordinary talents had indicated." And in mid-November of 1966 Schonberg reaffirmed this opinion: "In the last two seasons—after his year's sabbatical—there have . . . been pronounced changes. Mr. Bernstein's conducting now seems more intent on substance and less on flashiness."

It must have been pleasant for Bernstein to have the critics quite regularly patting him on the back at last, instead of slapping him down, but it cannot have been of great practical importance to him; for, all the while that his critical fortunes had been fluctuating, he had managed to achieve the greatest popular success in the history of symphonic music in America. His formal critics had been irritated by the uncontrolled abandon with which he plunged into his performances, by his unashamed anxiousness to please. They had cried "vulgarity . . . vanity . . . distortion." But to a very large public—large enough to keep the concert halls filled to overflowing, the TV dials tuned to his shows, and the royalties pouring in—these same passionate qualities meant other things. They meant artistic temperament, and creativity, and sexiness, and glamour, and magic virtuosity, and the wondrous mystery of what gives one person more musical talent than another. Even when the critics were against him, their city editors were for him—there was always a story or a picture in Leonard Bernstein because the musical love that flowed out of him sought and found people.

On November 2, 1966, it was announced that Leonard Bernstein would leave his post of Music Director of the New York Philharmonic when his contract expired in the spring of 1969. Bernstein would continue to have an important association with the orchestra after that date, explained Amyas Ames, President of the Philharmonic; the title of Laureate Conductor (for life) was being created especially for him and in that capacity he would conduct a number of weeks of the regular season and would take part in recording and television activities, particularly the Young People's Concerts. The New York *Times*'s front-page story on the news conference attributed Bernstein's leaving chiefly to his desire to devote himself to composing. "A time is arriving in my life," it quoted him as saying, "when I must concentrate maximally on composing, and this cannot be done while retaining the great responsibilities inherent in the Philharmonic post, which is a full-time commitment, and indeed, more than that." He wanted especially to write for the musical theater and perhaps also to have the time to do some opera conducting.

Wild speculation ensued about who would be Bernstein's successor. Since his resignation was announced in 1966 but was not to take effect until 1969, there was plenty of time for guessing. Everyone who accepted a guest-conducting engagement with the Philharmonic was assumed to be taking an audition. "I don't like to use the word candidates," said David Keiser, chairman of the Philharmonic's Board of Directors, according to *Newsweek* magazine, "but all the guest conductors will be listened to with the future in mind." Five conductors, all of them active on the international concert circuit, and all of them in their thirties or early forties, were repeatedly mentioned in the press as the principal contenders: Zubin Mehta (of India, but resident in the United States), Lorin Maazel (of the United States, but resident in Germany), Pierre Boulez (of France, but resident in Germany), Seiji Ozawa (of Japan, but resident in Canada), and Colin Davis (of England). Others who were thought at one time or another to be possibilities were the Italians Claudio Abbado and Carlo Maria Giulini, the Hungarian Istvan Kertesz, and the Pole Stanislaw Skrowaczewski. It was not long, however, before Mehta, one of the leading nominees for the position, was out of the running. In two interviews, one reported in the New York *Times* and the other in *Newsweek,* in December 1967, he was quoted as saying that his own Los Angeles orchestra was better than the New York Philharmonic and that he would not conduct the Philharmonic as a guest in 1968–69 if it meant that he was a candidate for the New York job. The Philharmonic men "step over" conductors, he was reported to have said. "A lot of us think why not send our worst enemy to the New York Philharmonic and finish him off once and for all." The New York musicians were indignant. Within a month Mehta was called before the executive board of Local 802 of the musicians' union to explain his remarks; he assured the board that he had meant only to express his pride in his own orchestra, not to disparage the New York orchestra. Even after this apology, musicians chuckled at the thought of what Mehta's first rehearsal with the Philharmonic would be like the next season, but it never came to a test: in April of 1968 the Philharmonic let it be known that his guest-conducting engagement had been indefinitely postponed.

Meanwhile, as a transitional measure, the Philharmonic Society repeated in 1967 what it had done after Rodzinski's resignation in 1947, when Bruno Walter had been named Musical Adviser for two years. It put off its final decision for a while by appointing George Szell Music Advisor [so spelled this time] and Senior Guest Conductor for 1969, while it continued its search for a Music Director.

George Szell—described by one of his Cleveland first-desk players as "a terrifying authoritarian of the old school, but . . . an artist of terrific ability"—was born in 1897 in Budapest and received his musical education in Vienna, under Reger, Mandyczewski, J. B. Foerster, and R. Robert. At the age of eleven he was presented as pianist and composer with sensational success, being hailed as a new Mozart. He was only twenty when he was engaged, at Richard Strauss's recommendation, as conductor at the Municipal Theater in Strasbourg. After that he held conducting positions in the theaters of Prague, Darmstadt, Düsseldorf, and Berlin, and with the Scottish Orchestra in Glasgow. From the age of thirty he had also been active as teacher, and when he settled in the United States at the outbreak of World War II, he taught at the New School for Social Research and the Mannes School of Music in New York. Beginning in 1942 he conducted at the Metropolitan Opera House. It was in 1946, when he took over the Cleveland Orchestra, that he had the opportunity to shape an orchestra according to his artistic ideals; he made of it one of the greatest orchestras in the world, acknowledged everywhere as a model of ensemble playing. "In Cleveland," he was quoted as saying, "we begin to rehearse when most orchestras leave off." Philharmonic audiences knew Szell as one of their most frequent guest conductors. He had first led the orchestra in two of its national broadcasts in the summer of 1943, and by the time of his appointment as Music Advisor in 1967 he had returned for more than two hundred performances in the regular subscription seasons. Since Szell was already Musical Director of the Cleveland Orchestra and would be seventy-two years old by the time he took over his Philharmonic office as Advisor in 1969, he was not interested in a full-time post in New York; he would serve as "caretaker" for the orchestra, he said, until a Music Director could be appointed.

When Bernstein gave his farewell concert as Music Director, on May 17, 1969, his public knew that he was not leaving for all time—as Laureate Conductor, he would probably be conducting Philharmonic concerts for many years to come—but it was nevertheless a deeply moving occasion for orchestra, conductor, and audience. Pleasure in honoring a remarkable artist for his achievements with the Society tempered sadness in marking the end of his directorship. Bernstein led a passionate performance of Mahler's Third Symphony, and the audience stood to cheer him for five minutes. Amyas Ames, the Society's President, announced three prizes or gifts appropriate for a new Laureate: in the tradition set by the ancient Greeks, a great laurel wreath; also in that tradition, a poet, Archibald MacLeish, to sing the praises of the honored one ("he is one of the few . . . who have truly *lived* an art in these years"); and, in a more modern tradition, a nineteen-foot motorboat named *The Laureate*.* The press summarized Bernstein's accomplishments and noted that he was relinquishing his post at the peak of the Society's success and his own artistry. "He leaves the orchestra," wrote Harold C. Schonberg in the *Times* on May 19, "with the comfortable feeling that he has been accepted not only by his public—which always was the case—but also by professionals and by music critics the world over."

A few weeks later, on June 10, 1969, the conductor chase came to an end. The French composer-conductor Pierre Boulez was named Music Director of the New York Philharmonic for a three-year term beginning with the season of 1971–72.[224] Until then, Szell would serve as Music Advisor and Senior Guest Conductor, but Boulez would already appear with the orchestra for five weeks of guest conducting in 1970–71 before assuming his title and responsibilities as Music Director.

Boulez, born at Montbrison in 1925, studied in Paris with Olivier Messiaen and René Leibowitz. As Music Director of Jean-Louis Bar-

* Yet surely, though the Philharmonic's Directors may not have been conscious of it, in the same spirit in which the Society's first conductor, Ureli Corelli Hill, had been given a gold snuffbox as a "tribute of merit" in 1847–48. What was certainly in a newer vein—typical of the sentimental humor that Bernstein shared with the orchestra players—was their presentation to him on the preceding day of a mezuzah, the little parchment roll containing the name of God and certain scriptural texts which is attached to the doorpost of a Jewish house according to biblical command.

rault's theater company, after 1948, he gained a reputation as a skillful and meticulous conductor, and it was as theater and ballet conductor that he visited the United States in the 1950s. At the same time he was becoming known as a leader in the cause of new music; with Barrault's help he founded the Domaine Musical concerts which became the focus for performances of new music in Paris. He had been writing music since his student days, but it was in the mid-1950s that he gained international attention with his cantata *Le Marteau sans Maître*. The New York Philharmonic gave the first United States performances of his two *Improvisations sur Mallarmé* in 1960 and 1961. Starting as a composer who conducted concerts only because he "couldn't find conductors to play my music," he became in the 1960s one of the busiest professional conductors on the international scene. From his headquarters in Baden-Baden (dissatisfied with the musical life in his native land, he had moved to Germany in 1959), he traveled throughout Europe, the United States, and Japan, his services in demand years in advance. At the time of his Philharmonic appointment, he had also been named Principal Guest Conductor of the Cleveland Orchestra (including its Blossom Music Festival in the summers) for the three years from 1969 to 1972, and Chief Conductor of the BBC Symphony Orchestra for the three seasons from 1971 to 1974.†

Wherever he went, Boulez was recognized as a man of original ideas and strong opinions. The Directors of the Philharmonic were aware that he would want to change much in the organization. But far from fearing this, they were counting on it. They agreed with Bernstein that his successor should not be forced to fit a preconceived idea of his qualifications; he should be chosen because he had strong qualities of his own that he could lend to the job.

For 1969–70, however, Boulez was not yet available, and Bernstein had already stepped down. It remained to be seen whether Bernstein's departure, like Toscanini's in 1936, would leave a personality vacuum behind it.

---

† When George Szell died in the summer of 1970, Boulez accepted yet another responsibility, as Music Adviser of the Cleveland Orchestra through the season of 1971–72, in addition to his position as Music Director of the New York Philharmonic.

Chapter 29

Philharmonic Hall
(1962–   )

The rebirth of the Philharmonic and the extension of its services had been made much easier by the orchestra's acquisition of a home of its own—Philharmonic Hall at Lincoln Center. Ground had barely been broken for the new hall in 1959 when the anticipated advantages were described in detail in a fund-raising brochure, *The Philharmonic at Lincoln Center:* "The Philharmonic . . . will be free to continue or expand its concerts for children and young people, to increase other educational services, to lengthen its regular season, to inaugurate a summer season of 'Pops' concerts, to expand its radio and television programs. . . . Air-conditioning will permit patrons to enjoy performances the year-round . . . Great summer music festivals at Philharmonic Hall are expected to enliven the New York scene—attracting thousands of visitors as well as New York residents."

Through all the years since its founding, the Philharmonic had had no home. After the early seasons in the Apollo Rooms (from 1842 to 1848 and from 1849 to 1851), the concerts had been given in a variety of halls. They make a picturesque list:

The Assembly Rooms of the Chinese Buildings, Broadway near Spring Street (two concerts in 1848–49)—host, in the very next season, to that prince of humbug, P. T. Barnum.

Niblo's Concert-Room and Garden, Broadway at Prince Street (seasons of 1851–53, 1854–56, and 1858–59)—celebrated for its gustatory as well as its musical refreshment.

Metropolitan Hall, Broadway and Bond Street (one concert in 1853)—newly outfitted in 1853, burned before the Philharmonic could give a second concert in it.

The Broadway Tabernacle, Broadway between Leonard and Worth Streets (January to April 1854)—originally a house of God, as its name suggests, but later used for every kind of show or meeting at which a very large crowd was expected (for example, the lottery drawings of the Art-Union).

The Academy of Music, Fourteenth Street and Irving Place (1856–58, 1859–61, 1863–66, and 1867–68)—then the site of New York's most fashionable opera performances, now the site of the Consolidated Edison Company's business office.

Irving Hall, Irving Place at Fifteenth Street (1861–63)—which began as a concert-lecture auditorium, but became in succession a home for performances of German plays, a burlesque house, and a moving-picture theater specializing in left-wing films, and is now—as the final stage in its rake's progress—a warehouse for the bargain basements of S. Klein's Department Store.

Steinway Hall, at 111 East Fourteenth Street, near Irving Place (1866–67)—the showroom for the piano company's artists, the scene of Anton Rubinstein's American debut and of many of Theodore Thomas's concerts. (The building no longer stands; in its place the pilgrim of today finds the 111 Delicatessen, "Highest Quality Food at Lowest Prices.")

In 1886 the concerts had moved to the new and elegant Metropolitan Opera House, at Broadway and Thirty-ninth Street, and in 1892 to Carnegie's even newer Music Hall, on Fifty-seventh Street at Seventh Avenue.

But the dream of a building designed especially for the Philharmonic had always been present. It went back as far as the orchestra itself. The Philharmonic was only four years old, in 1846, when it presented at Castle Garden its "Grand Concert, in Aid of the Fund for the Erection of the Philharmonic Hall." (See page 103.) The proceeds, unfortunately were only $390, and four years later the prospects of collecting enough additional money to erect a hall seemed so dim that the trustees who had been appointed to receive the money turned it back to the Society for general charitable purposes.* Still, the orchestra's ambition to have a hall of its own kept surfacing bravely every few years. It was whispered around town, early in 1856, that the Philharmonic had bought Philip Hone's house, at Broadway and Great Jones Street, and proposed to erect a music hall there. Nothing came of this, but in 1859, provoked by the previous year's difficulties in leasing the Academy of Music, the Philharmonic made another attempt at a building, this time by the formation of a stock company. That plan also fell through. And when George Templeton Strong was President of the Philharmonic in 1871, he recorded in his Diary (his tone implying that he considered the proposition a wild one) that he had had a visit from "Gissner of the Philharmonic [this was George Gipner, one of the Directors] to discuss the feasibility of raising half a million or so to build a grand Philharmonic music hall."

Even when the orchestra was comfortably acclimated to Carnegie Hall, after 1892, the vision of a Philharmonic Hall did not fade. When Dr. R. Ogden Doremus, the patriarchal former President of the Society, was asked to address the audience at a Philharmonic concert in 1902, he urged wealthy New Yorkers to give their money for an orchestra building that would house both an auditorium and a school of music: "Citizens of New York who have inherited or acquired those parallelogrammatic pieces of cellular tissue, tinted with the hydrated sesquioxide of chromium,† vulgarly, 'Greenbacks,' should unite in constructing an edifice for this grand association. It should be a splendid building, ornate, like 'frozen music,' with a large auditorium arranged on acoustic principles, with suitable conveniences for the orchestra and a chorus and a grand organ."[225] In 1914, during Stransky's regime, there was another "Proposal for a Philharmonic Building"; it had to be abandoned the

---

* At least one Philharmonic member had been afraid, from the beginning, that the Society might be biting off more than it could chew. Ritter, in his *Music in America,* quotes from a complaint addressed to the members by "A Member Looker-on": "As for the proposal of erecting a building with the denomination of the Philharmonic Hall, . . . if the present members of the Philharmonic Society of New York were *to be forced by* some *quibble of the law* to become responsible for the fulfilment of the engagements that such an undertaking would require, we should all of us be *compelled by our own elected officers of the government* to work during eight or ten years to come, that but *one-tenth* perhaps of the present might enjoy the produce of this establishment hereafter, at the expense of the folly and loss of time of those gone by." (Italics his.)

† This long-winded phrase was an inside joke—the audience knew Doremus as a distinguished chemist.

next year because of the unfavorable conditions caused by the European war, but not before architects' plans had been drawn up and published in a handsome brochure. On the orchestra's seventy-fifth anniversary, in 1917, the memorial book prepared for the occasion reminded the reader that the Philharmonic needed "but a home of its own, a home that it can name—Philharmonic Hall." And the similar book issued on the one hundredth anniversary in 1942, when the orchestra had been in Carnegie Hall for half a century, remarked wistfully that "no hall at any time, not even now, has quite measured up to the Philharmonic's ideals."

Then in 1955–56, after 110 years of frustration, the Philharmonic was able to announce that the projected Lincoln Center for the Performing Arts would include a new concert hall for the orchestra, to be located on Broadway at Sixty-fifth Street. The officers of the Society had been taking part, since 1953, in the planning for what was then spoken of as a Fine Arts and Music Center in New York. At first the discussions had moved so slowly that President Floyd G. Blair had had to report in 1954, with evident impatience, that "those interested in the establishment of such a center have not yet been able to secure the funds needed to make even preliminary studies and surveys." The tension had increased the next year, when Carnegie Hall, which was to be sold and torn down, had notified the Philharmonic that it would be without a home by 1959. But in 1955–56 things began to happen. This was the year when the newspaper critics vivisected the Philharmonic in public, the year when the Philharmonic reshuffled its officers and its management—"a year of self-examination," as the Annual Report described it. And one of the most important acts of the new officers, led by David M. Keiser, was to get the planning and the building of the new concert hall under way. President Eisenhower broke ground for the building on May 14, 1959, at a ceremony in which several of the future constituents of Lincoln Center—the Philharmonic, the Metropolitan Opera, the Juilliard School—were represented.

There was still the problem of where the Philharmonic would play between the closing of Carnegie Hall in 1960 (it had been postponed from 1959) and the anticipated completion of the new building in the autumn of 1961. Complicated arrangements had already been made for transferring the concerts to the Hunter College Auditorium, when it was learned that the "Save Carnegie Hall" campaign, captained by Isaac Stern, the violinist, had succeeded—in June of 1960 the City of

New York agreed to buy Carnegie Hall and lease it to a Carnegie Hall Corporation so that the historic building would not have to be torn down. The Philharmonic had an auditorium in which to give its concerts until its own hall was ready.

As the construction of Philharmonic Hall at Lincoln Center proceeded (the opening had been put off from the fall of 1961 to the fall of 1962), a steady flow of information about it reached the public through all the communications and advertising media. The Manhattan telephone directory carried a drawing of the exterior of the hall on its cover. Magazines, newspapers, radio, and television discussed the building's problems as they arose and their solutions as they were found: the architects were planning wider seats with more leg room because studies showed "that the average American in the past fifty years has become progressively larger in stature" (presumably at the bottom); the acoustical consultants were making actual tests of the world's leading concert halls; elevators would permit enlarging the stage and would also descend to the basement level to help in converting the auditorium from conventional seating to restaurant style for "pops" concerts. It was first announced that "acoustics and comfort" had determined the seating capacity of the hall at 2,400 seats, but so many protests were received from those who found it undemocratic or otherwise objectionable that the auditorium should seat so few people (Carnegie Hall's capacity was 2,760) that the plan was modified to raise the seating to something over 2,600. Most important of all, the new home would give the Philharmonic the working conditions it had needed for so long: under one roof it would have its air-conditioned concert hall for year-round use, proper facilities for rehearsal, recording, and broadcasting, office space for its management, modern box-office arrangements, a lounge and tuning room for the orchestra players, and adequate housing for the music library.

The inauguration of Philharmonic Hall was accompanied by much pomp and ceremony. In celebration of its first season in the hall, the Philharmonic commissioned new works of ten composers: Samuel Barber, Leonard Bernstein, Carlos Chávez, Aaron Copland, Alberto Ginastera, Hans Werner Henze, Paul Hindemith, Darius Milhaud, Francis Poulenc, and William Schuman. The brilliant inaugural concert on September 23, 1962, was the Philharmonic's party, with Leonard Bernstein conducting, but the entire opening week, from September 23 through 30, was treated as a festive demonstration of the Hall's uses;

there were performances by the Philharmonic, the Boston Symphony Orchestra, the Philadelphia Orchestra, the Cleveland Orchestra, the Juilliard Orchestra, the Metropolitan Opera, the Juilliard String Quartet, the New York Pro Musica, and the duo-pianists Gold and Fizdale. Unconsciously echoing the rhetoric of 1846, which had proclaimed the Philharmonic's fund-raising concert "an era in the musical world," the *Herald Tribune* of 1962 greeted the opening of Philharmonic Hall as "a new era in the cultural life of New York City."

Then came the one big disappointment. As the concerts continued, everyone—conductors, performers, critics, audiences—began to complain about the acoustics of Philharmonic Hall. "Listening to the music in Philharmonic Hall on its opening night," wrote Paul Henry Lang in the *Herald Tribune,* "was like hearing a giant Hi-Fi set, with the characteristic shrill and hard high frequencies so dear to Hi-Fi buffs . . . the quiet and moderately loud passages played by the large orchestras were satisfactorily projected, but substantial volumes of sound were not; the hall seemed not large enough to accommodate them." Harold C. Schonberg in the New York *Times* called the hall "inconsistent," its characteristics varying from one location to another—dry and thin, with a weak bass, in some areas, yet full and almost too live in others. Experienced conductors, listening as members of the audience, generally found the brass instruments to sound overresonant, passages for the full orchestra to run together muddily, and even chamber-orchestra groups to sound more like good broadcast or recorded tone than like clear live tone. At least as serious was the complaint of the orchestra musicians that they could not hear each other as they played on stage. Leo L. Beranek, president of Bolt, Beranek and Newman, the firm of acoustical engineers that was supervising the tuning of the hall, asked for patience: "I predicted in the beginning that it would take a year to get the hall into its ultimate condition," he said, "and I stick to that."

But the public was impatient. Musicians in particular seemed to take a vengeful glee in the discomfort of all these engineering experts who had given the impression that they were substituting efficient technology for subjective artistic judgment, and who, it now appeared, had patently and publicly goofed. So much fuss had been made in advance about the preparation of the hall's acoustic wonders that it all seemed rather ludicrous in retrospect. There had been a Tuning Week in May 1962, in which the architect and the acoustical engineers had given the orders. It was described in the sumptuous blue and gold souvenir booklet, *Opening Week of Lincoln Center for the Performing Arts:* "Symphonies were started and abruptly stopped on command. Music composed especially for acoustical testing was played. Blank cartridges were fired. Gongs struck. Reverberation time was measured. Soloists performed. Silence was called for continually so that acoustical experts in the highest terrace locations and in the remotest corners of the auditorium could give instructions. A whole symphony was recorded and played back." Lincoln Center had let it be known that, in planning the design of Philharmonic Hall, sixty concert halls in twenty countries, "as far east as Moscow, as far north as Helsinki and Turku in Finland, and as far south as Buenos Aires," had been studied, using modern acoustical instruments, and twenty-seven of the world's foremost conductors and twenty-five professional music critics had been interviewed. A great deal of publicity had been given to the 136 gold clouds suspended from the ceiling and to the artificial audience of fiber glass "people" with which the seats had been filled during tests to simulate concert conditions. "A modern concert hall," Leo Beranek, the acoustician, had said, "needn't sound like a hall of 1850." Now Paul Henry Lang retorted in the *Herald Tribune:* "Curious, how these old theaters and halls, including those in this country that we still manage to keep from the wreckers, are so excellent for all kinds of music without the performance by engineers and acousticians of superstitious rites just short of slaughtering animals." If, as the fund-raising brochures had insisted, "Good acoustics has been the major consideration," it looked as though Lincoln Center and the Philharmonic might end up with a $20,000,000 lemon on their hands.

By December the rumors were epidemic. It was whispered that microphones were being used to amplify all events in the new hall, that the Philadelphia Orchestra would go back to Carnegie Hall the next season, and that Columbia Records had refused to record the Philharmonic any longer in Philharmonic Hall. The wags-about-town circulated a story that Isaac Stern (the hero of the campaign that had saved Carnegie Hall from demolition) had decided after opening night that it was time to start a "Save Philharmonic Hall" movement.

William Schuman, President of Lincoln Center, acted as a wise executive, who was also an experienced musician, had to act. "We are proceeding," he said, "on the assumption that the hall is fine but has problems. We expect to take care of those problems without being stampeded into hasty action." In December 1962 Beranek's firm of acoustical engineers made their recommendations for improving the hall, but they were not carried out. Instead Schuman invited four acousticians, Heinrich Keilholz, Paul S. Veneklasen, Vern O. Knudsen, and Manfred R. Schroeder, to investigate the problem and submit their opinions. They recommended extensive alterations in the overhead clouds or acoustic panels, the stage itself, and the walls of the auditorium; these changes, which were referred to as Phase I and Phase II, were carried out during certain weeks of the summer of 1963 when the hall was not in use.

Having spent hundreds of thousands of dollars on these cosmetic improvements, the officials of Lincoln Center hoped that the music community would now be satisfied. George Szell, conductor of the Cleveland Orchestra, who was guest conductor of the Philharmonic in the hall for several weeks in November and December of 1963, gave his judgment in the form of a comparison: "Imagine a woman, lame, a hunchback, cross-eyed and with two warts. They've removed the warts." Erich Leinsdorf, conductor of the Boston Symphony Orchestra, expressed what the New York *Times* called a positive attitude, although the architects might have found it at least obliquely negative: "You have to take the historic view," he said. "When the famous old Vienna Opera House opened, one of the two architects committed suicide." Almost all of the Philharmonic orchestra players were still dissatisfied with the acoustics. From the listener's viewpoint, however, there must have been some improvement, for Carlos Moseley, the Philharmonic's Managing Director, who had had to deal with the letters of complaint the year before, reported that there was not a single one in the fall of 1963.

In the summers of 1964 and 1965, on the recommendation of Heinrich Keilholz, the new acoustical expert, further changes were made, providing the stage in effect with a plywood acoustical shell, altering the cloud ceiling, removing the carpets from the aisles, replacing the stuffed chairs with wooden-backed ones, paneling the walls of the auditorium in acacia wood, breaking up the surfaces with curved reflecting panels, and making the air conditioning quieter. Moreover, with a stroke of high managerial talent, while the seats in the auditorium were being changed, 178 new ones were added, making a seating capacity of 2,836 for the hall; the revenue from these seats would serve to pay off, perhaps even within five years, the renovation costs of approximately

$470,000, so that no funds contributed to the Society or to Lincoln Center would have to be involved in the most recent phase of acoustic improvements.

Critics and listeners now began to voice their approval of the hall's acoustics, at first with a few cautious reservations, but as time went by with fuller acceptance. Amyas Ames, President of the New York Philharmonic, was able to say, late in 1965, at the annual luncheon of the Friends of the Philharmonic, that even George Szell (he of the "two warts"), whom he characterized as "the Hall's severest critic and a man of such musical integrity that his words carry much weight," had made a statement of endorsement:

> The recent phase of repairs at Philharmonic Hall has led to a most significant and gratifying improvement. Almost miraculously an acoustically impossible hall has been changed into an acoustically very possible, acceptable one. The hope now seems justified that as plans are carried forward—it will be able to take its place among the finest halls of the world.

Was the battle of Philharmonic Hall won? No! It was only a short time before the firing resumed—not so heavy as before, but still on target. All the defects were *somewhat* improved, it seemed, but none was completely eliminated. In the summer of 1969 the Philharmonic Society spent three months and a million and a quarter dollars in carrying out more of Keilholz's recommendations: the hexagonal clouds, which, in the original plan of the auditorium, were supposed to permit its tuning, were replaced by a thick wooden ceiling; a new air-conditioning system was installed to reduce noise; and the lighting and the color scheme were brightened for "psycho-acoustic" ends, that is, to make the audience *feel* happier about the sound.

The test came on September 23, 1969, and it was a double one. The orchestra had a rehearsal in the morning, for which the hall would be almost empty, and a gala benefit concert in the evening, for which it would be packed with people. Now, a full auditorium sounds very different from an empty one, because the bodies absorb sound, but a fine concert hall must give satisfaction under both conditions. The double test of Philharmonic Hall would show whether the orchestra players would be able to hear each other in rehearsals and whether the audience would be able to hear them in concerts.

NEW PHILHARMONIC SOUND GLOWS, was the good news on the front page of the New York *Times* the next morning. "Philharmonic Hall from now on is going to be a happy auditorium," said Harold Schonberg, who had been one of the hall's most persistent critics. The acoustic jinx had been exorcised, he said. The musicians could hear each other well enough for the finest ensemble playing, the strings were silken and warm, the winds came through in all their color and clarity, the echoes and the hi-fi shrillness were gone, and the sections of the orchestra blended well with each other.

Science, art, patience, and money—and apparently voodoo—had triumphed. Looking about them in happy exhaustion, the Philharmonic and its public could recognize with satisfaction that the orchestra finally had a home of its own, a handsome building that sheltered performance, administration, library, and even refreshment under one roof, a building thronged with an eager public from one end of the year to the other, and named—as the farsighted founders had proposed in 1846—Philharmonic Hall.‡

‡ But not for long! It has just been announced, as this book is prepared for the printer, that, in recognition of "a major gift" to Lincoln Center from Avery Fisher, the name of Philharmonic Hall has been changed to Avery Fisher Hall.

Chapter 30

Interregnum
(1969–71)

Now that Bernstein was no longer Music Director, could the public interest in the Philharmonic be sustained?

To the calm observer, the answer had been clear for several years. Bernstein and the Philharmonic had built so well, during the decade before his leaving, that the Society was able to carry on its expanded activities—including the summer concerts, the educational work, and the touring—without any significant weakening of morale or support, even when he was away. This had already been demonstrated in 1964–65, Bernstein's sabbatical year, which had been one of the most successful in Philharmonic history despite his absence. That was the year when the great free concerts in the parks had been started, when the summer festivals had begun, and when all-time records had been set for the season's attendance and the number of concerts given (906,000 people at 199 performances). It was a sign of the Philharmonic's public strength that its doings were front-page news. The first free concert for an audience of seventy thousand in Central Park, conducted by Steinberg, and the first success of the reworked acoustics of Philharmonic Hall, in a concert conducted by Ozawa, were front-page picture stories in the New York *Times,* even though Bernstein was not involved.

In 1969–70, moreover, Bernstein *was* still involved. He was on hand for five weeks of the subscription season as Laureate, he did two special non-subscription concerts, and he was still Music Director for the Young People's Concerts. His following in the concert hall and on television was not lost. And Szell's strong hand was there as Music Advisor to hold the whole season together.

In the interregnum between Music Directors that the Philharmonic went through, from 1969 to 1971, it still carried the new stamp and style that it had taken on after 1958. It was in the summers, we said in describing the changes of those years, that the reborn Philharmonic had shown its new face most clearly. But the summer activities were the ones that depended least on Bernstein's personal participation. The free concerts in the city's parks, for example, owed their character as much to Carlos Moseley, the Managing Director of the orchestra, who had nursed them into being in the several years before 1965, as to any man. The whole series of twelve Park Concerts was given in the summer of 1969, and another series of twelve in 1970. The conductors the first year were Josef Krips, Efrem Kurtz, and Karel Ancerl; the second year they were Dean Dixon, Sixten Ehrling, and Rafael Frühbeck de Burgos. As in the past, the Schlitz Brewing Company and the City of New York came through with large grants toward the expenses. ("Schlitz beer is New York Philharmonic beer," Amyas Ames told the Central Park audience at the opening concert of the 1970 park series. "Good people make good beer.") As the novelty of these outdoor concerts wore off, and as some less celebrated conductors were employed, the audiences could be expected to drop somewhat from the massive turnout of the first summer, but the steep decline that the attendance records seemed to show—

475,000 in 1965
390,000 in 1966
316,000 in 1967
273,000 in 1968
185,000 in 1969

—did not have to be taken too seriously. Most of it apparently was due to a streak of bad weather—the bane of outdoor performances—for three years in a row. In spite of the downpours, audiences of 30,000, 50,000, and sometimes 70,000 persons were frequent. The summer of

1970, when the weather was more reasonable, became by that fact a sort of test. The opening night in Central Park, in perfect weather, was led by the American (Negro) conductor Dean Dixon, returning to conduct in the city of his birth after twenty-one years abroad; it attracted an audience that the Philharmonic and the police estimated to be 70,000, though Harold Schonberg of the *Times* put it at "75,000, at the very least." And the attendance at the whole set of twelve concerts in the five boroughs of the city came to 358,000. This could be taken as a fair gauge of the drawing power of the Park Concerts for the immediate future. Although it would probably take an exceptional stirring-up—like the novelty of Boulez's first appearances in the parks, or the return of Bernstein—and a strong publicity campaign to raise the figures to the level of that first summer of 1965, there was every reason to expect that, for the next few years, first-night crowds would sometimes reach 50,000 or even 75,000, and totals for the season 300,000 or more.[226]* It is easy to forget that we are talking here about average audiences of 25,000 or 30,000 for a single concert—about ten times the number that would hear a concert at Philharmonic Hall.

Turning to another of the Philharmonic's summer presentations, the Promenades, we recognize that these concerts, too, had never been dependent on Bernstein. It was André Kostelanetz who introduced the Promenades in 1963 and who served as their Artistic Director every summer thereafter. There were nineteen Promenade concerts in 1969 and nineteen more in 1970. More than 40 per cent of the available seats were taken by organizations that bought blocks of tickets in advance. This practice had been growing steadily in popularity; the number of groups that took tickets mounted from 63 in 1965 to 125 in 1970. The Promenades seemed to be flourishing during the interregnum.

Only one of the summer activities had to be abandoned, but that happened before Bernstein's resignation and had nothing to do with it. It had been hoped in 1965 that the Philharmonic, either alone or in conjunction with Lincoln Center, would be able to attract a new public for annual "summer festivals." For a long time before that, there had been suggestions that the Philharmonic should have a country home outside New York for the summers. "Perhaps," said President Floyd Blair in 1955, "as was the case with the organization of Tanglewood

---

* Backnote 226 and several others for this chapter indicate changes that occurred between the period that the chapter describes and the time of printing of this book.

and Aspen, one of our music-loving citizens will make a gift of his country estate to the Society." Caumsett, the 1,400-acre Long Island estate of the late Marshall Field, who had been President of the Philharmonic for many years, seemed a possibility around 1960, and both the Saratoga Spa Center in New York and the Interlochen Music Camp in Michigan were still being considered in 1963. But when the modern Philharmonic Hall at Lincoln Center made it possible to give summer concerts in air-conditioned comfort, the new President, Amyas Ames, indicated that the Philharmonic would concentrate its activities in the city—it would give *indoor* summer festivals that could be expected to find an inexhaustible reservoir of listeners among the New Yorkers who stayed in the city during the summer months and the tourists who flowed in from every part of the world. That was the idea behind the French-American Festival and the Stravinsky Festival that were given in the summers of 1965 and 1966, under Lukas Foss's direction, and the multifaceted Lincoln Center festivals of 1967 and 1968, in which the Philharmonic participated on a smaller scale. Unfortunately, the kind of public that had been expected failed to materialize. The festivals did not attract a national or an international audience; a survey conducted by Lincoln Center during the summers of 1967 and 1968 showed that the nucleus of the audience came from within a three-mile radius of the Center, and that it was made up of "the usual New York patrons." Consequently, when they started going away on vacation in July, attendance dropped markedly. The Lincoln Center festivals of 1967 and 1968 incurred losses of $750,000 in each year, and early in 1969 it was announced that the Center was in such financial straits that it would not be able to present a festival in either 1969 or 1970. Since Philharmonic Hall was undergoing the last phase of its acoustic overhauling during three months of the summer of 1969, the orchestra could not offer a festival then, anyway. Instead, the Philharmonic went out of town, after all, in the summer of 1969 (and again in 1970), to take part in the Garden State Festival at the new covered amphitheater, built and run by the State Highway Authority, at Telegraph Hill Park in New Jersey. For the time being, then, the Philharmonic was not sponsoring summer festivals at Philharmonic Hall, but there were many who thought that the results of the experiments of 1965–68 were not conclusive (the Philharmonic gave only two concerts in the Lincoln Center festival of 1968, but they were both sold out), and that a new audience might yet be developed for such events if the festivals were started up again.

When Lincoln Center tightened its financial belt in 1969, it bravely resolved not to curtail the ambitious educational program that had been established under William Schuman's leadership. This meant that the Philharmonic Society could continue, in 1969–70, the educational benefits that it had dispensed under the Lincoln Center Student Program. The Center underwrote the costs of four low-priced Philharmonic concerts for high school students, and it paid for Student Awards of free Philharmonic tickets to one thousand junior high and senior high school students. The Philharmonic also continued its own educational projects: the Young People's Concerts, the student tickets at reduced rates, and the three assistant conductorships awarded to the winners of the Mitropoulos International Music Competition. The Young People's Concerts, as in previous years, consisted of four different programs, each performed twice on the same day in the concert hall, and, as in previous years, both series were completely sold out by subscription. Bernstein chose to conduct only two of the four programs of 1969–70 —of the others, one was taken by Aaron Copland, and another was shared by Peter Ustinov, the actor, and Alfredo Bonavera, one of the Assistant Conductors—but they were all televised, in color, by CBS-TV on a nationwide hookup. Although Bernstein's face and style had come to be associated in the popular mind with the Philharmonic's educational work, there seemed to be no falling off of interest in the two programs that were conducted by other people. Of course, if Bernstein were to drop out of the series completely (he left his position as Philharmonic Music Director, after all, to gain time for his other interests), the televising of the Young People's Concerts might eventually be discontinued. But for the moment, that had not happened, and for the live concerts in Philharmonic Hall, prospective subscribers in 1970–71 had a waiting period of three years.[227]

The heart of the orchestra's schedule was still the subscription concerts, of which there were 115 in the season of 1969–70, just as there had been under Bernstein's directorship. Szell, the Senior Guest Conductor, had the longest stretch in the 1969–70 season, eight weeks; Bernstein, as Laureate Conductor, was scheduled for only five weeks; and five guest conductors, each taking two to five weeks of concerts, covered the rest of the subscription series. In the 1950s the pre-season prospectus had usually carried a plea to the patrons to subscribe for the whole season in advance; but in 1969–70, as in the years of Bernstein's directorship, the Philharmonic did not even bother to list subscription prices in its pre-season announcements of the concert programs— there were simply no subscriptions to be had at any price by the time the programs could be announced. Anyone who wanted to take out a new subscription could expect to wait a long time for it; for the Saturday night series the waiting period was six years! What with Bernstein's admirers, Szell's admirers, and the orchestra's admirers—and New York's habituation to sold-out houses over the past decade—the Philharmonic appeared to be in no danger of losing its public.[228]

And yet, with Szell's personality replacing Bernstein's in the dominant position in the season, some difference could be expected. Szell had a reputation, which he found it difficult to escape, as an interpreter of German-Austrian music from Haydn to Mahler, and as a precision expert in his control of orchestral ensemble. Both parts of this reputation were certainly warranted, but Szell's glorifiers as well as his detractors tended to speak as though those two specialties represented the sum total of his qualities. Since he was a man of encyclopedic knowledge not only in music but, it sometimes seemed, in all branches of human study—he could discuss the fine points of a line of Shakespeare, and he could tell you that in Huntington, West Virginia, Victor's Delicatessen on Sixth Avenue was the place to buy imported cheeses— he was often impatient with such crude categorizations of his talents, but they persisted among professional musicians as well as among concertgoers. The acid-tongued Igor Stravinsky, surveying the whole conducting situation in *The New York Review of Books* on March 14, 1968, that is, before Szell had even begun to function as Music Advisor, referred to him as "the ombudsman-elect" of the New York Philharmonic and criticized his advice in advance: "But I fail in the first place to see," he said, "how a musician based almost exclusively in last-century repertory can ombudsmanize the affairs of the fast-getting-on present one . . . As for the Philharmonic I think it might do better in the Yellow Pages." And Harold Schonberg complained in the *Times* throughout the season that the programs were too tame and predictable. Szell's own programs were undeniably staid in 1969–70, but like Bruno Walter two decades earlier, he obtained variety in the season by allowing for the other conductors' leanings—for Ozawa's interest in Copland, Prokofiev, Riegger, Ibert, Orff, Kirchner, Ligeti, Scriabin, and a blues-based concerto by Russo, and for Bernstein's taste for Nielsen,

Schuman, and Carter. Moreover, that part of the audience that held Beethoven to be Allah and Szell the Prophet was delighted with his attention to the monuments of an older art. For an all-Beethoven program on April 9, 1970, the *Times* reported, "there was not a vacant seat in the house, and outside Philharmonic Hall people were pleading for tickets."

As this summary has shown, the orchestra continued, in 1969–70, without diminution—though occasionally with a shade of difference in style or manner—the principal services, both winter and summer, that the city had grown accustomed to.

Outside New York, the Philharmonic continued to go in person to other audiences on its tours. Bernstein's resignation from the position of Music Director did not interfere with the traveling. In late August and September of 1969 the Philharmonic made a tour of twenty concerts in the United States and Canada, under Seiji Ozawa and Karel Ancerl. And for the same season of the year in 1970, Bernstein, sharing the conducting with Ozawa, took the orchestra to Japan for performances at Expo '70 and other locations, with stopovers on the way back for a number of concerts in the United States. The brief out-of-town trips to nearby cities survived too. In May 1970, for instance, the orchestra went to Washington, D.C., for two concerts under Maazel.

One department that *had* depended on the Bernstein magic, between 1958 and 1969, was the making of phonograph recordings. Despite the serious competition that all American orchestras encountered from imported recordings, made under cheaper labor conditions (a perennial point of protest by the musicians' union), the sales of Bernstein's recordings with the New York Philharmonic on the Columbia label rose to 400,000 albums a year by 1969. When the musicians and the management of the Philharmonic negotiated their three-year contract in 1967, both sides were so confident of the continued demand for recordings that they wrote into the contract a guarantee that each man in the orchestra would receive $1,000 per year in recording fees. "The first thing the orchestra felt when it heard Lenny was leaving," one of the players told a *Times* reporter in 1969, "was, there goes the recording work." In 1969–70, however, the recordings brought in just about the same amount in royalties as they had been earning before Bernstein's resignation. One reason for this was that Columbia Records was still keeping in print almost two hundred of the albums that Bernstein had made for them (an astonishing stability in the ephemeral record market). Another was that Bernstein continued to record with the Philharmonic as Laureate Conductor. When Bernstein began to turn more of his attention to recording opera in Europe, as he was expected to do in the next few years, his recordings with the Philharmonic might well go down in number. By that time the new Music Director, Pierre Boulez, would have stepped into the picture. How well his recordings would sell, nobody knew, but it was unlikely that they would have the magic appeal to the public that Bernstein's had had. Columbia Records was letting it be known, moreover, that regardless of who was conducting, the high costs of recording in New York City might soon force a reduction in the making of records by the Philharmonic.† To be realistic about it, it could be expected that the number of new Philharmonic recordings would diminish in the next few years, and that the sales of Philharmonic records would go down somewhat, too, as the Bernstein backlog was depleted. Still, the orchestra players' fears of losing the recording work seemed not yet to be coming true in September 1970 when the new three-year contract between the Philharmonic Society and its orchestra continued the recording guarantee of $1,000 a year for each musician.

When the plans for the season of 1970–71 were announced, they depicted, almost in the fashion of a charade, the transition from one director to another. At the beginning of the season, Leonard Bernstein, the former Music Director, would conduct the first five weeks of subscription programs; then he would step out and George Szell, the "caretaker" of these transitional years, would conduct five weeks of concerts; and at the end of the season, Pierre Boulez, the incoming Music Director, would enter for the final five weeks. (For the intervening weeks of the season there would be a number of guest conductors.) The death of George Szell on July 30, 1970, forced a modification of the plan. His share of the concerts was divided among another group of guest conductors. But the significance of the season's plan as a connecting link between Bernstein and Boulez remained the same. Bernstein's metamorphosis from Music Director to Laureate Conductor

† This argument aroused the indignation of President Max Arons of the musicians' union, who claimed that the players in the great American orchestras had the right to expect salaries commensurate with their artistic achievements. The truth was, he said, that the big recording companies *preferred* to use cheap foreign labor. And the Copyright Act, by denying musicians fair royalty payments for the commercial use of their recordings, forced them to charge initial recording rates high enough to compensate for the inequity.

may have reduced his personal share in the orchestra's doings, but the marks of the decade in which his musical zeal was complemented by the social concern of the Philharmonic's officers and Directors were still visible. The expanded schedule of services was continuing—the Park Concerts, the Promenades, the educational activities—and the orchestra, busy all year round in its fifty-two-week contract, had a sense of its importance in the community that it had never had before the 1960s. If a few of the outlets that were closely connected with Bernstein's personal activity might be in danger of narrowing—the televised Young People's Concerts, the intensive recording program, the multiple Assistant Conductors—the Philharmonic in 1970–71 still seemed committed to the policy of wider service to a wider public that it had acquired in the Bernstein era.

It is easy enough to talk about "wider service" and "wider public" but somebody has to find the money and the time to do all that widening. The two problems—how to finance the expanded Philharmonic, and how to divide the responsibility for running and directing it—had been looming over the Society for some years. They reached a danger point in 1969. To cover the gap between the cost of running the orchestra and the amount that it earned by its performances and recordings, the Philharmonic had relied on a combination of sources of income: its endowment funds, gifts from individuals and corporations, the annual campaign of the Friends of the Philharmonic, and grants from government and philanthropic foundations. In the last few years, however, and particularly since the orchestra's fifty-two-week contracts had increased the basic costs, it had been harder and harder to make ends meet. Back in 1953 Floyd G. Blair, then President of the Philharmonic-Symphony Society, though strongly opposed to government subsidies for orchestras, had anticipated that municipal funds might be required for school or park concerts and federal funds for overseas tours; but "difficult as the financial problems of our orchestras may be," he had said in his Annual Report to the Society, "they still should be met by each community which the orchestra serves and not solved by grants from Washington." This stage the Philharmonic had now gone through —its great Park Concerts aided by the city, its grand tours by the nation —but the Philharmonic's remarkable growth in the 1960s made it more difficult to maintain the independence that Blair had cherished, and by the end of the Bernstein era Amyas Ames and other Directors were thinking longingly of those "grants from Washington" that Blair had eschewed.

To help pay for the year-round activities, the Philharmonic had opened a 125th Anniversary Fund Campaign in 1967. Of its $10-million goal, about three quarters had been realized when the campaign was closed in 1969; like many other cultural institutions, including its "landlord," Lincoln Center, the Philharmonic found that large contributions were becoming harder to get, perhaps because donors were giving higher priorities to urban, racial, and educational problems. Early in 1969 the nation's "Big Five" symphony orchestras—the New York Philharmonic, the Boston Symphony Orchestra, the Chicago Symphony Orchestra, the Cleveland Orchestra, and the Philadelphia Orchestra—alarmed at their accelerating economic difficulties, engaged McKinsey & Co., Inc., management consultants, to analyze the financial situation. The McKinsey Report (as it came to be called, in half-conscious imitation of the Kinsey Report on human sexual response) warned that the situation would worsen rapidly in the next few years, becoming dangerous by 1971–72. Inflation would swell costs, while broadcast and recording income seemed to be going down or, at best, holding constant, and concert revenues could not be expected to increase very much since most concerts were already sold out and orchestra managements were reluctant to raise ticket prices to the point where they would exclude many people from the concert halls. The report hinted that the orchestra musicians and their unions should be made to understand the magnitude of the crisis so that they would cooperate in controlling costs while funds were being found. It also pointed out that the five orchestras had been, and would continue to be, unable to handle these difficulties separately, and therefore recommended that they establish "an ongoing committee," consisting of their presidents and general managers—later, other orchestras could be invited to participate—to exchange ideas and to seek funds *as a group,* rather than as individual orchestras, from the Federal government, foundations, and businesses.

Although the New York Philharmonic was in the best financial shape of the five (it earned more than the others from its concerts and royalties, and was the only one that had a small surplus, rather than a deficit, after gifts and other non-operating income had been counted), Amyas Ames and the Philharmonic promptly took a leading role in the movement. In November of 1969 the Philharmonic acted as host in

PHILHARMONIC SOCIETY.

FIRST CONCERT,—FIRST SEASON.

Apollo Rooms, 7th Dec. 1842.

TO COMMENCE AT 8 O'CLOCK PRECISELY.

PART I.

GRAND SYMPHONY IN C MINOR. - - - - BEETHOVEN.

SCENA, *from Oberon.* - - - - - - - - WEBER.

MADAME OTTO.

QUINTETTE IN D MINOR. - - - - - - - HUMMEL.

PART II.

OVERTURE TO OBERON. - - - - - - - - WEBER.

DUETT—*from Armida.* - - - - - - - ROSSINI.

MADAME OTTO AND MR. C. E. HORN.

SCENA, *from Fidelio.* - - - - - - - BEETHOVEN.

MR. C. E. HORN.

ARIA BRAVURA—*from Belmont and Constantia.* MOZART.

MADAME OTTO.

NEW OVERTURE IN D. - - - - - - - KALLIWODA.

The Vocal Music will be directed by Mr. Timm.

Wm. C. Martin, Printer, 111 John st.

1. Program of the first concert of the New York Philharmonic, 1842.

PART I.

GRAND SYMPHONY IN C. MINOR. - - - - BEETHOVEN.
CONDUCTED BY U. C. HILL.

FIRST MOVEMENT, - - - - - - - ALLEGRO CON BRIO.
SECOND, " - - - - - - - ANDANTE.
THIRD, " - - - - - - - MINUET AND TRIO.
FINALE, - - - - - - - - - - - ALLEGRO MAESTOSO.

SCENA, *from the Opera of Oberon.* - - - - - WEBER.
MADAME OTTO.

REIZA, the Heroine of the Opera, has been wrecked with her husband, SIR HUON; he leaves her to seek assistance, and she describes the storm in an address to Ocean.

The waves gradually rising until in utmost fury, the sun breaking thro' the clouds, as well as the other incidents of a storm at sea are described by the Orchestra with that dramatic vividness, for which Weber is so celebrated.

RECITATIVE.

Ocean! thou mighty monster that liest curled,

Like a green serpent, round about the world,

To musing eye thou art an awful sight,

When calmly sleeping in the morning light:

But when thou risest in thy wrath, as now,

And fling'st thy folds around some fated prow,

Crushing the strong-ribb'd bark as 'twere a reed,

Then, Ocean, art thou terrible indeed.

AIR.

Still I see thy billows flashing,

Through the gloom their white foam flinging,

And the breaker's sullen dashing

In mine ear hope's knell is ringing.

But lo! methinks a light is breaking

Slowly o'er the distant deep,

Like a second morn awaking,

Pale and feeble from its sleep.

Brighter now, behold, 'tis beaming
  On the storm whose misty train,
Like some shatter'd flag is streaming,
  Or a wild steed's flying mane.

RECITATIVE.

And now the sun bursts forth, the wind is lulling fast
And the broad wave but pants from fury past.

AIR.

Cloudless o'er the blushing water,
  Now the setting sun is burning,
Like a victor red with slaughter,
  To his tent in triumph turning.
Ah! perchance these eyes may never
  Look upon his light again.
Fare thee well, bright orb, for ever,
  Thou for me wilt rise in vain.
But what gleams so white and fair,
  Heaving with the heaving billow.
'Tis a sea-bird wheeling there
  O'er some wretch's wat'ry pillow;
No! it is no bird I mark,
  Joy! it is a boat—a sail;
And yonder rides a gallant bark,
  Uninjured by the gale.

O transport! my Huon! haste down to the shore;
  Quick, quick; for a signal this scarf shall be wav'd:
They see me, they answer, they ply the strong oar,
  My husband! my love! we are sav'd! we are sav'd!

QUINTETTE IN D. MINOR, - - - - - - - HUMMEL.

Piano Forte, Violin, Viola, Violoncello, and Double Bass.

MESSRS. SCHARFENBERG, HILL, DERWORT, BOUCHER AND ROSIER.

(4)

PART II.

OVERTURE TO OBERON. - - - - - - - - WEBER.
CONDUCTED BY MR. ETIENNE.

DUETT.   *From the Opera of Armida.*   ROSSINI.

MADAME OTTO AND MR. C. E. HORN.

SCENA, *from the Opera of Fidelio.*   BEETHOVEN.

MR. C. E. HORN.

ARIA BRAVURA.   } *From the Opera of Belmont and Constantia.* {   MOZART.

MADAME OTTO.

ADAGIO.

Before I knew what love was, I had vowed affection and yielded up a faithful heart.

ARIA.

But too soon this gladness departed. Cruel Fate has separated us. Joy is banished from my eyes, and sorrow will soon break my heart.

NEW OVERTURE IN D. - - - - - - - - KALLIWODA.
CONDUCTED BY MR. TIMM.

Wm. C. Martin, Printer, 113 Fulton Street.

2. Ureli Corelli Hill, "chief begetter of the
New York Philharmonic," first of the three
conductors on its opening program in 1842,
President of the Society during its first six seasons, and active in its affairs as officer and violinist for three decades.

3. Henry C. Timm, conductor of part of the Philharmonic's first concert on December 1842, and successor to U. C. Hill as President of the Society. Timm was elected President fifteen consecutive seasons, from 1848 to 18__ the period of the Philharmonic's consolidation

4. William Scharfenberg, one of the founding members of the New York Philharmonic, pianist in the Hummel Quintette on the first program, and President of the Society from 1863 to 1866. The music shop of "Luis and Scharfenberg" was for many years one of the principal stores of its kind in the city.

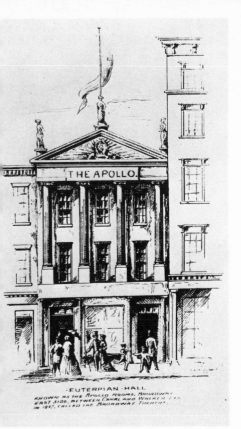

5. Exterior of the Apollo Rooms, the building in which the Philharmonic gave most of its concerts during the first nine seasons of its existence, from 1842 to 1851. The Apollo was at 410 Broadway, between Canal and Walker Streets.

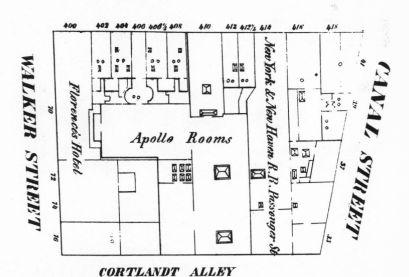

6. Map of the city block that contained the Apollo Rooms, showing how the structure flared out behind the narrow facade of 410 Broadway to make room for a large hall. (From W. Perris, *Maps of the City of New York*, 1853.)

7. The New York of the 1840s, the period of the Philharmonic's founding, had a varied and vigorous artistic life. In this painting of 1849, entitled *Kindred Spirits,* Asher B. Durand depicted the friendship between the poet Bryant and the painter Cole, whom he represented looking out over just such a wild American landscape as both loved to choose for the subjects of their works.

PHILHARMONIC SOCIETY.

———ooo●ooo———

LAST GRAND CONCERT,

FOR THIS SEASON.

Thursday Evening, April 5th, 1827.

PART I.

1. OVERTURE.—" L'Italiana in Algieri," ....*Rossini.*
2. SONG.—Mr. Howard.
3. CONCERTO.— Clarionet —Mr Mertens. ....*Krommer.*
4 SONG.—" The Rose and the Lily,"—Mr. Boyle.. ....*Martini.*
5. CAVATINA.—" Di tanti Palpiti," Madame Brichta..............*Rossini.*
6. SONG.—Mr. Boyle, accompanied by himself on the Piano.
7. OVERTURE,—" D'une Folie," ....*Méhul*

PART II.

1. OVERTURE.—" Chaperon Rouge," ....*Boieldieu.*
2. DUO.—" D'al campo," (from the opera of Tancredi,) Madame Brichta, and Signor Constantini,..............*Rossini.*
3. VARIATIONS.—Guitar—Mr. Martines.
4. SONG.—" Last words of Marmion," Mr. Boyle,..............*Dr. Clarke.*
5. QUINTETT.—Clarionet principal—Violin—Two Tenors,
   and Violincello,..*Kuffner.*
6. SONG.—Mr. Howard.
7. OVERTURE.—Del Irato.....................................*Méhul.*

——●◉●——

☞ **MR. GEAR,** principal double bass of the Society, gives a CONCERT on the 19th of April.

8. Program of a concert given in 1827 by the "second" Philharmonic Society of New York (which antedated the present, or "third" Philharmonic).

GRAND
MUSICAL FESTIVAL.

MR. A. P. HEINRICH

RESPECTFULLY ANNOUNCES TO HIS FRIENDS AND THE PUBLIC IN GENERAL
THAT HIS

GRAND MUSICAL FESTIVAL

WILL TAKE PLACE AT THE

Broadway Tabernacle,

ON

Thursday Evening, 16th June, 1842.

PRINCIPAL PERFORMERS.

MADAME OTTO,	**MRS. STRONG,**
MADAME SPOHR-ZAHN,	**MISS PEARSON,**
MRS. OUTCALT, *(her first appearance.)*	**MR. S. PEARSON,**
MRS. HARDWICK,	**MR. PEARSON,**
MR. SCHARFENBERG,	**MR. MASSETT,**
MR. E. R. HANSEN, *(from Philadelphia.)*	**MR. TIMM,**
MR. H. B. DODWORTH,	**MR. BOUCHER,**

LEOPOLD HERWIG, *(from Boston.)*

The ORCHESTRA will be NUMEROUS and POWERFUL; consisting of all the available
Professors in the city: together with upwards of 60 efficient voices.

Instrumental Leader, ... Mr. U. C. HILL.
Vocal Conductor, ... Mr. J. PEARSON.

General Director, ... *A. P. HEINRICH,*
Who will preside at the Piano-Forte.

E. HODGES, (Mus. Doc.) MR. WM. ALPERS & MR. D. R. HARRISON,
Will preside at the Organ alternately.

PROGRAMME.
PART I.
OPENING OF THE FESTIVAL.

I. The Grand Overture to the Pilgrim Fathers, ... A. P. Heinrich.
ITEMS:
> *Adagio Ottetto.*—The Genius of Freedom slumbering in the Forest shades of America.
> *Adagio Secondo*—Full Orchestra—She is awakened into life and action by those moving melodies with which Nature regales her solitudes.
> *Marcia.*—The efforts of Power to clip the wing of the young Eagle of Liberty.
> *Finale Allegrissimo.*—The joyous reign of universal Intelligence and universal Freedom.

II. *Concertante.*—Santa Maria. { *Mrs. Strong, Miss Pearson, Mr. S. Pearson, and Mr. Pearson,* } A. P. Heinrich.

III. *Song.*—Sweet is the Balm. *Mrs. Outcalt,* (her first appearance.) . . . A. P. Heinrich.

IV. *Duetto.*—From the Opera of Tancredi. *Md'me Spohr-Zahn & Md'me Otto.* Rossini.

V. { *Recit.*—" A chrystal pavement lies," *Aria.*—" The traveller stands perplex'd," } *Mr. S. Pearson.* . . . Haydn's Seasons.

VI. The Biographical " *Log-House Song.*" *Mrs. Strong.* . . . . A. P. Heinrich.
Piano-Forte Obligato,—*Mr. Scharfenberg.*

VII. *Grand Chorus Canonicale.*—From the Pilgrim Fathers. . . . . A. P. Heinrich.

PART II.

VIII. *Grand Solo* or *Concerto.* *Mr. Leopold Herwig.* . . . . . . —————

IX. *Aria, with Chorus.*—From Rossini's celebrated Stabet-Mater—"In flammatus et accensus. *Madame Otto.* . . . . Rossini.

X. *Duett.*—The Stranger's Requiem. *Mrs. Strong & Miss Pearson.* . . A. P. Heinrich.

XI. *Song.*—" Thy mighty power." *Mrs. Hardwick,* Contra-Basso. Obligato,—*Mr. Rosier.* V. Novello.

XII. *Quintetto.*—The Death of a Christian. { *Mrs. Strong, Miss Pearson, Mr. S. Pearson, Mr. Pearson and Mr. Massett.* } A. P. Heinrich.

XIII. *Finale.*—Beethoven's Grand Hallelujah to the Father. . . . . . Beethoven.

Doors will be opened at half past 6 o'clock; Performance will commence at 8.

SINGLE TICKETS, 1 DOLLAR; Tickets to admit a Lady and Gentleman, $1.50; to admit two Ladies and a Gentleman, $2. To be had at the Music stores, at the Book store of Dayton & Newman, at Saxton & Miles's, Broadway, at Mr. J. A. Sparks's office, 111 Nassau street, up stairs, and at the door on the evening of performance.

WM. C. MARTIN, PRINTER, 113 FULTON STREET, N. Y.

9. Program of Heinrich's Grand Musical Festival, 1842.

10. Anthony Philip Heinrich, eccentric but brilliant composer, whose Grand Musical Festival, on June 16, 1842, was one of the principal steppingstones on the way to the Philharmonic's first concert. (Picture from *The Atlas,* New York, about 1846.)

CONSTITUTION

OF THE

Philharmonic Society of New-York,

ADOPTED, APRIL, 1842.

I. That the name of the Association shall be the " PHILHARMONIC SOCIETY OF NEW-YORK," and its object the advancement of Instrumental Music.

II. That the members shall be professors of music and be limited to seventy.

III. That the Philharmonic Orchestra shall consist of fifty-three members.

LEADER.

10 First Violins.	2 Oboes.
9 Second "	2 Clarinets.
6 Tenors.	2 Bassoons.
4 Violoncellos.	4 Horns.
4 Basses.	3 Trombones.
2 Flutes.	2 Trumpets.
1 Picolo.	1 Drums.

IV. That the remaining members shall consist of Pianists, and professors of instruments not specified in the above, who shall be liable to be called upon by the government to play at any concert, on such terms as may be agreed upon.

V. That all candidates for admission shall be proposed at one meeting before their election, and be chosen by at least three-fourths of the members present.

VI. That every member shall sign the following declaration, " I promise to conform to the constitution of the Philharmonic Society of New-York."

VII. That the government shall be vested in a committee, consisting of a President, Vice-President, Secretary, Librarian and Treasurer, and two other members, to be elected annually ; five to constitute a quorum. Their duties shall be such as usually appertain to those offices, and the Treasurer shall be required to give bonds to the amount of $500, to be increased from time to time as the government shall see fit.

VIII. That the Society shall meet for practice and other business every alternate Saturday, from October 1st to June 30th inclusive, at 4 o'clock, to terminate at 6, and that every member of the orchestra not present at 4 o'clock, or absenting himself before 6 o'clock, shall be fined fifty cents.

IX. That three concerts shall be given annually by the Society, on evenings appointed by the government, and that any member not being present at the same, if required, shall be fined $5:

X. That each member of the orchestra shall receive $25 for his services, at all the concerts and rehearsals during the season.

XI. That the subscription to the concerts of the Society shall be $10 annually, payable on delivery of the tickets for the first concert, entitling the subscriber to four admissions to each. Each subscriber to be allowed two tickets extra at any concert, at $1.50 each.

XII. That every member shall be allowed to purchase two tickets for each concert, at one dollar each.

XIII. That no debts shall be incurred unless funds are in the hands of the Treasurer to meet them : to prevent which the government shall have the power of levying a tax, not exceeding twenty-five cents per month, for a room, the purchase of music, and other incidental expenses.

XIV. That no stranger shall be admitted during the rehearsals of the Society, except by permission from the government.

XV. That the situations of the members in the Orchestra, at the rehearsals and concerts of the Society, shall be assigned by the government.

XVI. That the Secretary shall, at the meeting following a concert, report on the same to the Society.

XVII. That an annual general meeting of the Society shall be held on the first Saturday in September, to receive the report of the government on the past season, elect officers for that ensuing, and on general business.

XVIII. That twenty members shall constitute a quorum of the Society, to do business.

XIX. That any member refusing to conform to the constitution and laws when required so to do, shall cease to be a member, and shall forfeit all claim to any portion of the property of the Society.

XX. That all elections shall be by ballot.

XXI. That no alteration in, or addition to the constitution and laws of the Society shall be made, unless the same shall be carried by a majority of three-fourths of the members at a special general meeting, to be convened for that purpose.

11. The original Constitution of the Philharmonic Society of New-York, as adopted in April 1842.

12. & 13. Joseph Burke, violinist, was elected an Honorary Member of the New York Philharmonic in its fourth season (1845–46), and played as soloist with the orchestra many times in the decade after that. In his boyhood, however, as "Master Burke, the Boy Phenomenon," he had been equally famous as an actor. The two pictures given here show him first as a boy, in the role of General Bombastes in *Bombastes Furioso,* and then as a mature young man, at about the time when he was appearing as soloist with the Philharmonic.

14. The mores of audiences at popular concerts in the middle of the nineteenth century can be observed in this picture of a Jullien concert at the Drury Lane Theatre in London in 1849. In the lower left corner, a pickpocket skillfully removes a man's handkerchief. In the center, immediately to the left of the orchestra, two men are fighting. The middle of the audience seems to be attentive, but the fringes are not, and there appears to be a considerable amount of talking and other social contact. The New York Philharmonic concerts, with their audiences of subscribers, were more staid in their atmosphere than were such popular entertainments, and one would not expect to encounter pickpockets or brawlers at a Philharmonic performance of the period. (Drawing by Richard Doyle, 1824–83.)

15. Broadway near Spring Street, as it looked at about the time when the Philharmonic played in the Chinese Buildings (third structure from the right) in 1848–49. (Lithograph after painting by Sébron, printed by Goupil, Paris and London, ca. 1855.)

16. & 17. William Henry Fry (top) and George F. Bristow, American composers, who protested in the press in 1854 that the New York Philharmonic
was not playing enough American music. Bristow's complaint gained special
weight from his relationship to the Philharmonic—he had been a violinist in
the orchestra since its second season, and had been elected an officer of the
Society only a few months before the public dispute flared up.

18. This picture has been printed many times with the erroneous title of "Founding Fathers." Actually it shows the Board of Directors of the Philharmonic for the sixteenth season, 1857–58. They are: (seated, left to right) L. Spier, Secretary and trombonist; H. C. Timm, President and occasionally pianist or trombonist; D. Walker, Treasurer and cellist; (standing, left to right) C. Brannes, Assistant on the Board and cellist; J. Noll, Assistant and violinist; T. Eisfeld, Vice-President and conductor; and C. Pazzaglia, Librarian and violinist. Only two of them, Timm and Walker, were among the founders of the Society in 1842.

19. Carl Bergmann, in the decade after the Civil War, built the Philharmonic into a great orchestra. By the spring of 1876, however, the talented conductor had sunk to such a state because of drunkenness and other problems that the Philharmonic had to ask for his resignation in mid-season.

20. Dr. R. Ogden Doremus, chemist, was the first President of the Philharmonic who was not a professional musician. In the three years of his presidency, from 1867 to 1870, the style of the Society changed rapidly, as the powers of money, glamour, and advertising were used to make the Philharmonic "catch on."

21.

FRANK LESLIE'S ILLUSTRATED NEWSPAPER. NEW YORK, OCTOBER 19, 1867.

SERENADE TO DR. DOREMUS BY THE MEMBERS OF THE N. Y. PHILHARMONIC SOCIETY, ON TUESDAY EVENING, SEPT. 24TH, AT HIS RESIDENCE, FOURTH AVENUE

22. George Templeton Strong, President of the Philharmonic Society from 1870 to 1874, whose urbane Diary is a rich source of information about New York's cultural life in his time. This portrait was made for a *carte de visite*, in 1860, by Rockwood and Rintoul, photographers.

23. José (Joseph) White, Negro violinist of Cuban birth, appeared as soloist with the Philharmonic in 1875–76, making such a success that he was engaged for a second concert in the same season.

24. Neither Leopold Damrosch nor his son Walter, who conducted the Philharmonic for one season each (Leopold in 1876–77 and Walter in 1902–3), was able to make a success with the orchestra. But their own Symphony Society—founded by Leopold in 1878 and carried on by Walter after 1885—was a serious rival to the Philharmonic until the two organizations merged in 1928. This photograph was taken around 1880, when Walter would have been eighteen years old and his father forty-eight.

25. Theodore Thomas, whose concerts with his own orchestra did much to shape the taste for symphonic music throughout the United States, took over the New York Philharmonic at a low point in its fortunes in the late 1870s and, in his thirteen seasons with the Society, gave it greater artistic and financial stability than it had ever enjoyed before.

26. Adolf Neuendorff, in the one season that he conducted the New York Philharmonic (1878–79, while Theodore Thomas was away), attracted the lowest box-office receipts that the orchestra had known in sixteen years. Neuendorff was an experienced conductor, but he could not match the hold that Thomas had gained on New York's musical life.

27. The oldest picture of the New York Philharmonic that has been found so far is this drawing of "A PHILHARMONIC CONCERT AT THE ACADEMY OF MUSIC, NEW YORK CITY," dating from 1884. The conductor is presumably Theodore Thomas. Pictures of the orchestra must have been made at an earlier date, but none has yet been recovered.

28. A page from *Harper's Weekly* marking the opening of Carnegie Hall in May 1891. [The drawings, by W. P. Snyder, show (1) the entrance, (2) the lobby, and (3) the interior.] It was not the New York Philharmonic that performed on this occasion, however, but its rival, Walter Damrosch's Symphony Society (which eventually merged with the Philharmonic, in 1928). The Philharmonic began to use Carnegie Hall for its concerts in 1892, and continued to play there for seventy years.

29. Anton Seidl could make the orchestra "sing and sigh and whisper, exult, plead and threaten, storm, rage and overwhelm, as no other conductor could," rhapsodized one New York critic. Given the challenging task of succeeding Theodore Thomas as conductor of the Philharmonic in 1891, Seidl led the orchestra through a period of unprecedented success and prosperity until his sudden death (from food poisoning) in 1898.

. Emil Paur was a respected conductor but had the almost impossible job of following e idolized Anton Seidl as conductor of the ilharmonic in 1898. He had a difficult time it, and was replaced in 1902 by Walter mrosch, who had an even more difficult e of it.

31. The oldest *photograph* of the New York Philharmonic that has been uncovered up to now: the orchestra under Walter Damrosch at Carnegie Hall in 1902.

32. Victor Herbert in the 1890s, when he played with the New York Philharmonic as cellist. On his return to the Philharmonic as guest conductor, in the 1903–4 season, he generously donated the fee he received to the orchestra's Pension Fund.

33. Richard Arnold was concertmaster and Vice-President of the Philharmonic in the difficult years before 1909, when the Society strove bravely but vainly to remain a cooperative. After the reorganization of the Philharmonic into a subsidized orchestra, Arnold was replaced as concertmaster but continued to hold the office of Vice-President until his death in 1918.

4. Vassily (or Wassily) Safonoff, fiery Russian conductor and pianist, was one of the earliest of the modern conductors to try conducting without a baton. He led the New York Philharmonic from 1906 to 1909. This photograph inscribed to Richard Arnold, who was conartmaster and Vice-President of the Philharonic during those years.

35. & 36. Two portrayals of Gustav Mahler, the great composer-conductor, who conducted the New York Philharmonic from 1909 to 1911: sculpture by Auguste Rodin (top), and photograph by W. A. Van Leer.

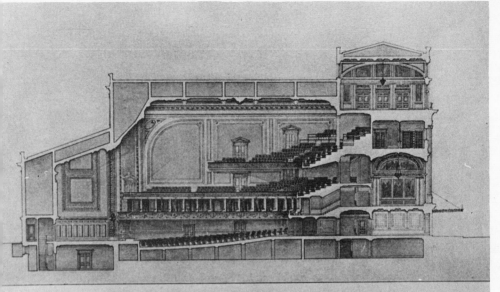

LONGITUDINAL SECTION
SCALE ONE INCH EQUALS EIGHT FEET
PROPOSED CONCERT HALL
FOR
NEW YORK PHILHARMONIC SOCIETY

37. A Philharmonic Hall that was never built. In 1914, during Josef Stransky's regime as conductor of the orchestra, a handsome brochure was prepared that presented the plans that had been drawn up by Parish and Schroeder, architects, for a "Philharmonic Building." Shown here is a longitudinal section of the proposed hall. The project had to be abandoned the next year because of unfavorable conditions attributed to the European war.

38. Josef Stransky, conductor of the New York Philharmonic from 1911 to 1923. He subsequently gave up his musical career and became a dealer in paintings.

39.. Members of the New York Philharmonic making recordings by the old acoustic process, about 1925, for Ginn and Company's Music Appreciation course. The conductor (upper left) is Henry Hadley.

40. In the summers, from 1922 to 1951, the Philharmonic was the official orchestra at the Stadium Concerts, given out of doors in Lewisohn Stadium of New York's City College. Tickets for these performances could be had for as little as 25¢. The photograph shows one of the largest audiences ever to attend a Stadium Concert—22,500 people, on July 17, 1939, for a Philharmonic-Symphony program conducted by André Kostelanetz, with Lily Pons as soloist.

41. "Minnie" Guggenheimer (Mrs. Charles S. Guggenheimer), who guided the Stadium Concerts for almost half a century, photographed appropriately against a Lewisohn Stadium background.

42. Ernest Schelling, who conducted the Children's and Young People's Concerts of the New York Philharmonic from 1923 to 1939, is shown with a group of youngsters at the store of the Aeolian piano company, in whose auditorium on Forty-second Street many of the Children's Concerts were given.

44. Mrs. Lytle Hull in 1961, when a chair was endowed in her honor in the soon-to-be-opened Philharmonic Hall. She is holding a token chair, presented to her by David M. Keiser, then the Philharmonic's President.

3. Mrs. Lytle Hull (the former Mrs. Vincent Astor) in the early 1920s, when she was the principal organizer for the Auxiliary Board of the Philharmonic. She was Chairman of the Auxiliary Board until 1961 and Honorary Chairman after that.

45. Simeon Bellison, principal clarinetist of the Philharmonic (first row, third from right), with the Clarinet Scholarship Ensemble in the late 1920s. For many years the women of the Philharmonic's Auxiliary Board raised the money to enable talented students of orchestral instruments to study free of charge with leading members of the orchestra. A number of these students, on various instruments, went on to become fine professionals.

46. Willem Mengelberg, either arriving from Europe or departing for it, as a Philharmonic conductor was expected to do each season.

47. In 1928, when Mengelberg and Toscanini were sharing the principal conducting duties of the Philharmonic, Mengelberg was given an honorary degree by Columbia University. Here he is being congratulated by Clarence Mackay, Chairman of the Philharmonic's Board of Directors.

48. Arturo Toscanini—already a legendary figure in his own lifetime—conducting the New York Philharmonic-Symphony, about 1936.

49. How Toscanini altered the orchestration of a page of Beethoven's Ninth Symphony (second movement) is shown by the ink markings in staves 9 to 11 (horns and trumpets) and 3 to 8 (woodwinds).

50. On April 23, 1930, the musicians of the Philharmonic-Symphony (and some of their wives) were photographed with Arturo Toscanini on the deck of the S.S. *DeGrasse* as the orchestra embarked on its first European tour. Toscanini (in cap and bow tie) is in the center of the first standing row.

51. Part of the line of people waiting outside Carnegie Hall for tickets to Toscanini's farewell concert with the Philharmonic-Symphony on April 29, 1936.

52. Wilhelm Furtwängler, about 1925, when he first worked with the Philharmonic as guest conductor. Furtwängler was announced as Toscanini's successor in 1936, but the apparent involvement of the Nazis in his affairs made his position in New York so awkward that he was unable to accept the appointment.

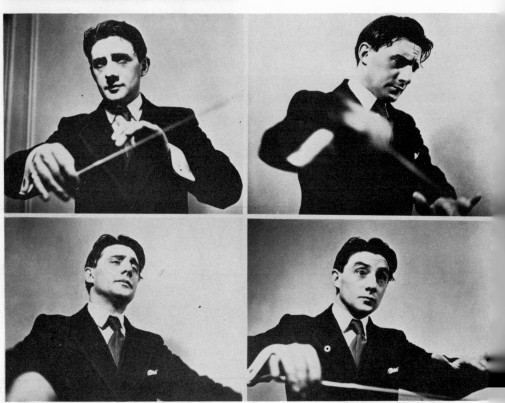

53. John Barbirolli was not yet thirty-seven years old when he succeeded Arturo Toscanini as a principal conductor of the New York Philharmonic-Symphony. This set of shots was taken in 1937 in connection with a Philharmonic broadcast.

54. In 1942, when Artur Rodzinski was one of the ten conductors engaged to lead the New York Philharmonic during its hundredth-anniversary season, he inscribed this photograph "To the Philharmonic-Symphony Society of New York with best wishes for the next Centennial."

55. Bruno Walter rehearsing the New York Philharmonic at Carnegie Hall in the 1940s. Walter led the orchestra frequently as guest conductor and from 1947 to 1949 held the title of Musical Adviser.

56. Leopold Stokowski was one of the two principal conductors of the Philharmonic for the 1949–50 season (the other was Dimitri Mitropoulos) and
made many appearances as guest conductor of the orchestra in other seasons. It is a tribute to the force of his personality, as well as to his sense of
humor, that he was able to sustain the mood of dedicated concentration in
this picture although his score (Schubert's "Unfinished" Symphony) was
upside down.

57. Dimitri Mitropoulos, at the piano, in rehearsal with members of the
New York Philharmonic in the 1950s in Carnegie Hall.

58. The marquee of the Roxy Theatre in September 1950 when the Philharmonic-Symphony played four concerts a day there, throughout a two-week period.

59. Arthur Judson (right) and Bruno Zirato (left), Managers of the Philharmonic, with Dimitri Mitropoulos, Musical Director, backstage at Carnegie Hall, in 1953. For almost half a century Judson was one of the most powerful figures in American music management.

60. Leonard Bernstein, "giving himself" to orchestra, audience, and music, in a typical gesture while conducting.

61. In 1958 Leonard Bernstein (right, in shirt-sleeves) had a special costume designed for the Philharmonic musicians to wear at the Preview concerts. It was intended to be less formal than full evening dress. The jackets and trousers were made of off-black tropical basket weave, the jackets with stand-up collars and white piping at the cuffs.

62. Leonard Bernstein conducting the New York Philharmonic at the Filarmoniya-Bolshoi Zal (large hall of the Philharmonic society) in Leningrad, 1959.

63. In February of 1961 Leonard Bernstein's three-year engagement as Music Director of the Philharmonic, due to expire at the end of that season, was extended for seven more years. With Bernstein at the signing of the agreement are George Judd, Jr. (center), Managing Director of the Philharmonic, and David M. Keiser (right), its President.

64. One of the largest audiences in the Philharmonic's history—estimates of its size ranged from 75,000 to 90,000 people—filled the Sheep Meadow in New York's Central Park on the evening of July 26, 1966, to hear Leonard Bernstein conduct Beethoven's *Eroica* Symphony and Stravinsky's *Rite of Spring*. (Even larger audiences assembled for Central Park concerts by the Philharmonic in the summers of 1972 and 1973.)

65. The title of Principal Guest Conductor the New York Philharmonic was given to D William Steinberg, conductor of the Pittsburg Symphony, for the seasons from 1966 to 196

66. George Szell, Musical Director of the Cleveland Orchestra, was guest conductor of the Philharmonic in hundreds of concerts between 1943 and his death in 1970. In 1969 he was named Music Advisor and Senior Guest Conductor of the Philharmonic.

67. Pierre Boulez, who was to become Music Director of the Philharmonic in the fall of 1971, discussing his plans for the orchestra at a press conference in January of 1971. Supporting him are Carlos Moseley (left), President of the Philharmonic, and Amyas Ames (right), Chairman of the Board of Directors.

68. The auditorium of Philharmonic Hall, at Lincoln Center in New York, just before its opening, in September 1962. The overhead clouds could be tilted, as needed, to help adjust the acoustics of the hall. Nevertheless, the acoustics were so generally criticized that radical changes had to be made in the auditorium between 1963 and 1969.

69. Philharmonic Hall after the alterations of 1969. The clouds have been replaced by a wooden ceiling, the walls have been covered with panels of acacia wood, and extensive changes have been made in the lighting, the stage, and other features of the auditorium.

70. & 71. Two views of the New York Philharmonic under Pierre Boulez. in 1972, at Philharmonic Hall:
(above) in a rehearsal with Christa Ludwig as vocal soloist
(below) in a concert

Philharmonic Hall at a two-day conference of 137 presidents, board chairmen, and managers of 77 orchestras, invited by the Big Five to discuss the financial problems. They decided to request the Federal government, for the first time in American history, to help the orchestras meet their deficits. An Ad Hoc Committee-of-the-Whole of Presidents of Symphony Orchestras was formed to work through the National Endowment for the Arts for the adoption of such a program by the government, and Amyas Ames was chosen as chairman of the committee. The total amount needed for all the orchestras of the United States in 1971–72 would be about $13 million. Ames found one of those happy phrases of comparison that people love to repeat when he pointed out that the $13 million was "just about half the cost of one modern traffic circle," like the $25-million Hawthorne traffic circle fifteen miles north of New York City. One of the speakers at the conference was Nancy Hanks, the new chairman of the National Endowment for the Arts, who must certainly have cited the Ad Hoc Committee as one of the evidences of the needs of the arts in presenting her budget proposals to President Nixon. On December 10, 1969, President Nixon asked Congress to approve $40 million, almost double the previous appropriation, for the National Foundation on the Arts and Humanities in the fiscal year 1971, half of this to be used for the arts and half for the humanities. Out of the arts half, the orchestras of the country could hope to receive about $3 million, which, since it would be required to generate additional sums on a matching basis, would go a long way toward helping them through their crisis. The $3 million to be divided among all the orchestras of the United States would be a paltry amount by comparison with European subsidies—the city of Hamburg gave more than that for its opera every year—but it would be much more than the American government had ever done before. The President's message was followed by a series of congressional hearings, at which Ames and other witnesses for the arts testified, and on July 21, 1970, President Nixon signed a bill making the National Foundation on the Arts and Humanities eligible to receive, for the next three years, $40 million the first year, $60 million the next year, and $80 million the year after that, half for the arts and half for the humanities. By the time Congress had made some cuts, the actual appropriation for the fiscal year 1971 was only $15 million of the $20 million that had been authorized for the arts, but this still represented an important increase in Federal support.

In a drive for state (as differentiated from Federal) money, Ames and others were just as active, and even more successful. They formed a Committee of Concerned Citizens for the Arts, with Ames as chairman, to support the request that Governor Rockefeller had made, in his annual message to the New York State Legislature on January 7, 1970, for $18 million in direct aid to non-profit cultural institutions in the state. On March 26 the legislature authorized the entire amount that the governor had asked for. So stunned were supporters of the arts at a state legislature's granting that much money to their cause, that one of them, Duane LaFlesche of Albany, cautioned the prospective beneficiaries to remember that their use of the money would be watched by the legislators. "We have received a golden egg," he said. "Please, please do not be so stupid as to think that it was a goose that laid it."‡

Following up these victories, Ames and other interested men and women from other parts of the country formed a Partnership for the Arts, in 1970–71, with the immediate aim of pressing Congress to appropriate the full $30 million that the arts were eligible to receive for the fiscal year 1972. A larger goal of the Partnership was the obtaining of a Federal funding of $200 million a year for the arts, which, it was pointed out, would mean only $1 per person in the United States, or (to look at it another way) only 1 per cent of what we spend each year on the building of roads and highways. And beyond that, the Partnership sought to encourage state and municipal legislatures, corporations, foundations, and individuals to increase their own financial contributions to the arts and to "[reject] the role of bystander to the maiming of our cultural heritage." When President Nixon, in January 1971, decided to ask Congress for the full $30 million, despite the economic stringency of the times, one of his aides indicated that the President had been influenced in his decision by the campaign carried on by Ames and the Partnership for the Arts.[229]

In these efforts Amyas Ames was acting in several capacities—as an altruistic citizen, as President of the New York Philharmonic, and as a director and chairman of the executive committee of the Lincoln Cen-

‡ The Philharmonic began to benefit from the new government appropriations before the end of 1970, when it was awarded grants from both the National Endowment for the Arts and the New York State Council on the Arts. One public-service project made possible by these grants was a joint venture with the New York City Central Labor Council AFL-CIO: a series of nine low-priced concerts, some in labor union halls and some at Philharmonic Hall, for union members and their families, in June 1971.

ter. He often spoke not just for the Philharmonic or for music but for all the arts. At the same time it was becoming increasingly difficult for the Music Director and the Managing Director of the Philharmonic to cope with their daily responsibilities to the orchestra and also give enough attention to the shaping of the Society's artistic and social policy. As the administrative problems grew in complexity, the Philharmonic Society, early in the spring of 1970, finally took a step that had become a necessity: it reorganized the highest ranks of its administrative officers.

In a bold and original move, planned largely by Amyas Ames and David M. Keiser, the Directors appointed a full-time, professional, salaried President. Since the days of Dr. R. Ogden Doremus in the 1860s, the Presidents of the Philharmonic (and of most other American orchestras) had been wealthy, public-spirited citizens, who had been willing to give their time, without any financial compensation, as a service to the community. Amyas Ames, too, had been an amateur President in that tradition. But it was he who now described the appointment of a professional President as "an administrative necessity." For the new position the Board of Directors chose Carlos Moseley, who had been Managing Director of the Society. Relieved of the day-by-day pressures of administrative chores, Moseley would concentrate on the long-range plans of the Philharmonic—"its musical functions, its educational and public service activity, its widening relationship in the community, its growing financial needs, its appeal for government support." The title of Managing Director was dropped, and duties of which Moseley had been relieved were turned over to a Manager, Helen M. Thompson, the first woman in the Philharmonic's history to hold that post. (According to the *Times,* an official of the Philharmonic was asked whether Mrs. Thompson's sex might not handicap her work, since orchestra musicians were accustomed to dealing with male managers. "The musicians of the Philharmonic," the official was quoted as replying severely, "are very gallant toward women.") Mrs. Thompson had not previously been a member of the Philharmonic staff, but she had collaborated with the Society on many a project in her capacity as Executive Vice-President and Treasurer of the American Symphony Orchestra League. She was respected and admired in the music world for her transformation of the League, between 1950 and 1970, from a modest association of community orchestras into the clearinghouse and central agency for the orchestras of America, in which the august

Philharmonic held membership alongside the humblest small-town ensemble. An untiring organizer and a persuasive advocate, she seemed
to succeed where others had failed in explaining to government officials
and foundation executives the problems of the symphony orchestras.
Her proven talents in this field promised to supplement Moseley's in a
new Philharmonic strategy: the orchestra would give more of its work
as a public service (free, or at low prices), and in return it would request more government and foundation funds to fortify its budget.

When Amyas Ames yielded the presidency to Carlos Moseley, he did
so not to lessen his own involvement in the Philharmonic's administration but to open up a higher level of activity for Moseley. Ames was
promptly elected Chairman of the Board. "As Chairman of the Board
of Directors," he reassured any who feared that the Philharmonic might
be losing one of its most effective officers, "I retain the senior authority
and responsibility of the Society and will devote just as much time and
effort to the affairs of the Society as in the past." That Ames was aug-
menting rather than diminishing his commitment to the arts was made
evident to all within the next two months when, in addition to his office
as Chairman of the Board of the Philharmonic, he also became Chairman of the Board of Lincoln Center, succeeding John D. Rockefeller
3rd. To make room for Ames as Philharmonic Chairman, David Keiser
had vacated that position, but had remained a member of the Board
and chairman of its Music Policy Committee; now, to honor Keiser for
his long association with the Society and to show him that he still held
a special place in its leadership, the Board created the new title of
Honorary Chairman for him. This gave the Philharmonic one of the
strongest administrative-managerial teams that it had ever enjoyed—
individually inventive, yet accustomed to working together—Amyas
Ames, David Keiser, Carlos Moseley, and Helen Thompson.[230]

In 1965, exhilarated by the success of the Park Concerts, the full
seasons, and the improved acoustics in Philharmonic Hall, Ames had
spoken to the Friends of the Philharmonic in a mood of bubbling enthusiasm. "The European orchestras," he had reminded them, "are
virtually totally supported by government grants, while, in this country,
the support is almost entirely from individuals . . . It is exciting that in
our affluent society the horizon of charitable giving has been increasingly extended to include the arts. The arts have always flourished
where they have interest and support."

In 1969, after the McKinsey study, Ames was a little less ebullient.

He wrote to the orchestra men that the Philharmonic faced troubled times in its finances. But his innate optimism prevailed. "We believe our problems are solvable," he said. "We are a productive people, who should be able to support the highest standards of artistic expression. Music cannot be given a second place in this country."

By 1970 his optimism was, to use his own adjective, "guarded." Without help from government, the orchestras of the country would wither, Ames wrote in an article entitled "The Silent Spring of Our Symphonies," in the *Saturday Review* of February 28, 1970. The orchestras had greatly expanded their public-service and educational work, but they had received little help. The various governments—Federal, state, and local, but especially the Federal—were failing to pay for what they were getting from the performing arts. That was why he and the Philharmonic's officers had become activists in a campaign for government subsidy of musical organizations, or at least of their public-service activities. The passage of the New York State and Federal bills aiding the arts, in the spring and summer of 1970, was an encouraging sign that government could be induced to help such organizations in their public work. "Our job," Ames had said when his Lincoln Center chairmanship was announced, "is to relate to the community and education." A similar belief was reflected in the addition of new members to the Philharmonic's Board of Directors in May 1970. Of the eight new Directors, almost all were already active in educational or community affairs (and in finding funds for them), one was the first Negro ever to be elected to the Board, one was a proponent of the business community's involvement in the arts, and several, in their late thirties and early forties, were younger than the directors of "establishment" cultural institutions had been wont to be.

"Public service" was not just a phrase for ceremonial occasions: it had become a goal that the Philharmonic could set itself—perhaps now *had* to set itself—for both practical and idealistic reasons. The Society could endorse the words of John D. Rockefeller 3rd that were inscribed on a bronze plaque that Philharmonic representatives helped to dedicate in his honor at Lincoln Center on June 23, 1970:

> The arts are not for the privileged few, but for the many. Their place is not on the periphery of daily life, but at its center.

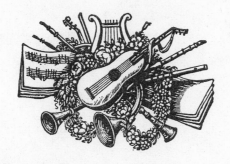

Epilogue

The Future

Leonard Bernstein's decision to leave the Philharmonic inevitably drew attention to his often-published opinions about the place of symphonic music in our times. They seemed to imply doubts that the Philharmonic's art was at the center of daily life, where John D. Rockefeller 3rd said it should be. CONDUCTOR THINKS SYMPHONY IS OUT OF DATE read a *Times* headline of an interview with Bernstein on April 28, 1965. "The symphony is not really in the mainstream of what is being written now in the world," he said on that occasion. "If this is true, it means that symphony orchestras have a museum function. A conductor is a kind of curator. He hangs symphonies up in the best possible lighting." If the Philharmonic were out of the mainstream, asked the reporter, would it last? "I give the Philharmonic forever," Bernstein replied. "It is a great curatorial institution." The idea that the symphony orchestra, particularly in America, was a musical anachronism or a music museum was a recurrent one in Bernstein's thinking. He was expounding it to his friends and pupils at Tanglewood before 1950. In 1954, in a witty article in *The Atlantic,* he allowed a fictional Broadway producer to persuade him to write for the musical theater rather than for the symphony orchestra: since the listener in America "doesn't give a damn about whether anyone is writing new symphonies or not," he has the producer argue, "there is no real vitality for him in our concert life, except the vitality of a visit to the museum." He summed up his viewpoints in an interview ("A Conversation with Leonard Bernstein") that was prepared in 1967 for a magazine called *Adventures in Sight & Sound* that Trans World Airlines distributed to its passengers:

The last important symphony I can think of is Stravinsky's "Symphony in Three Movements" which was written in 1945. Since the war, there has been virtually nothing important of a symphonic nature.

I think that is one of the reasons I am giving up the Music Directorship of the Philharmonic. It's very hard to continue in this role when you don't feel a vital bloodstream of new music coming in . . . you don't really have anyone to champion . . .

So, I am going to turn to other things.[231]

Bernstein's pessimism in these statements (and in similar ones that he has made since then) seems at variance with the thriving condition of the Philharmonic domain. Can the expansion of the Philharmonic be only an illusion? Is not the orchestra deeply involved in the current "cultural expansion" or "cultural boom"? If so, how can it be considered out of date and a museum of the past? Obviously the future of the organization hangs upon the answers to these questions.

They are questions that must be answered on several different levels.

First, there is no doubt of the reality of the Philharmonic's expansion of its activities since World War II. Nobody knows this better than the orchestra players who are now working all year round—for the first time in their history—to meet the demand for their services. And their paychecks are tangible evidence that those services are more appreciated than they used to be. In the late 1940s the minimum salary for a Philharmonic musician was between $3,000 and $4,000 a year; the 1970 contract made $16,860 the lowest salary in the orchestra and raised the minimum to $18,160 for the third year of the contract. Even after allowance has been made for the decline in the purchasing power of the dollar, the orchestra musician's income comes out more than double what it was right after the war. The music lover, too, trying to get a seat in Philharmonic Hall, or crowding onto the Central Park meadow with seventy thousand of his fellows, will testify to the growth of the Philharmonic's audiences, summer and winter.

There is no doubt, then, that an expansion of the Philharmonic's operations has taken place. But on another level of evaluation, it is equally beyond doubt that the character and dimensions of the expansion have been more modest than the shouts of "boom" and "explosion" suggest. There are built-in bounds to some aspects of the growth of a symphony orchestra, and the Philharmonic was not far from those bounds even before its recent flowering. For example, the number of rehearsals and performances that an orchestra can carry is not un-limited. During, and just after, World War II, the number of concerts that the Philharmonic gave ranged from 111 to 140 per season, includ-ing tours; in the 1960s this was raised to around 185 or 195, but it is not likely to go much higher since the players are now fully employed all year round. Nor could the number of persons attending the regular winter concerts be increased, once sold-out houses were achieved early in Bernstein's tenure; the best size for an auditorium, the acoustic ex-perts said, should not go much beyond a seating capacity of 2,500 or 2,800, and the new Philharmonic Hall, therefore, was built to accom-modate no more listeners than the old Carnegie Hall had held. In other words, except for the outdoor concerts in Central Park, there has not been a great deal of room for the Philharmonic to expand in, and some of the data confirm that there has been little change in the number and social strata of the audiences: The Subscription Series still make up the core of the orchestra's schedule, 123 concerts (includ-ing the eight Young People's Concerts) out of about 190. This is significant because it means that the largest part of the Philharmonic's work is directed toward an audience that totals only 28,000 persons over the whole year (that is how many subscribers there have been in the last few seasons) out of New York's 8,000,000 inhabitants—hardly the mass public that many imagine in a cultural explosion. For the sum-mer festivals that ended in 1968, as has been mentioned in the preced-ing chapter, a Lincoln Center evaluation indicated that the audience had consisted primarily of "the usual New York patrons"—in fact, it at-tributed the failure of the festivals to the tendency of too many of that class to leave the city on vacation after the Fourth of July every year. It is not known to what extent the Promenade audiences have been new listeners who were not acquainted with the Philharmonic before, but in any case they cannot be thought of as "the masses." Ticket prices ranging from $3 to $6.50 are moderate by recent New York stand-ards, but they are not for poor people; neither are the refreshments that one can enjoy in relaxation at the Promenades, at 50¢ for a Coca-Cola and $9 to $15 for a bottle of champagne. The old summer concerts at the Lewisohn Stadium may well have reached a broader public; two or three hit nights there (the capacity was about twenty-two thousand) could bring the Philharmonic as many listeners as a whole season of Prom-enade programs at Philharmonic Hall, and at ticket prices as low as 28¢. Only the Park Concerts, which are absolutely free, have permitted all to attend without financial problem, and even that audience, although showing more of a cross section of the city's population, strikes most observers as being a surprisingly select and affluent one. It seems to fit the pattern found in a recent sampling of free, outdoor performances of the New York Shakespeare Festival and the Philadelphia Robin Hood Dell Concerts: "Even at free performances the audience is relatively well educated, of relatively comfortable means, and is composed primarily of members of the professions."[232]

It is a temptation at this point to conclude that the magnitude of the cultural boom has been exaggerated as far as music is concerned. Indeed, some observers discount the extent of the explosion in all the performing arts. Professors William J. Baumol and William G. Bowen, Princeton University economists, who have made the most systematic investigation to date of the financial problems of performing groups in the arts, find evidence of only "a modest expansion in performing arts activity, one which, though by no means negligible, is far from universal and can hardly be called a cultural explosion."[233] But it would be an error to accept their evaluation without question. To do so would be to ignore the evidence of our senses—which see and hear the ferment of artistic activity and consumption going on all around us—and to misconstrue, as I believe Baumol and Bowen have done, the message that cries out from their beautifully collected and lucidly presented data. It is that there has, indeed, been an explosion or boom (call it what you will) of wide distribution in our society, *but that this revolution has taken place largely outside the established channels of institutions like the Philharmonic and the Metropolitan Opera.* Baumol and Bowen give hints from time to time that they know this to be so, but they doggedly devote almost all of their attention to the areas least touched by the boom that they claim to be investigating. They admit in advance that their subject matter in music has been defined to include only live professional performance of concert music and opera, excluding all the mass media, all amateur performance, and all "popular" music. But admitting it does not make the procedure more valid. They are studying change by looking at the least changed regions.

Meanwhile, our music world has been exploding in every direction, from the vernacular to the esoteric. # There is the tuned-in radio of every turned-on teen-ager. # There is the exportation to all the world of the American musical theater, from *Finian's Rainbow* and *West Side Story* to *Hair* and beyond. # There is the whole expanse of jazz, from the traditional folk-rooted varieties to the most abstruse and pretentious intellectualizations—all international commodities. # There is the musical fare on television, often limited in artistic variety, but unquestionably constituting an explosion in its dissemination by methods that were simply not available twenty-five years ago. # There is the musical fare on LP records and tape, almost *un*limited in variety, representing an explosion not only in the scope of the repertory but also in the value to the purchaser—a long-playing record may seem to cost a bit more in real dollars than one of the old 78-rpm recordings (though some actually cost less) but it contains five times as much music. Recordings have reshaped the musical tastes of a large segment of the population. The music of Telemann is still practically unknown on Philharmonic or Boston Symphony programs, but in the Schwann catalogue of LP records Telemann is a major composer, with well over 150 listings to his name. Many a year goes by at the Philharmonic without a Vivaldi performance, but Vivaldi now has as much space in the record catalogue as Brahms or Wagner. # There is the discovery or rediscovery by a broad public of whole epochs of old music not suited for performance by symphony orchestras—particularly the Baroque and the Renaissance, but also the Middle Ages—and the development of special ensembles, both professional and amateur, for the performance of such music: the mushrooming chamber orchestras and madrigal clubs and choral societies, the polished touring ensembles (like the Pro Musica Antiqua) that reproduce the music of the past, and the *collegia musica* of the universities. # There are the new ears of the West for oriental music, from the koto of Japan to the sitar of India (as many sitars are now sold each year in the United States as in India). # There is the huge expansion of music in all corridors of the educational world, the greatest such expansion in the entire history of our music education, which has made an introductory course in music a requirement for every college undergraduate, no matter what his major field of study, which has roused up hundreds of thousands of singers and players in our junior high and senior high schools, and which has created in our universities libraries and centers for musicological research, enclaves of composers and performers "in residence," and a circuit of paying audiences that sustains 70 per cent of the professional concert activity in the United States. # There is the incubation by philanthropic foundations of the avant-garde chamber-music groups, with their small but fanatic followings. # There is the financial support, for the first time in modern American history, of music and the other arts by Federal and state governments. # There have been the explosions of the folk-music movement, rhythm-and-blues, rock, the country style, the new pop music, and all their various blendings and cross-fertilizations—embracing the revival of authentic old songs and instrumental pieces, the creation of a literature of new ones, the epidemic spread of the guitar and of electrically amplified sounds, and the emergence of schools of poet-composer-performers, armies of active amateurs, and a worldwide audience of devotees. The folk, blues, country, pop, and rock artists of America have seen mountains of their recordings bought by the youth not only of their own country but of half the world; it is not uncommon for one of them to sell five million records in a year. When they give live concerts in New York, they often use the same Philharmonic Hall and Carnegie Hall that the symphony orchestras do, and they fill them with appreciative audiences, at prices at least as high as the orchestras charge. A star who can do even better than that at the box office may risk the acoustics of Madison Square Garden (capacity twenty thousand). The gigantic rock and pop "festivals," which are as much festive pilgrimages of the youth cult as they are festive performances of music, must be held in open country to accommodate their vast throngs—100,000 or 200,000 people have turned out for some of these festivals, and for the Woodstock Festival at Bethel, New York, in 1969, there were 300,000. But it is not just a matter of crowds and numbers; it is also a matter of communication. On a single day in January 1967, the New York *Times* was moved to describe the Carnegie Hall appearance of Tom Paxton, young singer-songwriter, as an example of how "our pop and folk music is speaking viably to and for a generation," and to praise the Philharmonic Hall performance of Simon and Garfunkel as embodying "artistry, depth, communication and musical expertise—all assimilated for an adulatory public." In the earnest, poetic songs of Joan Baez, Bob Dylan, and Simon and Garfunkel, a generation has found cultural mottoes, political dissent, and moral "right rules" of life. B. B. King, black blues singer and guitarist, is understood by listeners—young and old, black and white—at a swanky Las Vegas night club, a one-night stand on the "chitlin' circuit" in the South, and a concert in New York or San Francisco. The rock group named Blood, Sweat & Tears intoxicates Romanian kids as completely as it does their American contemporaries. And Johnny Cash, composer and performer of country music, after taking his songs to the inmates of Folsom Prison, is invited by the President of the United States to perform at the White House. # And could anyone in the 1960s really have missed THE BEATLES?

In sum, the most characteristic aspect of the boom has been its pluralism—the simultaneous existence of so many and such varied musical currents. They range in quality from superb artistry to ridiculous nonsense. Some of the results are less exciting than the propaganda about them. But many of them appeal widely to the young and they are very real, with a reality that is backed up by money. For the young people of New York, as of much of America, have been subsidized in their entertainment and their cultural indulgences by the rich society in and on which they live. "A Growing Audience of Swinging Young Spenders," hawked the New York *Post* in the promotion material for the entertainment advertising section with which it cashed in on this market in a recent summer.

It was something of all this lively variety that Leonard Bernstein seems to have had in mind when he weighed the world of symphonic music against the worlds of popular music and musical theater, and found the first to be a praiseworthy museum piece but lacking the innate vitality of the others. It may well have been something of this that led him to retain the Young People's Concerts, with their mass TV audience, as his chief connection with the Philharmonic when he took his sabbatical in 1964–65, and to emphasize television and phonograph recordings for the Laureate years following his relinquishing of the Music Director's post in 1969. It was probably something of this that lay behind his confession, in the summer of 1966, "that at this moment, as of this writing, God forgive me, I have far more pleasure in following the musical adventures of Simon & Garfunkel or of the Association singing 'Along Comes Mary' than I have in most of what is being written now by the whole community of 'avant-garde' composers . . . Pop music seems to be the only area where there is to be found unabashed vitality, the fun of invention, the feeling of fresh air. Everything else suddenly seems old-fashioned: electronic music, serialism, chance music—they have already acquired the musty odor of academicism. Even jazz seems to have ground to a painful halt. And tonal music lies in abeyance, dormant."[234] On January 13, 1967, Howard Taubman published an interview with Bernstein in the New York *Times*. "He regards the opera and the symphony as all but impossible to encompass for the contemporary composer," Taubman reported. "In the theater, he feels, it is possible, at least for him, to be true to himself and the spirit of his time . . . he believes it is time to take a step—then another and another—toward a marriage of our vernacular and music that reflects our time and place."

Bernstein's analysis of the musical scene may have been right for him, but what was the Philharmonic to do when it lost its spectacular-conductor, who had roused up the public and rebuilt the morale of the Society and its standing in the city? In tackling the problem of who could succeed Bernstein, the Philharmonic's administration had to re-consider the social and financial position of the Society, and its rela-tionship to the cultural upheaval that we have been discussing. The first reaction was one of cautious flexibility—the Philharmonic had to be ready, in these unpredictably changing times, to follow whatever path proved the necessary one. Carlos Moseley, then Managing Direc-tor, when asked (in interviews with the author of this book, at the time when Bernstein's resignation was announced) to comment on the future of the Philharmonic, suggested that some *retrenchment* might be the sensible step in the not too distant future. In explaining why the Phil-harmonic might be wise to reduce its operations at the moment of its greatest success, Moseley made some common-sense points, with which many orchestra managers and directors would still agree:

1. The symphonic repertory, as Bernstein had said repeatedly, was not being replenished in our time. In the earlier part of this century, at least Stravinsky, Hindemith, Bartók, Prokofiev, Copland, and a number of other composers, were adding to the list of viable works, but it seemed doubtful that Stockhausen and his contemporaries would fill the need for fresh symphonic material that could be welcomed by a concert-going public.

Yet, more music was being demanded for more and more concerts. Everywhere in the United States orchestras were expanding in size and lengthening their seasons, and the trend was being accelerated by the financial aid of foundations and government agencies. The supply and the demand were out of balance.

2. Big conductors and soloists who could capture the public in a world with so many distractions were fewer than formerly. And those who were available were performing less because of the income tax situation in this country.

3. The economics of the orchestral world had become even more difficult than before. The stars mentioned in the preceding paragraph received fees

of $4,000 to $6,000 for a performance, and the market was kept up by a Europe grown rich enough to compete for their services. The Philharmonic's orchestra players, who for most of the Society's history had "subsidized" it by taking less than a living wage, finally had fifty-two-week contracts at substantial salaries, and with improved fringe benefits; this was no more than they were entitled to, but the burden on the Society's finances was tremendous. The Philharmonic's operating budget in 1965–66 was $3.3 million, and even with sold-out houses the orchestra earned only about 80 per cent of it from ticket sales, recording royalties, and broadcasting fees. This ratio of earnings to expenses was considered very good by comparison with other orchestras, but it nevertheless left a deficit of $700,000 that had to be made up from contributions and special grants.

4. The subscription public was absolutely necessary for financial security—in 1965–66, the 28,787 subscribers to regular and Young People's series accounted for 65 per cent of the orchestra's concert receipts—but it tended to be a conservative public, notoriously difficult to warm up. One heard frequent talk of the new public in the city; it was true that there were *many* new publics, but not necessarily for symphonic music— they seemed to be attracted by the "cute little concert ideas" that were offered them on every hand, with everyone competing to outdo the others in novelty. The Philharmonic did seem to have found a new summer public, different from the winter one and quick to respond with enthusiasm; it provided an encouragement and perhaps a promise for the future, but for the present it was a financial liability rather than a help, since the Park Concerts were given free of charge; and in any case the summer public could not carry the bulk of the year's activities.

These were some of the reasons for Carlos Moseley's thinking in 1966 that a certain amount of retrenchment might be healthier for the New York Philharmonic than the continued expansion that most people seem to expect of an institution that is vested with a public interest. Perhaps for some cities that were at an earlier stage in their orchestral evolution there would still be room for further expansion, but it seemed unlikely to him that New York and the other very big ones would find the new repertory and the paying public to support constant enlargement of the orchestra's operations.

The situation had grown even more difficult by 1970. The Philharmonic's deficit had swollen in four years from $700,000 to $1,500,000. And the prospect of bringing together a fresh repertory and a fresh public was at least as remote as before: the season subscribers, whose conservatism had been blamed for slowing change, were more firmly intrenched than ever—their contribution had risen to 69 per cent of all concert receipts.

Yet the Philharmonic did not retrench, after all—and it has not done so to the present day. Instead, as was explained in the last chapter, Moseley, Ames, and the Directors of the Society have had the flexibility to try a different strategy. They have deliberately set out to widen the orchestra's services to the community, rather than to contract them, joining with the other orchestras of the country in pressing for government funds to make this possible. It would be easier to retrench: the Philharmonic could honorably confine itself to being the "great curatorial institution" that Bernstein has seen in it, the museumlike repository of a repertory drawn largely from the past. If this role were acted with conviction, the orchestra could occupy a small but secure place in our pluralistic culture. But curtailment would be a choice that would be out of tune with the current needs and style of the community, and it would not in itself solve the financial problems—less activity would mean less expense but it would also mean less income. Another choice might be to maintain the present level of the offering, including the summer events, the telecasts, and the educational activities, without any further expansion. But it should not be imagined that freezing the level of activity would also freeze the size of the budget. Unfortunately, as Moseley and Ames have explained, income from the fixed number of performances can be increased only slightly, while salaries and other operating expenses are sure to rise much more rapidly. Baumol and Bowen, in the study referred to above, propose as one of their principal theses that the "technology" of live performance, since it leaves little room for increasing productivity by labor-saving innovations, dooms it to an ever-widening gap between costs and income. Merely to keep up things as they are would require not the same but *much greater* support from philanthropic and government sources.

The Philharmonic's courageous decision neither to retreat nor merely to hold the line, but on the contrary to enlarge the orchestra's services, may yet prove to be as practical as it seems to be idealistic. It could conceivably make the orchestra important to enough people so that new sources of support—spiritual and economic—would be generated. But by what devices could such a broadening proceed? Potentially, as the prognosticators have been telling us for twenty-five years, a huge expansion should be possible by means of television, radio, and recordings, which could spread the present performances to great audiences outside the concert hall; but the realistic truth is that so far all these media together have contributed only a small share of the Philharmonic's income—about 8½ per cent in recent years. And plans for closed-circuit transmission, which might reach a large paying public, have not yet been consummated either, though they were proposed as early as the 1930s by Arthur Judson, the Philharmonic's Manager. The Philharmonic has not specified what other directions it may explore. But there are several imaginative possibilities that it must sooner or later investigate—possibilities for broadening its scope and rooting itself more organically in the city by being more things to more people —and ever since the Society's officers began to talk of "its widening relationship in the community," Philharmonic-watchers have been waiting for one or more such proposals to be publicly discussed:

1. For part of each season, the full orchestra could be divided into two or more chamber orchestras, which would tap the large new public that has shown more interest in such ensembles than in the full symphony orchestra. These chamber orchestras would bring a number of benefits with them. By giving parallel series of performances, they could accommodate twice as many paying subscribers, during their portion of the season, as the single large orchestra could. One or more of the chamber orchestras could also be available for student concerts. And many a second-desk player would gain in experience, morale, and prestige by having to function as a principal player in one of the chamber orchestras.*

2. The educational services of the orchestra could—some would say *must*—be expanded. For years the Philharmonic has recognized that the live audience reached by its educational activities represented only a tiny fraction of the student population of the city. As for the television audience, nobody knows how many viewers return from one program to the next and how many surmount the distractions of home television-watching; in any case, four concerts a year, fascinating as they may be, are hardly an educational program. In 1957 the Philharmonic's Coordinating Committee for Music Education, under Mrs. Melvin E. Sawin, proposed several excellent plans for giving Student Con-

* It is a satisfaction to note that, since the time when this paragraph was written, the Philharmonic has taken up the idea of dividing the orchestra into smaller orchestras for part of the season. For the Rug Concerts of June 1973 the Philharmonic was split into ensembles of seventy and thirty-five musicians, and for the Neighborhood Concerts in the same month into two fifty-member groups.

certs in series extended enough to have a real educational value—a concert every week throughout the entire Philharmonic season was one recommendation—but financial problems prevented their realization. Today, by taking advantage of the economy represented by the chamber-orchestra plan and by exploiting to the full whatever Federal, state, and municipal funds are available, the Philharmonic may be able to come closer to an adequate educational program.†

3. A century ago, that Philharmonic pioneer, Ureli Corelli Hill, dreaming of a grand celebration in honor of Beethoven, conceived the idea of a building that would seat 40,000, with standing room for 10,-000 more, and space for a chorus of 30,000.[235] Today, the Philharmonic need not go to such extremes, but it could well study the possibility of a giant structure, accommodating perhaps 30,000 listeners at a sitting. The acoustic problems would certainly be easier of solution than those of Sheep Meadow in Central Park, where 75,000 auditors have enjoyed themselves. Such an auditorium, perhaps of the geodesic structure that R. Buckminster Fuller and Geometrics Inc. have used with success, would have its own conceptual attraction. When the Philharmonic could give performances all year round for audiences of 30,000 at a time, with a really low admission price, it could begin to talk in a new sense about "the public."

4. The restoration of the Philharmonic's radio broadcasts, which have not been given since 1967, would be expected to have a high priority. Since the amount on which the dropping of the broadcasts hinged was said to be less than $150,000, it is hard for the public to understand that it should be allowed to interfere with so great a good. That amount is contributed every summer for the Park Concerts (which benefit a much smaller number of listeners than the broadcasts did) by the City of New York and the Jos. Schlitz Brewing Company. Surely some similar supporters should be discoverable for one of the orchestra's most important public services.

5. If any enlargement is attempted, or even if the present level is maintained, the Music Director of the Philharmonic may need a junta of sub-Music-Directors under him—one for educational activities, one for pop concerts, one for chamber orchestra work, and so on. This would represent an extension of the Philharmonic's recent practice of

† The appointment of Dr. Leon Thompson as Director of a Department of Educational Activities, in October 1970, may presage an enlargement of the Philharmonic's educational program.

dividing up the season among several directors, but the coordination would be more systematic under a master plan on a long-term basis.

In the broadest view, however, it is hard to see how a genuine expansion of the Philharmonic's sphere of effectiveness can succeed unless the audience base can be fundamentally altered to include a large part of the "ordinary" or "general" public, beyond the special small public on which it now depends. This cannot be done by fiat or legislation. For the Philharmonic to expand in this sense, its relationship to its society must warrant the expansion. The separation in America between plain people and fancy symphonic music has been a profound one. It may well be that the Philharmonic draws only 8½ per cent of its income from the popular media—radio, recordings, television, and films—because only 8½ per cent of its communication is to the part of the public that is reached by those media. The Philharmonic's community could probably be widened quantitatively if its offering were liberalized aesthetically by carrying even further—*much* further— Bernstein's leaning toward the American element, his tendency to derive style and practice from a national or local tradition. In an age when intellectuals incline toward internationalism, the Philharmonic still needs to be an *American* orchestra, not out of patriotism, but to avoid the wasteful and senseless anti-Americanism that still hampers the natural development of our musical art. Dr. William Schuman, when he was President of Lincoln Center, spoke angrily of this persistent national neurosis:

> This country has proven that it is capable of producing and appreciating great art. It is also capable of neurotic self-effacement in this regard. It has a lingering penchant for self-criticism and self-doubt that in artistic matters concedes us to be barbarous country cousins to our European relatives. And if this view is also widely held in Europe, then it is because it is so deeply ingrained at home.
>
> America as a nation has not understood the importance and grandeur of its artists or their work. And since we can really be no more than what we believe ourselves to be, America has robbed herself of her rightful honors and demeaned her position of artistic pre-eminence.[236]

Examples can be given by the hundreds. The American National Opera Company, despite its flag-waving name, devoted its first season entirely to Verdi, Puccini, and Berg, without anyone remarking that it had not presented a single American national opera. The Juilliard School dedicated its new building at Lincoln Center, in the presence of the wife of the President of the United States, before a nationwide television audience, with a concert that contained no American music. The Executive Director of the New York State Council on the Arts, in a booklet offering the services of young musical artists, had to take the American public to task for the way it treated its artists: "A persistently embarrassing feature of our national attitude toward the arts has been the necessity of American concert artists to acquire a reputation in Europe in order to be recognized in the United States."

As far as the Philharmonic is concerned, the call is not for the performance of a few more American pieces or the engagement of some lucky American conductor for a week of concerts. It is for a revolution in attitude and orientation sufficient to bring in some part of the great population still not involved with the Philharmonic, and to win back the brainwashed "cultivated" public to a natural and healthy relationship with the artists of their own community. It is for an employment of the richly available native talent on a scale massive enough to make up for a century and a quarter of America's undiscriminating submission to the European indoctrination. When this is done, what unsuspected treasures of musical composition and performance will be uncovered! How the repertory will be replenished when there is an inducement for doing so! How the radio listeners and the record listeners and the summer listeners will sustain their orchestra when it speaks their language! How new music will be created and old revitalized for the living culture that requires it! This is not rhetorical speculation about the future; every competent observer knows what superior musical artists exist everywhere in the United States at this very moment, smothered under what William Schuman calls our "intellectual, artistic and cultural masochism." As the Philharmonic sets out on its avowed mission to broaden its public, it must be understood that "broadening" can no longer mean merely teaching more people to adapt to the old imported culture; it can no longer mean merely conditioning another generation of defenseless school children to believe that something called "good" music, which comes from distant climes and times, must be prophylactically separated from their own vernacular idiom, which they can then hardly fail to identify, either guiltily or rebelliously, as "bad" music. The Philharmonic must continue to educate and elevate its public by the quality of its work, but unless the orchestra is brought closer to the local and national heritage, unless it *learns* at the same time that it *teaches,* the balance may be redressed in the wrong direction.‡

How far Pierre Boulez, the Philharmonic's new Music Director, will move in the necessary direction remains to be seen. There was encouragement in the statement that he made in accepting his appointment on June 10, 1969: "I hope that this collaboration will give us the opportunity to bring creators and interpreters together in a joint search for solutions for today and perhaps for the future." Presumably, if creators and interpreters are to be brought together in New York, at least some of them will be home-grown. But the first responses of many American musicians to Boulez's designation as Music Director were understandably wary because of his background and his public pronouncements. Since 1957, Bernstein's appointment had been celebrated as a sign that America was now mature enough musically to name as head of the Philharmonic a musician born and trained in this country. But Boulez was a French musician with a marked penchant for German-Austrian music, who had openly expressed his doubts about the future of American music. Had the country suddenly lapsed back into immaturity? Newspaper stories cannot be accepted as infallibly accurate, but the remarks attributed to Boulez in the press went so consistently in certain directions that their drift could not be mistaken. In a much quoted interview with Joan Peyser, printed in the New York *Times* on March 9, 1969, three months before his appointment to the Philharmonic post, he gave his opinion of the current quality of American composition: "They have no one in America as good as Hans Werner Henze," he said, referring to a German composer whom he had once described as producing musical garbage, "and that is not setting your sights very high. A composer the stature of Stockhausen they have not." American musicians and music journalists replied in kind. Leon Kirchner, composer, in a pretended interview in the *Times* of June 22, 1969, wrote sarcastically that he "would in general agree with Boulez that

‡ What can William Steinberg—Music Director of the Boston Symphony Orchestra, Conductor of the Pittsburgh Symphony Orchestra, and former Principal Guest Conductor of the Philharmonic—be thinking of when he says: "We have tried for years to keep the attention of the young by mixing the old and the new. In addition to Mozart and Beethoven we brought in the works of Bruckner, Mahler and Reger, which had been inexplicably neglected" (New York *Times,* June 23, 1969)? Young Americans may love Bruckner, Mahler, and Reger, as they do Mozart and Beethoven, but how can he really believe that that triumvirate represents "the new" to them?

'A composer the stature of Stockhausen (we) have not.' When you come right down to it, there are a few things for which we can be grateful." A year later a group of American avant-garde composers attacked Boulez in another of his many capacities, as conductor of the Ojai Festival in California, for not having included a single American work among the nineteen that he programmed, though he was doing two of his own compositions and one of Stockhausen's. Boulez's reply that "nationalism of this sort is destructive of life" did nothing to counter the charge that to perform no American music at all in an American music festival was a *negative nationalism* of the most absolute kind, which might not be destructive of life but might well be destructive of American music.

In spite of Boulez's awkward start in musical diplomacy, however, the press and the public have been appreciative of his performances and receptive to his projects, as he made the transition from guest conductor to Music Director of the Philharmonic in New York. His professional mastery has been universally acclaimed. And no one doubts that, with his spirited personality and creative talents, he will be able to stir up the musical and intellectual life of New York and to provide the cultural leadership that the city and the nation expect of the Philharmonic's Music Director. It is not necessary, even today, to be born and trained in the United States in order to be sensitive to its artistic needs; the Russian-born Koussevitzky was able to invigorate American music from Boston as a center, and it is possible that Boulez, though he comes a generation later in the historical evolution, may be able to do as much from New York.

In the meantime, it would seem that the least the Philharmonic can do—emulating the example that Koussevitzky set at Tanglewood—is to help train and encourage some prospective American successors to Boulez, so that New York may one day emerge from its musical colonialism. In 1965 Amyas Ames proudly gave New Yorkers "a little background" on their musical progress. "It was not long ago," he told them, "that we looked to Europe as the center of classical music and drew from it our conductors and our musicians, but times have changed. To make a quick comparison—there are only two professional symphony orchestras in France outside of Paris, . . . whereas some thirty of our largest cities have orchestras of stature. The Vienna Philharmonic gives twenty-three concerts a year . . . , the New York Philharmonic about two hundred. The total attendance at symphony concerts in France is 200,000 a year . . . a small fraction of the 5,700,000 who attends concerts annually in this country."[237] Yet when the flourishing Philharmonic needed a Music Advisor in 1967 it apparently had to engage Szell, trained in concert-poor Vienna, and when it needed a Music Director in 1969 it had to engage Boulez, trained in orchestra-poor France. Had the times changed back again since 1965? When, in the summer of 1969, two Negro musicians alleged before the New York Commission on Human Rights that the Philharmonic had discriminated against them in auditions, the deputy counsel for the Commission characterized the racial imbalance in all American orchestras as "grotesque" and commented that the Philharmonic had only one Negro member, the only one it has had during its more than 125 years of existence. He did not even notice the more grotesque circumstance that the Philharmonic has also had only one American Music Director in all that time—and now has none. We would have to forgive an objective observer if he concluded that all our American conservatories and schools of music were misleading their conducting students. For they have all been training would-be conductors for years and years—in some cases, for generations—without succeeding in having them taken seriously as candidates for the major American orchestras. In 1973, little more than a third of the major American orchestras were led by American-trained conductors. We can no longer hide behind the old excuse that we are a young country musically. Ozawa of Japan and Mehta of India come from countries that are much younger in the Western musical tradition. Besides, it is worth remembering that Columbus found these shores back in the middle of the Renaissance, the Pilgrims came here early in the Baroque, we achieved our independence at the height of the Classic era, and we have had all the time we deserve since then to grow up musically. Are we really to believe, then, that Americans are born with talents for singing, composing, and playing all known instruments, but not for conducting? It would take more than Gregor Mendel to explain that one genetically. No, the truth of the matter is that talented American conductors are everywhere around us—they have only to be recognized and given their opportunities. The problem lies not with the conservatories and colleges but with our symphony orchestras, which must accept the responsibility of engaging enough American conductors often enough to make a difference. For the Philharmonic a good place to begin would be with its own guest conductors and Assistant Conductors, who in the past decade have too rarely had Americans among them.

The Philharmonic's relationship to the community in which it functions has changed many times since those days of innocent optimism in 1842 when the launching of the Philharmonic was hailed as "a New Musical Era in this western world." There was a brief moment, early in the Philharmonic's life, when it was hoped and even assumed that it would one day grow to be the great central agent of American musical art, the instrument to express the indigenous music that our native creators would make with the materials that they inherited from the Old World, the distributor to a democratic society of the benefits of musical culture. But over the next half century, as we have seen, the Philharmonic had forgotten that an indigenous culture was possible, and by 1908 it had almost starved to death by trying to eat elegantly. Little by little, from 1909 to the present, it inched its way back toward the purposes and the people that could have sustained it in much earlier days—remembering that there was a whole society ready to be served by it instead of an isolated and now uncertain elite, and that all the talents of a creative nation were waiting to use it and be used by it. Today the Philharmonic is certainly closer to those ideals than it ever was. But the interested minority, though it is larger in the 1970s than it has ever been, is still a long way—in numbers and in commitment—from being "the community" of the idealists' dreams. The viability of symphony orchestras of the future, wrote Nancy Hanks, Chairman of the National Endowment for the Arts, in 1970, depends less on money than on "whether there is proper attention paid to the needs—and indeed the rights—of the community."[238]

Several hundred pages ago, this book took as its starting point the correction of Huneker's much-quoted assertion that "the history of the Philharmonic Orchestra is the history of music in America." Never has the fallacy of that viewpoint been more dramatically demonstrated than by Leonard Bernstein's leaving the Philharmonic to devote himself to branches of music-making—the theatrical and the vernacular—outside the orchestra's tradition. It is an act that forces the Philharmonic, after a century and a quarter of heroic struggle for the cause of symphonic music, to face its reality: at a time that the officers of the Society identify consciously as one of crisis and transition, they must decide to what extent the future of the Philharmonic will be the future of music in America.

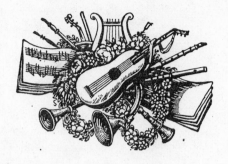

Backnotes

Each note in this section is preceded by a page number in parentheses, which indicates the text page to which the note refers.

(p. 17)
1. The Olympic was at 442–444 Broadway, between Howard and Grand Streets; the Park Theatre was at 21 Park Row, near Ann Street; the Bowery Theatre at 46 Bowery, south of Canal Street; and the Chatham at No. 143 on the southeast side of Chatham Street, between Roosevelt and James Streets. Just up the street from the Chatham, at No. 175, stood the 1,500-seat Franklin, where the German company played.

For casts of plays and other factual information about the New York theaters of 1841–42 see Odell's *Annals,* Vol. IV, pp. 529–602.

(p. 17)
2. *As You Like It, Coriolanus, Hamlet, Henry IV, Henry VIII, Julius Caesar, King John, King Lear, Macbeth, The Merry Wives of Windsor, A Midsummer Night's Dream, Othello, Richard III, Romeo and Juliet,* and *The Tempest.*

(p. 17)
3.   Cast of Characters

SHAKESPEARE's *Richard III*	OLYMPIC's *Richard No. III*
Richard, Duke of Gloucester, afterwards King Richard III	Richard, cad to Omnibus No. 3, afterwards driver
King Edward	Henry King, an old Omnibus driver
Duke of Buckingham	Bucky Gammon, an Omnibus driver
Henry, Earl of Richmond	Richmud, a Cab driver
Lord Stanley	Stand and Lie, an Omnibus driver
Sir William Catesby	Catspaw, Cad to No. 3
Sir Richard Ratcliff	Rarcliffe
Lady Anne	Sally Ann
Elizabeth, queen to King Edward IV	Mrs. McQueen
Duchess of York	Dutch Bess of New York

(p. 21)

4. Emerson's *Journals,* March 18, 1842: "Home from New York where I read six lectures on the Times, viz., Introductory; The Poet; The Conservative; The Transcendentalist; Manners; Prospects. They were . . . attended by three or four hundred persons . . ."

(p. 26)

5. See E. A. Poe, "The Literati of New York City: Sarah Margaret Fuller" (*Complete Works,* ed. 1965, Vol. XV), in which Poe grumbles at the "indiscriminate approbation" of Longfellow's work.

(p. 26)

6. Philip Hone, MS Diary, entry of October 13, 1841. (Excerpts from Hone's Diary are also available in published form; when reference is made to them, the title is given in italics as *Diary.*)

(p. 26)

7. G. T. Strong, *Diary,* entry of November 19, 1843. (The published *Diary* consists of four volumes of excerpts from Strong's MS Diary. When the title is given in italics, it refers to the published volumes.)

(p. 28)

8. It was not finished when he died in 1843. Allston lived in Cambridgeport, Massachusetts, but well-informed New Yorkers were familiar with his work and waited as patiently as Bostonians for the completion of *Belshazzar's Feast,* which it was hoped would be "a national specimen of American art."

(p. 28)

9. Cole had eventually decided to go to Europe for further study and Bryant cautioned him in a sonnet, as graceful as it is profound, not to let the Old World's beauties dim his vision of the American landscape:

> *Thine eyes shall see the light of distant skies:*
> *Yet, COLE! thy heart shall bear to Europe's strand*
> *A living image of thy native land,*
> *Such as on thy own glorious canvas lies.*
> *Lone lakes—savannas where the bison roves—*
> *Rocks rich with summer garlands—solemn streams—*
> *Skies, where the desert eagle wheels and screams—*
> *Spring bloom and autumn blaze of boundless groves.*
> *Fair scenes shall greet thee where thou goest—fair,*
> *But different—everywhere the trace of men,*
> *Paths, homes, graves, ruins, from the lowest glen*
> *To where life shrinks from the fierce Alpine air.*
> *Gaze on them, till the tears shall dim thy sight,*
> *But keep that earlier, wilder image bright.*

(Reprinted here from *Poems,* Boston, 1834; originally appeared in *The Talisman,* 1830. Later printings sometimes altered the phrase "thy native land" to "our own bright land.")

(p. 30)

10. Even the hastiest characterization of Charles Willson Peale (1741–1827) cannot fail to convey his ebullient creativity—Maryland saddler, Revolutionary

soldier, admired portrait painter of Washington and other illustrious personages, creator of huge street paintings and of "moving picture" shows, founder of one of the world's first museums of natural history and of the Pennsylvania Academy of Fine Arts, inventor of stoves and false teeth, bicyclist, first exhumer of a mastodon skeleton, friend of Tom Paine, and father of seventeen children, including the four painters whom he taught so well.

(p. 44)

11. It is impossible to pass over Hermann Zedtwitz without mentioning that, a few years later, when the American Revolution broke out, he was commissioned a lieutenant colonel, fought under Montgomery at Quebec, and was about to be given an important command near New York when a treasonous letter from him to the British governor was intercepted; after being cashiered and imprisoned, he escaped, but was picked up on his way to New York, "dressed in Woman's clothes." (See O. Sonneck, *Early Concert Life in America*, pp. 166, 170, 171, 175.)

(p. 46)

12. Isaac G. Ogden, the Secretary of the St. Cecilia Society, had taken over the same office in the new Philharmonic. His successor the next year, Robert McMennomy, had also been a St. Cecilia Secretary.

(p. 49)

13. The whole list contains 118 Governors and 74 Subscribers. Other Governors: Charles A. Davis (a thriving merchant), James W. Gerard (noted lawyer), Samuel Howland (the shipping merchant), Dominick Lynch, Jr. (wine merchant and musical amateur), James K. Paulding (man of letters), John C. Stevens (of the famous engineering family), General Joseph G. Swift (the military engineer, who had also been President of the New York Handel and Haydn Society), Fanning C. Tucker (who in 1820 had helped General Swift raise $11,000 for charity with an "oratorio" performance by the Handel and Haydn Society), Johnston Verplanck (of an old and respected New York family—and one of the original founders of the New York *American*), H. C. DeRham, Goold Hoyt, William Renwick, and Sam Ward, Jr. Even among the Subscribers there were a Cottenet, three more Delafields, a DePeyster, a Goelet, another Rhinelander, and Jones Schermerhorn (later to marry Philip Hone's daughter).

Among the Subscribers (though not the Governors) were several professional and amateur musicians: Denis Etienne, pianist and conductor, Edward C. Riley, violinist and conductor, J. A. Boocock and P. F. Gentil, cellists, P. H. Taylor, flutist, James M. Quin, N. Dumahault, William Taylor, Henry Lynch, violinists.

(p. 50)

14. Both New York Philharmonics were precocious in this regard. The 1799 Philharmonic had appointed a Leader (principal violinist) for the whole season. The London Philharmonic, in contrast, continued until 1846 to name a leader and a conductor for each separate concert.

Several other points invite comparison between the two cities. London also had its versions of the "death benefit" project and the "local composer" project. In 1827, three years later than the New York experiment, the London Philharmonic enacted a Law providing that, upon a member's death, his legal representatives would receive a share of the Society's funds (the funds being divided into as many shares as there were members at the time). This Law was attacked by some as a "wretched division of the spoil," and after three years it was rescinded. (See R. Elkin, *Royal Philharmonic*, pp. 12–13, and P. M. Young, *The Concert Tradition*, pp. 170–72.) And in its earliest years the London Philharmonic seems to have planned "trials" of music by local composers—as the second New York Philharmonic was to do in 1824—but, as Elkin remarks (pp. 17–18), "This admirable scheme . . . does not seem to have been put into practice."

The New York society followed the London society closely in one item of orchestral routine—the provision that "no distinction of rank" would be recognized, i.e., that no player would automatically be entitled to a special position in his section but would have to accept the one assigned to him by the conductor or leader.

These similarities may represent communication in both directions across the Atlantic.

(p. 50)

15. Odell, in his *Annals of the New York Stage,* refers to the Beethoven composition in the 1824 Philharmonic concert as "the finale of Beethoven's 'Sinfonie' in D," but it was not necessarily that movement that was played. The word "finale" in programs of this period in the United States and England usually refers to the place of the piece on the program, not to the movement in the symphony. In other words, it means simply that it was the last number on the program, but it may have been any one or more movements of the composition.

(p. 50)

16. The conductor of the Choral Society, James H. Swindells, who happened also to be the editor of *The Lyre: New-York Musical Journal,* went out of his way to demonstrate his friendship in the pages of his periodical. "It has been insinuated," he wrote in the issue of August 1, 1824, "that the Philharmonic and Choral Societies are clashing against each other in their interests; than which nothing was farther from the views of the original founders. The object of the Philharmonic is Secular Music, and that of the Choral Sacred. Let them both persevere in their praiseworthy intentions, and they will act as handmaids to each other . . ." After devoting several pages to an almost verbatim presentation of the Constitution and By-Laws of the Philharmonic Society, he concluded: "If the original plan of the Society is *strictly* adhered to, it will ultimately result in the general good of the profession." If the italicized *"strictly"* in that last sentence has a touch of the backhand in it, it would nevertheless be churlish to doubt Swindells's motives.

(p. 54)

17. New York *Mirror,* Vol. VII, No. 2, July 18, 1829, p. 15. "Who does not recollect," reminisced the *Mirror,* "the time when the nasal twang of the village precentor might be recognized, not only in the imitative efforts made in his appropriate sphere [the church] . . . but also, in the less sacred and lighter attempts to 'soothe the savage breast,' in drawing-rooms and parlours? . . . The teachers of music to the fair dames of Gotham were, with one or two exceptions, the masters of what were called *singing schools,* and their primitive and characteristic style— it is impossible to describe it—gave the tone to musical taste."

(p. 55)

18. Ibid., No. 4, August 1, 1829, p. 29.

(p. 58)
19. Ibid.

(p. 59)
20. J. N. Ireland, *Records of the New York Stage,* Vol. I, p. 528.

(p. 59)
21. In addition to operas and ballets, the French companies that came to New York presented important dramatic works from their national culture, including Molière's *Tartuffe* and Racine's *Andromaque.* The social historian cannot fail to observe that it was in the same period that another pillar of French civilization, its cuisine, became better known to New Yorkers, particularly through the efforts of Delmonico's restaurant, with its remarkable menu of close to four hundred dishes and its innovation of printing that menu in both French and English.

(p. 60)
22. For an amusing commentary on the ups and downs of Wagnerian opera at the Metropolitan in the 1880s, see *My Adventures in the Golden Age of Music,* pp. 202ff., by Henry T. Finck, who had been music critic of the New York *Evening Post.* "[It] was no secret that most of the wealthy boxholders did not really care for this kind of opera," recalled Finck, himself an ardent Wagnerian, ". . . Yet for seven years they patiently paid the piper and allowed themselves to be bored to death by music they did not understand. / In truth, these society leaders were in a way heroes and heroines—martyrs in the cause of highbrow music."

(p. 60)
23. Some of these productions were adaptations or pastiches, it is true, but this was not a peculiarity of New York; the adaptation practice is characteristic of the popular musical theaters of most ages and places and was exported to this country from the great capitals of Europe. In England, Sir Henry Bishop and Thomas Cooke built honored careers (honored enough to earn Sir Henry his title) on such double talents for composition and arrangement.

(p. 62)
24. If it seems strange to be making so much of class differences in the era of Jacksonian democracy, it must be emphasized that, contrary to general belief, New York had a highly class-conscious society in that era. The Jacksonian democracy, by its very insistence on the rights of the common man, recognized that he was of a separate class from the wealthy few. This sensitivity to class had become so strong by 1840 that politicians were able to make it the chief (though phony) issue in the presidential election: Van Buren, the incumbent and a wealthy New Yorker, was the candidate of the Democrats; he was depicted by his Whig enemies as an aristocrat who ate French food and wore a ruffled shirt, and the regal splendor of his life in the President's "Palace" was contrasted with the log-cabin simplicity that was said to satisfy the Whig candidate, William Henry Harrison. (Meanwhile Harrison, that simple frontiersman—who really came of one of the first families of Virginia—was living in a sixteen-room mansion on his 3,000-acre farm at North Bend, Ohio.)

(p. 64)
25. Other members of the second Philharmonic who played for García were W. Taylor, a fine violinist (he became Leader at the new Bowery Theatre the next

season, when Signorina García sang there), U. C. Hill and Dumahault, also violinists, Boocock and Gentil, cellists, and P. Taylor, flutist. The entire orchestra, which, at García's insistence, was larger than the Park Theatre usually employed, consisted of seven violins, two violas, three cellos, two basses, two flutes, two clarinets, one bassoon, two horns, two trumpets, and one kettledrummer—twenty-five men in all, counting Etienne at the piano.

(p. 65)

26.   Ritter (*Music in America,* p. 210) says 25, but then proceeds to list 27 instruments. The *American Musical Journal,* however, in February 1835 (Vol. I, No. 3, p. 61), gives the orchestra in detail and the total does seem to be 27 instruments:

7 violins	2 clarinets
2 violas	1 bassoon
2 violoncellos	2 horns
2 contrabasses	2 trumpets
2 flutes	3 trombones
1 do. for the oboe	drums

(p. 66)

27.   I say "at least forty musicians" for the 1839 Euterpean concert because Ritter lists forty-two (*Music in America,* pp. 224–25), Krehbiel forty (*The Philharmonic Society,* p. 31), and Howard, with some obvious slips, thirty-five (*Our American Music,* p. 158); the contemporary account in the New York *Musical Review* suggests that forty is about right, but in any case the same point is made for our illustration of sizable orchestras. Ritter is a bit off on the date and place of the concert—it was January 30 at the City Hotel, not June 30 at City Hall. The data for the concerts of the Musical Fund and Sacred Music Societies can be found in the *American Musical Journal,* Vol. I, Nos. 1 and 2 (1834), pp. 20, 45.

(p. 69)

28.   Daniel Schlesinger, born in Hamburg in 1799, studied in London with Beethoven's friend Moscheles and Beethoven's pupil Ries. He appeared as piano soloist with the London Philharmonic Society in 1827 with very great success, holding his own with the young Franz Liszt, who made his Philharmonic debut later in the same year. Within half a year after his arrival in New York in the fall of 1836, Schlesinger had earned a special place in the city's musical circles by his romantic consecration to his art, his great personal charm, his brilliant technique at the piano, and especially his dazzling talent in improvising on any themes given him. He was an enthusiast for chamber music and played regularly with several of the city's musicians in private homes. Some of his own compositions began to be heard. He became director of the German Concordia society. And he acquired a reputation as one of New York's finest teachers. He was considered to be at the peak of his powers when he died in 1839.

(p. 69)

29.   J. T. Howard, *Our American Music,* p. 154. Similar versions of the story are to be found in Ritter's *Music in America,* and in the Philharmonic books of Krehbiel and Erskine. Howard also asserts (p. 151) that "from this concert, largely orchestral in character, the idea of a permanent, professional orchestra was born."

(p. 70)

30. The only novelty among the orchestral pieces was Schlesinger's own Overture, included to honor his memory, but it seems to have made no particular effect on the hearers. This "Grand Overture—Full Orchestra . . . Composed expressly for the London Philharmonic Society" was probably the same piece of Schlesinger's that the London Philharmonic had scheduled for performance in 1835; it had been withdrawn, however, when the composer objected to its being placed at the end of the program (presumably because some listeners, in London as elsewhere, tended to leave before a concert was over). It affords a vicarious consolation to find it performed *first* on the program at his funeral concert in New York.

(The information about Schlesinger's London activities I glean from several of his autograph letters, of which Dr. C. B. Oldman, Honorary Librarian of the Royal Philharmonic Society, has kindly sent me copies. In M. B. Foster's history of the London Philharmonic, Schlesinger is repeatedly referred to by the initial of L., instead of D., but there is no question that the same man is intended: two of the autograph letters from D. Schlesinger accept engagements on the same dates in 1827 and 1829 that Foster records for L. Schlesinger.)

(p. 70)

31. See R. Osgood Mason, *Sketches and Impressions,* p. 168. For the concertgoer of 1839, moreover, the Solemnity held as many reminders of the past as promises of the future. Who should be listed in the program as "Director of the Concert, . . . Who will preside at the Piano-forte" but Etienne, quondam conductor of the second Philharmonic! And among the fifteen gentlemen who made up the Committee of Arrangements for the Solemnity were at least three Governors and a Subscriber of the departed Philharmonic—Henry Brevoort, Jr., Robert L. Stevens, Samuel E. Ward, Jr., and J. Boocock. Such relationships between the Schlesinger Solemnity of 1839 and the Philharmonic Society of 1824 confirm once again what we have been demonstrating all along—the essential continuity of New York's orchestral development over several decades.

(p. 70)

32. MS Diary, entry of June 25, 1839.

(p. 72)

33. As Theodore Hach of Boston reported in his *Musical Magazine* of March 27, 1841.

(p. 74)

34. The life of the eccentric but lovable Anthony Philip Heinrich—simply "Father" Heinrich to the broad musical public, but the "Beethoven of America" to his warmest admirers—had been all extremes. Born in Bohemia in 1781, he had been a successful businessman, even a millionaire according to some accounts, playing the violin and piano as a beloved avocation. But the loss of his fortune in the Austrian financial crash of 1811 led him to use his music professionally when he settled in the United States. He was already thirty-seven years old when he wrote his first piece of music—in a Kentucky log cabin where he had secluded himself as a starving fiddler to perfect his musicianship; he was fifty when he ventured on his first orchestral compositions. Yet, despite this late start, he managed to turn out a mountain of music (much of it now in the Library of Congress), including more than forty large orchestral scores, many of them for para-Berliozian forces. The

titles alone were enough to lift some eyebrows: *Manitou Mysteries; or The Voice of the Great Spirit: Gran Sinfonia Misteriosa-Indiana*. Or *The New England Feast of Shells. Divertimento pastorale oceanico,* containing a "Finale brillante—The Romantic 'Love Feast,' Resulting in the Destruction of the 'Bivalves' at the 'Sacrifice of Shells,' *vulgate* 'Clam Bake.'" The titles may be fanciful, but the music itself, though prolix, is always artistically conceived, technically expert, and filled with a dynamic and original personality. Heinrich spent some time in Philadelphia, in Boston, in London, and at various places on the European continent; but after 1837 he settled in New York where, working in a garret at 41 Liberty Street that became for New Yorkers the romantic symbol of the artist's purification through poverty, he gave lessons to earn a meager living while he continued to issue his stream of extravagant compositions. After a last vigorous attempt to impress Europe in a two-year tour (at the age of seventy-eight), he returned to New York, where he died, highly regarded but miserably rewarded, in 1861 at the age of eighty.

(p. 74)
35. A. P. Heinrich, Scrapbook (Library of Congress), p. 879.

(p. 75)
36. Heinrich's biographer, William Treat Upton, has too little confidence in his hero when he cautions (p. 163): "It is much to be doubted that this complete orchestra was realized, for the figures given vary from a hundred performers down to forty." Upton's doubts are occasioned by a review of the concert which refers to "a powerful orchestra consisting of at least forty instruments." But observe that the reviewer does not speak of forty players, but of forty *instruments,* and Heinrich, like many composers of his time, customarily indicated the size of his orchestrations by counting the number of instrumental parts or lines in the score rather than the total number of players (since one never knew exactly how many of each stringed instrument there would be). Actually, the list of seventy-nine *players* quoted adds up to exactly forty instrumental *parts,* the number mentioned by the reviewer!

(p. 75)
37. Heinrich was a pioneer in the presentation of Beethoven's music in America. His performance of the First Symphony on November 12, 1817, in Lexington, Kentucky, is the earliest American performance of a Beethoven symphony that has been uncovered so far. The entire "Grand Concert" on that occasion was a model of balance and variety for its time. After the Beethoven it contained instrumental and vocal works by Mozart, Dibdin, Viotti, Fiorillo, Pleyel, Gyrowetz, Giornovichi (Jarnovic), Kreutzer, Himmel, and Haydn, as well as English glees and catches.

(p. 75)
38. A. P. Heinrich, Scrapbook (Library of Congress), pp. 50, 1053. The names of the periodicals and the exact dates are not given, but the opening phrases of the reviews indicate that they were written within a few days of the concert.

(p. 76)
39. We can guess even before we look at the program that Heinrich's concert, like most other progressive concerts in the city, had U. C. Hill as leader of the or-

chestra. Madame Otto, soon to be the Philharmonic's first soloist, brightened the program with the Rossini "Inflammatus." Boucher played cello and Rosier double bass, Timm and Scharfenberg served at the piano, and at least one Dodworth was listed. Of the three organists who, it was announced, would "preside at the Organ alternately," two were future Philharmonic men: E. Hodges (Mus. Doc.) and W. Alpers.

(p. 80)
40. Charles H. Haswell, in his *Reminiscences*, described the attempt (shortly before the time of the Philharmonic's debut) of Simpson, the manager of the Park Theatre, to exclude unaccompanied females. "The operation of such a proceeding cannot be fully understood at this day," he explained. "The third tier of boxes, or gallery, with its foyer and a bar-room, was wholly given up to women and those who sought their company or visited there as spectators. Unfortunately the small size of audiences at theatres at this period, except upon occasions of special attraction, coupled with the loss of the many men who were attracted solely by the presence of the women, proved too powerful to permit the restriction of women, whereupon Simpson was criticized by the press and contributors to it."

(p. 80)
41. Letter dated July 12, 1844 (Second Series, p. 170). Also morally unimpeachable were Niblo's Saloon and Garden. The *Mirror* of July 6, 1839, complimented the proprietor on their respectability: "many, who object to attending our theatres on account of the tolerated infamy of a portion of the audience, may be seen at Niblo's with their families, without the apprehension of disagreeable contact." Niblo succeeded in maintaining that respectability; in later years (1851–53, 1854–56, and 1858–59) the Philharmonic Society would hold its concerts at his establishment.

(p. 82)
42. More than forty years later, Thomas Goodwin (1799–1886), one of the original members of the Philharmonic, tried to recall the events that led to this historic meeting: Some time after the Schlesinger Solemnity of 1839, he is reported to have said, Hill and a number of the other professional musicians who had taken part in it (among them Horn, Scharfenberg, Dodworth, Timm, Rosier, Otto, Reiff, Sr., and Boucher) happened to meet after their evening engagements and stopped off for refreshment at a restaurant known as The Shakespeare, in Park Row. With the success of the Solemnity still in their memories, they discussed the possibility of a "large and permanent" orchestral society. Next, an exploratory meeting of about ten musicians, mostly the same ones who had been at The Shakespeare, was held at Hill's house, and a committee was appointed to prepare for a general organizational meeting. The general meeting was postponed several times because of the skepticism of many of the needed musicians, but eventually it was possible to gather a sufficient number at the successful meeting of April 2, 1842.

This account, as given in R. O. Mason's *Sketches and Impressions . . . from the After-Dinner Talk of Thomas Goodwin* (pp. 170ff.), seems to be reliable, but it should not be taken as verbatim testimony by Goodwin himself. It was published in 1887, when Goodwin was already dead, by his son-in-law, Dr. Rufus Osgood Mason, who took the liberty of writing in Goodwin's name, and in the first person.

Many of the accounts of the Philharmonic's conception and derivation must be somewhat discounted to allow for accumulated myth or special bias. Krehbiel and Ritter, who issued their histories between 1883 and 1892, could still consult with a few surviving members of the founding group of 1842 (Scharfenberg, Timm, Ensign, Helfenritter, and Johnson) and with the son of the Philharmonic's first Vice-President, Reiff. But this advantage had its disadvantages. These loved and venerable figures, reminiscing in old age about events of fifty years earlier, tended to color their memories with their personal prejudices.* For example, there were conflicting versions of the way in which the idea for such a Philharmonic Society first occurred to U. C. Hill. William Scharfenberg, who came from Kassel in Germany, was sure, of course, that Hill had drawn his inspiration from Kassel, where he had studied with Spohr; but Anthony Reiff, Jr., was equally sure that it was his father, Anthony Reiff, Sr., who had worked out the plan with Hill during the voyage to Europe which they had made together. No one had stopped to reflect that Hill, as youth and young man, had known two Philharmonic Societies in New York before he crossed the Atlantic.

Nor did it require fifty years for historical uncertainty to creep in. In 1852, only ten years after the Philharmonic's establishment, there were already so many claims and counterclaims in connection with the genesis of the Society that the Philharmonic's Committee of Management "thought it a favorable time to give a brief account of the formation of the Society, *in order to . . . refresh the memories of the older members.*" (Italics mine.) And that committee, although six of its seven members were founding fathers, was so vague in its memories by 1852 that it could not refer to the date of the Schlesinger Solemnity more precisely than as "two or three years" previous to April 1842.

At the moment of the Philharmonic's founding, in 1842, some of the connecting threads with the past were still visible, but even at that close distance the assumptions about the origins of the new Society varied with the personal background and the age group of the observer. The very English and the very young assumed that the entire apparatus was borrowed wholesale from London. Those who remembered the second Philharmonic from the 1824–27 period could recognize the debt owed to that older epoch. Still others knew that a well-organized Philo-Harmonic Society had functioned in Boston for many years beginning around 1809,† and that Philadelphia had also founded a Philharmonic Society around 1833. Practically everyone connected with the new Philharmonic had had something to do with the Euterpean Society, the Sacred Music Society, the Schlesinger Solemnity, the German Society, or Heinrich's Grand Musical Festival, and could —with justice—attribute some of the Philharmonic's qualities to one or more of these sources.

---

* H. C. Timm, superb musicianship and genial personality notwithstanding, had an especially untrustworthy memory. In an autobiographical sketch that he prepared for Ritter, he made an error of two years in the date of his own presidency of the Philharmonic, gave the wrong conductor for the most sensational success in the orchestra's early history (the New York premiere of the *Tannhäuser* Overture under Bergmann), and awarded the credit for being the original Figaro in Rossini's *Barber of Seville* to his friend De Begnis, instead of to Luigi Zamboni, who was entitled to it.

† Anthony Philip Heinrich, who was chairman of the organizational meeting of the third New York Philharmonic on April 2, 1842, had enjoyed a benefit concert under the patronage of the Boston Society in 1823.

(p. 84)

43. The writer who undertakes to give Hill the long overdue recognition of a full-length biography must hope for the aid of Harold Lineback of St. Louis, who has painstakingly collected practically all the necessary materials, including Hill's autograph diary. Many of the details in my sketch of Hill's life are taken from materials that Mr. Lineback has sent me (including copies of Hill's farewell letters, and an article in the New York *Atlas* of February 8, 1846, entitled "President of the Philharmonic Society," which seems to be based at least in part on an interview with Hill) and from a glimpse that he afforded me of Hill's diary of his European tour.

Other information has been drawn from H. E. Krehbiel's article, "Founder of the Philharmonic," in the New York *Daily Tribune* of October 29, 1905, and from the countless newspaper reports of Hill's activities that appeared during his own lifetime. The remarks about the Tremont Theatre in Boston are derived from the New York *Mirror* of January 3, 1835, in which an informative article, signed "BY A MAN ABOUT TOWN," gives a critical survey of the orchestras of New York, Boston, Philadelphia, and Baltimore.

(p. 84)

44. Photocopies of the first two versions of the Laws of the Philharmonic Society of London, believed to date from 1813 and 1818, were kindly obtained for me from the British Museum by Dr. C. B. Oldman of the Royal Philharmonic Society. A facsimile of the 1842 Constitution of the New York Philharmonic—the original printing is so rare that even the Philharmonic Society does not own a copy—was given me by Harold Lineback. The Constitution and Bye-Laws of the (first) New York Philharmonic Society (1799, amended 1801), the Constitution, By-Laws, and Regulations of the (second) New York Philharmonic Society (1824), and the Constitution and By-Laws of the (third) New York Philharmonic Society (as amended 1846) were studied in the collections of the New-York Historical Society and the New York Public Library.

(p. 84)

45. The kinship among the three New York societies extended also to certain parliamentary proprieties. The Constitution of 1799, for example, specified that "twenty of the Resident Members shall constitute a quorum and have power to transact any business of the Society," and it is startling to find not just the thought and the expression but also the exact number echoed in 1842. Such traditions may have been perpetuated in New York, over the forty-three-year period from 1799 to 1842, through the constitutions of the many short-lived musical societies that rose and fell every few years in a dotted line of history.

(p. 85)

46.   LEADER.

10 First Violins.	2 Oboes.
9 Second ″	2 Clarinets.
6 Tenors [Violas].	2 Bassoons.
4 Violoncellos.	4 Horns.
4 Basses.	3 Trombones.
2 Flutes.	2 Trumpets.
1 Piccolo.	1 Drums.

When the Constitution was amended, shortly thereafter, the specification of the orchestra's size was very sensibly changed from fifty-three to "at least fifty-three." At the same time three other adjustments were made: the title of Leader was changed to Director, the number of second violins was raised from nine to ten (could this reflect the Leader's return to his ancestral place as a violinist?), and the phrase "1 Drums" (i.e., one man playing drums) became the more grammatical but less accurate "1 Drum."

(p. 85)
47. This extract is taken from the only copy of the Philharmonic's first prospectus that I have ever seen. It is reprinted for the first time in this book thanks to the generosity of its owner, Harold Lineback. Another excerpt is given in Chapter 9 on page 91.

(p. 88)
48. "The introduction of Handel's music into a composition of Rossini is of questionable propriety," opined the *Mirror,* "but presented most satisfactory apologies in the grand chorus of 'He gave them hailstones for rain,' and the graceful melody of 'Angels ever bright and fair.'" The *Mirror's* man was probably unaware that Handel, for his part, had introduced other composers' music freely into his *Israel in Egypt.* (For an enlightening discussion of the aesthetic and ethical significance of Handel's extensive borrowings, see Paul Henry Lang, *George Frideric Handel,* pp. 310–14 and 559–69.)

Although *The Israelites* had been given in London under very high auspices as long ago as 1833, apparently there were some who challenged the very idea of the theatrical presentation of a scriptural subject. "In answer to those who have questioned the propriety of such a production," countered the libretto in holy witness, "let it suffice to say, that the Author has been made acquainted with several instances of persons having been led by it alone to consult the Bible, who never opened Bible before. That single fact speaks its greatest panegyric."

(p. 88)
49. In the following list of "PRINCIPAL INSTRUMENTAL PERFORMERS" named in the libretto, I have marked with an * those definitely known to have been active in Philharmonic affairs in the first year: Chubb,* Meyer, Phillips,* Meyrer,* Appelles,* Herzog,* Shell, Gunter,* Chatel,* Chevalier, Goodwin,* Heinrich,* Lo Bianco, Rosier,* Jacoby,* Lehman,* Botsford, Woehning,* Nidds,* Mason,* Wolter,* Wiese,* Spier, Wrench, Laure, Rebhun, Wallace, Groenevelt,* Hegelund,* Walker,* Duckworth, Murray, Wood,* King,* Williams.

The production was part of a little opera season that included also Handel's *Acis and Galatea,* Rossini's *Barber of Seville,* and Bellini's *La Sonnambula*—all in English, and featuring the fine English singers Mr. and Mrs. Edward Seguin.

(p. 91)
50. There were other personal links between the second and third Philharmonics. J. A. Boocock, the cellist, who had been a subscribing member of the second Philharmonic in 1824, was elected to the third Philharmonic in 1846; he may also have been the "Mr. Boocock" who thought enough of the new Society in its first year to donate to it a fine collection of orchestral music. E. C. Riley and Dr. J. M. Quin, skilled violinists who had been subscribing members of the 1824 society, joined the new Philharmonic as Actual and Associate Member respectively,

in its third season; Dr. Quin had also been a subscriber from the very first season in 1842. James W. Gerard—mentioned above as a distinguished subscriber of 1842—who had been a Governor of the 1824 Philharmonic, contributed his services as lawyer to the third Philharmonic in 1845–46 when it was seeking an act of incorporation from the New York State Legislature. Such carry-overs, from the second Philharmonic to the third, seem less surprising when we recollect that only fifteen years had elapsed between the two societies. Many New Yorkers of 1842, watching Etienne and U. C. Hill conduct the new orchestra, could easily remember them as musicians of the older Philharmonic of 1824–27.

(p. 91)
51. Hundreds of copies of the prospectus must have been printed in 1842, but the only extant copy that I know of is owned by Harold Lineback of St. Louis, whose kindness enables me to reprint the list here for the first time.

Strictly speaking, the prospectus shows us those who intended to be Members, rather than those who actually were. No official roster for the first season is known, the minutes and other pertinent records of the Society's earliest meetings having unfortunately been lost some time during the nineteenth century. When Krehbiel was preparing his memorial history of the Philharmonic for publication in 1892, he consulted Samuel Johnson, one of the original viola players of 1842, who had also been Secretary from 1881 to 1883. Johnson claimed that he had seen the Philharmonic's first roll, containing the signatures of the original members, twelve or fifteen years before the time of Krehbiel's writing, but could not find it when he became Secretary in 1881.

F. L. Ritter in his *Music in America* (p. 275) presents a "list of members of the first season," but as Krehbiel points out with some sharpness, it seems unlikely that it can be correct since it includes the names of several musicians who are known to have been elected after the first season, and does not include several who are known to have been members during the first season.

There may still be a way to put together a roster for the whole of the first season, however, and certainly the Philharmonic's pioneers deserve that tribute. The list of members for the *second* season has been preserved in the Second Annual Report of the Society, and Krehbiel has proposed that it should be possible to reconstruct the first year's roster from it by subtracting the known names of those who joined in the second year and adding the known names of those who left before that time. I have performed those operations (in the presence of the reader, as it were) in Appendix II, pp. 489–92. The resulting list, it will be observed, differs somewhat from the one in the per-season prospectus, as given on page 91.

(p. 93)
52. At first view, this seems to detract somewhat from the value of the $25 dividend, which the player now appears to have been paying out of one of his pockets into another. But he took the subscriptions and tickets voluntarily, and received something of high value in return—admission to the concerts for his family or guests. Only the annual tax of $3, required of all Actual Members, could possibly be construed as reducing the dividend (though obviously necessary for the administration and maintenance of the Society).

(p. 93)
53. Erskine (*The New York Philharmonic-Symphony*, p. 42) is confused when he speaks of the Mendelssohn overture "on the first Philharmonic program." It was given on the third and last concert of the season, April 22, 1843.

(p. 99)

54. *Letters from New York,* second series, p. 170 (letter dated July 12, 1844).

(p. 102)

55. U. C. Hill was still trying, at the beginning of the next season, to talk Ole Bull into giving his services at a concert, as can be seen from a typically Hillian letter—frank yet slick—in the Philharmonic's Archives. The Philharmonic Society, he wrote to Bull on December 30, 1844,

> . . . would be pleased beyond measure to have your participation with them in lending your invaluable talents at their next concert . . . This is a national institution which is doing great good—the concerts are very liberally supported by subscription—but as the expenses of the Society particularly in its infancy are very heavy they could not offer you anything in the way of *terms* that would be worthy of consideration to one holding the rank you do in your profession— . . . We have a very large orchestra for this latitude numbering nearly 60 performers, and it would be a great source of pleasure to us all to have your coopperation [sic] in the cause which we are espousing and we are sure your heart is with us even if your assistance cannot be obtained—we should be pleased to [see?] you at our Society at least if you are in town—we meet at the Apollo rooms No 410. B.way at 4. oclock every Saturday afternoon. . . .

Even this skillful approach, however, seems to have been slow in succeeding— Bull did not appear with the Philharmonic until 1869.

(p. 102)

56. The sinking fund "for the relief of distressed members" was set up by one of several amendments to the 1842 Constitution that bring to mind a professional musicians' union of today. Another is the provision that members not included in the basic orchestra of about fifty-three players, if called upon to perform, would be paid "at Orchestral rates for each Concert." The feeling of "unionized" protection of mutual interests is intensified in several bylaws that were passed by 1846: "Every performing or actual member shall have his name regularly printed upon the Concert Bills"—here is professional pride in one's work and the practical advertising value of a program credit. "All Music intended to be performed at the Society's Concerts, shall be examined, revised, corected [sic!] and properly marked by a standing committee of three"—not just by a librarian. "At all rehearsals, the Symphonies, Overtures, or Grand Orchestral Pieces shall be performed first"—as a defense against the inroads of soloists, perhaps? "Seats shall be provided for the Orchestra at Rehearsals and Concerts, whenever practicable" —the seats not considered a necessity while playing, as the phrase "whenever practicable" implies, but rather as a comfort or convenience *between* playings; as we know, all the musicians except the cellists normally stood when performing,* but they liked to have chairs available for use between numbers and while soloists were singing or playing.

---

* This was so in German and English, as well as American, orchestras throughout the 1840s and in some cases even later. Richard Hoffman, the British-born New York pianist, said that in his youth [shortly before 1847, when he came to New York at the age of sixteen] "English orchestra players always stood while playing." The *Illustrated London News* in June 1843 shows the "orchestra of the Hanover Square Concert Rooms" standing while playing. The Gewandhaus Orchestra of Leipzig stood in its performances until 1905.

(p. 102)

57. On two occasions there were even compositions by New York Philharmonic members—an overture by Loder and a cornet duet by Dodworth. Other composers who were performed during the first four years were Sterndale Bennett, de Beriot, Bochsa, Cherubini, Heller, Hérold, Hummel, Kalliwoda, Kreutzer, Lindpaintner, Marschner, Méhul, Mercadante, Meyerbeer, Reicha, Reissiger, Ries, Romberg, Vieuxtemps. If some of them are almost forgotten today, they were nonetheless favorites in Europe as well as in America in the 1840s, and the neglect that is now their lot is certainly further from a just evaluation of their merits than the esteem in which they were held in their own day.

(p. 103)

58. Spohr's letter to Hill, dated January 4, 1845, is given in English translation (from the original German) by H. E. Krehbiel in his article "Founder of the Philharmonic" in the New York *Daily Tribune,* October 29, 1905.

The Mendelssohn letter to Hill (autograph), which is in the collection of the Music Division of the New York Public Library, has not previously been published. It reads:

U. C. Hill
    Esqre
no. 59 Franklin Street
    New=York
———————————————————————
      (America)

                          Frankfurt 30 Jan. 1845
Dear Sir
   I beg to return my best & most sincere thanks for your letter. Indeed I may say that I felt truly proud in receiving so kind & so highly flattering an invitation, and the offer itself as well as the friendly words in which you couched it will always continue a source of pride & true gratification, for which I shall feel sincerely indebted to you!

But it is not in my power to accept that invitation although I am sure it would have been the greatest treat to me, if I could have done so. My health has *seriously* suffered during the last year and a journey like that to your Country, which I would have been most happy to undertake some 3 or 4 years' ago is at present beyond my reach. Even the shorter trips which I used to make to England or the South of Germany have become too fatiguing to me and it will require a few years' perfect rest before I shall again be able to undertake the direction of a musical festival even in my own Country. I need not tell you how much I regret to find it utterly impossible to come & to thank you in person for all the kindness & friendship which your letter contains.

Accept then my written thanks which are certainly not less sincere & heartfelt; and pray let the Committee know with how great a gratification & how thankfully I heard of their kind intentions towards me, & how deeply I regret not to be able to avail myself of so much kindness! Should you ever visit Europe & my Country again I hope you will not forget me & give me an opportunity of renewing your acquaintance & of expressing to you once more how deeply I feel indebted to you. I shall always remain dear Sir
                             yours most truly
                      Felix Mendelssohn Bartholdy

That Mendelssohn's expressions of regret were sincere is confirmed by an unpublished letter to his brother Paul: "I recently received an invitation to a music festival which flattered me so much that I even *look* flattered since then . . . To New York, it is . . . What a pity that for me it is as impossible as a trip to the moon. But that I am flattered (and grateful) is not to be denied . . ." (See Eric Werner, *Mendelssohn: A New Image*, pp. 431, 454.)

(p. 104)

59. This place of entertainment, at the southern tip of Manhattan, had been built as a twenty-eight-gun fort, known as Southwest Battery, between 1807 and 1811. It was to have a career full of changes. For a while it was called Fort Clinton and then Castle Clinton, in honor of New York's mayor DeWitt Clinton. In 1824 it opened, under the name of Castle Garden, as an amphitheater capable of seating six thousand persons; it was here that great celebrations for the Marquis de Lafayette were held in 1824 and 1825, and that Jenny Lind sang in 1850. From 1855 to 1892 the building was part of the immigration station through which passed millions of new Americans. From 1896 to 1941 it housed New York's municipal aquarium. And it is now (having come almost full circle) being reconstructed as an early-nineteenth-century fort under the name of Castle Clinton National Monument.

(p. 105)

60.   CONDUCTORS OF THE NEW YORK PHILHARMONIC
                                     1842–53

                                     NOTES

1. For seasons shared by two or more conductors, number in parentheses ( ) after conductor's name shows number of programs he conducted, if other than one.
2. A few special cases, e.g., of composers who conducted their own works, are not covered in this list.

Season		Conductors
1st	(1842–43)	U. C. Hill (½+⅓), D. G. Etienne (⅓), H. C. Timm (⅓), W. Alpers (½), A. Boucher (½), G. Loder (½)
2nd	(1843–44)	U. C. Hill, D. G. Etienne, G. Loder, W. Alpers
3rd	(1844–45)	U. C. Hill (2), G. Loder, L. Wiegers
4th	(1845–46)	G. Loder, U. C. Hill, A. Boucher, H. C. Timm (U. C. Hill and G. Loder also shared extra Festival Concert)
5th	(1846–47)	G. Loder, H. C. Timm, A. Boucher, U. C. Hill
6th	(1847–48)	G. Loder (3), H. C. Timm
7th	(1848–49)	G. Loder (2), T. Eisfeld, M. Maretzek
8th	(1849–50)	T. Eisfeld (3), G. Loder
9th	(1850–51)	T. Eisfeld (3), G. Loder
10th	(1851–52)	T. Eisfeld (3), G. Loder
11th	(1852–53)	T. Eisfeld

(p. 106)

61. To be perfectly accurate about it, one of the Associate Members, Dr. J. M. Quin, was legally an amateur, but an exception had been made to admit him because he had for years played the violin as a colleague with the professors of the city.

(p. 114)
62. W. T. Upton, *William Henry Fry*, pp. 137–38.

(p. 114)
63. "Mr. Fry and His Critics," *Dwight's Journal*, Boston, February 4, 1854. The name Jonathan in the last sentence of the quotation is a variant of "Brother Jonathan," a colloquial designation for the United States and its people.

(p. 116)
64. Giovanni Bottesini (1821–89) had appeared in New York as early as 1848, and had returned in 1850 with Marty's Havana Opera Company, serving as leader (i.e., concertmaster) with his double bass. He was also a gifted composer and conductor; in the latter capacity he was to have an important career in several European cities, and was entrusted by Verdi with the premiere of *Aïda* in Cairo in 1871.

Antoine-Joseph Lavigne (1816–86) had settled in England in 1841, playing first in the Drury Lane Promenade Concerts. He was later to join Hallé's famous orchestra in Manchester. It was Lavigne who applied Böhm's ring-key system to the oboe. He died, it is sad to note, in the poorhouse at Manchester.

Others in the orchestra that Jullien brought to New York were Koenig the cornetist, Wuille the clarinetist and saxophonist, Reichert the flutist, and Hardy the bassoonist. In the violin section were the Mollenhauer brothers, Eduard and Friedrich, who liked the United States so well that they stayed behind after Jullien's departure, founding a musical dynasty in Brooklyn with the aid of their brother Henry, a cellist, and appearing frequently as soloists with the New York Philharmonic, of which Eduard was a member for many years.

Among the New York residents that Jullien incorporated into his orchestra was the young Theodore Thomas, later to be a powerful influence on the development of the New York Philharmonic and of orchestral music throughout the United States.

(p. 118)
65. Jullien has suffered unjustly from a double standard of criticism from his own day to the present. No one could deny the superb professionalism of his performances, but there was something about his personality and his flamboyant showmanship that led some of the "serious" critics of his own and later days to exaggerate the negative side of his work at the expense of its commendable qualities. Grove's Dictionary, for example, tells us that "all pieces of Beethoven's were conducted with a jewelled baton, and in a pair of clean kid gloves, handed him at the moment on a silver salver." Somehow this comment manages to convey an atmosphere of frivolousness, distracting the reader from the more important observation that Jullien, after all, was playing Beethoven (as he did regularly also Mozart and Mendelssohn) and making a ceremonial gesture of theatrical, but nevertheless marked, respect. The Penguin New Dictionary of Music has the following entry for Jullien:

JULLIEN, LOUIS GEORGES MAURICE ADOLPHE ROCH ALBERT ABEL ANTONIO ALEXANDRE NOÉ JEAN LUCIEN DANIEL EUGÈNE JOSEPH-LE-BRUN JOSEPH-BARÊME THOMAS THOMAS THOMAS-THOMAS PIERRE CERBON PIERRE-MAUREL BARTHÉLEMI ARTUS ALPHONSE BERTRAND ÉMANUEL DIEUDONNÉ JOSUÉ VINCENT LUC MICHEL JULES-DE-LA-PLANE JULES-BAZIN JULIO-CÉSAR (1812–60), French conductor, more than anyone else responsible for the establishment of promenade concerts in London; also composer of quadrilles and other light music, and of opera 'Peter the Great.' (That his name was as above is alleged in a contemporary magazine article; another source gives his surname as originally 'Julien' and his baptismal names simply as 'Louis Antoine.' He was anyway known by his surname only.) He became insane shortly before his death.

This is all amusing, but not quite cricket. After seducing us with the fantastic list of thirty-five names the lexicographer admits in a parenthetical sentence that this is only Jullien's name as *alleged* (obviously for humorous ends) in a contemporary magazine article, and that he was usually known only by his surname. For many people the final sentence, telling us that he became insane, since it comes at the end of the entry, will leave more of an impression than the brief phrases about his compositions and his responsibility for the establishment of promenade concerts in London.

This is the sort of treatment that Jullien has regularly received. Theodore Thomas, who played under Jullien in New York, refers to him in his *Autobiography* (Vol. I, p. 26) as "the musical charlatan of all ages, who, nevertheless, exerted some useful influence upon orchestral music"; he then goes on to smile impatiently at some of Jullien's superficialities, never hinting at the huge debt that his own program-making and orchestral understanding owed to the French conductor. George P. Upton, the adoring editor of Thomas's *Autobiography,* feels obliged to add a footnote about Jullien, kicking him once or twice, as long as the master has him down: "Mr. Thomas's sharp characterization of him is warranted by his many eccentricities, sensations, and extravagances, as well as by his affected deportment at the conductor's desk, which at times reached the extreme height of silliness. He was fond of prodigious effects. Upon one occasion in London he used six military bands in addition to his permanent orchestra, and in a 'musical congress' announced 'six grand musical fêtes, with four hundred instrumentalists, three distinct choruses, and three distinct military bands.'" Yet when it is a matter of discussing Thomas's own monster Festival of 1882 in New York, using a chorus of three thousand and an orchestra of three hundred, Upton, George William Curtis of *Harper's Magazine,* and Thomas himself have only admiration for Thomas's musical elephantiasis.

Jullien's approach was actually an educational one of a high order, which Theodore Thomas adopted in all its essentials when he had the opportunity some years later. The advance advertisements for Jullien's concerts made this clear from the beginning:

> The selections of music, in addition to those of a lighter character, will embrace the grander compositions of the great masters, the gradual introduction of which, with their complete and effective style of performance, cannot fail, it is believed, to contribute to the enhancement of musical taste . . . The programme (which will be changed every evening) will be selected from a Repertoire of/ TWELVE HUNDRED PIECES/ and will include a Classical Overture and two Movements of a Symphony by one of the great masters, a grand Operatic Selection, together with Quadrilles, Waltzes, Mazurkas, Polkas, Schottisches, Tarantelles, Galops, etc. . . .

And, as John Tasker Howard has said, "the amazing part was that it was all true."

(p. 118)

66. Fry's brilliant plan could serve as the outline for an educational series even today, with modifications only for the contributions of detail that musicology has made since his time in the various areas that he so intelligently mapped out. He

dealt with scales, intervals, melody, harmony, counterpoint, chords, rhythm, pitch, dynamics, the minor mode, the chromatic scale, simple and compound time. In a panoramic coverage of the general history of music, he discussed, with illustrations, ancient Chinese notation, instruments, and scales, with an ancient Chinese hymn performed by the orchestra and the chorus *in Chinese* (a translation of the text was given in the program), Siamese, East Indian, Egyptian, Hebrew, Greek, and early Christian musical art—all contrasted with instrumental and vocal music of more modern times. He had examples of the music of Egypt, collected while Napoleon was there, of ancient Greek hymns rendered into modern notation, of continental European music of the Middle Ages (Boethius, Hucbald, Guido d'Arezzo, the troubadours), of part-music from medieval England, of selections from Queen Elizabeth's music book. He had copies of a tenth-century illuminated manuscript from the monastery of St. Gall, and other materials illustrating the history of musical notation from the ancient Greeks to his own time. He had a Palestrina Mass, part of Gluck's *Orpheus* and of an opera of Le Sueur, as well as of Spontini's *Vestale*, Félicien David's *Christopher Columbus,* and Meyerbeer's *Le Prophète.* He treated of such subjects as acoustics, the human voice, the ballad, national songs, the orchestra and the history of the use of instruments by composers, the symphony and overture, the ballet, military music, church music, chamber music, the styles of different composers, and melodic phraseology. He discussed the difference "between formal and inspired music," in connection with such composers as Palestrina, Jommelli, Purcell, Gluck, Handel, Piccini, Haydn, Mozart, Beethoven, and Rossini. He considered the lyrical drama, including the origins of opera and its progress on the Italian, German, French, and English stages. He expressed his passionate convictions concerning the importance of the proper use of the English language for the musical theater if a broadly based musical art was to develop in this English-speaking country. And his tenth lecture, concerned with the connection of literature and oratory with music, treated of music as a part of collegiate education, of "music and its public diffusion with the national taste in other arts," with health and morals, with family life and society, and of the relation of the artist to private and public life. This of course led him to what, in a sense, was the core of his approach throughout the series—the question of the future of American music and the American artist.

(p. 119)
67. See Upton, *A. P. Heinrich,* pp. 163, 181, 193, and 216ff. A dissertation on "The Symphonies of Anthony Philip Heinrich Based on American Themes" is being prepared by Wilbur R. Maust, who has generously shared with me materials on Heinrich's dealings with the Philharmonic that he has collected for his study.

(p. 120)
68. Yet Mueller says inexplicably (*The American Symphony Orchestra,* facing p. 102, with facsimile of the Dodworth program) that "Dodworth was a violinist in the New York Philharmonic Orchestra, and his programs can hardly be distinguished from those of the Philharmonic." [!]

Strictly speaking, there was still another New York composition on the Dodworth program, a basset-horn solo written and played by Xavier Kiefer. Kiefer, an excellent clarinetist, was to settle in New York and serve as a Philharmonic member from 1854–55 until his death in the 1858–59 season. I have not counted him as a fifth New York composer in the Dodworth concert, however, because at the time of that concert in 1852 he was a relative newcomer to the city, still referred to in the program as "Herr Kiefer."

(p. 123)
69. George Templeton Strong, *Diary,* entry of November 22, 1856.

(p. 123)
70.   PHILHARMONIC SOCIETY OF NEW YORK
                                  NUMBERS OF MEMBERS, 1842–57

Season	Actual Members[1]	Associate Members	Professional Members	Subscribing Members[4]
1st (1842–43)	64(?)			139
2nd (1843–44)	63	5		204
3rd (1844–45)	63	12		220
4th (1845–46)	68	56		210
5th (1846–47)	70	93[2]		180
6th (1847–48)	72	132[3]		113
7th (1848–49)	80	193		57
8th (1849–50)	80	226		67
9th (1850–51)	81	288		67
10th (1851–52)	84	317		59
11th (1852–53)	85	489	58	68
12th (1853–54)	89	555	116	62
13th (1854–55)	89	747	166	59
14th (1855–56)	94	1,091	144	51
15th (1856–57)	97	1,773	213	48

NOTES

1. The number of Actual Members is larger each year than the number that really played in the orchestra, since it includes some "non-performing" members, particularly older ones, no longer active as players.
2. Divided into 22 professionals and 71 amateurs.
3. Divided into 20 professionals, 93 amateurs, and 19 ladies.
4. Entitled to four tickets each during the 1842–43 season, and three each during all subsequent seasons.

(p. 128)
71.   PHILHARMONIC SOCIETY OF NEW YORK
                                  MOVE TO IRVING HALL, 1861–63

Hall	Season	Subscriptions of All Kinds	Receipts
Academy of Music	1860–61	1,701	$10,557
Irving Hall	1861–62	1,040	$ 6,111
Irving Hall	1862–63	889	$ 6,597

(p. 128)
72. A Philharmonic concert given expressly as a wartime benefit, however, on April 2, 1864, was not a practical success. It was an extra concert in aid of the great Metropolitan Fair which was raising money for the Sanitary Commission. "There were not 150 people in all the vast auditorium [the Academy of Music]," reported George Templeton Strong in his Diary. (Strong was Treasurer of the Sanitary Commission, and his wife of the Metropolitan Fair.) Nevertheless, the

Philharmonic did not permit its artistic standards to be dampened, "Eisfeld and his battalion [coming] manfully up to their work." The program on this patriotic occasion was distinguished by two American compositions, a *Columbus* Overture by Bristow and a *Hail, Columbia* Overture by Hohnstock.

(p. 129)

73. Krehbiel is in error (*The Philharmonic Society of New York*, pp. 67, 130) in indicating the Philharmonic concerts of 1867–68 as being given in Steinway Hall. Actually they were back in the Academy of Music again for that season. The error has been carried over by John Erskine in his book on the Philharmonic.

(p. 129)

74.

TICKET RECEIPTS AND NUMBER OF MEMBERS
NEW YORK PHILHARMONIC, 1861–68

Season	Total Ticket Receipts	Number of Members[1]	Income From Extra Tickets	
20th (1861–62)	$ 6,111	1,040	$1,408	(23% of total income)
21st (1862–63)	$ 6,597	889	$1,982	(30% of total income)
22nd (1863–64)	$11,632	1,339[2]	$3,388	(29% of total income)
23rd (1864–65)	$13,463	1,001[3]	$5,273	(39% of total income)
24th (1865–66)	$13,926	874	$6,794	(49% of total income)
25th (1866–67)	$ 9,520[4]	658	$4,158[4]	(44% of total income)
26th (1867–68)	$14,061	457[5]	$9,194	(65% of total income)

NOTES

1. Including Associate, Professional, and Subscribing Members.

2. This is the season (1863–64) when the orchestra's moving from Irving Hall to the roomier and more attractive Academy of Music held off briefly the drop in season memberships that was threatened by an increase in subscription prices (from $5 to $6 for Associate Members and from $10 to $12 for Subscribers).

3. In this season (1864–65) prices were raised further, to $8 for Associate Members and $15 for Subscribing Members, and the ranks of the members began to thin.

4. This is the season (1866–67) when the enforced move to the smaller Steinway Hall slowed for one season the rises in total receipts and sales of extra tickets.

5. In 1867–68 the cost of the Associate Membership was raised even further, from $8 to $10.

(p. 131)

75. The financial inflation connected with the Civil War contributed, of course, to these rises in Philharmonic expenditures, but it was responsible for only a small part of them. The inflation of New York prices was of the order of 80 or 90 per cent in the years during which the Philharmonic's allotment for advertising went up by 300 per cent (from $164 to $608) and its allotment for "extra professional services" by 800 per cent (from $298 to $2,686). As a matter of fact, the price index was already beginning to go *down* again after the War, in 1865–66, while the Philharmonic's expenditures continued to climb.

(p. 133)

76. Not May 24, as Krehbiel says in *The Philharmonic Society*, p. 72.

(p. 134)
77.   SIZE OF ORCHESTRA
                          NEW YORK PHILHARMONIC, 1864–70

Seasons	Actual Members		
Before Doremus	Performing	Non-Performing	Total
1864–65	78	16	94
1865–66	81	15	96
1866–67	81	12	93
Under Doremus			
1867–68	99	18	117
1868–69	106	17	123
1869–70	103	13	116

(p. 136)
78. So conservative were the artistic habits of the Philharmonic, where conducting was concerned, that as late as 1867 it was still employing the outmoded expression "preside at the piano," a survival from the days when part of the direction of a concert had been entrusted to a respected musician at the keyboard, especially in vocal music. "MR. J. MOSENTHAL WILL PRESIDE AT THE PIANO" it was announced for the Grand Concert in celebration of the Society's twenty-fifth anniversary, on May 4, 1867. Apparently Mosenthal worked at the piano with the German Liederkranz in their choral number in the concert, but in 1867 "preside at the piano" was already an old-fashioned way of describing that function. It is even stranger, in the program of April 20, 1867, to read in capital letters at the foot of the page, "MR. H. C. TIMM WILL PRESIDE AT THE PIANO," because the concert does not even offer the excuse of including vocal music and it is hard to imagine how Timm occupied himself at the keyboard in Mozart's *Jupiter* Symphony, Wagner's *Tannhäuser* Overture, and an orchestral excerpt from Berlioz's *Romeo and Juliet* Symphony. All he was doing, it turns out (from a Philharmonic letter of thanks, dated April 27, 1867), was substituting at the piano for a missing harp player in the Berlioz excerpt!

(p. 136)
79. Eisfeld (1816–82) had studied with Rossini in Italy and with Reissiger in Germany, had conducted with distinction in Wiesbaden and in Paris, and had been elected an honorary member of the St. Cecilia Academy of Rome.

(p. 138)
80. Max Goldstein, "Der Stand der oeffentlichen Musikpflege in den Vereinigten Staaten."

(p. 141)
81. For a description of a New York musical production in the 1790s, see Julian Mates, *The American Musical Stage Before 1800*.

(p. 143)
82. Max Goldstein, op. cit.

(p. 144)
83. Ibid.

(p. 145)
84. Theodore Thomas, *Autobiography,* Vol. I, p. 3.

(p. 147)
85. *Diary,* IV, pp. 257–58, entry of October 17, 1869. For the other Strong quotations in this chapter, see the appropriate dates in the *Diary.*

(p. 153)
86. One of the most surprising of these was the case of Dr. James Pech, who had been conductor of Strong's Church Music Association, one of the conductors of Schermerhorn's chamber-orchestra matinees, and a participant in many other of the city's most respected musical activities. In 1872 the Church Music Association accused Pech of certain irregularities, including mismanagement of funds; he was also said to have made off with a good part of their library of music. When he was dismissed, he brought suit against the Association for about $5,000. It was then alleged that he was not really named Pech, but Peck, that he was an Englishman who had "Germanified" himself when he came to the United States (so complete was the German control of music here that it was apparently an advantage for an artist to be taken for German), that he was not really entitled to the Oxford doctor's degree that he had been using, and that he was a bigamist for whose apprehension a reward had been offered in 1860 in London where he had deserted his wife and children. In 1913, in his old age, Pech generously presented his library of music and books about music to Columbia University. I have often wondered, as I used the Pech collection at Columbia, whether any of it stems from the library that he was accused of taking from the Church Music Association in 1872.

(p. 154)
87. The Philharmonic in 1873 was not officially a unionized organization, but it is probably fair to say that most of the men were sympathetic to the idea of organized labor. Unionization efforts had been advancing among New York musicians since about 1860, first through the Aschenbrödel Society (i.e., "Cinderella" Society, a German-American musicians' organization that was at once a cultural, a benevolent, a social, and a labor association), and later through the M.M.P.U. (Musical Mutual Protective Union). In 1872, for example, the M.M.P.U. had tried to put pressure on the wealthy Trinity Church in connection with the orchestra engaged for Easter Sunday; the church, however, which had regarded this as an attempt "to extort money," had easily put together an orchestra from outside the union instead. But the Panic of 1873, with its attendant unemployment, encouraged unionism, and by 1876 the celebrated French composer Jacques Offenbach, for whose New York appearances a hundred-piece orchestra was assembled, could tell how he had won the affection of the players by merely volunteering to join their union. Most of the Philharmonic men were members of the Aschenbrödel Society or of the M.M.P.U., and the Philharmonic meetings were sometimes held at the Aschenbrödel clubhouse on East Fourth Street.

(p. 154)
88. August 10, 1876, not August 16 as most reference works indicate. The *Tribune* obituary is reproduced in *Dwight's Journal* of August 19, 1876 (Vol. 36, No. 10, p. 287).

(p. 155)

89. Three months later, Bergmann's admirers made an effort to do justice to his memory. On November 2, 1876, a Memorial Concert was held in his honor at Steinway Hall by the Philharmonic, the Leiderkranz, the Männergesangverein Arion, and the Sängerrunde, with Dr. Doremus as eloquent eulogist. Dr. Doremus's tribute—more than two columns of it—was printed in the *American Art Journal* on November 18 and in *Dwight's Journal* on December 9, 1876.

(p. 157)

90. T. Thomas, *Autobiography,* Vol. I, pp. 153–54.

(p. 158)

91. Ibid., p. 74.

(p. 158)

92. Erskine (*The Philharmonic-Symphony Society,* p. 18) says 1877–78, but he is in error.

(p. 158)

93. Krehbiel (*The Philharmonic Society,* p. 136) lists the concert on May 7, as does the Philharmonic's Twenty-ninth Annual Report, but the correct date is Saturday, May 6. Damrosch played a cadenza of his own composition in the Beethoven Concerto, but did not otherwise appear as composer, or as conductor, on this program, as has sometimes been stated.

(p. 160)

94. Born in Hamburg in 1843, Neuendorff had come to the United States as a boy of eleven or twelve, and had completed his musical education under German musicians in America. In addition to working as conductor or music director for theaters (especially German ones) in Milwaukee, New York, and Boston, he was very active as a theater manager, presenting many seasons of German plays in New York in the years between 1871 and 1885. In Boston, he was the first conductor of the Music Hall Promenade Concerts (later the Boston Pops). After some work in Berlin and Vienna, he returned to New York where he became music director of Temple Emanu-El in 1896, the year before his death.

(p. 166)

95. See T. Thomas, *Autobiography,* Vol. I, p. 74. Also Rose Fay Thomas, *Memoirs of Theodore Thomas,* pp. 192–94.

(p. 166)

96. "The laurel wreath which the musicians of the Philharmonic orchestra gave him on this occasion," his widow still recalled twenty years later, "was taken to Chicago, and hung on the wall of his library until its leaves dried and crumbled into dust, and the golden-lettered white ribbon with which it was tied, though now yellow and time-worn, is preserved there still, bound across the arms of his vacant chair." (R. F. Thomas, *Memoirs of Theodore Thomas,* p. 358.)

(p. 167)

97. *Autobiography,* Vol. I, p. 127, and Vol. II, p. 3 (as a sort of motto for the volume).

(p. 167)
98. Ibid., Vol. I, p. 157.

(p. 168)
99. Ibid., p. 152.

(p. 169)
100.   THEODORE THOMAS'S PROGRAMS
          WITH THE NEW YORK PHILHARMONIC, 1877–91

Composer	Perform-ances	Composer	Perform-ances	Composer	Perform-ances
Beethoven	56	Spohr	4	Bruckner	1
Wagner	34	Bargiel	3	Franchetti	1
Schumann	27	Cherubini	3	Fuchs, R.	1
Schubert	20	Cowen	3	Grädener	1
Mozart	17	Gluck	3	Grétry	1
Rubinstein	17	Reinhold	3	Huber	1
Brahms	16	Bruch	2	Jensen	1
Bach	13	Franz	2	Joachim	1
Liszt	12	Goetz	2	Lassus	1
Berlioz	11	Handel	2	Marschner	1
Dvořák	10	Henselt	2	Moszkowski	1
Weber	10	Krug	2	Paine	1
Haydn	7	Mackenzie	2	Reyer	1
Tchaikovsky	7	Massenet	2	Scharwenka	1
Mendelssohn	6	Nicodé	2	Scholz	1
Raff	5	Rheinberger	2	Stanford	1
Chopin	4	Saint-Saëns	2	Strauss, R.	1
Goldmark	4	Volkmann	2	Svendsen	1

(p. 170)
101. J. Mueller, *The American Symphony Orchestra*, p. 112.

(p. 170)
102. R. F. Thomas, *Memoirs*, pp. 110ff.

(p. 172)
103. G. P. Upton (ed.), *Theodore Thomas: A Musical Autobiography*, Vol. I,
pp. 243 and 217–19.

(p. 172)
104. J. Offenbach, *Offenbach en Amérique*, pp. 156–58.

(p. 172)
105. *The American Symphony Orchestra*, p. 106.

(p. 173)
106. *Autobiography*, Vol. II, p. 32.

(p. 173)

107. See *Autobiography*, Vol. I, pp. 210ff., and R. F. Thomas, *Memoirs*, pp. 200–2, 218–21, and 497. Mrs. Thomas gives the date of the New York Philharmonic performance of *Ein feste Burg* as February 14, but it was actually February 12, 1881.

(p. 173)

108. *Autobiography*, Vol. II, p. 32.

(p. 174)

109. These performances took place at the Seventh Regiment Armory in New York as part of Thomas's Musical Festival of May 2 to 6, 1882. See his *Autobiography*, Vol. I, pp. 90 and 284, and R. F. Thomas, *Memoirs*, pp. 221ff.

(p. 176)

110. *Autobiography*, Vol. I, pp. 99–100.

(p. 178)

111. F. L. Ritter, *Music in America*, new ed., p. 482.

(p. 178)

112. H. E. Krehbiel, *The Philharmonic Society*, p. 9.

(p. 179)

113. O. Šourek, *Dvořák: Sein Leben und Sein Werk*, p. 58, and *Dvořák: Letters and Reminiscences*, p. 174.

The late Miss Agnes Blatt of New York City told me in 1961 that she had been present on this historic occasion and she added the information that, in response to the ovation, Dvořák left the box in which he was seated and conducted the Largo himself as an encore. Since I had not found this detail in other contemporary reports, I asked Miss Blatt whether she might not have confused it in her memory with the performance of Dvořák's Symphony No. 1, Op. 60, which the records indicate that the composer conducted with the Philharmonic the year before, on December 16 and 17, 1892. She assured me that she had a perfectly clear recollection of the whole evening—December 16 was her birthday, and she had dined at the Waldorf before going to the concert. Dvořák sat in Box 10 with Mr. Thurber, the wholesale grocer (whose wife Jeanette was President of the National Conservatory where Dvořák taught), and Miss Blatt was in Row F below. At the end of the symphony Dvořák had come up to the podium; Seidl had then handed him his baton and Dvořák had conducted the Largo.

(p. 179)

114. *The Philharmonic Society of New York*, p. 14.

(p. 180)

115. F. L. Ritter, *Music in America*.

(p. 182)
116.   Data on which graph on page 182 is based.
COMPARISON OF TICKET SALES FOR AFTERNOON AND
EVENING PERFORMANCES
NEW YORK PHILHARMONIC, 1883–1909

Season	Subscriptions, Public Rehearsals	Subscriptions, Concerts	Extra Tickets, Public Rehearsals	Extra Tickets, Concerts
42nd (1883–84)	$10,299	$11,796	$1,133	$1,052
		+ 46		
43rd (1884–85)	11,956	13,562	882	792
44th (1885–86)	11,748	13,202	639	753
45th (1886–87)	12,731	14,348	527	838
46th (1887–88)	11,598	11,883	804	1,150
		+173		
47th (1888–89)	12,871	11,915	1,325	1,583
48th (1889–90)	13,255	12,111	1,399	1,734
49th (1890–91)	13,515	11,727	1,331	1,683
50th (1891–92)[1]	14,148	12,523	1,101	1,527
51st (1892–93)	15,469	12,868	1,719	2,519
52nd (1893–94)	14,533	11,355	1,731	2,495
53rd (1894–95)	15,257	11,236	2,468	3,700
54th (1895–96)	16,739	11,640	2,327	4,134
55th (1896–97)	16,876	11,593	2,328	3,527
56th (1897–98)[2]	24,914	16,351	2,280	6,046
		+100		
57th (1898–99)	22,272	12,837	2,186	3,630
58th (1899–1900)	18,947	11,077	3,095	4,592
59th (1900–1)	17,083	9,918	3,124	4,564
60th (1901–2)	15,294	9,681	4,023	6,624
61st (1902–3)	12,912	8,305	3,331	3,942
62nd (1903–4)	12,399	9,851	6,045	7,794[3]
63rd (1904–5)	16,265	13,963	6,523[4]	8,501[5]
64th (1905–6)	17,394	13,985	5,477[6]	6,275[7]
65th (1906–7)	19,953	17,038	4,680[8]	5,047[9]
66th (1907–8)	19,782	14,497	3,932[10]	4,037[11]
67th (1908–9)	18,475	9,858	4,195[12]	4,572[13]

NOTES

1. 1891–92, figures do not include three extra concerts of Semi-Centennial Anniversary.

2. 1897–98, the number of performances was increased from six concerts and six public rehearsals to eight of each.

3. 1903–4, $2,572 above the given figure was brought in by an additional special concert.

4, 5. 1904–5, add $1,900 and $3,021 respectively for special public rehearsal and concert.

6, 7. 1905–6, public rehearsals began to be called afternoon concerts. Add $2,918 and $3,693 for extra afternoon and evening concerts.

8, 9. 1906–7, add $2,689 and $3,728 for extra pair of concerts. Other additional concerts for special sponsors, add $2,201 more.

10, 11. 1907–8, add $2,161 and $2,273 for extra pair of concerts, and $2,935 for other special concerts.

12, 13. 1908–9, figures not available for two extra performances under Mahler.

(p. 183)

117. Reprinted in: A. Carnegie, *The Gospel of Wealth, and Other Timely Essays.*

(p. 184)

118. The Philharmonic named Mrs. Shaw an Honorary Associate Member in 1899—the only woman to be so honored. The list at that time included only six other names, which were given in the Annual Report as follows:

R. Ogden Doremus, M.D.	1868
*Edwin Booth, Tragedian	1869
*Geo. T. Strong, Esq.	1872
*E. H. Schermerhorn, Esq.	1879
E. Francis Hyde, Esq.	1892
Elkan Naumburg, Esq.	1892

*(*Deceased.*)

(p. 185)

119. "Poisoning from partaking of preserved fish" is the prosaic explanation in *Riemanns Musik Exikon.* Seidl's devoted supporter, Henry T. Finck, tells us more specifically (*My Adventures,* p. 247) that the several physicians who had been summoned "agreed that the immediate cause of death was some irritant poison, probably ptomain, but they also found cirrhosis of the liver and other degenerative changes which indicated that the acute attack had simply accelerated the advent of death which could not have been long delayed."

(p. 185)

120. See H. T. Finck, *My Adventures,* pp. 246–49.

(p. 186)

121. Van der Stucken, born in Texas in 1858, was an early champion of the American composer. In the 1880s he conducted American orchestral works in New York, at the Paris Exposition, and in Germany. As a young man he had studied in Antwerp and Leipzig (under Grieg) and had been engaged as theater conductor in Breslau. After serving in New York as conductor of the Arion Society, which he took on tour to Europe in 1892, he did important work in Cincinnati as director of the College of Music and conductor of the Cincinnati Symphony Orchestra. From 1908 on, however, he spent most of his time in Europe, and he died in Hamburg in 1929.

(p. 187)

122. The Romanian-Austro-German Paur, born in 1855, was "successor to everybody" in the course of his career: to Nikisch in Boston, to Seidl at the Philharmonic in New York, to Dvořák at the National Conservatory in New York, and to Muck in Berlin. He had had a brilliant student career in Vienna as both violinist and pianist, but had already become a professional conductor by the time he was twenty-one, working successively at important posts in Kassel, Königsberg, Mannheim, and Leipzig, before taking over the Boston Symphony Orchestra in 1893. After leaving the New York Philharmonic, he led the Pittsburgh Symphony Orchestra from 1904 until its dissolution in 1910 (it was not revived until 1937), and then became Kapellmeister at the Royal Opera in Berlin for a short time. He died in Czechoslovakia in 1932.

(p. 188)

123. Walter Johannes Damrosch, born in Breslau in 1862, had been brought to the United States as a boy of nine. After his father's death in 1885, he had become conductor of the Oratorio Society and the Symphony Society, and had continued as assistant for the German repertory at the Metropolitan Opera. Then, in 1894, he had organized a company that had presented German opera, chiefly Wagner, in many cities of the United States (including the first American performance of *Parsifal,* in concert form, in 1896). At the time when he became conductor of the Philharmonic, in 1902, he had also been conducting Wagner at the Metropolitan again. We will have many occasions to refer to his subsequent career in the chapters that follow. He died in New York, at the age of eighty-eight, in 1950.

(p. 189)

124. The story, as reconstructed here, can be traced in the Minutes of the Philharmonic's meetings for 1902–3, which fill in much that Damrosch omits in the account that he gives in his autobiography *(My Musical Life,* pp. 206–9).

(p. 192)

125. Carnegie and Rockefeller were rewarded by being named Honorary Associate Members in 1905.

(p. 192)

126. Victor Herbert, returning as successful composer and conductor to the orchestra in which he had once been a cellist, donated to the Philharmonic's Pension Fund the $400 salary that he received for his pair of performances.

(p. 195)

127. In his sensitivity about the position of the American composer, MacDowell hated to be given musical alms. When the well-meaning conductor Felix Mottl announced an "American composer's concert" in 1904, MacDowell wrote him a proud and angry letter:

> I see by the morning papers a so-called American composers' concert advertised for tomorrow evening at the Metropolitan Opera House.
> I have for years taken a strong stand against such affairs, and although I have not seen the program, fearing that there may be something of mine on it, I write to protest earnestly and strongly against the lumping together of American composers. Unless we are worthy of being put on programs with other composers to stand or fall, leave us alone. By giving such a concert you tacitly admit that we are too inferior to stand comparison with the composers of Europe. If my name is on the program and it is too late to have new ones printed, I beg you to have a line put through the number, crossing it off the program. If necessary, I will pay the expense of having it done. Hoping that this may not be necessary and that my name has not been added to the list of American composers whose works you have selected, believe me, very truly yours,
>
> Edward MacDowell

(See *Musical Courier,* February 17, 1904.)

(p. 201)

128. *The American Symphony Orchestra,* p. 46.

(p. 201)
129. Ibid., p. 50.

(p. 201)
130.   ACTUAL MEMBERS PERFORMING
                                    and
                    EXPENDITURES FOR SUBSTITUTES

                New York Philharmonic, 1867–70, 1870–75, 1883–1909
                        (Orchestra of about 100 players)

A	B	C	D	E
		Actual		
	Actual	Members	Spent for Sub-	
Season	Members	Performing	stitutes	Conductor
1867–68	117	99	$ 823	Bergmann
1868–69	123	106	1,158	"
1869–70	116	103	1,764	"
1870–71	111	96	2,588	"
1871–72	105	92	2,388	"
1872–73	104	92	2,590	"
1873–74	106	94	2,276	"
1874–75	98	82	2,466	"
1883–84	92	81	2,068	Thomas
1884–85	93	79	2,876	"
1885–86	92	73	2,748	"
1886–87	92	71	4,744	"
1887–88	95	77	3,422	"
1888–89	94	73	3,274	"
1889–90	90	69	3,436	"
1890–91	90	66	3,543	"
1891–92	96	67	3,705	Seidl
1892–93	94	64	3,692	"
1893–94	92	62	4,016	"
1894–95	93	61	4,270	"
1895–96	76	62	4,970	"
1896–97	77	64	4,129	"
1897–98	75	59	6,501	"
1898–99	73	62	5,637	Paur
1899–1900	74	62	5,277	"
1900–1	71	59	6,826	"
1901–2	73	58	6,742	"
1902–3	73	59	6,069	W. Damrosch
1903–4	73	56	6,634*	Guest Conductors
1904–5	68	56	6,882*	" "
1905–6	70	54	7,998*	" "
1906–7	65	55	6,575*	Safonoff
1907–8	63	50	7,041*	"
1908–9	57	37	8,406*	"

* These figures are for the regular concert series. Additional sums were spent for
substitutes for *extra* concerts in each season from 1903 to 1909.

(p. 204)
131. R. F. Thomas, *Memoirs,* p. 324.

(p. 207)
132. *The American Symphony Orchestra,* p. 51.

(p. 208)
133. The letter on which this condensed summary is based is entered in the Minutes of the Annual Meetings of the Philharmonic Society of New York, 1904–32, pp. 84–91 (meeting of February 12, 1909).

(p. 210)
134. For a brief interlude from 1910 to 1912 Loudon Charlton replaced Leifels as Manager, though not as Secretary. That interlude invites a word of comment. Leifels had been appointed Manager for 1910–11 at the apparently generous salary of $7,000 (considering that he had been paid $2,000 for the previous year). But there were a few strings attached: "Subject to the control and approval of the Committee," ran the agreement, "he shall at his own expense employ and pay a competent and efficient deputy and assistant, and all necessary stenographers and office boys, hire and pay the rent of a suitable office for the Society, and supply all necessary articles and things connected with or used in and about said office except a telephone and stationery." And all of this out of the $7,000 that constituted his annual salary! It is a relief to one who has acquired friendly feelings toward Leifels, as a result of tracing his efforts on behalf of the Philharmonic, to find that at the next meeting of the Committee he obtained the cancellation of his contract. It was agreed to accept Loudon Charlton as Manager instead. One feels less concern for Charlton, who was already engaged in the managerial business on his own and probably knew how to take care of himself. Leifels continued as personnel manager of the orchestra, however, even during the period when Charlton supplanted him as business manager.

(p. 210)
135. Spiering, though of American birth (he was born in St. Louis in 1871), studied in Berlin under Joachim and chose to live and work in Germany for considerable portions of his career. Before his appointment as Mahler's concertmaster in New York, he had already held important teaching and playing positions in Berlin (the Stern Conservatory) as well as in Chicago (the Thomas Orchestra, his own quartet, the Chicago Conservatory and Chicago Musical College). After his Philharmonic service he settled in Berlin again for a while, before returning to New York in 1914. In both countries he earned for himself a respected name as a teacher, performer, and conductor. He died in Munich in 1925.

(p. 213)
136. New York *Tribune,* November 11, 1909.

(p. 213)
137. Ibid., December 13, 1909.

(p. 213)
138. Ibid., January 15, 1910.

(p. 214)
139. Ibid., December 17, 1909.

(p. 214)
140. Ibid.

(p. 214)
141. New York *World*, December 18, 1909.

(p. 214)
142. See Ernst Krenek, "Gustav Mahler," in Bruno Walter's *Gustav Mahler*, p. 187.

(p. 216)
143. From an unpublished letter, a copy of which has been sent me by Spiering's daughter, Miss Lenore Spiering, of Burbank, California. The original is in German, and the translation is mine.

(p. 216)
144. Minutes of the Guarantors' Committee, New York Philharmonic Society, 1911.

(p. 217)
145. H. Shanet, "Mahler as Conductor—An Interview with Mrs. Alma Mahler Werfel," in *Notes on the Programs*, New York Philharmonic, February 4, 1960.

(p. 217)
146. Weiss did not play at the concert, but neither did Yolanda Merö who had been called in to replace him; on the morning of the day on which she was to perform, she discovered that she had injured her hand in practicing, and Paolo Gallico bravely substituted for her on a few hours' notice.

(p. 220)
147. The Minutes of the Annual Meetings of the Philharmonic Society show that, as of March 16, 1912, the Board of Directors consisted of: Richard Arnold (Vice-President), Felix F. Leifels (Secretary), Henry P. Schmitt (Treasurer), Carl Hauser, August Kalkhof, Alexander Laurendeau, August Roebbelen, and Frank Ruhlender. Andrew Carnegie, the President, and one other member of the Board had resigned, and had not been replaced; except for them, the Board was identical with that given three years earlier in the Annual Report of 1909.

(p. 222)
148. The Philharmonic's first performances in Canada were two concerts with the Toronto Oratorio Society in Stransky's first year, 1911–12. They marked the debut of the Oratorio Society.* The orchestra returned to Canada under Stransky's direction on subsequent occasions, including the grand coast-to-coast tour of the spring of 1921.

---

* Not the inauguration of Massey Hall, as implied by Erskine (*The Philharmonic-Symphony Society*, p. 46). Massey Hall had been opened in 1894.

(p. 225)
149. The documents relevant to the Pulitzer bequest are contained in the Minutes of the Meetings of the Board of Directors of the Philharmonic Society, 1903–12 (following p. 178), and the Minutes of the Annual Meetings of the Philharmonic Society, 1904–32 (following p. 96).

(p. 226)
150. See the five-page statement by the Directors in the program booklet for January 22, 1914.

(p. 230)
151. The Andante of Beethoven's Fifth seems to have been the first Philharmonic recording issued, but not the first one made. At the initial session on January 22, 1917, Thomas's *Raymond* Overture and Weber's *Freischütz* Overture were recorded, and it was not until the third session, on January 24, that the Beethoven was done. Columbia Records and Dr. A. F. R. Lawrence have supplied me with the complete list of the first Philharmonic recordings, which are given here in the order in which they were made:

1917
Raymond Overture—Thomas
Der Freischütz Overture—Weber [never published]
Largo from *New World* Symphony—Dvořák
Malagueña from Ballet Suite *Boabdil*—Moszkowski
Andante from Fifth Symphony—Beethoven
Marche Militaire from *Suite Algérienne*—Saint-Saëns
Capriccio Espagnol—Rimsky-Korsakov
1918
American Fantaisie—Victor Herbert
Martha Overture—Flotow
Light Cavalry Overture—Suppé
Stradella Overture—Flotow
Hungarian Dances No. 5 and No. 6—Brahms
L'Estudiantina, Waltz—Waldteufel
Hungarian Rhapsody No. 2—Liszt
Waltz of the Flowers, *Nutcracker* Suite—Tchaikovsky
1919
Hungarian March from *Damnation of Faust*—Berlioz
Mlle. Modiste Overture—Victor Herbert
Polonaise [Chopin?]
March of the Sardar from *Caucasian Sketches*—Ippolitov-Ivanov
Pomp and Circumstance March No. 1—Elgar [never published]
Andante from "Surprise" Symphony—Haydn
Angelus from *Scènes Pittoresques*—Massenet
Turkish March from Sonata in A Major—Mozart
Mikado Overture—Sullivan
Spanish Dance—[?]

(p. 230)
152. H. T. Finck, *My Adventures,* p. 421.

(p. 231)
153. Ibid., p. 422.

(p. 231)
154. See, for example, R. Schickel, *The World of Carnegie Hall,* passim.

(p. 232)
155. For a copy of the printed program for Varèse's concert of April 11, 1919, including the prospective programs for April 25–26 and May 9–10 (the two that were not given), I am indebted to Chou Wen-chung, who is preparing a biography of Varèse.

(p. 234)
156.   CONDUCTORS, NEW YORK PHILHARMONIC, 1921–30

1921–22	STRANSKY	*Associate Conductor:*	HADLEY	
	Guest Conductors: Mengelberg, Bodansky			
1922–23	STRANKSY, MENGELBERG	"	"	"
	Guest Conductor: van Hoogstraten			
1923–24	MENGELBERG, VAN HOOGSTRATEN	"	"	"
1924–25	MENGELBERG, VAN HOOGSTRATEN	"	"	"
	Guest Conductors: Stravinsky, Furtwängler			
1925–26	MENGELBERG, FURTWÄNGLER	"	"	"
	Guest Conductors: Toscanini, Reiner			
1926–27	MENGELBERG, FURTWÄNGLER	"	"	"
	Guest Conductors: Toscanini, Lange, Reiner, Georgesco			
1927–28	MENGELBERG, TOSCANINI			
	Guest Conductors: Beecham, Molinari			
1928–29	MENGELBERG, TOSCANINI			
	Guest Conductors: Damrosch, Gabrilowitsch, Honegger, Krauss, Molinari, Reiner	*Assistant Conductor:*	Lange	
1929–30	TOSCANINI, MENGELBERG, MOLINARI	"	"	"
	Tour Conductor: TOSCANINI			

(p. 238)
157. The quotation is from the companion volume to the set of sixty records, *Music Appreciation in the Schoolroom* (p. 4), by Thaddeus P. Giddings, Will Earhart, Ralph L. Baldwin, and Elbridge W. Newton. This was part of a Music Education Series put out by Ginn & Company. The authors were all respected music educators: Giddings was Director of School Music in Minneapolis, Earhart

in Pittsburgh, and Baldwin in Hartford; Newton was Managing Editor. My attention was steered to the Philharmonic's role in this project by Dr. A. F. R. Lawrence of New York and Donald Y. Gardner, formerly Head of the Music Department of Ginn & Company. Dr. Lawrence adds the information that a set of electrical recordings may have been issued subsequently, in addition to the original acoustic ones.

(p. 238)

158. Sophie Guggenheimer Untermeyer is the Philharmonic's Fund Raising Director and a member of the Board of Directors and the Auxiliary Board. Her collaborator on the book was Alix Williamson, for many years Director of Publicity for Stadium Concerts.

(p. 239)

159. The last summer of symphony concerts at the Stadium was 1964 (after that the Metropolitan Opera took over the Stadium for concert versions of opera) and Mrs. Guggenheimer ran all but the last two seasons, when her illness made it necessary for her daughter, Mrs. Untermeyer, to replace her. Mrs. Guggenheimer was also a Director of the Philharmonic-Symphony Society for many years and Vice-Chairman of the Philharmonic's Auxiliary Board from its earliest days until her death in 1966. In her honor the mobile trailer-stage created for the Philharmonic's outdoor concerts in the New York parks has been named by the city the "Minnie" Guggenheimer Shell.

(p. 240)

160. Judson was the Philharmonic's Manager until 1956 but stayed with the Stadium only until 1942; van Hoogstraten, on the other hand, held the regular Philharmonic post only until 1925, when he left to take over the Portland Symphony Orchestra in Oregon, but continued to do the Stadium seasons every summer until 1938. (Van Hoogstraten, for that matter, had already conducted the Philharmonic in half a Stadium season in 1922 and a very brief stint as guest conductor in January 1923.)

(p. 240)

161. J. Erskine, *The Philharmonic-Symphony Society*, p. 32.

(p. 240)

162. Ernest Schelling (1876–1939), whom we have already had occasion to mention as a member of the Guarantors' Committee that reorganized the Philharmonic in 1909, was a man of remarkably varied talents and background. At the age of four he was presented as a child prodigy, playing the piano, in public concert in Philadelphia. He then studied in Europe with some of the best-known pedagogues of the time, who made him heir to the principal musical traditions of the nineteenth century: Mathias (pupil of Chopin), Leschetizky (pupil of Czerny), Pruckner (pupil of Liszt), Barth (pupil of von Bülow), Moszkowski, Goetschius, Hans Huber, and Paderewski. After touring Europe and the Americas as pianist, he settled in the United States, and continued to tour widely in the triple role of pianist, composer, and conductor. In World War I he was commissioned Captain of Infantry, serving as Assistant Military Attaché to the American Legation in Switzerland, carrying out diplomatic missions in many countries of Europe, and earning decorations not only from his own country,

but from France and Poland as well; when he was discharged in 1920, he held the rank of major. Both before and after the war, his compositions were performed by the most distinguished conductors—Nikisch, Richter, Toscanini, Mottl, Fiedler, Muck, Pfitzner, Mengelberg, Stokowski, Stock, Damrosch. In addition to his work with the New York Philharmonic, he was conductor of the Baltimore Symphony Orchestra in 1936 and 1937, and guest conductor of many orchestras in Europe and America. Schelling had almost as many interests and activities outside music as within it. He was a collector of arms and armor, a connoisseur of books, prints, and objects of art, an expert swimmer, and a devotee of boating. Charming, handsome, intelligent, fluent in five languages, he was active in a dozen organizations, ranging from the Military Intelligence Reserve Society to the MacDowell Association (as President of the latter, during the last decade of his life, doing much to help the artists' colony maintained by the Association at Peterborough, New Hampshire).

(p. 241)
163. The Damrosch quotation is from *My Musical Life*, p. 268. The Schelling quotations in this and the succeeding paragraphs are from the following documents, preserved in the Ernest Schelling Archives at 863 Park Avenue in New York City:
Statement, dated March 16, 1933, prepared by Schelling on the death of Mrs. Harriman.
Talk by Schelling, Women's City Club, New York, February 18, 1931.
Analytical Notes, written by Schelling for Philharmonic Children's Concerts of February 9 and 11, 1924.
Address by Schelling, Principals' Association, Eastern High School, Baltimore, February 7, 1936.

(p. 241)
164. Letter, dated November 5, 1924, from Mrs. Charles E. Mitchell, chairman of the Philharmonic Children's Concerts, to Mrs. J. F. Cosgrave, The Lenox School, New York City. (The Ernest Schelling Archives.)

(p. 242)
165. Part of the expansion of the educational concerts must be attributed to the amalgamation of the Philharmonic with Walter Damrosch's Symphony Society in 1928; indeed, Damrosch was given eleven of the season's sixteen concerts to conduct in 1928–29. But Damrosch participated as conductor in only that one season; and, in the next two years, when Schelling took over all the concerts, the annual number of performances was sustained at fifteen.

(p. 242)
166. Letter, dated 18 October 1931, signed F. Weingartner. (The Ernest Schelling Archives. Original in German; English translation supplied by the Archives.)

(p. 248)
167. Minutes of the City Symphony Orchestra (Musical Society of the City of New York), 1922–23, now in the Archives of the New York Philharmonic.
The principal backers of the City Symphony, in addition to Senator (also known as General) DuPont, had been Bartlett Arkell, Manton B. Metcalf, and Ralph Pulitzer, and the counsel for the organization had been Louis W. Stotesbury.

(p. 249)

168. Willem Mengelberg (1871–1951) was born in Holland of a German family and studied both in Holland and in Germany. At the age of twenty he was already municipal music director in Lucerne and at the age of twenty-four took over the Concertgebouw Orchestra in Amsterdam. He was soon an admired guest conductor in the music capitals of Europe and America; we have already mentioned his appearance with the New York Philharmonic in 1905, and he was regularly engaged in Frankfurt, London, Moscow, St. Petersburg, Rome, and Naples. He was said to have been offered the conductorship of the Boston Symphony Orchestra in 1919, and to have turned it down. After his work in New York with the National Symphony Orchestra and the Philharmonic, Columbia University gave him an honorary degree (1928). During the German occupation of Holland in World War II, Mengelberg made no secret of his approval of the Nazis, and in 1945, after the liberation, he was found guilty of collaborating with them, and was barred from conducting in the Netherlands. He died in Switzerland in 1951.

(p. 250)

169. The first phrase is taken from Richard Aldrich's comment in the New York *Times* on a New York Philharmonic concert of November 10, 1905; the second from M. B. Foster's enthralled description, in his 1912 *History*, of Mengelberg's London Philharmonic concert of November 11, 1911; and the third from Winthrop Sargeant's 1949 reminiscences of his days as a Philharmonic violinist under Mengelberg in the late 1920s (*Geniuses, Goddesses, and People*, p. 94).

(p. 250)

170. *Geniuses, Goddesses, and People*, p. 94.

(p. 251)

171. H. T. Finck, *My Adventures*, p. 423. V. Sheean, *First and Last Love*, p. 67. Sheean, adopting the opinion that cultured New Yorkers were expected to hold, refers to the Philharmonic under Stransky as "moribund," but he is so unfamiliar with the subject that he spells the conductor's name "Strusky" and confuses the Philharmonic-National merger of 1921 with the Philharmonic-Symphony merger of 1928.

(p. 251)

172. Similarly, in Amsterdam, where Mengelberg was monarch of the Concertgebouw Orchestra, he allotted a substantial part of each season (the months when he was in New York) first to Karl Muck and later to Pierre Monteux. Though Mengelberg was feared in some quarters as the "terror of the orchestra world," he behaved unselfishly toward Monteux, allowing him wide freedom in choosing repertory and in changing orchestra players. Doris Monteux, speaking for her husband as well as for herself, has described the complicated tangle that was Mengelberg's personality: "He was at the same time kind and generous, unkind and small, bombastic yet gentle, childishly naive, foolishly proud and pompous, yet ridden with a feeling of unworthiness, religious yet at times positively hedonistic." Yet Monteux considered Mengelberg "a wonderful colleague" and insisted that, in the ten years of their association, there was never a problem of "getting along." (D. Monteux, *It's All in the Music*, pp. 136–41.)

(p. 253)

173. OPERATING EXPENSES, NEW YORK PHILHARMONIC, 1909–28
(selected seasons)

Season	Amount	Conductor(s)
1909–10	about $183,000	Mahler
1916–17	about $224,000	Stransky
1919–20	about $262,000	Stransky
1921–22	about $421,000	Stransky, with Mengelberg and Bodanzky as guest conductors (first year of merger with National Symphony Orchestra)
1922–23	about $450,000	Mengelberg and Stransky, with van Hoogstraten as guest conductor
1923–24	about $451,000	Mengelberg and van Hoogstraten
1924–25	about $487,000	Mengelberg and van Hoogstraten, with Stravinsky and Furtwängler as guests
1925–26	about $587,000	Mengelberg and Furtwängler, with Toscanini as guest
1926–27	about $625,000	Mengelberg and Furtwängler, with Toscanini, Reiner, and others as guests
1927–28	almost $700,000	Mengelberg and Toscanini, with Beecham and Molinari as guests

(p. 253)

174. Flagler came close to being a full-time music patron. Inheritor of an oil, hotel, and railroad fortune, he gave not only his money but also most of his personal attention to the cause of music. A brief declaration that was carried year after year in Who's Who in America reveals how he saw his role:

Although not a professional musician has devoted time largely for yrs. to promotion of music in New York; a reorganizer of Symphony Soc. of New York and served as v.p., now pres.; assumed entire financial backing of the society, 1914.

Flagler had shown his friendship for Damrosch as early as 1903, when, as Secretary of the Permanent Orchestra Fund, he had tried to help the conductor in his unsuccessful plan (of which we have traced the vicissitudes in Chapter 18 above) for subsidizing the Philharmonic as a permanent orchestra.

(p. 254)

175. Taft was a member of the respected law firm of Cadwalader, Wickersham and Taft, and thereby, one might say, a "descendant-at-law" of George Templeton Strong, President of the Philharmonic from 1870 to 1874, to whose law firm (Strong, Bidwell, and Strong) Taft's was the successor. Indeed, it was Taft who brought about the publication of Strong's Diary, to which frequent reference has been made in this book; in 1938, he mentioned the Diary to President Nicholas Murray Butler of Columbia University, who had been his fellow member on the Philharmonic's Board, and Butler transmitted the information to Professors Allan Nevins and Milton Thomas, who spent more than a decade in preparing and editing the four published volumes of excerpts from the Diary.

Rice, who had served for ten years as Treasurer of Damrosch's Symphony Society, was also a diligent amateur cellist and the paladin of the city's chamber-music forces. For an extraordinary musical lawsuit, Rice's defense of the famous

Flonzaley Quartet against an all-out legal attack by its own violist—a case in which affidavits were taken from Mengelberg, Schelling, Victor Herbert, and a dozen more of the best-known figures in the world of the Philharmonic and of New York music—see Rice's *Musical Reminiscences,* pp. 93–102.

(p. 255)
176. "With characteristic modesty," recounts Edwin T. Rice, who had been chairman of the Symphony Society's pension fund, "President Flagler did not sign the disbursing checks, but allowed me to perform that agreeable duty as Treasurer of the Symphony Society." (*Musical Reminiscences,* pp. 118–19.)

(p. 255)
177. *Geniuses, Goddesses, and People,* pp. 74, 78.

(p. 255)
178. *The American Symphony Orchestra,* p. 56.

(p. 258)
179. A brief résumé of the career around which the legend was woven may prove helpful for the reader of this chapter:

Arturo Toscanini (1867–1957) was born in Parma, Italy, and educated at the conservatory there, studying chiefly cello but also piano and composition. He won his spurs as a conductor in 1886, at the age of nineteen, while serving as cellist in an Italian opera company in Rio de Janeiro, when he was unexpectedly required to step in as substitute conductor in a performance of *Aïda* and carried it off with brilliant success. For more than two decades after that he worked as opera and concert conductor in the principal Italian cities, conducting, among other important works, the first performances of Leoncavallo's *Pagliacci* and Puccini's *La Bohème,* and serving, between 1898 and 1908, as chief conductor at La Scala in Milan. He first came to New York to conduct at the Metropolitan Opera in 1908, and although his relationships with some of the Met officials and personnel were stormy, he stayed for seven seasons, until 1915. Except for his American tour with the orchestra of La Scala in 1920–21, he did not work in New York again until his Philharmonic engagements as guest conductor in 1926 and 1927, but after that he was one of the Society's principal conductors in every year until 1936. He never gave his full time to the Philharmonic, however, even after relinquishing his duties as artistic director of La Scala in 1929; from 1930 on, at the height of his New York success, he was making notable appearances in Bayreuth, Vienna, Salzburg, London, and Palestine. He left the Philharmonic-Symphony in 1936, though he returned as guest conductor in 1942 and 1945. Meanwhile, in 1937, the National Broadcasting Company had persuaded him to come back to New York where a new orchestra, the NBC Symphony, was organized principally for him; he conducted this orchestra in almost every year until 1954, touring South America with it in 1940 and the United States in 1950 (at the age of eighty-three!). He died in New York only a couple of months before his ninetieth birthday.

(p. 261)
180. Toscanini's added kettledrum appears at first to be justifiable from another viewpoint: since Beethoven does use the kettledrum in a parallel passage earlier in the overture (mm. 92–95), it seems probable that he omits it the second time only because the key has changed and the hand-tuned pair of drums of his day couldn't

play the notes of the new key comfortably, as modern mechanical drums can. But to excuse the touching up, as some defenders of such changes do, on the grounds that "Beethoven would have done it this way if he had had our modern instruments," opens up a Pandora's box that Toscanini himself warned against on other occasions. Next one would have to rewrite Beethoven's horn and trumpet parts to take advantage of the invention of valves, his woodwind parts to allow for Böhm's improvements, his string parts to exploit the increased facility in high positions . . .

(p. 262)

181. Samuel Chotzinoff (*Toscanini: An Intimate Portrait*, pp. 133–34) says that it was he who ultimately discouraged Toscanini from using this change. He also implies that it was in the mid-1940s, as conductor of the NBC Symphony, that the Maestro tried it for the first time; but this is not correct—Toscanini had had the Philharmonic's timpanist, Saul Goodman, play the doubling too.

(p. 262)

182. The Wagner-Toscanini alterations in this passage have been drummed so unceasingly into the ears of musicians and listeners by the most influential conductors that they have come to be accepted as part of the sound of Beethoven's Ninth. But they are open to serious argument. Beethoven's woodwind scoring is admittedly too weak to balance a large body of strings, but it can be strengthened in performance simply by using more woodwinds of the same kinds that the score calls for—without resorting to all the added brass. The heavy additions, it can be argued further, turn the passage into the wrong kind of tutti—too powerful for what comes before or after it, it creates a premature climax that unbalances the formal structure of the movement.

One of the strangest of Toscanini's liberties with Beethoven's Ninth has been described (in B. H. Haggin's *The Toscanini Musicians Knew*, p. 109) by Jan Peerce, who was a favorite singer of the Maestro's. In the final vocal quartet of the Ninth Symphony, he said, Toscanini once altered the most conspicuous notes of the soprano part. "This man," exclaimed Peerce, "who kept saying, '*Canta come è scritto*' and 'Is written this way; sing it the way is written'—this man changed the B-naturals in the last quartet for the soprano!" One guesses that the unnamed soprano couldn't manage the high notes. But what remains puzzling to any musician who was not there is the unanswered question: *To what* could Toscanini have changed those two notoriously awkward and unconcealable high B's, as familiar to the world's ears as any favorite quotation from Shakespeare?! Peerce, questioned recently, could not remember, though he did recall that the Maestro had also altered the tenor part to conform to the change in the soprano. "The result couldn't have been too bad," he commented, "because I don't think there were any complaints."

(p. 262)

183. *Musical America*, September 1939. Toscanini's name was so readily associated with the quest for musical authenticity that the New York Public Library made plans in 1936 to establish an Arturo Toscanini Collection of Musical Autographs in Microfilm Reproduction as an appropriate tribute to him upon his retirement from the Philharmonic-Symphony. Though the project had Toscanini's enthusiastic approval, it did not come to realization until 1965, eight years after his death, when it took shape as the Toscanini Memorial Archives in the Music Division of the New York Public Library at Lincoln Center. (For information

about the history of the Archives, and generous aid in their use, I thank the Curator, Susan Thiemann Sommer.)

(p. 265)
184. In a somewhat similar case, an earlier Philharmonic conductor, Theodore Thomas, was also credited with supernatural powers because of a cello incident. It took place at a rehearsal of "Wotans Abschied" (from Wagner's *Die Walküre*) with a three-hundred-piece festival orchestra in 1882. A player at the last stand of the cellos read a passage in bass clef instead of tenor clef, and Thomas suspected the nature of the error not just from hearing it but from seeing the position of the man's hand. Now, there were thirty-six cellists in the three-hundred-piece orchestra and the last stand was eighty feet from the conductor, so when Thomas stepped down from the podium and walked all the way to the erring musician to point out his mistake, the orchestra was understandably impressed with the keenness of his hearing. Thomas tells the story in his *Autobiography* (Vol. I, pp. 89–90), concluding with a becoming mixture of modesty and pride that "the conductor sometimes hears with his eyes as well as his ears."

(p. 265)
185. (1) Paul Stefan, *Toscanini* (English translation), p. 58.
    (2) Winthrop Sargeant, *Geniuses, Goddesses, and People*, p. 175.
    (3) Howard Taubman, *The Maestro*, p. 262.

(p. 268)
186.

NEW YORK PHILHARMONIC

EARNED INCOME AND DEFICITS DURING THE TOSCANINI ERA

Season	Conductors	Earned Income	Deficit
1927–28	Mengelberg, Toscanini, and guests	$588,572	$110,628
1928–29*	Mengelberg, Toscanini, and guests	744,541	121,521
1929–30	Toscanini, Mengelberg, Molinari	755,652	117,867
1930–31	Toscanini, Molinari, Kleiber, and guest	732,813	142,818
1931–32	Toscanini, Kleiber, Walter, and guests	663,323	137,534
1932–33	Toscanini, Walter, and guest	611,836	184,270
1933–34	Toscanini, Walter, Lange	535,218	141,465
1934–35	Toscanini, Janssen, Klemperer, Lange, Rodzinski, Walter	530,955	178,652
1935–36	Toscanini, Klemperer, Lange, Beecham	548,345	176,669

(p. 270)
187. *Musical Courier*, Vol. CIX, No. 15, December 22, 1934.

(p. 271)
188. The plainness and heavy-handedness of Damrosch's conducting style prevented him from being considered by the public in the same class with such dazzling stars as Toscanini, Koussevitzky, and Stokowski, but he was a musician of

---

* First year of the merger of the Philharmonic and Symphony Societies to form the Philharmonic-Symphony Society.

wide experience and understanding, and in the years before his Symphony Society was absorbed into the Philharmonic, he brought a remarkable variety of music to New York audiences—and for that matter to the whole nation, for Damrosch was the most assiduous tourer since Theodore Thomas. Although Damrosch was born in Germany and brought up in the thickest German musical tradition, he played the Russians and the English too, and he began to give New York the modern French composers even before World War I made them fashionable. As for American music, he played even some for which he may have had no strong personal sympathy. There is a well-known story about Damrosch turning around to say to the audience, when he did the Copland *Organ* Symphony on January 11, 1925: "If a young man at the age of twenty-five can write a symphony like that, in five years he will be ready to commit murder." I have long wondered how a conductor who had undertaken to give the world premiere of a work could make that sort of wisecrack about it immediately after performing it. In response to my inquiry, Mr. Copland has supplied the following explanation:

> He had agreed to do the piece in the first place at the request of Nadia Boulanger, who was performing it that day [as organ soloist]. There was no question as to whether he liked it or not, since he had agreed in advance to play it. He was a great friend of Nadia and, you might say, was stuck with the thing. My idea is that he made the little speech in order to calm the nerves of the elderly ladies in his audience, of whom there were plenty, — and in order to imply that he was on their side of the fence. . . . Incidentally, in later years, he always seemed embarrassed when he met me, and more than once said to me, "*You* understood what I meant by that remark, didn't you?" As a matter of fact, he didn't hesitate to recommend me enthusiastically to the Guggenheim Foundation a few months later, even making complimentary remarks about the Organ Symphony. Perhaps this was just to salve his conscience, but at any rate it did help me to get a (the)* first Guggenheim. May he rest in peace!

Damrosch's performances of Gershwin's music constitute another case in point. Though he was not enthusiastic about jazz, believing that it "appeals to the nerves but never to the head or the heart" (*The Literary Digest,* February 17, 1934), he invited Gershwin to write a piano concerto with jazz elements and he gave its first performance with the Symphony Society in 1925, as he did of the same composer's *American in Paris* in 1928.

(p. 271)
189.   J. H. Mueller, *The American Symphony Orchestra,* pp. 59–60.

(p. 274)
190.   In Pound's pen name of William Atheling, under cover of which he wrote about music for several years, "Atheling" must surely be an anagram of "G. Antheil."

(p. 276)
191.   D. G. Mason, *Tune In, America,* pp. 36–48.

(p. 277)
192.   *The Philharmonic-Symphony Society,* p. 35. The broadcasts were carried first by WEAF (1922–26), then by WOR (1927–30), and after 1930 by the Columbia Broadcasting System on WABC.

---

* Copland was the first composer to be awarded a Guggenheim Fellowship.

(p. 277)
193. Quoted in *The Literary Digest*, February 17, 1934, p. 24.

(p. 277)
194. In punishment for his temerity, Moore was handled roughly in the columns of the New York *Herald Tribune* by Lawrence Gilman, the Philharmonic's program annotator, who had the advantage of being also the *Herald Tribune*'s music critic. My quotations are taken from the *Herald Tribune* of February 2, February 18, and March 11, 1934, and from the correspondence between the two men, which the late Professor Moore permitted me to examine.

(p. 282)
195. One is surprised, in the 1935–36 season, to find the regular Philharmonic-Symphony subscription concerts including works by such composers as Otto Luening, Robert McBride, Bernard Rogers, Carl Ruggles, and William Grant Still —until one notices that it was not Toscanini but Lange who conducted them. A definite influence of the Chamber Orchestra on the Philharmonic-Symphony programs during that season could be recognized in two compositions, one very old and one very new: four of Henry Purcell's Fantasias for Strings and parts of Carl Ruggles's *Men and Mountains*, which Lange played first with the Chamber Orchestra, found their way not long afterward onto programs that he conducted with the Philharmonic-Symphony.

(p. 283)
196. *Two Worlds of Music*, p. 19. Dr. Geissmar was not only Furtwängler's secretary but manager of the Berlin Philharmonic Orchestra for many years. In 1936 she became Sir Thomas Beecham's secretary and organizing manager of the London Philharmonic Orchestra.

(p. 283)
197. Geissmar, op. cit., pp. 159–60.

(p. 287)
198. For a summary of the work of the Composers' Forum-Laboratory, including a list of the composers performed, see Ashley Pettis, "The WPA and The American Composer," in *The Musical Quarterly*, January 1940.

(p. 288)
199.   NEW YORK PHILHARMONIC
                  CONCERTS AND EXPENDITURES, 1935–41

Season	Number of Concerts	Budget	Principal Conductors	
1935–36	122	$725,000	Toscanini and Klemperer	
1936–37	92	534,000	Barbirolli and Rodzinski	
1937–38	108	598,000	Barbirolli	A Special Campaign
1938–39	113	636,000	"	in 1938–39 brought
1939–40	128	743,000	"	in $107,000
1940–41	131	690,000	"	

(p. 301)

200. When some of the more sensational stories were revived in 1968 in John Gruen's *The Private World of Leonard Bernstein,* Rodzinski's son Richard complained, in a dignified letter to the New York *Times,* of the tastelessness of publishing such confidential details when his father was "no longer around to defend himself," and Leonard Bernstein, agreeing, deplored "the offense to Dr. Rodzinski's memory" (New York *Times Book Review,* December 22, 1968).

(p. 302)

201. Mishel Piastro, the concertmaster of the Philharmonic-Symphony orchestra since 1931–32, had been given the additional title of Assistant Conductor during the two years 1941–43, but no one had held the position as a full-time job since Lange's departure.

(p. 302)

202.   NEW YORK PHILHARMONIC
                        TOTAL EXPENSES, 1943–47

1943–44	$782,918
1944–45	$881,606
1945–46	$916,761
1946–47	$1,077,843

(p. 304)

203. New York *Herald Tribune,* February 9, 1947.

(p. 305)

204. The late Mishel Piastro, reminiscing in 1970, told me that at the time when Rodzinski fired him from the Philharmonic in 1943, he was in Chicago for a guest appearance as violinist and learned of his dismissal only by reading a review of his concert in the Chicago *Daily Tribune,* the next day, under the headline PIASTRO FIDDLES WHILE RODZINSKI WIRES BURN. A little research into the files of the *Tribune* (with the help of the newspaper's librarian, David Mendenhall) reveals that Piastro's memory was accurate in all but two details: the date of the headline was not 1943 but 1947, and the departure from the Philharmonic that it dealt with was not his own but Rodzinski's!

Halfway through his first year in Chicago, Rodzinski became involved in a dispute not unlike the one he had had in New York, and by January 1948 he had to leave the Chicago orchestra too. It was ten years before he conducted in the United States again. Meanwhile he worked in Europe and South America. He died in Boston in 1958.

(p. 310)

205. Dimitri Mitropoulos, born in Athens in 1896, studied at the Athens Conservatory and then in Brussels and Berlin (with Busoni). After working as a *répétiteur* (opera coach and assistant conductor) in Berlin from 1921 to 1925, he conducted in his native Greece for a number of years. Mitropoulos, who was a first-rate pianist, attracted special attention in 1930 when, as guest conductor with the Berlin Philharmonic, he substituted for the soloist of his concert (who had fallen ill) in Prokofiev's Piano Concerto No. 3, conducting from the keyboard. This was a stunt that he repeated in Paris and elsewhere in later years. He made his American debut with the Boston Symphony Orchestra in 1936, and then conducted the Minneapolis Symphony Orchestra for twelve years, from 1937 to 1949.

It was during this period that his guest engagements with the New York Philharmonic-Symphony occurred.

(p. 311)

206. The guest conductors who led the other concerts of those seasons were:
   1949–50. Bruno Walter, Leonard Bernstein, and Victor de Sabata.
   1950–51. Walter, Bernstein, de Sabata, and George Szell.
   1951–52. Walter, Szell, and Guido Cantelli.

A few concerts in each season were taken by the Italian-American conductor Franco Autori, who succeeded Walter Hendl as Associate Conductor of the Philharmonic-Symphony in 1949. (Hendl had been called Assistant Conductor but Autori was given the grander title of Associate, probably because he was older and had more of a conducting career behind him.)

(p. 318)

207. On the Edinburgh trip of 1951, made without government subsidy, there had also been some American compositions (Gould and Swanson) and soloists (Leonard Rose, John Corigliano, Harold Gomberg, and William Polisi, of the orchestra's first-desk players, and—for Beethoven's Ninth Symphony—Frances Yeend, Martha Lipton, David Lloyd, and Mack Harrell). But that had been a more limited project, not so much a tour as a visit to one city, which the Philharmonic had been able to undertake without government aid because the Edinburgh Festival had paid all the orchestra's expenses, including round-trip transportation.

(p. 319)

208. Milton Cross was later (1963–67) to be added to the list of radio commentators.

(p. 320)

209. ATTENDANCE AT PHILHARMONIC SUBSCRIPTION CONCERTS
IN NEW YORK

1949–50	252,369
1950–51	247,297
1951–52	238,888
1952–53	240,840
1953–54	232,279
1954–55	230,485
1955–56	228,308

For the effects of the mass media on audiences for all live performance, see Baumol and Bowen, *Performing Arts*, pp. 243–48.

(p. 321)

210. R. Gelatt, *The Fabulous Phonograph*, p. 302.

(p. 321)

211. After Schelling's death Rudolph Ganz had led the Young People's Concerts from 1940 to 1947. Then had come several seasons of guest conductors. In 1950 Igor Buketoff had been put in charge. And in 1953 Pelletier had succeeded him.

Rudolph Ganz (1877–1972) had a varied background and career. Born in Switzerland, he studied there, in Alsace, and in Germany, and made public appearances in his youth as cellist, pianist, and composer. He was twenty-four years old, in 1901, when he was put in charge of advanced piano instruction at the Chicago Musical College. From 1905 on, he toured widely as piano virtuoso. He was conductor of the St. Louis Symphony from 1921 to 1927, and director of the Chicago Musical College from 1929 to 1954. Ganz was responsible for the first performances of many works by contemporary composers. It was not until 1969, when he was ninety-two years old, that he retired completely from his musical activities. He died in Chicago in 1972.

Igor Buketoff, born in Hartford, Connecticut, in 1915, studied at the University of Kansas and the Juilliard School, and then taught conducting at the Juilliard. In 1942 he won the first Alice M. Ditson Award for American conductors. After touring as conductor of Menotti's operas *The Telephone* and *The Medium,* he was engaged for one concert in the Philharmonic's Young People's series of 1948–49. Meanwhile he had become conductor of the Fort Wayne Philharmonic Orchestra in 1948. In the next year the New York Philharmonic gave him four of the Young People's Concerts to conduct, and it was in the following season that he was put in charge of all the Philharmonic's children's concerts.

Wilfrid Pelletier was born in 1896 in Montreal, and at the age of seventeen was already an assistant conductor at the opera in that city. Soon thereafter he went to Paris, where he studied with Philipp and Widor. He came to the Metropolitan Opera in New York as an opera coach in 1917, and in the next fifteen years worked his way up to the positions of assistant conductor and conductor. During this period he also conducted for the Ravinia Opera and the San Francisco Opera. After 1935 he was as active in his native land as he was in New York; he founded the Concerts Symphoniques in Montreal, became director of the Montreal Conservatory in 1942 and of a music school in Quebec in 1943, and was named conductor of the Orchestre Symphonique in Quebec in 1951. When he was appointed conductor of the Philharmonic's Young People's Concerts in 1953, the announcements emphasized his experience with youth concerts in Montreal and Quebec.

Over the years, from Schelling's time to Pelletier's, the number of concerts in the Young People's seasons fluctuated somewhat. Schelling, in his first ten years, was able to give two series of five or six concerts in each season (in the 1928–31 period there were three series each year, but those were the exceptional seasons immediately after the merger with the Symphony Society); from 1933 to 1939, however, he presented only one series of six each year. Ganz's schedule from 1940 to 1947 was planned to include both an elementary series of three at Town Hall and the usual six at Carnegie, but the elementary ones were suspended in 1942 because of the war. Elementary or introductory concerts were resumed in 1947—at first two and then, from 1949 on, three per season—but at the same time the Carnegie Hall series for the older children was cut from six to five concerts. In Pelletier's last season, 1956–57, the introductory series was dropped again.

There were also a few children's concerts that were given in other places than Carnegie Hall. Beginning in 1952–53, Franco Autori, the orchestra's Associate Conductor, took the Philharmonic-Symphony to certain Long Island towns for a North Shore Series, usually of just two Young People's Concerts per season. The Philharmonic had a precedent for such educational concerts "away from home": in the years between 1926 and 1929 Schelling had given additional concerts, usually in series of four, in the Bronx, Brooklyn, and Newark.

(p. 325)
212. Judson's business affiliations had also been undergoing some changes. In 1950 he had been voted out of the presidency of CAMI (Columbia Artists

Management, Inc.) though he remained active in the subdivision of it known as Judson, O'Neill, and Judd. He continued to work within CAMI until 1963 when, as the result of a disagreement, he left to head the new firm of Judson, O'Neill, Beall, and Steinway (known in the trade as "JOBS"). Upon the departure of Frederick Steinway from the firm, in 1969, its name was changed to Arthur Judson Management, Inc., and Judson was still running it, in 1972, at the age of ninety-one.

(p. 325)

213. There were—all of them for short periods—four Europeans of reputation who had never before conducted the Philharmonic-Symphony (Rafael Kubelik, Fernando Previtali, André Cluytens, and Ernest Ansermet) and five other conductors, several of them of American birth, who were already familiar to New York audiences (Robert Shaw, Thomas Schippers, Aaron Copland to conduct some of his own works, André Kostelanetz to continue the popular Saturday night concerts that he had given for the preceding four years, and Franco Autori, still the orchestra's Associate Conductor).

(p. 326)

214. Among the compositions that Mitropoulos had introduced to the orchestra in his eight years as a principal conductor of the Philharmonic-Symphony were works of Reger, Schoenberg, Berg, Webern, Krenek, Wolpe, von Einem, Liebermann, Blacher, Hindemith, Satie, Milhaud, Roussel, Martin, Busoni, Malipiero, Sessions, Thomson, Dello Joio, Berger, Rochberg, Kirchner, Gould, Shulman, Harris, Mennin, Kubik, Weber (Ben), Barber, Read, Starer, Meyerowitz, Foss, Koutzen, Walton, Dohnányi, de Falla, Prokofiev, and Shostakovich. This is a selected list; the complete list would be three times as long.

(p. 329)

215. A heart attack prevented Mitropoulos from giving his share of the 1958–59 programs but he returned to the Philharmonic as guest conductor in 1959–60. He was scheduled to appear again in 1960–61, but he died on November 2, 1960, in Milan, while rehearsing the orchestra of La Scala in a Mahler symphony. In his memory Bernstein performed at the four New York Philharmonic concerts that week a movement from Mahler's *Resurrection* Symphony.

(p. 342)

216. An alphabetical list of some of the added names (not at all complete—intended only to show the range of the selection) includes:

Abbado	Davis	Maazel	Sargent
Allers	Ehrling	Morel	Semkow
Ancerl	Foss	Munch	Skrowaczewski
Ansermet	Giulini	Ozawa	Solomon
Barbirolli	Gould	Previn	Steinberg (Principal Guest
Böhm	von Karajan	Reiner	Conductor, 1966–68)
Boulanger	Krips	Rosbaud	Stokowski
Boulez	Kurtz	Rudel	Wallenstein
Carvalho			

Among the composer-conductors there would be Chávez, Copland, Ellington, Hindemith, Milhaud, and Schuller.

(p. 343)

217. The eleven composers whose commissioned works received their first performances during the anniversary celebrations were:

Richard Rodney Bennett	Symphony No. 2
Aaron Copland	*Inscape*
Roberto Gerhard	Symphony 4 (*New York*)
Howard Hanson	Symphony No. 6
Roy Harris	Eleventh Symphony: 1967
Nicholas Nabokov	Third Symphony (A Prayer)
Walter Piston	*Ricercare*
Roger Sessions	Symphony No. 8
Rodion Shchedrin	*The Chimes* (*Zvony*), Concerto No. 2 for Orchestra
Toru Takemitsu	*November Steps*
Virgil Thomson	*Shipwreck and Love Scene* (Juan and Haidee) from Byron's *Don Juan*

The seven other composers, whose commissioned works had to be scheduled for later seasons, were:

Milton Babbitt	*Relata II*
Luciano Berio	*Sinfonia*
Elliott Carter	*Concerto for Orchestra*
Leon Kirchner	*Music for Orchestra*
Fredric Myrow	(untitled)
William Schuman	*To Thee Old Cause*
Karlheinz Stockhausen	*Hymnen*

In addition, Lincoln Center commissioned works by Ned Rorem (*Sun*, for Soprano and Orchestra) and Gunther Schuller (*Triplum*) for performance by the Philharmonic during the Center's 1967 Summer Festival. Two premieres took place during the 1967 summer Promenades, just before the official opening of the anniversary year: Alan Hovhaness's *To Vishnu*, commissioned by the Philharmonic, and Ezra Laderman's *Magic Prison*, commissioned by André Kostelanetz.

(p. 345)

218. PROGRAM ANNOTATORS, NEW YORK PHILHARMONIC

1887–96	Arthur Mees
1896–1912	Henry E. Krehbiel
1912–21	William H. Humiston
1921–39	Lawrence Gilman
1939–41 (March)	Pitts Sanborn
1941 (March)–49	Robert Bagar and Louis Biancolli
1949–53	Herbert F. Peyser
1953–59	Irving Kolodin
1959–60	Howard Shanet
1960–	Edward O. Downes

Of those before 1959, all but Mees and Humiston were music critics and journalists by profession.

There were no regular program notes until 1887–88. Before that time there were only occasional "descriptive programmes," either unsigned or merely initialed, for individual pieces that seemed to invite verbal explanation.

(p. 346)

219. In *Allegro* (official publication of Local 802, Associated Musicians of Greater New York), July 1959.

(p. 346)

220. A big help to the Society in financing the new concert activities and the new orchestra benefits came from two Ford Foundation grants, each well over a million dollars—the first, in 1963, designed expressly for new activities, the second, in 1966, made up partly of endowment and partly of expendable funds. The terms of both grants required the Society to raise very large sums in "matching" funds and it succeeded in doing so.

(p. 347)

221. In the summer of 1969 two Negro musicians, Earl Madison, cellist, and J. Arthur Davis, bass player, brought charges against the Philharmonic before the New York City Commission on Human Rights for allegedly discriminating against them on racial grounds in auditions for Philharmonic vacancies. The Commission, in a decision rendered on October 29, 1970, found that the Philharmonic had not discriminated against Madison and Davis in their applications for permanent employment, but that it had engaged in discriminatory practices in the hiring of substitute and extra musicians. The orchestra was ordered, therefore, to offer Madison and Davis employment as substitutes or extras at the first available opportunity, and also to submit to the Commission a plan that would give "black and other minority instrumentalists" an equal opportunity to work as substitutes and extras and that would encourage them to apply for permanent jobs.

As for women in the Philharmonic orchestra, their number was brought to four in December 1970 by the appointment of Toby Saks, cello, and Michele Saxon, double bass, and to six in 1971–72 by the addition of Marilyn Dubow and Hanna Lachert, violins.

(p. 348)

222. The pattern was continued in 1971 when Nadien was succeeded by Rafael Druian, who, though born abroad, had been brought to the United States when he was only ten years old and had received his musical education and professional experience in this country.

(p. 356)

223.   CHRONOLOGY OF BERNSTEIN'S CAREER

Born in Lawrence, Massachusetts, August 25, 1918.

1931–35 Student at Boston Latin School.

1935–39 Student at Harvard University.

1939–41 Student at Curtis Institute of Music.

1940–42 (summers) Koussevitzky's pupil and assistant at Berkshire Music Center, Tanglewood.

1941 Clarinet Sonata.

1943 Appointed Assistant Conductor of New York Philharmonic-Symphony; November 14, debut as substitute for Bruno Walter. *I Hate Music: Five Kid Songs.*

1944 *Jeremiah* Symphony (New York Music Critics' Circle Award). *Fancy Free,* ballet. *On the Town,* musical comedy.

1945–47 Conductor of New York City Symphony (City Center of Music and Drama).

1946 Conducted at International Music Festival, Prague. *Facsimile*, ballet.

1947 Tour in Europe and Palestine. *La Bonne Cuisine*.

1949 *Age of Anxiety*, for piano and orchestra.

1950 Incidental music, *Peter Pan*.

1951 Married Felicia Montealegre, actress.

1951–55 Head of Orchestral Conducting Department at Tanglewood.

1951–56 Faculty of Brandeis University.

1952 *Trouble in Tahiti*, one-act opera.

1953 *Wonderful Town*, musical comedy. Conducted Cherubini's *Medea* at La Scala, Milan.

1954 *Serenade* for violin, strings, and percussion. Began "Omnibus" television programs. Score for film, *On the Waterfront*.

1956 *Candide*, musical comedy.

1957–58 Conductor (with Mitropoulos) of New York Philharmonic-Symphony; Young People's Concerts on television; tour of South America. *West Side Story*, musical comedy. Incidental music, *The Lark*.

1958 Music Director, New York Philharmonic-Symphony; began television series, "Leonard Bernstein and the New York Philharmonic." Ditson Award for service to American music.

1959 Tour of Russia, Europe, and Near East with Philharmonic. Book, *The Joy of Music*.

1960 Tour of Japan, Alaska, Canada, with Philharmonic.

1961 Moving picture of *West Side Story*. Philharmonic contract extended seven years.

1962 Publication of *Leonard Bernstein's Young People's Concerts* (scripts and recordings).

1963 *Kaddish*, oratorio (Symphony No. 3). Conducted Verdi's *Falstaff* at Metropolitan Opera, New York.

1964–65 Sabbatical leave from New York Philharmonic (extending seven-year contract one year, to end of 1968–69 season).

1965 *Chichester Psalms*.

1966 Book, *The Infinite Variety of Music*. Resignation from position of Music Director of New York Philharmonic announced, to take effect at end of 1968–69.

1969 Resigned as Music Director of New York Philharmonic; named Laureate Conductor for life.

1971 *Mass*, for opening of Kennedy Center for the Performing Arts in Washington, D.C. Conducted one thousandth concert with New York Philharmonic.

(p. 365)

224. It was actually in April 1969 that Boulez had been invited to become Music Director, but it had taken two months for his acceptance and the approval of the Philharmonic's Board of Directors to come through.

(p. 369)

225. "Address of Ex-President Prof. R. Ogden Doremus" (last concert of the sixtieth season, April 5, 1902, at Carnegie Hall), published in *American Art Journal*, April 12, 1902, pp. 18–20.

(p. 379)

226. Rain dampened the attendance (250,000) in 1971, when three performances had to be canceled. But in the summer of 1972 Boulez's first Central Park concert

drew an audience of 65,000, and on August 8, 1972, the confluence of perfect weather, an all-Tchaikovsky program, including the *1812* Overture with fireworks, Gary Graffman as pianist, and Henry Lewis as conductor, attracted more than 90,000 people. The total attendance for all the Park Concerts of that summer was 415,000. On July 31, 1973, another Tchaikovsky program drew the largest audience in Philharmonic history—the estimate was 110,000 people. The number of concerts in the series was increased from twelve to fifteen in 1973.

(p. 381)

227. In June 1972 the Philharmonic announced that Michael Tilson Thomas, twenty-seven-year-old Music Director of the Buffalo Philharmonic and Principal Guest Conductor of the Boston Symphony, would be Director and Conductor of the Young People's Concerts for the next two seasons. By 1973, although the subscription of Philharmonic Hall for the Young People's Concerts was still close to full, there was no longer the waiting period of several years that had been a mark of the Bernstein era.

(p. 382)

228. Only two years later, however, by 1973, the long waiting periods for subscriptions no longer applied.

(p. 388)

229. The President continued to request, and the Congress continued to appropriate, increased amounts from year to year: by 1973 the appropriation for the arts had reached $38 million.

(p. 390)

230. The Philharmonic's compulsory retirement system required Helen Thompson to leave the post of Manager on July 15, 1973. (She remained as a consultant, however, after that date.) Harold Lawrence was named her successor.

(p. 396)

231. Puzzled viewers read these lines, scotch-taped to a manuscript sketch from Elliott Carter's *Concerto for Orchestra*, on display in a glass case at the Library and Museum of the Performing Arts at Lincoln Center as part of an exhibition called "The New York Philharmonic: A Birthday Salute" in 1967–68. Inquiry revealed that Carter had happened to come across the published interview on a TWA flight, and had been irritated by the lines quoted here, because the Philharmonic had commissioned his *Concerto* for its 125th anniversary and now Bernstein was saying that "nothing important of a symphonic nature" was being written these days. When the Library asked Carter for a page of manuscript for display in the Philharmonic exhibition, he taped the offending lines to it for all to see. The *Concerto for Orchestra* had its world premiere by the Philharmonic, conducted by Bernstein, on February 5, 1970—Carter was late in finishing it—and the press reported that it received a warm welcome from many in the audience "who thought the wait well worth while," and from Bernstein, who "looked happy and embraced all within reach."

(p. 398)

232. Baumol and Bowen, *Performing Arts*, pp. 282–84.

(p. 398)
233. Op. cit., pp. 36, 8, 68.

(p. 401)
234. *The Infinite Variety of Music,* p. 10.

(p. 406)
235. *American Art Journal,* New York, April 12, 1902, p. 20.

(p. 407)
236. Speech before Friends of the Kennedy Center, Smithsonian Institution, Washington, D.C., May 19, 1967.

(p. 411)
237. Speech to the Friends of the Philharmonic's 15th Annual Luncheon, reprinted in New York Philharmonic program of December 29, 1965.

(p. 412)
238. "Music and Money," in *International Musician,* June 1970.

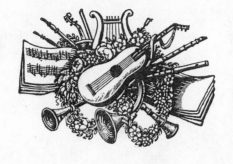

Bibliography

This Bibliography is divided into four sections:

BOOKS AND ARTICLES
PERIODICALS
DICTIONARIES, ENCYCLOPEDIAS, AND DIRECTORIES
MANUSCRIPTS AND OTHER MATERIALS IN SPECIAL COLLECTIONS

Individual concert programs and music scores are not included in the Bibliography, but their sources are generally indicated in the text or Backnotes when they are discussed.

LIST OF ABBREVIATIONS

JAMS *Journal of the American Musicological Society*, Richmond (Va.), 1948ff.
MA *Musical America*, New York, 1898ff.
MQ *The Musical Quarterly*, New York, 1915ff.
ALS autograph letter, signed
TLS typewritten letter, signed

BOOKS AND ARTICLES

The three principal studies of the New York Philharmonic, before this one, have been:

Krehbiel, Henry Edward. *The Philharmonic Society of New York: A Memorial; Published on the Occasion of the Fiftieth Anniversary of the Founding of the*

Philharmonic Society, New York and London, Novello, Ewer & Co., 1892. This book consists of 85 pages of history and 87 pages of program listings and other records.

Huneker, James Gibbon. *The Philharmonic Society of New York and Its Seventy-Fifth Anniversary: A Retrospect,* no imprint, no date, but presumably published in New York for the Society in 1917. This book consists of 36 pages of history, 83 pages of program listings and other records, 7 pages of pictures, and 10 pages devoted to the anniversary address delivered by Oswald Garrison Villard.

Erskine, John. *The Philharmonic-Symphony Society of New York: Its First Hundred Years,* New York, The Macmillan Company, 1943. This book consists of 60 pages of history, 107 pages of program listings, and 6 pages of pictures.

Other books and articles consulted were:

Allen, Warren Dwight. *Philosophies of Music History: A Study of General Histories of Music,* New York, 1939, 1962.

———. "The Value of Musicology to the Performer," *MA,* Vol. LIX, No. 14, Sept. 1939.

Ames, Amyas. "The Danger of Mediocrity," *Music Journal,* Vol. XXVIII, No. 1, New York, Jan. 1970.

———. "The Silent Spring of Our Symphonies," *Saturday Review,* New York, Feb. 28, 1970.

———. "A Year of Adventure," Speech to the Friends of the Philharmonic at their 15th Annual Luncheon, reprinted in New York Philharmonic program, Dec. 29, 1965.

Antek, Samuel. *This Was Toscanini,* New York, 1963.

Arion Society, New York. *Arion New York von 1854 bis 1904,* New York, 1904.

Baerman, Henry B. "American Symphony Orchestras," *Musical Courier,* Vol. 20, No. 6, Feb. 10, 1915.

Barker, Virgil. *American Painting: History and Interpretation,* New York, 1950.

Barzun, Jacques. *Berlioz and the Romantic Century,* Boston, 1950.

———. *The House of Intellect,* New York, 1959.

———. *Music in American Life,* Gloucester (Mass.), 1958.

Barzun, Jacques, and Graff, Henry F. *The Modern Researcher,* New York, 1957.

Baumol, William J., and Bowen, William G. *Performing Arts—The Economic Dilemma: A Study of Problems Common to Theater, Opera, Music and Dance,* New York, 1966.

Beach, Moses Y. *Wealth and Pedigree of the Wealthy Citizens of New York City,* 4th ed., New York, 1842; 12th ed. (entitled *The Wealthy Citizens of the City of New York*), 1855.

Bean, Betty Randolph. *The New York Philharmonic-Symphony Orchestra* (souvenir book), New York, 1955.

Berg, Adolph, and Mosby, Olav. *Musikselskabet Harmonien, 1765–1945,* Bergen (Norway), ca. 1945.

Berg, Alban. *Alban Berg: Letters to His Wife,* ed. and tr. Bernard Grun, New York, 1971.

Berger, Max. *The British Traveller in America, 1836–1860,* New York, 1943.

Berlioz, Hector. *Le Musicien Errant, 1842–1852; correspondance publiée par Julien Tiersot,* Paris, 1919.

———. *Voyage Musical en Allemagne et en Italie,* Paris, 1844.

Bernstein, Leonard. "A Conversation with Leonard Bernstein," *Adventures in Sight & Sound,* Trans World Airlines, Inc., New York, Summer 1967.
———. *The Infinite Variety of Music,* New York, 1966.
———. *The Joy of Music,* New York, 1959.
Blau, Joseph S., and Baron, Salo W. *The Jews of the United States, 1790–1840: A Documentary History,* New York and London, 1963.
Bowen, Frank C. *A Century of Atlantic Travel, 1830–1930,* Boston, 1930.
Brown, T. Allston. *A History of the New York Stage,* New York, 1903.
Bryant, William Cullen. *Poems,* Boston, 1834.
Butler, Nicholas Murray. "Columbia and the Department of Music" (statement reprinted from the New York *Times,* Feb. 8, 1904), New York, 1904.
The Cambridge History of American Literature, eds. William P. Trent, John Erskine, Stuart P. Sherman, and Carl Van Doren, New York, 1917, 1954.
Carnegie, Andrew. *The Gospel of Wealth, and Other Timely Essays,* New York, 1900.
Chase, Gilbert. *America's Music: From the Pilgrims to the Present,* New York, 1955.
Child, Lydia Maria. *Letters from New York,* New York, 1845.
Chotzinoff, Samuel. *Toscanini: An Intimate Portrait,* New York, 1956.
Ciano, (Count) Galeazzo. *Ciano's Hidden Diary: 1937–38,* tr. and ed. Andreas Mayor, New York, 1953.
Commager, Henry Steele. *The American Mind: An Interpretation of American Thought and Character since the 1880's,* New Haven, 1950.
Cone, John F. *Oscar Hammerstein's Manhattan Opera Company,* Norman (Okla.), 1966.
Creuzberg, Eberhard. *Die Gewandhaus-Konzerte zu Leipzig, 1781–1931,* Leipzig, 1931.
Crickmore, K. E. *Finance and the Permanent Symphony Orchestras,* Manchester (Eng.), 1956.
Curti, Merle. *The Growth of America,* 3rd ed., New York, 1964.
Damrosch, Walter. *My Musical Life,* New York, 1926.
Dickens, Charles. *American Notes and Pictures from Italy,* London, 1957 (orig. 1842).
———. *The Life and Adventures of Martin Chuzzlewit,* London, 1844, and Leipzig, 1844.
Diether, Jack. "Beethoven out of Mahler by Steinberg," *The American Record Guide,* Vol. 33, No. 5, New York, Jan. 1967.
Doremus, R. Ogden. "Address of Ex-President Prof. R. Ogden Doremus," *American Art Journal,* New York, Apr. 12, 1902.
Downes, Olin. *Ten Operatic Masterpieces,* introd. by Dimitri Mitropoulos, New York, 1952.
Dunlap, William, *Diary of William Dunlap (1766–1839),* ed. Dorothy C. Barck, New York, 1930.
———. *A History of the American Theatre,* New York, 1832.
———. *A History of the Rise and Progress of the Arts of Design in the United States,* Boston, 1918 (orig. New York, 1834).
Elkin, Robert. *Royal Philharmonic: The Annals of the Royal Philharmonic Society,* London, 1946.
Elson, Louis C. *The History of American Music,* rev. ed., New York, 1915.
———. *The National Music of America and Its Sources,* Boston, 1899 (5th printing, 1911).

Emerson, Ralph Waldo. *Essays,* Boston and New York, 1865 (orig. 1841).
———. *Journals,* Boston, 1911.
Eyer, Ronald F. "America's Notable Orchestras," *MA,* Vols. 56, 57, New York, 1936–37.
Farwell, Arthur. *A Letter to American Composers,* Newton Center (Mass.), 1903.
Finck, Henry T. *My Adventures in the Golden Age of Music,* New York and London, 1926.
Fisher, William Arms. "The Great American Symphony," *Proceedings of the Music Teachers National Association, 53rd Year, 1927,* pp. 61–68, Oberlin (Ohio), 1930.
Flexner, James Thomas. *A Short History of American Painting,* Boston, 1950.
Foster, Myles Birket. *History of the Philharmonic Society of London: 1813–1912,* London, 1912.
Fox, Dixon Ryan, and Schlesinger, Arthur M. (and others). *A History of American Life,* New York, 1927–44.
Freer, Eleanor Everest. *Recollections and Reflections of an American Composer,* no imprint, 1929.
Geissmar, Berta. *Two Worlds of Music,* New York, 1946.
Gelatt, Roland. *The Fabulous Phonograph: From Tin Foil to High Fidelity,* Philadelphia and New York, 1955.
"German Music," *The Euterpeiad: An Album of Music, Poetry, and Prose,* Vol. 1, No. 4, New York, June 1, 1830.
Giddings, Thaddeus P.; Earhart, Will; Baldwin, Ralph L.; and Newton, Elbridge W. *Music Appreciation in the Schoolroom,* Boston, 1926.
Gilbert, Henry F. "The American Composer," *MQ,* Vol. I, No. 2, pp. 169–80, Apr. 1915.
Gilman, Lawrence. *Notes on the Programmes of The New Symphony Orchestra (Season 1919–20),* New York and Boston, 1920.
———. *Toscanini and Great Music,* New York, 1938.
Goerges, Horst, ed. *125 Jahre Philharmonie,* Hamburg, ca. 1953.
Goldstein, Max. "Der Stand der oeffentlichen Musikpflege in den Vereinigten Staaten von Nord-Amerika," *Sammlung Musikalischer Vorträge,* Bd. 2, ed. Paul Graf Waldersee, Leipzig, 1880.
Gouge, Henry A. *New System of Ventilation . . . A Book for the Household,* New York, 1870.
Grant, Margaret, and Hettinger, Herman S. *America's Symphony Orchestras,* New York, 1940.
Griggs, John Cornelius. *Studien über die Musik in Amerika,* Leipzig, 1894.
Grout, Donald Jay. *A History of Western Music,* New York, 1960, rev. ed. 1973.
Gruenberg, Louis. "For an American Gesture," *Modern Music,* Vol. I, New York, 1924.
Haggin, B. H. *Conversations with Toscanini,* Garden City (New York), 1959.
———. *The Toscanini Musicians Knew,* New York, 1967.
Handlin, Oscar. *This Was America,* Cambridge (Mass.), ca. 1949.
Hanks, Nancy. "Music and Money," *International Musician,* Newark (New Jersey), June 1970.
Hanslick, Eduard. *Aus dem Tagebuch eines Musikers,* 3rd ed., Berlin, 1892.
———. *Geschichte des Concertwesens in Wien,* Vienna, 1869.
Harding, Chester. *A Sketch of Chester Harding, Artist, Drawn by his Own Hand,* ed. Margaret E. White, Cambridge (Mass.), 1929.
Haswell, Charles H. *Reminiscences of an Octogenarian of the City of New York,* New York, 1896.

Hatch, Christopher. "Music for America: A Critical Controversy of the 1850s," *American Quarterly*, XIV, Minneapolis, Winter 1962.

Heffner, Richard D. *A Documentary History of the United States*, New York, 1956.

Hennenberg, Fritz. *The Leipzig Gewandhaus Orchestra*, Leipzig, 1962.

Hewitt, John Hill. *Shadows on the Wall*, Baltimore, 1877.

Hoffman, Richard. *Some Musical Recollections of Fifty Years*, New York, 1910.

Hone, Philip. *The Diary of Philip Hone, 1828–1851*, ed. Allan Nevins, new ed., New York, 1936. (See also the entry for Hone's MS Diary under MANU-SCRIPTS below.)

Howard, John Tasker. *Our American Music: Three Hundred Years of It*, 3rd ed., with supplementary chapters by James Lyons, New York, 1954.

———. *A Program Outline of American Music*, New York, 1931.

Hubbard, Nathaniel T. *Autobiography of N. T. Hubbard*, New York, 1875.

Huneker, James Gibbons. *Painted Veils*, New York, 1920, reprinted 1964.

Ireland, Joseph N. *Records of the New York Stage, from 1750 to 1860*, New York, 1866–67.

Isham, Samuel. *The History of American Painting*, New York, 1942.

Jenkins, Stephen. *The Greatest Street in the World*, New York and London, 1911.

Johnson, H. Earle. "The Adams Family and Good Listening," *JAMS*, Summer-Fall 1958.

———. *Musical Interludes in Boston, 1795–1830*, New York, 1943.

Jones, F. O. *A Handbook of American Music and Musicians*, Buffalo, 1887.

Judson, Arthur. "American Orchestras," *MA*, Vol. 71, Feb. 1951.

Kanny, Mark N. "Two Views of the Nine Beethoven Symphonies," *The American Record Guide*, Vol. 33, No. 8, New York, Apr. 1967.

Kay, Ulysses (in cooperation with the American Symphony Orchestra League). *BMI Orchestral Program Survey*, New York, 1960–70.

Keppel, Frederick P., and Duffus, R. L. *The Arts in American Life*, New York and London, 1933.

Kerman, Joseph. "A Profile for American Musicology," *JAMS*, Vol. XVIII, No. 1, Spring 1965.

———. A communication in reply to Edward Lowinsky's "Character and Purposes of American Musicology," *JAMS*, Vol. XVIII, No. 3, Fall 1965.

Kinkeldey, Otto. "Beginnings of Beethoven in America," *MQ*, XIII, 1927.

Kipper-Köln, Hermann. "Das Kölner Gürzenich-Orchester," *Die Musik*, Jahrg. I, Berlin, Nov. 1901.

Kneschke, Emil. *Die hundertundfünfzigjährige Geschichte der Leipziger Gewand-haus-Concerte, 1743–1893*, Leipzig and New York, 1893.

Kobbé, Gustave. *The Complete Opera Book*, New York and London, 1919.

Kohn, Hans. *American Nationalism: An Interpretative Essay*, New York, 1957, 1961.

Korosi, Joseph. *Statistique Internationale des Grandes Villes*, Budapest, 1876.

Kouwenhoven, John Atlee. *Made in America: The Arts in Modern Civilization*, Garden City (New York), 1948, 1962.

Kralik, Heinrich. *The Great Orchestra*, Vienna, 1955.

Krehbiel, Henry Edward. "Founder of the Philharmonic," *New York Daily Tribune*, Oct. 29, 1905.

———. *How to Listen to Music: Hints and Suggestions to Untaught Lovers of the Art*, 19th ed., London, 1914 (1st ed., New York, 1896).

Krenek, Ernst. "Gustav Mahler," in Bruno Walter's *Gustav Mahler*, New York, 1941.

Kupferberg, Herbert. *Those Fabulous Philadelphians: The Life and Times of a Great Orchestra,* New York, 1969.

Lacy, M. Rophino. *The Israelites in Egypt* (libretto), New York, 1842.

Lahee, Henry C. *Annals of Music in America,* Boston, 1922.

Lang, Paul Henry. "Background Music for 'Mein Kampf,'" *Saturday Review,* New York, Jan. 20, 1945.

———. *George Frideric Handel,* New York, 1966.

———. *Music in Western Civilization,* New York, 1941.

———, ed. *One Hundred Years of Music in America,* New York, 1961.

Lansdale, Nelson, ed. *New York Philharmonic* (souvenir book), New York, 1960.

Larkin, Oliver W. *Art and Life in America,* New York, 1949.

Laser, Arthur. "Die Geschichte der Philharmonischen Gesellschaft von New-York," *Die Musik,* II. Jahrg., Berlin and Leipzig, 1903.

Levant, Oscar. *The Memoirs of an Amnesiac,* New York, 1965.

Levy, Lester S. *Grace Notes in American History: Popular Sheet Music from 1820 to 1900,* Norman (Okla.), 1967.

Lewis, Henry. *Making a Motion Picture in 1848,* ed. Bertha L. Heilbron, St. Paul (Minn.), 1936.

Lincoln Center for the Performing Arts. *The Philharmonic at Lincoln Center,* New York, ca. 1959.

Liverpool Philharmonic Society, Limited. *The Liverpool Philharmonic Society Limited,* Liverpool, 1951.

Loesser, Arthur. *Men, Women, and Pianos: A Social History,* New York, 1954.

Lourié, Arthur. *Sergei Koussevitzky and His Epoch,* tr. S. W. Pring, New York, 1931.

Lowens, Irving. *Music and Musicians in Early America,* New York, 1964.

———. "Writings about Music in the Periodicals of American Transcendentalism (1835–50)," *JAMS,* Vol. X, No. 2, Summer 1957.

Lowinsky, Edward E. "Character and Purposes of American Musicology: A Reply to Joseph Kerman," *JAMS,* Vol. XVIII, No. 2, Summer 1965.

Madeira, Louis C. (compiler). *Annals of Music in Philadelphia and History of the Musical Fund Society,* ed. Philip H. Goepp, Philadelphia, 1896.

Maretzek, Max. *Crotchets and Quavers; or Revelations of an Opera Manager in New York,* New York, 1855.

Mason, Daniel Gregory. *The Dilemma of American Music, and other essays,* New York, 1928.

———. *Tune In, America: A Study of Our Musical Independence,* New York, 1931.

Mason, Rufus Osgood. *Sketches and Impressions, Musical, Theatrical, and Social (1799–1885) including a sketch of the Philharmonic Society of New York; from the After-Dinner Talk of Thomas Goodwin, music librarian,* New York, 1887.

Mason, William. *Memories of a Musical Life,* New York, 1902.

Mates, Julian. *The American Musical Stage Before 1800,* New Brunswick (New Jersey), 1962.

McCorkle, Donald M. "Finding a Place for American Studies in American Musicology," *JAMS,* Vol. XIX, No. 1, Spring 1966.

McDermott, John F. "How Goes the Harding Fever?", *Bulletin of the Missouri Historical Society,* St. Louis, Oct. 1951.

———. *The Lost Panoramas of the Mississippi,* Chicago, 1958.

McMaster, John Bach. *A History of the People of the United States, from the Revolution to the Civil War,* New York and London, 1924.

Mellers, Wilfred H. "American Music (An English Perspective)," *The Kenyon Review*, Vol. 5, No. 3, Gambier (Ohio), Summer 1943.

Mittag, Erwin. *The Vienna Philharmonic*, tr. J. R. L. Orange and G. Morice, Vienna, 1950.

Monteux, Doris G. *It's All in the Music*, New York, 1965.

Moody, Richard, ed. *Dramas from the American Theatre, 1762–1909*, Boston, 1966.

Mott, Hopper Striker. *The New York of Yesterday—Bloomingdale*, New York, 1908.

Mueller, John H. *The American Symphony Orchestra: A Social History of Musical Taste*, Bloomington (Ind.), 1951.

The Musical Fund Society of Philadelphia. *The Musical Fund Society of Philadelphia*, Philadelphia, 1910.

"Music and Musicians in New York," *Harper's New Monthly Magazine*, Vol. LXII, No. 372, New York, May 1881.

"Music in New York Thirty Years Ago," *Harper's New Monthly Magazine*, Vol. LVII, No. 337, New York, 1878.

Music Performance Trust Funds. *Forty-Second Report and Statement*, New York, 1970.

Nettel, Reginald. *The Orchestra in England—A Social History*, London, 1946.

Nevins, Allan, ed. *America Through British Eyes*, New York, 1948.

New York State Council on the Arts. *Annual Reports*, New York, 1960–70.

NHK Symphony Orchestra, ed. *The NHK Symphony Orchestra*, Tokyo, 1964.

Odell, George C. D. *Annals of the New York Stage*, New York, 1927–49.

Offenbach, Jacques. *Offenbach en Amérique: Notes d'un musicien en voyage*, 2nd ed., Paris, 1877.

O'Handley, Marie. "Early Music Periodicals in New York City," *Listen*, New York, May–June 1964.

O'Neill, Rosetta. "The Dodworth Family and Ballroom Dancing in New York," *Dance Index*, Vol. 2, No. 4, New York, Apr. 1943.

"On the Evidences of Musical Taste," *American Musical Journal*, Vol. I, No. 1, New York, 1834.

Pan American Union (Library of Congress, co-sponsor). *Bio-Bibliographical Index of Musicians in the United States of America from Colonial Times*, Washington, 1941.

Perkins, Francis D. "Favorites of 25 Years on Orchestral Programs in New York," *MA*, Vol. 70, No. 3, Feb. 1960.

Perris, William. *Maps of the City of New York*, Vol. III, New York, 1853.

Pettis, Ashley. "The WPA and the American Composer," *MQ*, Vol. XXVI, No. 1, Jan. 1940.

Pfohl, Ferdinand. *Arthur Nikisch*, Hamburg, 1925.

Pichierri, Louis. *Music in New Hampshire, 1623–1800*, New York, 1960.

"Places of Public Amusement," *Putnam's Monthly*, Vol. III, No. 14, New York, Feb. 1854.

Poe, Edgar Allan. *Complete Works of Edgar Allan Poe*, ed. James A. Harrison, New York, 1965.

Pomerantz, Sidney I. *New York: An American City, 1783–1803. A Study of Urban Life*, New York, 1938.

"Portraits of the People.—No. 226.: President of the Philharmonic Society," *The Atlas*, Vol. VIII, No. 36, New York, Feb. 8, 1846.

Pound, Ezra. *Antheil and the Treatise on Harmony*, Paris, n.d., Chicago, 1927, and New York, 1968.

Rice, Edwin T. *Musical Reminiscences,* New York, 1943.

———. "Personal Recollections of Leopold Damrosch," *MQ,* Vol. 28, No. 3, July 1942.

Ritter, Frédéric Louis. *Music in America,* New York, 1883, new ed. 1895.

Rockefeller Brothers Fund, Inc. *The Performing Arts, Problems and Prospects: Rockefeller Panel Report on the future of theatre, dance, music in America,* New York, 1965.

———. *Prospect for America: The Rockefeller Panel Reports,* Garden City (New York), 1961.

The Royal Philharmonic Society (London). *Memorandum and Articles of Association of the Royal Philharmonic Society,* London, ca. 1955.

Russell, Charles Edward. *The American Orchestra and Theodore Thomas,* New York, 1927.

Russell, Thomas. *Philharmonic,* London, New York, Melbourne, 1942.

Ryan, Thomas. *Recollections of an Old Musician,* New York, 1899.

Salter, Sumner. "Early Encouragements to American Composers," *MQ,* Jan. 1932.

Sargeant, Winthrop. *Geniuses, Goddesses, and People,* New York, 1949.

Schickel, Richard. *The World of Carnegie Hall,* New York, 1960.

Scholes, Percy A. *The Mirror of Music, 1844–1944,* London, 1947.

Schonberg, Harold C. *The Great Conductors,* New York, 1967.

———. *The Great Pianists,* New York, 1963.

Schumann, Robert. *Gesammelte Schriften über Musik und Musiker,* 5th ed., ed. Martin Kreisig, Leipzig, 1914.

Seltsam, William H. (compiler) *Metropolitan Opera Annals,* New York, 1947.

Sessions, Roger. *Reflections on the Music Life in the United States,* New York, 1956.

Shanet, Howard. *Notes on the Programs* (New York Philharmonic), New York, 1959–60.

Sheean, Vincent. *First and Last Love,* New York, 1956.

Sittard, Josef. *Geschichte des Musik- und Concertwesens in Hamburg,* Altona and Leipzig, 1890.

Smith, Cecil. *Worlds of Music,* Philadelphia and New York, 1952.

Smith, J. Calvin, *Harper's Statistical Gazetteer of the World,* New York, 1855.

Sommer, Susan Thiemann. "Toscanini Memorial Archives," *Fontes Artis Musicae,* Kassel, Mar. 1969.

Sonneck, Oscar G. *Early Concert Life in America, 1731–1800,* Leipzig, 1907.

———. *A Survey of Music in America; Read before the "Schola Cantorum,"* at New York City, April 11, 1913, no imprint, n.d.

Šourek, Otakar. *Antonín Dvořák: Letters and Reminiscences,* tr. Roberta Finlayson Samsour, Prague, 1954.

———. *Antonín Dvořák: Sein Leben und Sein Werk,* tr. Pavel Eisner, Prague, 1953 (Eng. version as *Antonín Dvořák: His Life and Works,* tr. not identified, New York, 1954).

Spalding, Walter R. "The War in its Relation to American Music," *MQ,* Vol. 4, No. 1, Jan. 1918.

Stefan, Paul. *Arturo Toscanini,* tr. Eden and Cedar Paul, New York, 1936.

Stephenson, Kurt. *Hundert Jahre Philharmonische Gesellschaft in Hamburg,* Hamburg, 1928.

Stewart, Estelle M., and Bowen, J. C. "History of Wages in the United States from Colonial Times to 1928," *Bulletin of the United States Bureau of Labor Statistics,* No. 604, Washington, 1934.

Stockbridge, John C. *Memorials of the Mauran Family*, Providence (Rhode Island), 1893.

Stoddard, Hope. *Subsidy Makes Sense*, Newark, ca. 1961.

Stokes, I. N. Phelps. *The Iconography of Manhattan Island*, New York, 1915–28.

Strong, George Templeton. *The Diary of George Templeton Strong*, eds. Allan Nevins and Milton Halsey Thomas, New York, 1952. (See also the entry for Strong's MS Diary under MANUSCRIPTS below.)

Swift, Joseph Gardener. *The Memoirs of Gen. Joseph Gardener Swift LL.D., U.S.A.*, Worcester (Mass.), 1890.

"Symphony Finance," *Fortune*, Vol XI, No. 3, New York, Mar. 1935.

Taubman, Howard. *The Maestro: The Life of Arturo Toscanini*, New York, 1951.

———. "Report on Orchestra Operations Abroad Under Government Subsidy," *Newsletter*, American Symphony Orchestra League, Inc., Vol. 20, No. 3–4, Vienna (Va.), 1969.

———. "Toscanini in America," *MQ*, Vol. 33, No. 2, Apr. 1947.

Tchaikovsky, Piotr Ilyitch. *The Diaries of Tchaikovsky*, ed. and tr. Wladimir Lakond, New York, 1945.

Thomas, Rose Fay. *Memoirs of Theodore Thomas*, New York, 1911.

Thomas, Theodore. *Theodore Thomas: A Musical Autobiography*, ed. George P. Upton, Chicago, 1905.

Thomas, Theodore; Paine, John Knowles; and Klauser, Karl, eds. *Famous Composers and Their Music*, Vol. II, Boston, 1901.

Thomson, Virgil. *Music Reviewed, 1940–1954*, New York, 1967.

———. *The State of Music*, New York, 1939, rev. 1962.

Tuthill, William Burnet. *Practical Acoustics: A Study of the Diagrammatic Preparation of a Hall of Audience*, Memphis (Tenn.), 1946 (written 1928).

Ulanov, Barry. *A History of Jazz in America*, New York, 1955.

United States Bureau of Census. *A Century of Population Growth in the United States, 1790–1900*, Washington, 1909.

United States Congress. *Ventilation, Heating, and Lighting of U. S. Capitol* (41st Congress, 3rd Session, House of Representatives: Report No. 49), Washington, 1871.

United States Department of Labor, Bureau of Labor Statistics. *The Consumer Price Index: a Short Description*, Washington, 1967.

———. *Consumer Price Index for Urban Wage Earners and Clerical Workers* (1913–70), Washington, 1970.

———. *Index of Estimated Cost of Living in U.S., 1820 to 1913*, Washington, 1955.

———. *Wholesale Price Index, 1720–1960*, Washington, 1960.

United States Works Progress Administration. *List of American Orchestral Works Recommended by WPA Music Project Conductors*, Washington, 1941.

Untermeyer, Sophie Guggenheimer, and Williamson, Alix. *Mother Is Minnie*, Garden City (New York), 1960.

Upton, William Treat. *Anthony Philip Heinrich: A Nineteenth-Century Composer in America*, New York, 1939.

———. "Our Musical Expatriates," *MQ*, Vol. XIV, No. 1, Jan. 1928.

———. *William Henry Fry: American Journalist and Composer-Critic*, New York, 1954.

Valentine, David Thomas. *Manual of the Corporation of the City of New York*, New York, 1842–68.

Vernon, Grenville. *Yankee Doodle-Doo*, New York, 1927.

Walter, Bruno. *Gustav Mahler,* New York, 1941.
Warren, George F., and Pearson, Frank A. *Prices,* 3rd printing, New York, 1933.
Weiss, Piero, ed. *Letters of Composers Through Six Centuries,* Philadelphia, 1967.
Weissmann, John S. "Orchestras in Budapest," *Hallé; A Magazine for the Music Lover,* No. 17, Manchester (England), 1949.
Werner, Eric. *Mendelssohn: A New Image of the Composer and His Age,* tr. Dika Newlin, London and New York, 1963.
Whitmer, Carl. "The Energy of American Crowd Music," *MQ,* Vol. 4, No. 1, Jan. 1918.
Wiener Philharmoniker, *Wiener Philharmoniker, 1842–1942,* Vienna, 1942.
Wilson, Edmund, ed. *The Shock of Recognition: The Development of Literature in the United States Recorded by the Men Who Made It,* New York, 1943, 1955.
Wister, Frances Anne. *Twenty-five Years of the Philadelphia Orchestra,* Philadelphia, 1925.
Young, Percy M. *The Concert Tradition,* London, 1965.

As this book goes to press, an important new work on a related subject has appeared: Philip Hart's *Orpheus in the New World: The Symphony Orchestra as an American Cultural Institution,* New York, 1973.

PERIODICALS

Publication dates given for a periodical in the following list generally indicate the issues or volumes actually consulted, rather than the complete run of the periodical. For a number of publications, however, which were used as general sources to be sampled at many points in the study (e.g., the New York *Times, The Musical Quarterly),* the dates may show the entire period of publication.

In addition to the periodicals listed, use was made of such recent or current New York newspapers and magazines as the *Brooklyn Eagle, Cue, Journal-American, Mirror, The New Yorker, PM, New Yorker Staats-Zeitung und Herold, Variety,* and *World-Telegram and Sun.*

The Albion or British, Colonial and Foreign Weekly Gazette, 4th series, Vols. I, XV, New York, 1842, 1856.
Allegro, Official Publication of Local 802 (Associated Musicians of Greater New York), A. F. of M., New York, 1921ff.
American Art Journal, New York, 1876, 1880, 1902.
The American Musical Directory, New York, 1861.
American Musical Journal, New York, 1834–35.
The American Record Guide, New York, 1944ff. (Previous titles: 1935–44, *The American Music Lover;* Sept. 1944, *The Listener's Record Guide.*)
The Atlas, Vol. VIII, No. 36, New York, Feb. 8, 1846.
Brother Jonathan: A Weekly Compend of Belles Lettres and the Fine Arts, Standard Literature, and General Intelligence, Vol. I, New York, 1842.
Bulletin of the American Art-Union, New York, Apr. 1851, and May 1853 (Supplementary).
Chicago Daily Tribune, Chicago, Feb. 4, 1947.
Commercial Advertiser, New York, 1799, 1839, 1842.

Daily Advertiser, New York, 1799.

Daily News, New York, 1943, 1950, 1951.

Dexter Smith's Musical, Literary, Dramatic and Art Paper, Vols. 3 and 4, Boston, Jan.–Dec. 1873.

Dwight's Journal of Music: A Paper of Art and Literature, Boston, 1852–81.

The Euterpeiad: An Album of Music, Poetry, and Prose, Vol. I, No. 4, New York, June 1, 1830.

Evening Post (now *New York Post*), New York, 1842, 1892, 1943, 1951, 1971. (Continuous, under various titles, since 1801. See also *New-York Evening Post.*)

The Globe, Toronto, Jan. 12, 1912.

Harper's New Monthly Magazine, New York, 1878, 1881.

Herald, New York, Mar. 24, 1837.

International Musician, Official Journal of the American Federation of Musicians of the United States and Canada, Newark (New Jersey), 1901ff. (Previous title, 1898, *American Musician.*)

Journal of the American Musicological Society, Richmond (Va.), 1948ff.

The Literary Digest, New York, Feb. 17, 1934.

The Lyre: New-York Musical Journal, ed. James H. Swindells, New York, 1824–25.

Music Journal, New York (originally East Stroudsburg, Pa.), 1943ff.

Musical America, New York, 1898ff.

Musical Courier, New York, 1888ff.

The Musical Magazine, ed. Thomas Hastings, New York, 1835–37.

The Musical Magazine, or Repository of Musical Science, eds. Theodore Hach and T. B. Hayward, Boston, 1839–42.

The Musical Quarterly, New York, 1915ff.

The Musical Review and Record of Musical Science, Literature, and Intelligence, New York, 1838–39.

The Musical World and Journal of the Fine Arts (after July 16, 1852, merged with *The Musical Times* to form *The Musical World and New York Musical Times*), New York, 1852 and 1853–54.

Die Musik, Berlin and Leipzig, 1901, 1903.

New-York American, New York, 1839, 1841, 1842.

New-York Evening Post, New York, Aug. 28 and Dec. 4, 1837. (See also *Evening Post.*)

New York Herald Tribune, New York, 1926–66.

The New-York Mirror [*and Ladies' Literary Gazette*], New York, 1823–42.

The New York Times, New York, 1851ff.

The New York Times Index (1851–1970), New York, 1913ff.

New(-)York Tribune, New York, 1842, 1909–10.

Newsletter [*of the*] *American Symphony Orchestra League, Inc.* (title formerly *News Letter of the American Symphony Orchestra League, Inc.*), Charleston (W. Va.) and Vienna (Va.), 1948ff.

Orpheonist and Philharmonic Journal (later *Philharmonic Journal and Orpheonist* and then *Philharmonic Journal and Advertiser*), New York, 1867–79.

The Pathfinder, Vol. I, New York, 1843.

Putnam's Monthly Magazine, New York, 1854.

Saroni's Musical Times, New York, 1849–52.

(The) Saturday Review, New York, 1945, 1959, 1970.

The Sun, New York, 1842, 1943.

Times-Star, Cincinnati, Oct. 8, 1943.
La Tribuna, Rome, May 6, 1930.
The Union, Vol. I, New York, 1842.
United States Magazine and Democratic Review, ed. Thomas Prentice Kettell, New York, 1847.
The World, New York, 1909.

DICTIONARIES, ENCYCLOPEDIAS, AND DIRECTORIES

American Authors, 1600–1900, eds. Stanley J. Kunitz and Howard Haycraft, New York, ca. 1938.
The American History and Encyclopedia of Music, ed. W. L. Hubbard, Vol. IV (*History of American Music*), New York, Toledo, Chicago, 1908.
Appleton's Cyclopaedia of American Biography, eds. James Grant Wilson and John Fiske, New York, 1888.
Baker's Biographical Dictionary of Musicians, 5th ed., rev. Nicolas Slonimsky, New York, 1958, 1965, 1971.
British Musical Biography, ed. James D. Brown and Stephen S. Stratton, Birmingham, 1897.
Bryan's Dictionary of Painters and Engravers, ed. George C. Williamson, London, 1904.
The Century Dictionary and Cyclopedia, New York, 1913.
Dictionary of American Biography, eds. Allen Johnson and Dumas Malone, New York, 1943–58.
Dictionary of National Biography, eds. Leslie Stephen and Sidney Lee, London, 1908–9.
The Encyclopedia of American Facts and Dates, ed. Gorton Carruth and Associates, 3rd ed., New York, 1962.
The Encyclopaedia Britannica, 11th ed., Cambridge (Eng.) and New York, 1910.
Fétis, François Joseph. *Biographie Universelle des Musiciens et Bibliographie Générale de la Musique,* 2nd ed., Paris, 1867–70.
Grove's Dictionary of Music and Musicians, London and New York, 1890; 2nd ed., ed. J. A. Fuller Maitland, New York, 1904; American Supplement, ed. Waldo Selden Pratt, New York, 1920; 5th ed., ed. Eric Blom, New York, 1955.
Hugo Riemanns Musik Lexikon, 11th ed., rev. Alfred Einstein, Berlin, 1929.
The International Cyclopedia of Music and Musicians, ed. Oscar Thompson, 6th ed. rev. (ed. Nicolas Slonimsky), New York, 1952; 9th ed. (ed. Robert Sabin), 1964.
Jacobs, Arthur. *A New Dictionary of Music,* London, 1958, 1970.
Longworth's New York City Directory (also *Longworth's New York Register and City Directory* and *Longworth's American Almanac, New-York Register and City Directory*), New York, 1836–41. (See also *The New York City Directory.*)
Moore, John W. *Complete Encyclopaedia of Music,* Boston, 1854 (*Appendix,* 1875).
———. *A Dictionary of Musical Information,* Boston, 1876.
Die Musik in Geschichte und Gegenwart, ed. Friedrich Blume, Kassel and Basel, 1949–68.
The National Cyclopaedia of American Biography, New York, 1892–1970.

The New York City Directory (also *The New-York City and Co-Partnership Directory, Doggett's New-York City Directory,* and *Rode's New York City Directory*), New York, 1842–52. (See also *Longworth's New York City Directory.*)

Pierre Key's International Music Year Book, New York, 1925–27, 1929–30, 1935, 1938.

Pierre Key's Musical Who's Who, ed. Pierre V. R. Key, New York, 1931.

Redway, Virginia Larkin. *Music Directory of Early New York City,* New York, 1941.

Webster's Biographical Dictionary, Springfield (Mass.), 1943.

Who's Who in America, Chicago, 1899ff.

Who Was Who in America, Vols. 1–3, Chicago, ca. 1943, 1950, 1960.

MANUSCRIPTS AND OTHER MATERIALS IN SPECIAL COLLECTIONS

A. IN THE COLUMBIA UNIVERSITY LIBRARY:

Seidl, Anton. MS Catalog der Musikalien-Bibliothek von Anton Seidl.

Stanford, David. Scrapbook of musical programs, 1839–80.

B. IN THE LIBRARY OF CONGRESS:

Heinrich, Anthony Philip. Scrapbook.

C. IN THE NEW-YORK HISTORICAL SOCIETY:

Hone, Philip. MS Diary (autograph).

The Philharmonic Society of New-York ("first"). *Constitution and Bye-Laws of the Philharmonic Society, As Amended 3d December, 1801,* New York, 1801 (original 1799).

Strong, George Templeton. MS Diary (autograph).

D. IN THE ARCHIVES AND OFFICES OF THE NEW YORK PHILHAR-MONIC (PHILHARMONIC-SYMPHONY SOCIETY OF NEW YORK, INC.):

Hill, Ureli Corelli. ALS, dated Dec. 30, 1844.

Musical Society of the City of New York, Inc. Minutes and Accounts (type-written), New York, 1922–23.

The Philharmonic Society of New York ("third"). *Charter and By-Laws of the Philharmonic Society of New York,* New York, ca. 1898.

————. *Constitution and By-Laws of the Philharmonic Society of New(-)York* (amended), New York, 1846, 1847, 1851, 1864, 1867, 1880, 1891, 1899.

————. MS Journal, 1856–70.

————. MS Ledger, 1857–70.

————. MS Letter Copy Book, 1864–88.

————. MS Library Records and Orchestration List, n.d.

————. MS Membership Book, 1867–1908.

————. MS Memorandum Book, n.d.

————. MS Minutes of the Committee of Guarantors of the Philharmonic Society of New York, 1909–11.

————. MS Minutes of the Conductors' Committee, No. 2, Season 1904–5.

————. MS Minutes of the Executive Committee meetings, 1911–12.

————. MS Minutes of the Meetings of the Directors of the Philharmonic Society, 1903–12, and miscellaneous Reports, 1908–12.

————. MS [record of] Repertoire, Conductors, Soloists, 1842–1912.

————. MS Secretary's Accounts, 1868–85.

————. MS "34th and 35th Season—Old Papers."

————. MS Treasurer's Accounts, 1852–70.

————. Treasurer's Report 1919/20 and Comparisons with Past Three Seasons (typewritten), New York, 1920.

The Philharmonic(-Symphony) Society of New York[, Inc.]. *Annual Reports,* New York, 1843–1970 (the reports for 1876 to 1883, and for a number of other years, are lacking).

————. *By-Laws of the Philharmonic(-Symphony) Society of New York (Incorporated),* New York, 1912; amended 1917, 1921, 1928, 1934.

————. *Certificate of Incorporation* (filed 1853; amended 1890, 1912, 1917, 1928, 1934, 1938, 1952), and *By-Laws* (rev. 1945; amended 1952, 1953, 1954, 1965, 1966), New York, n.d.

————. Correspondence files (selected).

————. Financial Report for 20th Century Fund's study of "Economics of the Performing Arts" (mimeographed), New York, ca. 1964.

————. MS Minutes of the Philharmonic(-Symphony) Society, 1850–1932.

————. Press Book (mimeographed), New York, 1960, 1961.

————. Press Clipping books and files, 1903–70 (many seasons lacking in period 1903–36), including Stadium Concerts Press Clippings, 1921–47, 1950–63.

————. *Programs,* New York, 1842–1971.

The Symphony Society of [the City of] New York. *Descriptive Notes,* New York, 1892–96.

————. *Programs,* New York, 1880–85, and miscellaneous others.

————. MS [record of] Repertoire, Conductors, Soloists, 1878–1928.

————. *Symphony Society Bulletin,* New York, 1907–28.

E. IN THE MUSIC DIVISION OF THE NEW YORK PUBLIC LIBRARY (LIBRARY AND MUSEUM OF THE PERFORMING ARTS):

Biographical notices of Daniel Schlesinger, the pianist (from *The New-York Mirror*), New York?, 1839?.

Fry, William Henry. *Program of the First Lecture of the Course of Ten Lectures—Metropolitan Hall Nov. 30, 1852,* New York, 1852.

Jullien's Concert Book: Programme of Jullien's 7th Grand Concert at Metropolitan Hall, Monday, October 3rd, 1853, New York, 1853.

Lind, Jenny. Concert Programs, New York and Boston, 1850–52.

Manhattan Symphony Orchestra. Concert Programs (selection), New York, 1929–32.

Maretzek, Max. Contract of Max Maretzek, director of the Italian Opera Company of America, with William Keim, chorus-singer, for four months, Nov. 1st, 1849 to March 1st, 1850. New York, 1849.

Mendelssohn-Bartholdy, Felix. ALS, dated Jan. 30, 1845.

Minor, Andrew C. "Piano Concerts in New York City, 1849–1965," thesis (typescript), University of Michigan, Ann Arbor, 1947.

Montague, Richard A. "Charles Edward Horn, His Life and Works, 1786–1849," thesis (typescript), Florida State University, Tallahassee, 1959.

New-York Sacred Music Society. *Charter and By-Laws,* New York, 1833.

Philadelphia Philharmonic Society. *Constitution and By-Laws of the Philadelphia Philharmonic Society,* Philadelphia, 1869.

Philharmonic Society of Brooklyn. *Programmes,* Brooklyn, 1858–59, 1861–62, 1864–67.

Philharmonic Society of New-York ("second"). *Constitution, By-Laws, and Regulations, of the Philharmonic Society, of the City of New-York. As Amended March 27, 1824,* New York, 1824.

Redway, Virginia Larkin. "Notices, Announcements, etc., on Music From the Commercial Advertiser, 1838" (photostatic reproduction of typewritten copy), New York, ca. 1941.

The Symphony Society of the City of New York. MS "Minutes of proceedings of the board of directors" (including Charter, Constitution, and By-Laws), New York, 1878–93.

F. IN THE RECORDS OF THE ROYAL PHILHARMONIC SOCIETY OF LONDON (INCLUDING THOSE DEPOSITED IN THE BRITISH MUSEUM):

Damrosch, Walter. TLS, dated July 7, 1908.

Horn, Charles Edward. ALS, dated Aug. 10, 1843.

Hyde, E. Francis. Two ALS, dated July 18, 1892, and July 13, 1897.

Philharmonic Society of London. *Laws of the Philharmonic Society,* London, 1813? and 1818?.

Schlesinger, Daniel. Four ALS, dated Feb. 12, 1827, Apr. 10, 1829, and Jan. 28 and Mar. 27, 1835.

G. IN VARIOUS PRIVATE COLLECTIONS:

Bunnell, Mrs. C. Sterling. *The Auxiliary Board of the New York Philharmonic* (pamphlet), New York, 1962.

The City Symphony Orchestra. *Prospectus: First Season 1922–1923,* New York, 1922.

Copland, Aaron. Private communication to the author, dated Dec. 13, 1966.

Hill, Ureli Corelli. MS Diary.

———. Typewritten copies of ALS, dated Sept. 2 and 3 [Hill committed suicide on Sept. 2!], 1875.

Mahler, Gustav. Typewritten copy of ALS, dated June 21, 1910.

Moore, Douglas S. Correspondence with Lawrence Gilman, 1934 (including ALS of Gilman, and carbon copies of TLS of Moore).

The New Symphony Orchestra, Inc. of the Musicians' New Orchestra Society. Photocopy of *Programme,* April 11, 1919 (including prospective programs for April 25 and May 9, 1919).

New York City Commission on Human Rights. "Decision and Order: Madison and Davis vs. The Philharmonic Symphony Society of New York, Inc." (mimeographed), New York, Oct. 29, 1970.

Philharmonic Society of New-York ("third"). *First Season, 1842–43* (Prospectus), New York, 1842.

———. *Constitution of the Philharmonic Society of New-York, Adopted, April, 1842,* New York, 1842.

The Philharmonic Society of New York. *Description of a Proposed Philharmonic Building* (brochure), New York, ca. 1914.

————. "The Reorganization of The New York Philharmonic Society" (leaflet), New York, ca. 1908–9.

————. Statement of educational policy (leaflet), New York, 1922.

————. "After 80 Years: The Philharmonic's New Activities" (leaflet), New York, 1922.

The Philharmonic-Symphony Chamber Orchestra. *Programs,* New York, 1935–36.

Rodzinski, Artur. Correspondence and papers.

Rosenbaum, Samuel R. MS Talk to Women's Committee, Cincinnati Symphony, Sept. 9, 1960.

Schelling, Ernest. MS speeches and other materials.

————. "Repertoire, Ernest Schelling's Children's and Young People's Concerts, 1924 through 1939–40" (typescript), n.d.

Schuman, William. MS Speech before Friends of the Kennedy Center, Smithsonian Institution, Washington, D.C., May 19, 1967.

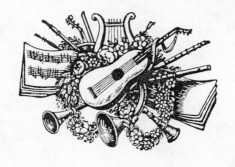

Appendices

Appendix I

Subscribers, New York Philharmonic Society
First Season, 1842–43
(as printed in the Third Annual Report, September 13, 1845)

Alsop,—
Allen,—
Anderson, Dr. F.
Boggs, Mrs.
Benson,
Brigham, J. T.
Boucher, A.*
Brooks, J.
Baur, G. Von
Borrowe, Dr. F. H.
Bunker, W.
Belmont, Aug.
Cushman, Don Alonzo
Canda, Chs.
Cottenet, F.
Cambreling, C.
Chegary, Mrs. 2
Christ,
Coster, Mrs.
Caswell,
Carville, C.

Coles, Mrs.
Delprat, J. C.
Durand, H.
Dodworth, A*
Dodworth, T.*
Derwort, G. H.*
Detmold, Dr.
Dorler,
Dubois, Wm.
Dunderdale, 2
Elliott, Dr.
Edgar, Wm.
Ensign, F. L.*
Ernst, P.*
Fendi & Zahn, 1
Field,
Gibbs, Mrs. L. W.
Gibbes, Th.
Gescheidt, Dr.
Gerard, J. W.
Hewitt, J. L.

Habicht, C. E.
Hill, U. C.*
Hills, Mrs. H. W.
Hope,
Horn C. E.*
Hudson, F.
Hoffman, L. M.
Herz, 2
Hastings, W.
Henschel, Dr.
Hoyer, C. F.
Henry, T.
Harms, J.
Jacoby, C.*
Judah, C.
Johnson, L.*
Jay, A.
Kane, D.
Kark,
Langley, H. G.
Langlois, Mrs. Chs.

Lacosse,
Luis, 2
Loomis, C.
Langley, W. C.
Lowe, Bauman
Lawrence, Mrs. J. T. } 1
 & Mrs. Coles,
Lewis, A. N.
Leroy, F. H.
DeLaunay, A.
DeLaunay, V. 2
Leavitt, J. W.
LeBarbier, A.
Moran, C.
Meyer,
Mauran, O.
Maroncelli, Piero
Moore, C. C.
Moore, Prest.
McCoun, W. T.
Mauran, Ths.
Markoe, Dr.
Moring,
Norrie, A.

Neilson, A. B.
Oppenhein,
Oakley, Mrs.
Oddie,
Pell,
Peers,
Payne, Ths.
Pyne, Rev. Dr.
Pease, W. H.
Parrish,
Pirsson, J.*
Quin, Dr. J. M.
DeRahm, C. H.
Rutherford,
Rosier, F. W.* 2
Rader, C. M.
Rhinelander, W. C.
Rhinelander, Mrs.
Raphael, Dr.
Reimer, C. F.
Remsen, S. H.
Rogers,
Stevens, R. L.
Stout, A. G.

Süs, A. W.
Swords, Chs. R.
Stodart, A.
Sandford, D. R.
Scharfenberg, W.*
Stevens, F. A.
Sheldon, H.
Sedgwick,
Stucken,
Sattler,
Schlesinger, Jr.
Scrimger,
Strong, P.
Sturges, F.
Strong, G.
Tucker, F. C.
Tredwell,
Waring, T. H.
Whiting, W. H.
Wurts, F.
Ward, Samuel
Wilkes,
Wilmerding, G.

Total number, 141.

The names with the asterisk are professional members.

Appendix II

Calculation of a *Possible List of Members* for the First Season of the New York Philharmonic, 1842–43

On page 490 I have reprinted the list of Actual Members as it appeared in the Second Annual Report, at the end of the 1843–44 season. Now, the same report indicates that nine of those members had been elected *during the second season.* Those nine, therefore, could not have been regular members during the first season, and we may remove their names from our working list; accordingly, we subtract Bristow, De Janon, Füllgraff (sometimes spelled Fülgraff, with one *l*), Stier, and Weiss from the violins, Chevalier and Schmeling (sometimes spelled Schmelling, with two *l*'s), from the violas, Lo Bianco from the double basses, and Wiese (sometimes spelled Weise) from the oboes. Further, the same report names ten musicians who had been members a year before, but who were no longer on the list as of September 1844: King and Rosier had resigned; Clapdor (Clapdau) and Broderson had died; and Kammerer, Hegelund, Lehman, Hansen, Kossowski, and Mason had left the city. By restoring these names to the roster, we obtain the Possible List of Members for the first season, as shown in the table on page 491. (See also pages 91–92 and Backnote 51.)

ACTUAL MEMBERS, NEW YORK PHILHARMONIC SOCIETY
SECOND SEASON, 1843–44

(as printed in the Second Annual Report, September 14, 1844)

VIOLIN.

Bristow, G. F.
De Luce, G.
Dodworth, A.
Dodworth, H. B.
De Janon, L.
Ensign, J. L.
Fulgraff, O. G.
Hill, U. C.
Herzog, C.
Hellwig,
Helfenritter,
Knæbel, S.
Marks, H.
Martini, L.
Meyrer, C. W.
Otto, H.
Sage, W. H.
Saur, C.
Stier, F.
Wiegers, L.
Weiss,
Woolf, E.

VIOLA.

Chevalier,
Derwort, G. H.
Grebner,
Goodwin, T.
Johnson, S.
Schmeling, P. A.

VIOLONCELLO.

Boucher, A.
Milon, S.
Musgriff, W.
Walker, D.

DOUBLE BASS.

Jacoby, C.
Loder, G.
Lo Bianco, G.
Pirsson, J.
Schneider.

OCTAVE FLUTE.

Dodworth, C. R.

FLUTE.

Ernst, P.
Gosden, J.
Kyle, J. A.

OBOE.

Stark,
Weise.

CLARINET.

Grœnevelt, T. W.
Gœller.

BASSOON.

Kyle, A.
Reiff, A.

HORN

Munson, R. Jr.
Nidds, W.
Trojsi, G.
Wœhning, C. F.

TRUMPET.

Wolter, J. F.

TROMBONE.

Dodworth, T.
Plain, W.
Schutz, C.

DRUMS.

Wood.

PIANO FORTE,—Metz, J.
       ″   or VIOLIN,—Scharfenberg, W.
       ″   ″   ″   Wallace,
       ″   ″ TROMBONE,—Timm, H. C.
       ″   ″ HORN,—Etienne, D.
       ″   ″ ORGAN,—Alpers, W.
       ″   ″   ″   Hodges, Dr.

TOTAL NUMBER OF ACTUAL MEMBER, 63.

At present the only vacancy is that of Second Trumpet.

POSSIBLE LIST OF MEMBERS
NEW YORK PHILHARMONIC
FIRST SEASON, 1842–43

VIOLIN

[Apelles (also clarinet)]
De Luce, G.
Dodworth, A.
Dodworth, H. B.
Ensign, J. L.
Hansen, E. R.
Hill, U. C.
Herzog, C.
Hellwig
Helfenritter
Knæbel, S.
Marks, H.
Martini, L.
Meyrer, C. W.
Otto, H.
Sage, W. H.
Saur, C.
Wiegers, L.
Woolf, E.

VIOLA

Clapdor
Derwort, G. H.
Grebner
Goodwin, T.
Johnson, S.

VIOLONCELLO

Boucher, A.
Milon, S.
Musgriff, W.
Walker, D.

DOUBLE BASS

Jacoby, C.
Loder, G.
Pirsson, J.
Rosier, F. W.
Schneider

OCTAVE FLUTE

Dodworth, C.

FLUTE

Ernst, P.
Gosden, J.
Kyle, J. A.
Lehman (or viola
or violin?)

OBOE

Stark

CLARINET

Goeller
Groenevelt, T. W.

BASSOON

Kyle, A.
Reiff, A.
Hegelund (also Vcl.)

HORN

Munson, R. Jr.
Nidds, W.
Trojsi, G.
Woehning, C. E.

TRUMPET

Mason, W.
Wolter, J. F.

TROMBONE

Dodworth, T.
Plain, W.
Schutz, C.

DRUMS

Wood, W.

PIANOFORTE: Metz, J.; King, W. A.; Kossowski, C.; Scharfenberg, W. (also Violin); Wallace, W. V. (also Violin); Timm, H. C. (also Trombone); Etienne, D. G. (also Horn); Alpers, W. (also Organ); Hodges, Dr. E. (also Organ). [Horn, C. E. (Pianoforte and Voice).]

INSTRUMENTS UNKNOWN: Broderson, Kammerer.

OTHER POSSIBLE MEMBERS: Penson, W., Violin.

Notes on POSSIBLE LIST OF MEMBERS, 1842–43

This list should be taken more as a rough sketch than an exact likeness, for several reasons: 1) It shows the total membership of the Society, but not the line-up of the musicians who actually played in each concert. 2) Many of the musicians doubled on several instruments and may have changed from one concert to the next, according to the needs of the Society. Stark (or Starck), for example, played both clarinet and oboe, and the Dodworths half a dozen instruments each. 3) When necessary, outsiders were paid as "ringers" to cover gaps in the instrumentation. Wiese, the oboist, who was not yet a member, was engaged for such professional services, and I should be very much surprised if Ribas, known as a fine performer on the same instrument (then rare in New

York), was not called in at some time during the first season. 4) We know that C. E. Horn took part in the organization of the Philharmonic, and that he sang in its first concert, but we also know that he was back in England by the summer of 1843, applying for membership in the London Philharmonic Society. His name does not occur in the Second Annual Report; yet he is mentioned in the Third Annual Report as one of several Actual Members who were stricken from the list, "having removed from the city, and having been absent for more than a year." So he must certainly have been one of the original members. Another in the same category was Apelles (who played second violin in U. C. Hill's string quartet and was also competent as a clarinetist), cited in the Third Annual Report as dropped, without there being any previous evidence of his having been picked up. Accordingly, I have added Apelles to the violinists and Horn to the pianists. 5) It is surprising, too, that Penson and Heinrich, both of whom had key roles in the organization of the Society, are not on the list. In Penson's case one can hazard the guess that he may have been too busy with his professional work. (I have put him under "Other Possible Members.") And the eccentric and opportunistic Heinrich may have resented not being elected an officer after having served as chairman of the organizational meeting; although he was listed in the prospectus as a violist, he sent in his resignation on September 20, 1842, before the first concert.

Appendix III

Critical Summary of the First Season of the New York Philharmonic

The Pathfinder, New York, May 6, 1843

(Vol. I, No. 11)

THE MUSICAL PATHFINDER.

NEW YORK PHILHARMONIC SOCIETY.—We do not think any thing has ever been attempted in this city, that will more conduce to the advancement of musical taste, than the formation of the above society, whose first season arrived at so successful a termination on Saturday week last.

One great cause, which has operated to check the onward march of music, has been that in the performances, usually placed before a New York audience, the chief object has been the pecuniary gain of the beneficiary; who, depending upon his connection and friends attending, whatever might be the quality of the Concert, has, generally speaking, given that most easily understood by uncultivated ears and obtainable at the most economical rate. This system has we trust received its deathblow, from the Association under consideration, and we sincerely hope that ere long "Grand Concerts," consisting of a few Songs and Ballads, with perhaps an instrumental solo, accompanied on the Piano Forte, will be looked upon as among "the things that were." Already has its influence been felt, not only in the quality of the music performed at the Concerts of Madam Otto, Messrs. Scharfenberg and Timm, but what is of more importance, its influence has been felt upon the public. We, ourselves, in many houses have seen Bethoven's [sic] Symphonies arranged as duetts on the Piano Fortes of young ladies, where we used to see Quicksteps and Gallops; and it has also been seen in the manner in which Concerts generally, have been patronised; during no season in our recollection has there been a larger number of Concerts, nor yet so well attended.

We can easily understand, that there must have been many difficulties to overcome, in the formation of the Society, from many circumstances, and we have heard much of its having originated in a *clique,* and of some professors not belonging to a particular *set,* having been neglected or excluded. The absurdity of these remarks, every one on looking at the list of talented artists enrolled, must acknowledge—as it embraces (with few exceptions) the best in the city. We say with exceptions, because there are some we know, whose names ought to be there, but we are not authorized on that account to suppose, they have been neglected; neglect in such a case, can only occur in the individual whose name is not there, for in starting a project like this, it must have its commencement somewhere, and we are convinced from the manly and independent tone of every act of the Society, that no one, however high in the profession he might stand, would be *solicited* to join it—the favor being one to be sought by the individual, not the body. In whatever manner it was begun, the result has proved of advantage in every respect, and we sincerely hope, that it will flourish more and more, as it grows older and older.

The music performed at the three Concerts given by the Society, has been of a character to elevate and improve the public taste, and though on neither occasion, has the evening's performance been entirely free from blemish, still the many beautiful effects, which have been for the first time heard by a New York audience, infinitely more than compensated for them. The chief defect of the Orchestra at present, is the want of a *pianissimo.* We think the nearest approach to this, was attained in the Symphony in C minor, played at the first Concert. We believe this was more often rehearsed, than any thing that has since been done; be that as it may, the first object of the Band should be, to attain this desirable effect. We can easily define several causes for the want of this—in the first place, there is an inherent desire in every man to distinguish himself, and we do not think musicians are much more free from this species of ambition, than the rest of the world, and secondly, the want of a pianissimo, may arise from the fact, that economy is so much a ruling principle with managers of Theatres and others who employ orchestral players, that one individual is generally expected to do the work (that is make the noise) of four, and we may say, en passant, in too many instances to be remunerated in an inverse ratio. These circumstances naturally tend towards a habit of rasping, which like most bad habits, is much more readily attained than discarded. There is one general rule however, that if followed will soon correct this, viz: "if a player in an orchestra hear his own instrument, he may form a shrewd suspicion, that he is playing too loud." This want of subduing the instruments, has been more felt in the accompaniments to the songs, than at any other time. We are of opinion, that the only song really well accompanied, was that of Spohi [Spohr], sung by Mrs. Loder at the third Concert, which was indeed almost a faultless performance, both as to singing and playing. It may be, (we fain hope it is not,) that the vocal part of the performance is looked upon by the Society as a secondary consideration, the object of the Association being "the advancement of *instrumental* music"; if it be so, it is not right, for whatever the Society does, should have the same pains bestowed upon it, to bring it as near perfection as possible; besides, it is hardly fair to the vocalist, as under any circumstances, they appear to disadvantage after a symphony, that species of composition being the production of the greatest efforts of the greatest minds. We would venture a slight hint as to the duration of any solo or concerted piece, which in our opinion should never be quite so long, as the unfortunate Septuor of Beethoven, perpetrated at the last Concert. —It would have been too long, even had it been as well played as in reality it was played badly, but under the latter disadvantage it "dragged its weary length most sluggishly along." We know this composition intimately; we had heard it in all shapes and arrangements; we know it to have been in the opinion of its immortal author his greatest work, and we looked at those who were about to perform it with confidence; candor, compels us to acknowledge our grievous disappointment. We will not say Mr. Hill *cannot,* but we certainly know, he *did not* play his part steadily; to this we must attribute the total want of "ensemble," perceptible throughout the whole of the performance. We were pleased with the tone of the wind instruments, and give them a decided meed of praise over the strings; the effect however, of the whole on us was the supposition, that the players were trying it for the first time. We hope the public will have an opportunity some day or other, to hear what this work really is, and we sincerely beg these artists not to discard it, as it was not the composition, but the execution that fatigued the audience.

We do not think we ever heard any thing that gave us greater delight than Mendelsohn's [sic] Overture to the Midsummer Night's Dream, and great credit is due to the violins, for the manner in which they executed their arduous part of imitating the buzzing of the fairies' wings. The wind instruments too, deserve great praise, with the exception of the second flute, which was much too sharp, (a fault often perceptible,) and must occasionally have seriously annoyed the first. The enthusiasm of the audience at the conclusion of the Jubilee Overture, exceeded every thing we recollect to have witnessed, many rising spontaneously to their feet, and the unanimous call for its repetition was promptly responded to by the Society, and thus concluded the first season of this very meritorious Association.

Appendix IV

Concerts and Repertory
Philharmonic-Symphony Society of
New York
1942–71*

The lists that constitute this appendix have been taken from the annual summaries issued by the New York Philharmonic, and the original style of spelling and punctuation (sometimes changing from year to year) have for the most part been preserved, even when they differed from those of the rest of this book. Obvious typographical errors have been corrected and a few adjustments have been made in the interests of clarity of presentation, but in general the phraseology of the annual summaries has been retained (including, for example, announcements that recordings "are now available").

---

*The record of the concerts and repertory of the New York Philharmonic for its first one hundred years, from 1842 to 1942, can be found in the three earlier books that have dealt with the Society's history:

For 1842–92: Krehbiel, Henry Edward. *The Philharmonic Society of New York: A Memorial*, pp. 95–163.
For 1892–1917: Huneker, James Gibbons. *The Philharmonic Society of New York and Its Seventy-Fifth Anniversary: A Retrospect*, pp. 49–130.
For 1917–42: Erskine, John. *The Philharmonic-Symphony Society of New York: Its First Hundred Years*, pp. 61–168.

1942–43 ONE HUNDRED FIRST SEASON

Conductors
(in Order of Appearance)

ARTURO TOSCANINI
BRUNO WALTER
HOWARD BARLOW
ARTUR RODZINSKI
DIMITRI MITROPOULOS
FRITZ REINER
JOHN BARBIROLLI
EFREM KURTZ

Concerts for Young People
Conductor
RUDOLPH GANZ

CONCERTS

1942

Arturo Toscanini, Conductor
Oct.   7—Ev'g.   Carnegie Hall
Oct.   9—Aft.   Carnegie Hall
Oct. 11—Aft.   Carnegie Hall

Bruno Walter, Conductor
†Oct. 12—Ev'g.   Carnegie Hall

Arturo Toscanini, Conductor
Oct. 14—Ev'g.   Carnegie Hall
Oct. 16—Aft.   Carnegie Hall
Oct. 18—Aft.   Carnegie Hall

Bruno Walter, Conductor
Oct. 22—Ev'g.   Carnegie Hall
Oct. 23—Aft.   Carnegie Hall
Oct. 24—Ev'g.   McCarter Theatre,
                        Princeton, N.J.
Oct. 25—Aft.   Carnegie Hall
Oct. 29—Ev'g.   Carnegie Hall
Oct. 30—Aft.   Carnegie Hall
*Oct. 31—Morn.   Carnegie Hall
Nov.   1—Aft.   Carnegie Hall

Howard Barlow, Conductor
Nov.   5—Ev'g.   Carnegie Hall
Nov.   6—Aft.   Carnegie Hall
Nov.   7—Ev'g.   Carnegie Hall
Nov.   8—Aft.   Carnegie Hall
Nov. 12—Ev'g.   Carnegie Hall
Nov. 13—Aft.   Carnegie Hall
Nov. 14—Ev'g.   Carnegie Hall
Nov. 15—Aft.   Carnegie Hall

Artur Rodzinski, Conductor
Nov. 18—Ev'g.   Carnegie Hall
Nov. 19—Ev'g.   Camp Joyce Kilmer,
                        New Brunswick, N.J.

1942
Nov. 20—Aft.   Carnegie Hall
Nov. 22—Aft.   Carnegie Hall
Nov. 26—Ev'g.   Carnegie Hall
Nov. 27—Aft.   Carnegie Hall
Nov. 29—Aft.   Carnegie Hall

Arturo Toscanini, Conductor
Nov. 30—Ev'g.   Carnegie Hall
            Benefit American Red Cross

Artur Rodzinski, Conductor
Dec.   3—Ev'g.   Carnegie Hall
Dec.   4—Aft.   Carnegie Hall
Dec.   5—Ev'g.   Carnegie Hall
Dec.   6—Aft.   Carnegie Hall
Dec.   7—Ev'g. U.S.S. "Prairie State"
                        New York, N.Y.
Dec. 10—Ev'g.   Carnegie Hall
Dec. 11—Aft.   Carnegie Hall
Dec. 12—Ev'g.   Carnegie Hall
Dec. 13—Aft.   Carnegie Hall

Dimitri Mitropoulos, Conductor
Dec. 17—Ev'g.   Carnegie Hall
Dec. 18—Aft.   Carnegie Hall
*Dec. 19—Morn.   Carnegie Hall
Dec. 20—Aft.   Carnegie Hall
Dec. 24—Ev'g.   Carnegie Hall
Dec. 25—Aft.   Carnegie Hall
Dec. 27—Aft.   Carnegie Hall
Dec. 29—Ev'g.   Mitchel Field,
                        Hempstead, L. I.
Dec. 31—Ev'g.   Carnegie Hall
1943
Jan.   1—Aft.   Carnegie Hall
Jan.   2—Ev'g.   Carnegie Hall
Jan.   3—Aft.   Carnegie Hall

† ALFREDO ANTONINI conductor for Nino Martini's aria.
* Concert for Young People, under the direction of RUDOLPH GANZ.

1943

Jan.	6—Ev'g.	Carnegie Hall
Jan.	8—Aft.	Carnegie Hall
Jan.	9—Ev'g.	Carnegie Hall
Jan.	10—Aft.	Carnegie Hall
Jan.	11—Ev'g.	Hotel Plaza, New York, N.Y.

Philharmonic-Symphony League

Fritz Reiner, Conductor

Jan.	14—Ev'g.	Carnegie Hall
Jan.	15—Aft.	Carnegie Hall
*Jan.	16—Morn.	Carnegie Hall
Jan.	17—Aft.	Carnegie Hall
Jan.	19—Ev'g.	Horace Bushnell Memorial Hall, Hartford, Conn.
Jan.	21—Ev'g.	Carnegie Hall
Jan.	22—Aft.	Carnegie Hall
Jan.	24—Aft.	Carnegie Hall

Bruno Walter, Conductor

Jan.	28—Ev'g.	Carnegie Hall
Jan.	29—Aft.	Carnegie Hall
Jan.	30—Ev'g.	Carnegie Hall
Jan.	31—Aft.	Carnegie Hall
Feb.	4—Ev'g.	Carnegie Hall
Feb.	5—Aft.	Carnegie Hall
Feb.	6—Ev'g.	Carnegie Hall
Feb.	7—Aft.	Carnegie Hall

John Barbirolli, Conductor

Feb.	11—Ev'g.	Carnegie Hall
Feb.	12—Aft.	Carnegie Hall
*Feb.	13—Morn.	Carnegie Hall
Feb.	13—Ev'g.	Carnegie Hall
Feb.	14—Aft.	Carnegie Hall
Feb.	15—Ev'g.	Fort Monmouth, Red Bank, N.J.
Feb.	16—Ev'g.	Hotel Plaza, New York, N.Y.

Philharmonic-Symphony League

1943

Feb.	18—Ev'g.	Carnegie Hall
Feb.	19—Aft.	Carnegie Hall
Feb.	21—Aft.	Carnegie Hall
Feb.	25—Ev'g.	Carnegie Hall
Feb.	26—Aft.	Carnegie Hall
Feb.	27—Ev'g.	Carnegie Hall
Feb.	28—Aft.	Carnegie Hall
Mar.	4—Ev'g.	Carnegie Hall
Mar.	5—Aft.	Carnegie Hall
Mar.	6—Ev'g.	Carnegie Hall
Mar.	7—Aft.	Carnegie Hall

Efrem Kurtz, Conductor

Mar.	10—Ev'g.	Carnegie Hall
Mar.	12—Aft.	Carnegie Hall
Mar.	14—Aft.	Carnegie Hall
Mar.	18—Ev'g.	Carnegie Hall
Mar.	19—Aft.	Carnegie Hall
*Mar.	20—Morn.	Carnegie Hall
Mar.	20—Ev'g.	Carnegie Hall
Mar.	21—Aft.	Carnegie Hall

Fritz Reiner, Conductor

Mar.	25—Ev'g.	Carnegie Hall
Mar.	26—Aft.	Carnegie Hall
Mar.	27—Ev'g.	Carnegie Hall
Mar.	28—Aft.	Carnegie Hall
Mar.	31—Ev'g.	Carnegie Hall
Apr.	2—Aft.	Carnegie Hall
Apr.	3—Ev'g.	Carnegie Hall
Apr.	4—Aft.	Carnegie Hall

Bruno Walter, Conductor

Apr.	6—Ev'g.	Academy of Music, Philadelphia, Pa.
Apr.	8—Ev'g.	Carnegie Hall
Apr.	9—Aft.	Carnegie Hall
Apr.	11—Aft.	Carnegie Hall
Apr.	15—Ev'g.	Carnegie Hall
Apr.	16—Aft.	Carnegie Hall
*Apr.	17—Morn.	Carnegie Hall
Apr.	18—Aft.	Carnegie Hall

COMPOSITIONS PERFORMED

(a) First performance anywhere.
(b) First performance in America.
(c) First performance in New York.
(d) First performance by the Society.
(e) First concert performance in America.
(f) First concert performance in New York.
(g) First performance in America in this arrangement.
(h) First performance in New York in this arrangement.

---

* Concert for Young People, under the direction of RUDOLPH GANZ.

ARENSKY—Variations on a Theme by Tschaikowsky for String Orchestra, Opus 35-A: Feb. 25, 26.

BACH—Aria from the Chorale-Prelude, "O Man Bewail Thy Grievous Sin" (Arranged for String Orchestra by Max Reger): Jan. 11.
Passion according to St. Matthew: Apr. 15, 16, 18.
Prelude and Fugue in B minor for Organ (Arranged for Orchestra by Dimitri Mitropoulos): Dec. 17 (h), 18, 20.
Prelude and Fugue in C minor (Transcribed for Orchestra by Llywelyn Gomer from the Six Suites for Solo 'Cello by Bach): Feb. 25 (c), 26.
Suite No. 3, in D major: Dec. 24, 25.

BARTOK—Concerto for Two Pianos with Orchestral Accompaniment: Jan. 21 (g), 22.

BATE—Concertante for Piano and String Orchestra: Jan. 30 (e).

BEETHOVEN—Concerto for Piano and Orchestra in C minor, No. 3. Opus 37: Nov. 5, 6.
Concerto for Piano and Orchestra in G major, No. 4, Opus 58: Jan. 2, 3.
Concerto for Piano and Orchestra in E-flat major, No. 5 ("Emperor"), Opus 73: Jan. 31.
Concerto for Violin and Orchestra in D major, Opus 61: Mar. 10, 12.
Overture to "Egmont," Opus 84: Oct. 12; Jan. 28, 30, 31.
Overture to "Fidelio," in E major, Opus 72: Jan. 21, 22.
Overture to "Leonore," No. 2, Opus 72: Oct. 22, 23, 24.
Overture to "Leonore," No. 3 in C major, Opus 72-A: Jan. 31.
Symphony in D major, No. 2, Opus 36: Nov. 18, 20, 22.
Symphony in C minor, No, 5, Opus 67: Nov. 19; Dec. 6, 7.
Symphony in A major, No. 7, Opus 92: Feb. 11, 12, 15.
Symphony in F major, No. 8. Opus 93: Jan. 31.

BENNETT, ROBERT RUSSELL—"Etudes": Nov. 5 (d), 6, 7.

BERLIOZ—Dramatic Symphony, "Romeo and Juliet," Opus 17: Oct. 7, 9, 11.
Dramatic Legend, "The Damnation of Faust," Opus 24: Dec. 10, 11.
Overture to "King Lear," Opus 4: Dec. 17, 18; Jan. 9, 10.
Overture, "The Roman Carnival," Opus 9: Oct. 7, 9, 11.
"Symphonie Fantastique," Opus 14-A: Jan. 28, 29, 30.
Three Excerpts from "The Damnation of Faust": Nov. 1.

BORODIN—Excerpts from "Prince Igor": Nov. 7, 8.

BRAHMS—Concerto for Piano and Orchestra in D minor, No. 1, Opus 15: Jan. 28, 29.
Concerto for Piano and Orchestra in B-flat major, No. 2, Opus 83: Nov. 8.
Concerto for Violin and Orchestra in D major, Opus 77: Dec. 12, 13; Mar. 25, 26, 28.
Four Hungarian Dances, Nos. 5, 6, 7, and 21: Jan. 21, 22.
Quartet in G minor for Piano and Strings, Op. 25, Transcribed for Orchestra by Arnold Schönberg: Nov. 26 (d), 27.
Symphony in C minor, No. 1, Opus 68: Dec. 12, 13.
Symphony in D major, No. 2, Opus 73: Feb. 21; Mar. 25, 26.
Symphony in F major, No. 3, Opus 90: Dec. 24, 25; Jan. 9, 10.
Symphony in E minor, No. 4, Opus 98: Oct. 29, 30; Nov. 1.

BRUCKNER—Symphony in E-flat major, No. 4 ("Romantic"): Feb. 4, 5.

CAILLIET—Fantasia and Fugue on "O Susanna": Mar. 6 (c), 7.

CARPENTER—Symphony No. 2: Oct. 22 (a), 23.

CHADWICK—Symphonic Sketch: "Jubilee": Nov. 12, 13.

CHASINS—"Parade": Feb. 13, 14.

CORELLI-BARBIROLLI—Concerto Grosso for String Orchestra in D major, freely transcribed by John Barbirolli from the Violin Sonatas of Arcangelo Corelli: Feb. 27 (a), 28.

COUPERIN—Prelude and Allegro (Arranged by Darius Milhaud): Mar. 10 (d), 12, 20.

CRESTON—Choric Dance No. 2: Mar. 18 (d), 19.
"Threnody": Mar. 6 (d).

DEBUSSY—Fantaisie for Piano and Orchestra: Mar. 4, 5.
"Ibéria": "Images" pour orchestre, No. 2: Mar. 31; Apr. 2.
"Petite Suite" (Orchestrated by Henri Busser): Feb. 16.
Prelude to "The Afternoon of a Faun": Feb. 6.

DELIUS—"A Song of Summer": Feb. 18, 19.

DVORAK—Concerto for Violin and Orchestra in A minor, Opus 53: Jan. 24.
Symphony in G major, No. 4, Opus 88: Feb. 4, 5, 6.
Two Movements from Symphony in E minor, No. 5, "From the New World," Opus 95: Dec. 6.

ELGAR—March, "Pomp and Circumstance": Dec. 29.
Variations on an Original Theme ("Enigma"), Opus 36: Mar. 4, 5.

FERNANDEZ—"Batuque," from the Suite "Reisado do Pastoreio": Mar. 21 (d).

FRANCK—Symphonic Variations for Piano and Orchestra: Nov. 14, 15.
Symphony in D minor: Feb. 13, 14.

GERSHWIN—"Porgy and Bess": A Symphonic Picture. Arranged for Orchestra by Robert Russell Bennett, Mar. 31 (c); Apr. 2, 3, 4.
"Rhapsody in Blue": Dec. 24 (d), 25, 27.

GLUCK—Overture to the Opera, "Alceste": Dec. 31; Jan. 1, 3.

GOLDMARK—Concerto for Violin and Orchestra in A minor, Opus 28: Nov. 1.

GOULD, MORTON—"American Symphonette," No. 2: Nov. 12 (d), 13.
"Spirituals for String Choir and Orchestra": Nov. 18 (d), 19, 20, 29; Dec. 7.

GRAINGER—Irish Tune from County Derry: Feb. 16.
"Molly on the Shore": Feb. 16.

GRIEG—String Quartet in G minor, Opus 27: Jan. 2 (d), 11.

HANDEL-BEECHAM—Suite from the Opera, "Il Pastor Fido" ("The Faithful Shepherd"): Dec. 3 (d), 4, 5.

HARRIS, ROY—Folk Song Symphony for Orchestra and Chorus, No. 4: Dec. 31 (g); Jan. 1.

HAYDN—Concerto for Violoncello and Orchestra, in D major, Opus 101: Apr. 11.
Symphony in D major, No. 10 (B. & H. No. 86): Apr. 6, 8, 9.
Symphony in G major, No. 13 (B. & H. No. 88): Mar 14.
Symphony in E-flat major (B. & H. No. 3 [99]): Oct. 14, 16, 18.
Symphony in G major, "Military" (B. & H. 100): Jan. 6, 8.
Symphony in B-flat, No. 102: Jan. 21, 22, 24.

HERRMANN—Symphony No. 1: Nov. 12 (e), 13.

IRELAND, JOHN—"Epic March": Feb. 18 (b), 19.

ITURBI—"Fantasy for Piano and Orchestra": Dec. 24 (c), 25, 27.

KABALEVSKY—Symphony No. 2, Opus 19: Mar. 10 (f), 12, 20.

KODALY—Suite, "Háry János": Nov. 12, 13, 14, 15.

KREISLER—Concerto in C major for Violin, String Orchestra, and Organ, in the Style of Antonio Vivaldi: Feb. 18 (d), 19.

KRENEK—Variations on a North Carolina Folk Song, "I Wonder As I Wander," Opus 94: Dec. 20 (c).

LISZT—Concerto for Piano and Orchestra, in E-flat major, No. 1: Mar. 6, 7.
Concerto for Piano and Orchestra in A major, No. 2: Nov. 14, 15.

LISZT-BYRNS—Grand Galop Chromatique: Mar. 14 (c).

MacDOWELL—Suite in E minor, No. 2, Opus 48 ("Indian"): Nov. 7.

MAHLER—Symphony in D major, No. 1: Oct. 22, 23, 24, 25.

MASON—"A Lincoln Symphony," Opus 35: Feb. 6.

McDONALD—Symphonic Poem, "Bataan": Dec. 6 (c).

MENDELSSOHN—Concerto for Violin and Orchestra, in E minor, Op. 64: Oct. 29, 30.
Overture, "The Wedding of Camacho": Mar. 20, 21.
Scherzo from the Music to "A Midsummer Night's Dream": Mar. 4, 5.
Symphony No. 3, in A minor, "Scotch," Op. 56: Dec. 27, 29.
Symphony in A major, No. 4, Opus 90 ("Italian"): Feb. 16; Apr. 3, 4.

MENOTTI—Overture to "The Old Maid and the Thief": Feb. 28.

MIASKOVSKY—Symphony No. 21: Nov. 5 (e), 6, 7, 8.

MOUSSORGSKY-RAVEL—"Pictures at an Exhibition": Jan. 14, 15, 17, 19.

MOZART—Concerto for Piano and Orchestra in F major, K. 459: Mar. 27.
"Eine kleine Nachtmusik," Serenade for String Orchestra (K. 525), Feb. 16; Mar. 27, 28.
Overture to the comedy, "Der Schauspieldirektor" ("The Impresario"), K. 486: Nov. 14, 15.
Overture to "The Magic Flute": Mar. 27.
Symphony in D major, No. 35, "Haffner" (K. 385): Feb. 7.
Symphony in E-flat major, No. 39, K. 543: Mar. 27.
Symphony in G minor, No. 40 (K. 550): Feb. 21.

NICOLAI—Overture to "The Merry Wives of Windsor": Feb. 13, 14, 15.

PAGANINI-WILHELMJ—Concerto for Violin and Orchestra, in One Movement: Oct. 12.

PAINE—Prelude to Sophocles' Tragedy, "Oedipus Tyrannus," Opus 35: Nov. 7 (d), 8.

PROKOFIEFF—"Classical" Symphony, Opus 25: Jan. 17, 19.
Concerto for Piano and Orchestra in C major, No. 3, Opus 26: Jan 6, 8.
Four Excerpts from the Ballet, "Romeo and Juliet": Mar. 21 (d).

PUCCINI—Aria, "Che gelida manina" from "La Bohème": Oct. 12.

RACHMANINOFF—Concerto for Piano and Orchestra in C minor, No. 2, Op. 18: Feb. 28.
Rhapsody on a Theme of Paganini, for Piano and Orchestra, Op. 43: Dec. 17, 18.
Symphonic Dances, Op. 45: Dec. 17 (d), 18, 20.

RAVEL—"Daphnis et Chloé," Ballet Suites Nos. 1 and 2: Feb. 25, 26, 27.
"Ma Mère L'Oye" ("Mother Goose"), Five Children's Pieces: Feb. 27, 28.

RESPIGHI—Symphonic Poem, "The Fountains of Rome": Feb. 13, 14.
Toccata for Piano and Orchestra: Jan. 11.

RIEGGER—Finale from "New Dance": Jan. 24.

RIMSKY-KORSAKOFF—Capriccio Espagnol, Op. 34: Feb. 27, 28.

ROSSINI—Overture to "L'Italiana in Algeri": Feb. 11, 12.
Overture to "William Tell": Oct. 12; Nov. 19; Dec. 7.

SAINT-SAENS—Concerto for 'Cello and Orchestra, in A minor, Opus 33: Feb. 27.

SCHÖNBERG—"Verklärte Nacht," for String Orchestra, Op. 4: Dec. 31; Jan. 1, 3.

SCHUBERT—Symphony in B-flat major, No. 2: Jan. 9, 10.
Symphony in C major, No. 7: Apr. 6, 8, 9, 11.
Symphony in B minor, No. 8 ("Unfinished"): Oct. 24, 25.

SCHUMAN, WILLIAM—"American Festival Overture": Nov. 5, 6.
"Prayer 1943": Mar. 25 (c), 26, 28.

SCHUMANN—Concerto for Violoncello and Orchestra in A minor, Op. 129:
Apr. 3, 4.
Symphony in D minor, No. 4, Opus 120: Mar. 18, 19, 20.

SCRIABIN—"Prometheus: The Poem of Fire," in F-sharp, Opus 60, for Orchestra
and Piano: Mar. 4, 5.

SHOSTAKOVICH—Polka and Dance from the Ballet, "The Golden Age," Opus
22: Jan. 17, 19.
Symphony No. 1, Opus 10: Nov. 26, 27, 29.
Symphony No. 5, Opus 47: Nov. 18, 20, 22.
Symphony No. 6, Opus 53: Jan. 14 (d), 15.
Symphony No. 7, Opus 60: Oct. 14 (f), 16, 18; Dec. 3, 4, 5.

SIBELIUS—Symphony in C major, No. 7, Op. 105: Oct. 29, 30.

SOUSA—March, "Stars and Stripes Forever": Nov. 19; Dec. 6, 7; Feb. 15.

STRAUSS, JOHANN—Waltz, "Tales from the Vienna Woods": Feb. 15, 16.
Waltz, "Wiener Blut" ("Vienna Blood"), Op. 354: Jan. 24.

STRAUSS, RICHARD—"Till Eulenspiegel's Merry Pranks," Op. 28: Apr. 11.
Tone Poem, "Don Juan," Opus 20: Jan. 21, 22, 24.

STRAVINSKY—Symphonic Poem, "Le Chant du Rossignol" ("The Nightingale's
Song"): Jan. 14, 15.

TANSMAN—"Polish Rhapsody": Jan. 2 (c), 3.

TAYLOR, DEEMS—"Marco Takes a Walk": Variations for Orchestra, Opus 25:
Nov. 14 (a), 15; Feb. 11, 12.

TOCH—"Big Ben": Variation-Fantasy on the Westminster Chimes: Feb. 18 (d),
19.

TSCHAIKOWSKY—"Capriccio Italien," Opus 45: Jan. 17, 19.
Concerto for Piano and Orchestra in B-flat minor, No. 1, Opus 23: Feb. 7.
Concerto for Violin and Orchestra in D major, Opus 35: Mar. 14.
Overture, "1812," Opus 49: Dec. 29.
Symphony in E minor, No. 5, Op. 64: Mar. 6, 7, 31; Apr. 2.
Symphony in B minor, No. 6 ("Pathetic"), Opus 74: Mar. 18, 19, 21.
Andante Lamentoso, only: Mar. 31.

VAUGHAN WILLIAMS—Fantasia on a Theme by Thomas Tallis, for Double
String Orchestra: Apr. 6, 8, 9.
Pastoral Symphony: Feb. 25, 26.
Symphony in F minor, No. 4: Jan. 6, 8.

VILLA-LOBOS—"Descobrimento do Brasil" ("Discovery of Brazil"), Suite No.
1: Feb. 11, 12.

VIOTTI—Concerto for Violin and Orchestra in A minor, No. 22: Feb. 18, 19.

WAGNER—"A Siegfried Idyl": Nov. 30.
Overture to "The Flying Dutchman": Nov. 30.
Daybreak and Siegfried's Rhine Journey from "Götterdämmerung": Nov. 30.
Funeral Music from "Götterdämmerung": Feb. 7.
Immolation Scene, from "Götterdämmerung": Nov. 30.
Prelude to "Lohengrin": Feb. 21.
Prelude to "Die Meistersinger": Nov. 30.
Overture to "Rienzi": Feb. 7.
Waldweben, from "Siegfried": Nov. 30.
Bacchanale from "Tannhäuser": Feb. 6, 7.
Overture to "Tannhäuser": Nov. 29.
Prelude and Liebestod (Love-death) from "Tristan und Isolde": Oct. 25; Nov.
30.

WALTON—"Scapino: A Comedy Overture": Mar. 10 (d), 12, 14.

WEBER—Overture to the Opera, "Euryanthe": Nov. 26, 27, 29.
Overture to the Opera, "Oberon": Dec. 6; Mar. 4, 5.

WEINBERGER—Polka and Fugue from "Schwanda": Nov. 5, 6; Feb. 13, 14.

SOLOISTS

PIANO

CLAUDIO ARRAU: Jan. 2, 3.
BÉLA BARTÓK: Jan. 21, 22.
DITTA PASZTORY-BARTÓK: Jan. 21, 22.
STANLEY BATE: Jan. 30.
ROBERT CASADESUS: Nov. 14, 15.
ARNALDO ESTRELLA: Feb. 7.
JOSÉ ITURBI: Dec. 24, 25, 27.
CORPORAL EDWARD KILENYI: Mar. 6, 7.
SERGEANT EUGENE LIST: Feb. 28.
DIMITRI MITROPOULOS: Jan. 6, 8, 11.
HORTENSE MONATH: Mar. 27.
SERGEI RACHMANINOFF: Dec. 17, 18.
NADIA REISENBERG: Mar. 4, 5.
ARTUR RUBINSTEIN: Nov. 5, 6, 8.
RUDOLF SERKIN: Jan. 28, 29, 31.

VIOLIN

JOHN CORIGLIANO: Jan. 24; April 15, 16, 18.
FRITZ KREISLER: Feb. 18, 19.
NATHAN MILSTEIN: Oct. 29, 30; Nov. 1.
MISHEL PIASTRO: Dec. 12, 13; April 15, 16, 18.
ALBERT SPALDING: Oct. 12.
JOSEPH SZIGETI: Mar. 25, 26, 28.
EFREM ZIMBALIST: Mar. 10, 12, 14.

VIOLA DA GAMBA

JANOS SCHOLZ: Apr. 15, 16, 18.

'CELLO

GREGOR PIATIGORSKY: Apr. 3, 4.
JOSEPH SCHUSTER: Feb. 27; Apr. 11.

FLUTE

JOHN WUMMER: April 15, 16, 18.

OBOE

BRUNO LABATE: April 15, 16, 18.

ORGAN

DR. ALEXANDER MCCURDY: Apr. 15, 16, 18.

HARPSICHORD

RALPH KIRKPATRICK: Apr. 15, 16, 18.

VOCAL

LORENZO ALVARY: Apr. 15, 16, 18.
NADINE CONNER: Apr. 15, 16, 18.
JACQUES GERARD: Oct. 7, 9, 11.
WILLIAM HAIN: Apr. 15, 16, 18.
MACK HARRELL: Apr. 15, 16, 18.
FREDERICK JAGEL: Dec. 10, 11.
HERBERT JANSSEN: Apr. 15, 16, 18.
NINO MARTINI: Oct. 12.
NICOLA MOSCONA: Oct. 7, 9, 11.
JARMILA NOVOTNA: Dec. 10, 11.
EZIO PINZA: Dec. 10, 11.
ABRASHA ROBOFSKY: Dec. 10, 11.
JENNIE TOUREL: Oct. 7, 9, 11.
HELEN TRAUBEL: Nov. 30.
WILLIAM VENTURA: Feb. 25, 26.
JEAN WATSON: Apr. 15, 16, 18.

CHORUS

COMBINED CHORUS FROM THE WASHINGTON IRVING AND BOYS' HIGH SCHOOLS: Dec. 31; Jan. 1.
JUNIOR CHOIRS OF THE PIUS X SCHOOL OF LITURGICAL MUSIC: Apr. 15, 16, 18.
THE WESTMINSTER CHOIR: Oct. 7, 9, 11; Dec. 10, 11; Apr. 15, 16, 18.

FIRST SUMMER SEASON
1943

Concerts sponsored by the United States Rubber Company
Broadcast over the coast-to-coast network of the
Columbia Broadcasting System
Sunday afternoons at 3:00 P.M. at Carnegie Hall

Conductors

Bruno Walter
May 23, 30.
Pierre Monteux
June 6, 13.
Eugene Ormandy
June 20, 27.
George Szell
July 4, 11.
Wilhelm Steinberg
July 18.

José Iturbi
July 25.
Fritz Reiner
Aug. 1, 8, 15.
Dimitri Mitropoulos
Aug. 22, 29; Sept. 5.
Howard Barlow
Sept. 12, 19.
Vladimir Golschmann
Sept. 26; Oct. 3.

SOLOISTS—SUMMER SEASON

PIANO
CLAUDIO ARRAU: Sept. 5.
ROBERT CASADESUS: Sept. 19.
JOSEF HOFMANN: Aug. 22.
JOSE ITURBI: July 25.
SGT. EUGENE LIST: July 11.
ARTUR RUBINSTEIN: June 27.
ARTUR SCHNABEL: June 13.

VIOLIN
ADOLF BUSCH: July 18.
JOHN CORIGLIANO: Aug. 8.
NATHAN MILSTEIN: Aug. 15.

CELLO
JOSEPH SCHUSTER: Sept. 25.

FLUTE
JOHN WUMMER: June 27.

VOCAL
MARJORIE LAWRENCE: Aug. 1.

COMPOSITIONS PERFORMED—SUMMER SEASON

ALBENIZ—"Ibéria," orchestrated by Enrique Fernandez Arbos: Oct. 3.

BEETHOVEN—Concerto for Piano and Orchestra in C minor, No. 3, Op. 37:
  June 27.
  Concerto for Piano and Orchestra in G major, No. 4, Op. 58: Aug. 22.
  Overture to "Leonore" No. 1: Sept. 19.
  Overture to "Leonore" No. 3, Op. 72A: May 23.
  Overture to "The Creatures of Prometheus," Op. 43: Aug. 8.
  Symphony in C minor, No. 5, Op. 67: May 23.
  Symphony in A major, No. 7, Op. 92: July 4.
  Symphony in F major, No. 8, Op. 93: May 23.

BRAHMS—Concerto for Violin and Orchestra in D major, Op. 77: July 18.
  Symphony in C minor, No. 1, Op. 68: Sept. 26.
  Symphony in F major, No. 3, Op. 90: July 18.
  Symphony in E minor, No. 4, Op. 98: June 20.

BRIDGE—Suite, "The Sea" (First time by the Society): Sept. 12.

CHAUSSON—Symphony in B-flat major, Op. 20: Aug. 29.

COPLAND—"El Salón México" (First time by the Society): Aug. 8.

DEBUSSY—"Dance" (orchestrated by Maurice Ravel): June 27.
"Images": Sept. 19.
Prelude to "The Afternoon of a Faun" (after the Eclogue of Stéphane Mallarmé): May 30.
Two Nocturnes for Orchestra: "Nuages" (Clouds), "Fêtes" (Festivals): June 6.
DVORAK—Symphony in G major, No. 4, Op. 88: May 30.
Symphony in E minor, No. 5, "From the New World," Op. 95: July 25.
DUKAS—"La Péri": A Danced Poem: Aug. 22.
FALLA—Dances from "The Three-Cornered Hat": June 27.
FRANCK—Symphony in D minor: June 6.
GERSHWIN—"Porgy and Bess": A Symphonic Picture (arranged for Orchestra by Robert Russell Bennett): Aug. 8.
"Rhapsody in Blue": July 11.
GRETRY—Suite from "Céphale et Procris," orchestrated by Felix Mottl: Sept. 26.
HANDEL—"The Faithful Shepherd" Suite, arranged by Sir Thomas Beecham: Oct. 3.
ITURBI—"Soliloquy" (First time by the Society): July 25.
KABALEVSKY—Overture to "Colas Breugnon" (First time by the Society): Aug. 15.
KENNAN—"Night Soliloquy" (First time by the Society): June 27.
LALO—Overture to "Le Roi d'Ys": Sept. 12.
LISZT—Concerto for Piano and Orchestra in E flat, No. 1: July 25.
Concerto for Piano and Orchestra in A major, No. 2: Sept. 5.
MENDELSSOHN—Concerto for Violin and Orchestra in E minor, Op. 64: Aug. 15.
Symphony in A major, No. 4, Op. 90, "Italian": July 11.
MILHAUD—"Suite Provençale": Sept. 5.
MOUSSORGSKY—"Pictures at an Exhibition," arranged for Orchestra by Maurice Ravel: Sept. 5.
MOZART—Concerto for Piano and Orchestra in C major, K. 467: Sept. 19.
PROKOFIEFF—"Classical" Symphony in D major, Op. 25: June 27.
RAVEL—"Daphnis and Chloe" Suite No. 2: June 20.
"La Valse," Choreographic Poem: Aug. 22.
SAINT-SAENS—Concerto for Violin and Orchestra in B minor, No. 3, Op. 61: Aug. 8.
Concerto for Violoncello and Orchestra in A minor, Op. 33: Sept. 26.
SCHUBERT—Symphony in B minor, No. 8 (Unfinished): May 30.
SCHUMANN—Concerto for Piano and Orchestra in A minor, Op. 54: June 13.
SHOSTAKOVICH—Symphony No. 5, Op. 47: Oct. 3.
Symphony No. 6, Op. 53: Aug. 15.
SINIGAGLIA—Overture to "Le Baruffe Chiozzotti," Op. 32: Aug. 22.
SMETANA—Symphonic Poem, "Vltava" ("The Moldau"): July 4.
SOUSA—March, "The Stars and Stripes Forever": July 4.
STRAUSS, RICHARD—Dance of the Seven Veils and Closing Scene from "Salome": Aug. 1.
"Till Eulenspiegel's Merry Pranks," Op. 28: June 20.
Tone-Poem, "Don Juan," Op. 20: July 11.
STRAVINSKY—Suite from "The Fire-Bird": Aug. 29.
TSCHAIKOWSKY—Symphony in F minor, No. 4, Op. 36: June 13.
VAUGHAN WILLIAMS—Fantasia on a Theme by Tallis: Aug. 29.

WAGNER—"A Siegfried Idyl": Sept. 12.
Introduction to Act III, "Lohengrin": Sept. 12.
Prelude to "Lohengrin": June 6.
Prelude to Act III, Dance of the Apprentices, Entrance of the Masters, from "Die Meistersinger": Sept. 12.
Prelude to "Parsifal": Aug. 1.
Overture to "Tannhaeuser": July 4.
Isolde's Narration from Act I, "Tristan and Isolde": Aug. 1.
Prelude and Liebestod from "Tristan and Isolde": Aug. 1.
WEBER—Overture to "Euryanthe": June 6, 11.

1943–44 ONE HUNDRED SECOND SEASON

Musical Director
ARTUR RODZINSKI

Guest Conductors
BRUNO WALTER
HOWARD BARLOW
WILHELM STEINBERG

Assistant Conductor
LEONARD BERNSTEIN

Concerts for Young People
Conductor
RUDOLPH GANZ

CONCERTS

1943   1943

Artur Rodzinski, Conductor

Oct.	7—Ev'g.	Carnegie Hall
Oct.	8—Aft.	Carnegie Hall
Oct.	10—Aft.	Carnegie Hall
Oct.	14—Ev'g.	Carnegie Hall
Oct.	15—Aft.	Carnegie Hall
Oct.	17—Aft.	Carnegie Hall
Oct.	21—Ev'g.	Carnegie Hall
Oct.	22—Aft.	Carnegie Hall
Oct.	23—Ev'g.	Carnegie Hall
Oct.	24—Aft.	Carnegie Hall
Oct.	28—Ev'g.	Carnegie Hall
Oct.	29—Aft.	Carnegie Hall
Oct.	30—Ev'g.	Carnegie Hall
Oct.	31—Aft.	Carnegie Hall

Bruno Walter, Conductor

Nov.	4—Ev'g.	Carnegie Hall
Nov.	5—Aft.	Carnegie Hall
Nov.	6—Ev'g.	Carnegie Hall
Nov.	7—Aft.	Carnegie Hall
Nov.	11—Ev'g.	Carnegie Hall
Nov.	12—Aft.	Carnegie Hall
*Nov.	13—Morn.	Carnegie Hall

Leonard Bernstein, Conductor

Nov.	14—Aft.	Carnegie Hall

Artur Rodzinski, Conductor

Nov.	17—Ev'g.	Carnegie Hall
Nov.	19—Aft.	Carnegie Hall
Nov.	20—Ev'g.	McCarter Theatre, Princeton, N. J.

Artur Rodzinski, Conductor

Nov.	21—Aft.	Carnegie Hall
Nov.	22—Ev'g.	Municipal Auditorium, Kingston, N. Y.
Nov.	25—Ev'g.	Carnegie Hall
Nov.	26—Aft.	Carnegie Hall
Nov.	27—Ev'g.	Carnegie Hall
Nov.	28—Aft.	Carnegie Hall
†Dec.	2—Ev'g.	Carnegie Hall
†Dec.	3—Aft.	Carnegie Hall
†Dec.	4—Ev'g.	Carnegie Hall
†Dec.	5—Aft.	Carnegie Hall
Dec.	9—Ev'g.	Carnegie Hall
Dec.	10—Aft.	Carnegie Hall

* Concert for Young People, under the direction of RUDOLPH GANZ.
† One number conducted by LEONARD BERNSTEIN.

1943

| Dec. 11—Ev'g. | New York City Center of Music and Drama |
| Dec. 12—Aft. | Carnegie Hall |

Leonard Bernstein, Conductor

Dec. 16—Ev'g.	Carnegie Hall
Dec. 17—Aft.	Carnegie Hall
*Dec. 18—Morn.	Carnegie Hall

Howard Barlow, Conductor

Sept. 23—Ev'g.	Poughkeepsie, N. Y.
Dec. 19—Aft.	Carnegie Hall
Dec. 23—Ev'g.	Carnegie Hall
Dec. 24—Aft.	Carnegie Hall
Dec. 25—Ev'g.	Carnegie Hall
Dec. 26—Aft.	Carnegie Hall

Artur Rodzinski, Conductor

| Dec. 30—Ev'g. | Carnegie Hall |
| Dec. 31—Aft. | Carnegie Hall |

1944

Jan. 1—Ev'g.	Carnegie Hall
Jan. 2—Aft.	Carnegie Hall
Jan. 3—Ev'g.	Halloran Hospital, Staten Island, N. Y.
Jan. 5—Ev'g.	Carnegie Hall
Jan. 7—Aft.	Carnegie Hall
Jan. 8—Ev'g.	Carnegie Hall
Jan. 9—Aft.	Carnegie Hall
Jan. 10—Ev'g.	Hotel Plaza New York, N. Y.

Philharmonic-Symphony League

Jan. 13—Ev'g.	Carnegie Hall
Jan. 14—Aft.	Carnegie Hall
Jan. 16—Aft.	Carnegie Hall
Jan. 18—Ev'g.	Camp Joyce Kilmer, New Brunswick, N. J.
Jan. 20—Ev'g.	Carnegie Hall
Jan. 21—Aft.	Carnegie Hall
*Jan. 22—Morn.	Carnegie Hall
Jan. 23—Aft.	Carnegie Hall

Wilhelm Steinberg, Conductor

Jan. 27—Ev'g.	Carnegie Hall
Jan. 28—Aft.	Carnegie Hall
Jan. 29—Ev'g.	Carnegie Hall
Jan. 30—Aft.	Carnegie Hall

Bruno Walter, Conductor

Feb. 3—Ev'g	Carnegie Hall
Feb. 4—Aft.	Carnegie Hall
Feb. 5—Ev'g.	Carnegie Hall
Feb. 6—Aft.	Carnegie Hall

Artur Rodzinski, Conductor

| Feb. 10—Ev'g. | Carnegie Hall |
| Feb. 11—Aft. | Carnegie Hall |

1944

*Feb. 12—Morn.	Carnegie Hall
Feb. 13—Aft.	Carnegie Hall
Feb. 14—Ev'g.	Hotel Plaza New York, N. Y.

Philharmonic-Symphony League

Feb. 17—Ev'g.	Carnegie Hall
Feb. 18—Aft.	Carnegie Hall
Feb. 20—Aft.	Carnegie Hall
Feb. 24—Ev'g.	Carnegie Hall
Feb. 25—Aft.	Carnegie Hall
Feb. 26—Ev'g.	Carnegie Hall
Feb. 27—Aft.	Carnegie Hall
Mar. 2—Ev'g.	Carnegie Hall
Mar. 3—Aft.	Carnegie Hall
Mar. 4—Ev'g.	Carnegie Hall
Mar. 5—Aft.	Carnegie Hall

Bruno Walter, Conductor

Mar. 8—Ev'g.	Carnegie Hall
Mar. 10—Aft.	Carnegie Hall
†Mar. 11—Ev'g.	War Dept. Theatre U. S. Military Academy West Point, N. Y.
Mar. 12—Aft.	Carnegie Hall
Mar. 16—Ev'g.	Carnegie Hall
Mar. 17—Aft.	Carnegie Hall
*Mar. 18—Morn.	Carnegie Hall
Mar. 19—Aft.	Carnegie Hall

Artur Rodzinski, Conductor

Mar. 23—Ev'g.	Carnegie Hall
Mar. 24—Aft.	Carnegie Hall
Mar. 25—Ev'g.	Carnegie Hall
Mar. 26—Aft.	Carnegie Hall

Leonard Bernstein, Conductor

Mar. 29—Ev'g.	Carnegie Hall
Mar. 31—Aft.	Carnegie Hall
Apr. 1—Ev'g.	Carnegie Hall

Artur Rodzinski, Conductor

| Apr. 2—Aft. | Carnegie Hall |
| Apr. 3—Ev'g. | Bushnell Memorial Hall, Hartford, Conn. |

Bruno Walter, Conductor

Apr. 6—Ev'g.	Carnegie Hall
Apr. 7—Aft.	Carnegie Hall
Apr. 9—Aft.	Carnegie Hall

Artur Rodzinski, Conductor

Apr. 13—Ev'g.	Carnegie Hall
Apr. 14—Aft.	Carnegie Hall
*Apr. 15—Morn.	Carnegie Hall
Apr. 16—Aft.	Carnegie Hall

* Concert for Young People, under the direction of RUDOLPH GANZ.
† Second half of concert conducted by LEONARD BERNSTEIN.

COMPOSITIONS PERFORMED

(a) First performance anywhere.
(b) First performance in the Western Hemisphere.
(c) First performance in New York.
(d) First performance by the Society.
(e) First performance of new version in New York.

BACH—Passion According to St. Matthew: Apr. 6, 7, 9.
Three Chorale-Preludes (Transcribed for Orchestra by Ottorino Resphigi):
"Nun komm', der Heiden Heiland": Oct. 14, 15.
"Meine Seele erhebt den Herren": Oct. 14, 15.
"Wachet auf, ruft uns die Stimme": Oct. 10, 14, 15.

BARBER—Symphony in One Movement: Mar. 8 (e), 10, 12.

BARTOK—Concerto for Violin and Orchestra: Oct. 14 (c), 15, 17.

BALAKIREFF—"Islamey," Oriental Fantasy (Orchestral version of piano original by Alfredo Casella): Dec. 23, 24.

BEETHOVEN—Concerto for Piano and Orchestra in G major, No. 4, Opus 58: Oct. 30, 31.
Concerto for Piano and Orchestra in E-flat major, No. 5 ("Emperor"), Opus 73: Dec. 30, 31; Jan. 2.
Concerto for Violin and Orchestra in D major, Opus 61: Dec. 16, 17, 19; Mar. 25, 26.
Overture to "Egmont," Opus 84: Nov. 7.
Overture to "Leonore," No. 3, Opus 72-A: Oct. 7, 8; Nov. 20, 22; Dec. 11.
Symphony in C major, No. 1, Opus 21: Apr. 13, 14, 16.
Symphony in C minor, No. 5, Opus 67: Oct. 17; Jan. 3; Mar. 11.
Symphony in F major, No. 6 ("Pastoral"), Opus 68: Nov. 11, 12.
Symphony in A major, No. 7, Opus 92: Jan. 27, 28, 29, 30.
Symphony in D minor, No. 9, with Final Chorus on Schiller's "Ode to Joy," Opus 125: Mar. 16, 17, 19.

BEREZOWSKY—"A Christmas Festival Overture," Opus 30, No. 2: Dec. 23 (a), 24, 25, 26.
"Soldier on the Town": Nov. 25 (a), 26, 27, 28.

BERLIOZ—"Symphonie Fantastique," Opus 14-A: Oct. 14, 15.
Two Movements from the "Symphonie Fantastique," Opus 14-A: Oct. 17.

BERNSTEIN—Symphony "Jeremiah": Mar. 29 (c), 31; Apr. 1.

BLOCH—"Three Jewish Poems": Dec. 2, 3, 4, 5.

BRAHMS—Concerto for Piano and Orchestra in B-flat major, No. 2, Opus 83: Nov. 21; Mar. 8, 10, 12.
Concerto for Violin and Orchestra in D major, Opus 77: Jan. 20, 21, 23.
Symphony in C minor, No. 1, Opus 68: Nov. 4, 5, 6, 7; Apr. 13, 14, 16.
Symphony in D major, No. 2, Opus 73: Oct. 7, 8, 10.
Symphony in F major, No. 3, Opus 90: Dec. 23, 24, 25, 26.
Symphony in E minor, No. 4, Opus 98: Feb. 24, 25, 26, 27; Apr. 3.
"Tragic Overture," Opus 81: Feb. 3, 4, 5.
Variations on a Theme by Haydn, Opus 56-A: Dec. 16, 17, 19.

BRUCKNER—"Te Deum Laudamus": Mar. 16 (d), 17.

CARPENTER—"The Anxious Bugler": Nov. 17 (a), 19, 20, 21, 22.

CHOPIN—Concerto for Piano and Orchestra in E minor, No. 1, Opus 11: Jan. 13, 14.
Concerto for Piano and Orchestra in F minor, No. 2, Opus 21: Dec. 9, 10; Feb. 26, 27.

COPLAND—"El Salón México": Mar. 29, 31; Apr. 1.

COUPERIN-STRAUSS—Dance Suite: Jan. 13, 14.

CRESTON—Concerto for Saxophone and Orchestra: Jan. 27 (a), 28; Feb. 13.

DEBUSSY—From "Nocturnes": "Nuages," "Fêtes": Jan. 27, 28.

DELIUS—"Paris, A Night Piece" ("The Song of a Great City"): Dec. 16, 17, 19.

DUKELSKY—Concerto for Violin and Orchestra in G minor: Jan. 5 (c), 7.

DVORAK—Aria from "Rusalka": Oct. 28, 29.
Piano Concerto in G minor, Opus 33 (First performance in New York in the edition of Vilem Kurz as authorized by the Composer): Oct. 28, 29.
"Songs My Mother Taught Me": Oct. 28, 29.
Symphony in E minor, No. 5, "From the New World," Opus 95: Jan. 5, 7, 8, 9.

ELGAR—"Falstaff": A Symphonic Study for full Orchestra: Oct. 7, 8, 10.

FERNANDEZ—"Batuque" from Suite "Reisado do Pastoreio": Mar. 2, 3, 4, 5.

FRANCK—Symphony in D minor: Mar. 23, 24, 25.

GERSHWIN—"An American in Paris": Nov. 17, 19, 20, 21, 22; Dec. 11; Jan. 3.

GLAZOUNOFF—Concerto for Violin and Orchestra in A minor, Opus 82: Nov. 27, 28.

GLIERE—Symphony in B minor, No. 3, Opus 42, "Ilya Mourometz": Nov. 25 (d), 26, 27, 28.

GUARNIERI—Two Brazilian Dances: Mar. 2 (d), 3, 4, 5.

HANDEL—Concerto for Oboe and Orchestra in G minor (First movement): Feb. 14.
Concerto for Orchestra and Organ, in D major (Transcribed by Sir Hamilton Harty): Jan. 20, 21, 23.

HANDEL-WILBER—Concerto-Piccolo, for Horn and Strings: Feb. 14.

HARRIS—"March in Time of War": Dec. 30 (a), 31; Jan. 1, 2.

HAYDN—Symphony in G major, No. 13 (B. & H. No. 88): Nov. 4, 5, 6, 7.
Symphony in F-sharp minor, No. 45 ("Farewell"): Feb. 14.

HERRMANN—"For the Fallen" (conducted by the Composer): Dec. 16 (a), 17, 19.

HINDEMITH—Symphonic Metamorphosis on Themes of C. M. von Weber: Jan. 20 (a), 21, 23.

KHATCHATOURIAN—Concerto for Piano and Orchestra: Dec. 12.

KODALY—Dances from "Galanta": Mar. 23, 24.

KOLAR—"Bagatelle," Flute solo with Strings and Harp: Feb. 14.

LALO—Overture to "Le Roi d'Ys": Sept. 23.
Concerto for Violoncello and Orchestra, in D minor: Jan. 29, 30.

LEKEU—"Fantaisie Contrapuntique sur un Cramignon Liégeois": Feb. 14.

LISZT—Concerto for Piano and Orchestra in E-flat major, No. 1: Nov. 17, 19.

LUTKIN—Benediction (chorus a cappella): Mar. 19.

MAHLER—Symphony in C minor, No. 2, for Orchestra, Soprano and Alto Solos, and Mixed Chorus: Dec. 2, 3, 4, 5.
Andante moderato from Symphony No. 2: Jan. 10.
Symphony in G, No. 4, Orchestra, with Soprano Solo: Feb. 3, 4, 5, 6.

MARTINU—"Memorial to Lidice": Oct. 28 (a), 29, 30, 31.
Symphony No. 2: Dec. 30 (c), 31; Jan. 1.

MASSENET—Aria, "Vision Fugitive" from "Hérodiade": Dec. 11.

MENDELSSOHN—Scherzo in G minor, from Octet for Strings, Opus 20: Feb. 17, 18, 20.
Symphony in A major, No. 4, Opus 90 ("Italian"): Mar. 29, 31; Apr. 1.

MIASKOVSKY—Sinfonietta for String Orchestra, No. 2, Opus 32: Feb. 10 (d), 11.

MILHAUD—"Cortège Funèbre": Mar. 23 (a), 24, 25.

MOZART—Concerto for Piano and Orchestra in C major (K. 467): Jan. 8, 9.
Overture to "The Marriage of Figaro": Nov. 21; Feb. 20; Mar. 29, 31; Apr. 1.
Symphony in D major, No. 35, "Haffner" (K. 385): Feb. 5, 6.
Symphony in G minor, No. 40 (K. 550): Jan. 10; Feb. 20, 24, 25.

MOZART-BELLISON—Concerto-Rondo, Adagio and Finale for Clarinet and Orchestra: Feb. 14.

NOSKOWSKI—Symphonic Poem, "The Steppe," Opus 66: Dec. 9 (d), 10, 12.

PROKOFIEFF—Concerto for Piano and Orchestra in C major, No. 3, Opus 26: Apr. 13, 14.
"Lieutenant Kije," Orchestral Suite, Opus 60: Dec. 23 (d), 24.

RACHMANINOFF—Concerto for Piano and Orchestra, in C minor, No. 2, Opus 18: Mar. 23, 24.
Concerto for Piano and Orchestra in D minor, No. 3, Opus 30: Nov. 25, 26.

RATHAUS—Polonaise Symphonique, Opus 52: Feb. 26 (a), 27.

RAVEL—"Daphnis et Chloé," Ballet Suite No. 2: Oct. 7, 9, 10.
"Rapsodie Espagnole": Jan. 13, 14, 16.

RIMSKY-KORSAKOFF—"Capriccio Espagnol," Opus 34: Nov. 27, 28.

ROGERS—"Invasion": Oct. 17 (a).

ROUSSEL—Symphony in G minor, No. 3, Opus 42: Jan. 13, 14, 16.

ROZSA—Theme, Variations and Finale, Opus 13: Nov. 4 (c), 5, 6, 14.

RUBINSTEIN—Concerto for Piano and Orchestra in G major, No. 3, Opus 45: Mar. 2, 3, 5.

SAINT-SAENS—Symphony in C minor, No. 3, Opus 78: Nov. 17, 19; Dec. 12.

SCARLATTI-BYRNS—Suite for Strings: Mar. 2 (d), 3, 4, 5.

SCHÖNBERG—"Verklärte Nacht" ("Transfigured Night") arranged for String Orchestra, Opus 4: Feb. 3, 4.

SCHREINER—"The Worried Drummer," Timpani Solo: Feb. 14.

SCHUBERT—Symphony No. 8 in B minor (Unfinished): Sept. 23.
Entr'acte and Ballet Music from "Rosamunde": Jan. 10.

SCHUBERT-CASSADO—Concerto for 'Cello and Orchestra in A major: Dec. 25, 26.

SCHUMAN, WILLIAM—William Billings Overture: Feb. 17 (a), 18; Apr. 2.

SCHUMANN—Overture to "Manfred," Opus 115: Nov. 11, 12, 14.
Symphony in B-flat major, No. 1, Opus 38: Mar. 2, 3, 4, 5.
Symphony in D minor, No. 4, Opus 120: Mar. 8, 10.
The Jolly Farmer (Arranged for Tuba Solo): Feb. 14.

SHOSTAKOVICH—Symphony No. 1, Opus 10: Feb. 10, 11.
Symphony No. 8, Opus 65: Apr. 2 (b).

SIBELIUS—Symphony in E-flat major, No. 5, Opus 82: Feb. 17, 18.

SMETANA—Lullaby, from the Opera "The Kiss": Oct. 28, 29.
Overture to "The Bartered Bride": Feb. 13.
String Quartet No. 1, in E minor "From My Life" (Orchestral Version by George Szell): Oct. 28, 29, 30, 31.
Symphonic Poem, "Blanik," from "Ma Vlast" (My Country): Oct. 28, 29, 30, 31.

SOUSA—March, "Stars and Stripes Forever": Nov. 22; Apr. 13, 14, 16.

STILL—"In Memoriam: The Colored Soldiers Who Died for Democracy": Jan. 5 (a), 7, 8, 9.

STRAUSS, JOHANN—Moto Perpetuo (Perpetual Motion): Jan. 10, 18.
Overture to "Die Fledermaus": Jan. 10, 18; Mar. 11.
Waltz, "Tales from the Vienna Woods": Jan. 10, 18.

STRAUSS, RICHARD—"Don Quixote" (Introduction, Theme with Variations and Finale); Fantastic Variations on a Theme of Knightly Character, Op. 35: Nov. 11, 12, 14.
Rondo, "Till Eulenspiegel's Merry Pranks," Opus 28: Dec. 30, 31; Jan. 1, 2.
Tone Poem, "Also Sprach Zarathustra" ("Thus Spake Zarathustra"), Opus 30: Feb. 24, 25; Mar. 4, 26.

STRAVINSKY—Suite from the Ballet, "The Fire Bird": Jan. 5, 7, 8, 9.

SUPPÉ—Overture to "The Beautiful Galathea": Jan. 10.

SZYMANOWSKI—Symphonie Concertante for Piano and Orchestra, Opus 60: Dec. 9 (d), 10, 12.

TANSMAN—Symphony in D minor, No. 5 (conducted by the Composer): Dec. 9 (c), 10.

TAYLOR, DEEMS—"A Christmas Overture" (conducted by the Composer): Dec. 23 (a), 24, 25.

TSCHAIKOWSKY—Andante Cantabile from String Quartet: Nov. 25.
Concerto for Piano and Orchestra in B-flat minor, No. 1, Opus 23: Jan. 16.
Concerto for Violin and Orchestra in D major, Opus 35: Oct. 21, 22, 24; Feb. 17, 18, 20.
Marche Slave, Opus 31: Jan. 16.
Overture-Fantasy, "Romeo and Juliet": Oct. 21, 22, 23; Mar. 11, 29, 31; Apr. 1, 3.
Polonaise from the Opera, "Eugene Onegin": Oct. 23.
Symphony in F minor, No. 4, Opus 36: Oct. 21, 22, 23, 24; Nov. 20, 22; Dec. 11; Jan. 18.
Scherzo; pizzicato ostinato; allegro, from Symphony No. 4: Jan. 3; Mar. 11.
Symphony in B minor, No. 6 (Pathetic), Opus 74: Feb. 10, 11, 13.

VIVALDI-SILOTI—Concerto Grosso in D minor, Opus 3, No. 11: Jan. 27 (d), 28.

WAGNER—Excerpts from "Die Meistersinger": Sept. 23; Jan. 20, 21, 23.
Prelude to "Die Meistersinger": Nov. 14; Apr. 16.
Prelude to "Lohengrin": Jan. 1, 2; Mar. 11; Apr. 3.
Prelude to "Lohengrin," Act III: Sept. 23; Mar. 12.
Prelude and Love-Death, "Tristan und Isolde": Jan. 1.
"A Siegfried Idyl": Sept. 23.

WEBER—Concerto for Bassoon and Orchestra (Second Movement): Feb. 14.
Overture to the Opera, "Der Freischütz": Mar. 19.
Overture to "Oberon": Jan. 3, 18, 29, 30; Apr. 3.

SOLOISTS

PIANO

ALEXANDER BRAILOWSKY: Jan. 13, 14, 16
ROBERT CASADESUS: Dec. 30, 31; Jan. 2.
RUDOLF FIRKUSNY: Oct. 28, 29.
JOSEF HOFMANN: Mar. 2, 3, 5.
VLADIMIR HOROWITZ: Nov. 25, 26.
EUGENE ISTOMIN: Nov. 21.
WILLIAM KAPELL: Mar. 23, 24.
WITOLD MALCUZYNSKI: Feb. 26, 27.
HORTENSE MONATH: Jan. 8, 9.

PVT. LEONARD PENNARIO: Nov. 17, 19.
NADIA REISENBERG: Apr. 13, 14.
ARTUR RUBINSTEIN: Dec. 9, 10, 12.
RUDOLF SERKIN: Mar. 8, 10, 12.
LEONARD SHURE: Oct. 30, 31.

VIOLIN

JOHN CORIGLIANO: Feb. 14; Mar. 25, 26; Apr. 6, 7, 9.
ZINO FRANCESCATTI: Oct. 21, 22, 24.
BRONISLAW HUBERMAN: Jan. 20, 21, 23.

NATHAN MILSTEIN: Feb. 17, 18, 20.
ERICA MORINI: Nov. 27, 28.
IMRE POGANY: Feb. 14.
RUTH POSSELT: Jan. 5, 7.
MICHAEL ROSENKER: Apr. 6, 7, 9.
ALBERT SPALDING: Dec. 16, 17, 19.
TOSSY SPIVAKOVSKY: Oct. 14, 15, 17.

VIOLA
WILLIAM LINCER: Nov. 11, 12, 14;
Feb. 14.

VIOLA DA GAMBA
JANOS SCHOLZ: Apr. 6, 7, 9.

'CELLO
LEONARD ROSE: Jan. 29, 30; Feb. 14.
JOSEPH SCHUSTER: Nov. 11, 12, 14;
Dec. 25, 26.

BASS
ANSELME FORTIER: Feb. 14.

FLUTE
JOHN WUMMER: Feb. 14; Apr. 6, 7, 9.

OBOE
HAROLD GOMBERG: Feb. 14; Apr. 6, 7,
9.

CLARINET
SIMEON BELLISON: Feb. 14.

BASSOON
WILLIAM POLISI: Feb. 14.

FRENCH HORN
WELDON WILBER: Feb. 14.

SAXOPHONE
VINCENT J. ABATO: Jan. 27, 28;
Feb. 13.

TUBA
WILLIAM BELL: Feb. 14.

TIMPANI
SAUL GOODMAN: Feb. 14.

ORGAN
EDOUARD NIES-BERGER: Jan. 20, 21,
23; Apr. 6, 7, 9.

HARPSICHORD
RALPH KIRKPATRICK: Apr. 6, 7, 9.

VOCAL
LORENZO ALVARY: Apr. 6, 7, 9.
NADINE CONNER: Apr. 6, 7, 9.
WILLIAM HAIN: Apr. 6, 7, 9.
DESI HALBAN: Feb. 3, 4, 5, 6.
MACK HARRELL: Apr. 6, 7, 9.
HERBERT JANSSEN: Apr. 6, 7, 9.
CHARLES KULLMAN: Mar. 16, 17, 19.
NICOLA MOSCONA: Mar. 16, 17, 19.
JARMILA NOVOTNA: Oct. 28, 29.
ELEANOR STEBER: Mar. 16, 17, 19.
ENID SZANTHO: Dec. 2, 3, 4, 5;
Mar. 16, 17, 19.
LAWRENCE TIBBETT: Dec. 11.
JENNIE TOUREL: Mar. 29, 31; Apr. 1.
ASTRID VARNAY: Dec. 2, 3, 4, 5.
JEAN WATSON: Apr. 6, 7, 9.

CHORUS
JUNIOR CHOIRS—BOYS AND GIRLS
TRAINED BY PIUS X SCHOOL OF
LITURGICAL MUSIC.
THE WESTMINSTER CHOIR: Dec. 2, 3,
4, 5; Mar. 16, 17, 19; Apr. 6, 7, 9.

●

SECOND SUMMER SEASON
1944

Concerts sponsored by the United States Rubber Company
Broadcast over the coast-to-coast network of the
Columbia Broadcasting System
Sunday Afternoons at 3:00 P.M. at Carnegie Hall

Conductors

Artur Rodzinski
Apr. 23, 30; May 21; Oct. 1 (Madison
Square Garden)
Vladimir Golschmann
May 28; June 4, 11; Sept. 10, 17, 24.

Bruno Walter
May 7, 14.
Fritz Reiner
June 18, 25; July 2, 16, 23.
Dimitri Mitropoulos
July 30; Aug. 6, 13, 20, 27; Sept. 3

SOLOISTS—SUMMER SEASON

PIANO
ALEXANDER BRAILOWSKY: Aug. 13.
ROBERT CASADESUS: May 28.
ANIA DORFMANN: June 25.
RUDOLF FIRKUSNY: Sept. 3.

VLADIMIR HOROWITZ: Apr. 23.
WILLIAM KAPELL: June 18.
BEVERIDGE WEBSTER: June 11.
SYLVIA ZAREMBA: May 21.
RUDOLF SERKIN: July 16.

VIOLIN
JOHN CORIGLIANO: July 9; Aug. 20.
CARROLL GLENN: Aug. 27.
NATHAN MILSTEIN: June 4.
ERICA MORINI: Sept. 17.
MICHAEL ROSENKER: July 9.
ISAAC STERN: Aug. 6.

CELLO
LEONARD ROSE: Aug. 20.

VOCAL
ALEXANDER KIPNIS: July 23.
HELEN TRAUBEL: Oct. 1.

NARRATOR
FRANK LUTHER: May 21.

COMPOSITIONS PERFORMED—SUMMER SEASON

BACH—Concerto for Two Violins and Orchestra in D minor: July 9.

BEETHOVEN—Concerto for Piano and Orchestra, No. 1, in C major, Opus 15: June 25.
Concerto for Piano and Orchestra, No. 3, in C minor, Opus 37: Aug. 13.
Concerto for Piano and Orchestra, No. 4, in G major, Opus 58: May 28.
Concerto for Piano and Orchestra, No. 5, in E-flat major, "Emperor," Opus 73: July 16.
Concerto for Violin and Orchestra in D major, Opus 61: Sept. 17.
Overture to "Coriolanus," Opus 62: May 28.
Overture to "Leonore," No. 3: Apr. 30.
Overture to "The Creatures of Prometheus," Opus 43: June 25.
Symphony in B-flat major, No. 4, Opus 60: June 25.
Symphony No. 5 in C minor, Opus 67: May 28; Oct. 1.
Symphony No. 6 in F major, Opus 68 ("Pastoral"): May 14.
Symphony No. 7 in A major, Opus 92: July 16.
Symphony No. 8 in F major, Opus 93: Sept. 17.

BLAND—Carry Me Back to Old Virginny: Oct. 1.

BRAHMS—Concerto for Piano and Orchestra, No. 1, in D minor, Opus 15: Sept. 3.
Concerto for Violin and Orchestra in D major, Opus 77: June 4.
Double Concerto for Violin, Cello and Orchestra in A minor, Opus 102: Aug. 20.
Symphony No. 1, in C minor, Opus 68: Sept. 24.
Symphony No. 2, in D major, Opus 73: Aug. 20.

COHAN—Over There: Oct. 1.

DEBUSSY—"La Mer," Three Symphonic Sketches: Sept. 10.

FRANCK—Symphony in D minor: Apr. 30.

GERSHWIN—"An American in Paris": Oct. 1.

GLINKA—Overture to "Russlan and Ludmilla": Sept. 10.

GOULD—"Symphony on Marching Tunes"
     I. March Variations   III. Quickstep
    II. Bivouac   IV. Memorial
       (First Performance) June 4.

LISZT—Symphonic Poem, "Les Préludes": Apr. 30.

MENDELSSOHN—Concerto for Violin and Orchestra in E minor, Opus 64: Aug. 27.
Symphony No. 3, in A minor ("Scotch"), Opus 56: Aug. 27.

MOUSSORGSKY—Excerpts from "Boris Godounoff," Orchestrated by Shostakovich:
  (A) Monologue and Hallucination Scene
  (B) Farewell of Boris:
     (First Performance) July 23.

MOZART—Symphony in E-flat major, No. 39 (K. 543): May 7.
Symphony No. 41 in C major, "Jupiter" (K. 551): July 9.

PROKOFIEFF—"Lieutenant Kije" Suite, Opus 60: June 18.
"Peter and the Wolf," Opus 67: May 21.

RACHMANINOFF—Concerto for Piano and Orchestra, No. 2, in C minor, Opus 18: June 18.
Concerto for Piano and Orchestra, No. 3, in D minor, Opus 30: Apr. 23.
Symphony No. 2, in E minor, Opus 27: July 30.
"The Isle of the Dead," Opus 29: July 30.

ROUGET DE LISLE—"La Marseillaise": Aug. 27.

SAINT-SAENS—Concerto for Piano, No. 2, in G minor, Opus 22: May 21.

SCHUBERT—Overture and Ballet Music Nos. 1 and 2 from "Rosamunde": May 7.
Symphony No. 5, in B-flat major: Sept. 3.

SCHUMANN—Concerto for Piano and Orchestra in A minor, Opus 54: June 11.
Overture to Byron's "Manfred," Opus 115: June 11.
Symphony No. 2, in C major, Opus 61: Aug. 13.
Symphony in D minor, No. 4, Opus 120: June 11.

SHOSTAKOVICH—Symphony No. 1, Opus 10: Apr. 23.

SIBELIUS—Concerto for Violin and Orchestra, in D minor, Opus 47: Aug. 6.
Symphony No. 1, in E minor, Opus 39: Aug. 6.

SOUSA—March, "The Stars and Stripes Forever": Oct. 1.

STRAUSS, JOHANN—"Emperor" Waltz: May 7.
Overture to "The Bat": May 7.
Overture to "The Gypsy Baron": May 7.

STRAUSS, RICHARD—"Till Eulenspiegel's Merry Pranks," Opus 28: July 9.
Waltzes from "Der Rosenkavalier": July 9.

STRAVINSKY—Suite from "The Fire Bird": June 18.

TSCHAIKOWSKY—Suite from the Ballet, "The Nutcracker," Opus 71-A: May 21.
Symphony No. 4, in F minor, Opus 36: Sept. 10.
Symphony No. 5, in E minor, Opus 64: July 23.

WAGNER—Immolation Scene, "The Dusk of the Gods": Oct. 1.
Excerpts from "Parsifal": July 2.
Excerpts from "The Mastersingers of Nuremberg": July 2.
Preludes to Acts 1 and 3, "Lohengrin": May 14.
Prelude and Love-Death, "Tristan and Isolde": May 14; Sept. 24.
Overture to "Rienzi": July 2.
Overture to "The Mastersingers of Nuremberg": Sept. 24.
Venusberg Music from "Tannhäuser": July 2.

1944–45 ONE HUNDRED THIRD SEASON

Musical Director
ARTUR RODZINSKI

Guest Conductors
PIERRE MONTEUX
GEORGE SZELL
ARTURO TOSCANINI
LEONARD BERNSTEIN
IGOR STRAVINSKY
BRUNO WALTER

Concerts for Young People
Conductor
RUDOLPH GANZ

CONCERTS

1944

Artur Rodzinski, Conductor

Oct.	5—Ev'g.	Carnegie Hall
Oct.	6—Aft.	Carnegie Hall
Oct.	8—Aft.	Carnegie Hall
Oct.	12—Ev'g.	Carnegie Hall
Oct.	13—Aft.	Carnegie Hall
Oct.	15—Aft.	Carnegie Hall
Oct.	19—Ev'g.	Carnegie Hall
Oct.	20—Aft.	Carnegie Hall
Oct.	21—Ev'g.	Carnegie Hall
Oct.	22—Aft.	Carnegie Hall
Oct.	26—Ev'g.	Carnegie Hall
Oct.	27—Aft.	Carnegie Hall
Oct.	28—Ev'g.	Carnegie Hall
Oct.	29—Aft.	Carnegie Hall

Pierre Monteux, Conductor

Nov.	2—Ev'g.	Carnegie Hall
Nov.	3—Aft.	Carnegie Hall
Nov.	4—Ev'g.	Carnegie Hall
Nov.	5—Aft.	Carnegie Hall
Nov.	9—Ev'g.	Carnegie Hall
Nov.	10—Aft.	Carnegie Hall
Nov.	11—Ev'g.	Carnegie Hall
Nov.	12—Aft.	Carnegie Hall

Artur Rodzinski, Conductor

Nov.	13—Ev'g.	Bushnell Memorial Hall, Hartford, Conn.
Nov.	16—Ev'g.	Carnegie Hall
Nov.	17—Aft.	Carnegie Hall
*Nov.	18—Morn.	Carnegie Hall
Nov.	19—Aft.	Carnegie Hall
Nov.	23—Ev'g.	Carnegie Hall
Nov.	24—Aft.	Carnegie Hall
Nov.	25—Ev'g.	McCarter Theatre, Princeton, N. J.
Nov.	26—Aft.	Carnegie Hall
Nov.	30—Ev'g.	Carnegie Hall
Dec.	1—Aft.	Carnegie Hall
Dec.	2—Ev'g.	Carnegie Hall
Dec.	3—Aft.	Carnegie Hall
Dec.	7—Ev'g.	Carnegie Hall
Dec.	8—Aft.	Carnegie Hall
Dec.	9—Ev'g.	Carnegie Hall
Dec.	10—Aft.	Carnegie Hall

George Szell, Conductor

Dec.	14—Ev'g.	Carnegie Hall
Dec.	15—Aft.	Carnegie Hall
*Dec.	16—Morn.	Carnegie Hall
Dec.	17—Aft.	Carnegie Hall
Dec.	19—Ev'g.	Camp Joyce Kilmer, New Brunswick, N. J.

1944

Dec.	21—Ev'g.	Carnegie Hall
Dec.	22—Aft.	Carnegie Hall
Dec.	24—Aft.	Carnegie Hall

Artur Rodzinski, Conductor

Dec.	28—Ev'g.	Carnegie Hall
Dec.	29—Aft.	Carnegie Hall
Dec.	30—Ev'g.	Carnegie Hall
Dec.	31—Aft.	Carnegie Hall

1945

Jan.	4—Ev'g.	Carnegie Hall
Jan.	5—Aft.	Carnegie Hall
Jan.	6—Ev'g.	Carnegie Hall
Jan.	7—Aft.	Carnegie Hall
Jan.	11—Ev'g.	Carnegie Hall
Jan.	12—Aft.	Carnegie Hall

Arturo Toscanini, Conductor

Jan.	13—Ev'g.	Carnegie Hall

Artur Rodzinski, Conductor

Jan.	14—Aft.	Carnegie Hall
Jan.	18—Ev'g.	Carnegie Hall
Jan.	19—Aft.	Carnegie Hall
*Jan.	20—Morn.	Carnegie Hall
Jan.	21—Aft.	Carnegie Hall
Jan.	22—Ev'g.	Mosque Theatre, Newark, N. J.

Leonard Bernstein, Conductor

Jan.	25—Ev'g.	Carnegie Hall
Jan.	26—Aft.	Carnegie Hall
Jan.	27—Ev'g.	Carnegie Hall
Jan.	28—Aft.	Carnegie Hall

Igor Stravinsky, Conductor

Feb.	1—Ev'g.	Carnegie Hall
Feb.	2—Aft.	Carnegie Hall
Feb.	3—Ev'g.	Carnegie Hall
Feb.	4—Aft.	Carnegie Hall

Artur Rodzinski, Conductor

†Feb.	8—Ev'g.	Carnegie Hall
†Feb.	9—Aft.	Carnegie Hall
*Feb.	10—Morn.	Carnegie Hall
Feb.	11—Aft.	Carnegie Hall
Feb.	13—Ev'g.	Hotel Plaza, New York, N. Y.

Philharmonic-Symphony League

Feb.	15—Ev'g.	Carnegie Hall
Feb.	16—Aft.	Carnegie Hall
Feb.	18—Aft.	Carnegie Hall
‡Feb.	22—Ev'g.	Carnegie Hall

---

* Concert for Young People, under the direction of RUDOLPH GANZ.

† Two numbers conducted by HEITOR VILLA-LOBOS.

‡ One number conducted by VIRGIL THOMSON.

1945

‡Feb. 23—Aft.	Carnegie Hall	
Feb. 24—Ev'g.	Carnegie Hall	
Feb. 25—Aft.	Carnegie Hall	
Mar. 1—Ev'g.	Carnegie Hall	
Mar. 2—Aft.	Carnegie Hall	
Mar. 3—Ev'g.	Carnegie Hall	
Mar. 4—Aft.	Carnegie Hall	

Bruno Walter, Conductor

Mar. 7—Ev'g.	Carnegie Hall

George Szell, Conductor

Mar. 8—Ev'g.	Carnegie Hall
Mar. 9—Aft.	Carnegie Hall
*Mar. 10—Morn.	Carnegie Hall
Mar. 11—Aft.	Carnegie Hall
Mar. 13—Ev'g.	Plaza Hotel, New York, N. Y.

Philharmonic-Symphony League

Mar. 15—Ev'g.	Carnegie Hall
Mar. 16—Aft.	Carnegie Hall
Mar. 18—Aft.	Carnegie Hall

1945

Artur Rodzinski, Conductor

§Mar. 22—Ev'g.	Carnegie Hall
§Mar. 23—Aft.	Carnegie Hall
Mar. 24—Ev'g.	Carnegie Hall
Mar. 25—Aft.	Carnegie Hall

Bruno Walter, Conductor

Mar. 29—Ev'g.	Carnegie Hall
Mar. 30—Aft.	Carnegie Hall
Mar. 31—Ev'g.	Carnegie Hall
Apr. 1—Aft.	Carnegie Hall

Artur Rodzinski, Conductor

Apr. 5—Ev'g.	Carnegie Hall
Apr. 6—Aft.	Carnegie Hall
*Apr. 7—Morn.	Carnegie Hall
Apr. 8—Aft.	Carnegie Hall
Apr. 9—Ev'g.	Carnegie Hall
**Apr. 12—Ev'g.	Carnegie Hall
Apr. 13—Aft.	Carnegie Hall
⚹Apr. 15—Aft.	Carnegie Hall

COMPOSITIONS PERFORMED

(a) First performance.
(b) First performance in North America.
(c) First performance in New York.
(d) First performance by the Society.
(e) First concert performance.
(f) First performance in this arrangement.

BACH—Passion According to St. Matthew: Mar. 29, 30, 31; Apr. 1.

BACH-RESPIGHI—Passacaglia in C minor: Oct. 5, 6.

BACH, C. P. E.—Concerto for Stringed Instruments in D major (Arranged by Maximilian Steinberg): Jan. 25, 26.

BARBER—"Second Essay": Dec. 21, 22.

BEETHOVEN—Concerto for Piano and Orchestra in C minor, No. 3, Opus 37: Jan. 18, 19; Apr. 5, 6, 8.
Concerto for Piano and Orchestra in G major, No. 4, Opus 58: Dec. 9, 10.
Concerto for Piano and Orchestra in E-flat major, No. 5 ("Emperor"), Opus 73: Mar. 22, 23; Apr. 9.
Concerto for Violin and Orchestra in D major, Opus 61: Jan. 11, 12, 14.
Overture, "Coriolanus," Opus 62: Apr. 5, 6, 8.
Overture to "Egmont," Opus 84: Dec. 9, 10; Apr. 9.
Overture to "Leonore," No. 3, Opus 72-A: Nov. 2, 3.
Overture to "Prometheus," Opus 43: Nov. 4, 5.
Quintet for Piano, Oboe, Clarinet, Bassoon and Horn in E-flat major, Opus 16: Mar. 13.
Romance, for Violin and Orchestra in G major, Opus 40: Mar. 18.
Symphony in C major, No. 1, Opus 21: Nov. 9, 10.

‡ One number conducted by VIRGIL THOMSON.
* Concert for Young People, under the direction of RUDOLPH GANZ.
§ One number conducted by ARTHUR KREUTZ.
** Concert canceled due to the death of President Franklin D. Roosevelt.
⚹ One number conducted by IGNACE STRASFOGEL.

Symphony in D major, No. 2, Opus 36: Jan. 25, 26, 27.
Symphony in E-flat major, No. 3 ("Eroica"), Opus 55: Dec. 14, 15.
First and Fourth Movements from Symphony No. 3: Dec. 19.
Symphony in C minor, No. 5, Opus 67: Mar. 8, 9, 11.
Symphony in A major, No. 7, Opus 92: Oct. 5, 6, 8; Nov. 13, 25; Jan. 22; Apr. 9.
Second Movement (Allegretto): Apr. 13, 15.

BERLIOZ—Overture to "Benvenuto Cellini," Opus 23: Nov. 11, 12.
Three Excerpts from "The Damnation of Faust":
    I. Ballet of the Sylphs: Oct. 28, 29; Nov. 13, 25; Jan. 22.
    II. Minuet of Will-o'-the-Wisps: Oct. 28, 29; Nov. 13, 25; Jan. 22.
    III. Rákóczy March: Oct. 28, 29; Nov. 25; Jan. 22.

BIZET—Symphony in C major: Oct. 26, 27, 28, 29.

BLOCH—"Schelomo" ("Solomon"), Hebrew Rhapsody for 'Cello and Orchestra: Nov. 26.
Symphony, "Israel," for Soprano, Contralto, Baritone and Women's Chorus: Dec. 28, 29, 30, 31.

BORODIN—Orchestral Sketch, "On the Steppes of Central Asia": Mar. 1, 2.
Symphony in B minor, No. 2, Opus 5: Oct. 12, 13.

BRAHMS—Concerto for Piano and Orchestra in D minor, No. 1, Opus 15: Nov. 4, 5.
Concerto for Violin and Orchestra in D major, Opus 77: Jan. 4, 5; Mar. 24, 25.
Symphony in C minor, No. 1, Opus 68: Jan. 4, 5, 6, 7; Mar. 7.
Symphony in D major, No. 2, Opus 73: Apr. 13, 15.
Symphony in F major, No. 3, Opus 90: Nov. 2, 3.
Symphony in E minor, No. 4, Opus 98: Dec. 21, 22, 24.
Variations on a Theme by Haydn, Opus 56-A: Jan. 4, 5.

BRUCH—Concerto for Violin and Orchestra in G minor, No. 1, Opus 26: Dec. 30, 31.

BRUCKNER—Symphony in E major, No. 7: Apr. 5, 6.

CARPENTER—"Sea Drift": Oct. 5 (f), 6, 8.

CHERUBINI—Overture to the Ballet-Opera, "Anacreon": Jan. 18, 19.

CLEMENTI-CASELLA—Symphony in D, No. 2: Nov. 16 (d), 17; Jan. 14.

COUPERIN—Prelude and Allegro (Arr. by Darius Milhaud): Oct. 26, 27, 28, 29.

CRESTON—Symphony No. 2: Feb. 15 (a), 16, 18.

DEBUSSY—"Images pour Orchestre": Nov. 2, 3.
"La Mer" ("The Sea"): Three Symphonic Sketches: Oct. 26, 27; Dec. 9, 10.
Prelude, "L'Après-Midi d'un Faune": Jan. 25, 26.
Two Nocturnes: "Nuages," "Fêtes": Nov. 4, 5.

DUKAS—Scherzo, "L'Apprenti Sorcier" (After a Ballad by Goethe): Feb. 15, 16, 18.

DVORAK—Concerto for 'Cello and Orchestra in B minor, Opus 104: Jan. 6, 7.
Slavonic Dances:
    Opus 46, Nos. 1 and 3: Dec. 19; Mar. 13.
    Opus 72, Nos. 2 and 7: Mar. 13.

ELGAR—March, "Pomp and Circumstance": Nov. 30; Dec. 1, 2, 3.

FALLA—Three Dances from "El Sombrero de Tres Picos" ("The Three-Cornered Hat"):
The Neighbors: Nov. 24, 25, 26.
The Miller's Dance: Nov. 24, 25.
Final Dance: Nov. 24, 25, 26.

FAURE—Ballade, for Piano and Orchestra in F-sharp major, Opus 19: Mar. 8 (d), 9.

FOSS—Ode for Orchestra: Mar. 15 (a), 16.
"The Prairie," a Cantata for Mixed Chorus, Four Solo Voices and Orchestra: Jan. 18 (d), 19, 21.

FRANCK-O'CONNELL—"Pièce Héroïque": Nov. 9 (d), 10.

GANZ—Percussional Melee: Feb. 13.

GERSHWIN-GOULD—"I Got Rhythm": Oct. 5 (e), 6, 8.

GLINKA—Overture to "Russlan and Ludmilla": Feb, 1, 2, 3, 4.

GOLDMARK—Concerto for Violin and Orchestra in A minor, Opus 28: Dec. 28, 29.

HANDEL-HARTY—"Water Music Suite": Oct. 19, 20, 21; Nov. 13, 25; Jan. 22.

HARRIS—Symphony No. 3 (In One Movement): Jan. 25 (d), 26, 27.

HAYDN—Concerto for 'Cello and Orchestra in D major, Opus 101: Nov. 23, 24.
Concerto for Harpsichord and Orchestra in D major: Feb. 22, 23.
Symphony in D major, No. 93 (Salomon No. 2): Feb. 15, 16, 24, 25.
Symphony in C major, B. & H. No. 97 (Salomon No. 1): Mar. 8, 9.
Symphony in D major, "Clock," No. 101: Jan. 13.
"Toy" Symphony: Feb. 8, 9, 11.

HINDEMITH—Symphony, "Mathis der Maler": Nov. 9, 10.

HUÉ—Fantasy for Flute: Feb. 13.

IBERT—"Escales" ("Ports of Call"): Feb. 22, 23, 24, 25.

KABALEVSKY—Overture to "Colas Breugnon": Mar. 1, 2.

KREUTZ—Music for Symphony Orchestra (conducted by the Composer): Mar. 22 (e), 23.

LALO—"Symphonie Espagnole," for Violin and Orchestra, Opus 21: Mar. 3, 4.

LEKEU—"Fantaisie Contrapuntique sur un Cramignon Liégeois": Feb. 13.

LISZT—"Mephisto Waltz": Feb. 8, 9, 11.

MAHLER—"Das Lied von der Erde" ("The Song of the Earth"): Nov. 16, 17, 19.

MENDELSSOHN—Concerto for Violin and Orchestra in E minor, Opus 64: Oct. 19, 20, 22; Mar. 7.
Overture, "Ruy Blas," Opus 95: Dec. 28, 29, 30; Feb. 18.
Scherzo in G minor, from Octet for Strings, Opus 20: Apr. 8.
Symphony in D major, No. 5, Opus 107 ("Reformation"): Mar. 22, 23, 24, 25.

MILHAUD—Suite Symphonique, No. 2, from the music to Paul Claudel's play, "Protée" ("Proteus"): Nov. 9 (d), 10.

MOORE—"In Memoriam": Jan. 11 (c), 12.

MOUSSORGSKY-RAVEL—"Pictures at an Exhibition": Mar. 1, 2, 3, 4.

MOZART—Concerto for Piano and Orchestra in F major (K. 413): Feb. 22 (d), 23.
Concerto for Piano and Orchestra in D minor (K. 466): Dec. 24.
Concerto for Piano and Orchestra in C minor (K. 491): Oct. 26, 27.
Concerto for Piano and Orchestra in C major (K. 503): Dec. 21 (d), 22.
"Eine Kleine Nachtmusik," Serenade for String Orchestra (K. 525): Nov. 19.
Serenade in B-flat major, for Thirteen Wind Instruments (K. 361): Mar. 13.
Symphonie Concertante for Violin and Viola with Orchestra, in E-flat major: Feb. 13.
Symphony in D major, No. 35, "Haffner" (K. 385): Nov. 23, 24, 26.
Symphony in G minor, No. 40 (K. 550): Apr. 13, 15.
Symphony in C major, "Jupiter" (K. 551): Mar. 7.

PAGANINI—Concerto for Violin and Orchestra in D major, Opus 6: Feb. 8, 9, 11.

PISTON—"Fugue on a Victory Tune": Oct. 21 (a), 22.

POPPER—Requiem, for Three 'Celli and Orchestra: Feb. 13.

PROKOFIEFF—Concerto for Violin and Orchestra, in D major, No. 1, Opus 19: Mar. 15, 16, 18.

PROKOFIEFF-BYRNS—"Suite Diabolique": Nov. 11 (f), 12.

RACHMANINOFF—Concerto for Piano and Orchestra in F-sharp minor, No. 1, Opus 1: Jan. 28.
Concerto for Piano and Orchestra, in C minor, No. 2, Opus 18: Jan. 21.
Symphony in E minor, No. 2, Opus 27: Jan. 11, 12.

RAVEL—Choreographic Poem for Orchestra, "La Valse"; Jan. 25, 26, 28.
"Daphnis et Chloé," Suite No. 2: Dec. 28, 29, 30, 31.
Introduction and Allegro, for Harp, Flute, Clarinet and Strings: Feb. 13, 15, 16.
"Rapsodie Espagnole": Nov. 11, 12.

RESPIGHI—Symphonic Poem, "The Pines of Rome": Nov. 2, 3; Jan. 13.

ROSSINI—Overture to "L'Italiana in Algeri": Feb. 22, 23, 24, 25.

SAINT-SAENS—Concerto for Piano and Orchestra in C minor, No. 4, Opus 44: Oct. 28, 29.

SCHÖNBERG—"Ode to Napoleon," Opus 41-B, for Recitation, Piano and String Orchestra: Nov. 23 (a), 24, 26.

SCHUMAN, WILLIAM—Symphony No. 3: Oct. 19 (d), 20, 21, 22.

SCHUMANN—Concerto for 'Cello and Orchestra in A minor, Opus 129: Feb. 24, 25.
Symphony in D minor, No. 4, Opus 120: Mar. 15, 16, 18.

SHOSTAKOVICH—Symphony No. 5, Opus 47: Jan. 27, 28.
Symphony No. 8, Opus 65: Oct. 12, 13, 15.

SIBELIUS—Concerto for Violin and Orchestra in D minor, Opus 47: Nov. 11, 12.
"The Swan of Tuonela" (Tone Poem): Jan. 13.

SMETANA—Symphonic Poem, "Vltava" ("The Moldau") from the Cycle, "Ma Vlast" ("My Fatherland"): Dec. 14, 15, 17, 19.

SOUSA—March, "Stars and Stripes Forever": Dec. 19.

STILL—Symphonic Poem, "Old California": Nov. 4 (c), 5.

STRAUSS, JOHANN—"Emperor" Waltz: Feb. 13.

STRAUSS, RICHARD—Burleske, for Piano and Orchestra in D minor: Mar. 8, 9, 11.
Suite from "Der Rosenkavalier": Oct. 5 (a), 6, 8; Nov. 13, 25; Jan. 22; Apr. 9.
"Till Eulenspiegel's Merry Pranks, After the Old-Fashioned Roguish Manner—In Rondo Form," Opus 28: Dec. 14, 15, 17.
Tone Poem, "Don Juan," Opus 20: Nov. 4, 5.

STRAVINSKY—Circus Polka: Feb. 1 (d), 2, 3, 4.
Concerto for Piano and Wind Orchestra (with Double-Basses and Timpani): Feb. 1, 2.
Four Norwegian Moods: Feb. 1 (d), 2, 3, 4.
"Ode" in Three Parts, for Orchestra: Feb. 1 (d), 2.
"Scènes de Ballet": Feb. 3 (e), 4.

TARTINI—Concerto in D minor, for Violin and String Orchestra: Mar. 15 (d), 16.

THOMSON—"Symphony on a Hymn Tune" (conducted by the Composer): Feb. 22 (a), 23.

TSCHAIKOWSKY—Concerto for Piano and Orchestra in B-flat minor, No. 1, Opus 23: Feb. 18.
Concerto for Violin and Orchestra in D major, Opus 35: Dec. 7, 8, 17.
"Overture, 1812," Opus 49: Oct. 15.
Overture-Fantasy, "Romeo and Juliet": Oct. 21; Feb. 15, 16; Apr. 8.

Suite "Mozartiana," Opus 61, No. 4: Dec. 7, 8; Feb. 11.
Symphony in C minor, No. 2, Opus 17: Feb. 1, 2, 3, 4.
Symphony in E minor, No. 5, Opus 64: Mar. 1, 2, 3, 4.
Symphony in B minor, No. 6, Opus 74 ("Pathetic"): Dec. 7, 8.
Third Movement from Symphony No. 6 ("Pathetic"): Dec. 9, 10.

VAUGHAN WILLIAMS—Symphony in D major, No. 5: Nov. 30 (b); Dec. 1, 2, 3.

VILLA-LOBOS—From "Bachianas Brasileiras," No. 2: Toccata ("Little Train of the Caipira"): Oct. 19 (d), 20, 21, 22.
"Bachianas Brasileiras," No. 5, for Eight 'Celli and Soprano: Oct. 19, 20, 21.
Choros No. 8, for Orchestra and Two Pianos (conducted by the Composer): Feb. 8 (d), 9.
Choros No. 9 for Orchestra (conducted by the Composer): Feb. 8 (b), 9.

WAGNER—Siegfried's Death and Funeral Music from "Götterdämmerung": Jan. 13.
Prelude to "Die Meistersinger": Jan. 6, 7; Mar. 15, 16, 18.
Transformation Scene; "Good Friday Spell" from "Parsifal": Mar. 22, 23, 24, 25.
Prelude and "Love-Death" from "Tristan and Isolde": Nov. 11, 12.

WALTON—"Belshazzar's Feast," for Baritone, Chorus and Orchestra: Nov. 30 (d); Dec. 1, 2, 3.

WEBER—Concertstück, for Piano and Orchestra in F minor, Opus 79: Mar. 11.
Overture to "Euryanthe": Jan. 13.
Overture, "Jubel" ("Jubilee"): Nov. 9, 10.
Overture to "Oberon": Dec. 14, 15, 17, 19.

WOLF-FERRARI—Overture to the Opera "The Secret of Suzanne": Jan. 14.

WOOLDRIDGE—"A Solemn Hymn to Victory": Nov. 30 (a), Dec. 1, 2.

SOLOISTS

PIANO
CLAUDIO ARRAU: Mar. 8, 9, 11.
ALEXANDER BRAILOWSKY: Jan. 18, 19, 21.
ROBERT CASADESUS: Oct. 26, 27, 28, 29; Apr. 9.
RUDOLF FIRKUSNY: Mar. 22, 23.
LEON FLEISHER: Nov. 4, 5.
EUGENE ISTOMIN: Dec. 9, 10.
WANDA LANDOWSKA: Feb. 22, 23.
ARTUR SCHNABEL: Dec. 21, 22, 24.
RUDOLF SERKIN: Apr. 5, 6, 8.
ZADEL SKOLOVSKY: Feb. 18.
RAOUL SPIVAK: Feb. 8, 9.
EDWARD STEUERMANN: Nov. 23, 24, 26.
IGNACE STRASFOGEL: Feb. 8, 9.
GEORGE SZELL: Mar. 13.
JEANNE THERRIEN: Jan. 28.
BEVERIDGE WEBSTER: Feb. 1, 2.

VIOLIN
JOHN CORIGLIANO: Feb. 13; Mar. 24, 25, 29, 30, 31; Apr. 1.
ZINO FRANCESCATTI: Feb. 8, 9, 11.
JASCHA HEIFETZ: Jan. 11, 12, 14.
FRITZ KREISLER: Jan. 4, 5.
YEHUDI MENUHIN: Oct. 19, 20, 22.

NATHAN MILSTEIN: Dec. 28, 29, 30, 31; Mar. 7.
ERICA MORINI: Dec. 17.
RICARDO ODNOPOSOFF: Mar. 3, 4.
MICHAEL ROSENKER: Nov. 11, 12; Mar. 29, 30, 31; Apr. 1.
ISAAC STERN: Dec. 7, 8.
JOSEPH SZIGETI: Mar. 15, 16, 18.

VIOLA
WILLIAM LINCER: Feb. 13.

VIOLA DA GAMBA
JANOS SCHOLZ: Mar. 29, 30, 31; Apr. 1.

'CELLO
NAOUM DINGER: Feb. 13.
GREGOR PIATIGORSKY: Nov. 23, 24, 26.
LEONARD ROSE: Jan. 6, 7; Feb. 13.
JOSEPH SCHUSTER: Feb. 24, 25.
CARL STERN: Feb. 13.

FLUTE
JOHN WUMMER: Feb. 13, 15, 16; Mar. 29, 30, 31; Apr. 1.

OBOE
HAROLD GOMBERG: Mar. 13, 29, 30, 31; Apr. 1.

ENGLISH HORN
MICHEL NAZZI: Jan. 13.

CLARINET
SIMEON BELLISON: Feb. 13, 15, 16; Mar. 13.

BASSOON
WILLIAM POLISI: Mar. 13.

FRENCH HORN
JOSEPH SINGER: Mar. 13.

PERCUSSION
SAM BORODKIN: Feb. 13.
SAUL GOODMAN: Feb. 13.
ARTHUR LAYFIELD: Feb. 13.
ALBERT RICH: Feb. 13.
JACOB WOLF: Feb. 13.

HARP
THEODORE CELLA: Feb. 13, 15, 16.

ORGAN
EDOUARD NIES-BERGER: Mar. 29, 30, 31; Apr. 1.

HARPSICHORD
RALPH KIRKPATRICK: Mar. 29, 30, 31; Apr. 1.
WANDA LANDOWSKA: Feb. 22, 23.

VOCAL
LORENZO ALVARY: Mar. 29, 30, 31; Apr. 1.
JOHN BROWNLEE: Nov. 30; Dec. 1, 2, 3.

NADINE CONNER: Mar. 29, 30, 31; Apr. 1.
TODD DUNCAN: Jan. 18, 19, 21.
WILLIAM HAIN: Jan. 18, 19, 21; Mar. 29, 30, 31; Apr. 1.
MACK HARRELL: Nov. 23, 24, 26; Mar. 29, 30, 31; Apr. 1.
DOROTHY KIRSTEN: Oct. 19, 20, 21; Jan. 18, 19, 21.
CHARLES KULLMAN: Nov. 16, 17, 19.
NEVILLE LANDOR: Dec. 28, 29, 30, 31.
NAN MERRIMAN: Jan. 18, 19, 21.
BARBARA STEVENSON: Dec. 28, 29, 30, 31.
KERSTIN THORBORG: Nov. 16, 17, 19.
MARCELLA UHL: Dec. 28, 29, 30, 31.
FRANCESO VALENTINO: Mar. 29, 30, 31; Apr. 1.
JEAN WATSON: Mar. 29, 30, 31; Apr. 1.

CHORUS
CHORAL ENSEMBLE FROM THE TEMPLE EMANU-EL CHOIR: Dec. 28, 29, 30, 31.
JUNIOR CHOIR OF ST. MARGARET'S CHURCH: Mar. 29, 30, 31; Apr. 1.
THE WESTMINSTER CHOIR: Nov. 30; Dec. 1, 2, 3; Jan. 18, 19, 21; Mar. 29, 30, 31; Apr. 1.

•

THIRD SUMMER SEASON
1945

Concerts sponsored by the United States Rubber Company
Broadcast over the coast-to-coast network of the
Columbia Broadcasting System
Sunday afternoons at 3:00 P.M. at Carnegie Hall

Conductors

Fritz Reiner
April 22, 29.
Bruno Walter
May 6, 13, 20, 27.
Eugene Ormandy
June 3, 10; July 22, 29.

George Szell
June 17, 24; July 8, 15.
Artur Rodzinski
July 1
Dimitri Mitropoulos
August 5, 12.

SOLOISTS—SUMMER SEASON

PIANO
ALEXANDER BRAILOWSKY: Aug. 5.
ROBERT CASADESUS: Apr. 29.
PIERRE LUBOSHUTZ and GENIA NEME-NOFF, Duo-Pianists: July 15.

ARTUR RUBINSTEIN: May 27.
GYORGY SANDOR: Aug. 12.
ARTUR SCHNABEL: June 17.
RUDOLF SERKIN: June 3.

VIOLIN   **VOCAL**
JOHN CORIGLIANO: May 20.   EILEEN FARRELL, Dramatic Soprano:
ERICA MORINI: July 22.   May 6.

COMPOSITIONS PERFORMED—SUMMER SEASON

BACH—Concerto for Violin and Orchestra, No. 2, in F major: May 20.
Fantasy and Fugue in G minor (Transcribed by Dimitri Mitropoulos): Aug. 5.
Toccata in C major (Transcribed for Orchestra by Eugene Ormandy): July 29.

BEETHOVEN—Concerto for Piano and Orchestra in C major, No. 1, Opus 15:
June 3.
Concerto for Piano and Orchestra in C minor, No. 3, Opus 37: June 17.
Concerto for Piano and Orchestra in G major, No. 4, Opus 58: May 27.
Concerto for Piano and Orchestra in E-flat major, No. 5 (Emperor), Opus 73:
April 29.
Overture to "Leonore," No. 3, Opus 72-A: May 13.
Overture to "The Creatures of Prometheus," Opus 43: June 17.
Symphony in B-flat major, No. 4, Opus 60: May 27.
Symphony in C minor, No. 5, Opus 67: July 29.
Symphony in F major, No. 8, Opus 93: June 17.

BERLIOZ—Overture to "Benvenuto Cellini," Opus 23: May 6.
Three Excerpts from "The Damnation of Faust": May 6.

BRAHMS—Symphony in C minor, No. 1, Opus 68: May 13.
Symphony in D major, No. 2, Opus 73: June 24.
Symphony in E minor, No. 4, Opus 98: May 6.
Variations on a Theme by Haydn, Opus 56-A: July 29.

DVORAK—Symphony in E minor, No. 5, "From the New World," Opus 95:
July 8.
Three Slavonic Dances: No. 3, in A-flat; No. 10, in E minor; No. 1, in C major:
July 8.

GLAZOUNOFF—Concerto for Violin and Orchestra in A minor, Opus 82: July
22.

GLUCK—Orpheus (Ballet Music): May 13.

HANDEL—Aria, "I Know That My Redeemer Liveth," from "Messiah": May 13.
Concerto for Orchestra, in D major (Transcribed by Eugene Ormandy): June
3.

HAYDN—Symphony in G major, No. 88 (B. & H. No. 13): June 3.

LISZT—Concerto for Piano and Orchestra in E-flat major, No. 1: Aug. 5.

MENDELSSOHN—Symphony in A major, No. 4, Opus 90 ("Italian"): July 15.

MILHAUD—"Fantaisie sur 'Le Boeuf Sur Le Toit' ": Aug. 5.

MOUSSORGSKY—Prelude to "Khovanshchina": July 22.

MOZART—Concerto for Two Pianos and Orchestra in E-flat major (K. 365):
July 15.
"Eine Kleine Nachtmusik," Serenade for String Orchestra (K. 525): July 1.
Overture to "The Marriage of Figaro": April 29.
Symphony in G minor, No. 40 (K. 550): June 24.

RACHMANINOFF—Concerto for Piano and Orchestra in C minor, No. 2, Opus
18: Aug. 12.

RAVEL—"Valses Nobles et Sentimentales": Aug. 5.

SCHUBERT—Symphony in B minor, No. 8 (Unfinished): May 20.

SMETANA—Symphonic Poem, "Vltava" ("The Moldau"): July 8.

STRAUSS, RICHARD—"Till Eulenspiegel's Merry Pranks," Opus 28: April 29.
Tone-Poem, "Death and Transfiguration," Opus 24: May 20.

STRAVINSKY—Suite From "The Fire-Bird": April 22.

TSCHAIKOWSKY—Symphony in F minor, No. 4, Opus 36: July 22.
Symphony in E minor, No. 5, Opus 64: July 1.
Symphony in B minor, No. 6, Opus 74, ("Pathétique") : April 22.

WAGNER—Excerpts from "Die Meistersinger": (A) Prelude to Act III, (B) Dance of the Apprentices, (C) Entrance of the Masters: June 10.
Overture to "Die Meistersinger": April 29.
Overture and Venusberg Scene from "Tannhäuser": June 10.
Prelude to "Die Meistersinger": July 1.
Prelude and Love-Death from "Tristan und Isolde": June 10.
Siegfried's Death and Funeral Music from "Gotterdämmerung": June 10.

WEBER—Overture to "Der Freischütz": July 15.

1945–46 ONE HUNDRED FOURTH SEASON

Musical Director
ARTUR RODZINSKI

Guest Conductors
GEORGE SZELL
BRUNO WALTER
HOWARD HANSON
IGOR STRAVINSKY

Assistant Conductor
WALTER HENDL

Concerts for Young People
Conductor
RUDOLPH GANZ

CONCERTS

1945

Artur Rodzinski, Conductor

Oct.	4—Ev'g.	Carnegie Hall
Oct.	5—Aft.	Carnegie Hall
Oct.	7—Aft.	Carnegie Hall
Oct.	11—Ev'g.	Carnegie Hall
Oct.	12—Aft.	Carnegie Hall
Oct.	14—Aft.	Carnegie Hall
Oct.	18—Ev'g.	Carnegie Hall
Oct.	19—Aft.	Carnegie Hall
Oct.	20—Ev'g.	Carnegie Hall
Oct.	21—Aft.	Carnegie Hall
Oct.	25—Ev'g.	Carnegie Hall
Oct.	26—Aft.	Carnegie Hall
Oct.	27—Ev'g.	Carnegie Hall
Oct.	28—Aft.	Carnegie Hall

George Szell, Conductor

Nov.	1—Ev'g.	Carnegie Hall
Nov.	2—Aft.	Carnegie Hall
Nov.	3—Ev'g.	Carnegie Hall
Nov.	4—Aft.	Carnegie Hall

1945

Nov.	8—Ev'g.	Carnegie Hall
Nov.	9—Aft.	Carnegie Hall
Nov.	10—Ev'g.	Carnegie Hall
Nov.	11—Aft.	Carnegie Hall

Artur Rodzinski, Conductor

Nov.	13—Ev'g.	Bushnell Memorial Hall, Hartford, Conn.
Nov.	15—Ev'g.	Carnegie Hall
Nov.	16—Aft.	Carnegie Hall
*Nov.	17—Morn.	Carnegie Hall
Nov.	18—Aft.	Carnegie Hall
Nov.	22—Ev'g.	Carnegie Hall
Nov.	23—Aft.	Carnegie Hall
Nov.	24—Ev'g.	McCarter Theatre, Princeton, N. J.
Nov.	25—Aft.	Carnegie Hall
Nov.	29—Ev'g.	Carnegie Hall
Nov.	30—Aft.	Carnegie Hall
Dec.	1—Ev'g.	Carnegie Hall
Dec.	2—Aft.	Carnegie Hall

* Concert for Young People, under the direction of RUDOLPH GANZ.

1945
†Dec. 6—Ev'g.   Carnegie Hall
†Dec. 7—Aft.   Carnegie Hall

Walter Hendl, Conductor
Dec. 8—Ev'g.   Carnegie Hall

Artur Rodzinski, Conductor
Dec. 9—Aft.   Carnegie Hall

Bruno Walter, Conductor
Dec. 13—Ev'g.   Carnegie Hall
Dec. 14—Aft.   Carnegie Hall
*Dec. 15—Morn.   Carnegie Hall
Dec. 16—Aft.   Carnegie Hall

Leopold Stokowski, Conductor
Dec. 18—Ev'g.   Madison Square
                       Garden

Bruno Walter, Conductor
Dec. 20—Ev'g.   Carnegie Hall
Dec. 21—Aft.   Carnegie Hall
Dec. 23—Aft.   Carnegie Hall

Artur Rodzinski, Conductor
Dec. 27—Ev'g.   Carnegie Hall
Dec. 28—Aft.   Carnegie Hall
Dec. 30—Aft.   Carnegie Hall

1946
Jan. 3—Ev'g.   Carnegie Hall
Jan. 4—Aft.   Carnegie Hall
*Jan. 5—Morn.   Carnegie Hall
Jan. 6—Aft.   Carnegie Hall
Jan. 10—Ev'g.   Carnegie Hall
Jan. 11—Aft.   Carnegie Hall
Jan. 12—Ev'g.   Carnegie Hall
Jan. 13—Aft.   Carnegie Hall

Howard Hanson, Conductor
Jan. 17—Ev'g.   Carnegie Hall
Jan. 18—Aft.   Carnegie Hall
Jan. 19—Ev'g.   Carnegie Hall
Jan. 20—Aft.   Carnegie Hall

Igor Stravinsky, Conductor
Jan. 24—Ev'g.   Carnegie Hall
Jan. 25—Aft.   Carnegie Hall
Jan. 26—Ev'g.   Carnegie Hall
Jan. 27—Aft.   Carnegie Hall

George Szell, Conductor
Jan. 31—Ev'g.   Carnegie Hall
Feb. 1—Aft.   Carnegie Hall
Feb. 2—Ev'g.   Carnegie Hall
Feb. 3—Aft.   Carnegie Hall

1946
Artur Rodzinski, Conductor
Feb. 7—Ev'g.   Carnegie Hall
Feb. 8—Aft.   Carnegie Hall
¶Feb. 8—Ev'g.   Carnegie Hall
*Feb. 9—Morn.   Carnegie Hall
Feb. 10—Aft.   Carnegie Hall
Feb. 11—Ev'g.   Hotel Plaza,
                       New York, N. Y.
Feb. 14—Ev'g.   Carnegie Hall
Feb. 15—Aft.   Carnegie Hall
Feb. 17—Aft.   Carnegie Hall
‡Feb. 21—Ev'g.   Carnegie Hall
‡Feb. 22—Aft.   Carnegie Hall
Feb. 23—Ev'g.   Carnegie Hall
§Feb. 23—Ev'g.   Town Hall
Feb. 24—Aft.   Carnegie Hall
Feb. 28—Ev'g.   Carnegie Hall
Mar. 1—Aft.   Carnegie Hall
Mar. 2—Ev'g.   Carnegie Hall
‡Mar. 3—Aft.   Carnegie Hall

Bruno Walter, Conductor
Mar. 7—Ev'g.   Carnegie Hall
Mar. 8—Aft.   Carnegie Hall
*Mar. 9—Morn.   Carnegie Hall
Mar. 10—Aft.   Carnegie Hall
Mar. 11—Ev'g.   Hotel Plaza,
                       New York, N. Y.
Mar. 14—Ev'g.   Carnegie Hall
Mar. 15—Aft.   Carnegie Hall
Mar. 17—Aft.   Carnegie Hall

Artur Rodzinski, Conductor
Mar. 21—Ev'g.   Carnegie Hall
Mar. 22—Aft.   Carnegie Hall
Mar. 23—Ev'g.   Carnegie Hall
Mar. 24—Aft.   Carnegie Hall
Mar. 28—Ev'g.   Carnegie Hall
Mar. 29—Aft.   Carnegie Hall
Mar. 30—Ev'g.   Carnegie Hall
Mar. 31—Aft.   Carnegie Hall
Apr. 3—Ev'g.   Carnegie Hall
Apr. 4—Ev'g.   Carnegie Hall
Apr. 5—Aft.   Carnegie Hall
*Apr. 6—Morn.   Carnegie Hall
Apr. 7—Aft.   Carnegie Hall
Apr. 11—Ev'g.   Carnegie Hall
Apr. 12—Aft.   Carnegie Hall
Apr. 14—Aft.   Carnegie Hall
Apr. 18—Ev'g.   Carnegie Hall

† Two numbers conducted by DARIUS MILHAUD.
* Concert for Young People, under the direction of RUDOLPH GANZ.
¶ Pension Fund Concert by SZIGETI, ARRAU AND STRAVINSKY.
‡ One number conducted by ROY HARRIS.
§ Pension Fund Concert by BUDAPEST STRING QUARTET AND SIMEON BELLISON.

COMPOSITIONS PERFORMED

(a) First performance.
(b) First performance in America.
(c) First performance in New York.
(d) First performance by the Society.
(e) First concert performance.
(f) First concert performance in New York.
(g) First performance in this arrangement.

ALBENIZ-ARBOS—"Fête-Dieu à Séville," from the Suite, "Ibéria": Nov. 15, 16, 18.

BACH—Passion According to St. Matthew: Mar. 7, 8.

BACH-BYRNS—Chorale, "Awake Us, Lord," from Cantata No. 22: Oct. 4 (g), 5; Nov. 13, 24.

BARRYMORE, LIONEL—"Partita": Mar. 30 (c), 31.

BARTOK—Concerto for Orchestra: Jan. 31 (d); Feb. 1, 3.

BEETHOVEN—Concerto for Piano and Orchestra in C major, No. 1, Op. 15: Nov. 8, 9, 11.
Concerto for Piano and Orchestra in C minor, No. 3, Op. 37: Dec. 20, 21.
Concerto for Piano and Orchestra in G major, No. 4, Op. 58: Nov. 15, 16, 18.
Concerto for Violin and Orchestra in D major, Op. 61: Dec. 6, 7, 9.
Overture to "Egmont," Op. 84: Jan. 3, 4, 6.
Overture to "Leonore," No. 2, Op. 72: Nov. 8, 9, 10; Mar. 17.
Overture to "Leonore," No. 3, Op. 72-A: Mar. 31; Apr. 11, 12, 14.
Overture to "Prometheus," Op. 43: Nov. 11.
Symphony in E-flat major, No. 3 ("Eroica"), Op. 55: Oct. 4, 5, 7.
Symphony in C minor, No. 5, Op. 67: Oct. 11, 12, 14; Nov. 13, 24.
Symphony in A major, No. 7, Op. 92: Jan. 3, 4, 6.
Symphony in F major, No. 8, Op. 93: Nov. 8, 9, 10, 11.
Symphony in D minor, No. 9 with Final Chorus on Schiller's "Ode to Joy," Op. 125: Apr. 11, 12, 14.

BERGSMA, WILLIAM—"Music on a Quiet Theme": Jan. 17 (c), 18.

BERLIOZ—Overture, "The Roman Carnival," Op. 9: Jan. 31; Feb. 1, 2.

BLOCH—"Schelomo" ("Solomon"), Hebrew Rhapsody for 'Cello and Orchestra: Nov. 29, 30.

BOCCHERINI—Symphony in A major: Jan. 10, 11.

BORODIN—Polovtsian Dances, from "Prince Igor": Mar. 30; Apr. 7.

BRAHMS—Concerto for Piano and Orchestra in D minor, No. 1, Op. 15: Feb. 7, 8, 10.
Concerto for Piano and Orchestra in B-flat major, No. 2, Op. 83: Feb. 28; Mar. 1.
Concerto for Violin and Orchestra in D major, Op. 77: Mar. 28, 29, 31.
Symphony in C minor, No. 1, Op. 68: Feb. 14, 15, 17.
Symphony in F major, No. 3, Op. 90: Jan. 31; Feb. 1, 2, 3.
Symphony in E minor, No. 4, Op. 98: Mar. 10.

BRUCKNER—Symphony in D minor, No. 9 (Unfinished): Mar. 14, 15, 17.

CARPENTER—"The Seven Ages": Symphonic Suite: Nov. 29 (a), 30; Dec. 1, 2.

CHABRIER—Rhapsody for Orchestra, "España": Feb. 11.

CHAUSSON—Symphony in B-flat major, Op. 20: Mar. 28, 29, 30; Apr. 7.

COPLAND—"A Lincoln Portrait": Feb. 14 (d), 15, 17.
Orchestral Suite from the Ballet, "Appalachian Spring": Oct. 4 (e), 5, 7.

CORELLI—"Christmas Concerto": Concerto Grosso in G minor, No. 8, Op. 6, "Fatto per la Notte di Natale": Dec. 13, 14, 16.
Suite for Strings (Arr. by Ettore Pinelli): Feb. 7, 8, 10.

DEBUSSY—"La Mer" ("The Sea"): Three Symphonic Sketches: Nov. 15, 16.
Prelude: "L'Après-Midi d'un Faune": Mar. 11.
Two Nocturnes: "Nuages," "Fêtes": Dec. 27, 28, 30.

DOHNANYI—Variations on a Nursery Air, for Orchestra and Piano Obbligato,
Op. 25: Feb. 17.

DONIZETTI—"O mio Fernando," from "La Favorita": Apr. 4, 5.

DVORAK—Three Slavonic Dances: (No. 1 in C major, Op. 46; No. 3 in A-flat,
Op. 46; No. 10 in E minor, Op. 72): Feb. 2.

ENESCO—Roumanian Rhapsody in A major, No. 1, Op. 11: Feb. 14, 15, 17.

FAURE—"Après un Rêve" (Transcribed for Violoncello): Feb. 11.
Élégie: Mar. 11.

FITELBERG, JERZY—Nocturne for Orchestra: Mar. 28 (a), 29.

FRANCK—Symphony in D minor: Dec. 27, 28, 30.

GERSHWIN—"An American in Paris": Apr. 18.
Concerto for Piano and Orchestra in F major: Jan. 3, 4, 6; Apr. 18.
"Rhapsody in Blue": Apr. 18.
Songs from Porgy and Bess: "Bess, You Is My Woman Now," "Buzzard Song,"
"I Got Plenty of Nuttin'," "It Ain't Necessarily So," "My Man's Gone Now,"
"Summertime": Apr. 18.

GERSHWIN-BENNETT—"Porgy and Bess": A Symphonic Picture: Jan. 3, 4, 6.

GLAZOUNOFF—Concerto for Violin and Orchestra in A minor, Op. 82: Feb. 2,
3.

GLINKA—Overture to "Russlan and Ludmilla": Oct. 25, 26, 27.

GOULD—Pavane, Second Movement, from Symphonette No. 2: Feb. 11.
"Spirituals for String Choir and Orchestra": April 4, 5, 7.

GRIFFES—"The White Peacock," Op. 7, No. 1: Jan. 17, 18, 19, 20.

GRUENBERG—Concerto for Violin and Orchestra, Op. 47: Apr. 3 (c).

HANSON—Symphony No. 2, "Romantic," Op. 30: Jan. 17, 18, 19, 20.

HARRIS—"Memories of a Child's Sunday" (conducted by the Composer): Feb.
21 (a), 22, 23; (omitting First Movement) Mar. 3.

HAYDN—Concerto for Harpsichord and Orchestra, in D major: Dec. 1, 2.
Minuet and Variations: Mar. 11.

HUMPERDINCK—Prelude to "Haensel und Gretel": Dec. 27, 28, 30.

IBERT—Festival Overture: Mar. 28 (b), 29.

JANACEK—Sinfonietta: Feb. 7, 8.

KABALEVSKY—Concerto for Piano and Orchestra in G minor, No. 2, Op. 23:
Oct. 11 (f), 12, 14.

KERN—Scenario for Orchestra, on Themes from "Showboat": Feb. 7, 8, 10.

LIADOFF—"The Enchanted Lake," Legend for Orchestra, Op. 62: Mar. 21, 22,
23.

LOEFFLER—"A Pagan Poem" (After Virgil) for Orchestra with Piano, English
Horn and Three Trumpets Obbligati, Op. 14: Jan. 17, 18.

LOPATNIKOFF—Concerto for Violin and Orchestra, Op. 26: Oct. 27 (d).

MAHLER—Lieder eines Fahrenden Gesellen ("Songs of a Wayfarer"): Apr. 4,
5.
Symphony in D major, No. 1: Oct. 18, 19, 20, 21.
Symphony No. 9: Dec. 20 (d), 21.

MENDELSSOHN—Concerto for Violin and Orchestra in E minor, Op. 64: Jan.
10, 11; Mar. 23; Apr. 3.
Excerpts from the Music to "A Midsummer Night's Dream":
Overture: Dec. 6, 7, 8, 9.

Nocturne: Dec. 6, 7, 9.
Intermezzo: Dec. 6, 7, 9.
Scherzo: Dec. 6, 7, 8, 9.

MENNIN, PETER—Folk Overture: Jan. 19 (c), 20.

MILHAUD—"Le Bal Martiniquais" (conducted by the Composer): Dec. 6 (a), 7.

Suite Française (conducted by the Composer): Dec. 6 (d), 7.

MOUSSORGSKY—Prelude to "Khovanshchina": Jan. 12, 13.

MOZART—Concerto for Piano and Orchestra in A major (K. 488): Mar. 3.
Concerto for Piano and Orchestra in E-flat major (K. 482): Dec. 1, 2.
Concerto for Violin and Orchestra in D major (K. 218): Dec. 16.
"Eine Kleine Nachtmusik," Serenade for String Orchestra (K. 525): Mar. 11.
Overture to "The Marriage of Figaro": Feb. 11.
Sinfonia Concertante for Violin and Viola with Orchestra in E-flat major (K. 364): Mar. 10.
Symphony in C major, "Jupiter" (K. 551): Nov. 1, 2, 3, 4.
Symphony in D major, No. 38 (K. 504): Mar. 11.
Symphony in E-flat major, No. 39 (K. 543): Dec. 23.

PFITZNER—Three Preludes from "Palestrina": Mar. 14, 15.

PISTON—Suite from the Ballet "The Incredible Flutist": Jan. 17 (d), 18, 19, 20.
Symphony No. 2: Nov. 15 (d), 16, 18.

POPPER—Vito, Op. 54, No. 5 (Spanish Dance): Feb. 11.

PROKOFIEFF—"Alexander Nevsky," Musical Pictures of Ancient Russian History: Dec. 18.
Concerto for Piano and Orchestra in D-flat major, No. 1, Op. 10: Mar. 30 (f).
Concerto for Piano and Orchestra in C major, No. 3, Op. 26: Oct. 20.
Concerto for Violin and Orchestra in G minor, No. 2, Op. 63: Jan. 12 (d), 13.
"Summer Day," Children's Suite for Little Symphony, Op. 65-B: Oct. 25 (b), 26, 27.
Symphony No. 5, Op. 100: Mar. 21 (d), 22, 23, 24.

PURCELL—Dido's Lament, from "Dido and Aeneas" (Transcribed for Viola): Feb. 11.

RACHMANINOFF—Concerto for Piano and Orchestra in C minor, No. 2, Op. 18: Dec. 8; Feb. 21, 22, 24.
Concerto for Piano and Orchestra in D minor, No. 3, Op. 30: Mar. 2.
Rhapsody on a Theme of Paganini, for Piano and Orchestra, Op. 43: Oct. 25, 26, 28.

RAVEL—Concerto in G major, for Piano and Orchestra: Feb. 11.
"Daphnis and Chloe": Ballet in One Act—Orchestral Excerpts; Second Suite: Oct. 4, 5, 7.
"La Valse," Choreographic Poem for Orchestra: Nov. 10.

ROGERS, BERNARD—"In Memory of Franklin Delano Roosevelt": Apr. 11 (a), 12, 14.

SAINT-SAENS—Allegro Appassionato: Feb. 11.
Introduction and Rondo Capriccioso: Feb. 11.

SCHELLING—"A Victory Ball," Fantasy for Orchestra: Oct. 11, 12, 14; Nov. 13, 24.

SCHOENBERG—Theme and Variations for Orchestra in G minor, Op. 43-B: Nov. 1 (c), 2, 3.

SCHUBERT—Symphony in C major, No. 7: Nov. 29, 30; Dec. 8.

SCHUMANN—Symphony in B-flat major, No. 1, Op. 38: Dec. 13, 14, 16.

SHOSTAKOVICH—Symphony No. 5, Op. 47: Feb. 21, 22, 23, 24.

SIBELIUS—Concerto for Violin and Orchestra in D minor, Op. 47: Apr. 7.
Symphony in A minor, No. 4, Op. 63: Feb. 28; Mar. 1, 2, 3.

SOUSA—March, "Stars and Stripes Forever": Mar. 3.

SPIRITUALS—"Sometimes I Feel like a Motherless Child": Apr. 4, 5.
"Ride On, King Jesus": Apr. 4, 5.

STILL—"In Memoriam: The Colored Soldiers Who Died for Democracy":
Nov. 3.
Poem for Orchestra: Apr. 4 (c), 5.

STRAUSS, JOHANN—Waltz, "Tales from the Vienna Woods": Nov. 13, 18, 24.

STRAUSS, RICHARD—"Don Quixote" (Introduction, Theme with Variations
and Finale); Fantastic Variations on a Theme of Knightly Character, Op. 35:
Nov. 1, 2, 4.
"Symphonia Domestica," Op. 53: Dec. 13, 14, 23.
"Till Eulenspiegel's Merry Pranks, After the Old-Fashioned Roguish Manner—
in Rondo Form," Op. 28: Oct. 11, 12, 14; Nov. 13, 24.

STRAVINSKY—Fair Scenes from "Petrouchka" (First and Last Tableaux):
Jan. 26, 27.
"Fireworks" ("Feu d'Artifice"), A Fantasy for Orchestra, Op. 4: Jan. 26, 27.
"Scènes de Ballet": Jan. 24, 25, 26, 27.
Suite from "The Firebird" ("L'Oiseau de Feu"): Nov. 10; New Augmented Ver-
sion: Jan. 24, 25.
Symphony in Three Movements: Jan. 24 (a), 25, 26, 27.

SZYMANOWSKI—Concerto for Violin and Orchestra in One Movement, Op.
35: Feb. 14 (d), 15.

TSCHAIKOWSKY—Concerto for Piano and Orchestra in B-flat minor, No. 1,
Op. 23: Mar. 21, 22, 24.
Concerto for Violin and Orchestra in D major, Op. 35: Oct. 18, 19, 21; Feb. 23.
"Marche Slave," Op. 31; Feb. 10.
Overture-Fantasy, "Romeo and Juliet": Mar. 3; Apr. 3, 4, 5.
Polonaise from the Opera "Eugene Onegin": Oct. 28.
Suite from the Ballet, "The Nutcracker," Op. 71-A: Dec. 27, 28, 30.
Suite "Mozartiana," Op. 61, No. 4: Dec. 1; Theme and Variations only, Dec. 2.
Symphony in F minor, No. 4, Op. 36: Jan. 10, 11, 12, 13.
Symphony in E minor, No. 5, Op. 64: Oct. 25, 26, 27, 28.

VAUGHAN WILLIAMS—Fantasia on a Theme by Thomas Tallis for Double
String Orchestra: Mar. 14, 15.

VIVALDI-SILOTI—Concerto Grosso in D minor, Op. 3, No. 11: Feb. 28; Mar.
1, 2.

WAGNER—"A Siegfried Idyl": Nov. 3.
Funeral Music, from "Goetterdaemmerung": Nov. 22, 23, 25.
Immolation Scene, from "Goetterdaemmerung": Nov. 22, 23, 25.
Prelude to "Lohengrin": Oct. 14.
Prelude to "Die Meistersinger": Dec. 9.
Entrance of the Gods into Valhalla, from "Das Rheingold": Nov. 22, 23, 25.
"Waldweben" ("Forest Murmurs"), from "Siegfried": Nov. 22, 23, 25.
Overture to "Tannhaeuser": Nov. 3, 4.
Act III, "Die Walkuere": Nov. 22, 23, 25.

WEBER—Overture to "Der Freischuetz": Apr. 3, 7.
Overture to "Oberon": Oct. 18, 19, 20, 21.

WIENIAWSKI—Concerto for Violin and Orchestra in D minor, No. 2, Op. 22:
Jan. 19, 20.

WOLF-FERRARI—Intermezzo from "Jewels of the Madonna": Feb. 11.
Overture to "The Secret of Suzanne": Nov. 29, 30.

SOLOISTS

PIANO
CLAUDIO ARRAU: Nov. 8, 9, 11.
ALEXANDER BRAILOWSKY: Feb. 21, 22, 24.
ROBERT CASADESUS: Nov. 15, 16, 18.
RUDOLF FIRKUSNY: Dec. 20, 21.
WALTER HENDL: Jan, 3, 4, 6, 17, 18; Feb. 11.
WILLIAM KAPELL: Oct. 25, 26, 28.
WANDA LANDOWSKA: Dec. 1, 2.
OSCAR LEVANT: Apr. 18.
LOUISE MEISZNER: Feb. 17.
MARISA REGULES: Mar. 2.
NADIA REISENBERG: Oct. 11, 12, 14.
ARTUR RUBINSTEIN: Mar. 21, 22, 24.
GYORGY SANDOR: Dec. 8.
ARTUR SCHNABEL: Feb. 28; Mar. 1, 3.
RUDOLF SERKIN: Feb. 7, 8, 10.
ZADEL SKOLOVSKY: Oct. 20.
HILDE SOMER: Mar. 30.

VIOLIN
JOHN CORIGLIANO: Feb. 11, 14, 15; Mar. 7, 8, 10.
ZINO FRANCESCATTI: Mar. 28, 29, 31.
JOSEPH FUCHS: Oct. 27.
JASCHA HEIFETZ: Apr. 3.
BRONISLAW HUBERMAN: Dec. 16.
FRITZ KREISLER: Jan. 10, 11.
YEHUDI MENUHIN: Dec. 6, 7, 9.
NATHAN MILSTEIN: Oct. 18, 19, 21.
MICHAEL ROSENKER: Feb. 2, 3; Mar. 7, 8.
ANGEL REYES: Mar. 23.
TOSSY SPIVAKOVSKY: Feb. 23.
ISAAC STERN: Jan. 19, 20.
PATRICIA TRAVERS: Jan. 12, 13.
CAMILLA WICKS: Apr. 7.

VIOLA
WILLIAM LINCER: Nov. 1, 2, 4; Feb. 11; Mar. 10.

VIOLA DA GAMBA
WALTER SCHEFFLER: Mar. 7, 8.

'CELLO
LEONARD ROSE: Nov. 1, 2, 4, 29, 30; Feb. 11; Mar. 11.

FLUTE
JOHN WUMMER: Mar. 7, 8.

OBOE
HAROLD GOMBERG: Mar. 7, 8.

ENGLISH HORN
MICHEL NAZZI: Jan. 17, 18.

TRUMPETS
WILLIAM VACCHIANO: Jan. 17, 18.
NATHAN PRAGER: Jan. 17, 18.
JAMES SMITH: Jan. 17, 18.

ORGAN
EDOUARD NIES-BERGER: Mar. 7, 8.

HARPSICHORD
WANDA LANDOWSKA: Dec. 1, 2.
YELLA PESSL: Mar. 7, 8.

VOCAL
THELMA ALTMAN: Nov. 22, 23, 25.
LORENZO ALVARY: Mar. 7, 8.
MARIAN ANDERSON: Apr. 4, 5.
ANNE BROWN: Apr. 18.
NADINE CONNER: Mar. 7, 8.
DONALD DAME: Apr. 11, 12, 14.
DORIS DOE: Nov. 22, 23, 25.
DORIS DOREE: Nov. 22, 23, 25.
TODD DUNCAN: Apr. 11, 12, 14, 18.
WELLINGTON EZEKIEL: Mar. 7, 8.
WILLIAM HAIN: Mar. 7, 8.
MACK HARRELL: Mar. 7, 8.
MARGARET HARSHAW: Nov. 22, 23, 25; Mar. 7, 8.
BEAL HOBER: Nov. 22, 23, 25.
HERBERT JANSSEN: Nov. 22, 23, 25.
DOROTHY KIRSTEN: Apr. 11, 12, 14.
NAN MERRIMAN: Apr. 11, 12, 14.
JEANNE PALMER: Nov. 22, 23, 25.
MAXINE STELLMAN: Nov. 22, 23, 25.
JENNIE TOUREL: Dec. 18.
HELEN TRAUBEL: Nov. 22, 23, 25.
THELMA VOTIPKA: Nov. 22, 23, 25.

SPEAKER
KENNETH SPENCER: Feb. 14, 15, 17

CHORUS
JUNIOR CHOIR OF ST. MARGARET'S CHURCH: Mar. 7, 8.
THE WESTMINSTER CHOIR: Dec. 18; Mar. 7, 8; Apr. 11, 12, 14.

SOLOISTS AT PENSION FUND CONCERTS OF CHAMBER MUSIC

CLAUDIO ARRAU
IGOR STRAVINSKY } Feb. 8
JOSEPH SZIGETI

SIMEON BELLISON
BUDAPEST STRING QUARTET } Feb. 23

1946–47 ONE HUNDRED FIFTH SEASON

Conductors
EFREM KURTZ
CHARLES MUENCH
ARTUR RODZINSKI
MANUEL ROSENTHAL
LEOPOLD STOKOWSKI
GEORGE SZELL
BRUNO WALTER

Assistant Conductor
WALTER HENDL

Concerts for Young People
Conductor
RUDOLPH GANZ

Guest Conductor, LEOPOLD STOKOWSKI

CONCERTS

1946

Artur Rodzinski, Conductor

Oct.	3—Ev'g.	Carnegie Hall
Oct.	4—Aft.	Carnegie Hall
Oct.	5—Ev'g.	Norwalk High School, Norwalk, Conn.
Oct.	6—Aft.	Carnegie Hall
Oct.	10—Ev'g.	Carnegie Hall
Oct.	11—Aft.	Carnegie Hall
Oct.	12—Ev'g.	McCarter Theatre, Princeton, N. J.
Oct.	13—Aft.	Carnegie Hall
Oct.	17—Ev'g.	Carnegie Hall
Oct.	18—Aft.	Carnegie Hall
Oct.	19—Ev'g.	Carnegie Hall
Oct.	20—Aft.	Carnegie Hall
Oct.	24—Ev'g.	Carnegie Hall
Oct.	25—Aft.	Carnegie Hall
Oct.	26—Ev'g.	Carnegie Hall
Oct.	27—Aft.	Carnegie Hall
Oct.	31—Ev'g.	Carnegie Hall
Nov.	1—Aft.	Carnegie Hall

Walter Hendl, Conductor

Nov.	2—Ev'g.	Carnegie Hall

Artur Rodzinski, Conductor

†Nov.	3—Aft.	Carnegie Hall
Nov.	7—Ev'g.	Carnegie Hall
Nov.	8—Aft.	Carnegie Hall
Nov.	9—Ev'g.	Carnegie Hall
Nov.	10—Aft.	Carnegie Hall
Nov.	14—Ev'g.	Carnegie Hall
Nov.	15—Aft.	Carnegie Hall

1946

Nov.	17—Aft.	Carnegie Hall
Nov.	19—Ev'g.	Bushnell Memorial Hall, Hartford, Conn.
Nov.	21—Ev'g.	Carnegie Hall
Nov.	22—Aft.	Carnegie Hall
*Nov.	23—Morn.	Carnegie Hall
Nov.	24—Aft.	Carnegie Hall
Nov.	28—Ev'g.	Carnegie Hall
Nov.	29—Aft.	Carnegie Hall
Nov.	30—Ev'g.	Carnegie Hall
Dec.	1—Aft.	Carnegie Hall

Manuel Rosenthal, Conductor

Dec.	5—Ev'g.	Carnegie Hall
Dec.	6—Aft.	Carnegie Hall

Artur Rodzinski, Conductor

Dec.	7—Ev'g.	Carnegie Hall
Dec.	8—Aft.	Carnegie Hall

George Szell, Conductor

Dec.	12—Ev'g.	Carnegie Hall
Dec.	13—Aft.	Carnegie Hall
*Dec.	14—Morn.	Carnegie Hall
Dec.	15—Aft.	Carnegie Hall
Dec.	16—Ev'g.	Hotel Plaza, New York, N. Y.
Dec.	19—Ev'g.	Carnegie Hall
Dec.	20—Aft.	Carnegie Hall
Dec.	22—Aft.	Carnegie Hall

Leopold Stokowski, Conductor

Dec.	26—Ev'g.	Carnegie Hall
Dec.	27—Aft.	Carnegie Hall
Dec.	29—Aft.	Carnegie Hall

† One number conducted by Walter Hendl.
* Concert for Young People, under the direction of Rudolph Ganz.

1947

Jan. 2—Ev'g. Carnegie Hall
Jan. 3—Aft. Carnegie Hall
*Jan. 4—Morn. Carnegie Hall
Jan. 5—Aft. Carnegie Hall
Jan. 9—Ev'g. Carnegie Hall
Jan. 10—Aft. Carnegie Hall
Jan. 11—Ev'g. Carnegie Hall
Jan. 12—Aft. Carnegie Hall
Jan. 16—Ev'g. Carnegie Hall
Jan. 17—Aft. Carnegie Hall
Jan. 18—Ev'g. Carnegie Hall
Jan. 19—Aft. Carnegie Hall

Charles Muench, Conductor

Jan. 23—Ev'g. Carnegie Hall
Jan. 24—Aft. Carnegie Hall
Jan. 25—Ev'g. Carnegie Hall
Jan. 26—Aft. Carnegie Hall
Jan. 30—Ev'g. Carnegie Hall
Jan. 31—Aft. Carnegie Hall
Feb. 1—Ev'g. Carnegie Hall
Feb. 2—Aft. Carnegie Hall

Bruno Walter, Conductor

Feb. 6—Ev'g. Carnegie Hall
Feb. 7—Aft. Carnegie Hall
*Feb. 8—Morn. Carnegie Hall
Feb. 9—Aft. Carnegie Hall
Feb. 11—Ev'g. Municipal Auditorium, Springfield, Mass.
Feb. 13—Ev'g. Carnegie Hall
Feb. 14—Aft. Carnegie Hall
Feb. 16—Aft. Carnegie Hall

Leopold Stokowski, Conductor

Feb. 20—Ev'g. Carnegie Hall
Feb. 21—Aft. Carnegie Hall
Feb. 22—Ev'g. Carnegie Hall
Feb. 23—Aft. Carnegie Hall

1947

Walter Hendl, Conductor

Feb. 27—Ev'g. Carnegie Hall
Feb. 28—Aft. Carnegie Hall
Mar. 1—Ev'g. Carnegie Hall
Mar. 2—Aft. Carnegie Hall

Leopold Stokowski, Conductor

Mar. 4—Ev'g. Memorial Auditorium, Worcester, Mass.

Bruno Walter, Conductor

Mar. 6—Ev'g. Carnegie Hall
Mar. 7—Aft. Carnegie Hall
*Mar. 8—Morn. Carnegie Hall
Mar. 9—Aft. Carnegie Hall

Leopold Stokowski, Conductor

Mar. 10—Ev'g. Hotel Plaza, New York, N. Y.
Mar. 13—Ev'g. Carnegie Hall
Mar. 14—Aft. Carnegie Hall
Mar. 16—Aft. Carnegie Hall

Efrem Kurtz, Conductor

Mar. 20—Ev'g. Carnegie Hall
Mar. 21—Aft. Carnegie Hall
Mar. 22—Ev'g. Carnegie Hall
Mar. 23—Aft. Carnegie Hall
Mar. 27—Ev'g. Carnegie Hall
Mar. 28—Aft. Carnegie Hall
Mar. 29—Ev'g. Carnegie Hall
Mar. 30—Aft. Carnegie Hall

Leopold Stokowski, Conductor

Apr. 3—Ev'g. Carnegie Hall
Apr. 4—Aft. Carnegie Hall
**Apr. 5—Morn. Carnegie Hall
Apr. 6—Aft. Carnegie Hall
Apr. 10—Ev'g. Carnegie Hall
Apr. 11—Aft. Carnegie Hall
Apr. 12—Ev'g. Carnegie Hall
Apr. 13—Aft. Carnegie Hall
‡May 5—Ev'g. Town Hall

COMPOSITIONS PERFORMED

(a) First performance anywhere.
(b) First performance in America.
(c) First performance in New York.
(d) First performance by the Society.
(e) First complete performance.
(f) First performance in New York in this version.

ALBENIZ—Fête-Dieu à Séville: Mar. 13, 14, 16.

BACH—Brandenburg Concerto in F major, No. 2, for Solo Flute, Oboe, Trumpet, Violin and String Orchestra: Jan. 16, 17, 18, 19.

---

* Concert for Young People, under the direction of Rudolph Ganz.
** Concert for Young People, under the direction of Leopold Stokowski.
‡ Pension Fund Concert by Casadesus and Francescatti.

Chorale-Prelude, "Christ lag in Todesbanden" ("In the bonds of death Christ lay"): Apr. 3, 4, 6.
Chorale-Prelude, "Ich ruf' zu dir": Jan. 19.
Chorale-Prelude, "Wir glauben all' an einen Gott": Dec. 26, 27, 29.
Fugue in G minor (the shorter): Jan. 16, 17, 19.
Geistliches Lied, "Komm süsser Tod": Jan. 16, 17, 18, 19; Mar. 4.
Geistliches Lied, "Mein Jesu": Mar. 10.
Passacaglia and Fugue in C minor: Jan. 16, 17, 19.
Preludio from the Partita in E major for String Orchestra: Jan. 19; Mar. 10.
Toccata and Fugue in D minor: Feb. 20, 21, 22; Mar. 4.

BACH-BLOOMFIELD—Toccata and Fugue, Intermezzo in C major: Oct. 3 (d), 4; only Fugue played: Oct. 5, 6, 12.

BACH-RESPIGHI—Chorale-Prelude, "Wachet auf, ruft uns die Stimme": Oct. 27.

BARBER—"Capricorn Concerto," Op. 21, for Flute, Oboe, Trumpet and Strings: Nov. 14 (d), 15.

BARRAUD—Concerto for Piano and Orchestra: Dec. 5 (b), 6.

BEETHOVEN—Concerto for Piano and Orchestra in C major, No. 1, Op. 15: Oct. 10, 11, 13.
Concerto for Piano and Orchestra in C minor, No. 3, Op. 37: Dec. 12, 13; Mar. 29.
Concerto for Piano and Orchestra in E-flat major, No. 5 ("Emperor"), Op. 73: Oct. 19.
Concerto for Violin and Orchestra in D major, Op. 61: Nov. 14, 15, 17.
Drei Equali, for Trombones: Mar. 10.
Marcia alla Turca, from the Music to the Play, "The Ruins of Athens," Op. 113: Nov. 17.
Overture, "Coriolanus": Jan. 30, 31; Feb. 1, 2.
Overture to "Egmont," Op. 84: Dec. 12, 13.
Overture to "Leonore," No. 3, Op. 72-A: Nov. 17, 19; Feb. 27, 28.
Overture to "Prometheus," Op. 43: Oct. 20, 24, 25, 26: Mar. 6, 7, 9.
Symphony in C major, No. 1, Op. 21: Oct. 10, 11; Nov. 17.
Symphony in D major, No. 2, Op. 36: Dec. 19, 20, 22.
Symphony in E-flat major, No. 3 ("Eroica"), Op. 55: Dec. 12, 13, 15.
Symphony in F major, No. 6 ("Pastoral"), Op. 68: Apr. 3, 4, 6.
Symphony in A major, No. 7, Op. 92: Feb. 11, 13, 14, 16.
Symphony in F major, No. 8, Op. 93: Jan. 16, 17, 18; Apr. 12.
Symphony in D minor, No. 9, Op. 125, with Final Chorus on Schiller's "Ode to Joy": Apr. 12.

BERLIOZ—Overture to "Benvenuto Cellini": Dec. 5, 6.
Symphonie Fantastique, No. 1, in C major, Op. 14-A: Jan. 30, 31.

BIZET—Suite from "L'Arlésienne," No. 1: Dec. 16.
Symphony in C major: Oct. 31; Nov. 1, 2, 3.

BRAHMS—Concerto for Violin and Orchestra in D major, Op. 77: Oct. 17, 18, 20; Jan. 30, 31.
Concerto for Violin and Violoncello with Orchestra, in A minor, Op. 102 (First Movement): Mar. 10.
Symphony in C minor, No. 1, Op. 68: Dec. 26, 27, 29.
Symphony in D major, No. 2, Op. 73: Oct. 3, 4, 5, 6, 12.
Symphony in F major, No. 3, Op. 90: Feb. 20, 21, 22, 23; Mar. 4.
Symphony in E minor, No. 4, Op. 98: Mar. 6, 7, 9.
Variations on a Theme by Joseph Haydn in B-flat major, Op. 56-A: Feb. 16.

CHOPIN—Concerto for Piano and Orchestra in E minor, No. 1, Op. 11: Feb. 6, 7, 9.
Concerto for Piano and Orchestra in F minor, No. 2, Op. 21: Nov. 9, 10.

CORELLI—"La Folia": Feb. 2.
Suite for String Orchestra (Arr. by Ettore Pinelli): Sarabande: Mar. 22, 23; Gigue: Mar. 22; Badinerie: Mar. 22, 23.

CRESTON—"Frontiers," Op. 34: Dec. 26 (d), 27; Mar. 4.

DEBUSSY—"Ibéria," Images pour Orchestre, No. 2: Jan. 23, 24, 25, 26.
"La Mer" ("The Sea"), Three Orchestral Sketches: Feb. 1, 2.
Excerpts from the Opera, "Pelléas et Mélisande": Oct. 31; Nov. 1.
Prelude to "The Afternoon of a Faun": Jan. 2, 3.
Soirée dans Grenade (Symphonic Transcription): Mar. 13, 14, 16.

DELIUS—Intermezzo, "The Walk to the Paradise Garden," from the Opera "A Village Romeo and Juliet": Oct. 20.

DELLO JOIO—Ricercari for Piano and Orchestra: Dec. 19 (a), 20.

DIAMOND, DAVID—Rounds for String Orchestra: Oct. 17 (d), 18, 19, 20.

FALLA—Suite from the Ballet-Pantomime, "El Amor Brujo" ("Love, the Sorcerer"): Jan. 5.

FRANCK—Symphonic Variations for Piano and Orchestra: Mar. 13, 14, 16.
Symphony in D minor: Nov. 2, 3.

GLAZOUNOFF—Concerto for Violin and Orchestra in A minor, Op. 82: Dec. 22.

GLINKA—"Memory of a Summer Night in Madrid": April 13.

HANDEL-HARTY—Suite, "Water Music": Jan. 23, 24, 25.

HAYDN—Serenade in C major: Mar. 10.
Symphony in G major, No. 13 (B. & H. No. 88): Mar. 20, 21, 30.
Symphony in G major, "Oxford" (B. & H. No. 92): Mar. 6, 7.

HINDEMITH—Symphony in E-flat, No. 1; Jan. 2, 3, 5.

HONEGGER—Symphony No. 3 for Large Orchestra, "Liturgique": Jan. 23 (b), 24, 26.

IBERT—"Escales" ("Ports of Call"): Oct. 24, 25, 26, 27.

d'INDY—Symphony for Orchestra and Piano on a French Mountain Song, Op. 25: Mar. 13, 14, 16.

KABALEVSKY—Overture to the Opera, "Colas Breugnon": Jan. 9, 10, 11, 12.

KHATCHATOURIAN—Concerto for Piano and Orchestra: Nov. 21, 22, 24.

KODALY—Suite from the Opera, "Háry János": Nov. 7, 8, 9, 10.

KORNGOLD—Concerto for Violin and Orchestra in D major, Op. 35: Mar. 27 (c), 28, 30.

LALO—Overture to the Opera, "Le Roi d'Ys": Oct. 31; Nov. 1, 10.
Symphonie Espagnole, for Violin and Orchestra, Op. 21: Jan. 2, 3, 5; Mar. 20, 21.

LISZT—Concerto for Piano and Orchestra in A major, No. 2: Dec. 15.

LULLY—Noce Villageoise (Adapted and orchestrated by Manuel Rosenthal): Dec. 5 (b), 6.

MAHLER—Symphony in D major, No. 1: Mar. 20, 21, 22, 23.
Symphony in C-sharp minor, No. 5: Feb. 6, 7.

MENDELSSOHN—Concerto for Violin and Orchestra in E minor, Op. 64: Mar. 6, 7, 9.
Overture and Scherzo from the Music to "A Midsummer Night's Dream": Nov. 7, 8, 9.

MENNIN—Symphony No. 3: Feb. 27 (a), 28.

MESSIAEN—"Hymne pour grand Orchestre": Mar. 13 (a), 14, 16.

MILHAUD—Concerto for Cello and Orchestra, No. 2: Nov. 28 (a), 29.
Saudades do Brasil: Jan. 2 (d), 3.

MOUSSORGSKY—"A Night on Bald Mountain," Fantasy for Orchestra: Apr. 10, 11, 13.
Entr'acte from the Opera, "Khovanshchina": Feb. 23.

MOZART—Concerto No. 3 for French Horn and Orchestra, in E-flat major (K. 447): Dec. 16.
Concerto for Piano and Orchestra in B-flat major (K. 595): Nov. 30; Dec. 1.
Concerto for Piano and Orchestra in C major (K. 415): Oct. 24 (d), 25, 27.
Concerto for Piano and Orchestra in F major, No. 19 (K. 459): Feb. 20, 21.
Concerto for Violin and Orchestra in D major, No. 4 (K. 218): Feb. 2.
Concerto for Violin and Orchestra in A major, No. 5 (K. 219): Mar. 27, 28, 30.
Funeral Music (K. 477): Dec. 19.
Overture to the Opera, "Don Giovanni": Jan. 2, 3, 5.
Symphony in G minor, No. 40 (K. 550): Nov. 28, 29.

POULENC—Concerto in G minor for Organ, String Orchestra and Kettle Drums: Jan. 25 (d).

PROKOFIEFF—Concerto for Violin and Orchestra in D major, No. 1, Op. 19: Mar. 22, 23.
"Scythian" Suite ("Ala and Lolli"), Op. 20: Apr. 10, 11, 13.
"Classical" Symphony in D major, Op. 25: Mar. 1, 2.
Symphony No. 5, Op. 100: Oct. 17, 18, 19.

RACHMANINOFF—Concerto for Piano and Orchestra in D minor, No. 3, Op. 30: Mar. 1, 2.
Symphonic Poem, "Isle of the Dead" ("Die Toteninsel"), Op. 29: Jan. 9, 10, 11, 12.

RAVEL—"Daphnis et Chloé," Suite No. 2: Jan. 23, 24, 25, 26; Mar. 27, 28, 29, 30.
Introduction and Allegro for Harp, Flute, Clarinet and Strings: Mar. 10.
"La Valse," Choreographic Poem for Orchestra: Mar. 13, 14, 16.

RESPIGHI—Symphonic Poem, "The Pines of Rome": Oct. 3, 4, 6.

RIMSKY-KORSAKOFF—Overture, "Russian Easter," Op. 36: Apr. 3, 4, 6.
Suite from the Opera, "Tsar Saltan": Nov. 21, 22, 30; Dec. 1.

RIVIER—Symphony No. 3, for Strings: Dec. 5 (d), 6.

ROSENTHAL—"La Fête du Vin": Dec. 5 (b), 6.
"Musique de Table," Orchestral Suite: Oct. 10 (b), 11, 13.

ROSSINI—Overture, "La Gazza Ladra": Mar. 23, 29.
Overture to the Opera, "Semiramide": Nov. 28, 29, 30; Dec. 1.

ROUSSEL—"Bacchus et Ariane," Suite No. 2, Op. 43: Feb. 1 (d), 2.
Symphony in G minor, No. 3, Op. 42: Feb. 1.

SAINT-SAENS—Concerto for 'Cello and Orchestra in A minor, Op. 33: Nov. 7, 8.
Excerpts from Septet for Solo Trumpet, Piano and Strings: Mar. 10.

SCHMITT—Poem for Oboe and Strings (Arr. by Hershey Kay): Mar. 10.

SCHUBERT—Entr'acte and Ballet Music from "Rosamunde": Dec. 16.
Symphony in B minor, No. 8 ("Unfinished"): Feb. 11.

SCHUMAN, WILLIAM—"Undertow," Choreographic Episodes for Orchestra: Oct. 3 (f), 4, 5, 6, 12.

SCHUMANN—Symphony in B-flat major, No. 1, Op. 38: Feb. 27, 28.
Symphony in C major, No. 2, Op. 61: Nov. 14, 15, 19.
Symphony in D minor, No. 4, Op. 120: Jan. 25, 26.

SHOSTAKOVICH—Concerto for Piano and Orchestra, Op. 35: Jan. 9, 10, 11, 12.
Symphony No. 1, Op. 10: Mar. 27, 28, 29.
Symphony No. 6, Op. 53: Apr. 10, 11, 13.
Symphony No. 9, Op. 70: Nov. 7 (c), 8, 9, 10, 19.

SIBELIUS—Symphony in C major, No. 3, Op. 52: Dec. 19, 20, 22.
Symphony in E-flat major, No. 5, Op. 82: Oct. 24, 25, 26, 27.
Tone Poem, "Finlandia," Op. 26, No. 7: Feb. 22, 23.
Tone Poem, "The Swan of Tuonela," Op. 22, No. 3: Dec. 26, 27.

SIEGMEISTER—"Harvest Evening" (Part 2 of "Prairie Legend"): Dec. 29 (a).
"Prairie Legend": Jan. 18 (e).

SMETANA—Furiant and Polka from "The Bartered Bride": Dec. 16.

STILL, WILLIAM GRANT—Festive Overture: Apr. 3 (c), 4, 6.

STRAUSS, JOHANN—Waltz, "The Beautiful Blue Danube": Dec. 16.

STRAUSS, RICHARD—Tone Poem, "Death and Transfiguration," Op. 24: Feb.
9, 11.
Tone Poem, "Don Juan," Op. 20: Mar. 1, 2.
Waltzes from "Der Rosenkavalier": Oct. 10, 11, 12, 13; Nov. 19.

STRAVINSKY—"Le Sacre du Printemps" ("The Consecration of the Spring"):
Nov. 28, 29, 30; Dec. 1.
Music from the Ballet Suite, "The Firebird": Apr. 10, 11, 13.
Suite from the Ballet, "Petrouchka": Feb. 27, 28.

STRIEGLER—Concerto for Timpani and Orchestra: Mar. 10.

TSCHAIKOWSKY—Concerto for Piano and Orchestra in B-flat minor, No. 1,
Op. 23: Feb. 22, 23.
Concerto for Violin and Orchestra in D major, Op. 35: Dec. 7, 8.
Marche Slave, Op. 31: Dec. 7, 8.
Overture-Fantasy, "Romeo and Juliet": Dec. 7, 8.
Solitude (Symphonic Transcription): Apr. 13.
Suite from the Ballet, "The Nutcracker," Op. 71-A (Arabian Dance omitted
at these performances): Dec. 7, 8.
Symphonic Poem, "Francesca da Rimini," Op. 32 (After Dante): Dec. 29.
Symphony in E minor, No. 5, Op. 64: Nov. 21, 22, 24.
Symphony in B minor, No. 6, Op. 74 ("Pathétique"): Jan. 9, 10, 11, 12.

TURNER—Fanfare, Chorale and Finale, for Four Horns, Three Trumpets, Three
Trombones and Tuba: Mar. 10.

VAUGHAN WILLIAMS—Symphony in D major, No. 5: Feb. 13, 14.

VICTORIA—Motet, "Jesu, Dulcis Memoria": Jan. 2, 3, 5.

VIEUXTEMPS—Concerto for Violin and Orchestra in D minor, No. 4, Op. 31:
Nov. 2, 3.

WAGNER—"A Faust Overture": Feb. 13, 14, 16.
Finale from "Goetterdaemmerung": Jan. 19.
Prelude to "Lohengrin": Feb. 20, 21.
Prelude to "Die Meistersinger": Mar. 1, 2.
Excerpts from "Die Meistersinger":
Prelude to Act III: Oct. 5, 20.
Dance of the Apprentices: Oct. 5, 12, 20; Nov. 19.
Entrance of the Masters: Oct. 5, 12, 20; Nov. 19.
Good Friday Music from "Parsifal": Apr. 3, 4, 6.
Finale of Act III, "Parsifal": Dec. 26, 27, 29.
Overture to "Tannhaeuser": Dec. 15.
Love Music from Acts II and III, "Tristan und Isolde": Jan. 16, 17, 18, 19;
Mar. 4.

WEBER—Overture to "Euryanthe": Oct. 13.
Overture to "Der Freischütz": Dec. 19, 20, 22.
Overture to the Opera, "Oberon": Feb. 9, 11.

WIENIAWSKI—Concerto for Violin and Orchestra in D minor, No. 2, Op. 22:
Oct. 26.

WOLF-FERRARI—Overture to the Opera, "The Secret of Suzanne": Nov. 2, 3.

SOLOISTS

PIANO
CLAUDIO ARRAU: Dec. 12, 13, 15.
ROBERT CASADESUS: Mar. 13, 14, 16.
NORMAN DELLO JOIO: Dec. 19, 20.
ANIA DORFMANN: Mar. 29.
WALTER HENDL: Mar. 10.
EUGENE ISTOMIN: Oct. 19.
MARYLA JONAS: Oct. 10, 11, 13.
WILLIAM KAPELL: Nov. 21, 22, 24.
WANDA LANDOWSKA: Oct. 24, 25, 27.
EUGENE LIST: Jan. 9, 10, 11, 12.
WITOLD MALCUZYNSKI: Mar. 1, 2.
HORTENSE MONATH: Feb. 20, 21.
ARTUR RUBINSTEIN: Feb. 6, 7, 9.
JESUS MARIA SANROMA: Feb. 22, 23.
E. ROBERT SCHMITZ: Dec. 5, 6.
ALEC TEMPLETON: Nov. 30; Dec. 1.
SYLVIA ZAREMBA: Nov. 9, 10.

VIOLIN
JOHN CORIGLIANO: Jan. 16, 17, 18, 19; Mar. 10, 20, 21.
MISCHA ELMAN: Nov. 14, 15, 17.
ZINO FRANCESCATTI: Mar. 6, 7, 9.
JOSEPH FUCHS: Dec. 7, 8.
JASCHA HEIFETZ: Mar. 27, 28, 30.
YEHUDI MENUHIN: Oct. 17, 18, 20.
DAVID NADIEN: Dec. 22.
MICHAEL ROSENKER: Nov. 2, 3.
ISAAC STERN: Mar. 22, 23.
HENRYK SZERYNG: Oct. 26.
JOSEPH SZIGETI: Jan. 30, 31; Feb. 2.
JACQUES THIBAUD: Jan. 2, 3, 5.

'CELLO
EDMUND KURTZ: Nov. 28, 29.
LEONARD ROSE: Nov. 7, 8; Mar. 10.

FLUTE
JOHN WUMMER: Nov. 14, 15; Jan. 16, 17, 18, 19; Mar. 10.

OBOE
HAROLD GOMBERG: Nov. 14, 15; Mar. 10.
FERDINAND PRIOR: Jan. 16, 17, 18, 19.

ENGLISH HORN
MICHEL NAZZI: Dec. 26, 27.

CLARINET
SIMEON BELLISON: Mar. 10.

FRENCH HORN
JAMES CHAMBERS: Dec. 16.

TRUMPET
WILLIAM VACCHIANO: Nov. 14, 15; Jan. 16, 17, 18, 19; Mar. 10.

TROMBONE
LEWIS VAN HANEY: Mar. 10.
ALLEN OSTRANDER: Mar. 10.
GORDON PULIS: Mar. 10.

TUBA
WILLIAM BELL: Mar. 10.

TYMPANI
SAUL GOODMAN: Mar. 10.

HARP
THEODORE CELLA: Mar. 10.

ORGAN
EDOUARD NIES-BERGER: Jan. 25.

VOCAL
CHARLOTTE BOERNER: Apr. 12.
DONALD DAME: Apr. 12.
TODD DUNCAN: Apr. 12.
RAOUL JOBIN: Oct. 31; Nov. 1.
NAN MERRIMAN: Jan. 5; Apr. 12.
MAGGIE TEYTE: Oct. 31, Nov. 1.

CHORUS
THE WESTMINSTER CHOIR: Apr. 12.

SOLOISTS AT PENSION FUND CONCERT OF CHAMBER MUSIC

ROBERT CASADESUS ⎱ May 5
ZINO FRANCESCATTI ⎰

•

SPRING TOUR OF 1947
Sponsored by the United States Rubber Company

Conductors

Leopold Stokowski
April 14 through April 24.
Eugene Ormandy
April 25, 26, 27, 28.

George Szell
April 29, 30; May 1, 2.
Dimitri Mitropoulos
May 3 through May 11.

SOLOIST—SPRING TOUR
HELEN TRAUBEL: April 28

CONCERTS—SPRING TOUR

Apr. 14	Baltimore Md.	Apr. 28	New Orleans, La.
Apr. 15	Norfolk, Va.	Apr. 29	Memphis, Tenn.
Apr. 16	Richmond, Va.	Apr. 30	Louisville, Ky.
Apr. 17	Raleigh, N. C.	May 1	St. Louis, Mo.
Apr. 18	Durham, N. C.	May 2	Chicago, Ill.
Apr. 19	Spartanburg, S. C.	May 3	Milwaukee, Wis.
*Apr. 20	Atlanta, Ga.	*May 4	Chicago, Ill.
Apr. 21	Atlanta, Ga.	May 5	Detroit, Mich.
Apr. 22	Knoxville, Tenn.	May 6	Dayton, O.
Apr. 23	Chattanooga, Tenn.	May 7	Charleston, W. Va.
Apr. 24	Birmingham, Ala.	May 8	Columbus, O.
Apr. 25	Montgomery, Ala.	May 9	Akron, O.
Apr. 26	New Orleans, La.	May 10	Buffalo N. Y.
*Apr. 27	New Orleans, La.	*May 11	Pittsburgh, Pa.

COMPOSITIONS PERFORMED—SPRING TOUR

BACH—Fugue in G minor (the shorter): April 15, 18, 19, 22.
Preludio from the Partita in E major for String Orchestra: April 16.
Toccata and Fugue in D minor: April 14, 17, 20, 24.

BEETHOVEN—Overture to "Leonore," No. 3, Op. 72-A: April 27.
Symphony in D major, No. 2, Op. 36: May 3, 5, 7, 8, 9, 11.
Symphony in A major, No. 7, Op. 92: April 14, 17, 24.

BRAHMS—Symphony in C minor, No. 1, Op. 68: April 15, 18, 19, 20, 22.
Symphony in D major, No. 2, Op. 73: April 29, 30; May 1, 2.
Symphony in E minor, No. 4, Op. 98: April 27.

CRESTON—"Frontiers": April 15, 18.

DEBUSSY—"La Mer" ("The Sea"), Three Symphonic Sketches: April 27.
Prelude, "L'Après-Midi d'un Faune" ("The Afternoon of a Faun"): April 14, 17, 20, 24.

IBERT—"Escales" ("Ports of call"): May 4, 6, 9, 11.

KABALEVSKY—Overture to the opera, "Colas Breugnon": April 16, 21, 23, 25, 26.

MOZART—Overture to the opera, "Don Giovanni": May 4, 6, 7, 10.

NOVACEK—"Perpetual Motion": April 14.

SHOSTAKOVICH—Symphony No. 6, Op. 53: April 25, 26.

SIBELIUS—Symphony in D major, No. 2, Op. 43: May 4, 6, 7, 10.

SIEGMEISTER—"Prairie Legend": April 16, 21, 23.

STRAUSS, RICHARD—Suite from "Der Rosenkavalier": April 27; May 4, 6, 9, 10, 11.

STRAVINSKY—Suite from the "Fire-bird": April 14, 17, 24.

STRINGFIELD—(A) Mountain song.
(B) Cripple Creek: April 19, 22.

TSCHAIKOWKSY—"Solitude" (Symphonic Transcription): April 14, 18, 19.
Symphony in E minor, No. 5, Op. 64: April 16, 21, 23, 25, 26; May 3, 5, 8.

* Concerts broadcast by the Columbia Broadcasting System over WCBS

WAGNER—"Du Bist Der Lenz" from "Die Walküre": April 28.
Elsa's Dream, from "Lohengrin": April 28.
Excerpts from "Götterdämmerung": April 28.
  Siegfried's Rhine Journey.
  Siegfried's Death and Funeral Music.
  Immolation and Closing Scene.
Finale of Act III, from "Parsifal": April 16, 21, 23.
Love-Music from Acts II and III of "Tristan und Isolde": April 15, 18, 19, 20, 22.
Overture to "Tannhäuser": April 29, 30; May 1, 2.
Prelude to "Die Meistersinger": April 28; May 10, 11.
Prelude to "Lohengrin," Act I: April 29, 30; May 1, 2.
Prelude and Love-Music, from "Tristan und Isolde": April 28, 29, 30; May 1, 2.

WEBER—Overture to "Der Freischütz": May 3, 5, 8, 9, 11.

1947–48 ONE HUNDRED SIXTH SEASON

Conductors
BRUNO WALTER

DIMITRI MITROPOULOS
CHARLES MUNCH
LEOPOLD STOKOWSKI
GEORGE SZELL

Assistant Conductor
WALTER HENDL

Concerts for Young People
Conductors
RUDOLPH GANZ
LEON BARZIN
WALTER HENDL
LEOPOLD STOKOWSKI
BRUNO WALTER

CONCERTS

1947

Leopold Stokowski, Conductor

Oct. 9—Ev'g.	Carnegie Hall
Oct. 10—Aft.	Carnegie Hall
Oct. 11—Ev'g.	Bushnell Memorial Hall, Hartford, Conn.
Oct. 12—Aft.	Carnegie Hall
Oct. 16—Ev'g.	Carnegie Hall
Oct. 17—Aft.	Carnegie Hall
*Oct. 18—Morn.	Town Hall
Oct. 19—Aft.	Carnegie Hall
Oct. 23—Ev'g.	Carnegie Hall
Oct. 24—Aft.	Carnegie Hall
Oct. 25—Ev'g.	Carnegie Hall
Oct. 26—Aft.	Carnegie Hall
Oct. 30—Ev'g.	Carnegie Hall
Oct. 31—Aft.	Carnegie Hall

1947

Nov. 1—Ev'g.	Carnegie Hall
Nov. 2—Aft.	Carnegie Hall

Charles Münch, Conductor

Nov. 6—Ev'g.	Carnegie Hall
Nov. 7—Aft.	Carnegie Hall
Nov. 8—Ev'g.	Carnegie Hall
Nov. 9—Aft.	Carnegie Hall
Nov. 13—Ev'g.	Carnegie Hall
Nov. 14—Aft.	Carnegie Hall
Nov. 15—Ev'g.	Carnegie Hall
Nov. 16—Aft.	Carnegie Hall

Dimitri Mitropoulos, Conductor

Nov. 20—Ev'g.	Carnegie Hall
Nov. 21—Aft.	Carnegie Hall
†Nov. 22—Morn.	Carnegie Hall

---

* Young People's Concert—WALTER HENDL, conductor
† Young People's Concert—RUDOLPH GANZ, conductor

1947			1948	
Nov. 23—Aft.	Carnegie Hall		Jan. 31—Ev'g.	Carnegie Hall
Nov. 27—Ev'g.	Carnegie Hall		Feb. 1—Aft.	Carnegie Hall
Nov. 28—Aft.	Carnegie Hall		Feb. 5—Ev'g.	Carnegie Hall
Nov. 30—Aft.	Carnegie Hall		Feb. 6—Aft.	Carnegie Hall
Dec. 4—Ev'g.	Carnegie Hall		Feb. 7—Ev'g.	Carnegie Hall
Dec. 5—Aft.	Carnegie Hall		Feb. 8—Aft.	Carnegie Hall
Dec. 6—Ev'g.	Carnegie Hall			
Dec. 7—Aft.	Carnegie Hall		**Bruno Walter, Conductor**	
Dec. 11—Ev'g.	Carnegie Hall		Feb. 12—Ev'g.	Carnegie Hall
Dec. 12—Aft.	Carnegie Hall		Feb. 13—Aft.	Carnegie Hall
Dec. 13—Ev'g.	Carnegie Hall		Feb. 14—Ev'g.	Mosque Theatre,
Dec. 14—Aft.	Carnegie Hall			Newark, N. J.

George Szell, Conductor

			Feb. 15—Aft.	Carnegie Hall
Dec. 18—Ev'g.	Carnegie Hall		Feb. 19—Ev'g.	Carnegie Hall
Dec. 19—Aft.	Carnegie Hall		Feb. 20—Aft.	Carnegie Hall
§Dec. 20—Morn.	Town Hall		*Feb. 21—Morn.	Carnegie Hall
Dec. 21—Aft.	Carnegie Hall		Feb. 22—Aft.	Carnegie Hall
Dec. 22—Ev'g.	Hotel Plaza,			
	New York, N. Y.		**George Szell, Conductor**	
Dec. 25—Ev'g.	Carnegie Hall		Feb. 26—Ev'g.	Carnegie Hall
Dec. 26—Aft.	Carnegie Hall		Feb. 27—Aft.	Carnegie Hall
Dec. 28—Aft.	Carnegie Hall		Feb. 28—Ev'g.	Carnegie Hall
			Feb. 29—Aft.	Carnegie Hall
1948			Mar. 4—Ev'g.	Carnegie Hall
			Mar. 5—Aft.	Carnegie Hall

Charles Münch, Conductor

			Mar. 6—Ev'g.	Carnegie Hall
Jan. 1—Ev'g.	Carnegie Hall		Mar. 7—Aft.	Carnegie Hall
Jan. 2—Aft.	Carnegie Hall			
Jan. 4—Aft.	Carnegie Hall		**Walter Hendl, Conductor**	
Jan. 8—Ev'g.	Carnegie Hall		Mar. 8—Ev'g.	Hotel Plaza,
Jan. 9—Aft.	Carnegie Hall			New York, N. Y.
†Jan. 10—Morn.	Carnegie Hall			
Jan. 11—Aft.	Carnegie Hall		**Leopold Stokowski, Conductor**	

Bruno Walter, Conductor

			Mar. 11—Ev'g.	Carnegie Hall
Jan. 15—Ev'g.	Carnegie Hall		Mar. 12—Aft.	Carnegie Hall
Jan. 16—Aft.	Carnegie Hall		†Mar. 13—Morn.	Carnegie Hall
			Mar. 14—Aft.	Carnegie Hall

Walter Hendl, Conductor

			Mar. 18—Ev'g.	Carnegie Hall
Jan. 17—Ev'g.	Carnegie Hall		Mar. 19—Aft.	Carnegie Hall
			Mar. 20—Ev'g.	Carnegie Hall

Bruno Walter, Conductor

			Mar. 21—Aft.	Carnegie Hall
Jan. 18—Aft.	Carnegie Hall		Mar. 25—Ev'g.	Carnegie Hall
Jan. 22—Ev'g.	Carnegie Hall		Mar. 26—Aft.	Carnegie Hall
Jan. 23—Aft.	Carnegie Hall		Mar. 27—Ev'g.	Carnegie Hall

Walter Hendl, Conductor

			Mar. 28—Aft.	Carnegie Hall
Jan. 24—Ev'g.	Carnegie Hall		Apr. 1—Ev'g.	Carnegie Hall
			Apr. 2—Aft.	Carnegie Hall

Bruno Walter, Conductor

			Apr. 3—Ev'g.	Carnegie Hall
Jan. 25—Aft.	Carnegie Hall		Apr. 4—Aft.	Carnegie Hall
			Apr. 6—Ev'g.	McCarter Theatre,

Charles Münch, Conductor

				Princeton, N. J.
Jan. 29—Ev'g.	Carnegie Hall			
Jan. 30—Aft.	Carnegie Hall			

§ Young People's Concert—LEON BARZIN, conductor
† Young People's Concert—RUDOLPH GANZ, conductor
* Young People's Concert—WALTER HENDL, conductor
(Feb. 21: One number conducted by BRUNO WALTER)

1948   1948

Bruno Walter, Conductor		Apr. 11—Aft.	Carnegie Hall
Apr. 8—Ev'g.	Carnegie Hall	Apr. 15—Ev'g.	Carnegie Hall
Apr. 9—Aft.	Carnegie Hall	Apr. 16—Aft.	Carnegie Hall
‡Apr. 10—Morn.	Carnegie Hall	Apr. 18—Aft.	Carnegie Hall

COMPOSITIONS PERFORMED

(a) First performance anywhere.
(b) First performance in America.
(c) First performance in North America.
(d) First performance in New York.
(e) First public performance in New York.
(f) First performance by the Society.
(g) First concert performance.
(h) First performance in this arrangement.

BACH—Chorale-Prelude, "Wachet auf, ruft uns die Stimme": Mar. 11, 12, 14; Apr. 6.
Prelude in E-flat minor: Oct. 23, 24, 25, 26.
Sinfonia from the Church Cantata, No. 156, "Ich Steh' mit einem Fuss im Grabe": Oct. 9, 10, 11, 12.

BACH-KAY—Chorale-Prelude, "Kyrie, Gott heiliger Geist": Jan. 17 (h).

BARBER—Concerto for Violoncello and Orchestra, Op. 22: Dec. 4 (f), 5, 7.
Suite from the Ballet, "Medea," Op. 23: Apr. 3 (f).

BARTOK—Dance Suite: Dec. 4 (f), 5, 6, 7.

BAUER—Tone Poem, "Sun Splendor", Op. 19: Oct. 25 (h).

BEETHOVEN—Concerto for Piano and Orchestra in G major, No. 4, Op. 58: Nov. 15, 16.
Concerto for Piano and Orchestra in E-flat major, No. 5 ("Emperor"), Op. 73: Feb. 19, 20, 22.
Concerto for Violin and Orchestra in D major, Op. 61: Dec. 25, 26.
"Missa Solemnis" in D major, Op. 123, for Orchestra, Chorus and Four Solo Voices: Apr. 15, 16, 18.
Overture to "Coriolanus," Op. 62: Nov. 20, 21; Dec. 13, 14, 25, 26.
Overture to "Leonore," No. 3, Op. 72-A: Jan. 18; Mar. 25, 26, 27.
Overture to "Prometheus," Op. 43: Apr. 11.
Symphony in B-flat major, No. 4, Op. 60: Jan. 15, 16, 25; Feb. 14.
Symphony in C minor, No. 5, Op. 67: Dec. 4, 5, 6, 7.
Symphony in F major, No. 6 ("Pastoral"), Op. 68: Dec. 25, 26, 28.
Symphony in A major, No. 7, Op. 92: Mar. 11, 12, 14; Apr. 6.
Symphony in F major, No. 8, Op. 93: Jan. 8, 9, 11.

BERLIOZ—Excerpts from "The Damnation of Faust": Jan. 25.
Overture to "Benvenuto Cellini': Feb. 8.
"Symphonie Fantastique," in C major, Op. 14-A: Jan. 29, 30, 31; Feb. 1.

BLOCH—Concerto Grosso for String Orchestra with Piano Obbligato: Feb. 5, 6, 7, 8.

BRAHMS—"Academic Festival Overture," Op. 80: Feb. 28, 29.
Allegro molto, from Serenade in D major, Op. 11: Mar. 8.
Concerto for Piano and Orchestra in B-flat major, No. 2, Op. 83: Apr. 8, 9.
Concerto for Violin and Orchestra in D major, Op. 77: Nov. 13, 14.
Symphony in C minor, No. 1, Op. 68: Oct. 11; Dec. 18, 19.
Symphony in D major, No. 2, Op. 73: Oct. 9, 10, 12; Apr. 8, 9.
Symphony in E minor, No. 4, Op. 98: Nov. 6, 7.
"Tragic" Overture, Op. 81: Apr. 8, 9.

---

‡ Young People's Concert—LEOPOLD STOKOWSKI, conductor

BRUCKNER—Symphony in C minor, No. 8: Jan. 22, 23.

CASADESUS—Concerto for Piano and Orchestra, Op. 37: Mar. 11 (d), 12, 14.

CHABRIER—"Joyeuse Marche": Jan. 31; Feb. 1.

CHOPIN—Concerto for Piano and Orchestra in E minor, No. 1, Op. 11: Feb. 28.
Concerto for Piano and Orchestra in F minor, No. 2, Op. 21: Mar. 6, 7.

COPLAND—Prairie Night and Celebration, from the Ballet Suite, "Billy the Kid": Oct. 25 (f).
Symphony No. 3: Dec. 18 (f), 19, 21.

COUPERIN-MILHAUD—Prelude and Allegro: Nov. 30.

DEBUSSY—"Claire de Lune" ("Moonlight"): Mar. 18, 19, 21.
"Danse": Mar. 8.
"Ibéria," Images pour Orchestre, No. 2: Nov. 23.
"La Damoiselle Élue" ("The Blessed Damozel"): Lyric Poem, after D. G. Rossetti, for Women's Voices (Soli and Chorus), with Orchestra: Mar. 20.
Nocturnes:
"Nuages," "Fêtes": Oct. 9, 10, 11, 12.
"Sirènes": Oct. 9, 10, 12.

DELLO JOIO—Concert Music for Orchestra: Mar. 14 (e).

DUKAS—Scherzo, "L'Apprenti Sorcier" ("The Sorcerer's Apprentice"): Feb. 5, 6, 7.

DVORAK—Concerto for Violin and Orchestra in A minor, Op. 53: Oct. 23, 24, 26.
Symphony in G major, No. 4, Op. 88: Feb. 12, 13, 14, 15.
Symphony in E minor, No. 5, "From the New World," Op. 95: Mar. 18, 19, 21.
Three Slavonic Dances:
No. 3 in A-flat, Op. 46: Feb. 15.
No. 2 in E minor, Op. 72: Feb. 15.
No. 1 in C major, Op. 46: Feb. 15.

FALLA—Ballet-Pantomime, "El Amor Brujo" ("Love, the Sorcerer"): Mar. 18, 19, 21.

FAURE—Ballade, for Piano and Orchestra in F-sharp major, Op. 19: Mar. 11, 12.
Suite from the incidental music to Maurice Maeterlinck's play, "Pelléas et Mélisande": Nov. 15, 16.

FERNANDEZ—"Batuque," Negro Dance from the Opera, "Malazarte": Mar. 21 (f).

FRANCK—Symphonic Poem, "Le Chasseur Maudit" ("The Accursed Huntsman"): Nov. 27, 28, 30.
Symphony in D minor: Nov. 13, 14; Feb. 28; Mar. 7.

GEORGE—Introduction and Allegro: Nov. 15 (f), 16.

GERSHWIN—Concerto for Piano and Orchestra in F major: Dec. 11, 12, 14.

GOULD—"Minstrel Show": Dec. 14 (f).

GRIEG—Concerto for Piano and Orchestra in A minor, Op. 16: Mar. 20.

GRIFFES—"The White Peacock," Op. 7, No. 1: Oct. 30, 31; Nov. 1, 2.

HANDEL—Concerto Grosso in A minor, Op. 6, No. 4: Nov. 13, 14, 15, 16.

HANDEL-CASADESUS—Concerto for Viola and Orchestra in B minor: Dec. 13 (f).

HANDEL-HARTY—Suite, "Water Music": Jan. 24.

HARRIS, ROY—Symphony No. 3 (In One Movement): Jan. 24.

HAYDN—Symphony in G major, "Oxford" (B. & H. No. 92): Mar. 4, 5.
Symphony in C minor (B. & H. No. 9 [95]): Jan. 25.
Symphony in B-flat major (B. & H. No. 102): Mar. 8.

HINDEMITH—Concert Music for Strings and Brass, Op. 50: Mar. 28 (f).
"Symphonia Serena": Feb. 12 (d), 13, 15.

HONEGGER—"Jeanne d'Arc au Bûcher": Jan. 1 (c), 2, 4.
Symphony No. 2, for Strings: Nov. 6 (d), 7, 8, 9.

KHACHATURIAN—"Masquerade," Suite from the Music for the Play of the
same name by Lermontov: Oct. 16 (d), 17, 19.
Russian Fantasy: Apr. 1 (b), 2, 3, 6.

KRENEK—Symphony No. 4: Nov. 27 (a), 28, 30.

LALO—"Symphonie Espagnole," for Violin and Orchestra, Op. 21: Feb. 26, 27,
29.

MAHLER—"Das Lied von der Erde" ("The Song of the Earth"): Jan. 15, 16,
18.
Symphony in A minor, No. 6: Dec. 11 (b), 12, 13.

MARTINU—Symphony No. 3: Jan. 8 (f), 9.

MASON—Symphony in A major, No. 2, Op. 30: Apr. 11.

MENDELSSOHN—Concerto for Violin and Orchestra in E minor, Op. 64:
Dec. 28.
Overture, "The Hebrides" ("Fingal's Cave"), Op. 26: Feb. 12, 13, 14, 15.
Scherzo in G minor, from Octet for Strings, Op. 20: Mar. 8.
Symphony in A minor, No. 3, "Scotch," Op. 56: Oct. 23, 24, 25, 26.
Symphony in A major, No. 4, "Italian," Op. 90: Jan. 24.

MENNIN—Fantasia for Strings: Jan. 17 (g).

MESSIAEN—"L'Ascension," Four Symphonic Meditations for Orchestra: Nov.
1 (f).

MILHAUD—Symphony No. 2: Feb. 5 (d), 6.

MOORE, DOUGLAS—Symphony in A major, No. 2: Feb. 19 (e), 20, 22.

MOUSSORGSKY—Excerpts from "Boris Godunoff": Oct. 16, 17, 19, 25.

MOZART—Adagio and Fugue in C minor, for String Orchestra (K. 546): Jan. 8,
9, 11.
Concerto for Piano and Orchestra in D minor (K. 466): Jan. 17.
Concerto for Piano and Orchestra in E-flat major (K. 449): Nov. 2 (f).
Concerto for Violin and Orchestra in A major, No. 5 (K. 219): Feb. 12, 13.
Overture to the Opera, "The Marriage of Figaro": Dec. 21.
Serenade in D major, No. 9, for Strings, Wind and Tympani (K. 320) (Four
movements): Feb. 26, 27.
Sinfonia Concertante for Violin and Viola with Orchestra, in E-flat major
(K. 364): Dec. 22.
Symphony in D major, No. 35, "Haffner" (K. 385): Dec. 22.
Symphony in D major, No. 38, "Prague" (K. 504): Jan. 11.
Symphony in C major, No. 41, "Jupiter" (K. 551): Mar. 25, 26, 27, 28.

PROKOFIEFF—Concerto for Piano and Orchestra in G minor, No. 2, Op. 16:
Jan. 31 (f); Feb. 1.

RAMEAU—Excerpts from Suites Nos. 1 and 2 from the Opera, "Dardanus":
Jan. 29, 30.

RAVEL—"Bolero": Feb. 8; Mar. 20.
"Daphnis et Chloé": Ballet in One Act—Orchestral Excerpts, Suite No. 2:
Oct. 9, 10, 11, 12; Jan. 11.
"La Valse," Choreographic Poem for Orchestra: Nov. 15, 16.
"Pavane pour une Infante défunte," for Small Orchestra: Mar. 8.
"Rapsodie Espagnole": Jan. 11.

REZNICEK—Overture to the Opera, "Donna Diana": Mar. 8.

RIMSKY-KORSAKOFF—Overture, "Russian Easter," Op. 36: Mar. 25, 26, 27,
28.

ROUSSEL—Suite in F major, Op. 33: Nov. 6, 7, 8.

SAINT-SAENS—Concerto for Violin and Orchestra in B minor, No. 3, Op. 61: Feb. 7, 8.
Symphony in C minor, No. 3, Op. 78, for Orchestra, Organ and Piano: Nov. 8, 9.

SCHUBERT—Symphony in B-flat major, No. 5: Feb. 5, 6, 7, 8.
Symphony in B minor, No. 8 ("Unfinished"): Dec. 21.

SCHUMAN, WILLIAM—"American Festival Overture": Mar. 18, 19.

SCHUMANN—Concerto for Piano and Orchestra in A minor, Op. 54: Oct. 30, 31; Jan. 29, 30.
Overture to "Manfred," Op. 115: Jan. 18.
Symphony in C major, No. 2, Op. 61: Feb. 26, 27, 29.
Symphony in D minor, No. 4, Op. 120: Nov. 20, 21; Dec. 6, 14.

SHOSTAKOVICH—Prelude in E-flat minor: Oct. 16 (f), 17, 19.
Symphony No. 5, Op. 47: Jan. 17.

SIBELIUS—Music from "Belshazzar's Feast": Apr. 1 (f), 2.

SIEGMEISTER—Symphony: Oct. 30 (a), 31; Nov. 1, 2.

SMETANA—Symphonic Poem, "Vltava" ("The Moldau") from the cycle, "Ma Vlast" ("My Fatherland"): Feb. 22.

STRAUSS, JOHANN—"Perpetual Motion": Dec. 22.
"Tritch-Tratch Polka": Dec. 22.
Waltz, "Wienerblut": Mar. 8.

STRAUSS, JOSEF—Waltz, "Village Swallows from Austria": Dec. 22.

STRAUSS, RICHARD—"Don Quixote" (Introduction, Theme with Variations and Finale); Fantastic Variations on a Theme of Knightly Character, Op. 35: Feb. 19, 20.
"Eine Alpensinfonie," Op. 64: Nov. 20, 21, 23.
"Metamorphosen," Study for 23 Solo String Instruments: Jan. 22 (f), 23.
Tone Poem, "Don Juan" (After Nicolaus Lenau), Op. 20: Dec. 28.
Tone Poem, "Till Eulenspiegel's Merry Pranks, After the Old-Fashioned Roguish Manner—in Rondo Form," Op. 28: Jan. 24.

STRAVINSKY—Concerto for Strings: Apr. 1 (d), 2, 4, 6.
"Pastorale," for Violin with Oboe, English Horn, Clarinet and Bassoon: Oct. 11 (f); Mar. 14.

THOMSON, VIRGIL—"The Seine at Night": Mar. 18 (d), 19, 21; Apr. 6.

TCHAIKOVSKY—Concerto for Piano and Orchestra in B-flat minor, No. 1, Op. 23: Nov. 30; Apr. 11.
Concerto for Violin and Orchestra in D major, Op. 35: Nov. 27, 28.
Music from the Ballet, "La belle au bois dormant" ("The Sleeping Beauty"): Mar. 20.
Symphonic Poem, "Francesca da Rimini," Op. 32 (After Dante): Oct. 23, 24, 26.
Symphony in F minor, No. 4, Op. 36: Apr. 1, 2, 3, 4.
Symphony in E minor, No. 5, Op. 64: Oct. 16, 17, 19.
Symphony in B minor, No. 6, "Pathetic," Op. 74: Mar. 4, 5, 6.
Variations on a Rococo Theme, for 'Cello and Orchestra, Op. 33: Jan. 8, 9.

VAUGHAN WILLIAMS—Fantasia on a Theme by Thomas Tallis, for Double String Orchestra: Mar. 25, 26, 27, 28.

VERDI—Overture to the Opera, "La Forza del Destino": Mar. 4 (f), 5, 6, 7.
Overture to the Opera, "I Vespri Siciliani": Dec. 4, 5, 6, 7.

WAGNER—"A Siegfried Idyl": Jan. 25; Feb. 14.
"Siegfried's Rhine Journey," from "Götterdämmerung": Mar. 11, 12, 14.
Music from Act III, "Parsifal": Mar. 25, 26, 27, 28.

Overture to "Rienzi": Mar. 20.
Overture to "Tannhäuser": Nov. 23.
Prelude and "Liebestod" ("Love-Death"), from "Tristan und Isolde": Apr. 1, 2, 3, 4, 6.
Wotan's Farewell to Brünnhilde and Magic Fire Music, from "Die Walküre": Oct. 30, 31; Nov. 1, 2.
WEBER—Overture to the Opera, "Euryanthe": Feb. 22.
Overture to the Opera, "Der Freischütz": Dec. 21.
Overture to the Opera, "Oberon": Nov. 9.

SOLOISTS

PIANO
JACQUES ABRAM: Nov. 15, 16.
ROBERT CASADESUS: Mar. 11, 12, 14.
CLIFFORD CURZON: Nov. 30.
WALTER HENDL: Jan. 17; Feb. 5, 6, 7, 8.
NICOLE HENRIOT: Jan. 29, 30.
MYRA HESS: Oct. 30, 31; Nov. 2.
VLADIMIR HOROWITZ: Apr. 8, 9, 11.
EUGENE ISTOMIN: Mar. 6, 7.
OSCAR LEVANT: Dec. 11, 12, 14.
MENAHEM PRESSLER: Mar. 20.
RUDOLF SERKIN: Feb. 19, 20, 22.
ZADEL SKOLOVSKY: Jan. 31; Feb. 1.
SIGI WEISSENBERG: Feb. 28.

VIOLIN
JOHN CORIGLIANO: Oct. 11; Dec. 22; Feb. 12, 13; Mar. 14.
MISCHA ELMAN: Nov. 27, 28.
YEHUDI MENUHIN: Feb. 26, 27, 29.
NATHAN MILSTEIN: Oct. 23, 24, 26.
ERICA MORINI: Dec. 25, 26, 28.
GINETTE NEVEU: Nov. 13, 14.
MICHAEL ROSENKER: Feb. 7, 8.

VIOLA
WILLIAM LINCER: Dec. 13, 22.
JOSEPH VIELAND: Feb. 19, 20.

'CELLO
RAYA GARBOUSOVA: Dec. 4, 5, 7.
LEONARD ROSE: Jan. 8, 9; Feb. 19, 20.

OBOE
HAROLD GOMBERG: Oct. 11; Mar. 14.

ENGLISH HORN
MICHEL NAZZI: Oct. 11; Mar. 14.

CLARINET
SIMEON BELLISON: Oct. 11; Mar. 14.

BASSOON
WILLIAM POLISI: Oct. 11; Mar. 14.

VOCAL
LORENZO ALVARY: Jan. 1, 2, 4; Apr. 15, 16, 18.
NADINE CONNER: Jan. 1, 2, 4.
KATHLEEN FERRIER: Jan. 15, 16, 18.
WILLIAM HAIN: Apr. 15, 16, 18.
JANE HOBSON: Mar. 20.
JOSEPH LADEROUTE: Jan. 1, 2, 4.
NAN MERRIMAN: Mar. 18, 19, 21; Apr. 15, 16, 18.
JARMILA NOVOTNA: Jan. 1, 2, 4.
BIDU SAYAO: Mar. 20.
ELEANOR STEBER: Apr. 15, 16, 18.
SET SVANHOLM: Jan. 15, 16, 18.
ENID SZANTHO: Jan. 1, 2, 4.

NARRATORS
RAYMOND GEROME: Jan. 1, 2, 4.
VERA ZORINA: Jan. 1, 2, 4.

CHORUS
THE WESTMINSTER CHOIR: Jan. 1, 2, 4; Apr. 15, 16, 18.
WOMEN'S CHORUS from THE WESTMINSTER CHOIR: Oct. 9, 10, 11; Mar. 20.

1948–49 ONE HUNDRED SEVENTH SEASON

Conductors
BRUNO WALTER
DIMITRI MITROPOULOS
CHARLES MUNCH
LEOPOLD STOKOWSKI
LEONARD BERNSTEIN

Assistant Conductor
WALTER HENDL

Conductors for Young People's Concerts
LEON BARZIN
IGOR BUKETOFF
WALTER HENDL
DIMITRI MITROPOULOS
LEOPOLD STOKOWSKI

CONCERTS

1948

Dimitri Mitropoulos, Conductor

Oct.	7—Ev'g.	Carnegie Hall
Oct.	8—Aft.	Carnegie Hall
Oct.	9—Ev'g.	Bushnell Memorial Hall, Hartford, Conn.
Oct.	10—Aft.	Carnegie Hall
Oct.	14—Ev'g.	Carnegie Hall
Oct.	15—Aft.	Carnegie Hall
*Oct.	16—Morn.	Town Hall
Oct.	17—Aft.	Carnegie Hall
Oct.	21—Ev'g.	Carnegie Hall
Oct.	22—Aft.	Carnegie Hall
Oct.	23—Ev'g.	Carnegie Hall
Oct.	24—Aft.	Carnegie Hall
Oct.	28—Ev'g.	Carnegie Hall
Oct.	29—Aft.	Carnegie Hall
Oct.	30—Ev'g.	Carnegie Hall
Oct.	31—Aft.	Carnegie Hall
Nov.	4—Ev'g.	Carnegie Hall
Nov.	5—Aft.	Carnegie Hall
Nov.	6—Ev'g.	Carnegie Hall
Nov.	7—Aft.	Carnegie Hall
Nov.	11—Ev'g.	Carnegie Hall
Nov.	12—Aft.	Carnegie Hall
Nov.	13—Ev'g.	McCarter Theatre, Princeton, N. J.
Nov.	14—Aft.	Carnegie Hall
Nov.	16—Ev'g.	Hotel Plaza
Nov.	18—Ev'g.	Carnegie Hall
Nov.	19—Aft.	Carnegie Hall
§Nov.	20—Morn.	Carnegie Hall
Nov.	21—Aft.	Carnegie Hall
Nov.	25—Ev'g.	Carnegie Hall
Nov.	26—Aft.	Carnegie Hall
Nov.	28—Aft.	Carnegie Hall

Bruno Walter, Conductor

Dec.	2—Ev'g.	Carnegie Hall
Dec.	3—Aft.	Carnegie Hall

Walter Hendl, Conductor

Dec.	4—Ev'g.	Carnegie Hall

1948

Bruno Walter, Conductor

Dec.	5—Aft.	Carnegie Hall
Dec.	9—Ev'g.	Carnegie Hall
Dec.	10—Aft.	Carnegie Hall

Walter Hendl, Conductor

Dec.	11—Ev'g.	Carnegie Hall

Bruno Walter, Conductor

Dec.	12—Aft.	Carnegie Hall
Dec.	14—Ev'g.	Mosque Theatre, Newark, N. J.

Charles Munch, Conductor

Dec.	16—Ev'g.	Carnegie Hall
Dec.	17—Aft.	Carnegie Hall
†Dec.	18—Morn.	Carnegie Hall
Dec.	19—Aft.	Carnegie Hall
Dec.	23—Ev'g.	Carnegie Hall
Dec.	24—Aft.	Carnegie Hall
Dec.	26—Aft.	Carnegie Hall
Dec.	27—Ev'g.	Hotel Plaza, New York, N. Y.
Dec.	30—Ev'g.	Carnegie Hall
Dec.	31—Aft.	Carnegie Hall

1949

Jan.	2—Aft.	Carnegie Hall
Jan.	6—Ev'g.	Carnegie Hall
Jan.	7—Aft.	Carnegie Hall
Jan.	8—Ev'g.	Carnegie Hall
Jan.	9—Aft.	Carnegie Hall

Leopold Stokowski, Conductor

Jan.	13—Ev'g.	Carnegie Hall
Jan.	14—Aft.	Carnegie Hall
Jan.	15—Ev'g.	Carnegie Hall
Jan.	16—Aft.	Carnegie Hall
Jan.	20—Ev'g.	Carnegie Hall
Jan.	21—Aft.	Carnegie Hall
Jan.	22—Ev'g.	Carnegie Hall
Jan.	23—Aft.	Carnegie Hall
Jan.	27—Ev'g.	Carnegie Hall
Jan.	28—Aft.	Carnegie Hall

* Young People's Concert—WALTER HENDL, Conductor
§ Young People's Concert—DIMITRI MITROPOULOS, Conductor
† Young People's Concert—IGOR BUKETOFF, Conductor

1949   1949

Walter Hendl, Conductor   **Bruno Walter, Conductor**
Jan. 29—Ev'g.   Carnegie Hall   Mar. 6—Aft.   Carnegie Hall
                                         Mar. 10—Ev'g.   Carnegie Hall
Leopold Stokowski, Conductor   Mar. 11—Aft.   Carnegie Hall
Jan. 30—Aft.   Carnegie Hall   ※Mar. 12—Morn.   Carnegie Hall
Feb. 3—Ev'g.   Carnegie Hall   Mar. 13—Aft.   Carnegie Hall
Feb. 4—Aft.   Carnegie Hall
                                         Walter Hendl, Conductor
Walter Hendl, Conductor   Mar. 14—Ev'g.   Hotel Plaza
Feb. 5—Ev'g.   Carnegie Hall
                                         Bruno Walter, Conductor
Leopold Stokowski, Conductor   Mar. 17—Ev'g.   Carnegie Hall
Feb. 6—Aft.   Carnegie Hall   Mar. 18—Aft.   Carnegie Hall
Feb. 10—Ev'g.   Carnegie Hall   Mar. 20—Aft.   Carnegie Hall
Feb. 11—Aft.   Carnegie Hall
Feb. 12—Ev'g.   Carnegie Hall   **Leopold Stokowski, Conductor**
Feb. 13—Aft.   Carnegie Hall   Mar. 24—Ev'g.   Carnegie Hall
Feb. 17—Ev'g.   Carnegie Hall   Mar. 25—Aft.   Carnegie Hall
Feb. 18—Aft.   Carnegie Hall   Mar. 26—Ev'g.   Carnegie Hall
*Feb. 19—Morn.   Carnegie Hall   Mar. 27—Aft.   Carnegie Hall
Feb. 20—Aft.   Carnegie Hall   Mar. 31—Ev'g.   Carnegie Hall
                                         Apr. 1—Aft.   Carnegie Hall
Bruno Walter, Conductor   Apr. 2—Ev'g.   Carnegie Hall
Feb. 24—Ev'g.   Carnegie Hall   Apr. 3—Aft.   Carnegie Hall
Feb. 25—Aft.   Carnegie Hall
                                         Bruno Walter, Conductor
Walter Hendl, Conductor   Apr. 5—Ev'g. Bushnell Memorial
Feb. 26—Ev'g.   Carnegie Hall   Hall, Hartford, Conn.
                                         Apr. 7—Ev'g.   Carnegie Hall
Bruno Walter, Conductor   Apr. 8—Aft.   Carnegie Hall
Feb. 27—Aft.   Carnegie Hall   ※Apr. 9—Morn.   Carnegie Hall
Mar. 3—Ev'g   Carnegie Hall   Apr. 10—Aft.   Carnegie Hall
Mar. 4—Aft.   Carnegie Hall   Apr. 14—Ev'g.   Carnegie Hall
                                         Apr. 15—Aft.   Carnegie Hall
Walter Hendl, Conductor   ‡Apr. 16—Morn.   Town Hall
Mar. 5—Ev'g.   Carnegie Hall   Apr. 17—Aft.   Carnegie Hall

FALL TOUR 1948

Leopold Stokowski, Conductor
Sept. 20   Syracuse, N. Y.   Sept. 27   East Lansing, Mich.
Sept. 21   Cleveland, Ohio   Sept. 28   Columbus, Ohio
Sept. 22   Detroit, Mich.   Sept. 29   Buffalo, N. Y.
Sept. 23   Chicago, Ill.   Sept. 30   Utica, N. Y.
Sept. 24   Chicago, Ill.   Oct. 1   Rochester, N. Y.
Sept. 25   Madison, Wis.   Oct. 2   Boston, Mass.
Sept. 26   Milwaukee, Wis.   Oct. 3   Portland, Maine

SPRING TOUR 1949

Leopold Stokowski, Conductor   Apr. 21   Atlanta, Ga.
Apr. 18   White Plains, N. Y.   Apr. 22   Spartanburg, S. C.
Apr. 19   Richmond, Va.   Apr. 23   Knoxville, Tenn.
Apr. 20   Columbia, S. C.   Apr. 24   Birmingham, Ala.

---

* Young People's Concert—WALTER HENDL, Conductor
※ Young People's Concert—LEOPOLD STOKOWSKI, Conductor
‡ Young People's Concert—LEON BARZIN, Conductor

Leonard Bernstein, Conductor		Apr. 28	Cincinnati, Ohio
Apr. 25	Chattanooga, Tenn.	Apr. 29	Toledo, Ohio
Bruno Walter, Conductor		Apr. 30	Pittsburgh, Pa.
Apr. 26	Roanoke, Va.	May 1	Washington, D. C.
Apr. 27	Bloomington, Ind.		

COMPOSITIONS PERFORMED

(a) First performance anywhere.
(b) First performance in America.
(c) First performance in New York.
(d) First concert performance in New York.
(e) First performance by the Society.
(f) First concert performance.
(g) First performance in this version.

BACH—Brandenburg Concerto No. 3 in G major: Jan. 6, 7, 8, 9.

Fugue in G minor (the shorter) (Transcription by Leopold Stokowski): Sept. 20, 23.

Three Chorale-Preludes (Transcription by Leopold Stokowski):
"Wir glauben all' an einen Gott": Jan. 15, 16; Feb. 20; Apr. 18, 19, 20, 24.
"Ich ruf' zu dir": Jan. 15, 16; Feb. 20; Apr. 24.
"Nun komm' der heiden Heiland": Jan. 15, 16; Apr. 24.

Preludio from the Partita in E major (Transcription by Leopold Stokowski): Feb. 20.

Air from Suite No. 3 in D: Dec. 4.

Toccata and Fugue in D minor (Transcription by Leopold Stokowski): Sept. 21, 22, 25, 26, 28, 30; Oct. 1, 2.

BACH-MITROPOULOS—Fantasia and Fugue in G minor: Oct. 23, 24; Nov. 18, 19.

BACH-RESPIGHI—Prelude and Fugue in D major; Oct. 7, 8, 9, 10.

BARON—"Ode to Democracy" (Gettysburg Address): Jan. 22 (a), 23.

BARTOK—Rhapsody No. 2 for Violin and Orchestra: Nov. 6 (e), 7.

BEETHOVEN—Concerto for Piano and Orchestra in C major, No. 1, Op. 15: Apr. 25.

Concerto for Piano and Orchestra in E-flat major, No. 5, Op. 73 ("Emperor"): Mar. 3, 4, 6.

Concerto for Violin and Orchestra in D major, Op. 61: Mar. 10, 11, 13.

Concerto for Violin, 'Cello and Piano with Orchestra in C major, Op. 56: Mar. 17, 18.

From "The Creatures of Prometheus," Op. 43:
Overture: Apr. 5, 7, 8, 10.
Adagio—Allegro molto: Apr. 7, 8, 10.
Allegretto: Finale: Apr. 7, 8, 10.

Overture to "Coriolanus," Op. 62: Apr. 14, 15, 17.
Overture to "Egmont," Op. 84: Feb. 24, 25, 27; Apr. 26, 29, 30; May 1.
Overture to "Leonore," No. 1: Mar. 20.
Overture to "Leonore," No. 2: Mar. 3, 4, 6.
Overture to "Leonore," No. 3, Op. 72A: Mar. 10, 11, 13; Apr. 25, 28.
Scena and Aria: "Ah, Perfido," Op. 65: Apr. 14, 15.
Symphony in C major, No. 1, Op. 21: Feb. 24, 25, 27; Apr. 5, 29.
Symphony in D major, No. 2, Op. 36: Mar. 3, 4, 6.
Symphony in E-flat major, No. 3, Op. 55 ("Eroica"): Feb. 24, 25, 27; Apr. 5, 29.
Symphony in B-flat major, No. 4, Op. 60: Mar. 17, 18, 20.
Symphony in C minor, No. 5, Op. 67: Apr. 7, 8, 10, 28.

Symphony in F major, No. 6, Op. 68 ("Pastorale"): Apr. 7, 8, 10, 28; May. 1.
Symphony in A major, No. 7, Op. 92: Sept. 22, 25, 28, 30; Oct. 1; Mar. 17, 18, 20; Apr. 25.
Symphony in F major, No. 8, Op. 93: Mar. 10, 11, 13.
Symphony in D minor, No. 9, Op. 125: Apr. 14, 15, 17.

BERLIOZ—Minuet of the Will-o'-the-Wisps and Rákóczy March from "The Damnation of Faust": Oct. 10.
Overture, "Carnaval Romain," Op. 9: Dec. 4.
Overture, "Benvenuto Cellini," Op. 23: Feb. 5.

BIZET—Overture, "La Patrie," Op. 19: Jan. 2.
Symphony in C major: Dec. 30, 31; Jan. 2.

BLOCH—"Schelomo" ("Solomon"): Hebrew Rhapsody for 'Cello and Orchestra: Jan. 30.
Suite for Viola and Orchestra: Oct. 23 (e).

BORODIN—Symphony in B minor, No. 2, Op. 5: Oct. 30, 31; Nov. 13.

BRAHMS—Concerto for Piano and Orchestra in D minor, No. 1, Op. 15: Feb. 3, 4.
Concerto for Piano and Orchestra in B-flat major, No. 2, Op. 83: Oct. 28, 29, 31.
Concerto for Violin and Orchestra in D major, Op. 77: Oct. 21, 22, 24; Dec. 4.
Concerto for Violin, 'Cello, and Orchestra, in A minor, Op. 102: Feb. 5.
Overture, "Academic Festival," Op. 80: Oct. 28, 29, 30, 31.
Overture, "Tragic," Op. 81: Dec. 2, 3.
"Schicksalslied" ("The Song of Destiny") for Chorus and Orchestra, Op. 54: Dec. 2, 3, 5.
Symphony in C minor, No. 1, Op. 68: Sept. 20, 21, 23, 26; Oct. 2, 7, 8, 10; Nov. 13; Apr. 18, 19, 20, 24, 26, 30.
Symphony in D major, No. 2, Op. 73: Nov. 25, 26, 28; Dec. 14; Mar. 5.
Symphony in F major, No. 3, Op. 90: Mar. 24, 25, 26, 27.
Symphony in E minor, No. 4, Op. 98: Jan. 13, 14, 15, 16.
Variations on a Theme by Haydn, Op. 56A: Apr. 27.

BRUCH—Concerto for Violin and Orchestra in D minor, Op. 44: Jan. 8.

BRUCKNER—Symphony in E-flat major, No. 4 ("Romantic"): Dec. 9, 10.

CHABRIER—"Bourrée Fantasque": Dec. 19.

CHARPENTIER—Orchestral Suite, "Impressions of Italy": Oct. 14, 15, 17 (Second movement omitted).

CHAUSSON—"Poème" for Violin and Orchestra, Op. 25: Dec. 30, 31; Jan. 2.
Symphony in B-flat major, Op. 20: Nov. 4, 5, 6, 7.

CHOPIN—Concerto for Piano and Orchestra, in E minor, No. 1, Op. 11: Feb. 26.

COPLAND—Prairie Night, Celebration Dance from the Ballet Suite, "Billy the Kid": Sept. 25, 28; Oct. 1.

COWELL—"American Piper": Jan. 22 (c), 23; Apr. 21, 22, 23.

DEBUSSY—"La Cathédrale Engloutie" (Symphonic transcription by Leopold Stokowski): Feb. 10, 11, 13.
"Au Clair de Lune" (Symphonic Transcription by Leopold Stokowski): Sept. 24, 27, 29, 30.
"Night in Granada" (Symphonic Transcription by Leopold Stokowski): Mar. 26, 27.
Two Nocturnes: "Nuages" and "Fêtes": Jan. 30.
Prelude, "L'Après-midi d'un Faune": Jan. 20, 21, 23.

DELLO JOIO—Variations, Chaconne and Finale: Dec. 9 (c), 10.

DIAMOND—Music for Shakespeare's "Romeo and Juliet": Dec. 4 (e).

DUBENSKY—Fugue for 34 Violins: Sept. 21, 24, 27, 29; Oct. 3.

DUKAS—Symphony in C major: Jan. 6, 7.

DVORAK—Symphony in G major, No. 4: Apr. 26, 30; May 1.
Two Slavonic Dances, Nos. 1 and 3, Op. 46: Nov. 16.

DYSON—Overture to the Cantata, "Canterbury Pilgrims" ("At the Tabard Inn"):
Feb. 10 (b), 11.

ENESCO—Roumanian Rhapsody in A major, No. 1: Feb. 17, 18, 20; Apr. 21, 22,
23.

FAURE—Suite from the incidental music to Maurice Maeterlinck's play, "Pelléas
et Mélisande": Dec. 27.

FITCH—"Terra Nova": Apr. 2 (a).

GERSHWIN—Concerto for Piano and Orchestra in F major: Jan. 27, 28.

GIBBONS-KAY—Suite for Orchestra: Dec. 11 (a).

GOULD—Philharmonic Waltzes: Nov. 16 (a).
Symphony No. 3: Oct. 28 (g), 29, 30.

GRETRY-MOTTL—Gigue from the opera "Céphale et Procris": Nov. 16.

GRIFFES—"The Pleasure-Dome of Kubla Khan": Jan. 22, 23.

HANDEL—Concerto Grosso in B minor, for String Orchestra, Op. 6, No. 12:
Jan. 29.

HANSON—Serenade for Flute, Harp and Strings: Mar. 26 (e), 27.

HAYDN—Symphony in D major, No. 10 (B. & H. No. 86): Dec. 9, 10, 12.
Symphony in G major, No. 13 (B. & H. No. 88): Mar. 14.
Symphony in D major (B. & H. No. 53), "Imperial": Feb. 17 (e), 18, 20.

HERRMANN—Suite from "The Devil and Daniel Webster": Feb. 10 (d), 11, 13.

HINDEMITH—Philharmonic Concerto (Variations for Orchestra): Jan. 13 (c),
14.
Overture, "Neues vom Tage": Feb. 26.

HONEGGER—Symphony No. 4: Dec. 30 (b), 31.

d'INDY—Symphony for Piano and Orchestra on a French Mountain Song: Dec.
16, 17, 19.

KHACHATURIAN—"Masquerade" from the music for the play of Lermontov:
Sept. 22, 25, 28; Oct. 1, 3.
Music from the Ballet Suite, "Gayaneh": Mar. 24, 25, 26, 27; Apr. 18, 19, 20.
Symphony No. 2: Sept. 24 (e); Jan. 20, 21, 22, 23.

KREUTZ—Music for Symphony Orchestra: Mar. 5 (g).

LALO—Overture to "Le Roi d'Ys": Dec. 23, 24, 26.
Symphonie Espagnole for Violin and Orchestra: Nov. 7.

LISZT—Concerto for Piano and Orchestra in A major, No. 2: Dec. 19.
Hungarian Rhapsody No. 2: Jan. 27, 28.

LUENING—"Pilgrim's Hymn": Jan. 23 (g).

MAGANINI—Suite, "Three Early American Pieces": Feb. 13 (d).

MAHLER—Symphony in C minor, No. 2, for Orchestra, Soprano and Alto Solos,
and Mixed Chorus: Dec. 2, 3, 5.
Symphony No. 7: Nov. 11, 12.

MASSENET—Aria from "Thaïs": Nov. 16.

MENDELSSOHN—Concerto for Violin and Orchestra in E minor, Op. 64:
Oct. 30.
Overture, "The Hebrides" ("Fingal's Cave"), Op. 26: Nov. 21.
Overture, "Ruy Blas," Op. 95: Nov. 11, 12, 13, 14.
From Music to "A Midsummer Night's Dream":
Overture and Scherzo: Dec. 12, 14.

Nocturne: Dec. 12.
Wedding March: Nov. 16.
Symphony in A minor, No. 3, Op. 56 ("Scotch"): Nov. 18, 19, 21.
Symphony in D major, No. 5, Op. 107 ("Reformation"): Jan. 6, 7, 8, 9.
MENOTTI—Concerto for Piano and Orchestra: Jan. 20 (c), 21.
Two Interludes from the Opera, "The Island God": Jan. 15 (e), 16; Apr. 21, 22, 23.
MESSIAEN—"L'Ascension," Four Symphonic Meditations for Orchestra: Sept. 21, 24, 27, 29, 30; Oct. 2.
MOERAN—"In the Mountain Country": Jan. 27 (b), 28, 30.
MOZART—Concerto for Piano and Orchestra in C major (K. 467): Dec. 16, 17; Feb. 6.
Concerto for Violin and Orchestra in G major, No. 3 (K. 216): Nov. 6.
Deutsche Tänze (K. 605), No. 3: Feb. 17, 18, 20.
Overture to the Opera, "Idomeneo": Mar. 5, 14.
Overture to the Opera, "The Marriage of Figaro": Oct. 21, 22.
Symphony in D major, No. 35 (K. 385) ("Haffner"): Dec. 19.
Symphony in D major, No. 38 (K. 504) ("Prague"): Dec. 27.
Symphony in G minor, No. 40 (K. 550): Mar. 31; Apr. 1, 2, 3.
MURADELI—Georgian Symphonic Dance: Jan. 20 (c), 21, 30.
PAGANINI—Concerto for Violin and Orchestra in D major, Op. 6: Nov. 28.
PANUFNIK—"Tragic" Overture: Mar. 24 (c), 25.
PERPESSA—Prelude and Fugue for Orchestra: Nov. 4 (b), 5, 6.
PORRINO—Sinfonia per una Fiaba: Sept. 20 (b), 23, 26.
POULENC—"Concert Champêtre" for Harpsichord (or Piano) and Orchestra: Nov. 11 (e), 12, 14.
PROKOFIEFF—Concerto for Piano and Orchestra in C major, No. 3, Op. 26: Feb. 20.
Concerto for Violin and Orchestra in G minor, No. 2: Nov. 25, 26.
PURCELL-WOOD—Suite in Five Movements: Mar. 31 (e); Apr. 1, 3.
RACHMANINOFF—Concerto for Piano and Orchestra in D minor, No. 3: Feb. 17, 18.
Rhapsody on a Theme of Paganini, for Piano and Orchestra, Op. 43: Jan. 9.
RAMEAU—Excerpts from Suites I and II from the Opera "Dardanus": Dec. 27.
Tambourin: Nov. 16.
RATHAUS—"Vision Dramatique": Nov. 18 (b), 19.
RAVEL—"Daphnis et Chloé" Suite No. 1: Jan. 8, 9.
"Daphnis et Chloé" Suite No. 2: Jan. 2; Feb. 5.
"Tzigane," Rhapsody for Violin and Orchestra: Dec. 30, 31; Jan. 2.
"Valses Nobles et Sentimentales": Dec. 23, 24, 26.
ROPARTZ—"La Chasse du Prince Arthur," Symphonic Etude: Dec. 16, 17.
ROUSSEL—Symphony No. 4, Op. 53: Dec. 23, 24, 26.
SAINT-SAENS—Concerto for Piano and Orchestra in G minor, No. 2, Op. 22: Jan. 22.
SATIE-DEBUSSY—Two "Gymnopédies": Nov. 21.
SCHNABEL—Rhapsody for Orchestra: Nov. 25 (c), 26.
SCHOENBERG—Five Pieces for Orchestra, Op. 16: Oct. 21, 22.
SCHUBERT—Symphony in C major, No. 7: Apr. 27.
SCHUMAN, W.—"Circus Overture" (A Side Show for Orchestra): Feb. 26 (e).
SCHUMANN, R.—Concerto for Piano and Orchestra in A minor, Op. 54: Nov. 18, 19, 21.
Concerto for Violoncello and Orchestra in A minor, Op. 129: Nov. 4, 5.

Symphony in B-flat major, No. 1, Op. 38: Jan. 29.

Symphony in C major, No. 2, Op. 61: Feb. 3, 4, 6.

Symphony in E-flat major, No. 3 ("Rhenish"), Op. 97: Oct. 21, 22, 23, 24.

SCOTT—"From the Sacred Harp": Jan. 30 (e).

SHOSTAKOVICH—Symphony No. 1, Op. 10: Dec. 11.

Symphony No. 9, Op. 70: Feb. 26.

SIBELIUS—Incidental Music from Maeterlinck's Drama, "Pelléas et Mélisande": Feb. 6; Apr. 24.

Concerto for Violin and Orchestra in D minor: Mar. 24, 25.

STAROKADOMSKY—Concerto for Orchestra, Op. 14: Feb. 5 (d).

STRAUSS, J.—Waltz, "The Beautiful Blue Danube": Dec. 27.

"Emperor" Waltz: Mar. 14.

Waltz, "Tales from the Vienna Woods": Nov. 16.

STRAUSS, R.—Tone Poem, "Also Sprach Zarathustra," Op. 30: Oct. 7, 8, 9.

Tone Poem, "Death and Transfiguration," Op. 24: Dec. 12, 14; Apr. 5.

Tone Poem, "Don Juan" (after Nicolaus Lenau), Op. 20: Oct. 10; Mar. 5.

STRAVINSKY—Music from "Petrouchka": Sept. 24, 27, 29; Oct. 3; Jan. 15, 16.

Suite from "The Fire-Bird": Dec. 4.

Suite for Small Orchestra, No. 2: Mar. 14 (e).

TCHAIKOVSKY—Concerto for Piano and Orchestra in B-flat minor, No. 1, Op. 23: Dec. 11.

Concerto for Violin and Orchestra in D major, Op. 35: Dec. 23, 24, 26.

Overture-Fantasy, "Romeo and Juliet": Jan. 29.

Symphonic Poem, "Francesca da Rimini," Op. 32: Apr. 18, 19, 20.

Symphony in F minor, No. 4, Op. 36: Sept. 27, 29; Oct. 3, 9, 14, 15, 17.

Symphony in E minor, No. 5, Op. 65: Nov. 14.

Symphony in B minor, No. 6 ("Pathétique"), Op. 74: Feb. 10, 11, 13; Apr. 21, 22, 23.

THOMSON—"The Seine at Night": Sept. 20, 22, 23, 26; Oct. 2.

Suite for Orchestra, "Louisiana Story": Jan. 29 (e).

"Wheat Field at Noon": Mar. 24 (c), 25, 26, 27; Apr. 18, 19, 20.

VAUGHAN WILLIAMS—Fantasia on a Theme of Thomas Tallis, for Double String Orchestra: Dec. 12, 14.

Symphony No. 6: Jan. 27 (c), 28, 30.

VERDI—Overture to the Opera "Nabucodonosor": Oct. 14 (e), 15, 17.

VIVALDI—Concerto Grosso in D minor, Op. 3, No. 11: Dec. 16, 17, 19 (Original version for Strings); Feb. 17, 18, 20 (Symphonic Transcription by Leopold Stokowski).

WAGNER—"A Siegfried Idyl": Mar. 14; Apr. 27.

Overture to "The Flying Dutchman": Jan. 13, 14; Apr. 21, 23.

Siegfried's Rhine Journey from "Götterdämmerung": Mar. 31; Apr. 1, 2, 3.

Siegfried's Death from "Götterdämmerung": Mar. 31; Apr. 1, 2, 3.

Brünnhilde's Immolation from "Götterdämmerung": Feb. 12; Mar. 31; Apr. 1, 2, 3.

Prelude to "Lohengrin": Nov. 4, 5, 6, 7.

Prelude to "Parsifal": Nov. 25, 26, 28.

Finale of the 3rd Act of "Parsifal": Sept. 20, 28; Oct. 1, 2.

Entrance of the Gods into Valhalla from "Das Rheingold": Feb. 12; Apr. 24.

Erda's Scene from "Das Rheingold": Feb. 12.

Overture to "Rienzi": Mar. 26, 27.

Forest Murmurs from "Siegfried": Feb. 12; Apr. 24.

Siegfried's Forging Song from "Siegfried": Feb. 12.

Love Music from Acts II and III from "Tristan und Isolde": Sept. 22, 23, 26.

Prelude and Love Death from "Tristan und Isolde": Sept. 21, 25, 30; Feb. 12, 26.

Wotan's Farewell and Magic Fire Music from "Die Walküre": Feb. 12; Apr. 21, 22, 23.

WALTON—"Spitfire" Prelude and Fugue from the Film "The First of the Few": Feb. 3 (d), 4, 6.

WEBERN—Passacaglia: Oct. 23 (e).

WEINBERGER—Polka and Fugue from the Opera "Schwanda": Jan. 13 (g), 14, 15, 16.

SOLOISTS

PIANO
LEONARD BERNSTEIN: Apr. 25.
ROBERT CASADESUS: Dec. 16, 17, 19.
CLIFFORD CURZON: Mar. 3, 4, 6.
RUDOLF FIRKUSNY: Jan. 20, 21.
JEAN GRAHAM: Jan. 22.
WALTER HENDL: Mar. 17, 18.
MYRA HESS: Feb. 3, 4, 6.
BYRON JANIS: Jan. 27, 28.
WILLIAM KAPELL: Feb. 17, 18, 20.
LUBKA KOLESSA: Feb. 26.
SEYMOUR LIPKIN: Jan. 9.
ARTURO MICHELANGELI: Nov. 18, 19, 21.
FRANCIS POULENC: Nov. 11, 12, 14.
RUDOLF SERKIN: Oct. 28, 29, 31.
HILDE SOMER: Dec. 11.

VIOLIN
JOHN CORIGLIANO: Mar. 17, 18, 24, 25.
ZINO FRANCESCATTI: Nov. 25, 26, 28.
SZYMON GOLDBERG: Dec. 4.
NATHAN MILSTEIN: Dec. 23, 24, 26.
ERICA MORINI: Mar. 10, 11, 13.
GINETTE NEVEU: Dec. 30, 31; Jan. 2.
DOROTHA POWERS: Oct. 30.
MICHAEL ROSENKER: Jan. 8; Feb. 5.
ISAAC STERN: Nov. 6, 7.
JOSEPH SZIGETI: Oct. 21, 22, 24.

VIOLA
WILLIAM LINCER: Oct. 23.

'CELLO
LEONARD ROSE: Nov. 4, 5; Jan. 30; Mar. 17, 18.
CARL STERN: Feb. 5.

FLUTE
JOHN WUMMER: Mar. 26, 27.

HARP
THEODORE CELLA: Mar. 26, 27.

ORGAN
EDOUARD NIES-BERGER: Mar. 31; Apr. 1, 3.

VOCAL
NADINE CONNER: Dec. 2, 3, 5.
MARY DAVENPORT: Feb. 12.
IRWIN DILLON: Feb. 12.
EILEEN FARRELL: Feb. 12.
MACK HARRELL: Apr. 14, 15, 17.
RAOUL JOBIN: Apr. 14, 15, 17.
NAN MERRIMAN: Apr. 14, 15, 17.
MICHAEL RHODES: Feb. 12.
MOLLY STARKMAN: Feb. 12.
ELEANOR STEBER: Apr. 14, 15, 17.
JEAN WATSON: Dec. 2, 3, 5.

CHORUS
SCHOLA CANTORUM (Chorus of Speakers): Jan. 22, 23.
WESTMINSTER CHOIR: Dec. 2, 3, 5; Apr. 14, 15, 17.

1949–50 ONE HUNDRED EIGHTH SEASON

Conductors
LEOPOLD STOKOWSKI   DIMITRI MITROPOULOS

Guest Conductors
BRUNO WALTER
VICTOR DE SABATA   LEONARD BERNSTEIN
WALTER HENDL

Associate Conductor
FRANCO AUTORI

Conductors of Young People's Concerts
LEOPOLD STOKOWSKI
IGOR BUKETOFF   DEAN DIXON
FRANCO AUTORI

CONCERTS

1949

Leopold Stokowski, Conductor

Oct. 13—Ev'g.	Carnegie Hall
Oct. 14—Aft.	Carnegie Hall

Bruno Walter, Conductor

Oct. 15—Ev'g.	Hunter College

Leopold Stokowski, Conductor

Oct. 16—Aft.	Carnegie Hall
Oct. 20—Ev'g.	Carnegie Hall
Oct. 21—Aft.	Carnegie Hall
*Oct. 22—Morn.	Town Hall
Oct. 23—Aft.	Carnegie Hall
Oct. 27—Ev'g.	Carnegie Hall
Oct. 28—Aft.	Carnegie Hall
Oct. 29—Ev'g.	Carnegie Hall
Oct. 30—Aft.	Carnegie Hall
Nov. 3—Ev'g.	Carnegie Hall
Nov. 4—Aft.	Carnegie Hall
Nov. 5—Ev'g.	Carnegie Hall
Nov. 6—Aft.	Carnegie Hall
Nov. 10—Ev'g.	Carnegie Hall
Nov. 11—Aft.	Carnegie Hall
Nov. 12—Ev'g.	Carnegie Hall
Nov. 13—Aft.	Carnegie Hall

Dimitri Mitropoulos, Conductor

Nov. 15—Ev'g.	High School Auditorium, Norwalk, Conn.

Leopold Stokowski, Conductor

Nov. 17—Ev'g.	Carnegie Hall
Nov. 18—Aft.	Carnegie Hall
‡Nov. 19—Morn.	Carnegie Hall
Nov. 20—Aft.	Carnegie Hall
Nov. 24—Eve.	Carnegie Hall
Nov. 25—Aft.	Carnegie Hall
Nov. 26—Ev'g.	Carnegie Hall
Nov. 27—Aft.	Carnegie Hall

Dimitri Mitropoulos, Conductor

Nov. 30—Ev'g.	Hotel Astor

Leopold Stokowski, Conductor

Dec. 1—Ev'g.	Carnegie Hall
Dec. 2—Aft.	Carnegie Hall
Dec. 3—Ev'g.	Carnegie Hall
Dec. 4—Aft.	Carnegie Hall

1949

Dimitri Mitropoulos, Conductor

Dec. 5—Ev'g.	Waldorf-Astoria Hotel
Dec. 8—Ev'g.	Carnegie Hall
Dec. 9—Aft.	Carnegie Hall
§Dec. 10—Morn.	Carnegie Hall
Dec. 11—Aft.	Carnegie Hall
Dec. 15—Ev'g.	Carnegie Hall
Dec. 16—Aft.	Carnegie Hall
§Dec. 17—Morn.	Town Hall
Dec. 18—Aft.	Carnegie Hall
Dec. 22—Ev'g.	Carnegie Hall
Dec. 23—Aft.	Carnegie Hall
Dec. 25—Aft.	Carnegie Hall
Dec. 27—Ev'g.	Bushnell Memorial Auditorium, Hartford, Conn.
Dec. 29—Ev'g.	Carnegie Hall
Dec. 30—Aft.	Carnegie Hall

1950

Jan. 1—Aft.	Carnegie Hall
Jan. 5—Ev'g.	Carnegie Hall
Jan. 6—Aft.	Carnegie Hall
Jan. 7—Ev'g.	Carnegie Hall
Jan. 8—Aft.	Carnegie Hall
Jan. 10—Ev'g.	Hotel Plaza
Jan. 12—Ev'g.	Carnegie Hall
Jan. 13—Aft.	Carnegie Hall
Jan. 14—Ev'g.	Carnegie Hall
Jan. 15—Aft.	Carnegie Hall
Jan. 19—Ev'g.	Carnegie Hall
Jan. 20—Aft.	Carnegie Hall
Jan. 21—Ev'g.	Carnegie Hall
Jan. 22—Aft.	Carnegie Hall
Jan. 26—Ev'g.	Carnegie Hall
Jan. 27—Aft.	Carnegie Hall
Jan. 28—Ev'g.	Carnegie Hall
Jan. 29—Aft.	Carnegie Hall
Jan. 31—Ev'g.	Mosque Theatre, Newark, N. J.

Bruno Walter, Conductor

Feb. 2—Ev'g.	Carnegie Hall
Feb. 3—Aft.	Carnegie Hall
*Feb. 4—Morn.	Carnegie Hall

---

* Young People's Concert—IGOR BUKETOFF, *Conductor*
‡ Young People's Concert—DEAN DIXON, *Conductor*
§ Young People's Concert—LEOPOLD STOKOWSKI, *Conductor*

1950

Feb. 5—Aft.	Carnegie Hall	
Feb. 9—Ev'g.	Carnegie Hall	
Feb. 10—Aft.	Carnegie Hall	

Franco Autori, Conductor

Feb. 11—Ev'g.   Carnegie Hall

Bruno Walter, Conductor

Feb. 12—Aft.   Carnegie Hall

Leonard Bernstein, Conductor

Feb. 16—Ev'g.	Carnegie Hall
Feb. 17—Aft.	Carnegie Hall
Feb. 18—Ev'g.	Carnegie Hall
Feb. 19—Aft.	Carnegie Hall
Feb. 23—Ev'g.	Carnegie Hall
Feb. 24—Aft.	Carnegie Hall
Feb. 25—Ev'g.	Carnegie Hall
Feb. 26—Aft.	Carnegie Hall
Feb. 28—Ev'g.	Academy of Music, Philadelphia, Penna.

Victor De Sabata, Conductor

March 2—Ev'g.	Carnegie Hall
March 3—Aft.	Carnegie Hall
※March 4—Morn.	Carnegie Hall
March 5—Aft.	Carnegie Hall
March 9—Ev'g.	Carnegie Hall
March 10—Aft.	Carnegie Hall
*March 11—Morn.	Carnegie Hall
March 12—Aft.	Carnegie Hall
March 16—Ev'g.	Carnegie Hall
March 17—Aft.	Carnegie Hall

1950

March 18—Ev'g.	Carnegie Hall
March 19—Aft.	Carnegie Hall
March 23—Ev'g.	Carnegie Hall
March 24—Aft.	Carnegie Hall
March 25—Ev'g.	Carnegie Hall
March 26—Aft.	Carnegie Hall

Leopold Stokowski, Conductor

March 30—Ev'g.	Carnegie Hall
March 31—Aft.	Carnegie Hall

Walter Hendl, Conductor

April 1—Ev'g.   Carnegie Hall

Leopold Stokowski, Conductor

April 2—Aft.   Carnegie Hall

Franco Autori, Conductor

April 3—Ev'g.   Hotel Plaza

Leopold Stokowski, Conductor

April 6—Ev'g.	Carnegie Hall
April 7—Aft.	Carnegie Hall
April 9—Aft.	Carnegie Hall

Dimitri Mitropoulos, Conductor

April 13—Ev'g.	Carnegie Hall
April 14—Aft.	Carnegie Hall
*April 15—Morn.	Carnegie Hall
April 16—Aft.	Carnegie Hall
April 20—Ev'g.	Carnegie Hall
April 21—Aft.	Carnegie Hall
April 22—Ev'g.	Carnegie Hall
April 23—Aft.	Carnegie Hall

COMPOSITIONS PERFORMED

(a) First performance.
(b) First performance in America.
(c) First performance in the United States.
(d) First performance in New York.
(e) First performance by the Society.
(f) First performance in this arrangement.

ARNELL—Prelude, *Black Mountain,* Opus 46: Oct. 29 (a).

AUBERT—*Offrande:* Nov. 17 (c), 18.

BACH—Brandenburg Concerto No. 3, G major: Jan. 10.
Concerto, G minor, for violin and orchestra: Dec. 15, 16, 18.
Overture, from Suite No. 3, D major: Feb. 11.
Sinfonia, from Cantata No. 21, *Ich hatte viel Bekümmernis:* Nov. 20 (f).
Sinfonia, from Cantata No. 156, *Ich steh' mit einem Fuss im Grabe:* Oct. 30.
Sinfonia, from Cantata No. 174, *Ich liebe den Höchsten:* Mar. 30, 31; Apr. 2.

BACH-MITROPOULOS—Fantasia and Fugue, G minor: Dec. 27.

BACH-REGER—Aria After the Chorale-Prelude, *O Man, Bewail Thy Grievous Sin:* Jan. 5, 6, 8.

※ Young People's Concert—FRANCO AUTORI, *Conductor*
* Young People's Concert—IGOR BUKETOFF, *Conductor*

BACH-STOKOWSKI—Bourrée, from English Suite No. 2, A minor, for clavier: Nov. 20 (f).
Chaconne, from Suite No. 2, D minor, for solo violin: Mar. 30 (f), 31.
Es ist vollbracht, from the *Passion According to St. John:* Mar. 30 (f), 31; Apr. 2.
Passacaglia and Fugue, C minor: Dec. 4.
Sacred Song, *Mein Jesu, was für Seelenweh:* Oct. 30 (f).
Sarabande, from Partita No. 1, D major, for solo violin: Nov. 20 (f).

BARTOK—Music for Strings, Percussion, and Celesta: Feb. 16, 17, 18, 19.

BEETHOVEN—Concerto No. 1, C major, Opus 15, for piano and orchestra: Feb. 18, 19, 28.
Concerto No. 2, B flat major, Opus 19, for piano and orchestra: Nov. 10, 11.
Concerto No. 4, G major, Opus 58, for piano and orchestra: Jan. 7, 8; Mar. 25.
Concerto No. 5, E flat major, Opus 73 ("Emperor"), for piano and orchestra: Jan. 26, 27, 29.
Concerto D major, Opus 61, for violin and orchestra: Jan. 14, 15.
Overture to *Egmont,* Opus 84: Oct. 15.
Overture, *Leonore,* No. 3, Opus 72a: Oct. 23; Feb. 26, 28.
Symphony No. 1, C major, Opus 21: Apr. 3.
Symphony No. 2, D major, Opus 36: Jan. 19, 20, 21, 22, 31.
Symphony No. 3, E flat major, Opus 55 ("Eroica"): Oct. 15; Nov. 15; Dec. 11.
Symphony No. 5, C minor, Opus 67: Mar. 18, 19.
Symphony No. 6, F major, Opus 68 ("Pastoral"): Oct. 27, 28, 30.
Symphony No. 8, F major, Opus 93: Feb. 23, 24, 25, 26, 28.

BENNETT—*Overture to an Imaginary Drama:* Nov. 26 (d).

BERG—Concerto for Violin and Orchestra: Dec. 15 (e), 16.

BERLIOZ—*Minuet of the Will-o'-the-Wisps,* from *The Damnation of Faust,* Opus 24: Nov. 30.
Overture, *The Roman Carnival,* Opus 9: Mar. 18, 19.
Rákóczy March, from *The Damnation of Faust,* Opus 24: Nov. 30.
Fantastic Symphony, Opus 14a: Mar. 2, 3.

BERNSTEIN—*The Age of Anxiety,* Symphony No. 2, for piano and orchestra (after W. H. Auden): Feb. 23 (d), 24, 26.

BLISS—Concerto, B flat major, for piano and orchestra: Jan. 21 (e).

BLOCH—Two Symphonic Interludes, from *Macbeth:* Nov. 3 (d), 4, 5, 6.

BORODIN—*Polovtsian Dances,* from *Prince Igor:* Nov. 26, 27.

BOYCE—Symphony No. 1, B flat major (arranged by Lambert): Apr. 3.

BRAHMS—Concerto No. 1, D minor, Opus 15, for piano and orchestra: Feb. 25; Apr. 1.
Concerto, D major, Opus 77, for violin and orchestra: Dec. 1, 2, 3; Mar. 16, 17, 19.
Symphony No. 1, C minor, Opus 68: Oct. 13, 14, 16.
Symphony No. 2, D major, Opus 73: Mar. 30, 31; Apr. 2.
Symphony No. 4, E minor, Opus 98: Nov. 15; Dec. 29, 30; Jan. 1, 31.
Variations on a Theme by Haydn, Opus 56a: Feb. 11.

BRITTEN—Concerto No. 1, D major, for Piano and Orchestra: Nov. 24 (d), 25, 26, 27.

BRUCKNER—Symphony No. 9, D minor ("Unfinished"): Feb. 2, 3.

CARPENTER—*Carmel Concerto:* Nov. 20 (a).

CHABRIER—*Joyeuse Marche:* Apr. 13, 14, 16.
Fête Polonaise, from *Le Roi Malgré Lui:* Apr. 13, 14, 16.

CHASINS—*Period Suite:* Apr. 20 (e), 21, 22; four movements of Suite: Apr. 23.

CHERUBINI—Overture to *Anacréon:* Jan. 26, 27, 29, 31.

CHOPIN—Concerto No. 1, E minor, Opus 11, for piano and orchestra: Apr. 22.

CHOPIN-STOKOWSKI—Mazurka, A minor, Opus 17, No. 4: Oct. 16 (f).

CLAPP—*Overture to a Comedy:* Dec. 29 (d), 30; Jan. 1.

CONRAD—*The Continental,* arranged for two pianos and orchestra by Whittemore and Lowe: Jan. 28 (e).

COPLAND—Children's Suite, from *The Red Pony:* Oct. 13 (d), 14, 16.
Outdoor Overture: Feb. 23 (e), 24, 26.

DEBUSSY—*La Mer (The Sea),* Three Orchestral Sketches: Oct. 13, 14.

DIAMOND—Overture to *The Tempest:* Nov. 3 (e), 4, 6.

DUBENSKY—Concerto Grosso for Three Solo Trombones, Tuba and Orchestra: Nov. 3 (a), 4.

DUKAS—Scherzo, *The Sorcerer's Apprentice:* Mar. 9, 10, 12.

DVORAK—Overture, *Carnival,* Opus 92: Nov. 30.
Symphony No. 5, E minor, Opus 95, *From the New World:* Mar. 23, 24, 25, 26.

ELGAR—Concerto, B minor, Opus 61, for violin and orchestra: Jan. 12, 13.

FALLA—*Nights in the Gardens of Spain,* Symphonic Impressions for Pianoforte and Orchestra: Nov. 13.
Three Dances from *The Three-Cornered Hat:* Jan. 19, 20, 21, 22.

FRANCK—Symphony, D minor: Mar. 9, 10, 12.

FRAZZI—*Preludio Magico:* Mar. 2 (d), 3.

GABRIELI—Canzon Quarti Toni a 15: Nov. 10 (e), 11.
In Ecclesiis Benedicite Domino, Ceremonial Music from *Symphoniae Sacrae:* Apr. 6 (e), 7, 9.

GERSHWIN—*I Got Plenty o' Nuttin',* from *Porgy and Bess:* Dec. 5.

GHEDINI—*Marinaresca e Baccanale:* Mar. 5 (d), 9, 10.

GLIERE—Symphony No. 3, B minor, Opus 42, *Ilya Mourometz:* Oct. 20, 21, 23, 29.

GOULD—*Philharmonic Waltzes:* Jan. 14, 15.
Spirituals for String Choir and Orchestra: Mar. 2, 3.

GOUNOD—*Jewel Song,* from *Faust:* Dec. 5.

HANDEL—Concerto, B flat major, Opus 4, No. 6, for harpsichord and orchestra: Nov. 17, 18, 20.
Concerto Grosso, G minor, Opus 6, No. 6, for string orchestra: Feb. 2, 3.

HAYDN—Concerto, C major, for violin and orchestra: Dec. 4.
Symphony No. 88, G major: Feb. 12.
Symphony No. 101, D major ("The Clock"): Nov. 3, 4, 5, 6.

HOLST—*St. Paul's Suite,* Opus 29, No. 1, for string orchestra: Jan. 10.

HONEGGER—Concertino, for piano and orchestra: Dec. 29, 30.
Summer Pastoral: Apr. 3.

IBERT—*Escales (Ports of Call):* Apr. 16.

IVANOV-RADKEVICH—*Russian Overture:* Nov. 13 (b).

KERN—*The Song is You,* arranged for two pianos and orchestra by Whittemore and Lowe: Jan. 28 (e).

KHACHATURIAN—Concerto, for piano and orchestra: Dec. 29, 30; Jan. 1.

KRENEK—Concerto No. 3, for piano and orchestra: Dec. 8 (d), 9, 11.

LEKEU—Adagio for Strings, Opus 83: Jan. 10.

LIEBERMANN—*Suite on Swiss Folk Melodies:* Oct. 16 (b).

LISZT—*A Faust Symphony:* Dec. 8, 9.

MAHLER—Symphony No. 1, D major: Feb. 9, 10, 12.
Symphony No. 8, E flat major: Apr. 6 (e), 7, 9.

MASSENET—*Pleurez, pleurez, mes yeux,* from *Le Cid:* Nov. 30.

MENDELSSOHN—Concerto, E minor, Opus 64, for violin and orchestra: Nov. 30; Mar. 18.
Overture to *A Midsummer Night's Dream,* Opus 21: Feb. 12.
Overture, *Ruy Blas,* Opus 95: Apr. 13, 14, 16.

MESSIAEN—*Trois Petites Liturgies de la Présence Divine:* Nov. 17 (b), 18.

MIASKOVSKY—*Slavic Rhapsody:* Oct. 20 (b), 21.

MOHAUPT—*Town Piper Music:* Jan. 5 (e), 6, 7.

MOZART—Concerto, E flat major, K. 271, for piano and orchestra: Oct. 29.
Concerto, D minor, K. 466, for piano and orchestra: Feb. 5.
Concerto, A major, K. 488, for piano and orchestra: Mar. 23, 24.
Concerto, G major, K. 216, for violin and orchestra: Dec. 18.
Eine Kleine Nachtmusik, K. 525: Nov. 27; Feb. 5.
Notturno, K. 286, for four orchestras: Oct. 20, 21, 23.
Overture to *The Abduction from the Seraglio:* Jan. 14, 15.
Overture to *The Magic Flute:* Nov. 15; Dec. 8, 9, 11.
Overture to *The Marriage of Figaro:* Mar. 9, 10.
Symphony, D major, K. 385 ("Haffner"): Nov. 17, 18, 20; Feb. 5.
Symphony, G minor, K. 550: Feb. 2, 3, 5.

PIKET—Overture, *Curtain Raiser to an American Play:* Jan. 7 (d), 8.

PORRINO—Symphonic Poem, *Sardegna:* Nov. 5 (b).

POULENC—*Concert Champêtre,* for harpsichord and orchestra: Nov. 17, 18, 20.
Concerto for Two Pianos and Orchestra: Jan. 28.

PROKOFIEFF—*Classical Symphony,* Opus 25: Nov. 30.
Symphony No. 5, Opus 100: Apr. 1.
Symphony No. 6, E flat minor, Opus 111: Nov. 24 (b), 25, 26; Dec. 4.

PURCELL-MITROPOULOS—Prelude and Death of Dido, from *Dido and Aeneas:* Jan. 10.

PURCELL-STOKOWSKI—Suite: Dec. 4 (f).

RABAUD—Symphonic Poem, *La Procession Nocturne:* Dec. 8, 9, 11.

RACHMANINOFF—Rhapsody on a Theme of Paganini, Opus 43, for piano and orchestra: Mar. 23, 24, 26.
Symphonic Dances, Opus 45: Jan. 26, 27, 29.

RAVEL—Bolero: Mar. 5.
Orchestral Fragments, Second Series, from *Daphnis et Chloé:* Mar. 16, 17.
Mother Goose, Five Children's Pieces: Mar. 25; three movements from Suite, Mar. 26.

REGER—Concerto, F minor, Opus 114, for piano and orchestra: Jan. 5 (e), 6.

RESPIGHI—Symphonic Poem, *Pines of Rome:* Mar. 12.

REVUELTAS—Symphonic Poem, *Sensemayá:* Nov. 13 (e).

RIEGGER—Canon and Fugue: Dec. 1 (d), 2, 3.

RIMSKY-KORSAKOFF—*Spanish Caprice,* Opus 34: Feb. 11.

RIVIER—Concertino for Viola and Orchestra: Nov. 5 (d).

RODGERS—*Falling in Love with Love,* arranged for two pianos and orchestra by Whittemore and Lowe: Jan. 28 (e).
Lover, arranged for two pianos and orchestra by Whittemore and Lowe: Jan. 28 (e).

ROSSINI—Overture to *La Gazza Ladra:* Mar. 2, 3, 5.

RUGGLES—*Organum:* Nov. 24 (a), 25.

SAINT-SAENS—Concerto No. 3, B minor, Opus 61, for violin and orchestra: Jan. 19, 20, 22.
Symphonic Poem, *Le Rouet d'Omphale,* Opus 31: Jan. 19, 20, 21, 22.

SCHOENBERG—*A Survivor from Warsaw,* Opus 46: Apr. 13 (d), 14.
Song of the Wood-Dove, from *Gurrelieder:* Oct. 27 (e), 28, 30.

SCHUBERT—Symphony No. 2, B flat major: Apr. 13, 14, 16.
Symphony No. 8, B minor ("Unfinished"): Nov. 27; Dec. 1, 2, 3.

SCHUMANN—Concerto, A minor, Opus 129, for violoncello and orchestra: Nov. 3, 4, 6.
Symphony No. 1, B flat major, Opus 38: Jan. 5, 6, 7, 8.
Symphony No. 3, E flat major, Opus 97 ("Rhenish"): Feb. 9, 10.
Symphony No. 4, D minor, Opus 120: Feb. 16, 17, 18.

SESSIONS—Symphony No. 2: Jan. 12 (d), 13, 14, 15.

SHAPERO—Adagietto, from *Symphony for Classical Orchestra:* Feb. 23 (d), 24, 25.

SHULMAN—Concerto for Violoncello and Orchestra: Apr. 13 (a), 14.

SIBELIUS—Symphony No. 1, E minor, Opus 39: Mar. 5.
Symphony No. 4, A minor, Opus 63: Apr. 20, 21, 23.

SINIGAGLIA–Overture to *Le Baruffe Chiozzotte:* Mar. 12.

SINIGAGLIA—Overture to *Le Baruffe Chiozzotte:* Mar. 12.

STRAUSS, J.—*Tritsch-Tratsch Polka:* Dec. 5.
Waltz, *On the Beautiful Blue Danube,* Opus 314: Oct 23.
Waltz, *Emperor,* Opus 437: Dec. 5.
Waltz, *Tales from the Vienna Woods,* Opus 325: Oct. 23; Apr. 3.
Waltz, *Voices of Spring,* Opus 410: Dec. 5.

STRAUSS, R.—*Elektra,* Tragedy in One Act: Dec. 22, 23, 25.
Symphonia Domestica, Opus 53: Apr. 20, 21, 22, 23.
Tone Poem, *Death and Transfiguration,* Opus 24: Oct. 20, 21, 29.

STRAVINSKY—Suite from *The Firebird:* Feb. 11.

TCHAIKOVSKY—Concerto No. 1, B flat major, Opus 23, for piano and orchestra: Feb. 11.
Overture-Fantasy, *Romeo and Juliet:* Nov. 24, 25.
Serenade, C major, Opus 48, for string orchestra: Jan. 10.
Symphonic Fantasy, *Francesca da Rimini,* Opus 32: Jan. 12, 13.
Symphony No. 5, E minor, Opus 64: Nov. 10, 11, 13.

THOMSON—Suite, *The Mother of Us All:* Mar. 30 (d), 31; three movements from Suite: Apr. 2.

VAUGHAN WILLIAMS—*English Folk-Song Suite:* Apr. 3 (e).
Symphony No. 4, F minor: Dec. 15, 16, 18.

VERDI—*O don fatale,* from Don Carlos: Nov. 30.
Overture to *The Sicilian Vespers:* Mar. 23, 24, 25, 26.

VILLA-LOBOS—Symphonic Poem, *Uirapurú:* Oct. 27 (e), 28, 30.

VIVALDI—Concerto Grosso, G minor, Opus 3, No. 2, for strings and cembalo: Nov. 5 (e), 6.

WAGNER—*A Siegfried Idyl:* Jan. 28.
Overture to *The Flying Dutchman:* Jan. 28.
Siegfried's Death and Funeral Music, from *Götterdämmerung:* Mar. 16, 17.
Siegfried's Rhine Journey, from *Götterdämmerung:* Mar. 16, 17.
Prelude to *Lohengrin:* Oct. 27, 28.
Introduction to Act III of *Lohengrin:* Jan. 12, 13.
Prelude to *Die Meistersinger:* Oct. 13, 14.
Good Friday Spell, from *Parsifal:* Mar. 9, 10, 18.

Siegfried's Ascent of the Mountain, Awakening of Brünnhilde, and Love Scene, from Act III of *Siegfried:* Nov. 12.
Bacchanale, from *Tannhäuser* (Paris version): Nov. 12.
Overture to *Tannhäuser:* Apr. 16.
Opening Scene, Garden Scene, and Closing Scene, from Act II of *Tristan und Isolde:* Nov. 12.
Prelude and Liebestod, from *Tristan und Isolde:* Dec. 1, 2, 3.
Ride of the Valkyries, from *Die Walküre:* Mar. 2, 3, 18.
Wotan's Farewell and Magic Fire Spell, from *Die Walküre:* Jan. 28.

WALTON—Concerto for Violin and Orchestra: Feb. 16 (e), 17.
Overture, *Portsmouth Point:* Apr. 1.

WEBER—Overture to *Euryanthe:* Feb. 9, 10, 19.
Overture to *Der Freischütz:* Dec. 15, 16, 18, 27.

WEBERN—Symphony, Opus 21: Jan. 26 (e), 27.

SOLOISTS

PIANISTS
JACQUES ABRAM: Nov. 24, 25, 26, 27.
JOSEPH BATTISTA: Apr. 1.
LEONARD BERNSTEIN: Feb. 18, 19.
ROBERT CASADESUS: Jan. 26, 27, 29.
RUDOLF FIRKUSNY: Feb. 5.
LUKAS FOSS: Feb. 23, 24, 26.
GARY GRAFFMAN: Feb. 25.
LEONID HAMBRO: Nov. 17, 18; Apr. 22.
EUGENE ISTOMIN: Oct. 29.
WILLIAM KAPELL: Nov. 10, 11, 13.
OSCAR LEVANT: Dec. 29, 30; Jan. 1.
MOURA LYMPANY: Mar. 25.
NIKITA MAGALOFF: Feb. 11.
DIMITRI MITROPOULOS: Dec. 8, 9, 11.
LEONARD PENNARIO: Jan. 21.
ARTUR RUBINSTEIN: Mar. 23, 24, 26.
RUDOLF SERKIN: Jan. 5, 6, 7, 8.

VIOLINISTS
JOHN CORIGLIANO: Jan. 12, 13; Feb. 2, 3.
ZINO FRANCESCATTI: Jan. 19, 20, 22.
SZYMON GOLDBERG: Jan. 14, 15.
JASCHA HEIFETZ: Feb. 16, 17.
NATHAN MILSTEIN: Mar. 16, 17, 19.
IMRE POGANY: Feb. 2, 3.
MIRIAM SOLOVIEFF: Mar. 18.
ISAAC STERN: Nov. 30; Dec. 1, 2, 3, 4.
JOSEPH SZIGETI: Dec. 15, 16, 18.

VIOLIST
WILLIAM LINCER: Nov. 5.

VIOLONCELLISTS
PIERRE FOURNIER: Nov. 3, 4, 6.
LEONARD ROSE: Feb. 2, 3; Apr. 13, 14

HARPSICHORDIST
WANDA LANDOWSKA: Nov. 17, 18, 20.

DUO-PIANISTS
ARTHUR WHITTEMORE and JACK LOWE: Jan. 28.

VOCALISTS
CARLOS ALEXANDER, Baritone: Apr. 6, 7, 9.
MARIAN ANDERSON, Contralto: Nov. 30.
ROBERT BERNAUER, Tenor: Nov. 12.
LOUISE BERNHARDT, Contralto: Apr. 6, 7, 9.
EUGENE CONLEY, Tenor: Nov. 12; Apr. 6, 7, 9.
BEVERLY DAME, Soprano: Dec. 22, 23, 25.
TODD DUNCAN, Baritone: Dec. 5.
EDITH EVANS, Soprano: Dec. 22, 23, 25.
UTA GRAF, Soprano: Apr. 6, 7, 9.
FREDERICK JAGEL, Tenor: Dec. 22, 23, 25.
HERBERT JANSSEN, Baritone: Dec. 22, 23, 25.
IRENE JESSNER, Soprano: Dec. 22, 23, 25.
MARTHA LIPTON, Mezzo-Soprano: Oct. 27, 28, 30; Apr. 6, 7, 9.
GEORGE LONDON, Bass-Baritone: Apr. 6, 7, 9.
MARIQUITA MOLL, Soprano: Nov. 12.
ELENA NIKOLAIDI, Contralto: Dec. 22, 23, 25.
JARMILA NOVOTNA, Soprano: Dec. 5.
VIRGINIA PARIS, Contralto: Nov. 12.
MICHAEL RHODES, Baritone: Dec. 22, 23, 25.
ELEANOR STEBER, Soprano: Dec. 5.
MIRIAM STOCKTON, Soprano: Dec. 22, 23, 25.

LAWRENCE TIBBETT, Baritone: Jan. 28.

ASTRID VARNAY, Soprano: Dec. 22, 23, 25.

ELINOR WARREN, Soprano: Dec. 22, 23, 25.

CAMILLA WILLIAMS, Soprano: Apr. 6, 7, 9.

FRANCES YEEND, Soprano: Apr. 6, 7, 9.

NARRATOR

ADOLPH ANDERSON: Apr. 13, 14.

ONDES MARTENOT

GINETTE MARTENOT: Nov. 17, 18.

CHORUSES

BOYS' CHORUS FROM PUBLIC SCHOOL NO. 12, MANHATTAN, Pauline L. Covner, Teacher: Apr. 6, 7, 9.

PRINCETON UNIVERSITY CHAPEL CHOIR, Carl Weinrich, Director: Apr. 13, 14.

SCHOLA CANTORUM, Hugh Ross, Director: Apr. 6, 7, 9.

WESTMINSTER CHOIR, John Finley Williamson, Director: Apr. 6, 7, 9.

WOMEN'S CHORUS FROM THE SCHOLA CANTORUM, Hugh Ross, Director: Nov. 12, 17, 18.

1950–51 ONE HUNDRED NINTH SEASON

Conductor
DIMITRI MITROPOULOS

Guest Conductors
BRUNO WALTER
VICTOR DE SABATA   GEORGE SZELL
LEONARD BERNSTEIN

Associate Conductor
FRANCO AUTORI

Conductor of Young People's Concerts
IGOR BUKETOFF

CONCERTS

1950

Dimitri Mitropoulos, Conductor

Oct. 12—Ev'g.	Carnegie Hall	
Oct. 13—Aft.	Carnegie Hall	
Oct. 15—Aft.	Carnegie Hall	
Oct. 17—Ev'g.	Rutgers University, New Brunswick, N.J.	
Oct. 19—Ev'g.	Carnegie Hall	
Oct. 20—Aft.	Carnegie Hall	
*Oct. 21—Aft.	Town Hall	
Oct. 22—Aft.	Carnegie Hall	
Oct. 26—Ev'g.	Carnegie Hall	
Oct. 27—Aft.	Carnegie Hall	
Oct. 28—Ev'g.	Carnegie Hall	
Oct. 29—Aft.	Carnegie Hall	
Nov. 2—Ev'g.	Carnegie Hall	
Nov. 3—Aft.	Carnegie Hall	
‡Nov. 4—Ev'g.	Carnegie Hall	
Nov. 5—Aft.	Carnegie Hall	
Nov. 7—Ev'g.	Bushnell Memorial Auditorium, Hartford, Conn.	

1950

Nov. 9—Ev'g.	Carnegie Hall
Nov. 10—Aft.	Carnegie Hall
Nov. 12—Aft.	Carnegie Hall
Nov. 13—Ev'g.	Carnegie Hall
Nov. 16—Ev'g.	Carnegie Hall
Nov. 17—Aft.	Carnegie Hall
*Nov. 18—Aft.	Town Hall
Nov. 19—Aft.	Carnegie Hall
Nov. 23—Ev'g.	Carnegie Hall
Nov. 24—Aft.	Carnegie Hall
Nov. 25—Ev'g.	Carnegie Hall
Nov. 26—Aft.	Carnegie Hall
Nov. 30—Ev'g.	Carnegie Hall
Dec. 1—Aft.	Carnegie Hall
Dec. 2—Ev'g.	Carnegie Hall
Dec. 3—Aft.	Carnegie Hall

George Szell, Guest Conductor

Dec. 7—Ev'g.	Carnegie Hall
Dec. 8—Aft.	Carnegie Hall

---

* Young People's Concert, conducted by Igor Buketoff.

‡ Conducted by Franco Autori, Associate Conductor.

1950			1951	
*Dec. 9—Morn.	Carnegie Hall		Feb. 22—Ev'g.	Carnegie Hall
Dec. 10—Aft.	Carnegie Hall		Feb. 23—Aft.	Carnegie Hall
Dec. 11—Ev'g.	Hotel Plaza		Feb. 24—Ev'g.	Carnegie Hall
Dec. 14—Ev'g.	Carnegie Hall		Feb. 25—Aft.	Carnegie Hall
Dec. 15—Aft.	Carnegie Hall			

Dimitri Mitropoulos, Conductor

*Dec. 16—Aft.	Town Hall		Mar. 1—Ev'g.	Carnegie Hall
Dec. 17—Aft.	Carnegie Hall		Mar. 2—Aft.	Carnegie Hall
Dec. 21—Ev'g.	Carnegie Hall		Mar. 3—Ev'g.	Carnegie Hall
Dec. 22—Aft.	Carnegie Hall		Mar. 4—Aft.	Carnegie Hall
Dec. 23—Ev'g.	Carnegie Hall		Mar. 8—Ev'g.	Carnegie Hall
Dec. 24—Aft.	Carnegie Hall		Mar. 9—Aft.	Carnegie Hall
Dec. 28—Ev'g.	Carnegie Hall		Mar. 10—Ev'g.	Carnegie Hall
Dec. 29—Aft.	Carnegie Hall		Mar. 11—Aft.	Carnegie Hall
Dec. 30—Ev'g.	Carnegie Hall			
Dec. 31—Aft.	Carnegie Hall			

Victor De Sabata, Guest Conductor

1951				
			Mar. 15—Ev'g.	Carnegie Hall
			Mar. 16—Aft.	Carnegie Hall
Jan. 4—Ev'g.	Carnegie Hall		*Mar. 17—Morn.	Carnegie Hall
Jan. 5—Aft.	Carnegie Hall		Mar. 18—Aft.	Carnegie Hall
*Jan. 6—Morn.	Carnegie Hall		Mar. 22—Ev'g.	Carnegie Hall
Jan. 7—Aft.	Carnegie Hall		Mar. 23—Aft.	Carnegie Hall
Jan. 11—Ev'g.	Carnegie Hall			

Jan. 12—Aft.	Carnegie Hall		**Dimitri Mitropoulos, Conductor**	
Jan. 14—Aft.	Carnegie Hall		Mar. 24—Aft.	Constitution Hall, Washington, D.C.

Bruno Walter, Guest Conductor

			Victor De Sabata, Guest Conductor	
Jan. 18—Ev'g.	Carnegie Hall		Mar. 25—Aft.	Carnegie Hall

Dimitri Mitropoulos, Conductor

Jan. 19—Aft.	Carnegie Hall			
Jan. 20—Ev'g.	Carnegie Hall		Mar. 29—Ev'g.	Carnegie Hall
Jan. 21—Aft.	Carnegie Hall		Mar. 30—Aft.	Carnegie Hall
Jan. 25—Ev'g.	Carnegie Hall		‡Mar. 31—Ev'g.	Carnegie Hall
Jan. 26—Aft.	Carnegie Hall		Apr. 1—Aft.	Carnegie Hall
Jan. 27—Ev'g.	Carnegie Hall		Apr. 5—Ev'g.	Carnegie Hall
Jan. 28—Aft.	Carnegie Hall		Apr. 6—Aft.	Carnegie Hall
Feb. 1—Ev'g.	Carnegie Hall		Apr. 7—Ev'g.	Carnegie Hall
Feb. 2—Aft.	Carnegie Hall		Apr. 8—Aft.	Carnegie Hall
*Feb. 3—Morn.	Carnegie Hall		Apr. 10—Ev'g.	Mosque Theatre, Newark, N.J.
Feb. 4—Aft.	Carnegie Hall			
Feb. 5—Ev'g.	Carnegie Hall		Apr. 12—Ev'g.	Carnegie Hall
Feb. 8—Ev'g.	Carnegie Hall		Apr. 13—Aft.	Carnegie Hall
Feb. 9—Aft.	Carnegie Hall		*Apr. 14—Morn.	Carnegie Hall
Feb. 11—Aft.	Carnegie Hall		Apr. 15—Aft.	Carnegie Hall

Leonard Bernstein, Guest Conductor

Feb. 15—Ev'g.	Carnegie Hall		Apr. 16—Ev'g.	Hotel Plaza
Feb. 16—Aft.	Carnegie Hall		Apr. 19—Ev'g.	Carnegie Hall
Feb. 17—Ev'g.	Carnegie Hall		Apr. 20—Aft.	Carnegie Hall
Feb. 18—Aft.	Carnegie Hall		Apr. 22—Aft.	Carnegie Hall

COMPOSITIONS PERFORMED

(a) First performance.
(b) First performance in America.
(c) First performance in New York.
(d) First performance by the Society.
(e) First concert performance in America.
(f) First complete performance by the Society.

---

* Young People's Concert, conducted by Igor Buketoff.
‡ Conducted by Franco Autori, Associate Conductor.

ALEXANDER—*Epitaphs* for Orchestra: March 8 (a), 9.

BABIN—Capriccio: Nov. 9 (a), 10.

BACH—Concerto, D minor, for Three Pianos and Strings: Nov. 23, 24, 26.
Concerto, A minor, for Violin with String Orchestra: March 1, 2.

BACH-CASELLA—Chaconne (Ciaccona): Oct. 12 (d), 13.

BACH-RESPIGHI—Passacaglia and Fugue, C minor: March 15, 16.

BACH-STOKOWSKI—*Komm, süsser Tod,* Geistliches Lied: March 31.

BARBER—First Essay for Orchestra: Dec. 7 (d), 8, 10, 23.
Overture, *The School for Scandal:* March 18.

BARTOK—Concerto No. 2 for Piano and Orchestra: March 31 (d).

BAX—*Overture to a Picaresque Comedy:* April 19, 20, 22.

BEETHOVEN—Concerto No. 3, C minor, Opus 37, for Piano and Orchestra:
April 7.
Concerto No. 4, G major, Opus 58, for Piano and Orchestra: April 22.
Concerto No. 5, E flat major, Opus 73 ("Emperor") for Piano and Orchestra:
Dec. 28, 29, 31.
Concerto, D major, Opus 61, for Violin and Orchestra: Dec. 21, 22, 30.
Overture, *Coriolanus,* Opus 65: Oct. 26, 27, 28, 29.
Overture to the ballet, *The Creatures of Prometheus,* Opus 43: Dec. 21, 22, 24.
Overture, *Leonore* No. 2, Opus 72-a: Oct. 15, 17; Feb. 5.
Scena and Aria, "Ah, Perfido!" Opus 62: Feb. 5.
Symphony No. 1, C major, Opus 21: Oct. 15.
Symphony No. 2, D major, Opus 36: Jan. 4, 5, 7.
Symphony No. 4, B flat major, Opus 60: Oct. 12, 13, 17; Nov. 7, 12; March 10,
24; April 10.
Symphony No. 6, F major, Opus 68 ("Pastoral"): Dec. 21, 22, 23, 24.
Symphony No. 7, A major, Opus 92: March 15, 16.
Symphony No. 8, F major, Opus 93: Feb. 5; March 18.

BERG—*Wozzeck,* Opera in 3 Acts, Opus 7 (in concert form): April 12 (f), 13,
15.

BERLIOZ—Excerpts from *The Damnation of Faust:* Minuet of the Will-o'-the-
Wisps: Nov. 12, 13; Dance of the Sylphs: Nov. 13; Rákóczy March: Nov. 12,
13.
Overture, *Rob Roy:* March 29 (d), 30; April 1.
Overture, *Roman Carnival:* Oct. 19, 20, 22.

BIZET—Suite, *Jeux d'Enfants,* Opus 22: April 16.
Symphony in C major: Oct. 28, 29; Nov. 7.

BLOCH—*Schelomo (Solomon),* Hebrew Rhapsody for Violoncello and Orchestra: April 5, 6, 8.

BOYCE—Symphony No. 1, B flat major (edited by Lambert): Nov. 4.

BRAHMS—Concerto, No. 1, D minor, Opus 15, for Piano and Orchestra: Jan.
25, 26, 27, 28.
Concerto, No. 2, B flat major, Opus 83, for Piano and Orchestra: Feb. 8, 9, 11;
April 19, 20.
Concerto, D major, Opus 77, for Violin and Orchestra: Jan. 18, 19, 20, 21.
Concerto, A minor, Opus 102, for Violin and Violoncello with Orchestra:
Feb. 1, 2, 4.
Four Hungarian Dances: No. 17, F sharp minor (orchestrated by Dvorak); No.
1, G minor; No. 3, F major (original edition by Brahms); No. 10, F major:
Feb. 4.
Overture, *Academic Festival,* Opus 80: Feb. 1, 2, 11.
Overture, *Tragic:* Jan. 18, 19, 20, 21.
Symphony No. 1, C minor, Opus 68: Jan. 18, 19, 20, 21.

Symphony No. 2, D major, Opus 73: Feb. 1, 2, 4.
Symphony No. 3, F major, Opus 90: Jan. 25, 26, 27, 28.
Symphony No. 4, E minor, Opus 98: Feb. 8, 9, 11.
Variations on a Theme by Haydn, Opus 56-a: Jan. 25, 26, 27, 28.
BRUCH—Concerto No. 1, G minor, Opus 26, for Violin and Orchestra: Nov. 4.
BRUCKNER—Symphony No. 8, C minor: Dec. 14, 15, 17.
CASADESUS—Concerto for Two Pianos and Orchestra: Nov. 25 (c).
CASELLA—*Paganiniana,* Divertimento for Orchestra on Themes of Niccoló
Paganini, Opus 65: Dec. 14 (c), 15, 17, 23.
CHERUBINI—Overture, *The Water-Carrier:* Nov. 30; Dec. 1, 2, 3.
CHOPIN—Concerto No. 2, F minor, Opus 21, for Piano and Orchestra: Jan. 7;
March 10.
COPLAND—*El Salón México:* Feb. 22, 23, 24, 25.
DEBUSSY—*Iberia:* Images pour Orchestre No. 2: March 15, 16, 18.
La Mer, Three Symphonic Sketches: Nov. 23, 24, 25, 26.
DELLO JOIO—*New York Profiles:* April 5 (c), 6, 7, 8.
DVORAK—Concerto, A minor, Opus 53, for Violin and Orchestra: March 1, 2,
4.
Concerto, B minor, Opus 104, for Violoncello and Orchestra: Nov. 9, 10, 12.
ELGAR—Variation No. 9 ("Nimrod") from Variations on an Original Theme,
Opus 36: Dec. 23.
FALLA—Three Dances from *The Three-Cornered Hat:* Nov. 7.
FRANCK—Symphonic Variations for Piano and Orchestra: Feb. 24, 25.
Symphony, D minor: March 31.
GLAZOUNOFF—Concerto, A minor, Opus 82, for Violin and Orchestra: Nov.
30; Dec. 1, 3.
GOLDMARK—Overture, *Sakuntala:* Nov. 9, 10, 12.
GRIEG—Concerto, A minor, Opus 16, for Piano and Orchestra: Dec. 2.
HAYDN—Sinfonia Concertante, B flat major, Opus 84, for Solo Violin, Violon-
cello, Oboe, Bassoon and Orchestra: Nov. 2, 3, 5; April 16.
Symphony, G major, No. 92 ("Oxford"): Jan. 11, 12.
IVES—Symphony No. 2: Feb. 22 (a), 23, 24, 25.
KOUTZEN—*Morning Music,* for Flute and String Orchestra: April 19 (a), 20,
22.
KRENEK—Symphonic Elegy for String Orchestra: March 29 (c), 30.
LALO—*Symphonie Espagnole,* Opus 21 (four movements) for Violin and Orches-
tra: Oct. 19, 20.
MALIPIERO—Concerto No. 4, for Piano and Orchestra: March 29 (b), 30;
April 1.
MARTIN—Concerto for Seven Wind Instruments, String Orchestra, Percussion,
and Timpani: Dec. 28 (b), 29, 30.
MENDELSSOHN—Concerto No. 1, G minor, Opus 25, for Piano and Orchestra:
Nov. 13; Jan. 14.
Overture, *The Hebrides (Fingal's Cave):* March 8, 9, 10, 11.
Overture, Scherzo, Notturno, Wedding March, from *A Midsummer Night's
Dream:* Jan. 4, 5.
Symphony No. 3, A minor ("Scotch"): April 5, 6, 7, 8.
MILHAUD—*Le Carnaval d'Aix,* Fantasy for Piano and Orchestra: Feb. 24, 25.
Music for the Play, *Les Choéphores* (The Libation-Bearers) by Aeschylus
(French version by Paul Claudel): Nov. 16 (b), 17.
MOZART—Adagio, K. 261; Rondo allegretto grazioso, K. 373: Nov. 30; Dec.
1, 3.

Concerto, G major, K. 453, for Piano and Orchestra: Feb. 22, 23.
Concerto, E flat major, K. 365, for Two Pianos and Orchestra: Nov. 23, 24, 25, 26.
Concerto No. 7, D major, K. 271-a, for Violin and Orchestra: Oct. 26, 27.
Concert-Rondo, for Piano and Orchestra, K. 382: Nov. 13 (d).
Overture to *Don Giovanni:* Feb. 22, 23, 24, 25.
Overture to *The Marriage of Figaro:* Nov. 13; April 10.
Suite from *Idomeneo:* March 1, 2, 3, 4, 24.
Symphony, D major, K. 385 ("Haffner"): Dec. 11.
Symphony No. 39, E flat major, K. 543: April 19, 20, 22.
The Village Musicians (A Musical Joke), K. 522: Dec. 11.
Three German Dances: No. 3, K. 605; No. 2, K. 602; No. 3, K. 602: Feb. 22, 23, 24, 25.

PAGANINI—Concerto, D major, Opus 6, for Violin and Orchestra: Oct. 22.

PERPESSA—*Christus Symphony:* Oct. 26 (a), 27; Dec. 2, 3.

PROKOFIEFF—Concerto No. 2, G minor, Opus 16, for Piano and Orchestra: March 3.
Concerto No. 3, C minor, Opus 26, for Piano and Orchestra: Feb. 15, 16.
Concerto No. 2, G minor, Opus 63, for Violin and Orchestra: Jan. 4, 5.
Symphony No. 5, Opus 100: Oct. 12, 13, 15, 17.

PURCELL—Prelude and Death of Dido, from *Dido and Aeneas* (arranged by Dimitri Mitropoulos): April 16.

RACHMANINOFF—Concerto No. 2, C minor, Opus 18, for Piano and Orchestra: Feb. 17, 18.
Symphony No. 2, E minor, Opus 27: March 29, 30; April 1, 10.

RAVEL—*Alborado del Grazioso:* Nov. 16, 17, 19.
L'Heure Espagnole (Spanish Time), Opera in One Act: Nov. 16 (d), 17, 19.
La Valse, Choreographic Poem for Orchestra: Oct. 26, 27, 28, 29.
Ma Mère l'Oye (Mother Goose), Five Children's Pieces: Nov. 19.
Pavane pour une Infante Défunte: Nov. 19.
Rapsodie Espagnole: Nov. 30; Dec. 1, 2, 3.

ROSSINI—Overture, *La Scala di Seta:* Dec. 28, 29, 31.

SAINT-SAENS—Concerto, A minor, Opus 33, for Violoncello and Orchestra: April 5, 6.
Danse Macabre, Opus 40: Oct. 28, 29.
Prelude to *Le Déluge:* April 5, 6, 7, 8, 16.

SCHOENBERG—Variations for Orchestra, Opus 31: Nov. 2 (d), 3, 5.

SCHUBERT—Entr'acte and Ballet Music No. 2, from *Rosamunde:* Dec. 11.
Symphony No. 9, C major: Jan. 11, 12, 14.

SCHUMANN—Concerto, A minor, Opus 54, for Piano and Orchestra: March 15, 16, 18.
Introduction and Allegro, D minor, for Piano and Orchestra: Nov. 13 (e).
Overture, Scherzo and Finale, Opus 52: March 10, 11.
Symphony No. 2, C major, Opus 61: Nov. 9, 10.

SIBELIUS—Concerto, D minor, Opus 47, for Violin and Orchestra: March 8, 9, 11.
Symphony No. 7, in One Movement, Opus 105: Dec. 7, 8, 10.

SMETANA—*From Bohemia's Fields and Groves,* from the Symphonic Cycle, *Ma Vlast (My Country)*: Dec. 28, 29, 30, 31.
Symphonic Poem, *Vltava (The Moldau)*: Jan. 7.

STRAUSS, J.—Waltz, *The Beautiful Blue Danube:* Dec. 11.

STRAUSS, R.—Burleske, for Piano and Orchestra: Nov. 13.
Tone Poem, *Don Juan*, Opus 20: March 31.

Tone Poem, *Don Quixote,* Opus 35: Dec. 7, 8, 10.
Tone Poem, *Ein Heldenleben,* Opus 40: Oct. 19, 20, 22.
STRAVINSKY—Ballet Music, *Petrouchka:* March 1, 2, 3, 4, 24.
Le Sacre du Printemps: Feb. 15, 16, 17, 18.
SWANSON—Short Symphony: Nov. 23 (a), 24, 25, 26.
TCHAIKOVSKY—Concerto No. 1, B flat minor, Opus 23, for Piano and Orchestra: Nov. 2, 3, 5.
Concerto, D major, Opus 35, for Violin and Orchestra: Dec. 24.
Overture-Fantasy, *Romeo and Juliet:* Feb. 15, 16, 17, 18.
Symphony No. 4, F minor, Opus 36: Dec. 31.
Symphony No. 6, B minor, Opus 74 ("Pathétique"): Nov. 4.
THOMSON—Symphony No. 2: Nov. 30 (d), Dec. 1.
VIEUXTEMPS—Concerto No. 4, D minor, Opus 31, for Violin and Orchestra: Oct. 28, 29.
WAGNER—Brünnhilde's Immolation, *Götterdämmerung:* March 25.
Siegfried's Death and Funeral Music, *Götterdämmerung:* Feb. 5.
Prelude to *Lohengrin:* Jan. 11, 12, 14.
Prelude to *Die Meistersinger:* Nov. 4; March 22, 23, 25.
Good Friday Spell, *Parsifal:* March 22, 23, 25.
Prelude to *Parsifal:* Feb. 5; March 22, 23, 25.
Forest Murmurs, *Siegfried:* March 25.
A Siegfried Idyl: March 22, 23.
Overture to *Tannhäuser:* March 22, 23.
Prelude and Liebestod, *Tristan und Isolde:* Feb. 5; March 22, 23, 25.
WEBER—Overture, *Euryanthe:* Nov. 2, 3, 5, 7.
Overture to *Oberon:* Dec. 7, 8, 10, 23.
Overture, *Ruler of the Spirits:* Nov. 23, 24, 25, 26.
Symphony No. 1, C major, Opus 19: March 8, 9, 11.

SOLOISTS

PIANO

CLAUDIO ARRAU: March 15, 16, 18.
LEONARD BERNSTEIN: Feb. 22, 23.
JORGE BOLET: March 3.
GABY CASADESUS: Nov. 23, 24, 25, 26.
JEAN CASADESUS: Nov. 23, 24, 26.
ROBERT CASADESUS: Nov. 23, 24, 25, 26.
ALDO CICCOLINI: Nov. 2, 3, 5.
CLIFFORD CURZON: Jan. 25, 26, 27, 28.
RICHARD FARRELL: Dec. 2.
RUDOLF FIRKUSNY: Jan. 14.
ANDOR FOLDES: March 31.
SIDNEY FOSTER: April 7.
MYRA HESS: Feb. 8, 9, 11.
WILLIAM KAPELL: Feb. 15, 16, 17, 18.
EUGENE LIST: Feb. 24, 25.
DIMITRI MITROPOULOS: March 29, 30; April 1.
GUIOMAR NOVAES: Jan. 7.
MENAHEM PRESSLER: March 10.
ARTUR RUBINSTEIN: April 19, 20, 22.
RUDOLF SERKIN: Nov. 13; Dec. 28, 29, 31.

VIOLIN

JOHN CORIGLIANO: Oct. 19, 20, 22; Nov. 2, 3, 5; Jan. 4, 5; Feb. 1, 2, 4; April 5, 6, 7, 8, 16.
ZINO FRANCESCATTI: Jan. 18, 19, 20, 21.
JASCHA HEIFETZ: March 8, 9, 11.
YEHUDI MENUHIN: Oct. 26, 27, 28, 29.
NATHAN MILSTEIN: Nov. 30; Dec. 1, 3.
ERICA MORINI: Dec. 21, 22, 24, 30.
YFRAH NEAMAN: Nov. 4.
OSSY RENARDY: Oct. 19, 20, 22.
ISAAC STERN: March 1, 2, 4.

VIOLA

WILLIAM LINCER: Dec. 7, 8, 10.

VIOLONCELLO

EDMUND KURTZ: Nov. 9, 10, 12.
LEONARD ROSE: Nov. 2, 3, 5; Dec. 7, 8, 10; Feb. 1, 2, 4; April 5, 6, 8, 16.

FLUTE

JOHN WUMMER: Dec. 28, 29, 30; April 19, 20, 22.

CLARINET
ROBERT MCGINNIS: Dec. 28, 29, 30.

OBOE
HAROLD GOMBERG: Nov. 2, 3, 5; Dec. 28, 29, 30; April 16.

BASSOON
WILLIAM POLISI: Nov. 2, 3, 5; Dec. 28, 29, 30; April 16.

FRENCH HORN
JAMES CHAMBERS: Dec. 28, 29, 30.

TRUMPET
WILLIAM VACCHIANO: Dec. 28, 29, 30.

TROMBONE
GORDON PULIS: Dec. 28, 29, 30.

TIMPANI
SAUL GOODMAN: Dec. 28, 29, 30.

PERCUSSION
ELDEN BAILEY: Dec. 28, 29, 30.
ARTHUR LAYFIELD: Dec. 28, 29, 30.
WALTER ROSENBERGER: Dec. 28, 29, 30.

VOCAL
ADOLPH ANDERSON, Baritone: Apr. 12, 13, 15.
EDWINA EUSTIS, Contralto: Nov. 16, 17; Apr. 12, 13, 15.

EILEEN FARRELL, Soprano: Nov. 16, 17; Mar. 25; Apr. 12, 13, 15.
KIRSTEN FLAGSTAD, Soprano: Feb. 5.
FRANCES GREER, Soprano: Nov. 16, 17, 19.
MACK HARRELL, Baritone: Nov. 16, 17, 19; Apr. 12, 13, 15.
RALPH HERBERT, Baritone: Nov. 16, 17, 19; Apr. 12, 13, 15.
BESS ANN HERDT, Soprano: Apr. 12, 13, 15.
FREDERICK JAGEL, Tenor: Apr. 12, 13, 15.
DAVID LLOYD, Tenor: Nov. 16, 17, 19; Apr. 12, 13, 15.
JOSEPH MORDINO, Tenor: Nov. 16, 17, 19; Apr. 12, 13, 15.
HUBERT NORVILLE, Baritone: Apr. 12, 13, 15.

NARRATOR
MADELEINE MILHAUD: Nov. 16, 17.

CHORUS
MEMBERS OF THE HIGH SCHOOL OF MUSIC AND ART CHORUS: April 12, 13, 15.
SCHOLA CANTORUM, Hugh Ross, Director: Apr. 12, 13, 15.
WESTMINSTER CHOIR, John Finley Williamson, Director: Nov. 16, 17.

1951–52 ONE HUNDRED TENTH SEASON

Musical Director: DIMITRI MITROPOULOS
Guest Conductors: BRUNO WALTER, GEORGE SZELL, GUIDO CANTELLI
Associate Conductor: FRANCO AUTORI
For Young People's Concerts: IGOR BUKETOFF

CONCERTS

1951

Dimitri Mitropoulos, Musical Director

Oct. 11—Ev'g.	Carnegie Hall
Oct. 12—Aft.	Carnegie Hall
Oct. 14—Aft.	Carnegie Hall
Oct. 16—Ev'g.	Academy of Music, Philadelphia, Pa.
Oct. 18—Ev'g.	Carnegie Hall
Oct. 19—Aft.	Carnegie Hall
*Oct. 20—Aft.	Town Hall
Oct. 21—Aft.	Carnegie Hall
Oct. 25—Ev'g.	Carnegie Hall

1951

Oct. 26—Aft.	Carnegie Hall
Oct. 27—Ev'g.	Carnegie Hall
Oct. 28—Aft.	Carnegie Hall
Nov. 1—Ev'g.	Carnegie Hall
Nov. 2—Aft.	Carnegie Hall
Nov. 3—Ev'g.	Carnegie Hall
Nov. 4—Aft.	Carnegie Hall
Nov. 6—Ev'g.	Constitution Hall, Washington, D.C.
Nov. 8—Ev'g.	Carnegie Hall
Nov. 9—Aft.	Carnegie Hall
Nov. 11—Aft.	Carnegie Hall

* Young People's Concert, conducted by Igor Buketoff.

1951

Nov. 12—Ev'g.	Hotel Plaza
Nov. 15—Ev'g.	Carnegie Hall
Nov. 16—Aft.	Carnegie Hall
*Nov. 17—Aft.	Town Hall
Nov. 18—Aft.	Carnegie Hall
Nov. 22—Ev'g.	Carnegie Hall
Nov. 23—Aft.	Carnegie Hall
Nov. 24—Ev'g.	Carnegie Hall
Nov. 25—Aft.	Carnegie Hall
Nov. 29—Ev'g.	Carnegie Hall
Nov. 30—Aft.	Carnegie Hall
Dec. 1—Ev'g.	Carnegie Hall
Dec. 2—Aft.	Carnegie Hall

George Szell, Guest Conductor

Dec. 6—Ev'g.	Carnegie Hall
Dec. 7—Aft.	Carnegie Hall
*Dec. 8—Morn.	Carnegie Hall
Dec. 9—Aft.	Carnegie Hall
Dec. 13—Ev'g.	Carnegie Hall
Dec. 14—Aft.	Carnegie Hall
*Dec. 15—Aft.	Town Hall
Dec. 16—Aft.	Carnegie Hall
Dec. 20—Ev'g.	Carnegie Hall
Dec. 21—Aft.	Carnegie Hall
Dec. 22—Ev'g.	Carnegie Hall
Dec. 23—Aft.	Carnegie Hall
Dec. 27—Ev'g.	Carnegie Hall
Dec. 28—Aft.	Carnegie Hall
Dec. 29—Ev'g.	Carnegie Hall
Dec. 30—Aft.	Carnegie Hall

1952

Guido Cantelli, Guest Conductor

Jan. 3—Ev'g.	Carnegie Hall
Jan. 4—Aft.	Carnegie Hall
*Jan. 5—Morn.	Carnegie Hall
Jan. 6—Aft.	Carnegie Hall

George Szell, Guest Conductor

Jan. 7—Ev'g.	Carnegie Hall
	(Pension Fund Benefit)

Franco Autori, Associate Conductor

Jan. 10—Ev'g.	Carnegie Hall
Jan. 11—Aft.	Carnegie Hall
Jan. 13—Aft.	Carnegie Hall

Guido Cantelli, Guest Conductor

Jan. 17—Ev'g.	Carnegie Hall
Jan. 18—Aft.	Carnegie Hall
Jan. 19—Ev'g.	Carnegie Hall
Jan. 20—Aft.	Carnegie Hall
Jan. 24—Ev'g.	Carnegie Hall
Jan. 25—Aft.	Carnegie Hall
Jan. 26—Ev'g.	Carnegie Hall
Jan. 27—Aft.	Carnegie Hall

1952

Dimitri Mitropoulos, Musical Director

Jan. 31—Ev'g.	Carnegie Hall
Feb. 1—Aft.	Carnegie Hall
*Feb. 2—Morn.	Carnegie Hall
Feb. 3—Aft.	Carnegie Hall
Feb. 7—Ev'g.	Carnegie Hall
Feb. 8—Aft.	Carnegie Hall
Feb. 10—Aft.	Carnegie Hall
Feb. 14—Ev'g.	Carnegie Hall
Feb. 15—Aft.	Carnegie Hall
Feb. 16—Ev'g.	Carnegie Hall
Feb. 17—Aft.	Carnegie Hall
Feb. 21—Ev'g.	Carnegie Hall
Feb. 22—Aft.	Carnegie Hall

Franco Autori, Associate Conductor

Feb. 23—Ev'g.	Carnegie Hall

Dimitri Mitropoulos, Musical Director

Feb. 24—Aft.	Carnegie Hall
Feb. 28—Ev'g.	Carnegie Hall
Feb. 29—Aft.	Carnegie Hall

Franco Autori, Associate Conductor

Mar. 1—Ev'g.	Carnegie Hall

Dimitri Mitropoulos, Musical Director

Mar. 2—Aft.	Carnegie Hall

George Szell, Guest Conductor

Mar. 6—Ev'g.	Carnegie Hall
Mar. 7—Aft.	Carnegie Hall
Mar. 8—Ev'g.	Carnegie Hall
Mar. 9—Aft.	Carnegie Hall

Franco Autori, Associate Conductor

Mar. 10—Ev'g.	Hotel Plaza

Bruno Walter, Guest Conductor

Mar. 13—Ev'g.	Carnegie Hall
Mar. 14—Aft.	Carnegie Hall
*Mar. 15—Morn.	Carnegie Hall
Mar. 16—Aft.	Carnegie Hall

Dimitri Mitropoulos, Musical Director

Mar. 18—Ev'g.	Bushnell Memorial Auditorium, Hartford, Conn.

Bruno Walter, Guest Conductor

Mar. 20—Ev'g.	Carnegie Hall
Mar. 21—Aft.	Carnegie Hall
Mar. 23—Aft.	Carnegie Hall

Dimitri Mitropoulos, Musical Director

Mar. 27—Ev'g.	Carnegie Hall
Mar. 28—Aft.	Carnegie Hall

* Young People's Concert, conducted by Igor Buketoff.

1952			1952		
Mar. 29—Ev'g.	Carnegie Hall		Apr. 13—Aft.	Carnegie Hall	
Mar. 30—Aft.	Carnegie Hall		Apr. 16—Ev'g.	Carnegie Hall	
Apr. 3—Ev'g.	Carnegie Hall			(Pension Fund Benefit)	
Apr. 4—Aft.	Carnegie Hall		Apr. 17—Ev'g.	Carnegie Hall	
Apr. 5—Ev'g.	Carnegie Hall		Apr. 18—Aft.	Carnegie Hall	
Apr. 6—Aft.	Carnegie Hall		Apr. 19—Ev'g.	RPI Field House,	
Apr. 10—Ev'g.	Carnegie Hall			Troy, New York	
Apr. 11—Aft.	Carnegie Hall		Apr. 20—Aft.	Carnegie Hall	
*Apr. 12—Morn.	Carnegie Hall				

COMPOSITIONS PERFORMED

(a) First performance.
(b) First performance in America.
(c) First performance in New York.
(d) First performance by the Society.
(e) First complete performance by the Society.
(f) First public performance.

BACH—*Brandenburg* Concerto No. 1, F major: Apr. 3, 4.
Air from Suite No. 3, D major: Oct. 11.
Suite No. 3, D major: Dec. 27, 28.

BACH-BOESSENROTH—Chorale-Prelude, *Credo* ("Wir glauben all' an einen Gott"): Nov. 25; Dec. 1.

BACH-SCHOENBERG—Two Chorale-Preludes ("Schmücke dich, O liebe Seele," "Komm, Gott, Schöpfer, heiliger Geist"): Nov. 15, 16, 18.

BALAKIREFF-CASELLA—*Islamey*, Oriental Fantasy: Nov. 22, 23, 25.

BARTOK—Divertimento for String Orchestra: Dec. 13 (d), 14, 16.

BEETHOVEN—Piano Concerto No. 3, C minor, Op. 37: Feb. 7, 8.
Piano Concerto No. 4, G major, Op. 58: Jan. 7.
Piano Concerto No. 5, E-flat major, Op. 73 ("Emperor"): Jan. 10, 11, 13.
Violin Concerto, D major, Op. 61: Dec. 20, 21, 22, 23.
Overture, *The Creatures of Prometheus*, Op. 43: Dec. 23.
Overture, *Fidelio*, E major, Op. 72: Feb. 28, 29.
Overture, *Leonore* No. 3, Op. 72: Dec. 20, 21, 22, 23; Mar. 8.
Symphony No. 1, C major, Op. 21: Nov. 24, 25.
Symphony No. 3, E-flat major, Op. 55 ("Eroica"): Feb. 14, 15, 16, 17.
Symphony No. 4, B-flat major, Op. 60: Mar. 6, 7.
Symphony No. 5, C minor, Op. 67: Jan. 3, 4, 6.
Symphony No. 6, F major, Op. 68 ("Pastoral"): Feb. 28, 29.
Symphony No. 8, F major, Op. 93: Dec. 20, 21, 22, 23.

BERLIOZ—Overture, *Beatrice and Benedict:* Mar. 27, 28, 29, 30.
Overture, *Roman Carnival:* Mar. 9.
Three Pieces from *The Damnation of Faust:* Oct. 14.

BOCCHERINI—'Cello Concerto, B-flat major, Op. 34: Nov. 12.

BRAHMS—*A German Requiem*, Op. 45: Mar. 13, 14, 16.
Piano Concerto No. 1, D minor, Op. 15: Nov. 22, 23, 25; Apr. 5.
Piano Concerto No. 2, B-flat major, Op. 83: Apr. 3, 4, 6.
Violin Concerto, D major, Op. 77: Dec. 6, 7, 9.
Song of Destiny (Schicksalslied), Op. 54: Mar. 13, 14.
Symphony No. 1, C minor, Op. 68: Nov. 29, 30; Dec. 1, 2.
Symphony No. 2, D major, Op. 73: Dec. 27, 28.
Symphony No. 3, F major, Op. 90: Apr. 17, 18, 20.
Symphony No. 4, E minor, Op. 98: Nov. 15, 16, 18, 24; Feb. 23.
Tragic Overture, Op. 81: Mar. 16.

---

* Young People's Concert, conducted by Igor Buketoff.

BRUCH—Violin Concerto No. 1, G minor, Op. 26: Jan. 31; Feb. 1.

BUSONI—*Arlecchino,* Theatrical Capriccio in One Act: Oct. 11 (b), 12, 14.
Berceuse élégiaque, Op. 42: Jan. 24, 25, 26, 27.

CASADESUS—Suite No. 2, B-flat major, Op. 26: Apr. 3 (a), 4.

CHOPIN—Piano Concerto No. 1, E minor, Op. 11: Oct. 27.
Piano Concerto No. 2, F minor, Op. 21: Dec. 16; Mar. 8.

CLAPP—Symphony No. 8, C major: Feb. 7 (f), 8.

COUPERIN-MILHAUD—Prelude and Allegro: Jan. 31; Feb. 1; Apr. 19.

DEBUSSY—*La Mer,* Three Symphonic Sketches: Dec. 6, 7, 9, 29.
Suite, *Children's Corner:* Nov. 12.
Two Nocturnes for Orchestra, *Nuages* and *Fêtes:* Mar. 1.

DEBUSSY-BUSSER—*Petite Suite:* Mar. 10.

DELLO JOIO—Variations, Chaconne and Finale: Jan. 10, 11.

DOHNANYI—Violin Concerto No. 2, C minor, Op. 43: Feb. 14 (c), 15.

DUKAS—*The Sorcerer's Apprentice:* Oct. 25, 26, 28.

DVORAK—'Cello Concerto, B minor, Op. 104: Mar. 27, 28.
Piano Concerto, G minor, Op. 33: Jan. 19, 20.

ELGAR—*Enigma* Variations, Op. 36: Mar. 6, 7, 8, 9.

FALLA—Three Dances from *The Three-Cornered Hat:* Oct. 14.

FRANCK—Symphonic Piece from *Redemption:* Nov. 1, 2, 3, 4.
Symphony, D minor: Jan. 31; Feb. 1, 3; Mar. 18; Apr. 19.

FRANCK-PIERNE—Prelude, Chorale and Fugue: Oct. 25, 26, 27, 28; Nov. 6.

FRESCOBALDI-GHEDINI—Four Pieces: Jan. 3 (d), 4, 6.

GEMINIANI—Andante: Jan. 10, 11, 13.

GLUCK—Overture, *Alceste:* Nov. 22, 23.

GOULD—Ballet Suite, *Fall River Legend:* Mar. 29 (c).

HANDEL—Organ Concerto No. 3, G minor, Op. 4: Apr. 17 (d), 18.

HAYDN—'Cello Concerto, D major, Op. 101: Nov. 1, 2.
Symphony No. 80, D minor: Oct. 21 (d); Nov. 12.
Symphony No. 86, D major: Apr. 5, 6.
Symphony No. 104, D major: Nov. 8, 9, 11.

HINDEMITH—Symphony, *Mathis der Maler:* Jan. 17, 18, 19, 20.

HONEGGER—*Pastorale d'Été:* Jan. 13.

d'INDY—Trilogy, *Wallenstein:* Oct. 25 (d), 26, 27, 28; Nov. 6.

KALLIWODA—Overture in D: Dec. 13.

KIRCHNER—Sinfonia in Two Parts: Jan. 31 (a); Feb. 1.

KODALY—*Dances from Galanta:* Mar. 27, 28, 29, 30; Apr. 19.

LALO—Symphonie Espagnole, Op. 21: Jan. 7, 24, 25.

LEHAR—Waltz, *Gold and Silver:* Mar. 10.

LISZT—Piano Concerto No. 1, E-flat major: Jan. 26, 27; Apr. 17, 18.
Piano Concerto No. 2, A major: Oct. 28.

MAHLER—Symphony No. 1, D major: Oct. 18, 19, 21.

MENDELSSOHN—Violin Concerto, E minor, Op. 64: Dec. 27, 28, 30.
Elijah, Dramatic Oratorio, Op. 70: Apr. 10 (e), 11, 13, 16.
Overture, Intermezzo and Scherzo, *A Midsummer Night's Dream:* Dec. 13, 14.
Scherzo, G minor, from Octet for Strings, Op. 20: Apr. 5.

MENOTTI—Piano Concerto, F major: Jan. 17, 18.

MILLS—Theme and Variations, Op. 81: Nov. 8 (a), 9, 11.

MOHAUPT—Symphony No. 1: Nov. 22, 23.

MONTEVERDI-GHEDINI—*Magnificat,* for Seven-Part Chorus, Organ and Orchestra: Jan. 3 (d), 4, 6.

MONTEVERDI-RESPIGHI—*Orfeo,* Opera in Three Acts: Feb. 21 (d), 22, 24.
MOUSSORGSKY-RAVEL—*Pictures at an Exhibition:* Jan. 24, 25, 26, 27.
MOZART—Piano Concerto, E-flat major, K. 271: Dec. 13, 14.
Piano Concerto, B-flat major, K. 595: Dec. 29.
Overture, *The Abduction from the Seraglio:* Oct. 11, 12, 14, 16.
Overture, *The Marriage of Figaro:* Dec. 30; Feb. 23.
Sinfonia Concertante for Oboe, Clarinet, Horn, Bassoon, with Orchestra Accompaniment, E-flat major, K. 297b: Oct. 11, 12.
Symphony No. 33, B-flat major, K. 319: Dec. 6, 7.
Symphony No. 35, D major, K. 385 ("Haffner"): Feb. 7, 8, 10.
PAGANINI—Violin Concerto No. 1, D major, Op. 6: Oct. 16; Nov. 29, 30.
PFITZNER—Preludes to Act I, II and III, *Palestrina:* Nov. 29, 30.
RACHMANINOFF—Piano Concerto No. 2, C minor, Op. 18: Feb. 23.
Piano Concerto No. 3, D minor, Op. 30: Nov. 6, 8, 9, 11.
Symphony No. 2, E minor, Op. 27: Oct. 16.
RESPIGHI—Toccata for Piano and Orchestra: Mar. 10.
RIMSKY-KORSAKOFF—*Capriccio Espagnol:* Nov. 3, 4.
RIVIER—Piano Concerto No. 1, C major: Mar. 6 (b), 7.
ROSSINI—Overture, *La Scala di Seta:* Nov. 8, 9, 11.
Overture, *Semiramide:* Jan. 24, 25, 26, 27.
RUBINSTEIN—Piano Concerto No. 4, D minor, Op. 70: Mar. 29, 30.
SAINT-SAENS—'Cello Concerto, A minor, Op. 33: Mar. 1.
Piano Concerto No. 5, F major, Op. 103: Nov. 24.
Symphony No. 2, A minor, Op. 55: Nov. 1, 2, 3; Mar. 2, 18.
SAMMARTINI, G. B.—Sinfonia No. 3, G major: Mar. 1, 10.
SATIE-DIAMOND—*Mass of the Poor:* Oct. 18 (c), 19.
Passacaglia: Oct. 18 (a), 19, 21.
SCHOENBERG—*Erwartung (Expectation),* Monodrama: Nov. 15 (b), 16, 18.
Verklärte Nacht (Transfigured Night), Op. 4: Mar. 27, 28, 30.
SCHUBERT—Symphony No. 2, B-flat major: Jan. 17, 18, 19.
Symphony No. 9, C major: Mar. 20, 21.
SCHUMANN—'Cello Concerto, A minor, Op. 129: Nov. 3, 4.
Piano Concerto, A minor, Op. 54: Oct. 25, 26; Feb. 10.
Overture, Scherzo and Finale, Op. 52: Feb. 14, 15, 16; Mar. 18.
SERLY—*American Elegy:* Feb. 23 (c).
SHULMAN—*A Laurentian Overture:* Jan. 17 (a), 18, 19, 20.
STRAUSS—*Till Eulenspiegel's Merry Pranks,* Op. 28: Dec. 14, 16, 29.
STRAVINSKY—Ballet Suite, *The Firebird:* Jan. 10, 11, 13.
Suite from *Petrouchka:* Feb. 7, 8, 10; Apr. 19.
SZYMANOWSKI—Violin Concerto in One Movement, No. 1, Op. 35: Oct. 18, 19.
Symphonie Concertante for Piano and Orchestra, No. 4, Op. 60: Apr. 17, 18.
TCHAIKOVSKY—Piano Concerto No. 1, B-flat minor, Op. 23: Mar. 9; Apr. 20.
Violin Concerto, D major, Op. 35: Feb. 3.
Symphony No. 4, F minor, Op. 36: Dec. 30; Mar. 1.
Symphony No. 5, E minor, Op. 64: Feb. 28, 29; Mar. 2.
Variations on a Rococo Theme, for 'Cello and Orchestra, Op. 33: Jan. 7.
TRAVIS—Symphonic Allegro: Dec. 1 (a).
VAUGHAN WILLIAMS—Two Piano Concerto, C major: Feb. 16 (c), 17.
WAGNER—Brünnhilde's Immolation, *Götterdämmerung:* Mar. 20, 21, 23.
Prelude, *Die Meistersinger:* Feb. 10; Mar. 23.
Prelude, *Parsifal:* Mar. 23.

Overture, *Rienzi:* Apr. 5, 6.
Overture, *Tannhäuser:* Feb. 17.
Bacchanale, *Tannhäuser:* Mar. 23.
Five *Wesendonck* Songs: Mar. 20, 21, 23.
WEBER—Overture, *Der Freischütz:* Dec. 6, 7, 9, 29; Jan. 7.
Overture, *Oberon:* Dec. 16; Jan. 7.
WIENIAWSKI—Violin Concerto No. 1, F-sharp minor, Op. 14: Dec. 1 (d), 2.
WOLF-FERRARI—Overture, *The Secret of Suzanne:* Nov. 12; Dec. 2.
WOLPE—First Ballet Suite, *The Man from Midian:* Nov. 1 (a), 2, 4.

SOLOISTS

PIANO
GINA BACHAUER: Nov. 6, 8, 9, 11.
MONIQUE DE LA BRUCHOLLERIE: Mar. 6, 7, 9.
JEAN CASADESUS: Nov. 24.
ROBERT CASADESUS: Apr. 3, 4, 6.
ALDO CICCOLINI: Oct. 25, 26, 28.
CLIFFORD CURZON: Jan. 10, 11, 13.
RUDOLF FIRKUSNY: Jan. 17, 18, 19, 20.
FRANK GLAZER: Feb. 23.
NICOLE HENRIOT: Jan. 26, 27.
MYRA HESS: Jan. 7; Feb. 7, 8, 10.
GRANT JOHANNESEN: Mar. 8.
CONSTANCE KEENE: Oct. 27.
OSCAR LEVANT: Mar. 29, 30.
WILLIAM MASSELOS: Apr. 5.
DIMITRI MITROPOULOS: Mar. 10.
HORTENSE MONATH: Dec. 29.
GUIOMAR NOVAES: Dec. 13, 14, 16.
ARTUR RUBINSTEIN: Apr. 17, 18, 20.
RUDOLF SERKIN: Nov. 22, 23, 25.
BRUNO WALTER: Mar. 20, 21, 23.
WHITTEMORE & LOWE: Feb. 16, 17.

VIOLIN
JOHN CORIGLIANO: Oct. 18, 19.
ZINO FRANCESCATTI: Jan. 31; Feb. 1, 3.
JASCHA HEIFETZ: Dec. 6, 7, 9.
FRANCES MAGNES: Feb. 14, 15.
NATHAN MILSTEIN: Dec. 20, 21, 22, 23; Jan. 7.
ERICA MORINI: Dec. 27, 28, 30.
MICHAEL RABIN: Oct. 16; Nov. 29, 30; Dec. 1, 2.
ISAAC STERN: Jan. 24, 25.

VIOLONCELLO
GREGOR PIATIGORSKY: Nov. 1, 2, 3, 4.
LEONARD ROSE: Jan. 7; Mar. 1, 27, 28.
LASZLO VARGA: Nov. 12, 15, 16, 18.

CLARINET
ROBERT MCGINNIS: Oct. 11, 12.

OBOE
HAROLD GOMBERG: Oct. 11, 12.

BASSOON
WILLIAM POLISI: Oct. 11, 12.

HORN
JAMES CHAMBERS: Oct. 11, 12.

ORGAN
EDOUARD NIES-BERGER: Apr. 17, 18.

VOCAL
MARDEN BATE, Baritone: Feb. 21, 22, 24.
NADINE CONNER, Soprano: Mar. 13, 14, 16.
DOROTHY DOW, Soprano: Nov. 15, 16, 18.
J. ALDEN EDKINS, Bass: Oct. 11, 12, 14; Feb. 21, 22, 24.
KIRSTEN FLAGSTAD, Soprano: Mar. 20, 21, 23.
FRANCES GREER, Soprano: Feb. 21, 22, 24; Apr. 10, 11, 13, 16.
MACK HARRELL, Baritone: Feb. 21, 22, 24; Mar. 13, 14, 16.
JANE HOBSON, Mezzo-Soprano: Feb. 21, 22, 24.
MARY HUMPHREY, Mezzo-Soprano: Feb. 21, 22, 24.
CHARLES KULLMAN, Tenor: Feb. 21, 22, 24.
DÉSIRÉ LIGETI, Bass-Baritone: Apr. 10, 11, 13, 16.
ELINOR LINK, Soprano: Feb. 21, 22, 24.
MARTHA LIPTON, Mezzo-Soprano: Oct. 11, 12, 14; Apr. 10, 11, 13.
DAVID LLOYD, Tenor: Oct. 11, 12, 14; Apr. 16.
WHITFIELD LLOYD, Contralto: Feb. 21, 22, 24.
JOHN MCCOLLUM, Tenor: Feb. 21, 22, 24.
JANICE MOUDRY, Mezzo-Soprano: Apr. 16.

JAMES PEASE, Baritone: Oct. 11, 12, 14.

RICHARD TUCKER, Tenor: Apr. 10, 11, 13.

WILLIAM WILDERMAN, Bass: Oct. 11, 12, 14.

NARRATOR

JOHN BROWNLEE: Oct. 11, 12, 14.

MIME

PAULINE POLISI: Oct. 11, 12, 14.

CHORUS

SCHOLA CANTORUM, Hugh Ross, Director: Feb. 21, 22, 24.

WESTMINSTER CHOIR, John Finley Williamson, Director: Jan. 3, 4, 6; Mar. 13, 14, 16; Apr. 10, 11, 13, 16.

●

CONCERTS
at the
INTERNATIONAL FESTIVAL OF MUSIC AND DRAMA
EDINBURGH 1951

Under the Direction of

Bruno Walter		Dimitri Mitropoulos	
Aug. 22—Ev'g.	Usher Hall	Aug. 23—Ev'g.	Usher Hall
Aug. 24—Ev'g.	Usher Hall	Aug. 25—Ev'g.	Usher Hall
Aug. 26—Ev'g.	Usher Hall	Aug. 27—Ev'g.	Usher Hall
Aug. 28—Ev'g.	Usher Hall	Aug. 29—Ev'g.	Usher Hall
Aug. 30—Ev'g.	Usher Hall	Aug. 31—Ev'g.	Usher Hall
Sept. 2—Ev'g.	Usher Hall	Sept. 1—Ev'g.	Usher Hall
Sept. 4—Ev'g.	Usher Hall	Sept. 3—Ev'g.	Usher Hall

BAX—*Overture to a Picaresque Comedy:* Aug. 31.

BEETHOVEN—Piano Concerto No. 4, G major, Op. 58: Aug. 25.
Piano Concerto No. 5, E-flat major, Op. 73 ("Emperor"): Aug. 29.
Violin Concerto, D major, Op. 61: Aug. 27.
Overture, *Coriolanus:* Aug. 23.
Overture, *Leonore* No. 2: Aug. 26.
Symphony No. 2, D major, Op. 36: Sept. 1.
Symphony No. 4, B-flat major, Op. 60: Aug. 23.
Symphony No. 9, D minor, Op. 125: Sept. 2, 4.

BERLIOZ—Overture, *Roman Carnival:* Sept. 3.
Three Pieces from *The Damnation of Faust:* Aug. 31.

BRAHMS—Piano Concerto No. 1, D minor, Op. 15: Aug. 31.
Tragic Overture, Op. 81: Aug. 24, 30.
Song of Destiny (Schicksalslied), Op. 54: Aug. 24, 30.
Symphony No. 2, D major, Op. 73: Aug. 24, 30.
Variations on a Theme by Haydn, Op. 56a: Aug. 24, 30.

BRUCKNER—Symphony No. 4, E-flat major ("Romantic"): Aug. 26.

CHERUBINI—Overture, *The Water-Carrier:* Sept. 1.

FALLA—Three Dances from *The Three-Cornered Hat:* Sept. 1.

GOULD—*Philharmonic Waltzes:* Aug. 29.

HANDEL—Concerto Grosso No. 6, G minor, Op. 6: Aug. 28.

HAYDN–Sinfonia Concertante for Solo Violin, 'Cello, Oboe, Bassoon and Orchestra, B-flat major, Op. 84: Aug. 25.
Symphony No. 88, G major: Aug. 26.

KRENEK—Symphonic Elegy for String Orchestra: Aug. 25.

MAHLER—Symphony No. 4, G major: Aug. 22.

MALIPIERO—Piano Concerto No. 4: Sept. 3.

MENDELSSOHN—Symphony No. 3, A minor, Op. 56 ("Scotch"): Aug. 29.

MOZART—Symphony No. 39, E-flat major, K. 543: Aug. 22.

PROKOFIEFF—Symphony No. 5, B-flat major, Op. 100: Aug. 23.

RACHMANINOFF—Symphony No. 2, E minor, Op. 27: Sept. 3.

SAINT-SAENS—'Cello Concerto, A minor, Op. 33: Sept. 3.

SCHUBERT—Symphony No. 9, C major: Aug. 28.

SCHUMANN—Piano Concerto, A minor, Op. 54: Sept. 1.
Overture, Scherzo and Finale, Op. 52: Aug. 25.

SWANSON—Short Symphony: Aug. 31.

VAUGHAN WILLIAMS—Fantasia on a Theme by Thomas Tallis: Sept. 2, 4.
Symphony No. 4, F minor: Aug. 27.

WAGNER—*A Siegfried Idyl:* Aug. 28.

WEBER—Overture, *Euryanthe:* Aug. 22.
Overture, *Der Freischütz:* Aug. 29.
Overture, *Ruler of the Spirits:* Aug. 27.

SOLOISTS—EDINBURGH

PIANO
ROBERT CASADESUS: Aug. 29.
MYRA HESS: Aug. 25; Sept. 1.
DIMITRI MITROPOULOS: Sept. 3.
SOLOMON: Aug. 31.

VIOLIN
JOHN CORIGLIANO: Aug. 25.
ZINO FRANCESCATTI: Aug. 27.

VIOLONCELLO
LEONARD ROSE: Aug. 25; Sept. 3.

OBOE
HAROLD GOMBERG: Aug. 25.

BASSOON
WILLIAM POLISI: Aug. 25.

VOCAL
MACK HARRELL, Baritone: Sept. 2, 4.
MARTHA LIPTON, Mezzo-Soprano: Sept. 2, 4.
DAVID LLOYD, Tenor: Sept. 2, 4.
IRMGARD SEEFRIED, Soprano: Aug. 22.
FRANCES YEEND, Soprano: Sept, 2, 4.

CHORUS
THE EDINBURGH ROYAL CHORAL UNION, Herrick Bunney, Director: Aug. 24, 30; Sept. 2, 4.

1952–53 ONE HUNDRED ELEVENTH SEASON

Musical Director: DIMITRI MITROPOULOS
Guest Conductors: BRUNO WALTER, GEORGE SZELL,
GUIDO CANTELLI
Associate Conductor: FRANCO AUTORI
For Young People's Concerts: IGOR BUKETOFF

CONCERTS

1952

**Dimitri Mitropoulos,
Musical Director**

Oct. 16—Ev'g.	Carnegie Hall
Oct. 17—Aft.	Carnegie Hall
Oct. 19—Aft.	Carnegie Hall
Oct. 21—Ev'g.	RPI Field House, Troy, New York
Oct. 23—Ev'g.	Carnegie Hall
Oct. 24—Aft.	Carnegie Hall

1952

*Oct. 25—Aft.	Town Hall
Oct. 26—Aft.	Carnegie Hall
**Oct. 29—Aft.	Great Neck Jr. High School, Great Neck, N. Y.
Oct. 30—Ev'g.	Carnegie Hall
Oct. 31—Aft.	Carnegie Hall
Nov. 1—Ev'g.	Carnegie Hall
Nov. 2—Aft.	Carnegie Hall
Nov. 6—Ev'g.	Carnegie Hall

* Young People's Concert, conducted by Igor Buketoff.
** Young People's Concert, conducted by Franco Autori.

1952		
Nov.	7—Aft.	Carnegie Hall
Nov.	8—Ev'g.	Carnegie Hall
Nov.	9—Aft.	Carnegie Hall
Nov.	13—Ev'g.	Carnegie Hall
Nov.	14—Aft.	Carnegie Hall
*Nov.	15—Morn.	Carnegie Hall
Nov.	16—Aft.	Carnegie Hall
Nov.	18—Ev'g.	Constitution Hall, Washington, D. C.
Nov.	20—Ev'g.	Carnegie Hall
Nov.	21—Aft.	Carnegie Hall
*Nov.	22—Aft.	Town Hall
Nov.	23—Aft.	Carnegie Hall
Nov.	27—Ev'g.	Carnegie Hall
Nov.	28—Aft.	Carnegie Hall
Nov.	29—Ev'g.	Carnegie Hall
Nov.	30—Aft.	Carnegie Hall
**Dec.	3—Aft.	Roslyn H. S., Roslyn, New York
Dec.	4—Ev'g.	Carnegie Hall
Dec.	5—Aft.	Carnegie Hall
*Dec.	6—Morn.	Carnegie Hall
Dec.	7—Aft.	Carnegie Hall

George Szell, Guest Conductor

Dec.	11—Ev'g.	Carnegie Hall
Dec.	12—Aft.	Carnegie Hall
Dec.	13—Ev'g.	Carnegie Hall
Dec.	14—Aft.	Carnegie Hall
Dec.	18—Ev'g.	Carnegie Hall
Dec.	19—Aft.	Carnegie Hall
Dec.	20—Ev'g.	Carnegie Hall
Dec.	21—Aft.	Carnegie Hall

Bruno Walter, Guest Conductor

Dec.	25—Ev'g.	Carnegie Hall
Dec.	26—Aft.	Carnegie Hall
*Dec.	27—Aft.	Town Hall
Dec.	28—Aft.	Carnegie Hall

1953

Bruno Walter, Guest Conductor

Jan.	1—Ev'g.	Carnegie Hall
Jan.	2—Aft.	Carnegie Hall

Franco Autori, Associate Conductor

Jan.	3—Ev'g.	Carnegie Hall

Bruno Walter, Guest Conductor

Jan.	4—Aft.	Carnegie Hall
Jan.	6—Ev'g.	Mosque Theatre, Newark, New Jersey

George Szell, Guest Conductor

Jan.	8—Ev'g.	Carnegie Hall
Jan.	9—Aft.	Carnegie Hall
Jan.	11—Aft.	Carnegie Hall
Jan.	12—Ev'g.	Carnegie Hall (Pension Fund Benefit)

1953		
Jan.	15—Ev'g.	Carnegie Hall
Jan.	16—Aft.	Carnegie Hall
*Jan.	17—Morn.	Carnegie Hall
Jan.	18—Aft.	Carnegie Hall

Vladimir Golschmann, Guest Conductor

Jan.	22—Ev'g.	Carnegie Hall
Jan.	23—Aft.	Carnegie Hall
Jan.	24—Ev'g.	Carnegie Hall
Jan.	25—Aft.	Carnegie Hall
Jan.	29—Ev'g.	Carnegie Hall
Jan.	30—Aft.	Carnegie Hall
Jan.	31—Ev'g.	Carnegie Hall
Feb.	1—Aft.	Carnegie Hall
Feb.	2—Ev'g.	Hotel Plaza

Efrem Kurtz, Guest Conductor

Feb.	5—Ev'g.	Carnegie Hall
Feb.	6—Aft.	Carnegie Hall
Feb.	8—Aft.	Carnegie Hall

Bruno Walter, Guest Conductor

Feb.	12—Ev'g.	Carnegie Hall
Feb.	13—Aft.	Carnegie Hall
*Feb.	14—Morn.	Carnegie Hall
Feb.	15—Aft.	Carnegie Hall
**Feb.	18—Aft.	R. K. Toaz Jr. H. S., Huntington, N. Y.
Feb.	19—Ev'g.	Carnegie Hall
Feb.	20—Aft.	Carnegie Hall

Franco Autori, Associate Conductor

Feb.	21—Ev'g.	Carnegie Hall

Bruno Walter, Guest Conductor

Feb.	22—Aft.	Carnegie Hall

Igor Stravinsky, Guest Conductor

Feb.	26—Ev'g.	Carnegie Hall
Feb.	27—Aft.	Carnegie Hall

Franco Autori, Associate Conductor

Feb.	28—Ev'g.	Carnegie Hall

Igor Stravinsky, Guest Conductor

Mar.	1—Aft.	Carnegie Hall

Bruno Walter, Guest Conductor

Mar.	2—Ev'g.	Carnegie Hall (Pension Fund Benefit)

Guido Cantelli, Guest Conductor

Mar.	5—Ev'g.	Carnegie Hall
Mar.	6—Aft.	Carnegie Hall
Mar.	7—Ev'g.	Carnegie Hall
Mar.	8—Aft.	Carnegie Hall
Mar.	12—Ev'g.	Carnegie Hall
Mar.	13—Aft.	Carnegie Hall
Mar.	14—Ev'g.	Carnegie Hall
Mar.	15—Aft.	Carnegie Hall

---

* Young People's Concert, conducted by Igor Buketoff.
** Young People's Concert, conducted by Franco Autori.

1953

Mar.	17—Ev'g.	Bushnell Memorial Auditorium, Hartford, Conn.
Mar.	19—Ev'g.	Carnegie Hall
Mar.	20—Aft.	Carnegie Hall
*Mar.	21—Morn.	Carnegie Hall
Mar.	22—Aft.	Carnegie Hall
Mar.	26—Ev'g.	Carnegie Hall
Mar.	27—Aft.	Carnegie Hall
Mar.	29—Aft.	Carnegie Hall

Dimitri Mitropoulos,
Musical Director

Apr.	2—Ev'g.	Carnegie Hall
Apr.	3—Aft.	Carnegie Hall
Apr.	4—Ev'g.	Carnegie Hall

1953

Apr.	5—Aft.	Carnegie Hall
Apr.	9—Ev'g.	Carnegie Hall
Apr.	10—Aft.	Carnegie Hall
Apr.	11—Ev'g.	Carnegie Hall
Apr.	12—Aft.	Carnegie Hall
†Apr.	13—Ev'g.	Hotel Plaza
	(Philharmonic Chamber Ensemble)	
Apr.	16—Ev'g.	Carnegie Hall
Apr.	17—Aft.	Carnegie Hall
Apr.	18—Ev'g.	Carnegie Hall
Apr.	19—Aft.	Carnegie Hall
Apr.	23—Ev'g.	Carnegie Hall
Apr.	24—Aft.	Carnegie Hall
Apr.	25—Ev'g.	Carnegie Hall
Apr.	26—Aft.	Carnegie Hall

†THREE SPECIAL CONCERTS

Nov. 17, 1952—Ev'g.
Federation of Jewish Philanthropies of New York, at Madison Square Garden; conducted by Dimitri Mitropoulos and Leon Barzin.

Dec. 14, 1952—Ev'g.
Yeshiva University, at the Waldorf-Astoria; conducted by André Kostelanetz.

Feb. 14, 1953—Ev'g.
"Queen's Fund for Greek Orphans Concert," at Carnegie Hall; conducted by Alec Sherman.

†FOUR CONCERTS FOR HIGH SCHOOL
STUDENTS OF NEW YORK CITY

Dec. 10, 1952—Aft.
Prospect Heights High School, Brooklyn, N. Y.; conducted by Wilfrid Pelletier.

Feb. 11, 1953—Aft.
Richmond Hill High School, Queens, N. Y.; conducted by Franco Autori.

Mar. 11, 1953—Aft.
Julia Richman High School, Manhattan, N. Y.; conducted by Wilfrid Pelletier.

Apr. 15, 1953—Aft.
DeWitt Clinton High School, Bronx, N. Y.; conducted by Wilfrid Pelletier.

REPERTOIRE FOR 1952–53

(a) First performance.
(b) First performance in America.
(c) First performance in New York.
(d) First performance by the Society.
(e) First American concert performance.
(f) First performance by the Society of some parts.

BACH—Sinfonia from the Christmas Oratorio, *And there were shepherds in the same country:* Dec. 25, 26.

BACH-MITROPOULOS—Fantasia and Fugue, G minor: Oct. 21; Nov. 13, 14, 16, 18.

BACH-ORMANDY—Chorale-Prelude, *Wachet auf, ruft uns die Stimme:* Apr. 4 (d), 5.

---

* Young People's Concert, conducted by Igor Buketoff.

† Programs for these concerts are included in the bound 1952–53 volumes of the Society, but not included in the repertoire.

BACH-RESPIGHI—Passacaglia and Fugue, C minor: Apr. 4, 5; Apr. 23, 24.
Prelude and Fugue, D major: Oct. 23, 24; Nov. 1, 2.

BACH-WEINER—Toccata and Fugue, C major: Dec. 4, 5, 7.

BARTOK—Concerto for Orchestra: Mar. 5, 6, 7, 8; Mar. 17.

BEETHOVEN—Piano Concerto No. 1, C major, Op. 15: Mar. 29.
Piano Concerto No. 3, C minor, Op. 37: Nov. 23; Dec. 11, 12.
Piano Concerto No. 4, G major, Op. 58: Dec. 20, 21; Mar. 12, 13.
Piano Concerto No. 5, E-flat major, Op. 73 ("Emperor"): Jan. 3; Feb. 8.
Violin Concerto, D major, Op. 61: Oct. 26; Feb. 15; Feb. 28.
Overture, *The Creatures of Prometheus,* Op. 43: Dec. 14.
Overture, *Egmont,* Op. 84: Dec. 11, 12; Dec. 20, 21.
Overture, *Fidelio,* E major, Op. 72: Oct. 16, 17, 19.
Overture, *Leonore* No. 1, C major, Op. 138: Nov. 27, 28, 29.
Overture, *Leonore* No. 3, C major, Op. 72A: Feb. 15.
Symphony No. 3, E-flat major, Op. 55 ("Eroica"): Jan. 29, 30.
Symphony No. 5, C minor, Op. 67: Dec. 7; Apr. 23, 24, 25.
Symphony No. 6, F major, Op. 68 ("Pastorale"): Dec. 11, 12.
Symphony No. 7, A major, Op. 92: Mar. 5, 6, 7, 8; Mar. 17.
Symphony No. 8, F major, Op. 93: Oct. 21; Nov. 16, 18.
Symphony No. 9, D minor, Op. 125: Mar. 2.

BERG—Three Orchestral Pieces, Op. 6: Nov. 20 (c), 21.

BERGER—*Ideas of Order:* Apr. 11 (a), 12.

BERLIOZ—Excerpts from the Dramatic Symphony, *Romeo and Juliet,* Op. 17:
Oct. 23, 24, 26.
Overture, *Benvenuto Cellini:* Nov. 20, 21; Apr. 25, 26.
Overture, *Roman Carnival:* Jan. 8, 9; Jan. 29, 30, 31; Feb. 1.
Fantastic Symphony, C major, Op. 14A: Feb. 5, 6.
Song Cycle, *Nuits d'Été (Summer Nights),* Op. 7: Apr. 4 (c), 5.

BOCCHERINI—Symphony, A major: Oct. 30, 31; Nov. 29, 30.

BORODIN—*On the Steppes of Central Asia:* Apr. 18, 19.
Polovtsian Dances, from *Prince Igor:* Nov. 23.

BOYCE-LAMBERT—Symphony No. 1, B-flat major: Feb. 28.

BRAHMS—Overture, *Academic Festival,* Op. 80: Dec. 13, 14.
Overture, *Tragic,* Op. 81: Mar. 5, 6, 7; Mar. 17.
Piano Concerto No. 1, D minor, Op. 15: Apr. 11, 12.
Piano Concerto No. 2, B-flat major, Op. 83: Jan. 8, 9, 11.
Violin Concerto, D major, Op. 77: Dec. 13, 14.
Symphony No. 1, C minor, Op. 68: Oct. 21; Nov. 27, 28; Feb. 21.
Symphony No. 2, D major, Op. 73: Oct. 30, 31; Nov. 1, 2; Jan. 6.
Symphony No. 3, F major, Op. 90: Dec. 13; Dec. 21.
Symphony No. 4, E minor, Op. 98: Jan. 31; Feb. 1.

BRAHMS-LEINSDORF—Chorale, *Oh God, Thou Holiest:* Apr. 16 (c), 17.

BRUCKNER—*Te Deum Laudamus:* Mar. 2.
Symphony No. 8, C minor: Dec. 25, 26.

CHAUSSON—Symphony, B-flat major, Op. 20: Apr. 25, 26.

CORELLI—Concerto Grosso No. 8, G minor, Op. 6, *Fatto per la Notte di
Natale:* Dec. 25, 26.

CRESTON—Two Choric Dances: Mar. 14 (f).

DEBUSSY—Excerpts from *Le Martyre de St. Sébastien:* Mar. 12 (f), 13, 14, 15.

DEBUSSY-AUTORI—*La Cathédrale Engloutie:* Jan. 3.

DVORAK—Two Slavonic Dances, Op. 46: No. 1, C major; No. 3, A-flat major:
Feb. 2.
Symphony No. 4, G major, Op. 88: Feb. 12, 13.

EINEM—*Orchestermusik,* Op. 9: Apr. 16 (b), 17.

FALLA—Interlude and Dance, *La Vida Breve:* Jan. 25 (d).
Three Dances from *The Three-Cornered Hat:* Nov. 16; Dec. 4, 5.

FAURE—Excerpts from Suite, *Pelléas et Mélisande:* Feb. 2.

FERGUSON—Concerto for Piano and String Orchestra, D major: Feb. 5 (b), 6.

FRANCK—Symphonic Variations for Piano and Orchestra: Dec. 4, 5; Apr. 19.

FRANCK-PIERNÉ—Prelude, Chorale and Fugue: Apr. 18, 19.

GABRIELI-GHEDINI—*La Battaglia:* Mar. 26 (b), 27.

GESENSWAY—*A Double Portrait:* Nov. 1 (a).

GHEDINI—*Concerto of the Albatross:* Mar. 19 (e), 20, 22.

HAYDN—Symphony No. 88, G major: Jan. 8, 9, 11.
Symphony No. 92, G major ("Oxford"): Jan. 22, 23, 24.
Symphony No. 100, G major ("Military"): Apr. 9, 10, 11.
Symphony No. 102, B-flat major: Feb. 19, 20.

HINDEMITH—'Cello Concerto: Jan. 22 (d), 23.

IPPOLITOV-IVANOV—*Caucasian Sketches:* Apr. 16, 17.

KODALY—Dances from *Galanta:* Nov. 29, 30.

LISZT—Piano Concerto No. 2, A major: Mar. 15.

LULLY—Minuet, *Le Bourgeois Gentilhomme:* Feb. 2 (d).

MAHLER—*Das Lied von der Erde (The Song of the Earth):* Feb. 19, 20, 22.
Songs for Soprano with Orchestra (1) "Ich bin der Welt abhanden gekommen"
(2) "Wo die schönen Trompeten blasen" (3) "Ich atmet' einen linden Duft"
(4) "Wer hat dies Liedlein erdacht": Jan. 1 (d), 2.
Symphony No. 4, G major, for Orchestra with Soprano Solo: Jan. 1, 2, 4.

MARTIN—Violin Concerto: Nov. 13 (b), 14, 16.

MARTINU—'Cello Concerto No. 1, D major: Oct. 30 (c), 31.

MENDELSSOHN—Violin Concerto, E minor, Op. 64: Nov. 1, 2; Apr. 26.
Overture, *A Midsummer Night's Dream:* Jan. 15, 16.
Overture, *Ruy Blas:* Nov. 23.
Symphony No. 4, A major, Op. 90 ("Italian"): Feb. 2.

MILHAUD—*Christophe Colomb,* Opera in Two Parts: Nov. 6 (b), 7, 8, 9.

MOUSSORGSKY—Excerpts from the opera, *Boris Godounoff:* Oct. 16, 17, 19.

MOUSSORGSKY-RAVEL—*Pictures at an Exhibition:* Mar. 26, 27, 29.

MOZART—Overture, *The Magic Flute:* Dec. 18, 19, 20.
Overture, *The Marriage of Figaro:* April 11, 12.
Piano Concerto, G major, K. 453: Nov. 27, 28.
Piano Concerto, D minor, K. 466: Jan. 31; Feb. 1; Mar. 26, 27.
Piano Concerto, B-flat major, K. 595: Feb. 21.
Violin Concerto No. 3, G major, K. 216: Jan. 15, 16, 18.
Symphonie Concertante for Violin and Viola with Orchestra, E-flat major,
K. 364: Feb. 12, 13.
Symphony, C major: Mar. 12 (b), 13, 14.
Symphony No. 35, D major, K. 385 ("Haffner"): Jan. 4.
Symphony No. 38, D major, K. 504 ("Prague"): Feb. 12, 13, 15.
Symphony No. 40, G minor, K. 550: Jan. 1, 2; Jan. 6.
Symphony No. 41, C major, K. 551 ("Jupiter"): Dec. 18, 19, 20.
The Village Musicians (A Musical Joke), K. 522: Mar. 19, 20, 22.

PIZZETTI—*Preludio a un Altro Giorno:* Mar. 26 (b), 27.

PROKOFIEFF—Piano Concerto No. 3, C major, Op. 26: Nov. 20, 21.
Violin Concerto No. 1, D major, Op. 19: Apr. 23, 24.
Violin Concerto No. 2, G minor, Op. 63: Oct. 23, 24.

Suite No. 2, from the Ballet *Romeo and Juliet,* Op. 64: Jan. 22 (f), 23, 24, 25.
Symphony No. 5, Op. 100: Apr. 2, 3.

PURCELL-MITROPOULOS—Prelude and Death of Dido, from *Dido and Aeneas:* Apr. 2, 3.

RACHMANINOFF—Piano Concerto No. 3, D minor, Op. 30: Apr. 18.

RAVEL—*Pavane pour une Infante défunte:* Feb. 2.
Rapsodie Espagnole: Jan. 24, 25.
Suite No. 2 from *Daphnis et Chloé:* Mar. 12, 13, 14, 15.
Tzigane, for Violin and Orchestra: Jan. 15, 16.
La Valse, Choreographic Poem for Orchestra: Jan. 22, 23; Apr. 25, 26.

RIMSKY-KORSAKOFF—*Capriccio Espagnol,* Op. 34: Dec. 7.

ROCHBERG—*Night Music:* April 23 (a), 24.

ROSSINI—Overture, *Il Signor Bruschino:* Mar. 29.
Overture, *Semiramide:* Feb. 8.

ROUSSEL—Piano Concerto, C major, Op. 36: Dec. 4 (c), 5.
Bacchus et Ariane, Suite No. 2, Op. 43: Feb. 8.

SAINT-SAENS—Piano Concerto No. 2, G minor, Op. 22: Apr. 19.
Piano Concerto No. 4, C minor, Op. 44: Dec. 7.
Suite Algérienne, Op. 60: Nov. 20, 21.

SCHOENBERG—Violin Concerto, Op. 36: Nov. 29 (c), 30.

SCHUBERT—Symphony No. 8, B minor ("Unfinished"): Dec. 14.

SCHUBERT-CASSADO—'Cello Concerto in A ("Arpeggione"): Apr. 9, 10.

SCHUMANN—Symphony No. 2, C major, Op. 61: Apr. 16, 17.
Symphony No. 4, D minor, Op. 120: Dec. 4, 5.

SCRIABIN—*Poem of Ecstasy,* Opus 54: Apr. 18, 19.
Poem of Fire: "Prometheus," Opus 60: Apr. 9, 10.

SHOSTAKOVICH—Symphony No. 5, Op. 47: Nov. 13, 14; Nov. 18.

SIBELIUS—Symphony No. 2, D major, Op. 43: Jan. 3; Jan. 15, 16, 18.

SOUSA—*The Stars and Stripes Forever:* Dec. 7.

STRAUSS—Dance of the Seven Veils and Closing Scene, from *Salome,* Op. 54: Dec. 18, 19.
Tone Poem, *Also Sprach Zarathustra,* Op. 30: Oct. 16, 17; Nov. 23.
Tone Poem, *Death and Transfiguration,* Op. 24: Dec. 28.
Tone Poem, *Don Juan,* Op. 20: Dec. 28; Jan. 6.
Tone Poem, *Till Eulenspiegel's Merry Pranks,* Op. 28: Jan. 8, 9, 11.

STRAVINSKY—Divertimento from *Le Baiser de la Fée* (*The Fairy's Kiss*): Feb. 26 (d), 27; Mar. 1.
Jeu de Cartes (*Card Game*), a Ballet in Three Deals: Feb. 26, 27; Mar. 1.
Lullaby and Finale from *L'Oiseau de Feu* (*The Firebird*): Feb. 26, 27; Mar. 1.
Suite from *Pulcinella* (after Pergolesi) for Small Orchestra: Feb. 26, 27; Mar. 1.
Quatre Etudes for Orchestra: Feb. 26 (d), 27.

TCHAIKOVSKY—Piano Concerto No. 1, B-flat minor, Op. 23: Jan. 12.
Violin Concerto, D major, Op. 35: Jan. 24, 25.
Symphony No. 4, F minor, Op. 36: Jan. 12.
Symphony No. 5, E minor, Op. 64: Feb. 28.

VAUGHAN WILLIAMS—Fantasia on a Theme by Thomas Tallis: Feb. 22.
Symphony No. 4, F minor: Apr. 2, 3, 4, 5.

VERDI—Overture, *La Forza del Destino:* Mar. 8; Mar. 14, 15; Mar. 17.

VIVALDI—Concerto Grosso for String Orchestra, No. 11, D minor, Op. 3: Feb. 5, 6, 8.

WAGNER—Siegfried's Rhine Journey, *Götterdämmerung:* Mar. 19, 20, 22.
Prelude, *Die Meistersinger:* Jan. 18.
Excerpts from *Die Meistersinger:* Feb. 21; Apr. 9, 10, 12.
Prelude to Act I, *Parsifal:* Dec. 28.
Overture, *Rienzi:* Nov. 2; Mar. 19, 20, 22.
Overture, *Tannhäuser:* Nov. 30.
Prelude and Love-Death, *Tristan und Isolde:* Dec. 28.
A Faust Overture: Mar. 19, 20, 22.
A Siegfried Idyl: Dec. 28.

WALTON—Violin Concerto: Jan. 29, 30.

WEBER—Overture, *Der Freischütz:* Jan. 6.

SOLOISTS

PIANO

CLAUDIO ARRAU: Mar. 12, 13, 15.
PAUL BADURA-SKODA: Feb. 21.
CLIFFORD CURZON: Jan. 8, 9, 11.
RUDOLF FIRKUSNY: Dec. 11, 12.
VERA FRANCESCHI: Jan. 31; Feb. 1.
LELIA GOUSSEAU: Dec. 4, 5, 7.
FRIEDRICH GULDA: Nov. 20, 21, 23.
LEONID HAMBRO: Mar. 19, 20, 22; Apr. 9, 10.
MYRA HESS: Feb. 5, 6, 8.
VLADIMIR HOROWITZ: Jan. 12.
EUGENE ISTOMIN: Jan. 3.
WILLIAM KAPELL: Nov. 27, 28; Apr. 11, 12.
GUIOMAR NOVAES: Dec. 20, 21.
ARTUR RUBINSTEIN: Apr. 19.
RUDOLF SERKIN: Mar. 26, 27, 29.
ANNA XYDIS: Apr. 18

VIOLA

WILLIAM LINCER: Feb. 12, 13.

VIOLIN

JOHN CORIGLIANO: Jan. 29, 30; Feb. 12, 13; Mar. 19, 20, 22.
MISCHA ELMAN: Jan. 24, 25.
ZINO FRANCESCATTI: Oct. 23, 24, 26.
ARTHUR GRUMIAUX: Jan. 15, 16, 18.
LOUIS KRASNER: Nov. 29, 30.
YEHUDI MENUHIN: Nov. 1, 2.
NATHAN MILSTEIN: Apr. 23, 24, 26.
JEANNE MITCHELL: Feb. 28.
ERICA MORINI: Dec. 13, 14.
JOSEPH SZIGETI: Nov. 13, 14, 16.
CAMILLA WICKS: Feb. 15.

VIOLONCELLO

PIERRE FOURNIER: Oct. 30, 31.
EDMUND KURTZ: Jan. 22, 23.
LASZLO VARGA: Mar. 19, 20, 22; Apr. 9, 10.

VOCAL

DOROTHY DOW, Soprano: Nov. 6, 7, 8, 9.
MACK HARRELL, Baritone: Nov. 6, 7, 8, 9; Mar. 2.
MARTHA LIPTON, Mezzo-Soprano: Mar. 2.
DAVID LLOYD, Tenor: Nov. 6, 7, 8, 9; Mar. 2.
WHITFIELD LLOYD, Contralto: Oct. 16, 17, 19.
GEORGE LONDON, Bass-Baritone: Oct. 16, 17, 19.
JOHN MCCOLLUM, Tenor: Oct. 16, 17, 19.
ELENA NIKOLAIDI, Contralto: Feb. 19, 20, 22.
MICHAEL RHODES, Baritone: Oct. 16, 17, 19.
NORMAN SCOTT, Bass: Nov. 6, 7, 8, 9.
IRMGARD SEEFRIED, Soprano: Jan. 1, 2, 4.
ELEANOR STEBER, Soprano: Apr. 4, 5.
SET SVANHOLM, Tenor: Dec. 18, 19; Feb. 19, 20, 22.
BLANCHE THEBOM, Mezzo-Soprano: Dec. 18, 19.
ASTRID VARNAY, Soprano: Dec. 18, 19.
FRANCES YEEND, Soprano: Mar. 2.

NARRATOR

ADOLPH ANDERSON: Nov. 6, 7, 8, 9; Mar. 19, 20, 22.
JOHN BROWNLEE: Nov. 6, 7, 8, 9.

CHORUS

SCHOLA CANTORUM, Hugh Ross, Director: Oct. 16, 17, 19.
SPECIAL CHORUS, Hugh Ross, Director: Nov. 6, 7, 8, 9.
THE WESTMINSTER CHOIR, Dr. John Finley Williamson, Director: Mar. 2.

1953–54 ONE HUNDRED TWELFTH SEASON

DIMITRI MITROPOULOS, *Musical Director*

Guest Conductors: BRUNO WALTER, GEORGE SZELL, GUIDO CANTELLI

Associate Conductor	Three Special Saturdays	Young People's Concerts
FRANCO AUTORI	ANDRE KOSTELANETZ	WILFRID PELLETIER

CONCERTS

1953

Dimitri Mitropoulos

Oct.	8—Ev'g.	Carnegie Hall
Oct.	9—Aft.	Carnegie Hall
*Oct.	10—Aft.	Town Hall
Oct.	11—Aft.	Carnegie Hall
Oct.	13—Ev'g.	Hartford, Conn.
Oct.	15—Ev'g.	Carnegie Hall
Oct.	16—Aft.	Carnegie Hall
Oct.	18—Aft.	Carnegie Hall
Oct.	19—Ev'g.	Carnegie Hall
		(Steinway Centenary—
		Pension Fund Benefit)
Oct.	22—Ev'g.	Carnegie Hall
Oct.	23—Aft.	Carnegie Hall
Oct.	24—Ev'g.	Carnegie Hall
Oct.	25—Aft.	Carnegie Hall
**Oct.	28—Aft.	Manhasset H. S.,
		Manhasset, L. I.
Oct.	29—Ev'g.	Carnegie Hall
Oct.	30—Aft.	Carnegie Hall
Oct.	31—Ev'g.	Carnegie Hall
Nov.	1—Aft.	Carnegie Hall
Nov.	5—Ev'g.	Carnegie Hall
Nov.	6—Aft.	Carnegie Hall
Nov.	7—Ev'g.	Carnegie Hall
Nov.	8—Aft.	Carnegie Hall
Nov.	12—Ev'g.	Carnegie Hall
Nov.	13—Aft.	Carnegie Hall
Nov.	14—Ev'g.	Carnegie Hall
Nov.	15—Aft.	Carnegie Hall
Nov.	19—Ev'g.	Carnegie Hall
Nov.	20—Aft.	Carnegie Hall
*Nov.	21—Aft.	Town Hall
Nov.	22—Aft.	Carnegie Hall
Nov.	26—Ev'g.	Carnegie Hall
Nov.	27—Aft.	Carnegie Hall
*Nov.	28—Morn.	Carnegie Hall
Nov.	29—Aft.	Carnegie Hall

George Szell

Dec.	3—Ev'g.	Carnegie Hall
Dec.	4—Aft.	Carnegie Hall
Dec.	5—Ev'g.	Carnegie Hall
Dec.	6—Aft.	Carnegie Hall
Dec.	10—Ev'g.	Carnegie Hall

1953

Dec.	11—Aft.	Carnegie Hall
Dec.	12—Ev'g.	Carnegie Hall
Dec.	13—Aft.	Carnegie Hall

Bruno Walter

Dec.	17—Ev'g.	Carnegie Hall
Dec.	18—Aft.	Carnegie Hall
*Dec.	19—Morn.	Carnegie Hall
Dec.	20—Aft.	Carnegie Hall
Dec.	24—Ev'g.	Carnegie Hall
Dec.	25—Aft.	Carnegie Hall
*Dec.	26—Aft.	Town Hall
Dec.	27—Aft.	Carnegie Hall

George Szell

Dec.	31—Ev'g.	Carnegie Hall

1954

George Szell

Jan.	1—Aft.	Carnegie Hall

Franco Autori

Jan.	2—Ev'g.	Carnegie Hall

George Szell

Jan.	3—Aft.	Carnegie Hall
Jan.	7—Ev'g.	Carnegie Hall
Jan.	8—Aft.	Carnegie Hall

Franco Autori

Jan.	9—Ev'g.	Carnegie Hall

George Szell

Jan.	10—Aft.	Carnegie Hall

Bruno Walter

Jan.	14—Ev'g.	Carnegie Hall
Jan.	15—Aft.	Carnegie Hall

André Kostelanetz

Jan.	16—Ev'g.	Carnegie Hall

Bruno Walter

Jan.	17—Aft.	Carnegie Hall
Jan.	18—Ev'g.	Hotel Plaza
(Philharmonic Chamber Ensemble)		
Jan.	21—Ev'g.	Carnegie Hall
Jan.	22—Aft.	Carnegie Hall
*Jan.	23—Morn.	Carnegie Hall
Jan.	24—Aft.	Carnegie Hall

* Young People's Concert, conducted by Wilfrid Pelletier.
** Young People's Concert, conducted by Franco Autori.

1954

Dimitri Mitropoulos

Jan. 28—Ev'g.	Carnegie Hall
Jan. 29—Aft.	Carnegie Hall
Jan. 30—Ev'g.	Carnegie Hall
Jan. 31—Aft.	Carnegie Hall
Feb. 4—Ev'g.	Carnegie Hall
Feb. 5—Aft.	Carnegie Hall
Feb. 6—Ev'g.	Carnegie Hall
Feb. 7—Aft.	Carnegie Hall
Feb. 11—Ev'g.	Carnegie Hall
Feb. 12—Aft.	Carnegie Hall

André Kostelanetz

Feb. 13—Ev'g.	Carnegie Hall

Dimitri Mitropoulos

Feb. 14—Aft.	Carnegie Hall
**Feb. 17—Aft.	Great Neck J. H. S.
	Great Neck, L. I.
Feb. 18—Ev'g.	Carnegie Hall
Feb. 19—Aft.	Carnegie Hall
*Feb. 20—Morn.	Carnegie Hall
Feb. 21—Aft.	Carnegie Hall

Guido Cantelli

Feb. 25—Ev'g.	Carnegie Hall
Feb. 26—Aft.	Carnegie Hall
Feb. 27—Ev'g.	Carnegie Hall
Feb. 28—Aft.	Carnegie Hall
Mar. 4—Ev'g.	Carnegie Hall
Mar. 5—Aft.	Carnegie Hall
Mar. 6—Ev'g.	Carnegie Hall
Mar. 7—Aft.	Carnegie Hall

1954

Mar. 11—Ev'g.	Carnegie Hall
Mar. 12—Aft.	Carnegie Hall

André Kostelanetz

Mar. 13—Ev'g.	Carnegie Hall

Guido Cantelli

Mar. 14—Aft.	Carnegie Hall
Mar. 15—Ev'g.	Hotel Plaza
Mar. 18—Ev'g.	Carnegie Hall
Mar. 19—Aft.	Carnegie Hall
*Mar. 20—Morn.	Carnegie Hall
Mar. 21—Aft.	Carnegie Hall

Dimitri Mitropoulos

Mar. 22—Ev'g.	Carnegie Hall
	(Pension Fund Benefit)
Mar. 25—Ev'g.	Carnegie Hall
Mar. 26—Aft.	Carnegie Hall
Mar. 27—Ev'g.	Carnegie Hall
Mar. 28—Aft.	Carnegie Hall
Apr. 15—Ev'g.	Carnegie Hall
Apr. 16—Aft.	Carnegie Hall
Apr. 17—Ev'g.	Carnegie Hall
Apr. 18—Aft.	Carnegie Hall
Apr. 22—Ev'g.	Carnegie Hall
Apr. 23—Aft.	Carnegie Hall
Apr. 24—Ev'g.	Carnegie Hall
Apr. 25—Aft.	Carnegie Hall
Apr. 28—Ev'g.	Corning, N. Y.
Apr. 29—Ev'g.	Carnegie Hall
Apr. 30—Aft.	Carnegie Hall
May 1—Ev'g.	Carnegie Hall
May 2—Aft.	Carnegie Hall

SPRING TOUR

Dimitri Mitropoulos

Mar. 29—Ev'g.	Huntington, W. Va.
Mar. 30—Ev'g.	Lexington, Ky.
Mar. 31—Ev'g.	Knoxville, Tenn.
Apr. 1—Ev'g.	Chattanooga, Tenn.
Apr. 2—Ev'g.	Birmingham, Ala.
Apr. 3—Ev'g.	Montgomery, Ala.
Apr. 4—Aft.	New Orleans, La.
Apr. 5—Ev'g.	Atlanta, Ga.
Apr. 6—Ev'g.	Clemson, S. C.
Apr. 7—Ev'g.	Columbia, S. C.
Apr. 8—Ev'g.	Charlotte, N. C.
Apr. 9—Ev'g.	Greensboro, N. C.
Apr. 10—Ev'g.	Roanoke, Va.
Apr. 11—Aft.	Washington, D. C.

TWO CONCERTS FOR HIGH SCHOOL
STUDENTS OF NEW YORK CITY

Mar. 3, 1954—Aft.
Prospect Heights High School, Brooklyn, New York; conducted by Franco Autori.

Apr. 14, 1954—Aft.
Julia Richman High School, Manhattan, New York; conducted by Wilfrid Pelletier.

NOTE: Programs for Young People's Concerts, the Two Concerts for High School Students of New York City, and the Members' Concert at the Hotel Plaza on Jan. 18 are included in the bound 1953–54 volumes of the Society, but not included in the repertoire.

** Young People's Concert, conducted by Franco Autori.
* Young People's Concert, conducted by Wilfrid Pelletier.

REPERTOIRE FOR 1953-54

(a) World premiere.
(b) American premiere.
(c) New York premiere.
(d) First performance by the Society.
(e) First New York concert performance.

Compositions marked with asterisk (*) are recorded by
The Philharmonic-Symphony Orchestra on Columbia Records

AUBERT—Fantaisie for Piano and Orchestra: Nov. 12 (c), 13.

BACH—Violin Concerto, A minor: Mar. 11, 12.
Suite No. 3, D major: Apr. 15, 16, 17, 18.

BACH-BOESSENROTH—Chorale-Prelude, Credo, "Wir glauben all' an einen
Gott, Schoepfer": Mar. 22.

BACH-HONEGGER—Suite: Jan. 30.

BACH-WEBERN—Ricercare No. 2 from the "Musical Offering": Nov. 29 (b).

BARTOK—Music for Strings, Percussion and Celesta: Feb. 25, 26, 28.
Rhapsody No. 2, for Violin and Orchestra: Oct. 15, 16, 18.

BEETHOVEN—Piano Concerto No. 4, G major, Op. 58: Dec. 12, 13; Jan. 28, 29;
Mar. 22.
*Piano Concerto No. 5, E-flat major, Op. 73 ("Emperor"): Feb. 27, 28.
*Violin Concerto, D major, Op. 61: Jan. 7, 8, 10.
*Triple Concerto, C major, Op. 56: Jan. 21, 22.
"Missa Solemnis," D major, Op. 123: Nov. 5, 6, 7, 8.
Overture to "Coriolanus": Jan. 21, 22.
Overture to "Egmont," Op. 84: Dec. 13; Jan. 7, 8.
Overture to "Prometheus," Op. 43: Dec. 20; Feb. 18, 19, 21.
Excerpts from the Ballet, "The Creatures of Prometheus," Op. 43: Feb. 18, 19,
21.
*Symphony No. 1, C major, Op. 21: Jan. 31; Mar. 31.
*Symphony No. 2, D major, Op. 36: Nov. 26, 27, 29; Jan. 9; Apr. 3, 7.
*Symphony No. 3, E-flat major, Op. 55 ("Eroica"): Jan. 21, 22.
*Symphony No. 5, C minor, Op. 67: Jan. 7, 8, 10.

BERLIOZ—*Overture, "Roman Carnival," Op. 9: Oct. 11; Jan. 16; Mar. 28, 29,
30; Apr. 8, 10, 11.
Symphony, "Harold in Italy," Op. 16: Oct. 8, 9, 11, 13.
Three Excerpts from "The Damnation of Faust": Dec. 5, 6.

BEZANSON—Piano Concerto: Nov. 12 (a), 13.

BIZET—*Symphony in C major: Apr. 22, 23, 24, 25, 28.

BLACHER—"Ornaments" for Orchestra: Nov. 19 (b), 20.

BLOCH—*"Schelomo," Hebrew Rhapsody for 'Cello and Orchestra: Nov. 26, 27.
"Sinfonia Breve": Dec. 10 (c), 11, 12.

BOCCHERINI—'Cello Concerto, B-flat major, Op. 34: Nov. 26, 27.

BORODIN—Symphony No. 2, B minor, Op. 5: Oct. 22, 23, 24.

BRAHMS—Piano Concerto No. 1, D minor, Op. 15: Dec. 31; Jan. 1, 3.
Piano Concerto No. 2, B-flat major, Op. 83: Dec. 3, 4; Jan. 9.
Violin Concerto, D major, Op. 77: Dec. 17, 18, 20.
*Overture, "Academic Festival," Op. 80: Dec. 20.
Overture, "Tragic," Op. 81: Nov. 12, 13, 14.
*Symphony No. 1, C minor, Op. 68: Jan. 17; Feb. 25, 26, 27.
*Symphony No. 2, D major, Op. 73: Dec. 3, 4.
Symphony No. 3, F major, Op. 90: Dec. 17, 18.

*Symphony No. 4, E minor, Op. 98: Nov. 12, 13, 22; Jan. 2; Mar. 30.
Variations on a Theme by Haydn, Op. 56-a: Dec. 17, 18.
BRUCKNER—Symphony No. 9, D minor: Dec. 24, 25, 27.
BUSONI—"Berceuse Élégiaque": Mar. 18, 19, 21.
"Dance-Waltz for Orchestra," Opus 53: Mar. 18 (d), 19, 21.
CHABRIER—"Fête Polonaise" from "Le Roi malgré Lui": Apr. 22, 23, 25.
CHERUBINI—Symphony in D major: Mar. 18, 19, 21.
CHOPIN—Piano Concerto No. 1, E minor, Op. 11: Mar. 22.
Piano Concerto No. 2, F minor, Op. 21: Apr. 22, 23.
CIMAROSA—Overture, "The Beautiful Grecian": Feb. 18 (d), 19, 21; Mar. 27; Apr. 1, 3, 6, 7, 10.
CONVERSE—"The Mystic Trumpeter," Opus 19: Apr. 22 (d), 23.
COPLAND—"Appalachian Spring," Orchestral Suite from the Ballet: Feb. 4, 5, 7; Mar. 31; Apr. 1, 6, 7.
DALGLEISH—Statement for Orchestra: May 1 (a).
DALLAPICCOLA—Symphonic Fragments from the Ballet, "Marsia": Mar. 4 (e), 5, 6, 7.
DEBUSSY—"Images for Orchestra": Feb. 4, 5.
"Iberia" from "Images for Orchestra": Feb. 6, 7.
Prelude, "The Afternoon of a Faun": Feb. 13.
*"La Mer," Three Symphonic Sketches: Mar. 4, 5, 6, 7.
DUKAS—Scherzo, "The Sorcerer's Apprentice": Feb. 13.
EINEM—"Capriccio": Oct. 15 (b), 16, 18.
ENESCO—*Roumanian Rhapsody No. 1, A major, Op. 11: Feb. 13.
FALLA—*Dances from "The Three-Cornered Hat": Oct. 19; Oct. 25; Mar. 30; Apr. 1, 2, 4, 5, 8, 9.
"Homenajes": Feb. 18 (b), 19, 21; Mar. 29; Apr. 10, 11.
*Interlude and Dance, "La Vida Breve": Oct. 29, 30, 31; Nov. 1.
FRANCK—Symphony in D minor: Dec. 5, 6.
FRESCOBALDI-AUTORI—"Bergamasca": Jan. 9 (c).
GABRIELI-GHEDINI—"Canzon for eight voices": Feb. 25 (e), 26, 28.
GERSHWIN—*"An American in Paris": Mar. 13.
GERSHWIN-BENNETT—"Porgy and Bess": A Symphonic Picture: Jan. 16.
GLAZOUNOFF—Violin Concerto, A minor, Op. 82: May 1, 2.
GOULD—"Dance Variations" for Two Pianos and Orchestra: Oct. 24 (a), 25.
"Inventions" for Four Pianos and Orchestra: Oct. 19 (a).
GROFE—"Grand Canyon Suite": Feb. 13 (Mov'ts. 3, 4, 5).
HAYDN—Overture for an English Opera: Nov. 19 (b), 20; Feb. 6, 7.
Symphony No. 80, D minor: Feb. 4, 5, 6, 7.
Symphony No. 88, G major: Jan. 24.
HELM—Piano Concerto in G: Apr. 24 (b).
HINDEMITH—Symphony, "Die Harmonie der Welt": Oct. 22 (c), 23, 25.
KASSERN—"Adagio" from Concerto for String Orchestra: Jan. 2 (c).
KODALY—"Dances of Galanta": Jan. 30, 31; Mar. 29; Apr. 8, 10, 11.
KRENEK—Concerto for Two Pianos and Orchestra: Oct. 24 (a).
LALO—'Cello Concerto, D minor: Mar. 27.
Overture to "Le Roi d'Ys": Apr. 22, 23, 24, 25, 28.
Symphonie Espagnole for Violin and Orchestra, Op. 21: Dec. 5, 6.
LIEBERMANN—"Furioso": Nov. 14 (c), 15.
MacDOWELL—Suite No. 2, E minor, Op. 48 ("Indian") (Movements 1, 3, 5): Oct. 19.

MAHLER—Symphony No. 1, D major: Jan. 24.

MALIPIERO—Vivaldiana: Oct. 22 (b), 23.

MENDELSSOHN—Piano Concerto No. 1, G minor, Op. 25: Feb. 6.
*Violin Concerto, E minor, Op. 64: Nov. 14, 15; Mar. 11, 12, 14.
Overture, "Calm Sea and Prosperous Voyage," Op. 27: Oct. 24; Nov. 1.
Overture, "Fingal's Cave," Op. 26: Oct. 29, 30; Nov. 15.
Overture, "Ruy Blas," Op. 95: Oct. 31; Apr. 2, 5, 9, 11.
Symphony No. 3, A minor, Op. 56 ("Scotch"): Oct. 31; Nov. 1.
*Symphony No. 4, A major, Op. 90 ("Italian"): Mar. 4, 5, 6, 7, 15.
*Symphony No. 5, D major, Op. 107 ("Reformation"): Oct. 15, 16, 18; Apr. 6, 10, 11.

MENNIN—Symphony No. 3: Jan. 30.

MENOTTI—Violin Concerto: Apr. 17 (d), 18.

MOHAUPT—Violin Concerto: Apr. 29 (a), 30.

MOUSSORGSKY—Prelude, "Khovanshchina": Dec. 10, 11, 12.

MOZART—Adagio in E major, for Violin and Orchestra, K. 261: Apr. 17, 18.
Divertimento No. 15, B-flat major, K. 287: Mar. 11, 12, 14.
Piano Concerto No. 9, E-flat major, K. 271: Jan. 14, 15.
Piano Concerto No. 14, E-flat major, K. 449: Jan. 17.
Piano Concerto No. 17, G major, K. 453: Jan. 28, 29.
*Piano Concerto No. 21, C major, K. 467: Oct. 31.
Piano Concerto No. 24, C minor, K. 491: Dec. 10, 11.
Overture to "The Abduction from the Seraglio": Jan. 28, 29, 31.
*Overture to "Cosí fan tutte": Jan. 17.
Overture to "The Marriage of Figaro": Mar. 13.
Mass in C minor, K. 427, "Et Incarnatus Est": Dec. 24, 25.
Motet, "Exsultate, Jubilate" for Soprano, Orchestra and Organ, K. 165: Dec. 24 (d), 25, 27.
Symphony No. 38, D major, K. 504 ("Prague"): Jan. 14, 15.
Symphony No. 39, E-flat major, K. 543: Dec. 20.
*Symphony No. 41, C major, K. 551 ("Jupiter"): Jan. 14, 15.
The Village Musicians, K. 522 (A Musical Joke): Mar. 15.

PROKOFIEFF—Piano Concerto No. 3, C major, Op. 26: Oct. 19 (Finale only); Jan. 2.
Symphony in D major, Op. 25 ("Classical"): Mar. 13.
*Symphony No. 5, Op. 100: Mar. 27, 31; Apr. 1, 2, 3, 4, 5, 8, 9, 15, 16.
"Wedding Suite" from the Ballet, "The Stone Flower": Jan. 16 (c).

RACHMANINOFF—*Piano Concerto No. 2, C minor, Op. 18: Nov. 22.
Piano Concerto No. 3, D minor, Op. 30: Jan. 30, 31.
Piano Concerto No. 4, G minor, Op. 40: Apr. 25 (d).
Rhapsody on a Theme of Paganini, Op. 43: Mar. 22.
Symphonic Dances, Op. 45: Nov. 19, 20; Nov. 22 (3rd Mov't.).
*Symphony No. 2, E minor, Op. 27: Apr. 28, 29, 30; May 1, 2.

RAVEL—"Alborada del Gracioso": Feb. 4, 5, 7.
Bolero: Jan. 16; Mar. 18, 19, 21.
"Mother Goose," Five Children's Pieces: Jan. 16.
Piano Concerto, G major: Nov. 29.
Rapsodie Espagnole: Nov. 26, 27, 29.

RIMSKY-KORSAKOFF—*"Capriccio Espagnol": Jan. 2.
Overture, "Russian Easter," Opus 26: Apr. 17, 18.

ROSSINI—Overture to "La Cenerentola": Mar. 4, 5; Mar. 15.
Overture to "La Gazza Ladra": Feb. 27.
Overture to "L'Italiana in Algeri": Mar. 6, 7.
Overture to "Semiramide": Feb. 28.

SAINT-SAENS—*Piano Concerto No. 4, C minor, Op. 44: Oct. 29, 30; Nov. 1.

SCHOENBERG—Piano Concerto: Feb. 6 (d).
Symphonic Poem, "Pelleas and Melisande," Opus 5: Oct. 29, 30.
SCHUBERT—Symphony No. 2, B-flat major: Feb. 18, 19; Mar. 28.
SCHUMANN—Piano Concerto in A minor, Op. 54: Feb. 21.
Symphony No. 1, B-flat major, Op. 38: Nov. 14, 15.
*Symphony No. 3, E-flat major, Op. 97 ("Rhenish"): Oct. 8, 9, 11, 13.
Symphony No. 4, D minor, Op. 120: Dec. 10, 11, 12, 13.
SOUSA-GOULD—"Stars and Stripes Forever": Oct. 19 (a).
STAMITZ—Symphonie Konzertante, in F: Oct. 8 (d), 9, 13.
STRAUSS—"Burleske" for Piano and Orchestra: Jan. 28, 29.
Festival Prelude, Op. 61: Feb. 14.
Prelude to Act III, "Arabella," Op. 79: Feb. 11 (d), 12, 14.
Fantasy from "Die Frau ohne Schatten": Feb. 11 (d), 12, 14.
Three Symphonic Interludes from "Intermezzo," Op. 72: Feb. 11, 12.
Waltzes from "Der Rosenkavalier": Jan. 16.
"Symphonia Domestica," Op. 53: Feb. 11, 12, 14.
*Tone Poem, "Death and Transfiguration," Opus 24: Mar. 18, 19, 21.
STRAVINSKY—*Suite from "The Firebird": Mar. 13.
TCHAIKOVSKY—Violin Concerto, D major, Op. 35: Mar. 25, 26, 28.
*Overture-Fantasy, "Romeo and Juliet": Mar. 13.
Introduction and Fugue from Suite No. 1, D minor, Op. 43: Mar. 25, 26, 28.
Suite for Orchestra, "Queen of Spades": Feb. 13 (c).
*Symphonic Fantasy, "Francesca da Rimini," Opus 32: Mar. 30; Apr. 2, 4, 5, 6, 7, 9, 24.
Symphony No. 5, E minor, Op. 64: Mar. 25, 26, 29.
VAUGHAN WILLIAMS—Fantasia on a Theme by Thomas Tallis: Apr. 15, 16, 17, 18.
VERDI—Overture to "Nabucco": Apr. 29, 30.
VIEUXTEMPS—Violin Concerto, D minor, Op. 31: Nov. 19, 20.
VIOTTI—Violin Concerto No. 22, A minor: Oct. 15, 16, 18.
VIVALDI-EPHRIKIAN—Concerto Grosso in A for Strings and Cembalo (F. 11, No. 4): Mar. 11 (d), 12, 14, 15.
WAGNER—Overture to "The Flying Dutchman": Dec. 31; Jan. 1, 3.
Prelude to "Die Meistersinger": Oct. 19, 25; Dec. 13; Dec. 31; Jan. 1.
Prelude to "Parsifal": Dec. 24, 25, 27.
*Overture to "Rienzi": Dec. 31; Jan. 1, 3.
Overture to "Tannhäuser": Dec. 31; Jan. 1, 3.
WEBER-BERLIOZ—"Invitation to the Dance": Feb. 13.
WEBER-SZELL—Perpetual Motion: May 1 (d), 2.

SOLOISTS

PIANO

JACQUES ABRAM: Jan. 9.
PAUL BADURA-SKODA: Dec. 10, 11.
JEAN CASADESUS: Oct. 31.
ROBERT CASADESUS: Oct. 29, 30; Nov. 1.
RUDOLF FIRKUSNY: Dec. 12, 13.
LEON FLEISHER: Dec. 31; Jan. 1, 3.
LELIA GOUSSEAU: Apr. 22, 23.
JOANNA GRAUDAN: Jan. 21, 22.
LEONID HAMBRO: Apr. 24, 25.
NICOLE HENRIOT: Nov. 29.

MYRA HESS: Jan. 14, 15, 17.
EUGENE ISTOMIN: Dec. 3, 4.
BYRON JANIS: Jan. 30, 31.
JACOB LATEINER: Jan. 2.
JAMES MACINNES: Feb. 6.
DIMITRI MITROPOULOS: Oct. 19.
ARTUR RUBINSTEIN: Mar. 22.
RUDOLF SERKIN: Jan. 28, 29; Feb. 27, 28.
JOHN SIMMS: Nov. 12, 13.
SORIANO: Feb. 21.
DANIEL WAYENBERG: Nov. 22.
WHITTEMORE & LOWE: Oct. 24, 25.

VIOLA
WILLIAM LINCER: Oct. 8, 9, 11, 13.

VIOLIN
ALFREDO CAMPOLI: Dec. 5, 6.
JOHN CORIGLIANO: Oct. 8, 9, 13; Nov. 19, 20; Jan. 21, 22.
MISCHA ELMAN: Nov. 14, 15.
ZINO FRANCESCATTI: Mar. 25, 26, 28.
JASCHA HEIFETZ: Mar. 11, 12, 14.
YEHUDI MENUHIN: Oct. 15, 16, 18.
ERICA MORINI: Dec. 17, 18, 20.
MICHAEL RABIN: Apr. 29, 30; May 1, 2.
TOSSY SPIVAKOVSKY: Apr. 17, 18.
ISAAC STERN: Jan. 7, 8, 10.

VIOLONCELLO
LEONARD ROSE: Nov. 26, 27.
LASZLO VARGA: Oct. 8, 9, 13; Jan. 21, 22; Mar. 27.

OBOE
HAROLD GOMBERG: Oct. 8, 9, 13.

FLUTE
JOHN WUMMER: Oct. 8, 9, 13.

CLARINET
ROBERT MCGINNIS: Oct. 8, 9, 13.

HORN
JAMES CHAMBERS: Oct. 8, 9, 13.
WILLIAM NAMEN: Oct. 8, 9, 13.

VOICE
MACK HARRELL, Bass: Nov. 5, 6, 7, 8.
IRMGARD SEEFRIED, Soprano: Dec. 24, 25, 27.
HARVEY SMITH-SPENCER, Tenor: Nov. 5, 6, 7, 8.
ELEANOR STEBER, Soprano: Nov. 5, 6, 7, 8.
NELL TANGEMAN: Mezzo-Soprano: Nov. 5, 6, 7, 8.

CHORUS
THE WESTMINSTER CHOIR, Dr. John Finley Williamson, Director: Nov. 5, 6, 7, 8.

1954–55 ONE HUNDRED THIRTEENTH SEASON

DIMITRI MITROPOULOS, *Musical Director*

Guest Conductors: BRUNO WALTER, GEORGE SZELL, GUIDO CANTELLI

Associate Conductor	*Three Special Saturdays*	*Young People's Concerts*
FRANCO AUTORI	ANDRE KOSTELANETZ	WILFRID PELLETIER

CONCERTS

1954

Dimitri Mitropoulos
Oct.	7—Ev'g.	Carnegie Hall
Oct.	8—Aft.	Carnegie Hall
*Oct.	9—Aft.	Town Hall
Oct.	10—Aft.	Carnegie Hall
Oct.	12—Ev'g.	Hartford, Conn.
Oct.	14—Ev'g.	Carnegie Hall
Oct.	15—Aft.	Carnegie Hall
Oct.	17—Aft.	Carnegie Hall
Oct.	21—Ev'g.	Carnegie Hall
Oct.	22—Aft.	Carnegie Hall
Oct.	23—Ev'g.	Carnegie Hall
Oct.	24—Aft.	Carnegie Hall

Leopold Stokowski
| Oct. | 26—Ev'g. | Carnegie Hall |

(Columbia University Bicentennial)

1954

Dimitri Mitropoulos
Oct.	28—Ev'g.	Carnegie Hall
Oct.	29—Aft.	Carnegie Hall
Oct.	30—Ev'g.	Carnegie Hall
Oct.	31—Aft.	Carnegie Hall
Nov.	4—Ev'g.	Carnegie Hall
Nov.	5—Aft.	Carnegie Hall

Franco Autori
| Nov. | 6—Ev'g. | Carnegie Hall |

Dimitri Mitropoulos
Nov.	7—Aft.	Carnegie Hall
Nov.	11—Ev'g.	Carnegie Hall
Nov.	12—Aft.	Carnegie Hall

Franco Autori
| Nov. | 13—Ev'g. | Carnegie Hall |

---

*Young People's Concert, conducted by Wilfrid Pelletier.

1954

Dimitri Mitropoulos
Nov. 14—Aft.   Carnegie Hall

Richard Rodgers
Nov. 15—Ev'g.   Carnegie Hall
                          (Pension Fund Benefit)

Bruno Walter
Nov. 18—Ev'g.   Carnegie Hall
Nov. 19—Aft.   Carnegie Hall
*Nov. 20—Morn.   Carnegie Hall
Nov. 21—Aft.   Carnegie Hall
Nov. 25—Ev'g.   Carnegie Hall
Nov. 26—Aft.   Carnegie Hall
*Nov. 27—Aft.   Town Hall

André Kostelanetz
Nov. 27—Ev'g.   Carnegie Hall

Bruno Walter
Nov. 28—Aft.   Carnegie Hall

George Szell
Dec. 2—Ev'g.   Carnegie Hall
Dec. 3—Aft.   Carnegie Hall
Dec. 4—Ev'g.   Carnegie Hall
Dec. 5—Aft.   Carnegie Hall
Dec. 9—Ev'g.   Carnegie Hall
Dec. 10—Aft.   Carnegie Hall
Dec. 11—Ev'g.   Carnegie Hall
Dec. 12—Aft.   Carnegie Hall

Bruno Walter
Dec. 16—Ev'g.   Carnegie Hall
Dec. 17—Aft.   Carnegie Hall
*Dec. 18—Aft.   Town Hall
Dec. 19—Aft.   Carnegie Hall
Dec. 23—Ev'g.   Carnegie Hall
Dec. 24—Aft.   Carnegie Hall

André Kostelanetz
Dec. 25—Ev'g.   Carnegie Hall

Bruno Walter
Dec. 26—Aft.   Carnegie Hall

André Kostelanetz
Dec. 29—Ev'g.   White Plains, N. Y.

George Szell
Dec. 30—Ev'g.   Carnegie Hall
Dec. 31—Aft.   Carnegie Hall

1955

George Szell
Jan. 2—Aft.   Carnegie Hall
Jan. 6—Ev'g.   Carnegie Hall
Jan. 7—Aft.   Carnegie Hall

1955

*Jan. 8—Morn.   Carnegie Hall
Jan. 9—Aft.   Carnegie Hall

Guido Cantelli
Jan. 13—Ev'g.   Carnegie Hall
Jan. 14—Aft.   Carnegie Hall
Jan. 15—Ev'g.   Carnegie Hall
Jan. 16—Aft.   Carnegie Hall
**Jan. 19—Aft.   Great Neck J. H. S.
                          Great Neck, L. I.
†Jan. 20—Ev'g.   Carnegie Hall

Franco Autori
Jan. 21—Aft.   Carnegie Hall
Jan. 22—Ev'g.   Carnegie Hall
Jan. 23—Aft.   Carnegie Hall

Guido Cantelli
Jan. 27—Ev'g.   Carnegie Hall
Jan. 28—Aft.   Carnegie Hall
Jan. 29—Ev'g.   Carnegie Hall
Jan. 30—Aft.   Carnegie Hall
Feb. 3—Ev'g.   Carnegie Hall
Feb. 4—Aft.   Carnegie Hall

Walter Hendl
Feb. 5—Ev'g.   Carnegie Hall

Guido Cantelli
Feb. 6—Aft.   Carnegie Hall

Dimitri Mitropoulos
Feb. 10—Ev'g.   Carnegie Hall
Feb. 11—Aft.   Carnegie Hall
*Feb. 12—Morn.   Carnegie Hall
Feb. 13—Aft.   Carnegie Hall
Feb. 14—Ev'g.   Hotel Plaza
    (Philharmonic Chamber Ensemble)
Feb. 17—Ev'g.   Carnegie Hall
Feb. 18—Aft.   Carnegie Hall
Feb. 19—Ev'g.   Carnegie Hall
Feb. 20—Aft.   Carnegie Hall
Feb. 24—Ev'g.   Carnegie Hall
Feb. 25—Aft.   Carnegie Hall
Feb. 26—Ev'g.   Carnegie Hall
Feb. 27—Aft.   Carnegie Hall
**Mar. 2—Aft.   Manhasset H. S.,
                          Manhasset, L. I.

Guido Cantelli
Mar. 3—Ev'g.   Carnegie Hall
Mar. 4—Aft.   Carnegie Hall

André Kostelanetz
Mar. 5—Ev'g.   Carnegie Hall

Guido Cantelli
Mar. 6—Aft.   Carnegie Hall
Mar. 10—Ev'g.   Carnegie Hall

---

* Young People's Concert, conducted by Wilfrid Pelletier.
** Young People's Concert, conducted by Franco Autori.
† Three works conducted by Franco Autori.

1955
Mar. 11—Aft.	Carnegie Hall
*Mar. 12—Morn.	Carnegie Hall
Mar. 13—Aft.	Carnegie Hall

André Kostelanetz

Mar. 14—Ev'g.	Hotel Plaza

Guido Cantelli

Mar. 17—Ev'g.	Carnegie Hall
Mar. 18—Aft.	Carnegie Hall
Mar. 19—Ev'g.	Carnegie Hall
Mar. 20—Aft.	Carnegie Hall
Mar. 24—Ev'g.	Carnegie Hall
Mar. 25—Aft.	Carnegie Hall

Thomas Schippers

Mar. 26—Ev'g.	Carnegie Hall

Guido Cantelli

Mar. 27—Aft.	Carnegie Hall

1955

Dimitri Mitropoulos

Mar. 30—Ev'g.	Riverside Church (Organ Dedication Concert)
Mar. 31—Ev'g.	Carnegie Hall
Apr. 1—Aft.	Carnegie Hall
Apr. 2—Ev'g.	Carnegie Hall
Apr. 3—Aft.	Carnegie Hall
Apr. 7—Ev'g.	Carnegie Hall
Apr. 8—Aft.	Carnegie Hall
Apr. 9—Ev'g.	Carnegie Hall
Apr. 10—Aft.	Carnegie Hall
Apr. 14—Ev'g.	Carnegie Hall
Apr. 15—Aft.	Carnegie Hall
*Apr. 16—Morn.	Carnegie Hall
Apr. 17—Aft.	Carnegie Hall

TWO CONCERTS FOR HIGH SCHOOL STUDENTS OF NEW YORK CITY

Mar. 16—Aft.
Julia Richman High School, Manhattan, New York; conducted by André Kostelanetz.

Mar. 23—Aft.
Prospect Heights High School, Brooklyn, New York; conducted by Thomas Schippers.

NOTE: Programs for Young People's Concerts, the Two Concerts for High School Students of New York City, and the Members' Concert at the Hotel Plaza on Feb. 14 are included in the bound 1954–55 volumes of the Society, but are not included in the repertoire.

REPERTOIRE FOR 1954–55

(a) World premiere.
(b) American premiere.
(c) New York premiere.
(d) First performance by the Society.

Compositions marked with asterisk (*) are recorded by
The Philharmonic-Symphony Orchestra on Columbia Records

BACH—Aria from Suite No. 3, D major: Mar. 24, 25.
Concerto for Organ and Orchestra, No. 1, D major: Mar. 30 (d).
Concerto for Violin and Orchestra, A minor: Dec. 2, 3.
Concerto for Violin and Orchestra, G minor: Dec. 23, 24.
BACH-MITROPOULOS—Fantasia and Fugue, G minor: Oct. 7, 8, 10.
BARBER—Adagio for Strings, Op. 11: Jan. 20, 21, 23; Mar. 19, 27.
BARTOK—Concerto for Violin and Orchestra: Feb. 24, 25.
"Deux Portraits" for Violin and Orchestra, Op. 5 (Andante only): Dec. 23 (d), 24.
Dance Suite: Oct. 26.
"Deux Images" for Orchestra, Op. 10: Mar. 26 (d).
BEETHOVEN—Concerto for Piano and Orchestra No. 3, C minor, Op. 37: Mar. 10, 11, 13.

---

* Young People's Concert, conducted by Wilfrid Pelletier.

Concerto for Piano and Orchestra No. 4, G major, Op. 58: Nov. 18, 19; Dec. 4, 5.
*Concerto for Piano and Orchestra No. 5, E-flat major, Op. 73 ("Emperor"): Oct. 21, 22; Jan. 15, 16.
*Concerto for Violin and Orchestra, D major, Op. 61: Dec. 30, 31; Jan. 22, 23.
Overture, "Egmont," Op. 84: Jan. 15.
Overture, "Leonore," No. 2: Oct. 21, 22, 24.
Overture, "Leonore," No. 3: Nov. 28; Dec. 30, 31; Jan. 2.
Overture, "Prometheus," Op. 43: Nov. 27; Feb. 5.
*Symphony No. 3, E-flat major, Op. 55 ("Eroica"): Oct. 23, 24; Mar. 31; Apr. 1.
*Symphony No. 6, F major, Op. 68 ("Pastoral"): Jan. 13, 14, 15.
*Symphony No. 7, A major, Op. 92: Mar. 24, 25, 27.
*Symphony No. 8, F major, Op. 93: Dec. 30, 31; Jan. 2.
*Symphony No. 9, D minor, Op. 125: Apr. 14, 15, 17.

BERLIOZ—Overture, "Roman Carnival," Op. 9: Dec. 2, 3, 5.
Symphonie Fantastique, C major, Op. 14-A: Nov. 18, 19, 21.

BLACHER—Variations on a Theme of Paganini, Opus 26: Dec. 2 (c), 3, 4, 5.

BONPORTI—Concerto Grosso No. 8, D major, Op. 11: Jan. 13 (b), 14.

BRAHMS—A German Requiem, Op. 45: Dec. 16, 17, 19.
Concerto for Piano and Orchestra No. 1, D minor, Op. 15: Feb. 10, 11, 13.
Concerto for Piano and Orchestra No. 2, B-flat major, Op. 83: Feb. 17, 18, 20.
Concerto for Violin and Orchestra, D major, Opus 77: Feb. 24, 25, 26, 27.
Concerto for Violin, Violoncello and Orchestra, A minor, Op. 102: Nov. 28.
*Overture, "Academic Festival," Op. 80: Nov. 6, 28.
*Overture, "Tragic," Op. 81: Dec. 19.
*Symphony No. 1, C minor, Op. 68: Mar. 17, 18, 19, 20.
*Symphony No. 2, D major, Op. 73: Nov. 11, 12.
*Symphony No. 3, F major, Op. 90: Jan. 20, 21.
*Symphony No. 4, E minor, Op. 98: Jan. 6, 7, 9; Feb. 5.
*Variations on a Theme by Haydn, B-flat major, Op. 56-A: Nov. 11, 12; Feb. 13.

BRUCH—*Concerto for Violin and Orchestra, No. 1, G minor, Op. 26: Dec. 2, 3.

BRUCKNER—Symphony No. 7, E major: Dec. 23, 24.

CAAMANO—Suite for Strings: Nov. 13 (c).

CHABRIER—"Fête Polonaise" from "Le Roi malgré Lui": Apr. 3.

CHAUSSON—"Poème" for Violin and Orchestra, Op. 25: Apr. 2.

CHOPIN—Concerto for Piano and Orchestra No. 1, E minor, Op. 11: Jan. 6, 7.
Concerto for Piano and Orchestra No. 2, F minor, Op. 21: Jan. 9.

CIMAROSA—Overture, "Il Fanatico per gli Antichi Romani": Feb. 10 (d), 11, 13.

COPLAND—"El Salón México": Mar. 10, 11, 13.

CORTEZ—Sinfonia Sacra: Apr. 9 (a).

COUPERIN-BAZELAIRE—Pièces en Concert, for Violoncello and Orchestra: Oct. 28, 29, 31.

COUPERIN-MILHAUD—*Prelude and Allegro, "La Sultane": Oct. 30, 31; Nov. 4, 5.

DEBUSSY—Nocturnes: "Clouds," "Festivals": Mar. 17, 18, 20. ("Festivals" only, Mar. 20).
Prelude, "L'Après-midi d'un Faune": Jan. 20, 21, 23.

DELLO JOIO—Variations, Chaconne and Finale: Nov. 6.

DUKAS—Scherzo, "The Sorcerer's Apprentice": Jan. 27, 28, 29, 30.

DVORAK—Overture, "Carnival," Op. 92: Nov. 14.
*Symphony No. 4, G major, Op. 88: Nov. 25, 26.

FALLA—*Three Dances from "The Three-Cornered Hat": Mar. 3, 4, 6.

FRANCK—Symphonic Variations for Piano and Orchestra: Mar. 3, 4.

GABURO—"On a Quiet Theme": Feb. 26 (a).

GERSHWIN—*"An American in Paris": Dec. 25, 29.
Cuban Overture: Dec. 25, 29.
"The Man I Love": Dec. 25, 29.
Rhapsody in Blue: Dec. 25, 29.

GERSHWIN-BENNETT—*"Porgy and Bess: A Symphonic Picture": Dec. 25, 29.

GHEDINI—Pezzo Concertante, for Two Violins and Viola obbligato: Jan. 27 (d), 28.

GLUCK—Overture, "Iphigenia in Aulis": Dec. 23, 24.

GOSSEC—Symphony in D major: Nov. 13 (d).

GOULD—Show Piece for Orchestra: Feb. 19 (c), 20; Apr. 7, 8.

GROFE—"Mississippi" Suite: Nov. 27.

HANDEL—"Largo" from "Xerxes": Mar. 27.

HANSON—Concerto for Organ, Strings and Harp: Mar. 30 (d).

HARRIS—Symphonic Epigram: Nov. 14 (a).

HAYDN—Concerto for 'Cello and Orchestra, D major, Op. 101: Jan. 29.
Symphony No. 88, G major: Mar. 14.
Symphony No. 93, D major: Mar. 3, 4, 6.
Symphony No. 96, D major: Nov. 21 (d).

JANACEK—Sinfonietta: Dec. 9, 10, 11.

JONGEN—Symphonie Concertante, Op. 81: Mar. 30 (d).

KABALEVSKY—Overture, "Colas Breugnon": Oct. 14, 15, 17.

KHATCHATOURIAN—*"Masquerade" Suite: Nov. 27.

LADMIRAULT—Variations sur des Airs de Biniou: Apr. 2, 3 (b).

LALO—Symphonie Espagnole for Violin and Orchestra, Op. 21: Apr. 2, 3.

LIADOFF—"The Enchanted Lake": Mar. 5.

LIEBERMANN—Concerto for Jazzband and Symphony Orchestra: Mar. 31 (c); Apr. 1.

LISZT—Symphonic Poem, "Les Préludes": Mar. 5.

LUENING—Symphonic Fantasia No. 2: Oct. 26 (d).

MacDOWELL—Concerto for Piano and Orchestra No. 2, D minor, Op. 23: Oct. 26.

MAHLER—Symphony No. 6, A minor: Apr. 7, 8, 10.

MARINUZZI—Fantasia quasi Passacaglia: Jan. 13 (b), 14.

MASON—Overture, "Chanticleer": Oct. 26.

MENDELSSOHN—Concerto for Piano and Orchestra No. 1, G minor, Op. 25: Oct. 30.
*Concerto for Violin and Orchestra, E minor, Op. 64: Nov. 11, 12; Jan. 2.
Overture, "The Wedding of Camacho": Feb. 17, 18.
Symphony No. 4, A major, Op. 90 ("Italian"): Mar. 26.
*Symphony No. 5, D major, Op. 107 ("Reformation"): Oct. 12; Nov. 14.

MENNIN—Symphony No. 6: Feb. 17 (c), 18, 20.

MEYEROWITZ—"The Glory Around His Head"—Cantata of the Resurrection: Apr. 14 (a), 15, 17.

MILHAUD—"Le Carnaval d'Aix," Fantasy for Piano and Orchestra: Oct. 23.
Suite Provençale: Feb. 26, 27; Mar. 31; Apr. 1.

MOORE—Symphony No. 2, A major: Oct. 26.

MOUSSORGSKY-RAVEL—*Pictures at an Exhibition: Jan. 13, 14, 16; Mar. 19.

MOZART—Concerto for Piano and Orchestra, C major, K. 467: Mar. 3, 4, 6.
Concerto for Piano and Orchestra, D major, K. 537: Oct. 21, 22.
Concerto for Violin and Orchestra, A major, K. 219: Nov. 13; Dec. 26.
Overture, "The Magic Flute": Oct. 23, 24.
Overture, "The Marriage of Figaro": Dec. 12; Jan. 16; Mar. 14.
Serenade, "Eine kleine Nachtmusik," K. 525: Mar. 5.
Symphony No. 29, A major, K. 201: Jan. 27, 28, 30.
Symphony No. 35, D major, K. 385 ("Haffner"): Dec. 4.
Symphony No. 38, D major, K. 504 ("Prague"): Nov. 25, 26, 28.
Symphony No. 39, E-flat major, K. 543: Dec. 26.

PAGANINI-MOLINARI—Moto Perpetuo: Nov. 7.

PAISIELLO—Overture, "Nina, o la Pazza per Amore": Jan. 29.

PISTON—Toccata: Mar. 10 (d), 11, 13.

PROKOFIEFF—Concerto for Piano and Orchestra No. 2, G minor, Op. 16:
Nov. 4, 5, 7.
Concerto for Piano and Orchestra, No. 3, C major, Op. 26: Dec. 11, 12.
"Scythian" Suite, Op. 20: Feb. 26, 27.
*Symphony No. 5, B-flat major, Op. 100: Oct. 12.

RACHMANINOFF—Rhapsody on a Theme of Paganini, Op. 43: Dec. 9, 10.
Vocalise: Feb. 24, 25, 27.

RAVEL—"Daphnis et Chloé," Suite No. 2: Dec. 2, 3, 4, 5; Mar. 17, 18, 20.
"Pavane pour une Infante défunte": Mar. 6.
"Tzigane," Rhapsody for Violin and Orchestra: Mar. 14.
"La Valse," Choreographic Poem for Orchestra: Jan. 20, 21, 22, 23.

RESPIGHI: Symphonic Poem, "The Fountains of Rome": Jan. 20, 21, 22.
Symphonic Poem, "The Pines of Rome": Mar. 24, 25, 27.
Symphonic Poem, "Roman Festivals": Feb. 5.

RIETI—Concerto for Violoncello and Orchestra No. 2: Oct. 28 (a), 29, 31.

RIMSKY-KORSAKOFF—"Scheherazade," Symphonic Suite, Op. 35: Nov. 27.

RODGERS—Selections from "Carousel," "Oklahoma!," "On Your Toes," "South
Pacific," "State Fair," "The King and I": Nov. 15 (d).
Victory at Sea—A Symphonic Scenario: Nov. 15 (a).
Waltzes for Orchestra: Nov. 15 (d).

ROSSINI—Overture, "L'Italiana in Algeri": Jan. 22, 23.
Overture, "The Siege of Corinth": Mar. 17, 18, 19, 20.

ROUSSEL—Symphony No. 3, G minor: Feb. 10, 11; Apr. 2, 3.

SCHOENBERG—"Verklaerte Nacht" (Transfigured Night) for String Orchestra,
Op. 4: Nov. 25, 26.

SCHUBERT—Marche Militaire: Mar. 5, 14.
Symphony No. 8, B minor ("Unfinished"): Dec. 16, 17.

SCHUBERT-LISZT—Fantasy, C major, Op. 15 ("Der Wanderer"): Oct. 23, 24.

SCHUMANN—Overture, "Julius Caesar," Op. 128: Oct. 28, 29.
Symphony No. 2, C major, Op. 61: Nov. 4, 5; Feb. 19.

SHOSTAKOVICH—*Symphony No. 10, E minor: Oct. 14 (b), 15, 30; Apr. 9.

SIBELIUS—Concerto for Violin and Orchestra, D minor, Op. 47: Feb. 19.
Symphony No. 2, D major, Op. 43: Dec. 9, 10, 11, 12.

SKALKOTTAS—Greek Dances: Nov. 4 (b), 5, 7; Apr. 9.

SMETANA—Overture, "The Bartered Bride": Jan. 6, 7, 9.

SOWERBY—Mediaeval Poem: Mar. 30 (d).

STRAUSS, Johann—Overture, "Die Fledermaus": Mar. 5.
Tritsch-Tratsch Polka: Mar. 14.

Waltz, "On the Beautiful Blue Danube": Mar. 14.
Waltz, "Tales of the Vienna Woods": Mar. 5.
STRAUSS, Josef and Johann—Pizzicato Polka: Mar. 5, 14.
STRAUSS, Richard—Waltzes from "Der Rosenkavalier": Mar. 5.
"Dance of the Seven Veils," from "Salome," Op. 54: Oct. 28, 29, 31.
*Tone Poem, "Death and Transfiguration": Nov. 13.
Tone Poem, "Till Eulenspiegel's Merry Pranks," Op. 28: Dec. 26.
STRAVINSKY—*Suite from "The Firebird": Mar. 26.
TCHAIKOVSKY—Concerto for Piano and Orchestra, No. 1, B-flat minor, Op. 23: Nov. 14.
*Concerto for Violin and Orchestra, D major, Op. 35: Oct. 14, 15, 17; Nov. 6.
*Suite No. 1, D minor, Op. 43: Oct. 17.
Symphony No. 4, F minor, Op. 36: Jan. 27, 28, 29, 30.
TOCH—"Circus," An Overture: Nov. 27 (c).
VAUGHAN WILLIAMS—Symphony No. 4, F minor: Oct. 28, 29, 31.
VERDI—Overture, "La Forza del Destino": Feb. 13.
Requiem, composed in Memory of Alessandro Manzoni: Feb. 3, 4, 6.
VILLA-LOBOS—Concerto for Violoncello and Orchestra, No. 2, A minor: Feb. 5 (a).
VIVALDI—Concerto Grosso, D minor, Op. 3, No. 11: Mar. 13.
"Autumn," "Winter," from "The Seasons": Mar. 24, 25.
"Spring," "Summer," from "The Seasons": Mar. 10, 11.
WAGNER—Act I, "Die Walkuere": Oct. 7, 8, 10.
Ride of the Valkyries, from "Die Walkuere": Jan. 2.
A Faust Overture: Nov. 18, 19.
*Overture, "Rienzi": Dec. 12.
*Overture, "Tannhaeuser": Nov. 6.
*Prelude, "Die Meistersinger": Dec. 26.
WALTON—Fanfare: Mar. 30 (d).
WEBER—Overture, "Euryanthe": Mar. 26.
*Overture, "Der Freischuetz": Oct. 7, 8, 10, 12; Apr. 9, 10.
WIDOR—Allegro moderato, from Symphony No. 6: Mar. 30 (d).

SOLOISTS

PIANO

CLAUDIO ARRAU: Jan. 6, 7, 9.
ROBERT CASADESUS: Oct. 21, 22; Jan. 15, 16.
VAN CLIBURN: Nov. 14.
CLIFFORD CURZON: Nov. 18, 19; Dec. 4, 5.
ANIA DORFMANN: Oct. 30.
RUDOLF FIRKUSNY: March 10, 11, 13.
WALTER GIESEKING: March 3, 4, 6.
GARY GRAFFMAN: Oct. 26; Dec. 11, 12.
MYRA HESS: Feb. 10, 11, 13.
GRANT JOHANNESEN: Oct. 23, 24.
EUGENE LIST: Dec. 25, 29.
PIETRO SCARPINI: Nov. 4, 5, 7.
RUDOLF SERKIN: Feb. 17, 18, 20.
DANIEL WAYENBERG: Dec. 9, 10.

VIOLIN

NORMAN CAROL: Nov. 13.
JOHN CORIGLIANO: Feb. 19; Mar. 14.
MISCHA ELMAN: Oct. 14, 15, 17.
ZINO FRANCESCATTI: Nov. 11, 12; Apr. 2, 3.
YEHUDI MENUHIN: Feb. 24, 25, 26, 27.
NATHAN MILSTEIN: Dec. 2, 3; Jan. 22, 23.
ERICA MORINI: Dec. 30, 31; Jan. 2.
RUGGIERO RICCI: Nov. 6.
ISAAC STERN: Nov. 28.
JOSEPH SZIGETI: Dec. 23, 24, 26.

VIOLONCELLO

RAYA GARBOUSOVA: Oct. 28, 29, 31.
ALDO PARISOT: Feb. 5.
LEONARD ROSE: Nov. 28.
LASZLO VARGA: Jan. 29.

ORGAN
VIRGIL FOX: Mar. 30.

VOICE
DAVIS CUNNINGHAM, Tenor: Nov. 15.
ANNAMARY DICKEY, Soprano: Nov. 15.
MACK HARRELL, Baritone: Apr. 14, 15, 17.
JEROME HINES, Bass: Feb. 3, 4, 6.
MARTHA LIPTON, Mezzo-Soprano: Apr. 14, 15, 17.
DAVID LLOYD, Tenor: Apr. 14, 15, 17.
GEORGE LONDON, Bass-Baritone: Dec. 16, 17, 19.
HERVA NELLI, Soprano: Feb. 3, 4, 6.
JOHN RAITT, Baritone: Nov. 15.
IRMGARD SEEFRIED, Soprano: Dec. 16, 17, 19.
RICHARD TUCKER, Tenor: Feb. 3, 4, 6.

CLARAMAE TURNER, Contralto: Nov. 15; Feb. 3, 4, 6.
ASTRID VARNAY, Soprano: Oct. 7, 8, 10.
LUBEN VICHEY, Bass: Oct. 7, 8, 10.
RAMON VINAY, Tenor: Oct. 7, 8, 10.
FRANCES YEEND, Soprano: Apr. 14, 15, 17.

CHORUS
THE WESTMINSTER CHOIR, Dr. John Finley Williamson, Director: Dec. 16, 17, 19; Feb. 3, 4, 6; Apr. 14, 15, 17.

BAND
SAUTER-FINEGAN ORCHESTRA: Mar. 31; Apr. 1.

●

SPRING TOUR 1955

Conductors

Dimitri Mitropoulos		Guido Cantelli	
Apr. 18—Ev'g.	Detroit, Mich.	Apr. 20—Ev'g.	Urbana, Ill.
Apr. 19—Ev'g.	Lafayette, Ind.	Apr. 22—Ev'g.	Topeka, Kan.
Apr. 21—Ev'g.	Kansas City, Mo.	Apr. 25—Ev'g	El Paso, Tex.
Apr. 24—Aft.	Albuquerque, N. M.	Apr. 26—Ev'g.	Tucson, Arizona
Apr. 27—Ev'g.	Phoenix, Ariz.	Apr. 29—Ev'g.	Los Angeles, Calif.
Apr. 28—Ev'g.	Pasadena, Calif.	Apr. 30—Ev'g.	San Diego, Calif.
May 1—Aft.	Santa Barbara, Calif.	May 5—Ev'g.	San Francisco, Calif.
May 2—Ev'g.	Fresno, Calif.	May 7—Ev'g.	Corvallis, Ore.
May 4—Ev'g.	San Francisco, Calif.	May 8—Ev'g.	Seattle, Wash.
May 6—Ev'g.	Eugene, Ore.	May 11—Ev'g.	Salt Lake City, Utah
May 8—Aft.	Seattle, Wash.	May 14—Ev'g.	Denver, Colo.
May 9—Ev'g.	Portland, Ore.	May 16—Ev'g.	Ames, Iowa
May 12—Ev'g.	Provo, Utah	May 18—Ev'g.	Madison, Wisc.
May 15—Aft.	Omaha, Neb.	May 21—Ev'g.	Chicago, Ill.
May 17—Ev'g.	Minneapolis, Minn.		
May 19—Ev'g.	Milwaukee, Wis.		
May 22—Aft.	Ann Arbor, Mich.		

REPERTOIRE—SPRING TOUR

* Recorded by the Philharmonic-Symphony Orchestra
on Columbia Records

BARBER—Adagio for Strings, Op. 11: Apr. 20, 22, 26, 29; May 7, 14, 18, 21.
BEETHOVEN—Concerto for Piano and Orchestra, No. 3, C minor, Op. 37: May 12.
*Symphony No. 7, A major, Op. 92: Apr. 22; May 7, 18, 21.
BRAHMS—*Symphony No. 1, C minor, Op. 68: Apr. 20, 21, 26, 29, 30; May 5, 8 (eve.), 11, 14, 16.

*Symphony No. 2, D minor, Op. 73: Apr. 21, 24, 27; May 2, 6.
*Variations on a Theme by Haydn, B-flat major, Op. 56-A: Apr. 18, 19, 28; May 4, 8 (aft.), 9, 15.
COPLAND—"El Salón México": Apr. 26.
DEBUSSY—Nocturnes: "Clouds," "Festivals": Apr. 25, 30; May 5, 8 (eve.), 11, 16.
GOULD—Show Piece for Orchestra: Apr. 19, 21, 27; May 9, 15, 22.
KABALEVSKY—Overture, "Colas Breugnon": Apr. 18, 28; May 1, 4, 17, 22.
MENDELSSOHN—Overture, "The Wedding of Camacho": Apr. 24; May 2, 6.
*Symphony No. 5, D major, Op. 107 ("Reformation"): May 1, 17, 19.
MOUSSORGSKY-RAVEL—*"Pictures at an Exhibition": Apr. 20, 22, 29; May 7, 14, 18, 21.
PROKOFIEFF—*Symphony No. 5, B-flat major, Op. 100: Apr. 24; May 2, 6, 8 (aft.), 12, 19.
RAVEL—"Daphnis et Chloé," Suite No. 2: Apr. 25, 26, 30; May 5, 8 (eve.), 11, 16.
RACHMANINOFF—Vocalise: Apr. 21; May 8 (aft.), 11.
ROSSINI—Overture, "The Siege of Corinth": Apr. 25, 26, 29, 30.
SCHUMANN—Symphony No. 2, C major, Op. 61: Apr. 19; May 9, 15.
SHOSTAKOVICH—*Symphony No. 10, E minor: Apr. 18, 28; May 1, 4, 17, 22.
SKALKOTTAS—Greek Dances: Apr. 18, 27, 28; May 4, 22.
VIVALDI—Concerto Grosso, D minor, Op. 3, No. 11: Apr. 20, 22; May 7, 8 (eve.), 14, 18, 21.
WEBER—*Overture, "Der Freischuetz": Apr. 19, 21, 27; May 8 (aft.), 9, 12, 15, 19.

SOLOIST—SPRING TOUR

GRANT JOHANNESEN, Piano: May 12.

1955–56 ONE HUNDRED FOURTEENTH SEASON

DIMITRI MITROPOULOS, *Musical Director*

Guest Conductors
BRUNO WALTER, PIERRE MONTEUX, GEORGE SZELL, GUIDO CANTELLI, MAX RUDOLF

Associate Conductor	*Four Special Saturdays*	*Young People's Concerts*
FRANCO AUTORI	ANDRE KOSTELANETZ	WILFRID PELLETIER

CONCERTS

1955			1955		
Dimitri Mitropoulos			‡Oct.	29—Morn.	Carnegie Hall
Oct. 20—Ev'g.		Carnegie Hall	Oct.	30—Aft.	Carnegie Hall
Oct. 21—Aft.		Carnegie Hall	Nov.	3—Ev'g.	Carnegie Hall
‡Oct. 22—Aft.		Town Hall	Nov.	4—Aft.	Carnegie Hall
Oct. 23—Aft.		Carnegie Hall			
Oct. 27—Ev'g.		Carnegie Hall		**Max Rudolf**	
Oct. 28—Aft.		Carnegie Hall	Nov.	5—Ev'g.	Carnegie Hall

‡ Young People's Concert, conducted by WILFRID PELLETIER.

1955

Dimitri Mitropoulos

Nov.	6—Aft.	Carnegie Hall
**Nov.	9—Aft.	Manhasset, H. S.
		Manhasset, L. I.
Nov.	10—Ev'g.	Carnegie Hall
Nov.	11—Aft.	Carnegie Hall
Nov.	12—Ev'g.	Carnegie Hall
Nov.	13—Aft.	Carnegie Hall

Pierre Monteux

Nov.	17—Ev'g.	Carnegie Hall
Nov.	18—Aft.	Carnegie Hall
Nov.	19—Ev'g.	Carnegie Hall
Nov.	20—Aft.	Carnegie Hall
Nov.	24—Ev'g.	Carnegie Hall
Nov.	25—Aft.	Carnegie Hall
Nov.	26—Ev'g.	Carnegie Hall
Nov.	27—Aft.	Carnegie Hall

George Szell

Dec.	1—Ev'g.	Carnegie Hall
Dec.	2—Aft.	Carnegie Hall
Dec.	3—Ev'g.	Carnegie Hall
Dec.	4—Aft.	Carnegie Hall
Dec.	8—Ev'g.	Carnegie Hall
Dec.	9—Aft.	Carnegie Hall
Dec.	10—Ev'g.	Carnegie Hall
Dec.	11—Aft.	Carnegie Hall
Dec.	15—Ev'g.	Carnegie Hall
Dec.	16—Aft.	Carnegie Hall
*Dec.	17—Aft.	Town Hall
Dec.	18—Aft.	Carnegie Hall

Dimitri Mitropoulos

Dec.	20—Ev'g.	Hartford, Conn.
Dec.	21—Ev'g.	Carnegie Hall
		(Pension Fund Benefit)

George Szell

Dec.	22—Ev'g.	Carnegie Hall
Dec.	23—Aft.	Carnegie Hall
Dec.	25—Aft.	Carnegie Hall

Dimitri Mitropoulos

Dec.	29—Ev'g.	Carnegie Hall
Dec.	30—Aft.	Carnegie Hall

André Kostelanetz

Dec.	31—Ev'g.	Carnegie Hall

1956

Dimitri Mitropoulos

Jan.	1—Aft.	Carnegie Hall
Jan.	5—Ev'g.	Carnegie Hall
Jan.	6—Aft.	Carnegie Hall

1956

*Jan.	7—Morn.	Carnegie Hall
Jan.	8—Aft.	Carnegie Hall

Max Rudolf

Jan.	12—Ev'g.	Carnegie Hall
Jan.	13—Aft.	Carnegie Hall

Franco Autori

Jan.	14—Ev'g.	Carnegie Hall
Jan.	15—Aft.	Carnegie Hall

Pierre Monteux

Jan.	19—Ev'g.	Carnegie Hall
Jan.	20—Aft.	Carnegie Hall
Jan.	21—Ev'g.	Carnegie Hall
Jan.	22—Aft.	Carnegie Hall

Dimitri Mitropoulos

†Jan.	26—Ev'g.	Carnegie Hall
†Jan.	27—Aft.	Carnegie Hall
*Jan.	28—Aft.	Town Hall
Jan.	28—Ev'g.	Carnegie Hall
†Jan.	29—Aft.	Carnegie Hall
**Jan.	30—Aft.	Great Neck J. H. S.
		Great Neck, L. I.
Feb.	2—Ev'g.	Carnegie Hall
Feb.	3—Aft.	Carnegie Hall

André Kostelanetz

Feb.	4—Ev'g.	Carnegie Hall

Dimitri Mitropoulos

Feb.	5—Aft.	Carnegie Hall
Feb.	9—Ev'g.	Carnegie Hall
Feb.	10—Aft.	Carnegie Hall
*Feb.	11—Morn.	Carnegie Hall
Feb.	12—Aft.	Carnegie Hall
Feb.	14—Ev'g.	Newark, N. J.
Feb.	16—Ev'g.	Carnegie Hall
Feb.	17—Aft.	Carnegie Hall

Franco Autori

Feb.	18—Ev'g.	Carnegie Hall

Dimitri Mitropoulos

Feb.	19—Aft.	Carnegie Hall
Feb.	23—Ev'g.	Carnegie Hall
Feb.	24—Aft.	Carnegie Hall
Feb.	25—Ev'g.	Carnegie Hall
Feb.	26—Aft.	Carnegie Hall

Bruno Walter

Mar.	1—Ev'g.	Carnegie Hall
Mar.	2—Aft.	Carnegie Hall

André Kostelanetz

Mar.	3—Ev'g.	Carnegie Hall

Bruno Walter

Mar.	4—Aft.	Carnegie Hall

** Young People's Concert, conducted by Franco Autori.
* Young People's Concert, conducted by Wilfrid Pelletier.
† Two works conducted by Carlos Chavez.

1956			1956		
Dimitri Mitropoulos			Mar. 31—Ev'g.		Carnegie Hall
Mar. 6—Ev'g.		Carnegie Hall	Apr. 1—Aft.		Carnegie Hall
		(Pension Fund Benefit)	Apr. 5—Ev'g.		Carnegie Hall
			Apr. 6—Aft.		Carnegie Hall
Bruno Walter					
Mar. 8—Ev'g.		Carnegie Hall	**André Kostelanetz**		
Mar. 9—Aft.		Carnegie Hall	Apr. 7—Ev'g.		Carnegie Hall
*Mar. 10—Morn.		Carnegie Hall			
Mar. 11—Aft.		Carnegie Hall	**Guido Cantelli**		
			Apr. 8—Aft.		Carnegie Hall
Guido Cantelli					
Mar. 15—Ev'g.		Carnegie Hall	**Dimitri Mitropoulos**		
Mar. 16—Aft.		Carnegie Hall	Apr. 12—Ev'g.		Carnegie Hall
			Apr. 13—Aft.		Carnegie Hall
Thomas Schippers			Apr. 14—Ev'g.		Carnegie Hall
Mar. 17—Ev'g.		Carnegie Hall	Apr. 15—Aft.		Carnegie Hall
			Apr. 19—Ev'g.		Carnegie Hall
Guido Cantelli			Apr. 20—Aft.		Carnegie Hall
Mar. 18—Aft.		Carnegie Hall	Apr. 21—Ev'g.		Carnegie Hall
Mar. 22—Ev'g.		Carnegie Hall	Apr. 22—Aft.		Carnegie Hall
Mar. 23—Aft.		Carnegie Hall	Apr. 26—Ev'g.		Carnegie Hall
Mar. 24—Ev'g.		Carnegie Hall	Apr. 27—Aft.		Carnegie Hall
Mar. 25—Aft.		Carnegie Hall	*Apr. 28—Morn.		Carnegie Hall
Mar. 29—Ev'g.		Carnegie Hall	Apr. 29—Aft.		Carnegie Hall
Mar. 30—Aft.		Carnegie Hall			

TWO CONCERTS FOR HIGH SCHOOL
STUDENTS OF NEW YORK CITY

Mar. 14—Aft.
Prospect Heights High School, Brooklyn, New York; conducted by Thomas Schippers.

Apr. 25—Aft.
Julia Richman High School, Manhattan, New York; conducted by Dimitri Mitropoulos.

NOTE: Programs for the Young People's Concerts and the two concerts for High School students of New York City, are included in the bound 1955–1956 volumes of the Society, but are not included in the repertoire.

REPERTOIRE FOR 1955–56

(a) World premiere.
(b) United States premiere.
(c) New York premiere.

Compositions marked with asterisk (*) are recorded by The Philharmonic-Symphony Orchestra on Columbia Records

BACH—Suite No. 3, D major: Nov. 26.
BACH-MITROPOULOS—Fantasia and Fugue in G minor: Feb. 19, 23, 24.
BACH-RESPIGHI—Prelude and Fugue, D major: Apr. 12, 13, 14, 22.
BARBER—Medea's Meditation and Dance of Vengeance, Opus 23-A: Feb. 2 (a), 3, 5.
Overture, "The School for Scandal": Jan. 12, 13.
BARTOK-SERLY—Mikrokosmos Suite: Jan. 14 (c), 15.

---

* Young People's Concert, conducted by WILFRID PELLETIER.

BEETHOVEN—Concerto for Piano and Orchestra, No. 2, B-flat major, Opus 19: Dec. 10, 11.
Concerto for Piano and Orchestra, No. 4, G major, Opus 58: Dec. 1, 2; Feb. 18; Mar. 15, 16, 18.
Concerto for Piano and Orchestra, No. 5, E-flat major, Opus 73 ("Emperor"): Mar. 22, 23, 25.
Concerto for Violin and Orchestra, D major, Opus 61: Feb. 9, 10, 12; Mar. 6.
Overture, "Coriolanus": Nov. 20; Dec. 1, 2.
*Overture, "Egmont": Nov. 27.
Overture, "Fidelio": Nov. 3, 4, 6.
Overture, "Leonore," No. 3: Dec. 3, 4.
*Symphony No. 2, D major, Opus 36: Jan. 12, 13.
*Symphony No. 6, F major, Opus 68 ("Pastoral"): Dec. 1, 2, 3, 4.

BERLIOZ—*Excerpts from the Dramatic Symphony, "Romeo and Juliet," Opus 17: Prelude—Love Scene—Queen Mab Scherzo—Romeo Alone—Festivities in Capulet's Palace: Nov. 24, 25. Romeo Alone—Festivities in Capulet's Palace: Nov. 26, 27.
Overture, "Benvenuto Cellini": Nov. 24, 25.
Rákóczy March from "The Damnation of Faust": Apr. 8.

BIZET—"L'Arlésienne," Suite No. 1: Dec. 31.
"Jeux d'Enfants," Suite, Opus 22: Jan. 29; Feb. 9, 10.
*Symphony in C major: Mar. 17.

BLOCH—"Schelomo," Hebrew Rhapsody for Violoncello and Orchestra: Feb. 16, 17, 19.

BRAHMS—Concerto for Piano and Orchestra, No. 1, D minor, Opus 15: Apr. 5, 6, 8.
Concerto for Violin and Orchestra, D major, Opus 77: Dec. 21; Jan. 21, 22; Feb. 2, 3.
Rhapsody for Alto Solo, Male Chorus and Orchestra, Opus 53: Mar. 29, 30, 31; Apr. 1.
*Symphony No. 1, C minor, Opus 68: Nov. 5; Jan. 15.
*Symphony No. 2, D major, Opus 73: Apr. 14, 19, 20, 29.
*Symphony No. 3, F major, Opus 90: Nov. 17, 18, 19, 20.

BRITTEN—Sinfonia da Requiem, Opus 20: Mar. 22, 23, 24.

BRUCH—*Concerto for Violin and Orchestra, No. 1, G minor, Opus 26: Nov. 17, 18.

BUXTEHUDE-CHAVEZ—Chaconne, E minor: Jan. 26, 27, 29.

CASADESUS—Concerto for Piano and Orchestra, E minor, Opus 37: Nov. 10, 11.

CHABRIER—"España" Rhapsody: Apr. 7.
"Fête Polonaise" from "Le Roi Malgré Lui": Feb. 5.

CHAUSSON—Symphony, B-flat major, Opus 20: Feb. 2, 3, 5, 14.

CHAVEZ—Symphony No. 3: Jan. 26 (b), 27, 29.

CHOPIN—Concerto for Piano and Orchestra, No. 2, F minor, Opus 21: Nov. 24, 25.

COPLAND—*"A Lincoln Portrait": Feb. 4.

COUPERIN-MILHAUD—*Prelude and Allegro, "La Sultane": Dec. 20.

CRESTON—"Dance Overture," Opus 62: Mar. 15 (c), 16, 18.
Symphony No. 2, Opus 35: Jan. 19, 20, 21, 22.

DEBUSSY—*"La Mer," Three Symphonic Sketches: Nov. 17, 18, 19, 20.

DEBUSSY-MOLINARI—"L'Isle Joyeuse": Apr. 19, 20, 21, 22.

DVORAK—Concerto for Violin and Orchestra, A minor, Opus 53: Jan. 5, 6.
Symphony No. 2, D minor, Opus 17: Dec. 15, 16, 18.

598 APPENDIX IV

ELGAR—March, "Pomp and Circumstance," Opus 39, No. 1: Apr. 7.
FALLA—*Two Dances from "The Three-Cornered Hat": Nov. 6.
FOSS—"Song of Songs," Biblical Solo Cantata for Soprano and Orchestra: Jan. 8.
FRANCK—Symphony, D minor: Jan. 14.
GLINKA—Overture, "Russlan and Ludmilla": Feb. 26; Apr. 7.
GROFE—"Hudson River" Suite: Feb. 4.
HALL—Elegy for Orchestra: Apr. 21 (a).
HANDEL—"Largo" from "Xerxes": Apr. 8.
HAYDN—Symphony No. 88, G major: Apr. 5, 6.
Symphony No. 103, E-flat major ("Drum Roll"): Feb. 9, 10, 12.
HINDEMITH—Concert Music for Strings and Brass, Opus 50: Apr. 5, 6, 8.
Symphony, "Mathis der Maler": Nov. 5.
d'INDY—*Symphony for Orchestra and Piano on a French Mountain Song, Opus 25: Nov. 26, 27.
KABALEVSKY—Overture, "Colas Breugnon": Feb. 4.
KAY—"Saturday Night": Dec. 31.
KERN—"Showboat" Scenario: Dec. 31.
KIRCHNER—Concerto for Piano and Orchestra: Feb. 23 (a), 24.
KODALY—Suite, "Háry János": Jan. 26, 27; Feb. 25.
"Intermezzo," "Entrance of the Emperor" only: Jan. 29.
KONOYE—"Etenraku": Dec. 31 (c).
LIEBERMANN—"Musique" for Narrator and Orchestra: Feb. 25 (b), 26.
LISZT—Mephisto Waltz: Feb. 25, 26.
Symphonic Poem, "Les Préludes": Feb. 16, 17, 26.
MAHLER—Symphony No. 3, D minor: April 12, 13, 15.
MENDELSSOHN—Concerto for Violin and Orchestra, E minor, Opus 64: Nov. 20; Mar. 6.
*Overture, "A Midsummer Night's Dream": Nov. 5.
Overture, "Ruy Blas": Mar. 6.
MENOTTI—Two Interludes from "The Island God": Mar. 17.
MIYAGI—"Sea of the Spring": Dec. 31 (c).
MONTEVERDI—Magnificat, for Seven-Part Chorus, Organ and Orchestra: Mar. 29, 30, 31; Apr. 1.
MOUSSORGSKY—Prelude, "Khovanshchina": Dec. 22, 23; Feb. 4.
MOZART—Adagio for Violin and Orchestra, No. 3, E major, K. 261: Dec. 3, 4.
Concerto for Piano and Orchestra, No. 16, D major, K. 451: Oct. 20, 21, 23.
Concerto for Piano and Orchestra, No. 17, G major, K. 453: Mar. 1, 2.
Concerto for Piano and Orchestra, No. 20, D minor, K. 466: Mar. 4.
Concerto for Piano and Orchestra, No. 22, E-flat major, K. 482: Nov. 3, 4, 6.
Concerto for Piano and Orchestra, No. 23, A major, K. 488: Oct. 20, 21.
Concerto for Piano and Orchestra, No. 24, C minor, K. 491: Nov. 26, 27.
Concerto for Piano and Orchestra, No. 25, C major, K. 503: Oct. 20, 21, 23.
Concerto for Two Pianos and Orchestra, E-flat major, K. 365: Nov. 13.
Concerto for Violin and Orchestra, No. 3, G major, K. 216: Dec. 3, 4; Jan. 12, 13.
Concerto for Violin and Orchestra, No. 5, A major, K. 219: Dec. 21; Jan. 1, 19, 20.
Concerto for Violin and Orchestra, No. 7, D major, K. 271-A: Jan. 28.
"Et Incarnatus Est," from the Mass in C minor, K. 427: Mar. 8, 9.
Suite from "Idomeneo": Jan. 28.
Overture, "The Abduction from the Seraglio": Oct. 20, 21.
Overture, "Don Giovanni": Dec. 29, 30; Jan. 1.

Requiem in D minor, K. 626: Mar. 8, 9, 11.
Sinfonia Concertante for Violin, Viola, Violoncello and Orchestra, K. Anh. 104: Oct. 23, 27, 28.
Symphony No. 25, G minor, K. 183: Mar. 8, 9, 11.
Symphony No. 29, A major, K. 201: Mar. 1, 2, 4.
Symphony No. 39, E-flat major, K. 543: Mar. 4.
*Symphony No. 41, C major, K. 551 ("Jupiter"): Mar. 1, 2.
OFFENBACH-ROSENTHAL—"Gaîté Parisienne": Dec. 31.
PIKET—"The Funnies," Suite for Orchestra: Feb. 18 (c).
PROKOFIEFF—Concerto for Piano and Orchestra, No. 3, C major, Opus 26: Jan. 26, 27, 29.
Concerto for Violin and Orchestra, No. 1, D major, Opus 19: Feb. 25, 26.
*Concerto for Violin and Orchestra, No. 2, G minor, Opus 63: Apr. 29.
Concerto for Violoncello and Orchestra, No. 1, E minor, Opus 58: Apr. 14.
Concerto for Violoncello and Orchestra, No. 2, Opus 125: Apr. 19 (b), 20.
Suite from "Lt. Kije," Opus 60: Jan. 5, 6.
RACHMANINOFF—Concerto for Piano and Orchestra, No. 3, D minor, Opus 30: Feb. 16, 17, 19.
Rhapsody on a Theme of Paganini, Opus 43: Feb. 5.
*Symphony No. 2, E minor, Opus 27: Apr. 26, 27.
RAVEL—"Alborada del Gracioso": Apr. 26, 27, 29.
Pavane pour une Infante défunte: Feb. 4.
*"La Valse," Choreographic Poem for Orchestra: Dec. 15, 16, 18; Feb. 4.
RIMSKY-KORSAKOFF—*Caprice Espagnole: Apr. 7.
Introduction and March from "Le Coq d'Or": Feb. 4.
ROSSINI—Overture, "L'Italiana in Algeri": Jan. 21, 22.
Overture, "La Scala di Seta": Dec. 8, 9.
Overture, "Semiramide": Mar. 24, 25.
SAINT-SAENS—Carnival of the Animals (Verses by Ogden Nash): Apr. 7.
Concerto for Piano and Orchestra, No. 2, G minor, Opus 22: Nov. 12, 13.
*Concerto for Violin and Orchestra, No. 3, B minor, Opus 61: Apr. 26, 27.
Concerto for Violoncello and Orchestra, A minor, Opus 33: Dec. 8, 9.
Symphonic Poem, "La Jeunesse d'Hercule": Jan. 1.
Symphonic Poem, "Phaëton," Opus 30: Jan. 8.
SCHUMAN—"Judith," Choreographic Poem: Nov. 10, 11, 12, 13.
SCHUMANN—Concerto for Piano and Orchestra, A minor, Opus 54: Nov. 19.
Symphony No. 1, B-flat major, Opus 38: Apr. 21, 22.
Symphony No. 2, C major, Opus 61: Jan. 5, 6, 28; Feb. 14.
Symphony No. 4, D minor, Opus 120: Mar. 15, 16, 18, 24.
SCOTT—Lotus Land: Apr. 7.
SHOSTAKOVICH—*Concerto for Violin and Orchestra, A minor, Opus 99: Dec. 29 (b), 30; Jan. 1.
Festival Overture: Feb. 16 (c), 17.
Symphony No. 1, Opus 10: Mar. 17.
*Symphony No. 10, E minor: Dec. 20.
SIBELIUS—Concerto for Violin and Orchestra, D minor, Opus 47: Dec. 15, 16, 18; Apr. 21, 22.
*Symphony No. 2, D major, Opus 43: Dec. 8, 9, 10, 11.
SKALKOTTAS—Greek Dances: Jan. 8.
STRAUSS, Johann—Waltz, "On the Beautiful Blue Danube": Apr. 7.
STRAUSS, Richard—"Dance of the Seven Veils" from "Salome," Opus 54: Nov. 12, 13.
An "Alpine" Symphony: Feb. 23, 24.
Tone Poem, "Also Sprach Zarathustra": Nov. 3, 4, 6.

*Tone Poem, "Don Juan," Opus 20: Mar. 22, 23, 25.
Tone Poem, "Ein Heldenleben," Opus 40: Jan. 19, 20.
Tone Poem, "Till Eulenspiegel's Merry Pranks," Opus 28: Jan. 12, 13.

TCHAIKOVSKY—Concerto for Violin and Orchestra, D major, Opus 35: Dec. 21, 22, 23, 25; Jan. 14, 15.
*"Nutcracker," Suite, Opus 71-A: Mar. 3.
*"Queen of Spades," Suite for Orchestra: Mar. 3.
*"Romeo and Juliet," Overture-Fantasy: Mar. 3.
"Sleeping Beauty" Ballet—Introduction and Waltz: Mar. 3.
"Swan Lake," Suite from the Ballet: Mar. 3.
Symphony No. 4, F minor, Opus 36: Dec. 22, 23, 25; Feb. 18.

THOMSON—Concerto for Flute, Strings and Percussion: Apr. 19 (c), 20.

VAUGHAN WILLIAMS—Symphony No. 4, F minor: Dec. 29, 30; Jan. 8.

VERDI—Overture, "Sicilian Vespers": Feb. 19.
Te Deum, for Double Chorus and Orchestra: Mar. 29, 30, 31; Apr. 1.

VILLA-LOBOS—Toccata, "Little Train of the Caipira," from "Bachianas Brasileiras," No. 2: Apr. 7.

VIVALDI—Concerto Grosso, D minor, Opus 3, No. 11: Mar. 24, 25.

WAGENAAR—Five Tableaux for Violoncello and Orchestra: Dec. 8 (b), 9.

WAGNER—"Die Goetterdaemmerung," Act III: Oct. 27, 28, 30.
"Good Friday Spell" from "Parsifal": Mar. 29, 30, 31; Apr. 1.
*Overture, "Rienzi": Feb. 12.
*Prelude, "Die Meistersinger": Mar. 17.
"Waldweben" from "Siegfried": Oct. 30.

WEBER, Ben—Prelude and Passacaglia, Opus 42: Nov. 3 (c), 4.

WEBER, Carl Maria—Konzertstueck for Piano and Orchestra, F minor, Opus 79: Nov. 10, 11.
Overture, "Euryanthe": Nov. 17, 18.
*Overture, "Der Freischuetz": Feb. 14.
*Overture, "Oberon": Dec. 10, 11.
Symphony No. 1, C major, Opus 19: Nov. 10, 11, 12; Dec. 20.

SOLOISTS

PIANO
GINA BACHAUER: Jan. 26, 27, 29.
WILHELM BACKHAUS: Mar. 15, 16, 18.
ALEXANDER BRAILOWSKY: Nov. 24, 25.
JOHN BROWNING: Feb. 5.
GABY CASADESUS: Nov. 13.
JEAN CASADESUS: Nov. 12, 13.
ROBERT CASADESUS: Nov. 10, 11, 13, 26, 27.
HENRI DEERING: Nov. 19.
RUDOLF FIRKUSNY: Apr. 5, 6, 8.
LEON FLEISHER: Dec. 10, 11.
WALTER GIESEKING: Mar. 22, 23, 25.
LEONID HAMBRO & JASCHA ZAYDE: Apr. 7.
MYRA HESS: Mar. 1, 2, 4.
EUGENE ISTOMIN: Dec. 1, 2.
LEON KIRCHNER: Feb. 23, 24.
WITOLD MALCUZYNSKI: Feb. 16, 17, 19.

PIETRO SCARPINI: Nov. 3, 4, 6.
RUDOLF SERKIN: Oct. 20, 21, 23.
VENTSIS YANKOFF: Feb. 18.

VIOLA
WILLIAM LINCER: Oct. 23, 27, 28.

VIOLIN
GIOVANNI BAGAROTTI: Jan. 28.
JOHN CORIGLIANO: Oct. 23, 27, 28; Jan. 19, 20.
MISCHA ELMAN: Nov. 17, 18, 20.
ZINO FRANCESCATTI: Apr. 26, 27, 29.
IVRY GITLIS: Dec. 15, 16, 18.
JASCHA HEIFETZ: Feb. 9, 10, 12.
YEHUDI MENUHIN: Mar. 6.
NATHAN MILSTEIN: Jan. 5, 6, 21, 22.
ERICA MORINI: Dec. 22, 23, 25.
DAVID OISTRAKH: Dec. 21, 29, 30; Jan. 1.
MISHEL PIASTRO: Jan. 14, 15.
MICHAEL RABIN: Feb. 2, 3.

TOSSY SPIVAKOVSKY: Apr. 21, 22.

ISAAC STERN: Jan. 12, 13; Feb. 25, 26.

JOSEPH SZIGETI: Dec. 3, 4.

VIOLONCELLO

EDMUND KURTZ: Dec. 8, 9.

MSTISLAV ROSTROPOVICH: Apr. 19, 20.

LASZLO VARGA: Oct. 23, 27, 28; Feb. 16, 17, 19; Apr. 14.

FLUTE

JOHN WUMMER: Dec. 31; Apr. 19, 20.

CIMBALOM

TONI KOVES: Jan. 26, 27, 29; Feb. 25.

KOTO

SHINICHI YUIZE: Dec. 31.

VOICE

LUCINE AMARA, Soprano: Oct. 27, 28, 30.

ELLABELLE DAVIS, Soprano: Jan. 8.

ROSALIND ELIAS, Mezzo-Soprano: Oct. 27, 28, 30.

HERTA GLAZ, Mezzo-Soprano: Oct. 27, 28, 30.

CLIFFORD HARVUOT, Baritone: Oct. 27, 28, 30.

BEATRICE KREBS, Mezzo-Contralto: Apr. 12, 13, 15.

MARTHA LIPTON, Mezzo-Soprano: Mar. 29, 30, 31; Apr. 1.

IRMGARD SEEFRIED, Soprano: Mar. 8, 9, 11.

LEOPOLD SIMONEAU, Tenor: Mar. 8, 9, 11.

JENNIE TOUREL, Mezzo-Soprano: Mar. 8, 9, 11.

ASTRID VARNAY, Soprano: Oct. 27, 28, 30.

SHAKEH VARTENISSIAN, Soprano: Oct. 27, 28, 30.

LUBEN VICHEY, Bass: Oct. 27, 28, 30.

RAMON VINAY, Tenor: Oct. 27, 28, 30.

WILLIAM WARFIELD, Baritone: Mar. 8, 9, 11.

NARRATOR

NOEL COWARD: Apr. 7.

CARL SANDBURG: Feb. 4.

VERA ZORINA: Feb. 25, 26.

CHORUS

THE WESTMINSTER CHOIR, Dr. John Finley Williamson, Director: Mar. 8, 9, 11, 29, 30, 31; Apr. 1, 12, 13, 15.

●

EUROPEAN TOUR 1955

Conductors

Dimitri Mitropoulos

Sept. 5—Ev'g.	Edinburgh	
Sept. 10—Ev'g.	Edinburgh	
Sept. 12—Ev'g.	Vienna	
Sept. 13—Ev'g.	Vienna	
Sept. 14—Ev'g.	Brussels	
Sept. 15—Ev'g.	Berlin	
Sept. 16—Ev'g.	Berlin	
Sept. 18—Ev'g.	Paris	
Sept. 21—Ev'g.	Basel	
Sept. 22—Ev'g.	Berne	
Sept. 23—Ev'g.	Zurich	
Sept. 26—Ev'g.	Milan	
Sept. 27—Ev'g.	Perugia	
Sept. 28—Ev'g.	Rome	

Sept. 29—Ev'g.	Naples
Oct. 1—Ev'g.	Athens
Oct. 2—Morn.	Athens
Oct. 2—Ev'g.	Athens
Oct. 4—Ev'g.	London
Oct. 5—Ev'g.	London

Guido Cantelli

Sept. 6—Ev'g.	Edinburgh
Sept. 7—Ev'g.	Edinburgh
Sept. 19—Ev'g.	Paris
Sept. 20—Ev'g.	Geneva
Sept. 25—Ev'g.	Milan

George Szell

Sept. 8—Ev'g.	Edinburgh
Sept. 9—Ev'g.	Edinburgh

REPERTOIRE—EUROPEAN TOUR

* Recorded by the Philharmonic-Symphony Orchestra
on Columbia Records

BARBER—Adagio for Strings, Opus 11: Sept. 7, 19, 20, 25.

BEETHOVEN—Concerto for Piano and Orchestra, No. 3, C minor, Opus 37: Sept. 5, 21, 22.

*Concerto for Piano and Orchestra, No. 5, E-flat major, Opus 73 ("Emperor"): Sept. 18.
*Symphony No. 3, E-flat major, Opus 55 ("Eroica"): Sept. 27; Oct. 2 (morn.).
*Symphony No. 7, A major, Opus 92: Sept. 7, 19, 20.
BRAHMS—Concerto for Piano and Orchestra, No. 1, D minor, Opus 15: Sept. 8; Oct. 4.
*Symphony No. 1, C minor, Opus 68: Sept. 6, 25.
*Symphony No. 2, D major, Opus 73: Sept. 10, 12, 14, 16, 28; Oct. 2 (ev'g.).
*Symphony No. 4, E minor, Opus 98: Sept. 8.
*Variations on a Theme by Haydn, B-flat major, Opus 56-A: Sept. 29; Oct. 2 (morn.).
COPLAND—"El Salón México": Sept. 7.
COUPERIN-MILHAUD—*Prelude and Allegro, "La Sultane": Sept. 13, 15, 23; Oct. 1.
DEBUSSY—Nocturnes: "Clouds," "Festivals": Sept. 6.
DVORAK—Concerto for Violin and Orchestra, A minor, Opus 53: Oct. 5.
GOULD—Show Piece for Orchestra: Sept. 5, 23, 29.
KABALEVSKY—Overture, "Colas Breugnon": Sept. 21.
MENDELSSOHN—*Symphony No. 5, D major, Opus 107 ("Reformation"): Sept. 10, 13, 15, 27, 28; Oct. 2 (ev'g.).
MOUSSORGSKY-RAVEL—*Pictures at an Exhibition: Sept. 7, 19, 20, 25.
PROKOFIEFF—*Symphony No. 5, B-flat major, Opus 100: Sept. 14, 15.
RAVEL—"Daphnis et Chloé," Suite No. 2; Sept. 6.
ROSSINI—Overture, "The Siege of Corinth": Sept. 6, 19, 20, 25.
SCHUMANN—Symphony No. 2, C major, Opus 61: Sept. 12, 16, 26; Oct. 1, 4.
SHOSTAKOVICH—*Symphony No. 10, E minor: Sept. 13, 18, 21, 22, 23, 26, 29; Oct. 1, 5.
SIBELIUS—Symphony No. 2, D major, Opus 43: Sept. 9.
SKALKOTTAS—Greek Dances: Sept. 10, 23, 28; Oct. 2 (morn. & ev'g.).
VAUGHAN WILLIAMS—Symphony No. 4, F minor: Sept. 5.
VERDI—Overture, "La Forza del Destino": Sept. 12, 22, 26, 27, 29; Oct. 2 (morn.), 5.
WAGNER—*Overture, "Rienzi": Sept. 9.
Prelude, "Lohengrin": Sept. 9.
*Prelude, "Die Meistersinger": Sept. 9.
Siegfried Idyl: Sept. 9.
WEBER—*Overture, "Der Freishuetz": Sept. 10, 14, 16, 18, 28; Oct. 2 (ev'g.), 4.

SOLOISTS—EUROPEAN TOUR

ROBERT CASADESUS: Sept. 18   BYRON JANIS: Sept. 22.
CLIFFORD CURZON: Sept. 8.   GRANT JOHANNESEN: Sept. 21.
MYRA HESS: Sept. 5; Oct. 4.   NATHAN MILSTEIN: Oct. 5.

1956–57 ONE HUNDRED FIFTEENTH SEASON

DIMITRI MITROPOULOS, *Musical Director*

Guest Conductors
LEONARD BERNSTEIN, PAUL PARAY, MAX RUDOLF, GEORG SOLTI
IGOR STRAVINSKY, HEITOR VILLA-LOBOS, BRUNO WALTER

Associate Conductor   *Four Special Saturday Nights*   *Young People's Concerts*
FRANCO AUTORI   ANDRE KOSTELANETZ   WILFRID PELLETIER

CONCERTS

1956

Dimitri Mitropoulos

Oct. 18—Eve.	Carnegie Hall
Oct. 19—Aft.	Carnegie Hall
Oct. 20—Eve.	Carnegie Hall
Oct. 21—Aft.	Carnegie Hall
Oct. 25—Eve.	Carnegie Hall
Oct. 26—Aft.	Carnegie Hall
Oct. 27—Eve.	Carnegie Hall
Oct. 28—Aft.	Carnegie Hall
Nov. 1—Eve.	Carnegie Hall
Nov. 2—Aft.	Carnegie Hall

André Kostelanetz

Nov. 3—Eve.	Carnegie Hall

Dimitri Mitropoulos

Nov. 4—Aft.	Carnegie Hall
Nov. 5—Eve.	Hartford, Conn.
Nov. 8—Eve.	Carnegie Hall
Nov. 9—Aft.	Carnegie Hall
Nov. 11—Aft.	Carnegie Hall

Paul Paray

Nov. 15—Eve.	Carnegie Hall
Nov. 16—Aft.	Carnegie Hall
Nov. 17—Eve.	Carnegie Hall
Nov. 18—Aft.	Carnegie Hall
Nov. 22—Eve.	Carnegie Hall
Nov. 23—Aft.	Carnegie Hall
Nov. 24—Eve.	Carnegie Hall
Nov. 25—Aft.	Carnegie Hall

Dimitri Mitropoulos

Nov. 29—Eve.	Carnegie Hall
Nov. 30—Aft.	Carnegie Hall
*Dec. 1—Morn.	Carnegie Hall
Dec. 2—Aft.	Carnegie Hall

Paul Paray

Dec. 6—Eve.	Carnegie Hall
Dec. 7—Aft.	Carnegie Hall
Dec. 8—Eve.	Carnegie Hall
Dec. 9—Aft.	Carnegie Hall
**Dec. 10—Aft.	Great Neck J.H.S.
	Great Neck, L. I.

Leonard Bernstein

Dec. 13—Eve.	Carnegie Hall
Dec. 14—Aft.	Carnegie Hall
Dec. 15—Eve.	Carnegie Hall
Dec. 16—Aft.	Carnegie Hall
Dec. 20—Eve.	Carnegie Hall
Dec. 21—Aft.	Carnegie Hall

1956

André Kostelanetz

Dec. 22—Eve.	Carnegie Hall

Leonard Bernstein

Dec. 23—Aft.	Carnegie Hall
Dec. 27—Eve.	Carnegie Hall
Dec. 28—Aft.	Carnegie Hall
Dec. 30—Aft.	Carnegie Hall

1957

Jan. 3—Eve.	Carnegie Hall
Jan. 4—Aft.	Carnegie Hall
Jan. 5—Eve.	Carnegie Hall
Jan. 6—Aft.	Carnegie Hall

Igor Stravinsky

Jan. 10—Eve.	Carnegie Hall
Jan. 11—Aft.	Carnegie Hall
*Jan. 12—Morn.	Carnegie Hall
Jan. 13—Aft.	Carnegie Hall

Leonard Bernstein

Jan. 17—Eve.	Carnegie Hall
Jan. 18—Aft.	Carnegie Hall

André Kostelanetz

Jan. 19—Eve.	Carnegie Hall

Leonard Bernstein

Jan. 20—Aft.	Carnegie Hall
Jan. 24—Eve.	Carnegie Hall
Jan. 25—Aft.	Carnegie Hall
Jan. 26—Eve.	Carnegie Hall
Jan. 27—Aft.	Carnegie Hall
**Jan. 30—Aft.	Manhasset H. S.
	Manhasset, L. I.

Dimitri Mitropoulos

Jan. 31—Eve.	Carnegie Hall
Feb. 1—Aft.	Carnegie Hall
Feb. 2—Eve.	Carnegie Hall
Feb. 3—Aft.	Carnegie Hall

Bruno Walter

Feb. 7—Eve.	Carnegie Hall
Feb. 8—Aft.	Carnegie Hall

André Kostelanetz

Feb. 9—Eve.	Carnegie Hall

Bruno Walter

Feb. 10—Aft.	Carnegie Hall
Feb. 14—Eve.	Carnegie Hall
Feb. 15—Aft.	Carnegie Hall
*Feb. 16—Morn.	Carnegie Hall
Feb. 17—Aft.	Carnegie Hall

* Young People's Concert, conducted by Wilfrid Pelletier.
** Young People's Concert, conducted by Franco Autori.

1957

1957

Dimitri Mitropoulos

Feb. 21—Eve.	Carnegie Hall
Feb. 22—Aft.	Carnegie Hall
Feb. 23—Eve.	Carnegie Hall
Feb. 24—Aft.	Carnegie Hall

Bruno Walter

Feb. 26—Eve.   Carnegie Hall
(Pension Fund Benefit)

Dimitri Mitropoulos

Feb. 28—Eve.   Carnegie Hall
Mar. 1—Aft.   Carnegie Hall

Max Rudolf

Mar. 2—Eve.   Carnegie Hall
Mar. 3—Aft.   Carnegie Hall

Dimitri Mitropoulos

Mar. 7—Eve.   Carnegie Hall
Mar. 8—Aft.   Carnegie Hall
Mar. 9—Morn.   Carnegie Hall
Mar. 10—Aft.   Carnegie Hall
Mar. 12—Eve.   Staten Island

Georg Solti

Mar. 14—Eve.   Carnegie Hall
Mar. 15—Aft.   Carnegie Hall
Mar. 17—Aft.   Carnegie Hall
Mar. 21—Eve.   Carnegie Hall
Mar. 22—Aft.   Carnegie Hall
Mar. 23—Eve.   Carnegie Hall
Mar. 24—Aft.   Carnegie Hall

Heitor Villa-Lobos

Mar. 28—Eve.   Carnegie Hall
Mar. 29—Aft.   Carnegie Hall

Franco Autori

Mar. 30—Eve.   Carnegie Hall
Mar. 31—Aft.   Carnegie Hall

Dimitri Mitropoulos

Apr. 3—Eve.   Carnegie Hall
(Pension Fund Benefit)

Paul Paray

Apr. 4—Eve.   Carnegie Hall
Apr. 5—Aft.   Carnegie Hall
Apr. 6—Eve.   Carnegie Hall
Apr. 7—Aft.   Carnegie Hall

Dimitri Mitropoulos

Apr. 25—Eve.   Carnegie Hall
Apr. 26—Aft.   Carnegie Hall

Franco Autori

Apr. 27—Eve.   Carnegie Hall

Dimitri Mitropoulos

Apr. 28—Aft.   Carnegie Hall
May 2—Eve.   Carnegie Hall
May 3—Aft.   Carnegie Hall

Franco Autori

May 4—Eve.   Carnegie Hall

Dimitri Mitropoulos

May 5—Aft.   Carnegie Hall
May 9—Eve.   Carnegie Hall
May 10—Aft.   Carnegie Hall
*May 11—Morn.   Carnegie Hall
May 12—Aft.   Carnegie Hall

SPRING TOUR

Dimitri Mitropoulos

Apr. 8—Eve.	Kingston, N. Y.
Apr. 9—Eve.	Schenectady, N. Y.
Apr. 10—Eve.	Utica, N. Y.
Apr. 11—Eve.	Syracuse, N. Y.
Apr. 12—Eve.	Buffalo, N. Y.
Apr. 13—Eve.	Toronto, Ont.
Apr. 14—Aft.	Rochester, N. Y.
Apr. 15—Eve.	Corning, N. Y.

TWO CONCERTS FOR HIGH SCHOOL STUDENTS OF NEW YORK CITY

Feb. 16—Aft.
Prospect Heights High School, Brooklyn, New York; conducted by Wilfrid Pelletier.

Mar. 5—Aft.
Carnegie Hall, conducted by Dimitri Mitropoulos.

REPERTOIRE FOR 1956–57

(a) World premiere.
(b) United States premiere.
(c) New York premiere.
(d) First concert performance in the United States.

* Young People's Concert, conducted by Wilfrid Pelletier.

Compositions marked with asterisk (*) are recorded by
The Philharmonic-Symphony Orchestra on Columbia Records

ALBENIZ-ARBOS—Fête-Dieu à Séville: Jan. 19.

BACH—Aria after the Chorale-Prelude, "O Mensch, bewein' dein Sünde gross": Nov. 8.
Suite No. 3, D major, for Three Trumpets, Timpani, Oboes and Strings: Nov. 29, 30; Mar. 10; May 4; "Air" only: Jan. 19.

BACH-RESPIGHI—Passacaglia and Fugue, C minor: Apr. 28.

BACH-STRAVINSKY—Chorale Variations on the Christmas Song, "Vom Himmel hoch da komm' ich her" for Chorus and Orchestra: Jan. 10 (c), 11, 13.

BARBER—"Capricorn Concerto," Opus 21, for Flute, Oboe, Trumpet and Strings: Oct. 18, 19, 20, 21; Nov. 5.

BARRAUD—"Offrande à une Ombre": Nov. 15 (c), 16.

BARTOK—Concerto No. 2 for Piano and Orchestra: Nov. 22, 23.
Dance Suite: Mar. 14, 15, 17.
Music for Strings, Percussion and Celesta: Jan. 3, 4, 5, 6.

BEETHOVEN—Concerto for Piano and Orchestra No. 1, C major, Opus 15: Oct. 20.
Concerto for Piano and Orchestra No. 2, B-flat major, Opus 19: Jan. 26, 27.
Concerto for Piano and Orchestra No. 3, C minor, Opus 37: Feb. 23, 24.
Concerto for Piano and Orchestra No. 4, G major, Opus 58: Feb. 26, 28; Mar. 1.
Concerto for Piano and Orchestra No. 5, E-flat major, Opus 73 ("Emperor"): Mar. 7, 8, 10.
Concerto for Violin and Orchestra, D major, Opus 61: Dec. 15.
Overture, "Coriolanus": Feb. 26.
Overture, "Leonore" No. 3: Mar. 10.
Overture, "Prometheus," Opus 43: Dec. 13, 14, 15, 16; Feb. 14, 15.
*Symphony No. 2, D major, Opus 36: Mar. 21, 22.
*Symphony No. 3, E-flat major, Opus 55 ("Eroica"), Funeral March only: Jan. 17, 18, 20.
*Symphony No. 4, B-flat major, Opus 60: Jan. 24, 25.
*Symphony No. 5, C minor, Opus 67: Oct. 18, 19, 20, 21; Mar. 12; Apr. 10.
*Symphony No. 6, F major, Opus 68 ("Pastoral"): Feb. 26.
*Symphony No. 8, F major, Opus 93: Apr. 8, 13, 25, 26; May 5.

BENTZON—Variazioni Brevi, Opus 75: May 9 (b), 10.

BERLIOZ—Overture, "Beatrice and Benedict": Feb. 23, 24.
Overture, "The Corsair": May 2, 3.
Rákóczy March from "The Damnation of Faust": Dec. 23.
Symphonie Fantastique, C major, Opus 14-A: Feb. 21, 22; Apr. 14.

BERNSTEIN—Overture, "Candide": Jan. 26, 27.

BOYCE—Symphony No. 1, B-flat major (trans. Lambert): Mar. 30, 31.

BRAHMS—Concerto for Piano and Orchestra No. 1, D minor, Opus 15: Mar. 23, 24.
Concerto for Piano and Orchestra No. 2, B-flat major, Opus 83: Apr. 25, 26, 28
Concerto for Violin and Orchestra, D major, Opus 77: Apr. 7, 8.
*Overture, "Academic Festival," Opus 80: Apr. 28.
*Symphony No. 1, C minor, Opus 68: Mar. 14, 15, 17.
*Symphony No. 2, D major, Opus 73: Apr. 8, 13, 27.
*Symphony No. 4, E minor, Opus 98: Oct. 25, 26, 27, 28; Nov. 5.
*Variations on a Theme by Haydn, B-flat major, Opus 56-A: Mar. 30.

BRUCKNER—Symphony No. 9, D minor: Feb. 7, 8, 10.

CARTER—Holiday Overture: Apr. 25, 26, 28.

CHABRIER—"España" Rhapsody: Nov. 17, 18.

CHERUBINI—Overture, "Anacréon": Dec. 20, 21.

CHOPIN—Concerto for Piano and Orchestra No. 2, F minor, Opus 21: Oct. 27; Apr. 4, 5.

COPLAND—Short Symphony: Jan. 24 (d), 25, 26, 27.

CORELLI—Suite for Strings: Nov. 3.

COWELL—Hymn and Fuguing Tune No. 2 for String Orchestra: Nov. 22, 23, 24, 25.

DALLAPICCOLA—Tartiniana: May 2, 3.

DEBUSSY—*"La Mer," Three Symphonic Sketches: Nov. 15, 16, 17, 18.
Nocturne, "Fêtes" (Festivals): Mar. 2.
Prelude, "The Afternoon of a Faun": Jan. 19.

DELLO JOIO—Concert Music for Orchestra: May 4.
Variations, Chaconne and Finale: Mar. 2, 3.

DUKAS—Scherzo, "The Sorcerer's Apprentice": Oct. 28.

DVORAK—Concerto for Violin and Orchestra, A minor, Opus 53: Dec. 6, 7.
Concerto for Violoncello and Orchestra, B minor, Opus 104: Nov. 24.

EGGE—Concerto for Violin and Orchestra, Opus 26: Apr. 27 (b).

EINEM—Orchestermusik, Opus 9: Mar. 21, 22.

FALLA—"Nights in the Gardens of Spain," Symphonic Impressions for Piano and Orchestra: Nov. 1, 2.
Pantomime and Ritual Fire Dance, "El Amor Brujo": Jan. 19.

FAURE—"Pelléas et Mélisande," Incidental Music: Nov. 25.

FOSS—"Psalms" for Chorus and Orchestra: May 9 (a), 10, 12.

FRANCK—Symphonic Variations for Piano and Orchestra: Dec. 9.

GERSHWIN—*An American in Paris: Dec. 22.
Cuban Overture: Dec. 22.

GERSHWIN-BENNETT—*"Porgy and Bess: A Symphonic Picture": Dec. 22.

GINASTERA—Overture to the Creole "Faust": Feb. 21, 22, 24; Apr. 9, 10, 11, 15.

GLAZOUNOFF—Concerto for Violin and Orchestra, A minor, Opus 82: Mar. 2, 3.
Overture on Greek Themes No. 1, G minor: Nov. 11.

GLUCK—Overture, "Alceste": Oct. 25, 26, 27.

GOLDMARK—Concerto for Violin and Orchestra, A minor, Opus 28: Jan. 31; Feb. 1, 3.

GOULD—Jekyll and Hyde Variations for Orchestra: Feb. 2 (a), 3.

GRANADOS—Intermezzo and Interlude, "Goyescas": Jan. 19.

GRIEG—Concerto for Piano and Orchestra, A minor, Opus 16: Mar. 30, 31.

GUARNIERI—Abertura Concertante: Mar. 28 (c), 29.

HANDEL—Concerto Grosso No. 2, B-flat major, Opus 3: Oct. 18, 19, 21; Nov. 5.
"Messiah": Dec. 27, 28, 30.

HARRIS—Symphony No. 3 (In One Movement): Jan. 24, 25, 26, 27.

HAYDN—Symphony No. 86, D major: Mar. 2, 3.
*Symphony No. 96, D major: Nov. 15, 16, 17, 18.
Symphony No. 100, G major ("Military"): Nov. 1, 2, 4.
*Symphony No. 102, B-flat major: Jan. 3, 4, 5, 6.

HEIDEN—"Euphorion," Scene for Orchestra: Apr. 4 (c), 5.

HINDEMITH—Symphonic Metamorphosis of Themes of Weber: Mar. 17.
Symphony, "Mathis der Maler": Dec. 20, 21, 23.

KODALY—"Psalmus Hungaricus" for Tenor, Chorus and Orchestra: May 9, 10, 12.

KUBIK—Symphony No. 3: Feb. 28 (a); Mar. 1.

LALO—Overture, "Le Roi d'Ys": Apr. 7, 8.
Symphonie Espagnole for Violin and Orchestra, Opus 21: Nov. 4; Feb. 21, 22.

LIADOFF—The Enchanted Lake: Feb. 9.

LISZT—Concerto for Piano and Orchestra No. 1, E-flat major: Nov. 25.
Symphonic Poem, "Les Préludes": Feb. 9.

LOEWE-BENNETT—Selections from "My Fair Lady": Jan. 19.

MAHLER—Songs for Soprano with Orchestra: "Wo die schönen Trompeten blasen," "Ich atmet' einen linden Duft," "Ich bin der Welt abhanden gekommen": Feb. 14, 15.
Symphony No. 2, C minor, for Orchestra, Soprano and Contralto Solos, and Mixed Chorus: Feb. 14, 15, 17.

MANN—Fantasy for Orchestra: Feb. 23 (a).

MARQUINA—España Cani: Jan. 19.

MENDELSSOHN—Concerto for Violin and Orchestra, E minor, Opus 64: Nov. 17, 18.
*Symphony No. 3, A minor, Opus 56 ("Scotch"): May 2, 3.

MEYEROWITZ—Symphony, "Midrash Esther": Jan. 31 (a); Feb. 1.

MOUSSORGSKY-RAVEL—*Pictures at an Exhibition: Mar. 30, 31.

MOZART—Concerto for Piano and Orchestra No. 20, D minor, K. 466: Nov. 15, 16.
Concerto for Piano and Orchestra No. 23, A major, K. 488: Dec. 8, 9; Mar. 14, 15.
Concerto for Piano and Orchestra No. 24, C minor, K. 491: Dec. 13, 14, 16.
Concerto for Violin and Orchestra No. 5, A major, K. 219: Mar. 21, 22.
Divertimento for Strings, Flute, Oboe, Bassoon and Four Horns No. 2, D major, K. 131: Jan. 31; Feb. 1, 2, 3; Mar. 12.
Overture, "La Clemenza di Tito"; Nov. 5, 8, 9, 11.
Overture, "The Marriage of Figaro": Mar. 23.
*Symphony No. 38, D major, K. 504 ("Prague"): Mar. 23, 24.

PORTER-BENNETT—"Kiss Me, Kate": Nov. 3.

PROKOFIEFF—Concerto for Violin and Orchestra No. 2, G minor, Opus 63: Jan. 17, 18, 20.
"Peter and the Wolf," Opus 67: Dec. 22.
"Classical" Symphony, D major, Opus 25: Dec. 6, 7, 8.
*Symphony No. 5, B-flat major, Opus 100: Nov. 29, 30; Dec. 2; Apr. 9, 11, 12, 15.
*Wedding Suite from "The Stone Flower": Nov. 3.

PUCCINI—Excerpts from Act I, "La Bohème" (Orch. trans.): Feb. 9.

RACHMANINOFF—Concerto for Piano and Orchestra No. 1, F-sharp minor, Opus 1: Nov. 8, 9.
Concerto for Piano and Orchestra No. 2, C minor, Opus 18: Jan. 3, 4.
Concerto for Piano and Orchestra No. 3, D minor, Opus 30: May 4.

RAVEL—Concerto for Piano and Orchestra, G major: Jan. 5, 6.
Piano Concerto for the Left hand: Nov. 1, 2.
"Daphnis et Chloé," Suite No. 2: Nov. 22, 23, 24, 25.
*"La Valse," Choreographic Poem for Orchestra: Dec. 13, 14, 15, 16.

READ—Toccata Giocosa, Opus 94: Oct. 25 (c), 26.

RODGERS-BENNETT—"South Pacific": Nov. 3.

ROSENTHAL—Ode: Jan. 24 (a), 25.

ROSSINI—Overture, "The Barber of Seville": Jan. 19.
Overture, "Semiramide": Dec. 2.

ROUSSEL—The Spider's Feast, Opus 17: Apr. 4, 5, 6.

SAMMARTINI—Symphony No. 3, G major: Apr. 27.

SCHMITT—"Salammbô," Suite No. 2: Mar. 28 (c), 29.

SCHUBERT—Symphony No. 5, B-flat major: Feb. 23, 24, 28; Mar. 1, 12; Apr. 10, 12.
  *Symphony No. 7, C major: Dec. 6, 7, 8, 9.
  Symphony No. 8, B minor ("Unfinished"): Feb. 7, 8.

SCHULLER—Dramatic Overture: Mar. 7 (b), 8, 10.
  Symphony for Brass and Percussion: Nov. 1, 2, 4.

SCHUMAN—Credendum (Article of Faith): Nov. 8, 9.
  New England Triptych, Three Pieces for Orchestra after William Billings: Nov. 3 (c).

SCHUMANN—Concerto for Violoncello and Orchestra, A minor, Opus 129: Feb. 2.
  Symphony No. 1, B-flat major, Opus 38: Nov. 8, 9, 11.
  Symphony No. 4, D minor, Opus 120: Nov. 22, 23, 24, 25.

SCRIABIN—*"The Poem of Ecstasy," Opus 54: Oct. 25, 26.

SHERWOOD—Introduction and Allegro: May 5 (a).

SIBELIUS—Symphony No. 5, E-flat major, Opus 82: Jan. 17, 18, 20.

STARER—Prelude and Rondo Giocoso: Oct. 27 (a), 28.

STRAUSS, Johann—*Waltz, "Tales from the Vienna Woods": Feb. 9.

STRAUSS, Josef and Johann—*Pizzicato Polka: Feb. 9.

STRAUSS, Richard—Dance of the Seven Veils, "Salome," Opus 54: Nov. 4.
  Sinfonia Domestica: Mar. 7, 8.
  *Tone Poem, "Death and Transfiguration," Opus 24: Nov. 29, 30; Dec. 2; Apr. 13, 14.
  *Tone Poem, "Don Juan," Opus 20: Oct. 18, 19, 28; Mar. 12; Apr. 8, 9, 10, 11, 12, 15.
  *Tone Poem, "Till Eulenspiegel's Merry Pranks," Opus 28: Mar. 21, 22, 23, 24.

STRAVINSKY—*Suite from "The Firebird": Jan. 19, 26, 27.
  "Persephone," Melodrama by André Gide for Narrator, Tenor and Chorus: Jan. 10, 11, 13.
  *Suite from "Petrouchka": Jan. 10, 11, 13.
  Symphonic Poem, "The Song of the Nightingale": Dec. 13, 14, 15, 16.

TCHAIKOVSKY—Capriccio Italien, Opus 45: Apr. 9, 11, 14, 15; May 5.
  Concerto for Piano and Orchestra No. 1, B-flat minor, Opus 23: Nov. 11.
  *Overture-Fantasy, "Romeo and Juliet": Jan. 5, 6.
  *Symphony No. 6, B minor, Opus 74 ("Pathétique"): Dec. 20, 21, 23.

VERDI—Aria, "Pace, pace" from "La Forza del Destino": Apr. 3.
  Arias, "Salce, salce" and "Ave Maria" from "Otello": Apr. 3.
  Aria, "Tacea la notte" from "Il Trovatore": Apr. 3.
  Ballet Music, "Macbeth": Apr. 3.
  Overture, "La Battaglia di Legnano": Apr. 3.
  Overture, "La Forza del Destino": Apr. 3.
  Overture, "Giovanna d'Arco": Apr. 3.
  Overture, "Nabucco": Apr. 3.
  Overture, "I Vespri Siciliani": Apr. 3.

VILLA-LOBOS—Bachianas Brasileiras No. 1 for Eight 'Celli (First Two Movements): Mar. 28, 29.
  Choros No. 6: Mar. 28, 29.
  "Mandú-Carará," Cantata Profana: Mar. 28 (c), 29.

VIVALDI—Concerto for Strings, Cembalo and Two Mandolins: Jan. 17, 18.

WAGNER—*Overture, "The Flying Dutchman": Mar. 2, 3.
  *Prelude, "Die Meistersinger": Mar. 31.
  Prelude and Love Death, "Tristan und Isolde": Apr. 4, 5, 6, 7.

Ride of the Valkyries, "Die Walkuere": Apr. 4, 5, 6, 7.
*A Siegfried Idyl: Feb. 10.
WALTON—"Belshazzar's Feast": May 9, 10, 12.
Concerto for Violoncello and Orchestra: May 2 (c), 3, 5.
Suite from "Facade": Feb. 9.
WEBER—*Invitation to the Dance: Nov. 3.
*Overture, "Der Freischuetz": Feb. 7, 8.
*Overture, "Oberon": Mar. 17.
WEINBERGER—Polka and Fugue, "Schwanda": Oct. 21.
WOLF-FERRARI—Overture, "The Secret of Suzanne": Feb. 9.
ZANDONAI—Symphonic Episode from "Giulietta e Romeo": Jan. 31; Feb. 1, 2, 3.

SOLOISTS

PIANO
GEZA ANDA: Nov. 22, 23, 25.
STANLEY BABIN: Oct. 20.
LEONARD BERNSTEIN: Jan. 5, 6.
ALEXANDER BRAILOWSKY: Jan. 3, 4.
JEAN CASADESUS: Feb. 23, 24.
ROBERT CASADESUS: Nov. 1, 2; Dec. 8, 9.
CLIFFORD CURZON: Mar. 14, 15, 30, 31.
RAY DUDLEY: May 4.
RUDOLF FIRKUSNY: Dec. 13, 14, 16.
GLENN GOULD: Jan. 26, 27.
CLARA HASKIL: Nov. 15, 16.
MYRA HESS: Feb. 26.
EUGENE ISTOMIN: Mar. 7, 8, 10.
BYRON JANIS: Nov. 8, 9.
LOUIS KENTNER: Apr. 25, 26, 28.
WITOLD MALCUZYNSKI: Apr. 4, 5.
RUDOLF SERKIN: Feb. 28; Mar. 1, 23, 24.
RUTH SLENCZYNSKA: Oct. 27.
ANNA XYDIS: Nov. 11.

VIOLIN
JOHN CORIGLIANO: Dec. 6, 7; May 2, 3.
ZINO FRANCESCATTI: Feb. 21, 22; Apr. 6, 7.
BETTY JEAN HAGEN: Nov. 4.
NATHAN MILSTEIN: Jan. 31; Feb. 1, 3.
ERICA MORINI: Mar. 2, 3, 21, 22.
OSCAR SHUMSKY: Dec. 15.
TOSSY SPIVAKOVSKY: Nov. 17, 18.
ISAAC STERN: Jan. 17, 18, 20.
CAMILLA WICKS: Apr. 27.

VIOLONCELLO
ALDO PARISOT: Nov. 24.
GREGOR PIATIGORSKY: May 2, 3, 5.
LASZLO VARGA: Feb. 2.

FLUTE
JOHN WUMMER: Oct. 18, 19, 20, 21; Nov. 5.

OBOE
HAROLD GOMBERG: Oct. 18, 19, 20, 21; Nov. 5.

TRUMPET
WILLIAM VACCHIANO: Oct. 18, 19, 20, 21; Nov. 5.

ZITHER
FRANZ DIETSCHMANN: Feb. 9.

VOICE
ADELE ADDISON, soprano: Dec. 27, 28, 30.
MAUREEN FORRESTER, contralto: Feb. 14, 15, 17.
DAVID LLOYD, tenor: Dec. 27, 28, 30; May 9, 10, 12.
RUSSELL OBERLIN, countertenor: Dec. 27, 28, 30.
RICHARD ROBINSON, tenor: Jan. 10, 11, 13.
MARIA STADER, soprano: Feb. 14, 15, 17.
RENATA TEBALDI, soprano: Apr. 3.
GIORGIO TOZZI, bass: May 9, 10, 12.
WILLIAM WARFIELD, baritone: Dec. 27, 28, 30.

NARRATOR
JOHN DALY: Dec. 22.
VERA ZORINA: Jan. 10, 11, 13.

CHORUS
GIRLS CHORUS from HIGH SCHOOL OF MUSIC AND ART, Chester Coleman, Director: Mar. 28, 29.
SCHOLA CANTORUM, Hugh Ross, Conductor: Mar. 28, 29; May 9, 10, 12.
THE WESTMINSTER CHOIR, Dr. John Finley Williamson, Director: Dec. 27, 28, 30; Jan. 10, 11, 13; Feb. 14, 15, 17.

610

1957–58 ONE HUNDRED SIXTEENTH SEASON

Principal Conductors
DIMITRI MITROPOULOS
LEONARD BERNSTEIN

Guest Conductors
ERNEST ANSERMET, ANDRE CLUYTENS, AARON COPLAND, RAFAEL KUBELIK
FERNANDO PREVITALI, THOMAS SCHIPPERS, ROBERT SHAW

Musical Director, Young People's Concerts
LEONARD BERNSTEIN

Associate Conductor
FRANCO AUTORI

Four Special Saturday Nights
ANDRE KOSTELANETZ

CONCERTS

1957

Dimitri Mitropoulos
Oct. 12—Eve.	Carnegie Hall
Oct. 13—Aft.	Carnegie Hall

Thomas Schippers
Oct. 17—Eve.	Carnegie Hall
Oct. 18—Aft.	Carnegie Hall
Oct. 19—Eve.	Carnegie Hall
Oct. 20—Aft.	Carnegie Hall
Oct. 24—Eve.	Carnegie Hall
Oct. 25—Aft.	Carnegie Hall
Oct. 26—Eve.	Carnegie Hall
Oct. 27—Aft.	Carnegie Hall

Dimitri Mitropoulos
Oct. 31—Eve.	Carnegie Hall
Nov. 1—Aft.	Carnegie Hall

André Kostelanetz
Nov. 2—Eve.	Carnegie Hall

Dimitri Mitropoulos
Nov. 3—Aft.	Carnegie Hall

André Cluytens
Nov. 7—Eve.	Carnegie Hall
Nov. 8—Aft.	Carnegie Hall
Nov. 9—Eve.	Carnegie Hall
Nov. 10—Aft.	Carnegie Hall
Nov. 14—Eve.	Carnegie Hall
Nov. 15—Aft.	Carnegie Hall
Nov. 16—Eve.	Carnegie Hall
Nov. 17—Aft.	Carnegie Hall
Nov. 21—Eve.	Carnegie Hall
Nov. 22—Aft.	Carnegie Hall
*Nov. 23—Noon	Carnegie Hall
Nov. 24—Aft.	Carnegie Hall
Nov. 28—Eve.	Carnegie Hall
Nov. 29—Aft.	Carnegie Hall

1957

André Kostelanetz
Nov. 30—Eve.	Carnegie Hall

André Cluytens
Dec. 1—Aft.	Carnegie Hall

Dimitri Mitropoulos
Dec. 3—Eve.	Hartford, Conn.

Fernando Previtali
Dec. 5—Eve.	Carnegie Hall
Dec. 6—Aft.	Carnegie Hall
Dec. 8—Aft.	Carnegie Hall
Dec. 12—Eve.	Carnegie Hall
Dec. 13—Aft.	Carnegie Hall
Dec. 14—Eve.	Carnegie Hall
Dec. 15—Aft.	Carnegie Hall
Dec. 19—Eve.	Carnegie Hall
Dec. 20—Aft.	Carnegie Hall

André Kostelanetz
Dec. 21—Eve.	Carnegie Hall

Fernando Previtali
Dec. 22—Aft.	Carnegie Hall

1958

Leonard Bernstein
Jan. 2—Eve.	Carnegie Hall
Jan. 3—Aft.	Carnegie Hall
Jan. 4—Eve.	Carnegie Hall
Jan. 5—Aft.	Carnegie Hall
Jan. 9—Eve.	Carnegie Hall
Jan. 10—Aft.	Carnegie Hall
Jan. 11—Eve.	Carnegie Hall
Jan. 12—Aft.	Carnegie Hall
Jan. 16—Eve.	Carnegie Hall
Jan. 17—Aft.	Carnegie Hall
**Jan. 18—Noon	Carnegie Hall

* Young People's Concert, conducted by Thomas Schippers.
** Young People's Concert, conducted by Leonard Bernstein.

1958

Jan. 19—Aft.	Carnegie Hall
Jan. 23—Eve.	Carnegie Hall
Jan. 24—Aft.	Carnegie Hall
Jan. 25—Eve.	Carnegie Hall
Jan. 26—Aft.	Carnegie Hall

Aaron Copland, Franco Autori

Jan. 30—Eve.	Carnegie Hall
Jan. 31—Aft.	Carnegie Hall
**Feb. 1—Noon	Carnegie Hall

Dimitri Mitropoulos

Feb. 2—Aft.	Carnegie Hall
Feb. 6—Eve.	Carnegie Hall
Feb. 7—Aft.	Carnegie Hall
Feb. 8—Eve.	Carnegie Hall
Feb. 9—Aft.	Carnegie Hall

Rafael Kubelik

Feb. 13—Eve.	Carnegie Hall
Feb. 14—Aft.	Carnegie Hall
Feb. 15—Eve.	Carnegie Hall
Feb. 16—Aft.	Carnegie Hall
***Feb. 17—Aft.	Garden City H. S. Garden City, N. Y.
Feb. 18—Eve.	Newark, N. J.
Feb. 20—Eve.	Carnegie Hall
Feb. 21—Aft.	Carnegie Hall

Franco Autori

| Feb. 22—Eve. | Carnegie Hall |

Rafael Kubelik

| Feb. 23—Aft. | Carnegie Hall |

Bruno Walter

| Feb. 26—Eve. | Carnegie Hall (Pension Fund Benefit) |

Dimitri Mitropoulos

Feb. 27—Eve.	Carnegie Hall
Feb. 28—Aft.	Carnegie Hall
Mar. 1—Eve.	Carnegie Hall
Mar. 2—Aft.	Carnegie Hall
Mar. 6—Eve.	Carnegie Hall
Mar. 7—Aft.	Carnegie Hall
**Mar. 8—Noon	Carnegie Hall
Mar. 9—Aft.	Carnegie Hall

Dimitri Mitropoulos, Danny Kaye

| Mar. 10—Eve. | Carnegie Hall (Pension Fund Benefit) |

1958

Dimitri Mitropoulos

| Mar. 13—Eve. | Carnegie Hall |
| Mar. 14—Aft. | Carnegie Hall |

André Kostelanetz

| Mar. 15—Eve. | Carnegie Hall |

Dimitri Mitropoulos

| Mar. 16—Aft. | Carnegie Hall |
| ***Mar. 17—Aft. | Great Neck J. H. S. Great Neck, N. Y. |

Ernest Ansermet

Mar. 20—Eve.	Carnegie Hall
Mar. 21—Aft.	Carnegie Hall
Mar. 22—Eve.	Carnegie Hall
Mar. 23—Aft.	Carnegie Hall
Mar. 27—Eve.	Carnegie Hall
Mar. 28—Aft.	Carnegie Hall

Franco Autori

| Mar. 29—Eve. | Carnegie Hall |

Ernest Ansermet

| Mar. 30—Aft. | Carnegie Hall |

Leonard Bernstein

| Apr. 2—Eve. | Brooklyn, N. Y. |

Robert Shaw

Apr. 3—Eve.	Carnegie Hall
Apr. 4—Aft.	Carnegie Hall
Apr. 6—Aft.	Carnegie Hall

Leonard Bernstein

Apr. 10—Eve.	Carnegie Hall
Apr. 11—Aft.	Carnegie Hall
Apr. 12—Eve.	Carnegie Hall
Apr. 13—Aft.	Carnegie Hall
Apr. 17—Eve.	Carnegie Hall
Apr. 18—Aft.	Carnegie Hall
**Apr. 19—Noon	Carnegie Hall
Apr. 20—Aft.	Carnegie Hall

André Kostelanetz

| Apr. 22—Eve. | White Plains, N. Y. |

Leonard Bernstein

Apr. 24—Eve.	Carnegie Hall
Apr. 25—Aft.	Carnegie Hall
Apr. 27—Aft.	Carnegie Hall

THREE CONCERTS IN CARNEGIE HALL FOR
HIGH SCHOOL STUDENTS OF NEW YORK CITY

Jan. 22—Leonard Bernstein, Conductor.   Mar. 12—Dimitri Mitropoulos, Conduc-
Feb. 12—Thomas Schippers, Conductor.   tor.

** Young People's Concert, conducted by Leonard Bernstein.
*** Young People's Concert, conducted by Franco Autori.

REPERTOIRE FOR 1957–58

(a) World premiere.
(b) First performance in the Western Hemisphere.
(c) First performance in the United States.
(d) First performance in New York.
(e) First concert performance in New York.

Compositions marked with asterisk (*) are recorded by
the New York Philharmonic on Columbia Records

ARLEN—Suite for Orchestra from "Blues Opera": Nov. 2 (d).

BACH—Concerto for Piano and Orchestra, D minor: Mar. 13, 14.
Concerto No. 2 for Violin and Orchestra, E major: Nov. 9, 10.
Suite No. 4, D major: Feb. 13, 14.

BACH-SCHOENBERG—Two Chorale Preludes: "Schmuecke dich, o liebe Seele"
and "Komm, Gott, Schoepfer, heiliger Geist": Feb. 27, 28; Mar. 1, 2
("Komm, Gott" only on Mar. 2).

BARBER—Adagio for Strings, Opus 11: Oct. 19, 20.
Medea's Meditation and Dance of Vengeance, Opus 23-A: Mar. 13, 14, 16.
Intermezzo from Act IV, "Vanessa": Mar. 15 (e).

BARTOK—Concerto for Orchestra: Feb. 13, 14.
Concerto No. 3 for Piano and Orchestra: Oct. 17, 18.
Concerto for Violin and Orchestra: Jan. 23, 24, 26.
Rhapsody No. 1 for Violin and Orchestra: Nov. 9, 10.

BEETHOVEN—Concerto No. 3 for Piano and Orchestra, C minor, Opus 37:
Mar. 20, 21, 23.
Concerto No. 4 for Piano and Orchestra, G major, Opus 58: Jan. 16, 17.
Concerto for Violin and Orchestra, D major, Opus 61: Jan. 9, 10.
Overture, "Egmont": Dec. 1.
Overture, "Leonore," No. 2: Feb. 2, 26.
Overture, "Leonore," No. 3: Nov. 14, 15, 16, 17.
*Symphony No. 2, D major, Opus 36: Feb. 2.
*Symphony No. 7, A major, Opus 92: Feb. 13, 14, 15, 16, 18.

BERLIOZ—Excerpts from "The Damnation of Faust": Nov. 30.
Overture, "Roman Carnival," Opus 9: Nov. 2.

BIZET—"Carmen," Suite for Orchestra: Nov. 30.
Symphony in C major: Nov. 28, 29.

BLITZSTEIN—"Lear: A Study": Feb. 27 (a), 28.

BLOCH—Concerto for Violin and Orchestra: Dec. 12, 13.

BOCCHERINI—Sinfonia in D major, Opus 16, No. 2: Dec. 14, 15.

BONDEVILLE—Symphonie Lyrique: Nov. 16 (c).

BORISHANSKY—Music for Orchestra: Apr. 17 (a), 18, 20.

BORODIN—Symphony No. 3, A minor (Unfinished): Mar. 27, 28.

BRAHMS—Concerto No. 2 for Piano and Orchestra, B-flat major, Opus 83: Apr.
17, 18.
*Overture, "Academic Festival," Opus 80: Feb. 9.
*Symphony No. 1, C minor, Opus 68: Dec. 19, 20, 22.
*Symphony No. 3, F major, Opus 90: Feb. 6, 7, 8, 9.
*Symphony No. 4, E minor, Opus 98: Nov. 7, 8, 9, 10.

BRITTEN—Concerto No. 1 for Piano and Orchestra, D major: Mar. 1.

BUSONI—Excerpts from the Suite, "Turandot," Opus 41: Dec. 5, 6, 8.

CASTRO—Corales Criollos: Mar. 20 (c), 21, 22, 23.

CHABRIER—Fête Polonaise from "Le Roi Malgré Lui": Nov. 24.
Habanera: Nov. 24.

CHAVEZ—Sinfonía India: Apr. 20.

CHERUBINI—Symphony in D major: Oct. 24, 25, 26.

CHOPIN—Concerto No. 2 for Piano and Orchestra, F minor: Nov. 21, 22.

COPLAND—A Lincoln Portrait: Mar. 15.
Excerpts from the Ballet, "Rodeo": Nov. 30.
An Outdoor Overture: Jan. 30, 31.
Third Symphony: Jan. 30, 31.

DEBUSSY—"La Damoiselle Élue": Nov. 14, 15, 16, 17.
*"La Mer," Three Symphonic Sketches: Mar. 20, 21, 22, 23.

DIAMOND—Symphony No. 4: Jan. 9, 10, 11.

DUKAS—"La Péri": Mar. 27, 28, 30.

DURUFLE—Andante and Scherzo, Opus 8: Nov. 21 (d), 22, 24 (Scherzo only on Nov. 24).

DUTILLEUX—Symphony: Nov. 21, 22, 24.

DVORAK—Slavonic Dances, Opus 72, Nos. 1, 2, 3, 7: Feb. 23.
Symphony No. 2, D minor, Opus 70: Feb. 20, 21, 23.

ELGAR—Variations on an Original Theme, "Enigma," Opus 36: Feb. 22.

FALLA—*Three Dances from "The Three-Cornered Hat": Mar. 1, 2, 10.

FOSS—"Song of Songs," Biblical Solo Cantata: Jan. 25, 26.

FRANCK—Symphonic Variations for Piano and Orchestra: Nov. 14, 15, 17.

GERSHWIN—*"An American in Paris": Apr. 20, 22.
Concerto for Piano and Orchestra, F major: Nov. 30; Apr. 22.

GIANNINI—Symphony No. 2: Feb. 22.

GLAZOUNOFF—Concerto for Violin and Orchestra, A minor, Opus 82: Apr. 12, 13.

GRETRY-MOTTL—Ballet Music from "Céphale et Procris": Mar. 15.

GROFE—Excerpts from "Grand Canyon Suite": Mar. 15.

GUARNIERI—Prologo e Fuga: Mar. 13, 14, 16.

HAIEFF—Ballet in E: Jan. 11 (d), 12 ("Amusements" only on Jan. 12).

HAYDN—Concerto for Violoncello and Orchestra, D major, Opus 101: Mar. 29.
"The Creation": Apr. 3, 4, 6.
Symphony No. 99, E-flat major: Feb. 20, 21.
Symphony No. 104, D major ("London"): Jan. 23, 24, 25; Apr. 2.

HINDEMITH—Concerto for Violoncello and Orchestra: Mar. 22.

HONEGGER—Concertino for Piano and Orchestra: Nov. 14, 15, 17.
"Joan of Arc at the Stake": Apr. 24, 25, 27.
Symphony No. 2 for String Orchestra: Nov. 7, 8.

KABALEVSKY—Symphony No. 4: Oct. 31 (b); Nov. 1, 2; Dec. 3.

LALO—Symphonie Espagnole for Violin and Orchestra, Opus 21: Jan. 30, 31.

LISZT—Concerto No. 1 for Piano and Orchestra, E-flat major: Jan. 19.
Concerto No. 2 for Piano and Orchestra, A major: Oct. 20.

MacDOWELL—Concerto No. 2 for Piano and Orchestra, D minor, Opus 23: Feb. 22.

MACERO—Fusion: Jan. 11, 12.

MAHLER—Symphony No. 10: Mar. 13 (d), 14, 16.

MANFREDINI—Sinfonia No. 10, E minor: Feb. 22.

MARKEVITCH—"Icare": Apr. 10 (c), 11, 12, 13.

MARTIN—Petite Symphonie Concertante for Harpsichord, Harp, Piano and Double String Orchestra: Mar. 27, 28, 30.

MARTINU—"Incantation" (Piano Concerto No. 4): Feb. 15, 16, 18.

MENDELSSOHN—Concerto No. 1 for Piano and Orchestra, G minor, Opus 25: Oct. 27.
Concerto for Two Pianos and Orchestra, A-flat major: Feb. 27 (d), 28; Mar. 1.
Concerto for Violin and Orchestra, E minor, Opus 64: Jan. 11, 12.
Overture, "Fingal's Cave," Opus 26: Mar. 20, 21, 22, 23.
*Symphony No. 3, A minor, Opus 56 ("Scotch"): Dec. 5, 6, 8.
Symphony No. 4, A major, Opus 90 ("Italian"): Jan. 9, 10, 12.

MENNIN—Concertato for Orchestra, "Moby Dick": Mar. 29.

MOUSSORGSKY—Prelude, "Khovanshchina": Nov. 14, 15.
"A Night on Bald Mountain," Fantasy for Orchestra: Nov. 3; Dec. 3.

MOUSSORGSKY-RAVEL—Pictures at an Exhibition: Nov. 28, 29; Dec. 1.

MOZART—Aria, "Per pietà," from "Così fan tutte": Dec. 5, 6, 8.
Concerto No. 17 for Piano and Orchestra, G major, K. 453: Oct. 12; Dec. 3.
Concerto No. 3 for Violin and Orchestra, G major, K. 216: Feb. 2.
Overture, "The Abduction from the Seraglio": Oct. 27.
Overture, "The Magic Flute": Feb. 2.
Sinfonia Concertante for Violin, Viola and Orchestra, E-flat major, K. 364: Feb. 20, 21, 23.
*Symphony No. 35, D major, K. 385 ("Haffner"): Nov. 14, 15, 16, 17.
Symphony No. 36, C major, K. 425 ("Linz"): Feb. 26.

PAGANINI—Concerto No. 1 for Violin and Orchestra, D major, Opus 6: Dec. 14, 15.

PETRASSI—Concerto No. 1 for Orchestra: Dec. 19, 20, 22.

PROKOFIEFF—Excerpts from the Ballet, "Romeo and Juliet": Oct. 31; Nov. 1, 3.
Concerto No. 3 for Piano and Orchestra, C major, Opus 26: Oct. 13; Jan. 4.
Symphony No. 1, D major, Opus 25 ("Classical"): Nov. 2; Apr. 10, 11, 13.
Symphony No. 5, B-flat major, Opus 100: Oct. 24, 25, 26, 27.

RACHMANINOFF—Rhapsody on a Theme of Paganini, Opus 43: Feb. 15, 16, 18.
Vocalise: Nov. 2.

RAVEL—Bolero: Jan. 23, 24, 25.
Concerto, G major, for Piano and Orchestra: Apr. 2.
"Daphnis it Chloé," Suite No. 2: Nov. 7, 8.
"Mother Goose" Suite: Dec. 12, 13, 14, 15.
Rapsodie Espagnole: Jan. 23, 24, 25, 26; Apr. 2.
"La Valse," Choreographic Poem for Orchestra: Jan. 2, 3, 4, 5; Apr. 2.

REGER—Concerto in F minor, Opus 114, for Piano and Orchestra: Feb. 8.

RIMSKY-KORSAKOFF—Overture, "Russian Easter," Opus 36: Apr. 13.

ROTA—Variazioni sopra un Tema Gioviale: Dec. 12 (c), 13.

ROUSSEL—"Bacchus et Ariane," Suite No. 2, Opus 43: Oct. 24, 25, 26.

SAINT-SAENS—Overture, "La Princesse Jaune": Nov. 30.

SAMMARTINI—Sinfonia No. 3, G major: Dec. 19, 20.

SCHOENBERG—Concerto for Piano and Orchestra: Mar. 13, 14, 16.
Verklaerte Nacht ("Transfigured Night") for String Orchestra, Opus 4: Feb. 27, 28; Mar. 1.

SCHUBERT—Symphony No. 8, B minor ("Unfinished"): Feb. 26.

SCHUMAN—New England Triptych, Three Pieces for Orchestra after William Billings: Mar. 15.
Symphony No. 6 (In One Movement): Apr. 17, 18, 20.

SCHUMANN—Concerto for Piano and Orchestra, A minor, Opus 54: Nov. 28, 29; Dec. 1.
Introduction and Allegro Appassionato for Piano and Orchestra, G major, Opus 92: Feb. 6, 7, 9.

Overture, "Manfred," Opus 115: Jan. 2, 3, 4, 5.

SHAPERO—Credo: Jan. 25 (d), 26.

SHOSTAKOVICH—Concerto No. 2 for Piano and Orchestra: Jan. 2 (b), 3, 5.
Symphony No. 1, Opus 10: Oct. 19.

SIBELIUS—Symphony No. 2, D major, Opus 43: Oct. 17, 18, 19, 20.
"The Death of Melisande" from the Incidental Music for "Pelléas et Mélisande": Oct. 12.

SICILIANOS—Symphony No. 1, Opus 14: Mar. 1 (a).

SMETANA—Symphonic Poem, "The Moldau" from the Cycle, "My Fatherland": Feb. 15, 16, 18.

STRAUSS—"Burleske" for Piano and Orchestra: Feb. 6, 7, 9.
*Dance of the Seven Veils, "Salome," Opus 54: Mar. 10.
"Elektra," Tragedy in One Act: Mar. 6, 7, 9.
Four Last Songs: Dec. 5, 6, 8.
*Tone Poem, "Don Juan," Opus 20: Nov. 21, 22, 24.
Tone Poem, "Don Quixote," Opus 35: Jan. 2, 3, 4, 5.

STRAVINSKY—"Le Sacre du Printemps": Jan. 16, 17, 19.
*Suite from "The Firebird": Dec. 12, 13, 14, 15.

TAYLOR—The White Knight, from the Suite, "Through the Looking Glass": Mar. 15.

TCHAIKOVSKY—Concerto No. 1 for Piano and Orchestra, B-flat minor, Opus 23: Dec. 21.
Concerto for Violin and Orchestra, D major, Opus 35: Mar. 27, 28, 30.
Marche Slave, Opus 31: Oct. 13.
"1812 Overture," Opus 49: Dec. 21; Apr. 22.
*Overture-Fantasy, "Romeo and Juliet": Dec. 21; Apr. 22.
Suite No. 1 from "The Nutcracker": Dec. 21.
Symphony No. 4, F minor, Opus 36: Apr. 10, 11, 12.
*Symphony No. 5, E minor, Opus 64: Mar. 29.
*Symphony No. 6, B minor, Opus 74 ("Pathétique"): Oct. 12.

TURNER—Encounter: Feb. 6 (d), 7.

VAUGHAN WILLIAMS—Fantasia on a Theme of Thomas Tallis for Double String Orchestra: Feb. 8.
*Symphony No. 4, F minor: Oct. 13.

VERDI—Overture, "I Vespri Siciliani": Mar. 16.

VILLA-LOBOS—Memories of Youth: Nov. 2 (d).

VIVALDI—Concerto, G minor: Oct. 12, 13.

WAGNER—*Overture, "Tannhaeuser": Oct. 17, 18.
*Prelude, "Die Meistersinger": Nov. 7, 8, 9, 10.
Siegfried Idyl: Feb. 26.

WEBER—Overture, "Euryanthe": Mar. 30.
*Overture, "Der Freischuetz": Dec. 22; Mar. 10.

WEBERN—Six Pieces for Orchestra, Opus 6: Jan. 16, 17, 19.

SOLOISTS

PIANO

JACQUES ABRAM: Mar. 1.
LEONARD BERNSTEIN: Jan. 2, 3, 5; Apr. 2.
JORGE BOLET: Jan. 16, 17, 19.
ALDO CICCOLINI: Nov. 14, 15, 17.
PHILIPPE ENTREMONT: Jan. 4.
RUDOLF FIRKUSNY: Feb. 15, 16, 18.

ARTHUR GOLD and ROBERT FIZDALE: Feb. 27, 28; Mar. 2.
GLENN GOULD: Mar. 13, 14, 16.
LEONID HAMBRO: Nov. 30; Apr. 22.
MYRA HESS: Mar. 20, 21, 23.
LILIAN KALLIR: Oct. 12; Dec. 3.
LOUIS KENTNER: Oct. 17, 18, 20.
ANTON KUERTI: Oct. 27.

EUGENE LIST: Dec. 21.

GUIOMAR NOVAES: Nov. 28, 29; Dec. 1.

BRUCE PRINCE-JOSEPH: Mar. 27, 28, 30.

ARTUR RUBINSTEIN: Apr. 17, 18.

RUDOLF SERKIN: Feb. 6, 7, 8, 9.

CLAUDETTE SOREL: Feb. 22.

ANDRE TCHAIKOWSKY: Oct. 13; Nov. 21, 22.

VIOLIN

JOHN CORIGLIANO: Apr. 12, 13.

MISCHA ELMAN: Jan. 9, 10, 11, 12.

JOSEPH FUCHS: Feb. 20, 21, 23.

LEONID KOGAN: Jan. 30, 31; Feb. 2.

JOHANNA MARTZY: Nov. 9, 10.

YEHUDI MENUHIN: Dec. 12, 13, 14, 15.

NATHAN MILSTEIN: Mar. 27, 28, 30.

ISAAC STERN: Jan. 23, 24, 26.

VIOLA

LILLIAN FUCHS: Feb. 20, 21, 23.

WILLIAM LINCER: Jan. 2, 3, 4, 5.

VIOLONCELLO

JOSEPH SCHUSTER: Mar. 29.

LASZLO VARGA: Jan. 2, 3, 4, 5; Feb. 27, 28; Mar. 1, 22.

HARPSICHORD

SYLVIA MARLOWE: Mar. 27, 28, 30.

HARP

CHRISTINE STAVRACHE: Mar. 27, 28, 30.

VOICE

ADELE ADDISON, soprano: Apr. 3, 4, 6, 24, 25, 27.

LORENZO ALVARY, bass-baritone: Apr. 24, 25, 27.

FRANCES BIBLE, mezzo-soprano: Apr. 24, 25, 27.

INGE BORKH, soprano: Mar. 6, 7, 9.

THOMAS FISHER, bass: Mar. 6, 7, 9.

MAUREEN FORRESTER, contralto: Nov. 14, 15, 16, 17.

MACK HARRELL, baritone: Apr. 3, 4, 6.

JUNE KELLY, soprano: Mar. 6, 7, 9.

DAVID LLOYD, tenor: Mar. 6, 7, 9; Apr. 24, 25, 27.

MARGERY MAYER, contralto: Mar. 6, 7, 9.

MARJORIE MCCLUNG, soprano: Mar. 6, 7, 9.

JOHN MCCOLLUM, tenor: Apr. 3, 4, 6.

LOUISE NATALE, soprano: Apr. 3, 4, 6.

LEONTYNE PRICE, soprano: Apr. 24, 25, 27.

LIZABETH PRITCHETT, mezzo-soprano: Mar. 6, 7, 9.

EVELYN SACHS, mezzo-soprano: Mar. 6, 7, 9.

BIDU SAYAO, soprano: Nov. 14, 15, 16, 17.

ELISABETH SCHWARZKOPF, soprano: Dec. 5, 6, 8.

BLANCHE THEBOM, mezzo-soprano: Mar. 6, 7, 9.

JENNIE TOUREL, mezzo-soprano: Jan. 25, 26.

GIORGIO TOZZI, bass: Mar. 6, 7, 9.

PAUL UKENA, baritone: Apr. 3, 4, 6.

FRANCES YEEND, soprano: Mar. 6, 7, 9.

NARRATOR

FELICIA MONTEALEGRE: Apr. 24, 25, 27.

CARL SANDBURG: Mar. 15.

MARTIAL SINGHER: Apr. 24, 25, 27.

BARBARA WOODS: Nov. 2.

CHORUS

COLUMBUS BOYCHOIR, Princeton, N. J., Directed and Trained by Paul Ziegler: Apr. 24, 25, 27.

ROBERT SHAW CHORALE: Apr. 3, 4, 6.

WOMEN'S CHORUS from the WESTMINSTER CHOIR, Dr. John Finley Williamson, Director: Nov. 14, 15, 16, 17.

THE WESTMINSTER CHOIR, Warren Martin, Director: Apr. 24, 25, 27.

●

LATIN-AMERICAN TOUR 1958

Conductors

Leonard Bernstein

Apr. 29	Panama City	May 7	Medellín
Apr. 30	Caracas	May 8	Cali
May 1	Caracas	May 9	Guayaquil
May 2	Caracas	May 11	Quito
May 3	Maracaibo	May 12	Lima
May 5	Bogotá	May 13	Lima
May 6	Bogotá	May 15	La Paz
		May 16	La Paz

May 17	Asunción	**Dimitri Mitropoulos**	
May 18	Asunción	May 31	Buenos Aires
May 20	Santiago	June 1	Montevideo
May 21	Viña del Mar	June 2	Buenos Aires
May 22	Santiago	June 3	Pôrto Alegre
May 23	Santiago	June 5	São Paulo
May 24	Mendoza	June 6	São Paulo
May 26	Montevideo	June 7	São Paulo (aft.)
May 27	Montevideo	June 7	São Paulo (eve.)
May 28	Buenos Aires	June 9	Rio de Janeiro
May 29	Córdoba	June 10	Rio de Janeiro
June 11	Rio de Janeiro	June 15	Mexico City
June 14	Mexico City		

SOLOIST—LATIN-AMERICAN TOUR

LEONARD BERNSTEIN, Piano: Apr. 29, 30; May 5, 8, 11, 12, 18, 23, 26, 28.

COMPOSITIONS PERFORMED—LATIN-AMERICAN TOUR

BARBER—Medea's Meditation and Dance of Vengeance: May 31; June 1, 3, 5, 10, 15.

BEETHOVEN—Symphony No. 2: May 31; June 1, 6, 10, 15.

BRAHMS—Academic Festival Overture: May 13, 28; June 1, 6, 7 (aft.), 11.
Symphony No. 2: May 22; June 6.
Symphony No. 3: June 3, 5.

CHAVEZ—Sinfonía India: May 2, 3, 6, 8†, 12†, 16, 22, 27†; June 11, 14.

COPLAND—Third Symphony: Apr. 29, 30; May 5, 11, 12, 18, 23, 26.

FALLA—"Three-Cornered Hat" Finale: May 31†; June 1†, 3†, 5†, 7 (aft.), 10†, 15†.

GERSHWIN—An American in Paris: May 1, 3, 6, 7, 9, 15, 17, 21, 22, 27; June 11, 14.

GINASTERA—Overture to the Creole Faust: May 31.

GUARNIERI—Prologo e Fuga: June 3, 5, 9.

HARRIS—Symphony No. 3: May 1, 3, 6, 7, 8, 9, 15, 17, 20, 24, 27, 28, 29; June 14.

HAYDN—Symphony No. 104 ("London"): May 1, 3, 7, 9, 11, 12, 15, 17, 20, 21, 24, 27, 29.

MENDELSSOHN—Symphony No. 4 ("Italian"): Apr. 29, 30; May 5, 7 (fourth movement)†, 16, 18, 23, 26.

PROKOFIEFF—Symphony No. 5: June 2, 7 (eve.), 9.

RAVEL—La Valse: May 1, 3, 7, 9, 13†, 15, 17, 22, 27; June 14†.
Piano Concerto: Apr. 29, 30; May 5, 8, 11, 12, 18, 23, 26, 28.

SCHOENBERG—Verklaerte Nacht: May 31; June 1, 3, 5, 10.

SCHUMAN—Symphony No. 6: May 2, 13.

STRAUSS—Don Juan: June 2, 7 (aft.), 7 (eve.), 9, 15.

TCHAIKOVSKY—Symphony No. 4: May 2, 6, 8, 11 (third movement)†, 13, 16, 20, 21, 24, 28, 29; June 11, 14.

TURNER—Encounter: June 2, 7 (aft.), 7 (eve.), 9.

VERDI—"Forza del Destino" Overture: June 2†, 6†, 7 (aft.), 15.
"Sicilian Vespers" Overture: June 7 (eve.)†.

WEBER—"Der Freischuetz" Overture: June 2, 7 (aft.), 7 (eve.), 10, 15.

National Anthems of Argentina, Bolivia, Brazil, Chile, Colombia, Ecuador, Panama, Paraguay, Peru, the United States, Uruguay, and Venezuela.

---

† As encore.

1958–59 ONE HUNDRED SEVENTEENTH SEASON

LEONARD BERNSTEIN, *Music Director*

Guest Conductors

SIR JOHN BARBIROLLI, HERBERT VON KARAJAN, PIERRE MONTEUX, JEAN MOREL
PAUL PARAY, THOMAS SCHIPPERS

Music Director, Young People's Concerts: LEONARD BERNSTEIN

Associate Conductor	*Three Special Sunday Nights*
FRANCO AUTORI	ANDRE KOSTELANETZ

CONCERTS

1958

Leonard Bernstein

Oct.	2—Eve.	Carnegie Hall
Oct.	3—Aft.	Carnegie Hall
Oct.	4—Eve.	Carnegie Hall
Oct.	5—Aft.	Carnegie Hall
Oct.	9—Eve.	Carnegie Hall
Oct.	10—Aft.	Carnegie Hall
Oct.	11—Eve.	Carnegie Hall
Oct.	12—Aft.	Carnegie Hall
Oct.	16—Eve.	Carnegie Hall
Oct.	17—Aft.	Carnegie Hall
Oct.	18—Eve.	Carnegie Hall
Oct.	19—Aft.	Carnegie Hall
Oct.	23—Eve.	Carnegie Hall
Oct.	24—Aft.	Carnegie Hall
Oct.	25—Eve.	Carnegie Hall
Oct.	26—Aft.	Carnegie Hall

Thomas Schippers

Oct.	30—Eve.	Carnegie Hall
Oct.	31—Aft.	Carnegie Hall
*Nov.	1—Noon	Carnegie Hall
Nov.	1—Eve.	Carnegie Hall
Nov.	2—Aft.	Carnegie Hall
Nov.	6—Eve.	Carnegie Hall
Nov.	7—Aft.	Carnegie Hall
Nov.	8—Eve.	Carnegie Hall
Nov.	9—Aft.	Carnegie Hall

Herbert von Karajan

Nov.	13—Eve.	Carnegie Hall
Nov.	14—Aft.	Carnegie Hall
Nov.	15—Eve.	Carnegie Hall
Nov.	16—Aft.	Carnegie Hall
Nov.	20—Eve.	Carnegie Hall
Nov.	21—Aft.	Carnegie Hall
Nov.	22—Eve.	Carnegie Hall
Nov.	23—Aft.	Carnegie Hall

Leonard Bernstein

Nov.	27—Eve.	Carnegie Hall
Nov.	28—Aft.	Carnegie Hall

1958

Nov.	29—Eve.	Carnegie Hall
Nov.	30—Aft.	Carnegie Hall
Dec.	4—Eve.	Carnegie Hall
Dec.	5—Aft.	Carnegie Hall
Dec.	6—Eve.	Carnegie Hall
Dec.	7—Aft.	Carnegie Hall
Dec.	10—Eve.	United Nations, N. Y.
Dec.	11—Eve.	Carnegie Hall
Dec.	12—Aft.	Carnegie Hall
**Dec.	13—Noon	Carnegie Hall
Dec.	13—Eve.	Carnegie Hall
Dec.	14—Aft.	Carnegie Hall
Dec.	18—Eve.	Carnegie Hall
Dec.	19—Aft.	Carnegie Hall
Dec.	20—Eve.	Carnegie Hall
Dec.	21—Aft.	Carnegie Hall

André Kostelanetz

Dec.	21—Eve.	Carnegie Hall

1959

Sir John Barbirolli

Jan.	1—Eve.	Carnegie Hall
Jan.	2—Aft.	Carnegie Hall
Jan.	3—Eve.	Carnegie Hall
Jan.	4—Aft.	Carnegie Hall
Jan.	8—Eve.	Carnegie Hall
Jan.	9—Aft.	Carnegie Hall
Jan.	10—Eve.	Carnegie Hall
Jan.	11—Aft.	Carnegie Hall
Jan.	15—Eve.	Carnegie Hall
Jan.	16—Aft.	Carnegie Hall
Jan.	17—Eve.	Carnegie Hall
Jan.	18—Aft.	Carnegie Hall
Jan.	22—Eve.	Carnegie Hall
Jan.	23—Aft.	Carnegie Hall
**Jan.	24—Noon	Carnegie Hall
Jan.	24—Eve.	Carnegie Hall
Jan.	25—Aft.	Carnegie Hall

Leonard Bernstein

Jan.	29—Eve.	Carnegie Hall
Jan.	30—Aft.	Carnegie Hall

* Young People's Concert, conducted by Thomas Schippers.
** Young People's Concert, conducted by Leonard Bernstein.

1959

Jan. 31—Eve.	Carnegie Hall
Feb. 1—Aft.	Carnegie Hall
Feb. 5—Eve.	Carnegie Hall
Feb. 6—Aft.	Carnegie Hall
Feb. 7—Eve.	Carnegie Hall
Feb. 8—Aft.	Carnegie Hall

André Kostelanetz

Feb. 8—Eve.	Carnegie Hall

Leonard Bernstein

Feb. 12—Eve.	Carnegie Hall
Feb. 13—Aft.	Carnegie Hall
Feb. 14—Eve.	Carnegie Hall
Feb. 15—Aft.	Carnegie Hall
Feb. 17—Eve.	Carnegie Hall
	(Pension Fund Benefit)
Feb. 19—Eve.	Carnegie Hall
Feb. 20—Aft.	Carnegie Hall
Feb. 21—Eve.	Carnegie Hall
Feb. 22—Aft.	Carnegie Hall

Pierre Monteux

Feb. 26—Eve.	Carnegie Hall
Feb. 27—Aft.	Carnegie Hall
**Feb. 28—Noon	Carnegie Hall
Feb. 28—Eve.	Carnegie Hall
Mar. 1—Aft.	Carnegie Hall
Mar. 5—Eve.	Carnegie Hall
Mar. 6—Aft.	Carnegie Hall
Mar. 7—Eve.	Carnegie Hall
Mar. 8—Aft.	Carnegie Hall

Jean Morel

Mar. 12—Eve.	Carnegie Hall
Mar. 13—Aft.	Carnegie Hall
Mar. 14—Eve.	Carnegie Hall
Mar. 15—Aft.	Carnegie Hall

1959

Paul Paray

Mar. 19—Eve.	Carnegie Hall
Mar. 20—Aft.	Carnegie Hall
Mar. 21—Eve.	Carnegie Hall
Mar. 22—Aft.	Carnegie Hall

André Kostelanetz

Mar. 22—Eve.	Carnegie Hall

Leonard Bernstein

Mar. 26—Eve.	Carnegie Hall
Mar. 27—Aft.	Carnegie Hall
**Mar. 28—Noon	Carnegie Hall
Mar. 28—Eve.	Carnegie Hall
Mar. 29—Aft.	Carnegie Hall
Mar. 31—Eve.	Englewood, N. J.
Apr. 2—Eve.	Carnegie Hall
Apr. 3—Aft.	Carnegie Hall
Apr. 4—Eve.	Carnegie Hall
Apr. 5—Aft.	Carnegie Hall
Apr. 8—Eve.	Carnegie Hall
	(Pension Fund Benefit)
Apr. 9—Eve.	Carnegie Hall
Apr. 10—Aft.	Carnegie Hall
Apr. 11—Eve.	Carnegie Hall
Apr. 12—Aft.	Carnegie Hall
Apr. 16—Eve.	Carnegie Hall
Apr. 17—Aft.	Carnegie Hall
Apr. 18—Eve.	Carnegie Hall
Apr. 19—Aft.	Carnegie Hall
Apr. 23—Eve.	Carnegie Hall
Apr. 24—Aft.	Carnegie Hall
Apr. 25—Eve.	Carnegie Hall
Apr. 26—Aft.	Carnegie Hall
Apr. 30—Eve.	Carnegie Hall
May 1—Aft.	Carnegie Hall
May 2—Eve.	Carnegie Hall
May 3—Aft.	Carnegie Hall

FALL TOUR

Leonard Bernstein

Sept. 24—Eve.	Springfield, Mass.	Sept. 26—Eve.	Boston, Mass.
Sept. 25—Eve.	Hartford, Conn.	Sept. 27—Eve.	Providence, R. I.
		Sept. 28—Aft.	Washington, D. C.

REPERTOIRE FOR 1958–59

(a) World premiere.
(b) First performance in the United States.
(c) First performance in New York.

Compositions marked with an asterisk (*) are recorded by
the New York Philharmonic on Columbia Records

ARNOLD—"Tam o'Shanter" Overture: Jan. 4 (c).

BACH—Cantata, "Jauchzet Gott in allen Landen," for Solo Soprano and Orchestra: Dec. 18, 19, 20, 21.
Concerto No. 1 in D minor for Piano and Orchestra: Dec. 18, 19, 20, 21.

** Young People's Concert, conducted by Leonard Bernstein.

Concerto No. 7 in G minor for Piano and Orchestra: Dec. 18, 19, 20, 21.
Concerto for Violin and Orchestra, D minor: Mar. 5, 6, 7.
Magnificat in D major: Dec. 18, 19, 20, 21.

BARBER—Concerto for Violoncello and Orchestra, Opus 22: Jan. 29, 30, 31.

BARBIROLLI—Elizabethan Suite (From the Fitzwilliam Virginal Book): Jan. 8, 9, 10, 11.

BECKER—"Symphonia Brevis" (No. 3): Oct. 16, 17, 18, 19.

BEETHOVEN—Concerto No. 3 for Piano and Orchestra, C minor, Opus 37: Dec. 4, 5, 6; Apr. 5.
Concerto No. 5 for Piano and Orchestra, E-flat major, Opus 73 ("Emperor"): Oct. 26; Feb. 26, 27, 28; Mar. 1.
Concerto for Violin and Orchestra, D major, Opus 61: Apr. 16, 17, 18, 19.
*Overture, "Leonore," No. 3: Dec. 10; Feb. 19, 20, 21; Mar. 31.
*Symphony No. 1, C major, Opus 21: Nov. 20, 21, 22, 23.
*Symphony No. 7, A major, Opus 92: Sept. 24, 27, 28; Oct. 2, 3, 4, 5.
*Symphony No. 9, D minor, Opus 125, with Final Chorus on Schiller's "Ode to Joy": Nov. 20, 21, 22, 23.

BEGLARIAN—Diversions for Orchestra: Apr. 12 (a).

BEN-HAIM—The Sweet Psalmist of Israel: Apr. 23 (b), 24, 25, 26.

BERLIOZ—Overture, "Roman Carnival," Opus 9: Sept. 24, 25, 26, 27, 28; Mar. 19, 20, 21, 22.
Rêverie et Caprice, Opus 8, for Violin and Orchestra: Mar. 5, 6, 7.
*Symphonie Fantastique, C major, Opus 14: Feb. 26, 27, 28; Mar. 1.

BRAHMS—Concerto No. 1 for Piano and Orchestra, D minor, Opus 15: Feb. 1.
Concerto No. 2 for Piano and Orchestra, B-flat major, Opus 83: Jan. 1, 2, 3, 4.
Concerto for Violin and Orchestra, D major, Opus 77: Jan. 15, 16, 17, 18.
*Symphony No. 1, C minor, Opus 68: Apr. 30; May 1, 2, 3.
*Symphony No. 2, D major, Opus 73: Nov. 6, 7, 8, 9.

BRITTEN—Scottish Ballad: Dec. 21 (eve.).

CASELLA—"Paganiniana," Divertimento on Themes of Paganini, Opus 65: Nov. 6, 7, 8, 9.

CHABRIER—Bourrée Fantasque: Mar. 19, 20, 21, 22.

CHADWICK—"Melpomene," Dramatic Overture: Oct. 23, 24, 25, 26.

CHOPIN—Concerto No. 2 for Piano and Orchestra, F minor, Opus 21: Oct. 9, 10, 11, 12.

COPLAND—Music for the Theatre: Dec. 4, 5, 6, 7.
Orchestral Variations: Dec. 4 (c), 5, 6.

COUPERIN-MILHAUD—Prelude and Allegro, "La Sultane": Feb. 26, 27, 28; Mar. 1.

CRESTON—"Frontiers," Opus 34: Dec. 21 (eve.).

DEBUSSY—Images pour Orchestre: Oct. 23, 24, 25, 26.
"Pelléas et Mélisande" (Concert Version): Mar. 12, 13, 14, 15.
Prelude, "L'Après-midi d'un Faune": Mar. 8.

DVORAK—Concerto for Violoncello and Orchestra, B minor, Opus 104: Dec. 7.
*Symphony No. 4, G major, Opus 88: Jan. 4.

ELGAR—"The Dream of Gerontius": Jan. 22, 23, 24, 25.
Introduction and Allegro for Strings (Quartet and Orchestra), Opus 47: Jan. 1, 2, 3.

FAURE—"Pelléas et Mélisande," Incidental Music: Mar. 19, 20, 21, 22.

FINE—"Serious Song," A Lament for String Orchestra: Apr. 16, 17, 18, 19.

FOOTE—"A Night Piece" for Flute and Strings: Oct. 23, 24, 25.

FOSS—Symphony of Chorales: Apr. 9 (c), 10, 11, 12.

FRANCK—Symphony in D minor: Jan. 29, 30, 31.

GABURO—Elegy: Apr. 2 (a), 3, 4, 5.

GERSHWIN—An American in Paris: Dec. 11, 12, 13, 14.
Rhapsody in Blue: Dec. 11, 12, 13, 14.

GILBERT—Comedy Overture on Negro Themes: Oct. 9, 10, 11, 12.

GROFE—"Mississippi" Suite: Dec. 21 (eve.).

HANDEL—Concerto for Harpsichord and Orchestra, F major ("The Cuckoo and the Nightingale"): Apr. 9, 10, 11.
Concerto for Harpsichord and Orchestra, G minor, Opus 4, No. 1: Apr. 23, 24, 25, 26.
Concerto for Organ and Orchestra, F major, Opus 4, No. 5: Mar. 26, 27, 28, 29.
Concerto Grosso, B minor, Opus 6, No. 12: Apr. 2, 3, 4, 5.
Ode for Saint Cecilia's Day: Apr. 30; May 1, 2, 3.
The Passion According to Saint John: Mar. 26, 27, 28, 29.

HARRIS—American Creed: Feb. 5, 6, 7.
American Overture, "When Johnny Comes Marching Home": Feb. 8.

HAYDN—Sinfonia Concertante in B-flat major, Opus 84, for Violin, Violoncello, Oboe, Bassoon and Orchestra: Jan. 29, 30, 31; Feb. 1; Mar. 31.
Symphony No. 88, G major: Jan. 8, 9, 10.

HOLST—Five Movements from "The Planets": Jan. 15, 16, 17, 18.

d'INDY—Prelude to "Fervaal": Mar. 8.

IVES—Symphony No. 2: Sept. 24, 25, 26, 27, 28; Oct. 2, 3, 4, 5.

LEHAR—"The Merry Widow," Suite for Orchestra: Dec. 21 (eve.).

LISZT—Concerto No. 1 for Piano and Orchestra, E-flat major: Oct. 30, 31; Nov. 1, 2.
Hungarian Fantasy for Piano and Orchestra: Oct. 30, 31; Nov. 1, 2.

MacDOWELL—Indian Suite No. 2 in E minor (Nos. 1, 4, 5): Oct. 9, 10, 11, 12.

MAHLER—*Symphony No. 1, D major: Jan. 8, 9, 10, 11.

MENDELSSOHN—Concerto for Violin and Orchestra, E minor, Opus 64: Dec. 11, 12, 13, 14.

MILHAUD—"La Création du Monde": Dec. 11, 12, 13, 14.

MOUSSORGSKY-RAVEL—Pictures at an Exhibition: Oct. 9, 10, 11, 12.

MOZART—Concerto No. 21 for Piano and Orchestra, C major, K. 467: Apr. 9, 10, 11, 12.
Concerto No. 24 for Piano and Orchestra, C minor, K. 491: April 2, 3, 4.
Concerto No. 25 for Piano and Orchestra, C major, K. 503: Feb. 17.
Overture, "The Marriage of Figaro": Dec. 21 (eve.).
*Symphony No. 41, C major, K. 551 ("Jupiter"): Nov. 13, 14, 15, 16.

PAGANINI—Concerto No. 1 for Violin and Orchestra, D major, Opus 6: Nov. 6, 7, 8.

PISTON—Concerto for Orchestra: Feb. 12, 13, 14, 15.

PROKOFIEFF—Concerto No. 2 for Piano and Orchestra, G minor, Opus 16: Nov. 27, 28, 29, 30.
Concerto No. 3 for Piano and Orchestra, C major, Opus 26, Feb. 17.
Symphony No. 5, B-flat major, Opus 100: Dec. 7, 10.

PUCCINI—"Mi chiamano Mimi" from "La Bohème": Dec. 10.

RACHMANINOFF—Concerto No. 2 for Piano and Orchestra, C minor, Opus 18: Feb. 8 (eve.).
Concerto No. 3 for Piano and Orchestra, C major, Opus 26: Feb. 17.
Second Movement (Allegro molto) from Symphony No. 2, E minor, Opus 27: Feb. 8 (eve.).
Vocalise, Opus 34, No. 14: Feb. 8 (eve.).

RAVEL—"Daphnis et Chloé," Suites Nos. 1 and 2: Mar. 5, 6, 7, 8.
*Rapsodie Espagnole: Mar. 5, 6, 7.
"Shéhérazade," Three Poems for Voice and Orchestra to Verses of Tristan Klingsor: Feb. 12, 13, 14.
Suite, "Le Tombeau de Couperin": Mar. 5, 6, 7, 8.
*"La Valse," Choreographic Poem for Orchestra: Mar. 19, 20, 21, 22.
RIEGGER—Music for Orchestra, Opus 50: Oct. 16, 17, 18, 19.
RIMSKY-KORSAKOFF—Capriccio Espagnol: Dec. 21 (eve.); Apr. 23, 24, 25, 26.
"Scheherazade," Symphonic Suite, Opus 35: Feb. 12, 13, 14, 15.
RODGERS—Selections from "Flower Drum Song": Feb. 8 (eve.).
ROREM—Symphony No. 3: Apr. 16 (a), 17, 18, 19.
ROSSINI—Overture, "The Siege of Corinth": Oct. 30, 31; Nov. 1, 2.
RUGGLES—Men and Mountains: Oct. 16, 17, 18, 19.
RUSSO—Symphony No. 2 in C—"Titans": Apr. 16 (a), 17, 18, 19.
SAINT-SAENS—Concerto No. 2 for Piano and Orchestra, G minor, Opus 22: Mar. 8.
Symphony No. 3, C minor, Opus 78: Mar. 19, 20, 21, 22.
SCHUMAN—American Festival Overture: Oct. 2, 3, 4, 5.
SCHUMANN—Concerto for Piano and Orchestra, A minor, Opus 54: Oct. 23, 24, 25; Feb. 17, 22.
Concerto for Violoncello and Orchestra, A minor, Opus 129: Feb. 5, 6, 7.
Symphony No. 4, D minor, Opus 120: Nov. 27, 28, 29, 30.
SESSIONS—Concerto for Violin and Orchestra: Feb. 19 (c), 20, 21.
SHOSTAKOVICH—*Symphony No. 5, Opus 47: Feb. 5, 6, 7, 8; Mar. 31.
STRAUSS, Richard—*Dance of the Seven Veils, "Salome": Feb. 8 (eve.).
Tone Poem, "Ein Heldenleben," Opus 40: Nov. 13, 14, 15, 16.
Tone Poem, "Till Eulenspiegel's Merry Pranks," Opus 28: Apr. 2, 3, 4, 5.
*Waltzes from "Der Rosenkavalier": Feb. 8 (eve.).
STRAVINSKY—Concerto for Piano and Wind Orchestra (with Double-Basses and Timpani): Feb. 8.
*Suite from "The Firebird": Oct. 30, 31; Nov. 1, 2.
TCHAIKOVSKY—Barcarolle ("June") from "The Months," Opus 37-A: Mar. 22 (eve.).
Concerto No. 1 for Piano and Orchestra, B-flat minor, Opus 23: Feb. 15.
Symphonic Fantasy, "Francesca da Rimini," Opus 32: Mar. 22 (eve.).
Pas de Deux and Valse-Finale from "The Nutcracker": Mar. 22 (eve.).
*Symphony No. 4, F minor, Opus 36: Sept. 25, 26.
*Symphony No. 5, E minor, Opus 64: Feb. 19, 20, 21, 22; Mar. 22 (eve.).
Three Waltzes (Valse Sentimentale, Opus 51, No. 6; Valse in E-flat major, Opus 39, No. 8; Loin du Bal, Opus 38, No. 3): Mar. 22 (eve.).
THOMSON—Suite, "The Mother of Us All": Feb. 22.
THOMPSON—Symphony No. 2, E minor: Feb. 1.
VARESE—Arcana: Nov. 27, 28, 29, 30.
VAUGHAN WILLIAMS—Symphony No. 8, D minor: Jan. 1, 2, 3.
VERDI—"Pace, pace, mio Dio," from "La Forza del Destino": Dec. 10.
VIVALDI—Concerto in C minor for Flute, Strings and Cembalo, F. VI, No. 11: Dec. 11, 12, 13.
Concerto in D minor for Oboe, Strings and Cembalo, F. VII, No. 1: Dec. 4, 5, 6.
Concerto in C major for Piccolo, Strings and Cembalo, F. VI, No. 4: Dec. 14.
Concerto in C major for Strings, Cembalo and Two Mandolins: Nov. 27, 28, 29, 30.

WAGNER—Overture, "Tannhäuser": Apr. 9, 10, 11, 12.
WALTON—Concerto for Violin and Orchestra: Jan. 11.
WEBER—Konzertstück for Piano and Orchestra, F minor, Opus 79: Feb. 8.
*Overture, "Der Freischütz": Jan. 15, 16, 17, 18.
WEBERN—Five Movements for String Orchestra, Opus 5: Nov. 13, 14, 15, 16.
WIENIAWSKI—Concerto No. 2 for Violin and Orchestra, D minor, Opus 22: Nov. 9; Apr. 23, 24, 25, 26.
ZAFRED—Symphony No. 4 ("In Honor of the Resistance"): Oct. 30 (b), 31; Nov. 1, 2.

SOLOISTS

PIANO

CLAUDIO ARRAU: Dec. 4, 5, 6.
VLADIMIR ASHKENAZY: Nov. 27, 28, 29, 30.
GINA BACHAUER: Jan. 1, 2, 3, 4.
LEONARD BERNSTEIN: Dec. 11, 12, 13, 14.
VAN CLIBURN: Oct. 16, 17, 18, 19; Feb. 17.
GYORGY CZIFFRA: Oct. 30, 31; Nov. 1, 2.
LUKAS FOSS: Apr. 9, 10, 11, 12.
GLENN GOULD: Apr. 2, 3, 4, 5.
GARY GRAFFMAN: Feb. 15.
EUGENE ISTOMIN: Oct. 23, 24, 25.
JACOB LATEINER: Feb. 22.
SEYMOUR LIPKIN: Feb. 8.
LEE LUVISI: Oct. 26.
WILLIAM MASSELOS: Mar. 8.
GUIOMAR NOVAES: Oct. 9, 10, 11, 12.
LEONARD PENNARIO: Feb. 8 (Eve.).
RUDOLF SERKIN: Feb. 26, 27, 28; Mar. 1.
RUSSELL SHERMAN: Feb. 1.
ROSALYN TURECK: Dec. 18, 19, 20, 21.
ARTHUR WHITTEMORE & JACK LOWE: Dec. 21 (Eve.).

VIOLIN

JACK BENNY: Apr. 8 (Pension Fund Benefit Concert).
JOHN CORIGLIANO: Jan. 11.
JOHANNA MARTZY: Dec. 11, 12, 13, 14.
ERICA MORINI: Apr. 23, 24, 25, 26.
RUGGIERO RICCI: Nov. 6, 7, 8.
BERL SENOFSKY: Jan. 15, 16, 17, 18.
TOSSY SPIVAKOVSKY: Feb. 19, 20, 21.
ARNOLD STEINHARDT: Nov. 9.
ISAAC STERN: Apr. 16, 17, 18, 19.
JOSEPH SZIGETI: Mar. 5, 6, 7.

VIOLONCELLO

MAURICE GENDRON: Feb. 5, 6, 7.
LEONARD ROSE: Jan. 29, 30, 31.
LASZLO VARGA: Dec. 7.

FLUTE

JOHN WUMMER: Oct. 23, 24, 25; Dec. 11, 12, 13.

OBOE

HAROLD GOMBERG: Dec. 4, 5, 6.

PICCOLO

F. WILLIAM HEIM: Dec. 14.

HARPSICHORD

LUKAS FOSS: Apr. 9, 10, 11.
SYLVIA MARLOWE: Apr. 23, 24, 25, 26.

ORGAN

BRUCE PRINCE-JOSEPH: Mar. 26, 27, 28, 29.

VOICE

ADELE ADDISON, soprano: Apr. 30; May 1, 2, 3.
MILDRED ALLEN, soprano: Mar. 12, 13, 14, 15.
PHYLLIS CURTIN, soprano: Mar. 12, 13, 14, 15.
NORMAN FARROW, baritone: Dec. 18, 19, 20, 21; Mar. 26, 27, 28, 29.
MAUREEN FORRESTER, contralto: Nov. 20, 21, 22, 23; Jan. 22, 23, 24, 25.
NICOLAI GEDDA, tenor: Mar. 12, 13, 14, 15.
MARGARET KALIL, soprano: Mar. 26, 27, 28, 29.
FLORENCE KOPLEFF, contralto: Dec. 18, 19, 20, 21.
RICHARD LEWIS, tenor: Jan. 22, 23, 24, 25.
DAVID LLOYD, tenor: Mar. 26, 27, 28, 29.
CALVIN MARSH, baritone: Mar. 12, 13, 14, 15.
JOHN MCCOLLUM, tenor: Apr. 30; May 1, 2, 3.
MORLEY MEREDITH, baritone: Jan. 22, 23, 24, 25; Mar. 26, 27, 28, 29.
RUSSELL OBERLIN, countertenor: Dec. 18, 19, 20, 21.

JAN PEERCE, tenor: Dec. 18, 19, 20, 21.

LEONTYNE PRICE, soprano: Nov. 20, 21, 22, 23.

REGINA RESNIK, mezzo-soprano: Mar. 12, 13, 14, 15.

NORMAN SCOTT, bass-baritone: Nov. 20, 21, 22, 23.

LEOPOLD SIMONEAU, tenor: Nov. 20, 21, 22, 23.

MARTIAL SINGHER, baritone: Mar. 12, 13, 14, 15.

KENNETH SMITH, bass: Mar. 12, 13, 14, 15.

MARIA STADER, soprano: Dec. 18, 19, 20, 21.

RENATA TEBALDI, soprano: Dec. 10.

JENNIE TOUREL, mezzo-soprano: Feb. 12, 13, 14.

ROBERT WHITE, countertenor: Mar. 26, 27, 28, 29.

CHORUS

RUTGERS UNIVERSITY CHOIR, F. Austin Walter, Director: Apr. 30; May 1, 2, 3.

SCHOLA CANTORUM, Hugh Ross, Director: Dec. 18, 19, 20, 21; Mar. 26, 27, 28, 29.

WESTMINSTER CHOIR, Warren Martin, Director: Nov. 20, 21, 22, 23; Jan. 22, 23, 24, 25.

1959–60 ONE HUNDRED EIGHTEENTH SEASON

LEONARD BERNSTEIN, *Music Director*

Guest Conductors
ELEAZAR DE CARVALHO, PAUL HINDEMITH,
DIMITRI MITROPOULOS, FRITZ REINER, THOMAS SCHIPPERS,
LEOPOLD STOKOWSKI, BRUNO WALTER

Young People's Concerts
LEONARD BERNSTEIN, *Music Director*
HOWARD SHANET, *Guest Conductor*

Special Holiday Series: ANDRE KOSTELANETZ

Assistant Conductors
SEYMOUR LIPKIN, STEFAN BAUER-MENGELBERG,
KENNETH SCHERMERHORN, ARNOLD GAMSON‡

CONCERTS

1959

André Kostelanetz

June	4—Eve.	Carnegie Hall
		(World Petroleum Congress)

Leonard Bernstein

Oct. 12—Eve.	Washington, D. C.
Oct. 15—Eve.	Carnegie Hall
Oct. 16—Aft.	Carnegie Hall
Oct. 17—Eve.	Carnegie Hall
Oct. 18—Aft.	Carnegie Hall
Oct. 19—Eve.	Springfield, Mass.
Oct. 20—Eve.	Boston, Mass.
Oct. 22—Eve.	Carnegie Hall
Oct. 23—Aft.	Carnegie Hall

1959

Eleazar de Carvalho

Oct. 24—Aft.	United Nations, N. Y.

Leonard Bernstein

Oct. 24—Eve.	Carnegie Hall
Oct. 25—Aft.	Carnegie Hall

Eleazar de Carvalho

Oct. 29—Eve.	Carnegie Hall
Oct. 30—Aft.	Carnegie Hall
Oct. 31—Eve.	Carnegie Hall
Nov. 1—Aft.	Carnegie Hall
Nov. 5—Eve.	Carnegie Hall
Nov. 6—Aft.	Carnegie Hall
Nov. 7—Eve.	Carnegie Hall
Nov. 8—Aft.	Carnegie Hall

‡ Appointed March 22, 1960, succeeding Mr. Schermerhorn.

1959

Thomas Schippers

Nov. 12—Eve.	Carnegie Hall
Nov. 13—Aft.	Carnegie Hall
Nov. 14—Eve.	Carnegie Hall
Nov. 15—Aft.	Carnegie Hall
Nov. 19—Eve.	Carnegie Hall
Nov. 20—Aft.	Carnegie Hall

Howard Shanet

*Nov. 21—Noon	Carnegie Hall

Thomas Schippers

Nov. 21—Eve.	Carnegie Hall
Nov. 22—Aft.	Carnegie Hall

Leonard Bernstein

Nov. 26—Eve.	Carnegie Hall
Nov. 27—Aft.	Carnegie Hall
Nov. 28—Eve.	Carnegie Hall
Nov. 29—Aft.	Carnegie Hall

André Kostelanetz

Nov. 29—Eve.	Carnegie Hall
Dec. 1—Eve.	Garden City, N. Y.

Leonard Bernstein

Dec. 3—Eve.	Carnegie Hall
Dec. 4—Aft.	Carnegie Hall
Dec. 5—Eve.	Carnegie Hall
Dec. 6—Aft.	Carnegie Hall
Dec. 7—Eve.	Worcester, Mass.
Dec. 8—Eve.	Bridgeport, Conn.
Dec. 10—Eve.	Carnegie Hall
Dec. 11—Aft.	Carnegie Hall
Dec. 12—Eve.	Carnegie Hall
Dec. 13—Aft.	Carnegie Hall
Dec. 17—Eve.	Carnegie Hall
Dec. 18—Aft.	Carnegie Hall
Dec. 19—Eve.	Carnegie Hall
Dec. 20—Aft.	Carnegie Hall

André Kostelanetz

Dec. 20—Eve.	Carnegie Hall

Dimitri Mitropoulos

Dec. 31—Eve.	Carnegie Hall

1960

Jan. 1—Aft.	Carnegie Hall
Jan. 2—Eve.	Carnegie Hall
Jan. 3—Aft.	Carnegie Hall
Jan. 7—Eve.	Carnegie Hall
Jan. 8—Aft.	Carnegie Hall
Jan. 9—Eve.	Carnegie Hall
Jan. 10—Aft.	Carnegie Hall
Jan. 14—Eve.	Carnegie Hall

1960

Jan. 15—Aft.	Carnegie Hall
Jan. 16—Eve.	Carnegie Hall
Jan. 17—Aft.	Carnegie Hall
Jan. 21—Eve.	Carnegie Hall
Jan. 22—Aft.	Carnegie Hall

Leonard Bernstein

*Jan. 23—Noon	Carnegie Hall

Dimitri Mitropoulos

Jan. 23—Eve.	Carnegie Hall
Jan. 24—Aft.	Carnegie Hall

Leonard Bernstein

Jan. 28—Eve.	Carnegie Hall
Jan. 29—Aft.	Carnegie Hall
Jan. 30—Eve.	Carnegie Hall
Jan. 31—Aft.	Carnegie Hall
Feb. 4—Eve.	Carnegie Hall
Feb. 5—Aft.	Carnegie Hall
Feb. 6—Eve.	Carnegie Hall
Feb. 7—Aft.	Carnegie Hall
Feb. 11—Eve.	Carnegie Hall
Feb. 12—Aft.	Carnegie Hall
**Feb. 13—Noon	Carnegie Hall
Feb. 13—Eve.	Carnegie Hall
Feb. 14—Aft.	Carnegie Hall
††Feb. 18—Eve.	Carnegie Hall
††Feb. 19—Aft.	Carnegie Hall
††Feb. 20—Eve.	Carnegie Hall
††Feb. 21—Aft.	Carnegie Hall

André Kostelanetz

Feb. 21—Eve.	Carnegie Hall

Paul Hindemith

Feb. 25—Eve.	Carnegie Hall
Feb. 26—Aft.	Carnegie Hall
Feb. 27—Eve.	Carnegie Hall
Feb. 28—Aft.	Carnegie Hall

Leopold Stokowski

Mar. 3—Eve.	Carnegie Hall
Mar. 4—Aft.	Carnegie Hall
Mar. 5—Eve.	Carnegie Hall
Mar. 6—Aft.	Carnegie Hall

Fritz Reiner

Mar. 10—Eve.	Carnegie Hall
Mar. 11—Aft.	Carnegie Hall
Mar. 12—Eve.	Carnegie Hall
Mar. 13—Aft.	Carnegie Hall
Mar. 17—Eve.	Carnegie Hall
Mar. 18—Aft.	Carnegie Hall
Mar. 19—Eve.	Carnegie Hall
Mar. 20—Aft.	Carnegie Hall

* Young People's Concert.
** Young People's Concert, with Seymour Lipkin, Stefan Bauer-Mengelberg and Kenneth Schermerhorn also conducting.
†† Seymour Lipkin also conducting.

1960   1960

Leonard Bernstein		Bruno Walter	
Mar. 24—Eve.	Carnegie Hall	Apr. 21—Eve.	Carnegie Hall
Mar. 25—Aft.	Carnegie Hall	**Leonard Bernstein**	
*Mar. 26—Noon	Carnegie Hall	Apr. 22—Aft.	Carnegie Hall
Mar. 26—Eve.	Carnegie Hall	*Apr. 23—Noon	Carnegie Hall
Mar. 27—Aft.	Carnegie Hall	Apr. 23—Eve.	Carnegie Hall
†Mar. 31—Eve.	Carnegie Hall	**Bruno Walter**	
†Apr. 1—Aft.	Carnegie Hall	Apr. 24—Aft.	Carnegie Hall
†Apr. 2—Eve.	Carnegie Hall	**Leonard Bernstein**	
†Apr. 3—Aft.	Carnegie Hall	Apr. 26—Eve.	Philadelphia, Pa.
Apr. 4—Eve.	Carnegie Hall	Apr. 28—Eve.	Carnegie Hall
	(Pension Fund Benefit)	Apr. 29—Aft.	Carnegie Hall
Apr. 5—Eve.	The White House	Apr. 30—Eve.	Carnegie Hall
Apr. 7—Eve.	Carnegie Hall	May 1—Aft.	Carnegie Hall
Apr. 8—Aft.	Carnegie Hall	May 5—Eve.	Carnegie Hall
Apr. 9—Eve.	Carnegie Hall	May 6—Aft.	Carnegie Hall
Apr. 10—Aft.	Carnegie Hall	May 7—Eve.	Carnegie Hall
Apr. 14—Eve.	Carnegie Hall	May 8—Aft.	Carnegie Hall
Bruno Walter		May 12—Eve.	Carnegie Hall
Apr. 15—Aft.	Carnegie Hall	May 13—Aft.	Carnegie Hall
Apr. 16—Eve.	Carnegie Hall	May 14—Eve.	Carnegie Hall
Leonard Bernstein		May 15—Aft.	Carnegie Hall
Apr. 17—Aft.	Carnegie Hall	May 15—Eve.	Carnegie Hall
Apr. 19—Eve.	Hartford, Conn.		(Pension Fund Benefit)

REPERTOIRE FOR 1959–60

    (a) World premiere.
    (b) First performance in the United States.
    (c) First performance in New York.

Compositions marked with an asterisk (*) are recorded by
the New York Philharmonic on Columbia Records

AMIROV—"Azerbaijan," Symphonic Suite: Mar. 3 (b), 4, 5, 6.

BACH—Brandenburg Concerto No. 1, F major: Dec. 13.
Brandenburg Concerto No. 2, F major: Nov. 29.
Brandenburg Concerto No. 3, G major: Nov. 26, 27, 28.
Brandenburg Concerto No. 4, G major: Dec. 10, 11, 12.
Brandenburg Concerto No. 5, D major: Dec. 3, 4, 5, 6, 7, 8.
Brandenburg Concerto No. 6, B-flat major: Dec. 17, 18, 19, 20.
Concerto for Three Pianos and Orchestra, C major: Dec. 17, 18, 19, 20.
Magnificat, D major: Dec. 17, 18, 19, 20.
Opening Chorus from the "Christmas Oratorio": "Jauchzet, frohlocket! auf,
preiset die Tage!": Dec. 17, 18, 19, 20.

BARBER—Second Essay for Orchestra, Opus 17: Oct. 12, 22, 23, 24, 25; Apr. 19,
26.
"Knoxville: Summer of 1915," for Voice and Orchestra, Opus 24: Nov. 12, 13,
14, 15.

BARTOK—Concerto No. 1 for Piano and Orchestra: Mar. 17, 18, 19.
Concerto for Orchestra: Nov. 26, 27, 28, 29; Dec. 7, 8.
Suite from the Pantomime, "The Miraculous Mandarin," Opus 19: Mar. 10, 11,
12, 13.

---

* Young People's Concert.
† Arnold Gamson, Seymour Lipkin, Stefan Bauer-Mengelberg and Howard
Shanet also conducting.

BEETHOVEN—Concerto No. 3 for Piano and Orchestra, C minor, Opus 37: Nov. 29.

Concerto No. 4 for Piano and Orchestra, G major, Opus 58: Nov. 5, 6, 7.

Concerto for Piano, Violin, Violoncello and Orchestra, C major, Opus 56: Oct. 12, 15, 16, 17, 18, 19, 20.

Concerto for Violin and Orchestra, D major, Opus 61: Nov. 26, 27, 28.

Fantasy, C minor, for Piano, Chorus and Orchestra: May 15 (eve.).

Grand Fugue, B-flat major, Opus 133: Dec. 31; Jan. 1, 2, 3.

Missa Solemnis, D major, Opus 123, for Four Solo Voices, Chorus and Orchestra: Apr. 14, 17, 22, 23.

*Overture, "Egmont," Opus 84: Oct. 15, 16, 17, 18, 19, 20.

Selections from the Ballet Suite "The Creatures of Prometheus," Opus 43: Apr. 28, 29, 30; May 1.

Symphony No. 1, C major, Opus 21: June 4.

*Symphony No. 5, C minor, Opus 67: Nov. 12, 13, 14, 15.

*Symphony No. 9, D minor, Opus 125, Final Movement only: Oct. 24 (aft.).

*Symphony No. 9, D minor, Opus 125: May 15 (eve.).

BERG—Violin Concerto: Dec. 3, 4, 5, 6.

BERLIOZ—From "Romeo and Juliet," Dramatic Symphony, Opus 17: Oct. 22, 23, 24, 25.

BERNSTEIN—Symphonic Suite from the film "On the Waterfront": May 12 (c), 13, 14, 15.

BLISS—Concerto for Piano and Orchestra: Jan. 7, 8, 9, 10.

BLOCH—Sacred Service (Avodath Hakodesh): A Sabbath Morning Service, for Baritone (Cantor), Chorus and Orchestra: Apr. 7, 8, 9, 10.

BOITO—"L'altra notte in fondo al mare," from "Mefistofele": Apr. 4.

Prologue to "Mefistofele": Apr. 5, 6, 7, 8.

BOULEZ—Improvisation sur Mallarmé I: Mar. 31 (b); Apr. 1, 2, 3.

BRAHMS—Concerto No. 1 for Piano and Orchestra, D minor, Opus 15: Mar. 24, 25, 26, 27.

*Concerto for Violin, Violoncello and Orchestra, A minor, Opus 102: Dec. 3, 4, 5, 6.

*Symphony No. 1, C minor, Opus 68: Dec. 7, 8; Apr. 19, 26.

*Symphony No. 2, D major, Opus 73: Mar. 10, 11, 12, 13.

BRANT—Antiphony One: Mar. 31; Apr. 1, 2, 3.

BRUBECK, H.—Dialogues for Jazz Combo and Orchestra: Dec. 10 (c), 11, 12, 13.

BRUCKNER—Symphony No. 7, E major: Feb. 25, 26, 27, 28.

CASADESUS, R.—Trois Danses, Opus 54: Nov. 5 (a), 6, 7.

CATALANI—"Ebben, ne andro lontana," from "La Wally": Apr. 4.

CHAVEZ—Sinfonía India: Oct. 24 (aft.).

Symphony No. 4 ("Sinfonía Romántica"): Feb. 4 (c), 5, 6, 7.

CHERUBINI—Overture, "Medea": Feb. 25, 26, 27, 28.

CILEA—From "Adriana Lecouvreur": "Io son l'umile ancella"; Introduction to Act IV; "Poveri fiori": Apr. 4.

COPLAND—Four Dance Episodes from the Ballet "Rodeo": Buckaroo Holiday, Corral Nocturne, Saturday Night Waltz, Hoe-Down: Apr. 28, 29, 30; May 1.

Corral Nocturne, Hoe-Down: Feb. 21 (eve.).

DEBUSSY—Festivals: Nov. 29 (eve.); Dec. 1.

Jeux, Poème dansé: Apr. 28, 29, 30.

DIAMOND—The World of Paul Klee: Feb. 18 (c), 19, 20, 21.

DURANTE—Concerto No. 1, F minor, for String Orchestra: Nov. 12, 13, 14, 15.

ENESCO—Roumanian Rhapsody No. 1, A major, Opus 11: June 4.

FOSS—"Introductions and Goodbyes": May 5 (a), 6, 7, 8.

FRANCK—Symphonic Variations: Oct. 24 (aft.).

GERSHWIN—Concerto in F for Piano and Orchestra: Feb. 21 (eve.).

GERSHWIN-BENNETT—"Porgy and Bess; A Symphonic Picture": June 4.

GLINKA—Overture, "Russlan and Ludmilla": Dec. 20 (eve.).

GRIEG—Concerto for Piano and Orchestra, A minor, Opus 16: Dec. 20 (eve.).

HANDEL—"Water Music" Suite (Arranged by Stokowski): Mar. 3, 4, 5, 6.

HANDEL-HARTY—"Water Music" Suite: Feb. 21 (eve.).

HAYDN—Symphony No. 88, G major: Nov. 29 (eve.); Dec. 1.
*Symphony No. 102, B-flat major: Nov. 19, 20, 21, 22.

HINDEMITH—Concerto for Violoncello and Orchestra (1940): Feb. 25, 26, 27, 28.
Three Duets from "Mathis der Maler": May 5, 6, 7, 8.

HUMPERDINCK—Children's Prayer from "Hansel and Gretel": Dec. 20 (eve.).

IVES—The Unanswered Question: Oct. 22, 23, 24, 25.

KABALEVSKY—Overture, "Colas Breugnon," Opus 24: Nov. 8.

KERN—Highlights from "Show Boat": Dec. 20 (eve.).

KODALY—Variations on a Hungarian Folk Song, "The Peacock": Mar. 10, 11, 12, 13.

LEHAR—"The Merry Widow," Suite for Orchestra: June 4.

LISZT—Concerto No. 1 for Piano and Orchestra, E-flat major: Jan. 14, 15, 16, 17.
Mephisto Waltz: Jan. 14, 15, 16, 17.

LUENING-USSACHEVSKY—Concerted Piece for Tape Recorder and Orchestra: Mar. 31; Apr. 1, 2, 3.

MAHLER—Das Lied von der Erde (The Song of the Earth): Apr. 15, 16, 21, 24.
Fünf Kindertotenlieder (Five Songs on the Death of Children): Feb. 11, 12, 13, 14.
Four Songs—(1) Ich atmet' einen linden Duft (2) Ich bin der Welt abhanden gekommen (3) Das irdische Leben (4) Um Mitternacht: Feb. 4, 5, 6, 7.
*Symphony No. 1, D major: Jan. 7, 8, 9, 10.
*Symphony No. 2, C minor, for Orchestra, Soprano and Contralto Solos, and Mixed Chorus: Feb. 18, 19, 20, 21.
*Symphony No. 4, G major, for Orchestra and Soprano Solo: Jan. 28, 29, 30, 31.
*Symphony No. 5, C-sharp minor: Dec. 31; Jan. 1, 2, 3.
Symphony No. 9: Jan. 21, 22, 23, 24.
Symphony No. 10 (Movement I): Jan. 14, 15, 16, 17.

MENDELSSOHN—Overture, Nocturne, Scherzo and Wedding March from "A Midsummer Night's Dream": May 12, 13, 14, 15.
*Symphony No. 4, A major, Opus 90 ("Italian"): Apr. 4.

MOZART—Concerto for Piano and Orchestra, E-flat major, K. 449: Feb. 11, 12, 13, 14.
Concerto for Piano and Orchestra, D major, K. 451: May 1.
Concerto for Piano and Orchestra, G major, K. 453: Apr. 19, 26.
Concerto for Piano and Orchestra, C major, K. 467: Mar. 20.
Concerto for Piano and Orchestra, A major, K. 488: Jan. 28, 29, 30, 31.
Concerto for Piano and Orchestra, B-flat major, K. 595: Mar. 31; Apr. 1, 2, 3.
Concerto for Two Pianos and Orchestra, E-flat major, K. 365: Dec. 10, 11, 12, 13.
Overture, "The Magic Flute," K. 620: Oct. 29, 30, 31; Nov. 1.
*Symphony No. 40, G minor, K. 550: Mar. 3, 4, 5, 6.

MUSSORGSKY-RAVEL—*Pictures from an Exhibition: Mar. 17, 18, 19, 20.
OFFENBACH-ROSENTHAL—Gaîté Parisienne: Nov. 29 (eve.); Dec. 1.
PERGOLESI (?)—Concertino for Strings, No. 3, A major: Mar. 24, 25, 26, 27.
Concertino for Strings, No. 4, F minor: Mar. 31; Apr. 1, 2, 3.
PERGOLESI—Stabat Mater: Apr. 7, 8, 9, 10.
PROKOFIEFF—Concerto No. 1 for Piano and Orchestra, D-flat major, Opus 10:
May 1.
Concerto No. 2 for Violin and Orchestra, G minor, Opus 63: Nov. 19, 20, 21,
22.
PUCCINI—Crisantemi: Nov. 29 (eve.); Dec. 1.
"Signore, ascolta!" from "Turandot": Apr. 4.
RACHMANINOFF—Concerto No. 2 for Piano and Orchestra, C minor, Opus
18: Feb. 4, 5, 6, 7.
Concerto No. 3 for Piano and Orchestra, D minor, Opus 30: Nov. 8.
RAVEL—*Bolero: Feb. 21 (eve.).
Concerto for the Left Hand, for Piano and Orchestra: Feb. 11, 12, 13, 14.
Tzigane, Rhapsody for Violin and Orchestra: Nov. 29 (eve.); Dec. 1.
ROSSINI—Overture, "La Gazza Ladra": Jan. 28, 29, 30, 31.
Overture, "L'Italiana in Algeri": Apr. 4.
Overture, "William Tell": Dec. 20 (eve.).
"Selva opaca" from "William Tell": Apr. 4.
SCHOENBERG—Kammersymphonie, E major, Opus 9b: Oct. 29, 30, 31; Nov. 1.
SCHUBERT—Symphony No. 8, B minor ("Unfinished"): Apr. 15, 16, 21, 24.
SCHULLER—Spectra: Jan 14 (a), 15, 16, 17.
SCHUMAN—Symphony for Strings (Symphony No. 5): Nov. 5, 6, 7.
SHOSTAKOVICH—Symphony No. 1, Opus 10: Mar. 3, 4, 5, 6.
*Symphony No. 5, Opus 47: Oct. 12, 15, 16, 17, 18, 19, 20.
SIBELIUS—The Swan of Tuonela, Opus 22, No. 3: Feb. 21 (eve.).
Symphony No. 7, in One Movement, Opus 105: Mar. 24, 25, 26, 27.
STARER—Concerto for Viola, Strings, and Percussion: Dec. 10 (b), 11, 12, 13.
STRAUSS—Also Sprach Zarathustra, Opus 30: Oct. 29, 30, 31; Nov. 1.
*Don Juan, Opus 20: Nov. 12, 13, 14, 15.
STRAVINSKY—Concerto for Piano and Wind Orchestra (with Double-Basses
and Timpani): Oct. 22, 23, 24, 25.
Divertimento (Suite from the Ballet "Le Baiser de la Fée"): Mar. 17, 18, 19, 20.
Petroushka, A Burlesque in Four Tableaux: Nov. 5, 6, 7, 8.
Suite from "Pulcinella" (after Pergolesi), for Small Orchestra: Mar. 24, 25, 26,
27.
SVENDSEN—Romance: Dec. 20 (eve.).
TCHAIKOVSKY—*Capriccio Italien, Opus 45: Feb. 11, 12, 13, 14; Apr. 4.
Marche Solennelle: Feb. 21 (eve.).
"Nutcracker" Suite, Opus 71a: Apr. 28, 29, 30.
*Symphony No. 5, E minor, Opus 64: May 12, 13, 14, 15.
THOMSON—Acts III and IV from "Four Saints in Three Acts": May 5, 6, 7, 8.
VILLA-LOBOS—Chôros No. 10, "Rasga o coracao," for Orchestra and Mixed
Chorus: Oct. 29, 30, 31; Nov. 1.
Descobrimento do Brasil: Oct. 24 (aft.).
WAGNER—*Prelude to "Die Meistersinger von Nürnberg": Nov. 19, 20, 21, 22.
Siegfried's Death and Funeral Music, from "Götterdämmerung": Nov. 19, 20,
21, 22.
Siegfried's Rhine Journey, from "Götterdämmerung": Nov. 19, 20, 21, 22.
WALDTEUFEL—Skaters' Waltz: Dec. 20 (eve.).

WALTON—Johannesburg Festival Overture: Nov. 29 (eve.); Dec. 1.
WEBER—Invitation to the Dance: June 4.
WEBERN—Passacaglia for Orchestra, Opus 1: Jan. 21, 22, 23, 24.
Christmas Carols: Dec. 20 (eve.).

SOLOISTS

PIANO
GINA BACHAUER: Jan. 7, 8, 9, 10.
DAVID BAR-ILLAN: Jan. 14, 15, 16, 17.
LEONARD BERNSTEIN: Oct. 12, 15, 16, 17, 18, 19, 20; Dec. 7, 8, 17, 18, 19, 20; Apr. 5, 19, 26.
JOHN BROWNING: Feb. 11, 12, 13, 14.
ROBERT CASADESUS: Oct. 24 (aft.); Nov. 5, 6, 7.
PHILIPPE ENTREMONT: Feb. 4, 5, 6, 7.
MALCOLM FRAGER: May 1.
CLAUDE FRANK: Nov. 29.
ARTHUR GOLD and ROBERT FIZDALE: Dec. 10, 11, 12, 13.
MIECZYSLAW HORSZOWSKI: Mar. 31; Apr. 1, 2, 3.
BYRON JANIS: Jan. 28, 29, 30, 31.
DAVID KEISER: Dec. 17, 18, 19, 20.
JACQUES KLEIN: Nov. 8.
SEYMOUR LIPKIN: Oct. 22, 23, 24, 25.
CARLOS MOSELEY: Dec. 17, 18, 19, 20.
ANDRE PREVIN: Feb. 21 (eve.).
RUDOLF SERKIN: Mar. 17, 18, 19, 20; May 15 (eve.).
LEONARD SHURE: Mar. 24, 25, 26, 27.
SYLVIA ZAREMBA: Dec. 20 (eve.).

VIOLIN
JOHN CORIGLIANO: Oct. 12, 15, 16, 17, 18, 19, 20; Nov. 29 (aft. and eve.); Dec. 1, 7, 8, 10, 11, 12.
ZINO FRANCESCATTI: Nov. 26, 27, 28.
TOSSY SPIVAKOVSKY: Nov. 19, 20, 21, 22.
ISAAC STERN: Dec. 3, 4, 5, 6.

VIOLA
WILLIAM LINCER: Dec. 10, 11, 12, 13.

VIOLONCELLO
ALDO PARISOT: Feb. 25, 26, 27, 28.
LEONARD ROSE: Dec. 3, 4, 5, 6.
LASZLO VARGA: Oct. 12, 15, 16, 17, 18, 19, 20.

FLUTE
ROBERT MORRIS: Dec. 10, 11, 12.
JOHN WUMMER: Nov. 29; Dec. 3, 4, 5, 6, 7, 8, 10, 11, 12.

OBOE
HAROLD GOMBERG: Nov. 29.

TRUMPET
WILLIAM VACCHIANO: Nov. 29.

HARPSICHORD
LEONARD BERNSTEIN: Dec. 3, 4, 5, 6, 7, 8.

VOICE
ADELE ADDISON, soprano: Apr. 7, 8, 9, 10.
BETTY ALLEN, mezzo-soprano: May 5, 6, 7, 8.
HERBERT BEATTIE, bass: May 5, 6, 7, 8.
MCHENRY BOATWRIGHT, baritone: May 5, 6, 7, 8.
KIM BORG, bass-baritone: Oct. 24 (aft.); Apr. 14, 17, 22, 23.
CHARLES BRESSLER, tenor: Dec. 17, 18, 19, 20.
PHYLLIS CURTIN, soprano: Feb. 18, 19, 20, 21.
ROBERT ECKERT, tenor: May 5, 6, 7, 8.
ROSALIND ELIAS, mezzo-soprano: May 15 (eve.).
EILEEN FARRELL, soprano: Apr. 14, 17, 22, 23.
NORMAN FARROW, baritone: Dec. 17, 18, 19, 20.
MAUREEN FORRESTER, contralto: Oct. 24 (aft.); Apr. 15, 16, 21, 24.
RERI GRIST, soprano: Jan. 28, 29, 30, 31.
IRENE JORDAN, soprano: May 5, 6, 7, 8.
RICHARD LEWIS, tenor: Apr. 14, 15, 16, 17, 21, 22, 23, 24.
ROBERT MERRILL, baritone: Apr. 7, 8, 9, 10.
MARNI NIXON, soprano: Mar. 31; Apr. 1, 2, 3.
RUSSELL OBERLIN, countertenor: Dec. 17, 18, 19, 20.
JAN PEERCE, tenor: Oct. 24 (aft.).
LEONTYNE PRICE, soprano: Nov. 12, 13, 14, 15.
JOHN REARDON, baritone: May 5, 6, 7, 8.
REGINA RESNIK, mezzo-soprano: Feb. 18, 19, 20, 21.

REGINA SARFATY, mezzo-soprano: Apr. 7, 8, 9, 10.
ELISABETH SCHWARZKOPF, soprano: Oct. 24 (aft.).
CAROL SMITH, contralto: Apr. 14, 17, 22, 23.
KENNETH SMITH, bass-baritone: May 15 (eve.).
GERARD SOUZAY, baritone: Feb. 11.
ELEANOR STEBER, soprano: May 15 (eve.).
BRIAN SULLIVAN, tenor: May 15 (eve.).
RENATA TEBALDI, soprano: Apr. 4.
JENNIE TOUREL, mezzo-soprano: Dec. 17, 18, 19, 20; Feb. 4, 5, 6, 7, 12, 13, 14.
LEE VENORA, soprano: Dec. 17, 18, 19, 20; May 5, 6, 7, 8.
ARNOLD VOKETAITIS, bass: May 5, 6, 7, 8.

CHORUS

BOYS' CHOIR of ST. PAUL'S CHURCH, Flatbush, Charles Ennis, Director: May 5, 6, 7, 8.

CHOIRS of the METROPOLITAN SYNAGOGUE and the COMMUNITY CHURCH of NEW YORK, Maurice Levine, Director: Apr. 7, 8, 9, 10.
CHORAL ART SOCIETY, William Jonson, Director: May 5, 6, 7, 8.
RUTGERS UNIVERSITY CHOIR, F. Austin Walter, Director: Feb. 18, 19, 20, 21.
SCHOLA CANTORUM, Hugh Ross, Director: Oct. 24 (aft.); Dec. 17, 18, 19, 20; May 15 (eve.).
SYMPHONIC CHOIR of the WESTMINSTER CHOIR COLLEGE, Warren Martin, Conductor: Oct. 29, 30, 31; Nov. 1; Apr. 14, 17, 22, 23.

NARRATOR

RABBI JUDAH CAHN: Apr. 7, 8, 9, 10.

JAZZ ENSEMBLE

DAVE BRUBECK QUARTET: Dec. 10, 11, 12, 13.

TAPE RECORDER

VLADIMIR USSACHEVSKY: Mar. 31; Apr. 1, 2, 3.

●

TOUR OF EUROPE AND NEAR EAST—1959

Conductors

Leonard Bernstein	
Aug. 5—Eve.	Athens
Aug. 11—Eve.	Istanbul
Aug. 12—Eve.	Istanbul
Aug. 13—Eve.	Salonika
Aug. 16—Eve.	Salzburg
Aug. 18—Eve.	Warsaw
Aug. 19—Eve.	Warsaw
Aug. 20—Eve.	Warsaw
Aug. 22—Eve.	Moscow
Aug. 23—Eve.	Moscow
Aug. 24—Eve.	Moscow
Aug. 25—Eve.	Moscow
Aug. 26—Eve.	Moscow
Aug. 28—Eve.	Leningrad
Aug. 29—Eve.	Leningrad
Aug. 30—Eve.	Leningrad
Sept. 6—Eve.	Kiev
Sept. 7—Eve.	Kiev
Sept. 11—Eve.	Moscow
Sept. 13—Eve.	Scheveningen
Sept. 20—Eve.	Paris
Sept. 21—Eve.	Basel
Sept. 22—Eve.	Munich
Sept. 23—Eve.	Belgrade
Sept. 24—Eve.	Zagreb
Sept. 26—Eve.	Venice

Sept. 28—Eve.	Milan
Sept. 29—Eve.	Milan
Sept. 30—Eve.	Hamburg
Oct. 1—Eve.	Berlin
Oct. 2—Eve.	Oslo
Oct. 4—Eve.	Helsinki
Oct. 5—Eve.	Turku (Abo)
Oct. 6—Eve.	Stockholm
Oct. 8—Eve.	Göteborg
Oct. 10—Eve.	London

Thomas Schippers	
Aug. 6—Eve.	Athens
Aug. 8—Eve.	Baalbek
Aug. 31—Eve.	Leningrad
Sept. 1—Eve.	Leningrad
Sept. 2—Eve.	Leningrad
Sept. 4—Eve.	Kiev
Sept. 5—Eve.	Kiev
Sept. 9—Eve.	Moscow
Sept. 10—Eve.	Moscow
Sept. 15—Eve.	Düsseldorf
Sept. 16—Eve.	Essen
Sept. 17—Eve.	Wiesbaden
Sept. 18—Eve.	Luxembourg

Seymour Lipkin	
Aug. 9—Eve.	Baalbek

TOUR REPERTOIRE

Compositions marked with an asterisk (*) are recorded by
the New York Philharmonic on Columbia Records

BARBER—Medea's Meditation and Dance of Vengeance, Opus 23-A: Aug. 6, 8,
31; Sept. 1, 4, 9, 10, 15, 16, 17, 18.
Second Essay for Orchestra, Opus 17: Aug. 5, 13, 16, 18, 22, 29; Sept. 6, 11, 22,
23, 26, 28, 29; Oct. 4, 5, 6, 10.

BEETHOVEN—Concerto for Piano, Violin, Violoncello and Orchestra, C major,
Opus 56: Aug. 24, 29; Sept. 6, 13, 23, 30; Oct. 6.
*Overture, "Egmont," Opus 84: Aug. 9, 13, 23, 28; Sept. 20.
*Overture, "Leonore," No. 3, Opus 72: Aug. 12, 20, 26; Sept. 7; Oct. 2.
*Symphony No. 7, A major, Opus 92: Aug. 9, 12, 26; Sept. 7, 11, 13, 20; Oct. 2.
Symphony No. 8, F major, Opus 93: Aug. 6, 8, 31; Sept. 1, 4, 9, 10, 15, 17.

BERLIOZ—From the Dramatic Symphony "Romeo and Juliet," Opus 17: Love
Scene—Queen Mab Scherzo—Romeo Alone—Festivities in Capulet's Palace:
Aug. 19, 24, 29; Sept. 6, 23.
Overture, "Roman Carnival," Opus 9: Aug. 20, 25, 30; Sept. 13, 24, 30; Oct. 1.

BERNSTEIN—*Symphony No. 2, "Age of Anxiety": Aug. 13, 16, 18, 23, 28;
Sept. 20, 26.

BRAHMS—*Symphony No. 1, C minor, Opus 68: Aug. 5, 11, 18, 23, 28; Sept. 21,
22, 28, 29; Oct. 4, 5, 8, 10.
*Symphony No. 2, D major, Opus 73: Sept. 2, 16, 18.

COPLAND—Ballet Suite: "Billy the Kid": Aug. 12, 20, 26; Sept. 7; Oct. 2.

DIAMOND—The World of Paul Klee: Sept. 2, 5.

GERSHWIN—*Rhapsody in Blue: Aug. 12, 20, 26; Sept. 7, 28, 29; Oct. 2.

IVES—The Unanswered Question: Aug. 25, 30; Sept. 13, 23, 26; Oct. 1, 10.

MOZART—Concerto for Piano and Orchestra, G major, K. 453: Aug. 5, 11, 19,
22; Sept. 21, 22, 24; Oct. 1, 4, 5, 8, 10.

PISTON—Concerto for Orchestra: Aug. 9, 11, 19, 24; Sept. 21, 24, 30; Oct. 1, 8.

RAVEL—*"La Valse," Choreographic Poem for Orchestra: Aug. 9, 20, 25, 30;
Sept. 20, 24; Oct. 1.

ROSSINI—Overture, "Siege of Corinth": Sept. 2, 5, 16, 18.

SHOSTAKOVICH—*Symphony No. 5, Opus 47: Aug. 13, 16, 22; Sept. 11, 26;
Oct. 6.

STRAUSS—Tone Poem, "Till Eulenspiegel's Merry Pranks," Opus 28: Sept. 30.

STRAVINSKY—Concerto for Piano and Wind Orchestra (with Double-Basses
and Timpani): Aug. 25, 30.
*"Le Sacre du Printemps": Aug. 25, 30.
*Suite from "The Firebird": Sept. 2, 5, 16, 18.

TCHAIKOVSKY—*Symphony No. 4, F minor, Opus 36: Aug. 6, 8, 31; Sept. 4,
9, 15, 17.

VIVALDI—*Concerto in C minor for Flute, Strings and Cembalo, F. VI, No. 11:
Sept. 28, 29.

WAGNER—*Overture, "Tannhaeuser": Sept. 1, 5, 10.
Prelude and Love Death, "Tristan und Isolde": Sept. 1, 5, 10.
Siegfried's Rhine Journey, "Götterdämmerung": Sept. 1, 5, 10.

TOUR SOLOISTS

LEONARD BERNSTEIN, piano: Aug. 5, 11, 12, 19, 20, 22, 24, 26, 29; Sept. 6, 7, 13, 21, 22, 23, 24, 28, 29, 30; Oct. 1, 2, 4, 5, 6, 8, 10.

JOHN CORIGLIANO, violin: Aug. 24, 29; Sept. 6, 13, 23, 30; Oct. 6.

SEYMOUR LIPKIN, piano: Aug. 13, 16, 18, 23, 25, 28, 30; Sept. 20, 26.

LASZLO VARGA, violoncello: Aug. 24, 29; Sept. 6, 13, 23, 30; Oct. 6.

JOHN WUMMER, flute: Sept. 28, 29.

1960–61 ONE HUNDRED NINETEENTH SEASON

LEONARD BERNSTEIN, *Music Director*

Guest Conductors
KARL BOEHM, CARLOS CHAVEZ, AARON COPLAND, VLADIMIR GOLSCHMANN,
PAUL PARAY, HANS ROSBAUD, THOMAS SCHIPPERS,
STANISLAW SKROWACZEWSKI, ALFRED WALLENSTEIN

Young People's Concerts	*Three Saturday Concerts*
LEONARD BERNSTEIN, *Music Director*	ANDRE KOSTELANETZ

Assistant Conductors
GREGORY MILLAR, ELYAKUM SHAPIRA, RUSSELL STANGER

CONCERTS

1960

Leonard Bernstein
Sept. 27—Eve.   Carnegie Hall
                       (Pension Fund Benefit)
Sept. 29—Eve.   Carnegie Hall
Sept. 30—Aft.   Carnegie Hall

Leonard Bernstein, Gregory Millar
Oct. 1—Eve.   Carnegie Hall

Gregory Millar, Elyakum Shapira, Russell Stanger
Oct. 2—Aft.   Carnegie Hall

Leonard Bernstein
Oct. 6—Eve.   Carnegie Hall
Oct. 7—Aft.   Carnegie Hall
Oct. 8—Eve.   Carnegie Hall
Oct. 9—Aft.   Carnegie Hall
Oct. 13—Eve.   Carnegie Hall
Oct. 14—Aft.   Carnegie Hall
Oct. 15—Eve.   Newark, N. J.
Oct. 16—Aft.   Carnegie Hall
Oct. 18—Eve.   Brooklyn, N. Y.
Oct. 20—Eve.   Carnegie Hall
Oct. 21—Aft.   Carnegie Hall

Leonard Bernstein, Russell Stanger
†Oct. 22—Noon   Carnegie Hall

1960

Leonard Bernstein
Oct. 23—Aft.   Carnegie Hall
Oct. 26—Eve.   White Plains, N. Y.
Oct. 27—Eve.   Carnegie Hall
Oct. 28—Aft.   Carnegie Hall
Oct. 29—Eve.   Carnegie Hall
Oct. 30—Aft.   Carnegie Hall
Nov. 3—Eve.   Carnegie Hall
Nov. 4—Aft.   Carnegie Hall
Nov. 5—Eve.   Carnegie Hall
Nov. 6—Aft.   Carnegie Hall
Nov. 8—Eve.   Brooklyn, N. Y.

Aaron Copland
Nov. 10—Eve.   Carnegie Hall
Nov. 11—Aft.   Carnegie Hall

Leonard Bernstein, Aaron Copland
†Nov. 12—Noon   Carnegie Hall

Aaron Copland
Nov. 13—Aft.   Carnegie Hall

Carlos Chávez
Nov. 17—Eve.   Carnegie Hall
Nov. 18—Aft.   Carnegie Hall
Nov. 19—Eve.   Carnegie Hall
Nov. 20—Aft.   Carnegie Hall

Hans Rosbaud
Nov. 24—Eve.   Carnegie Hall
Nov. 25—Aft.   Carnegie Hall

† Young People's Concert.

1960

André Kostelanetz
Nov. 26—Eve.   Carnegie Hall

Hans Rosbaud
Nov. 27—Aft.   Carnegie Hall
Nov. 30—Eve.   Hartford, Conn.
Dec. 1—Eve.   Carnegie Hall
Dec. 2—Aft.   Carnegie Hall
Dec. 4—Aft.   Carnegie Hall

Karl Boehm
Dec. 8—Eve.   Carnegie Hall
Dec. 9—Aft.   Carnegie Hall
Dec. 10—Eve.   United Nations, N. Y.
Dec. 11—Aft.   Carnegie Hall

Gregory Millar, Russell Stanger
Dec. 15—Eve.   Carnegie Hall
Dec. 16—Aft.   Carnegie Hall

**Gregory Millar, Elyakum Shapira,
Russell Stanger**
Dec. 17—Eve.   Brooklyn, N. Y.

Gregory Millar, Russell Stanger
Dec. 18—Aft.   Carnegie Hall

Leonard Bernstein
Dec. 18—Eve.   Carnegie Hall
                    (Pension Fund Benefit)

Stanislaw Skrowaczewski
Dec. 29—Eve.   Carnegie Hall
Dec. 30—Aft.   Carnegie Hall

Skitch Henderson
Dec. 31—Eve.   Carnegie Hall
          (Special New Year's Eve Concert)

1961

Stanislaw Skrowaczewski
Jan. 1—Aft.   Carnegie Hall
Jan. 5—Eve.   Carnegie Hall
Jan. 6—Aft.   Carnegie Hall
Jan. 7—Eve.   Carnegie Hall
Jan. 8—Aft.   Carnegie Hall

Paul Paray
Jan. 12—Eve.   Carnegie Hall
Jan. 13—Aft.   Carnegie Hall
Jan. 14—Eve.   Brooklyn, N. Y.
Jan. 15—Aft.   Carnegie Hall
Jan. 19—Eve.   Carnegie Hall
Jan. 20—Aft.   Carnegie Hall
Jan. 21—Eve.   Carnegie Hall
Jan. 22—Aft.   Carnegie Hall

Alfred Wallenstein
Jan. 26—Eve.   Carnegie Hall
Jan. 27—Aft.   Carnegie Hall
Jan. 28—Eve.   Brooklyn, N. Y.
Jan. 29—Aft.   Carnegie Hall

1961

Peter Herman Adler
Jan. 31—Eve.   Carnegie Hall
          (Arthur Judson Foundation Concert)

Alfred Wallenstein
Feb. 2—Eve.   Carnegie Hall
Feb. 3—Aft.   Carnegie Hall

André Kostelanetz
Feb. 4—Eve.   Carnegie Hall

Alfred Wallenstein
Feb. 5—Aft.   Carnegie Hall

Thomas Schippers
Feb. 9—Eve.   Carnegie Hall
Feb. 10—Aft.   Carnegie Hall
Feb. 11—Eve.   Carnegie Hall
Feb. 12—Aft.   Carnegie Hall

**Aaron Copland, Lukas Foss,
Vladimir Golschmann,
Yuri Krasnopolsky**
Feb. 13—Eve.   Carnegie Hall
                    (Pension Fund Benefit)

Thomas Schippers
Feb. 16—Eve.   Carnegie Hall
Feb. 17—Aft.   Carnegie Hall
Feb. 18—Eve.   Newark, N. J.
Feb. 19—Aft.   Carnegie Hall

Vladimir Golschmann
Feb. 23—Eve.   Carnegie Hall
Feb. 24—Aft.   Carnegie Hall
Feb. 25—Eve.   Brooklyn, N. Y.
Feb. 26—Aft.   Carnegie Hall

Leonard Bernstein
Mar. 2—Eve.   Carnegie Hall
Mar. 3—Aft.   Carnegie Hall

André Kostelanetz
Mar. 4—Eve.   Carnegie Hall

Leonard Bernstein
Mar. 5—Aft.   Carnegie Hall

André Kostelanetz
Mar. 7—Eve.   Queens, N. Y.

Leonard Bernstein
Mar. 9—Eve.   Carnegie Hall
Mar. 10—Aft.   Carnegie Hall
Mar. 11—Eve.   Newark, N. J.
Mar. 12—Aft.   Carnegie Hall

André Kostelanetz
Mar. 14—Eve.   Staten Island, N. Y.

Leonard Bernstein, Gregory Millar
Mar. 16—Eve.   Carnegie Hall
Mar. 17—Aft.   Carnegie Hall

1961

**Leonard Bernstein, Gregory Millar,
Elyakum Shapira, Russell Stanger**
†Mar. 18—Noon   Carnegie Hall

Leonard Bernstein, Russell Stanger
Mar. 18—Eve.   Carnegie Hall

Leonard Bernstein, Gregory Millar
Mar. 19—Aft.   Carnegie Hall

Leonard Bernstein
Mar. 23—Eve.   Carnegie Hall
Mar. 24—Aft.   Carnegie Hall
Mar. 25—Eve.   Carnegie Hall
Mar. 26—Aft.   Carnegie Hall
Mar. 30—Eve.   Carnegie Hall
Mar. 31—Aft.   Carnegie Hall
Apr. 1—Eve.   Carnegie Hall
Apr. 2—Aft.   Carnegie Hall

1961

Leonard Bernstein, Elyakum Shapira
Apr. 6—Eve.   Carnegie Hall
Apr. 7—Aft.   Carnegie Hall

Leonard Bernstein
†Apr. 8—Noon   Carnegie Hall
Apr. 8—Eve.   Carnegie Hall
Apr. 9—Aft.   Carnegie Hall

Leonard Bernstein, Seiji Ozawa
Apr. 13—Eve.   Carnegie Hall
Apr. 14—Aft.   Carnegie Hall

Leonard Bernstein
Apr. 15—Eve.   Brooklyn, N. Y.

Leonard Bernstein, Seiji Ozawa
Apr. 16—Aft.   Carnegie Hall

REPERTOIRE FOR 1960–61

(a) World premiere.
(b) First performance in the United States.
(c) First performance in New York.

Compositions marked with an asterisk (*) are recorded by the New York Philharmonic on Columbia Records and now available; those with two asterisks (**) will be released by Columbia Records in the near future.

ALBENIZ-ARBOS—"Fête-Dieu à Séville" from "Iberia" Suite: Feb. 4.

BACH—Concerto for Violin and Orchestra, No. 2, E major: Nov. 3, 4, 5, 6, 8.

BARBER—Concerto for Violin and Orchestra, Opus 14: Oct. 13, 14, 16.

BARTOK—*Concerto for Orchestra: Feb. 16, 17, 18, 19.
Music for Strings, Percussion and Celesta: Mar. 16, 17, 18, 19.

BEETHOVEN—Concerto No. 1 for Piano and Orchestra, C major, Opus 15: Sept. 29, 30; Oct. 1, 15, 18, 26.
Concerto No. 4 for Piano and Orchestra, G major, Opus 58: Mar. 16, 17, 19.
*Concerto for Violin and Orchestra, D major, Opus 61: Sept. 27; Nov. 24, 25, 27.
*Overture, "Leonore," No. 3, Opus 72A: Sept. 29, 30; Oct. 1, 2, 15, 18, 26.
Symphony No. 1, C major, Opus 21: Nov. 26.
Symphony No. 2, D major, Opus 36: Jan. 19, 20, 21, 22.
Symphony No. 3, E flat major, Opus 55 ("Eroica"): Feb. 2, 3, 5.
*Symphony No. 7, A major, Opus 92: Oct. 15, 18, 26; Mar. 18.

BERG—Three Orchestral Pieces, Opus 6: Mar. 2, 3, 5.

BERLIOZ—*Overture, "Benvenuto Cellini," Opus 23: Oct. 27, 28, 29, 30.
Romeo and Juliet, a Dramatic Symphony, Opus 17: Jan. 26, 27, 28, 29.
*Symphonie Fantastique, C major, Opus 14: Jan. 5, 6, 7, 8.
Three Excerpts from "The Damnation of Faust": Jan. 12, 13, 14, 15.

BERNSTEIN—Overture to "Candide": Sept. 27; Feb. 13.
Selections from "Candide," "Fancy Free," "On the Town," "West Side Story," "Wonderful Town": Feb. 13.
Symphony No. 1 ("Jeremiah"): Feb. 13.
**Symphonic Dances from "West Side Story": Feb. 13 (a).

BORODIN—*Polovetsian Dances from "Prince Igor": Mar. 4, 7, 14.

---

† Young People's Concert.

BOULEZ—Improvisation on Mallarmé, No. 2, "Une Dentelle s'abolit": Mar. 16 (b), 17, 19.

BRAHMS—Concerto No. 1 for Piano and Orchestra, D minor, Opus 15: Nov. 30; Dec. 1, 2, 4.
Concerto for Violin and Orchestra, D major, Opus 77: Apr. 13, 14, 16.
*Symphony No. 3, F major, Opus 90: Dec. 29, 30; Jan. 1.
*Symphony No. 4, E minor, Opus 98: Dec. 8, 9, 11, 17.

CASTELLANOS—La Morena de mi Copla: Feb. 4.

CARTER—Holiday Overture: Nov. 17, 18, 19, 20.

CHABRIER—"España," Rhapsody for Orchestra: Feb. 4.

CHAVEZ—Sinfonía India: Apr. 6, 7, 8, 9, 15.

CHOU Wen-chung—"And the Fallen Petals," a Triolet for Orchestra: Jan. 5 (c), 6, 7, 8.

COPLAND—El Salón México: Nov. 10, 11, 13.
Symphonic Ode: Nov. 10, 11, 13.

CRESTON—Janus, Opus 77: Mar. 18 (c).

DEBUSSY—"La Mer," Three Symphonic Sketches: Feb. 23, 24, 25, 26.
Nocturnes: Nuages, Fêtes, Sirènes: Feb. 9, 10, 11, 12.
Prelude to the Afternoon of a Faun: Oct. 2.

DVORAK—Concerto for Violin and Orchestra, A minor, Opus 53: Nov. 10, 11, 13.
Scherzo Capriccioso, Opus 66: Jan. 31.

FALLA—*Suite, "The Three-Cornered Hat": Feb. 4.

FOSS—Time Cycle (for Soprano and Orchestra): Oct. 20 (a), 21, 23.

FRANCHETTI—Largo for Strings, in Memoriam: Nov. 10 (c), 11, 13.

FRANCK—Symphonic Poem, "Psyché": Jan. 19, 20, 21, 22.

GIORDANO—"La Mamma Morta" from "Andrea Chénier": Dec. 10.

GLAZUNOFF—Fourth tableau from "The Seasons": Dec. 31.

GLUCK—Overture, "Iphigénie en Aulide": Nov. 10, 11, 13.

GOULD—Dialogues for Piano and String Orchestra: Jan. 12, 13, 14, 15.

GRANADOS—Interludio and Aria ("The Lady and the Nightingale") from "Goyescas": Feb. 4.

HANDEL—Concerto Grosso, B flat major, Opus 3, No. 1: Nov. 24, 25, 27.

HARRIS—Symphony No. 3 (in One Movement): Sept. 27.

HAYDN—Symphony No. 85, B flat major ("La Reine"): Feb. 2, 3, 5.

HEROLD—Overture, "Zampa": Dec. 31.

HINDEMITH—Concert Music for Strings and Brass, Opus 50: Mar. 9, 10, 12.
Concerto for Orchestra, Opus 38: Nov. 30; Dec. 1, 2, 4.
Symphonic Metamorphosis of Themes by Carl Maria von Weber: Dec. 8, 9, 11.

IVES—*Symphony No. 2: Mar. 2, 3, 5.

KERN—Portrait for Orchestra: Mark Twain: Mar. 4, 7, 14.

KERN-BENNETT—Jerome Kern—A Portrait in Music: Nov. 26.

KHACHATURIAN—Concerto for Piano and Orchestra: Apr. 6, 7, 8, 9, 15.
Concerto for Violoncello and Orchestra: Jan. 5, 6, 7, 8.

LARA—Granada: Feb. 4.

LISZT—Concerto No. 1 for Piano and Orchestra, E flat major: Mar. 4, 7, 14.
Concerto No. 2 for Piano and Orchestra, A major: Dec. 18 (eve.).
A Faust Symphony in Three Character Pictures (after Goethe): Nov. 3, 4, 5, 6, 8.
Tone Poem, "Hunnenschlacht" (Battle of the Huns): Dec. 18 (eve.).

LOPATNIKOFF—Festival Overture: Jan. 19 (c), 20, 21, 22.

LUTOSLAWSKI—Concerto for Orchestra: Dec. 29 (c), 30; Jan. 1.

MAHLER—*Fourth Movement ("Urlicht") from Symphony No. 2 ("Resurrection"): Nov. 3, 4, 5, 6.
Symphony No. 3, D minor: Mar. 30, 31; Apr. 1, 2.

MARQUINA—España Cani: Feb. 4.

MAYUZUMI—Bacchanale: Apr. 13 (c), 14, 16.

MENDELSSOHN—*Overture, "Ruy Blas": Oct. 20, 21, 23.
*Symphony No. 4, A major, Opus 90 ("Italian"): Feb. 23, 24, 25, 26.

MOUSSORGSKY—Dance of the Persian Slaves from "Khovanshchina": Nov. 26.

MOUSSORGSKY-RAVEL—*Pictures at an Exhibition: Feb. 23, 24, 25, 26.

MOZART—Concerto for Piano and Orchestra, D minor, K. 466: Oct. 6, 7, 8, 9.
Symphony No. 23, D major, K. 181: Mar. 4, 7, 14.
Symphony No. 29, A major, K. 201: Dec. 29, 30; Jan. 1.
Symphony No. 34, C major, K. 338 (with Minuet, K. 409): Dec. 8, 9, 10, 11, 17.
Symphony No. 36, C major, K. 425 ("Linz"): Mar. 2, 3, 5, 11.
*Symphony No. 39, E flat major, K. 543: Mar. 23, 24, 25, 26.
*Symphony No. 40, G minor, K. 550: Nov. 20.
*Symphony No. 41, C major, K. 551 ("Jupiter"): Nov. 24, 25, 27, 30.

PONCE—Estrellita: Feb. 4.

PROKOFIEFF—Cantata, "Alexander Nevsky," Opus 78: Feb. 9, 10, 11, 12.
Concerto No. 3 for Piano and Orchestra, C major, Opus 26: Jan. 19, 20, 21, 22.
Concerto No. 5 for Piano and Orchestra, G major, Opus 55: Oct. 27, 28, 29, 30.
Suite, "Winter Holiday": Dec. 31.
Symphony No. 5, B flat major, Opus 100: Apr. 6, 7, 8, 9, 15.

RACHMANINOFF—Concerto No. 2 for Piano and Orchestra, C minor, Opus 18: Nov. 26.
Rhapsody on a Theme of Paganini for Piano and Orchestra, Opus 43: Feb. 16, 17, 18, 19.

RAVEL—**"Daphnis and Chloé" (Complete Ballet): Mar. 9, 10, 11, 12.
"Daphnis and Chloé," Suite No. 2: Sept. 27.
"Mother Goose" Suite: Mar. 4, 7, 14.
*"La Valse," a Choreographic Poem for Orchestra: Nov. 26.

RIEGGER—Variations for Piano and Orchestra, Opus 54: Oct. 6, 7, 8, 9.

RIMSKY-KORSAKOFF—*Capriccio Espagnol, Opus 34: Feb. 4.
"Cortège" and "Danse des bouffons" from "Snegurochka" (The Snow Maiden): Dec. 31.

RODGERS—*Ballet Music from "On Your Toes": Mar. 4, 7, 14.

ROSSINI—Overture, "La scala di seta": Jan. 12, 13, 14, 15.
"Una voce poco fa," from "The Barber of Seville": Feb. 4.

SAINT-SAENS—Overture to "The Yellow Princess": Nov. 26.

SCHOENBERG—Five Pieces for Orchestra, Opus 16: Dec. 1, 2, 4.

SCHUBERT—Symphony No. 4, C minor ("Tragic"): Feb. 9, 10, 11, 12.

SCHUMAN—**Symphony No. 3 (in Two Parts, and Four Movements): Oct. 13, 14, 16.

SCHUMANN—Concerto for Piano and Orchestra, A minor, Opus 54: Nov. 17, 18, 19; Jan. 31.
Concerto for Violoncello and Orchestra, A minor, Opus 129: Oct. 20, 21, 23.
Symphony No. 1, B flat major, Opus 38 ("Spring"): Oct. 27, 28, 29, 30.
Symphony No. 2, C major, Opus 61: Oct. 6, 7, 8, 9.

Symphony No. 3, E flat major, Opus 97 ("Rhenish"): Oct. 13, 14, 16.
**Symphony No. 4, D minor, Opus 120: Sept. 29, 30; Oct. 1, 2.
SIBELIUS—Concerto for Violin and Orchestra, D minor, Opus 47: Jan. 31.
Symphony No. 2, D major, Opus 43: Jan. 12, 13, 14, 15.
Symphony No. 5, E flat major, Opus 82: Mar. 23, 24, 25, 26.
STRAUSS—*Don Juan, Opus 20: Dec. 15, 16, 18.
"Don Quixote" (Introduction, Theme with Variations, and Finale), Fantastic
    Variations on a Theme of Knightly Character, Opus 35: Nov. 17, 18, 19, 20.
Final Scene from "Capriccio," Opus 85: Dec. 15, 16, 17, 18.
Symphonia Domestica, Opus 53: Dec. 15, 16, 18.
STRAVINSKY—Concerto for Violin and Orchestra, D major: Feb. 2, 3, 5.
*Le Sacre du Printemps: Apr. 13, 14, 16.
*Suite from "The Firebird": Oct. 2.
Symphony of Psalms: Mar. 9, 10, 12.
TANSMAN—Suite Baroque: Feb. 23 (b), 24, 25, 26.
TCHAIKOVSKY—Concerto No. 1 for Piano and Orchestra, B flat minor, Opus
    23: Dec. 18 (eve.).
Marche Solennelle: Mar. 7, 14.
**Symphonic Fantasy, "Francesca da Rimini," Opus 32: Oct. 27, 28, 29, 30.
*Symphony No. 4, F minor, Opus 36: Dec. 10.
TOCH—Circus Overture: Mar. 4.
WAGNER—"Liebestod" from "Tristan und Isolde": Dec. 10.
*Overture, "Tannhäuser": Feb. 16, 17, 18, 19.
*Siegfried Idyll: Oct. 20, 21, 23.
WALDTEUFEL—Skaters' Waltz: Dec. 31.
WEBER—Overture, "Der Freischütz": Jan. 31.
*Overture, "Oberon": Oct. 6, 7, 8, 9.
WEBER, B.—Concerto for Piano and Orchestra, Opus 52: Mar. 23 (a), 24, 25,
    26.
WEBERN—Six Pieces for Orchestra, Opus 6: Dec. 1, 2, 4.

SOLOISTS

PIANO

LEONARD BERNSTEIN: Sept. 29, 30;
    Oct. 1, 15, 18, 26.
ZITA CARNO: Oct. 6, 7, 8, 9.
IVAN DAVIS: Jan. 31.
RUDOLF FIRKUSNY: Nov. 30; Dec. 1,
    2, 4.
LEON FLEISHER: Feb. 16, 17, 18, 19.
SAMSON FRANÇOIS: Oct. 27, 28, 29,
    30.
GLENN GOULD: Mar. 16, 17, 19.
MORTON GOULD: Jan. 12, 13, 14, 15.
LORIN HOLLANDER: Apr. 6, 7, 8, 9, 15.
MOURA LYMPANY: Nov. 26.
OZAN MARSH: Mar. 4, 7, 14.
WILLIAM MASSELOS: Mar. 23, 24, 25,
    26.
GUIOMAR NOVAES: Nov. 17, 18, 19.
SVIATOSLAV RICHTER: Dec. 18.
ZADEL SKOLOVSKY: Jan. 19, 20, 21, 22.

VIOLIN

JOHN CORIGLIANO: Nov. 10, 11, 13.
CHRISTIAN FERRAS: Nov. 3, 4, 5, 6, 8.
ZINO FRANCESCATTI: Apr. 13, 14, 16.
ERIC FRIEDMAN: Jan. 31.
LEONID KOGAN: Nov. 24, 25, 27.
AARON ROSAND: Oct. 13, 14, 16.
ISAAC STERN: Sept. 27.
ZVI ZEITLIN: Feb. 2, 3, 5.

VIOLA

WILLIAM LINCER: Nov. 17, 18, 19, 20.

VIOLONCELLO

ROHAN DE SARAM: Jan. 5, 6, 7, 8.
LEONARD ROSE: Oct. 20, 21, 23.
LASZLO VARGA: Nov. 17, 18, 19, 20.

VOICE

ADELE ADDISON, soprano: Oct. 20, 21,
    23.
CHARLES BRESSLER, tenor: Nov. 3, 4,
    5, 6, 8.

LILI CHOOKASIAN, contralto: Feb. 9, 10, 11, 12.

LISA DELLA CASA, soprano: Dec. 15, 16, 17, 18.

DONALD GRAMM, bass-baritone: Jan. 27, 28, 29.

MARTHA LIPTON, mezzo-soprano: Mar. 30, 31; Apr. 1, 2.

NAN MERRIMAN, mezzo-soprano: Jan. 26, 27, 28, 29.

MARNI NIXON, soprano: Mar. 16, 17, 19.

LEONIE RYSANEK, soprano: Dec. 10.

BEVERLY SILLS, soprano: Feb. 4.

LEOPOLD SIMONEAU, tenor: Jan. 26, 27, 28, 29.

JENNIE TOUREL, mezzo-soprano: Nov. 3, 4, 5, 6; Feb. 13.

CHESTER WATSON, bass-baritone: Jan. 26.

CHORUS

BOYS' CHOIR from THE LITTLE CHURCH AROUND THE CORNER, Stuart Gardner, Director: Mar. 30, 31; Apr. 1, 2.

CHORAL ART SOCIETY, William Jonson, Director: Nov. 3, 4, 5, 6, 8.

JUILLIARD CHORUS, Frederick Prausnitz, Conductor; Abraham Kaplan, Associate Conductor: Jan. 26, 27, 28, 29.

SCHOLA CANTORUM OF NEW YORK, Hugh Ross, Director: Mar. 9, 10, 11, 12; Women's Chorus only: Mar. 30, 31; Apr. 1, 2.

SYMPHONIC CHOIR of the WESTMINSTER CHOIR COLLEGE, Warren Martin, Conductor: Feb. 9, 10, 11, 12.

ENSEMBLE

LUKAS FOSS IMPROVISATION CHAMBER ENSEMBLE: Oct. 20, 21, 23.

Participants in Pension Fund Concert, Feb. 13:

EDIE ADAMS, BETTY COMDEN, BARBARA COOK, ADOLPH GREEN, CAROL LAWRENCE, ANNA MOFFO, ELAINE STRITCH, JENNIE TOUREL, RICHARD TUCKER, members of AMERICAN BALLET THEATRE.

●

TOUR OF CONTINENTAL UNITED STATES, HAWAII, CANADA, AND WEST BERLIN—1960

Conductors

Leonard Bernstein

Aug. 10—Eve.	Atlantic City, N.J.
Aug. 11—Eve.	Detroit, Mich.
Aug. 13—Eve.	Denver, Colo.
Aug. 15—Eve.	Vancouver, B.C.

Leonard Bernstein, Russell Stanger

*Aug. 16—Aft.	Vancouver, B.C.

Leonard Bernstein

Aug. 16—Eve.	Vancouver, B.C.
Aug. 18—Eve.	Seattle, Wash.
Aug. 19—Eve.	Seattle, Wash.
Aug. 20—Eve.	Portland, Ore.
Aug. 22—Eve.	Honolulu, Hawaii
Aug. 23—Eve.	Honolulu, Hawaii
Aug. 26—Eve.	San Francisco, Cal.
Aug. 27—Eve.	San Francisco, Cal.

Leonard Bernstein, Russell Stanger

Aug. 28—Aft.	Berkeley, Cal.

Leonard Bernstein

Aug. 29—Eve.	Las Vegas, Nev.
Aug. 30—Eve.	San Diego, Cal.

Sept. 1—Eve.	Santa Barbara, Cal.
Sept. 2—Eve.	Hollywood, Cal.
Sept. 4—Eve.	Hollywood, Cal.
Sept. 5—Eve.	Hollywood, Cal.
Sept. 7—Eve.	Salt Lake City, Utah
Sept. 9—Eve.	Chicago, Ill.

Leonard Bernstein, Russell Stanger

*Sept. 10—Aft.	Chicago, Ill.

Leonard Bernstein

Sept. 10—Eve.	Chicago, Ill.

Leonard Bernstein, Russell Stanger

Sept. 11—Aft.	St. Louis, Mo.

Leonard Bernstein

Sept. 12—Eve.	Memphis, Tenn.
Sept. 13—Eve.	New Orleans, La.
Sept. 15—Eve.	Atlanta, Ga.
Sept. 16—Eve.	Chattanooga, Tenn.
Sept. 17—Eve.	Birmingham, Ala.
Sept. 18—Aft.	Charlotte, N.C.
Sept. 22—Eve.	West Berlin
Sept. 23—Eve.	West Berlin
Sept. 25—Aft.	Washington, D.C.

* Young People's Concert.

TOUR REPERTOIRE

Compositions marked with an asterisk (*) are recorded by
the New York Philharmonic on Columbia Records

BARTOK—*Concerto for Orchestra: Aug. 16, 19, 26, 29; Sept. 2, 7, 10, 15, 17, 23, 25.

BEETHOVEN—Concerto No. 1 for Piano and Orchestra, C major, Opus 15: Aug. 16, 19, 26, 29; Sept. 1, 2, 7, 10, 11, 15, 17, 23.
*Symphony No. 7, A major, Opus 92: Aug. 28; Sept. 9, 12, 13.

BERLIOZ—Overture, "Roman Carnival," Opus 9: Aug. 15, 19, 26, 29; Sept. 1, 2, 10, 11, 15, 17.

BERNSTEIN—Overture to "Candide": Aug. 13, 20, 22, 27, 30; Sept. 4, 7, 9, 16, 22, 25.

BRAHMS—Concerto for Violin and Orchestra, D major, Opus 77: Sept. 4.
*Symphony No. 1, C minor, Opus 68: Aug. 13; Sept. 16.

COPLAND—El Salón México: Aug. 13, 20, 22, 27, 30; Sept. 4, 16, 22, 25.

DEBUSSY—Nocturnes: Nuages, Fêtes: Aug. 11; Sept. 12.
Prelude to the Afternoon of a Faun: Aug. 28; Sept. 13, 18.

FRANCK—*Symphony in D minor: Aug. 10, 11, 15, 18, 23; Sept. 18.

HARRIS—Symphony No. 3 (in One Movement): Aug. 13, 20, 22, 27, 30; Sept. 1, 4, 11, 16, 22, 25.

RAVEL—"Daphnis and Chloé," Suite No. 2: Aug. 10, 15, 18, 23; Sept. 1, 5, 9, 11.

ROSSINI—*Overture, "Semiramide": Aug. 10, 11, 15, 18, 23, 28; Sept. 12, 13, 18, 23.

STRAUSS—*Tone Poem, "Till Eulenspiegel's Merry Pranks," Opus 28: Aug. 10, 15, 18, 23; Sept. 5, 9.

STRAVINSKY—*Suite from "The Firebird": Aug. 28; Sept. 13, 18.

TCHAIKOVSKY—Capriccio Italien, Opus 45: Aug. 11; Sept. 12.
*Symphony No. 5, E minor, Opus 64: Aug. 20, 22, 27, 30; Sept. 5, 22.

TOUR SOLOISTS

LEONARD BERNSTEIN, piano: Aug. 16, 19, 26, 29; Sept. 1, 2, 7, 10, 11, 15, 17, 23.
JASCHA HEIFETZ, violin: Sept. 4.

1961–62 ONE HUNDRED TWENTIETH SEASON

LEONARD BERNSTEIN, *Music Director*

Guest Conductors

NADIA BOULANGER	GEORG SOLTI
JOSEF KRIPS	WILLIAM STEINBERG
PAUL PARAY	LEOPOLD STOKOWSKI
THOMAS SCHIPPERS	ALFRED WALLENSTEIN

Young People's Concerts   *Three Special Saturday Concerts*
LEONARD BERNSTEIN, *Music Director*   ANDRE KOSTELANETZ

Assistant Conductors
JOHN CANARINA, SEIJI OZAWA, MAURICE PERESS

Naumburg Foundation Concerts   *Lincoln Center Student Concerts*
WERNER TORKANOWSKY   IZLER SOLOMON

CONCERTS

1961

Leonard Bernstein

Sept. 26—Eve.	Carnegie Hall	
	(Pension Fund Benefit)	
Sept. 28—Eve.	Carnegie Hall	
Sept. 29—Aft.	Carnegie Hall	
Sept. 30—Eve.	Carnegie Hall	
Oct. 1—Aft.	Carnegie Hall	
Oct. 12—Eve.	Carnegie Hall	
Oct. 13—Aft.	Carnegie Hall	
*Oct. 14—Aft.	Carnegie Hall	
Oct. 14—Eve.	Carnegie Hall	
Oct. 15—Aft.	Carnegie Hall	
Oct. 19—Eve.	Carnegie Hall	
Oct. 20—Aft.	Carnegie Hall	
Oct. 21—Eve.	Carnegie Hall	
Oct. 22—Aft.	Carnegie Hall	
Oct. 26—Eve.	Carnegie Hall	
Oct. 27—Aft.	Carnegie Hall	
Oct. 28—Eve.	Carnegie Hall	
Oct. 29—Aft.	Carnegie Hall	
Nov. 2—Eve.	Carnegie Hall	
Nov. 3—Aft.	Carnegie Hall	
Nov. 4—Eve.	Carnegie Hall	
Nov. 5—Aft.	Carnegie Hall	
Nov. 7—Eve.	White Plains, N. Y.	

Paul Paray

Nov. 9—Eve.	Carnegie Hall
Nov. 10—Aft.	Carnegie Hall

Leonard Bernstein

*Nov. 11—Aft.	Carnegie Hall

Paul Paray

Nov. 11—Eve.	Carnegie Hall
Nov. 12—Aft.	Carnegie Hall
Nov. 16—Eve.	Carnegie Hall
Nov. 17—Aft.	Carnegie Hall
Nov. 18—Eve.	Carnegie Hall
Nov. 19—Aft.	Carnegie Hall

Josef Krips

Nov. 23—Eve.	Carnegie Hall
Nov. 24—Aft.	Carnegie Hall
Nov. 25—Eve.	Carnegie Hall
Nov. 26—Aft.	Carnegie Hall
Nov. 30—Eve.	Carnegie Hall
Dec. 1—Aft.	Carnegie Hall
Dec. 2—Eve.	Carnegie Hall
Dec. 3—Aft.	Carnegie Hall
Dec. 7—Eve.	Carnegie Hall
Dec. 8—Aft.	Carnegie Hall
Dec. 9—Eve.	Carnegie Hall
Dec. 10—Aft.	Carnegie Hall

1961

Dec. 14—Eve.	Carnegie Hall
Dec. 15—Aft.	Carnegie Hall
Dec. 16—Eve.	Carnegie Hall
Dec. 17—Aft.	Carnegie Hall

Werner Torkanowsky

Dec. 28—Eve.	Carnegie Hall
Dec. 30—Eve.	Carnegie Hall
	(Naumburg Foundation Concerts)

1962

Georg Solti

Jan. 4—Eve.	Carnegie Hall
Jan. 5—Aft.	Carnegie Hall
Jan. 6—Eve.	Carnegie Hall
Jan. 7—Aft.	Carnegie Hall
Jan. 11—Eve.	Carnegie Hall
Jan. 12—Aft.	Carnegie Hall
Jan. 13—Eve.	Carnegie Hall
Jan. 14—Aft.	Carnegie Hall

Thomas Schippers

Jan. 18—Eve.	Carnegie Hall
Jan. 19—Aft.	Carnegie Hall
Jan. 20—Eve.	Carnegie Hall
Jan. 21—Aft.	Carnegie Hall
Jan. 25—Eve.	Carnegie Hall
Jan. 26—Aft.	Carnegie Hall
Jan. 27—Eve.	Carnegie Hall
Jan. 28—Aft.	Carnegie Hall
Feb. 1—Eve.	Carnegie Hall
Feb. 2—Aft.	Carnegie Hall
Feb. 3—Eve.	Carnegie Hall
Feb. 4—Aft.	Carnegie Hall
Feb. 8—Eve.	Carnegie Hall
Feb. 9—Aft.	Carnegie Hall

André Kostelanetz

Feb. 10—Eve.	Carnegie Hall

Thomas Schippers

Feb. 11—Aft.	Carnegie Hall

Nadia Boulanger

Feb. 15—Eve.	Carnegie Hall
Feb. 16—Aft.	Carnegie Hall

**Leonard Bernstein, John Canarina,
Seiji Ozawa, Maurice Peress**

Feb. 17—Aft.	Troy, N. Y.
	(Concert for Young People)

Nadia Boulanger

Feb. 17—Eve.	Carnegie Hall
Feb. 18—Aft.	Carnegie Hall

Alfred Wallenstein

Feb. 22—Eve.	Carnegie Hall
Feb. 23—Aft.	Carnegie Hall

* Young People's Concert.

1962

Feb. 24—Eve.	Carnegie Hall
Feb. 25—Aft.	Carnegie Hall

Leopold Stokowski

Mar. 1—Eve.	Carnegie Hall
Mar. 2—Aft.	Carnegie Hall

André Kostelanetz

Mar. 3—Eve.	Carnegie Hall

Leopold Stokowski

Mar. 4—Aft.	Carnegie Hall

Alfred Wallenstein

Mar. 8—Eve.	Carnegie Hall
Mar. 9—Aft.	Carnegie Hall

André Kostelanetz

Mar. 10—Eve.	Carnegie Hall

Alfred Wallenstein

Mar. 11—Aft.	Carnegie Hall

William Steinberg

Mar. 15—Eve.	Carnegie Hall
Mar. 16—Aft.	Carnegie Hall
Mar. 17—Eve.	Carnegie Hall
Mar. 18—Aft.	Carnegie Hall
Mar. 22—Eve.	Carnegie Hall
Mar. 23—Aft.	Carnegie Hall

Leonard Bernstein

*Mar. 24—Aft.	Carnegie Hall

William Steinberg

Mar. 24—Eve.	Carnegie Hall
Mar. 25—Aft.	Carnegie Hall

Leonard Bernstein

Mar. 29—Eve.	Carnegie Hall
Mar. 30—Aft.	Carnegie Hall
Mar. 31—Eve.	Carnegie Hall
Apr. 1—Aft.	Carnegie Hall
Apr. 5—Eve.	Carnegie Hall
Apr. 6—Aft.	Carnegie Hall

1962

Leonard Bernstein, John Canarina, Seiji Ozawa, Maurice Peress

*Apr. 7—Aft.	Carnegie Hall

Leonard Bernstein

Apr. 7—Eve.	Carnegie Hall
Apr. 8—Aft.	Carnegie Hall
Apr. 10—Eve.	Newark, N. J.
Apr. 12—Eve.	Carnegie Hall
Apr. 13—Aft.	Carnegie Hall
Apr. 14—Eve.	Carnegie Hall
Apr. 15—Aft.	Carnegie Hall
Apr. 19—Eve.	Carnegie Hall
Apr. 20—Aft.	Carnegie Hall
Apr. 21—Eve.	Carnegie Hall
Apr. 22—Aft.	Carnegie Hall
Apr. 26—Eve.	Carnegie Hall
Apr. 27—Aft.	Carnegie Hall
Apr. 28—Eve.	Carnegie Hall
Apr. 29—Aft.	Carnegie Hall

Leonard Bernstein, Seiji Ozawa, Maurice Peress

May 3—Eve.	Carnegie Hall
May 4—Aft.	Carnegie Hall
May 5—Eve.	Carnegie Hall
May 6—Aft.	Carnegie Hall

Izler Solomon
8 Lincoln Center Student Concerts
(Two each afternoon)

May 8—Aft.	Carnegie Hall
May 9—Aft.	Carnegie Hall
May 10—Aft.	Carnegie Hall
May 11—Aft.	Carnegie Hall

Leonard Bernstein

May 17—Eve.	Carnegie Hall
May 18—Aft.	Carnegie Hall
May 19—Aft.	Carnegie Hall
May 20—Aft.	Carnegie Hall

REPERTOIRE FOR 1961–62

(a) World premiere.
(b) First performance in the United States.
(c) First performance in New York.
(d) First performance of orchestral version.

Compositions marked with an asterisk (*) are recorded by the New York Philharmonic on Columbia Records and now available; those with two asterisks (**) will be released by Columbia Records in the near future.

BACH—Concerto for Violin, Oboe, and Orchestra, D minor: Dec. 30.
The Passion of Our Lord According to Saint Matthew: Apr. 19, 20, 21, 22.
Suite No. 4, D major, BWV 1069: Jan. 18, 19, 20, 21.

---

* Young People's Concert.

BARBER—Adagio for Strings: Feb. 1, 2, 3, 4.
Medea's Meditation and Dance of Vengeance, Opus 23-A: Jan. 25, 26, 27, 28.

BARTOK—**Rhapsody No. 1 for Violin and Orchestra: Apr. 12, 13.
**Rhapsody No. 2 for Violin and Orchestra: Apr. 14, 15.
Suite, "The Wonderful Mandarin": Jan. 11, 12, 13, 14.

BEETHOVEN—Concerto No. 2 for Piano and Orchestra, B-flat major, Opus 19: Mar. 22, 23, 24, 25.
**Concerto No. 5 for Piano and Orchestra, E-flat major, Opus 73 ("Emperor"): Apr. 26, 27, 28, 29.
Fantasy for Piano, Chorus, and Orchestra, C minor, Opus 80: Apr. 26, 27, 28, 29.
Overture, "Coriolanus": Nov. 30; Dec. 1, 2, 3.
*Overture, "Leonore," No. 2, Opus 72-A: Dec. 28.
Symphony No. 4, B-flat major, Opus 60: Apr. 26, 27, 28, 29.
*Symphony No. 5, C minor, Opus 67: Sept. 26; Nov. 7.
Symphony No. 6, F major, Opus 68, ("Pastorale"): Nov. 9, 10, 11, 12.
*Symphony No. 9, with Final Chorus on Schiller's Ode "To Joy," D minor, Opus 125: Dec. 14, 15, 16, 17.

BERLIOZ—Cléopâtre: Sept. 28, 29, 30; Oct. 1.
**Harold in Italy, Symphony in Four Movements with Viola Solo, Opus 16: Oct. 19, 20, 21, 22.

BLOCH—"Schelomo," Hebrew Rhapsody for Violoncello and Orchestra: Nov. 2, 3, 4, 5, 7.

BOULANGER, L.—Psalm 24, "La terre appartient à l'Eternel": Feb. 15, 16, 17, 18.
Psalm 129, "Ils m'ont assez opprimé": Feb. 15, 16, 17, 18.
Psalm 130, "Du fond de l'abîme": Feb. 15, 16, 17, 18.

BRAHMS—*Academic Festival Overture, Opus 80: Mar. 8, 9, 11.
Concerto No. 1 for Piano and Orchestra, D minor, Opus 15: Apr. 5, 6, 8.
Concerto No. 2 for Piano and Orchestra, B-flat major, Opus 83: Mar. 8, 9, 11.
Concerto for Violin and Orchestra, D major, Opus 77: Dec. 7, 8, 9, 10.
*Symphony No. 1, C minor, Opus 68: Nov. 23, 24, 25, 26; Apr. 7, 10.
*Symphony No. 2, D major, Opus 73: May 17, 18, 19, 20.
*Symphony No. 3, F major, Opus 90: Mar. 8, 9, 11.
*Symphony No. 4, E minor, Opus 98: Feb. 8, 9, 11.

BRUCH—**Concerto for Violin and Orchestra, No. 1, G minor, Opus 26: Jan. 20.

BRUCKNER—Symphony No. 8, C minor: Nov. 30; Dec. 1, 2, 3.
Symphony No. 9, D minor: Mar. 29, 30, 31; Apr. 1.

CHERUBINI—Overture, "Médée": Feb. 1, 2, 3, 4.

CHOPIN—Concerto No. 2 for Piano and Orchestra, F minor, Opus 21: Nov. 16, 17, 18, 19.

COPLAND—**Suite from the Ballet "Appalachian Spring": Sept. 28, 29; Oct. 1.

DEBUSSY—"La Mer," Three Symphonic Sketches: Oct. 12, 13, 14, 15.
Rhapsody for Clarinet and Orchestra: Oct. 12, 13, 14, 15; Nov. 7.

DIAMOND—Symphony No. 8: Oct. 26 (a), 27, 28, 29.

DVORAK—**Symphony No. 5, "From the New World," E minor, Opus 95: Apr. 12, 13, 14, 15.

FALLA—*Three Dances from "The Three-Cornered Hat": Nov. 2, 3, 4, 5, 7.

FAURE—**Ballade for Piano and Orchestra, F-sharp major, Opus 19: Oct. 26, 27, 28, 29.
Requiem Mass, Opus 48: Feb. 15, 16, 17, 18.

FOSS—A Parable of Death: Dec. 14, 15, 16, 17.

HARRIS—Symphony No. 7 (In one movement): Oct. 19, 20, 21, 22.

HAYDN—Symphony No. 22, E-flat major ("The Philosopher"): Mar. 22, 23, 24, 25.
   Symphony No. 82, C major ("L'Ours"): May 3, 4, 5, 6.
   Symphony No. 83, G minor ("La Poule"): Mar. 29, 30, 31; Apr. 1, 7, 10.

HINDEMITH—Symphonic Metamorphosis of Themes by Carl Maria von Weber: Dec. 30.
   Symphony, "Mathis der Maler": Mar. 22, 23, 24, 25.

HONEGGER—Symphony No. 2, for String Orchestra: Dec. 7, 8, 9, 10.

IVES—Central Park in the Dark: May 3, 4, 5, 6.

JANACEK—Sinfonietta: Jan. 4, 5, 6, 7.

KURKA—Julius Caesar (A Symphonic Epilogue after Shakespeare's Play): Mar. 1 (c), 2, 4.

LEHAR—Serenade from "Frasquita": Feb. 10.
   Suite, "The Merry Widow": Feb. 10.
   "Yours Is My Heart Alone" from "The Land of Smiles": Feb. 10.

MAHLER—*Symphony No. 1, D major: May 3, 4, 5, 6.
   *Symphony No. 4, G major, for Orchestra and Soprano Solo: Jan. 11, 12, 13, 14.
   Symphony No. 7: Mar. 15, 16, 17, 18.

MENDELSSOHN—Overture, "The Hebrides" (Fingal's Cave), Opus 26: Nov. 16, 17, 18, 19.

MENNIN—*Symphony No. 3: Feb. 1, 2, 3, 4.

MENOTTI—Overture, "Amelia Goes to the Ball": Feb. 8, 9, 11.

MESSIAEN—Trois Petites Liturgies de la Présence Divine (Three Little Liturgies of the Divine Presence): Nov. 2, 3, 4, 5.

MILHAUD—**Les Choéphores ("The Libation Bearers"): Oct. 12, 13, 14, 15.

MOZART—Adagio and Rondo from Serenade No. 10, for Thirteen Woodwinds, B-flat major, K. 361: Apr. 12, 13, 14, 15.
   "Alleluia" from the motet "Exsultate, Jubilate," K. 165: Feb. 10.
   Aria, "Voi che sapete," from "The Marriage of Figaro": Feb. 10.
   Concerto for Piano and Orchestra, B-flat major, K. 450: Jan. 4, 5, 6, 7.
   Concerto No. 1 for Violin and Orchestra, B-flat major, K. 207: Apr. 12, 13, 14, 15.
   Concerto No. 5 for Violin and Orchestra, A major, K. 219: Dec. 30.
   Overture, "The Magic Flute": Nov. 9, 10, 11, 12.
   Overture, "The Marriage of Figaro": Feb. 10.
   Symphony No. 24, B-flat major, K. 182: Feb. 10.
   Symphony No. 35, D major, "Haffner," K. 385: Nov. 23, 24, 25, 26.

NIELSEN—Overture, "Maskarade": Apr. 5, 6, 8.
   Symphony No. 5, Opus 50: Apr. 5, 6, 8.

PISTON—Concerto No. 2 for Violin and Orchestra: May 17 (c), 18, 19, 20.

POULENC—Concerto for Two Pianos and Orchestra, D minor: Oct. 19, 20, 21, 22.

PROKOFIEV—Concerto No. 2 for Piano and Orchestra, G minor, Opus 16: Nov. 23, 24, 25, 26.
   Concerto No. 3 for Piano and Orchestra, C major, Opus 26: Jan. 27.
   Concerto No. 2 for Violin and Orchestra, G minor, Opus 63: Jan. 18, 19, 21.
   Symphony No. 3, C minor, Opus 44: Dec. 28.
   Symphony No. 7, C sharp minor, Opus 131: Feb. 22, 23, 24, 25.

PURCELL—Dido's Lament, from "Dido and Aeneas": Jan. 11, 12, 13, 14.

RACHMANINOFF—Concerto No. 3 for Piano and Orchestra, D minor, Opus 30: Feb. 8, 9, 11.

RAVEL—*Bolero: Nov. 16, 17, 18, 19.
*"Daphnis et Chloé," Suite No. 2: Sept. 28, 29; Oct. 1.

RESPIGHI—Symphonic Poem, "The Pines of Rome": Nov. 9, 10, 11, 12.

RIEGGER—Study in Sonority for Ten Violins or Any Multiple Thereof, Opus 7: Mar. 29, 30, 31; Apr. 1.

ROCHBERG—Symphony No. 2: Dec. 30.

ROSSINI—Act 1, "Il Conte Ory": Feb. 1, 2, 3, 4.

ROUSSEL—Symphony No. 3, G minor, Opus 42: Sept. 28, 29, 30; Oct. 1.

SAINT-SAENS—**Concerto No. 4 for Piano and Orchestra, C minor, Opus 44: Oct. 26, 27, 28, 29.

SATIE—Parade: Oct. 26, 27, 28, 29.

SCHUBERT—Symphony No. 3, D major: Mar. 15, 16, 17, 18.
Symphony No. 9, C major: Feb. 22, 23, 24, 25.

SCHUMAN—*New England Triptych: Three Pieces for Orchestra after William Billings: Dec. 28.

SCHUMANN—Symphony No. 2, C major, Opus 61: Nov. 16, 17, 18, 19.
*Symphony No. 4, D minor, Opus 120: Jan. 4, 5, 6, 7.

SHOSTAKOVICH—Concerto No. 1 for Piano and Orchestra, Opus 35: Apr. 7, 10.
Symphony No. 1, Opus 10: Jan. 25, 26, 28.
*Symphony No. 5, Opus 47: Mar. 1, 2, 4.

SMIT—Capriccio for Strings: Nov. 2 (c), 3, 4, 5.

STRAUS, O.—"My Hero" from "The Chocolate Soldier": Feb. 10.

STRAUSS, J.—Excerpts from "Die Fledermaus": Feb. 10.
"On the Beautiful Blue Danube," Waltz, Opus 314: Feb. 10.

STRAUSS, R.—*Don Juan, Tone Poem after Nicolaus Lenau, Opus 20: Sept. 26; Mar. 22, 23, 24, 25.
Suite, "Der Rosenkavalier," Opus 59: Dec. 28.
*Tone Poem, "Death and Transfiguration," Opus 24: Jan. 25, 26, 27, 28.
Waltzes from "Der Rosenkavalier": Feb. 10.

STRAVINSKY—Capriccio for Piano and Orchestra: May 17, 18, 19, 20.
*Fireworks, Fantasy for Large Orchestra, Opus 4: May 17, 18, 19, 20.
Greeting Prelude: May 17, 18, 19, 20.
*Suite from "The Firebird" (1919 Version): Dec. 7, 8, 9, 10.

TCHAIKOVSKY—**Concerto No. 1 for Piano and Orchestra, B-flat minor, Opus 23: Sept. 30.
Excerpts from the Ballet "Swan Lake": Mar. 10.
Overture Solennelle "1812," Opus 49: Mar. 10.
*"Romeo and Juliet," Fantasy Overture, after Shakespeare: Mar. 3.
Serenade, C major, Opus 48, for String Orchestra: Mar. 10.
*Suite from the Ballet "The Nutcracker," Opus 71A: Mar. 3.
*Suite, "Queen of Spades": Mar. 10.
*Symphony No. 5, E minor, Opus 64: Mar. 3.
*Symphony No. 6, B minor, Opus 74 ("Pathétique"): Jan. 18, 19, 20, 21.

THOMSON—A Solemn Music: Feb. 15 (d), 16, 17, 18.
The Seine at Night: Oct. 12, 13, 14, 15.

VAUGHAN WILLIAMS—*Fantasia on a Theme by Thomas Tallis, for Double String Orchestra: Mar. 1, 2, 4.

VERDI—Overture, "La Forza del Destino": Jan. 25, 26, 27, 28.

WAGNER—A Faust Overture: Feb. 22, 23, 24, 25.
**Brünnhilde's Immolation Scene from "Götterdämmerung": Sept. 26.
**Five Wesendonck Songs: Sept. 26.

*Overture, "The Flying Dutchman": Nov. 9, 10, 11, 12.
Prelude, "Lohengrin": Nov. 9, 10, 11, 12.
Scenes from Act III, "Parsifal": Mar. 1, 2, 4.
WEBERN—Passacaglia for Orchestra, Opus 1: Nov. 30; Dec. 1, 2, 3.
WOLF—Mignon's Song, "Kennst du das Land?": Jan. 11, 12, 13, 14.

SOLOISTS

PIANO
GINA BACHAUER: Jan. 27.
JOHN BROWNING: Jan. 4, 5, 6, 7.
ROBERT CASADESUS: Oct. 26, 27, 28, 29.
SHURA CHERKASSKY: Nov. 23, 24, 25, 26.
VAN CLIBURN: Mar. 8, 9, 11.
PHILIPPE ENTREMONT: Sept. 30.
MALCOLM FRAGER: Mar. 22, 23, 24, 25.
ARTHUR GOLD and ROBERT FIZDALE: Oct. 19, 20, 21, 22.
GLENN GOULD: Apr. 5, 6, 8.
PAUL JACOBS: Nov. 2, 3, 4, 5.
SEYMOUR LIPKIN: May 17, 18, 19, 20.
ANDRE PREVIN: Apr. 7, 10.
RUDOLF SERKIN: Apr. 26, 27, 28, 29.
ABBEY SIMON: Feb. 8, 9, 11.
FOU TS'ONG: Nov. 16, 17, 18, 19.

VIOLIN
JOHN CORIGLIANO: Mar. 10; Apr. 19, 20, 21, 22.
ZINO FRANCESCATTI: Jan. 18, 19, 20, 21.
JOSEPH FUCHS: May 17, 18, 19, 20.
JOSEPH SILVERSTEIN: Dec. 30.
TOSSY SPIVAKOVSKY: Dec. 7, 8, 9, 10.
ISAAC STERN: Apr. 12, 13, 14, 15.

VIOLA
WILLIAM LINCER: Oct. 19, 20, 21, 22.

VIOLONCELLO
ZARA NELSOVA: Nov. 2, 3, 4, 5, 7.
CARL STERN: Apr. 19, 20, 21, 22.
LASZLO VARGA: Mar. 10.

DOUBLE BASS
CARLO RAVIOLA: Apr. 19, 20, 21, 22.

FLUTE
JOHN WUMMER: Apr. 19, 20, 21, 22.

OBOE
HAROLD GOMBERG: Dec. 30; Apr. 19, 20, 21, 22.

OBOE D'AMORE
ENGELBERT BRENNER: Apr. 19, 20, 21, 22.
ALBERT GOLTZER: Apr. 19, 20, 21, 22.

CLARINET
STANLEY DRUCKER: Oct. 12, 13, 14, 15; Nov. 7.

TRUMPET
WILLIAM VACCHIANO: Apr. 7, 10.

HARPSICHORD
LEONID HAMBRO: Apr. 19, 20, 21, 22.

ORGAN
VERNON de TAR: Feb. 15, 16, 17, 18.
BRUCE PRINCE-JOSEPH: Apr. 19, 20, 21, 22.

ONDES MARTENOT
JOHN CANARINA: Nov. 2, 3, 4, 5.

VOICE
ADELE ADDISON, soprano: Apr. 19, 20, 21, 22.
BETTY ALLEN, mezzo-soprano: Apr. 19, 20, 21, 22.
VIRGINIA BABIKIAN, soprano: Oct. 12, 13, 14, 15.
DONALD BELL, bass-baritone: Apr. 19, 20, 21, 22.
GIMI BENI, bass-baritone: Feb. 1, 2, 3, 4.
MCHENRY BOATWRIGHT, baritone: Oct. 12, 13, 14, 15.
CHARLES BRESSLER, tenor: Apr. 19, 20, 21, 22.
PHYLLIS CURTIN, soprano: Feb. 10.
ROBERT ECKERT, tenor: Feb. 15, 16, 17, 18.
EILEEN FARRELL, soprano: Sept. 26.
NORMAN FARROW, bass-baritone: Dec. 14, 15, 16, 17.
DONALD GRAMM, baritone: Feb. 15, 16, 17, 18.
RERI GRIST, soprano: Feb. 15, 16, 17, 18.
IRENE JORDAN, soprano: Oct. 12, 13, 14, 15.
WILMA LIPP, soprano: Dec. 14, 15, 16, 17.
DAVID LLOYD, tenor: Apr. 19, 20, 21, 22.
MARGUERITE PAQUET, mezzo-soprano: Feb. 15, 16, 17, 18.

RUDOLF PETRAK, tenor: Dec. 14, 15, 16, 17.

FRANK PORRETTA, tenor: Feb. 1, 2, 3, 4.

JUDITH RASKIN, soprano: Feb. 1, 2, 3, 4.

IRMGARD SEEFRIED, soprano: Jan. 11, 12, 13, 14.

CAROL TOSCANO, soprano: Feb. 1, 2, 3, 4.

JENNIE TOUREL, mezzo-soprano: Sept. 28, 29, 30; Oct. 1.

NORMAN TREIGLE, bass-baritone: Feb. 1, 2, 3, 4.

HELEN VANNI, mezzo-soprano: Feb. 1, 2, 3, 4.

SHIRLEY VERRETT-CARTER, mezzo-soprano: Dec. 14, 15, 16, 17; Feb. 1, 2, 3, 4.

WILLIAM WILDERMAN, bass: Apr. 19, 20, 21, 22.

CHORUS

BOYS' CHOIR from THE LITTLE CHURCH AROUND THE CORNER, Stuart Gardner, Director: Apr. 19, 20, 21, 22.

CHORAL ART SOCIETY, William Jonson, Director: Feb. 15, 16, 17, 18; Women's Choir only: Nov. 2, 3, 4, 5.

CHORUS, Walter Baker, Director: Feb. 1, 2, 3, 4.

COLLEGIATE CHORALE, Abraham Kaplan, Director: Apr. 19, 20, 21, 22.

SCHOLA CANTORUM OF NEW YORK, Hugh Ross, Director: Oct. 12, 13, 14, 15.

WESTMINSTER SYMPHONIC CHOIR, Warren Martin, Director: Dec. 14, 15, 16, 17; Apr. 26, 27, 28, 29.

DANCERS

PATRICIA WILDE: Mar. 10.

CONRAD LUDLOW: Mar. 10.

NARRATOR

FELICIA MONTEALEGRE: Dec. 14, 15, 16, 17.

OGDEN NASH: Mar. 3.

VERA ZORINA: Oct. 12, 13, 14, 15.

•

FALL TOUR 1961

Leonard Bernstein, Conductor

Sept. 21—Eve.	Philadelphia	Sept. 23—Eve.	Richmond
Sept. 22—Eve.	Baltimore	Sept. 24—Aft.	Washington, D. C.

TOUR REPERTOIRE

* Recorded by the New York Philharmonic on Columbia Records and now available.
** Recording will be released by Columbia Records in the near future.

BEETHOVEN—*Symphony No. 5, Opus 67: Sept. 21, 23, 24.

RAVEL—*"Daphnis et Chloé," Suite No. 2: Sept. 22, 23.

ROUSSEL—Symphony No. 3, G minor, Opus 42: Sept. 21, 22, 24.

STRAUSS—*Don Juan, Tone Poem after Nicolaus Lenau, Opus 20: Sept. 22, 23.

WAGNER—**Brünnhilde's Immolation, from "Götterdämmerung": Sept. 21, 22.
**Five Wesendonck Songs: Sept. 23, 24.

TOUR SOLOIST

EILEEN FARRELL, soprano: Sept. 21, 22, 23, 24.

1962–63 ONE HUNDRED TWENTY-FIRST SEASON

LEONARD BERNSTEIN, *Music Director*

Guest Conductors

SIR JOHN BARBIROLLI	PAUL HINDEMITH	THOMAS SCHIPPERS
KARL BOEHM	LORIN MAAZEL	GEORGE SZELL

Young People's Concerts
LEONARD BERNSTEIN, Music Director

Pension Fund Benefit, Lincoln Center Student Concerts, Introduction to Lincoln Center Concert
ANDRE KOSTELANETZ

Assistant Conductors
SERGE FOURNIER, YURI KRASNOPOLSKY, ZOLTAN ROZSNYAI

CONCERTS

1962

Leonard Bernstein
Sept. 23—Eve.   Philharmonic Hall
    (Inaugural Concert)
Sept. 26—Eve.   Philharmonic Hall
    (Special Concert During Opening
        Week)
Sept. 30—Aft.   Philharmonic Hall
Oct. 4—Eve.   Philharmonic Hall
Oct. 5—Aft.   Philharmonic Hall
Oct. 6—Eve.   Philharmonic Hall
Oct. 7—Aft.   Philharmonic Hall
Oct. 11—Eve.   Philharmonic Hall
Oct. 12—Aft.   Philharmonic Hall
Oct. 13—Aft.   Philharmonic Hall
    (Young People's Concert)
Oct. 13—Eve.   Philharmonic Hall
    (Invitational Program for Young
        People)
Oct. 14—Aft.   Philharmonic Hall
Oct. 18—Eve.   Philharmonic Hall
Oct. 19—Aft.   Philharmonic Hall

**Leonard Bernstein, Serge Fournier,
Zoltan Rozsnyai, Yuri Krasnopolsky**
Oct. 20—Eve.   Philharmonic Hall
Oct. 21—Aft.   Philharmonic Hall

Leonard Bernstein
Oct. 25—Eve.   Philharmonic Hall
Oct. 26—Aft.   Philharmonic Hall
Oct. 27—Eve.   Philharmonic Hall
Oct. 28—Aft.   Philharmonic Hall

Karl Boehm
Nov. 1—Eve.   Philharmonic Hall
Nov. 2—Aft.   Philharmonic Hall

1962

Leonard Bernstein
Nov. 3—Aft.   Philharmonic Hall
    (Young People's Concert)

Karl Boehm
Nov. 3—Eve.   Philharmonic Hall
Nov. 4—Aft.   Philharmonic Hall
Nov. 8—Eve.   Philharmonic Hall
Nov. 9—Aft.   Philharmonic Hall
Nov. 10—Eve.   Philharmonic Hall
Nov. 11—Aft.   Philharmonic Hall
Nov. 15—Eve.   Philharmonic Hall
Nov. 16—Aft.   Philharmonic Hall
Nov. 17—Eve.   Philharmonic Hall
Nov. 18—Aft.   Philharmonic Hall
Nov. 22—Eve.   Philharmonic Hall
Nov. 23—Aft.   Philharmonic Hall
Nov. 24—Eve.   Philharmonic Hall
Nov. 25—Aft.   Philharmonic Hall

Sir John Barbirolli
Nov. 29—Eve.   Philharmonic Hall
Nov. 30—Aft.   Philharmonic Hall
Dec. 1—Eve.   Philharmonic Hall
Dec. 2—Aft.   Philharmonic Hall
Dec. 6—Eve.   Philharmonic Hall
Dec. 7—Aft.   Philharmonic Hall
Dec. 8—Eve.   Philharmonic Hall
Dec. 9—Aft.   Philharmonic Hall

Lorin Maazel
Dec. 13—Eve.   Philharmonic Hall
Dec. 14—Aft.   Philharmonic Hall
Dec. 15—Eve.   Philharmonic Hall
Dec. 16—Aft.   Philharmonic Hall
Dec. 20—Eve.   Philharmonic Hall
Dec. 21—Aft.   Philharmonic Hall
Dec. 22—Eve.   Philharmonic Hall
Dec. 23—Aft.   Philharmonic Hall

Concerts and Repertory, 1962–63

1963

Leonard Bernstein

Jan.	3—Eve.	Philharmonic Hall
Jan.	4—Aft.	Philharmonic Hall
Jan.	5—Eve.	Philharmonic Hall
Jan.	6—Aft.	Philharmonic Hall
Jan.	10—Eve.	Philharmonic Hall
Jan.	11—Aft.	Philharmonic Hall
Jan.	11—Aft.	Philharmonic Hall

Leonard Bernstein, Serge Fournier, Zoltan Rozsnyai, Yuri Krasnopolsky

Jan. 12—Aft.   Philharmonic Hall
(Young People's Concert)

Leonard Bernstein

Jan.	12—Eve.	Philharmonic Hall
Jan.	13—Aft.	Philharmonic Hall
Jan.	17—Eve.	Philharmonic Hall
Jan.	18—Aft.	Philharmonic Hall
Jan.	19—Eve.	Philharmonic Hall
Jan.	20—Aft.	Philharmonic Hall

André Kostelanetz

Jan. 22—Eve.   Philharmonic Hall
(Pension Fund Benefit)

Leonard Bernstein

Jan.	24—Eve.	Philharmonic Hall
Jan.	25—Aft.	Philharmonic Hall
Jan.	26—Eve.	Philharmonic Hall
Jan.	27—Aft.	Philharmonic Hall
Jan.	31—Eve.	Philharmonic Hall
Feb.	1—Aft.	Philharmonic Hall
Feb.	2—Eve.	Philharmonic Hall
Feb.	3—Aft.	Philharmonic Hall
Feb.	7—Eve.	Philharmonic Hall
Feb.	8—Aft.	Philharmonic Hall
Feb.	9—Aft.	Philharmonic Hall

(Young People's Concert)

Feb.	9—Eve.	Philharmonic Hall
Feb.	10—Aft.	Philharmonic Hall

George Szell

Feb.	28—Eve.	Philharmonic Hall
Mar.	1—Aft.	Philharmonic Hall
Mar.	2—Eve.	Philharmonic Hall
Mar.	3—Aft.	Philharmonic Hall
Mar.	7—Eve.	Philharmonic Hall
Mar.	8—Aft.	Philharmonic Hall
Mar.	9—Eve.	Philharmonic Hall
Mar.	10—Aft.	Philharmonic Hall
Mar.	14—Eve.	Philharmonic Hall
Mar.	15—Aft.	Philharmonic Hall
Mar.	16—Eve.	Philharmonic Hall
Mar.	17—Aft.	Philharmonic Hall
Mar.	21—Eve.	Philharmonic Hall
Mar.	22—Aft.	Philharmonic Hall
Mar.	23—Eve.	Philharmonic Hall
Mar.	24—Aft.	Philharmonic Hall

1963

Leonard Bernstein

Mar. 26—Eve.   Philharmonic Hall
(Pension Fund Benefit)

André Kostelanetz
6 Lincoln Center Student Concerts
(2 each afternoon)

Mar.	26—Aft.	Philharmonic Hall
Mar.	28—Aft.	Philharmonic Hall
Mar.	29—Aft.	Philharmonic Hall

André Kostelanetz

Mar. 30—Aft.   Philharmonic Hall
(Introduction to Lincoln Center Concert)

Thomas Schippers

Apr.	4—Eve.	Philharmonic Hall
Apr.	5—Aft.	Philharmonic Hall
Apr.	6—Eve.	Philharmonic Hall
Apr.	7—Aft.	Philharmonic Hall

Claudio Abbado, Pedro Calderon, Zdenek Kosler*

Apr. 7—Eve.   Philharmonic Hall
(Concert for winners of Dimitri Mitropoulos International Music Competition)

Thomas Schippers

Apr.	11—Eve.	Philharmonic Hall
Apr.	12—Aft.	Philharmonic Hall
Apr.	13—Eve.	Philharmonic Hall
Apr.	14—Aft.	Philharmonic Hall

Paul Hindemith

Apr.	18—Eve.	Philharmonic Hall
Apr.	19—Aft.	Philharmonic Hall
Apr.	20—Eve.	Philharmonic Hall
Apr.	21—Aft.	Philharmonic Hall
Apr.	25—Eve.	Philharmonic Hall
Apr.	26—Aft.	Philharmonic Hall
Apr.	27—Eve.	Philharmonic Hall
Apr.	28—Aft.	Philharmonic Hall

Leonard Bernstein

May	2—Eve.	Philharmonic Hall
May	3—Aft.	Philharmonic Hall
May	4—Eve.	Philharmonic Hall
May	5—Aft.	Philharmonic Hall

Leonard Bernstein, Serge Fournier, Zoltan Rozsnyai, Yuri Krasnopolsky

May	9—Eve.	Philharmonic Hall
May	10—Aft.	Philharmonic Hall
May	11—Aft.	Philharmonic Hall

(Student Concert, presented by New York State Council on the Arts and The Lincoln Center Fund)

May	11—Eve.	Philharmonic Hall
May	12—Aft.	Philharmonic Hall

* Assistant Conductors 1963–64.

Leonard Bernstein   May 24—Aft.   Philharmonic Hall
May 16—Eve.   Philharmonic Hall   May 25—Eve.   Philharmonic Hall
May 17—Aft.   Philharmonic Hall   May 26—Aft.   Philharmonic Hall
May 18—Eve.   Philharmonic Hall
May 19—Aft.   Philharmonic Hall

REPERTOIRE

(a) World première: commissioned by the New York Philharmonic in celebration of its opening season in Lincoln Center for the Performing Arts.
(b) First performance in the United States.
(c) First performance in New York.

Compositions marked with an asterisk (*) are recorded by the New York Philharmonic on Columbia Records and now available; those with two asterisks (**) will be released by Columbia Records in the near future.

BACH, J. C.—Symphony in G minor, Op. 6, No. 6: Nov. 8, 9, 10, 11.

BACH, J. S.—Brandenburg Concerto No. 6, B-flat major, BWV 1051: Oct. 11, 12, 13, 14.
Concerto for Four Claviers and String Orchestra, A minor, BWV 1065: Sept. 26.

BARBER—Andromache's Farewell: Apr. 4 (a), 5, 6, 7.

BEETHOVEN—*Concerto No. 1 for Piano and Orchestra, C major, Opus 15: March 14, 15, 16, 17.
Concerto No. 3 for Piano and Orchestra, C minor, Opus 37: March 7, 8, 9, 10.
*Concerto No. 4 for Piano and Orchestra, G major, Opus 58: Nov. 29, 30; Dec. 1, 2.
*Concerto No. 5 for Piano and Orchestra, E-flat major, Opus 73 ("Emperor"): Feb. 28; March 1, 2, 3.
*Gloria, from Missa Solemnis in D major, Opus 123: Sept. 23.
Overture, "The Consecration of the House," Opus 124: Oct. 4, 5, 6, 7.
Overture to "The Creatures of Prometheus," Opus 43: Mar. 7, 8, 9, 10.
*Overture to "Egmont," Opus 84: Feb. 28; Mar. 1, 2, 3.
Symphony No. 2, D major, Opus 36: Feb. 28; Mar. 1, 2, 3.
Symphony No. 3, E-flat major, Opus 55 ("Eroica"): Mar. 7, 8, 9, 10.
*Symphony No. 5, C minor, Opus 67: Dec. 13, 14, 15, 16.
Symphony No. 6, F major, Opus 68 ("Pastoral"): May 9, 10, 11, 12.
*Symphony No. 7, A major, Opus 92: Nov. 22, 23, 24, 25.

BERG—*Concerto for Violin and Orchestra: Dec. 13, 14, 15, 16.

BERLIOZ—*Overture, "The Roman Carnival," Opus 9: Jan. 22; Mar. 23, 24.
*Symphonie Fantastique, Opus 14: May 23, 24, 25, 26.

BERNSTEIN—*Symphonic Dances from "West Side Story": Feb. 7, 8, 9, 10.

BIZET—Symphony in C major: May 23, 24, 25, 26.

BRAHMS—Concerto No. 2 for Piano and Orchestra, B-flat major, Opus 83: Oct. 25, 26, 27, 28.
*Concerto for Violin, Violoncello and Orchestra, A minor, Opus 102: Nov. 8, 9, 10, 11.
*Symphony No. 2, D major, Opus 73: Nov. 29, 30; Dec. 1, 2.
*Symphony No. 3, F major, Opus 90: Mar. 21, 22, 23, 24.
*Symphony No. 4, E minor, Opus 98: Oct. 4, 5, 6, 7.
*Tragic Overture, Opus 81: Mar. 21, 22, 23, 24.

BRITTEN—Spring Symphony, Opus 44: May 2, 3, 4, 5.
Variations on a Theme by Frank Bridge, Opus 10: Apr. 4, 5, 6, 7.

BRUCH—*Concerto No. 1 for Violin and Orchestra, G minor, Opus 26: Mar. 23, 24.

BRUCKNER—Psalm 150: Apr. 18, 19, 20, 21.
Symphony No. 7, E major: Nov. 1, 2, 3, 4.

CHOPIN—Concerto No. 1 for Piano and Orchestra, E minor, Opus 11: Jan. 17, 18, 19.

COPLAND—*Connotations for Orchestra: Sept. 23 (a); Jan. 31; Feb. 1, 2.

DEBUSSY—Ibéria from *"Images pour orchestre": May 16, 17, 18, 19.
Rondes de Printemps from *"Images pour orchestre": May 9, 10, 11, 12.
The Martyrdom of Saint Sebastian: Oct. 18, 19, 20, 21.

DELIUS—Intermezzo from "Fennimore and Gerda": Nov. 29, 30; Dec. 1, 2.
On Hearing the First Cuckoo in Spring: May 9, 10, 11, 12.

DVORAK—Symphony No. 2, D minor, Opus 70: Jan. 24, 25, 26, 27; Feb. 3.

EINEM—Suite, "Dantons Tod," Opus 6A: Nov. 22 (c), 23, 24, 25.

ELGAR—"Cockaigne (In London Town)," Concert Overture, Opus 40: Feb. 7, 8, 9, 10.

ETLER—Concerto for Wind Quintet and Orchestra (1960): Oct. 25 (b), 26, 27, 28.

FALLA—*Three Dances from "The Three-Cornered Hat": Jan. 22.

FINE—Adagio, from Notturno for Strings and Harp: Oct. 4, 5, 6, 7.

GERHARD—Symphony No. 1: Jan. 10 (b), 11, 12, 13.

HARRIS—Kentucky Spring: May 9, 10, 11, 12.

HAYDN—Concerto No. 2 for Violoncello and Orchestra, D major, Opus 101: Dec. 6, 7, 8, 9.
Sinfonia Concertante for Violin, Violoncello, Oboe, Bassoon and Orchestra, B-flat major, Opus 84: Sept. 26.
Symphony No. 88, G major: Jan. 3, 4, 5, 6.
*Symphony No. 102, B-flat major: Oct. 25, 26, 27, 28.

HENZE—Symphony No. 5: May 16 (a), 17, 18, 19.

HINDEMITH—Concerto for Organ and Orchestra: Apr. 25 (a), 26, 27, 28.
**When Lilacs Last in the Dooryard Bloom'd: A Requiem "For Those We Love": Apr. 18, 19, 20, 21

HONEGGER—Three Symphonic Movements: Rugby, Pastorale d'Eté, Pacific 231: Oct. 18, 19, 20, 21.

IVES—Decoration Day: May 23, 24, 25, 26.

JANACEK—Slavonic Mass: Jan. 24, 25, 26, 27.

LISZT—*Concerto No. 1 for Piano and Orchestra, E-flat major: Jan. 31; Feb. 1.

MAHLER—*Symphony No. 5: Jan. 3, 4, 5, 6.
*Symphony No. 8, E-flat major, Part One (Veni, Creator Spiritus): Sept. 23.
Symphony No. 9, D major: Dec. 6, 7, 8, 9.

MARTINU—String Quartet with Orchestra: Jan. 17, 18, 19, 20.

MENDELSSOHN—*Concerto for Violin and Orchestra, E minor, Opus 64: Nov. 15, 16, 17, 18.
*Symphony No. 5, D minor, Opus 107 ("Reformation"): Dec. 13, 14, 15, 16.

MENNIN—Concertato for Orchestra: "Moby Dick": Jan. 17, 18, 19, 20.

MILHAUD—Ouverture Philharmonique: Nov. 29 (a), 30; Dec. 1, 2.

MOUSSORGSKY-RAVEL—*Pictures at an Exhibition: Dec. 20, 21, 22, 23.

MOZART—Concerto for Piano and Orchestra, D major, K. 537 ("Coronation"): Jan. 20.
Concerto for Violin and Orchestra No. 5, A major, K. 219: May 16, 17, 18, 19.
Serenade No. 8, D major, for Four Orchestras, K. 286: Dec. 20, 21, 22, 23.
Symphony No. 38, D major, K. 504 ("Prague"): April 11, 12, 13, 14.
*Symphony No. 40, G minor, K. 550: May 16, 17, 18, 19.
*Symphony No. 41, C major, K. 551 ("Jupiter"): Nov. 1, 2, 3, 4.

POULENC—Concerto for Organ, String Orchestra and Timpani, G minor: April 11, 12, 13, 14.
Sept Répons des Ténèbres: April 11 (a), 12, 13, 14.

PUCCINI—Aria, "Vissi d'arte," from "Tosca": Jan. 22.

RAVEL—Concerto for Piano and Orchestra, G major: Feb. 2, 3.
"Mother Goose" Suite: Jan. 22.
*La Valse: Jan. 17, 18, 19, 20.

REGER—Variations and Fugue on a Merry Theme of Johann Adam Hiller, Opus 100: Apr. 25, 26, 27, 28.

ROSSINI—Aria, "Bel raggio," from "Semiramide": Mar. 26.
Overture, "The Barber of Seville": Mar. 26.
Overture, "La Scala di Seta": Jan. 10, 11, 12, 13.

SCHUBERT—Symphony No. 5, B-flat major: Jan. 31; Feb. 1, 2, 3.
*Symphony in B minor ("Unfinished"): Mar. 26.

SCHUMAN—*New England Triptych: Three Pieces for Orchestra after William Billings: Jan. 22.
Symphony No. 8: Oct. 4 (a), 5, 6, 7.

SCHUMANN—Concerto for Piano and Orchestra, A minor, Opus 54: Nov. 22, 23, 24, 25.
Symphony No. 1, B-flat major, Opus 38 ("Spring"): May 2, 3, 4, 5.
Symphony No. 2, C major, Opus 61: Dec. 20, 21, 22, 23.
*Symphony No. 3, E-flat major, Opus 97 ("Rhenish"): Mar. 14, 15, 16, 17.

SHOSTAKOVICH—Symphony No. 7, Opus 60 ("Leningrad"): Oct. 11, 12, 13, 14.

SIBELIUS—Concerto for Violin and Orchestra, D minor, Opus 47: Jan. 10, 11, 12, 13.
Symphony No. 2, D major, Opus 43: April 4, 5, 6, 7.

SMETANA—Overture, "The Bartered Bride": Jan. 24, 25, 26, 27.

STRAUSS, R.—*Dance of the Seven Veils, from "Salome": Jan. 22.
*Don Juan, Tone Poem after Nikolaus Lenau, Opus 20: Jan. 31; Feb. 1, 2.
*Festival Prelude for Large Orchestra and Organ, Opus 61: Sept. 26.
Final Scene from "Salome": Jan. 22.
*Till Eulenspiegel's Merry Pranks, After Old-Time Roguish Fashion—In Rondeau Form, Opus 28: Jan. 10, 11, 12, 13.
Tone Poem, "Also Sprach Zarathustra," Opus 30: Nov. 8, 9, 10, 11.
Tone Poem, "Ein Heldenleben," Opus 40: Nov. 15, 16, 17, 18.

STRAVINSKY—*Le Sacre du Printemps: Sept. 26.

TCHAIKOVSKY—*Concerto for Violin and Orchestra, D major, Opus 35: Mar. 21, 22.
*Symphony No. 4, F minor, Opus 36: Feb. 7, 8, 9, 10.

THOMAS—Mad Scene from "Hamlet": Mar. 26.
Overture to "Mignon": Mar. 26.

VAUGHAN WILLIAMS—*Serenade to Music: Sept. 23.

VERDI—Aria, "Madre, pietosa vergine," from "La Forza del Destino": Jan. 22.
Recitative and Aria, "Ernani, involami," from "Ernani": Mar. 26.

VIVALDI—*Concerto, E major, Opus 8, No. 1 ("Spring"), from "The Four Seasons": May 9, 10, 11, 12.
Concerto for Four Violins and String Orchestra, B minor, Opus 3, No. 10: Sept. 26.

WAGNER—Prelude to "Die Meistersinger von Nürnberg": Apr. 11, 12, 13, 14.
Prelude to "Lohengrin": Mar. 14, 15, 16, 17.

WEBER—Cavatina: "Und ob die Wolke," from "Der Freischütz": Mar. 26.
Overture to "Der Freischütz": Mar. 26.
Overture to "Euryanthe": Apr. 25, 26, 27, 28.
*Overture to "Oberon": Nov. 15, 16, 17, 18.

SOLOISTS

PIANO

GINA BACHAUER: Nov. 29, 30; Dec. 1, 2.

LEONARD BERNSTEIN: Feb. 2, 3.

MICHEL BLOCK: Jan. 20.

CLIFFORD CURZON: Feb. 28; Mar. 1, 2, 3.

RUDOLF FIRKUSNY: Mar. 7, 8, 9, 10.

LEON FLEISHER: Sept. 26; Mar. 14, 15, 16, 17.

MALCOLM FRAGER: Sept. 26.

GARY GRAFFMAN: Sept. 26.

EUGENE ISTOMIN: Sept. 26; Oct. 25, 26, 27, 28.

JULIUS KATCHEN: Nov. 22, 23, 24, 25.

ROSINA LHEVINNE: Jan. 17, 18, 19.

ANDRE WATTS: Jan. 31; Feb. 1.

VIOLIN

JOHN CORIGLIANO: Sept. 26; Nov. 8, 9, 10, 11, 15, 16, 17, 18; May 9, 10, 11, 12.

CHRISTIAN FERRAS: Dec. 13, 14, 15, 16.

JOSEPH FUCHS: Sept. 26.

ZINO FRANCESCATTI: Jan. 10, 11, 12, 13.

SZYMON GOLDBERG: Sept. 26.

FRANK GULLINO: Sept. 26.

ERICA MORINI: Mar. 21, 22, 23, 24.

RUGGIERO RICCI: Nov. 15, 16, 17, 18.

TOSSY SPIVAKOVSKY: Sept. 26.

ISAAC STERN: May 16, 17, 18, 19.

VIOLONCELLO

ALDO PARISOT: Dec. 6, 7, 8, 9.

LASZLO VARGA: Nov. 8, 9, 10, 11.

CARL STERN: Sept. 26.

FLUTE

JOHN WUMMER: Oct. 25, 26, 27, 28.

OBOE

HAROLD GOMBERG: Sept. 26; Oct. 25, 26, 27, 28.

CLARINET

STANLEY DRUCKER: Oct. 25, 26, 27, 28.

BASSOON

MANUEL ZEGLER: Sept. 26; Oct. 25, 26, 27, 28.

FRENCH HORN

JAMES CHAMBERS: Oct. 25, 26, 27, 28.

ORGAN

E. POWER BIGGS: Sept. 26.

ANTON HEILLER: Apr. 25, 26, 27, 28.

BRUCE PRINCE-JOSEPH: Jan. 24, 25, 26, 27; Apr. 18, 19, 20, 21.

THOMAS SCHIPPERS: Apr. 11, 12, 13, 14.

ENSEMBLE

JUILLIARD STRING QUARTET: Jan. 17, 18, 19, 20.

VOICE

ADELE ADDISON, soprano: Sept. 23; Oct. 18, 19, 20, 21.

LUCINE AMARA, soprano: Sept. 23.

MARTINA ARROYO, soprano: Apr. 4, 5, 6, 7, 18, 19, 20, 21.

VIRGINIA BABIKIAN, soprano: Oct. 18, 19, 20, 21.

DONALD BELL, bass-baritone: Sept. 23.

CHARLES BRESSLER, tenor: Sept. 23.

LILI CHOOKASIAN, mezzo-soprano: Sept. 23.

EILEEN FARRELL, soprano: Sept. 23.

EZIO FLAGELLO, bass-baritone: Sept. 23.

GEORGE GAYNES, bass: Jan. 24, 25, 26, 27.

NICOLAI GEDDA, tenor: Jan. 24, 25, 26, 27.

MARLENA KLEINMAN, mezzo-soprano: Oct. 18, 19, 20, 21.

RICHARD LEWIS, tenor: May 2, 3, 4, 5.

GEORGE LONDON, bass-baritone: Sept. 23; Apr. 18, 19, 20, 21.

JANIS MARTIN, contralto: Jan. 24, 25, 26, 27.

JEFFREY MEYER, boy soprano: Apr. 11, 12, 13, 14.

BIRGIT NILSSON, soprano: Jan. 22.

LOUISE PARKER, contralto: Apr. 18, 19, 20, 21.

HELGA PILARCZYK, soprano: Jan. 24, 25, 26, 27.

REGINA SARFATY, mezzo-soprano: May 2, 3, 4, 5.

JOANNA SIMON, mezzo-soprano: Oct. 18, 19, 20, 21.

JOAN SUTHERLAND, soprano: Mar. 26.

JENNIE TOUREL, mezzo-soprano: Sept. 23.

RICHARD TUCKER, tenor: Sept. 23.

SHIRLEY VERRETT-CARTER, mezzo-soprano: Sept. 23.

JON VICKERS, tenor: Sept. 23.

JENNIFER VYVYAN, soprano: May 2, 3, 4, 5.

CHORUS

BOYS' CHOIR from THE LITTLE CHURCH AROUND THE CORNER, Stuart Gardner, Director: Apr. 11, 12, 13, 14; May 2, 3, 4, 5.

BOYS' CHOIR from ST. PAUL'S CHURCH, Flatbush, Charles Ennis, Director: Apr. 11, 12, 13, 14.

BOYS' CHOIR from ST. PAUL'S CHURCH, Westfield, N. J., Richard Connelly, Director: May 2, 3, 4, 5.

CHORAL ART SOCIETY, William Jonson, Director: Oct. 18, 19, 20, 21.

COLLEGIATE CHORALE, Abraham Kaplan, Director: May 2, 3, 4, 5.

COLUMBUS BOYCHOIR, Donald Bryant, Director: Sept. 23.

JUILLIARD CHORUS, Abraham Kaplan, Director: Sept. 23.

SCHOLA CANTORUM of NEW YORK, Hugh Ross, Director: Sept. 23; Apr. 18, 19, 20, 21.

WALTER BAKER CHORUS: Apr. 11, 12, 13, 14.

WESTMINSTER CHOIR, Elaine Brown, Director: Jan. 24, 25, 26, 27.

NARRATORS

FELICIA MONTEALEGRE: Oct. 18, 19, 20, 21.

FRITZ WEAVER: Oct. 18, 19, 20, 21.

•

TOUR TO ENGLAND AND FLORIDA—WINTER, 1963

Leonard Bernstein, Conductor

Feb. 13—Eve.	London	Feb. 19—Eve.	Miami Beach
Feb. 14—Aft.	London	Feb. 20—Eve.	Miami
	(Concert for Young People)	Feb. 21—Eve.	Miami Beach
Feb. 14—Eve.	London	Feb. 22—Eve.	Ft. Lauderdale
Feb. 16—Eve.	Manchester	Feb. 23—Eve.	Miami Beach

TOUR REPERTOIRE

*Recorded by the New York Philharmonic on Columbia Records and now available.

BEETHOVEN—*Overture, "Leonore," No. 3, Opus 72A: Feb. 19, 22, 23.

BERLIOZ—*Overture, "Roman Carnival," Opus 9: Feb. 21.

BERNSTEIN—*Symphonic Dances from "West Side Story": Feb. 14 (eve.), 16, 19, 20, 22, 23.

BRAHMS—*Symphony No. 4, E minor, Opus 98: Feb. 19.

COPLAND—*Connotations for Orchestra: Feb. 13.

DVORAK—Symphony No. 2, D minor, Opus 70: Feb. 13, 20, 21.

ELGAR—"Cockaigne (In London Town)," Concert Overture, Opus 40: Feb. 13.

RAVEL—Concerto for Piano and Orchestra, G major: Feb. 13, 21.

ROSSINI—Overture, "La scala di seta": Feb. 14 (eve.), 16.

SCHUBERT—Symphony No. 5, B-flat major: Feb. 14 (eve.), 16, 20, 21.

TCHAIKOVSKY—*Symphony No. 4, F minor, Opus 36: Feb. 14 (eve.), 16, 22, 23.

TOUR SOLOIST

LEONARD BERNSTEIN, pianist: Feb. 13, 21.

•

NEW YORK PHILHARMONIC "PROMENADES"
FIRST SEASON   1963   PHILHARMONIC HALL

Conductors

André Kostelanetz
May 29, 30, 31; June 1, 2; June 5, 6, 7, 8, 9 (Eves.).

André Previn
June 12, 13, 14, 15, 16 (Eves.).

Morton Gould
June 19, 20, 21, 22, 23 (Eves.).

REPERTOIRE—"PROMENADES"

Compositions marked with an asterisk (*) are recorded by the New York Philharmonic on Columbia Records and now available.

CANTELOUBE—Songs of the Auvergne: June 15, 16.

COPLAND—Dance Symphony: June 22, 23.
 Hoe-Down, from *"Rodeo": May 29, 30.
 *A Lincoln Portrait: May 29, 30.
 Suite, "The Red Pony": June 12, 13, 14.

DEBUSSY—*Nocturnes: Nuages, Fêtes: June 15, 16.

FALLA—Ballet-Pantomime, "El Amor Brujo": June 19, 20, 21.

FERNANDEZ—"Batuque" from the Suite "Reisado do Pastoreio": June 19, 20, 21.

GERSHWIN—*An American in Paris: June 15, 16.
 Catfish Row—Suite from "Porgy and Bess" (orchestrated by the composer): May 29 (First New York performance), 30.
 Gershwin on Broadway (Overture to "Girl Crazy"; The Man I Love; Fascinating Rhythm; Strike Up the Band): June 5, 6, 9.
 Promenade: May 29 (First New York performance), 30.
 Rhapsody in Blue: June 5, 6, 9.
 Three Preludes (piano solo): June 5, 6, 9.

GLAZOUNOV—Excerpts from the Ballet "Raymonda": June 22, 23.

GOTTSCHALK—The Banjo (arranged by Maganini): May 29, 30.

GOTTSCHALK-KAY—Grand Tarantelle for Piano and Orchestra: May 29, 30.

GOULD—Latin-American Symphonette: June 19, 20, 21.

KAY—Saturday Night, from "Western Symphony": May 29, 30.

KERN—Music from "Show Boat": May 29, 30.

KORNGOLD—Marietta's Song, from "The Dead City": May 31; June 1, 2.

LEHAR—Orchestral Suite from "The Merry Widow": May 31; June 1, 2.
 Yours Is My Heart Alone, from "The Land of Smiles": May 31; June 1, 2.

MENOTTI—Overture, "Amelia Goes to the Ball": June 22, 23.

MOZART—"Alleluia" from the motet "Exsultate, Jubilate," K. 165: May 31; June 1, 2.
 Aria, "Martern aller Arten," from "The Abduction from the Seraglio": May 31; June 1, 2.
 Overture, "The Marriage of Figaro": May 31; June 1, 2.
 Symphony No. 24, B-flat major, K. 182: May 31; June 1, 2.

MILHAUD—Suite Française: June 15, 16.

OFFENBACH-ROSENTHAL—Gaîté Parisienne: June 15, 16.

PREVIN—Overture to a Comedy: June 12 (First New York performance), 13, 14.

PROKOFIEV—Symphony No. 1, D major, Opus 25 ("Classical"): June 12, 13, 14.

RAVEL—Pavane pour une Infante défunte: June 22, 23.
*La Valse: June 22, 23.

RIMSKY-KORSAKOV—*Capriccio Espagnol, Opus 34: June 19, 20, 21.

SCHUMAN—*New England Triptych: Three Pieces for Orchestra after William Billings: May 29, 30.

SOUSA—The Stars and Stripes Forever: May 29, 30.

STRAUSS, J.—Czardas, from "Die Fledermaus": May 31; June 1, 2.
"Straussiana" (Voices of Spring, Perpetuum Mobile, Pizzicato Polka, Tritsch-Tratsch Polka, On the Beautiful Blue Danube): May 31; June 1, 2.

STRAUSS, R.—Waltzes from "Der Rosenkavalier": May 31; June 1, 2.

TCHAIKOVSKY—Excerpts from "Eugene Onegin": June 7, 8.
Excerpts from the Ballet "Swan Lake": June 7, 8.
*Marche Slave, Opus 31: June 7, 8.
Suite from the Ballet "The Nutcracker," Opus 71a, with verses by Ogden Nash: June 7, 8.

TURINA—La Oración del Torero: June 19, 20, 21.

WEBER—Invitation to the Dance: June 22, 23.

Jazz Improvisations on Themes from Leonard Bernstein's "West Side Story" (Jazz combo only): June 12, 13, 14.

SOLOISTS—"PROMENADES"

PIANO
AGUSTIN ANIEVAS: June 5, 6, 9.
THEODORE LETTVIN: May 29, 30.
ANDRE PREVIN: June 12, 13, 14.

DOUBLE BASS
RED MITCHELL: June 12, 13, 14.

PERCUSSION
SHELLY MANNE: June 12, 13, 14.

VOICE
MCHENRY BOATWRIGHT, baritone: June 5, 6, 9.
CAROL BRICE, contralto: June 19, 20, 21.
MARNI NIXON, soprano: June 15, 16.
ARLENE SAUNDERS, soprano: June 7, 8.
BEVERLY SILLS, soprano: May 31; June 1, 2.
VERONICA TYLER, soprano: June 5, 6, 9.

CHORUS
SCHOLA CANTORUM of NEW YORK, HUGH ROSS, Director: June 5, 6, 9.

NARRATOR
OGDEN NASH: June 7, 8.
CARL SANDBURG: May 29, 30.

DANCERS
BALLET ESPAÑOL XIMENEZ-VARGAS: June 19, 20, 21.
DANNY DANIELS: June 22, 23.
ROYES FERNANDEZ: June 22, 23.
THE ROBERT HERGET DANCERS: May 31; June 1, 2.
CONRAD LUDLOW: June 7, 8.
PATRICIA WILDE: June 7, 8, 22, 23.

1963–64 ONE HUNDRED TWENTY-SECOND SEASON

LEONARD BERNSTEIN, *Music Director*

Guest Conductors
JOSEF KRIPS   GEORGE SZELL

LUKAS FOSS	ROBERT LA MARCHINA	ALFRED WALLENSTEIN
Lincoln Center	AMERIGO MARINO	*Pension Fund*
Student Concerts	*Conductors Selected Under*	*Benefit Concert*
	American Conductors Project	

LEONARD BERNSTEIN
Music Director,
Young People's Concerts

ANDRE KOSTELANETZ
Special Saturday Night
Concerts

CLAUDIO ABBADO, PEDRO CALDERON, ZDENEK KOSLER
Assistant Conductors

CONCERTS

1963

Leonard Bernstein
Sept. 24—Eve.   Philharmonic Hall
       (Pension Fund Benefit)
Sept. 26—Eve.   Philharmonic Hall
Sept. 27—Aft.   Philharmonic Hall
Sept. 28—Eve.   Philharmonic Hall
Sept. 29—Aft.   Philharmonic Hall
Oct. 3—Eve.   Philharmonic Hall
Oct. 4—Aft.   Philharmonic Hall
Oct. 5—Eve.   Philharmonic Hall
Oct. 6—Aft.   Philharmonic Hall
Oct. 10—Eve.   Philharmonic Hall
Oct. 11—Aft.   Philharmonic Hall
Oct. 12—Eve.   Philharmonic Hall
Oct. 13—Aft.   Philharmonic Hall

Leonard Bernstein,
Zdenek Kosler
Oct. 17—Eve.   Philharmonic Hall
Oct. 18—Aft.   Philharmonic Hall
Oct. 19—Eve.   Philharmonic Hall
Oct. 20—Aft.   Philharmonic Hall

Josef Krips
Oct. 24—Eve.   Philharmonic Hall
Oct. 25—Aft.   Philharmonic Hall
Oct. 26—Eve.   Philharmonic Hall
Oct. 27—Aft.   Philharmonic Hall
Oct. 31—Eve.   Philharmonic Hall
Nov. 1—Aft.   Philharmonic Hall

Leonard Bernstein
Nov. 2—Aft.   Philharmonic Hall
       (Young People's Concert)

Josef Krips
Nov. 2—Eve.   Philharmonic Hall
Nov. 3—Aft.   Philharmonic Hall
Nov. 7—Eve.   Philharmonic Hall

1963
Nov. 8—Eve.   Philharmonic Hall
Nov. 9—Eve.   Philharmonic Hall
Nov. 10—Aft.   Philharmonic Hall
Nov. 14—Eve.   Philharmonic Hall
Nov. 15—Aft.   Philharmonic Hall
Nov. 16—Eve.   Philharmonic Hall
Nov. 17—Aft.   Philharmonic Hall

George Szell
Nov. 21—Eve.   Philharmonic Hall
Nov. 22—Aft.   Philharmonic Hall
Nov. 23—Eve.   Philharmonic Hall
Nov. 24—Aft.   Philharmonic Hall
Nov. 28—Eve.   Philharmonic Hall

Leonard Bernstein,
Claudio Abbado,
Pedro Calderon,
Zdenek Kosler
Nov. 29—Aft.   Philharmonic Hall
Nov. 30—Aft.   Philharmonic Hall
       (Young People's Concert)

André Kostelanetz
Nov. 30—Eve.   Philharmonic Hall

George Szell
Dec. 1—Aft.   Philharmonic Hall
Dec. 5—Eve.   Philharmonic Hall
Dec. 6—Aft.   Philharmonic Hall
Dec. 7—Eve.   Philharmonic Hall
Dec. 8—Aft.   Philharmonic Hall
Dec. 12—Eve.   Philharmonic Hall
Dec. 13—Aft.   Philharmonic Hall
Dec. 14—Eve.   Philharmonic Hall
Dec. 15—Aft.   Philharmonic Hall

Robert La Marchina
Dec. 19—Eve.   Philharmonic Hall
Dec. 20—Aft.   Philharmonic Hall

1963

Amerigo Marino

Dec. 21—Eve.	Philharmonic Hall
Dec. 22—Aft.	Philharmonic Hall

1964

Leonard Bernstein

Jan. 2—Eve.	Philharmonic Hall
Jan. 3—Eve.	Philharmonic Hall
Jan. 4—Eve.	Philharmonic Hall
Jan. 5—Aft.	Philharmonic Hall
Jan. 9—Eve.	Philharmonic Hall
Jan. 10—Aft.	Philharmonic Hall
Jan. 11—Eve.	Philharmonic Hall
Jan. 12—Aft.	Philharmonic Hall

**Leonard Bernstein,
Stefan Bauer-Mengelberg**

Jan. 16—Eve.	Philharmonic Hall
Jan. 17—Aft.	Philharmonic Hall
Jan. 18—Eve.	Philharmonic Hall
Jan. 19—Aft.	Philharmonic Hall

Leonard Bernstein

Jan. 23—Eve.	Philharmonic Hall
Jan. 24—Aft.	Philharmonic Hall
Jan. 25—Aft.	Philharmonic Hall

(Young People's Concert)

Jan. 25—Eve.	Philharmonic Hall
Jan. 26—Aft.	Philharmonic Hall

Claudio Abbado

Jan. 30—Eve.	Philharmonic Hall
Jan. 31—Aft.	Philharmonic Hall

Pedro Calderon

Feb. 1—Eve.	Philharmonic Hall
Feb. 2—Aft.	Philharmonic Hall

**Leonard Bernstein,
Earle Brown**

Feb. 6—Eve.	Philharmonic Hall
Feb. 7—Aft.	Philharmonic Hall

**Leonard Bernstein,
Gunther Schuller**

Feb. 8—Aft.	Philharmonic Hall

(Young People's Concert)

**Leonard Bernstein,
Earle Brown**

Feb. 8—Eve.	Philharmonic Hall
Feb. 9—Aft.	Philharmonic Hall

Josef Krips

Feb. 13—Eve.	Philharmonic Hall
Feb. 14—Aft.	Philharmonic Hall
Feb. 15—Eve.	Philharmonic Hall
Feb. 16—Aft.	Philharmonic Hall
Feb. 20—Eve.	Philharmonic Hall

1964

Feb. 21—Aft.	Philharmonic Hall
Feb. 22—Eve.	Philharmonic Hall
Feb. 23—Aft.	Philharmonic Hall
Feb. 27—Eve.	Philharmonic Hall
Feb. 28—Aft.	Philharmonic Hall
Feb. 29—Eve.	Philharmonic Hall
Mar. 1—Aft.	Philharmonic Hall
Mar. 5—Eve.	Philharmonic Hall
Mar. 6—Aft.	Philharmonic Hall
Mar. 7—Eve.	Philharmonic Hall
Mar. 8—Aft.	Philharmonic Hall

George Szell

Mar. 12—Eve.	Philharmonic Hall
Mar. 13—Aft.	Philharmonic Hall

André Kostelanetz

Mar. 14—Eve.	Philharmonic Hall

George Szell

Mar. 15—Aft.	Philharmonic Hall
Mar. 19—Eve.	Philharmonic Hall
Mar. 20—Aft.	Philharmonic Hall
Mar. 21—Eve.	Philharmonic Hall
Mar. 22—Aft.	Philharmonic Hall
Mar. 26—Eve.	Philharmonic Hall
Mar. 27—Aft.	Philharmonic Hall
Mar. 28—Eve.	Philharmonic Hall
Mar. 29—Aft.	Philharmonic Hall
Apr. 2—Eve.	Philharmonic Hall
Apr. 3—Aft.	Philharmonic Hall
Apr. 4—Eve.	Philharmonic Hall
Apr. 5—Aft.	Philharmonic Hall

Alfred Wallenstein

Apr. 7—Eve.	Philharmonic Hall

(Pension Fund Benefit)

Leonard Bernstein

Apr. 9—Eve.	Philharmonic Hall
Apr. 10—Aft.	Philharmonic Hall
Apr. 11—Eve.	Philharmonic Hall
Apr. 12—Aft.	Philharmonic Hall
Apr. 14—Eve.	Philharmonic Hall

**Lukas Foss,
Claudio Abbado,
Zdenek Kosler**

8 Lincoln Center Student Concerts
(2 each afternoon)

Apr. 14—Aft.	Philharmonic Hall
Apr. 15—Aft.	Philharmonic Hall
Apr. 16—Aft.	Philharmonic Hall
Apr. 17—Aft.	Philharmonic Hall

Leonard Bernstein

Apr. 23—Eve.	Philharmonic Hall
Apr. 24—Aft.	Philharmonic Hall
Apr. 25—Eve.	Philharmonic Hall
Apr. 26—Aft.	Philharmonic Hall

1964

Apr. 30—Eve.	Philharmonic Hall	
May 1—Aft.	Philharmonic Hall	
May 2—Eve.	Philharmonic Hall	
May 3—Aft.	Philharmonic Hall	

**Leonard Bernstein,
Zdenek Kosler**

May 7—Eve.	Philharmonic Hall
May 8—Aft.	Philharmonic Hall

1964

May 9—Eve.	Philharmonic Hall
May 10—Aft.	Philharmonic Hall

Leonard Bernstein

May 14—Eve.	Philharmonic Hall
May 15—Aft.	Philharmonic Hall
May 16—Eve.	Philharmonic Hall
May 17—Aft.	Philharmonic Hall

REPERTOIRE

* Recorded by the New York Philharmonic on Columbia Records.

(a) World première.
(b) First performance in the United States.
(c) First performance in New York.

AUSTIN—Improvisations for Orchestra and Jazz Soloists: Jan. 9 (c), 10, 11, 12.

BACH—Suite No. 3, D major, BWV 1068: Dec. 5, 6, 7, 8.

BAIRD—Four Essays for Orchestra: Nov. 28 (b), 29; Dec. 1.

BARBER—Concerto for Violin and Orchestra, Opus 14: Apr. 23, 24, 25, 26.
Piano Concerto, Opus 38: Nov. 7, 8, 9, 10.

BARTOK—Concerto No. 2 for Piano and Orchestra: Oct. 24, 25, 26, 27.

BEETHOVEN—Concerto No. 3 for Piano and Orchestra, C minor, Opus 37: Jan. 16, 17, 18, 19.
Concerto No. 4 for Piano and Orchestra, G major, Opus 58: Nov. 21, 23, 24.
Concerto for Violin and Orchestra, D major, Opus 61: Dec. 21, 22.
*"Leonore" Overture No. 3, C major, Opus 72A: Nov. 21, 22.
Symphony No. 1, C major, Opus 21: Jan. 16, 17, 18, 19.
Symphony No. 2, D major, Opus 36: Jan. 2, 3, 4, 5.
Symphony No. 3, E flat major, Opus 55 ("Eroica"): Jan. 23, 24, 25, 26; *Marcia funebre* only: Nov. 23, 24.
*Symphony No. 5, C minor, Opus 67: Nov. 21, 23, 24.
*Symphony No. 7, A major, Opus 92: Oct. 24, 25, 26, 27; Apr. 30; May 1, 2, 3.
Symphony No. 8, F major, Opus 93: Oct. 3, 4, 5, 6.
*Symphony No. 9, with Final Chorus on Schiller's Ode "To Joy," D minor, Opus 125: May 14, 15, 16, 17.

BERLIOZ—Overture, "The Corsair," Opus 21: Dec. 19, 20.

BERNSTEIN—*Symphony No. 3: "Kaddish," for Orchestra, Mixed Chorus, Boys' Choir, Speaker (Woman) and Soprano Solo: Apr. 9 (c), 10, 11, 12, 14.

BRAHMS—Concerto No. 1 for Piano and Orchestra, D minor, Opus 15: Feb. 13, 14, 15, 16; Apr. 7.
Concerto No. 2 for Piano and Orchestra, B flat major, Opus 83: Apr. 7.
*Symphony No. 2, D major, Opus 73: Mar. 12, 13, 15.
*Symphony No. 3, F major, Opus 90: April 9, 10, 11, 12, 14.
*Symphony No. 4, E minor, Opus 98: Oct. 31; Nov. 1, 2, 3.
*Tragic Overture, Opus 81: Apr. 9, 10, 11, 12, 14.

BROWN—Available Forms II, for Orchestra Four Hands: Feb. 6 (b), 7, 8, 9.

BRUCKNER—Symphony No. 4, E flat major ("Romantic"): Mar. 5, 6, 7, 8.
Symphony No. 7, E major: Mar. 26, 27, 28, 29.

CAGE—Atlas Eclipticalis with Winter Music (Electronic Version): Feb. 6, 7, 8, 9.

CHAUSSON—Poème for Violin and Orchestra, Opus 25: Jan. 2, 3, 4, 5.
Symphony in B flat major, Op. 20: May 7, 8, 9, 10.

CHAVEZ—Symphony No. 6 (Commissioned by the New York Philharmonic):
May 7 (a), 8, 9, 10.

COPLAND—Concerto for Piano and Orchestra: Jan. 9, 10, 11, 12.

CRESTON—Frontiers, Opus 34: Nov. 30.

DALLAPICCOLA—An Mathilde: May 14, 15, 16, 17.

DEBUSSY—"Ibéria," from *"Images pour orchestre": Sept. 24.
"La Mer," Three Symphonic Sketches: Dec. 12, 13, 14, 15.
*Prelude to "The Afternoon of a Faun": Dec. 12, 13, 14, 15.

DVORAK—*Symphony No. 4, G major, Opus 88: Nov. 28, 29; Dec. 1.

FELDMAN—. . . Out of 'Last Pieces': Feb. 6, 7, 8, 9.

FRANCK—*Symphony in D minor: Dec. 19, 20.

GINASTERA—Concerto for Violin and Orchestra (Commissioned by the New
York Philharmonic): Oct. 3 (a), 4, 5, 6.

GLINKA—Overture, "Russlan and Ludmilla": Oct. 10, 11, 12, 13; Mar. 14.

HAIEFF—Symphony No. 2: Nov. 7, 8, 9, 10.

HAYDN—Symphony No. 83, G minor ("La Poule"): Feb. 1, 2.
Symphony No. 93, D major: Dec. 12, 13, 14, 15.
Symphony No. 94, G major ("Surprise"): Nov. 14, 15, 16, 17.

HINDEMITH—Concerto for Violin and Orchestra: Apr. 23, 24, 25, 26.
"The Entombment," from "Mathis der Maler": Jan. 2.
Symphonia Serena: Dec. 21, 22.
Symphonic Metamorphosis of Themes by Carl Maria von Weber: Mar. 5, 6, 7,
8.

KABALEVSKY—Symphony No. 2, Opus 19: Nov. 30.

LA MONTAINE—Fragments from "The Song of Songs," Opus 29: Feb. 27 (c),
28, 29; Mar. 1.

LIGETI—Atmosphères: Jan. 2 (b), 3, 4, 5.

LISZT—Concerto No. 2 for Piano and Orchestra, A major: Dec. 12, 13, 14, 15.

LUTOSLAWSKI—Funeral Music, for String Orchestra: Mar. 12 (c), 13, 15.

MAHLER—Das Lied von der Erde: Feb. 20, 21, 22, 23.
*Symphony No. 2, C minor, for Orchestra, Soprano and Contralto Solos, and
Mixed Chorus: Sept. 26, 27, 28, 29.

MARTIN—Concerto for Violin and Orchestra: Dec. 19, 20.

MENDELSSOHN—Concerto for Violin and Orchestra, E minor, Opus 64: Dec.
5, 6, 7, 8.
Overture to "A Midsummer Night's Dream": Apr. 2, 3, 4, 5.
*Symphony No. 3, A minor, Opus 56 ("Scotch"): Jan. 9, 10, 11, 12.
*Symphony No. 4, A major, Opus 90 ("Italian"): Sept. 24.

MENNIN—Symphony No. 7 in One Movement ("Variation Symphony"): Apr. 2,
3, 4, 5.

MOZART—Aria, "Aer tranquillo," from "Il Rè pastore": Mar. 12, 13, 15.
Aria, "Zeffiretti lusinghieri," from "Idomeneo": Mar. 12, 13, 15.
Concerto No. 3 for Violin and Orchestra, G major, K. 216: Jan. 30, 31.
Eine kleine Nachtmusik, K. 525: Mar. 19, 20, 21, 22.
Motet, "Ave verum corpus," K. 618: Feb. 27, 28, 29; Mar. 1.
Motet, "Exsultate, jubilate," K. 165: Mar. 12, 13, 15.
Overture, "The Abduction from the Seraglio": Nov. 30; Mar. 5, 6, 7, 8.
Overture, "The Impresario": Jan. 30, 31.
Overture, "The Magic Flute": Feb. 27, 28, 29; Mar. 1.
*Requiem, D minor, K. 626: Feb. 27, 28, 29; Mar. 1.

Symphony No. 36, C major, K. 425 ("Linz"): May 7, 8, 9, 10.
*Symphony No. 41, C major, K. 551 ("Jupiter"): Nov. 7, 8, 9, 10.

PROKOFIEFF—Scythian Suite ("Ala and Lolli"), Opus 20: Apr. 30; May 1, 2, 3.
Suite from the Ballet "Chout" ("The Buffoon"), Opus 21a: Jan. 30, 31.
Wedding Suite, from "The Stone Flower," Opus 126: Mar. 14.

RACHMANINOFF—Concerto No. 3 for Piano and Orchestra, D minor, Opus 30: Oct. 10, 11, 12, 13.
Rhapsody on a Theme of Paganini, for Piano and Orchestra, Opus 43: Apr. 30; May 1, 2, 3.

RAVEL—"Daphnis and Chloé," Suite No. 2: Apr. 2, 3, 4, 5.
"Shéhérazade," Three Poems for Voice and Orchestra to Verses by Tristan Klingsor: Nov. 30.
Tzigane, Concert Rhapsody for Violin and Orchestra: Jan. 2, 3, 4, 5.

REVUELTAS—*Sensemayá: Oct. 3, 4, 5, 6.

RIMSKY-KORSAKOFF—*Symphonic Suite, "Scheherazade," Opus 35: Mar. 14.

ROSSINI—*Overture, "Semiramide": Feb. 1, 2.
Sonata No. 3, C major: Dec. 21, 22.

SAINT-SAENS—Introduction and Rondo Capriccioso for Violin and Orchestra, Opus 28: Jan. 2, 3, 4, 5.

SCHUBERT—*Symphony No. 8, B minor ("Unfinished"): Feb. 20, 21, 22, 23.
Symphony No. 9, C major: Nov. 14, 15, 16, 17.

SCHUMAN—*Symphony No. 3 (in Two Parts, Four Movements): Oct. 31; Nov. 1, 2, 3.

SCHUMANN—Concerto for Piano and Orchestra, A minor, Opus 54: Apr. 2, 3, 4, 5.
*Overture, "Genoveva," Opus 81: Oct. 3, 4, 5, 6.
*Symphony No. 2, C major, Opus 61: Dec. 5, 6, 7, 8.

SHOSTAKOVICH—Concerto for Violoncello and Orchestra, Opus 107: Mar. 19 (c), 20, 21, 22.
Symphony No. 1, Opus 10: Feb. 1, 2.
Symphony No. 6, Opus 53: Oct. 10, 11, 12, 13.

SIBELIUS—Symphonic Fantasia: "Pohjola's Daughter," Opus 49: Apr. 23, 24, 25, 26.

STRAUSS, R.—*Don Juan, Tone Poem after Nicolaus Lenau, Opus 20: Oct. 24, 25, 26, 27.
"Don Quixote," (Introduction, Theme with Variations, and Finale), Fantastic Variations on a Theme of Knightly Character, Opus 35: Mar. 19, 20, 21, 22.
Scenes from "Der Rosenkavalier": Sept. 24.
*Till Eulenspiegel's Merry Pranks, after Old-Time Roguish Fashion—in Rondeau Form, Opus 28: Nov. 14, 15, 16, 17.

STRAVINSKY—*Suite from "The Firebird" (1919 Version): Mar. 14.
Symphony in C: Oct. 17, 18, 19, 20.
*Symphony in Three Movements: Oct. 17, 18, 19, 20.
Symphony of Psalms: Oct. 17, 18, 19, 20.

SZYMANOWSKI—Concerto No. 2 for Violin and Orchestra, Opus 61: Feb. 1, 2.

TCHAIKOVSKY—Concerto No. 1 for Piano and Orchestra, B flat minor, Opus 23: Nov. 28, 29; Dec. 1.
Symphony No. 2, C minor, Opus 17 ("Little Russian"): Jan. 30, 31.
*Symphony No. 6, B minor, Opus 74 ("Pathétique"): Feb. 6, 7, 8, 9.

VARESE—Déserts: Jan. 23, 24, 25, 26.

VIVALDI—Concerto for Violin and Orchestra, G minor, Opus 8, No. 2 ("Summer"), from *"The Four Seasons": Jan. 23, 24, 25, 26.
Concerto for Violin and Orchestra, F major, Opus 8, No. 3 ("Fall"), from

*"The Four Seasons": Feb. 6, 7, 8, 9.
Concerto for Violin and Orchestra, F minor, Opus 8, No. 4 ("Winter"), from
*"The Four Seasons": Jan. 9, 10, 11, 12.
WAGNER—"Die Meistersinger von Nürnberg," Prelude to Act I, Prelude to
Act III, Dance of the Apprentices and Entrance of the Mastersingers:
Apr. 23, 24, 25, 26.
Prelude and Good Friday Music from "Parsifal": Mar. 26, 27, 28, 29.
WALTON—"Façade"—excerpts, Suites I, II: Nov. 30.
Johannesburg Festival Overture: Nov. 30.
"Scapino," A Comedy Overture: Oct. 31; Nov. 1, 2, 3.
Symphony No. 1: Feb. 13, 14, 15, 16.
WEBER—Overture, "Euryanthe": Feb. 13, 14, 15, 16.
WOLPE—Symphony No. 1 (Movements I and II): Jan. 16 (a), 17, 18, 19.
XENAKIS—Pithoprakta: Jan. 2 (b), 3, 4, 5.

SOLOISTS

PIANO
CLAUDIO ARRAU: Feb. 13, 14, 15, 16.
JOHN BROWNING: Nov. 7, 8, 9, 10.
ROBERT CASADESUS: Nov. 21, 22, 23, 24.
AARON COPLAND: Jan. 9, 10, 11, 12.
JEANNE-MARIE DARRE: Dec. 12, 13, 14, 15.
JAKOV FLIERE: Oct. 10, 11, 12, 13.
CLAUDE FRANK: Apr. 2, 3, 4, 5.
GARY GRAFFMAN: Apr. 30; May 1, 2, 3.
JEROME LOWENTHAL: Oct. 24, 25, 26, 27.
LEV OBORIN: Nov. 28, 29; Dec. 1.
ARTUR RUBINSTEIN: Apr. 7.
RUDOLF SERKIN: Jan. 16, 17, 18, 19.
DAVID TUDOR: Feb. 6, 7, 8, 9.

VIOLIN
JOHN CORIGLIANO: Jan. 9, 10, 11, 12, 23, 24, 25, 26; Feb. 6, 7, 8, 9; Mar. 14.
ZINO FRANCESCATTI: Jan. 2, 3, 4, 5.
ERICA MORINI: Dec. 5, 6, 7, 8.
RUGGIERO RICCI: Oct. 3, 4, 5, 6.
TOSSY SPIVAKOVSKY: Dec. 19, 20, 21, 22.
ISAAC STERN: Apr. 23, 24, 25, 26.
CHARLES TREGER: Jan. 30, 31; Feb. 1, 2.

VIOLA
WILLIAM LINCER: Mar. 19, 20, 21, 22.

VIOLONCELLO
PIERRE FOURNIER: Mar. 19, 20, 21, 22.

JAZZ ENSEMBLE: Jan. 9, 10, 11, 12.
(DON ELLIS, trumpet; BARRE PHILLIPS, bass; JOE COCUZZO, percussion).

VOICE
ADELE ADDISON, soprano: Feb. 27, 28, 29; Mar. 1.
MARTINA ARROYO, soprano: May 14, 15, 16, 17.
PHYLLIS CURTIN, soprano: Sept. 24.
NICHOLAS DI VIRGILIO, tenor: May 14, 15, 16, 17.
MAUREEN FORRESTER, contralto: Feb. 20, 21, 22, 23.
DONALD GRAMM, bass-baritone: Feb. 27, 28, 29; Mar. 1.
RICHARD LEWIS, tenor: Feb. 20, 21, 22, 23.
LOUISE PARKER, contralto: Feb. 27, 28, 29; Mar. 1.
JUDITH RASKIN, soprano: Sept. 24.
REGINA SARFATY, mezzo-soprano: Sept. 24; May 14, 15, 16, 17.
NORMAN SCOTT, bass: May 14, 15, 16, 17.
LEOPOLD SIMONEAU, tenor: Feb. 27, 28, 29; Mar. 1.
MARIA STADER, soprano: Mar. 12, 13, 15.
BLANCHE THEBOM, mezzo-soprano: Nov. 30.
JENNIE TOUREL, mezzo-soprano: Sept. 26, 27, 28, 29; Apr. 9, 10, 11, 12, 14.
LEE VENORA, soprano: Sept. 26, 27, 28, 29.

CHORUS
CAMERATA SINGERS, Abraham Kaplan, Director: Apr. 9, 10, 11, 12, 14.
CHORAL ART SOCIETY, William Jonson, Director: Oct. 17, 18, 19, 20.

COLLEGIATE CHORALE, Abraham Kaplan, Director: Sept. 26, 27, 28, 29.
COLUMBUS BOYCHOIR, Donald Bryant, Director: Apr. 9, 10, 11, 12, 14.
JUILLIARD CHORUS, Abraham Kaplan, Director: May 14, 15, 16, 17.

SCHOLA CANTORUM OF NEW YORK, Hugh Ross, Director: Feb. 27, 28, 29; Mar. 1.

SPEAKER
FELICIA MONTEALEGRE: Apr. 9, 10, 11, 12, 14.

●

TOUR OF THE UNITED STATES—AUTUMN 1963

Conductors

Leonard Bernstein, Seiji Ozawa
Aug. 29—Eve.   Hollywood, Cal.

Leonard Bernstein
Aug. 30—Eve.   Hollywood, Cal.
Aug. 31—Eve.   Monterey, Cal.
Sept. 1—Eve.   Hollywood, Cal.

Leonard Bernstein, Seiji Ozawa
Sept. 5—Eve.   Denver, Colo.

Leonard Bernstein
Sept. 6—Eve.   Milwaukee, Wis.
Sept. 7—Eve.   Chicago, Ill.

Leonard Bernstein, Seiji Ozawa
Sept. 8—Aft.   Chicago, Ill.
Sept. 8—Eve.   Chicago, Ill.

Leonard Bernstein
Sept. 11—Eve.   Ann Arbor, Mich.

Leonard Bernstein, Seiji Ozawa
Sept. 12—Eve.   Detroit, Mich.

Leonard Bernstein
Sept. 13—Eve.   Columbus, Ohio
Sept. 14—Eve.   Cleveland, Ohio

Leonard Bernstein, Seiji Ozawa
Sept. 15—Aft.   Pittsburgh, Pa.

Leonard Bernstein
Sept. 16—Eve.   Philadelphia, Pa.
Sept. 19—Eve.   Reading, Pa.

Leonard Bernstein, Seiji Ozawa
Sept. 20—Eve.   Baltimore, Md.

Leonard Bernstein
Sept. 21—Eve.   Washington, D.C.

Leonard Bernstein, Seiji Ozawa
Sept. 22—Aft.   Washington, D.C.

TOUR REPERTOIRE

* Recorded by the New York Philharmonic on Columbia Records.

BEETHOVEN—*Symphony No. 5, C minor, Opus 67: Aug. 29; Sept. 5, 6, 7, 12, 15, 20.

BERLIOZ—*Overture, "Roman Carnival," Opus 9: Sept. 13.

BRAHMS—*Academic Festival Overture, Opus 80: Sept. 1, 8 (Aft.), 11, 14, 16, 22.
Concerto for Violin, Cello and Orchestra, A minor, Opus 102: Sept. 1.
*Symphony No. 4, E minor, Opus 98: Aug. 31; Sept. 1, 8 (Eve.), 11, 13, 16, 19.

DEBUSSY—Ibéria, from *"Images pour orchestre": Aug. 30; Sept. 7, 14, 19, 21.

LISZT—*Concerto for Piano and Orchestra, No. 1, E flat major: Aug. 29; Sept. 8 (Aft.), 22.

MENDELSSOHN—*Symphony No. 4, A major, Opus 96 ("Italian"): Aug. 30; Sept. 5, 6, 7, 8 (Eve.), 12, 15, 20, 21.

ROSSINI—"Una voce poco fa," from "The Barber of Seville": Aug. 30.

SCHUMAN—*Symphony No. 3: Aug. 29; Sept. 8 (Aft.), 11, 13, 14, 16, 22.

STRAUSS, R.—Scenes from "Der Rosenkavalier": Sept. 21.

STRAVINSKY—*Suite from "The Firebird": Aug. 31; Sept. 5, 6, 8 (Eve.), 12, 15, 20, 22.

TCHAIKOVSKY—*Symphonic Fantasy, "Francesca da Rimini," Opus 32: Aug. 30, 31; Sept. 8 (Aft.), 14, 19.

VERDI—"Ah, fors'e lui . . . Sempre libera," from "La Traviata": Aug. 30.

TOUR SOLOISTS

PHYLLIS CURTIN, soprano: Sept. 21.
JASCHA HEIFETZ, violinist: Sept. 1.
ANNA MOFFO, soprano: Aug. 30.
GREGOR PIATIGORSKY, violoncellist: Sept. 1.
JUDITH RASKIN, soprano: Sept. 21.
REGINA SARFATY, mezzo-soprano: Sept. 21.
ANDRE WATTS, pianist: Aug. 29; Sept. 8 (Aft.), 22.

•

NEW YORK PHILHARMONIC "PROMENADES"
SECOND SEASON   1964   PHILHARMONIC HALL

Conductors

André Kostelanetz
May 20, 21, 23, 24, 27, 28, 29, 30, 31; June 10, 11, 12, 13, 14 (Eves.).

Sir Malcolm Sargent
June 3, 4, 5, 6, 7 (Eves.).

REPERTOIRE—"PROMENADES"

Compositions marked with an asterisk (*) are recorded by the New York Philharmonic on Columbia Records and now available.

ARLEN—"Blues Opera"—Suite for Orchestra: May 29, 30, 31.
BRITTEN—*Variations and Fugue on a Theme of Purcell, Opus 34: June 3, 4, 5. "Soirées Musicales," Opus 9 (after Rossini), preceded by an overture, "Passo a sei" (ballet music from Rossini's "William Tell"): May 22, 23, 27, 28.
CHABRIER—"España," Rhapsody for Orchestra: June 13, 14.
GARDINER—"Shepherd Fennel's Dance": June 3, 4, 5.
GERSHWIN—Concerto for Piano and Orchestra in F major: May 29, 30, 31.
GILBERT AND SULLIVAN—Recitative and Song, "Though Tear and Long-Drawn Sigh," from "The Yeomen of the Guard."
Song, "The Moon and I," from "The Mikado": June 3, 4, 5.
HOLST—Mars, Venus, Jupiter, from "The Planets": June 3, 4, 5.
HOVHANESS—"Meditations of Orpheus"—Choreographed by Norman Walker (First New York Performances): May 20, 21, 24.
Meditation on Orpheus (same music as above, without dance): June 13, 14.
IVES-SCHUMAN—Variations on "America" (World Premiere): May 20, 21, 24.
KERN—"Mark Twain"—Portrait for Narrator and Orchestra: May 29, 30, 31.
KHACHATURIAN—Waltz, from "Masquerade" Suite: May 20, 21, 24.
MENDELSSOHN—Excerpts from "A Midsummer Night's Dream": June 6, 7.
OFFENBACH-ROSENTHAL—Gaîté Parisienne: June 10, 11, 12, 13, 14.
POULENC—Concerto for Piano and Orchestra: June 10, 11, 12.
PUCCINI—Excerpts from the Opera, "La Rondine": May 22, 23, 27, 28.
QUILTER—Three Shakespeare Songs: June 6, 7.
RAVEL—Concerto for Piano and Orchestra, G major: May 20, 21, 24.
Une barque sur l'océan (First Performances in New York of Orchestral Version): June 10, 11, 12.

RESPIGHI—Pines of Rome: May 22, 23, 27, 28.

SAINT-SAENS—Overture, "The Yellow Princess": June 10, 11, 12.

"SALUTE TO BROADWAY"—Excerpts from PORTER's "Kiss Me Kate," RODGERS' "South Pacific," LOEWE's "My Fair Lady": May 20, 21, 24.

SCHUMAN—The Orchestra Song (First Performances in New York): May 29, 30, 31.

SHOSTAKOVICH—Excerpts from the Opera, "Lady Macbeth of Mtsensk": May 20, 21, 24 (Orchestral Interludes & Aria); June 13, 14 (Orchestral Interludes only).

SOUSA—The Stars and Stripes Forever: May 29, 30, 31.

SULLIVAN—Overture, "Di Ballo": June 3, 4, 5.

TCHAIKOVSKY—Concerto for Violin and Orchestra, D major, Opus 35: June 13, 14.

*Fantasy Overture, "Romeo and Juliet": June 6, 7.

VAUGHAN WILLIAMS—Serenade to Music: June 6, 7.

VERDI—Overture, "La Forza del destino": May 22, 23, 27, 28.

WAGNER, Roger, arr.—Folk Songs of France (First Performances in New York of this arrangement): June 10, 11, 12.

WALTON—"Façade," excerpts from Suites I and II: June 3, 4, 5.

WALTON-SARGENT—Fanfare from "Hamlet": June 6, 7.

SOLOISTS—"PROMENADES"

PIANO
JOHN BROWNING: May 20, 21, 24.
LORIN HOLLANDER: May 29, 30, 31.
OZAN MARSH: June 10, 11, 12.

VIOLIN
TOSHIYA ETO: June 13, 14.

VOICE
RICHARD CASSILLY, tenor: June 6, 7.
PHYLLIS CURTIN, soprano: May 22, 23, 27, 28.
JOSHUA HECHT, bass-baritone: June 6, 7.
MARY HENSLEY, mezzo-soprano: June 6, 7.
FRANK PORRETTA, tenor: May 22, 23, 27, 28
JOAN SENA, soprano: May 20, 21, 24.
VERONICA TYLER, soprano: June 6, 7.
LEE VENORA, soprano: June 3, 4, 5.

CHORUS
SCHOLA CANTORUM OF NEW YORK, Hugh Ross, Director: June 6, 7, 10, 11, 12.

NARRATOR
MARC CONNELLY: May 29, 30, 31.

DANCERS
NORMAN WALKER, CORA CAHAN: May 20, 21, 24.
PATRICIA WILDE & COMPANY: May 22, 23, 27, 28.

1964-65 ONE HUNDRED TWENTY-THIRD SEASON

LEONARD BERNSTEIN, *Music Director*
(On Sabbatical Leave, 1964–65)

Guest Conductors
JOSEF KRIPS LORIN MAAZEL THOMAS SCHIPPERS WILLIAM STEINBERG

DANNY KAYE	GEORGE CLEVE
Pension Fund	ELYAKUM SHAPIRA
Benefit Concert	*Conductors selected under*
	American Conductors Project

LEONARD BERNSTEIN	ANDRE KOSTELANETZ
Music Director,	*Special Saturday*
Young People's Concerts	*Night Concerts*

SEIJI OZAWA
Assistant Conductor

CONCERTS

1964

Josef Krips

Sept. 29—Eve.	Philharmonic Hall
(Pension Fund Benefit)	
Oct. 1—Eve.	Philharmonic Hall
Oct. 2—Aft.	Philharmonic Hall
Oct. 3—Eve.	Philharmonic Hall
Oct. 4—Aft.	Philharmonic Hall
Oct. 8—Eve.	Philharmonic Hall
Oct. 9—Aft.	Philharmonic Hall
Oct. 10—Eve.	Philharmonic Hall
Oct. 11—Aft.	Philharmonic Hall
Oct. 15—Eve.	Philharmonic Hall
Oct. 16—Aft.	Philharmonic Hall

Leonard Bernstein

Oct. 17—Aft.	Philharmonic Hall
(Young People's Concert)	

Josef Krips

Oct. 17—Eve.	Philharmonic Hall
Oct. 18—Aft.	Philharmonic Hall
Oct. 22—Eve.	Philharmonic Hall
Oct. 23—Aft.	Philharmonic Hall
Oct. 24—Eve.	Philharmonic Hall
Oct. 25—Aft.	Philharmonic Hall

Arthur Fiedler

Oct. 27—Eve.	Philharmonic Hall
(Special Concert in Honor of the	
American Academy of Pediatrics)	

Josef Krips

Oct. 29—Eve.	Philharmonic Hall
Oct. 30—Aft.	Philharmonic Hall
Nov. 1—Aft.	Philharmonic Hall
Nov. 5—Eve.	Philharmonic Hall
Nov. 6—Aft.	Philharmonic Hall
Nov. 7—Eve.	Philharmonic Hall
Nov. 8—Aft.	Philharmonic Hall

1964

William Steinberg

Nov. 12—Eve.	Philharmonic Hall
Nov. 13—Aft.	Philharmonic Hall
Nov. 14—Eve.	Philharmonic Hall
Nov. 15—Aft.	Philharmonic Hall
(Lincoln Center Student Program)	
Nov. 19—Eve.	Philharmonic Hall
Nov. 20—Aft.	Philharmonic Hall

Leonard Bernstein

Nov. 21—Aft.	Philharmonic Hall
(Young People's Concert)	

William Steinberg

Nov. 21—Eve.	Philharmonic Hall
Nov. 22—Aft.	Philharmonic Hall
Nov. 26—Eve.	Philharmonic Hall
Nov. 27—Aft.	Philharmonic Hall
Nov. 28—Eve.	Philharmonic Hall
Nov. 29—Aft.	Philharmonic Hall

William Steinberg, Leon Kirchner

Dec. 3—Eve.	Philharmonic Hall
Dec. 4—Aft.	Philharmonic Hall
(Lincoln Center Student Program)	
Dec. 5—Eve.	Philharmonic Hall
Dec. 6—Aft.	Philharmonic Hall

William Steinberg

Dec. 10—Eve.	Philharmonic Hall
Dec. 11—Aft.	Philharmonic Hall
Dec. 12—Eve.	Philharmonic Hall

James De Preist, Edo de Waart, Ricardo del Carmen, Jacques Houtmann, Lawrence L. Smith, Niklaus Wyss

Dec. 13—Eve.	Philharmonic Hall
(Mitropoulos International Music	
Competition)	

1964

William Steinberg

Dec. 17—Eve.	Philharmonic Hall
Dec. 18—Aft.	Philharmonic Hall
Dec. 19—Eve.	Philharmonic Hall
Dec. 20—Aft.	Philharmonic Hall

Thomas Schippers

Dec. 31—Eve.	Philharmonic Hall

1965

Jan. 1—Aft.	Philharmonic Hall
Jan. 2—Eve.	Philharmonic Hall
Jan. 3—Aft.	Philharmonic Hall
Jan. 7—Eve.	Philharmonic Hall
Jan. 8—Aft.	Philharmonic Hall
Jan. 9—Eve.	Philharmonic Hall
Jan. 10—Aft.	Philharmonic Hall
Jan. 14—Eve.	Philharmonic Hall
Jan. 15—Aft.	Philharmonic Hall

André Kostelanetz

Jan. 16—Eve.	Philharmonic Hall

Thomas Schippers

Jan. 17—Aft.	Philharmonic Hall
Jan. 21—Eve.	Philharmonic Hall
Jan. 22—Aft.	Philharmonic Hall

Leonard Bernstein

Jan. 23—Aft.	Philharmonic Hall
(Young People's Concert)	

Thomas Schippers

Jan. 23—Eve.	Philharmonic Hall
Jan. 24—Aft.	Philharmonic Hall
Jan. 28—Eve.	Philharmonic Hall
Jan. 29—Eve.	Philharmonic Hall
Jan. 30—Eve.	Philharmonic Hall
Jan. 31—Aft.	Philharmonic Hall
Feb. 4—Eve.	Philharmonic Hall
Feb. 5—Aft.	Philharmonic Hall
Feb. 6—Eve.	Philharmonic Hall
Feb. 7—Aft.	Philharmonic Hall

Josef Krips

Feb. 11—Eve.	Philharmonic Hall
Feb. 12—Aft.	Philharmonic Hall

Leonard Bernstein

Feb. 13—Aft.	Philharmonic Hall
(Young People's Concert)	

Josef Krips

Feb. 13—Eve.	Philharmonic Hall
Feb. 14—Aft.	Philharmonic Hall
Feb. 18—Eve.	Philharmonic Hall
Feb. 19—Aft.	Philharmonic Hall
Feb. 20—Eve.	Philharmonic Hall
Feb. 21—Aft.	Philharmonic Hall
Feb. 25—Aft.	Philharmonic Hall
(Lincoln Center Student Program)	

1965

Feb. 26—Aft.	Philharmonic Hall
Feb. 27—Eve.	Philharmonic Hall
Feb. 28—Aft.	Philharmonic Hall
Mar. 4—Eve.	Philharmonic Hall
Mar. 5—Aft.	Philharmonic Hall

André Kostelanetz

Mar. 6—Eve.	Philharmonic Hall

Josef Krips

Mar. 7—Aft.	Philharmonic Hall

Elyakum Shapira

Mar. 11—Eve.	Philharmonic Hall

George Cleve

Mar. 12—Eve.	Philharmonic Hall
(Cornell Centennial Concert)	
Mar. 13—Eve.	Philharmonic Hall

Elyakum Shapira

Mar. 14—Aft.	Philharmonic Hall

Seiji Ozawa

Mar. 18—Aft.	Philharmonic Hall
(Lincoln Center Student Program)	
Mar. 19—Aft.	Philharmonic Hall
Mar. 20—Eve.	Philharmonic Hall
Mar. 21—Aft.	Philharmonic Hall

Lorin Maazel

Mar. 25—Eve.	Philharmonic Hall
Mar. 26—Aft.	Philharmonic Hall
Mar. 27—Eve.	Philharmonic Hall
Mar. 28—Aft.	Philharmonic Hall

**Danny Kaye,
Seiji Ozawa**

Mar. 29—Eve.	Philharmonic Hall
(Pension Fund Benefit)	

Lorin Maazel

Apr. 1—Eve.	Philharmonic Hall
Apr. 2—Aft.	Philharmonic Hall
(Lincoln Center Student Program)	
Apr. 3—Eve.	Philharmonic Hall
Apr. 4—Aft.	Philharmonic Hall
Apr. 8—Eve.	Philharmonic Hall
Apr. 9—Aft.	Philharmonic Hall
Apr. 10—Eve.	Philharmonic Hall
Apr. 11—Aft.	Philharmonic Hall
Apr. 15—Eve.	Philharmonic Hall
Apr. 16—Aft.	Philharmonic Hall
Apr. 17—Eve.	Philharmonic Hall
Apr. 18—Aft.	Philharmonic Hall

William Steinberg

Apr. 22—Eve.	Philharmonic Hall
Apr. 23—Aft.	Philharmonic Hall
Apr. 24—Eve.	Philharmonic Hall
Apr. 25—Aft.	Philharmonic Hall

1965		1965	
Apr. 29—Eve.	Philharmonic Hall	May 15—Eve.	Philharmonic Hall
Apr. 30—Aft.	Philharmonic Hall	May 16—Aft.	Philharmonic Hall
May 1—Eve.	Philharmonic Hall	May 20—Eve.	Philharmonic Hall
May 2—Aft.	Philharmonic Hall	May 21—Aft.	Philharmonic Hall
May 6—Eve.	Philharmonic Hall	May 22—Eve.	Philharmonic Hall
May 7—Aft.	Philharmonic Hall	May 23—Aft.	Philharmonic Hall
May 8—Eve.	Philharmonic Hall	May 27—Eve.	Philharmonic Hall
May 9—Aft.	Philharmonic Hall	May 28—Aft.	Philharmonic Hall
May 13—Eve.	Philharmonic Hall	May 29—Eve.	Philharmonic Hall
May 14—Aft.	Philharmonic Hall	May 30—Aft.	Philharmonic Hall

REPERTOIRE

*Recorded by the New York Philharmonic on Columbia Records.

(a) World premiere.
(b) First performance in the United States.
(c) First performance in New York.

BACH, C. P. E.—Concerto for Two Pianos and Orchestra, F major: Jan. 7, 8, 9, 10.

BACH, J. S.—Brandenburg Concerto No. 3, G major, BWV 1048: Apr. 1, 2, 3, 4.
Brandenburg Concerto No. 5, D major, BWV 1050: Feb. 11, 12, 13, 14.
Concerto for Violin and Orchestra, A minor, BWV 1041: Oct. 15, 16, 17, 18.
Concerto for Violin and Orchestra, E major, BWV 1042: Oct. 15, 16, 17, 18.
Mass in B minor, BWV 232: May 27, 28, 29, 30.

BARBER—Adagio for Strings: Jan. 30.
Medea's Meditation and Dance of Vengeance, Opus 23A: Jan. 21, 22.
Overture to "The School for Scandal": Jan. 21, 22, 23, 24.
Second Essay for Orchestra, Opus 17: Jan. 23, 24.

BARTOK—*Concerto for Orchestra: Apr. 8, 9, 10, 11.
Concerto No. 2 for Violin and Orchestra: May 13, 14, 15, 16.
Dance Suite: Mar. 11, 14.
Scherzo for Piano and Orchestra, Opus 2: Dec. 17 (b), 18, 19, 20.

BEETHOVEN—"Ah, perfido!" Opus 65: Feb. 4, 5, 6, 7.
Cantata on the Death of Emperor Joseph II: Jan. 14, 15, 17.
Concerto No. 4 for Piano and Orchestra, G major, Opus 58: May 6, 7, 8.
Concerto No. 5 for Piano and Orchestra, E flat major, Opus 73 ("Emperor"):
    Feb. 18, 19, 20, 21.
*Overture to "Egmont," Opus 84: Feb. 18, 19, 20, 21.
Overture to "The Ruins of Athens": Jan. 14, 15, 17.
Symphony No. 3, E flat major, Opus 55 ("Eroica"): May 13, 14, 15, 16.
Symphony No. 4, B flat major, Opus 60: Jan. 21, 22, 23, 24.
*Symphony No. 5, C minor, Opus 67: Oct. 27.
*Symphony No. 6, F major, Opus 68 ("Pastoral"): Oct. 8, 9, 10, 11.

BERG—"Lulu" Suite: Jan. 7, 8, 9, 10.

BERLIOZ—Overture to "Beatrice and Benedict": May 13, 14, 15, 16.
*Overture, "The Roman Carnival," Opus 9: Mar. 29.
*Symphonie fantastique, Opus 14: Mar. 12, 13.
Symphonie funèbre et triomphale, Opus 15: Dec. 3, 4, 5, 6.
Three Excerpts from Dramatic Legend, "La Damnation de Faust": Dec. 3, 4, 5, 6.

BIZET—Symphony in C major: Dec. 31; Jan. 1, 2, 3.

BRAHMS—Concerto for Violin and Orchestra, D major, Opus 77: Apr. 1, 3, 4.
*Symphony No. 1, C minor, Opus 68: Jan. 28, 29, 30, 31.

*Symphony No. 2, D major, Opus 73: Oct. 1, 2, 3, 4.
*Symphony No. 3, F major, Opus 90: Mar. 25, 26, 27, 28; Apr. 2.
*Symphony No. 4, E minor, Opus 98: Nov. 12, 13, 14.
*Variations on a Theme by Haydn, Opus 56A: Oct. 29, 30; Nov. 1.

BRITTEN—Sinfonia da Requiem: Oct. 22, 23, 24, 25.

BRUCH—Concerto No. 1 for Violin and Orchestra, G minor, Opus 26: May 9.

BRUCKNER—Mass No. 3, F minor (with Ave Maria): Mar. 4, 5, 7.
Symphony No. 3, D minor: Oct. 15, 16, 17, 18.
Symphony No. 5, B flat major: May 20, 21, 22, 23.
Symphony No. 6, A major: Dec. 17, 18, 19, 20.
Symphony No. 8, C minor: Nov. 19, 20, 21, 22.
Symphony No. 9, D minor: Feb. 11, 12, 13, 14.

CHOPIN—Concerto No. 2 for Piano and Orchestra, F minor, Opus 21: Jan. 21, 22, 23, 24.

COPLAND—Nonet for Strings: Nov. 19, 20, 21, 22.
Quiet City: Oct. 29, 30; Nov. 1.

DALLAPICCOLA—Variations for Orchestra: Mar. 25, 26, 27, 28; Apr. 2.

DEBUSSY—*Prelude to "The Afternoon of a Faun": Mar. 25, 26, 27, 28.

DVORAK—Concerto for Violoncello and Orchestra, B flat major, Opus 104: Oct. 22, 23, 24, 25.

ELGAR—Variations on an Original Theme ("Enigma"), Opus 36: Nov. 26, 27, 28, 29; "Nimrod" only: Jan. 10.

FAURE—Nocturne from "Shylock": Feb. 4, 5, 6, 7.

GLUCK—Overture to "Iphigenia in Aulis": May 20, 21, 22, 23.

HAYDN—Symphony No. 49, F minor ("La Passione"): Apr. 29, 30; May 1, 2.
Symphony No. 99, E flat major: Nov. 26, 27, 28, 29.
The Seasons: Apr. 15, 16, 17, 18.

HINDEMITH—Symphony, "Mathis der Maler": Oct. 8, 9, 10, 11.

HOVHANESS—Floating World—Ukiyo (Ballade for Orchestra), Opus 209: Mar. 6 (c).

HUMPERDINCK—Prelude to "Hansel and Gretel": Oct. 27.

KABALEVSKY—Overture to "Colas Breugnon": Jan. 16.

KIRCHNER—Concerto No. 2 for Piano and Orchestra: Dec. 3 (c), 4, 5, 6.

LEES—Profile for Orchestra: Jan. 28, 29, 30, 31.

LIADOFF—"The Enchanted Lake," Legend for Orchestra, Opus 62: Jan. 16.

LISZT—Concerto No. 1 for Piano and Orchestra, E flat major: Oct. 27; Mar. 12, 13.
*Symphonic Poem, "Les Préludes": Oct. 27; Mar. 6.

LOPATNIKOFF—Variazioni Concertanti, Opus 38: Nov. 5, 6, 7, 8.

MAHLER—Kindertotenlieder: Oct. 8, 9, 10, 11.
Songs of a Wayfarer: Nov. 26, 27.
*Symphony No. 4, G major, for Orchestra and Soprano Solo: Feb. 25, 26, 27, 28.
Symphony No. 6, A minor: Apr. 29, 30; May 1, 2.

MARTINU—Concerto No. 3 for Piano and Orchestra: Feb. 25, 26, 27, 28.

MENDELSSOHN—Concerto No. 1 for Piano and Orchestra, G minor, Opus 25: Apr. 22, 23, 24, 25.
Concerto No. 2 for Piano and Orchestra, D minor, Opus 40: Apr. 22, 23, 24, 25.
Scherzo (from Octet, Opus 20): Apr. 22, 23, 24, 25.
*Symphony No. 4, A major, Opus 90 ("Italian"): Apr. 22, 23, 24, 25.

MENOTTI—Overture to "The Old Maid and the Thief": Jan. 7, 8, 9, 10.

MOUSSORGSKY-RAVEL—*Pictures at an Exhibition: Jan. 7, 8, 9, 10.

MOZART—Concerto for Flute and Orchestra, D major, K. 314: Apr. 8, 9, 10, 11.
Concerto for Piano and Orchestra, C major, K. 467: Mar. 18, 19, 20, 21.
Concerto for Piano and Orchestra, E flat major, K. 482: Nov. 28, 29.
Concerto for Piano and Orchestra, C minor, K. 491: Nov. 5, 6, 7, 8.
Overture to "The Impresario": Apr. 8, 9, 10, 11.
Overture to "The Marriage of Figaro": Oct. 27.
Symphony No. 31, D major, K. 297 ("Paris"): Feb. 18, 19, 20, 21.
Symphony No. 32, G major, K. 318: Mar. 12, 13.

PALMER—A Centennial Overture: Mar. 12 (a), 13.

PERRY—Study for Orchestra: May 6, 7, 8, 9.

PISTON—Concerto for Viola and Orchestra: Feb. 18, 19, 20, 21.
Symphony No. 4: Mar. 11, 14.

PROKOFIEFF—Classical Symphony, D major, Opus 25: Nov. 5, 6, 7, 8; Mar. 6.
Concerto No. 2 for Piano and Orchestra, G minor, Opus 16: Oct. 29, 30; Nov. 1.
Concerto No. 3 for Piano and Orchestra, C major, Opus 26: Mar. 11, 14.
Symphony No. 5, Opus 100: Mar. 18, 19, 20, 21.

RACHMANINOFF—Concerto No. 1 for Piano and Orchestra, F sharp minor, Opus 1: Jan. 16.

RAVEL—"Shéhérazade," Three Poems for Voice and Orchestra to Verses by Tristan Klingsor: Feb. 4, 5, 6, 7.

REZNICEK—Overture to "Donna Diana": Feb. 4, 5, 6, 7.

ROSSINI—Stabat Mater: Jan. 14, 15, 17.

SAINT-SAENS—Concerto No. 5 for Piano and Orchestra, F major, Opus 103: Dec. 31; Jan. 1, 2, 3.

SALIERI—Overture to "Axur, rè d'Ormus": Dec. 31; Jan. 1, 2, 3.

SCHUBERT—Symphony No. 2, B flat major: Dec. 3, 4, 5, 6.
Symphony No. 6, C major: Sept. 29.

SCHUMAN—Credendum: Oct. 1, 2, 3, 4.

SCHUMANN—Concerto for Violoncello and Orchestra, A minor, Opus 129: Apr. 8, 9, 10, 11.
*Symphony No. 4, D minor, Opus 120: Oct. 29, 30; Nov. 1

SCRIABIN—*Poem of Ecstasy, Opus 54: Mar. 25, 26, 27, 28; Apr. 2.

SIBELIUS—Symphony No. 1, E minor, Opus 39: Apr. 1, 3, 4.

SMETANA—Overture to "The Bartered Bride": Feb. 25, 26, 27, 28.

STRAUSS, Johann—On the Beautiful Blue Danube: Sept. 29.
Overture to "Die Fledermaus": Sept. 29.
Two Arias from "Die Fledermaus": Mein Herr Marquis; Spiel' ich die Unschuld vom Lande: Sept. 29.
Overture to "The Gypsy Baron": Sept. 29.
"Perpetuum mobile," Musical Jest: Sept. 29.
The Pizzicato Polka (with Josef Strauss): Sept. 29.
Tales from the Vienna Woods: Sept. 29.
Voices of Spring: Sept. 29.

STRAUSS, Richard—"Also sprach Zarathustra," Tone Poem (freely after Friedrich Nietzsche), for Large Orchestra, Opus 30: Nov. 12, 13, 14.
"Death and Transfiguration," Tone Poem, Opus 24: Nov. 5, 6, 7, 8.
"Don Juan," Tone Poem, Opus 20: Sept. 29.
"Elektra," Tragedy in One Act: Dec. 10, 11, 12.
"Le Bourgeois Gentilhomme," Orchestral Suite, Opus 60: Oct. 1, 2, 3, 4.
*Till Eulenspiegel's Merry Pranks, after Old-Time Roguish Fashion, in Rondeau Form, Opus 28: Mar. 11, 14.

STRAVINSKY—"Petrouchka" Suite: Dec. 31; Jan. 1, 2, 3.
The Song of the Nightingale: May 6, 7, 8, 9.

TAKEMITSU—Requiem, for String Orchestra: Mar. 18 (c), 19, 20, 21.

TCHAIKOVSKY—*Concerto for Violin and Orchestra, D major, Opus 35: Jan. 28, 29, 31.
*Symphony No. 4, F minor, Opus 36: Feb. 4, 5, 6, 7.
*Symphony No. 5, E minor, Opus 64: Mar. 6.
*Symphony No. 6, B minor, Opus 74 ("Pathétique"): Jan. 16.

VERDI—Quartet for Strings, E minor: May 6, 7, 8, 9.

WAGNER—Prelude and Love-Death, from "Tristan and Isolde": Mar. 4, 5, 7.

WALTON—Symphony No. 2: Oct. 22, 23, 24, 25.

WEBER—*Overture to "Oberon": Dec. 17, 18, 19, 20.

WEBERN—Six Pieces for Orchestra, Opus 6: Nov. 12, 13, 14.

WIENIAWSKI—Concerto No. 2 for Violin and Orchestra, D minor, Opus 22: Jan. 30.

WOLF—Harfenspieler Lieder: Nov. 26, 27.

SOLOISTS

PIANO

GINA BACHAUER: Feb. 18, 19, 20, 21.
DANIEL BARENBOIM: Nov. 28, 29.
YARA BERNETTE: Mar. 11, 14.
BARBARA BLEGEN: Jan. 7, 8, 9, 10.
JORGE BOLET: Mar. 12, 13.
ROBERT CASADESUS: Nov. 5, 6, 7, 8.
VAN CLIBURN: May 6, 7, 8.
JEANNE-MARIE DARRE: Dec. 31; Jan. 1, 2, 3.
RUDOLF FIRKUSNY: Feb. 25, 26, 27, 28.
LEON FLEISHER: Dec. 3, 4, 5, 6.
LORIN HOLLANDER: Oct. 29, 30; Nov. 1.
THEODORE LETTVIN: Dec. 17, 18, 19, 20.
OZAN MARSH: Oct. 27.
LEONARD PENNARIO: Jan. 16.
THOMAS SCHIPPERS: Jan. 7, 8, 9, 10.
RUDOLF SERKIN: Apr. 22, 23, 24, 25.
ABBEY SIMON: Mar. 18, 19, 20, 21.
ANDRE WATTS: Jan. 21, 22, 23, 24.

HARPSICHORD

RALPH KIRKPATRICK: Feb. 11, 12, 13, 14.

VIOLIN

JOHN CORIGLIANO: Feb. 11, 12, 13, 14.
ZINO FRANCESCATTI: Jan. 28, 29, 31.
SIDNEY HARTH: Jan. 30.
YEHUDI MENUHIN: Oct. 15, 16, 17, 18.
NATHAN MILSTEIN: Apr. 1, 3, 4.
EDITH PEINEMANN: May 13, 14, 15, 16.
ITZHAK PERLMAN: May 9.

VIOLA

WALTER TRAMPLER: Feb. 18, 19, 20, 21.

VIOLONCELLO

LORNE MUNROE: Oct. 22, 23, 24, 25.
LESLIE PARNAS: Apr. 8, 9, 10, 11.

FLUTE

JOHN WUMMER: Feb. 11, 12, 13, 14; Apr. 8, 9, 10, 11.

INSTRUMENTAL ENSEMBLE

UNITED STATES MILITARY ACADEMY BAND, WEST POINT, Lt. Col. William H. Schempf, Director.

VOICE

PIERRETTE ALARIE, soprano: Feb. 25, 26, 27, 28.
MARTINA ARROYO, soprano: Jan. 14, 15, 17.
CHARLES BRESSLER, tenor: Apr. 15, 16, 17, 18; May 27, 28, 29, 30.
WALTER CASSEL, baritone: Dec. 10, 11, 12.
REGINE CRESPIN, soprano: Feb. 4, 5, 6, 7.
PHYLLIS CURTIN, soprano: Dec. 10, 11, 12.
TITO DEL BIANCO, tenor: Jan. 14, 15, 17.
JUSTINO DIAZ, bass: Jan. 14, 15, 17.
JOHN FIORITO, baritone: Dec. 10, 11, 12.
DIETRICH FISCHER-DIESKAU, baritone: Nov. 26, 27.
MAUREEN FORRESTER, contralto: Oct. 8, 9, 10, 11.

LILLIAN GARABEDIAN, mezzo-soprano: Dec. 10, 11, 12.

DONALD GRAMM, bass-baritone: Mar. 4, 5, 7.

LAUREL HURLEY, soprano: Apr. 15, 16, 17, 18.

LOIS MARSHALL, soprano: May 27, 28, 29, 30.

MARY BETH PEIL, soprano: Dec. 10, 11, 12.

ROBERTA PETERS, soprano: Sept. 29.

NELL RANKIN, mezzo-soprano: Mar. 4, 5, 7.

REGINA RESNIK, mezzo-soprano: Dec. 10, 11, 12.

MARGARET ROGGERO, mezzo-soprano: Dec. 10, 11, 12.

HELEN ROSENGREN, soprano: Dec. 10, 11, 12.

JOSEPH ROULEAU, bass: Apr. 15, 16, 17, 18.

ARTURO SERGI, tenor: Dec. 10, 11, 12.

LEOPOLD SIMONEAU, tenor: Mar. 4, 5, 7.

KENNETH SMITH, bass-baritone: May 27, 28, 29, 30.

MARIA STADER, soprano: Mar. 4, 5, 7.

ASTRID VARNAY, soprano: Dec. 10, 11, 12.

SHIRLEY VERRETT, mezzo-soprano: May 27, 28, 29, 30.

BEVERLY WOLFF, mezzo-soprano: Jan. 14, 15, 17.

LOU ANN WYCKOFF, soprano: Dec. 10, 11, 12.

CHORUS

AMERICAN CONCERT CHOIR, Margaret Hillis, Director: May 27, 28, 29, 30.

CAMERATA SINGERS, Abraham Kaplan, Director: Jan. 14, 15, 17.

THE COLLEGIATE CHORALE, Abraham Kaplan, Director: Mar. 4, 5, 7.

SCHOLA CANTORUM OF NEW YORK, Hugh Ross, Director: Apr. 15, 16, 17, 18.

•

TOUR—AUTUMN, 1964

Josef Krips, Conductor

Sept. 23—Eve.	Kingston, N.Y.	Sept. 26—Eve.	Montreal, Que.
Sept. 24—Eve.	Albany, N.Y.	Sept. 27—Aft.	Montreal, Que.
Sept. 25—Eve.	Newark, N.J.		

TOUR REPERTOIRE

* Recorded by the New York Philharmonic on Columbia Records.

BEETHOVEN—Symphony No. 8, F major, Opus 93: Sept. 24, 27.

BRAHMS—*Symphony No. 2, D major, Opus 73: Sept. 23, 26.

HINDEMITH—Symphonic Metamorphosis on Themes of Carl Maria von Weber: Sept. 24, 25, 27.

SCHUBERT—Symphony No. 6, C major: Sept. 23, 25, 26.

STRAUSS, R.—"Don Juan," Tone Poem, Opus 20: Sept. 23, 25, 26.

STRAVINSKY—*Suite from "The Firebird": Sept. 24, 25, 27.

WAGNER—Prelude to "Die Meistersinger von Nürnberg": Sept. 24, 27.

•

NEW YORK PHILHARMONIC "PROMENADES"
THIRD SEASON   1965   PHILHARMONIC HALL

Conductors

André Kostelanetz
June 2, 3, 4, 5, 8, 9, 10, 11, 12, 22, 23, 24, 25, 26; July 2, 3 (Eves.).

Sir Malcolm Sargent
June 15, 16, 17, 18, 19 (Eves.).

Franz Allers
June 29, 30; July 1 (Eves.).

REPERTOIRE—"PROMENADES"

* Compositions marked with an asterisk are recorded by the New York
Philharmonic on Columbia Records and now available.

CASTELLANOS—"La Morena de mi copla": June 2, 3, 4, 5.

CHAPI—Overture and Aria, "Por qué sin motivos," from "La Revoltosa": June 2,
3, 4, 5.

CHAUSSON—"Poème" for Violin and Orchestra: June 15, 16.

DEBUSSY—*"L'après-midi d'un Faune": June 17, 18, 19.

DELIUS—La Calinda: June 17, 18, 19.

FALLA—*Excerpts from "The Three Cornered Hat": June 2, 3, 4, 5.

FAURE—Pavane: June 15, 16.

GERSHWIN—Cuban Overture, Mine, Promenade, "Porgy and Bess" Concert
Version, Second Rhapsody for Piano and Orchestra, Strike up the Band:
June 25, 26; July 2, 3.

GRANADOS—Interlude and Aria, "The Maja and the Nightingale," from
"Goyescas": June 2, 3, 4, 5.

GRIEG—Piano Concerto: June 17, 18, 19.

KREISLER—Caprice Viennoise, "Ich wär so gern" from "Sissy," Liebesfreud,
Liebesleid: June 11, 12.

LEHAR—"Ich bin verliebt" from "Schön ist die Welt," Suite from "The Count of
Luxemburg": June 11, 12.

MARQUINA—España cani: June 2, 3, 4, 5.

MOZART—Eine kleine Nachtmusik; Aria, "Martern aller Arten," from "The
Abduction from the Seraglio": June 11, 12.

OFFENBACH—Music from "La belle Hélène," "La Vie Parisienne," "Orpheus in
the Underworld": June 29, 30; July 1.

RAVEL—Alborada del gracioso, *Bolero: June 2, 3, 4, 5.

RESPIGHI—The Fountains of Rome: June 15, 16.

REZNICEK—Overture to "Donna Diana": June 11, 12.

ROSSINI—Overture to "William Tell": June 17, 18, 19.

ROSSINI-RESPIGHI—La Boutique Fantasque: June 15, 16.

SIBELIUS—Finlandia: June 15, 16.

STRAUS, O.—"Leise, ganz leise" from "Walzertraum": June 11, 12.

STRAUSS, R.—Waltzes from "Der Rosenkavalier": June 11, 12.

STRAVINSKY—*"Firebird Suite": June 17, 18, 19.

TCHAIKOVSKY—"At the Ball" (ballet choreographed by Patricia Wilde); Children's Suite, "Between Birthdays" with verses by Ogden Nash; *Francesca da Rimini; Serenade for Strings: June 8, 9, 10.

Marche Solennelle, *Overture "1812," Scenes from "The Queen of Spades," Suite from "The Sleeping Beauty": June 22, 23, 24.

TURINA—La Oración del torero, Cantares: June 2, 3, 4, 5.

VAUGHAN WILLIAMS—The Lark Ascending: June 15, 16.

WAGNER—Prelude to Act III, "Lohengrin": June 17, 18, 19.

SOLOISTS—"PROMENADES"

NARRATOR
DAVID WAYNE: June 8, 9, 10.

CHORUSES
CHORAL ART SOCIETY, William Jonson, director: June 29, 30; July 1.
SCHOLA CANTORUM, Hugh Ross, director: June 25, 26; July 2, 3.

DANCERS
PATRICIA WILDE & COMPANY: June 8, 9, 10.

PIANO
THEODORE LETTVIN: June 25, 26; July 2, 3.
MOURA LYMPANY: June 17, 18, 19.

VIOLIN
CARROLL GLENN: June 11, 12.
RUGGIERO RICCI: June 15, 16.

VOICE
PHYLLIS CURTIN, soprano: June 22, 23, 24.

LAUREL HURLEY, soprano: June 11, 12.

MARNI NIXON, soprano: June 29, 30; July 1.

TERESA STRATAS, soprano: June 2, 3, 4, 5.

VERONICA TYLER, soprano: June 25, 26; July 2, 3.

BARBARA CROUCH, mezzo-soprano: June 22, 23, 24.

ANITA DARIAN, mezzo-soprano: June 29, 30; July 1.

RICHARD CASSILLY, tenor: June 22, 23, 24.

LOREN DRISCOLL, tenor: June 29, 30; July 1.

ROBERT MOSLEY, baritone: June 25, 26; July 2, 3.

JOHN REARDON, baritone: June 29, 30; July 1.

•

NEW YORK PHILHARMONIC FRENCH-AMERICAN FESTIVAL
1965—PHILHARMONIC HALL

LUKAS FOSS, *Artistic Director for the Festival*

Conductors

Charles Munch
July 14, 17, 21, 22.

Leonard Bernstein
July 15, 16.

Aaron Copland
July 28.

Lukas Foss,
Darius Milhaud
July 24.

Lukas Foss,
Duke Ellington
July 30, 31.

Chamber Music Concerts
July 19, 20, 23, 26.

REPERTOIRE—FRENCH-AMERICAN FESTIVAL

(a) World premiere.
(b) First performance in the United States.
(c) First performance in New York.

* Recorded by the New York Philharmonic on Columbia Records.

ORCHESTRAL:

BERLIOZ—"The Damnation of Faust": July 21, 22; *Roman Carnival Overture: July 24.
BERNSTEIN—"The Age of Anxiety," *"Chichester Psalms" (a), Serenade for Violin solo, strings and percussion: July 15, 16.
CASADESUS—Concerto for Three Pianos (a): July 24.
COPLAND—Preamble for a Solemn Occasion: July 30, 31; "The Tender Land" (Concert Version): July 28.
DEBUSSY—Fanfare: July 14, 17; *Nocturnes: July 24.
ELLINGTON—"New World A'Coming," "The Golden Broom and the Green Apple" (a): July 30, 31.
IVES—"From the Steeples and the Mountains" (a): July 30, 31.
MacDOWELL—Piano Concerto No. 2: July 31.
MESSIAEN—"Strophe et Antistrophe" from "Chronochromie" (b): July 24.
MILHAUD—"Death of a Great Chief of State" (c), Symphony No. 10 (c): July 24.
POULENC—Gloria: July 14, 17.
RAVEL—*"Daphnis and Chloé" Suites 1 & 2: July 14, 17; Piano Concerto for the Left Hand: July 14.
SAINT-SAENS—Violin Concerto No. 3: July 17.
SCHUMAN—"A Song of Orpheus": July 30.
WUORINEN—Orchestral and Electronic Exchanges (a): July 30, 31.

CHAMBER MUSIC:

BARBER—Dover Beach: July 26.
BOULEZ—Improvisations sur Mallarmé, No. II: July 23.
CAGE—Variations V, Choreographed by Merce Cunningham (a): July 23.
CARTER—Quartet No. 2: July 23.
CHAUSSON—Concerto for piano, violin and string quartet: July 20.
DEBUSSY—Sonata for violin and piano: July 20.
DIAMOND—Nonet: July 26.
FAURE—Sonata, Opus 13: July 20.
FOSS—Time Cycle (chamber version): July 26.
IVES—Largo: July 26.
KIRCHNER—Concerto for violin, cello, ten winds and percussion: July 26.
RAMEAU—Pièces de Clavecin en Concerts (Premier Concert, Cinquième Concert); "L'Impatience"; Pièces de Clavecin; "Le Berger fidèle": July 19.
VARESE—Hyperprism: July 23.

SOLOISTS—FRENCH-AMERICAN FESTIVAL

PIANO
ROBERT, JEAN and GABY CASADESUS
VAN CLIBURN
PHILIPPE ENTREMONT

CHORUSES
CAMERATA SINGERS, Abraham Kaplan, director
CHORAL ART SOCIETY, William Jonson, director

VIOLIN
ZINO FRANCESCATTI

CELLO
LEONARD ROSE

HARPSICHORD
RALPH KIRKPATRICK

VOICE
ADELE ADDISON, soprano
MARTINA ARROYO, soprano
BETHANY BEARDSLEE, soprano
JOY CLEMENTS, soprano
JENNIE TOUREL, mezzo-soprano

CLARAMAE TURNER, mezzo-soprano
RICHARD CASSILLY, tenor
LEOPOLD SIMONEAU, tenor
RICHARD VERREAU, tenor
LAWRENCE BOGUE, baritone
RICHARD FREDRICKS, baritone
THEODOR UPPMAN, baritone
NORMAN TREIGLE, bass-baritone

ENSEMBLES
LENOX QUARTET
THE GROUP FOR CONTEMPORARY MUSIC AT COLUMBIA UNIVERSITY, Harvey Sollberger and Charles Wuorinen, Directors (Richard Dufallo, Conductor)
CHAMBER ENSEMBLE from the MARLBORO MUSIC FESTIVAL, Rudolf Serkin, Artistic Director

DANCERS
MERCE CUNNINGHAM AND DANCE COMPANY, John Cage, Music Director

●

LONG ISLAND FESTIVAL
1965—C. W. POST COLLEGE, BROOKVILLE, NEW YORK

Charles Munch, Conductor
August 6, 7.

REPERTOIRE—LONG ISLAND FESTIVAL

* Compositions marked with an asterisk are recorded by the New York Philharmonic on Columbia Records.

BEETHOVEN—Concerto No. 3 for Piano and Orchestra, C minor, Op. 37: August 6, 7.
BERLIOZ—*Symphonie fantastique, Op. 14: August 7.
BRAHMS—*Symphony No. 2, D major, Op. 73: August 6.
RAVEL—"Daphnis and Chloé," Suite No. 2: August 6.
ROUSSEL—"Bacchus et Ariane," Suite No. 2, Op. 43: August 7.

SOLOIST—LONG ISLAND FESTIVAL

GARY GRAFFMAN, piano: August 6, 7.

●

NEW YORK PHILHARMONIC OUTDOOR CONCERTS IN THE
PARKS OF THE CITY OF NEW YORK
FIRST SEASON (1965)

Conductors

William Steinberg
August 10, 11, 13, 14.

Seiji Ozawa
August 17, 18, 20, 21.

Alfred Wallenstein
August 24, 25, 27, 28.

REPERTOIRE—PARK CONCERTS

* Compositions marked with an asterisk are recorded by
the New York Philharmonic on Columbia Records.

BEETHOVEN—*Symphony No. 9, D minor, Op. 125: August 10, 11, 13, 14.
BRAHMS—*Symphony No. 1, C minor, Op. 68: August 17, 18, 20, 21.
COPLAND—*Concerto for Piano and Orchestra: August 24, 25, 27, 28.
HARRIS—American Overture, "When Johnny Comes Marching Home": August
17, 18, 20, 21.
MOZART—Concerto for Clarinet and Orchestra, A major, K. 622: August 17,
18, 20, 21.
SCHUMAN—Philharmonic Fanfare (first performances): August 10, 11, 13, 14.
STRAUSS, R.—*"Don Juan," Op. 20: August 24, 25, 27, 28.
TCHAIKOVSKY—*Symphony No. 4, F minor, Op. 36: August 24, 25, 27, 28.
WAGNER—Prelude to Act I, "Die Meistersinger": August 10, 11, 13, 14.

SOLOISTS—PARK CONCERTS

PIANO
AARON COPLAND: August 24, 25, 27,
28.
CLARINET
BENNY GOODMAN: August 17, 18, 20,
21.
VOICE
ELLA LEE, soprano: August 10, 11,
13, 14.

JOANNA SIMON, mezzo-soprano: August 10, 11, 13, 14.
RICHARD CASSILLY, tenor: August 10,
11, 13, 14.
JOHN WEST, bass: August 10, 11,
13, 14.
CHORUS
MANHATTAN CHORUS, Hugh Ross, Director: August 10, 11, 13, 14.

1965–66 ONE HUNDRED TWENTY-FOURTH SEASON

LEONARD BERNSTEIN, *Music Director*

Guest Conductors
LUKAS FOSS   THOMAS SCHIPPERS   WILLIAM STEINBERG   GEORGE SZELL

LEONARD BERNSTEIN	ANDRE KOSTELANETZ
Music Director	*Special Saturday Night Concerts*
Young People's Concerts	

JAMES DEPREIST   EDO DE WAART   JACQUES HOUTMANN
Assistant Conductors

CONCERTS

1965

Leonard Bernstein

Sept. 28—Eve.	Philharmonic Hall
(Pension Fund Benefit)	
Sept. 30—Eve.	Philharmonic Hall
Oct. 1—Aft.	Philharmonic Hall
Oct. 2—Eve.	Philharmonic Hall
Oct. 4—Eve.	Philharmonic Hall
Oct. 7—Eve.	Philharmonic Hall
Oct. 8—Aft.	Philharmonic Hall
Oct. 9—Eve.	Philharmonic Hall
Oct. 11—Eve.	Philharmonic Hall
Oct. 14—Eve.	Philharmonic Hall
Oct. 15—Aft.	Philharmonic Hall
Oct. 16—Eve.	Philharmonic Hall
Oct. 18—Eve.	Philharmonic Hall
Oct. 20—Eve.	Philharmonic Hall
Oct. 23—Aft.(2)	Philharmonic Hall
(Young People's Concerts)	
Oct. 24—Aft.	United Nations
Oct. 25—Eve.	Newark, N.J.

George Szell

Oct. 28—Eve.	Philharmonic Hall
Oct. 29—Aft.	Philharmonic Hall
Oct. 30—Eve.	Philharmonic Hall
Nov. 1—Eve.	Philharmonic Hall
Nov. 4—Eve.	Philharmonic Hall
Nov. 5—Aft.	Philharmonic Hall
Nov. 6—Eve.	Philharmonic Hall
Nov. 8—Eve.	Philharmonic Hall
Nov. 11—Eve.	Philharmonic Hall
Nov. 12—Aft.	Philharmonic Hall

André Kostelanetz

Nov. 13—Eve.	Philharmonic Hall

George Szell

Nov. 15—Eve.	Philharmonic Hall
Nov. 18—Eve.	Philharmonic Hall
Nov. 19—Aft.	Philharmonic Hall

Leonard Bernstein

Nov. 20—Aft.(2)	Philharmonic Hall
(Young People's Concerts)	

1965

George Szell

Nov. 20—Eve.	Philharmonic Hall
Nov. 22—Eve.	Philharmonic Hall

Leonard Bernstein

Nov. 25—Eve.	Philharmonic Hall
Nov. 26—Aft.	Philharmonic Hall
Nov. 27—Eve.	Philharmonic Hall

**Leonard Bernstein,
Edo de Waart**

Nov. 29—Eve.	Philharmonic Hall

Leonard Bernstein

Dec. 2—Eve.	Philharmonic Hall
Dec. 3—Aft.	Philharmonic Hall
Dec. 4—Eve.	Philharmonic Hall

**Leonard Bernstein,
Jacques Houtmann**

Dec. 6—Eve.	Philharmonic Hall

Leonard Bernstein

Dec. 9—Eve.	Philharmonic Hall
Dec. 10—Aft.	Philharmonic Hall
Dec. 11—Eve.	Philharmonic Hall
Dec. 13—Eve.	Philharmonic Hall
Dec. 15—Eve.	Philharmonic Hall
Dec. 18—Aft.(2)	Philharmonic Hall
(Young People's Concerts)	

William Steinberg

Dec. 29—Eve.	Philharmonic Hall
Dec. 30—Eve.	Philharmonic Hall
Dec. 31—Aft.	Philharmonic Hall

1966

Jan. 1—Eve.	Philharmonic Hall
Jan. 3—Eve.	Philharmonic Hall
Jan. 6—Eve.	Philharmonic Hall
Jan. 7—Aft.	Philharmonic Hall
Jan. 8—Eve.	Philharmonic Hall
Jan. 10—Eve.	Philharmonic Hall
Jan. 13—Eve.	Philharmonic Hall

1966

Jan.	14—Aft.	Philharmonic Hall
Jan.	15—Eve.	Philharmonic Hall
Jan.	17—Eve.	Philharmonic Hall

Sylvia Caduff, Walter Gillessen, Juan Pablo Izquierdo, Alain Lombard

Jan.	19—Eve.	Philharmonic Hall

(Mitropoulos International Music Competition)

William Steinberg

Jan.	20—Eve.	Philharmonic Hall
Jan.	21—Aft.	Philharmonic Hall
Jan.	22—Eve.	Philharmonic Hall
Jan.	24—Eve.	Philharmonic Hall

Leonard Bernstein

Jan.	25—Eve.	Philharmonic Hall

(Pension Fund Benefit)

Jan.	27—Eve.	Philharmonic Hall
Jan.	28—Aft.	Philharmonic Hall
Jan.	29—Eve.	Philharmonic Hall

Leonard Bernstein, James DePreist

Jan.	31—Eve.	Philharmonic Hall

Leonard Bernstein

Feb.	3—Eve.	Philharmonic Hall
Feb.	4—Aft.	Philharmonic Hall
Feb.	5—Eve.	Philharmonic Hall
Feb.	7—Eve.	Philharmonic Hall
Feb.	10—Eve.	Philharmonic Hall
Feb.	11—Aft.	Philharmonic Hall
Feb.	12—Eve.	Philharmonic Hall
Feb.	14—Eve.	Philharmonic Hall
Feb.	16—Eve.	Philharmonic Hall

Leonard Bernstein, James DePreist, Edo de Waart, Jacques Houtmann

Feb.	19—Aft.(2)	Philharmonic Hall

(Young People's Concerts)

Leonard Bernstein

Feb.	21—Aft.	Washington, D.C.

Thomas Schippers

Feb.	24—Eve.	Philharmonic Hall
Feb.	25—Aft.	Philharmonic Hall
Feb.	26—Eve.	Philharmonic Hall
Feb.	28—Eve.	Philharmonic Hall
Mar.	3—Eve.	Philharmonic Hall
Mar.	4—Aft.	Philharmonic Hall
Mar.	5—Eve.	Philharmonic Hall
Mar.	7—Eve.	Philharmonic Hall
Mar.	10—Eve.	Philharmonic Hall
Mar.	11—Aft.	Philharmonic Hall

1966

André Kostelanetz

Mar.	12—Eve.	Philharmonic Hall

Thomas Schippers

Mar.	14—Eve.	Philharmonic Hall
Mar.	17—Eve.	Philharmonic Hall
Mar.	18—Aft.	Philharmonic Hall
Mar.	19—Eve.	Philharmonic Hall

Lukas Foss, James DePreist

(Six Lincoln Center Student Programs)

Mar.	23—Aft.(2)	Philharmonic Hall
Mar.	24—Aft.(2)	Philharmonic Hall
Mar.	25—Eve.(1)	Philharmonic Hall
Mar.	26—Aft.(1)	Philharmonic Hall

Thomas Schippers

Mar.	28—Eve.	Philharmonic Hall

Lukas Foss

Mar.	31—Eve.	Philharmonic Hall
Apr.	1—Aft.	Philharmonic Hall
Apr.	2—Eve.	Philharmonic Hall
Apr.	4—Eve.	Philharmonic Hall
Apr.	7—Eve.	Philharmonic Hall
Apr.	8—Aft.	Philharmonic Hall
Apr.	9—Eve.	Philharmonic Hall
Apr.	11—Eve.	Philharmonic Hall
Apr.	14—Eve.	Philharmonic Hall
Apr.	15—Aft.	Philharmonic Hall
Apr.	16—Eve.	Philharmonic Hall
Apr.	18—Eve.	Philharmonic Hall
Apr.	21—Eve.	Philharmonic Hall
Apr.	22—Aft.	Philharmonic Hall
Apr.	23—Eve.	Philharmonic Hall
Apr.	25—Eve.	Philharmonic Hall

Leonard Bernstein, David Diamond

Apr.	28—Eve.	Philharmonic Hall
Apr.	29—Aft.	Philharmonic Hall
Apr.	30—Eve.	Philharmonic Hall
May	2—Eve.	Philharmonic Hall

Leonard Bernstein

May	3—Eve.	Philharmonic Hall

(International Savings Bankers Congress Concert)

May	5—Eve.	Philharmonic Hall
May	6—Aft.	Philharmonic Hall
May	7—Eve.	Philharmonic Hall
May	9—Eve.	Philharmonic Hall
May	12—Eve.	Philharmonic Hall
May	13—Aft.	Philharmonic Hall
May	14—Eve.	Philharmonic Hall
May	16—Eve.	Philharmonic Hall
May	18—Eve.	Philharmonic Hall
May	21—Eve.	Philharmonic Hall

REPERTOIRE

* Recorded by the New York Philharmonic on Columbia Records.

(a) World premiere.
(b) First performance in the United States.
(c) First performance in New York.

BACH, J. S.—Concerto for Violin and Orchestra, E major, BWV 1042: Feb. 3, 4, 5, 7.
Concerto for Violin, Oboe, and Orchestra, C minor, BWV 1060: Feb. 3, 4, 5, 7.
St. John Passion: Apr. 7, 8, 9, 11.
BARTOK—Concerto for Two Pianos, Percussion, and Orchestra: May 3, 5, 6, 7, 9.
BEETHOVEN—Concerto No. 5 for Piano and Orchestra, E flat major, Opus 73 ("Emperor"): Jan. 6, 7, 8, 10.
Grosse Fuge for Strings, B flat major, Opus 133: Mar. 31; Apr. 1, 2, 4.
*Leonore Overture No. 3, Opus 72A: Oct. 24, 25; Mar. 31; Apr. 1, 2, 4.
"Meeresstille und glückliche Fahrt," Cantata for Chorus and Orchestra, Opus 112: Jan. 13, 14, 15, 17.
Military Marches for Winds: Mar. 31; Apr. 1, 2, 4.
*Symphony No. 5, C minor, Opus 67: Jan. 27, 28, 29, 31.
Symphony No. 9, D minor, Opus 125, Finale, "Ode to Joy": Oct. 24.
BERG—Ostinato and Adagio from "Lulu": Apr. 21, 22, 23, 25.
*Three Excerpts from "Wozzeck": Apr. 21, 22, 23, 25.
Three Songs from "Seven Early Songs": Apr. 21, 22, 23, 25.
BERLIOZ—*"Harold in Italy," for Viola and Orchestra, Opus 16: Nov. 11, 12, 15.
*Overture, "The Roman Carnival," Opus 9: May 3.
BERNSTEIN—Serenade for Solo Violin, String Orchestra, Harps, and Percussion (after Plato's "Symposium"): Feb. 10, 11, 12, 14.
*Symphonic Dances from "West Side Story": Nov. 13.
*Three Dances from "Fancy Free," Galop-Waltz-Danzon: Sept. 28.
BRAHMS—Concerto No. 2 for Piano and Orchestra, B flat major, Opus 83: Jan. 25.
Hungarian Dance No. 6: Sept. 28.
Serenade No. 2, A major, Opus 16: Jan. 25.
*Symphony No. 1, C minor, Opus 68: April 21, 22, 23, 25.
*Symphony No. 2, D major, Opus 73: May 21.
Variations on a Theme by Haydn, Opus 56A: Jan. 20, 21, 22, 24.
BRUCKNER—Symphony No. 7, E major: Nov. 4, 5, 6, 8.
BUSONI—Tanzwalzer, Opus 53: Dec. 29, 30, 31; Jan. 1, 3.
CHAVEZ—Concerto for Violin and Orchestra: Oct. 7 (c), 8, 9, 11.
COPLAND—Statements for Orchestra: Mar. 17, 18, 19.
Third Symphony: Feb. 10, 11, 12, 14, 16, 21.
DEBUSSY—*Prelude to "The Afternoon of a Faun": Mar. 12.
DIAMOND—Piano Concerto: Apr. 28 (a), 29, 30; May 2.
Symphony No. 5: Apr. 28 (a), 29, 30; May 2.
DUKAS—La Péri: Mar. 3, 4, 5, 7.
The Sorcerer's Apprentice, Scherzo after a Ballad of Goethe: Mar. 12.
DVORAK—"Carnival" Overture, Opus 92: Nov. 18, 19, 20, 22.
Concerto for Cello and Orchestra, B minor, Opus 104: Nov. 18, 19, 20, 22.
Slavonic Dance, Opus 46, No. 1: Sept. 28.
*Symphony No. 2, D minor, Opus 70 (No. 7 new): Nov. 18, 19, 20, 22.
ELGAR—Symphony No. 2, E flat major, Opus 63: Jan. 6, 7, 8, 10.

FALLA—Excerpts from "La Vida Breve": Aria, "Vivan los que rien"; Danza; Aria, "Allí está! Riyendo!": Nov. 13.
"Nights in the Gardens of Spain," Symphonic Impressions for Piano and Orchestra: Mar. 3, 4, 5, 7.
Spanish Dance from "La Vida Breve": Sept. 28.

FAURE—"Pelléas et Mélisande," Orchestral Suite, Opus 80: Nov. 11, 12, 15.

FOSS—Elytres: Apr. 14, 15, 16, 18.

GINASTERA—Canción al arbol del olvido: Nov. 13.

GLUCK—Overture to "Iphigenia in Aulis": Mar. 3, 4, 5, 7.

GRIEG—Norwegian Dance, A major, Opus 35, No. 2: Sept. 28.

HANDEL-HARTY—Suite, "Water Music": Nov. 13.

HARRIS—*Symphony No. 3: May 21.

HAYDN—Symphony No. 84, E flat major: May 5, 6, 7, 9.
Symphony No. 85, B flat major, "La Reine": May 21.
Symphony No. 92, G major, "Oxford": Mar. 10, 11, 14.
The Creation: May 12, 13, 14, 16, 18.

HOVHANESS—Fantasy on Japanese Woodprints, for Xylophone and Orchestra: Mar. 12 (c).

IVES—*Symphony No. 3, "The Camp Meeting": Nov. 25, 26, 27, 29.

KILAR—Riff 62: Apr. 14 (c), 15, 16, 18.

LISZT—"Totentanz," for Piano and Orchestra: Sept. 28.

LALO—"Symphonie espagnole," for Violin and Orchestra, Opus 21: Jan. 20, 21, 22, 24.

MacDOWELL—Concerto No. 2 for Piano and Orchestra, D minor, Opus 23: Mar. 10, 11, 14.

MAHLER—Symphony No. 7: Dec. 2, 3, 4, 6.
Symphony No. 8, E flat major ("Symphony of a Thousand"): Dec. 9, 10, 11, 13, 15.
Symphony No. 9, D major: Nov. 25, 26, 27, 29.

MENDELSSOHN—"Elijah," Opus 70: Feb. 24, 25, 26, 28.
Overture, "The Hebrides," Opus 26: Feb. 16, 21.

MENOTTI—Apocalypse: Mar. 10, 11, 14.

MONTSALVATGE—Canción de cuna para dormir a un negrito; Canto negro: Nov. 13.

MOUSSORGSKY—"Khovanshchina," Dance of the Persian Slaves and Break of Day: Mar. 12.
Prelude to "Khovanshchina": Oct. 28, 29, 30; Nov. 1.

MOZART—Concerto for Piano and Orchestra, D minor, K. 466: Mar. 3, 4, 5, 7.
Concerto for Piano and Orchestra, A major, K. 488: Dec. 29, 30, 31; Jan. 1, 3.
Concerto for Piano and Orchestra, C minor, K. 491: Apr. 14, 15, 16, 18.
Concerto for Piano and Orchestra, B flat major, K. 595: Nov. 4, 5, 6, 8.
German Dance, C major, K. 605: Sept. 28.
Overture to "The Marriage of Figaro": Nov. 4, 5, 6, 8.

NIELSEN—Concerto for Flute and Orchestra: Jan. 27, 28, 29, 31.
Symphony No. 3, "Sinfonia espansiva," Opus 27: Sept. 30; Oct. 1, 2, 4.

PROKOFIEFF—Concerto No. 2 for Piano and Orchestra, G minor, Opus 16: Mar. 28.
Concerto No. 3 for Piano and Orchestra, C major, Opus 26: Oct. 28, 29, 30; Nov. 1.
Symphony No. 5, B flat major, Opus 100: Feb. 3, 4, 5, 7.

RACHMANINOFF—Concerto No. 3 for Piano and Orchestra, D minor, Opus 30: Feb. 16, 21.
Symphonic Dances, Opus 45: Dec. 29, 30, 31; Jan. 1, 3.

RAVEL—Concerto for Piano and Orchestra, G major: Nov. 11, 12, 15.
*Daphnis et Chloé, Suite No. 2: Nov. 13.
*Rapsodie espagnole: Mar. 17, 18, 19.
RESPIGHI—Symphonic Poem, "The Pines of Rome": Mar. 12.
ROSSINI—*Overture to "La gazza ladra": Mar. 17, 18, 19, 28.
SAINT-SAENS—Symphony No. 3, C minor, Opus 78: Oct. 7, 8, 9, 11, 20.
SCHUBERT—Symphony No. 5, B flat major: Dec. 29, 30, 31; Jan. 1, 3.
SCHUMANN—*Symphony No. 2, C major, Opus 61: Mar. 17, 18, 19, 28.
*Symphony No. 4, D minor, Opus 120: Oct. 14, 15, 16, 18, 25.
SHOSTAKOVICH—Excerpts from "Katerina Ismailova": Nov. 13.
Symphony No. 9, Opus 70: Oct. 14, 15, 16, 18, 20, 24.
SIBELIUS—*Symphony No. 2, D major, Opus 43: Apr. 28, 29, 30; May 2, 3.
Symphony No. 3, C major, Opus 52: Sept. 30; Oct. 1, 2, 4.
Symphony No. 4, A minor, Opus 63: Jan. 27, 28, 29, 31.
*Symphony No. 5, E flat major, Opus 82: May 5, 6, 7, 9.
Symphony No. 7, C major, Opus 105: Oct. 7, 8, 9, 11.
Songs for Soprano and Orchestra: Sept. 30; Oct. 1, 2, 4.
"Luonnatar" for Soprano and Orchestra, Opus 70: Sept. 30; Oct. 1, 2, 4.
SMIT—Symphony No. 2, in Six Movements: Feb. 10 (c), 11, 12, 14.
STRAUSS, Johann—"Artist's Life": Sept. 28.
STRAUSS, Richard—*Dance of the Seven Veils from "Salome": Sept. 28.
"Ein Heldenleben," Tone Poem, Opus 40: Jan. 20, 21, 22, 24.
STRAVINSKY—Concerto for Violin and Orchestra, D major: Oct. 20.
Russian Dance from "Petrouchka": Sept. 28.
Symphonies of Wind Instruments: Apr. 14, 15, 16, 18.
TCHAIKOVSKY—*Francesca da Rimini, Opus 32: Apr. 14, 15, 16, 18.
*Symphony No. 5, E minor, Opus 64: Oct. 28, 29, 30; Nov. 1.
TURINA—Cantares; La Giralda from "Cantos a Sevilla": Nov. 13.
TURNER—The Marriage of Orpheus: Mar. 3 (a), 4, 5, 7.
VAUGHAN WILLIAMS—Symphony No. 4, F minor: Oct. 14, 15, 16, 18, 25.
VERDI—Messa da Requiem: Jan. 13, 14, 15, 17.
WAGNER—Final Scene from "Siegfried": Mar. 31; Apr. 1, 2, 4.
WEBER—Invitation to the Dance: Sept. 28.
WEBERN—Five Pieces for Orchestra, Opus 10: Apr. 21, 22, 23, 25.
Symphony, Opus 21: Dec. 2, 3, 4, 6.

SOLOISTS

PIANO

VAN CLIBURN: Mar. 10, 11, 14.
CLIFFORD CURZON: Nov. 4, 5, 6, 8.
IVAN DAVIS: Sept. 28; Mar. 23, 24, 25, 26.
ALICIA DE LARROCHA: Dec. 29, 30, 31; Jan. 1, 3.
ARTHUR GOLD and ROBERT FIZDALE, duo-pianists: May 3, 5, 6, 7, 9.
GARY GRAFFMAN: Oct. 28, 29, 30; Nov. 1.
TONG IL HAN: Mar. 28.
GRANT JOHANNESEN: Nov. 11, 12, 15.
LEON KIRCHNER: Apr. 14, 15, 16, 18.

JEROME LOWENTHAL: Feb. 16, 21.
ARTURO BENEDETTI MICHELANGELI: Jan. 6, 7, 8, 10.
GUIOMAR NOVAES: Mar. 3, 4, 5, 7.
THOMAS SCHUMACHER: Apr. 28, 29, 30; May 2.
RUDOLF SERKIN: Jan. 25.

VIOLIN

JOHN CORIGLIANO: Jan. 20, 21, 22, 24.
ZINO FRANCESCATTI: Feb. 10, 11, 12, 14.
JAMES OLIVER BUSWELL IV: Oct. 20.
ISAAC STERN: Feb. 3, 4, 5, 7.
HENRYK SZERYNG: Oct. 7, 8, 9, 11.

VIOLA
WILLIAM LINCER: Nov. 11, 12, 15.

VIOLONCELLO
MSTISLAV ROSTROPOVICH: Nov. 18, 19, 20, 22.

FLUTE
JULIUS BAKER: Jan. 27, 28, 29, 31.

OBOE
HAROLD GOMBERG: Feb. 3, 4, 5, 7.

VIOLA DA GAMBA
JUDITH DAVIDOFF: Apr. 7, 8, 9, 11.

HARPSICHORD
ALBERT FULLER: Apr. 7, 8, 9, 11.

ORGAN
BRUCE PRINCE-JOSEPH: Feb. 24, 25, 26, 28; Apr. 7, 8, 9, 11.

LUTE
STANLEY SILVERMAN: Apr. 7, 8, 9, 11.

XYLOPHONE
YOICHI HIRAOKA: Mar. 12.

VOICE
BETTY ALLEN, mezzo-soprano: Apr. 7, 8, 9, 11.

MARTINA ARROYO, soprano: Oct. 24; Jan. 13, 14, 15, 17.

CAROL BAUER, mezzo-contralto: Feb. 24, 25, 26, 28.

JOHN BOYDEN, baritone: Dec. 9, 10, 11, 13, 15.

CHARLES BRESSLER, tenor: Apr. 7, 8, 9, 11.

GENE BULLARD, tenor: Feb. 24, 25, 26, 28.

STEVEN CHALL, boy-soprano: Feb. 24, 25, 26, 28.

PHYLLIS CURTIN, soprano: Sept. 30; Oct. 1, 2, 4.

JUSTINO DIAZ, bass: Oct. 24.

SARAMAE ENDICH, soprano: Dec. 9, 10, 11, 13, 15.

GARY FINKELSTEIN, boy-soprano: Apr. 21, 22, 23, 25.

EZIO FLAGELLO, bass: Dec. 9, 10, 11, 13, 15; Jan. 13, 14, 15, 17.

MAUREEN FORRESTER, mezzo-soprano: Jan. 13, 14, 15, 17.

FLOR GARCIA, soprano: Nov. 13.

GRAYSON HIRST, tenor: Feb. 24, 25, 26, 28.

MARILYN HORNE, soprano: Apr. 21, 22, 23, 25.

GLADYS KUCHTA, soprano: Mar. 31; Apr. 1, 2, 4.

ELLA LEE, soprano: Dec. 9, 10, 11, 13, 15.

RICHARD LEWIS, tenor: Jan. 13, 14, 15, 17; Apr. 7, 8, 9, 11.

JANE MARSH, soprano: Feb. 24, 25, 26, 28.

DONALD MCINTYRE, bass: Feb. 24, 25, 26, 28.

TERESA MONTES DE OCA, soprano: Feb. 24, 25, 26, 28.

TICHO PARLY, tenor: Mar. 31; Apr. 1, 2, 4.

THOMAS PAUL, bass: Apr. 7, 8, 9, 11.

JUDITH RASKIN, soprano: May 12, 13, 14, 16, 18.

JOHN REARDON, baritone: May 12, 13, 14, 16, 18.

REGINA RESNIK, mezzo-soprano: Oct. 24.

GEORGE SHIRLEY, tenor: Dec. 9, 10, 11, 13, 15.

JENNIE TOUREL, mezzo-soprano: Dec. 9, 10, 11, 13, 15.

JON VICKERS, tenor: Oct. 24.

VERONICA TYLER, soprano: Apr. 7, 8, 9, 11.

WILLIAM WARFIELD, baritone: Apr. 7, 8, 9, 11.

BEVERLY WOLFF, mezzo-soprano: Dec. 9, 10, 11, 13, 15; Feb. 24, 25, 26, 28.

ALEXANDER YOUNG, tenor: May 12, 13, 14, 16, 18.

CHORUS
BROWNING SCHOOL BOYS' CHOIR, Stuart Gardner, Director: Apr. 7, 8, 9, 11.

CAMERATA SINGERS, Abraham Kaplan, Director: Feb. 24, 25, 26, 28; May 12, 13, 14, 16, 18.

COLLEGIATE CHORALE, Abraham Kaplan, Director: Jan. 13, 14, 15, 17.

BOYS' CHOIR from THE LITTLE CHURCH AROUND THE CORNER, Stuart Gardner, Director: Apr. 7, 8, 9, 11.

ST. KILIAN BOYCHOIR, Arpad Darazs, Director: Dec. 9, 10, 11, 13, 15.

ST. LUKE'S CHAPEL CHOIR, Clifford Clark, Director: Apr. 7, 8, 9, 11.

SCHOLA CANTORUM OF NEW YORK, Hugh Ross, Director: Oct. 24; Apr. 7, 8, 9, 11.

WESTMINSTER CHOIR, George Lynn, Director: Dec. 9, 10, 11, 13, 15.

NEW YORK PHILHARMONIC "PROMENADES"
FOURTH SEASON   1966   PHILHARMONIC HALL

Conductors

André Kostelanetz
May 25, 26, 27, 28, 31; June 1, 2, 3, 4, 10, 11, 14, 15, 16, 17, 18.

Morton Gould
June 7, 8, 9.

Sir Malcolm Sargent
June 21, 22, 23, 24, 25.

REPERTOIRE—"PROMENADES"

* Compositions marked with an asterisk are recorded by the New York
Philharmonic on Columbia Records and now available.

(c) First performance in New York.

ALBENIZ—Fête-Dieu à Séville from the suite "Iberia": June 14, 15, 16.

BARBER—Essay No. 1: June 7, 8, 9.

BERNSTEIN—*Suite from "West Side Story": June 17, 18.

BERLIOZ—*Roman Carnival Overture: June 23, 24, 25.

BIZET—L'Arlésienne Suite: June 23, 24, 25.

CHABRIER—Fête Polonaise: June 23, 24, 25.

COPLAND—Old American Songs: June 7, 8, 9.

DEBUSSY—*"Nuages" and "Fêtes": June 23, 24, 25.

DUKAS—The Sorcerer's Apprentice: June 21, 22.

ELGAR—Wand of Youth Suite No. 2: June 21, 22.

ENESCO—Rumanian Rhapsody No. 1: June 14, 15, 16.

GERSHWIN-GOULD—"Porgy and Bess" Suite: June 7, 8, 9.

GOTTSCHALK-SHANET—Night of the Tropics: June 3, 10, 11.

GOULD—Interplay for Piano and Orchestra: June 7, 8, 9.

GROFE—*Painted Desert, On the Trail, from "Grand Canyon" Suite: June 7,
8, 9.

GUARNIERI—Brazilian Dance: June 14, 15, 16.

KALMAN—Entrance of Maritza and "Sag' ja" from "Countess Maritza": May
31; June 1, 2, 4.

MENDELSSOHN—Violin Concerto in E minor: June 21, 22.

MIYAGI—Sea of the Spring: June 3, 10, 11.

MOZART—Symphony No. 23: May 31; June 1, 2, 4.
"Voi che sapete" from "The Marriage of Figaro": May 31; June 1, 2, 4.
"Alleluja" from the Motet "Exsultate, Jubilate": May 31; June 1, 2, 4.
Contra-Dance and Dances: May 31; June 1, 2, 4.

PROKOFIEFF—Classical Symphony: May 25, 26, 27, 28.

RACHMANINOFF—Piano Concerto No. 2: June 17, 18.

RIMSKY-KORSAKOFF—Excerpts from the Opera, "The Tsar's Bride": May 25,
26, 27, 28.
Suite from "Le Coq d'Or": June 3, 10, 11.

SAINT-SAENS—*Carnival of the Animals: June 3, 10, 11.
Piano Concerto No. 2: June 23, 24, 25.

SCHUMAN—American Festival Overture: June 7, 8, 9.

SHOSTAKOVICH—Festival Fantasy: May 25 (c), 26, 27, 28; June 17, 18.

SMETANA—From Bohemia's Woods and Fields: June 21, 22.

STRAUSS, J.—Czardas from "Die Fledermaus": May 31; June 1, 2, 4.
Overture to "Die Fledermaus": May 31; June 1, 2, 4.
Tales from the Vienna Woods: May 31; June 1, 2, 4.

STRAVINSKY—*"Firebird" Suite: June 3, 10, 11.

TCHAIKOVSKY—Cossack Dance from "Mazeppa": May 25, 26, 27, 28.
Variations on a Rococo Theme: May 25, 26, 27, 28.

VILLA-LOBOS—Memories of Youth: June 17, 18.
Little Train of the Caipira: June 14, 15, 16.

WALTON—Johannesburg Festival Overture: June 14, 15, 16.

WEBER—Invitation to the Dance: June 17, 18.
*"Oberon" Overture: June 21, 22.

Fado—The Songs of Portugal, for voice and guitars: June 14, 15, 16.

Folk Songs of Portugal, for voice and orchestra: June 14, 15, 16.

SOLOISTS—"PROMENADES"

NARRATORS
SONNY FOX: June 3, 10, 11.
LISA MARGERY SCHEIN: June 17, 18.

DANCERS
PATRICIA WILDE: May 31; June 1, 2, 4.
MICHAEL MAULE: May 31; June 1, 2, 4.
TONY MONTANARO, Mime: May 31; June 1, 2, 4.

PIANO
MORTON GOULD: June 7, 8, 9.
GRANT JOHANNESEN: June 17, 18.
MOURA LYMPANY: June 23, 24, 25.
LEONID HAMBRO & JASCHA ZAYDE: June 3, 10, 11.

VIOLIN
JAMES OLIVER BUSWELL IV: June 21, 22.

CELLO
LORNE MUNROE: May 25, 26, 27, 28.

VOICE
SARAMAE ENDICH, soprano: May 31; June 1, 2, 4.
AMALIA RODRIGUES, mezzo-soprano: June 14, 15, 16.
EILEEN SCHAULER, soprano: May 25, 26, 27, 28.
THEODOR UPPMAN, baritone: June 7, 8, 9.

•

A FESTIVAL OF STRAVINSKY: HIS HERITAGE AND HIS LEGACY
1966—PHILHARMONIC HALL

LUKAS FOSS, *Artistic Director for the Festival*

Conductors

Ernest Ansermet
July 9, 12.

Leonard Bernstein
June 30; July 5.

Kiril Kondrashin
July 14, 16.

Robert Craft
July 23.

Igor Stravinsky
July 23.

Lukas Foss
July 7, 20, 21, 22.

Richard Dufallo
July 22.

Chamber Music Concerts
July 13, 15, 22.

REPERTOIRE—STRAVINSKY FESTIVAL

* Recorded by the New York Philharmonic on Columbia Records.

BABBITT—Ensembles for Synthesizer: July 22.
BARBER—Capricorn Concerto: June 30; July 5.
BOULEZ—Eclat (New York Premiere): July 22.
BRITTEN—Six Hölderlin Fragments: July 13.
CARTER—Etudes and Fantasy: July 22.
COPLAND—Dance Symphony: June 30; July 5.
FOSS—Echoi: July 22.
GABRIELI—Canzona noni toni a 12: July 20, 21.
GESUALDO—Motet: "Aestimatus sum": July 20, 21.
MACHAUT—Hoquetus: July 9, 12.
MONTEVERDI—Arianna's Lament: "Lasciatemi morire": July 20, 21.
MOUSSORGSKY—Gathering Mushrooms, Cradle Song, Little star, where art thou?: July 13.
MOZART—Eine kleine deutsche Kantate, Abendempfindung, Meine Wünsche: July 13.
   "Per Pietà" and "E amore un ladroncello" from "Così fan tutte": July 7.
POULENC—Organ Concerto: July 9, 12.
RACHMANINOFF—The Harvest of Sorrow, The Little Island, Before my Window, To the Children: July 13.
REVUELTAS—*Sensemayá: June 30; July 5.
RIMSKY-KORSAKOV—Piano Concerto in C sharp minor: July 14, 16.
STRAVINSKY—Star-Spangled Banner (harmonized and orchestrated by Igor Stravinsky): June 30; July 5.
   Elégie: July 15.
   Excerpts from "Le Baiser de la fée": July 15.
   Fanfare for two trumpets: July 22.
   Der Faun und die Schäferin: July 13.
   Fireworks: July 14, 16.
   L'Histoire du Soldat: July 15.
   Introitus: July 22. (First performance in New York).
   *Le Sacre du printemps: June 30; July 5.
   Oedipus Rex: July 20, 21.
   Pastorale: July 13.
   *Perséphone: July 9, 12.
   Petrouchka: July 14, 16.
   Piano Rag Music: July 15.
   Prelude and Bedlam Scene from "The Rake's Progress": July 7.
   Pulcinella (after Pergolesi): July 7.
   The Star Visaged: July 9, 12.
   Symphony in three movements: July 23.
   Symphony of Psalms: July 23.
   Symphonies of Wind Instruments: July 9, 12.
   The Flood: July 23 (First New York concert performance).
   The Cloister: July 13.
   Ragtime: July 15.

TCHAIKOVSKY—The Tempest: July 14, 16.
Nur wer die Sehnsucht kennt, Warum?, Pimpinella: July 13.
VARESE—Octandre: July 22.
VERDI—Te Deum: July 20, 21.
WEBERN—Kinderstück (World Premiere): July 22.
String Trio (American Premiere): July 22.

SOLOISTS—STRAVINSKY FESTIVAL

PIANO
CAREN GLASSER: July 22.
RALPH VOTAPEK: July 15.
ANDRE WATTS: July 14, 16.
VIOLIN
JAIME LAREDO: July 15.
CHARLES HAUPT: July 22.
VIOLA
JESSE LEVINE: July 15, 22.
CELLO
ROBERT MARTIN: July 22.
ORGANIST
PIERRE COCHEREAU: July 9, 12.
PERCUSSION
JAN WILLIAMS: July 22.
CHAMBER ENSEMBLES
MEMBERS of the DORIAN QUINTET: July 22.
CHAMBER ENSEMBLE: July 15, 22. (Richard Dufallo, conductor).
CHAMBER ENSEMBLE: July 15, 22. (Lukas Foss, conductor).
VOICE
RICHARD FRISCH, baritone: July 23.
ERNST HAEFLIGER, tenor: July 20, 21.
ROLLAND HURST, bass: July 23.
RAYMOND MICHALSKI, bass: July 7.
THOMAS PAUL, bass: July 20, 21.

HEINZ REHFUSS, bass-baritone: July 20, 21.
ELISABETH SCHWARZKOPF, soprano: July 7, 13.
RICHARD SHADLEY, tenor: July 20, 21, 23.
LEOPOLD SIMONEAU, tenor: July 7, 9, 12.
SHIRLEY VERRETT, mezzo-soprano: July 20, 21.
CHORUS
CAMERATA SINGERS, Abraham Kaplan, Director: July 7, 9, 12, 20, 21, 22, 23.
CHOREOGRAPHER
GEORGE BALANCHINE: July 15.
DANCERS
SUZANNE FARRELL: July 15.
ARTHUR MITCHELL: July 15.
NARRATORS
JOHN CAGE: July 15.
ELLIOTT CARTER: July 15.
AARON COPLAND: July 15.
JOHN HOLLANDER: July 23.
YVETTE MIMIEUX: July 9, 12.
JASON ROBARDS: July 20, 21.
VISUAL PRESENTATION
LARRY RIVERS: July 20, 21.

●

NEW YORK PHILHARMONIC OUTDOOR CONCERTS
IN THE PARKS OF THE CITY OF NEW YORK
SECOND SEASON (1966)

Conductors

Leonard Bernstein
July 26, 29.

Lukas Foss
August 2, 4, 6, 8, 10.

Alfred Wallenstein
August 12, 14, 16, 18, 20.

REPERTOIRE—PARK CONCERTS

* Compositions marked with an asterisk are recorded by
the New York Philharmonic on Columbia Records.

BARBER—Overture to "The School for Scandal": August 12, 14, 16, 18, 20.
BEETHOVEN—*Symphony No. 3, E flat major, Op. 55: July 26, 29.
BRAHMS—Concerto No. 1 for Piano and Orchestra, D minor, Op. 15: August 12, 14, 16, 18, 20.
COPLAND—A Lincoln Portrait: August 2, 4, 6, 8, 10.
MENDELSSOHN—*Symphony No. 4, A major, Op. 90: August 12, 14, 16, 18, 20.
MOZART—Symphony No. 40, G minor, K. 550: August 2, 4, 6, 8, 10.
RAVEL—*"Daphnis and Chloé," Suite No. 2: August 2, 4, 6, 8, 10.
STRAVINSKY—*"Le Sacre du printemps": July 26, 29.
TCHAIKOVSKY—*Francesca da Rimini, Op. 32: August 2, 4, 6, 8, 10.

SOLOISTS—PARK CONCERTS

RUDOLF FIRKUSNY, piano: August 12, 14, 16, 18, 20.
MARIAN ANDERSON, narrator: August 2, 4, 6, 8, 10.

●

LONG ISLAND FESTIVAL
1966—C. W. POST COLLEGE, BROOKVILLE, NEW YORK

Leonard Bernstein, Conductor
July 30.

REPERTOIRE—LONG ISLAND FESTIVAL

* Recorded by the New York Philharmonic on Columbia Records.

BEETHOVEN—*Symphony No. 3, E flat major, Op. 55.
STRAVINSKY—*Le Sacre du printemps.

1966–67 ONE HUNDRED TWENTY-FIFTH SEASON

LEONARD BERNSTEIN, *Music Director*

Guest Conductors

WILLIAM STEINBERG	LORIN MAAZEL	CHARLES MUNCH
	ALFRED WALLENSTEIN	

LEONARD BERNSTEIN
Music Director
Young People's Concerts

ANDRE KOSTELANETZ
Special Saturday Night Concerts

SYLVIA CADUFF   JUAN PABLO IZQUIERDO   ALAIN LOMBARD
Assistant Conductors

CONCERTS

1966   1966

Leonard Bernstein

Sept.	28—Eve.	Philharmonic Hall

(Pension Fund Benefit)

Sept.	29—Eve.	Philharmonic Hall
Sept.	30—Aft.	Philharmonic Hall
Oct.	1—Eve.	Philharmonic Hall
Oct.	3—Eve.	Philharmonic Hall
Oct.	6—Eve.	Philharmonic Hall
Oct.	7—Aft.	Philharmonic Hall
Oct.	8—Eve.	Philharmonic Hall
Oct.	10—Eve.	Philharmonic Hall
Oct.	13—Eve.	Philharmonic Hall
Oct.	14—Aft.	Philharmonic Hall
Oct.	15—Eve.	Philharmonic Hall
Oct.	17—Eve.	Philharmonic Hall
Oct.	19—Eve.	Philharmonic Hall
Oct.	22—Aft. (2)	Philharmonic Hall

(Young People's Concerts)

Oct.	24—Eve.	Newark, N. J.
Oct.	27—Eve.	Philharmonic Hall
Oct.	28—Aft.	Philharmonic Hall
Oct.	29—Eve.	Philharmonic Hall
Oct.	31—Eve.	Philharmonic Hall

Lorin Maazel

Nov.	3—Eve.	Philharmonic Hall
Nov.	4—Aft.	Philharmonic Hall
Nov.	5—Eve.	Philharmonic Hall
Nov.	7—Eve.	Philharmonic Hall
Nov.	10—Eve.	Philharmonic Hall
Nov.	11—Aft.	Philharmonic Hall
Nov.	12—Eve.	Philharmonic Hall
Nov.	14—Eve.	Philharmonic Hall

Sir Malcolm Sargent

Nov.	15—Eve.	Philharmonic Hall

(American Bible Society)

Lorin Maazel

Nov.	17—Eve.	Philharmonic Hall
Nov.	18—Aft.	Philharmonic Hall

(Lincoln Center Student Program)

Nov.	19—Eve.	Philharmonic Hall
Nov.	21—Eve.	Philharmonic Hall

William Steinberg

Nov.	23—Aft.	Philharmonic Hall

(Lincoln Center Student Program)

Nov.	25—Aft.	Philharmonic Hall
Nov.	26—Eve.	Philharmonic Hall
Nov.	28—Eve.	Philharmonic Hall
Dec.	1—Eve.	Philharmonic Hall
Dec.	2—Aft.	Philharmonic Hall
Dec.	3—Eve.	Philharmonic Hall
Dec.	5—Eve.	Philharmonic Hall
Dec.	8—Eve.	Philharmonic Hall
Dec.	9—Aft.	Philharmonic Hall

André Kostelanetz

Dec.	10—Eve.	Philharmonic Hall

William Steinberg

Dec.	12—Eve.	Philharmonic Hall
Dec.	15—Eve.	Philharmonic Hall
Dec.	16—Aft.	Philharmonic Hall
Dec.	17—Eve.	Philharmonic Hall

**Leonard Bernstein,
Sylvia Caduff, Juan
Pablo Izquierdo**

Dec.	17—Aft. (2)	Philharmonic Hall

(Young People's Concerts)

Leonard Bernstein

Dec.	28—Eve.	Philharmonic Hall
Dec.	29—Eve.	Philharmonic Hall
Dec.	30—Aft.	Philharmonic Hall
Dec.	31—Eve.	Philharmonic Hall

1967

Jan.	2—Eve.	Philharmonic Hall
Jan.	5—Eve.	Philharmonic Hall
Jan.	6—Aft.	Philharmonic Hall
Jan.	7—Eve.	Philharmonic Hall
Jan.	9—Eve.	Philharmonic Hall
Jan.	12—Eve.	Philharmonic Hall
Jan.	13—Aft.	Philharmonic Hall
Jan.	14—Eve.	Philharmonic Hall
Jan.	16—Eve.	Philharmonic Hall
Jan.	18—Eve.	Philharmonic Hall
Jan.	21—Aft. (2)	Philharmonic Hall

(Young People's Concerts)

**Paul Capolongo,
Enrique Garcia-Asensio,
Helen Quach, Alois
Springer**

Jan.	23—Eve.	Philharmonic Hall

(Mitropoulos International Music Competition)

Leonard Bernstein

Jan.	24—Eve.	White Plains, N.Y.

William Steinberg

Jan.	26—Eve.	Philharmonic Hall
Jan.	27—Aft.	Philharmonic Hall
Jan.	28—Eve.	Philharmonic Hall
Jan.	30—Eve.	Philharmonic Hall
Feb.	2—Eve.	Philharmonic Hall
Feb.	3—Aft.	Philharmonic Hall
Feb.	4—Eve.	Philharmonic Hall
Feb.	6—Eve.	Philharmonic Hall
Feb.	9—Eve.	Philharmonic Hall
Feb.	10—Aft.	Philharmonic Hall

(Lincoln Center Student Program)

André Kostelanetz
Feb. 11—Eve.   Philharmonic Hall

William Steinberg
Feb. 13—Eve.   Philharmonic Hall

**Alfred Wallenstein,
Anis Fuleihan**
Feb. 16—Eve.   Philharmonic Hall
Feb. 17—Aft.   Philharmonic Hall
Feb. 18—Eve.   Philharmonic Hall
Feb. 20—Eve.   Philharmonic Hall

Charles Munch
Feb. 23—Eve.   Philharmonic Hall
Feb. 24—Aft.   Philharmonic Hall

Leonard Bernstein
Feb. 25—Aft. (2) Philharmonic Hall
(Young People's Concerts)

Charles Munch
Feb. 25—Eve.   Philharmonic Hall
Feb. 27—Eve.   Philharmonic Hall

Leonard Bernstein
Mar. 2—Eve.   Philharmonic Hall
Mar. 3—Aft.   Philharmonic Hall
Mar. 4—Eve.   Philharmonic Hall
Mar. 6—Eve.   Philharmonic Hall
Mar. 9—Eve.   Philharmonic Hall
Mar. 10—Eve.   Philharmonic Hall
(Lincoln Center Student Program)
Mar. 11—Eve.   Philharmonic Hall
Mar. 13—Eve.   Philharmonic Hall
Mar. 15—Eve.   Philharmonic Hall
Mar. 17—Aft.   Philharmonic Hall
Mar. 18—Eve.   Philharmonic Hall
Mar. 20—Eve.   Philharmonic Hall

**Sylvia Caduff, Juan
Pablo Izquierdo, Alain
Lombard**
Mar. 23—Eve.   Philharmonic Hall
Mar. 24—Aft.   Philharmonic Hall

Leonard Bernstein
Mar. 25—Eve.   Philharmonic Hall
(Pension Fund Benefit)

**Sylvia Caduff, Juan
Pablo Izquierdo, Alain
Lombard**
Mar. 27—Eve.   Philharmonic Hall

William Steinberg
Mar. 30—Eve.   Philharmonic Hall
Mar. 31—Aft.   Philharmonic Hall
Apr. 1—Eve.   Philharmonic Hall
Apr. 3—Eve.   Philharmonic Hall
Apr. 6—Eve.   Philharmonic Hall
Apr. 7—Aft.   Philharmonic Hall
Apr. 8—Aft.   Philharmonic Hall
(Lincoln Center Student Program)
Apr. 10—Eve.   Philharmonic Hall
Apr. 13—Eve.   Philharmonic Hall
Apr. 14—Aft.   Philharmonic Hall
Apr. 15—Eve.   Philharmonic Hall
Apr. 17—Eve.   Philharmonic Hall
Apr. 20—Eve.   Philharmonic Hall
Apr. 21—Aft.   Philharmonic Hall
Apr. 22—Eve.   Philharmonic Hall
Apr. 24—Eve.   Philharmonic Hall

Leonard Bernstein
Apr. 27—Eve.   Philharmonic Hall
Apr. 28—Aft.   Philharmonic Hall
Apr. 29—Eve.   Philharmonic Hall
May 1—Eve.   Philharmonic Hall
May 4—Eve.   Philharmonic Hall
May 5—Aft.   Philharmonic Hall
May 6—Eve.   Philharmonic Hall
May 8—Eve.   Philharmonic Hall
May 11—Eve.   Philharmonic Hall
May 12—Aft.   Philharmonic Hall
May 13—Eve.   Philharmonic Hall
May 18—Eve.   Philharmonic Hall
May 19—Aft.   Philharmonic Hall
May 20—Eve.   Philharmonic Hall

REPERTOIRE

* Recorded by the New York Philharmonic on Columbia Records.

    (a) World premiere.
    (b) First performance in the United States.
    (c) First performance in New York.

ALBENIZ-ARBOS—Excerpts from the Suite, "Iberia": Feb. 11.
AMRAM—King Lear Variations: March 23, 24, 27.
BACH, J. S.—Suite No. 3, D major, BWV 1068: Nov. 10, 11, 12, 14, 18.
BARBER—Toccata Festiva, Opus 36: Nov. 23, 25, 26, 28.

BARTOK—Concerto No. 2 for Piano and Orchestra: Jan. 18.
Concerto No. 3 for Piano and Orchestra: Jan. 12, 13, 14, 16.
Concerto for Violin and Orchestra, No. 2: May 11, 12, 13.
"The Miraculous Mandarin" Suite: Nov. 3, 4, 5, 7.

BEETHOVEN—Concerto for Piano and Orchestra, No. 3, C minor, Opus 37:
Oct. 27, 28, 29, 31.
Concerto No. 5 for Piano and Orchestra, E-flat major, Opus 73 ("Emperor"):
Nov. 17, 19, 21.
Concerto for Violin and Orchestra, D major, Opus 61: Nov. 3, 4, 5, 7.
*Missa Solemnis, D major, Opus 123, for Four Solo Voices, Chorus and
Orchestra: Dec. 8, 9, 12.
Overture to "The Creatures of Prometheus," Opus 43: Dec. 10.
Overture to "Egmont," Opus 84: Nov. 3, 4, 5, 7.
Overture to "Fidelio," E major, Opus 72: Jan. 5, 6, 7, 9.
Overture to "King Stephen," Opus 117: Sept. 29, 30; Oct. 1, 3.
*Symphony No. 3, E-flat major, Opus 55 ("Eroica"): Jan. 5, 6, 7, 9, 24.
*Symphony No. 7, A major, Opus 92: Dec. 1, 2, 3, 5; Apr. 8.
Symphony No. 8, F major, Opus 93: Apr. 6, 7, 10.
Symphony No. 9, D minor, with Final Chorus on Schiller's "Ode to Joy," Opus
125: Nov. 10, 11, 12, 14.

BERLIOZ—*Overture, "Benvenuto Cellini," Opus 23: Jan. 26, 27, 28, 30; Feb.
10.
Scenes from "Romeo and Juliet": May 4, 5, 6, 8.

BERNSTEIN—*"Chichester Psalms," for Chorus and Orchestra (1965): Dec.
28, 29, 30, 31.

BLITZSTEIN—"The Airborne" Symphony: Oct. 13, 14, 15, 17.

BLOMDAHL—Forma Ferritonans: Mar. 9 (b), 10, 11, 13, 15.

BRAHMS—Concerto No. 1 for Piano and Orchestra, D minor, Opus 15: Oct. 19,
24; Dec. 15, 16, 17.
Concerto for Violin and Orchestra, D major, Opus 77: Jan. 26, 27, 28, 30.
*Symphony No. 1, C minor, Opus 68: Nov. 23, 25, 26, 28.
*Symphony No. 2, D major, Opus 73: Nov. 17, 18, 19, 21.

BRITTEN—"War Requiem," for soprano, tenor and baritone solos, mixed
chorus, boys' choir, full orchestra and chamber orch., Opus 66 (1962): Apr.
20, 21, 22, 24.

BRUCKNER—Symphony No. 4, E-flat major ("Romantic"): Feb. 2, 3, 4, 6.
Symphony No. 8, C minor (original version of 1890): Apr. 6, 7, 10.

COPLAND—"Lincoln Portrait": Feb. 11.
Short Symphony (No. 2): Dec. 15, 16, 17.
Symphony for Organ and Orchestra: Dec. 28, 29, 30, 31; Jan. 2.

COWELL—Hymn and Fuguing Tune No. 16: Oct. 6 (a), 7, 8, 10.

DEBUSSY—*"La Mer," Three Symphonic Sketches: Mar. 23, 24, 27.
*Prelude to "The Afternoon of a Faun": Feb. 23, 24, 25, 27.

DENISOV—Crescendo and Diminuendo: May 18 (b), 19, 20.

DVORAK—Concerto for Violin and Orchestra, A minor, Opus 53: Feb. 2, 3, 4, 6.

ELGAR—Concerto for Violoncello and Orchestra, E minor, Opus 85: Mar. 30,
31; Apr. 1, 3, 8.

FAURE—"Pelléas et Mélisande," Orchestral Suite, Opus 80: Feb. 23, 24, 25, 27.

FINE—Symphony (1962): Oct. 27, 28, 29, 31.

FOSS—"Phorion": Apr. 27 (a), 28, 29; May 1.

FULEIHAN—Symphony No. 2; Feb. 16 (a), 17, 18, 20.

GARRIDO-LECCA—"Elegía a Machu Picchu": Mar. 23 (c), 24, 27.

HANDEL—Concerto for Organ and Orchestra, F major, No. 13 ("The Cuckoo and the Nightingale"): Jan. 2.
Messiah: Nov. 15.

HANDEL-HARTY—Concerto for Orchestra with Organ, D major: Feb. 11.

HAYDN—Symphony No. 55 ("The Schoolmaster") in E-flat major: Dec. 1, 2, 3, 5.
Symphony No. 86, D major: Mar. 2, 3, 4, 6.
Symphony No. 87, A major: Mar. 17, 18, 20.

HINDEMITH—Pittsburgh Symphony: Apr. 13, 14, 15, 17.
Symphony in E-flat major: Mar. 2, 3, 4, 6.

HONEGGER—Symphony No. 2 for String Orchestra: Feb. 23, 24, 25, 27.
Symphony No. 5 ("di tre re"): Dec. 15, 16, 17.

JANACEK—Sinfonietta: Jan. 26, 27, 28, 30; Feb. 10.

LISZT—*"Les Préludes": Feb. 11.

MAHLER—*Das Lied von der Erde ("The Song of the Earth"): Mar. 17, 18, 20.
Symphony No. 1, D major: Sept. 29, 30; Oct. 1, 3.
Symphony No. 6, A minor: Apr. 27, 28, 29; May 1.

MARTIRANO—Contrasto: Nov. 17 (c), 18, 19, 21.

MENDELSSOHN—Overture and Incidental Music for Shakespeare's "A Midsummer Night's Dream": Mar. 30, 31; Apr. 1, 3.
Symphony No. 5, D minor, Opus 107 ("Reformation"): Dec. 28, 29, 30, 31; Jan. 2, 24.

MOUSSORGSKY—Scenes from "Boris Godunov": Sept. 28.

MOZART—Concerto for Piano and Orchestra, No. 15, B-flat major, K. 450: May 4, 5, 6, 8.
Concerto for Piano and Orchestra, D minor, K. 466: Dec. 1, 2, 3, 5.
Overture to "Così fan tutte": Feb. 2, 3, 4, 6.
Overture to "The Magic Flute": Oct. 27, 28, 29, 31.
Sinfonia Concertante, for Oboe, Clarinet, Horn, Bassoon with Orchestra Accompaniment, K. 297b, in E-flat major: Oct. 6, 7, 8, 10.
Symphony No. 41, C major, K. 551 ("Jupiter"): Feb. 16, 17, 18, 20.

MOZART-WERNER—Fantasy for a Mechanical Organ, K. 608: Dec. 10.

NIELSEN—Concerto for Clarinet and Orchestra, Opus 57: Mar. 9, 10, 11, 13, 15.

POULENC—Concerto for Piano and Orchestra: Dec. 10.

PROKOFIEV—Concerto No. 4 for Piano and Orchestra, Left Hand, Opus 53: May 18, 19, 20.

RACHMANINOFF—Concerto No. 3 for Piano and Orchestra, D minor, Opus 30: Feb. 16, 17, 18, 20.

RAVEL—*"La Valse": Dec. 10; Mar. 23, 24, 27.
"Mother Goose" Suite: Nov. 3, 4, 5, 7.
Une Barque sur l'océan: Dec. 10.
Tzigane, Concert Rhapsody for Violin and Orchestra: Feb. 11.

RESPIGHI—Symphonic Poem, "The Fountains of Rome": Nov. 23, 25, 26, 28.

REGER—Variations and Fugue for Orchestra on a Theme by Mozart, Opus 132: Feb. 9, 10, 13.

RIMSKY-KORSAKOV—*Capriccio espagnol: Sept. 28; Oct. 19, 24.
Suite from "Le Coq d'or": Dec. 10.

ROUSSEL—*Symphony No. 3, G minor, Opus 42: Feb. 23, 24, 25, 27.

SCHUBERT—Overture, "Des Teufels Lustschloss": Jan. 12, 13, 14, 16, 18.
Symphony No. 6, C major, Opus 140: Apr. 13, 14, 15, 17.
Symphony No. 9, C major: Jan. 12, 13, 14, 16, 18.

SCHUMAN—Symphony for Strings (Symphony No. 5): Sept. 29, 30; Oct. 1, 3, 19, 24.

SCHUMANN—Concerto for Violoncello and Orchestra, A minor, Opus 129: Mar. 2, 3, 4, 6.
Concerto for Piano and Orchestra, A minor, Opus 54: Apr. 13, 14, 15, 17.
*Symphony No. 4, D minor, Opus 120: Mar. 23, 24, 27.

SCHOENBERG—Chamber Symphony No. 2, Opus 38: Oct. 13, 14, 15, 17.
"A Survivor from Warsaw": Oct. 13, 14, 15, 17.
Concerto for Violin and Orchestra, Opus 36: Jan. 5, 6, 7, 9.

SHAPERO—Adagietto from Symphony for Classical Orchestra: Oct. 27, 28, 29, 31.

SHCHEDRIN—Mischievous Folk Ditties: May 18, 19, 20.

SHOSTAKOVICH—*Symphony No. 5, Opus 47: May 11, 12, 13.

SIBELIUS—Symphony No. 1, E minor, Opus 39: Mar. 9, 10, 11, 13, 15.
Symphony No. 6 in D minor, Opus 104: May 4, 5, 6, 8.
Incidental Music for Shakespeare's "The Tempest": Feb. 11.

SUPPE—Overture, "Die schöne Galatea": Jan. 24.

TCHAIKOVSKY—*Concerto for Violin and Orchestra, D major, Opus 35: Oct. 6, 7, 8, 10.
"Manfred" Symphony in Four Tableaux, after the dramatic poem of Byron, Opus 58: Feb. 9, 13.
*Overture-Fantasy, "Romeo and Juliet": Sept. 28.
*Symphony No. 4 in F, Opus 36: May 18, 19, 20.

VARESE—Intégrales: Oct. 6, 7, 8, 10.

VERDI—Messa da Requiem, for soloists, chorus and orchestra: Mar. 25.

WAGNER—Siegfried's Rhine Journey, from "Götterdämmerung": Jan. 26, 27, 28, 30; Feb. 10.

WEBER—Overture to "Der Freischütz": Mar. 30, 31; Apr. 1, 3, 8.

SOLOISTS

PIANO
VLADIMIR ASHKENAZY: Apr. 13, 14, 15, 17.
DAVID BARENBOIM: Dec. 15, 16, 17.
DAVID BAR-ILLAN: May 18, 19, 20.
PHILIPPE ENTREMONT: Jan. 12, 13, 14, 16, 18.
RUDOLF FIRKUSNY: Dec. 1, 2, 3, 5.
EMIL GILELS: Nov. 17, 19, 21.
GARY GRAFFMAN: Oct. 19, 24.
WILHELM KEMPFF: Oct. 27, 28, 29, 31.
EUGENE LIST: Dec. 10.
PETER SERKIN: May 4, 5, 6, 8.
ALEXIS WEISSENBERG: Feb. 16, 17, 18, 20.

VIOLIN
ZINO FRANCESCATTI: Jan. 26, 27, 28, 30.
ARTHUR GRUMIAUX: Nov. 3, 4, 5, 7.
DAVID NADIEN: Oct. 6, 7, 8, 10; Feb. 11.

EDITH PEINEMANN: Feb. 2, 3, 4, 6.
ISAAC STERN: May 11, 12, 13.
ZVI ZEITLIN: Jan. 5, 6, 7, 9.

VIOLONCELLO
JACQUELINE DU PRE: Mar. 2, 3, 4, 6.
LORNE MUNROE: Mar. 30, 31; Apr. 1, 3, 8.

CLARINET
STANLEY DRUCKER: Mar. 9, 10, 11, 13, 15.

ORGAN
E. POWER BIGGS: Dec. 28, 29, 30, 31; Jan. 2.
CATHARINE CROZIER: Nov. 23, 25, 26, 28.
BRUCE PRINCE-JOSEPH: Feb. 11.

NARRATORS
ROBERT HOOKS: Oct. 13, 14, 15, 17.
MAYOR JOHN V. LINDSAY: Feb. 11.
NANCY MARCHAND: Mar. 30, 31; Apr. 1, 3.

JULIAN MILLER: Mar. 30, 31; Apr. 1, 3.

PAUL SPARER: Mar. 30, 31; Apr. 1, 3.

VERA ZORINA: Oct. 13, 14, 15, 17.

VOICE

LILI CHOOKASIAN, contralto: Dec. 8, 9, 12.

JUSTINO DIAZ, bass: Mar. 25.

SARAMAE ENDICH, soprano: Nov. 10, 11, 12, 14, 15.

SIMON ESTES, bass-baritone: Nov. 15.

DIETRICH FISCHER-DIESKAU, baritone: Mar. 17, 18, 20.

CARROLL BENTON FREEMAN, alto: Dec. 28, 29, 30, 31.

NICOLAI GHIAUROV, bass: Sept. 28.

MARILYN HORNE, mezzo-soprano: Mar. 25.

STANLEY KOLK, tenor: Dec. 8, 9, 12.

GLADYS KUCHTA, soprano: Dec. 8, 9, 12.

ELLA LEE, soprano: Apr. 20, 21, 22, 24.

JOHN MCCOLLUM, tenor: Nov. 15.

THOMAS PAUL, bass: Dec. 8, 9, 12.

GEORGE SHIRLEY, tenor: Nov. 10, 11, 12, 14.

JOANNA SIMON, mezzo-soprano: Mar. 30, 31; Apr. 1, 3.

GERARD SOUZAY, baritone: Apr. 20, 21, 22, 24.

YI-KWEI SZE, bass: Nov. 10, 11, 12, 14.

JESS THOMAS, tenor: Mar. 17, 18, 20.

RICHARD TUCKER, tenor: Mar. 25.

ANDREA VELIS, tenor: Oct. 13, 14, 15, 17.

SHIRLEY VERRETT, mezzo-soprano: Nov. 10, 11, 12, 14.

JON VICKERS, tenor: Apr. 20, 21, 22, 24.

GALINA VISHNEVSKAYA, soprano: Mar. 25.

DAVID WATSON, baritone: Oct. 13, 14, 15, 17.

NADJA WITKOWSKA, soprano: Mar. 30, 31; Apr. 1, 3.

BEVERLY WOLFF, mezzo-soprano: Nov. 15.

CHORUS

CAMERATA SINGERS, Abraham Kaplan, Director: Sept. 28; Dec. 28, 29, 30, 31; Mar. 25, 30, 31; Apr. 1, 3.

CHORAL ART SOCIETY, William Jonson, Director: Oct. 13, 14, 15, 17.

COLLEGIATE CHORALE, Abraham Kaplan, Director: Nov. 10, 11, 12, 14.

JUILLIARD CHORUS, Abraham Kaplan, Director: Apr. 20, 21, 22, 24.

ST. KILIAN BOYCHOIR, Herman Furthmoser, Director: Apr. 20, 21, 22, 24.

WESTMINSTER CHOIR, George Lynn, Director: Nov. 15; Dec. 8, 9, 12.

●

TOUR—AUTUMN, 1966

Leonard Bernstein, Conductor

Sept. 13—Eve.	Philadelphia, Pa.	Sept. 21—Eve.	Storrs, Conn.
Sept. 16—Eve.	Villanova, Pa.	Sept. 22—Eve.	Springfield, Mass.
Sept. 17—Eve.	Richmond, Va.	Sept. 24—Eve.	Providence, R.I.
Sept. 18—Aft.	Washington, D.C.	Sept. 25—Aft.	Boston, Mass.
Sept. 20—Eve.	Hartford, Conn.		

TOUR REPERTOIRE

* Recorded by the New York Philharmonic.

BEETHOVEN—Overture to "King Stephen," Opus 117: Sept. 13, 16, 17, 18, 20, 21, 22, 25.

BERLIOZ—*Overture, "The Roman Carnival," Opus 9: Sept. 24.

COPLAND—Dance Symphony: Sept. 13, 18, 25.

MAHLER—Symphony No. 1, D major: Sept. 13, 16, 17, 18, 20, 21, 22, 24, 25.

TCHAIKOVSKY—*Fantasy Overture, "Romeo and Juliet": Sept. 16, 17, 20, 21, 22, 24.

NEW YORK PHILHARMONIC "PROMENADES"
FIFTH SEASON 1967 PHILHARMONIC HALL

Conductor
André Kostelanetz
May 24–June 17.

REPERTOIRE—"PROMENADES"

* Compositions marked with an asterisk are recorded by the New York
Philharmonic on Columbia Records and are now available.

(a) World premiere.
(c) First performance in New York.

BACHELET—Chère Nuit: June 16, 17.
BELLINI—"Casta Diva" from *Norma:* June 16, 17.
BERLIOZ—Three Excerpts from the Dramatic Legend, "La Damnation de Faust":
June 12, 14, 15.
CHAGRIN—Romanian Fantasy for Harmonica and Orchestra: May 30 (c), 31;
June 1, 3.
DEBUSSY—*"Fêtes," from *Nocturnes:* June 2, 9, 10.
Lia's Aria from *The Prodigal Son:* June 16, 17.
FLOYD—"Ain't it a Pretty Night?" from *Susannah:* June 16, 17.
GINASTERA—Canción al arbol del olvido: June 16, 17.
GLINKA—Overture, "Russlan and Ludmilla": June 6, 7, 8.
HOVHANESS—"To Vishnu": June 2 (a), 9, 10.
IBERT—Divertissement: June 6, 7, 8.
Ports of Call (Escales): May 30, 31; June 1, 3.
ITURBI—"Seguidillas": June 16 (c), 17.
KHACHATURIAN—Suite from the Ballet, "Gayne": May 24, 25, 26, 27; June
16, 17.
KODALY—Dances from *Galanta:* June 16, 17.
LIADOFF—"The Enchanted Lake," Legend for Orchestra, Opus 62: May 24,
25, 26, 27.
MacLEISH-LADERMAN—"Magic Prison," for two narrators and orchestra:
June 12 (a), 14, 15.
MOUSSORGSKY—"Daybreak" from *Khovanshchina:* June 2, 9, 10.
MOZART—Overture, "The Abduction from the Seraglio": June 12, 14, 15.
Symphony No. 24, B-flat major, K. 182: June 6, 7, 8.
POULENC-FRANCAIX—The Story of Babar, the Little Elephant: June 6 (c),
7, 8.
PROKOFIEV—Wedding Suite from "The Stone Flower," Opus 126: May 24,
25, 26, 27.
PUCCINI—Crisantemi: May 24, 25, 26, 27.
Excerpts from "La Rondíne": May 24, 25, 26, 27.
REIZENSTEIN—"Concerto Populare" for Piano and Orchestra: June 6 (c), 7, 8.
RODRIGO—De los alamos vengo: June 16, 17.
SKALKOTTAS—Greek Dances: May 30, 31; June 1, 3.
STRAUS, Oscar—"Leise, ganz leise" from *Ein Walzertraum:* June 16, 17.

STRAUSS—*"Dance of the Seven Veils" from *Salome:* June 2, 9, 10.

TCHAIKOVSKY—Concerto for Violin and Orchestra, D major, Opus 35: June 2, 9, 10.

*Fantasy Overture, "Romeo and Juliet": June 12, 14, 15.

VERDI—Ballet from Act III of "Otello": May 24, 25, 26, 27.

Songs of Israel: May 30, 31; June 1, 3.

SOLOISTS—"PROMENADES"

NARRATORS

MARC CONNELLY: June 6, 7, 8.

ANNE DRAPER: June 12, 14, 15.

E. G. MARSHALL: June 12, 14, 15.

PIANO

LEONID HAMBRO: June 6, 7, 8.

VIOLIN

GLENN DICTEROW: June 2, 9, 10.

HARMONICA

LARRY ADLER: May 30, 31; June 1, 3.

VOICE

PHYLLIS CURTIN, soprano: June 16, 17.

SHOSHANA DAMARI, contralto: May 30, 31; June 1, 3.

MICHELE MOLESE, tenor: May 24, 25, 26, 27.

TERESA STRATAS, soprano: May 24, 25, 26, 27.

●

NEW YORK PHILHARMONIC: LINCOLN CENTER FESTIVAL '67
1967—PHILHARMONIC HALL

Conductors

Karel Ancerl
July 1, 5.

Leonard Bernstein
June 22, 24, 28, 30.

Seiji Ozawa
July 7, 8.

REPERTOIRE—LINCOLN CENTER FESTIVAL

* Compositions marked with an asterisk are recorded by the New York Philharmonic on Columbia Records and are now available.

(a) World premiere.

DVORAK—*Symphony No. 9 (formerly No. 5), E minor, Opus 95, "From the New World": July 1, 5.

HONEGGER—"Joan of Arc at the Stake," Dramatic Oratorio by Paul Claudel (English translation by Dennis Arundell): July 7, 8.

JANACEK—Taras Bulba: July 1, 5.

MAHLER—*Symphony No. 2, C minor, for Orchestra, Soprano and Contralto Solos and Mixed Chorus: June 22, 24.

RACHMANINOFF—Piano Concerto No. 3, D minor, Opus 30: June 28, 30.

ROREM—Sun, for Soprano and Orchestra: July 1 (a), 5.

SCHULLER—Triplum: June 28 (a), 30.

STRAVINSKY—Symphony in Three Movements: June 28, 30.

SOLOISTS—LINCOLN CENTER FESTIVAL

PIANO

VAN CLIBURN: June 28, 30.

VOICE

STANLEY KOLK, tenor: July 7, 8.

JANE MARSH, soprano: July 1, 5.

RAYMOND MICHALSKI, bass: July 7, 8.

MARY MORRISON, soprano: July 7, 8.

LOUISE PARKER, soprano: July 7, 8.

LILIAN SUKIS, soprano: July 7, 8.

JENNIE TOUREL, mezzo-soprano: June 22, 24.

VERONICA TYLER, soprano: June 22, 24.

NARRATORS

JANET DOWD: July 7, 8.

EARL MONTGOMERY: July 7, 8.

REX ROBBINS: July 7, 8.

MICHAEL WAGER: July 7, 8.

VERA ZORINA: July 7, 8.

CHORUS

CAMERATA SINGERS, Abraham Kaplan, Director, July 7, 8.

ST. KILIAN BOYCHOIR, Herman Furthmoser, Director, July 7, 8.

SCHOLA CANTORUM, Hugh Ross, Director, June 22, 24.

•

THE LONG ISLAND FESTIVAL
1967—C. W. POST COLLEGE, GREENVALE, NEW YORK

Alfred Wallenstein, Conductor
July 14, 15.

REPERTOIRE—LONG ISLAND FESTIVAL

* Compositions marked with an asterisk are recorded by the New York Philharmonic on Columbia Records and are now available.

BEETHOVEN—Symphony No. 8, F major, Opus 93: July 15.

DEBUSSY—*"La Mer," Three Symphonic Sketches: July 15.

GLINKA—Overture, "Russlan and Ludmilla": July 14.

MENDELSSOHN—Concerto for Violin and Orchestra, E minor, Opus 64: July 15.

RACHMANINOFF—Concerto for Piano and Orchestra, No. 2, C minor, Opus 18: July 14.

TCHAIKOVSKY—*Symphony No. 4, F minor, Opus 36: July 14.

WAGNER—Prelude to "Die Meistersinger von Nürnberg": July 15.

SOLOISTS—LONG ISLAND FESTIVAL

MICHAEL RABIN, violinist: July 15.   ANDRE WATTS, pianist: July 14.

•

NEW YORK PHILHARMONIC OUTDOOR CONCERTS IN THE PARKS OF THE CITY OF NEW YORK
THIRD SEASON (1967)

Conductors

Sixten Ehrling
July 25, 27, 29.

Lorin Maazel
July 18, 20, 22.

Seiji Ozawa
August 1, 3, 5, 6.

Alfred Wallenstein
August 9, 10.

REPERTOIRE—PARK CONCERTS

* Compositions marked with an asterisk are recorded by the New York Philharmonic on Columbia Records and are now available.

BEETHOVEN—*Symphony No. 7, A major, Opus 92: July 25, 27, 29.

BLOCH—"Schelomo," Hebrew Rhapsody for Violoncello and Orchestra: August 10, 11.

BRAHMS—*Symphony No. 4, E minor, Opus 98: August 9, 10, 11.

MENDELSSOHN—Concerto for Violin and Orchestra, E minor, Opus 64: July 18, 20, 22.

RACHMANINOFF—Concerto No. 2 for Piano and Orchestra, C minor, Opus 18: July 25, 27, 29.

RAVEL—*La Valse: August 9, 10, 11.

SHOSTAKOVICH—*Symphony No. 5, Opus 47: July 18, 20, 22.

STRAUSS, R.—*"Till Eulenspiegel's Merry Pranks," Opus 28: July 25, 27, 29.

WEBER—*Overture to "Oberon": July 18, 20, 22.

SOLOISTS—PARK CONCERTS

PIANO
ANDRE WATTS: July 25, 27, 29.

VIOLIN
MICHAEL RABIN: July 18, 20, 22.

CELLO
LORNE MUNROE: August 9, 10.

VOICE
JENNIE TOUREL, mezzo-soprano: August 1, 3, 5, 6.

1967–68 ONE HUNDRED TWENTY-SIXTH SEASON

LEONARD BERNSTEIN, *Music Director*

Guest Conductors
WILLIAM STEINBERG, *Principal Guest Conductor*

CLAUDIO ABBADO	SIR JOHN BARBIROLLI	SEIJI OZAWA
THOMAS SCHIPPERS	LEOPOLD STOKOWSKI	GEORGE SZELL

LEONARD BERNSTEIN
Music Director
Young People's Concerts

ANDRE KOSTELANETZ
Special Saturday Night Concerts
ALFRED WALLENSTEIN
Lincoln Center Student Concerts

PAUL CAPOLONGO   HELEN QUACH   ALOIS SPRINGER
Assistant Conductors

CONCERTS

1967

Leonard Bernstein
Oct. 5—Eve.   Philharmonic Hall
Oct. 6—Aft.   Philharmonic Hall
Oct. 7—Eve.   Philharmonic Hall
Oct. 9—Eve.   Philharmonic Hall

1967

Leonard Bernstein,
Karl Boehm
Oct. 12—Eve.   Philharmonic Hall

Leonard Bernstein,
Helen Quach
Oct. 13—Aft.   Philharmonic Hall

1967

**Leonard Bernstein,
Paul Capolongo**
Oct. 14—Eve.   Philharmonic Hall

**Leonard Bernstein,
Alois Springer**
Oct. 16—Eve.   Philharmonic Hall

Leonard Bernstein
Oct. 19—Eve.   Philharmonic Hall
Oct. 20—Aft.   Philharmonic Hall
Oct. 21—Eve.   Philharmonic Hall
Oct. 23—Eve.   Philharmonic Hall
Oct. 25—Eve.   Philharmonic Hall
Oct. 28—Aft.(2)   Philharmonic Hall
(Young People's Concerts)
Oct. 30—Eve.   Washington, D.C.

Claudio Abbado
Nov. 2—Eve.   Philharmonic Hall
Nov. 3—Aft.   Philharmonic Hall
Nov. 4—Eve.   Philharmonic Hall
Nov. 6—Eve.   Philharmonic Hall

Seiji Ozawa
Nov. 9—Eve.   Philharmonic Hall
Nov. 10—Aft.   Philharmonic Hall
Nov. 11—Eve.   Philharmonic Hall
Nov. 13—Eve.   Philharmonic Hall

William Steinberg
Nov. 16—Eve.   Philharmonic Hall
Nov. 17—Eve.   Philharmonic Hall
Nov. 18—Eve.   Philharmonic Hall
Nov. 20—Eve.   Philharmonic Hall
Nov. 23—Eve.   Philharmonic Hall
Nov. 24—Aft.   Philharmonic Hall
Nov. 25—Eve.   Philharmonic Hall
Nov. 27—Eve.   Philharmonic Hall
Nov. 30—Eve.   Philharmonic Hall
Dec. 1—Aft.   Philharmonic Hall
Dec. 2—Eve.   Philharmonic Hall
Dec. 4—Eve.   Philharmonic Hall

Alfred Wallenstein
Dec. 5—Aft.   Philharmonic Hall
(Lincoln Center Student Program)

Leonard Bernstein
Dec. 7—Eve.   Philharmonic Hall
(125th Anniversary Year Concert)

Alfred Wallenstein
Dec. 8—Aft.   Philharmonic Hall
(Lincoln Center Student Program)

William Steinberg
Dec. 9—Eve.   Half Hollow Hills
Audit. (Hunting-
ton/Babylon)

1967
Dec. 11—Eve.   Philharmonic Hall
Dec. 14—Eve.   Philharmonic Hall
Dec. 15—Aft.   Philharmonic Hall
Dec. 16—Eve.   Philharmonic Hall
Dec. 18—Eve.   Philharmonic Hall
Dec. 21—Eve.   Philharmonic Hall
Dec. 22—Aft.   Philharmonic Hall
Dec. 23—Eve.   Philharmonic Hall

1968

Leonard Bernstein
Jan. 4—Eve.   Philharmonic Hall
Jan. 5—Aft.   Philharmonic Hall

**Leonard Bernstein,
Paul Capolongo**
Jan. 6—Aft.(2)   Philharmonic Hall
(Young People's Concerts)

Leonard Bernstein
Jan. 8—Eve.   Philharmonic Hall
Jan. 11—Eve.   Philharmonic Hall
Jan. 12—Aft.   Philharmonic Hall
Jan. 13—Eve.   Philharmonic Hall
Jan. 15—Eve.   Philharmonic Hall
Jan. 18—Eve.   Philharmonic Hall
Jan. 19—Aft.   Philharmonic Hall
Jan. 20—Eve.   Philharmonic Hall
Jan. 22—Eve.   Philharmonic Hall
Jan. 24—Eve.   Philharmonic Hall

**Leonard Bernstein,
Helen Quach,
Alois Springer**
Jan. 27—Aft.(2)   Philharmonic Hall
(Young People's Concerts)

**Boris Brott,
Gaetano Delogu,
François Huybrechts,
Farhad Mechkat**
Jan. 29—Eve.   Philharmonic Hall
(Mitropoulos International Music
Competition)

William Steinberg
Feb. 1—Eve.   Philharmonic Hall
Feb. 2—Aft.   Philharmonic Hall
Feb. 3—Eve.   Philharmonic Hall
Feb. 5—Eve.   Philharmonic Hall

**William Steinberg,
Roy Harris**
Feb. 8—Eve.   Philharmonic Hall
Feb. 9—Aft.   Philharmonic Hall

André Kostelanetz
Feb. 10—Eve.   Philharmonic Hall

1968   1968

William Steinberg,
Roy Harris
Feb. 12—Eve.   Philharmonic Hall

William Steinberg
Feb. 15—Eve.   Philharmonic Hall
Feb. 16—Aft.   Philharmonic Hall
Feb. 17—Eve.   Philharmonic Hall
Feb. 19—Eve.   Philharmonic Hall
Feb. 22—Eve.   Philharmonic Hall
Feb. 23—Aft.   Philharmonic Hall

Leonard Bernstein
Feb. 24—Aft.(2)   Philharmonic Hall
  (Young People's Concerts)

William Steinberg
Feb. 24—Eve.   Philharmonic Hall
Feb. 26—Eve.   Philharmonic Hall

Leonard Bernstein,
Howard Hanson
Feb. 29—Eve.   Philharmonic Hall
Mar. 1—Aft.   Philharmonic Hall
Mar. 2—Eve.   Philharmonic Hall
Mar. 4—Eve.   Philharmonic Hall

Leonard Bernstein
Mar. 7—Eve.   Philharmonic Hall
Mar. 8—Aft.   Philharmonic Hall
Mar. 9—Eve.   Philharmonic Hall
Mar. 11—Eve.   Philharmonic Hall
Mar. 14—Eve.   Philharmonic Hall
Mar. 15—Aft.   Philharmonic Hall
Mar. 16—Eve.   Philharmonic Hall
Mar. 18—Eve.   Philharmonic Hall
Mar. 20—Eve.   Philharmonic Hall

André Kostelanetz
Mar. 22—Aft.   Philharmonic Hall
  (Lincoln Center Student Program)
Mar. 23—Eve.   Philharmonic Hall

Leonard Bernstein
Mar. 25—Eve.   Philharmonic Hall
  (Lincoln Center Student Program)

Skitch Henderson,
Richard Rodgers
Mar. 26—Eve.   Philharmonic Hall
  (Pension Fund Benefit)

George Szell
Mar. 28—Eve.   Philharmonic Hall
Mar. 29—Aft.   Philharmonic Hall
Mar. 30—Eve.   Philharmonic Hall
Apr. 1—Eve.   Philharmonic Hall

Sir John Barbirolli
Apr. 4—Eve.   Philharmonic Hall
Apr. 5—Aft.   Philharmonic Hall
Apr. 6—Eve.   Philharmonic Hall
Apr. 8—Eve.   Philharmonic Hall

Leopold Stokowski
Apr. 11—Eve.   Philharmonic Hall
Apr. 12—Aft.   Philharmonic Hall
Apr. 13—Eve.   Philharmonic Hall
Apr. 15—Eve.   Philharmonic Hall

William Steinberg
Apr. 18—Eve.   Philharmonic Hall
Apr. 19—Aft.   Philharmonic Hall
Apr. 20—Eve.   Philharmonic Hall
Apr. 22—Eve.   Philharmonic Hall
Apr. 25—Eve.   Philharmonic Hall
Apr. 26—Aft.   Philharmonic Hall
Apr. 27—Eve.   Philharmonic Hall
Apr. 29—Eve.   Philharmonic Hall
May 2—Eve.   Philharmonic Hall
May 3—Aft.   Philharmonic Hall
May 4—Eve.   Philharmonic Hall
May 6—Eve.   Philharmonic Hall

Thomas Schippers
May 9—Eve.   Philharmonic Hall
May 10—Aft.   Philharmonic Hall
May 11—Eve.   Philharmonic Hall
May 13—Eve.   Philharmonic Hall

Leonard Bernstein
May 16—Eve.   Philharmonic Hall
May 17—Aft.   Philharmonic Hall
May 18—Eve.   Philharmonic Hall
May 23—Eve.   Philharmonic Hall
May 24—Aft.   Philharmonic Hall
May 25—Eve.   Philharmonic Hall

REPERTOIRE

* Recorded by the New York Philharmonic on Columbia Records.

(a) First performance anywhere; commissioned by the New York Philharmonic
      for its 125th Anniversary year.
(b) First performance in the United States.
(c) First performance in New York.

BACH, J. S.—Concerto for Violin and Orchestra, No. 2, E major, BWV 1042: Feb. 1, 2, 3, 5.

BARBER—*Second Essay for Orchestra: Apr. 18, 19, 20, 22.

BARTOK—*Music for Strings, Percussion and Celesta: Nov. 30; Dec. 1, 2, 4, 11.

BEETHOVEN—*Concerto for Piano and Orchestra, No. 1, C major, Opus 15: Jan. 4, 5, 8.

*Concerto for Piano and Orchestra, No. 4, G major, Opus 58: Feb. 19.

"In des Lebens Frühlingstagen," from *Fidelio:* Dec. 7.

Grand Fugue in B-flat major, Opus 133 (Edited for String Orchestra by Felix Weingartner): Feb. 22, 23, 24, 26.

*Symphony No. 2, D major, Opus 36: Nov. 9, 10, 11, 13.

*Symphony No. 4, B-flat major, Opus 60: Dec. 14, 15, 16, 18.

*Symphony No. 5, C minor, Opus 67: Dec. 7.

*Symphony No. 7, A major, Opus 92: May 9, 10, 11, 13.

*Symphony No. 8, F major, Opus 93: Nov. 17; Mar. 28, 29, 30; Apr. 1.

*Symphony No. 9, D minor, Opus 125: May 16, 17, 18.

BENNETT, Richard R.—Symphony No. 2: Jan. 18 (a), 19, 20, 22, 24.

BERG—Three Orchestral Pieces, Opus 6: Nov. 2, 3, 4, 6.

Three Fragments for Voice and Orchestra, from *Wozzeck,* Opus 7: Feb. 22, 23, 24, 26.

BERLIOZ—The Damnation of Faust, Dramatic Legend, Opus 24: Nov. 16, 17, 18, 20.

*Symphonie fantastique, Opus 14: Feb. 29; Mar. 1, 2, 4, 25.

BLOCH—Schelomo, Hebrew Rhapsody for Violoncello and Orchestra: Dec. 5, 8.

BRAHMS—*Academic Festival Overture, Opus 80: Nov. 2, 3, 4, 6.

*Concerto for Piano and Orchestra, No. 2, B-flat major, Opus 83: Jan. 18, 19, 20, 22, 24.

*Symphony No. 4, E minor, Opus 98: Nov. 30; Dec. 1, 2, 4, 5, 8, 9, 11.

BRITTEN—Les Illuminations, Opus 18: Feb. 10.

Sinfonia da Requiem, Opus 20: Jan. 18, 19, 20, 22, 24.

BRUCH—*Concerto for Violin and Orchestra, No. 1, G minor, Opus 26: Dec. 14, 15, 16, 18.

Scottish Fantasy for Violin and Orchestra, Opus 46: May 4.

BRUCKNER—Symphony No. 7, E major: Feb. 8, 9, 12.

CHOPIN—Concerto for Piano and Orchestra, No. 1, E minor, Opus 11: May 2, 3, 6.

COPLAND—*Suite from *Appalachian Spring:* Dec. 21, 22, 23.

Inscape: Oct. 19, 20, 21, 23, 25, 30.

DEBUSSY—*Prelude to the Afternoon of a Faun: Feb. 10.

*Images: Mar. 7, 8, 9, 11, 25.

*Rhapsody for Clarinet and Orchestra: May 9, 10, 11, 13.

DVORAK—*Symphony No. 7 (No. 2), D minor, Opus 70: Apr. 4, 5, 6, 8.

Symphony No. 8 (No. 4), G major, Opus 88: Nov. 2, 3, 4, 6.

ELGAR—Concerto for Violin and Orchestra, C minor, Opus 68: Nov. 23, 24, 25, 27.

Falstaff, Symphonic Study for Orchestra, C minor, Opus 68: Feb. 1, 2, 3, 5.

Military March, Pomp and Circumstance, No. 2, A minor, Opus 39: Feb. 1, 2, 3, 5.

GERHARD—Symphony 4 (New York): Dec. 14 (a), 15, 16, 18.

GERSHWIN—*An American in Paris: Mar. 23.

Concerto in F: Mar. 22, 23.

GOLDMARK—Symphony, A Rustic Wedding, Opus 26: Mar. 7, 8, 9, 11.

GRETRY-MOTTL—Suite from *Céphale et Procris:* Feb. 10.

HANDEL—Concerto Grosso, D minor, Opus 6, No. 10: Apr. 18, 19, 20, 22.

HANSON—Symphony No. 6: Feb. 29 (a); Mar. 1, 2, 4.

HARRIS—Symphony No. 3: May 23, 24, 25.
Eleventh Symphony—1967: Feb. 8 (a), 9, 12.

HINDEMITH—Symphony, Mathis der Maler: Nov. 9, 10, 11, 13.
Symphonic Metamorphosis of Themes by Weber: Jan. 4, 5, 8.

HUMMEL—Piano Quintet in D minor (1st movement), Opus 87: Dec. 7.

d'INDY—Symphony on a French Mountain Air, Opus 25: Dec. 21, 22, 23.

IVES—*Symphony No. 2: Oct. 5, 6, 7, 9, 30.
Thanksgiving and Forefathers' Day: Feb. 29; Mar. 1, 2, 4.

KALLIWODA—Overture No. 1, D minor: Dec. 7.

KODALY—Suite, *Háry János:* Feb. 10; Mar. 22.
Psalmus Hungaricus, Opus 13: Apr. 18, 19, 20, 22.

MAHLER—The Boy's Magic Horn: Oct. 12, 13, 14, 16.
*Symphony for Orchestra and Soprano Solo, No. 4, G major: Oct. 5, 6, 7, 9.
*Symphony No. 5, C-sharp minor: Oct. 19, 20, 21, 23, 25.
Symphony No. 10, F-sharp major (Cooke Performing Version): Apr. 25, 26, 27, 29.

MENDELSSOHN—Concerto for Piano and Orchestra, No. 1, G minor, Opus 25: Feb. 22, 23, 24, 26.
Concerto for Violin and Orchestra, E minor, Opus 64: Nov. 30; Dec. 1, 2, 4, 11.
*Overture, The Hebrides (Fingal's Cave), Opus 26: Feb. 15, 16, 17.
Symphony No. 5, D major, Opus 107 (Reformation): Jan. 29.

MILHAUD—Concerto for Two Pianos and Orchestra: Mar. 14, 15, 16, 18, 20.

MITROPOULOS—Concerto Grosso: Mar. 14 (b), 15, 16, 18, 20.

MOZART—Concerto for Piano and Orchestra, No. 24, C minor, K. 491: Feb. 15, 16, 17.
Concerto for Piano and Orchestra, No. 27, B-flat major, K. 595: Dec. 21, 22, 23.
Concerto for Three Pianos and Orchestra, F major, K. 242: Mar. 14, 15, 16, 18, 20.
Overture to *The Impresario:* Apr. 25, 26, 27, 29.
Marches, K. 335, No. 1, D major and K. 408, No. 3, C major: Mar. 28, 29, 30; Apr. 1.
"Ach ich liebte" from *The Abduction from the Seraglio,* K. 384: Dec. 7.
Symphony No. 29, A major, K. 201: Jan. 29.
Symphony No. 34, C major, K. 338: Nov. 23, 24, 25, 27; Dec. 9.
Symphony No. 35, D major (Haffner), K. 385: Oct. 12, 13, 14, 16.
Symphony No. 41, C major (Jupiter), K. 551: Jan. 11, 12, 13, 15.

NABOKOV—Third Symphony (A Prayer): Jan. 4 (a), 5, 8.

PISTON—Ricercare: Mar. 7 (a), 8, 9, 11.

PROKOFIEV—*Symphony No. 5, B-flat major, Opus 100: Mar. 28, 29, 30; Apr. 1.

RAVEL—*Alborada del Gracioso: Mar. 22, 23.
*Daphnis and Chloé, Suite No. 2: Jan. 29.
*La Valse: Dec. 5, 8, 21, 22, 23.
Mother Goose Suite: Jan. 29.

RAWSTHORNE—Overture, Street Corner: Apr. 4, 5, 6, 8.

RESPIGHI—Symphonic Poem, Roman Festivals: Mar. 14, 15, 16, 18, 20.

RIMSKY-KORSAKOV—Overture, The Great Russian Easter, Opus 36: Apr. 11, 12, 13, 15.
*Scheherazade, Opus 35: May 2, 3, 4, 6.

RODGERS and HAMMERSTEIN—*Oklahoma!:* Mar. 26.

ROSSINI—"Grata quest' alma!" from *Armida:* Dec. 7.

SCHUMANN—Concerto for Violin and Orchestra, D minor, Opus Posth.: Feb. 1, 2, 3, 5.
Introduction and Allegro Appassionato for Piano and Orchestra, G major, Opus 92: Feb. 22, 23, 24, 26.
*Manfred Overture, Opus 115: May 9, 10, 11, 13.

SESSIONS—Symphony No. 8: May 2 (a), 3, 4, 6.

SHCHEDRIN—The Chimes (Zvony): Concerto No. 2 for Orchestra: Jan. 11 (a), 12, 13, 15.

SHOSTAKOVICH—Concerto for Violin and Orchestra, No. 2: Jan. 11 (b), 12.
Symphony No. 6, Opus 54: Apr. 11, 12, 13, 15.

SIBELIUS—Swan of Tuonela, Opus 22, No. 3: Mar. 22, 23.

STARER—Samson Agonistes: Apr. 25 (c), 26, 27, 29.

STRAUSS—Tone Poem, Death and Transfiguration, Opus 24: Nov. 23, 24, 25, 27; Dec. 9.
Four Last Songs (1948), Opus 33: May 16, 17, 18.
*Till Eulenspiegel's Merry Pranks, Opus 28: Nov. 2, 3, 4, 6.

STRAVINSKY—Symphony in Three Movements: May 9, 10, 11, 13.

TAKEMITSU—November Steps: Nov. 9 (a), 10, 11, 13.

TCHAIKOVSKY—*Concerto for Piano and Orchestra, No. 1, B-flat minor, Opus 23: Jan. 13, 15.
*Fantasy Overture, Romeo and Juliet: Dec. 14, 15, 16, 18.
Marche Solennelle: Feb. 10.
Symphony No. 2, C minor (Little Russian), Opus 17: Oct. 12, 13, 14, 16, 30.
Symphony No. 6, B minor (Pathétique), Opus 74: Feb. 15, 16, 17, 19.

THOMSON—Shipwreck and Love Scene (Juan and Haidee), from Byron's *Don Juan:* Apr. 11 (a), 12, 13, 15.

VAUGHAN WILLIAMS—Symphony No. 2 (London): Apr. 4, 5, 6, 8.

WAGNER—Overture to *The Flying Dutchman:* Feb. 22, 23, 24, 26.
Symphonic Excerpts, *Parsifal,* Act III: Apr. 11, 12, 13, 15.
Die Walküre, Act I: May 23, 24, 25.

WALTON—Belshazzar's Feast: Apr. 18, 19, 20, 22.

WEBER—Overture to *Euryanthe:* Jan. 4, 5, 8.
*Overture to *Oberon:* Dec. 7.
"Ozean, du Ungeheuer" from *Oberon:* Dec. 7.

SOLOISTS

PIANO
GINA BACHAUER: Feb. 15, 16, 17.
LEONARD BERNSTEIN: Dec. 7; Jan. 4, 5, 8; Mar. 14, 15, 16, 18, 20.
ROBERT CASADESUS: Dec. 21, 22, 23.
VAN CLIBURN: May 2, 3, 6.
ANTHONY DI BONAVENTURA: Feb. 22, 23, 24, 26.
MISHA DICHTER: Jan. 13, 15.
ARTHUR GOLD and ROBERT FIZDALE: Mar. 14, 15, 16, 18, 20.
LORIN HOLLANDER: Mar. 22, 23.
RUDOLF SERKIN: Feb. 19.
ANDRE WATTS: Jan. 18, 19, 20, 22, 24.

VIOLIN
PINA CARMIRELLI: Nov. 30; Dec. 1, 2, 4, 11.
YEHUDI MENUHIN: Nov. 23, 24, 25, 27.
DAVID NADIEN: Dec. 7, 14, 15, 16, 18.
DAVID OISTRAKH: Jan. 11, 12.
HENRYK SZERYNG: Feb. 1, 2, 3, 5.
KYUNG WHA CHUNG: May 4.

VIOLONCELLO
LORNE MUNROE: Dec. 5, 7, 8.

VIOLA
WILLIAM LINCER: Dec. 7.

DOUBLE BASS
ROBERT BRENNAND: Dec. 7.

CLARINET
STANLEY DRUCKER: May 9, 10, 11, 13.

BIWA
KINSHI TSURUTA: Nov. 9, 10, 11, 13.

SHAKUHACHI:
KATSUYA YOKOYAMA: Nov. 9, 10, 11, 13.

VOICE
JOHN ALEXANDER, tenor: May 16, 17, 18.
BETTY ALLEN, contralto: May 16, 17, 18.
WALTER BERRY, baritone: Oct. 12, 13, 14, 16.
MCHENRY BOATWRIGHT, bass: May 16, 17, 18.
JOE BOVA: Mar. 26.
PHYLLIS CURTIN, soprano: Feb. 10.
HOWARD DA SILVA: Mar. 26.
JOHN DAVIDSON: Mar. 26.
EILEEN FARRELL, soprano: Dec. 7; May 23, 24, 25.
EZIO FLAGELLO, baritone: Nov. 18, 20.
NICOLAI GEDDA, tenor: Dec. 7.
ANITA GILLETTE: Mar. 26.
RERI GRIST, soprano: Dec. 7.
ERNST HAEFLIGER, tenor: Nov. 16, 17, 18, 20.

MARGARET HAMILTON: Mar. 26.
SENA JURINAC, soprano: May 16, 17, 18.
JAMES KING, tenor: May 23, 24, 25.
RICHARD KNESS, tenor: Apr. 11, 12, 13, 15.
MICHAEL LANGDON, bass: May 23, 24, 25.
CHRISTA LUDWIG, mezzo-soprano: Oct. 12, 13, 14, 16.
RAYMOND MICHALSKI, bass: Nov. 16, 17, 18, 20.
TICHO PARLY, tenor: Apr. 18, 19, 20, 22.
EILEEN SCHAULER, soprano: Feb. 22, 23, 24, 26.
GERARD SOUZAY, baritone: Nov. 16.
CONSTANCE TOWERS: Mar. 26.
ARNOLD VOKETAITIS, bass: Apr. 18, 19, 20, 22.
BEVERLY WOLFF, mezzo-soprano: Nov. 16, 17, 18, 20.
JEANNETTE ZAROU, soprano: Oct. 5, 6, 7, 9.

CHORUS
CAMERATA SINGERS, Abraham Kaplan, Director: Feb. 29; Mar. 1, 2, 4, 26; Apr. 18, 19, 20, 22.
SCHOLA CANTORUM, Hugh Ross, Director: May 16, 17, 18.
WESTMINSTER CHOIR, George Lynn, Director: Nov. 16, 17, 18, 20.

●

TOUR—AUTUMN, 1967

Conductors

Leonard Bernstein

Sept. 12—Eve.	Ann Arbor, Mich.
Sept. 13—Eve.	Ann Arbor, Mich.
Sept. 14—Eve.	Chicago, Ill.
Sept. 15—Eve.	Chicago, Ill.
Sept. 17—Aft.	Urbana-Champaign, Ill.
Sept. 19—Eve.	Calgary (Alberta), Canada
Sept. 20—Eve.	Vancouver (B. C.), Canada

Leonard Bernstein, Alois Springer

Sept. 21—Eve.	Vancouver (B. C.), Canada

Leonard Bernstein

Sept. 22—Eve.	Edmonton (Alberta), Canada
Sept. 23—Eve.	Winnipeg (Manitoba), Canada
Sept. 25—Eve.	London (Ontario), Canada
Sept. 26—Eve.	Toronto (Ontario), Canada
Sept. 27—Eve.	Ottawa (Ontario), Canada
Sept. 29—Eve.	Montreal (Quebec), Canada
Sept. 30—Eve.	Montreal (Quebec), Canada
Oct. 2—Eve.	Halifax (Nova Scotia), Canada

TOUR REPERTOIRE

* Recorded by the New York Philharmonic.

(a) First performance anywhere; commissioned by the New York Philharmonic for its 125th Anniversary year.

BEETHOVEN—*Symphony No. 8, F major, Opus 93: Sept. 13, 15, 17, 21, 22, 23, 26, 30; Oct. 2.

BERNSTEIN—*Overture to *Candide:* Sept. 13.

COPLAND—Inscape: Sept. 13 (a), 15, 17, 21, 22, 23, 26, 30; Oct. 2.

IVES—*Symphony No. 2: Sept. 12, 14, 19, 20, 25, 27, 29.

MAHLER—*Symphony No. 4, G major, for Orchestra and Soprano Solo: Sept. 12, 14, 19, 20, 25, 27, 29.

TCHAIKOVSKY—Symphony No. 2 (Little Russian), C minor, Opus 17: Sept. 13, 15, 17, 21, 22, 23, 26, 30; Oct. 2.

TOUR SOLOIST

JEANNETTE ZAROU, soprano: Sept. 12, 14, 19, 20, 25, 27, 29.

●

NEW YORK PHILHARMONIC "PROMENADES"
SIXTH SEASON   1968   PHILHARMONIC HALL

Conductor

André Kostelanetz
May 29–June 22.

REPERTOIRE—"PROMENADES"

* Compositions marked with an asterisk are recorded by the New York Philharmonic.

(c) First performance in New York.
(t) Two-piano solo, performed with orchestral accompaniment.

ALBENIZ-ARBOS—Excerpts from the Suite, "Ibéria": June 18, 19.

BERLIOZ—*Overture, The Roman Carnival, Opus 9: June 12, 13, 14, 15.

BERNSTEIN—*Overture and "Glitter and Be Gay" from "Candide": June 20, 21, 22.

BIZET—Excerpts from "L'Arlésienne": June 7, 8, 11.

BRAHMS—(t) Three Waltzes, E major, B minor, A-flat major, Opus 39: June 18, 19.

BRITTEN—Scottish Ballad, Opus 26: June 18, 19.

CHAPI—Overture from the zarzuela, "La Revoltosa" ("The Revolutionary Girl"): June 12, 13, 14, 15.

CRESTON-COWELL—Images in Flight: June 20 (c), 21, 22.

DUKAS—The Sorcerer's Apprentice: June 7, 8, 11.

HAYDN—Symphony No. 88, G major: May 29, 30, 31; June 1.

HOVHANESS—Floating World—Ukiyo (Ballade for Orchestra, Opus 209): June 20, 21, 22.

KABALEVSKY—Overture to "Colas Breugnon": June 4, 5, 6.

KALMAN—Entrance of Maritza, from "Countess Maritza": May 29, 30, 31; June 1.

KORNGOLD—Marietta's Lied, from "The Dead City": May 29, 30, 31; June 1.

KREISLER—Kreisleriana: May 29, 30, 31; June 1.

LEHAR—Suite, from "The Merry Widow": May 29, 30, 31; June 1.

MENOTTI—Excerpts from "The Telephone": June 20, 21, 22.

MILHAUD—Le Boeuf sur le toit ("The Nothing-Doing Bar"): June 7, 8, 11.

MOORE—Willow Song from "The Ballad of Baby Doe": June 20, 21, 22.

MOZART—Martern aller Arten, from "The Abduction from the Seraglio": May 29, 30, 31; June 1.

RACHMANINOFF—Excerpts from "Aleko": May 29, 30, 31; June 1.
"In the Silent Night," Opus 4, No. 3: May 29, 30, 31; June 1.

RAVEL—(t) Bolero: June 18, 19.
Mother Goose Suite (Ma Mère l'Oye): June 7, 8, 11.

REGER—(t) Valse d'Amour, Opus 130, No. 5: June 18, 19.

ROSSINI-BRITTEN—Soirées Musicales, Opus 9: June 18, 19.

SCHUBERT—Overture to "The Devil's Pleasure Palace": May 29, 30, 31; June 1.

SCHUMAN—New England Triptych: Three Pieces for Orchestra after William Billings: June 20, 21, 22.

SHOSTAKOVICH—Symphonic Excerpts, "Katerina Ismailova": June 4, 5, 6.

STRAUSS, R.—"Breit über mein Haupt" and "Amor": May 29, 30, 31; June 1.

TCHAIKOVSKY—Ballet from Suites for Orchestra, No. 1, Opus 43, No. 2, Opus 53: June 4, 5, 6.
*Francesca da Rimini, Opus 32: June 4, 5, 6.

TOCH—Circus Overture: June 20, 21, 22.

VERDI—Overture from "La forza del destino": June 12, 13, 14, 15.

WAGNER—Prelude, "Die Meistersinger von Nürnberg"; Liebestod (Love-Death), from "Tristan und Isolde"; Ride of the Valkyries, from "Die Walküre": June 18, 19.

WALTON—"Façade," excerpts from Suites I and II: June 12, 13, 14, 15.

Etenraku (Music Coming Through from Heaven): June 12, 13, 14, 15.
Portuguese Folksongs for Voice and Orchestra: June 12, 13, 14, 15.
Fado of Lisbon, for Voice and Guitars: June 12, 13, 14, 15.

SOLOISTS—"PROMENADES"

NARRATOR
OGDEN NASH: June 7, 8, 11.

DUO-PIANISTS
ARTHUR WHITTEMORE and JACK LOWE: June 18, 19.

DANCE
MELISSA HAYDEN and JACQUES D'AMBOISE: June 4, 5, 6.

MIME
CLAUDE KIPNIS: June 7, 8, 11.

VOICE
MARY COSTA, soprano: June 20, 21, 22.

SIMON ESTES, bass-baritone: June 4, 5, 6.

AMALIA RODRIGUES, mezzo-soprano: June 12, 13, 14, 15.

BEVERLY SILLS, soprano: May 29, 30, 31; June 1.

NEW YORK PHILHARMONIC: LINCOLN CENTER FESTIVAL '68
1968—PHILHARMONIC HALL

Conductors

Leonard Bernstein, Aaron Copland, Gunther Schuller
June 27, 28.

REPERTOIRE—LINCOLN CENTER FESTIVAL

* Compositions marked with an asterisk are recorded by the
New York Philharmonic.

(a) World premiere.

BERNSTEIN—*Serenade for Solo Violin, String Orchestra, Harp and Percussion
(After Plato's "Symposium"): June 27, 28.
COPLAND—*Third Symphony: June 27, 28.
SCHULLER—Concerto for Double Bass and Chamber Orchestra: June 27 (a),
28.

SOLOISTS—LINCOLN CENTER FESTIVAL

JAMES OLIVER BUSWELL IV, violin-   GARY KARR, double-bassist: June 27,
ist: June 27, 28.   28.

●

NEW YORK PHILHARMONIC OUTDOOR CONCERTS IN THE
PARKS OF THE CITY OF NEW YORK
FOURTH SEASON (1968)

Conductors

Joseph Krips
July 30; August 1, 3, 4.

Lorin Maazel
August 6, 8, 9, 10.

Julius Rudel
August 13, 15, 16.

REPERTOIRE—PARK CONCERTS

* Compositions marked with an asterisk are recorded by
the New York Philharmonic.

BEETHOVEN—*Symphony No. 8, F major, Opus 93: August 13, 15, 16.
BERLIOZ—Overture, "Le Corsaire": July 30; August 1, 3, 4.
GLINKA—*Overture, "Russlan and Ludmilla": August 6, 8, 9, 10.
ORFF—Carmina Burana: August 13, 15, 16.
PAGANINI—Concerto No. 1 for Violin and Orchestra, D major, Opus 6:
August 6, 8, 9, 10.
SCHUMAN—*Symphony No. 3: July 30; August 1, 3, 4.

STRAUSS—"Rosenkavalier" Suite: July 30; August 1, 3, 4.
STRAVINSKY—*"Firebird" Suite: July 30; August 1, 3, 4.
TCHAIKOVSKY—*Symphony No. 5, E minor, Opus 64: August 6, 8, 9, 10.

SOLOISTS—PARK CONCERTS

VIOLIN
RUGGIERO RICCI: August 6, 8, 9, 10.

VOICE
PATRICIA BROOKS, soprano: August 13, 15, 16.
DOMINIC COSSA, baritone: August 13, 15, 16.

WILLIAM DU PREE, tenor: August 13, 15, 16.

CHORUS
ALL-CITY HIGH SCHOOL CHORUS, John Motley, Director: August 13, 15, 16.

1968–69 ONE HUNDRED TWENTY-SEVENTH SEASON

LEONARD BERNSTEIN, *Music Director*

Guest Conductors

PIERRE BOULEZ   COLIN DAVIS   CARLO MARIA GIULINI
SEIJI OZAWA   GEORG SEMKOW   STANISLAW SKROWACZEWSKI
                       GEORGE SZELL

LEONARD BERNSTEIN
Music Director
Young People's Concerts

ANDRE KOSTELANETZ
Special Saturday Night Concerts

BORIS BROTT
FRANCOIS HUYBRECHTS

GAETANO DELOGU
FARHAD MECHKAT

Assistant Conductors

CONCERTS

1968

Leonard Bernstein

Oct. 3—Eve.	Philharmonic Hall
Oct. 4—Aft.	Philharmonic Hall
Oct. 5—Eve.	Philharmonic Hall
Oct. 7—Eve.	Philharmonic Hall

**Leonard Bernstein,
Luciano Berio**

Oct. 10—Eve.	Philharmonic Hall
Oct. 11—Aft.	Philharmonic Hall
Oct. 12—Eve.	Philharmonic Hall
Oct. 14—Eve.	Philharmonic Hall

Leonard Bernstein

Oct. 17—Eve.	Philharmonic Hall
Oct. 18—Aft.	Philharmonic Hall
Oct. 19—Eve.	Philharmonic Hall
Oct. 21—Eve.	Philharmonic Hall
Oct. 23—Eve.	Philharmonic Hall
Oct. 26—Aft.(2)	Philharmonic Hall

(Young People's Concerts)

Oct. 28—Eve.	Philharmonic Hall

1968

Colin Davis

Oct. 31—Eve.	Philharmonic Hall
Nov. 1—Aft.	Philharmonic Hall
Nov. 2—Eve.	Philharmonic Hall
Nov. 4—Eve.	Philharmonic Hall
Nov. 7—Eve.	Philharmonic Hall
Nov. 8—Aft.	Philharmonic Hall
Nov. 9—Eve.	Philharmonic Hall
Nov. 11—Eve.	Philharmonic Hall
Nov. 14—Eve.	Philharmonic Hall
Nov. 15—Aft.	Philharmonic Hall
Nov. 16—Eve.	Philharmonic Hall
Nov. 18—Eve.	Philharmonic Hall
Nov. 21—Aft.	Philharmonic Hall

(Lincoln Center Student Program)

Nov. 22—Aft.	Philharmonic Hall
Nov. 23—Eve.	Philharmonic Hall
Nov. 25—Eve.	Philharmonic Hall

1968

Stanislaw Skrowaczewski

Nov.	27—Eve.	Philharmonic Hall
Nov.	29—Aft.	Philharmonic Hall
Nov.	30—Eve.	Philharmonic Hall
Dec.	2—Eve.	Philharmonic Hall
Dec.	5—Eve.	Philharmonic Hall
Dec.	6—Aft.	Philharmonic Hall

André Kostelanetz

Dec.	7—Eve.	Philharmonic Hall

Stanislaw Skrowaczewski

Dec.	9—Eve.	Philharmonic Hall

Carlo Maria Giulini

Dec.	12—Eve.	Philharmonic Hall
Dec.	13—Aft.	Philharmonic Hall
Dec.	14—Eve.	Philharmonic Hall
Dec.	16—Eve.	Philharmonic Hall
Dec.	19—Eve.	Philharmonic Hall
Dec.	20—Aft.	Philharmonic Hall
Dec.	21—Eve.	Philharmonic Hall
Dec.	30—Eve.	Philharmonic Hall

1969

Jan.	2—Eve.	Philharmonic Hall
Jan.	3—Aft.	Philharmonic Hall
Jan.	4—Eve.	Philharmonic Hall
Jan.	6—Eve.	Philharmonic Hall
Jan.	9—Eve.	Philharmonic Hall
Jan.	10—Aft.	Philharmonic Hall

Leonard Bernstein

Jan.	11—Aft.(2)	Philharmonic Hall

(Young People's Concerts)

Carlo Maria Giulini

Jan.	11—Eve.	Philharmonic Hall
Jan.	13—Eve.	Philharmonic Hall

Leonard Bernstein

Jan.	16—Eve.	Philharmonic Hall

**Leonard Bernstein,
Boris Brott**

Jan.	17—Aft.	Philharmonic Hall

Leonard Bernstein

Jan.	18—Eve.	Philharmonic Hall

**Leonard Bernstein,
Boris Brott**

Jan.	20—Eve.	Philharmonic Hall

Leonard Bernstein

Jan.	23—Eve.	Philharmonic Hall
Jan.	24—Aft.	Philharmonic Hall
Jan.	25—Eve.	Philharmonic Hall
Jan.	27—Eve.	Philharmonic Hall
Jan.	30—Eve.	Philharmonic Hall
Jan.	31—Aft.	Philharmonic Hall

1969

Feb.	1—Eve.	Philharmonic Hall
Feb.	3—Eve.	Philharmonic Hall
Feb.	5—Eve.	Philharmonic Hall

**Leonard Bernstein,
Leopold Stokowski**

Feb.	8—Aft.(2)	Philharmonic Hall

(Young People's Concerts)

Leonard Bernstein

Feb.	10—Eve.	West Palm Beach

Seiji Ozawa

Feb.	13—Eve.	Philharmonic Hall
Feb.	14—Aft.	Philharmonic Hall
Feb.	15—Eve.	Philharmonic Hall
Feb.	17—Eve.	Philharmonic Hall
Feb.	20—Eve.	Philharmonic Hall
Feb.	21—Aft.	Philharmonic Hall
Feb.	22—Eve.	Philharmonic Hall
Feb.	24—Eve.	Philharmonic Hall

Leonard Bernstein

Feb.	26—Eve.	Philharmonic Hall

(Pension Fund Benefit)

Seiji Ozawa

Feb.	27—Eve.	Philharmonic Hall
Feb.	28—Aft.	Philharmonic Hall

(Lincoln Center Student Program)

Mar.	1—Eve.	Philharmonic Hall
Mar.	3—Eve.	Philharmonic Hall
Mar.	6—Eve.	Philharmonic Hall
Mar.	7—Aft.	Philharmonic Hall

André Kostelanetz

Mar.	8—Eve.	Philharmonic Hall

Seiji Ozawa

Mar.	10—Eve.	Philharmonic Hall

André Kostelanetz

Mar.	11—Aft.	Philharmonic Hall

(Lincoln Center Student Program)

Pierre Boulez

Mar.	13—Eve.	Philharmonic Hall
Mar.	14—Aft.	Philharmonic Hall
Mar.	15—Eve.	Philharmonic Hall
Mar.	17—Eve.	Philharmonic Hall
Mar.	20—Eve.	Philharmonic Hall
Mar.	21—Aft.	Philharmonic Hall
Mar.	22—Eve.	Philharmonic Hall
Mar.	24—Eve.	Philharmonic Hall
Mar.	27—Eve.	Philharmonic Hall
Mar.	28—Aft.	Philharmonic Hall
Mar.	29—Eve.	Philharmonic Hall
Mar.	31—Eve.	Philharmonic Hall
Apr.	3—Eve.	Philharmonic Hall
Apr.	4—Aft.	Philharmonic Hall
Apr.	5—Eve.	Philharmonic Hall
Apr.	7—Eve.	Philharmonic Hall

1969   1969

George Szell
Apr. 8—Eve.   Philharmonic Hall
(Pension Fund Benefit)

Georg Semkow
Apr. 10—Eve.   Philharmonic Hall
Apr. 11—Aft.   Philharmonic Hall
Apr. 12—Eve.   Philharmonic Hall
Apr. 14—Eve.   Philharmonic Hall
Apr. 17—Eve.   Philharmonic Hall
Apr. 18—Eve.   Philharmonic Hall

Leonard Bernstein
Apr. 19—Aft.(2)   Philharmonic Hall
(Young People's Concerts)

Georg Semkow
Apr. 21—Eve.   Philharmonic Hall

Leonard Bernstein
Apr. 24—Eve.   Philharmonic Hall
Apr. 25—Aft.   Philharmonic Hall
Apr. 26—Eve.   Philharmonic Hall
Apr. 28—Eve.   Philharmonic Hall

Farhad Mechkat,
François Huybrechts
May 1—Eve.   Philharmonic Hall
May 2—Aft.   Philharmonic Hall
May 3—Eve.   Philharmonic Hall
May 5—Eve.   Philharmonic Hall

Leonard Bernstein
May 8—Eve.   Philharmonic Hall
May 9—Aft.   Philharmonic Hall
May 10—Eve.   Philharmonic Hall
May 15—Eve.   Philharmonic Hall
May 16—Aft.   Philharmonic Hall
May 17—Eve.   Philharmonic Hall

REPERTOIRE

* Recorded by the New York Philharmonic.
** Recorded by the New York Philharmonic and soon to be released.

(a) First performance anywhere; commissioned by the Orchestra
for its 125th Anniversary.
(c) First performance in New York.

BABBITT—Relata II: Jan. 16 (a), 17, 18, 20.
BACH, J. S.—Brandenburg Concerto No. 3, G major: Nov. 7, 8, 9, 11.
Brandenburg Concerto No. 5, D major: Jan. 16, 17, 18, 20.
Brandenburg Concerto No. 6, B-flat major: May 8, 9, 10.
Toccata and Fugue in D minor, BWV 565 (Bach-Skrowaczewski): Dec. 5, 6, 9.
BARTOK—*Concerto for Orchestra: Feb. 27, 28; Mar. 1, 3.
Concerto for Piano and Orchestra, No. 1: Mar. 20, 21, 22, 24.
Concerto for Piano and Orchestra, No. 2: Nov. 14, 15, 16, 18.
*Music for Strings, Percussion and Celesta: Mar. 20, 21, 22, 24.
BEETHOVEN—*Concerto No. 4 for Piano and Orchestra, G major, Op. 58:
Oct. 10, 11, 12, 14.
*Concerto No. 5 for Piano and Orchestra, E-flat major, Op. 73 ("Emperor"):
Feb. 20, 21, 22, 24.
*Missa solemnis in D major for Four Solo Voices, Chorus and Orchestra, Op.
123: Jan. 30, 31; Feb. 1, 3.
*Symphony No. 3, E-flat major, Op. 55 ("Eroica"): Nov. 7, 8, 9, 11.
BERG—*Concerto for Violin and Orchestra: Mar. 13, 14, 15, 17.
BERIO—**Sinfonia: Oct. 10 (a), 11, 12, 14.
BERNSTEIN—*Overture, "Candide": Feb. 10.
*Symphony No. 1 ("Jeremiah"): May 8, 9, 10.
BERLIOZ—*"Cléopâtre": Oct. 31; Nov. 1, 2, 4.
*Excerpts from "Romeo and Juliet": Oct. 31; Nov. 1, 2, 4.
Three Excerpts from the Dramatic Legend, "La Damnation de Faust": Mar. 8,
11.
Overture to "Beatrice and Benedict": Nov. 14, 15, 16, 18.

Overture to "King Lear," Op. 4: Nov. 21, 22, 23, 25.
Overture, "Les Francs-Juges": Oct. 31; Nov. 1, 2, 4.
*Overture, "Le Carnaval romain," Op. 9: Mar. 8, 11.
Requiem (Grande Messe des Morts), Op. 5: Feb. 13, 14, 15, 17.
*"Symphonie fantastique," Op. 14: Oct. 3, 4, 5, 7, 23, 28.

BONPORTI—Concerto a Quattro, D major, Op. 11, No. 2: Jan. 2, 3, 4, 6.

BRAHMS—*Symphony No. 2, D major, Op. 73: Nov. 14, 15, 16, 18.
*Symphony No. 1, C minor, Op. 68: Dec. 19, 20, 21, 30.

BRUCKNER—**Symphony No. 9, D minor: Jan. 23, 24, 25, 27; Feb. 5.

CASELLA—"La giara" (Suite sinfonica): Jan. 9, 10, 11, 13.

CHOPIN—*Concerto No. 2 for Piano and Orchestra, F minor, Op. 21: Dec. 5, 6, 9.

CORELLI—Suite for String Orchestra (arranged by Ettore Pinelli): Dec. 7.

DEBUSSY—*"Jeux," Poème dansé: Mar. 13, 14, 15, 17.
*"La Mer," Three Symphonic Sketches: Mar. 13, 14, 15, 17.

ELGAR—Symphony No. 1, A-flat major, Op. 55: Nov. 21, 22, 23, 25.
Variations on an Original Theme ("Enigma"), Op. 36: Mar. 6, 7, 10.

GINASTERA—Dances from the Ballet "Estancia": Feb. 20, 21, 22, 24.

GOTTSCHALK-KAY—"Grand Tarantella" for Piano and Orchestra: Mar. 8, 11.

GOTTSCHALK-SHANET—"Night of the Tropics": Mar. 8, 11.

GRIEG—Concerto in A minor for Piano and Orchestra, Op. 16: Dec. 7.

HAYDN—Symphony No. 48, C major, ("Maria Theresia"): Apr. 10, 11, 12, 14.
*Symphony No. 87, A major: Oct. 17, 18, 19, 21, 23, 28.
Symphony No. 89, F major: Mar. 20, 21, 22, 24.
Symphony No. 91, E-flat major: Mar. 27, 28, 29, 31.
Symphony No. 94, G major ("Surprise"): Jan. 9, 10, 11, 13.

HINDEMITH—Concert Music for Strings and Brass, Op. 50: Dec. 19, 20, 21, 30.

IVES—Symphony No. 4: Feb. 20, 21, 22, 24.
"Three Places in New England": Mar. 27, 28, 29, 31.

LISZT—*Concerto No. 1 for Piano and Orchestra, E-flat major: Mar. 8, 11.

LUTOSLAWSKI—Funeral Music for String Orchestra: Nov. 27, 29, 30; Dec. 2.

MAHLER—*"Kindertotenlieder": Oct. 23, 28.
*Symphony No. 3: May 15, 16, 17.

MARTINU—Concerto for Piano and Orchestra, No. 2: Dec. 19, 20, 21, 30.

MENDELSSOHN—**Concerto for Violin and Orchestra, E minor, Op. 64: Feb. 5, 10; Apr. 10, 11, 12, 14.

MOZART—Concerto for Piano and Orchestra, D minor, K. 466; Dec. 12, 13, 14, 16; Apr. 8.
Concerto for Piano and Orchestra, No. 9, E-flat major, K. 271: Jan. 23, 24, 25, 27.
Divertimento in D major, K. 251 (4 movements only): Dec. 12, 13, 14, 16.
Masonic Funeral Music, K. 477: Dec. 12, 13, 14, 16.
Overture, "The Abduction from the Seraglio": Feb. 20, 21, 22, 24.
Sonata for Piano and Violin, B-flat major, K. 378: Jan. 16, 17, 18, 20.
Symphony No. 36, C major, K. 425 ("Linz"): Feb. 27, 28; Mar. 1, 3.
*Symphony No. 40, G minor, K. 550: Dec. 12, 13, 14, 16.

NIELSEN—Violin Concerto, Op. 33: Mar. 6 (c), 7, 10.

PROKOFIEV—Concerto for Violin and Orchestra, No. 1, D major, Op. 19: Jan. 16, 17, 18, 20.

PURCELL—Five Fantazias (No. 1, D minor; No. 4, F major; No. 6, E minor; No. 8, G minor; No. 15, G minor, "In Nomine"): Apr. 3, 4, 5, 7.

RACHMANINOFF—Concerto No. 1 for Piano and Orchestra, F-sharp minor, Op. 1: Nov. 21, 22, 23, 25.

RAVEL—*"Rapsodie espagnole": Mar. 6, 7, 10.
*"Shéhérazade," Three Poems for Voice and Orchestra to Verses by Tristan Klingsor: Mar. 27, 28, 29, 31.

RIMSKY-KORSAKOV—*"Scheherazade," Op. 35: Dec. 7.

ROSSINI—Sonata a Quattro: Apr. 17, 18, 21.

SCHOENBERG—Five Pieces for Orchestra, Op. 16: Mar. 27, 28, 29, 31.

SCHUBERT—Symphony No. 4, C minor ("Tragic"): Jan. 2, 3, 4, 6.

SCHUMAN, William—**"To Thee Old Cause," Evocation for Oboe, Brass, Timpani, Piano and Strings: Oct. 3 (a), 4, 5, 7.
*Symphony No. 3: Oct. 3, 4, 5, 7.

SCHUMANN—Concerto for Piano and Orchestra, A minor, Op. 54: Apr. 8.
*Symphony No. 3, E-flat major, Op. 97 ("Rhenish"): Jan. 9, 10, 11, 13.
*Symphony No. 2, C major, Op. 61: May 8, 9, 10.

SCRIABIN—Symphony No. 2, C minor, Op. 29: Apr. 10, 11, 12, 14.

SHOSTAKOVICH—*Symphony No. 5, Op. 47: Dec. 5, 6, 9.

STRAUSS—*"Don Juan," Tone Poem after Nicolaus Lenau, Op. 20: Apr. 8.
**"Don Quixote," Op. 35: Oct. 17, 18, 19, 21.

STRAVINSKY—"Agon": Oct. 10, 11, 12, 14, 28.
*"Firebird" Suite: May 1, 2, 3, 5.
Four Etudes: May 1, 2, 3, 5.
"Jeu de cartes": Apr. 17, 18, 21.
Octet for Wind Instruments: May 1, 2, 3, 5.
**"Petrouchka": May 1, 2, 3, 5.
*"Rite of Spring": Apr. 3, 4, 5, 7.
Symphonies of Winds: Apr. 3, 4, 5, 7.
Symphony in C: Nov. 7, 8, 9, 11.

SZYMANOWSKI—Symphony No. 2, Op. 19: Nov. 27, 29, 30; Dec. 2.

TCHAIKOVSKY—*Symphony No. 4, F minor, Op. 36: Nov. 27, 29, 30; Dec. 2.
*Symphony No. 5, E minor, Op. 64: Apr. 17, 18, 21.

THOMPSON, R.—**Symphony No. 2, E minor: Oct. 17, 18, 19, 21.

VARESE—"Intégrales": Mar. 13, 14, 15, 17.

VERDI—Four Sacred Pieces: Jan. 2, 3, 4, 6.
Messa da Requiem, for soloists, chorus and orchestra: Apr. 24, 25, 26, 28.

VILLA-LOBOS—"Little Train of the Caipira" from "Bachianas Brasileiras," No. 2: Mar. 8.
"Modinha" (Preludio) from "Bachianas Brasileiras," No. 1: Mar. 8.

WAGNER—Scenes from "Tristan und Isolde": Feb. 26.

WALTON, W.—Capriccio burlesco: Dec. 7 (a).

WEBERN—Six Pieces for Orchestra, Op. 6: Apr. 3, 4, 5, 7.

XENAKIS—"Eonta": Feb. 27, 28; Mar. 1, 3.

SOLOISTS

PIANO
VLADIMIR ASHKENAZY: Feb. 20, 21, 22, 24.
LEONARD BERNSTEIN: Jan. 16, 17, 18, 20.
STEPHEN BISHOP: Nov. 14, 15, 16, 18.
JOHN BROWNING: Jan. 23, 24, 25, 27.

RUDOLF FIRKUSNY: Dec. 19, 20, 21, 30.
MALCOLM FRAGER: Mar. 20, 21, 22, 24.
ROBERT GOLDSAND: Nov. 21, 22, 23, 25.

EUGENE ISTOMIN: Oct. 10, 11, 12, 14.

PAUL JACOBS: Feb. 20, 21, 22, 24.

GRANT JOHANNESEN: Dec. 7.

ARTURO BENEDETTI MICHELANGELI: Dec. 12, 13, 14, 16.

ARTUR RUBINSTEIN: Apr. 8.

YUJI TAKAHASHI: Feb. 27, 28; Mar. 1, 3.

ALEXIS WEISSENBERG: Dec. 5, 6, 9.

VIOLIN

ALBERTO LYSY: Mar. 13, 14, 15, 17.

DAVID NADIEN: Jan. 30, 31; Feb. 1, 3; Apr. 10, 11, 12, 14; Oct. 17, 18, 19, 21.

TOSSY SPIVAKOVSKY: Mar. 6, 7, 10.

ISAAC STERN: Jan. 16, 17, 18, 20.

PINCHAS ZUKERMAN: Feb. 5.

VIOLA

WILLIAM LINCER: Oct. 17, 18, 19, 21.

CELLO

LORNE MUNROE: Oct. 17, 18, 19, 21.

FLUTE

JULIUS BAKER: Jan. 16, 17, 18, 20.

ENGLISH HORN

ENGELBERT BRENNER: Feb. 8.

OBOE

HAROLD GOMBERG: Oct. 3, 4, 5, 7.

POST HORN

JOHN WARE: May 15, 16, 17.

VOICE

BETTY ALLEN, mezzo-soprano: May 15, 16, 17.

MARTINA ARROYO, soprano: Apr. 24, 25, 26, 28.

EILEEN FARRELL, soprano: Feb. 26.

DIETRICH FISCHER-DIESKAU, baritone: Oct. 23, 28.

MARILYN HORNE, mezzo-soprano: Apr. 24, 25, 26, 28.

WALDEMAR KMENTT, tenor: Jan. 30, 31; Feb. 1, 3.

PILAR LORENGAR, soprano: Jan. 30, 31; Feb. 1, 3.

JUDITH RASKIN, soprano: Mar. 27, 28, 29, 31.

GEORGE SHIRLEY, tenor: Apr. 24, 25, 26, 28.

CESARE SIEPI, bass: Apr. 24, 25, 26, 28.

JOANNA SIMON, mezzo-soprano: Feb. 26.

LEOPOLD SIMONEAU, tenor: Feb. 13, 14, 15, 17.

JESS THOMAS, tenor: Feb. 26.

JENNIE TOUREL, mezzo-soprano: May 8, 9, 10.

NORMAN TREIGLE, bass: Jan. 30, 31; Feb. 1, 3.

HELEN WATTS, contralto: Jan. 30, 31; Feb. 1, 3.

BEVERLY WOLFF, mezzo-soprano: Oct. 31; Nov. 1, 2, 4.

CHORUS

BOYS' CHOIR from BROWNING SCHOOL, Stuart Gardner, Director: May 15, 16, 17.

BOYS' CHOIR from LITTLE CHURCH AROUND THE CORNER, Stuart Gardner, Director: May 15, 16, 17.

CAMERATA SINGERS, Abraham Kaplan, Director: Jan. 2, 3, 4, 6; Apr. 24, 25, 26, 28.

COLLEGIATE CHORALE, Abraham Kaplan, Director: Feb. 13, 14, 15, 17.

SCHOLA CANTORUM, Hugh Ross, Director (Women's Chorus only): May 15, 16, 17.

SWINGLE SINGERS: Oct. 10, 11, 12, 14.

WESTMINSTER CHOIR, George Lynn, Director: Jan. 30, 31; Feb. 1, 3.

●

1968 TOUR OF EUROPE AND ISRAEL

Leonard Bernstein, Conductor
Alain Lombard, Associate Tour Conductor

Aug. 24—Eve.	Ghent	Sept. 5—Eve.	Vienna
Aug. 25—Eve.	Brussels	Sept. 7—Eve.	Venice†
Aug. 27—Eve.	Lucerne	Sept. 8—Eve.	Venice
Aug. 29—Eve.	Jerusalem	Sept. 10—Eve.	Monte Carlo
Aug. 31—Eve.	Caesarea	Sept. 12—Eve.	Montreux
Sept. 2—Eve.	Florence	Sept. 13—Eve.	Montreux†
Sept. 4—Eve.	Vienna	Sept. 14—Eve.	Milan

† Schuman Symphony conducted by Mr. Lombard.

Sept. 15—Eve.	Milan	Sept. 23—Eve.	West Berlin†
Sept. 17—Eve.	Munich	Sept. 24—Eve.	West Berlin
Sept. 18—Eve.	Bonn	Sept. 25—Eve.	Copenhagen
Sept. 19—Eve.	Hoechst	Sept. 26—Eve.	London
Sept. 20—Eve.	Amsterdam	Sept. 29—Aft.	Washington, D.C.
Sept. 22—Eve.	West Berlin		

TOUR REPERTOIRE

* Recorded by the New York Philharmonic.

BERLIOZ—*"Symphonie fantastique": Aug. 27; Sept. 2, 4, 7, 10, 13, 17, 18, 19, 20, 23, 25, 26.

HARRIS—*Symphony No. 3: Aug. 25, 27, 29; Sept. 8, 10, 14, 15, 18, 19, 20, 24, 25, 26.

HAYDN—*Symphony No. 87: Aug. 24, 27, 31; Sept. 5, 10, 12, 18, 19, 20, 22, 25, 26, 29.

MAHLER—*Symphony No. 5: Aug. 24, 29, 31; Sept. 5, 8, 12, 14, 15, 22, 24, 29.

ROSSINI—*Overture, "L'Italiana in Algeri": Aug. 25; Sept. 2, 4, 7, 13, 14, 15, 17, 23.

SCHUMAN, William—*Symphony No. 3: Sept. 2, 4, 7, 13, 17, 23.

•

NEW YORK PHILHARMONIC "PROMENADES"
SEVENTH SEASON   1969   PHILHARMONIC HALL

Conductor

André Kostelanetz
May 21–June 14

REPERTOIRE—"PROMENADES"

* Compositions marked with an asterisk are recorded by the
New York Philharmonic.

(pa) Works for piano alone.

BORODIN—Excerpts from "Prince Igor": May 23, 27, 28, 29.

BRITTEN—Excerpts from Act II, scene 2, "The Prince of the Pagodas": June 10, 11.

CASALS—Sardana for Cello Orchestra: May 21, 22, 24.
"Song of the Birds": May 21, 22, 24.
"Sant Martí del Canigó": May 21, 22, 24.

CHAPI—"Por qué sin motivos" from "La Revoltosa": May 21, 22, 24.

DEBUSSY—"Printemps," Suite symphonique: June 5, 6, 7.

DELIUS—"On Hearing the First Cuckoo in Spring": June 5, 6, 7.

DUPARC—"L'Invitation au voyage": June 12, 13, 14.
"Phydilé": June 12, 13, 14.

FALLA—*Three Dances from "The Three-Cornered Hat": May 21, 22, 24.
Excerpts from "La Vida breve": May 21, 22, 24.

GERSHWIN—"Porgy and Bess," Concert Version: May 30, 31; June 3, 4.

† Schuman Symphony conducted by Mr. Lombard.

GLINKA—*Overture, "Russlan and Ludmilla": May 23, 27, 28, 29.

GOTOVAC—"Kolo" from the opera, "Ero the Joker": May 30, 31; June 3, 4.

HANDEL-HARTY—"Water Music" Suite: May 30, 31; June 3, 4.

HOLST—Excerpts from "The Planets," Opus 32: June 10, 11.

LIADOV—The Enchanted Lake: May 28, 29.

LISZT—"Liebestraum": Notturno No. 3, A-flat major: May 30, 31; June 3, 4 (pa).

LITOLFF—Scherzo from Symphonic Concerto for Piano and Orchestra, No. 4, D minor, Opus 102: May 30, 31; June 3, 4.

OFFENBACH—Overture, "La Belle Hélène": June 12, 13, 14.
Aria, "Le vrai, je ne suis pas," from "La Belle Hélène": June 12, 13, 14.
Arias, "Ah, que j'aime les militaires," and "Dites-lui" from "La Grande Duchesse de Gérolstein": June 12, 13, 14.
Aria, "C'est ici l'endroit," from "La Vie parisienne": June 12, 13, 14.

OFFENBACH-ROSENTHAL—"Gaîté parisienne": June 12, 13, 14.

PROKOFIEV—Toccata for Piano Solo, Opus 11: May 30, 31; June 3, 4 (pa).

RAVEL—Concerto for Piano and Orchestra, G major: June 10, 11.
La Valse: June 12, 13, 14.

RESPIGHI—Symphonic Poem, "Pines of Rome": June 10, 11.

RIMSKY-KORSAKOV—*"Capriccio espagnol," Opus 34: May 21, 22, 24.
Suite from "Le Coq d'Or": June 10, 11.

SAINT-SAENS—Introduction and Rondo capriccioso for Violin and Orchestra, Opus 28: June 5, 6, 7.
"La Princesse jaune," Overture: June 12, 13, 14.

SARASATE—"Zigeunerweisen," Opus 20: June 5, 6, 7.
Introduction and Tarantella, Opus 43: June 5, 6, 7.

SERRANO—"Marinella" from the zarzuela, "Canción del olvido": May 21, 22, 24.

SHOSTAKOVICH—"Carnaval fantastique": May 23, 27, 28, 29.

STRAVINSKY—*Suite from "The Firebird": June 5, 6, 7.

TCHAIKOVSKY—*"Capriccio italien," Opus 45: May 23, 27, 28, 29.

WALTON—"Capriccio burlesco": June 5, 6, 7.

SOLOISTS—"PROMENADES"

PIANO
DAVID BAR-ILLAN: June 10, 11.
THEODORE LETTVIN: May 30, 31; June 3, 4.

VIOLIN
MICHAEL RABIN: June 5, 6, 7.

VOICE
DAVID CLATWORTHY, baritone: May 28, 29.
ROSALIND ELIAS, mezzo-soprano: June 12, 13, 14.
DONALD GRAMM, bass-baritone: May 23, 27.

ROBERT MOSLEY, baritone: May 30, 31; June 3, 4.
MARALIN NISKA, soprano: May 22, 24.
NED STYRES, baritone: May 22, 24.
VERONICA TYLER, soprano: May 30, 31; June 3, 4.

CHORUS
SCHOLA CANTORUM: May 30, 31; June 3, 4.

MARIONETTE COMPANY
THE BIL BAIRD MARIONETTES: May 23, 27, 28, 29.

NEW YORK PHILHARMONIC: GARDEN STATE ARTS CENTER, 1969

Conductors

Karel Ancerl, Aaron Copland, Stanislaw Skrowaczewski
June 19, 21, 26, 27, 28; August 13, 14

REPERTOIRE—GARDEN STATE CONCERTS

* Compositions marked with an asterisk are recorded by
the New York Philharmonic.

BEETHOVEN—Concerto for Piano and Orchestra, No. 3, C minor, Opus 37:
    August 13.
BERLIOZ—Overture, "The Corsair," Opus 21: June 26, 27, 28.
BERNSTEIN—*Overture to "Candide": June 19, 21.
COPLAND—*"Billy the Kid," Ballet Suite: June 19, 21.
    Concerto for Clarinet and String Orchestra with Harp and Piano: June 19, 21.
DVORAK—*"Carnival" Overture, Opus 92: August 13, 14.
    *Symphony No. 9 ("New World"): August 14.
FRANCK—*Symphony in D minor: August 13, 14.
IVES—*Decoration Day: June 19, 21.
LISZT—Concerto No. 1 for Piano and Orchestra, E-flat major: June 26, 27, 28.
SHOSTAKOVICH—Symphony No. 9, Opus 70: June 19, 21.
TCHAIKOVSKY—*Symphony No. 5, E minor, Opus 64: June 26, 27, 28.

SOLOISTS—GARDEN STATE CONCERTS

VAN CLIBURN, pianist, June 26, 27, 28.
BENNY GOODMAN, clarinetist: June 19, 21.
BYRON JANIS, pianist: August 13.

●

NEW YORK PHILHARMONIC OUTDOOR CONCERTS IN THE
PARKS OF THE CITY OF NEW YORK
FIFTH SEASON (1969)

Conductors

Karel Ancerl
August 12, 15, 16, 21, 22.

Josef Krips
July 30, 31; August 1.

Efrem Kurtz
August 5, 6, 7, 9.

REPERTOIRE—PARK CONCERTS

* Compositions marked with an asterisk are recorded by
the New York Philharmonic.

BARBER—Piano Concerto, Opus 38: July 30, 31; August 1.
BEETHOVEN—Overture to "Egmont," Opus 84: July 30, 31; August 1.

Concerto for Piano and Orchestra, No. 3, C minor, Opus 37: August 12, 15, 16, 21, 22.

COPLAND—Concerto for Clarinet and String Orchestra with Harp and Piano: August 5, 6, 7, 9.

DVORAK—*"Carnival" Overture, Opus 92: August 12, 15, 16, 21, 22.

FRANCK—*Symphony in D minor: August 12, 15, 16, 21, 22.

PROKOFIEV—*"Romeo and Juliet" Excerpts: August 5, 6, 7, 9.

ROSSINI—Overture to "Il viaggio a Reims": August 5, 6, 7, 9.

SCHUBERT—Symphony No. 9, C major: July 30, 31; August 1.

TCHAIKOVSKY—*Symphony No. 6, B minor, Opus 74 ("Pathétique"): August 5, 6, 7, 9.

SOLOISTS—PARK CONCERTS

CLARINET
STANLEY DRUCKER: August 5, 6, 7, 9.

PIANO
JOHN BROWNING: July 30, 31; August 1.
BYRON JANIS: August 12.
GRANT JOHANNESEN: August 15, 16, 21, 22.

1969–70 ONE HUNDRED AND TWENTY-EIGHTH SEASON

GEORGE SZELL, *Music Advisor and Senior Guest Conductor*
Laureate Conductor: LEONARD BERNSTEIN

Guest Conductors: CLAUDIO ABBADO, RAFAEL FRUEHBECK DE BURGOS, ISTVAN KERTESZ, LORIN MAAZEL, SEIJI OZAWA

Special Saturday Evenings: ANDRE KOSTELANETZ

Young People's Concerts: LEONARD BERNSTEIN, *Music Director;*
AARON COPLAND and PETER USTINOV, *Guest Conductors*

Assistant Conductors: ALFREDO BONAVERA, MESRU M. MEHMEDOV, URI SEGAL

CONCERTS

1969

Seiji Ozawa
Sept. 23—Eve.   Philharmonic Hall
(Opening Night Benefit Concert)
Sept. 25—Eve.   Philharmonic Hall
Sept. 26—Aft.   Philharmonic Hall
Sept. 27—Eve.   Philharmonic Hall
Sept. 29—Eve.   Philharmonic Hall
Oct. 2—Eve.   Philharmonic Hall
Oct. 3—Aft.   Philharmonic Hall
Oct. 4—Eve.   Philharmonic Hall
Oct. 6—Eve.   Philharmonic Hall
Oct. 9—Eve.   Philharmonic Hall
Oct. 10—Aft.   Philharmonic Hall
Oct. 11—Eve.   Philharmonic Hall
Oct. 13—Eve.   Philharmonic Hall

1969

**Seiji Ozawa,
Leon Kirchner**
Oct. 16—Eve.   Philharmonic Hall
Oct. 17—Aft.   Philharmonic Hall
Oct. 18—Eve.   Philharmonic Hall
Oct. 20—Eve.   Philharmonic Hall

Seiji Ozawa
Oct. 23—Eve.   Philharmonic Hall
Oct. 24—Aft.   Philharmonic Hall
(Lincoln Center Student Program)

André Kostelanetz
Oct. 25—Eve.   Philharmonic Hall

Seiji Ozawa
Oct. 27—Eve.   Philharmonic Hall
Oct. 30—Eve.   Philharmonic Hall
Oct. 31—Aft.   Philharmonic Hall

1969

Aaron Copland
Nov. 1—Aft. (2) Philharmonic Hall
(Young People's Concert)

George Szell
Nov. 10—Eve.   Philharmonic Hall
(Pension Fund Benefit)
Nov. 13—Eve.   Philharmonic Hall
Nov. 14—Aft.   Philharmonic Hall
Nov. 15—Eve.   Philharmonic Hall
Nov. 17—Eve.   Philharmonic Hall
Nov. 20—Eve.   Philharmonic Hall
Nov. 21—Aft.   Philharmonic Hall
Nov. 22—Eve.   Philharmonic Hall
Nov. 24—Eve.   Philharmonic Hall
Nov. 26—Eve.   Philharmonic Hall
Nov. 28—Aft.   Philharmonic Hall
Nov. 29—Eve.   Philharmonic Hall
Dec. 1—Eve.   Philharmonic Hall
Dec. 4—Eve.   Philharmonic Hall
Dec. 5—Aft.   Philharmonic Hall
Dec. 6—Eve.   Philharmonic Hall
Dec. 8—Eve.   Philharmonic Hall

István Kertész
Dec. 11—Eve.   Philharmonic Hall
Dec. 12—Aft.   Philharmonic Hall
Dec. 13—Eve.   Philharmonic Hall
Dec. 15—Eve.   Philharmonic Hall
Dec. 18—Eve.   Philharmonic Hall
Dec. 19—Aft.   Philharmonic Hall
Dec. 20—Eve.   Philharmonic Hall

Rafael Frühbeck de Burgos
Dec. 31—Eve.   Philharmonic Hall

1970

Jan. 1—Eve.   Philharmonic Hall
Jan. 2—Aft.   Philharmonic Hall
Jan. 3—Eve.   Philharmonic Hall
Jan. 5—Eve.   Philharmonic Hall
Jan. 8—Eve.   Philharmonic Hall
Jan. 9—Aft.   Philharmonic Hall

Leonard Bernstein
Jan. 10—Aft. (2) Philharmonic Hall
(Young People's Concert)

Rafael Frühbeck de Burgos
Jan. 12—Eve.   Philharmonic Hall

Leonard Bernstein
Jan. 15—Eve.   Philharmonic Hall
Jan. 16—Aft.   Philharmonic Hall
Jan. 17—Eve.   Philharmonic Hall
Jan. 19—Eve.   Philharmonic Hall
Jan. 22—Eve.   Philharmonic Hall
Jan. 23—Aft.   Philharmonic Hall

1970
Jan. 24—Eve.   Philharmonic Hall
Jan. 26—Eve.   Philharmonic Hall

**Philippe Bender,
Mario Benzecry,
David Gilbert**
Jan. 28—Eve.   Philharmonic Hall
(Mitropoulos International Music
Competition)

Leonard Bernstein
Jan. 29—Eve.   Philharmonic Hall
Jan. 30—Aft.   Philharmonic Hall
Jan. 31—Eve.   Philharmonic Hall
Feb. 2—Eve.   Philharmonic Hall
Feb. 5—Eve.   Philharmonic Hall
Feb. 6—Aft.   Philharmonic Hall
Feb. 7—Eve.   Philharmonic Hall
Feb. 9—Eve.   Philharmonic Hall
Feb. 11—Eve.   Philharmonic Hall
Feb. 14—Aft. (2) Philharmonic Hall
(Young People's Concert)
Feb. 16—Eve.   Philharmonic Hall

Claudio Abbado
Feb. 19—Eve.   Philharmonic Hall
Feb. 20—Aft.   Philharmonic Hall

André Kostelanetz
Feb. 21—Eve.   Philharmonic Hall

Claudio Abbado
Feb. 23—Eve.   Philharmonic Hall
Feb. 26—Eve.   Philharmonic Hall
Feb. 27—Aft.   Philharmonic Hall
Feb. 28—Eve.   Philharmonic Hall
Mar. 2—Eve.   Philharmonic Hall
Mar. 3—Eve.   Philharmonic Hall
(Pension Fund Benefit)
Mar. 5—Eve.   Philharmonic Hall
Mar. 6—Aft.   Philharmonic Hall
Mar. 7—Eve.   Philharmonic Hall
Mar. 9—Eve.   Philharmonic Hall
Mar. 12—Eve.   Philharmonic Hall
Mar. 13—Aft.   Philharmonic Hall
(Lincoln Center Student Program)
Mar. 14—Eve.   Philharmonic Hall
Mar. 16—Eve.   Philharmonic Hall

George Szell
Mar. 19—Eve.   Philharmonic Hall
Mar. 20—Aft.   Philharmonic Hall
Mar. 21—Eve.   Philharmonic Hall
Mar. 23—Eve.   Philharmonic Hall
Mar. 26—Eve.   Philharmonic Hall
Mar. 27—Aft.   Philharmonic Hall
Mar. 28—Eve.   Philharmonic Hall
Mar. 30—Eve.   Philharmonic Hall
Apr. 2—Eve.   Philharmonic Hall

1970

Apr.	3—Aft.	Philharmonic Hall
Apr.	4—Eve.	Philharmonic Hall
Apr.	6—Eve.	Philharmonic Hall
Apr.	9—Eve.	Philharmonic Hall
Apr.	10—Aft.	Philharmonic Hall
Apr.	11—Eve.	Philharmonic Hall
Apr.	13—Eve.	Philharmonic Hall

Lorin Maazel

Apr.	16—Eve.	Philharmonic Hall
Apr.	17—Aft.	Philharmonic Hall
Apr.	18—Eve.	Philharmonic Hall
Apr.	20—Aft.	Philharmonic Hall
(Lincoln Center Student Program)		
Apr.	23—Eve.	Philharmonic Hall
Apr.	24—Aft.	Philharmonic Hall
Apr.	25—Eve.	Philharmonic Hall
Apr.	27—Eve.	Philharmonic Hall
Apr.	30—Eve.	Philharmonic Hall
May	1—Aft.	Philharmonic Hall
(Lincoln Center Student Program)		

1970

May	2—Eve.	Philharmonic Hall
May	4—Eve.	Philharmonic Hall
May	6—Eve.	Washington, D.C.
May	7—Eve.	Washington, D.C.

**Peter Ustinov,
Alfredo Bonavera**

May	9—Aft. (2)	Philharmonic Hall
(Young People's Concert)		

Lorin Maazel

May	11—Eve.	Philharmonic Hall
May	14—Eve.	Philharmonic Hall
May	15—Aft.	Philharmonic Hall
May	16—Eve.	Philharmonic Hall
May	18—Eve.	Philharmonic Hall
May	21—Eve.	Philharmonic Hall
May	22—Aft.	Philharmonic Hall
May	23—Eve.	Philharmonic Hall

REPERTOIRE

* Recorded by the New York Philharmonic.

(a) First performance anywhere; commissioned by the New York Philharmonic
for its 125th Anniversary Year.
(b) First performance anywhere.
(c) First New York performance.

BACH, J. C.—Symphony Op. 18, No. 4, D major: Sept. 25, 26, 27, 29.

BACH, J. S.—Concerto for Two Violins and Orchestra, D minor, BWV 1043:
Apr. 30; May 1, 2, 4, 7, 11.

BARTOK—"Bluebeard's Castle," Opus 11: Dec. 11, 12, 13, 15.

BEETHOVEN—Concerto for Piano and Orchestra, No. 4, G major, Op. 58:
Nov. 10; Apr. 9, 10, 11, 13.
Concerto for Violin and Orchestra, D major, Op. 61: Oct. 30, 31; Mar. 3.
"Fidelio" (Concert version): Jan. 15, 16, 17, 19.
"Leonore" Overture No. 2: Nov. 13, 14, 15, 17.
Overture to "The Creatures of Prometheus," Op. 43: Apr. 9, 10, 11, 13.
*Symphony No. 1, C major, Op. 21: Oct. 9, 10, 11, 13.
*Symphony No. 5, C minor, Op. 67: Dec. 31; Jan. 1, 2, 3, 5.
*Symphony No. 7, A major, Op. 92: Apr. 9, 10, 11, 13.
*Symphony No. 9, D minor, with final chorus on Schiller's "Ode to Joy," Opus
125: Nov. 13, 14, 15, 17.

BERG—"Lulu Suite": Feb. 26, 27, 28; Mar. 2.

BERLIOZ—*Overture, "Benvenuto Cellini," Op. 23: Mar. 19, 20, 21, 23.
*Overture, "Le Carnaval romain": Mar. 5, 6, 7, 9.

BRAHMS—Serenade No. 1, D major, Op. 11: Dec. 18, 19, 20.
*Symphony No. 2, D major, Op. 73: Mar. 5, 6, 7, 9.
*Symphony No. 4, E minor, Op. 98: Mar. 26, 27, 28, 30.

BRUCKNER—Symphony No. 1, C minor (Linz version): Feb. 26, 27, 28;
Mar. 2.

CARTER—Concerto for Orchestra: Feb. 5 (a), 6, 7, 9.

CASADESUS—Suite No. 2, B-flat major, Op. 26: Nov. 26, 28, 29; Dec. 1.

CHOPIN—Concerto No. 1 for Piano and Orchestra, E minor, Op. 11: Oct 16, 17, 18, 20.

COPLAND—Concerto for Clarinet and String Orchestra with Harp and Piano: Sept. 23.

DEBUSSY—*"La Mer," Three Symphonic Sketches: Sept. 23.

DELIUS—Prelude, "Irmelin": Mar. 19, 20, 21, 23.

DVORAK—Concerto for Cello and Orchestra, B minor, Op. 104: Dec. 4, 5, 6, 8.
*Symphony No. 8, G major, Op. 88: Mar. 19, 20, 21, 23.
*Symphony No. 9, E minor, Op. 95, "From the New World": Dec. 18, 19, 20.

FALLA—"El amor brujo": Dec. 31; Jan. 1, 2, 3, 5.

FAURE—"Pelléas et Mélisande," Op. 80: May 14, 15, 16, 18.

FRANCK—*Symphony in D minor: Apr. 2, 3, 4, 6.

HAYDN—Piano Concerto in D major: May 14, 15, 16, 18.
*Symphony No. 88, G major: Nov. 26, 28, 29; Dec. 2.
Symphony No. 101, D major, "The Clock": Jan. 29, 30, 31; Feb. 2.
Symphony No. 103, E-flat major, "The Drumroll": Feb. 5, 6, 7, 9.

HINDEMITH—Symphonic Metamorphosis of Themes by Carl Maria von Weber: Feb. 19, 20, 23; Mar. 3.

HOVHANESS—"Meditation on Orpheus": Oct. 25.

IBERT—Divertissement: Oct. 2, 3, 4, 6.
"Ports of Call" ("Escales"): Feb. 21.

KIRCHNER—Music for Orchestra: Oct. 16 (a), 17, 18, 20.

KODALY—Dances from Galánta: Oct. 25.

LALO—Concerto for Cello and Orchestra, D minor: Oct. 23, 24, 27.
"Symphonie espagnole," for Violin and Orchestra, Op. 21: Mar. 19, 20, 21, 23.

LIGETI—*"Atmosphères": Oct. 23, 24, 27, 30, 31.

MacLEISH-LADERMAN–"Magic Prison": Feb. 21.

MAHLER—*Symphony No. 1, D major: Jan. 8, 9, 12.
*Symphony No. 4, G major, for Orchestra and Soprano Solo: Apr. 16, 17, 18, 20; May 6.
*Symphony No. 6, A minor: Nov. 20, 21, 22, 24.

MENDELSSOHN—*Symphony No. 4, A major, Op. 90 ("Italian"): Oct. 23, 24, 27, 30, 31.

MOUSSORGSKY—Four Choruses: Mar. 12, 13, 14, 16.

MOZART—Aria: "Vorrei spiegarvi, oh Dio!" K. 418: Feb. 26, 27, 28; Mar. 2.
Concerto for Piano and Orchestra, No. 18, B-flat major, K. 456: Apr. 2, 3, 4, 6.
Concerto for Piano and Orchestra, No. 21, C major, K. 467: Nov. 10.
Concerto for Piano and Orchestra, No. 24, C minor, K. 491: Apr. 23, 24, 25, 27.
Concerto for Piano and Orchestra, No. 26, D major, K. 536 ("Coronation"): Nov. 26, 28, 29; Dec. 1.
Concerto for Two Pianos and Orchestra, No. 10, E-flat major, K. 365: Feb. 11, 16.
Concerto for Violin and Orchestra, No. 3, G major, K. 216: Apr. 30; May 2, 4, 7, 11.
Concerto for Violin and Orchestra, No. 4, D major, K. 218: Mar. 3.
Concerto for Violin and Orchestra, No. 5, A major, K. 219: Mar. 26, 27, 28, 30.
Overture, "The Marriage of Figaro": Oct. 25.
Serenade No. 10, B-flat major, K. 361: Dec. 11, 12, 13, 15.
Symphony No. 23, D major, K. 181: Oct. 25.
Symphony No. 25, G minor, K. 183: Jan. 8, 9, 12.
Symphony No. 29, A major, K. 201: Apr. 23, 24, 25, 27.

Symphony No. 32, G major, K. 318: Oct. 16, 17, 18, 20.
Symphony No. 38, D major, K. 504 ("Prague"): Apr. 23, 24, 25, 27; May 6.
*Symphony No. 40, G minor, K. 550: Nov. 10.

NIELSEN—Symphony No. 4, Op. 29, "The Inextinguishable": Jan. 29, 30, 31; Feb. 2.
*Symphony No. 5, Op. 50: Oct. 9, 10, 11, 13.

ORFF—"Carmina Burana": Oct. 2, 3, 4, 6.

PROKOFIEV—*"Classical" Symphony, Op. 25: Feb. 21.
Concerto No. 3 for Piano and Orchestra, C major, Op. 26: Sept. 23; Feb. 19, 20, 23.
*"Romeo and Juliet," Excerpts: Sept. 23; Mar. 12, 13, 14, 16.

RACHMANINOFF—Concerto No. 1 for Piano and Orchestra, F-sharp minor, Op. 1: Oct. 25.
Concerto No. 4 for Piano and Orchestra, G minor, Op. 40: Dec. 31; Jan. 1, 2, 3, 5.

RAVEL—*"Daphnis and Chloé" Suite No. 2: Nov. 26, 28, 29; Dec. 1.
*"La Valse": Apr. 16, 17, 18, 20; May 7.

RESPIGHI—Symphonic Poem, "The Pines of Rome": Oct. 16, 17, 18, 20.

RIEGGER—Study in Sonority, Op. 7: Oct. 2, 3, 4, 6.

ROSSINI—*Overture, "L'Italiana in Algeri": Jan. 8, 9, 12.
Overture, "Il Viaggio a Reims": Mar. 26, 27, 28, 30.

RUSSO—Three Pieces for Blues Band and Symphony Orchestra, Op. 50: Oct. 9 (c), 10, 11, 13.

SAINT-SAENS—Concerto for Cello and Orchestra, A minor, Op. 33: Mar. 5, 6, 7, 9.

SCHUMAN, W.—"In Praise of Shahn," Canticle for Orchestra: Jan. 29 (b), 30, 31; Feb. 2, 11.

SCHUMANN—Concerto for Piano and Orchestra, A minor, Op. 54: Sept. 25, 26, 27, 29.
"Das Paradies und die Peri": May 21, 22, 23.

SCRIABIN—"Prometheus, the Poem of Fire," Op. 60: Oct. 23, 24, 27.

SIBELIUS—*Symphony No. 4, A minor, Op. 63: Dec. 4, 5, 6, 8.
*Symphony No. 5, E-flat major, Op. 82: May 14, 15, 16, 18.

STRAUSS—Burleske in D minor for Piano and Orchestra: May 14, 15, 16, 18.

STRAVINSKY—"Oedipus Rex": Mar. 12, 13, 14, 16.
"L'Histoire du Soldat": Apr. 30; May 1, 2, 4, 11.
Petite Suite No. 1: Apr. 30; May 1, 2, 4, 11.
"The Song of the Nightingale": Apr. 16, 17, 18, 20; May 7.

TCHAIKOVSKY—*"Francesca da Rimini," Op. 32: Feb. 21.
Symphony No. 1, G minor, Op. 13, "Winter Dreams": Sept. 25, 26, 27, 29.
Symphony No. 3, D major, Op. 29, "Polish": Feb. 5, 6, 7, 9, 11, 16.
*Symphony No. 5, E minor, Op. 64: Feb. 19, 20, 23.

VERDI—Overture, "La forza del destino": Dec. 4, 5, 6, 8.

VIVALDI—Concerto in G minor, P. 383: Mar. 5, 6, 7, 9.

WAGNER—Scenes from "Götterdämmerung": Jan. 22, 23, 24, 26.

WALTON—Variations on a Theme by Hindemith: Apr. 2, 3, 4, 6.

SOLOISTS

PIANO
ALEGRIA ARCE: Oct. 25.
MARTHA ARGERICH: Feb. 19, 20, 23.
ROBERT CASADESUS: Nov. 26, 28, 29; Dec. 1.

CLIFFORD CURZON: Apr. 9, 10, 13.
CLAUDE FRANK: Apr. 2, 3, 4, 6.
NELSON FREIRE: Dec. 31; Jan. 1, 2, 3, 5.
PAUL JACOBS: Oct. 23, 27.

BYRON JANIS: Sept. 23.

ALICIA DE LARROCHA: Sept. 25, 26, 27, 29.

ISRAELA MARGALIT: May 14, 15, 16, 18.

MAURIZIO POLLINI: Oct. 16, 17, 18, 20.

RUDOLF SERKIN: Nov. 10.

ANDRE WATTS: Apr. 23, 24, 25, 27.

JOSEPH KALICHSTEIN: Apr. 11.

DUO-PIANISTS

ARTHUR GOLD and ROBERT FIZDALE: Feb. 11, 16.

VIOLIN

LORIN MAAZEL: Apr. 30; May 1, 2, 4, 7, 11.

DAVID NADIEN: Oct. 30, 31; Apr. 30; May 1, 2, 4, 7, 11.

DAVID OISTRAKH: Mar. 3.

EDITH PEINEMANN: Mar. 26, 27, 28, 30.

ITZHAK PERLMAN: Mar. 19, 20, 21, 23.

CELLO

JACQUELINE DU PRE: Mar. 5, 6, 7, 9.

PIERRE FOURNIER: Dec. 4, 5, 6, 8.

LORNE MUNROE: Oct. 23, 27.

CLARINET

STANLEY DRUCKER: Sept. 23.

BLUES BAND

CORKY SIEGEL BLUES BAND: Oct. 9, 10, 11, 13.

VOICE

JACQUELYN BENSON, soprano: Jan. 15.

ROBERT BENTON, baritone: Jan. 15, 16, 17, 19.

HELGE BRILIOTH, tenor: May 21, 22, 23.

PATRICIA BROOKS, soprano: Oct. 2, 3, 4, 6.

LOUISA BUDD, soprano: Jan. 16, 19.

DAVID CUMBERLAND, bass-baritone: Jan. 15, 17.

ANITA DARIAN, soprano: Jan. 15, 17.

RYAN EDWARDS, bass-baritone: Jan. 16, 19.

KEITH ENGEN, bass-baritone: May 21, 22, 23.

SIMON ESTES, bass-baritone: Mar. 12, 13, 14, 16.

ANDRAS FARAGO, baritone: Dec. 11, 12, 13, 15.

EILEEN FARRELL, soprano: Jan. 22, 23, 24, 26.

ALPHA FLOYD, soprano: Jan. 16, 19.

CATHERINE GAYER, soprano: Feb. 26, 27, 28; Mar. 2.

DAVID HALL, tenor: Jan. 15, 17.

ERNST HAFFLIGER, tenor: Nov. 13, 14, 15, 17.

HEATHER HARPER, soprano: Nov. 13, 14, 15, 17.

JANE HOBSON, mezzo-soprano: Nov. 13, 14, 15, 17.

WERNER HOLLWEG, tenor: Mar. 12, 13, 14, 16.

GUNDULA JANOWITZ, soprano: May 21, 22, 23.

NORMA LERER, contralto: Dec. 31; Jan. 1, 2, 3, 5.

JANE MARSH, soprano: Apr. 16, 17, 18, 20; May 6.

RAYMOND MICHALSKI, bass-baritone: Mar. 12, 13, 14, 16.

JOHN MACK OUSLEY, bass: Jan. 16, 19.

THOMAS PAUL, bass: Nov. 13, 14, 15, 17.

JOHN REARDON, baritone: Oct. 2, 3, 4, 6.

HOWARD ROSS, bass: Jan. 15, 17.

CAROL SMITH, mezzo-soprano: May 21, 22, 23.

FRANK SPOTE, tenor: Jan. 16, 19.

OLGA SZONYI, mezzo-soprano: Dec. 11, 12, 13, 15.

JESS THOMAS, tenor: Jan. 22, 23, 24, 26.

ELIZABETH THOMPSON, soprano: Jan. 17.

TATIANA TROYANOS, mezzo-soprano: Mar. 12, 13, 14, 16.

ANASTASIOS VRENIOS, tenor: Oct. 2, 3, 4, 6.

FOREST WARREN, tenor: Jan. 15, 16, 17, 19.

NARRATOR

DOUGLAS FAIRBANKS, JR.: Mar. 12, 13, 14, 16.

E. G. MARSHALL: Feb. 21.

FRANCES STERNHAGEN: Feb. 21.

CHORUS

CAMERATA SINGERS, Abraham Kaplan, Director: Nov. 13, 14, 15, 17; Mar. 12, 13, 14, 16.

JUILLIARD CHORUS, Abraham Kaplan, Director: Jan. 15, 16, 17, 19.

SCHOLA CANTORUM, Hugh Ross, Director: Oct. 2, 3, 4, 6.

WESTMINSTER CHOIR, Robert Carwithen, Director: May 21, 22, 23.

1969 TRANSCONTINENTAL U.S. TOUR

Conductors

Karel Ancerl			
Aug. 26—Eve.	Ottawa, Canada	Sept. 4—Eve.	Los Angeles
Aug. 28—Eve.	Rochester	Sept. 6—Eve.	Los Angeles
	(Meadowbrook)	Sept. 7—Aft.	Santa Barbara
Aug. 29—Eve.	Rochester	Sept. 9—Eve.	Ames
	(Meadowbrook)	Sept. 10—Eve.	Ames
		Sept. 11—Eve.	Ames
Seiji Ozawa		Sept. 13—Eve.	Ames
Aug. 30—Eve.	Rochester	Sept. 14—Aft.	Ames
	(Meadowbrook)	Sept. 15—Eve.	Wheaton
Aug. 31—Eve.	Rochester	Sept. 18—Eve.	Madison
	(Meadowbrook)	Sept. 19—Eve.	Milwaukee
Sept. 2—Eve.	San Francisco	Sept. 20—Eve.	Chicago
Sept. 3—Eve.	San Francisco	Sept. 21—Aft.	Ann Arbor

TOUR REPERTOIRE

BARTOK—*Concerto for Orchestra: Sept. 4, 11, 14, 16, 18, 21.

BEETHOVEN—Concerto for Piano and Orchestra, No. 3, C minor, Op. 37: Aug. 26, 28, 29.
Concerto for Piano and Orchestra, No. 5, E-flat major, Op. 73: Sept. 19.

COPLAND—Clarinet Concerto: Sept. 3, 7, 9, 18.

DEBUSSY—*"La Mer": Aug. 30, 31; Sept. 3, 9, 13, 19.
*"Prelude to the Afternoon of a Faun": Sept. 11, 14.

FRANCK—*Symphony in D minor: Aug. 26, 28, 29.

GINASTERA—"Estancia" Suite: Aug. 30, 31; Sept. 3, 9, 19.

GLINKA—*"Russlan and Ludmilla" Overture: Aug. 30, 31; Sept. 2, 4, 10, 19, 20.

GRIEG—Piano Concerto: Sept. 6.

DVORAK—*"Carnival Overture": Aug. 26, 28, 29.

LISZT—Piano Concerto No. 1, E-flat major: Sept. 13.

MENDELSSOHN—*"Italian" Symphony: Sept 3, 7, 9, 18.

MOZART—Arias: "Aer tranquillo," "Ruhe sanft," "Zeffiretti lusinghieri": Sept. 11, 14.
Overture, "The Abduction from the Seraglio": Sept. 21.

POULENC—Gloria in G: Sept. 11, 14.

PROKOFIEV—Concerto No. 3 for Piano and Orchestra, C major, Op. 26: Sept. 10.

RACHMANINOFF—Concerto No. 3 for Piano and Orchestra, D minor, Op. 30: Aug. 30, 31; Sept. 2, 4, 20, 21.

SCHUBERT—*Symphony No. 8 in B minor, "Unfinished": Sept. 6.

TCHAIKOVSKY—*Symphony No. 4, F minor, Op. 36: Sept. 2, 6, 7, 10, 13, 16, 20.

TOUR SOLOISTS

VAN CLIBURN, pianist: Sept. 19.

STANLEY DRUCKER, clarinetist: Sept. 3, 7, 9, 18.

BYRON JANIS, pianist: Aug. 28, 29; Sept. 10.

GRANT JOHANNESEN, pianist: Aug. 26.

LEONARD PENNARIO, pianist: Sept. 6.

EUGENE PRIDINOFF, pianist: Sept. 13.

JUDITH RASKIN, soprano: Sept. 11, 14.

ANDRE WATTS, pianist: Aug. 30, 31; Sept. 2, 4, 20, 21.

CHORUS

IOWA STATE SINGERS AND ORATORIO CHORUS: Sept. 11, 14.

NEW YORK PHILHARMONIC "PROMENADES"
EIGHTH SEASON   1970   PHILHARMONIC HALL

Conductor

André Kostelanetz
May 27–June 20

REPERTOIRE—"PROMENADES"

(a) World premiere.
(pa) Works for piano alone.
(sg) Soprano and guitar alone.

* Compositions marked with an asterisk are recorded by the
New York Philharmonic.

ALFVEN—"Midsummer Vigil," Swedish Rhapsody No. 2: June 5, 6, 9, 10.

BERNSTEIN—*Overture to "Candide": May 29, 30; June 2.

CHARPENTIER—Depuis le jour, from "Louise": June 18, 19, 20.

DVORAK—Slavonic Dances, Op. 46, Nos. 1, 2; Op. 72, Nos. 2, 7: June 16, 17.

ENESCO—Roumanian Rhapsody No. 1, A major, Op. 11: June 16, 17.

FALLA—Allí está! Riyendo!, from "La Vida breve": June 18, 19, 20.
    Suite from "El amor brujo": June 18, 19, 20.

GLINKA—Jota Aragonesa: May 27, 28; June 3, 4.

GOTTSCHALK-SHANET—"Night of the Tropics": June 11, 12, 13.

GRANADOS—The Maja and the Nightingale, from "Goyescas": June 18, 19, 20.

GRIEG—"The Swan"; "Spring"; "A Dream": June 5, 6, 9, 10.
    "Shapes and Motions": June 5, 6, 9, 10.
    Symphonic Dance, Op. 64, No. 2: June 5, 6, 9, 10.

HOVHANESS—"And God Created Great Whales": June 11 (a), 12, 13.

LEHAR—Suite from "Count of Luxembourg": June 16, 17.

LISZT—Hungarian Fantasy for Piano and Orchestra: June 16, 17.
    Three Grand Etudes after Paganini: June 16, 17 (pa).

MOUSSORGSKY—Excerpts from "Khovanshchina": May 27, 28; June 3, 4.

NIELSEN—Overture, "Maskarade": June 5, 6, 9, 10.

PROKOFIEV—"Peter and the Wolf": May 29, 30; June 2.

PUCCINI—Waltz, from "La Rondine": May 29, 30; June 2.

RACHMANINOFF—Waltz, from "Aleko": May 29, 30; June 2.

RANGSTROM—"A Dance Rhythm": June 5, 6, 9, 10.

RAVEL—*"Boléro": June 11, 12, 13.
    *"Daphnis et Chloé," Suite No. 2: June 18, 19, 20.

REZNICEK—*Overture to "Donna Diana": June 16, 17.

RODRIGO—Concierto de Aranjuez: May 27, 28; June 3, 4.

ROSSINI-BRITTEN—*Soirées musicales, Op. 9: May 29, 30; June 2.

SIBELIUS—Incidental Music for Shakespeare's "The Tempest": June 5, 6, 9, 10.
    Tone Poem, "Finlandia," Op. 26, No. 7: June 5, 6, 9, 10.
    "Was It A Dream": June 5, 6, 9, 10.

SKALKOTTAS—Greek Dances: June 18, 19, 20.

STRAUSS—Waltz, from "Der Rosenkavalier": May 29, 30; June 2.

TCHAIKOVSKY—*"1812 Overture," Op. 49: May 27, 28; June 3, 4.
*Fantasy Overture, "Romeo and Juliet": May 29, 30; June 2.
 Serenade for Strings, C major, Op. 48: June 11, 12, 13.
 Prince Yeletsky's Aria from "The Queen of Spades": May 27, 28; June 3, 4.
VERDI—Ballet from Act III of "Otello": June 18, 19, 20.

ENCORES:

BRAHMS—Hungarian Dance No. 5: June 16, 17.
DINICU—Hora Staccato: June 16, 17.
GERSHWIN—"Strike Up The Band": May 29, 30; June 2.
GRIEG—Norwegian Dance No. 2: June 5, 6, 9, 10.
LIADOV—"Music Box": May 28; June 3, 4.
OFFENBACH—"Can-Can": June 19.
PRESS—Wedding Dance: June 18.
SHOSTAKOVICH—"Folk Festival": May 27, 28; June 3, 4.
 Galop No. 8: June 5, 6, 9, 10.
SOUSA—"Stars and Stripes": June 20.
TCHAIKOVSKY—"None But the Lonely Heart": May 27, 28; June 3, 4.
TUCCI—"Bamba de Vera Cruz": June 11, 12, 13.
WEILL—"Mack The Knife": May 29, 30; June 2.

Traditional—"El Vita": June 18, 19, 20 (sg).

SOLOISTS—"PROMENADES"

BALLET
  JOHNNA KIRKLAND: June 11, 12, 13.
  EDWARD VILLELLA: June 11, 12, 13.
CONCERTINA
  BORIS MATUSEWITCH: June 11, 12, 13.
GUITAR
  ALIRIO DIAZ: May 27, 28; June 3, 4.
NARRATOR
  CYRIL RITCHARD: May 29, 30; June 2.
MARIONETTE COMPANY
  THE BIL BAIRD MARIONETTES: June
  5, 6, 9, 10.

PIANO
  EARL WILD: June 16, 17.
VOICE
  PILAR LORENGAR, soprano: June 18,
  19, 20.
  SHERRILL MILNES, baritone: May 27,
  28; June 3, 4.
  CAROL NEBLETT, soprano: June 5, 6,
  9, 10.
  WILLIAM SCHUSTIK, baritone: June 11,
  12, 13.

●

NEW YORK PHILHARMONIC OUTDOOR CONCERTS IN THE
PARKS OF THE CITY OF NEW YORK
SIXTH SEASON (1970)

Conductors

Dean Dixon
July 21, 23, 25.

Sixten Ehrling
July 28, 31; August 1, 2.

Rafael Frühbeck de Burgos
August 11, 14, 16, 17, 18.

SOLOISTS—PARK CONCERTS

PIANO
ALICIA DE LARROCHA: August 11, 14, 16, 17, 18.
EARL WILD: July 28, 31; August 1, 2.

VIOLIN
JAMES OLIVER BUSWELL, IV: July 21, 23, 25.

REPERTOIRE—PARK CONCERTS

* Compositions marked with an asterisk are recorded by
the New York Philharmonic.

BEETHOVEN—*Symphony No. 5, C minor, Opus 67: August 11, 14, 16, 17, 18.

BRAHMS—*Symphony No. 2, D major, Opus 73: July 21, 23, 25.

DEBUSSY—*"Prelude to The Afternoon of a Faun": July 28, 31; August 1, 2.

FALLA—"Nights in the Gardens of Spain," for Piano and Orchestra: August 11, 14, 16, 17, 18.

HENZE—Trois Pas des Tritons, from "Undine": July 21, 23, 25.

MOUSSORGSKY-RAVEL—*"Pictures at an Exhibition": July 28, 31; August 1, 2.

RACHMANINOFF—*Rhapsody on a Theme of Paganini, for Piano and Orchestra, Opus 43: July 28, 31; August 1, 2.

RAVEL—Concerto for Piano and Orchestra, G major: August 11, 14, 16, 17, 18.

ROSSINI—*Overture, "L'Italiana in Algeri": August 11, 14, 16, 17, 18.

SCHUMAN—"American Festival Overture": July 28, 31; August 1, 2.

SIBELIUS—Concerto for Violin and Orchestra, D minor, Opus 47: July 21, 23, 25.

●

NEW YORK PHILHARMONIC: GARDEN STATE ARTS CENTER 1970

Conductors

Sixten Ehrling
July 29, 30.

André Kostelanetz
August 12, 15.

SOLOISTS—GARDEN STATE CONCERTS

VLADIMIR ASHKENAZY: July 29, 30.   LORIN HOLLANDER: August 12, 15.

REPERTOIRE—GARDEN STATE CONCERTS

* Compositions marked with an asterisk are recorded by
the New York Philharmonic.

BEETHOVEN—Concerto No. 5 for Piano and Orchestra, E flat major, Opus 73 ("Emperor"): July 29, 30.

KHACHATURIAN—Suite from the Ballet, "Gayne": August 12, 15.

MOUSSORGSKY-RAVEL—*"Pictures at an Exhibition": July 29, 30.

PROKOFIEFF—*Classical Symphony, Opus 25: August 12, 15.

RACHMANINOFF—Concerto No. 2 for Piano and Orchestra, C minor, Opus 18: August 12, 15.

SCHUMAN—American Festival Overture: July 29, 30.

STRAVINSKY—*Suite from "The Firebird": August 12, 15.

1970-71 ONE HUNDRED AND TWENTY-NINTH SEASON

Laureate Conductor: LEONARD BERNSTEIN

Guest Conductors: DANIEL BARENBOIM, KARL BOEHM, PIERRE BOULEZ,
ALDO CECCATO, AARON COPLAND, DEAN DIXON,
MILTON KATIMS, SEIJI OZAWA, ROBERT SHAW,
STANISLAW SKROWACZEWSKI, KARLHEINZ STOCKHAUSEN

Special Saturday Evenings: ANDRE KOSTELANETZ

Young People's Concerts: LEONARD BERNSTEIN, *Music Director;*
DEAN DIXON and YEHUDI MENUHIN, *Guest Conductors*

Assistant Conductors: PHILIPPE BENDER, MARIO BENZECRY, DAVID GILBERT

CONCERTS

1970

Leonard Bernstein

Sept. 22—Eve.	Philharmonic Hall	
(Opening Night Benefit Concert)		
Sept. 24—Eve.	Philharmonic Hall	
Sept. 25—Aft.	Philharmonic Hall	
Sept. 26—Aft. (2)	Philharmonic Hall	
(Young People's Concert)		
Sept. 28—Eve.	Philharmonic Hall	
Oct. 1—Eve.	Philharmonic Hall	
Oct. 2—Aft.	Philharmonic Hall	
Oct. 3—Eve.	Philharmonic Hall	
Oct. 5—Eve.	Philharmonic Hall	
Oct. 8—Eve.	Philharmonic Hall	
Oct. 9—Aft.	Philharmonic Hall	
Oct. 10—Eve.	Philharmonic Hall	
Oct. 12—Eve.	Philharmonic Hall	
Oct. 15—Eve.	Philharmonic Hall	
Oct. 16—Aft.	Philharmonic Hall	
Oct. 17—Eve.	Philharmonic Hall	
Oct. 19—Eve.	Philharmonic Hall	
Oct. 21—Eve.	Philharmonic Hall	
Oct. 24—Aft. (2)	Philharmonic Hall	
(Young People's Concert)		
Oct. 26—Eve.	Philharmonic Hall	

Aaron Copland

Oct. 29—Eve.	Philharmonic Hall
Oct. 30—Aft.	Philharmonic Hall
Oct. 31—Eve.	Philharmonic Hall
Nov. 2—Eve.	Philharmonic Hall

1970

Aldo Ceccato

Nov. 5—Eve.	Philharmonic Hall
Nov. 6—Aft.	Philharmonic Hall
Nov. 7—Eve.	Philharmonic Hall
Nov. 9—Aft.	Philharmonic Hall
(Lincoln Center Student Program)	

Milton Katims

Nov. 12—Eve.	Philharmonic Hall
Nov. 13—Aft.	Philharmonic Hall
Nov. 14—Eve.	Philharmonic Hall
Nov. 16—Eve.	Philharmonic Hall

Robert Shaw

Nov. 19—Eve.	Philharmonic Hall
Nov. 20—Aft.	Philharmonic Hall
Nov. 21—Eve.	Philharmonic Hall
Nov. 23—Eve.	Philharmonic Hall

Dean Dixon

Nov. 25—Eve.	Philharmonic Hall
Nov. 27—Aft.	Philharmonic Hall
Nov. 28—Eve.	Philharmonic Hall
Nov. 30—Eve.	Philharmonic Hall

Stanislaw Skrowaczewski

Dec. 3—Eve.	Philharmonic Hall
Dec. 4—Aft.	Philharmonic Hall
Dec. 5—Eve.	Philharmonic Hall
Dec. 7—Eve.	Philharmonic Hall
Dec. 10—Eve.	Philharmonic Hall
Dec. 11—Aft.	Philharmonic Hall

1970

André Kostelanetz
Dec. 12—Eve.   Philharmonic Hall

Stanislaw Skrowaczewski
Dec. 14—Eve.   Philharmonic Hall
Dec. 17—Eve.   Philharmonic Hall
Dec. 18—Aft.   Philharmonic Hall
Dec. 19—Eve.   Philharmonic Hall

Daniel Barenboim
Dec. 30—Eve.   Philharmonic Hall
Dec. 31—Eve.   Philharmonic Hall
1971
Jan. 1—Aft.   Philharmonic Hall
Jan. 2—Eve.   Philharmonic Hall
Jan. 4—Eve.   Philharmonic Hall

Leonard Bernstein,
James DePreist,
Mesru Mehmedov
Jan. 5—Eve.   Felt Forum
(Mitropoulos International Music Competition)

Daniel Barenboim
Jan. 7—Eve.   Philharmonic Hall
Jan. 8—Aft.   Philharmonic Hall
Jan. 9—Eve.   Philharmonic Hall
Jan. 11—Aft.   Philharmonic Hall
(Lincoln Center Student Program)
Jan. 14—Eve.   Philharmonic Hall
Jan. 15—Aft.   Philharmonic Hall
Jan. 16—Eve.   Philharmonic Hall
Jan. 18—Eve.   Philharmonic Hall
Jan. 20—Eve.   Philharmonic Hall
(Pension Fund Benefit)
Jan. 21—Eve.   Philharmonic Hall
Jan. 22—Aft.   Philharmonic Hall

Dean Dixon
Jan. 23—Aft. (2)   Philharmonic Hall
(Young People's Concert)

Daniel Barenboim
Jan. 25—Eve.   Philharmonic Hall

Seiji Ozawa
Jan. 28—Eve.   Philharmonic Hall
Jan. 29—Eve.   Queens College
Jan. 30—Eve.   Philharmonic Hall
Feb. 1—Eve.   Philharmonic Hall
Feb. 4—Eve.   Philharmonic Hall
Feb. 5—Eve.   Philharmonic Hall
Feb. 6—Eve.   Philharmonic Hall
Feb. 8—Eve.   Philharmonic Hall
Feb. 11—Eve.   Philharmonic Hall
Feb. 12—Aft.   Philharmonic Hall
Feb. 13—Eve.   Philharmonic Hall
Feb. 15—Eve.   Philharmonic Hall

1971
Feb. 18—Eve.   Philharmonic Hall
Feb. 19—Aft.   Philharmonic Hall
Feb. 20—Eve.   Philharmonic Hall
Feb. 22—Eve.   Philharmonic Hall

Karlheinz Stockhausen
Feb. 25—Eve.   Philharmonic Hall

Philippe Bender,
Mario Benzecry,
David Gilbert
Feb. 26—Aft.   Philharmonic Hall
(Lincoln Center Student Program)
Feb. 27—Eve.   Philharmonic Hall
Mar. 2—Aft.   Philharmonic Hall
(Lincoln Center Student Program)

Karl Böhm
Mar. 4—Eve.   Philharmonic Hall
Mar. 5—Aft.   Philharmonic Hall
Mar. 6—Eve.   Philharmonic Hall
Mar. 8—Eve.   Philharmonic Hall
Mar. 11—Eve.   Philharmonic Hall
Mar. 12—Aft.   Philharmonic Hall

André Kostelanetz
Mar. 13—Eve.   Philharmonic Hall

Karl Böhm
Mar. 15—Eve.   Philharmonic Hall
Mar. 18—Eve.   Philharmonic Hall
Mar. 19—Aft.   Philharmonic Hall
Mar. 20—Eve.   Philharmonic Hall
Mar. 22—Eve.   Philharmonic Hall

Stanislaw Skrowaczewski
Mar. 25—Eve.   Philharmonic Hall
Mar. 26—Aft.   Philharmonic Hall

Yehudi Menuhin
Mar. 27—Aft. (2)   Philharmonic Hall
(Young People's Concert)

Stanislaw Skrowaczewski
Mar. 29—Eve.   Philharmonic Hall
Apr. 1—Eve.   Philharmonic Hall
Apr. 2—Aft.   Philharmonic Hall
(Lincoln Center Student Program)
Apr. 3—Eve.   Philharmonic Hall
Apr. 5—Eve.   Philharmonic Hall
Apr. 8—Eve.   Philharmonic Hall
Apr. 9—Aft.   Philharmonic Hall
Apr. 10—Eve.   Philharmonic Hall
Apr. 12—Eve.   Philharmonic Hall

Pierre Boulez
Apr. 15—Eve.   Philharmonic Hall
Apr. 16—Aft.   Philharmonic Hall
Apr. 17—Eve.   Philharmonic Hall

1971		1971	
Apr. 19—Eve.	Philharmonic Hall	May 3—Eve.	Philharmonic Hall
Apr. 22—Eve.	Philharmonic Hall	May 6—Eve.	Philharmonic Hall
Apr. 23—Aft.	Philharmonic Hall	May 7—Aft.	Philharmonic Hall
Apr. 24—Eve.	Philharmonic Hall	May 8—Eve.	Philharmonic Hall
Apr. 26—Eve.	Philharmonic Hall	May 10—Eve.	Washington, D.C.
Apr. 29—Eve.	Philharmonic Hall	May 13—Eve.	Philharmonic Hall
Apr. 30—Aft.	Philharmonic Hall	May 14—Aft.	Philharmonic Hall
May 1—Eve.	Philharmonic Hall	May 15—Eve.	Philharmonic Hall

REPERTOIRE

(a) First New York performance of completed version.
(b) First New York performance.
(c) First performance anywhere of orchestral version, commissioned by the New York Philharmonic.
(d) First performance in the United States.

* Recorded by the New York Philharmonic.

BACH, J. S.—Suite No. 3, D major, BWV 1068: Apr. 1, 3, 5 (Overture and Air: Apr. 2).

BARBER—"Medea's Dance of Vengeance," Opus 23A: Dec. 17, 18, 19.

BARTOK—Concerto No. 3 for Piano and Orchestra: Nov. 5, 6, 7, 9.
Concerto No. 2 for Violin and Orchestra: Jan. 28, 29, 30; Feb. 1.
Divertimento for Strings: Apr. 1, 3, 5 (First and Third Movements: Apr. 2).
"The Miraculous Mandarin": May 6, 7, 8.

BEETHOVEN—Concerto No. 1 for Piano and Orchestra, C major, Opus 15: Feb. 4, 5, 6, 8.
Concerto No. 3 for Piano and Orchestra, C minor, Opus 37: Nov. 12, 13, 14, 16.
Concerto No. 4 for Piano and Orchestra, G major, Opus 58: Jan. 20.
Concerto for Violin and Orchestra, D major, Opus 61: Nov. 25, 27, 28, 30.
"Coriolanus" Overture, Opus 62: Nov. 25, 27, 28, 30.
*Overture to "Egmont," Opus 84: Sept. 22.
*Symphony No. 3, E-flat major, Opus 55 ("Eroica"): Dec. 30, 31; Jan. 1, 2, 4.
*Symphony No. 4, B-flat major, Opus 60: Sept. 22; Jan. 28, 29, 30; Feb. 1.
*Symphony No. 6, F major, Opus 68 ("Pastoral"): Nov. 25, 27, 28, 30.
*Symphony No. 8, F major, Opus 93: Nov. 12, 13, 14, 16.

BERG—"Five Orchestral Songs after Picture Postcard Texts by Peter Altenberg," Opus 4: Apr. 15, 16, 17, 19.
"Seven Early Songs": Apr. 15, 16, 17, 19.
Three Orchestral pieces, Opus 6: Apr. 15, 16, 17, 19.

BERLIOZ—"Nuits d'été," Opus 7: Jan. 14, 15, 16, 18.
Overture and Scenes from "Béatrice et Bénédict": Apr. 22, 23, 24, 26; May 10 (Overture alone).

BERNSTEIN—*Symphonic Dances from "West Side Story": Jan. 28, 29, 30; Feb. 1.

BERIO—*Sinfonia (in five sections): Oct. 8 (a), 9, 10, 12.

BRAHMS—Concerto No. 1 for Piano and Orchestra, D minor, Opus 15: Jan. 20.
Concerto for Piano and Orchestra, No. 2, B-flat major, Opus 83: Mar. 4, 5, 6, 8.
"A German Requiem," Opus 45: Nov. 19, 20, 21, 23.
"Tragic Overture," Opus 81: Nov. 19, 20, 21, 23.
*Symphony No. 1, C minor, Opus 68: Jan. 7, 8, 9, 11.

*Symphony No. 3, F major, Opus 90: Feb. 26, 27; Mar. 2.
*Symphony No. 4, E minor, Opus 98: Mar. 18, 19, 20, 22.
BRITTEN—"Les Illuminations," Opus 18: Mar. 13.
BRUCKNER—Symphony No. 5, B-flat major (Original Version): Dec. 3, 4, 5, 7.
Symphony No. 8, C minor: Mar. 11, 12, 15.
"Te Deum": Jan. 14, 15, 16, 18.
CHOPIN—Concerto No. 2 for Piano and Orchestra, F minor, Opus 21: Jan. 21, 22, 25.
COPLAND—*"El Salón México": Oct. 29, 30, 31; Nov. 2.
*"Inscape": Oct. 29, 30, 31; Nov. 2.
*"Music for the Theatre": Oct. 29, 30, 31; Nov. 2.
Short Symphony (No. 2): Oct. 29, 30, 31; Nov. 2.
*Suite from the Ballet "Appalachian Spring": Oct. 29, 30, 31; Nov. 2.
DALLAPICCOLA—Variations for Orchestra: Nov. 5, 6, 7, 9.
DEBUSSY—"Khamma," Légende dansée: Feb. 26 (b), 27; Mar. 2.
*"La Mer," Three Symphonic Sketches: Jan. 5.
"Printemps," Suite symphonique: Mar. 13.
*Rhapsody for Clarinet and Orchestra: May 13, 14, 15.
Three Images: May 13, 14, 15.
DELIUS—"On Hearing the First Cuckoo in Spring": Mar. 13.
DVORAK—Symphony No. 6, D major, Opus 60: Dec. 17, 18, 19.
GABRIELI—"Sacrae symphoniae" (sections): May 13, 14, 15.
GINASTERA—Estudios sinfónicos, Opus 35: Dec. 10 (b), 11, 14.
GOEHR—Concerto for Violin and Orchestra: Dec. 30 (b), 31; Jan. 1, 2, 4.
GRIEG—Concerto for Piano and Orchestra, A minor, Opus 16: Dec. 12.
HANDEL—Concerto Grosso, B minor, Opus 6, No. 12: Feb. 4, 5, 6, 8.
HAYDN—Mass, D minor, "Nelson": Apr. 8, 9, 10, 12.
Symphony No. 90, C major: Feb. 18, 19, 20, 22.
Symphony No. 95, C minor: Jan. 14, 15, 16, 18.
Symphony No. 99, E-flat major: Oct. 1, 2, 3, 5.
Symphony No. 100, G major ("Military"): Oct. 8, 9, 10, 12.
KABALEVSKY—Symphony No. 2, Opus 19: Dec. 12.
LUTOSLAWSKI—Concerto for Orchestra: Feb. 18, 19, 20, 22.
MAHLER—"Songs of a Wayfarer": May 6, 7, 8.
*Symphony No. 1, D major: Feb. 11, 12, 13, 15.
*Symphony No. 3, D minor (Finale): Jan. 5.
*Symphony No. 9, D major: Sept. 24, 25, 28.
MAYUZUMI—"Mandala" Symphony: Apr. 8, 9, 10, 12.
MENDELSSOHN—*Overture, "Ruy Blas," Opus 95: Dec. 30, 31; Jan. 1, 2, 4.
Symphony No. 1, C minor, Opus 11: Apr. 1, 2, 3, 5.
*Symphony No. 3, A minor, Opus 56 ("Scottish"): Jan. 5.
MENNIN—Sinfonia for Orchestra: Mar. 25 (b), 26, 29.
MESSIAEN—"Oiseaux exotiques," for Piano and Orchestra: Apr. 22, 23, 24, 26.
MOZART—Concerto No. 9 for Piano and Orchestra, E-flat major, K. 271: Dec. 3, 4, 5, 7.
Concerto No. 25, for Piano and Orchestra, C major, K. 503: Jan. 7, 8, 9, 11.
Divertimento No. 1, D major, K. 136: Feb. 11, 12, 13, 15.
"The Abduction from the Seraglio," Overture, K. 384: Dec. 12.
"Don Giovanni," Overture, K. 527: Feb. 26, 27; Mar. 2.
Symphony No. 28, C major, K. 200: Mar. 4, 5, 6, 8.
Symphony No. 33, B-flat major, K. 319: Mar. 11, 12, 15.

POUSSEUR—"Couleurs croisées": May 13 (d), 14, 15.

PROKOFIEV—Concerto No. 3 for Piano and Orchestra, Opus 26: Nov. 12, 13, 14, 16.
Concerto for Violin and Orchestra, No. 2, G minor, Opus 63: Mar. 25, 26, 29.

RACHMANINOFF—Piano Concerto No. 3, D minor, Opus 30: Sept. 22.

RAVEL—Concerto for Piano and Orchestra, G major: Feb. 11, 12, 13, 15.
"Mother Goose" Suite: Feb. 4, 5, 6, 8.
"Le Tombeau de Couperin": Apr. 22, 23, 24, 26.
*"La Valse": Dec. 12.

ROSSINI—"Tancredi" Overture: Nov. 5, 6, 7, 9.

SAINT-SAENS—"Omphale's Spinning Wheel" ("Le Rouet d'Omphale"): Dec. 12.

SCHOENBERG—Concerto for Piano and Orchestra, Opus 42: Feb. 18, 19, 20, 22.
Lieder, Opus 22: May 6, 7, 8.
*"Verklärte Nacht" ("Transfigured Night"), Opus 4: Apr. 15, 16, 17, 19.

SCHUBERT—Symphony No. 3, D major: Jan. 21, 22, 25.
Symphony No. 6: May 6, 7, 8.

SCHUMAN, W.—Fantasy for Cello and Orchestra: "A Song of Orpheus": Dec. 17, 18, 19.

SCHUMANN—*Symphony No. 1, B-flat major, Opus 38: Mar. 25, 26, 29.
*Symphony No. 4, D minor, Opus 120: Mar. 18, 19, 20, 22.

SHOSTAKOVICH—Symphony No. 1, Opus 10: Nov. 5, 6, 7, 9.

SIBELIUS—*Symphony No. 2, D major, Opus 43: Dec. 10, 11, 14.

STOCKHAUSEN—"Hymnen": Feb. 25 (c and d).

STRAUSS—*"Also sprach Zarathustra," Opus 30: Oct. 1, 2, 3, 5.
*"Don Juan," Tone Poem after Nicolaus Lenau, Opus 20: Feb. 26, 27; Mar. 2.
*"Don Quixote" (Introduction, Theme with Variations and Finale), Fantastic Variations on a Theme of Knightly Character, Opus 35: Oct. 21, 26.

STRAVINSKY—Concerto in D for String Orchestra: Jan. 7, 8, 9, 11.
"Les Noces" ("Svádebka"): Oct. 1, 2, 3, 5.
"Petrushka" (Complete 1911 Version): Apr. 29, 30; May 1, 3, 10.
"Pulcinella": Apr. 29, 30; May 1, 3.
"Requiem Canticles": Apr. 29, 30; May 1, 3.
*Suite from "The Firebird" (1919 Version): Mar. 4, 5, 6, 8.

SZYMANOWSKI—"Stabat Mater," Opus 53: Apr. 8, 9, 10, 12.

TAKEMITSU—"The Dorian Horizon": Feb. 4, 5, 6, 8.

TCHAIKOVSKY—*"Capriccio italien," Opus 45: Mar. 13.
"Hamlet," Fantasy-Overture after Shakespeare, Opus 67: Oct. 15, 16, 17, 19.
Serenade in C major for String Orchestra, Opus 48: Oct. 15, 16, 17, 19.
*Symphony No. 1, G minor, Opus 13 ("Winter Dreams"): Oct. 15, 16, 17, 19, 21, 26.
*Symphony No. 4, F minor, Opus 36: Jan. 21, 22, 25.

VARESE—"Ionisation": Apr. 22, 23, 24, 26.

WALTON—"Capriccio burlesco": Mar. 13.

WEBER—Overture, "Der Beherrscher der Geister" ("The Ruler of the Spirits"): Dec. 10, 11, 14.
Overture to "Euryanthe": Jan. 20.

WEBERN—Five Pieces for Orchestra, Opus 10: Jan. 14, 15, 16, 18.
Passacaglia, Opus 1: Apr. 15, 16, 17, 19.

XENAKIS—"Akrata," for Sixteen Wind Instruments: Apr. 1, 2, 3, 5.

SOLOISTS

PIANO
MITCHELL ANDREWS: Oct. 1, 2, 3, 5.
CLAUDIO ARRAU: Mar. 4, 5, 6, 8.
VLADIMIR ASHKENAZY: Jan. 21, 22, 25.
GINA BACHAUER: Nov. 12, 13, 14, 16.
ALFRED BRENDEL: Jan. 7, 8, 9, 11.
RUDOLF FIRKUSNY: Dec. 3, 4, 5, 7.
BRUNO LEONARDO GELBER: Feb. 11, 12, 13, 15.
PAUL JACOBS: Oct. 1, 2, 3, 5; Apr. 22, 23, 24, 26.
GILBERT KALISH: Oct. 1, 2, 3, 5.
ROBERT MILLER: Oct. 1, 2, 3, 5.
GARRICK OHLSSON: Feb. 4, 5, 6, 8.
LEONARD PENNARIO: Dec. 12.
ARTUR RUBINSTEIN: Jan. 20.
PETER SERKIN: Feb. 18, 19, 20, 22.
ALEXANDER SLOBODYANIK: Sept. 22.
TAMAS VASARY: Nov. 5, 6, 7, 9.

VIOLIN
FRANK GULLINO: Oct. 21, 26.
DAVID NADIEN: Mar. 25, 26, 29.
RUGGIERO RICCI: Dec. 30, 31; Jan. 1, 2, 4.
HENRYK SZERYNG: Nov. 25, 27, 28, 30.
MASUKO USHIODA: Jan. 28, 29, 30; Feb. 1.

VIOLA
WILLIAM LINCER: Oct. 21, 26.

CELLO
LORNE MUNROE: Dec. 17, 18, 19.
GREGOR PIATIGORSKY: Oct. 21, 26.

CLARINET
STANLEY DRUCKER: May 13, 14, 15.

SPECIAL ELECTRONIC GROUP
GROUP STOCKHAUSEN: Feb. 25.

VOICE
MILDRED ALLEN, soprano: Oct. 1, 2, 3, 5.
SHEILA ARMSTRONG, soprano: Jan. 14, 15, 16, 18.
JANET BAKER, mezzo-soprano: Jan. 14, 15, 16, 18.
ELAINE BONAZZI, mezzo-soprano: Oct. 1, 2, 3, 5; Apr. 29, 30; May 1, 3.
STUART BURROWS, tenor: Jan. 14, 15, 16, 18.
PHYLLIS CURTIN, soprano: Mar. 13.

BIRGIT FINNILA, contralto: Apr. 8, 9, 10, 12.
HEATHER HARPER, soprano: Apr. 15, 16, 17, 19.
JERRY JENNINGS, tenor: Apr. 22, 23, 24, 26.
GWENDOLYN KILLEBREW, contralto: Apr. 22, 23, 24, 26.
TOM KRAUSE, baritone: Nov. 19, 20, 21, 23.
EVELYN LEAR, soprano: Apr. 8, 9, 10, 12.
WILLIAM METCALF, baritone: Oct. 1, 2, 3, 5.
RAYMOND MICHALSKI, bass: Apr. 29, 30; May 1, 3.
SHERRILL MILNES, baritone: Apr. 8, 9, 10, 12.
YVONNE MINTON, mezzo-soprano: May 6, 7, 8.
PAUL PLISHKA, bass: Jan. 14, 15, 16, 18.
JUDITH RASKIN, soprano: Nov. 19, 20, 21, 23; Apr. 22, 23, 24, 26.
KENNETH RIEGEL, tenor: Apr. 29, 30; May 1, 3.
RICHARD SHADLEY, tenor: Oct. 1, 2, 3, 5.
JOHN STEWART, tenor: Apr. 8, 9, 10, 12.
BENITA VALENTE, soprano: Apr. 29, 30; May 1, 3.
JOSEPHINE VEASEY, mezzo-soprano: Apr. 22, 23, 24, 26.

CHORUS
CAMERATA SINGERS, Abraham Kaplan, Director: Oct. 1, 2, 3, 5; Nov. 19, 20, 21, 23; Apr. 29, 30; May 1, 3.
MANHATTAN SINGERS and MASTER CHORALES OF WESTCHESTER AND LONG ISLAND, Hugh Ross, Director, Carl Druba, Associate Director: Jan. 14, 15, 16, 18.
SCHOLA CANTORUM, Hugh Ross, Director: May 6, 7, 8.
SWINGLE SINGERS: Oct. 8, 9, 10, 12.
WESTMINSTER CHOIR, Robert Carwithen, Director: Apr. 8, 9, 10, 12.

1970 TOUR OF JAPAN AND SOUTHERN U.S.A.

Conductors

Leonard Bernstein		**Seiji Ozawa**	
Aug. 29—Eve.	Osaka	Sept. 8—Eve.	Tokyo
Aug. 30—Eve.	Osaka		
		Leonard Bernstein	
Seiji Ozawa		Sept. 9—Eve.	Tokyo
Aug. 31—Eve.	Osaka		
		Seiji Ozawa	
Leonard Bernstein		Sept. 10—Eve.	Sapporo
Sept. 1—Eve.	Osaka	Sept. 16—Eve.	Raleigh
Sept. 3—Eve.	Fukuoka	Sept. 17—Eve.	Raleigh
Sept. 4—Eve.	Kyoto	Sept. 18—Eve.	Atlanta
Sept. 5—Eve.	Nagoya	Sept. 19—Eve.	Greenville
Sept. 7—Eve.	Tokyo	Sept. 20—Aft.	Charlotte

TOUR REPERTOIRE

BEETHOVEN—*"Egmont" Overture, Opus 84: Sept. 1, 5.
*"Symphony No. 4, B-flat major, Opus 60: Sept. 1, 3, 4, 5.
*Symphony No. 5, C minor, Opus 67: Sept. 1, 5.

BERLIOZ—*"Symphonie fantastique," Opus 14: Aug. 30; Sept. 3, 4, 9.

COPLAND—Concerto for Clarinet and Orchestra: Aug. 30; Sept. 9, 16, 17, 18, 19, 20.

HAYDN—Symphony No. 101, D major ("The Clock"): Aug. 30; Sept. 9.

MAHLER—*Symphony No. 9, D major: Aug. 29, Sept. 7.

MENDELSSOHN—*Symphony No. 4, A major, Opus 90 ("Italian"): Aug. 31; Sept. 8, 10, 16, 17, 18, 19, 20.

MOUSSORGSKY-RAVEL—*"Pictures at an Exhibition": Aug. 31; Sept. 8, 10, 16, 17, 18, 19, 20.

TAKEMITSU—"November Steps" No. 1: Aug. 31; Sept. 8, 10.

TOUR SOLOISTS

STANLEY DRUCKER, clarinet: Aug. 30; Sept. 9, 16, 17, 18, 19, 20.
KINSHI TSURUTA, biwa: Aug. 31; Sept. 8, 10.
KATSUYA YOKOYAMA, shakuhachi: Aug. 31; Sept. 8, 10.

●

NEW YORK PHILHARMONIC "PROMENADES"
NINTH SEASON   1971   PHILHARMONIC HALL

Conductor

André Kostelanetz
May 19–22, 25–29; June 1–5, 8–12

REPERTOIRE—"PROMENADES"

(a) First performances in New York.
(b) World premiere.
(pa) Work for piano alone.

* Compositions marked with an asterisk are recorded by
the New York Philharmonic.

ALBENIZ—"Fête-Dieu à Séville," from "Ibéria" Suite: June 2, 3, 5.

BACHELET—"Chère nuit": June 10, 11, 12.

BELLINI—Recitative and Aria, "Oh quante volte," from "I Capuleti e i Montecchi": May 19, 20, 26.

BERLIOZ—*Overture, "Le Carnaval romain" ("The Roman Carnival"), Opus 9: June 2, 3, 5.

CHOPIN—Etude, E major, Opus 10, No. 3 (pa): May 21, 22, 25.

COPLAND—*"Corral Nocturne" and "Hoe-Down," from "Rodeo": May 27, 28, 29; June 1.

DEBUSSY—*Prelude to "The Afternoon of a Faun": June 10, 11, 12.

DOHNANYI—Capriccio in F minor (pa): May 21, 22, 25.

FAURE—Incidental Music to "The Merchant of Venice," Opus 57: May 19, 20, 26.

GERSHWIN—*"An American in Paris": June 2, 3, 5.

GLAZUNOV—Suite from "The Seasons": May 27, 28, 29; June 1.

GLIERE—Concerto for Coloratura Soprano and Orchestra, Opus 82 (a): June 10, 11, 12.

GLIERE-LEWENTHAL—Paraphrase on the "Russian Sailor's Dance" from "The Red Poppy" (pa): May 21, 22, 25.

GOTTSCHALK-KAY—"Grand Tarantella," for Piano and Orchestra: June 2, 3, 5.

KODALY—"Háry János" Suite: May 21, 22, 25.

MENDELSSOHN—Barcarole in F-sharp minor from "Songs without Words," Opus 30, No. 6 (arr. for violin and orchestra by Charles Lichter): May 19, 20, 26.

NASH—"Carnival of Marriage" (b): June 2, 3, 5.

OFFENBACH—Overture to "La Belle Hélène": June 10, 11, 12.

PAGANINI-ERNST—"Carnival of Venice": May 19, 20, 26.

PONCHIELLI—*"The Dance of the Hours," from "La Gioconda": May 19, 20, 26.

PROKOFIEV—*"Romeo and Juliet" Excerpts: June 4, 8, 9.
Wedding Suite from "The Stone Flower," Opus 126: June 10, 11, 12.

RACHMANINOFF—Concerto No. 2 for Piano and Orchestra, C minor, Opus 18: June 4.
"Floods of Spring," Opus 14, No. 11: June 8, 9.
Intermezzo and Gypsy Dance from "Aleko": June 4, 8, 9.
"O, Cease thy Singing, Maiden Fair," Opus 4, No. 4: June 8, 9.
"Vocalise," Opus 34, No. 14: June 8, 9.

ROSSINI—*"Pas de six" and Overture from "William Tell": June 10, 11, 12.

SCHARWENKA—"Allegro non troppo" (Finale) from Concerto No. 2 for Piano and Orchestra, C minor: May 21, 22, 25.

SCRIABIN—Nocturne for the Left Hand, D-flat major, Opus 9 (pa): May 21, 22, 25.

SHOSTAKOVICH—"Folk Festival": May 27, 28, 29; June 1.

SMETANA—*Three Dances from "The Bartered Bride": May 21, 22, 25.

STRAVINSKY—*Dances from "Petrushka": May 27, 28, 29; June 1.

TCHAIKOVSKY—"The Sleeping Beauty" Suite, Opus 66A: May 21, 22, 26.

THOMAS—"Mad Scene" from "Hamlet": June 10, 11, 12.

VERDI—Recitative and Aria: "D'Amor sull'ali rosee," from "Il Trovatore": June 8, 9.

Recitative and Aria, "Ernani, involami," from "Ernani": May 19, 20, 26.
Ballet from Act III of "Otello": May 19, 20, 26.
Ballet from Act III of "Otello": May 19, 20, 26

VILLA-LOBOS—"Bachianas Brasileiras" No. 5: June 8, 9.
"Little Train of the Caipira," from "Bachianas Brasileiras" No. 2: June 4, 8, 9.
"Modinha" (Preludio), from "Bachianas Brasileiras" No. 1: June 4, 8, 9.

WEBER—"Invitation to the Dance": May 27, 28, 29; June 1.

WOLF-FERRARI—Orchestral Suite from "The Jewels of the Madonna": May 19, 20, 26.

ENCORES:

BACH-BUSONI—Chorale Prelude (pa): June 2, 3, 5.

BIZET—"Dance of the Toreadors" from "Carmen": June 10, 11, 12.

BRAHMS—Hungarian Dance No. 5: June 10, 11.

CHAPI—Aria from "La Revoltosa": June 8, 9.

DELIBES—Pizzicato Polka: May 27, 28, 29; June 1.

GERSHWIN—"Bess, Where's my Bess": June 2, 3, 5.

KHACHATURIAN—Aysha's Dance: June 4, 8, 9.
Lezgenka from "Gayne": May 27, 28, 29; June 1.

MENDELSSOHN—Barcarole No. 2: May 19, 20, 26.

OFFENBACH—"Barcarole" from "Tales of Hoffman": May 19, 20, 26.
Cancan: June 2, 3, 5.

PRESS—Wedding Dance: June 8.

PROKOFIEV—Prelude, Opus 12, No. 7 (pa): June 2, 3, 5.

PUCCINI—Doretta's Aria from "La Rondine": June 10, 11, 12.
"O mio Babbino caro": May 19, 20, 26.

ROSSINI—"Semiramide": May 19, 20, 26.

SOUSA—"Stars and Stripes Forever": June 10, 11, 12.

TCHAIKOVSKY—"Danse des coupes" from "Swan Lake": May 21, 22, 25.
"Pas de Quatre" from "Sleeping Beauty": May 21, 22, 25.

TUCCI—"La Bamba de Vera Cruz": June 4, 8, 9.

SOLOISTS—"PROMENADES"

BALLET
ANNA ARAGNO: May 27, 28, 29; June 1.
EDWARD VILLELLA: May 27, 28, 29; June 1.

CIMBALOM
TONI KOVES-STEINER: May 21, 22, 25.

NARRATOR
TONY RANDALL: June 2, 3, 5.

PIANO
MISHA DICHTER: June 4.
THEODORE LETTVIN: June 2, 3, 5.
RAYMOND LEWENTHAL: May 21, 22, 25.

VIOLIN
AARON ROSAND: May 19, 20, 26.

CELLO
LORNE MUNROE: May 27, 28, 29; June 1, 8, 9.

VOICE
PATRICIA BROOKS, soprano: June 10, 11, 12.
ANNA MOFFO, soprano: May 19, 20, 26.
MARALIN NISKA, soprano: June 8, 9.

NEW YORK PHILHARMONIC AND AFL-CIO
"EXPERIENCE IN MUSIC" 1971

Conductors

Aaron Copland   June 20   National Maritime Union
June 17   Co-op City   June 24   Philharmonic Hall
June 18   Electric Industry Center
June 23   Philharmonic Hall   **Michael Tilson Thomas**
                                        June 25   Philharmonic Hall
Robert Shaw   June 26   Co-op City
June 19   Electric Industry Center   June 27   Philharmonic Hall

REPERTOIRE—AFL-CIO CONCERTS

* Compositions marked with an asterisk are recorded
by the New York Philharmonic.

BEETHOVEN—Concerto No. 1 for Piano and Orchestra, C major, Opus 15:
June 25, 26, 27.
*Overture to "Egmont," Opus 84: June 19, 20, 24.
BERNSTEIN—*Symphonic Dances from "West Side Story": June 25, 26, 27.
BRUCH—Concerto No. 1 for Violin and Orchestra, G minor, Opus 26: June
17, 18, 23.
COPLAND—*"Danzón cubano": June 17, 18, 23.
"Old American Songs": June 17, 18, 23.
FAURE—"Pelléas et Mélisande," Orchestral Suite, Opus 80: June 17, 18, 23.
GLINKA—*Overture, "Russlan and Ludmilla": June 17, 18, 23.
HANDEL—"Water Music" Suite: June 25, 26, 27.
IVES—*"The Unanswered Question": June 25, 26, 27.
PROKOFIEV—*"Classical" Symphony, Opus 25: June 17, 18, 23.
RACHMANINOFF—Rhapsody on a Theme of Paganini, for Piano and Orches-
tra, Opus 43: June 19, 20, 24.
SCHUBERT—*Symphony No. 8, B minor ("Unfinished"): June 19, 20, 24.
STRAVINSKY—*Suite from "The Firebird": June 19, 20, 24.

SOLOISTS—AFL-CIO CONCERTS

PIANO
MISHA DICHTER: June 25, 26, 27.
LORIN HOLLANDER: June 19, 20, 24.
VIOLIN
MICHAEL RABIN: June 17, 23, 28.

VOICE
WILLIAM WARFIELD, baritone: June
17, 18, 23.

•

NEW YORK PHILHARMONIC OUTDOOR CONCERTS
IN THE PARKS OF THE CITY OF NEW YORK
SEVENTH SEASON (1971)

Conductors

István Kertész
August 4, 5, 7.

Aldo Ceccato
August 10, 13, 17; September 3, 4.

James De Preist
August 20, 21, 24, 25.

REPERTOIRE—PARK CONCERTS

(a) First performance in the United States.

* Compositions marked with an asterisk are recorded by
the New York Philharmonic.

BRAHMS—*Symphony No. 3, F major, Opus 90: Aug. 10, 13, 17; Sept. 3, 4.
Three Hungarian Dances: Aug. 10, 13, 17; Sept. 3, 4.

DVORAK—Symphony No. 6, D major, Opus 60: Aug. 4, 5, 7.

GRIEG—Concerto for Piano and Orchestra, A minor, Opus 16: Aug. 10, 13, 17;
Sept. 3, 4.

PAGANINI—Concerto No. 4 for Violin and Orchestra, D minor: Aug. 20 (a),
21, 24, 25.

PROKOFIEV—Concerto No. 2 for Piano and Orchestra, G minor, Opus 16:
Aug. 4, 5, 7.

ROSSINI—*Overture to "La gazza ladra": Aug. 10, 13, 17; Sept. 3, 4.

SIBELIUS—*Symphony No. 1, E minor, Opus 39: Aug. 20, 21, 24, 25.

SMITH, HALE—"Contours": Aug. 20, 21, 24, 25.

WEBER—Overture to "Euryanthe": Aug. 4, 5, 7.

SOLOISTS—PARK CONCERTS

PIANO
LORIN HOLLANDER: Aug. 4, 5, 7.
GINA BACHAUER: Aug. 10, 13, 17;
Sept. 3, 4.

VIOLIN
RUGGIERO RICCI: Aug. 20, 21, 24, 25.

NEW YORK PHILHARMONIC: GARDEN STATE ARTS CENTER 1971

Conductors

André Kostelanetz
August 11, 12.

Aldo Ceccato
September 1, 2.

REPERTOIRE—GARDEN STATE CONCERTS

(pa) Works for piano alone.

* Compositions marked with an asterisk are recorded by
the New York Philharmonic.

ALBENIZ—Excerpts from the Suite "Ibéria": "Fête-Dieu à Séville," "Triana":
Aug. 11, 12.

BERLIOZ—*Overture, "Le Carnaval romain," Opus 9: Aug. 11, 12.

BRAHMS—*Symphony No. 3, F major, Opus 90: Sept. 1, 2.
Three Hungarian Dances: Sept. 1, 2.

GRIEG—Concerto for Piano and Orchestra, A minor, Opus 16: Sept. 1, 2.

LISZT—Hungarian Fantasy: Aug. 11, 12.
Three Grand Etudes after Paganini, Nos. 3, 5, 2: Aug. 11, 12 (pa).

RESPIGHI—*Symphonic Poem, "The Pines of Rome": Aug. 11, 12.

ROSSINI—*Overture to "La gazza ladra": Sept. 1, 2.

SOLOISTS—GARDEN STATE CONCERTS

PIANO
GINA BACHAUER: Sept. 1, 2.
EARL WILD: Aug. 11, 12.

●

Appendix V

Personnel
New York Philharmonic Orchestra
1973–74†

PIERRE BOULEZ, *Music Director*

Violins

Rafael Druian
Concertmaster
Frank Gullino
Associate Concertmaster
Kenneth Gordon
Assistant Concertmaster
William Dembinsky
Bjoern Andreasson
Alfio Micci
Enrico Di Cecco
Max Weiner
Carlo Renzulli
Leon Rudin
Newton Mansfield
William Nowinski
Nathan Goldstein
Gino Sambuco
Theodor Podnos

Gabriel Banat
Allan Schiller
Sanford Allen
Marc Ginsberg, *Principal*
Oscar Weizner
Jacques Margolies
Eugene Bergen
Luigi Carlini
Martin Eshelman
William Barbini
Bernard Robbins
Richard Simon
Oscar Ravina
Matitiahu Braun
Michael Gilbert
Marilyn Dubow
Donald Whyte
Hanna Lachert
Barry Finclair

† The latest roster available at time of printing.

Violas
Sol Greitzer, *Principal*
Leonard Davis*
David Kates
Ralph Mendelson
Selig Posner
Eugene Becker
Robert Weinrebe
Henry Nigrine
Larry Newland
William Carboni
Raymond Sabinsky
Barry Lehr

Cellos
Lorne Munroe, *Principal*
Nathan Stutch*
Bernardo Altmann
Gerald K. Appleman
George Feher
Lorin Bernsohn
Paul Clement
Avram A. Lavin
Thomas Liberti
Evangeline Benedetti
Asher Richman
Toby Saks

Basses
Walter Botti
John Schaeffer, *Principal*
Jon Deak*
Homer R. Mensch
Orin O'Brien
James V. Candido
Lew Norton
Michele Saxon
Robert Brennand

Flutes
Julius Baker, *Principal*
Robert Morris
Paige Brook*

Piccolo
F. William Heim

Oboes
Harold Gomberg, *Principal*‡
Jerome Roth
Albert Goltzer*

English Horn
Thomas Stacy

Clarinets
Stanley Drucker, *Principal*
Michael Burgio
Peter Simenauer*

E-flat Clarinet
Peter Simenauer

Bass Clarinet
Stephen Freeman

Bassoons
Manuel Zegler, *Principal*
Leonard Hindell
Harold Goltzer*

Contrabassoon
Bert Bial

Horns
Joseph Singer, *Principal*
John Cerminaro*
L. William Kuyper
John Carabella
Ranier De Intinis
Aubrey Facenda

Trumpets
John Ware, *Co-Principal*
Gerard Schwarz, *Co-Principal*
Carmine Fornarotto
James Smith

Trombones
Edward Herman, Jr., *Principal*
Gilbert Cohen
Allen Ostrander
Edward Erwin*

Tuba
Joseph Novotny, *Principal*

Timpani
Roland Kohloff, *Principal*
Morris Lang*

Percussion
Walter Rosenberger, *Principal*
Elden Bailey
Morris Lang

Harp
Myor Rosen, *Principal*

Organ, Harpsichord
Bruce Prince-Joseph

Piano, Celeste
Paul Jacobs

Orchestra
Personnel Manager
James Chambers

Assistant Personnel Mgr.
John Schaeffer

Librarians
Louis Robbins, *Principal*
Robert De Celle*

Stage Representative
Francis Nelson

---

* Associate or Assistant Principal.
‡ On leave 1973–74; during his absence oboe section headed by Albert Goltzer and Ronald Roseman.

Appendix VI

Officers, Directors, Trustees and Administration
The Philharmonic-Symphony Society of New York, Inc.
1973—74†

OFFICERS AND DIRECTORS

Chairman
Amyas Ames

Honorary Chairman
David M. Keiser

President
Carlos Moseley

Vice-Chairmen
Mrs. Lytle Hull
Mrs. Robert L. Hoguet
Ethan A. Hitchcock

Treasurer
Sampson R. Field

Assistant Treasurers
William Rosenwald
Anthony P. Terracciano
Maynard Steiner

Secretary
Peter Heller

Mrs. William C. Breed
Lee H. Bristol, Jr.
Mrs. C. Sterling Bunnell
Benjamin J. Buttenwieser

Mrs. George A. Carden
Mrs. Charles A. Dana
Maitland A. Edey
Gianluigi Gabetti
Francis Goelet
Wm. Rogers Herod
J. Buckhout Johnston
Philip R. Kiendl
Mrs. Hampton S. Lynch
John Macomber
Mrs. Flagler Matthews
Howard Phipps, Jr.
Harvey Picker
Francis T. P. Plimpton
Mrs. Robert H. Preiskel
Luis Quero-Chiesa
Richard Rodgers
Axel G. Rosin
Carleton Sprague Smith
Albert C. Stewart
Mrs. John W. Straus
Miss Alice Tully
Robert A. Uihlein, Jr.
Mrs. Sophie G. Untermeyer

† The latest roster available at time of printing.

Appendix VII

Benefactors and Patrons
New York Philharmonic
1973–74†

BENEFACTORS

Miss Mathilde E. Weber
Mr. and Mrs. Edward R. Wardwell
Mr. and Mrs. David Rockefeller
The Ford Foundation
Mr. and Mrs. John Holbrook
Jos. Schlitz Brewing Company
Mrs. John D. Rockefeller, Jr.
Mr. and Mrs. Amyas Ames
Rockefeller Brothers Fund
Constans-Culver Foundation
Francis Goelet
Lauder Greenway
Mr. and Mrs. David M. Keiser
Mrs. Lytle Hull
Mr. and Mrs. Sampson R. Field

Alice Tully
Mr. and Mrs. Arthur A. Houghton, Jr.
Avalon Foundation
Mrs. Elbridge Gerry Chadwick
Old Dominion Foundation
Mr. and Mrs. William S. Beinecke
Mrs. Mellon Bruce
Glen Alden Corporation
Trans World Airlines
Mr. and Mrs. W. Van Alan Clark
Mr. and Mrs. Robert L. Hoguet
Mr. and Mrs. Nathan Cummings
Mrs. Charles A. Dana
Cecile Lehman Mayer*
The Andrew W. Mellon Foundation

GUARANTORS, SPONSORS, AND PATRONS/1973–74

Mr. Winthrop W. Aldrich
Mr. and Mrs. Amyas Ames
Mr. and Mrs. George L. Armour
Mr. and Mrs. Robert H. Arnow

Mrs. April Axton
The Theodore H. Barth Foundation
Mr. Redfield D. Beckwith
Mr. and Mrs. William S. Beinecke

---

† The latest roster available at time of printing.
* In Memoriam.

Mr. and Mrs. George F. Berlinger
Mr. and Mrs. Leonard Bernstein
Mr. and Mrs. Abraham L. Bienstock
Mrs. William C. Breed
Mrs. Samuel N. Brimberg
Dr. and Mrs. Lee Hastings Bristol, Jr.
Mr. and Mrs. Edgar M. Bronfman
Mr. and Mrs. Harry A. Brooks
Mrs. Alvin G. Brush
Mr. and Mrs. C. Sterling Bunnell
Mr. and Mrs. Robert L. Burch III
Mrs. Chester G. Burden
Mr. and Mrs. Benjamin J. Buttenwieser
Mr. and Mrs. Samuel R. Callaway
Dr. and Mrs. George A. Carden
Mary Flagler Cary Charitable Trust
CBS Foundation, Inc.
Mrs. Elbridge Gerry Chadwick
Mrs. Gilbert W. Chapman
Mrs. William H. Conroy
Mr. and Mrs. Gardner Cowles
Mrs. Cornelius Crane
Mrs. Joseph F. Cullman III
Charles E. Culpeper Foundation, Inc.
Constans-Culver Foundation
Mrs. Allerton Cushman
Mr. and Mrs. Leonard Dalsemer
Mrs. Charles A. Dana
Mr. Arthur H. Dean
Mr. and Mrs. Aaron Diamond
Mr. and Mrs. Maitland A. Edey
Mr. Dean E. Eggertsen
Mr. and Mrs. Frederick L. Ehrman
Mrs. Morton Fearey
Mr. and Mrs. Sampson R. Field
The Frazer Foundation
Mrs. Jack M. Goddard
Mr. Francis Goelet
Mrs. Robert W. Goelet
Mr. and Mrs. Edward Goldberger
Mr. and Mrs. Peter C. Golffing
Mr. and Mrs. Joshua A. Gollin
Mr. and Mrs. William W. Golub
Mrs. Louis A. Green
Mr. and Mrs. David J. Greene
Mrs. Alfred Harcourt
George D. Harris Foundation, Inc.
Mr. and Mrs. Peter S. Heller
Mr. and Mrs. William R. Herod
Mr. and Mrs. Leon Hess
Mr. and Mrs. Ethan A. Hitchcock
Miss Priscilla B. Hoefer
Mrs. Robert L. Hoguet
Barbara F. Hooker
Mrs. Lytle Hull
Mr. and Mrs. Adrian C. Israel
Mrs. Henry Ittleson, Jr.

Mr. and Mrs. Kenneth A. Ives
Mr. and Mrs. J. Buckhout Johnston
Mr. and Mrs. Alfred Winslow Jones
Mr. and Mrs. Leonard S. Kandell
The J. M. Kaplan Fund Inc.
Mrs. Irving D. Karpas
Mr. and Mrs. David M. Keiser
Mrs. William S. Kies
Mr. David Klee
Mr. and Mrs. H. Frederick Krimendahl II
Lanvin-Charles of the Ritz
Mr. and Mrs. Stanley S. Lasdon
Mr. and Mrs. William Lasdon
Mrs. Leon Lauterstein
Hon. and Mrs. Peter I. B. Lavan
Hon. and Mrs. Samuel J. LeFrak
Mr. and Mrs. George J. Leness
Mrs. Edgar M. Leventritt
Mrs. Philip J. Levin
Mr. and Mrs. Gustave L. Levy
Mr. and Mrs. Henry A. Loeb
Mr. and Mrs. John L. Loeb
Mrs. Milton B. Loeb
Mr. and Mrs. John Lubell
Mr. and Mrs. Hampton S. Lynch
Mr. Frasier McCann
Mrs. Joseph V. McMullan
James A. Macdonald Foundation
Mrs. William G. Maguire
Mr. and Mrs. Raphael B. Malsin
Mr. and Mrs. Hubert T. Mandeville
Mr. and Mrs. Frits Markus
Mrs. George R. Martin
Mr. and Mrs. H. Bradley Martin
Mrs. Robert W. Martin, Jr.
Mr. and Mrs. Leonard M. Marx
Mrs. Flagler Matthews
Dr. Edgar Mayer
The Andrew W. Mellon Foundation
Mr. and Mrs. Stanley R. Miller
Mrs. Joseph A. Neff
Mr. and Mrs. Albert Nerken
Alice and Fred Netter Foundation, Inc.
Mrs. Donald M. Oenslager
Louise L. Ottinger Charitable Trust
Mrs. Walter N. Pharr
Mr. and Mrs. Howard Phipps, Jr.
Mr. and Mrs. Harvey D. Picker
Mr. and Mrs. Ned L. Pines
Mr. and Mrs. Francis T. P. Plimpton
Mr. and Mrs. Saul Poliak
Mrs. H. Irving Pratt
Mrs. Richardson Pratt
Mr. Francis F. Randolph
Mr. C. Frank Reavis

Mr. Charles Revson
Mr. John L. Riegel
Mr. William C. Riker
Mrs. Karl Robbins
Mrs. George Roberts
Mr. and Mrs. David Rockefeller
Rockefeller Brothers Fund, Inc.
Mr. and Mrs. Richard Rodgers
Mr. and Mrs. Harold L. Rosenthal
Mr. Axel G. Rosin
Mr. Louis Rosoff
Mrs. Harry J. Rudick
The Fan Fox and Leslie R. Samuels
  Foundation, Inc.
The Scherman Foundation
Mrs. J. Myer Schine
Jos. Schlitz Brewing Co.
Mrs. M. Lincoln Schuster
Bernard and Irene Schwartz
Mr. & Mrs. Joseph E. Shorin
Mr. and Mrs. Daniel H. Silberberg
J. Sidney Silberman Foundation, Inc.
Mrs. Leo Simon
Mr. and Mrs. John H. Slade
Mr. Rudolph G. Sonneborn
Mr. and Mrs. Charles G. Stachelberg

The STARR Foundation
Mr. and Mrs. Theodore E. Stebbins
Steinway and Sons
Mrs. Carl Stern
Mr. and Mrs. H. Peter Stern
Mrs. John P. Stevens, Jr.
Mr. and Mrs. John W. Straus
The Stuart Foundation, Inc.
Miss Jean Tennyson
Mr. and Mrs. Emanuel M. Terner
Mrs. Carll Tucker
Miss Alice Tully
Mr. and Mrs. Robert Uihlein, Jr.
Mr. Chauncey L. Waddell
The Walters Family Foundation
Mr. and Mrs. Edward R. Wardwell
Mr. and Mrs. Frank T. Weston
Mrs. Alexander M. White
Mr. and Mrs. John Hay Whitney
Mr. Robert I. Wishnick
Mr. and Mrs. Sidney H. Witty
Mr. and Mrs. James D. Wolfensohn
Mr. and Mrs. Alfred J. Yardley
Mr. Benjamin C. Zitron and Family
Anonymous Patrons

Appendix VIII

The Auxiliary Board of the New York Philharmonic 1973–74†

† The latest roster available at time of printing.

JUNIOR MEMBERS

Mrs. Christopher Elkus	Mrs. A. Slade Mills, Jr.
Miss Barbara Gaylord	Mrs. Leon Root
Mrs. Edward A. Hansen	Mrs. J. Harden Rose
Mrs. James Hellmuth	Mrs. William T. Seed
Mrs. Charles M. Lewis	Mrs. Michael A. Sennott
	Mrs. Hamilton Southworth, Jr.

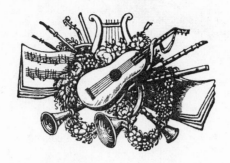

Index

Index

In this Index the term Philharmonic, when not otherwise qualified, refers to the "third" New York Philharmonic (founded in 1842 as the Philharmonic Society of New-York and reorganized in 1928 as the present Philharmonic-Symphony Society of New York). The terms "first" New York Philharmonic and "second" New York Philharmonic refer to the two previous Philharmonic Societies of New York, founded in 1799 and 1824 respectively. The Philharmonic societies of other cities are identified by the names of their cities.

Men and Moutains (Ruggles), 457
Mendel, Gregor, 411
Mendelssohn, Felix, 24*n.*, 37, 66, 81, 83, 85, 93, 95, 96, 102, 103, 109, 116, 117, 120, 125*n.*, 140, 169, 227, 237, 347*n.*, 427; letter of, to Hill, 429–30
Mendelssohn, Paul, 430
Mendelssohn: A New Image (Werner), 430
Mendenhall, David, 458
Mengelberg, Willem, 192, 232–35 *passim*, 237, 246–47, 249–52 *passim*, 256, 257, 281*n.*, 282, 450, 451, 452, 453, 455; *illus.*, Figs. 46, 47
Mennin, Peter, 308, 461
Menotti, Gian Carlo, 307, 460
Mercadante, Saverio, 429
Mercati, Countess. *See* Edgar, Mrs. N. L.
Mercury, 44
Merger, with the Philharmonic, of the City Symphony Orchestra, 247–49, 255, 450; of the National Symphony Orchestra, 233–36, 239, 239*n.*, 244–47, 249, 253, 254, 255, 451, 452; proposed, of the Metropolitan Opera, 268–70, 272; of the Symphony Society of New York, 253–56 *passim*, 450, 451, 455*n.*, 456, 460
Merö, Yolanda, 446
Messiaen, Olivier, 307, 365
Messiah (Handel), 39, 66, 83, 117*n.*
Metcalf, Manton B., 450
Metropolitan Fair, Philharmonic concert in aid of, 434
Metropolitan Hall, 119, 120, 368
Metropolitan Opera (Association), 34, 148–49, 199, 200, 210, 215, 215*n.*, 232, 245*n.*, 259, 267, 268, 269, 272, 306, 312, 322, 325, 364, 370, 372, 443, 453, 464; orchestra of the, 239, 267, 268–69, 345–46, 453. *See also* Metropolitan Opera House
Metropolitan Opera Association Protective Committee, 269
Metropolitan Opera House, 165, 181, 185, 244, 269–70, 364, 368, 443. *See also* Metropolitan Opera (Association)
Metropolitan Theatre, 137
Metz, J., 92
Meyer (orchestra musician), 426
Meyerbeer, Giacomo, 60, 150, 429, 433
Meyerowitz, Jan, 461
Meyrer, C. W., 91, 426
Mezuzah, given to Bernstein by Philharmonic musicians, 365*n.*
Microfilm Reproduction, Arturo Toscanini Collection of Musical Autographs in, 454
Middle Ages, music of the, 399, 433
Midsummer Night's Dream (Mendelssohn), 93, 96, 237
Midwest, tours of the Philharmonic to the, 222, 318, 339
Miguel, F. E., 113
Mihalovici, Marcel, 287
Milan, 13, 14; Philharmonic tour to, 318
Milhaud, Darius, 251, 300, 307, 313, 371, 461
Military-band music, 8, 118, 433; in Philharmonic programs, 342. *See also* Dodworth's Band

Military Intelligence Reserve Society, 450
Milon, S., use of two cellos by, 8
Milstein, Nathan, 303, 318
Milwaukee, Philharmonic concerts in, 335, 336, 339
Minneapolis Symphony Orchestra, 241, 253, 458
Minnesota, University of, 345
"Minnie" Guggenheimer Shell, 336, 449
Minutes of the Annual Meetings of the Philharmonic, 445
Mirror, New York. *See:* New York *Mirror*
Missa Solemnis (Beethoven), 359
Mississippi River, panoramas of, by J. Banvard and J. R. Smith, 32
Mitchell, Mrs. Charles E., 240, 450
Mitchell, William, 17, 20, 35, 38*n.*
Mitropoulos, Dimitri, 289, 291, 292, 303, 304, 307, 309, 310–14 *passim*, 316, 318, 321, 323–29 *passim*, 338, 340, 342, 350, 356, 458–59, 461; *illus.*, Figs. 57, 59
Mitropoulos International Music Competition, 344, 348, 381
Moldau, The (Smetana), 263
Molière (Jean Baptiste Poquelin), 419
Molinari, Bernardino, 455
Mollenhauer, Eduard, 431
Mollenhauer, Friedrich, 431
Mollenhauer, Henry, 431
Monroe, Vaughan, and his orchestra, 304
Monster Music Festival (of music by Wagner and Tchaikovsky), 226
Montealegre, Felicia (Mrs. Leonard Bernstein), 464
Monteux, Doris, 451
Monteux, Pierre, 271, 300, 303, 342, 451
Monteverdi, Claudio, 245*n.*, 313
Monthly Concerts, of the "first" New York Philharmonic, 45
Montreal, Concerts Symphoniques in, 460
Montreal Conservatory, 460
Montresor's Italian opera company, 64, 65
Monumental Symphony—"To the Spirit of Beethoven," A (Heinrich), 119
Moore, Clement C., 49, 91
Moore, Douglas, 275, 277, 306, 308, 457
Moore, Thomas, 23
Moral Re-Armament movement, 301
Morel, Jean, 461
Morgan, J. P., 197, 208
Morini, Erika, 303
Morning Chronicle, 47
Morris, George P., 35, 56
Morris, Harold, 227
Morros, Boris, 304
Morse, Samuel F. B., 27, 28, 29, 31, 32
Morse code, and Beethoven's Fifth Symphony, 291
Moscheles, Ignaz, 420
Moscow, 8, 14
Moscow Conservatory, 193
Moseley, Carlos du Pre, vii, ix, 334–36 *passim*, 348, 374, 378, 389, 390, 402–3, 404; *illus.*, Fig. 67
Mosenthal, J., 436
Moszkowski, Moritz, 230, 449
"Motetto Concertante" (Heinrich), 75
Mother Is Minnie (Untermeyer), 238
Motley, John L., 26
Mottl, Felix, 443, 450

PHOTO CREDITS

Howard Shanet is Chairman of the Department of Music of Columbia University and Conductor of the University Orchestra, which, under his guidance, has gained a reputation for the daring and unconventinal programs it offers the public. He has been guest conductor of the New York Philharmonic in its Young People's series, the Boston Symphony Orchestra at Tanglewood, and orchestras in Holland, Israel, and elsewhere. Before that, he was assistant conductor to Leonard Bernstein and to the late Dr. Serge Koussevitzky. His book *Learn to Read Music,* which has been widely used for many years in its American and British editions, has been translated into Norwegian and is being translated into Italian and Czechoslovakian.